BRITISH POLITICAL FACTS 1900 – 1985

BY

DAVID BUTLER

AND

GARETH BUTLER

SIXTH EDITION

M

MACMILLAN

First edition 1963
Reprinted with corrections 1964
Second edition 1968
Third edition 1969
Fourth edition 1975
Fifth edition 1980
Sixth edition 1986

Published by
THE MACMILLAN PRESS LTD
Houndmills, Basingstoke, Hampshire RG21 2XS
and London
Companies and representatives
throughout the world

Printed in Hong Kong

British Library Cataloguing in Publication Data
Butler, David, *1924–*
British political facts, 1900–1985. – 6th ed.
1. Great Britain – Politics and government – 20th century
I. Title II. Butler, Gareth III. Butler,
David. British political facts, 1900–1979
320.941 JN231
ISBN 0–333–39948—X (hc)
ISBN 0–333–39949—8 (pbk)

CONTENTS

INTRODUCTION to the Sixth Edition xv

I. MINISTRIES

Complete Ministries 1
Ministerial Salaries 67
Opposition Salaries 67
Ministerial Offices: the Offices 68
the Holders 70
Leaders of the House of Commons and the House of Lords 81
Size of Cabinets and Governments 82
Social and Educational Composition of Cabinets 83
Durability of Prime Ministers 84
Long Tenure of Office 84
Oldest and Youngest Ministers 84
Cabinet Members Dying in Office 85
Cabinet Members Suffering Electoral Defeat 85
Ministerial Resignations 85
Parliamentary Private Secretaries to Prime Ministers 87
Biographical Notes on Prime Ministers, Chancellors of the Exchequer, Foreign Secretaries, and Leaders of the Opposition 88
Index of Ministers 95

II. PARTIES

Conservative Party:
Leaders and Deputy Leaders of the Party 135
Leaders in the House of Lords 135
Party Officials 135
Chief Whips in the House of Commons and House of Lords 136
Chairmen of the 1922 Committee 137
Shadow Cabinets 137
Party Membership 139
Party Finance 139
Party Conferences and their Chairmen 140

Labour Party:
Leaders and Deputy Leaders of the Party 142
Election of Leaders 142
Leaders in the House of Lords 143
Chief Whips in the House of Commons and House of Lords 144
Labour Representation Committee and National Executive Committee Office-holders 144
Parliamentary Labour Party 145
Parliamentary Committee Chairmen 149
Party Conferences and Party Chairmen 149

Party Membership Statistics 151
Labour Party Organisation and Constitutions 152
Sponsored M.P.s 154
Party Finance 157

Liberal Party:
Leaders and Deputy Leaders of the Party 158
Leaders in the House of Lords 158
Principal Office-holders 158
Chief Whips in the House of Commons and House of Lords 159
Party Conferences and their Presidents 159

Minor Parties:
Minor Parties Contesting Elections 162
Common Wealth 164
Communist Party 164
Co-operative Party 164
Independent Labour Party 165
Irish Nationalist Party up to 1922 166
Irish Parties since 1922 166
Liberal National Party 167
Liberal Unionist Party 168
National Democratic Party 168
National Front 169
National Party 169
National Labour Party 169
New Party, British Union of Fascists, Union Movement 169
Plaid Cymru 170
Scottish Labour Party 171
Scottish National Party 171
Social Democratic Party 171
Independent M.P.s 172
Representation of Minor Parties in the House of Commons 173

III. PARLIAMENT

House of Commons:
Speakers and their Deputies 175
Officers of the House of Commons 176
Parliamentary Sessions 176
Parliamentary Hours of Sitting 176
Government and Private Members' Time 176
Broadcasting of Parliament 177
Main Occupation of M.P.s 178
Education of M.P.s 179
Dates of Sessions, Use of Parliamentary Time, Parliamentary Bills, and Questions to Ministers 180
Fathers of the House of Commons 183
Long-service M.P.s 184
Oldest and Youngest M.P.s 184
Family Connections of M.P.s 185

Spouse's Succession 186
Filial Succession 186
Critical Votes in the House of Commons 188
Confidence Motions since 1945 191
Guillotine Motions since 1945 191
Suspension of M.P.s 191
Regnal Years 192
Select Committees: 192
Powers 193
Chairmen 193
Chairmen's Liaison Committee 193
Selection 194
Public Accounts 195
Estimates 196
National Expenditure 197
Expenditure 197
Nationalised Industries 197
Agriculture 198
Science and Technology 198
Education and Science 198
Race Relations and Immigration 198
Overseas Aid, Overseas Development 199
Scottish Affairs 199
European Secondary Legislation 199
Procedure 200
House of Commons Services 200
Privileges 201
Statutory Instruments 205
Public Petitions 206
Parliamentary Commissioner for Administration 207
House of Commons Commission 208
Public Accounts Commission 208
Specialist Select Committees since 1979 209
Payment of M.P.s 210
Seats Forfeited 211
House of Lords:
Lord Chairmen of Committees 213
Officers of the House of Lords 213
Composition of the House of Lords 213
Creation of Peerages 214
Party Organisation 214
Party Strengths 215
Attendance 215
Sittings and Business 216
Critical Votes 218
Reform of the House of Lords 218

IV. ELECTIONS

General Election Statistics 223
1975 E.E.C. Referendum Result 229
Direct Elections to European Parliament 229

General Election Results by Regions 230
Party Changes between Elections 232
M.P.s' Changes of Allegiance 233
M.P.s Denied Renomination 239
By-elections 241
Seats Changing Hands at By-elections 241
M.P.s seeking Re-election 244
Ministers seeking Re-election 245
Electoral Administration, Franchise and Redistribution 245
Election Expenses 247
European Referendum Expenses 248
Lost Deposits 249
Women Candidates and M.P.s 249
Election Petitions 250
Sources on Electoral Matters 250
Public Opinion Polling Organisations 252
Polls on Voting Intention 254
Accuracy of Forecasts in General Elections 264

V. POLITICAL ALLUSIONS

Political Place-names 267
Political Quotations 270
Political Scandals 280
Major Civil Disturbances and Demonstrations 281
Political Assassinations 281

VI. CIVIL SERVICE

Heads of Departments and Public Offices 283
Top Civil Service Salary Level 288
Prime Minister's Staff 289
Political Advisers 290
Size of Civil Service 290

VII. ROYAL COMMISSIONS, COMMITTEES OF INQUIRY AND TRIBUNALS

Investigatory Processes 293
Royal Commissions:
Royal Commissions Listed Chronologically 294
Permanent and Operating Commissions 297
Other Crown Committees 298
Irish Vice-Regal Commissions 299
Departmental Committees 299
Select Chronological List 300
Inquiries Held under the Tribunals of Inquiry (Evidence) Act, 1921 302
Tribunals and Commissions 304
Political Honours Scrutiny Committee 304

VIII. ADMINISTRATION OF JUSTICE

Criminal Justice Legislation 307
Legislation Relating to Administration of Civil Justice 310

Cases of Political Significance 311
Principal Judges 315
Other Legal and Law Enforcement Officials 317
Judge Power by Type of Judge and Population 318
Volume of Civil Proceedings 318
Appeal Proceedings 319
Criminal Statistics:
Higher Courts 319
Summary Courts: Indictable Offences 319
Non-indictable Offences 320
Prison Sentences and Prison Populations 320
Parole Board 321
Police Force 321

IX. SOCIAL CONDITIONS

Population:
U.K. Population 1901- 323
Intercensal Changes in Population 323
Population of Components of U.K. 324
Birth Rates, Death Rates, and Marriages in the U.K. 324
Age Distribution of the Population of the U.K. 325
Expectation of Life 325
Main Causes of Death 325
Average Age at First Marriage 326
Divorces 326
Net Emigration from Great Britain and Ireland 326
People Born Overseas 327
Naturalisation 327
Commonwealth Immigration:
Annual Net Commonwealth Immigration 328
Commonwealth Immigrants in the U.K. 329
Race Relations Legislation 329
Housing:
Major Housing Acts 330
Major Rent and Mortgage Interest Restriction Acts 331
Permanent Dwellings Completed 332
Number of Houses 333
Tenancy 334
Social Security:
Legislation 334
Old Age Pensions 337
Women's Rights 337
Maternity and Child Welfare 339
Legal Abortions 340
Education:
Legislation 340
Pupils in Schools 342
Percentage Receiving Full-time Education 342
Students in Full-time Higher Education 342
Expenditure on Education 343

- Public Library Service 344
- Pressure Groups 344
- Transport and Communications:
  - Current Vehicle Licences 347
  - Driving Licences, Road Deaths, and Traffic Offences 347
  - Railways 348
  - Shipping 348
  - Volume of Postal Traffic 348
  - Cost of Letter Mail 349
  - Telephones 349

X. EMPLOYMENT AND TRADE UNIONS

- Major Employment and Trade Union Legislation 351
- Major Trade Union Litigation 355
- Earnings and Hours Worked 357
- Size of Labour Force 359
- Rates of Unemployment Benefit 359
- Industrial Analysis of the Occupied Population 360
- Trades Union Congresses, with Presidents and General Secretaries 361
- The Largest Unions:
  - Formation and Officers 362
  - Membership Figures 366
- Income, Expenditure and Funds of Registered Trade Unions 368
- Density of Union Membership in Total Labour Force 368
- White-Collar Unions 369
- Major Industrial Disputes 369
- Emergency Powers 371
- Unemployment, Industrial Disputes, and Trade Union Statistics 372

XI. THE ECONOMY

- Some Landmarks in British Economic Policy 375
- Sources of Government Economic Advice:
  - Economic Section of the Cabinet Office 377
  - Economic Adviser to the Government 377
  - Head of Government Economic Service 378
  - Bank of England 378
  - Economic Advisory Council 378
  - Import Duties Advisory Council 378
  - Economic Planning Board 378
  - National Economic Development Office 378
  - Council on Pay, Productivity and Incomes 378
  - National Incomes Commission 378
  - Prices and Incomes Board 378
  - Prices Commission 378
  - Pay Board 379
  - Industrial Adviser to the Government 379
- Economic Interest Groups 379
- Statistics:
  - National Income 380
  - Income Tax 380

Wholesale and Retail Price Indices 380
Purchasing Power of the Pound in 1900 Terms 380
Real Gross Domestic Product per head 380
Indices of Industrial Production 383
Coal and Steel Production 383
Raw Cotton Consumption 383
Agriculture, Output and Employment 383
Agriculture: Cultivated Areas, Cattle, and Sheep 383
Price of 2½% Consols 383
Bank Rate 383
Net Balance of Payments 385
Terms of Trade 385
Imports and Exports: Volume Indices 385
Foreign Exchange Rates 385
Total National Revenue 387
Main Sources of Revenue 387
Main Heads of Expenditure 389
Specimen Tariffs 389
National Debt 389
Percentage Shares in Net National Income 392
Selected Items of Consumer Expenditure 392
Income Distribution after Tax 392
Percentage of Personal Net Capital owned by Groups of Population 393
Output per Man 393
Industrial Output of the U.K. 393
Surtax 394
Estate Duty 394
Death Duty 394
Capital Transfer Tax 394
Hire Purchase 395
Budget Dates 395

XII. NATIONALISATION

Main Landmarks 397
Privatisation 398
Nationalised Industries: Chairmen and Responsible Ministers 399
Nationalised Industries: Assets and Employees, 1950– 408
Inquiries into Nationalised Industries 408
Select Committee on Nationalised Industries Reports 409
Other Public Corporations 410
Central Government Trading Bodies 411
Other Quasi-governmental Organisations 411
White Papers on Nationalised Industry Policy 412

XIII. ROYALTY

British Kings and Queens 415
Use of Royal Power 415
Regency Acts 416
The Royal Family 416

Private Secretaries to the Sovereign 419
Lord Chamberlains 419
Poets Laureate 419
Civil List of the Crown 419

XIV. BRITISH ISLES
Scotland 421
Wales 422
Ireland 1900-1922 423
Northern Ireland 1922-1972 424
Governors and Prime Ministers of Northern Ireland 426
Northern Ireland Ministers 1921-72 426
General Elections of Northern Ireland 1921-69 427
Northern Ireland 1972- 427
Channel Islands 429
Isle of Man 431
Devolution 432

XV. LOCAL GOVERNMENT
Structure 435
Number of Councils 435
Local Government Finance 436
Major Legislation Affecting Local Government 436
Local Authority Interest Groups 440
New Towns 441
Local Government Elections: 442
Borough Council Election Results 1949-72 442
Party Control in Major Cities 1945- 443
Local Government Elections 1973- 445
Party Representation on the London County Council and Greater London Council 447

XVI. THE COMMONWEALTH
Main Territories under British Rule since 1900 449
Independent Self-Governing Members of the Commonwealth 454
Commonwealth Prime Ministers' Meetings 455
Commonwealth Secretariat 456
Viceroys and Governors-General 456

XVII. INTERNATIONAL RELATIONS
Major Treaties and Documents Subscribed to by Britain 459
League of Nations 461
United Nations 461
Foreign Affairs Pressure Groups 461
British Ambassadors to Leading Powers and International Organisations 461

XVIII. BRITAIN AND EUROPE
A Chronology of Events 465

European Organisations with British Membership 466
European Parliament 469
European Court of Justice 469
British Representation in Europe 470

XIX. ARMED FORCES

Service Chiefs 471
Defence Organisation:
Committee of Imperial Defence 472
Ministry of Defence 472
Defence Pressure Groups 473
Total Forces Serving 473
Total Expenditure on Defence 473
Conscription 474
Rationing 474
Principal Military Operations, with Costs and Casualties 475
Major War Commanders 478

XX. THE PRESS

National Daily Newspapers 481
National Sunday Newspapers 486
London Evening Newspapers 488
National Newspapers Printing in More than One City 491
Partisan Tendencies in General Elections 492
Circulations 494
Provincial Morning Daily Newspapers 495
Main Political Weeklies 498
Newspaper Readership 499
The Press Council 499

XXI. BROADCASTING AUTHORITIES

The British Broadcasting Corporation: 501
British Broadcasting Company Board 501
British Broadcasting Corporation Board 501
B.B.C. Radio 503
B.B.C. Television 504
Licences and Expenditure 504
Independent Broadcasting 505
Members of the Independent Television Authority 505
Programme Contracting Companies—Television 506
Independent Television News Ltd. 509
Programme Contracting Companies—Radio 509
Inquiries into Broadcasting 510

XXII. RELIGION

Church Membership Statistics 511
The Church of England: 512
Membership Statistics 512
Archbishops and Leading Bishops of the Five Principal Dioceses in the Church of England 513

The Church in Wales 513
Episcopal Church in Scotland 514
Baptist Union 514
Congregational Union 514
Presbyterian Church 515
United Reformed Church 515
Methodist Church 515
The Church of Scotland 516
The Roman Catholic Church 516
Northern Ireland, Religious Affiliations 517
Other Christian Denominations 517
The Jewish Community 517
Buddhists, Hindus, Muslims and Sikhs 518
Marriages by Manner of Solemnisation 518

XXIII. BIBLIOGRAPHICAL NOTE 519

INDEX 523

INTRODUCTION TO THE SIXTH EDITION

THE table of contents offers the simplest justification for this book—but inevitably it is a book that must justify itself in different ways to different readers. The scholar, the journalist, the politician and the everyday pedant were each in the authors' minds at some point during its compilation. Some of those who look at this book will, we hope, be delighted to find in compact and reliable form data that might still have eluded them after searching through a dozen standard works of reference; others will at least discover from our pages where the information they seek may be found; a few, we fear, will be infuriated by our omissions and, despite all our efforts at checking, by our errors.

The idea of writing this book grew gradually in the mind of one of its authors as, in the course of his years as a student and a teacher at Nuffield College (which is devoted to research in contemporary subjects), he noticed the amount of time that he and others wasted in searching for seemingly obvious facts about twentieth-century Britain. If, therefore, any one reader has been especially in our minds, he is the graduate student writing a thesis on any domestic theme in the last eighty years. We hope he will find here not only an expeditious way of checking basic facts but also, if he finds time to browse through our lists and tables, a stimulating reminder of people and considerations that must have played a part, perhaps only as background, in the situations he is analysing.

But we are not concerned solely with academic needs. Experience of checking facts in newspaper offices and broadcasting studios, and the anecdotes of friends in Whitehall and Westminster, have made plain to us how much elementary political data is annoyingly elusive. Many admirable works of reference exist but the right one is not always to hand; most of them, moreover, are compiled on an annual basis—which can be very frustrating for those who are trying to trace an office or a statistic over a number of years.

The compiler of any work of reference is limited by space and time. How much data shall be included? How far shall other works be duplicated? How many hours is it worth devoting to any particular entry? In this book we have had to exclude interesting information either because it would fill a disproportionate number of pages or because it could not be obtained without more labour than we thought justified. We have consoled ourselves for setting out data in abbreviated form by giving exact references to more exhaustive sources.

Indeed, since the compilation of reference books is, even more than other research, systematised plagiarism, perhaps the most valuable part of these pages lies in these citations. We have not attempted an exhaustive bibliography—except for a compilation of bibliographies and general reference books—but we have throughout tried to list all major authorities.

The title, *British Political Facts 1900-1985*, provides a reasonably close delimitation of the scope of this book. *British* indicates that we have been concerned with the domestic history of the United Kingdom. But it is not possible to set precise boundaries to the term ' domestic ' and we have perhaps strayed beyond them by listing Colonies, Governors-General, and some Ambassadors, as well as including a chapter on Britain's relations with Europe.

Political is potentially ambiguous, but we have used it to stress that our interest is in the power of the state. We have tried to list the principal people who were involved in the government of Britain at any moment in this century; we have recorded election results—as providing the basis for political authority—and major legislation—as representing its use; we have assembled, in summary form, statistical data which show some of the social and economic background to all political action.

Facts indicates that we have tried to eschew political judgements as far as possible. Some value judgements may be implicit in our selection of material, but we believe that virtually everything here would be acceptable as non-controversial evidence in debates over the nature of twentieth-century British history. It is a waste of time to argue about verifiable questions of fact. But it is also a waste of time to assemble facts except as a basis for argument. Because in this book we have stuck rigidly to facts, it does not mean that we overrate them. Analysis of our past and present situation is far more important than mere fact-gathering. Unlike Martha we are fully aware which is the better part.

1900-1985 is a somewhat arbitrary period—but any historical period must be arbitrary. Our terminal date is simply as near to the present as publishing allows. Our opening date was a numerological accident—but it would be hard to find a better watershed without going back at least to 1885, which because of space, and still more because of the availability of data, was impracticable. We have endeavoured to treat every one of our eighty-five years equally, providing as full and exact data about 1901 as about 1981. With some statistics this has proved impossible and some of our time-series are regrettably discontinuous. But in general it will be found that we have resisted the temptation to make a special favourite of the more recent past; it is not our fault that there were no Gallup polls before 1938 and that local election results cannot usefully be pursued very far back.

In compiling this book we have become very conscious of the strengths and weaknesses of other reference books—and particularly of the importance of pedantic accuracy and clear presentation. We have certainly not avoided all the pitfalls into which we have observed others falling; therefore, by way both of excuse and of warning, it may be worth describing a few of the difficulties we have faced.

The general problems of finding exact data on British politics were best exemplified in the gathering of complete lists of ministries over the last eighty-five years—the most time-consuming of all our operations. There are a number of publications which purport to list all ministerial appointments—the most useful of these are the two Parliamentary handbooks, *Dod* and *Vacher*. There is also the Stationery Office publication *H.M. Ministers and Heads of Public Departments* which used to appear four or five times a year. Lists of ministers are also printed in *Hansard* once a fortnight during sessions. But all these sources have the same disadvantage—no indication is given of the date when a minister was appointed or left office. A man may indeed be appointed and leave office between the publication of these lists, so that there is no record whatever of his elevation. *Keesing's Contemporary Archives* have since 1931 recorded most government appointments—but they depend solely on newspaper sources and are not altogether infallible. The *Indexes* to *The Times* are the best means of checking on ministerial changes, though here too there are problems. *Palmer's Index to the Times* which was not superseded by the *Official Index* until 1906 is far from satisfactory; under the heading 'Official Appointments' is the depressing injunction 'See every issue'. From 1906 the *Official Index* is much more thorough, although misprints and references to different editions of the paper do occur. Even *The Times*, moreover, has occasionally missed a minor government change. An additional complication lies in the range of possible days which might be considered the date of appointment: there is the announcement from Downing Street, the press report the following day, the official gazetting a week or more later, the exchange of seals and the kissing of hands. None of these may represent the precise date on which the new minister took over his duties, but, wherever possible, we have used the date of *The Times* report, as being the earliest and most public announcement; however, when, as has happened more and more since 1960, a resignation or reshuffle has been well publicised on the air on the previous evening, and where *The Times* reports the announcement as having been made 'yesterday', we have used the earlier date. Peerages sometimes cause further confusion, since weeks usually elapse before a newly elevated minister's title is announced. Care has also to be taken when a familiar minister disappears behind a new name—the fact that Mr Ivor Guest, Lord Ashby St Ledgers, and Viscount Wimborne were one and the same person is not immediately apparent. Another snag arises, particularly in wartime and since the late 1960s, when the titles and functions of ministries change kaleidoscopically.

In many other fields the sources of confusion were almost equally numerous. The search for reliable and consistent evidence about newspaper circulations, religious affiliations and trade disputes caused us particular trouble. But it would be tedious to quote all the gaps in existing works of reference which we have—with very varying success—tried to fill. We must, however, mention the complications which arise from the structure of the United Kingdom. The changes in Ireland in 1922 inevitably cause a break in all national statistical time-series and since then many tables have, perforce, to exclude Northern Ireland as well as Eire; but the administrative separation of Scotland causes almost as many difficulties. Statistics are compiled independently north and south of the Border, quite often on different bases. Sometimes this arises from the different legal or administrative systems—as with education; but in the case of population and vital statistics the Registrars-General seem unnecessarily perverse in presenting their census findings in differing forms.

This book was first compiled at the beginning of the 1960s. It has been checked, updated and modified through successive editions in response to the reactions of its readers. It is the people who have used the book most—academics, civil servants, librarians, journalists, party officials and officers of the Houses of Parliament—who have been its keenest and most constructive critics.

The preparation and revision of this book has indeed depended on a vast amount of help from many quarters, ranging from scholars and friends who have spent many hours assisting us to check on obscure details, to unidentified voices at the end of official telephones. We must thank above all Jennie Freeman, who in 1961 bore so much of the brunt of preparing the First Edition, and Anne Sloman who co-authored the Fourth and Fifth editions, introducing valuable new features. After them come the Warden, Fellows and Students of Nuffield College, who have made so many contributions over the years. But we owe a deep debt of gratitude to officials in Parliament, in Party Headquarters, in Government Departments and in newspaper offices, to many colleagues in the academic world and in the B.B.C., especially to those in News Information and the Reference Library, to complete strangers who have sent us corrections and suggestions, and to our publishers. We must also acknowledge what we owe to anonymous compilers of the many works of reference from which we have so freely drawn. We give here an incomplete list of those who have supplied information or emendations in the preparation of one or more of the successive editions of this book and, although many have given unstinted help, we must draw special attention to the encyclopaedic precision of Mr S. M. Lees which has saved us from so many errors.

P. Addison
R. K. Alderman
R. F. Allen
J. M. Austen
G. S. Bain
Miss P. Baines
F. M. Barlow
C. J. Bartlett
E. Batstone
D. Beamish
M. Beloff
F. Berman
H. B. Berrington
N. Birnbaum
N. Blewett
G. D. M. Block
V. Bogdanor
J. M. Bowen
M. G. Brock
P. A. Bromhead
E. E. Butler
R. Butt
P. Campbell
T. J. M. Cartwright
A. N. Cass
J. Chesshire
Sir N. Chester
D. M. Clark
H. A. Clegg
P. C. Collison
Miss S. J. Conwill
D. Cowling
F. W. S. Craig
J. A. Cross
S. Cursley
J. K. Curtice
P. Davies
C. Dawson
N. Deakin
A. Deyermond
C. Dobson
Mrs M. Dowley
G. Drewry
C. Driver
B. Dye
Miss D. Edmunds
N. D. Ellis
Sir T. Evans
H. R. M. Farmer
Sir E. Fellowes
A. Flanders
A. Fox
Lord Fraser of Kilmorack
Yash Ghai
M. Gilbert
S. Gordon
B. Gosschalk
A. H. Halsey
T. Harris
M. Harrison
A. J. Hastings
S. C. Hawtrey
A. Hayes
C. G. Hazlehurst
D. Heald
J. Hemingway
R. J. Hetherington
A. E. Holmans
C. C. Hood
A. Hunt
R. J. Jackson
D. Jeffcock
Miss J. Jeger
R. Jenkins
L. Keillor
B. Keith-Lucas
A. S. King
U. W. Kitzinger
A. L. Lamaison
F. Lawson
S. M. Lees
T. O. Lloyd
A. B. Lyons
Lord MacCarthy
J. C. McCrudden
K. MacDonald
Sir D. MacDougall
A. MacIntyre
R. McKibbin
A. F. Madden
G. Marshall
J. Maule

Miss E. Meehan
J. S. Milner
B. R. Mitchell
Miss J. P. Morgan
J. Morland Craig
D. L. Munby
R. Neuss
H. G. Nicholas
P. Norton
C. O'Leary
P. Oppenheimer
J. Palmer
Lord Pannell
J. Paxton
H. Pelling
Dame M. Perham
M. Pinto-Duschinsky
A. M. Potter
D. Prysor-Jones
G. Pyatt
C. Raphael
R. A. Rempel
N. Rees
Miss A. Rhodes
P. G. Richards
Mrs P. Ryan
M. Ryle
J. C. Sainty
S. Sargent
Miss K. Schott
Miss O. Seligman
C. Seymour-Ure
D. M. Shapiro
L. J. Sharpe
Mrs A. Skeats
R. J. A. Skidelsky
M. G. M. Sloman
M. Steed
D. Stephen
S. Symes
Mrs A. Taylor
A. J. P. Taylor
P. C. Thompson
Mrs I. Wagner
R. Walford
N. D. Walker
W. Wallace
A. H. Warren
Miss N. Watts
P. Way
Mrs J. Wigan
P. M. Williams
Mrs B. Williamson
T. Wilson
R. Worcester
R. Wybrow

While we could not have completed this book without these far-flung helpers (not to mention the indefatigable assistance of our secretaries) we should stress our sole responsibility for its inevitable errors. Our readers are earnestly invited to let us know of any that they may detect.

DAVID BUTLER
GARETH BUTLER

NUFFIELD COLLEGE, OXFORD
January 1985

I
MINISTRIES

THE following list contains all holders of paid and political ministerial offices since 1900. It leaves out some office-holders, since various offices in the Royal Household have during the past century ceased to be political appointments. The list also omits some politicians with governmental posts, since various other offices such as the Church Estates Commissioners are at times filled by M.P.s who are not regarded as part of the Ministry. Assistant Government Whips were unpaid until the 1964 Parliament and are not listed until then. Parliamentary Private Secretaries are also unlisted.

The problems of compiling this list are discussed on p. xvi. The dates are as far as possible the dates on which the announcement of the appointment appeared in *The Times*, except where it is plain that the news received wide publicity the previous day. Where more than one person holds the same title starting and finishing dates are given. In almost all other cases it may be assumed that the date of the new appointment represents the vacating of the office. **Ministers** in the cabinet are printed throughout this section in heavy type. MINISTERS outside the cabinet and Ministers of State are printed in capitals. Junior Ministers are in ordinary print. The seven leading offices are placed first in each Ministry; the remainder are arranged alphabetically, except the law offices and the political appointments to the Royal Household, which are placed at the end, together with the Treasury appointments which are held by Whips. In these tables (and throughout the book) titles are placed in brackets if acquired during the tenure of a particular office or on transfer to the next office. U-S. denotes Under-Secretary; F.S. Financial Secretary; P.S. Parliamentary Secretary.

This section has been sub-divided chronologically at changes of Prime Minister, except when few other offices changed hands, as in 1902, 1923, 1937, 1955, 1963, and 1976; further sub-divisions are made for the drastic reconstructions of 1915, 1931, and May 1945.

CONSERVATIVE GOVERNMENT, 1900-1905

	MINISTERS IN CABINET		JUNIOR MINISTERS ATTACHED
P.M.	**M of Salisbury (3rd)**	1900-11 Jul 02	
	A. Balfour	12 Jul 02-4 Dec 05	
1st Ld of Treasury[1]	**A. Balfour**	1900	
	(office combined with P.M. when Balfour succeeded Salisbury)		
Ld Pres.	**D of Devonshire**	1900	
	M of Londonderry	13 Oct 03	
Ld Chanc.	**E of Halsbury**	1900	
Privy S.	**Vt Cross**	1900	
	M of Salisbury (3rd) (P.M.)	1 Nov 00	
	A. Balfour (P.M.)	12 Jul 02	
	M of Salisbury (4th)	11 Oct 03	

[1] The only occasion in this century when 1st Ld of Treasury was not combined with P.M.

CONSERVATIVE GOVERNMENT, 1900-1905 *(contd.)*

	MINISTERS IN CABINET			JUNIOR MINISTERS ATTACHED	
Exch.	**Sir M. Hicks Beach**	1900	*Treasury:*		
	C. Ritchie	8 Aug 02	*F.S.*	R. Hanbury	1900
	A. Chamberlain	6 Oct 03		A. Chamberlain	7 Nov 00
				W. Hayes Fisher	8 Aug 02
				A. Elliot	10 Apr 03
				V. Cavendish	9 Oct 03
For. O.	**M of Salisbury (3rd) (P.M.)**	1900	*U-S.*	St J. Brodrick	1900
	M of Lansdowne	1 Nov 00		Vt Cranborne[1] *(4th M of Salisbury)*	7 Nov 00
				Earl Percy[1]	9 Oct 03
Home O.	**Sir M. White Ridley**	1900	*U-S.*	J. Collings	1900
	C. Ritchie	1 Nov 00		T. Cochrane	8 Aug 02
	A. Akers-Douglas	8 Aug 02			
Admir.	**G. Goschen**	1900	*P. & F.S.:*		
	E of Selborne	1 Nov 00		Sir W. Macartney	1900
	Earl Cawdor	5 Mar 05		H. Arnold-Forster	7 Nov 00
				E. Pretyman	11 Oct 03
			Civil Ld:		
				A. Chamberlain	1900
				E. Pretyman	7 Nov 00
				A. Lee	11 Oct 03
Bd Ag. & Fish.	**W. Long**	1900			
	R. Hanbury	14 Nov 00			
	E of Onslow	19 May 03			
	A. Fellowes	12 Mar 05			
Col. O.	**J. Chamberlain**	1900	*U-S.*	E of Selborne	1900
	A. Lyttelton	6 Oct 03		E of Onslow	12 Nov 00
				D of Marlborough	23 Jul 03
	(office not established)				
Bd Educ.	**D of Devonshire**	1 Apr 00		*Vice-President of Committee of Council on Education*—Sir J. Gorst	1900
	M of Londonderry	8 Aug 02		*(office abolished 8 Aug 02)*	
			P.S.	Sir W. Anson	8 Aug 02
India O.	**Ld G. Hamilton[1]**	1900	*U-S.*	E of Onslow	1900
	St J. Brodrick	6 Oct 03		E of Hardwicke	12 Nov 00
				Earl Percy[1]	8 Aug 02
				E of Hardwicke	15 Oct 03
				M of Bath	19 Jan 05
Chief Sec. Ireland	*(office not in cabinet)*		*V. Pres. Dept. Agric. for Ireland:*		
	G. Wyndham	8 Aug 02		(Sir) H. Plunkett	1900
	W. Long	12 Mar 05			
Ld Chanc. Ireland	**Ld Ashbourne**	1900			
Ld Lieut. Ireland	**Earl Cadogan**	1900			
	(E of Dudley 8 Aug 02 & office not in cabinet)				
D. Lanc.	**Ld James of Hereford**	1900			
	(Sir W. Walrond 8 Aug 02 & office not in cabinet)				
Loc. Govt. Bd	**H. Chaplin**	1900	*P.S.*	T. Russell	1900
	W. Long	7 Nov 00		(Sir) J. Lawson	11 Nov 00
	G. Balfour	12 Mar 05		A. Jeffreys	27 Jun 05
Postm.-Gen.	*(office not in cabinet)*				
	M of Londonderry	7 Nov 00			
	A. Chamberlain	8 Aug 02			
	Ld Stanley[1]	6 Oct 03			
Scotland	**Ld Balfour of Burleigh**	1900			
	A. Murray	6 Oct 03			
	M of Linlithgow	2 Feb 05			

[1] M.P. not a member of the House of Lords.

CONSERVATIVE GOVERNMENT, 1900-1905 *(contd.)*

MINISTERS IN CABINET			JUNIOR MINISTERS ATTACHED		
B.o.T.	**C. Ritchie**	1900	*P.S.*	E of Dudley	1900
	G. Balfour	7 Nov 00		A. Bonar Law	8 Aug 02
	M of Salisbury (4th)	12 Mar 05			
War O.	**M of Lansdowne**	1900	*F.S.*	J. Powell Williams	1900
	St J. Brodrick	1 Nov 00		Ld Stanley[1]	7 Nov 00
	H. Arnold-Forster	6 Oct 03		W. Bromley-Davenport	11 Oct 03
			U-S.	G. Wyndham	1900
				Ld Raglan	12 Nov 00
				E of Hardwicke	8 Aug 02
				E of Donoughmore	15 Oct 03
1st C. Works	**A. Akers-Douglas**	1900			
	(Ld Windsor 8 Aug 02 & Office out of cabinet)				

MINISTERS NOT IN CABINET					
Chief Sec. Ireland	G. BALFOUR	1900	*(for Junior Ministers see above)*		
	G. WYNDHAM	7 Nov 00			
	(8 Aug 02 office in cabinet)				
D. Lanc.	*(office in cabinet)*				
	SIR W. WALROND	8 Aug 02			
Paym.-Gen.	D OF MARLBOROUGH	1900			
	SIR S. CROSSLEY	11 Mar 02			
Postm.-Gen.	D OF NORFOLK	1900			
	M OF LONDONDERRY	2 Apr 00			
	(7 Nov 00 office in cabinet)				
1st C. Works	*(office in cabinet)*				
	LD WINDSOR	8 Aug 02			
Law Officers:			*P.S. to Treasury:*		
Att.-Gen.	SIR R. WEBSTER	1900		Sir W. Walrond	1900
	SIR R. FINLAY	7 May 00		Sir A. Acland Hood	8 Aug 02
Sol.-Gen.	SIR R. FINLAY	1900	*Junior Lds of Treasury:*		
	SIR E. CARSON	7 May 00		W. Hayes Fisher	1900-8 Aug 02
Ld Advoc.	A. MURRAY	1900		H. Anstruther	1900-11 Oct 03
	S. DICKSON	18 Oct 03		Ld Stanley[1]	1900-7 Nov 00
Sol.-Gen. Scotland	S. DICKSON	1900		A. Fellowes	7 Nov 00-15 Mar 05
	D. DUNDAS	18 Oct 03		H. Forster	8 Aug 02-4 Dec 05
	E. SALVESEN	30 Jan 05		Ld Balcarres[1]	11 Oct 03-4 Dec 05
	J. CLYDE	16 Oct 05		G. Loder	29 Mar 05-8 Apr 05
Att.-Gen. Ireland	J. ATKINSON	1900		Ld E. Talbot[1]	16 Jun 05-4 Dec 05
	J. CAMPBELL	4 Dec 05	*Lds in Waiting:*		
Sol.-Gen. Ireland	D. BARTON	1900		E of Clarendon	1900-30 Oct 00
	G. WRIGHT	30 Jan 00		Ld Harris	1900-4 Dec 00
	J. CAMPBELL	8 Jul 03		Ld Churchill (Vt)	1900-4 Dec 05
H.M. Household:				Ld Lawrence	1900-4 Dec 05
Treas.	VT CURZON[1] (Earl Howe)	1900		E of Kintore	1900-4 Dec 05
	V. CAVENDISH	3 Dec 00		Ld Bagot	1900-2 Jul 1901
	M OF HAMILTON[1]	11 Oct 03		E of Denbigh	1900-4 Dec 05
Comptr.	VT VALENTIA[1]	1900		Earl Howe	30 Oct 00-1 Oct 03
V. Chamb.	A. FELLOWES	1900		Ld Kenyon	4 Dec 00-4 Dec 05
	SIR A. ACLAND HOOD	3 Dec 00		E of Erroll	19 Oct 03-4 Dec 05
	LD WOLVERTON	17 Nov 02			
Ld Chamb.	E OF HOPETOUN	1900			
	E OF CLARENDON	12 Nov 00			
Ld Steward	E OF PEMBROKE & MONTGOMERY	1900			

[1] M.P. Not a member of the House of Lords.

CONSERVATIVE GOVERNMENT, 1900-1905 *(contd.)*

MINISTERS NOT IN CABINET

Capt. Gents at Arms	LD BELPER	1900
Capt. Yeomen of Guard	EARL WALDEGRAVE	1900
Master of Horse	D OF PORTLAND	1900
Master of Buckhounds	E OF COVENTRY	1900
	LD CHESHAM	2 Nov 00
	(office abolished 1901)	

LIBERAL GOVERNMENT, 1905-1908

	MINISTERS IN CABINET			JUNIOR MINISTERS ATTACHED	
P.M.	**Sir H. Campbell-Bannerman**	5 Dec 05-5 Apr 08			
Ld Pres.	**E of Crewe**	10 Dec 05			
Ld Chanc.	**Sir R. Reid** (*Ld Loreburn*)	10 Dec 05			
Privy S.	**M of Ripon**	10 Dec 05			
Exch.	**H. Asquith**	10 Dec 05	*Treasury:* *F.S.*	R. McKenna	12 Dec 05
				W. Runciman	29 Jan 07
For. O.	**Sir E. Grey**	10 Dec 05	*U-S.*	Ld E. Fitzmaurice[1] (Ld)	18 Dec 05
Home O.	**H. Gladstone**	10 Dec 05	*U-S.*	H. Samuel	12 Dec 05
Admir.	**Ld Tweedmouth**	10 Dec 05	*P. & F.S.:*	E. Robertson	12 Dec 05
			Civil Ld:	G. Lambert	18 Dec 05
Bd Ag. & Fish.	**Earl Carrington**	10 Dec 05			
Col. O.	**E of Elgin**	10 Dec 05	*U-S.*	W. Churchill	12 Dec 05
Bd Educ.	**A. Birrell**	10 Dec C5	*P.S.*	T. Lough	18 Dec 05
	R. McKenna	23 Jan 07			
India O.	**J. Morley**	10 Dec 05	*U-S.*	J. Ellis	12 Dec 05
				C. Hobhouse	29 Jan 07
Chief Sec. Ireland	**J. Bryce**	10 Dec 05	*Vice-Pres. Dept. Agric. for Ireland:*	Sir H. Plunkett	12 Dec 05
	A. Birrell	23 Jan 07		T. Russell	21 May 07
D. Lanc.	**Sir H. Fowler**	10 Dec 05			
Loc. Govt. Bd.	**J. Burns**	10 Dec 05	*P.S.*	W. Runciman	18 Dec 05
				T. Macnamara	29 Jan 07
Postm.-Gen.	**S. Buxton**	10 Dec 05			
Scotland	**J. Sinclair**	10 Dec 05			
B.o.T.	**D. Lloyd George**	10 Dec 05	*P.S.*	H. Kearley	18 Dec 05
War O.	**R. Haldane**	10 Dec 05	*U-S.*	E of Portsmouth	12 Dec 05
			F.S.	T. Buchanan	14 Dec 05
1st C. Works	*(office not in cabinet)*				
	L. Harcourt	27 Mar 07			

MINISTERS NOT IN CABINET

Paym.-Gen.	R. CAUSTON	12 Dec 05
1st C. Works	L. HARCOURT	10 Dec 05
	(27 Mar 07 office in cabinet)	

[1]M.P. Not a member of the House of Lords.

LIBERAL GOVERNMENT, 1905-1908 *(contd.)*

MINISTERS NOT IN CABINET

Law Officers:		
Att.-Gen.	SIR J. WALTON	12 Dec 05
	SIR W. ROBSON	28 Jan 08
Sol.-Gen.	SIR W. ROBSON	12 Dec 05
	SIR S. EVANS	28 Jan 08
Ld Advoc.	T. SHAW	12 Dec 05
Sol.-Gen. Scotland	A. URE	18 Dec 05
Att.-Gen. Ireland	R. CHERRY	20 Dec 05
Sol.-Gen. Ireland	R. BARRY	20 Dec 05
H.M. Household:		
Treas.	SIR E. STRACHEY	18 Dec 05
Comptr.	MASTER OF ELIBANK	18 Dec 05
V. Chamb.	W. BEAUMONT (*Ld Allendale*)	18 Dec 05
	J. FULLER	27 Feb 07
Ld Chamb.	VT ALTHORP	18 Dec 05
Ld Steward	LD HAWKESBURY (*1st E of Liverpool*)	18 Dec 05
	EARL BEAUCHAMP	31 Jul 07
Master of Horse	E OF SEFTON	18 Dec 05
	E OF GRANARD	6 Sep 07
Capt. Gents at Arms	EARL BEAUCHAMP	18 Dec 05
	LD DENMAN	31 Jul 07
Capt. Yeomen of Guard	D OF MANCHESTER	18 Dec 05
	LD ALLENDALE	29 Apr 07

P.S. to Treasury:	
G. Whiteley	12 Dec 05
Junior Lds of Treasury:	
H. Lewis	18 Dec 05-5 Apr 08
J. Pease	18 Dec 05-5 Apr 08
F. Freeman-Thomas	21 Dec 05-2 Feb 06
C. Norton	21 Dec 05-5 Apr 08
J. Fuller	2 Feb 06-27 Feb 07
J. Whitley	27 Feb 07-5 Apr 08
Lds in Waiting:	
Ld Denman	18 Dec 05-31 Jul 07
E of Granard	18 Dec 05-21 Aug 07
Ld Acton	18 Dec 05-5 Apr 08
Earl Granville	18 Dec 05-5 Apr 08
Ld Hamilton of Dalzell	18 Dec 05-5 Apr 08
Ld Colebrooke	20 Dec 05-5 Apr 08
Ld Herschell	31 Jul 07-5 Apr 08
Ld O'Hagan	1 Nov 07-5 Apr 08

LIBERAL GOVERNMENT, 1908-1915

	MINISTERS IN CABINET			JUNIOR MINISTERS ATTACHED	
P.M.	**H. Asquith**	5 Apr 08-25 May 15			
Ld Pres.	**Ld Tweedmouth**	12 Apr 08			
	Vt Wolverhampton	13 Oct 08			
	Earl Beauchamp	16 Jun 10			
	Vt Morley	3 Nov 10			
	Earl Beauchamp	5 Aug 14			
Ld Chanc.	**Ld Loreburn (Earl)**	12 Apr 08			
	Vt Haldane	10 Jun 12			
Privy S.	**M of Ripon**	12 Apr 08			
	E of Crewe	9 Oct 08			
	Earl Carrington	23 Oct 11			
	M of Crewe	13 Feb 12			
Exch.	**D. Lloyd George**	12 Apr 08	*Treasury:*		
			F.S.	C. Hobhouse	12 Apr 08
				T. McKinnon Wood	23 Oct 11
				C. Masterman	13 Feb 12
				E. Montagu	11 Feb 14
				F. Acland	3 Feb 15
For. O.	**Sir E. Grey**	12 Apr 08	*U-S.*	Ld Fitzmaurice	12 Apr 08
				T. McKinnon Wood	19 Oct 08
				F. Acland	23 Oct 11
				N. Primrose	4 Feb 15

LIBERAL GOVERNMENT, 1908-1915 *(contd.)*

	MINISTERS IN CABINET			JUNIOR MINISTERS ATTACHED	
Home O.	**H. Gladstone**	12 Apr 08	*U-S.*	H. Samuel	12 Apr 08
	W. Churchill	14 Feb 10		C. Masterman	7 Jul 09
	R. McKenna	23 Oct 11		E. Griffith	19 Feb 12
				C. Harmsworth	4 Feb 15
Admir.	**R. McKenna**	12 Apr 08	*P. & F.S.:*	T. Macnamara	13 Apr 08
	W. Churchill	23 Oct 11	*Civil Ld:*	G. Lambert	12 Apr 08
Bd Ag. & Fish.	**Earl Carrington**	12 Apr 08	*P.S.*	*(post not established)*	
				Sir E. Strachey (*Ld Strachie*)	20 Dec 09
	W. Runciman	23 Oct 11		Ld Lucas	23 Oct 11
	Ld Lucas	6 Aug 14		Sir H. Verney	10 Aug 14
Att. Gen.	*(office not in cabinet)*				
	Sir R. Isaacs	4 Jun 12			
	Sir J. Simon	19 Oct 13			
Col. O.	**E of Crewe**	12 Apr 08	*U-S.*	J. Seely	12 Apr 08
	L. Harcourt	3 Nov 10		Ld Lucas	23 Mar 11
				Ld Emmott	23 Oct 11
				Ld Islington	10 Aug 14
Bd Educ.	**W. Runciman**	12 Apr 08	*P.S.*	T. McKinnon Wood	13 Apr 08
	J. Pease	23 Oct 11		C. Trevelyan	19 Oct 08
				C. Addison	10 Aug 14
India O.	**J. Morley (Vt)**	12 Apr 08	*U-S.*	T. Buchanan	12 Apr 08
	E of Crewe	3 Nov 10		Master of Elibank	25 Jun 09
	Vt Morley	7 Mar 11		E. Montagu	20 Feb 10
	E of Crewe (M)	25 May 11		C. Roberts	17 Feb 14
Chief Sec. Ireland	**A. Birrell**	12 Apr 08	*V. Pres. Dept. Agric. Ireland*	T. Russell	12 Apr 08
D. Lanc.	**Sir H. Fowler** (*Vt Wolverhampton*)	12 Apr 08			
	Ld Fitzmaurice	13 Oct 08			
	H. Samuel	25 Jun 09			
	J. Pease	14 Feb 10			
	C. Hobhouse	23 Oct 11			
	C. Masterman	11 Feb 14			
	E. Montagu	3 Feb 15			
Loc. Govt. Bd	**J. Burns**	12 Apr 08	*P.S.*	C. Masterman	12 Apr 08
	H. Samuel	11 Feb 14		H. Lewis	7 Jul 09
Postm.-Gen.	**S. Buxton**	12 Apr 08	*Ass.*	*(post not established)*	
	H. Samuel	14 Feb 10		Sir H. Norman	3 Jan 10
	C. Hobhouse	11 Feb 14		C. Norton	20 Feb 10
Scotland	**J. Sinclair** (*Ld Pentland*)	12 Apr 08			
	T. McKinnon Wood	13 Feb 12			
B.o.T.	**W. Churchill**	12 Apr 08	*P.S.*	(Sir) H. Kearley	12 Apr 08
	S. Buxton	14 Feb 10		H. Tennant	10 Jan 09
	J. Burns	11 Feb 14		J. Robertson	25 Oct 11
	W. Runciman	5 Aug 14			
War O.	**R. Haldane (Vt)**	12 Apr 08	*F.S.*	F. Acland	12 Apr 08
	J. Seely	12 Jun 12		C. Mallet	4 Mar 10
	H. Asquith (P.M.)	30 Mar 14		F. Acland	31 Jan 11
	Earl Kitchener	5 Aug 14		H. Tennant	25 Oct 11
				H. Baker	14 Jun 12
			U-S.	Ld Lucas	12 Apr 08
				J. Seely	23 Mar 11
				H. Tennant	14 Jun 12
1st C. Works	**L. Harcourt**	12 Apr 08			
	Earl Beauchamp	3 Nov 10			
	Ld Emmott	6 Aug 14			

LIBERAL GOVERNMENT, 1908-1915 *(contd.)*

MINISTERS NOT IN CABINET

Paym.-Gen.	R. Causton (*Ld Southwark*)	12 Apr 08
	I. Guest (*Ld Ashby St Ledgers*)	23 Feb 10
	Ld Strachie	23 May 12
Law Officers:		
Att.-Gen.	Sir W. Robson	12 Apr 08
	Sir R. Isaacs	7 Oct 10
	(*4 Jun 12 office in cabinet*)	
Sol.-Gen.	Sir S. Evans	12 Apr 08
	Sir R. Isaacs	6 Mar 10
	Sir J. Simon	7 Oct 10
	Sir S. Buckmaster	19 Oct 13
Ld Advoc.	T. Shaw	12 Apr 08
	A. Ure	14 Feb 09
	R. Munro	30 Oct 13
Sol.-Gen. Scotland	A. Ure	12 Apr 08
	A. Dewar	18 Feb 09
	W. Hunter	18 Apr 10
	A. Anderson	3 Dec 11
	T. Morison	30 Oct 13
Att.-Gen. Ireland	R. Cherry	12 Apr 08
	R. Barry	2 Dec 09
	C. O'Connor	26 Sep 11
	I. O'Brien	24 Jun 12
	T. Molony	10 Apr 13
	J. Moriarty	20 Jun 13
	J. Pim	1 Jul 14
Sol.-Gen. Ireland	R. Barry	12 Apr 08
	C. O'Connor	2 Dec 09
	I. O'Brien	19 Oct 11
	T. Molony	24 Jun 12
	J. Moriarty	25 Apr 13
	J. Pim	20 Jun 13
	J. O'Connor	1 Jul 14
H.M. Household:		
Treas.	Sir E. Strachey	12 Apr 08
	W. Dudley Ward	20 Dec 09
	F. Guest	21 Feb 12
Comptr.	Master of Elibank	12 Apr 08
	E of Liverpool (2nd)	12 Jul 09
	Ld Saye & Sele	1 Nov 12
V. Chamb.	(Sir) J. Fuller	12 Apr 08
	G. Howard	6 Feb 11
Ld Chamb.	Vt Althorp (*Earl Spencer*)	12 Apr 08
	Ld Sandhurst	14 Feb 12
Ld Steward	Earl Beauchamp	12 Apr 08
	E of Chesterfield	22 Jun 10
Master of Horse	E of Granard	12 Apr 08
Capt. Gents at Arms	Ld Denman	12 Apr 08
	Ld Colebrooke	26 Jun 11
Capt. Yeomen of Guard	Ld Allendale (Vt)	12 Apr 08
	E of Craven	2 Oct 11

JUNIOR MINISTERS ATTACHED

P.S. to Treasury:		
	G. Whiteley	12 Apr 08
	J. Pease	3 Jun 08
	Master of Elibank	14 Feb 10
	P. Illingworth	7 Aug 12
	J. Gulland	24 Jan 15
Junior Lds of Treasury:		
	J. Pease	12 Apr 08-3 Jun 08
	H. Lewis	12 Apr 08-7 Jul 09
	C. Norton	12 Apr 08-20 Feb 10
	J. Whitley	12 Apr 08-20 Feb 10
	O. Partington	6 Jul 09-19 Jan 11
	J. Gulland	7 Jul 09-24 Jan 15
	W. Benn	20 Feb 10-25 May 15
	E. Soares	20 Feb 10-16 Apr 11
	P. Illingworth	28 Feb 10-7 Aug 12
	W. Jones	19 Jan 11-25 May 15
	F. Guest	16 Apr 11-21 Feb 12
	Sir A. Haworth	23 Feb 12-16 Apr 12
	H. Webb	16 Apr 12-25 May 15
	C. Beck	3 Feb 15-25 May 15
	W. Rea	3 Feb 15-25 May 15
Lds in Waiting:		
	Ld O'Hagan	12 Apr 08-15 Apr 10
	Ld Hamilton of Dalzell	12 Apr 08-2 Oct 11
	Ld Colebrooke	12 Apr 08-26 Jun 11
	Ld Herschell	12 Apr 08-25 May 15
	Ld Acton	12 Apr 08-25 May 15
	Earl Granville	12 Apr 08-25 May 15
	Ld Tweedmouth	15 Apr 10-4 Dec 11
	Ld Willingdon	19 Jul 11-31 Jan 13
	Vt Allendale	2 Oct 11-25 May 15
	Ld Loch	4 Dec 11-1 May 14
	Ld Ashby St Ledgers (*Ld Wimborne*)	31 Jan 13-8 Feb 15
	Ld Stanmore	1 May 14-25 May 15
	Ld Ranksborough	8 Feb 15-25 May 15

COALITION GOVERNMENT, 1915-1916

	MINISTERS IN CABINET			JUNIOR MINISTERS ATTACHED	
P.M.	**H. Asquith** (Lib)	25 May 15-5 Dec 16			
Ld Pres.	**M of Crewe** (Lib)	25 May 15			
Ld Chanc.	**Ld Buckmaster** (Lib)	25 May 15			
Privy S.	**Earl Curzon** (C)	25 May 15			
Exch.	**R. McKenna** (Lib)	25 May 15	*Treasury:*		
			F.S.	E. Montagu (Lib)	26 May 15
				(also D. Lanc., in cabinet from 11 Jan 16)	
				T. McKinnon Wood (Lib)	9 Jul 16
				(also D. Lanc. in cabinet)	
For. O.	**Sir E. Grey** (Lib) **(Vt)**	25 May 15	*U-S.*	Ld R. Cecil[1] (C)	30 May 15
				(also Blockade, in cabinet from 23 Feb 16)	
			Ass.	Ld Newton (C)	18 Aug 16
Home O.	**Sir J. Simon** (Lib)	25 May 15	*U-S.*	W. Brace (Lab)	30 May 15
	Sir H. Samuel (Lib)	10 Jan 16			
Admir.	**A. Balfour** (C)	25 May 15	*P. & F.S.:*	T. Macnamara (Lib)	30 May 15
			Civil Ld:	D of Devonshire (C)	9 Jun 15
				E of Lytton (C)	26 Jul 16
Bd Ag. & Fish.	**E of Selborne** (C)	25 May 15	*P.S.*	F. Acland (Lib)	30 May 15
	E. of Crawford (C)	11 Jul 16			
Att.-Gen.	**Sir E. Carson** (C)	25 May 15			
	Sir F. Smith (C)	3 Nov 15			
Blockade	**Ld R. Cecil**[1] (C)	23 Feb 16			
	(also U-S. at F.O.)				
Col. O.	**A. Bonar Law** (C)	25 May 15	*U-S.*	A. Steel-Maitland (C)	30 May 15
Bd Educ.	**A. Henderson** (Lab)	25 May 15	*P.S.*	H. Lewis (Lib)	30 May 15
	M of Crewe (Lib)	18 Aug 16			
Health & Loc. Govt Bd	**W. Long** (C)	25 May 15	*P.S.*	W. Hayes Fisher (C)	30 May 15
India O.	**A. Chamberlain** (C)	25 May 15	*U-S.*	Ld Islington (Lib)	30 May 15
Chief Sec. Ireland	**A. Birrell** (Lib)	25 May 15	*V. Pres. Dept. Agric. & Technical Instruction Ireland:*		
	(office vacant 3 May 16)			T. Russell (Lib)	30 May 15
	H. Duke (C)	31 Jul 16			
D. Lanc.	**W. Churchill** (Lib)	25 May 15			
	H. Samuel (Lib)	25 Nov 15			
	E. Montagu (Lib)	11 Jan 16			
	(also F.S. at Treasury)				
	T. McKinnon Wood (Lib)	9 Jul 16			
	(also F.S. at Treasury)				
Munitions	**D. Lloyd George** (Lib)	25 May 15	*P.S.*	C. Addison (Lib)	30 May 15-8 Dec 16
	E. Montagu (Lib)	9 Jul 16		A. Lee (C)	11 Nov 15[2]-9 Jul 16
Paym.-Gen.	*(office not in cabinet)*				
	A. Henderson (Lab)	18 Aug 16			
Min. without Portfolio	**M of Lansdowne** (C)	25 May 15			
Scotland	**T. McKinnon Wood** (Lib)	25 May 15			
	H. Tennant (Lib)	9 Jul 16			
B.o.T.	**W. Runciman** (Lib)	25 May 15	*P.S.*	E. Pretyman (C)	30 May 15
War O.	**Earl Kitchener**	25 May 15	*U-S.*	H. Tennant (Lib)	30 May 15
	D. Lloyd George (Lib)	6 Jul 16		E of Derby (C)	6 Jul 16
			F.S.	H. Forster (C)	30 May 15
1st C. Works	**L. Harcourt (Vt)** (Lib)	25 May 15			

[1] M.P. Not a member of the House of Lords.
[2] Date of first reply in Commons as *Parliamentary (Military) Secretary to the Munitions Department.*

COALITION GOVERNMENT, 1915-1916 *(contd.)*

MINISTERS NOT IN CABINET

Paym.-Gen.	Ld Newton (C) (*A. Henderson* 18 *Aug* 16 *&* *office in cabinet)*	9 Jun 15
Postm.-Gen.	H. Samuel (Lib) J. Pease (Lib)	26 May 15 18 Jan 16
Law Officers:		
Att.-Gen.	*(office in cabinet)*	
Sol.-Gen.	Sir F. Smith (C) (Sir) G. Cave (C)	2 Jun 15 8 Nov 15
Ld Advoc.	R. Munro (Lib)	8 Jun 15
Sol.-Gen. Scotland	T. Morison (Lib)	8 Jun 15
Att.-Gen. Ireland	J. Gordon (C) J. Campbell (C)	8 Jun 15 9 Apr 16
Sol.-Gen. Ireland	J. O'Connor (Nat)	8 Jun 15
H.M. Household:		
Treas.	J. Hope (C)	30 May 15
Comptr.	C. Roberts (Lib)	30 May 15
V. Chamb.	C. Beck (Lib)	30 May 15
Ld Chamb.	Ld Sandhurst (Lib)	9 Jun 15
Ld Steward	Ld Farquhar (C)	9 Jun 15
Master of Horse	E of Chesterfield (Lib)	9 Jun 15
Capt. Gents at Arms	Ld Colebrooke (Lib)	9 Jun 15
Capt. Yeomen of Guard	Ld Suffield (C)	9 Jun 15

JUNIOR MINISTERS ATTACHED

Ass.	H. Pike Pease (C)	30 May 15
P.S. to Treasury:		
	J. Gulland (Lib)	30 May 15-5 Dec 16
	Ld E. Talbot[1] (C)	30 May 15-5 Dec 16
Junior Lds of Treasury:		
	G. Howard (Lib)	27 May 15-5 Dec 16
	G. Roberts (Lab)	27 May 15-5 Dec 16
	W. Bridgeman (C)	27 May 15-5 Dec 16
	W. Rea (Lib)	27 May 15-5 Dec 16
Lds in Waiting:		
	Ld Herschell (Lib)	9 Jun 15-5 Dec 16
	Vt Allendale (Lib)	9 Jun 15-5 Dec 16
	Ld Stanmore (Lib)	9 Jun 15-5 Dec 16
	Ld Ranksborough (Lib)	9 Jun 15-5 Dec 16
	Vt Valentia[1] (C)	9 Jun 15-5 Dec 16
	Ld Hylton (C)	9 Jun 15-5 Dec 16

COALITION GOVERNMENT, 1916-1922

From 6 Dec 1916 to 31 Oct 1919 there was an inner war cabinet of 5-7 ministers. **D. Lloyd George, Earl Curzon,** and **A. Bonar Law** were members throughout; the other members were,

A. Henderson (Lab) 10 Dec 16-12 Aug 17
Vt Milner (C) 10 Dec 16-18 Apr 18
J. Smuts[2] 22 Jun 17-10 Jan 19
G. Barnes (Lab) 29 May 17-3 Aug 17, 13 Aug 17-10 Jan 19
A. Chamberlain (C) 18 Apr 18-31 Oct 19
Sir E. Geddes (C) 10 Jan 19-31 Oct 19

MINISTERS IN CABINET

P.M.	**D. Lloyd George** (Lib)	6 Dec 16-19 Oct 22
Ld Pres.	**Earl Curzon** (C) **A. Balfour** (C)	10 Dec 16 23 Oct 19
Ld Chanc.	**Ld Finlay** (C) **Ld Birkenhead (Vt)** (C)	10 Dec 16 10 Jan 19
Privy S.	**E of Crawford** (C) **A. Bonar Law** (C) **A. Chamberlain** (C)	15 Dec 16 10 Jan 19 23 Mar 21
Exch.	**A. Bonar Law** (C) **A. Chamberlain** (C) **Sir R. Horne** (C)	10 Dec 16 10 Jan 19 1 Apr 21

JUNIOR MINISTERS ATTACHED

Treasury:		
F.S.	Sir H. Lever (Lib)	15 Dec 16-19 May 19
	S. Baldwin (C)	18 Jun 17-1 Apr 21
	E. Young (Lib)	1 Apr 21-19 Oct 22

[1]M.P. Not a member of the House of Lords.
[2]Not a member of the House of Commons.

COALITION GOVERNMENT, 1916-1922 *(contd.)*

	MINISTERS IN CABINET			JUNIOR MINISTERS ATTACHED	
For. O.	**A. Balfour** (C)	10 Dec 16	*U-S.*	Ld R. Cecil[1] (C)	10 Dec 16
	Earl Curzon (C)	23 Oct 19		C. Harmsworth (Lib)	10 Jan 19
	(**Marquess**)		*Ass. U-S.*		
				Ld Newton (C)	10 Dec 16
				(*post abolished* 10 *Jan* 1919)	
Home O.	**Sir G. Cave** (**Vt**) (C)	10 Dec 16	*U-S.*	W. Brace (Lab)	10 Dec 16
	E. Shortt (Lib)	10 Jan 19		Sir H. Greenwood (Lib)	10 Jan 19
				(Sir) J. Baird (C)	29 Apr 19
Admir.	**Sir E. Carson** (C)	10 Dec 16	*P. & F.S.:*		
	Sir E. Geddes (C)	17 Jul 17		T. Macnamara (Lib)	10 Dec 16
	W. Long (C)	10 Jan 19		Sir J. Craig (C)	2 Apr 20
	Ld Lee (C)	13 Feb 21		L. Amery (C)	1 Apr 21
			P.S. Addit.:		
				E of Lytton (C)	7 Feb 17
				(*post abolished* 27 *Jan* 1919)	
			Civil Ld:		
				E. Pretyman (C)	14 Dec 16
				E of Lytton (C)	27 Jan 19
				E of Onslow (C)	26 Oct 20
				B. Eyres-Monsell (C)	1 Apr 21
			2nd Civil Ld:		
				A. Pease (C)	10 Dec 16
				(*post abolished* 10 *Jan* 1919)	
Bd Ag. & Fish.	**R. Prothero** (C)	10 Dec 16	*P.S.*	Sir R. Winfrey (Lib)	14 Dec 16-10 Jan 19
	(*Ld Ernle*)			D of Marlborough (C)	18 Feb 17-21 Mar 18
	Ld Lee (C)	15 Aug 19		Vt Goschen (C)	26 Mar 18-18 Jun 18
	(*Bd renamed Min.* 15 *Aug* 19)			Ld Clinton (C)	18 Jun 18-10 Jan 19
	Sir A. Griffith-Boscawen (C)	13 Feb 21		Sir A. Griffith-Boscawen (C)	10 Jan 19-13 Feb 21
				(*& Dep. Min. Fisheries* 18 *Nov* 19)	
				E of Onslow (C)	5 Apr 21-7 Apr 21
				E of Ancaster (C)	7 Apr 21-19 Oct 22
				(*& Dep. Min. Fisheries* 28 *Oct* 21)	
Att. Gen.	(*office not in cabinet*)				
	Sir G. Hewart (Lib)	7 Nov 21			
	(*Sir E. Pollock* (*C*) 6 *Mar* 22 *& office not in cabinet*)				
Col. O.	**W. Long** (C)	10 Dec 16	*U-S.*	(Sir) A. Steel-Maitland (C)	10 Dec 16
	Vt Milner (C)	10 Jan 19		W. Hewins (C)	26 Sep 17
	W. Churchill (Lib)	13 Feb 21		L. Amery (C)	10 Jan 19
				E. Wood (C)	1 Apr 21
Bd Educ.	**H. Fisher** (Lib)	10 Dec 16	*P.S.*	(Sir) H. Lewis (Lib)	10 Dec 16
Health	(*Dept. under Loc. Govt Bd: see below*)		*P.S.* (*Loc. Govt Bd*):		
				W. Hayes Fisher (C)	10 Dec 16
	C. Addison (Lib)	24 Jun 19		S. Walsh (Lab)	28 Jun 17
	Sir A. Mond (Lib)	1 Apr 21		W. Astor (Vt) (C)	27 Jan 19
				E of Onslow (C)	7 Apr 21
India O.	**A. Chamberlain** (C)	10 Dec 16	*U-S.*	Ld Islington (Lib)	10 Dec 16
	E. Montagu (Lib)	17 Jul 17		Ld Sinha (Lib)	10 Jan 19
	Vt Peel (C)	19 Mar 22		E of Lytton (C)	22 Sep 20
				Earl Winterton[1] (C)	20 Mar 22
Chief Sec. Ireland	**(Sir) H. Duke** (C)	10 Dec 16	*V. Pres. Dept. Agric. & Technical Instruction for Ireland:*		
	E. Shortt (Lib)	5 May 18			
	I. Macpherson (Lib)	10 Jan 19		(Sir) T. Russell (Lib)	10 Dec 16
	Sir H. Greenwood (Lib)	2 Apr 20		H. Barrie (C)	15 Jan 19
Ld Lieut. Ireland	**Vt French** (*E of Ypres*)	6 May 18			
	(*Not usually ministerial office. In cabinet only* 28 *Oct* 19-2 *Apr* 21)				

[1]M.P. Not a member of the House of Lords.

COALITION GOVERNMENT, 1916-1922 *(contd.)*

	MINISTERS IN CABINET	JUNIOR MINISTERS ATTACHED
Lab.	**J. Hodge** (Lab) 10 Dec 16 **G. Roberts** (Lab) 17 Aug 17 **Sir R. Horne** (C) 10 Jan 19 **T. Macnamara** (Lib) 19 Mar 20	*P.S.* W. Bridgeman (C) 22 Dec 16 G. Wardle (Lab) 10 Jan 19 Sir A. Montague-Barlow (C) 2 April 20
D. Lanc.	**Sir F. Cawley** (Lib) 10 Dec 16 **Ld Beaverbrook** (C) 10 Feb 18 *(& Min. of Propaganda/Information)* **Ld Downham** (C) 4 Nov 18 *(E of Crawford (C) 10 Jan 19 & office not in cabinet)*	
Loc. Govt. Bd	**Ld Rhondda** (Lib) 10 Dec 16 **W. Hayes Fisher** (C) 28 Jun 17 *(Ld Downham)* **Sir A. Geddes** (C) 4 Nov 18 **C. Addison** (Lib) 10 Jan 19 *(24 Jun 19 became Min. of Health: see above)*	*(for Junior Ministers see above, under Health)*
Munitions (Supply)	**C. Addison** (Lib) 10 Dec 16 **W. Churchill** (Lib) 17 Jul 17 *(Ld Inverforth Min. of Supply 10 Jan 19 & office not in cabinet)*	*P.S.* Sir L. Worthington-Evans (C) 14 Dec 16-30 Jan 18 F. Kellaway (Lib) 14 Dec 16-1 Apr 20 J. Seely (Lib) 10 Jul 18-10 Jan 19 J. Baird (C) 10 Jan 19-27 Jan 19 *P. & F.S.:* Sir L. Worthington-Evans (C) 30 Jan 18-18 Jul 18 J. Hope (C) 27 Jan 19-31 Mar 21
Min. without Portfolio	**A. Henderson** (Lab) 10 Dec 16-12 Aug 17 **Vt Milner** (C) 10 Dec 16-18 Apr 18 **J. Smuts**[1] 22 Jun 17-10 Jan 19 **Sir E. Carson** (C) 17 Jul 17-21 Jan 18 **G. Barnes** (Lab) 13 Aug 17-27 Jan 20 **A. Chamberlain** (C) 18 Apr 18-10 Jan 19 **Sir E. Geddes** (C) 10 Jan 19-19 May 19 **Sir L. Worthington-Evans** (C) 2 Apr 20-13 Feb 21 **C. Addison** (Lib) 1 Apr 21-14 Jul 21	
Scotland	**R. Munro** (Lib) 10 Dec 16	*P.S. Min. of Health for Scotland:* (Sir) J. Pratt (Lib) 8 Aug 19
B.o.T.	**Sir A. Stanley** (Lib) 10 Dec 16 **Sir A. Geddes** (C) 26 May 19 **Sir R. Horne** (C) 19 Mar 20 **S. Baldwin** (C) 1 Apr 21	*P.S.* G. Roberts (Lab) 14 Dec 16 G. Wardle (Lab) 17 Aug 17 W. Bridgeman (C) 10 Jan 19 Sir P. Lloyd-Greame (C) 22 Aug 20 Sir W. Mitchell-Thomson (C) 1 Apr 21 *Sec. Dept. Overseas Trade:* Sir A. Steel-Maitland (C) 14 Sep 17 Sir H. Greenwood (Lib) 29 Apr 19 F. Kellaway (Lib) 2 Apr 20 Sir P. Lloyd-Greame (C) 1 Apr 21 *(Director Overseas Trade Dept.)* *P.S. Mines Dept.:* W. Bridgeman (C) 22 Aug 20

[1] Not a member of the House of Commons.

COALITION GOVERNMENT, 1916-1922 *(contd.)*

	MINISTERS IN CABINET			JUNIOR MINISTERS ATTACHED	
Transp.	*(office not established)*		*P.S.*	Sir R. Williams (Lib)	23 Sep 19
	Sir E. Geddes (C)	19 May 19		A. Neal (Lib)	28 Nov 19
	(Vt Peel 7 Nov 21 & office not in cabinet)				
	E of Crawford (C)	12 Apr 22			
War O.	**E of Derby** (C)	10 Dec 16	*U-S.*	I. Macpherson (Lib)	14 Dec 16
	Vt Milner (C)	18 Apr 18		Vt Peel (C)	10 Jan 19
	(10 *Jan* 19 *War O. & Air Min. combined)*			Sir R. Sanders (C)	1 Apr 21
			F.S.	H. Forster (Ld) (C)	10 Dec 16
	W. Churchill (Lib)	10 Jan 19		Sir A. Williamson (Lib)	18 Dec 19
	(13 *Feb* 21 *War O. only)*			G. Stanley (C)	1 Apr 21
	Sir L. Worthington-Evans (C)	13 Feb 21	*P.S.*	Earl Stanhope (C)	14 Dec 16
				(post abolished 10 *Jan* 1919)	
1st C. Works	*(office not in cabinet)*				
	E of Crawford (C)	7 Apr 22			

	MINISTERS NOT IN CABINET			JUNIOR MINISTERS ATTACHED	
Air	Ld Cowdray (Lib)	3 Jan 17	*P.S. Air Council:*		
	Ld Rothermere (Lib)	26 Nov 17		J. Baird (C)	14 Dec 16
	Ld Weir (Lib)	26 Apr 18		*(post abolished* 10 *Jan* 19)	
	(War O. & Air Min. combined 10 *Jan* 19, *see above)*		*U-S.*	J. Seely (Lib)	10 Jan 19
	W. Churchill (Lib)	10 Jan 19		G. Tryon (C)	22 Dec 19
	F. Guest (Lib)	1 Apr 21		M of Londonderry (C)	2 Apr 20
				Ld Gorell (Lib)	18 Jul 21
Blockade	Ld R. Cecil[1] (C)	10 Dec 16	*P.S.*	F. Leverton Harris (C)	22 Dec 16
	(also U-S. at F.O.)			*(post abolished* 10 *Jan* 19)	
	Sir L. Worthington-Evans (C)	18 Jul 18			
	(office abolished 10 *Jan* 1919)				
Food Control	Vt Devonport (Lib)	10 Dec 16	*P.S.*	(Sir) C. Bathurst (C)	12 Dec 16
	Ld Rhondda (Vt) (Lib)	19 Jun 17		J. Clynes (Lab)	2 Jul 17
	J. Clynes (Lab)	9 Jul 18		W. Astor (C)	18 Jul 18
	G. Roberts (Lab)	10 Jan 19		C. McCurdy (Lib)	27 Jan 19
	C. McCurdy (Lib)	19 Mar 20		Sir W. Mitchell-Thomson (C)	19 Apr 20
	(office abolished 31 *Mar* 21)				
Ld Chanc. Ireland	Sir I. O'Brien (Lib)	10 Dec 16			
	Sir J. Campbell (C)	4 Jun 18			
	Sir J. Ross (C)	27 Jun 21			
D. Lanc.	*(office of cabinet rank see above)*				
	E of Crawford (C)	10 Jan 19			
	Vt Peel (C)	1 Apr 21			
	Sir W. Sutherland (Lib)	7 Apr 22			
Nat. S.	N. Chamberlain	19 Aug 16	*P.S.*	S. Walsh (Lab)	17 Mar 17-28 Jun 17
	Sir A. Geddes (C)	17 Aug 17		C. Beck (Lib)	28 Jun 17-19 Dec 19
	(office held jointly with Reconstruction Jan-May 19 *and with B of Trade May-Aug* 19 *and formally abolished* 19 *Dec* 19)			Vt Peel (C)	15 Apr 18-10 Jan 19
				(post abolished 19 *Dec* 19)	
Paym.-Gen.	Sir J. Compton-Rickett (Lib)	15 Dec 16			
	Sir T. Walters (Lib)	26 Oct 19			
Pensions	G. Barnes (Lab)	10 Dec 16	*P.S.*	Sir A. Griffith-Boscawen (C)	22 Dec 16
	J. Hodge (Lab)	17 Aug 17		Sir J. Craig (C)	10 Jan 19
	Sir L. Worthington-Evans (C)	10 Jan 19		G. Tryon (C)	2 Apr 20
	I. Macpherson (Lib)	2 Apr 20			
Postm.-Gen.	A. Illingworth (Lib)	10 Dec 16	*Ass.*	H. Pike Pease (C)	10 Dec 16
	F. Kellaway (Lib)	1 Apr 21			
Reconstruction	C. Addison (Lib)	17 Jul 17		*(for Junior Ministers see above, under National Service & Reconstruction)*	
	(office combined with Nat.S. 10 *Jan* 19)				

[1]M.P. Not a member of the House of Lords.

COALITION GOVERNMENT, 1916-1922 *(contd.)*

MINISTERS NOT IN CABINET		
Shipping	SIR J. MACLAY (LD) (Lib)	10 Dec 16
	(*office abolished* 31 *Mar* 21)	
Supply	LD INVERFORTH (C)	10 Jan 19
	(*office abolished* 31 *Mar* 21)	
Transp.	(*office in cabinet* 19 *May* 19-7 *Nov* 21)	
	VT PEEL (C)	7 Nov 21
	(*E of Crawford* 12 *Apr* 22 *& office in cabinet*)	
1*st C. Works*	SIR A. MOND (Lib)	10 Dec 16
	E OF CRAWFORD (C)	1 Apr 21
	(*office in cabinet* 7 *Apr* 22)	

JUNIOR MINISTERS ATTACHED		
P.S.	Sir L. Chiozza Money (Lib)	22 Dec 16
	L. Wilson (C)	10 Jan 19
	(*for Junior Ministers see above*)	

Law Officers:

Att.-Gen.	SIR F. SMITH (C) (*Ld Birkenhead*)	10 Dec 16
	SIR G. HEWART (Lib)	10 Jan 19
	(*office in cabinet* 7 *Nov* 21)	
	SIR E. POLLOCK (C)	6 Mar 22
Sol.-.Gen.	SIR G. HEWART (Lib)	10 Dec 16
	SIR E. POLLOCK (C)	10 Jan 19
	(SIR) L. SCOTT (C)	6 Mar 22
Ld Advoc.	J. CLYDE (C)	10 Dec 16
	T. MORISON (Lib)	25 Mar 20
	C. MURRAY (C)	5 Mar 22
Sol.-Gen. Scotland	T. MORISON (Lib)	10 Dec 16
	C. MURRAY (C)	25 Mar 20
	A. BRIGGS CONSTABLE (C)	16 Mar 22
	W. WATSON (C)	24 Jul 22
Att.-Gen. Ireland	J. CAMPBELL (C)	20 Dec 16
	J. O'CONNOR (Nat)	8 Jan 17
	A. SAMUELS (C)	7 Apr 18
	D. HENRY (C)	6 Jul 19
	T. BROWN (C)	5 Aug 21
	(*office vacant from* 16 *Nov* 21)	
Sol.-Gen. Ireland	J. CHAMBERS (C)	19 Mar 17
	A. SAMUELS (C)	12 Sep 17
	J. POWELL[2] (C)	7 Apr 18
	D. HENRY (C)	27 Nov 18
	D. WILSON (C)	6 Jul 19
	T. BROWN (C)	12 Jun 21
	(*office vacant from* 5 *Aug* 21)	

P.S. to Treasury:

Ld E. Talbot[1] (C)	14 Dec 16-1 Apr 21
N. Primrose (Lib)	14 Dec 16-2 Mar 17
F. Guest (Lib)	2 Mar 17-1 Apr 21
C. McCurdy (Lib)	1 Apr 21-19 Oct 22
L. Wilson (C)	1 Apr 21-19 Oct 22

Junior Lds of Treasury:

J. Hope (C)	14 Dec 16-27 Jan 19
J. Pratt (Lib)	14 Dec 16-8 Aug 19
S. Baldwin (C)	29 Jan 17-18 Jun 17
J. Parker (Lab)	29 Jan 17-19 Oct 22
J. Towyn Jones (Lib)	29 Jan 17-4 Jul 22
(Sir) R. Sanders (C)	5 Feb 19-1 Apr 21
Sir G. Collins (Lib)	8 Aug 19-10 Feb 20
W. Edge (Lib)	18 Aug 19-1 Aug 22
Sir W. Sutherland (Lib)	15 Feb 20-7 Apr 22
Sir J. Gilmour (C)	1 Apr 21-19 Oct 22
T. Lewis (Lib)	4 Jul 22-26 Jul 22

H.M. Household:

Treas.	(SIR) J. CRAIG (C)	14 Dec 16
	(*office vacant* 22 *Jan* 18)	
	R. SANDERS (C)	11 Jun 18
	B. EYRES-MONSELL (C)	5 Feb 19
	G. GIBBS (C)	1 Apr 21
Comptr.	SIR E. CORNWALL (Lib)	14 Dec 16
	G. STANLEY (C)	28 Feb 19
	H. BARNSTON (C)	7 Apr 21
V. Chamb.	C. BECK (Lib)	14 Dec 16
	W. DUDLEY WARD (Lib)	9 Dec 17
Ld Chamb.	LD SANDHURST (Vt) (Lib)	14 Dec 16
	D OF ATHOLL (C)	20 Nov 21
Ld Steward	LD FARQUHAR (Vt) (C)	14 Dec 16
Master of Horse	E OF CHESTERFIELD (Lib)	14 Dec 16
Capt. Gents at Arms	LD COLEBROOKE (Lib)	14 Dec 16

Lds in Waiting:

Ld Herschell (Lib)	14 Dec 16-11 Feb 19
Ld Stanmore (Lib)	14 Dec 16-19 Oct 22
Ld Ranksborough (Lib)	14 Dec 16-4 Apr 21
Vt Valentia[1] (C)	14 Dec 16-19 Oct 22
Ld Hylton (C)	14 Dec 16-18 May 18
Ld Kenyon (C)	14 Dec 16-11 Sep 18
Ld Somerleyton (C)	18 May 18-19 Oct 22
E of Jersey (C)	11 Jan 19-17 Aug 19
E of Bradford (C)	11 Feb 19-19 Oct 22
E of Onslow (C)	17 Aug 19-21 Nov 20
E of Lucan (C)	12 Nov 20-19 Oct 22
E of Clarendon (C)	7 Apr 21-19 Oct 22

[1]M.P. Not a member of the House of Lords. Viscount Valentia became a U.K. Peer (Ld Annesley) in 1917.
[2]Not a member of the House of Commons.

COALITION GOVERNMENT, 1916-1922 (*contd.*)

	MINISTERS NOT IN CABINET			JUNIOR MINISTERS ATTACHED	
H.M. Household:					
Capt.	Ld Suffied (C)	14 Dec 16			
Yeomen of Guard	Ld Hylton (C)	21 May 18			

CONSERVATIVE GOVERNMENT, 1922-1924

	MINISTERS IN CABINET			JUNIOR MINISTERS ATTACHED	
P.M.	**A. Bonar Law**	23 Oct 22-20 May 23			
	S. Baldwin	22 May 23-22 Jan 24			
Ld Pres.	**M of Salisbury**	24 Oct 22			
Ld Chanc.	**Vt Cave**	24 Oct 22			
Privy S.	(*office vacant*)				
	Ld R. Cecil[1]	25 May 23			
Exch.	**S. Baldwin**	24 Oct 22	*Treasury:*		
	(*& P.M. from 22 May* 23)		*F.S.*	J. Hills	6 Nov 22
	N. Chamberlain	27 Aug 23		A. Boyd-Carpenter	12 Mar 23
F.S. to Treasury	(*office not in cabinet*)			(*Sir W. Joynson-Hicks* 25 *May* 23 *& seat in cabinet*)	
	Sir W. Joynson-Hicks	25 May 23			
	(*W. Guinness* 5 *Oct* 23 *& office not in cabinet*)			W. Guinness	5 Oct 23
For. O.	**Marquess Curzon**	24 Oct 22	*U-S.*	R. McNeill	31 Oct 22
Home O.	**W. Bridgeman**	24 Oct 22	*U-S.*	G. Stanley	31 Oct 22
				G. Locker-Lampson	12 Mar 23
Admir.	**L. Amery**	24 Oct 22	*P. & F.S.:*		
				B. Eyres-Monsell	31 Oct 22
				A. Boyd-Carpenter	25 May 23
			Civil Ld:		
				M of Linlithgow	31 Oct 22
Ag. & Fish.	**Sir R. Sanders**	24 Oct 22	*P.S. Ag. & Deputy Min. Fisheries:*		
				E of Ancaster	31 Oct 22
Air	(*office not in cabinet*)		*U-S.*	D of Sutherland	31 Oct 22
	Sir S. Hoare	25 May 23			
Col. O.	**D of Devonshire**	24 Oct 22	*U-S*	W. Ormsby-Gore	31 Oct 22
Bd Educ.	**E. Wood**	24 Oct 22	*P.S.*	Ld E. Percy[1]	21 Mar 23
				E of Onslow	25 May 23
Health	**Sir A. Griffith-Boscawen**	24 Oct 22	*P.S.*	E of Onslow	31 Oct 22
				Ld E. Percy[1]	25 May 23
	N. Chamberlain	7 Mar 23			
	Sir W. Joynson-Hicks	27 Aug 23			
India O.	**Vt Peel**	24 Oct 22	*U-S.*	Earl Winterton[1]	31 Oct 22
Lab.	**Sir A. Montague-Barlow**	31 Oct 22	*P.S.*	A. Boyd-Carpenter	6 Nov 22
				H. Betterton	12 Mar 23
D. Lanc.	**M of Salisbury**	24 Oct 22			
	(*J. Davidson & office not in cabinet* 25 *May* 23)				
Postm.-Gen.	(*office not in cabinet*)				
	Sir L. Worthington-Evans	28 May 23			
Scotland	**Vt Novar**	24 Oct 22	*P.S. Min. of Health for Scotland:*		
				J. Kidd	31 Oct 22
				W. Elliot	15 Jan 23

[1] M.P. Not a member of the House of Lords.

CONSERVATIVE GOVERNMENT, 1922-1924 *(contd.)*

MINISTERS IN CABINET

B.o.T.	**Sir P. Lloyd-Greame**	24 Oct 22
War O.	**E of Derby**	24 Oct 22

JUNIOR MINISTERS ATTACHED

P.S.	Vt Wolmer[1]	31 Oct 22
Sec. Overseas Trade Dept.:	Sir W. Joynson-Hicks	31 Oct 22-12 Mar 23
	A. Buckley	12 Mar 23-18 Nov 23
P.S. Mines Dept.:	G. Lane-Fox	6 Nov 22
U-S.	W. Guinness	31 Oct 22
	W. Ashley	8 Oct 23
F.S.	S. Jackson	31 Oct 22
	R. Gwynne	15 Mar 23

MINISTERS NOT IN CABINET

Air	Sir S. Hoare	31 Oct 22
	(office in cabinet 25 *May* 23)	
D. Lanc.	*(office in cabinet)*	
	J. Davidson	25 May 23
Paym.-Gen.	*(office vacant)*	
	N. Chamberlain	5 Feb 23
	Sir W. Joynson-Hicks	15 Mar 23
	A. Boyd-Carpenter	25 May 23
Pensions	G. Tryon	31 Oct 22
Postm.-Gen.	N. Chamberlain	31 Oct 22
	Sir W. Joynson-Hicks	7 Mar 23
	(*Sir L. Worthington-Evans & office in cabinet* 28 *May* 23)	
Transp.	Sir J. Baird	31 Oct 22
1st C. Works	Sir J. Baird	31 Oct 22

JUNIOR MINISTERS ATTACHED

P.S. (Pensions)	C. Craig	13 Feb 23
P.S. Office of Works & Min. of Transp.:	W. Ashley	31 Oct 22
	J. Moore-Brabazon	8 Oct 23
	(to Min. Transp. only)	

Law Officers:

Att.-Gen.	Sir D. Hogg	24 Oct 22
Sol.-Gen.	Sir T. Inskip	31 Oct 22
Ld Advoc.	W. Watson	24 Oct 22
Sol.-Gen. Scotland	D. Fleming[2]	6 Nov 22
	F. Thomson	5 Apr 23

P.S. to Treasury:

L. Wilson	31 Oct 22
B. Eyres-Monsell	25 Jul 23

Junior Lds of Treasury:

D. King	31 Oct 22-22 Jan 24
A. Buckley	31 Oct 22-12 Mar 23
G. Hennessy	11 Dec 22-22 Jan 24
F. Thomson	7 Feb 23-10 Apr 23
W. Cope	20 Mar 23-22 Jan 24
P. Ford	10 Apr 23-20 Dec 23
Sir J. Gilmour	20 Dec 23-22 Jan 24

H.M. Household:

Treas.	G. Gibbs	6 Nov 22
Comptr.	H. Barnston	31 Oct 22
V. Chamb.	D. Hacking	20 Nov 22
Ld Chamb.	E of Cromer	20 Nov 22
Ld Steward	E of Shaftesbury	20 Nov 22
Master of Horse	M of Bath	20 Nov 22
Capt. Gents at Arms	E of Clarendon	20 Nov 22
Capt. Yeomen of Guard	Ld Hylton	20 Nov 22

Lds in Waiting:

Vt Valentia	20 Nov 22-22 Jan 24
Ld Somerleyton	20 Nov 22-22 Jan 24
E of Bradford	20 Nov 22-22 Jan 24
E of Lucan	20 Nov 22-22 Jan 24
E of Malmesbury	20 Nov 22-22 Jan 24
E of Albemarle	20 Nov 22-22 Jan 24

[1] M.P. Not a member of the House of Lords.
[2] Not a member of the House of Commons.

LABOUR GOVERNMENT, 1924

MINISTERS IN CABINET			JUNIOR MINISTERS ATTACHED		
P.M.	**R. MacDonald**	22 Jan 24-3 Nov 24			
Ld Pres.	**Ld Parmoor**	22 Jan 24			
Ld Chanc.	**Vt Haldane**	22 Jan 24			
Privy S.	**J. Clynes**	22 Jan 24			
Exch.	**P. Snowden**	22 Jan 24	*Treasury:*		
			F.S.	W. Graham	23 Jan 24
For O.	**R. MacDonald (P.M.)**	22 Jan 24	*U-S.*	A. Ponsonby	23 Jan 24
Home O.	**A. Henderson**	22 Jan 24	*U-S.*	R. Davies	23 Jan 24
Admir.	**Vt Chelmsford**	22 Jan 24	*P. & F.S.:*	C. Ammon	23 Jan 24
			Civil Ld:	F. Hodges	24 Jan 24
Ag. & Fish.	**N. Buxton**	22 Jan 24	*P.S.*	W. Smith	23 Jan 24
Air	**Ld Thomson**	22 Jan 24	*U-S.*	W. Leach	23 Jan 24
Col. O.	**J. Thomas**	22 Jan 24	*U-S.*	Ld Arnold	23 Jan 24
Bd Educ.	**C. Trevelyan**	22 Jan 24	*P.S.*	M. Jones	23 Jan 24
Health	**J. Wheatley**	22 Jan 24	*P.S.*	A. Greenwood	23 Jan 24
India O.	**Ld Olivier**	22 Jan 24	*U-S.*	R. Richards	23 Jan 24
Lab.	**T. Shaw**	22 Jan 24	*P.S.*	Miss M. Bondfield	23 Jan 24
D. Lanc.	**J. Wedgwood**	22 Jan 24			
Postm.-Gen.	**V. Hartshorn**	22 Jan 24			
Scotland	**W. Adamson**	22 Jan 24	*P.S. Health for Scotland:*	J. Stewart	23 Jan 24
B.o.T.	**S. Webb**	22 Jan 24	*P.S.*	A. Alexander	23 Jan 24
			P.S. Overseas Trade Dept.:	W. Lunn	23 Jan 24
			P.S. Mines Dept.:	E. Shinwell	23 Jan 24
War O.	**S. Walsh**	22 Jan 24	*U-S.*	C. Attlee	23 Jan 24
			F.S.	J. Lawson	23 Jan 24
1st C. Works	**F. Jowett**	22 Jan 24			

MINISTERS NOT IN CABINET			JUNIOR MINISTERS ATTACHED		
Paym.-Gen.	H. Gosling	6 May 24	*P.S.*	J. Muir	28 Jan 24
Pensions	F. Roberts	23 Jan 24	*P.S.*	(*vacant*)	
Transp.	H. Gosling	24 Jan 24			
Law Officers:			*P.S. to Treasury:*	B. Spoor	23 Jan 24
Att.-Gen.	Sir P. Hastings	23 Jan 24	*Junior Lds of Treasury:*	F. Hall	2 Feb 24
Sol.-Gen.	Sir H. Slesser	23 Jan 24		T. Kennedy	2 Feb 24
Ld Advoc.	H. Macmillan[1]	8 Feb 24		J. Robertson	2 Feb 24
Sol.-Gen. Scotland	J. Fenton[1]	18 Feb 24		G. Warne	24 Feb 24
H.M. Household:			*Lds in Waiting:*	Earl De La Warr	8 Feb 24
Treas.	T. Griffiths	2 Feb 24		Ld Muir-Mackenzie	8 Feb 24
Comptr.	J. Parkinson	2 Feb 24			
V. Chamb.	J. Davison	2 Feb 24			

[1] Non-political appointments. Not members of the House of Commons.

CONSERVATIVE GOVERNMENT, 1924-1929

	MINISTERS IN CABINET			JUNIOR MINISTERS ATTACHED	
P.M.	**S. Baldwin**	4 Nov 24-4 Jun 29			
Ld Pres.	**Marquess Curzon**	6 Nov 24			
	E of Balfour	27 Apr 25			
Ld Chanc.	**Vt Cave**	6 Nov 24			
	Ld Hailsham (Vt)	28 Mar 28			
Privy S.	**M of Salisbury**	6 Nov 24			
Exch.	**W. Churchill**	6 Nov 24	*Treasury:*		
			F.S.	W. Guinness	11 Nov 24
				R. McNeill (*Ld Cushendun*)	5 Nov 25
				A. Samuel	1 Nov 27
For. O.	**(Sir) A. Chamberlain**	6 Nov 24	*U-S.*	R. McNeill	11 Nov 24
				G. Locker-Lampson	7 Dec 25
Home O.	**Sir W. Joynson-Hicks**	6 Nov 24	*U-S.*	G. Locker-Lampson	11 Nov 24
				D. Hacking	8 Dec 25
				Sir V. Henderson	9 Nov 27
Admir.	**W. Bridgeman**	6 Nov 24	*P. & F.S.:*		
				J. Davidson	11 Nov 24
				C. Headlam	16 Dec 26
			Civil Ld:		
				Earl Stanhope	11 Nov 24
Ag. & Fish.	**E. Wood**	6 Nov 24	*P.S. Ag. .& Deputy Min. of Fisheries:*		
	W. Guinness	4 Nov 25		Ld Bledisloe	11 Nov 24
				E of Stradbroke	5 Feb 28
Air	**Sir S. Hoare**	6 Nov 24	*U-S.*	Sir P. Sassoon	11 Nov 24
Att.-Gen.	**Sir D. Hogg** (*Ld Hailsham*) (28 *Mar* 28 *Sir T. Inskip & office not in cabinet*)	6 Nov 24			
Col. O.	**L. Amery**	6 Nov 24	*U-S.*	W. Ormsby-Gore	12 Nov 24
Dom. O.	**L. Amery**	11 Jun 25	*U-S.*	E of Clarendon	5 Aug 25
				Ld Lovat	5 May 27
				E of Plymouth	1 Jan 29
Bd Educ.	**Ld E. Percy**[1]	6 Nov 24	*P.S.*	Duchess of Atholl	11 Nov 24
Health	**N. Chamberlain**	6 Nov 24	*P.S.*	Sir K. Wood	11 Nov 24
India O.	**E of Birkenhead**	6 Nov 24	*U-S.*	Earl Winterton[1]	11 Nov 24
	Vt Peel	18 Oct 28			
Lab.	**Sir A. Steel-Maitland**	6 Nov 24	*P.S.*	H. Betterton	11 Nov 24
D. Lanc.	**Vt Cecil of Chelwood**	10 Nov 24			
	Ld Cushendun	19 Oct 27			
Scot. O.	**Sir J. Gilmour** (*became Sec. of State for Scotland* 15 *Jul* 26)	6 Nov 24	*U-S.*	W. Elliot	26 Jul 26
			P.S. Health for Scotland:		
				W. Elliot (*post abolished* 26 *Jul* 26)	11 Nov 24
B.o.T.	**Sir P. Lloyd-Greame** (*changed name to Sir P. Cunliffe-Lister* 27 *Nov* 24)	6 Nov 24	*P.S.*	Sir B. Chadwick	11 Nov 24
				H. Williams	13 Jan 28
			P.S. Overseas Trade Dept.:		
				A. Samuel	11 Nov 24
				D. Hacking	9 Nov 27
			P.S. Mines Dept.:		
				G. Lane-Fox	11 Nov 24
				D. King	13 Jan 28
War O.	**Sir L. Worthington-Evans**	6 Nov 24	*U-S.*	E of Onslow	11 Nov 24
				D of Sutherland	2 Dec 28
			F.S.	D. King	11 Nov 24
				A. Duff Cooper	13 Jan 28
1st C. Works	**Vt Peel**	10 Nov 24			
	M of Londonderry	18 Oct 28			

[1]M.P. Not a member of the House of Lords.

CONSERVATIVE GOVERNMENT, 1924-1929 *(contd.)*

MINISTERS NOT IN CABINET

Paym.-Gen.	*(office vacant)*	
	D of Sutherland	28 Jan 25
	E of Onslow	2 Dec 28
Pensions	G. Tryon	11 Nov 24
Postm.-Gen	Sir W. Mitchell-Thomson	11 Nov 24
Transp.	W. Ashley	11 Nov 24
Law Officers:		
Att.-Gen.	*(office in cabinet)*	
	Sir T. Inskip	28 Mar 28
Sol.-Gen.	Sir T. Inskip	11 Nov 24
	Sir F. Merriman	28 Mar 28
Ld Advoc.	W. Watson	11 Nov 24
	A. MacRobert	23 Apr 29
Sol.-Gen. Scotland	D. Fleming	11 Nov 24
	A. MacRobert	30 Dec 25
	W. Normand	23 Apr 29
H.M. Household:		
Treas.	G. Gibbs	13 Nov 24
	Sir G. Hennessy	13 Jan 28
Comptr.	Sir H. Barnston	13 Nov 24
	Sir W. Cope	13 Jan 28
V. Chamb.	D. Hacking	13 Nov 24
	(Sir) G. Hennessy	10 Dec 25
	(Sir) F. Thomson	13 Jan 28
Capt. Gents at Arms	E of Clarendon	1 Dec 24
	E of Plymouth	26 Jun 25
	E of Lucan	1 Jan 29
Capt. Yeomen of Guard	Ld Desborough	1 Dec 24

JUNIOR MINISTERS ATTACHED

P.S.	G. Stanley	11 Nov 24
Ass.	Vt Wolmer[1]	11 Nov 24
P.S.	J. Moore-Brabazon	11 Nov 24
	(post vacant from 14 *Jan* 27)	
P.S. to Treasury:		
	B. Eyres-Monsell	7 Nov 24
Junior Lds of Treasury:		
	G. Hennessy	13 Nov 24-10 Dec 25
	Ld Stanley[1]	13 Nov 24-9 Nov 27
	F. Thomson	13 Nov 24-14 Jan 28
	(Sir) W. Cope	13 Nov 24-14 Jan 28
	Vt Curzon[1]	13 Nov 24-15 Jan 29
	D. Margesson	28 Aug 26-4 Jun 29
	G. Bowyer	28 Dec 27-4 Jun 29
	F. Penny	13 Jan 28-4 Jun 29
	M of Titchfield[1]	13 Jan 28-4 Jun 29
	E. Wallace	1 Jan 29-4 Jun 29
Lds in Waiting:		
	Vt Gage	1 Dec 24-4 Jun 29
	Ld Somers	1 Dec 24-23 Mar 26
	E of Lucan	1 Dec 24-1 Jan 29
	E of Airlie	1 Apr 26-4 Jun 29
	Ld Templemore	1 Jan 29-4 Jun 29

LABOUR GOVERNMENT, 1929-1931

MINISTERS IN CABINET

P.M.	**R. MacDonald**	5 Jun 29-24 Aug 31
Ld Pres.	**Ld Parmoor**	7 Jun 29
Ld Chanc.	**Ld Sankey**	7 Jun 29
Privy S.	**J. Thomas**	7 Jun 29
	V. Hartshorn	5 Jun 30
	T. Johnston	24 Mar 31
Exch.	**P. Snowden**	7 Jun 29
For. O.	**A. Henderson**	7 Jun 29
Home O.	**J. Clynes**	7 Jun 29
Admir.	**A. Alexander**	7 Jun 29
Ag. & Fish.	**N. Buxton**	7 Jun 29
	C. Addison	5 Jun 30

JUNIOR MINISTERS ATTACHED

Treasury:		
F.S.	F. Pethick-Lawrence	11 Jun 29
U-S.	H. Dalton	11 Jun 29
U-S.	A. Short	11 Jun 29
P. & F.S.:		
	C. Ammon	11 Jun 29
Civil Ld:		
	G. Hall	11 Jun 29
P.S.	C. Addison	11 Jun 29
	Earl De La Warr	5 Jun 30

[1]M.P. Not a member of the House of Lords.

LABOUR GOVERNMENT, 1929-1931 *(contd.)*

	MINISTERS IN CABINET			JUNIOR MINISTERS ATTACHED	
Air	**Ld Thomson**	7 Jun 29	*U-S.*	F. Montague	11 Jun 29
	Ld Amulree	14 Oct 30			
Col. O.	**Ld Passfield**	7 Jun 29	*U-S.*	W. Lunn	11 Jun 29
				D. Shiels	1 Dec 29
Dom. O.	**Ld Passfield**	7 Jun 29	*U-S.*	A. Ponsonby	11 Jun 29
	J. Thomas	5 Jun 30		W. Lunn	1 Dec 29
Bd Educ.	**Sir C. Trevelyan**	7 Jun 29	*P.S.*	M. Jones	11 Jun 29
	H. Lees-Smith	2 Mar 31			
Health	**A. Greenwood**	7 Jun 29	*P.S.*	Miss S. Lawrence	11 Jun 29
India O.	**W. Benn**	7 Jun 29	*U-S.*	D. Shiels	11 Jun 29
				Earl Russell	1 Dec 29
				Ld Snell	13 Mar 31
Lab.	**Miss M. Bondfield**	7 Jun 29	*P.S.*	J. Lawson	11 Jun 29
Scot. O.	**W. Adamson**	7 Jun 29	*U-S.*	T. Johnston	7 Jun 29
				J. Westwood	25 Mar 31
B.o.T.	**W. Graham**	7 Jun 29	*P.S.*	W. Smith	11 Jun 29
			P.S. Overseas Trade Dept.:		
				G. Gillett	7 Jul 29
			P.S. Mines Dept.:		
				B. Turner	1 Jun 29
				E. Shinwell	5 Jun 30
Transp.	*(office not in cabinet)*		*P.S.*	Earl Russell	11 Jun 29
	H. Morrison	19 Mar 31		A. Ponsonby (Ld)	1 Dec 29
				J. Parkinson	1 Mar 31
War O.	**T. Shaw**	7 Jun 29	*U-S.*	Earl De La Warr	11 Jun 29
				Ld Marley	5 Jun 30
			F.S.	E. Shinwell	11 Jun 29
				W. Sanders	5 Jun 30
1st C. Works	**G. Lansbury**	7 Jun 29			

	MINISTERS NOT IN CABINET			JUNIOR MINISTERS ATTACHED	
D. Lanc.	Sir O. Mosley	7 Jun 29			
	C. Attlee	23 May 30			
	Ld Ponsonby	13 Mar 31			
Paym.-Gen.	Ld Arnold	7 Jun 29			
	(office vacant 6 *Mar* 31)				
Pensions	F. Roberts	7 Jun 29	*P.S.*	*(post vacant)*	
Postm.-Gen.	H. Lees-Smith	7 Jun 29	*Ass.*	S. Viant	7 Jul 29
	C. Attlee	2 Mar 31			
Transp.	H. Morrison	7 Jun 29		*(for Junior Ministers see above)*	
	(office in cabinet 19 *Mar* 31)				
Law Officers:			*P.S. to Treasury:*		
Att.-Gen.	Sir W. Jowitt	7 Jun 29		T. Kennedy	14 Jun 29
Sol.-Gen.	Sir J. Melville	7 Jun 29	*Junior Lds of Treasury:*		
	Sir S. Cripps	22 Oct 30		J. Parkinson	11 Jun 29-13 Mar 31
Ld Advoc.	C. Aitchison	17 Jun 29		C. Edwards	11 Jun 29-24 Aug 31
Sol.-Gen. Scotland	J. Watson[1]	17 Jun 29		A. Barnes	11 Jun 29-23 Oct 30
				W. Whiteley	27 Jun 29-24 Aug 31
				W. Paling	27 Jun 29-24 Aug 31
				E. Thurtle	23 Oct 30-24 Aug 31
				H. Charleton	13 Mar 31-23 Aug 31
H.M. Household:			*Lds in Waiting:*		
Treas.	B. Smith	24 Jun 29		Earl De La Warr	18 Jul 29-24 Aug 31

[1] Not a member of the House of Commons.

LABOUR GOVERNMENT, 1929-1931 *(contd.)*

	MINISTERS NOT IN CABINET		JUNIOR MINISTERS ATTACHED	
H.M. Household:				
Comptr.	T. HENDERSON	24 Jun 29	Ld Muir-Mackenzie	18 Jul 29-22 May 30
V. Chamb.	J. HAYES	24 Jun 29	Ld Marley	17 Jan 30-24 Aug 31

NATIONAL GOVERNMENT, 1931-1935

	MINISTERS IN CABINET			JUNIOR MINISTERS ATTACHED	
P.M.	**R. MacDonald** (N. Lab)	24 Aug 31-7 Jun 35			
Ld Pres.	**S. Baldwin** (C)	25 Aug 31			
Ld Chanc.	**Ld Sankey** (Vt) (N. Lab)	25 Aug 31			
Privy S.	*(office not in cabinet)*				
	Vt Snowden (N. Lab)	5 Nov 31			
	S. Baldwin (C)	29 Sep 32			
	(31 *Dec* 33 *A. Eden & office not in cabinet)*		*Treasury:*		
Exch.	**P. Snowden (Vt)** (N. Lab)	25 Aug 31	*F.S.*	W. Elliot (C)	3 Sep 31
	N. Chamberlain (C)	5 Nov 31		L. Hore-Belisha (L. Nat)	29 Sep 32
				A. Duff Cooper (C)	29 Jun 34
For. O.	**M of Reading** (Lib)	25 Aug 31	*U-S.*	A. Eden (C)	3 Sep 31
	Sir J. Simon (L. Nat)	5 Nov 31		Earl Stanhope (C)	18 Jan 34
Home O.	**Sir H. Samuel** (Lib)	25 Aug 31	*U-S.*	O. Stanley (C)	3 Sep 31
	Sir J. Gilmour (C)	28 Sep 32		D. Hacking (C)	22 Feb 33
				H. Crookshank (C)	29 Jun 34
Admir.	*(office not in cabinet)*		*P. & F.S.:*		
	Sir B. Eyres-Monsell (C)	5 Nov 31		Earl Stanhope (C)	3 Sep 31
				Ld Stanley[1] (C)	10 Nov 31
			Civil Ld:		
				E. Wallace (C)	10 Nov 31
Ag. & Fish.	*(office not in cabinet)*		*P.S.*	*(vacant)*	
	Sir J. Gilmour (C)	5 Nov 31		Earl De La Warr (N. Lab)	10 Nov 31
	W. Elliot (C)	28 Sep 32			
Air	*(office not in cabinet)*		*U-S.*	Sir P. Sassoon (C)	3 Sep 31
	M of Londonderry (C)	5 Nov 31			
Col. O.	**J. Thomas** (N. Lab)	25 Aug 31	*U-S.*	Sir R. Hamilton (Lib)	3 Sep 31
	Sir P. Cunliffe-Lister (C)	5 Nov 31		E of Plymouth (C)	29 Sep 32
Dom. O.	**J. Thomas** (N. Lab)	25 Aug 31	*U-S.*	M. MacDonald (N. Lab)	3 Sep 31
Bd Educ.	*(office not in cabinet)*		*P.S.*	Sir K. Wood (C)	3 Sep 31
	Sir D. Maclean (Lib)	5 Nov 31		H. Ramsbotham (C)	10 Nov 31
	Ld Irwin (*Vt Halifax*) (C)	15 Jun 32			
Health	**N. Chamberlain** (C)	25 Aug 31	*P.S.*	E. Simon (Lib)	22 Sep 31
	Sir E. Young (C)	5 Nov 31		E. Brown (L. Nat.)	10 Nov 31
				G. Shakespeare (L. Nat)	30 Sep 32
India O.	**Sir S. Hoare** (C)	25 Aug 31	*U-S.*	*(vacant)*	
				M of Lothian (Lib)	10 Nov 31
				R. Butler (C)	29 Sep 32
Lab.	*(office not in cabinet)*		*P.S.*	M. Gray (Lib)	3 Sep 31
	Sir H. Betterton (C)	5 Nov 31		R. Hudson (C)	10 Nov 31
	O. Stanley (C)	29 Jun 34			
Postm.-Gen.	*(office not in cabinet)*		*Ass.*	G. White (Lib)	3 Sep 31
	Sir K. Wood (C)	20 Dec 33		Sir E. Bennett (N. Lab)	21 Oct 32
Scot. O.	*(office not in cabinet)*		*U-S.*	N. Skelton (C)	3 Sep 31
	Sir A. Sinclair (Lib)	5 Nov 31			
	Sir G. Collins (L. Nat)	28 Sep 32			

[1]M.P. Not a member of the House of Lords.

NATIONAL GOVERNMENT, 1931-1935 *(contd.)*

	MINISTERS IN CABINET			JUNIOR MINISTERS ATTACHED	
B.o.T.	**Sir P. Cunliffe-Lister** (C)	25 Aug 31	*P.S.*	G. Lloyd-George (Lib)	3 Sep 31
	W. Runciman (L. Nat)	5 Nov 31		L. Hore-Belisha (L. Nat)	10 Nov 31
				L. Burgin (L. Nat)	29 Sep 32
			P.S. Overseas Trade Dept.:		
				Sir E. Young (C)	3 Sep 31
				J. Colville (C)	10 Nov 31
			P.S. Mines Dept.:		
				I. Foot (Lib)	3 Sep 31
				E. Brown (L. Nat)	30 Sep 32
War O.	*(office not in cabinet)*		*U-S.*	*(vacant)*	
	Vt Hailsham (C)	5 Nov 31		Earl Stanhope (C)	10 Nov 31
				Ld Strathcona & Mount Royal (C)	24 Jan 34
			F.S.	A. Duff Cooper (C)	3 Sep 31
				D. Hacking (C)	29 Jun 34
1st C. Works	*(office not in cabinet)*				
	W. Ormsby-Gore (C)	5 Nov 31			

	MINISTERS NOT IN CABINET			JUNIOR MINISTERS ATTACHED	
Admir.	Sir A. Chamberlain (C)	25 Aug 31		*(for Junior Ministers see above)*	
	(5 Nov 31 Sir B. Eyres-Monsell & office in cabinet)				
Ag. & Fish.	Sir J. Gilmour (C)	25 Aug 31		*(for Junior Ministers see above)*	
	(5 Nov 31 office in cabinet)				
Air	Ld Amulree (N. Lab)	25 Aug 31		*(for Junior Ministers see above)*	
	(5 Nov 31 M of Londonderry & office in cabinet)				
Bd Educ.	Sir D. Maclean (Lib)	25 Aug 31		*(for Junior Ministers see above)*	
	(5 Nov 31 office in cabinet)				
Lab.	Sir H. Betterton (C)	25 Aug 31		*(for Junior Ministers see above)*	
	(5 Nov 31 office in cabinet)				
D. Lanc.	M of Lothian (Lib)	25 Aug 31			
	(Sir) J. Davidson (C)	10 Nov 31			
Paym.-Gen.	Sir T. Walters (Lib)	4 Sep 31			
	Ld Rochester (N. Lab)	23 Nov 31			
Pensions	G. Tryon (C)	3 Sep 31	*P.S.*	*(vacant)*	
				C. Headlam (C)	10 Nov 31
				(vacant from 29 Sep 32)	
Postm.-Gen.	W. Ormsby-Gore (C)	3 Sep 31		*(for Junior Ministers see above)*	
	Sir K. Wood (C)	10 Nov 31			
	(20 *Dec 33 office in cabinet)*				
Privy S.	Earl Peel (C)	3 Sep 31			
	(5 *Nov 31 Vt Snowden & office in cabinet)*				
	A. Eden (C)	31 Dec 33			
Scot. O.	Sir A. Sinclair (Lib)	25 Aug 31		*(for Junior Ministers see above)*	
	(5 Nov 31 office in cabinet)				
Transp.	J. Pybus (L. Nat)	3 Sep 31	*P.S.*	(Sir) G. Gillett (N. Lab)	4 Sep 31
	O. Stanley (C)	22 Feb 33		E of Plymouth (C)	25 Nov 31
	L. Hore-Belisha (L. Nat)	29 Jun 34		C. Headlam (C)	29 Sep 32
				(5 Jul 34 vacant)	
				A. Hudson (C)	12 Apr 35
War O.	M of Crewe (Lib)	26 Aug 31		*(for Junior Ministers see above)*	
	(5 Nov 31 Vt Hailsham & office in cabinet)				
1st C. Works	M of Londonderry (C)	25 Aug 31			
	(5 *Nov 31 W. Ormsby-Gore & office in cabinet)*				
Law Officers:			*P.S. to Treasury:*		
Att.-Gen.	Sir W. Jowitt (N. Lab)	3 Sep 31		Sir B. Eyres-Monsell (C)	3 Sep 31
	Sir T. Inskip (C)	26 Jan 32		D. Margesson (C)	10 Nov 31

NATIONAL GOVERNMENT, 1931-1935 *(contd.)*

MINISTERS NOT IN CABINET

Sol.-Gen.	SIR T. INSKIP (C)	3 Sep 31
	SIR F. MERRIMAN (C)	26 Jan 32
	SIR D. SOMERVELL (C)	29 Sep 33
Ld Advoc.	C. AITCHISON (N. Lab)	3 Sep 31
	W. NORMAND (C)	2 Oct 33
	D. JAMIESON (C)	28 Mar 35
Sol.-Gen. Scotland	J. WATSON[1] (N. Lab)	4 Sep 31
	W. NORMAND (C)	10 Nov 31
	D. JAMIESON (C)	2 Oct 33
	T. COOPER (C)	15 May 35
H.M. Household:		
Treas.	SIR G. HENNESSY (C)	3 Sep 31
	SIR F. THOMSON (C)	12 Nov 31
	SIR F. PENNY (C)	1 May 35
Comptr.	G. OWEN (Lib)	14 Sep 31
	W. REA (Lib)	12 Nov 31
	SIR F. PENNY (C)	30 Sep 32
	SIR V. WARRENDER (C)	1 May 35
V. Chamb.	SIR F. THOMSON (C)	3 Sep 31
	SIR F. PENNY (C)	12 Nov 31
	SIR V. WARRENDER (C)	30 Sep 32
	SIR L. WARD (C)	1 May 35
Capt. Gents at Arms	E OF LUCAN (C)	12 Nov 31
Capt. Yeomen of Guard	LD STRATHCONA & MOUNT ROYAL (C)	12 Nov 31
	LD TEMPLEMORE (C)	24 Jan 34

JUNIOR MINISTERS ATTACHED

Junior Lds of Treasury:	
D. Margesson (C)	26 Aug 31-10 Nov 31
Sir F. Penny (C)	3 Sep 31-12 Nov 31
A. Glassey (Lib)	14 Sep 31-12 Nov 31
M of Titchfield[3] (C)	3 Sep 31-12 Nov 31
E. Wallace (C)	3 Sep 31-12 Nov 31
(Sir) W. Womersley (C)	12 Nov 31-7 Jun 35
Sir V. Warrender (C)	12 Nov 31-30 Sep 32
G. Shakespeare (L. Nat)	12 Nov 31-30 Sep 32
A. Hudson (C)	12 Nov 31-12 Apr 35
Sir L. Ward (C)	12 Nov 31-1 May 35
G. Davies (C)	11 Oct 32-7 Jun 35
J. Blindell (L. Nat)	30 Sep 32-7 Jun 35
J. Stuart (C)	1 May 35-7 Jun 35
A. Southby (C)	23 Apr 35-7 Jun 35
Lds in Waiting:	
Ld Templemore (C)	12 Nov 31-24 Jan 34
Vt Gage (C)	12 Nov 31-7 Jun 35
Vt Allendale (Lib)	12 Nov 31-28 Sep 32
E of Munster (C)	24 Jan 34-7 Jun 35
E of Feversham (C)	24 Jan 34-7 Jun 35

NATIONAL GOVERNMENT, 1935-1940

MINISTERS IN CABINET

P.M.	**S. Baldwin**	7 Jun 35-28 May 37
	[2]**N. Chamberlain**	28 May 37-10 May 40
Ld Pres.	**R. MacDonald**	7 Jun 35
	Vt Halifax	28 May 37
	Vt Hailsham	9 Mar 38
	Vt Runciman	31 Oct 38
	Earl Stanhope	3 Sep 39
Ld Chanc.	**Vt Hailsham**	7 Jun 35
	Ld Maugham	9 Mar 38
	Vt Caldecote	3 Sep 39
Privy S.	**M of Londonderry**	7 Jun 35
	Vt Halifax	22 Nov 35
	Earl De La Warr	28 May 37
	Sir J. Anderson	31 Oct 38
	[2]**Sir S. Hoare**	3 Sep 39
	Sir K. Wood	3 Apr 40

[1] Not a member of the House of Commons.
[2] Denotes member of the War Cabinet. Following the British declaration of war against Germany on 3 Sep 39, all members of the cabinet formally surrendered their portfolios to the P.M.; in the evening of the same day the formation of a war cabinet was announced.
[3] M.P. Not a member of the House of Lords.

NATIONAL GOVERNMENT, 1935-1940 *(contd.)*

	MINISTERS IN CABINET			JUNIOR MINISTERS ATTACHED	
Exch.	**N. Chamberlain**	7 Jun 35	*Treasury:*		
	[2]Sir J. Simon	28 May 37	*F.S.*	A. Duff Cooper	18 Jun 35
				W. Morrison	22 Nov 35
				J. Colville	29 Oct 36
				E. Wallace	16 May 38
				H. Crookshank	21 Apr 39
For. O.	**Sir S. Hoare**	7 Jun 35	*U-S.*	Earl Stanhope	18 Jun 35-16 Jun 36
	A. Eden	22 Dec 35		Vt Cranborne[1]	6 Aug 35-20 Feb 38
	[2]Vt Halifax	21 Feb 38		*(for League of Nations Affairs)*	
				E of Plymouth	30 Jul 36-12 May 39
				R. Butler	25 Feb 38-10 May 40
Home O.	**Sir J. Simon**	7 Jun 35	*U-S.*	E. Wallace	18 Jun 35
	Sir S. Hoare	28 May 37		G. Lloyd	28 Nov 35
	Sir J. Anderson	3 Sep 39		O. Peake	21 Apr 39
			P.S. Min. Home Security:		
				A. Lennox-Boyd	6 Sep 39
				W. Mabane	24 Oct 39
Admir.	**Sir B. Eyres-Monsell**	7 Jun 35	*P. & F.S.:*		
	(Vt Monsell)			Sir V. Warrender	18 Jun 35
	Sir S. Hoare	5 Jun 36		Ld Stanley[1]	28 Nov 35
	A. Duff Cooper	28 May 37		G. Shakespeare	28 May 37
	Earl Stanhope	27 Oct 38		Sir V. Warrender	3 Apr 40
	[2]W. Churchill	3 Sep 39	*Civil Ld:*		
				K. Lindsay	18 Jun 35
				J. Llewellin	28 May 37
				A. Hudson	14 Jul 39
Ag. & Fish.	**W. Elliot**	7 Jun 35	*P.S.*	Earl De La Warr	18 Jun 35
	W. Morrison	29 Oct 36		H. Ramsbotham	28 Nov 35
	Sir R. Dorman-Smith	29 Jan 39		E of Feversham	30 Jul 36
				Ld Denham	19 Sep 39
Air	**Sir P. Cunliffe-Lister**		*U-S.*	Sir P. Sassoon	18 Jun 35
	(Vt Swinton)	7 Jun 35		A. Muirhead	28 May 37
	[2]Sir K. Wood	16 May 38		H. Balfour	16 May 38
	Sir S. Hoare	3 Apr 40			
Col. O.	**M. MacDonald**	7 Jun 35	*U-S.*	E of Plymouth	18 Jun 35
	J. Thomas	22 Nov 35		Earl De La Warr	30 Jul 36
	W. Ormsby-Gore	28 May 36		M of Dufferin & Ava	28 May 37
	M. MacDonald	16 May 38			
Min. for Co-ordination of Defence	*(office not established)*				
	Sir T. Inskip	13 Mar 36			
	[2]Ld Chatfield	29 Jan 39			
	(office abolished 3 *Apr* 40)				
Dom. O.	**J. Thomas**	7 Jun 35	*U-S.*	Ld Stanley[1]	18 Jun 35
	M. MacDonald	22 Nov 35		D. Hacking	28 Nov 35
	Ld Stanley[1]	16 May 38		M of Hartington[1]	4 Mar 36
	M. MacDonald	31 Oct 38		*(D of Devonshire)*	
	Sir T. Inskip	29 Jan 39			
	(Vt Caldecote)				
	A. Eden	3 Sep 39			
Bd Educ.	**O. Stanley**	7 Jun 35	*P.S.*	H. Ramsbotham	18 Jun 35
	Earl Stanhope	28 May 37		Earl De La Warr	28 Nov 35
	Earl De La Warr	27 Oct 38		G. Shakespeare	30 Jul 36
	H. Ramsbotham	3 Apr 40		K. Lindsay	28 May 37
Food	*(combined with D. Lanc.* 4 *Sep* 39)		*P.S.*	A. Lennox-Boyd	11 Oct 39
	Ld Woolton	3 Apr 40			
Health	**Sir K. Wood**	7 Jun 35	*P.S.*	G. Shakespeare	18 Jun 35
	W. Elliot	16 May 38		R. Hudson	30 Jul 36
				R. Bernays	28 May 37
				Miss F. Horsbrugh	14 Jul 39

[1] M.P. Not a member of the House of Lords.

[2] Denotes member of the War Cabinet. Following the British declaration of war against Germany on 3 Sep 39, all members of the cabinet formally surrendered their portfolios to the P.M.; in the evening of the same day the formation of a war cabinet was announced.

NATIONAL GOVERNMENT, 1935-1940 *(contd.)*

	MINISTERS IN CABINET			JUNIOR MINISTERS ATTACHED	
India O. (*& Burma O.* 1937-)	**M of Zetland**	7 Jun 35	*U-S.*	R. Butler	18 Jun 35
				Ld Stanley[1]	28 May 37
				A. Muirhead	16 May 38
				Sir H. O'Neill	11 Sep 39
Information	*(office not established)*		*P.S.*	Sir E. Grigg	19 Sep 39
	Ld Macmillan	4 Sep 39		*(office vacant* 3 *Apr* 40)	
	Sir J. Reith	5 Jan 40			
Lab.	**E. Brown**	7 Jun 35	*P.S.*	A. Muirhead	18 Jun 35
	(3 *Sep* 39 *Lab. & Nat S.*)			R. Butler	28 May 37
				A. Lennox-Boyd	25 Feb 38
				R. Assheton	6 Sep 39
D. Lanc.	*(office not in cabinet)*				
	Earl Winterton[1]	11 Mar 38			
	W. Morrison	29 Jan 39			
	(4 *Sep* 39-3 *Apr* 40 *combined with Min. of Food)*				
	G. Tryon	3 Apr 40			
Min. without Portfolio for League of Nations Affairs	**A. Eden**	7 Jun 35-22 Dec 35			
Min. without Portfolio	**Ld E. Percy**[1]	7 Jun 35-31 Mar 36			
	L. Burgin	21 Apr 39-14 Jul 39			
	[2]**Ld Hankey**	3 Sep 39-10 May 40			
Scot. O.	**Sir G. Collins**	7 Jun 35	*U-S.*	N. Skelton	18 Jun 35
	W. Elliot	29 Oct 36		J. Colville	28 Nov 35
	J. Colville	16 May 38		H. Wedderburn	29 Oct 36
				J. McEwen	6 Sep 39
Shipping	*(office not established)*		*P.S.*	Sir A. Salter	13 Nov 39
	Sir J. Gilmour	13 Oct 39			
	R. Hudson	3 Apr 40			
Supply	*(office not established)*		*P.S.*	J. Llewellin	14 Jul 39
	L. Burgin	14 Jul 39			
B.o.T.	**W. Runciman**	7 Jun 35	*P.S.*	L. Burgin	18 Jun 35
	O. Stanley	28 May 37		E. Wallace	28 May 37
	Sir A. Duncan	5 Jan 40		R. Cross	16 May 38
				G. Lloyd-George	6 Sep 39
			P.S. Overseas Trade Dept.:		
				J. Colville	18 Jun 35
				E. Wallace	28 Nov 35
				R. Hudson	28 May 37
				G. Shakespeare	3 Apr 40
			P.S. Mines Dept.:		
				H. Crookshank	18 Jun 35
				G. Lloyd	21 Apr 39
Transp.	*(office not in cabinet)*		*P.S.*	A. Hudson	18 Jun 35
	L. Hore-Belisha	29 Oct 36		R. Bernays	14 Jul 39
	L. Burgin	28 May 37			
	E. Wallace	21 Apr 39			
War O.	**Vt Halifax**	7 Jun 35	*U-S.*	Ld Strathcona & Mount Royal	18 Jun 35
	A. Duff Cooper	22 Nov 35		E of Munster	29 Jan 39
	[2]**L. Hore-Belisha**	28 May 37		Vt Cobham	19 Sep 39
	O. Stanley	5 Jan 40	*F.S.*	D. Hacking	18 Jun 35
				Sir V. Warrender	28 Nov 35
				Sir E. Grigg	3 Apr 40

[1] M.P. Not a member of the House of Lords.
[2] Denotes member of the War Cabinet. Following the British declaration of war against Germany on 3 Sep 39, all members of the cabinet formally surrendered their portfolios to the P.M.; in the evening of the same day the formation of a war cabinet was announced.

NATIONAL GOVERNMENT, 1935-1940 *(contd.)*

MINISTERS IN CABINET

1st C. Works	**W. Ormsby-Gore**	7 Jun 35
	Earl Stanhope	16 Jun 36
	(28 *May* 37 *Sir P. Sassoon & office out of cabinet)*	

MINISTERS NOT IN CABINET

Econ. Warfare	R. Cross	3 Sep 39
D. Lanc.	Sir J. Davidson	18 Jun 35
	Earl Winterton[1]	28 May 37
	(*office in cabinet* 11 *Mar* 38)	
Paym.-Gen.	Ld Rochester	18 Jun 35
	Ld Hutchison	6 Dec 35
	E of Munster	2 Jun 38
	Earl Winterton[1]	29 Jan 39
	(*office vacant from Nov* 39)	
Pensions	R. Hudson	18 Jun 35
	H. Ramsbotham	30 Jul 36
	Sir W. Womersley	7 Jun 39
Postm.-Gen.	G. Tryon	7 Jun 35
	W. Morrison	3 Apr 40
Transp.	L. Hore-Belisha	18 Jun 35
	(*office in cabinet 29 Oct* 36)	
1st C. Works	*(office in cabinet)*	
	Sir P. Sassoon	28 May 37
	H. Ramsbotham	7 Jun 39
	Earl De La Warr	3 Apr 40
Law Officers:		
Att.-Gen.	Sir T. Inskip	18 Jun 35
	Sir D. Somervell	18 Mar 36
Sol.-Gen.	Sir D. Somervell	18 Jun 35
	Sir T. O'Connor	19 Mar 36
Ld Advoc.	D. Jamieson	18 Jun 35
	T. Cooper	25 Oct 35
Sol.-Gen. Scotland	T. Cooper	18 Jun 35
	A. Russell[2]	29 Nov 35
	J. Reid	25 Jun 36

JUNIOR MINISTERS ATTACHED

Ass. (Postm.-Gen.)	Sir E. Bennett	18 Jun 35
	Sir W. Womersley	6 Dec 35
	W. Mabane	7 Jun 39
	C. Waterhouse	24 Oct 39
P.S. to Treasury:	D. Margesson	18 Jun 35
Junior Lds of Treasury:	J. Stuart	18 Jun 35-10 May 40
	(Sir) A. Southby	18 Jun 35-28 May 37
	Sir W. Womersley	18 Jun 35-6 Dec 35
	G. Davies	18 Jun 35-6 Dec 35
	(Sir) J. Blindell	18 Jun 35-28 May 37
	A. Hope	6 Dec 35-28 May 37
	(Sir) H. Morris-Jones	6 Dec 35-28 May 37
	C. Kerr	28 May 37-4 Apr 39
	T. Dugdale	28 May 37-12 Feb 40
	C. Waterhouse	28 May 37-18 Oct 37
	R. Cross	28 May 37-18 Oct 37
	P. Munro	18 Oct 37-10 May 40
	R. Grimston	18 Oct 37-18 May 38
	S. Furness	20 May 38-10 May 40
	Sir J. Edmondson	4 Apr 39-13 Nov 39
	P. Buchan-Hepburn	13 Nov 39-10 May 40
	W. Boulton	12 Feb 40-10 May 40

[1] M.P. Not a member of the House of Lords.
[2] Not a member of the House of Commons.

NATIONAL GOVERNMENT, 1935-1940 *(contd.)*

MINISTERS NOT IN CABINET

H.M. Household:

Treas.	Sir F. Penny	18 Jun 35
	Sir L. Ward	28 May 37
	A. Hope	18 Oct 37
	C. Waterhouse	4 Apr 39
	R. Grimston	12 Nov 39
Comptr.	Sir G. Bowyer	21 Jun 35
	Sir L. Ward	6 Dec 35
	Sir G. Davies	28 May 37
	C. Waterhouse	18 Oct 37
	C. Kerr	4 Apr 39
V. Chamb.	Sir L. Ward	18 Jun 35
	(Sir) G. Davies	6 Dec 35
	A. Hope	28 May 37
	R. Cross	18 Oct 37
	R. Grimston	18 May 38
	Sir J. Edmondson	12 Nov 39
Capt. Gents at Arms	E of Lucan	18 Jun 35
Capt. Yeomen of Guard	Ld Templemore	18 Jun 35

JUNIOR MINISTERS ATTACHED

Lds in Waiting:

Vt Gage	18 Jun 35-11 Apr 39
E of Munster	18 Jun 35-2 Jun 38
E of Feversham	18 Jun 35-30 Jul 36
M of Dufferin & Ava	29 Oct 36-28 May 37
E of Erne	29 Oct 36-25 Jul 39
Earl Fortescue	26 Aug 37-10 May 40
E of Birkenhead	12 Jul 38-10 May 40
Vt Bridport	11 Apr 39-10 May 40
Ld Ebury	25 Jul 39-10 May 40

COALITION GOVERNMENT, 1940-1945

MINISTERS IN WAR CABINET

P.M.	**W. Churchill** (C)	10 May 40-23 May 45
Ld Pres.	**N. Chamberlain** (C)	11 May 40
	Sir J. Anderson (Nat)	3 Oct 40
	C. Attlee (Lab)	24 Sep 43
Ld Chanc.	*(office not in war cabinet)*	
Privy S.	**C. Attlee** (Lab)	11 May 40
	Sir S. Cripps (Lab)	19 Feb 42
	(*Vt Cranborne 22 Nov 42 & office not in war cabinet)*	
Exch.	*(office not in war cabinet)*	
	Sir K. Wood (C)	3 Oct 40
	(19 *Feb* 42 *office not in war cabinet)*	
	Sir J. Anderson (Nat)	24 Sep 43
For. O.	**Vt Halifax** (C)[1]	11 May 40
	A. Eden (C)	22 Dec 40
Min. of State	**Ld Beaverbrook** (C)	1 May 41
	O. Lyttelton (C)	29 Jun 41
	(*became Min. of Production* 12 *Mar* 42 *& remained in war cabinet)*	
Home O. & Home Security	*(office not in war cabinet)*	
	H. Morrison (Lab)	22 Nov 42
Aircraft Production	*(office not in war cabinet)*	
	Ld Beaverbrook (C)	2 Aug 40
	(*J. Moore-Brabazon* 1 *May* 41 *& office not in war cabinet)*	
Def.	**W. Churchill (P.M.)** (C)	10 May 40

JUNIOR MINISTERS ATTACHED

Treasury:

F.S.	H. Crookshank (C)	15 May 40
	R. Assheton (C)	7 Feb 43
	O. Peake (C)	29 Oct 44
Min. of State:	R. Law[2] (C)	24 Sep 43
U-S.	R. Butler (C)	15 May 40
	R. Law (C)	20 Jul 41
	G. Hall (Lab)	25 Sep 43
U-S.	O. Peake (C)	15 May 40
	E of Munster (C)	31 Oct 44
P.S. Home Security:	W. Mabane (L. Nat)	15 May 40-3 Jun 42
	Miss E. Wilkinson (Lab)	8 Oct 40-23 May 45

(for Junior Ministers see below)

[1] Although Vt Halifax became Ambassador to the United States 24 Jan 41, he remained nominally a member of the War Cabinet until 1945.
[2] This office was not formally under the Foreign Office but was more akin to Minister without Portfolio.

COALITION GOVERNMENT, 1940-1945 *(contd.)*

Office	Ministers in War Cabinet		Junior Ministers Attached		
Dom. O.	*(office not in war cabinet)*			*(for Junior Ministers see below)*	
	C. Attlee (Lab)	19 Feb 42			
	(Vt Cranborne 24 Sep 43 & office not in war cabinet)				
Lab. & Nat. S.	*(office not in war cabinet)*		*P.S.*	R. Assheton (C)	15 May 40-4 Feb 42
	E. Bevin (Lab)	3 Oct 40		G. Tomlinson (Lab)	8 Feb 41-23 May 45
				M. McCorquodale (C)	4 Feb 42-23 May 45
Min. resident in Mid. East	**O. Lyttelton** (C)	19 Feb 42	*Deputy Min. of State:*	Ld Moyne (C)	27 Aug 42-28 Jan 44
	R. Casey[1]	19 Mar 42			
	(office not in war cabinet 23 Dec 43)				
Min. without Portfolio	**A. Greenwood** (Lab)	11 May 40-22 Feb 42			
	(Sir W. Jowitt appointed 30 Dec 42 not in war cabinet)				
Reconstruction	*(office not established)*				
	Ld Woolton (C)	11 Nov 43			
Supply	*(office not in war cabinet)*			*(for Junior Ministers see below)*	
	Ld Beaverbrook (C)	29 Jun 41			
	(Sir A. Duncan & office not in war cabinet 4 Feb 42)				
(War) Production	*(office not established)*		*P.S.*	G. Garro-Jones (Lab)	10 Sep 42
	Ld Beaverbrook (C)	4 Feb 42			
	(office vacant 19 Feb 42)				
	O. Lyttelton (C)	12 Mar 42			
	(Minister of Production)				

Office	Ministers not in War Cabinet		Junior Ministers Attached		
Admir.	A. Alexander (Lab)	11 May 40	*P. & F.S.:*	Sir V. Warrender (C) *(Ld Bruntisfield)*	17 May 40
			Civil Ld:	A. Hudson (C)	15 May 40
				R. Pilkington (C)	4 Mar 42
			F.S.	G. Hall (Lab)	4 Feb 42
				J. Thomas (C)	25 Sep 43
Ag. & Fish.	R. Hudson (C)	14 May 40	*P.S.*	Ld Moyne (C)	15 May 40-8 Feb 41
				T. Williams (Lab)	15 May 40-23 May 45
				D of Norfolk (C)	8 Feb 41-23 May 45
Air	Sir A. Sinclair (Lib)	11 May 40	*P.S.*	H. Balfour (C)	15 May 40-21 Nov 44
				Ld Sherwood (Lib)	20 Jul 41-23 May 45
				R. Brabner (C)	21 Nov 44-27 Mar 45
				Q. Hogg (C)	12 Apr 45-23 May 45
Aircraft Production	Ld Beaverbrook (C)	14 May 40	*P.S.*	J. Llewellin (C)	15 May 40
	(office in war cabinet 2 Aug 40)			F. Montague (Lab)	1 May 41
	J. Moore-Brabazon (C)	1 May 41		B. Smith (Lab)	4 Mar 42
	J. Llewellin (C)	22 Feb 42		A. Lennox-Boyd (C)	11 Nov 43
	Sir S. Cripps (Lab)	22 Nov 42			
Civil Av.	*(office not established)*		*P.S.*	R. Perkins (C)	22 Mar 45
	Vt Swinton (C)	8 Oct 44			
Col. O.	Ld Lloyd (C)	12 May 40	*U-S.*	G. Hall (Lab)	15 May 40
	Ld Moyne (C)	8 Feb 41		H. Macmillan (C)	4 Feb 42
	Vt Cranborne (C)	22 Feb 42		D of Devonshire (C)	1 Jan 43
	O. Stanley (C)	22 Nov 42			

[1] Not a member of the House of Commons.

COALITION GOVERNMENT, 1940-1945 *(contd.)*

MINISTERS NOT IN WAR CABINET			JUNIOR MINISTERS ATTACHED		
Dom. O.	Vt Caldecote (C)	14 May 40	*U-S.*	G. Shakespeare (L. Nat)	15 May 40
	Vt Cranborne[1] (C)	3 Oct 40		P. Emrys-Evans (C)	4 Mar 42
	(C. Attlee 19 Feb 42 & office in war cabinet)				
	Vt Cranborne (C)	24 Sep 43			
Economic Warfare	H. Dalton (Lab)	15 May 40	*P.S.*	D. Foot (Lib)	17 May 40
	Vt Wolmer[1] *(E of Selborne)*	22 Feb 42			
Bd Educ.	H. Ramsbotham (C)	14 May 40	*P.S.*	C. Ede (Lab)	15 May 40
	R. Butler (C)	20 Jul 41			
	(3 Aug 44 becomes Min. of Educ.)				
Exch.	Sir K. Wood (C)	12 May 40		*(for Financial Secretary to Treasury see above)*	
	(3 Oct 40 office in war cabinet, 19 Feb 42 out of war cabinet again)				
	(24 Sep 43 Sir J. Anderson & office in war cabinet)				
Food	Ld Woolton (C)	13 May 40	*P.S.*	R. Boothby (C)	15 May 40
	J. Llewellin (C)	11 Nov 43		G. Lloyd-George (Ind. L)	22 Oct 40
				W. Mabane (L. Nat)	3 Jun 42
Fuel, Light & Power	*(office not established)*		*P.S.*	G. Lloyd (C)	3 Jun 42-23 May 45
	G. Lloyd-George (Ind L.)	3 Jun 42		T. Smith (Lab)	3 Jun 42-23 May 45
Health	M. MacDonald (N. Lab)	13 May 40	*P.S.*	Miss F. Horsbrugh (C)	15 May 40
	E. Brown (L. Nat)	8 Feb 41			
	H. Willink (C)	11 Nov 43			
Home O. & Home Security	Sir J. Anderson (Nat)	12 May 40		*(for Junior Ministers see above)*	
	H. Morrison (Lab)	3 Oct 40			
	(22 Nov 42 office in war cabinet)				
India & Burma O.	L. Amery (C)	13 May 40	*P.S.*	D of Devonshire (C)	17 May 40
				E of Munster (C)	1 Jan 43
				E of Listowel (Lab)	31 Oct 44
Information	A. Duff Cooper (C)	12 May 40	*P.S.*	H. Nicolson (N. Lab)	17 May 40
	(attended war cabinet from 28 May 40)			E. Thurtle (Lab)	20 Jul 41
	B. Bracken (C)	20 Jul 41			
Lab. & Nat. S.	E. Bevin (Lab)	13 May 40		*(for Junior Ministers see above)*	
	(office in war cabinet 3 Oct 40)				
D. Lanc.	Ld Hankey (Ind)	14 May 40			
	A. Duff Cooper (C)	20 Jul 41			
	E. Brown (L. Nat)	11 Nov 43			
Ld Chanc.	Vt Simon (L. Nat)	12 May 40			
Min. resident at Allied H.Q. in N.W. Africa	H. Macmillan (C)	30 Dec 42			
Min. resident in Washington for Supply	J. Llewellin (C)	22 Nov 42			
	B. Smith (Lab)	11 Nov 43			
Min. resident in W. Africa	Vt Swinton (C)	8 Jun 42			
	H. Balfour (C)	21 Nov 44			
Min. of State in Mid. East	*(office in war cabinet)*			*(for Junior Ministers see above)*	
	Ld Moyne (C)	28 Jan 44			
	Sir E. Grigg (C)	21 Nov 44			

[1] M.P. Not a member of the House of Lords. Viscount Wolmer was moved to the House of Lords by writ of acceleration in October 1940. The same was done for Viscount Cranborne in January 1941.

COALITION GOVERNMENT, 1940-1945 *(contd.)*

	MINISTERS NOT IN WAR CABINET			JUNIOR MINISTERS ATTACHED	
Paym.-Gen.	Vt Cranborne[1] (C)	15 May 40			
	(*office vacant* 3 *Oct* 40)				
	Ld Hankey (Ind)	20 Jul 41			
	Sir W. Jowitt (Lab)	4 Mar 42			
	Ld Cherwell (C)	30 Dec 42			
Pensions	Sir W. Womersley (C)	15 May 40	*P.S.*	Miss E. Wilkinson (Lab)	17 May 40
				Ld Tryon (C)	8 Oct 40
				W. Paling (Lab)	8 Feb 41
Min. without Portfolio	(*in war cabinet* 11 *May* 40-22 *Feb* 42)				
	Sir W. Jowitt (Lab)	30 Dec 42-8 Oct 44			
Postm.-Gen.	W. Morrison (C)	15 May 40	*Ass.*	C. Waterhouse (C)	17 May 40
	H. Crookshank (C)	7 Feb 43		A. Chapman (C)	1 Mar 41
				R. Grimston (C)	4 Mar 42
Privy S.	(*office in war cabinet*)				
	Vt Cranborne (C)	22 Nov 42			
	Ld Beaverbrook (C)	24 Sep 43			
Scot. O.	E. Brown (L. Nat)	14 May 40	*P.S.*	J. Westwood (Lab)	17 May 40-23 May 45
	T. Johnston (Lab)	8 Feb 41		H. Wedderburn (C)	8 Feb 41-4 Mar 42
				A. Chapman (C)	4 Mar 42-23 May 45
Shipping	R. Cross (C)	14 May 40	*P.S.*	Sir A. Salter (Ind)	15 May 40
	(1 *May* 41 *combined with Min. of Transport, as Min. of War Transport see below*)				
Soc. Insur.	(*office not established*)		*P.S.*	C. Peat (C)	22 Mar 45
	Sir W. Jowitt (Lab)	8 Oct 44			
	(*renamed National Insurance* 17 *Nov* 44)				
Supply	H. Morrison (Lab)	12 May 40	*P.S.*	H. Macmillan (C)	15 May 40-4 Feb 42
	Sir A. Duncan (C)	3 Oct 40		Ld Portal (C)	4 Sep 40-4 Mar 42
	(*Ld Beaverbrook 29 Jun* 41 *& office in war cabinet*)			R. Assheton (C)	4 Feb 42-7 Feb 43
	Sir A. Duncan (C)	4 Feb 42		C. Peat (C)	4 Mar 42-22 Mar 45
				D. Sandys (C)	7 Feb 43-21 Nov 44
				J. Wilmot (Lab)	21 Nov 44-23 May 45
				J. de Rothschild (Lib)	22 Mar 45-23 May 45
T. & C. Planning	(*office not established*)		*P.S.*	H. Strauss (C)	30 Dec 42
	W. Morrison (C)	30 Dec 42		A. Jenkins (Lab)	22 Mar 45
	(*Minister designate until* 7 *Feb* 43)				
B.o.T.	Sir A. Duncan (C)	12 May 40	*P.S.*	G. Lloyd-George (Ind L.)	15 May 40
	O. Lyttelton (C)	3 Oct 40		(*& P.S. Food* 22 *Oct* 40)	
	Sir A. Duncan (C)	29 Jun 41		C. Waterhouse (C)	8 Feb 41
	J. Llewellin (C)	4 Feb 42	*Sec. Bd Overseas Trade:*		
	H. Dalton (Lab)	22 Feb 42		H. Johnstone (Lib)	15 May 40
				S. Summers (C)	22 Mar 45
			Mines Dept.:		
				D. Grenfell (Lab)	15 May 40
			Sec. Petrol Dept.:		
				G. Lloyd (C)	15 May 40-3 Jun 42
				(3 *Jun* 42 *combined in Min. of Fuel, Light & Power*)	
Transp.	Sir J. Reith (Nat)	14 May 40		(*for Junior Ministers see below, under War Transport*)	
	J. Moore-Brabazon (C)	3 Oct 40			
	(1 *May* 41 *became Min. of War Transport, see below*)				

[1] M.P. Not a member of the House of Lords.

COALITION GOVERNMENT, 1940-1945 *(contd.)*

MINISTERS NOT IN WAR CABINET

War O.	A. EDEN (C)	11 May 40
	D. MARGESSON (C)	22 Dec 40
	SIR J. GRIGG (Nat)	22 Feb 42
War Transp.	LD LEATHERS (C)	1 May 41
1st C. Works	LD TRYON (C)	18 May 40
	SIR J. REITH (LD) (Nat)	3 Oct 40
	(*Min. of Works & Buildings & 1st C. Works* 3 *Oct* 40)	
	LD PORTAL (C)	22 Feb 42
	(*Min. of Works and Planning* 11 *Feb* 42. *Min. of Works Feb* 43)	
	D. SANDYS (C)	21 Nov 44
Law Officers:		
Att.-Gen.	SIR D. SOMERVELL (C)	15 May 40
Sol.-Gen.	SIR W. JOWITT (Lab)	15 May 40
	SIR D. MAXWELL FYFE (C)	4 Mar 42
Ld Advoc.	T. COOPER (C)	15 May 40
	J. REID (C)	5 Jun 41
Sol.-Gen. Scotland	J. REID (C)	15 May 40
	(SIR) D. MURRAY (C)	5 Jun 41
H.M. Household:		
Treas.	R. GRIMSTON (C)	17 May 40
	SIR J. EDMONDSON (C)	12 Mar 42
Comptr.	W. WHITELEY (Lab)	17 May 40
	W. JOHN (Lab)	12 Mar 42
	G. MATHERS (Lab)	2 Oct 44

JUNIOR MINISTERS ATTACHED

U-S.	Sir H. Page Croft (C) (*Ld Croft*)	17 May 40-23 May 45
	Sir E. Grigg (C)	17 May 40-4 Mar 42
	A. Henderson (Lab)	4 Mar 42-7 Feb 43
F.S.	R. Law (C)	17 May 40
	D. Sandys (C)	20 Jul 41
	A. Henderson (Lab)	7 Feb 43
P.S.	F. Montague (Lab)	18 May 40-1 May 41
	(*renamed War Transport* 1 *May* 41)	
	J. Llewellin (C)	1 May 41-4 Feb 42
	Sir A. Salter (Ind)	29 Jun 41-4 Feb 42
	P. Noel-Baker (Lab)	4 Feb 42-23 May 45
P.S.	G. Hicks (Lab)	19 Nov 40-23 May 45
	H. Strauss (C)	4 Mar 42-30 Dec 42
P.S. to Treasury:		
	D. Margesson (C)	17 May 40-22 Dec 40
	Sir C. Edwards (Lab)	17 May 40-12 Mar 42
	J. Stuart (C)	14 Jan 41-23 May 45
	W. Whiteley (Lab)	12 Mar 42-23 May 45
Junior Lds of Treasury:		
	S. Furness (L. Nat)	12 May 40-18 May 40
	J. Stuart (C)	12 May 40-14 Jan 41
	P. Munro (C)	12 May 40-13 Mar 42
	P. Buchan-Hepburn (C)	12 May 40-26 Jun 40
	W. Boulton (C)	12 May 40-13 Mar 42
	W. Paling (Lab)	18 May 40-8 Feb 41
	J. Thomas (C)	26 Jun 40-25 Sep 43
	T. Dugdale (C)	8 Feb 41-23 Feb 42
	W. Adamson (Lab)	1 Mar 41-2 Oct 44
	A. Young (C)	23 Feb 42-3 Jul 44
	J. McEwen (C)	13 Mar 42-6 Dec 44
	L. Pym (C)	13 Mar 42-23 May 45
	A. Beechman (L. Nat)	25 Sep 43-23 May 45
	C. Drewe (C)	3 Jul 44-23 May 45
	W. John (Lab)	2 Oct 44-23 May 45
	P. Buchan-Hepburn (C)	6 Dec 44-23 May 45
Lds in Waiting:		
	Earl Fortescue (C)	31 May 40-22 Mar 45
	Vt Clifden (Lib)	31 May 40-23 May 45
	Ld Alness (L. Nat)	31 May 40-23 May 45
	M of Normanby (C)	22 Mar 45-23 May 45

COALITION GOVERNMENT, 1940-1945 *(contd.)*

MINISTERS NOT IN WAR CABINET			JUNIOR MINISTERS ATTACHED
V. Chamb.	SIR J. EDMONDSON (C)	17 May 40	
	W. BOULTON (C)	12 Mar 42	
	A. YOUNG (C)	13 Jul 44	
Capt. Gents at Arms	LD SNELL (Lab)	31 May 40-21 Apr 44	
	EARL FORTESCUE (C)	22 Mar 45	
Capt. Yeomen of Guard	LD TEMPLEMORE (C)	31 May 40	

CARETAKER GOVERNMENT, 1945

MINISTERS IN CABINET			JUNIOR MINISTERS ATTACHED		
P.M.	**W. Churchill**	23 May 45-26 Jul 45			
Ld Pres.	**Ld Woolton**	25 May 45			
Ld Chanc.	*(office not in cabinet)*				
Privy S.	**Ld Beaverbrook**	25 May 45			
Exch.	**Sir J. Anderson**	25 May 45	*Treasury:*		
			F.S.	O. Peake	26 May 45
For. O.	**A. Eden**	25 May 45	*Min. of State:*		
				W. Mabane[1]	25 May 45
			U-S.	Ld Dunglass[2]	26 May 45
				Ld Lovat	26 May 45
Home O.	**Sir D. Somervell**	25 May 45	*U-S.*	E of Munster	26 May 45
Admir.	**B. Bracken**	25 May 45	*P. & F.S.:*		
				Ld Bruntisfield	26 May 45
			Civil Ld:		
				R. Pilkington	26 May 45
			F.S.	J. Thomas	26 May 45
Ag. & Fish.	**R. Hudson**	25 May 45	*P.S.*	D of Norfolk	26 May 45
				D. Scott	26 May 45
Air	**H. Macmillan**	25 May 45	*U-S.*	Q. Hogg	26 May 45
				Earl Beatty	26 May 45
Col. O.	**O. Stanley**	25 May 45	*U-S.*	D of Devonshire	26 May 45
Def.	**W. Churchill (P.M.)**	25 May 45			
Dom. O.	**Vt Cranborne**	25 May 45	*U-S.*	P. Emrys-Evans	26 May 45
India & Burma O.	**L. Amery**	25 May 45	*P.S.*	E of Scarbrough	26 May 45
Lab. & Nat. S.	**R. Butler**	25 May 45	*P.S.*	M. McCorquodale	26 May 45
Production	**O. Lyttelton** *(& Pres. B.o.T.)*	25 May 45	*P.S.*	J. Maclay	28 May 45
Scot. O.	**E of Rosebery**	25 May 45	*P.S.*	A. Chapman	26 May 45
				T. Galbraith	26 May 45
B.o.T.	**O. Lyttelton** *(& Min. of Production)*	25 May 45	*P.S.*	C. Waterhouse	26 May 45
			Sec. Bd Overseas Trade:		
				S. Summers	26 May 45
War O.	**Sir J. Grigg**	25 May 45	*U-S.*	Ld Croft	26 May 45
			F.S.	M. Petherick	26 May 45

MINISTERS NOT IN CABINET			JUNIOR MINISTERS ATTACHED		
Aircraft Production	E. BROWN	25 May 45	*P.S.*	A. Lennox-Boyd	26 May 45

[1] This office was not formally under the Foreign Office but was more akin to Minister without Portfolio.
[2] M.P. Not a member of the House of Lords.

CARETAKER GOVERNMENT, 1945 *(contd.)*

MINISTERS NOT IN CABINET			JUNIOR MINISTERS ATTACHED		
Civil Av.	Vt Swinton	25 May 45	*P.S.*	R. Perkins	26 May 45
Educ.	R. Law	25 May 45	*P.S.*	Mrs T. Cazalet-Keir	26 May 45
Food	J. Llewellin	25 May 45	*P.S.*	Miss F. Horsbrugh	26 May 45
Fuel & P.	G. Lloyd-George	25 May 45	*P.S.*	Sir A. Hudson	26 May 45
Health	H. Willink	25 May 45	*P.S.*	H. Kerr	26 May 45
Information	G. Lloyd	25 May 45			
D. Lanc.	Sir A. Salter	25 May 45			
Ld Chanc.	Vt Simon	25 May 45			
Min. resident in Mid. East	Sir E. Grigg	25 May 45			
Min. resident in W. Africa	H. Balfour	25 May 45			
Nat. Ins.	L. Hore-Belisha	25 May 45	*P.S.*	C. Peat	26 May 45
Paym.-Gen.	Ld Cherwell	25 May 45			
Pensions	Sir W. Womersley	25 May 45	*P.S.*	W. Sidney (*Ld De L'Isle)*	26 May 45
Postm.-Gen.	H. Crookshank	25 May 45	*Ass.*	W. Anstruther-Gray	26 May 45
Supply	Sir A. Duncan	25 May 45	*P.S.*	R. Grimston	26 May 45
T. & C. Planning	W. Morrison	25 May 45	*P.S.*	R. Tree	26 May 45
War Transp.	Ld Leathers	25 May 45	*P.S.*	P. Thorneycroft	26 May 45
Works	D. Sandys	25 May 45	*P.S.*	R. Manningham-Buller	26 May 45
Law Officers:			*P.S. to Treasury:*		
Att.-Gen.	Sir D. Maxwell Fyfe	25 May 45		J. Stuart	26 May 45
Sol.-Gen.	Sir W. Monckton[1]	25 May 45	*Junior Lds of Treasury:*		
Ld Advoc.	J. Reid	25 May 45		A. Beechman	28 May 45
Sol.-Gen. Scotland	Sir D. Murray	25 May 45		C. Drewe	25 May 45
				P. Buchan-Hepburn	25 May 45
				R. Cary	28 May 45
				C. Mott-Radclyffe	28 May 45
H.M. Household:			*Lds in Waiting:*		
Treas.	Sir J. Edmondson	28 May 45		Ld Alness	28 May 45
Comptr.	L. Pym	28 May 45		M of Normanby	28 May 45
V. Chamb.	A. Young	28 May 45		D of Northumberland	28 May 45
Capt. Gents at Arms	Earl Fortescue	28 May 45			
Capt. Yeomen of Guard	Ld Templemore	28 May 45			

LABOUR GOVERNMENT, 1945-1951

MINISTERS IN CABINET			JUNIOR MINISTERS ATTACHED
P.M.	**C. Attlee**	26 Jul 45-26 Oct 51	
Ld Pres.	**H. Morrison**	27 Jul 45	
	Vt Addison	9 Mar 51	
Ld Chanc.	**Ld Jowitt**	27 Jul 45	

[1]M.P. Not a member of the House of Commons.

LABOUR GOVERNMENT, 1945-1951 *(contd.)*

	MINISTERS IN CABINET			JUNIOR MINISTERS ATTACHED	
Privy S.	**A. Greenwood**	27 Jul 45			
	Ld Inman	17 Apr 47			
	Vt Addison	7 Oct 47			
	E. Bevin	9 Mar 51			
	R. Stokes	26 Apr 51			
	(*also Min. of Materials from* 6 *Jul* 51)				
Exch.	**H. Dalton**	27 Jul 45	*Min. Econ. Affairs:*		
	Sir S. Cripps	13 Nov 47		H. GAITSKELL	28 Feb 50-19 Oct 50
	H. Gaitskell	19 Oct 50			
Min. Econ. Affairs	*(office not established)*		*Treasury:*		
	Sir S. Cripps	29 Sep 47	*F.S.*	W. Glenvil Hall	4 Aug 45
	(*office combined with Exch.* 13 *Nov* 47)			D. Jay	2 Mar 50
			Econ S.:		
				D. Jay	5 Dec 47
				(*office vacant* 2 *Mar* 50)	
				J. Edwards	19 Oct 50
For. O.	**E. Bevin**	27 Jul 45	*Min. of State:*[1]		
	H. Morrison	9 Mar 51		P. NOEL-BAKER	3 Aug 45
				H. MCNEIL	4 Oct 46
				K. YOUNGER	28 Feb 50
			U-S.	H. McNeil	4 Aug 45-4 Oct 46
				C. Mayhew	4 Oct 46-2 Mar 50
				Ld Henderson	7 Jun 48-26 Oct 51
				E. Davies	2 Mar 50-26 Oct 51
Home O.	**C. Ede**	3 Aug 45	*U-S.*	G. Oliver	4 Aug 45
				K. Younger	7 Oct 47
				G. de Freitas	2 Mar 50
Admir.	**A. Alexander**	3 Aug 45		(*for Junior Ministers see below*)	
	(*Vt Hall* 4 *Oct* 46 *& office not in cabinet*)				
Ag. & Fish.	**T. Williams**	3 Aug 45	*P.S.*	E of Huntingdon	4 Aug 45-22 Nov 50
				P. Collick	5 Sep 45-7 Oct 47
				G. Brown	7 Oct 47-26 Apr 51
				E of Listowel	22 Nov 50-26 Oct 51
				A. Champion	26 Apr 51-26 Oct 51
Air	**Vt Stansgate**	3 Aug 45		(*for Junior Ministers see below*)	
	(*P. Noel-Baker* 4 *Oct* 46 *& office not in cabinet*)				
Civil Av.	(*office not in cabinet*)		*P.S.*	I. Thomas	10 Aug 45
	Ld Pakenham	31 May 48		G. Lindgren	4 Oct 46
	(*office not in cabinet* 28 *Feb* 50)			F. Beswick	2 Mar 50
Col. O.	**G. Hall**	3 Aug 45	*Min.*	E OF LISTOWEL	4 Jan 48
	A. Creech Jones	4 Oct 46		J. DUGDALE	28 Feb 50
	J. Griffiths	28 Feb 50	*U-S.*	A. Creech Jones	4 Aug 45
				I. Thomas	4 Oct 46
				D. Rees-Williams	7 Oct 47
				T. Cook	2 Mar 50
C.R.O.	(*office not established*)		*Min.*	A. HENDERSON	14 Aug 47-7 Oct 47
	Vt Addison	7 Jul 47			
	P. Noel-Baker	7 Oct 47	*U-S.*	A. Bottomley	7 Jul 47
	P. Gordon Walker	28 Feb 50		P. Gordon Walker	7 Oct 47
				Ld Holden	2 Mar 50
				D. Rees-Williams (*Ld Ogmore*)	4 Jul 50
				E of Lucan	1 Jun 51
Def.	**C. Attlee (P.M.)**	27 Jul 45			
	A. Alexander (Vt)	20 Dec 46			
	E. Shinwell	28 Feb 50			
Dom. O.	**Vt Addison**	3 Aug 45	*U-S.*	J. Parker	4 Aug 45
	(*became C.R.O.* 7 *Jul* 47 *see above*)			A. Bottomley	10 May 46
Educ.	**Miss E. Wilkinson**	3 Aug 45	*P.S.*	A. Jenkins	4 Aug 45
	G. Tomlinson	10 Feb 47		D. Hardman	30 Oct 45

[1] This office was not formally under the Foreign Office until 1950.

LABOUR GOVERNMENT, 1945-1951 *(contd.)*

	MINISTERS IN CABINET			JUNIOR MINISTERS ATTACHED	
Fuel & P.	**E. Shinwell**	3 Aug 45		*(for Junior Ministers see below)*	
	(H. Gaitskell 7 Oct 47 & office not in cabinet)				
Health	**A. Bevan**	3 Aug 45	*P.S.*	C. Key	4 Aug 45
	(H. Marquand 17 Jan 51 & office not in cabinet)			J. Edwards	12 Feb 47
				A. Blenkinsop	1 Feb 49
India O. &	**Ld Pethick-Lawrence**	3 Aug 45	*U-S.*	A. Henderson	4 Aug 45-14 Aug 47
Burma O.	**E of Listowel**	17 Apr 47			
	(14 Aug 47 & 4 Jan 48 offices abolished)				
Lab. &	**G. Isaacs**	3 Aug 45	*P.S.*	N. Edwards	4 Aug 45
Nat. S.	**A. Bevan**	17 Jan 51		F. Lee	2 Mar 50
	A. Robens	24 Apr 51			
D. Lanc.	*(office not in cabinet)*				
	H. Dalton	31 May 48			
	Vt Alexander	28 Feb 50			
Paym.-Gen.	*(office vacant)*				
	A. Greenwood	9 Jul 46			
	(H. Marquand 5 Mar 47 & office not in cabinet)				
	Vt Addison	2 Jul 48			
	(Ld Macdonald 1 Apr 49 & office not in cabinet)				
Min. without Portfolio	**A. Alexander**	4 Oct 46-20 Dec 46			
	A. Greenwood	17 Apr 47-29 Sep 47			
Scot. O.	**J. Westwood**	3 Aug 45	*U-S.*	G. Buchanan	4 Aug 45-7 Oct 47
	A. Woodburn	7 Oct 47		T. Fraser	4 Aug 45-26 Oct 51
	H. McNeil	28 Feb 50		J. Robertson	7 Oct 47-2 Mar 50
				Miss M. Herbison	2 Mar 50-26 Oct 51
T. & C. Planning	*(office not in cabinet)*		*P.S.*	F. Marshall	10 Aug 45
	H. Dalton	28 Feb 50		E. King	7 Oct 47
	(recast as Local Government & Planning 31 Jan 51)			G. Lindgren	2 Mar 50
B.o.T.	**Sir S. Cripps**	27 Jul 45	*P.S.*	E. Smith	4 Aug 45
	H. Wilson	29 Sep 47		J. Belcher	12 Jan 46
	Sir H. Shawcross	24 Apr 51		J. Edwards	1 Feb 49
				H. Rhodes	2 Mar 50
			Sec. Overseas Trade Dept.:		
				H. Marquand	4 Aug 45
				H. Wilson	5 Mar 47
				A. Bottomley	7 Oct 47
War O.	**J. Lawson**	3 Aug 45		*(for Junior Ministers see below)*	
	(F. Bellenger 4 Oct 46 & office not in cabinet)				

	MINISTERS NOT IN CABINET			JUNIOR MINISTERS ATTACHED	
Admir.	*(office in cabinet)*		*P. & F.S.:*		
	VT HALL	4 Oct 46		J. Dugdale	4 Aug 45
	LD PAKENHAM	24 May 51		J. Callaghan	2 Mar 50
			Civil Ld:		
				W. Edwards	4 Aug 45
Air	*(office in cabinet)*		*U-S.*	J. Strachey	4 Aug 45
	P. NOEL-BAKER	4 Oct 46		G. de Freitas	27 May 46
	A. HENDERSON	7 Oct 47		A. Crawley	2 Mar 50
Aircraft Production	J. WILMOT	4 Aug 45	*P.S.*	A. Woodburn	4 Aug 45
	(office abolished 1 Apr 46)				
Civil Av.	LD WINSTER	4 Aug 45		*(for Junior Ministers see above)*	
	LD NATHAN	4 Oct 46			
	(Ld Pakenham 31 May 48 & office in cabinet)				
	LD PAKENHAM	28 Feb 50			
	LD OGMORE	1 Jun 51			

LABOUR GOVERNMENT, 1945-1951 *(contd.)*

	MINISTERS NOT IN CABINET			JUNIOR MINISTERS ATTACHED	
Food	Sir B. Smith	3 Aug 45	*P.S.*	Edith Summerskill	4 Aug 45
	J. Strachey	27 May 46		S. Evans	2 Mar 50
	M. Webb	28 Feb 50		F. Willey	18 Apr 50
Fuel & P.	*(office in cabinet)*		*P.S.*	W. Foster	4 Aug 45
	H. Gaitskell	7 Oct 47		H. Gaitskell	10 May 46
	P. Noel-Baker	28 Feb 50		A. Robens	7 Oct 47
				H. Neal	26 Apr 51
Health	*(office in cabinet)*			*(for Junior Ministers see above)*	
	H. Marquand	17 Jan 51			
Information	E. Williams	4 Aug 45			
	E. of Listowel	26 Feb 46			
	(office wound up 31 *Mar* 46)				
D. Lanc.	J. Hynd	4 Aug 45			
	Ld Pakenham	17 Apr 47			
	(*H. Dalton* 31 *May* 48 *& office in cabinet)*				
Nat. Ins.	J. Griffiths	4 Aug 45	*P.S.*	G. Lindgren	4 Aug 45
	Edith Summerskill	28 Feb 50		T. Steele	4 Oct 46
				H. Taylor	2 Mar 50
Paym.-Gen.	*(office in cabinet)*				
	H. Marquand	5 Mar 47			
	(*Vt Addison* 2 *Jul* 48 *& office in cabinet)*				
	Ld Macdonald of Gwaenysgor	1 Apr 49			
Pensions	W. Paling	3 Aug 45	*P.S.*	Mrs J. Adamson	4 Aug 45
	J. Hynd	17 Apr 47		A. Blenkinsop	10 May 46
	G. Buchanan	7 Oct 47		C. Simmons	1 Feb 49
	H. Marquand	2 Jul 48			
	G. Isaacs	17 Jan 51			
Postm.-Gen.	E of Listowel	4 Aug 45	*Ass.*	W. Burke	10 Aug 45
	W. Paling	17 Apr 47		C. Hobson	7 Oct 47
	N. Edwards	28 Feb 50			
Supply	J. Wilmot	3 Aug 45	*P.S.*	W. Leonard	4 Aug 45-7 Oct 47
	G. Strauss	7 Oct 47		A. Woodburn	1 Apr 46-7 Oct 47
				J. Freeman	7 Oct 47-2 Mar 50
				J. Jones	7 Oct 47-2 Mar 50
				J. Freeman	2 Mar 50-2 May 51
				M. Stewart	2 May 51-26 Oct 51
T. & C. Planning	L. Silkin	4 Aug 45		*(for Junior Ministers see above)*	
	(H. Dalton 28 *Feb* 50 *& office in cabinet)*				
Transp.[1]	A. Barnes	3 Aug 45	*P.S.*	G. Strauss	4 Aug 45
				J. Callaghan	7 Oct 47
				Ld Lucas of Chilworth	2 Mar 50
War O.	*(office in cabinet)*		*U-S.*	Ld Nathan	4 Aug 45
	F. Bellenger	4 Oct 46		Ld Pakenham	4 Oct 46-17 Apr 47
	E. Shinwell	7 Oct 47	*F.S.*	F. Bellenger	4 Aug 45
	J. Strachey	28 Feb 50		J. Freeman	4 Oct 46-17 Apr 47
			U. & F.S.	J. Freeman	17 Apr 47
				M. Stewart	7 Oct 47
				W. Wyatt	2 May 51
Works	G. Tomlinson	4 Aug 45	*P.S.*	H. Wilson	4 Aug 45
	C. Key	10 Feb 47		E. Durbin	5 Mar 47
	R. Stokes	28 Feb 50		Ld Morrison	26 Sep 48
	G. Brown	26 Apr 51			
Law Officers:			*P.S. to Treasury:*		
Att.-Gen.	Sir H. Shawcross	4 Aug 45		W. Whiteley	3 Aug 45
	Sir F. Soskice	24 Apr 51	*Junior Lds of Treasury:*		
				R. Taylor	4 Aug 45-26 Oct 51
Sol.-Gen.	Sir F. Soskice	4 Aug 45		J. Henderson	4 Aug 45-1 Jan 50
	Sir L. Ungoed-Thomas	24 Apr 51		M. Stewart	10 Aug 45-30 Mar 46

[1] Ministry of War Transport until 6 Mar 46.

LABOUR GOVERNMENT, 1945-1951 *(contd.)*

MINISTERS NOT IN CABINET

Law Officers:

Ld Advoc.	G. Thomson	10 Aug 45
	J. Wheatley	7 Oct 47
Sol.-Gen. Scotland	D. Blades[1]	10 Sep 45
	J. Wheatley	19 Mar 47
	D. Johnston	24 Oct 47

H.M. Household:

Treas.	G. Mathers	4 Aug 45
	A. Pearson	30 Mar 46
Comptr.	A. Pearson	4 Aug 45
	M. Stewart	30 Mar 46
	F. Collindridge	9 Dec 46
V. Chamb.	J. Snow	10 Aug 45
	M. Stewart	9 Dec 46
	E. Popplewell	16 Oct 47
Capt. Gents at Arms	Ld Ammon	4 Aug 45
	Ld Shepherd	18 Oct 49
Capt. Yeomen of Guard	Ld Walkden	4 Aug 45
	Ld Shepherd	6 Jul 49
	Ld Lucas of Chilworth	18 Oct 49
	E of Lucan	5 Mar 50
	Ld Archibald	8 Jun 51

JUNIOR MINISTERS ATTACHED

	A. Blenkinsop	10 Aug 45-10 May 46
	F. Collindridge	10 Aug 45-9 Dec 46
	C. Simmons	30 Mar 46-1 Feb 49
	W. Hannan	10 May 46-26 Oct 51
	J. Snow	9 Dec 46-3 Mar 50
	R. Adams	1 Feb 49-23 Apr 50
	W. Wilkins	1 Jan 50-26 Oct 51
	H. Bowden	3 Mar 50-26 Oct 51
	C. Royle	23 Apr 50-26 Oct 51
Lds in Waiting:		
	Ld Westwood	10 Sep 45-17 Jan 47
	Ld Pakenham	14 Oct 45-4 Oct 46
	Ld Henderson	21 Oct 45-7 Jun 48
	Ld Chorley	11 Oct 46-31 Mar 50
	Ld Morrison	17 Jan 47-26 Sep 48
	Ld Lucas of Chilworth	9 Jul 48-18 Oct 49
	Ld Shepherd	14 Oct 48-6 Jul 49
	Ld Kershaw	6 Jul 49-26 Oct 51
	Ld Darwen	18 Oct 49-26 Dec 50
	Ld Burden	31 Mar 50-26 Oct 51
	Ld Haden-Guest	13 Feb 51-26 Oct 51

CONSERVATIVE GOVERNMENT, 1951-1957

MINISTERS IN CABINET			JUNIOR MINISTERS ATTACHED		
P.M.	**(Sir) W. Churchill**	26 Oct 51-5 Apr 55			
	Sir A. Eden	6 Apr 55-9 Jan 57			
Ld Pres.	**Ld Woolton**	28 Oct 51			
	M of Salisbury	24 Nov 52			
Ld Chanc.	**Ld Simonds**	30 Oct 51			
	Vt Kilmuir	18 Oct 54			
Privy S.	**M of Salisbury**	28 Oct 51			
	H. Crookshank	7 May 52			
	R. Butler	20 Dec 55			
Exch.	**R. Butler**	28 Oct 51	*Min. Econ. Affs.*		
	H. Macmillan	20 Dec 55		Sir A. Salter	31 Oct 51
				(24 *Nov* 52 *office abolished)*	
			Treasury:		
			F.S.	J. Boyd-Carpenter	31 Oct 51
				H. Brooke	28 Jul 54
			Econ. S.:	R. Maudling	24 Nov 52
				Sir E. Boyle	7 Apr 55
				D. Walker-Smith	11 Nov 56
For. O.	**(Sir) A. Eden**	28 Oct 51	*Min. of State*	S. Lloyd	30 Oct 51-18 Oct 54
	H. Macmillan	7 Apr 55		M of Reading	11 Nov 53-9 Jan 57
	S. Lloyd	20 Dec 55		A. Nutting	18 Oct 54-3 Nov 56
				A. Noble	9 Nov 56-9 Jan 57
			U-S.	M of Reading	31 Oct 51-11 Nov 53
				A. Nutting	31 Oct 51-18 Oct 54
				D. Dodds-Parker	11 Nov 53-18 Oct 54
				R. Turton	18 Oct 54-20 Dec 55
				D. Dodds-Parker	20 Dec 55-9 Jan 57

(continued)

[1] Not a member of the House of Commons.

CONSERVATIVE GOVERNMENT, 1951-1957 *(contd.)*

	MINISTERS IN CABINET			JUNIOR MINISTERS ATTACHED	
				Ld J. Hope[1]	18 Oct 54-9 Nov 56
				D. Ormsby-Gore	9 Nov 56-9 Jan 57
Home O. & Welsh Affs.	**Sir D. Maxwell Fyfe (Vt Kilmuir)**	28 Oct 51	*U-S.*	D. Llewellyn	5 Nov 51-14 Oct 52
	G. Lloyd-George	18 Oct 54		Sir H. Lucas-Tooth	3 Feb 52-20 Dec 55
				Ld Lloyd	24 Nov 52-18 Oct 54
				Ld Mancroft	18 Oct 54-9 Jan 57
				W. Deedes	20 Dec 55-9 Jan 57
Ag. & Fish.	*(office not in cabinet)*				
	Sir T. Dugdale	3 Sep 53	*P.S.*	Ld Carrington	5 Nov 51-18 Oct 54
	D. Heathcoat Amory	28 Jul 54		R. Nugent	5 Nov 51-9 Jan 57
	(18 *Oct* 54 *Min. of Ag. & Fish. combined with Min. of Food)*			Earl St Aldwyn	18 Oct 54-9 Jan 57
				H. Nicholls	7 Apr 55-9 Jan 57
Col. O.	**O. Lyttelton**	28 Oct 51	*Min.*	A. Lennox-Boyd	2 Nov 51
	A. Lennox-Boyd	28 Jul 54		H. Hopkinson	7 May 52
				J. Hare	20 Dec 55
				J. Maclay	18 Oct 56
			U-S.	E of Munster	5 Nov 51
				Ld Lloyd	18 Oct 54
C.R.O.	**Ld Ismay**	28 Oct 51	*U-S.*	J. Foster	3 Nov 51
	M of Salisbury	12 Mar 52		D. Dodds-Parker	18 Oct 54
	Vt Swinton	24 Nov 52		A. Noble	20 Dec 55
	E of Home	7 Apr 55		Ld J. Hope[1]	9 Nov 56
Co-ordination of Transport, Fuel & Power	**Ld Leathers**	30 Oct 51			
	(3 *Sep* 53 *office abolished)*				
Def.	**W. Churchill (P.M.)**	28 Oct 51	*P.S.*	N. Birch	28 Feb 52
	Earl Alexander of Tunis	1 Mar 52		Ld Carrington	18 Oct 54
	H. Macmillan	18 Oct 54		E of Gosford	26 May 56
	S. Lloyd	7 Apr 55			
	Sir W. Monckton	20 Dec 55			
	A. Head	18 Oct 56			
Educ.	*(office not in cabinet)*		*P.S.*	K. Pickthorn	5 Nov 51
	Miss F. Horsbrugh	3 Sep 53		D. Vosper	18 Oct 54
	Sir D. Eccles	18 Oct 54			
Food	*(office not in cabinet)*				
	G. Lloyd-George	3 Sep 53	*P.S.*	C. Hill	31 Oct 51
	D. Heathcoat Amory	18 Oct 54			
	(& combined with Min. of Ag. & Fish.)				
Health	**H. Crookshank**	30 Oct 51	*P.S.*	Miss P. Hornsby-Smith	3 Nov 51
	(*I. Macleod* 7 *May* 52 *& office not in cabinet)*				
Housing & Loc. Govt.	**H. Macmillan**	30 Oct 51	*P.S.*	E. Marples	3 Nov 51
	D. Sandys	18 Oct 54		W. Deedes	18 Oct 54
				E. Powell	20 Dec 55
Lab. & Nat. S.	**Sir W. Monckton**	28 Oct 51	*P.S.*	Sir P. Bennett	31 Oct 51
	I. Macleod	20 Dec 55		H. Watkinson	28 May 52
				R. Carr	20 Dec 55
D. Lanc.	*(office not in cabinet)*				
	Ld Woolton (Vt)	24 Nov 52			
	(3 *Sep* 53-16 Aug 54 *also Min. of Materials)*				
	E of Selkirk	20 Dec 55			
Paym.-Gen.	**Ld Cherwell**	30 Oct 51			
	(11 *Nov* 53 *E of Selkirk & office not in cabinet)*				
	Sir W. Monckton	18 Oct 56			
Pensions & Nat. Ins.	*(office not in cabinet)*			*(for Junior Ministers see below)*	
	O. Peake	18 Oct 54			
	(20 *Dec* 55 *J. Boyd-Carpenter & office not in cabinet)*				

[1] M.P. Not a member of the House of Lords.

CONSERVATIVE GOVERNMENT, 1951-1957 *(contd.)*

	MINISTERS IN CABINET			JUNIOR MINISTERS ATTACHED	
Scot. O.	**J. Stuart**	30 Oct 51	*Min.*	E of Home	2 Nov 51
				T. Galbraith *(Ld Strathclyde)*	7 Apr 55
			U-S.	T. Galbraith	2 Nov 51-5 Apr 55
				W. Snadden	2 Nov 51-13 Jun 55
				J. Henderson Stewart	4 Feb 52-9 Jan 57
				J. Browne	7 Apr 55-9 Jan 57
				N. Macpherson	13 Jun 55-9 Jan 57
B.o.T.	**P. Thorneycroft**	30 Oct 51	*Min.*	D. Heathcoat Amory	3 Sep 53
				T. Low	28 Jul 54
			P.S.	H. Strauss	3 Nov 51
				D. Kaberry	7 Apr 55
				D. Walker-Smith	19 Oct 55
				F. Erroll	11 Nov 56
			Sec. Overseas Trade:		
				H. Hopkinson	3 Nov 51
				H. Mackeson	28 May 52
				(3 Sep 53 office abolished, Min. of State established)	
Works	*(office not in cabinet)*			*(for Junior Ministers see below)*	
	P. Buchan-Hepburn	20 Dec 55			
	MINISTERS NOT IN CABINET			JUNIOR MINISTERS ATTACHED	
Admir.	J. Thomas *(Vt Cilcennin)*	31 Oct 51	*P. & F.S.:*		
				A. Noble	5 Nov 51
	Vt Hailsham	2 Sep 56		G. Ward	20 Dec 55
			Civil Ld:		
				S. Wingfield Digby	5 Nov 51
Ag. & Fish.	Sir T. Dugdale *(3 Sep 53 office in cabinet)*	31 Oct 51		*(for Junior Ministers see above)*	
Air	Ld De L'Isle and Dudley	31 Oct 51	*U-S.*	N. Birch	3 Nov 51
				G. Ward	29 Feb 52
	N. Birch	20 Dec 55		C. Soames	20 Dec 55
Educ.	Miss F. Horsbrugh *(3 Sep 53 office in cabinet)*	2 Nov 51		*(for Junior Ministers see above)*	
Food	G. Lloyd-George *(3 Sep 53 office in cabinet)*	31 Oct 51		*(for Junior Ministers see above)*	
Fuel & P.	G. Lloyd	31 Oct 51	*P.S.*	L. Joynson-Hicks	5 Nov 51
	A. Jones	20 Dec 55		D. Renton	20 Dec 55
Health	*(office in cabinet)*			*(for Junior Ministers see above)*	
	I. Macleod	7 May 52			
	R. Turton	20 Dec 55			
D. Lanc.	Vt Swinton *(also Min. of Materials; 24 Nov 52, Ld Woolton became D. Lanc. & office in cabinet)*	31 Oct 51-24 Nov 52			
Materials	Vt Swinton *(also D. Lanc.)*	31 Oct 51-24 Nov 52			
	Sir A. Salter *(1 Sep 53-16 Aug 54 Ld Woolton combined Materials with D. Lanc. in cabinet. 16 Aug 54 Min. of Materials wound up)*	24 Nov 52-1 Sep 53			
Min. without Portfolio	E of Munster	18 Oct 54-9 Jan 57			
Nat. Ins.	O. Peake *(3 Sep 53 combined with Min. of Pensions, see below)*	31 Oct 51	*P.S.*	R. Turton	5 Nov 51-3 Sep 53
Paym.-Gen.	*(office in cabinet)*				
	E of Selkirk *(20 Dec 55 office vacant, Sir W. Monckton 18 Oct 56 & office in cabinet)*	11 Nov 53			

CONSERVATIVE GOVERNMENT, 1951-1957 *(contd.)*

MINISTERS NOT IN CABINET

Pensions (& Nat. Ins.)	D. HEATHCOAT AMORY	5 Nov 51
	(1 *Sep* 53 *combined Min. of Pensions & National Insurance)*	
	O. PEAKE	3 Sep 53
	(18 *Oct* 54 *office in cabinet)*	
	J. BOYD-CARPENTER	20 Dec 55
Postm.-Gen.	EARL DE LA WARR	5 Nov 51
	C. HILL	7 Apr 55
Power	*(see Fuel & Power above)*	
Supply	D. SANDYS	31 Oct 51
	S. LLOYD	18 Oct 54
	R. MAUDLING	7 Apr 55
Transp. (& Civil Av.)	J. MACLAY	31 Oct 51
	A. LENNOX-BOYD	7 May 52
	(*Ministries of Transport & Civil Aviation merged* 1 *Oct* 53)	
	J. BOYD-CARPENTER	28 Jul 54
	H. WATKINSON	20 Dec 55
War O.	A. HEAD	31 Oct 51
	J. HARE	18 Oct 56
Works	(SIR) D ECCLES	1 Nov 51
	N. BIRCH	18 Oct 54
	(20 *Dec* 55 *P. Buchan-Hepburn & office in cabinet)*	
Law Officers:		
Att.-Gen.	SIR L. HEALD	3 Nov 51
	SIR R. MANNINGHAM-BULLER	18 Oct 54
Sol.-Gen.	SIR R. MANNINGHAM-BULLER	3 Nov 51
	SIR H. HYLTON-FOSTER	18 Oct 54
Ld Advoc.	J. CLYDE	2 Nov 51
	W. MILLIGAN	30 Dec 54
Sol.-Gen. Scotland	W. MILLIGAN[1]	3 Nov 51
	W. GRANT	10 Jan 55
H.M. Household:		
Treas.	(SIR) C. DREWE	7 Nov 51
	T. GALBRAITH (JNR)	13 Jun 55
Comptr.	R. CONANT	7 Nov 51
	T. GALBRAITH (JNR)	7 Jun 54
	H. OAKSHOTT	13 Jun 55
V. Chamb.	H. STUDHOLME	7 Nov 51
	R. THOMPSON	8 Apr 56
Capt. Gents ar Arms	EARL FORTESCUE	5 Nov 51
Capt. Yeomen of Guard	E OF ONSLOW	5 Nov 51

JUNIOR MINISTERS ATTACHED

P.S.	J. Smyth	5 Nov 51-20 Dec 55
	R. Turton	3 Sep 53-18 Oct 54
	E. Marples	18 Oct 54-20 Dec 55
	Miss E. Pitt	20 Dec 55-9 Jan 57
	R. Wood	20 Dec 55-9 Jan 57
Ass.	D. Gammans	5 Nov 51
	C. Alport	20 Dec 55
P.S.	T. Low	3 Nov 51
	Sir E. Boyle	28 Jul 54
	F. Erroll	7 Apr 55
	I. Harvey	11 Nov 56
P.S.	J. Braithwaite	5 Nov 51-1 Nov 53
	R. Maudling	18 Apr 52-24 Nov 52
	J. Profumo	24 Nov 52-9 Jan 57
	H. Molson	11 Nov 53-9 Jan 57
U-S. & F.S.		
	J. Hutchison	5 Nov 51
	F. Maclean	18 Oct 54
P.S.	H. Molson	3 Nov 51
	R. Bevins	11 Nov 53
P.S. to Treasury:		
	P. Buchan-Hepburn	30 Oct 51
	E. Heath	30 Dec 55
Junior Lds of Treasury:		
	H. Mackeson	7 Nov 51-28 May 52
	(Sir) H. Butcher	7 Nov 51-3 Jul 53
	E. Heath	7 Nov 51-20 Dec 55
	T. Galbraith (Jnr)	7 Nov 51-4 Jun 54
	D. Vosper	7 Nov 51-18 Oct 54
	H. Oakshott	28 May 52-13 June 55
	M. Redmayne	3 Jul 53-9 Jan 57
	R. Thompson	28 Jul 54-8 Apr 56
	G. Wills	26 Oct 54-9 Jan 57
	P. Legh	13 Jun 55-9 Jan 57
	E. Wakefield	24 Jan 56-9 Jan 57
	H. Harrison	8 Apr 56-9 Jan 57
Lds in Waiting:		
	E of Birkenhead	5 Nov 51-28 Jan 55
	E of Selkirk	5 Nov 51-11 Nov 53
	Ld Lloyd	7 Nov 51-24 Nov 52
	Ld Mancroft	15 Dec 52-18 Oct 54
	Ld Hawke	11 Nov 53-9 Jan 57
	Ld Fairfax	18 Oct 54-9 Jan 57
	Ld Chesham	28 Jan 55-9 Jan 57

[1] Not a member of the House of Commons.

CONSERVATIVE GOVERNMENT, 1957-1964

	MINISTERS IN CABINET			JUNIOR MINISTERS ATTACHED	
P.M.	**H. Macmillan**	10 Jan 57-13 Oct 63			
	Sir A. Douglas-Home (*formerly E of Home*)	18 Oct 63-16 Oct 64			
First Sec. of State	**R. Butler**	13 Jul 62			
	(*office wound up* 18 *Oct* 63)				
Ld Pres.	**M of Salisbury**	13 Jan 57			
	E of Home	29 Mar 57			
	Vt Hailsham	17 Sep 57			
	E of Home	14 Oct 59			
	Vt Hailsham *(Q. Hogg)* (*also Min. for Science*)	27 Jul 60			
Ld Chanc.	**Vt Kilmuir**	14 Jan 57			
	Ld Dilhorne	13 Jul 62			
Privy S.	**R. Butler** (*also Home Sec.*)	13 Jan 57			
	Vt Hailsham (*also Min. for Science*)	14 Oct 59			
	E. Heath	27 Jul 60			
	S. Lloyd	20 Oct 63			
Exch.	**P. Thorneycroft**	13 Jan 57	*Treasury:*		
	D. Heathcoat Amory	6 Jan 58	*F.S.*	E. Powell	16 Jan 57
	S. Lloyd	27 Jul 60		J. Simon	6 Jan 58
	R. Maudling	13 Jul 62		Sir E. Boyle	22 Oct 59
	(*see also Paymaster-General*)			A. Barber	16 Jul 62
				A. Green	23 Oct 63
			Econ. S.:		
				N. Birch	16 Jan 57
				(*office vacant* 6 *Jan* 58)	
				F. Erroll	23 Oct 58
				A. Barber	22 Oct 59
				E. du Cann	16 Jul 62
				M. Macmillan	21 Oct 63
For. O.	**S. Lloyd**	14 Jan 57	*Min. of State:*		
	E of Home	27 Jul 60		A. NOBLE	16 Jan 57-16 Jan 59
	R. Butler	20 Oct 63		D. ORMSBY-GORE	16 Jan 57-27 Jun 61
				J. PROFUMO	16 Jan 59-27 Jul 60
				J. GODBER	27 Jun 61-27 Jun 63
				E OF DUNDEE	9 Oct 61-16 Oct 64
				P. THOMAS	27 Jun 63-16 Oct 64
			U-S.	E of Gosford	18 Jan 57-23 Oct 58
				I. Harvey	18 Jan 57-24 Nov 58
				M of Lansdowne	23 Oct 58-20 Apr 62
				J. Profumo	28 Nov 58-16 Jan 59
				R. Allan	16 Jan 59-7 Oct 60
				J. Godber	28 Oct 60-27 Jun 61
				P. Thomas	27 Jun 61-27 Jun 63
				(*office left vacant*)	
				P. Smithers	16 Jul 62-29 Jan 64
				R. Mathew	30 Jan 64-16 Oct 64

CONSERVATIVE GOVERNMENT, 1957–1964 *(contd.)*

	MINISTERS IN CABINET		JUNIOR MINISTERS ATTACHED		
Home O.	**R. Butler**	13 Jan 57	*Min. Home Affs.:*		
	H. Brooke	13 Jul 62		D. Vosper	28 Oct 60
				D. Renton	27 Jun 61
				Earl Jellicoe	17 Jul 62
				Ld Derwent	21 Oct 63
			U-S.	Miss P. Hornsby-Smith	18 Jan 57-22 Oct 59
				J. Simon	18 Jan 57-6 Jan 58
				D. Renton	17 Jan 58-27 Jun 61
				D. Vosper	22 Oct 59-28 Oct 60
				Earl Bathurst	8 Feb 61-16 Jul 62
				C. Fletcher-Cooke	27 Jun 61-27 Feb 63
				C. Woodhouse	16 Jul 62-16 Oct 64
				Miss M. Pike	1 Mar 63-16 Oct 64
Ag. Fish. & Food	**D. Heathcoat Amory**	14 Jan 57	*P.S.*	Earl St Aldwyn	18 Jan 57-27 Jun 58
	J. Hare	6 Jan 58		J. Godber	18 Jan 57-28 Oct 60
	C. Soames	27 Jul 60		Earl Waldegrave	27 Jun 58-16 Jul 62
				W. Vane	28 Oct 60-16 Jul 62
				Ld St. Oswald	16 Jul 62-16 Oct 64
				J. Scott-Hopkins	16 Jul 62-16 Oct 64
Aviation	*(see Transp. & Civil Av.)*			*(for Junior Ministers see below Transp. & Civil Aviation)*	
	D. Sandys	14 Oct 59			
	P. Thorneycroft	27 Jul 60	*P.S.*	G. Rippon	22 Oct 59
	(J. Amery and office not in cabinet 16 Jul 62)			C. Woodhouse	9 Oct 61
				B. de Ferranti	16 Jul 62
				N. Marten	3 Dec 62
Col. O.	**A. Lennox-Boyd**	14 Jan 57	*Min.*	E of Perth	16 Jan 57
	I. Macleod	14 Oct 59		M of Lansdowne	20 Apr 62
	R. Maudling	9 Oct 61		*(joint with C.R.O. 21 Oct 63)*	
	(joint minister with C.R.O. 13 Jul 62)		*U-S.*	J. Profumo	18 Jan 57
	D. Sandys	13 Jul 62		J. Amery	28 Nov 58
				H. Fraser	28 Oct 60
				N. Fisher	16 Jul 62-16 Oct 64
				R. Hornby	24 Oct 63-16 Oct 64
				(joint with C.R.O. 21 Oct 63)	
C.R.O.	**E of Home**	14 Jan 57	*Min.*	C. Alport	22 Oct 59-8 Feb 61
	D. Sandys	27 Jul 60		D of Devonshire	6 Sep 62-16 Oct 64
	(joint minister with Col. O. 13 Jul 62)			*(joint with Col. O. 21 Oct 63)*	
			U-S.	C. Alport	18 Jan 57
				R. Thompson	22 Oct 59
				D of Devonshire	28 Oct 60-6 Sep 62
				B. Braine	8 Feb 61-16 Jul 62
				J. Tilney	16 Jul 62-16 Oct 64
				(joint with Col. O. 21 Oct 63)	
Defence	**D. Sandys**	13 Jan 57	*P.S.*	Ld Mancroft	18 Jan 57
	H. Watkinson	14 Oct 59		*(11 Jun 57 office vacant)*	
	P. Thorneycroft	13 Jul 62		*(reorganisation 1 Apr 64)*	
			Ministers of State:		
			Air	H. Fraser	1 Apr 64
			Army	J. Ramsden	1 Apr 64
			Navy	Earl Jellicoe	1 Apr 64
			U-S. Air Force	J. Ridsdale	1 Apr 64
			U-S. Army	P. Kirk	1 Apr 64
			U-S. Navy	J. Hay	1 Apr 64
Educ.	**Vt Hailsham**	13 Jan 57	*P.S.*	Sir E. Boyle	18 Jan 57
	G. Lloyd	17 Sep 57		K. Thompson	22 Oct 59

CONSERVATIVE GOVERNMENT, 1957–1964 *(contd.)*

	MINISTERS IN CABINET			JUNIOR MINISTERS ATTACHED	
	Sir D. Eccles	14 Oct 59		C. Chataway	16 Jul 62
	Sir E. Boyle	13 Jul 62		*(reorganisation* 1 *Apr* 64)	
	(*Educ. & Science* 1 *Apr* 64)		*Ministers of State:*		
	Q. Hogg	1 Apr 64		*(Sir E. Boyle, and seat in cabinet)*	1 Apr 64
	(formerly Vt Hailsham)				
Min. of State Educ.	**Sir E. Boyle**	1 Apr 64		Ld Newton	1 Apr 64
			U-S.	E of Bessborough	1 Apr 64
				C. Chataway	1 Apr 64
				(for Junior Ministers see below)	
Health	*(office not in cabinet)*				
	E. Powell	13 Jul 62			
	A. Barber	20 Oct 63			
			Min. of State for Welsh Affairs:		
Housing, Loc. Govt. & Welsh Affs.	**H. Brooke**	13 Jan 57		Ld Brecon	12 Dec 57
	C. Hill	9 Oct 61	*P.S.*	R. Bevins	18 Jan 57
	Sir K. Joseph	13 Jul 62		Sir K. Joseph	22 Oct 59-9 Oct 61
				Earl Jellicoe	27 Jun 61-16 Jul 62
				G. Rippon	9 Oct 61-16 Jul 62
				F. Corfield	16 Jul 62-16 Oct 64
				Ld Hastings	3 Dec 62-16 Oct 64
Lab. & Nat. S.	**I. Macleod**	14 Jan 57	*P.S.*	R. Carr	19 Jan 57
	E. Heath	14 Oct 59		R. Wood	14 Apr 58
	(12 *Nov* 59—*Min. of Labour)*			P. Thomas	22 Oct 59
	J. Hare	27 Jul 60		A. Green	27 Jun 61
	J. Godber	20 Oct 63		W. Whitelaw	16 Jul 62
D. Lanc.	**C. Hill**	13 Jan 57			
	I. Macleod	9 Oct 61			
	Vt Blakenham (*J. Hare)*	20 Oct 63			
Paym.-Gen.	*(office not in cabinet)*				
	R. Maudling	17 Sep 57			
	Ld Mills	14 Oct 59			
	(after 9 *Oct* 61 *Chief Sec. to Treasury & Paymaster-General)*				
	H. Brooke	9 Oct 61			
	J. Boyd-Carpenter	13 Jul 62			
Min. without Portfolio	*(office not in cabinet)*				
	Ld Mills	9 Oct 61-14 Jul 62			
	W. Deedes	13 Jul 62-16 Oct 64			
	Ld Carrington	20 Oct 63-16 Oct 64			
Power	**Ld Mills**	13 Jan 57	*P.S.*	D. Renton	18 Jan 57
	(14 *Oct* 59 *R. Wood & office not in cabinet)*			Sir I. Horobin	17 Jan 58
				J. George	22 Oct 59
	F. Erroll	20 Oct 63		J. Peyton	25 Jun 62
Science	**Vt Hailsham**	14 Oct 59	*P.S.*	D. Freeth	8 Feb 61
	(1 *Apr* 64 *Educ. & Science)*			E of Bessborough	24 Oct 63
				(1 *Apr* 64, *Educ. & Science)*	
Scot. O.	**J. Maclay**	13 Jan 57	*Min.*	Ld Strathclyde	17 Jan 57
	M. Noble	13 Jul 62		Ld Forbes	23 Oct 58
				J. Browne (*Ld Craigton)*	22 Oct 59
			U-S.	J. Browne	18 Jan 57-22 Oct 59
				N. Macpherson	19 Jan 57-28 Oct 60
				Ld J. Hope	18 Jan 57-22 Oct 59
				T. Galbraith	22 Oct 59-8 Nov 62
				G. Leburn	22 Oct 59-15 Aug 63
				R. Brooman-White	28 Oct 60-12 Dec 63
				Lady Tweedsmuir	3 Dec 62-16 Oct 64
				A. Stodart	19 Aug 63-16 Oct 64
				G. Campbell	12 Dec 63-16 Oct 64

CONSERVATIVE GOVERNMENT, 1957–1964 *(contd.)*

	MINISTERS IN CABINET			JUNIOR MINISTERS ATTACHED	
B.o.T.	**Sir D. Eccles**	13 Jan 57	*Min.*	D. Walker-Smith	16 Jan 57
	R. Maudling	14 Oct 59		J. Vaughan-Morgan	17 Sep 57
	F. Erroll	9 Oct 61		F. Erroll	22 Oct 59
	E. Heath	20 Oct 63		Sir K. Joseph	9 Oct 61
	(also Sec. of State for Industry,			A. Green	16 Jul 62-23 Oct 63
	Trade & Regional Development)			Ld Derwent	6 Sep 62-23 Oct 63
				Ld Drumalbyn	23 Oct 63-16 Oct 64
				(formerly N. Macpherson)	
				E. du Cann	21 Oct 63-16 Oct 64
			P.S.	F. Erroll	18 Jan 57
				J. Rodgers	24 Oct 58
				N. Macpherson	28 Oct 60
				D. Price	17 Jul 62
Transp. & Civil Av.	**H. Watkinson**	13 Jan 57	*P.S.*	R. Nugent	18 Jan 57-22 Oct 59
	(14 Oct 59 Min. of Transp. only)			A. Neave	18 Jan 57-16 Jan 59
	E. Marples	14 Oct 59		J. Hay	16 Jan 59-3 May 63
	(see above, Min. of Aviation)			Ld Chesham	22 Oct 59-16 Oct 64
				J. Hughes-Hallett	26 Apr 61-16 Oct 64
				T. Galbraith	3 May 63-16 Oct 64
				(for Junior Ministers see below)	
Works	*(office not in cabinet)*				
	G. Rippon	20 Oct 63			
	(Min. of Public Building & Works)				

	MINISTERS NOT IN CABINET			JUNIOR MINISTERS ATTACHED	
Admir.	E of Selkirk	16 Jan 57	*P. & F.S.*	C. Soames	18 Jan 57
	Ld Carrington	16 Oct 59		R. Allan	17 Jan 58
	Earl Jellicoe	22 Oct 63		C. Orr Ewing	16 Jan 59
	(1 Apr 64, reorganised under Min. of Defence)			*(16 Oct 59 office vacant)*	
			Civil Ld:	T. Galbraith	18 Jan 57
				C. Orr Ewing	16 Oct 59
				J. Hay	3 May 63
Air	G. Ward	16 Jan 57	*U-S.*	C. Orr Ewing	18 Jan 57
	J. Amery	28 Oct 60		A. Neave	16 Jan 59
	H. Fraser	16 Jul 62		W. Taylor	16 Oct 59
	(1 Apr 64, reorganised under Min. of Defence)			J. Ridsdale	16 Jul 62
Aviation	*(office in cabinet)*				
	J. Amery	16 Jul 62		*(for Junior Ministers see above)*	
Health	D. Vosper	16 Jan 57	*P.S.*	J. Vaughan-Morgan	18 Jan 57
	D. Walker-Smith	17 Sep 57		R. Thompson	17 Sep 57
	E. Powell	27 Jul 60		Miss E. Pitt	22 Oct 59
	(13 Jul 62 E. Powell & office in cabinet)			B. Braine	16 Jul 62-16 Oct 64
				Ld Newton	6 Sep 62-1 Apr 64
				M of Lothian	24 Mar 64-16 Oct 64
Paym.-Gen.	R. Maudling	16 Jan 57			
	(17 Sep 57 office in cabinet)				
Pensions & Nat. Ins.	J. Boyd-Carpenter	16 Jan 57	*P.S.*	Miss E. Pitt	19 Jan 57-22 Oct 59
	N. Macpherson	16 Jul 62		R. Wood	19 Jan 57-14 Apr 58
	R. Wood	21 Oct 63		W. Vane	14 Apr 58-28 Oct 60
				Miss P. Hornsby-Smith	22 Oct 59-31 Aug 61
				B. Braine	28 Oct 60-8 Feb 61
				R. Sharples	8 Feb 61-16 Jul 62
				Mrs M. Thatcher	9 Oct 61-16 Oct 64
				S. Maydon	16 Jul 62-16 Oct 64
Min. without Portfolio	E of Munster	16 Jan 57			
	Ld Mancroft	11 Jun 57			
	E of Dundee	23 Oct 58			
	(9 Oct 61 Ld Mills & office in cabinet)				

CONSERVATIVE GOVERNMENT, 1957–1964 *(contd.)*

MINISTERS NOT IN CABINET			JUNIOR MINISTERS ATTACHED		
Postm.-Gen.	E. Marples	16 Jan 57	*Ass.*	K. Thompson	18 Jan 57
	R. Bevins	22 Oct 59		Miss M. Pike	22 Oct 59
				R. Mawby	1 Mar 63
Power	*(office in cabinet)*			*(for Junior Ministers see above)*	
	R. Wood	14 Oct 59			
	(20 *Oct* 63, *F. Erroll & office in cabinet)*				
Supply	A. Jones	16 Jan 57	*P.S.*	W. Taylor	18 Jan 57
	(office wound up 22 *Oct* 59)			*(office wound up* 22 *Oct* 59)	
Technical Cooperation	*(office not established)*				
	D. Vosper	27 Jun 61			
	R. Carr	9 May 63			
War O.	J. Hare	16 Jan 57	*U-S. & F.S.:*		
	C. Soames	6 Jan 58		J. Amery	18 Jan 57
	J. Profumo	27 Jul 60		H. Fraser	28 Nov 58
	J. Godber	27 Jun 63		J. Ramsden	28 Oct 60
	J. Ramsden	21 Oct 63		P. Kirk	24 Oct 63
	(1 *Apr* 64, *reorganised under Min. of Defence)*				
Works	H. Molson	16 Jan 57	*P.S.*	H. Nicholls	18 Jan 57
	Ld J. Hope	22 Oct 59		R. Thompson	28 Oct 60
	(16 *Jul* 62, *Min. of Public Building & Works)*			R. Sharples	16 Jul 62
	G. Rippon	16 Jul 62			
	(20 *Oct* 63, *office in cabinet)*				
Law Officers:			*P.S. to Treasury:*		
Att.-Gen.	Sir R. Manningham-Buller	17 Jan 57		E. Heath	17 Jan 57
	Sir J. Hobson	16 Jul 62		M. Redmayne	14 Oct 59
			Junior Lds of Treasury:		
Sol.-Gen.	Sir H. Hylton-Foster	17 Jan 57		M. Redmayne	21 Jan 57-14 Oct 59
	Sir J. Simon	22 Oct 59		P. Legh	21 Jan 57-17 Sep 57
	Sir J. Hobson	8 Feb 62		E. Wakefield	21 Jan 57-23 Oct 58
	Sir P. Rawlinson	19 Jul 62		H. Harrison	21 Jan 57-16 Jan 59
Ld. Advoc.	W. Milligan	17 Jan 57		A. Barber	9 Apr 57-19 Feb 58
	W. Grant	5 Apr 60		R. Brooman-White	28 Oct 57-21 Jun 60
	I. Shearer[1]	12 Oct 62		P. Bryan	19 Feb 58-9 Feb 61
				M. Hughes-Young	23 Oct 58-6 Mar 62
				G. Finlay	16 Jan 59-28 Oct 60
Sol.-Gen. Scotland	W. Grant	17 Jan 57		D. Gibson-Watt	22 Oct 59-29 Nov 61
	D. Anderson	11 May 60		R. Chichester-Clark	21 Jun 60-29 Nov 61
	N. Wylie[1]	27 Apr 64		J. Hill	28 Oct 60-16 Oct 64
				W. Whitelaw	6 Mar 61-16 Jul 62
				J. Peel	29 Nov 61-16 Oct 64
				M. Noble	29 Nov 61-13 Jul 62
				F. Pearson	6 Mar 62-19 Oct 63
				G. Campbell	6 Sep 62-12 Dec 63
				M. Hamilton	6 Sep 62-16 Oct 64
				M. McLaren	21 Nov 63-16 Oct 64
				I. MacArthur	12 Dec 63-16 Oct 64
H.M. Household:			*Lds in Waiting:*		
Treas.	H. Oakshott	19 Jan 57		Ld Hawke	21 Jan 57-11 Jun 57
	P. Legh (*Ld Newton)*	16 Jan 59		Ld Fairfax	21 Jan 57-21 Jun 57
	E. Wakefield	21 Jun 60		Ld Chesham	21 Jan 57-22 Oct 59
	M. Hughes-Young	6 Mar 62		M of Lansdowne	11 Jun 57-23 Oct 58

[1] Not a member of the House of Commons.

CONSERVATIVE GOVERNMENT, 1957–1964 *(contd.)*

MINISTERS NOT IN CABINET

Comptr.	(Sir) G. Wills	19 Jan 57
	E. Wakefield	23 Oct 58
	H. Harrison	16 Jan 59
	R. Chichester-Clark	29 Nov 61
V. Chamb.	R. Thompson	21 Jan 57
	P. Legh	17 Sep 57
	E. Wakefield	16 Jan 59
	R. Brooman-White	21 Jun 60
	G. Finlay	28 Oct 60
Capt. Gents at Arms	Earl Fortescue	21 Jan 57
	Earl St Aldwyn	27 Jun 58
Capt. Yeomen of Guard	E of Onslow	21 Jan 57
	Ld Newton	28 Oct 60
	Vt Goschen	6 Sep 62

JUNIOR MINISTERS ATTACHED

Earl Bathurst	17 Sep 57-8 Feb 61
E of Gosford	23 Oct 58-22 Oct 59
Ld St Oswald	22 Oct 59-16 Jul 62
Earl Jellicoe	8 Feb 61-27 Jun 61
Ld Hastings	6 Mar 61-3 Dec 62
Ld Denham	27 Jun 61-16 Oct 64
M of Lothian	6 Sep 62-3 Mar 64
Earl Ferrers	3 Dec 62-10 Oct 64

LABOUR GOVERNMENT, 1964-1970

MINISTERS IN CABINET

P.M.	**H. Wilson**	16 Oct 64-19 Jun 70
First Sec. of State	**G. Brown**	16 Oct 64
	M. Stewart	11 Aug 66-18 Mar 68
	(*office linked to Min. of Econ. Affairs* 16 *Oct* 64-29 *Aug* 67)	
	Mrs B. Castle	6 Apr 68
	(*office linked to Min. of Employment*)	
Ld Pres.	**H. Bowden**	16 Oct 64
	R. Crossman	11 Aug 66
	F. Peart	18 Oct 68
Ld Chanc.	**Ld Gardiner**	16 Oct 64
Privy S.	**E of Longford**	18 Oct 64
	Sir F. Soskice	23 Dec 65
	E of Longford	6 Apr 66
	Ld Shackleton	16 Jan 68
	F. Peart	6 Apr 68
	Ld Shackleton	18 Oct 68
Exch.	**J. Callaghan**	16 Oct 64
	R. Jenkins	30 Nov 67
Treasury: Chief Sec. (office not in cabinet)		
	J. Diamond	1 Nov 68
Econ. Affs.	**G. Brown**	16 Oct 64
	M. Stewart	11 Aug 66
	P. Shore	29 Aug 67
	(*office abolished* 6 *Oct* 69)	

JUNIOR MINISTERS ATTACHED

Treasury: Chief Sec.		
	J. Diamond	20 Oct 64
	(1 *Nov* 68 *office in cabinet*)	
Min. of State		
	D. Taverne	6 Apr 68
	W. Rodgers	13 Oct 69
F.S.	N. MacDermot	21 Oct 64
	H. Lever	29 Aug 67
	D. Taverne	13 Oct 69
Econ. S.	A. Crosland	19 Oct 64
	(*de facto Min. of State, Econ. Affs. Office abolished* 22 *Dec* 64)	
Min. of State		
	A. Crosland	20 Oct 64
	(*until* 22 *Dec* 64 *nominally Econ. Sec. to Treas.*)	
	A. Albu	27 Jan 65-7 Jan 67
	T. Urwin	6 Apr 68-6 Oct 69
U-S.	M. Foley	21 Oct 64-6 Apr 66
	W. Rodgers	21 Oct 64-7 Jan 67
	H. Lever	7 Jan 67-29 Aug 67
	P. Shore	7 Jan 67-29 Aug 67
	A. Williams	29 Aug 67-6 Oct 69
	E. Dell	29 Aug 67-6 Apr 68

LABOUR GOVERNMENT, 1964-1970 *(contd.)*

	MINISTERS IN CABINET			JUNIOR MINISTERS ATTACHED	
For. O.	**P. Gordon Walker**	16 Oct 64	*Min. of State:*		
(& Comm.	**M. Stewart**	22 Jan 65		Ld Caradon	16 Oct 64-19 Jun 70
O.)	**G. Brown**	11 Aug 66		G. Thomson	19 Oct 64-6 Apr 66
	M. Stewart	16 Mar 68			7 Jan 67-29 Aug 67
	(*merged with Comm. O.* 17 *Oct* 68)			W. Padley	19 Oct 64-7 Jan 67
				Ld Chalfont	23 Oct 64-19 Jun 70
				Mrs E. White	11 Apr 66-7 Jan 67
				F. Mulley	7 Jan 67-6 Oct 69
				G. Roberts	29 Aug 67-13 Oct 69
				Ld Shepherd	17 Oct 68-19 Jun 70
			U-S.	Ld Walston	20 Oct 64-7 Jan 67
				W. Rodgers	7 Jan 67-3 Jul 68
				M. Foley	3 Jul 68-19 Jun 70
				W. Whitlock	17 Oct 68-13 Oct 69
				E. Luard	13 Oct 69-19 Jun 70
Home O.	**Sir F. Soskice**	18 Oct 64	*Min. of State*		
	R. Jenkins	23 Dec 65		Miss A. Bacon	19 Oct 64
	J. Callaghan	30 Nov 67		Ld Stonham	29 Aug 67
				Mrs S. Williams	13 Oct 69
			U-S.	Ld Stonham	20 Oct 64-29 Aug 67
				G. Thomas	20 Oct 64-6 Apr 66
				M. Foley	6 Apr 66-7 Jan 67
				D. Taverne	6 Apr 66-6 Apr 68
				D. Ennals	7 Jan 67-1 Nov 68
				E. Morgan	6 Apr 68-19 Jun 70
				M. Rees	1 Nov 68-19 Jun 70
Ag. Fish.	**F. Peart**	18 Oct 64	*P.S.*	J. Mackie	20 Oct 64-19 Jun 70
& Food	**C. Hughes**	6 Apr 68		J. Hoy	21 Oct 64-19 Jun 70
Col. O.	**A. Greenwood**	18 Oct 64	*U-S.*	Mrs E. White	20 Oct 64-11 Apr 66
	E of Longford	23 Dec 65		Ld Taylor	20 Oct 64-11 Oct 65
	F. Lee	6 Apr 66		Ld Beswick	11 Oct 65-1 Aug 66
	(*came under Dept. of Commonwealth Affs. 1 Aug 66. Office abolished* 7 *Jan* 67)			(*Ld Taylor & Ld Beswick were also U-S. at C.R.O.)*	
				J. Stonehouse	6 Apr 66-7 Jan 67
C.R.O.	**A. Bottomley**	18 Oct 64	*Min.*	C. Hughes	19 Oct 64-6 Apr 66
	(*re-named Commonwealth*		*of*	Mrs J. Hart	6 Apr 66-26 Jul 67
	Affairs 1 *Aug* 66)		*State*	G. Thomas	7 Jan 67-6 Apr 68
	H. Bowden	11 Aug 66		Ld Shepherd	26 Jul 67
	G. Thomson	29 Aug 67	*U-S.*	Ld Taylor	20 Oct 64
	(*merged with For. O.* 17 Oct 68)			Ld Beswick	11 Oct 65
				(*held jointly with U-S. at Col. O. until* 1 *Aug* 66)	
				W. Whitlock	26 Jul 67
Def.	**D. Healey**	16 Oct 64	*Min.*	F. Mulley	19 Oct 64
			Army	G. Reynolds	24 Dec 65
			& Dep. Sec. of State	(*no Dep. Sec. of State after* 24 *Dec* 65. *Office abolished* 7 *Jan* 67)	
			U-S.	G. Reynolds	20 Oct 64
			for	M. Rees	24 Dec 65
			Army	D. Ennals	6 Apr 66
				J. Boyden	7 Jan 67
				I. Richard	13 Oct 69
			Min.	C. Mayhew	19 Oct 64
			for	J. Mallalieu	19 Feb 66
			Navy	(*office abolished* 7 *Jan* 67)	
			U-S.	J. Mallalieu	21 Oct 64
			for	Ld Winterbottom	6 Apr 66
			Navy	M. Foley	7 Jan 67
				D. Owen	3 Jul 68
			Min.	Ld Shackleton	19 Oct 64
			for Air Force	(*office abolished* 7 *Jan* 67)	
			U-S.	B. Millan	20 Oct 64
			for Air	M. Rees	6 Apr 66
			Force	Ld Winterbottom	1 Nov 68

LABOUR GOVERNMENT, 1964-1970 *(contd.)*

	MINISTERS IN CABINET			JUNIOR MINISTERS ATTACHED	
			Min.	G. Reynolds	7 Jan 67
			of Defence for Administration		
				R. Hattersley	15 Jul 69
			Min.	R. Mason	7 Jan 67
			of Defence for Equipment		
				J. Morris	6 Apr 68
Educ. & Science	**M. Stewart**	18 Oct 64	*Min. of State*	Ld Bowden	19 Oct 64-11 Oct 65
	A. Crosland	22 Jan 65		R. Prentice	20 Oct 64-6 Apr 66
	P. Gordon Walker	29 Aug 67		E. Redhead	11 Oct 65-7 Jan 67
	E. Short	6 Apr 68		G. Roberts	6 Apr 66-29 Aug 67
				Mrs S. Williams	7 Jan 67-13 Oct 69
				Miss A. Bacon	29 Aug 67-19 Jun 70
				G. Fowler	13 Oct 69-19 Jun 70
			Min. of State (Arts)		
				Miss J. Lee	17 Feb 67-19 Jun 70
			U-S.	J. Boyden	20 Oct 64-24 Feb 65
				D. Howell	20 Oct 64-13 Oct 69
				Miss J. Lee *(Arts)*	24 Feb 65-17 Feb 67
				Miss J. Lestor	13 Oct 69-19 Jun 70
Emp. & Productivity	**Mrs B. Castle**	6 Apr 68	*Min. of State*	E. Dell	13 Oct 69
			U-S.	E. Fernyhough	6 Apr 68-13 Oct 69
				R. Hattersley	6 Apr 68-15 Jul 69
				H. Walker	6 Apr 68-19 Jun 70
Health &[1] *Soc. Sec.*	**R. Crossman**	1 Nov 68	*Min. of State*	S. Swingler	1 Nov 68-19 Feb 69
				D. Ennals	1 Nov 68-19 Jun 70
				Lady Serota	25 Feb 69-19 Jun 70
			U-S.	N. Pentland	1 Nov 68-13 Oct 69
				C. Loughlin	1 Nov 68-20 Nov 68
				J. Snow	1 Nov 68-13 Oct 69
				B. O'Malley	13 Oct 69-19 Jun 70
				J. Dunwoody	13 Oct 69-19 Jun 70
Housing & Local Govt.	**R. Crossman**	18 Oct 64	*Min. of State*	F. Willey	17 Feb 67
	A. Greenwood	11 Aug 66		N. MacDermot	29 Aug 67-28 Sep 68
	(*office out of cabinet* 6 *Oct* 69)				
			Min. for Planning and Land	K. Robinson	1 Nov 68
				(*office abolished* 6 *Oct* 69)	
			P.S.	R. Mellish	18 Oct 64-29 Aug 67
				J. MacColl	20 Oct 64-13 Oct 69
				Ld Kennet	6 Apr 66-13 Oct 69
				A. Skeffington	17 Feb 67-13 Oct 69
Labour	**R. Gunter**	18 Oct 64	*P.S.*	R. Marsh	20 Oct 64-11 Oct 65
	(6 *Apr* 68 *reorganised as Min. of Employment & Productivity)*			E. Thornton	21 Oct 64-6 Apr 66
				Mrs S. Williams	6 Apr 66-7 Jan 67
				E. Fernyhough	7 Jan 67-6 Apr 68
				R. Hattersley	7 Jan 67-6 Apr 68
D. Lanc.	**D. Houghton**	18 Oct 64			
	(*G. Thomson* 6 *Apr* 66 *& office not in cabinet)*				
	G. Thomson	6 Oct 69			
Local Govt. & Regional Planning	(*office created* 6 *Oct* 69)		*Min. of State*	T. Urwin	6 Oct 69
	A. Crosland	6 Oct 69			
Overseas Development	**Mrs B. Castle**	18 Oct 64	*P.S.*	A. Oram	21 Oct 64
	A. Greenwood	23 Dec 65			
	A. Bottomley	11 Aug 66			
	(*R. Prentice* 29 *Aug* 67 *& office not in cabinet)*				
Paym.-Gen.	(*office not in cabinet)*				
	Ld Shackleton	6 Apr 68			
	Mrs J. Hart	1 Nov 68			
	H. Lever	6 Oct 69			

[1]The Secretary of State at this department became officially known as the Secretary of State for Social Services.

LABOUR GOVERNMENT, 1964-1970 *(contd.)*

	MINISTERS IN CABINET			JUNIOR MINISTERS ATTACHED	
Min. without Portfolio	**D. Houghton**	6 Apr 66-7 Jan 67			
	P. Gordon Walker	7 Jan 67-21 Aug 67			
	G. Thomson	17 Oct 68-6 Oct 69			
	P. Shore	6 Oct 69-19 Jun 70			
Power	**F. Lee**	18 Oct 64	*P.S.*	J. Morris	21 Oct 64
	R. Marsh	6 Apr 66		Ld Lindgren	10 Jan 66
	R. Gunter	6 Apr 68		J. Bray	6 Apr 66
	R. Mason	1 Jul 68		R. Freeson	7 Jan 67
	(*office abolished* 6 *Oct* 69)				
Scot.O.	**W. Ross**	18 Oct 64	*Min. of State*		
				G. WILLIS	20 Oct 64-7 Jan 67
				D. MABON	7 Jan 67-19 Jun 70
				LD HUGHES	13 Oct 69-19 Jun 70
			U-S.	Ld Hughes	21 Oct 64-13 Oct 69
				Mrs J. Hart	20 Oct 64-6 Apr 66
				D. Mabon	21 Oct 64-7 Jan 67
				B. Millan	6 Apr 66-19 Jun 70
				N. Buchan	7 Jan 67-19 Jun 70
Tech.	**F. Cousins**	18 Oct 64	*Min. of State*		
	A. Benn	4 Jul 66		J. STONEHOUSE	15 Feb 67-1 Jul 68
				J. MALLALIEU	1 Jul 68-13 Oct 69
				R. PRENTICE	6 Oct 69-10 Oct 69
				LD DELACOURT-SMITH	13 Oct 69-19 Jun 70
				E. VARLEY	13 Oct 69-19 Jun 70
			P.S.	Ld Snow	19 Oct 64-6 Apr 66
				R. Marsh	11 Oct 65-6 Apr 66
				P. Shore	6 Apr 66-7 Jan 67
				E. Dell	6 Apr 66-29 Aug 67
				J. Bray	7 Jan 67-24 Sep 69
				G. Fowler	29 Aug 67-13 Oct 69
				A. Williams	6 Oct 69-19 Jun 70
				N. Carmichael	13 Oct 69-19 Jun 70
				E. Davies	13 Oct 69-19 Jun 70
B.o.T.	**D. Jay**	18 Oct 64	*Min. of State*	G. DARLING	20 Oct 64-6 Apr 68
	A. Crosland	29 Aug 67		E. REDHEAD	20 Oct 64-11 Oct 65
	R. Mason	6 Oct 69		R. MASON	20 Oct 64-7 Jan 67
				LD BROWN	11 Oct 65-19 Jun 70
				J. MALLALIEU	7 Jan 67-1 Jul 68
				E. DELL	6 Apr 68-13 Oct 69
				W. RODGERS	1 Jul 68-13 Oct 69
				G. ROBERTS	13 Oct 69-19 Jun 70
			P.S.	Ld Rhodes	20 Oct 64
				Ld Walston	7 Jan 67
				Mrs G. Dunwoody	29 Aug 67
Transport	**T. Fraser**	18 Oct 64	*Min. of State*	S. SWINGLER	29 Aug 67-1 Nov 68
	Mrs B. Castle	23 Dec 65			
	R. Marsh	6 Apr 68	*P.S.*	Ld Lindgren	20 Oct 64-10 Jan 66
	(*F. Mulley* 6 *Oct* 69 *& office not in cabinet*)			S. Swingler	20 Oct 64-29 Aug 67
				J. Morris	10 Jan 66-6 Apr 68
				N. Carmichael	29 Aug 67-13 Oct 69
				R. C. Brown	6 Apr 68-19 Jun 70
				A. Murray	13 Oct 69-19 Jun 70
Wales	**J. Griffiths**	18 Oct 64	*Min. of State*	G. ROBERTS	20 Oct 64
	C. Hughes	6 Apr 66		G. THOMAS	6 Apr 66
	G. Thomas	6 Apr 68		MRS E. WHITE	7 Jan 67
			U-S.	H. Finch	21 Oct 64
				I. Davies	6 Apr 66
	MINISTERS NOT IN CABINET			E. Rowlands	13 Oct 69
Aviation	R. JENKINS	18 Oct 64	*P.S.*	J. Stonehouse	20 Oct 64-7 Jan 67
	F. MULLEY	23 Dec 65		J. Snow	6 Apr 66-7 Jan 67
	J. STONEHOUSE	7 Jan 67			
	(*office abolished* 15 *Feb* 67)				

LABOUR GOVERNMENT, 1964-1970 *(contd.)*

	MINISTERS NOT IN CABINET			JUNIOR MINISTERS ATTACHED	
D. Lanc.	*(office in cabinet)*				
	G. Thomson	6 Apr 66			
	F. Lee	7 Jan 67			
	(G. Thomson 6 Oct 69 & office in cabinet)				
Health	K. Robinson	18 Oct 64	*P.S.*	Sir B. Stross	20 Oct 64
	(office abolished 1 Nov 68)			C. Loughlin	24 Feb 65
				J. Snow	7 Jan 67
Housing &	*(office in cabinet)*		*Min.*	D. Howell	13 Oct 69
Local Govt.	A. Greenwood	6 Oct 69	*of State*		
	R. Mellish	31 May 70	*P.S.*	A. Skeffington	13 Oct 69-19 Jun 70
				Ld Kennet	13 Oct 69-19 Jun 70
				R. Freeson	13 Oct 69-19 Jun 70
Land &	F. Willey	18 Oct 64	*P.S.*	Ld Mitchison	20 Oct 64-6 Apr 66
Nat. Res.	*(office wound up 17 Feb 67)*			A. Skeffington	21 Oct 64-17 Feb 67
Overseas	*(office in cabinet)*				
Dev.	R. Prentice	29 Aug 67	*P.S.*	A. Oram	29 Aug 67
	Mrs J. Hart	6 Oct 69		B. Whitaker	13 Oct 69
Paym.-Gen.	G. Wigg	19 Oct 64-12 Nov 67			
	(office vacant 12 Nov 67)				
	(Ld Shackleton 6 Apr 68 & office in cabinet)				
Pensions &	Miss M. Herbison	18 Oct 64	*P.S.*	H. Davies	20 Oct 64-6 Aug 66
Nat. Ins. (6 Aug 66 became Min. of Social Security)				N. Pentland	21 Oct 64-6 Aug 66
Min.	Sir E. Fletcher	19 Oct 64-6 Apr 66			
without	Ld Champion	21 Oct 64-7 Jan 67			
Portfolio	Ld Shackleton	7 Jan 67-16 Jan 68			
Postm.-Gen.	A. Benn	19 Oct 64	*Ass.*	J. Slater	20 Oct 64
	E. Short	4 Jul 66			
	R. Mason	6 Apr 68			
	J. Stonehouse	1 Jul 68			
	(1 Oct 69 Post Office became a Public Corporation)				
Posts &	J. Stonehouse	1 Oct 69	*P.S.*	J. Slater	1 Oct 69
Telecommunications				N. Pentland	13 Oct 69
Public	C. Pannell	19 Oct 64	*P.S.*	Miss J. Lee *(Arts)*	20 Oct 64
Building	R. Prentice	6 Apr 66		J. Boyden	24 Feb 65
& Works	R. Mellish	29 Aug 67		Ld Winterbottom	7 Jan 67
	J. Silkin	30 Apr 69		C. Loughlin	20 Nov 68
Social	Miss M. Herbison	6 Aug 66	*P.S.*	H. Davies	6 Aug 66-7 Jan 67
Security	Mrs J. Hart	26 Jul 67		N. Pentland	6 Aug 66-1 Nov 68
	(office abolished 1 Nov 68, see Health & Social Security)			C. Loughlin	7 Jan 67-1 Nov 68
Transport	*(office in cabinet)*		*(for Junior Ministers see above)*		
	F. Mulley	6 Oct 69			
Law Officers:			*P.S. to Treasury:*		
Att.-Gen.	Sir E. Jones	18 Oct 64		E. Short	18 Oct 64
				J. Silkin	4 Jul 66
Sol.-Gen.	Sir D. Foot	18 Oct 64		R. Mellish	30 Apr 69
	Sir A. Irvine	24 Aug 67		*(office vacant 31 May 70)*	
Ld Advoc.	G. Stott[1]	20 Oct 64			
	H. S. Wilson (Ld)[1]	26 Oct 67	*Junior Lds of Treasury:*		
Sol.-Gen.	J. Leechman[1]	20 Oct 64		G. Rogers	21 Oct 64-11 Jan 66
Scotland	H. S. Wilson[1]	11 Oct 65		G. Lawson	21 Oct 64-1 Apr 67
	E. Stewart[1]	26 Oct 67		J. McCann	21 Oct 64-11 Apr 66
					29 Jul 67-13 Oct 69
				I. Davies	21 Oct 64-6 Apr 66
				Mrs H. Slater	21 Oct 64-6 Apr 66
				J. Silkin	11 Jan 66-11 Apr 66
				A. Fitch	16 Apr 66-13 Oct 69
				J. Harper	16 Apr 66-19 Jun 70
				W. Whitlock	11 Apr 66-7 Jul 66
					1 Apr 67-28 Jul 67

[1] Not a member of the House of Commons.

LABOUR GOVERNMENT, 1964-1970 *(contd.)*

MINISTERS NOT IN CABINET

H.M. Household:

Treas.	S. Irving	21 Oct 64
	J. Silkin	11 Apr 66
	C. Grey	7 Jul 66
	C. Morris	13 Oct 69
Comptr.	C. Grey	21 Oct 64
	W. Whitlock	7 Jul 66
	W. Howie	1 Apr 67
	I. Evans	6 Feb 68
V. Chamb.	W. Whitlock	21 Oct 64
	J. McCann	11 Apr 66
	C. Morris	29 Jul 67
	A. Fitch	13 Oct 69
Capt. Gents at Arms	Ld Shepherd	21 Oct 64
	Ld Beswick	29 Jul 67
Capt. Yeomen of Guard	Ld Bowles	28 Dec 64

JUNIOR MINISTERS ATTACHED

W. Howie	16 Apr 66-1 Apr 67
H. Gourlay	7 Jul 66-29 Oct 68
B. O'Malley	1 Apr 67-13 Oct 69
W. Harrison	29 Oct 68-19 Jun 70
N. McBride	13 Oct 69-19 Jun 70
E. Perry	13 Oct 69-19 Jun 70
E. Armstrong	13 Oct 69-19 Jun 70

Asst. Govt. Whips:

A. Fitch	22 Oct 64[1]-16 Apr 66
H. Gourlay	22 Oct 64[1]-7 Jul 66
J. Harper	22 Oct 64[1]-16 Apr 66
W. Howie	22 Oct 64[1]-16 Apr 66
B. O'Malley	22 Oct 64[1]-1 Apr 67
J. Silkin	22 Oct 64[1]-11 Jan 66
C. Morris	25 Jan 66-29 Jul 67
E. Bishop	16 Apr 66-1 Apr 67
R. W. Brown	16 Apr 66-20 Jan 67
W. Harrison	16 Apr 66-28 Oct 68
N. McBride	16 Apr 66-13 Oct 69
I. Evans	7 Jul 66-6 Feb 68
E. Armstrong	20 Jan 67-13 Oct 69
H. Walker	1 Apr 67-5 Apr 68
E. Varley	29 Jul 67-30 Nov 68
E. Perry	6 Feb 68-13 Oct 69
D. Concannon	11 Apr 68-19 Jun 70
M. Miller	29 Oct 68-13 Oct 69
T. Boston	13 Oct 69-19 Jun 70
J. Hamilton	13 Oct 69-19 Jun 70
R. Dobson	13 Oct 69-19 Jun 70
W. Hamling	13 Oct 69-19 Jun 70

Lds in Waiting:

Ld Hobson	21 Oct 64-17 Feb 66
Ld Beswick	28 Dec 64-11 Oct 65
Ld Sorensen	28 Dec 64-20 Apr 68
Lady Phillips	10 Dec 65-19 Jun 70
Ld Hilton	6 Apr 66-19 Jun 70
Lady Serota	23 Apr 68-25 Feb 69
Lady Llewelyn-Davies	13 Mar 69-19 Jun 70

CONSERVATIVE GOVERNMENT, 1970-1974

MINISTERS IN CABINET

P.M.	**E. Heath**	19 Jun 70-4 Mar 74
Ld Pres.	**W. Whitelaw**	20 Jun 70
	R. Carr	7 Apr 72
	J. Prior	5 Nov 72

JUNIOR MINISTERS ATTACHED

P.S. Civil Service Dept.

D. Howell[2]	23 Jun 70-26 Mar 72
K. Baker	7 Apr 72-4 Mar 74
G. Johnson-Smith	5 Nov 72-4 Mar 74

[1] The appointment of Assistant Government Whips as paid Ministers of the Crown dates technically from 12 Nov 64.
[2] Also Junior Ld of Treasury 24 Jun 70-6 Jan 71, P.S. Dept. of Employment 5 Jan 71-26 Mar 72.

CONSERVATIVE GOVERNMENT, 1970-1974 *(contd.)*

	MINISTERS IN CABINET		JUNIOR MINISTERS ATTACHED		
Ld. Chanc.	**Q. Hogg (Ld Hailsham)**	20 Jun 70			
Privy S.	**Earl Jellicoe**	20 Jun 70			
	Ld Windlesham	5 Jun 73			
Exch.	**I. Macleod**	20 Jun 70	*Treasury: Chief Sec.*		
	A. Barber	25 Jul 70		M. Macmillan	23 Jun 70
				P. Jenkin	7 Apr 72
				T. Boardman	8 Jan 74
			Min. of State		
				T. Higgins	23 Jun 70
				J. Nott	7 Apr 72
			F.S.	P. Jenkin	23 Jun 70
				T. Higgins	7 Apr 72
For. & Comm. O.	**Sir A. Douglas-Home**	20 Jun 70			
			Min. of State		
				J. Godber	23 Jun 70-5 Nov 72
				Lady Tweedsmuir	7 Apr 72-4 Mar 74
				J. Amery	5 Nov 72-4 Mar 74
				Ld Balniel[2]	5 Nov 72-4 Mar 74
			U-S.	M of Lothian	24 Jun 70-7 Apr 72
				A. Royle	24 Jun 70-8 Jan 74
				A. Kershaw	15 Oct 70-5 Jun 73
				P. Blaker	8 Jan 74-4 Mar 74
			Min. for Overseas Development[1]		
				R. Wood	15 Oct 70
Home O.	**R. Maudling**	20 Jun 70	*Min. of State*		
	R. Carr	18 Jul 72		R. Sharples	23 Jun 70-7 Apr 72
				Ld Windlesham	23 Jun 70-26 Mar 72
				M. Carlisle	7 Apr 72-4 Mar 74
				Vt Colville	21 Apr 72-4 Mar 74
			U-S.	M. Carlisle	24 Jun 70
				D. Lane	7 Apr 72
Ag., Fish. & Food	**J. Prior**	20 Jun 70	*Min. of State*		
	J. Godber	5 Nov 72		A. Stodart	7 Apr 72
			P.S.	A. Stodart	24 Jun 70-7 Apr 72
				P. Mills	7 Apr 72-5 Nov 72
				Mrs P. Fenner	5 Nov 72-4 Mar 74
				Earl Ferrers	8 Jan 74-4 Mar 74
Defence	**Ld Carrington**	20 Jun 70	*Min. of State*		
	I. Gilmour	8 Jan 74		Ld Balniel[2]	23 Jun 70
				I. Gilmour	5 Nov 72
				G. Younger	8 Jan 74
			Min. of State for Procurement		
				I. Gilmour	7 Apr 71
				(*office abolished* 5 *Nov* 72)	
			U-S. for Navy		
				P. Kirk	24 Jun 70
				A. Buck	5 Nov 72
			U-S. for Air Force		
				Ld Lambton	24 Jun 70
				A. Kershaw	5 Jun 73
				Ld Strathcona & Mount Royal	8 Jan 74
			U-S. for Army		
				I. Gilmour	24 Jun 70
				G. Johnson-Smith	7 Apr 71
				P. Blaker	5 Nov 72
				D. Smith	8 Jan 74

[1] The Ministry of Overseas Development formally came under the F.O. 12 Nov 70.
[2] M.P. Not a member of the House of Lords.

CONSERVATIVE GOVERNMENT, 1970-1974 *(contd.)*

Office	Ministers in Cabinet		Junior Ministers Attached		
Educ. & Science	**Mrs M. Thatcher**	20 Jun 70	*Min. of State (Arts)*		
				N. St. John-Stevas	2 Dec 73
			U-S.	Ld Belstead	24 Jun 70-5 Jun 73
				W. Van Straubenzee	24 Jun 70-5 Nov 72
				N. St. John-Stevas	5 Nov 72-2 Dec 73
				Ld Sandford	5 Jun 73-4 Mar 74
				T. Raison	2 Dec 73-4 Mar 74
Employment (& Productivity till 12 Nov 70)	**R. Carr**	20 Jun 70	*Min. of State*		
	M. Macmillan	7 Apr 72		P. Bryan	23 Jun 70
	W. Whitelaw	2 Dec 73		R. Chichester-Clark	7 Apr 72
			U-S.	D. Smith	24 Jun 70-8 Jan 74
				D. Howell[2]	5 Jan 71-26 Mar 72
				N. Scott	8 Jan 74-4 Mar 74
Energy	**Ld Carrington**	8 Jan 74	*Min.*	P. Jenkin	8 Jan 74
			Min. of State		
				D. Howell	8 Jan 74
			U-S.	P. Emery	8 Jan 74
Environment	**P. Walker**	15 Oct 70	*Min. for Local Govt. & Development*		
	G. Rippon	5 Nov 72		G. Page	15 Oct 70
			Min. for Housing & Construction		
				J. Amery	15 Oct 70
				P. Channon	5 Nov 72
			Min. for Transport Industries		
				J. Peyton	15 Oct 70
			U-S.	E. Griffiths	15 Oct 70-4 Mar 74
				P. Channon	15 Oct 70-26 Mar 72
				M. Heseltine	15 Oct 70-7 Apr 72
				Ld Sandford	15 Oct 70-5 Jun 73
				K. Speed	7 Apr 72-4 Mar 74
				R. Eyre	7 Apr 72-4 Mar 74
				Lady Young	5 Jun 73-4 Mar 74
				H. Rossi	8 Jan 74-4 Mar 74
Health &[2] Social Security	**Sir K. Joseph**	20 Jun 70	*Min. of State*		
				Ld Aberdare	23 Jun 70-8 Jan 74
			P.S.	P. Dean	24 Jun 70-4 Mar 74
				M. Alison	24 Jun 70-4 Mar 74
Housing & Local Govt.	**P. Walker**	20 Jun 70-15 Oct 70[1]	*Min. of State*		
	(15 *Oct* 70 *office reorganised under Environment)*			G. Page	23 Jun 70-15 Oct 70
			P.S.	P. Channon	24 Jun 70-15 Oct 70
				E. Griffiths	24 Jun 70-15 Oct 70
				Ld Sandford	24 Jun 70-15 Oct 70
D. Lanc. (with special responsibility for Europe)	**A. Barber**	20 Jun 70			
	G. Rippon	28 Jul 70			
	J. Davies	5 Nov 72			
Northern Ireland	**W. Whitelaw**	24 Mar 72	*Min. of State*		
	F. Pym	2 Dec 73		P. Channon	26 Mar 72-5 Nov 72
				Ld Windlesham	26 Mar 72-5 Jun 73
				W. Van Straubenzee	5 Nov 72-4 Mar 74
				D. Howell	5 Nov 72-8 Jan 74
			U-S.	D. Howell	26 Mar 72-5 Nov 72
				P. Mills	5 Nov 72-4 Mar 74
				Ld Belstead	5 Jun 73-4 Mar 74
Paymaster-General	*(office not in cabinet)*				
	M. Macmillan	2 Dec 73			
Scot. O.	**G. Campbell**	20 Jun 70	*Min. of State*		
				Lady Tweedsmuir	23 Jun 70
				Ld Polwarth	7 Apr 72

[1] Formally the changes took effect on 12 Nov 70.
[2] See footnote on p.47

CONSERVATIVE GOVERNMENT, 1970-1974 *(contd.)*

MINISTERS IN CABINET			JUNIOR MINISTERS ATTACHED		
			U-S.	A. Buchanan-Smith	24 Jun 70-4 Mar 74
				G. Younger	24 Jun 70-8 Jan 74
				E. Taylor	24 Jun 70-28 Jul 71
				H. Monro	28 Jul 71-4 Mar 74
				E. Taylor	8 Jan 74-4 Mar 74
Tech.	**G. Rippon**	20 Jun 70	*Min. of State:*		
	J. Davies	28 Jul 70-15 Oct 70		Sir J. Eden	23 Jun 70-15 Oct 70
	(15 *Oct* 70 *office reorganised under Trade and Industry)*			E of Bessborough	24 Jun 70-15 Oct 70
			P.S.	D. Price	24 Jun 70-15 Oct 70
				N. Ridley	24 Jun 70-15 Oct 70
B.ofT.	**M. Noble**	20 Jun 70-15 Oct 70	*Min. of State:*	F. Corfield	24 Jun 70-15 Oct 70
			P.S.	A. Grant	24 Jun 70-15 Oct 70
Trade and Industry	**J. Davies**	15 Oct 70	*Min. for Trade:*	M. Noble	15 Oct 70
	P. Walker	5 Nov 72		(*Sir G. Howe & in cabinet* 5 *Nov* 72)	
Trade and Consumer Affairs	**Sir G. Howe**	5 Nov 72	*U-S.*	A. Grant	15 Oct 70
				E of Limerick	7 Apr 72
			Min. for Industry:		
				Sir J. Eden	15 Oct 70
				T. Boardman	7 Apr 72-8 Jan 74
			U-S.	N. Ridley	15 Oct 70
				P. Emery	7 Apr 72-8 Jan 74
			Min. for Aerospace (*and Shipping* 5 *Nov* 72):		
				F. Corfield	1 May 71
				M. Heseltine	7 Apr 72
			U-S.	D. Price	1 May 71
				C. Onslow	7 Apr 72
			Min. for Industrial Development:		
				C. Chataway	7 Apr 72
			U-S.	A. Grant	7 Apr 72
Wales	**P. Thomas**	20 Jun 70	*Min. of State:*	D. Gibson-Watt	23 Jun 70

MINISTERS NOT IN CABINET					
Aviation Supply	F. Corfield	15 Oct 70	*P.S.*	D. Price	15 Oct 70-1 May 71
	(abolished 1 *May* 71 *and responsibilities transferred to Procurement Executive, Min. of Defence)*				
Overseas Development	R. Wood	23 Jun 70-15 Oct 70[1]			
	*(*15 *Oct* 70[1] *came under Foreign Office)*				
Paym.-Gen.	Vt Eccles *(Min. for Arts)*	23 Jun 70			
	(*M. Macmillan & office in cabinet* 2 *Dec* 73)				
Min. without Portfolio	Ld Drumalbyn	15 Oct 70			
	Ld Aberdare	8 Jan 74			
Posts & Tel.	C. Chataway	24 Jun 70			
	Sir J. Eden	7 Apr 72			
Public Buildings & Works	J. Amery	23 Jun 70-15 Oct 70	*P.S.*	A. Kershaw	24 Jun 70-15 Oct 70[1]
	*(*15 *Oct* 70[1] *office reorganised under Dept. of Environment)*				
Transport	J. Peyton	23 Jun 70-15 Oct 70[1]	*P.S.*	M. Heseltine	24 Jun 70-15 Oct 70[1]
Law Officers:			*P.S. to Treasury:*		
Att.-Gen.	Sir P. Rawlinson	23 Jun 70		F. Pym	20 Jun 70
Sol.-Gen.	Sir G. Howe	23 Jun 70		H. Atkins	2 Dec 73
	Sir M. Havers	5 Nov 72			

[1] Formally the changes took effect on 12 Nov 70.

CONSERVATIVE GOVERNMENT, 1970-1974 *(contd.)*

MINISTERS NOT IN CABINET

Ld Advoc.	N. WYLIE	23 Jun 70
Sol.-Gen.	D. BRAND[1]	23 Jun 70
Scotland	I. STEWART[1]	5 Nov 72

H.M. Household:

Treas.	H. ATKINS	24 Jun 70
	B. WEATHERILL	2 Dec 73
Comptr.	W. ELLIOTT	24 Jun 70
	R. EYRE	24 Sep 70
	B. WEATHERILL	7 Apr 72
	W. CLEGG	2 Dec 73
V. Chamb.	J. MORE	24 Jun 70
	B. WEATHERILL	17 Oct 71
	W. CLEGG	7 Apr 72
	P. HAWKINS	2 Dec 73
Capt. Gents at Arms	EARL ST ALDWYN	24 Jun 70
Capt. Yeomen of Guard	VT GOSCHEN	24 Jun 70
	LD DENHAM	20 Nov 71

JUNIOR MINISTERS ATTACHED

Junior Lds of Treasury:

R. Eyre	24 Jun 70-23 Sep 70
D. Howell[2]	24 Jun 70-6 Jan 71
H. Monro	24 Jun 70-28 Jul 71
B. Weatherill	24 Jun 70-17 Oct 71
W. Clegg	24 Jun 70-7 Apr 72
V. Goodhew	21 Oct 70-9 Oct 73
P. Hawkins	5 Jan 71-2 Dec 73
T. Fortescue	8 Nov 71-21 Sep 73
K. Speed	8 Nov 71-7 Apr 72
H. Rossi	7 Apr 72-8 Jan 74
O. Murton	7 Apr 72-30 Oct 73
M. Jopling	30 Oct 73-4 Mar 74
H. Gray	30 Oct 73-4 Mar 74
J. Thomas	30 Oct 73-4 Mar 74
M. Fox	2 Dec 73-4 Mar 74
K. Clarke	8 Jan 74-4 Mar 74

Asst. Govt. Whips:

V. Goodhew	29 Jun 70-21 Oct 70
P. Hawkins	29 Jun 70-5 Jan 71
T. Fortescue	29 Jun 70-8 Nov 71
K. Speed	29 Jun 70-8 Nov 71
H. Rossi	21 Oct 70-7 Apr 72
H. Gray	8 Nov 71-30 Oct 73
J. Thomas	8 Nov 71-30 Oct 73
M. Jopling	8 Nov 71-30 Oct 73
O. Murton	8 Nov 71-7 Apr 72
M. Fox	13 Apr 72-2 Dec 73
K. Clarke	13 Apr 72-8 Jan 74
D. Walder	30 Oct 73-4 Mar 74
A. Hall-Davis	30 Oct 73-4 Mar 74
R. Hicks	30 Oct 73-4 Mar 74
A. Butler	8 Jan 74-4 Mar 74
C. Parkinson	8 Jan 74-4 Mar 74

Lds in Waiting:

Ld Mowbray	24 Jun 70-4 Mar 74
Ld Denham	24 Jun 70-20 Nov 71
Ld Bethell	24 Jun 70-5 Jan 71
Earl Ferrers	5 Jan 71-8 Jan 74
M of Lothian	7 Apr 72-27 Jul 73
E of Gowrie	7 Apr 72-4 Mar 74
Lady Young	21 Apr 72-5 Jun 73
Ld Strathcona & Mount Royal	27 Jun 73-8 Jan 74
Ld Sandys	8 Jan 74-4 Mar 74
Earl Cowley	8 Jan 74-4 Mar 74
Earl Alexander of Tunis	8 Jan 74-4 Mar 74

[1] Not a member of the House of Commons.
[2] Also P.S. Civil Service Dept. 23 Jun 70-26 Mar 72.

LABOUR GOVERNMENT, 1974–1979

	MINISTERS IN CABINET			JUNIOR MINISTERS ATTACHED	
P.M.	**H. Wilson**	4 Mar 74-5 Apr 76	*Civil Service Dept. Min. of State:*		
	J. Callaghan	5 Apr 76-4 May 79		R. Sheldon	7 Mar 74
				C. Morris	18 Oct 74
			P.S.	J. Grant	7 Mar 74-18 Oct 74
Ld Pres.	**E. Short**	5 Mar 74	*Privy Council Office, Min. of State:*		
	M. Foot	8 Apr 76		G. Fowler	18 Oct 74
Ld Chanc.	**Ld Elwyn-Jones**	5 Mar 74		Ld Crowther-Hunt	23 Jan 76
Privy S.	**Ld Shepherd**	7 Mar 74		J. Smith	8 Apr 76
	Ld Peart	10 Sep 76		Lady Birk	3 Jan 79
			P.S.	W. Price	18 Oct 74
Exch.	**D. Healey**	5 Mar 74	*Paym.-Gen.*		
				E. Dell	7 Mar 74
P.S. to Treasury	*(office not in cabinet)* **R. Mellish**	26 Jul 74-8 Apr 76		(*Mrs S. Williams and office combined with Prices & Consumer Protection* 8 *Apr* 76 *and then with Education* 10 *Sep* 76)	
Chief Sec.	*(office not in cabinet)* **J. Barnett**	21 Feb 77	*Chief Sec.*		
				J. Barnett	7 Mar 74
				(*office in cabinet* 21 *Feb* 77)	
			F.S.	J. Gilbert	7 Mar 74
				R. Sheldon	17 Jun 75
			Min. of State:		
				R. Sheldon	18 Oct 74
				D. Davies	17 Jun 75
For. & Comm. O.	**J. Callaghan**	5 Mar 74	*Min. of State:*		
	A. Crosland	8 Apr 76		D. Ennals	7 Mar 74-8 Apr 76
	D. Owen	21 Feb 77		R. Hattersley	7 Mar 74-10 Sep 76
				Ld Goronwy-Roberts	4 Dec 75-4 May 79
				E. Rowlands	14 Apr 76-4 May 79
				D. Owen	10 Sep 76-21 Feb 77
				F. Judd	21 Feb 77-4 May 79
			U-S.	Miss J. Lestor	8 Mar 74-12 Jun 75
				Ld Goronwy-Roberts	8 Mar 74-4 Dec 75
				E. Rowlands	12 Jun 75-14 Apr 76
				J. Tomlinson	17 Mar 76-4 May 79
				(*see also Overseas Development*)	
				E. Luard	14 Apr 76-4 May 79
Home O.	**R. Jenkins**	5 Mar 74	*Min. of State:*		
	M. Rees	10 Sep 76		Ld Harris	8 Mar 74-3 Jan 79
				A. Lyon	8 Mar 74-14 Apr 76
				B. John	14 Apr 76-4 May 79
				Ld Boston	3 Jan 79-4 May 79
			U-S.	Dr S. Summerskill	8 Mar 74
Ag., Fish. and Food	**F. Peart**	5 Mar 74	*Min. of State:*		
	J. Silkin	10 Sep 76		N. Buchan	8 Mar 74
				E. Bishop	18 Oct 74
			P.S.	R. Moyle	11 Mar 74
				E. Bishop	28 Jun 74
				G. Strang	18 Oct 74

LABOUR GOVERNMENT, 1974-1979 *(contd.)*

	MINISTERS IN CABINET		JUNIOR MINISTERS ATTACHED		
Defence	**R. Mason**	5 Mar 74	*Min. of State:*		
	F. Mulley	10 Sep 76		W. RODGERS	8 Mar 74
				J. GILBERT	10 Sep 76
			U-S. for Navy		
				F. Judd	8 Mar 74
				P. Duffy	14 Apr 76
			U-S. for Army		
				Ld Brayley	8 Mar 74
				R. C. Brown	18 Oct 74
			U-S. for Air Force		
				B. John	8 Mar 74
				J. Wellbeloved	14 Apr 76
Educ. & Science	**R. Prentice**	5 Mar 74	*Min. of State:*		
	F. Mulley	10 Jun 75		G. FOWLER	8 Mar 74
	Mrs S. Williams	10 Sep 76		LD CROWTHER-HUNT	18 Oct 74
				G. FOWLER	23 Jan 76
				G. OAKES	10 Sep 76
			Min. of State (Arts)		
				LD DONALDSON	14 Apr 76
			U-S.	E. Armstrong	7 Mar 74-12 Jun 75
			(Arts)	H. Jenkins	8 Mar 74-14 Apr 76
				Miss J. Lestor	12 Jun 75-21 Feb 76
				Miss M. Jackson	12 Mar 76-4 May 79
Employment	**M. Foot**	5 Mar 74	*Min. of State:*		
	A. Booth	8 Apr 76		A. BOOTH	8 Mar 74
				H. WALKER	14 Apr 76
			U-S.	J. Fraser	8 Mar 74-14 Apr 76
				H. Walker	11 Mar 74-14 Apr 76
				J. Grant	14 Apr 76-4 May 79
				J. Golding	14 Apr 76-4 May 79
Energy	**E. Varley**	5 Mar 74	*Min. of State:*		
	A. Benn	10 Jun 75		LD BALOGH	7 Mar 74
				J. SMITH	4 Dec 75
				D. MABON	14 Apr 76
			U-S.	G. Strang	7 Mar 74-18 Oct 74
				A. Eadie	7 Mar 74-4 May 79
				J. Smith	18 Oct 74-4 Dec 75
				Ld Lovell-Davis	4 Dec 75-14 Apr 76
				G. Oakes	14 Apr 76-10 Sep 76
				J. Cunningham	10 Sep 76-4 May 79
Environment	**A. Crosland**	5 Mar 74	*Min. for Transport:*		
	P. Shore	8 Apr 76		F. MULLEY	7 Mar 74
				J. GILBERT	12 Jun 75
				(separate Department and office in cabinet 10 *Sep* 76*)*	
Planning & Local Govt. (in Dept. of Environment)	*(office not in cabinet)*		*Min. for Planning & Local Govt.*		
	J. Silkin	18 Oct 74		J. SILKIN	7 Mar 74
	(office abolished 10 *Sep* 76*)*			*(office in cabinet* 18 *Oct* 74*)*	
			Min. for Housing & Construction:		
				R. FREESON	7 Mar 74
			Min. of State (Urban Affs.):		
				C. MORRIS	7 Mar 74
				(post abolished 18 *Oct* 74*)*	
			Min. of State (Sport and Recreation (and Water Resources 24 *Aug* 76*))*		
				D. HOWELL	7 Mar 74
			U-S.	N. Carmichael	8 Mar 74-4 Dec 75
				G. Kaufman	8 Mar 74-12 Jun 75
				G. Oakes	8 Mar 74-14 Apr 76
				Lady Birk	18 Oct 74-3 Jan 79
				E. Armstrong	12 Jun 75-4 May 79

LABOUR GOVERNMENT, 1974-1979 *(contd.)*

	MINISTERS IN CABINET			JUNIOR MINISTERS ATTACHED	
				K. Marks	5 Dec 75-4 May 79
				G. Barnett	14 Apr 76-4 May 79
				Lady Stedman	3 Jan 79-4 May 79
Health & Social Security (Social Services)	**Mrs B. Castle**	5 Mar 74	*Min. of State:*		
	D. Ennals	8 Apr 76		B. O'Malley	8 Mar 74-6 Apr 76
				D. Owen	26 Jul 74-10 Sep 76
				S. Orme	8 Apr 76-10 Sep 76
				R. Moyle	10 Sep 76-4 May 79
			U-S.	D. Owen	8 Mar 74-26 Jul 74
				R. C. Brown	8 Mar 74-18 Oct 74
				A. Jones	18 Oct 74-12 Jun 75
				M. Meacher	12 Jun 75-14 Apr 76
				E. Deakins	14 Apr 76-4 May 79
				Ld Wells-Pestell	3 Jan 79-4 May 79
			U-S. (Disabled):		
				A. Morris	11 Mar 74-4 May 79
Industry	**A. Benn**	5 Mar 74	*Min. of State:*		
	(also 7 Mar 74-29 Mar 74 Min. for Posts and Telecommunications)			E. Heffer	7 Mar 74-9 Apr 75
				Ld Beswick	11 Mar 74-4 Dec 75
	E. Varley	10 Jun 75		G. Mackenzie	10 Jun 75-14 Apr 76
				G. Kaufman	4 Dec 75-4 May 79
				A. Williams	14 Apr 76-4 May 79
			U-S.	G. Mackenzie	7 Mar 74-10 Jun 75
				M. Meacher	7 Mar 74-12 Jun 75
				G. Kaufman	12 Jun 75-4 Dec 75
				Ld Melchett	4 Dec 75-10 Sep 76
				N. Carmichael	4 Dec 75-14 Apr 76
				L. Huckfield	14 Apr 76-4 May 79
				R. Cryer	10 Sep 76-20 Nov 78
D. Lanc.	**H. Lever**	5 Mar 74			
Northern Ireland	**M. Rees**	5 Mar 74	*Min. of State:*		
	R. Mason	10 Sep 76		S. Orme	7 Mar 74-8 Apr 76
				R. Moyle	27 Jun 74-10 Sep 76
				D. Concannon	14 Apr 76-4 May 79
				Ld Melchett	10 Sep 76-4 May 79
			U-S.	Ld Donaldson	11 Mar 74-14 Apr 76
				D. Concannon	27 Jun 74-14 Apr 76
				J. Dunn	14 Apr 76-4 May 79
				R. Carter	14 Apr 76-4 May 79
				T. Pendry	11 Nov 78-4 May 79
Overseas Development	*(Mrs J. Hart and office not in cabinet)*				
	R. Prentice	10 Jun 75	*(for Junior Ministers see below)*		
	(F. Judd and office not in cabinet 21 Dec 76)				
Prices & Consumer Protection	**Mrs S. Williams**	5 Mar 74	*Min. of State:*		
	R. Hattersley	10 Sep 76		A. Williams	8 Mar 74
				J. Fraser	14 Apr 76
			U-S.	R. Maclennan	11 Mar 74
Scot. O.	**W. Ross**	5 Mar 74	*Min. of State:*		
	B. Millan	8 Apr 76		B. Millan	8 Mar 74-8 Apr 76
				Ld Hughes	8 Mar 74-8 Aug 75
				Ld Kirkhill	8 Aug 75-15 Dec 78
				G. Mackenzie	14 Apr 76-4 May 79
			U-S.	R. Hughes	11 Mar 74-22 Jul 75
				H. Brown	28 Jun 74-4 May 79
				H. Ewing	18 Oct 74-4 May 79
				F. McElhone	12 Sep 75-4 May 79
Social Security (in Dept. of Health & Soc. Security)	*(office not in cabinet)*				
	S. Orme	10 Sep 76			

LABOUR GOVERNMENT, 1974-1979 *(contd.)*

MINISTERS IN CABINET			JUNIOR MINISTERS ATTACHED		
Trade	**P. Shore**	5 Mar 74	*U-S.*	E. Deakins	8 Mar 74-14 Apr 76
	E. Dell	8 Apr 76		S. Clinton Davis	8 Mar 74-4 May 79
	J. Smith	11 Nov 78		M. Meacher	14 Apr 76-4 May 79
Transport	*(office not in cabinet)*		*U-S.*	J. Horam	12 Sep 76
	W. Rodgers	10 Sep 76			
Wales	**J. Morris**	5 Mar 74	*U-S.*	E. Rowlands	7 Mar 74-12 Jun 75
				B. Jones	7 Mar 74-4 May 79
				A. Jones	12 Jun 75-4 May 79
MINISTERS NOT IN CABINET			**JUNIOR MINISTERS ATTACHED**		
Overseas Development[1]	MRS J. HART	7 Mar 74	*P.S.*	W. Price	11 Mar 74
	(R. Prentice & office in cabinet 10 Jun 75-21 Dec 76)			J. Grant	18 Oct 74
				F. Judd	14 Apr 76
				J. Tomlinson *(also at F.O.)*	13 Jan 77
	F. JUDD	21 Dec 76			
	MRS J. HART	21 Feb 77			
Law Officers:					
Att.-Gen.	S. SILKIN	7 Mar 74	*P.S.*	A. Davidson	26 Jul 74
Sol.-Gen.	P. ARCHER	7 Mar 74			
Ld Advoc.	R. K. MURRAY	8 Mar 74			
Sol.-Gen. Scotland	J. MCCLUSKEY[2] (LD)	14 Mar 74			

P.S. to Treasury:

R. MELLISH	5 Mar 74
(*office in cabinet* 26 *Jul* 74-8 *Apr* 76)	
M. COCKS	8 Apr 76

Junior Lds of Treasury:

D. Coleman	8 Mar 74-6 Jul 78
J. Dunn	8 Mar 74-14 Apr 76
J. Golding	8 Mar 74-18 Oct 74
T. Pendry	8 Mar 74-18 Jan 77
J. Hamilton	8 Mar 74-28 Jun 74
M. Cocks	28 Jun 74-8 Apr 76
J. Dormand	18 Oct 74-4 May 79
D. Stoddart	14 Apr 76-18 Nov 77
E. Graham	14 Apr 76-4 May 79
T. Cox	19 Jan 77-4 May 79
P. Snape	23 Nov 77-4 May 79
A. Stallard	5 Jul 78-17 Jan 79
A. Bates	17 Jan 79-4 May 79

Asst. Govt. Whips:

M. Cocks	8 Mar 74-24 Jun 74
T. Cox	8 Mar 74-19 Jan 77
E. Perry	8 Mar 74-24 Oct 74
J. Dormand	14 Mar 74-18 Oct 74
L. Pavitt	14 Mar 74-5 Feb 76
W. Johnson	22 Jun 74-23 Jan 75
Miss B. Boothroyd	24 Oct 74-4 Nov 75
J. Ellis	24 Oct 74-8 Nov 76
Miss M. Jackson	27 Jan 75-12 Mar 76
D. Stoddart	27 Jan 75-14 Apr 76
P. Snape	20 Nov 75-23 Nov 77
A. Stallard	5 Feb 76-5 Jul 78
A. Bates	12 Mar 76-17 Jan 79
F. White	14 Apr 76-31 Oct 78
J. Tinn	16 Jun 76-4 May 79
J. Ashton	8 Nov 76-9 Nov 77
Mrs A. Taylor	19 Jan 77-4 May 79
J. Marshall	23 Nov 77-4 May 79
J. Dean	6 Jul 78-4 May 79
J. Evans	31 Oct 78-4 May 79
B. Davies	17 Jan 79-4 May 79

[1] Formally under Foreign Office until 27 Jun 74. From 10 Jun 75 the post of Minister of Overseas Development was taken by the Foreign Secretary. The Minister in charge of the Department became the Minister for Overseas Development.

[2] Not a member of the House of Commons.

LABOUR GOVERNMENT, 1974-1979 *(contd.)*

MINISTERS NOT IN CABINET

H.M. Household:		
Treas.	W. HARRISON	7 Mar 74
Comptr.	J. HARPER	8 Mar 74
	J. HAMILTON	5 Jul 78
V. Chamb.	D. CONCANNON	8 Mar 74
	J. HAMILTON	28 Jun 74
	D. COLEMAN	5 Jul 78
Capt. Gents at Arms	BARONESS LLEWELYN-DAVIES	11 Mar 74
Capt. Yeomen of the Guard	LD STRABOLGI	11 Mar 74

JUNIOR MINISTERS ATTACHED

Lds in Waiting:	
Ld Jacques	14 Mar 74-19 Jan 77
Ld Garnsworthy	14 Mar 74-4 Sep 74
Lady Birk	14 Mar 74-18 Oct 74
Ld Wells-Pestell	14 Mar 74-3 Jan 79
Ld Winterbottom	29 Oct 74-27 Oct 78
Ld Lovell-Davis	29 Oct 74-4 Dec 75
Ld Melchett	29 Oct 74-4 Dec 75
Lady Stedman	4 Dec 75-3 Jan 79
Ld Oram	23 Jan 76-23 Mar 78
Ld Wallace of Coslany	28 Feb 77-4 May 79
Lady David	27 Oct 78-4 May 79
Ld Leonard	27 Oct 78-4 May 79
Ld Jacques	11 Jan 79-4 May 79

CONSERVATIVE GOVERNMENT, 1979-

MINISTERS IN CABINET

P.M.	**Mrs M. Thatcher**	4 May 79
Ld Pres.	**Ld Soames**	5 May 79
	F. Pym	14 Sep 81
	J. Biffen	5 Apr 82
	Vt Whitelaw	11 Jun 83
Ld Chanc.	**Ld Hailsham**	5 May 79
Privy S.	**Sir I. Gilmour**	5 May 79
	H. Atkins	14 Sep 81
	Lady Young	6 Apr 82
	J. Biffen	11 Jun 83
Exch.	**Sir G. Howe**	5 May 79
	N. Lawson	11 Jun 83
Chief Sec.	**J. Biffen**	5 May 79
	L. Brittan	5 Jan 81
	P. Rees	11 Jun 83
For. & Comm. O.	**Ld Carrington**	5 May 79
	F. Pym	6 Apr 82
	Sir G. Howe	11 Jun 83

JUNIOR MINISTERS ATTACHED

Min. of State Civil Service Dept:		
	P. CHANNON	7 May 79
	B. HAYHOE	5 Jan 81
	(*Department abolished 12 Nov 81*)	
Min. of State, Privy Council Office		
	E. OF GOWRIE	13 Jun 83
	(*office vacant 11 Sept 84*)	
F.S.	N. LAWSON	6 May 79
	N. RIDLEY	14 Sep 81
	J. MOORE	18 Oct 83
Econ. S		
	J. BRUCE-GARDYNE	11 Nov 81
	J. MOORE	13 Jun 83
	I. STEWART	18 Oct 83
Min. of State:		
	P. REES	6 May 79-14 Sep 81
	LD. COCKFIELD	6 May 79-6 Apr 82
	J. BRUCE-GARDYNE	15 Sep 81-11 Nov 81
	B. HAYHOE	11 Nov 81-
	J. WAKEHAM	6 Apr 82-13 Jun 83
Min. of State:		
	D. HURD	6 May 79-13 Jun 83
	N. RIDLEY	6 May 79-14 Sep 81
	P. BLAKER	6 May 79-29 May 81
	R. LUCE	14 Sep 81-5 Apr 82
	LD BELSTEAD	5 Apr 82-13 Jun 83
	C. ONSLOW	5 Apr 82-13 Jun 83
	LADY YOUNG	13 Jun 83-
	M. RIFKIND	13 Jun 83-
	R. LUCE	13 Jun 83-
Min. of State (Overseas Development):		
	N. MARTEN	6 May 79
	T. RAISON	6 Jan 83
U-S.	R. Luce	6 May 79
	Ld Trefgarne	14 Sep 81
	M. Rifkind	6 Apr 82
	R. Whitney	13 Jun 83
	T. Renton	11 Sep 84

CONSERVATIVE GOVERNMENT, 1979- (*contd.*)

MINISTERS IN CABINET			JUNIOR MINISTERS ATTACHED		
Home O.	**W. Whitelaw**	5 May 79	*Min. of State:*		
	L. Brittan	11 Jun 83		T. Raison	6 May 79-6 Jan 83
				L. Brittan	6 May 79-5 Jan 81
				P. Mayhew	5 Jan 81-13 Jun 83
				D. Waddington	6 Jun 83-
				D.Hurd	13 Jun 83-11 Sep 84
				Ld Elton	11 Sep 84-27 Mar 85
				G. Shaw	11 Sep 84-
			U-S.	Ld Belstead	7 May 79-6 Apr 82
				Ld Elton	6 Apr 82-11 Sep 84
				D. Mellor	6 Jan 83-
				Ld Glenarthur	27 Mar 85-
Ag., Fish. & Food	**P. Walker**	5 May 79	*Min. of State:*		
	M. Jopling	11 Jun 83		Earl Ferrers	7 May 79-13 Jun 83
				A. Buchanan-Smith	7 May 79-13 Jun 83
				J. MacGregor	13 Jun 83-
				Ld Belstead	13 Jun 83-
			P.S.	J. Wiggin	7 May 79
				Mrs. P. Fenner	14 Sep 81
Defence	**F. Pym**	5 May 79	*Min. of State:*		
	J. Nott	5 Jan 81		Ld Strathcona	6 May 79
	M. Heseltine	6 Jan 83		Vt Trenchard	5 Jan 81-29 May 81
			Min. of State (Armed Forces):		
				P. Blaker	29 May 81
				J. Stanley	13 Jun 83
			Min. of State (Defence Procurement):		
				Ld Trenchard	29 May 81
				G. Pattie	6 Jan 83
				A. Butler	11 Sep 84
			U-S. (Army)		
				B. Hayhoe	6 May 79
				P. Goodhart	5 Jan 81
			U-S. (Navy)		
				K. Speed	6 May 79-18 May 81
			U-S. (Air)		
				G. Pattie	6 May 79-29 May 81
				(Defence Department reorganised)	
			U-S. (Armed Forces)		
				P. Goodhart	29 May 81
				J. Wiggin	15 Sep 81
				Ld Trefgarne	13 Jun 83
			U-S. (Procurement)		
				G. Pattie	29 May 81
				I. Stewart	6 Jan 83
				J. Lee	18 Oct 83
Educ. & Science	**M. Carlisle**	5 May 79	*Min. of State:*		
	Sir K. Joseph	14 Sep 81		Lady Young	7 May 79-14 Sep 81
				P. Channon	5 Jan 81-13 Jun 83
			U-S.	R. Boyson	7 May 79-13 Jun 83
				N. Macfarlane	7 May 79-15 Sep 81
				W. Shelton	15 Sep 81-13 Jun 83
				W. Waldegrave	15 Sep-13 Jun 83
				P. Brooke	13 Jun 83-
				R. Dunn	13 Jun 83-
Employment	**J. Prior**	5 May 79	*Min. of State:*		
	N. Tebbit	14 Sep 81		E of Gowrie	7 May 79-15 Sep 81
	T. King	16 Oct 83		M. Alison	15 Sep 81-13 Jun 83
				P. Morrison	13 Jun 83-
				J. S. Gummer	18 Oct 83-11 Sep 84
			U-S.	J. Lester	7 May 79-5 Jan 81
				P. Mayhew	7 May 79-5 Jan 81
				D. Waddington	5 Jan 81-6 Jan 83
				P. Morrison	5 Jan 81-13 Jun 83
				J. S. Gummer	6 Jan 83-18 Oct 83
				A. Clarke	13 Jun 83-
				P. Bottomley	11 Sep 84-

CONSERVATIVE GOVERNMENT, 1979- (*contd.*)

	MINISTERS IN CABINET		JUNIOR MINISTERS ATTACHED		
Energy	**D. Howell**	5 May 79	*Min. of State:*		
	N. Lawson	14 Sep 81		H. GRAY	7 May 79
	P. Walker	11 Jun 83		A. BUCHANAN-SMITH	13 Jun 83
			U-S.	N. Lamont	7 May 79-5 Sep 81
				J. Moore	7 May 79-13 Jun 83
				D. Mellor	15 Sep 81-6 Jan 83
				E of Avon	6 Jan 83-11 Sep 84
				G. Shaw	13 Jun 83-11 Sep 84
				A. Goodlad	11 Sep 84-
				D. Hunt	11 Sep 84-
Environment	**M. Heseltine**	5 May 79	*Min. of State (Local Government):*		
	T. King	6 Jan 83		T. KING	6 May 79
	P. Jenkin	11 Jun 83		LD BELLWIN	6 Jan 83
				K. BAKER	11 Sep 84
			Min. of State (Housing and Construction):		
				J. STANLEY	7 May 79
				I. GOW	13 Jun 83
			Min. of State		
				LD ELTON	27 Mar 85
			U-S.	M. Fox	7 May 79-5 Jan 81
				G. Finsberg	7 May 79-15 Sep 81
				Ld Bellwin	7 May 79-6 Jan 83
				H. Monro	7 May 79-15 Sep 81
				G. Shaw	5 Jan 81-13 Jun 83
				N. MacFarlane	15 Sep 81-
				Sir G. Young	15 Sep 81-
				W. Waldegrave	13 Jun 83-
				E of Avon	11 Sep 84-27 Mar 85
Health & Social Security (Social Services)	**P. Jenkin**	5 May 79	*Min. of State (Health):*		
	N. Fowler	14 Sep 81		G. VAUGHAN	7 May 79
				K. CLARKE	5 Mar 82
			Min. of State (Social Security):		
				R. PRENTICE	7 May 79
				H. ROSSI	5 Jan 81
				R. BOYSON	12 Jun 83
				A. NEWTON	11 Sep 84
			U-S.	Sir G. Young	7 May 79-15 Sep 81
				Mrs. L. Chalker	7 May 79-5 Mar 82
				G. Finsberg	15 Sep 81-14 Jun 83
				Ld Elton	15 Sep 81-6 Apr 82
				A. Newton	5 Mar 82-11 Sep 84
				Ld Trefgarne	6 Apr 82-14 Jun 83
				J. Patten	14 Jun 83-
				Ld Glenarthur	14 Jun 83-26 Mar 85
				R. Whitney	11 Sep 84-
				Lady Trumpington	30 Mar 85-
Industry	**Sir K. Joseph**	7 May 79	*Min. of State:*		
	P. Jenkin	14 Sep 81		A. BUTLER	6 May 79-5 Jan 81
				VT TRENCHARD	6 May 79-5 Jan 81
	(12 Jun 83 office reorganised as Trade and Industry)			N. TEBBIT	5 Jan 81-14 Sep 81
				N. LAMONT	14 Sep 81-12 Jun 83
			Min. of State (Industry & Information Technology):		
				K. BAKER	5 Jan 81-12 Jun 83
			U-S.	D. Mitchell	6 May 79-5 Jan 81
				M. Marshall	6 May 79-15 Sep 81
				J. MacGregor	5 Man 81-14 Jun 83
				J. Wakeham	15 Sep 81-6 Apr 82
				J. Butcher	6 Apr 82-14 Jun 83
D. Lanc.	**N. St John Stevas**	5 May 79			
	F. Pym	5 Jan 81			
	Lady Young	14 Sep 81			
	C. Parkinson	6 Apr 82			
	Ld Cockfield	11 Jun 83			
	E of Gowrie	11 Sep 84			

CONSERVATIVE GOVERNMENT, 1979- (*contd.*)

	MINISTERS IN CABINET			JUNIOR MINISTERS ATTACHED	
Northern Ireland	**H. Atkins**	5 May 79	*Min. of State:*		
	J. Prior	14 Sep 81		M. Alison	7 May 79-15 Sep 81
	D. Hurd	11 Sep 84		H. Rossi	7 May 79-5 Jan 81
				A. Butler	5 Jan 81-11 Sep 84
				E of Gowrie	15 Sep 81-13 Sep 83
				E of Mansfield	13 Jun 83-12 Apr 84
				R. Boyson	11 Sep 84-
			U-S.	Ld Elton	7 May 79-15 Sep 81
				P. Goodhart	7 May 79-5 Jan 81
				G. Shaw	7 May 79-5 Jan 81
				D. Mitchell	5 Jan 81-13 Jun 83
				J. Patten	5 Jan 81-13 Jun 83
				N. Scott	15 Sep 81-
				C. Patten	14 Jun 83-
				Ld Lyell	12 Apr 84
Paym. -Gen.	**A. Maude**	5 May 79			
	F. Pym	5 Jan 81			
	C. Parkinson	14 Sep 81			
	(office vacant 11 Jun 83)				
	(J. Gummer 11 Sep 84 and office not in cabinet)				
Scot. O.	**G. Younger**	5 May 79	*Min. of State:*		
				E of Mansfield	7 May 79
				Ld Gray of Contin	13 Jun 83
			U-S.	A. Fletcher	7 May 79-14 Jun 83
				R. Fairgrieve	7 May 79-15 Sep 81
				M. Rifkind	7 May 79-14 Jun 83
				A. Stewart	15 Sep 81-
				J. Mackay	6 Apr 82-
				M. Ancram	13 June 83-
Trade	**J. Nott**	5 May 79	*Min. for Consumer Affairs:*		
	J. Biffen	5 Jan 81		Mrs S. Oppenheim	6 May 79
	Ld Cockfield	6 Apr 82		G. Vaughan	5 Mar 82
			Min. for Trade:		
				C. Parkinson	7 May 79
				P. Rees	14 Sep 81
			U-S.	N. Tebbit	7 May 79-5 Jan 81
				R. Eyre	7 May 79-5 Mar 82
				Ld Trefgarne	5 Jan 81-15 Sep 81
				I. Sproat	15 Sep 81-12 Jun 83
	(12 Jun 83 office reorganised as Trade and Industry)				
Trade & Industry	**C. Parkinson**	12 Jun 83	*Min. for Trade:*		
	N. Tebbit	16 Oct 83		P. Channon	13 Jun 83-
			Min. for Industry & Information Technology:		
				K. Baker	13 Jun 83
				G. Pattie	11 Sep 84-
			Min. of State for Industry:		
				N. Lamont	13 Jun 83-
			U-S.	J. Butcher	14 Jun 83-
				A. Fletcher	14 Jun 83-
				D. Trippier	14 Jun 83-
				Ld Lucas of Chilworth	11 Sep 84-
Transport	*(office not in cabinet)*				
	N. Fowler	5 Jan 81	*Min. of State:*		
	D. Howell	14 Sep 81		Mrs L. Chalker	18 Oct 81-
	T. King	11 Jun 83	*P.S.*	K. Clarke	7 May 79-5 Jan 81
	N. Ridley	16 Oct 83	*U-S.*	K. Clarke	5 Jan 81-5 Mar 82
				Mrs. L. Chalker	5 Mar 82-18 Oct 83
				R. Eyre	5 Mar 82-13 Jun 83
				D. Mitchell	13 Jun 83-
				M. Spicer	11 Sep 84-
Wales	**N. Edwards**	5 May 79	*Min. of State*		
				J. S. Thomas	17 Feb 83-
			U-S.	M. Roberts	7 May 79-10 Feb 83
				W. Roberts	7 May 79-

CONSERVATIVE GOVERNMENT, 1979- (*contd.*)

MINISTERS IN CABINET

Min. without Portfolio	**Ld Young of Graffham**	11 Sep 84

MINISTERS NOT IN CABINET

Ministers responsible for the Arts	*(N. St John-Stevas and office in cabinet 5 May 79-5 Jan 81)*	
	P. CHANNON	5 Jan 81
	E OF GOWRIE	13 Jun 83
	(office in cabinet 11 Sep 84)	
Paym. Gen.	*(office in cabinet till* 11 *Jun 83 then vacant)*	
	J. S. GUMMER	11 Sep 84
Transport	N. FOWLER	11 May 79
	(office in cabinet 5 Jan 81)	
Law officers:		
Att.-Gen.	SIR M. HAVERS	6 May 79
Sol.-Gen.	SIR I. PERCIVAL	6 May 79
	SIR P. MAYHEW	13 Jun 83
Ld Advoc.	J. MACKAY (LD)	7 May 79
	LD CAMERON OF LOCHBROOM	16 May 84
Sol.-Gen. Scotland	N. FAIRBAIRN	7 May 79
	P. FRASER	28 Jan 82

JUNIOR MINISTERS ATTACHED

(for Junior Ministers see above)

P.S. to Treasury:	
M. JOPLING	5 May 79
J. WAKEHAM	11 Jun 83
Junior Lds of Treasury:	
C. Mather	7 May 79-1 Oct 81
P. Morrison	7 May 79-5 Jan 81
Ld J. Douglas-Hamilton[1]	7 May 79-1 Oct 81
J. MacGregor	7 May 79-5 Jan 81
D. Waddington	16 May 79-5 Jan 81
R. Boscawen	9 Jan 81-17 Feb 83
J. Wakeham	9 Jan 81-15 Sep 81
J. Cope	9 Jan 81-13 Jun 83
A. Newton	1 Oct 81-5 Mar 82
P. Brooke	1 Oct 81-13 Jun 83
J. S. Gummer	1 Oct 81-6 Jan 83
A. Goodlad	16 Mar 82-10 Sep 84
D. Thompson	14 Jan 83-
D. Hunt	23 Feb-10 Sep 84
I. Lang	13 Jun 83-
T. Garel-Jones	13 Jun 83-
J. Major	3 Oct 84-
A. Hamilton	3 Oct 84-
Ass. Govt. Whips:	
R. Boscawen	16 May 79-9 Jan 81
J. Cope	16 May 79-9 Jan 81
A. Newton	16 May 79-30 Sep 81
J. Wakeham	16 May 79-9 Jan 81
P. Brooke	16 May 79-30 Sep 81
J. S. Gummer	9 Jan 81-30 Sep 81
A. Goodlad	9 Jan 81-16 Mar 82
D. Thompson	9 Jan 81-14 Jan 83
N. Budgen	30 Sep 81-11 May 82
D. Hunt	30 Sep 81-22 Feb 83
I. Lang	30 Sep 81-13 Jun 83
T. Garel-Jones	16 Mar 82-13 Jun 83
A. Hamilton	11 May 82-3 Oct 84
J. Major	14 Jan 83-3 Oct 84
D. Hogg	17 Feb 83-3 Oct 84
M. Neubert	15 Jun 83-

[1] Not a member of the House of Lords.

CONSERVATIVE GOVERNMENT, 1979- (*contd.*)

MINISTERS NOT IN CABINET

H.M. Household:		
Treas.	J. S. THOMAS	6 May 79
	A. BERRY	17 Feb 83
	J. COPE	13 Jun 83
Comptr.	S. LE MARCHANT	7 May 79
	A. BERRY	30 Sep 81
	C. MATHER	17 Feb 83
V. Chamb.	A. BERRY	7 May 79
	C. MATHER	30 Sep 81
	R. BOSCAWEN	17 Feb 83
Capt. Gents at Arms	LORD DENHAM	6 May 79
Capt. Yeomen of the Guard	LD SANDYS	16 May 79
	E OF SWINTON	3 Nov 82

JUNIOR MINISTERS ATTACHED

	T. Sainsbury	15 Jun 83-
	T. Durant	3 Oct 84-
	P. Lloyd	3 Oct 84-
	M. Lennox-Boyd	3 Oct 84-
Lds in Waiting:		
	Ld Mowbray and Stourton	9 May 79-22 Sep 80
	Vt Long	9 May 79-
	Ld Lyell	9 May 79-12 Apr 84
	Ld Cullen of Ashbourne	9 May 79-7 Jun 82
	Ld Trefgarne	9 May 79-5 Jan 81
	E of Avon	22 Sep 80-6 Jan 83
	Ld Skelmersdale	5 Jan 81-
	Ld Glenarthur	7 Jun 82-14 Jun 83
	Ld Lucas of Chilworth	6 Jan 83-11 Sep 84
	Lady Trumpington	13 Jun 83-30 Mar 85
	E of Caithness	8 May 84-
	Ld Brabazon of Tara	2 Sep 84-
	Lady Cox	6 Apr 85-

(for addenda)

(for addenda)

Ministerial Salaries

	Prime Minister[1]	Lord Chancellor[2]	Secretaries of State[1]	Other Dept. Ministers[1]
1831	£5,000	£14,000	£5,000	£2,000
1937	£10,000	£10,000	£5,000	£5,000
1954	£10,000	£12,000	£5,000	£5,000
1965	£14,000	£14,500	£8,500	£8,500
1972	£20,000	£20,000	£13,000	£7,500
1978	£22,000	£22,228	£14,300	£8,250
1979[3]	£22,000 (£33,000)	£22,228 (£37,000)	£19,650	£12,625
1980	£23,500 (£34,650)	£23,500 (£40,000)	£23,500	£16,250
1981	£27,825 (£36,725)	£27,825 (£44,500)	£27,825	£19,775
1982	£28,950 (£38,200)	£28,950 (£52,500)	£28,950	£20,575
1983	£29,367 (£38,987)	£30,110 (£58,500)	£29,367	£20,867
1984	£30,304 (£40,424)	£31,680 (£62,000)	£30,304	£21,364
1985	£31,271 (£42,980)	£33,250 (£65,900)	£31,271	£21,881

[1] Ministers and other paid office-holders who are Members of the House of Commons received a reduced Parliamentary salary (in 1985 £11,709) in addition to their Ministerial or official salary. The salaries shown in the table represent the Ministerial or official salary only.

[2] The Lord Chancellor receives a Judicial salary from the Consolidated Fund and a salary as speaker of the House of Lords from the House of Lords vote. The salaries shown in the table represent the total salary payable to the Lord Chancellor.

[3] After taking up office in 1979, the Prime Minister and Lord Chancellor elected to receive the same salary as their Cabinet colleagues. When Ministerial salaries were increased in 1979 the Prime Minister and Lord Chancellor decided to forgo the increase. This enabled their Cabinet colleagues to catch up. Following the 1980 salary increase, the Prime Minister's and Lord Chancellor's salaries were the same as their Cabinet colleagues. The salaries shown in brackets are the full Ministerial salaries which the Prime Minister and Lord Chancellor are entitled to receive.

Opposition Salaries

	Leader of the Opposition	Chief Opposition Whip	
		House of Commons	House of Lords
1937	£2,000	—	—
1957	£3,000	—	—
1965	£4,500	£3,750	£1,500
1972	£9,500	£7,500	£2,500
1978	£10,450	£8,250	£3,248
1979	£16,225	£12,625	£7,124
1980	£20,950	£16,250	£9,950
1981	£25,550	£19,775	£16,275
1982	£26,575	£20,575	£16,925
1983	£26,947	£20,867	£17,840
1984	£27,764	£21,364	£18,770
1985	£28,601	£25,881	£19,710

Ministerial Offices, 1900-

This list includes all specifically named ministerial offices held by Ministers or Ministers of State, apart from appointments in the Royal Household or after 1950 Ministers of State without a functional title. It does not include offices held by junior ministers.

Admiralty. First Lord of the Admiralty, 1900-64
Aerospace. Minister, 1971-72
Aerospace and Shipping, 1972-74
Agriculture. President of the Board of Agriculture, 1900-3; President of the Board of Agriculture and Fisheries, 1903-19; Minister of Agriculture and Fisheries, 1919-1955; Minister of Agriculture, Fisheries and Food, 1955-
Air. President of the Air Board, 1917; President of the Air Council, 1917-1918; Secretary of State, 1918-64
Aircraft Production. Minister, 1940-1946
***Armed Forces*. Minister of State, 1981-**
Arts. Under Secretary of State, 1965-67; Minister of State, 1967-70; (Paymaster-General, 1970-73); Minister of State, 1973-74; Under Secretary of State, 1974-76; Minister of State, 1976-79; Minister for Arts 1979-
Attorney-General, 1900-
Attorney-General for Ireland, 1900-22
Aviation. Minister, 1959-67 (see *Civil Aviation)*
Aviation Supply. Minister, 1970-71
Blockade. Minister, 1916-19
Burma. Secretary of State for India and Burma, 1937-47; Secretary of State for Burma, 1947-48
Civil Aviation. Minister, 1944-53; Minister of Transport and Civil Aviation, 1953-59; Minister of Aviation, 1959-67
Civil Service. Minister for the, 1968-
Colonies. Secretary of State, 1900-67
Commonwealth. Secretary of State for Dominions, 1925-47; Secretary of State for Commonwealth Relations, 1947-66; Secretary of State for Commonwealth Affairs, 1966-68
Co-ordination of Defence. Minister, 1936-40
Co-ordination of Transport, Fuel and Power. Secretary of State, 1951-53
Defence. Minister, 1940-64[1]; Secretary of State, 1964-
***Defence Procurement*. Minister of State, 1971-72, 1981-**
Defence for Administration. Minister of, 1967-70
Defence for Air Force. Minister of, 1964-67
Defence for Army. Minister of, 1964-67
Defence for Equipment. Minister of, 1967-70
Defence for Navy. Minister of, 1964-67
Dominions. Secretary of State, 1925-47
Duchy of Lancaster. Chancellor, 1900-
Economic Affairs. Minister, Sep-Nov 1947, Feb-Oct 1950, 1951-52; Secretary of State, 1964-69
Economic Warfare. Minister, 1939-45
Education. President of the Board of Education, 1900-44; Minister of Education, 1944-64; Secretary of State for Education and Science, 1964-
Employment and Productivity. Secretary of State, 1968-70
Employment. Secretary of State, 1970-
Energy. Secretary of State, 1974-; *also* Minister for, Jan-Mar 1974
Environment. Secretary of State, 1970-
First Secretary of State. 1962-63, 1964-1970
Food. Minister, 1916-21, and 1939-55 (see *Agriculture)*
***Foreign Affairs*. Secretary of State, 1900-68**
Foreign and Commonwealth Affairs. Secretary of State, 1968-
Fuel and Power. Minister, 1944-57 (see *Power)*
Fuel, Light and Power. Minister, 1942-44 (see *Fuel and Power)*
Health. Minister, 1919-68; Minister of State, 1968-70, 1979-
Health and Social Security (see *Social Services)*
Home Affairs. Secretary of State, 1900-
Home Security. Ministers, 1939-45
Housing and Local Government. Minister of Town and Country Planning, 1943-51; Minister of Local Government and Planning, 1951; Minister of Housing and Local Government, 1951-70 (see *Local Government)*
Housing and Construction. Minister, 1970-
***India*. Secretary of State for India, 1900-37; Secretary of State for India and Burma, 1937-47**
Industrial Development. Minister, 1972-74
Industry. Minister, 1970-74; Secretary of State, 1974-
Industry, Trade and Regional Development. Secretary of State, 1963-64
Information. Minister, Mar-Nov 1918 and 1939-46
***Information Technology*. Minister for Industry and Information Technology, 1981-3; Minister for Information Technology, 1983-**
Ireland. Chief Secretary to the Lord Lieutenant of Ireland, 1900-22 (*Irish Office wound up 1924)*
Labour. Minister of Labour, 1916-39; Minister of Labour and National Service, 1939-59; Minister of Labour, 1959-68

[1]From 1940 to 1946 and from 1951 to 1952 the office was held by the Prime Minister. A permanent department for Defence was not established until 1946.

Land and Natural Resources. Minister, 1964-67
Local Government. President of the Local Government Board, 1900-19 (see *Housing and Local Government*)
Local Government and Environmental Services. Minister, 1979-
Local Government and Development. Minister, 1970-74
Local Government and Planning. Minister, 1951 (see *Housing and Local Government*)
Local Government and Regional Planning, Secretary of State, 1969-70 (see *Planning and Local Government*)
Lord Advocate, 1900-
Lord Chancellor, 1900-
Lord Chancellor of Ireland, 1900-22
Lord President of the Council, 1900-
Lord Privy Seal, 1900-
Materials. Minister, 1951-54
Mines. Secretary for Mines Department, 1920-42
Ministers Resident Overseas. Allied H.Q., North Africa, 1942-5; Washington for Supply, 1942-5; West Africa, 1942-5; Middle East, 1942-3, 1944-5.
Munitions. Minister, 1915-19 (see *Supply*)
National Insurance. Minister, 1944-53; Minister of Pensions and National Insurance, 1953-66
National Service. Minister, 1917-19; Minister of Labour and National Service, 1939-59
Northern Ireland. Secretary of State, 1972-
Overseas Development. Minister, 1964-
Overseas Trade. Secretary for Overseas Trade, 1917-53
Paymaster-General, 1900-
Pensions. Minister of Pensions, 1916-53; Minister of Pensions and National Insurance, 1953-66
Petroleum. Secretary for Petroleum Department, 1940-42
Planning and Land. Minister, 1968-69
Planning and Local Government. Minister for Planning and Local Government, 1974-76
Portfolio. Minister without portfolio, 1915-21, 1935-36, 1939-42, 1942-44, 1946, 1947, 1954-68, 1968-74
Post Office. Postmaster-General, 1900-69
Post and Telecommunications. Minister, 1969-74
Power. Minister, 1957-69 (see *Fuel and Power*)
Prices and Consumer Protection. Secretary of State, 1974-79
Prime Minister, 1900-
Privy Council Office. Minister of State, 1974-79
Production. Minister, 1942-45
Public Building and Works. Minister, 1962-70 (see *Housing and Construction*)
Reconstruction. Minister, 1917-19 and 1944-45
Science. Minister, 1959-64
Scotland. Secretary, 1900-26; Secretary of State, 1926-
Shipping. Minister, 1916-21 and 1939-41 (see *War Transport*)
Social Insurance. Minister, Oct-Nov 1944 (see *National Insurance*)
Social Security. Minister, 1966-68, 1976-
Social Services. Secretary of State, 1968-
Solicitor-General, 1900-
Solicitor-General for Ireland, 1900-22
Solicitor-General for Scotland, 1900-
Sport (and Recreation). Minister of State, 1974-79
State. Minister of, 1941-42, 1943-50; First Secretary of, 1962-63, 1964-70
Supply. Minister, 1919-21 and 1939-59
Technical Cooperation. Secretary for, 1961-64
Technology. Minister, 1964-70
Town and Country Planning. Minister of Town and Country Planning, 1943-51 (see *Local Government and Planning*)
Trade. President of the Board of Trade, 1900-70; Secretary of State of Trade and Industry, 1970-74, 1983-; Secretary of State for Trade, 1974-83, *also* Minister for Trade, 1970-72; Minister for Trade and Consumer Affairs, 1972-74; Minister for Trade, 1983-
Transport. Minister of Transport, 1919-41; Minister of War Transport, 1941-46; Minister of Transport, 1946-53; Minister of Transport and Civil Aviation, 1953-59; Minister of Transport, 1959-70; Minister for Transport Industries, 1970-74; Minister for Transport, 1974-76; Secretary of State, 1976-79, 1981-; Minister of Transport, 1979-81
Treasury. Chancellor of the Exchequer, 1900-; Chief Secretary, 1961-; Financial Secretary, 1900-; Economic Secretary, 1947-50, 1950-51, 1952-8, 1958-64, 1981-; Minister of State, 1964-9, 1970-
Urban Affairs. Minister of State, 1974-74
Wales. Minister for Welsh Affairs, 1951-64; Secretary of State for Wales, 1964-; *also* Minister of State for Welsh Affairs, 1957-64
War. Secretary of State, 1900-64
War Transport. Minister, 1941-46 (see *Shipping* and *Transport*)
Works. First Commissioner of Works, 1900-40; Minister of Works and Buildings, 1940-42; Minister of Works and Planning, 1942-43; Minister of Works, 1943-62; Minister of Public Building and Works, 1962-70

SOURCE.—For a full table of changes within the central administration between 1914-56 see *The Organisation of British Central Government, 1914-1956*, by D. N. Chester and F. M. G. Willson (1957), especially Appendix C, pp. 385-420.

Holders of Ministerial Offices

Prime Minister

1900		M of Salisbury (3rd)
12 Jul	02	A. Balfour
5 Dec	05	Sir H. Campbell-Bannerman
5 Apr	08	H. Asquith
6 Dec	16	D. Lloyd George
23 Oct	22	A. Bonar Law
22 May	23	S. Baldwin
22 Jan	24	R. MacDonald
4 Nov	24	S. Baldwin
5 Jun	29	R. MacDonald
7 Jun	35	S. Baldwin
28 May	37	N. Chamberlain
10 May	40	W. Churchill
26 Jul	45	C. Attlee
26 Oct	51	(Sir) W. Churchill
6 Apr	55	Sir A. Eden
10 Jan	57	H. Macmillan
18 Oct	63	Sir A. Douglas-Home
16 Oct	64	H. Wilson
19 Jun	70	E. Heath
4 Mar	74	H. Wilson
5 Apr	76	J. Callaghan
4 May	79	Mrs M. Thatcher

Lord President of the Council

1900		D of Devonshire
13 Oct	03	M of Londonderry
10 Dec	05	E of Crewe
12 Apr	08	Ld Tweedmouth
13 Oct	08	Vt Wolverhampton
16 Jun	10	Earl Beauchamp
3 Nov	10	Vt Morley
5 Aug	14	Earl Beauchamp
25 May	15	M of Crewe
10 Dec	16	Earl Curzon
23 Oct	19	(Sir) A. Balfour (E of Balfour)
24 Oct	22	M of Salisbury (4th)
22 Jan	24	Ld Parmoor
6 Nov	24	Marquess Curzon
27 Apr	25	E of Balfour
7 Jun	29	Ld Parmoor
25 Aug	31	S. Baldwin
7 Jun	35	R. MacDonald
28 May	37	Vt Halifax
9 Mar	38	Vt Hailsham (1st)
31 Oct	38	Vt Runciman
3 Sep	39	Earl Stanhope
11 May	40	N. Chamberlain
3 Oct	40	Sir J. Anderson
24 Sep	43	C. Attlee
25 May	45	Ld Woolton
27 Jul	45	H. Morrison
9 Mar	51	Vt Addison
28 Oct	51	Ld Woolton
24 Nov	52	M of Salisbury (5th)
29 Mar	57	E of Home
17 Sep	57	Vt Hailsham (2nd)
14 Oct	59	E of Home
27 Jul	60	Vt Hailsham (2nd) (Q. Hogg)
16 Oct	64	H. Bowden
11 Aug	66	R. Crossman
18 Oct	68	F. Peart
20 Jun	70	W. Whitelaw
7 Apr	72	R. Carr
5 Nov	72	J. Prior
5 Mar	74	E. Short
8 Apr	76	M. Foot
5 May	79	Ld Soames
14 Sep	**81**	**F. Pym**
5 Apr	**82**	**J. Biffen**
11 Jun	**83**	**Vt Whitelaw**

Lord Chancellor

1900		E of Halsbury
10 Dec	05	Ld Loreburn (E)
10 Jun	12	Vt Haldane
25 May	15	Ld Buckmaster
10 Dec	16	Ld Finlay
10 Jan	19	Ld Birkenhead (Vt)
24 Oct	22	Vt Cave
22 Jan	24	Vt Haldane
6 Nov	24	Vt Cave
28 Mar	28	Ld Hailsham (Vt)
7 Jun	29	Ld Sankey (Vt)
7 Jun	35	Vt Hailsham
9 Mar	38	Ld Maugham (Vt)
3 Sep	39	Vt Caldecote
12 May	40	Vt Simon
27 Jul	45	Ld Jowitt
30 Oct	51	Ld Simonds
18 Oct	54	Vt Kilmuir
13 Jul	62	Ld Dilhorne
16 Oct	64	Ld Gardiner
20 Jun	70	Ld Hailsham
5 Mar	74	Ld Elwyn-Jones
5 May	79	Ld Hailsham

Lord Privy Seal

1900		Vt Cross
1 Nov	00	M of Salisbury (3rd)
12 Jul	02	A. Balfour
11 Oct	03	M of Salisbury (4th)
10 Dec	05	M of Ripon
9 Oct	08	E of Crewe
23 Oct	11	Earl Carrington
13 Feb	12	M of Crewe
25 May	15	Earl Curzon
15 Dec	16	E of Crawford
10 Jan	19	A. Bonar Law
23 Mar	21	A. Chamberlain
24 Oct	22	(*office vacant)*
25 May	23	Ld R. Cecil
22 Jan	24	J. Clynes
6 Nov	24	M of Salisbury (4th)
7 Jun	29	J. Thomas
5 Jun	30	V. Hartshorn
24 Mar	31	T. Johnston
3 Sep	31	Earl Peel
5 Nov	31	Vt Snowden
29 Sep	32	S. Baldwin
31 Dec	33	A. Eden
7 Jun	35	M of Londonderry
22 Nov	35	Vt Halifax
28 May	37	Earl De La Warr
31 Oct	38	Sir J. Anderson
3 Sep	39	Sir S. Hoare
3 Apr	40	Sir K. Wood
11 May	40	C. Attlee
19 Feb	42	Sir S. Cripps
22 Nov	42	Vt Cranborne (5th M of Salisbury)
24 Sep	43	Ld Beaverbrook
27 Jul	45	A. Greenwood
17 Apr	47	Ld Inman
7 Oct	47	Vt Addison
9 Mar	51	E. Bevin
26 Apr	51	R. Stokes
28 Oct	51	M of Salisbury (5th)
7 May	52	H. Crookshank
20 Dec	55	R. Butler
14 Oct	59	Vt Hailsham
27 Jul	60	E. Heath
20 Oct	63	S. Lloyd
18 Oct	64	E of Longford
23 Dec	65	Sir F. Soskice
6 Apr	66	E of Longford
16 Jan	68	Ld Shackleton
6 Apr	68	F. Peart
18 Oct	68	Ld Shackleton
20 Jun	70	Earl Jellicoe
5 Jun	73	Ld Windlesham
7 Mar	74	Ld Shepherd
10 Sep	76	Ld Peart
5 May	79	Sir I. Gilmour
14 Sep	**81**	**H. Atkins**
6 Apr	82	Lady Young
11 Jun	83	J. Biffen

Secretary of State for Economic Affairs

16 Oct	64	G. Brown
11 Aug	66	M. Stewart
29 Aug	67	P. Shore

(*office abolished* 8 *Oct* 69)

Chancellor of the Exchequer

1900		Sir M. Hicks-Beach
8 Aug	02	C. Ritchie
6 Oct	03	A. Chamberlain
10 Dec	05	H. Asquith
12 Apr	08	D. Lloyd-George
25 May	15	R. McKenna
10 Dec	16	A. Bonar Law

10 Jan	19	A. Chamberlain
1 Apr	21	Sir R. Horne
24 Oct	22	S. Baldwin
27 Aug	23	N. Chamberlain
22 Jan	24	P. Snowden
6 Nov	24	W. Churchill
7 Jun	29	P. Snowden
5 Nov	31	N. Chamberlain
28 May	37	Sir J. Simon
12 May	40	Sir K. Wood
24 Sep	43	Sir J. Anderson
27 Jul	45	H. Dalton
13 Nov	47	Sir S. Cripps
19 Oct	50	H. Gaitskell
28 Oct	51	R. Butler
20 Dec	55	H. Macmillan
13 Jan	57	P. Thorneycroft
6 Jan	58	D. Heathcoat Amory
27 Jul	60	S. Lloyd
13 Jul	62	R. Maudling
16 Oct	64	J. Callaghan
30 Nov	67	R. Jenkins
20 Jun	70	I. Macleod
25 Jul	70	A. Barber
5 Mar	74	D. Healey
5 May	79	Sir G. Howe
11 Jun	**83**	**N. Lawson**

Secretary of State for Foreign Affairs

1900		M of Salisbury (3rd)
1 Nov	00	M of Lansdowne
10 Dec	05	Sir E. Grey (Vt)
10 Dec	16	A. Balfour
23 Oct	19	Earl Curzon (M)
22 Jan	24	R. MacDonald
6 Nov	24	(Sir) A. Chamberlain
7 Jun	29	A. Henderson
25 Aug	31	M of Reading
5 Nov	31	Sir J. Simon
7 Jun	35	Sir S. Hoare
22 Dec	35	A. Eden
21 Feb	38	Vt Halifax
22 Dec	40	A. Eden
27 Jul	45	E. Bevin
9 Mar	51	H. Morrison
28 Oct	51	(Sir) A. Eden
7 Apr	55	H. Macmillan
20 Dec	55	S. Lloyd
27 Jul	60	E of Home
20 Oct	63	R. Butler
16 Oct	64	P. Gordon Walker
22 Jan	65	M. Stewart
11 Aug	66	G. Brown
16 Mar	68	M. Stewart

(Secretary of State for Foreign and Commonwealth Affairs)

17 Oct	68	M. Stewart
20 Jun	70	Sir A. Douglas-Home
5 Mar	74	J. Callaghan
8 Apr	76	A. Crosland
21 Feb	77	D. Owen
5 May	79	Ld Carrington
5 Apr	**82**	**F. Pym**
11 Jun	**83**	**Sir G. Howe**

Secretary of State for the Home Department

1900		Sir M. White-Ridley
1 Nov	00	C. Ritchie
8 Aug	02	A. Akers-Douglas
10 Dec	05	H. Gladstone
14 Feb	10	W. Churchill
23 Oct	11	R. McKenna
25 May	15	Sir J. Simon
10 Jan	16	Sir H. Samuel
10 Dec	16	Sir G. Cave (Vt)
10 Jan	19	E. Shortt
24 Oct	22	W. Bridgeman
22 Jan	24	A. Henderson
6 Nov	24	Sir W. Joynson-Hicks
7 Jun	29	J. Clynes
25 Aug	31	H. Samuel
28 Sep	32	Sir J. Gilmour
7 Jun	35	Sir J. Simon
28 May	37	Sir S. Hoare
3 Sep	39	Sir J. Anderson
3 Oct	40	H. Morrison
25 May	45	Sir D. Somervell
3 Aug	45	C. Ede
28 Oct	51	Sir D. Maxwell-Fyfe
18 Oct	54	G. Lloyd-George
13 Jan	57	R. Butler
13 Jul	62	H. Brooke
18 Oct	64	Sir F. Soskice
23 Dec	65	R. Jenkins
30 Nov	67	J. Callaghan
20 Jun	70	R. Maudling
19 Jul	72	R. Carr
5 Mar	74	R. Jenkins
10 Sep	76	M. Rees
5 May	79	W. Whitelaw
11 Jun	**83**	**L. Brittan**

First Lord of the Admiralty

1900		G. Goschen
1 Nov	00	E of Selborne
5 Mar	05	Earl Cawdor
10 Dec	05	Ld Tweedmouth
12 Apr	08	R. McKenna
23 Oct	11	W. Churchill
25 May	15	A. Balfour
10 Dec	16	Sir E. Carson
17 Jul	17	Sir E. Geddes
10 Jan	19	W. Long
13 Feb	21	Ld Lee
24 Oct	22	L. Amery
22 Jan	24	Vt Chelmsford
6 Nov	24	W. Bridgeman
7 Jun	29	A. Alexander
25 Aug	31	Sir A. Chamberlain
5 Nov	31	Sir B. Eyres-Monsell (Vt Monsell)
5 Jun	36	Sir S. Hoare
28 May	37	A. Duff Cooper
27 Oct	38	Earl Stanhope
3 Sep	39	W. Churchill
11 May	40	A. Alexander
25 May	45	B. Bracken
3 Aug	45	A. Alexander
4 Oct	46	Vt Hall
24 May	51	Ld Pakenham
31 Oct	51	J. Thomas (Vt Cilcennin)
2 Sep	56	Vt Hailsham
16 Jan	57	E of Selkirk
16 Oct	59	Ld Carrington
22 Oct	63	Earl Jellicoe

(*office abolished* 1 *Apr* 64)

Minister for Aerospace (and Shipping)

1 May	71	F. Corfield
7 Apr	72	M. Heseltine

(*office abolished* 5 *Mar* 74)

President of the Board of Agriculture (and Fisheries 1903)

1900		W. Long
14 Nov	00	R. Hanbury
19 May	03	E of Onslow
12 Mar	05	A. Fellowes
10 Dec	05	Earl Carrington
23 Oct	11	W. Runciman
6 Aug	14	Ld Lucas
25 May	15	E of Selborne
11 Jul	16	E of Crawford
10 Dec	16	R. Prothero (Ld Ernle)

(Minister of Agriculture and Fisheries)

(*and Food, since* 18 *Oct* 54)

15 Aug	19	Ld Lee
13 Feb	21	Sir A. Griffith-Boscawen
24 Oct	22	Sir R. Sanders
22 Jan	24	N. Buxton
6 Nov	24	E. Wood
4 Nov	25	W. Guinness
7 Jun	29	N. Buxton
5 Jun	30	C. Addison
25 Aug	31	Sir J. Gilmour
28 Sep	32	W. Elliot
29 Oct	36	W. Morrison
29 Jan	39	Sir R. Dorman-Smith
14 May	40	R. Hudson
3 Aug	45	T. Williams
31 Oct	51	Sir T. Dugdale
28 Jul	54	D. Heathcoat Amory
6 Jan	58	J. Hare
27 Jul	60	C. Soames
18 Oct	64	F. Peart

6 Apr	68	C. Hughes
20 Jun	70	J. Prior
5 Nov	72	J. Godber
5 Mar	74	F. Peart
10 Sep	76	J. Silkin
5 May	79	P. Walker
11 Jun	**83**	**M. Jopling**

President of the Air Board

3 Jan	17	Ld Cowdray

(President of the Air Council)

26 Nov	17	Ld Rothermere
26 Apr	18	Ld Weir

(Secretary of State for Air)

10 Jan	19	W. Churchill
1 Apr	21	F. Guest
31 Oct	22	Sir S. Hoare
22 Jan	24	Ld Thomson
6 Nov	24	Sir S. Hoare
7 Jun	29	Ld Thomson
14 Oct	30	Ld Amulree
5 Nov	31	M of Londonderry
7 Jun	35	Sir P. Cunliffe-Lister (Vt Swinton)
16 May	38	Sir K. Wood
3 Apr	40	Sir S. Hoare
11 May	40	Sir A. Sinclair
25 May	45	H. Macmillan
3 Aug	45	Vt Stansgate
4 Oct	46	P. Noel-Baker
7 Oct	47	A. Henderson
31 Oct	51	Ld De L'Isle
20 Dec	55	N. Birch
16 Jan	57	G. Ward
28 Oct	60	J. Amery
16 Jul	62	H. Fraser

(*office abolished* 1 *Apr* 64)

Minister of Aircraft Production

14 May	40	Ld Beaverbrook
1 May	41	J. Moore-Brabazon
22 Feb	42	J. Llewellin
22 Nov	42	Sir S. Cripps
25 May	45	E. Brown
4 Aug	45	J. Wilmot

(*office abolished* 1 *Apr* 46)

Minister of State for the Armed Forces

29 May	**81**	**P. Blaker**
13 Jun	**83**	**J. Stanley**

Minister for the Arts

20 Oct	64	Miss J. Lee[1]
17 Feb	67	Miss J. Lee[2]
23 Jun	70	Vt Eccles[3]
2 Dec	73	N. St John-Stevas[2]
8 Mar	74	H. Jenkins[1]
14 Apr	76	Ld Donaldson[2]
5 May	79	N. St John-Stevas[4]
5 Jun	**81**	**P. Channon[2]**
13 Jun	**83**	**E of Gowrie[2,3]**

[1] P.S. then U-S.
[2] Minister of State
[3] Paymaster-General
[4] Chancellor of the Duchy of Lancaster

Attorney-General

1900		Sir R. Webster
7 May	00	Sir R. Finlay
12 Dec	05	Sir J. Walton
28 Jan	08	Sir W. Robson
7 Oct	10	Sir R. Isaacs
19 Oct	13	Sir J. Simon
25 May	15	Sir E. Carson
3 Nov	15	Sir F. Smith
10 Jan	19	Sir G. Hewart
6 Mar	22	Sir E. Pollock
24 Oct	22	Sir D. Hogg
23 Jan	24	Sir P. Hastings
6 Nov	24	Sir D. Hogg
28 Mar	28	Sir T. Inskip
7 Jun	29	Sir W. Jowitt
26 Jan	32	Sir T. Inskip
18 Mar	36	Sir D. Somervell
25 May	45	Sir D. Maxwell Fyfe
4 Aug	45	Sir H. Shawcross
24 Apr	51	Sir F. Soskice
3 Nov	51	Sir L. Heald
18 Oct	54	Sir R. Manningham-Buller
16 Jul	62	Sir J. Hobson
1 Oct	64	Sir E. Jones
23 Jun	70	Sir P. Rawlinson
7 Mar	74	S. Silkin
5 May	79	Sir M. Havers

Minister of Blockade

10 Dec	16	Ld R. Cecil
18 Jul	18	Sir L. Worthington-Evans

(*office abolished* 10 *Jan* 19)

Minister of Civil Aviation

8 Oct	44	Vt Swinton
4 Aug	45	Ld Winster
4 Oct	46	Ld Nathan
31 May	48	Ld Pakenham
1 Jun	51	Ld Ogmore
31 Oct	51	J. Maclay
7 May	52	A. Lennox-Boyd

(Minister of Transport and Civil Aviation)

1 Oct	53	A. Lennox-Boyd
28 Jul	54	J. Boyd-Carpenter
20 Dec	55	H. Watkinson

(Minister of Aviation)

14 Oct	59	D. Sandys
27 Jul	60	P. Thorneycroft
16 Jul	62	J. Amery
18 Oct	64	R. Jenkins
23 Dec	65	F. Mulley
7 Jan	67	J. Stonehouse

(*office absorbed into Ministry of Technology* 15 *Feb* 67)

Minister of Aviation Supply

15 Oct	70	F. Corfield

(*office absorbed into Ministry of Defence* 1 *May* 71)

Minister for the Civil Service

1 Nov	68	H. Wilson
19 Jun	70	E. Heath
4 Mar	74	H. Wilson
5 Apr	76	J. Callaghan
4 May	79	Mrs M. Thatcher

Secretary of State for the Colonies

1900		J. Chamberlain
6 Oct	03	A. Lyttelton
10 Dec	05	E of Elgin
12 Apr	08	E of Crewe
3 Nov	10	L. Harcourt
25 May	15	A. Bonar Law
10 Dec	16	W. Long
10 Jan	19	Vt Milner
13 Feb	21	W. Churchill
24 Oct	22	D of Devonshire
22 Jan	24	J. Thomas
6 Nov	24	L. Amery
7 Jun	29	Ld Passfield
25 Aug	31	J. Thomas
5 Nov	31	Sir P. Cunliffe-Lister
7 Jun	35	M. MacDonald
22 Nov	35	J. Thomas
28 May	36	W. Ormsby-Gore
16 May	38	M. MacDonald
12 May	40	Ld Lloyd
8 Feb	41	Ld Moyne
22 Feb	42	Vt Cranborne
22 Nov	42	O. Stanley
3 Aug	45	G. Hall
4 Oct	46	A. Creech Jones
28 Feb	50	J. Griffiths

28 Oct	51	O. Lyttelton
28 Jul	54	A. Lennox-Boyd
14 Oct	59	I. Macleod
9 Oct	61	R. Maudling
13 Jul	62	D. Sandys
18 Oct	64	A. Greenwood
23 Dec	65	E of Longford
6 Apr	66	F. Lee

(*office came under Commonwealth Affairs* 1 *Aug* 66 *and abolished* 6 *Jan* 67)

Minister for Co-ordination of Defence

13 Mar	36	Sir T. Inskip
29 Jan	39	Ld Chatfield

(Minister of Defence)

10 May	40	W. Churchill
27 Jul	45	C. Attlee
20 Dec	46	A. Alexander
28 Feb	50	E. Shinwell
28 Oct	51	W. Churchill
1 Mar	52	Earl Alexander of Tunis
18 Oct	54	H. Macmillan
7 Apr	55	S. Lloyd
20 Dec	55	Sir W. Monckton
18 Oct	56	A. Head
13 Jan	57	D. Sandys
14 Oct	59	H. Watkinson
13 Jul	62	P. Thorneycroft

(Secretary of State)

1 Apr	64	P. Thorneycroft
16 Oct	64	D. Healey
20 Jun	70	Ld Carrington
8 Jan	74	I. Gilmour
5 Mar	74	R. Mason
10 Sep	76	F. Mulley
5 May	79	F. Pym
5 Jan	**81**	**J. Nott**
8 Jan	**83**	**M. Heseltine**

Minister of State for Defence Procurement

7 Apr	71	I. Gilmour

(*office vacant* 5 *Nov* 72)

29 May	**81**	**Ld Trenchard**
6 Jan	**83**	**G. Pattie**
11 Sep	84	A. Butler

Minister of Defence for Administration

7 Jan	67	G. Reynolds
15 Jul	69	R. Hattersley

(*office abolished* 19 *Jun* 70)

Minister of Defence for Air Force

1 Apr	64	H. Fraser
19 Oct	64	Ld Shackleton

(*office abolished* 7 *Jan* 67)

Minister of Defence for Army

1 Apr	64	J. Ramsden
19 Oct	64	F. Mulley
24 Dec	65	G. Reynolds

(*office abolished* 7 *Jan* 67)

Minister of Defence for Navy

1 Apr	64	Earl Jellicoe
19 Oct	64	C. Mayhew
19 Feb	66	J. Mallalieu

(*office abolished* 7 *Jan* 67)

Minister of Defence for Equipment

7 Jan	67	R. Mason
6 Apr	68	J. Morris

(*office abolished* 19 *Jun* 70)

Secretary of State for Dominion Affairs

11 Jun	25	L. Amery
7 Jun	29	Ld Passfield
5 Jun	30	J. Thomas
22 Nov	35	M. MacDonald
16 May	38	Ld Stanley
31 Oct	38	M. MacDonald
29 Jan	39	Sir T. Inskip (Vt Caldecote)
3 Sep	39	A. Eden
14 May	40	Vt Caldecote
3 Oct	40	Vt Cranborne
19 Feb	42	C. Attlee
24 Sep	43	Vt Cranborne
3 Aug	45	Vt Addison

(Secretary of State for Commonwealth Relations)

7 Jul	47	Vt Addison
7 Oct	47	P. Noel-Baker
28 Feb	50	P. Gordon Walker
28 Oct	51	Ld Ismay
12 Mar	52	M of Salisbury
24 Nov	52	Vt Swinton
7 Apr	55	E of Home
27 Jul	60	D. Sandys
18 Oct	64	A. Bottomley

(Secretary of State for Commonwealth Affairs)

1 Aug	66	A. Bottomley
11 Aug	66	H. Bowden
29 Aug	67	G. Thomson

(17 *Oct* 68 *office merged with Foreign Office*)

Minister of Economic Warfare

3 Sep	39	R. Cross
15 May	40	H. Dalton
22 Feb	42	Vt Wolmer (E of Selborne)

(*office wound up* 23 *May* 45)

President of the Board of Education

1 Jan	00	D of Devonshire
8 Aug	02	M of Londonderry
10 Dec	05	A. Birrell
23 Jan	07	R. McKenna
12 Apr	08	W. Runciman
23 Oct	11	J. Pease
25 May	15	A. Henderson
18 Aug	16	M of Crewe
10 Dec	16	H. Fisher
24 Oct	22	E. Wood
22 Jan	24	C. Trevelyan
6 Nov	24	Ld E. Percy
7 Jun	29	Sir C. Trevelyan
2 Mar	31	H. Lees-Smith
25 Aug	31	Sir D. Maclean
15 Jun	32	Ld Irwin (Vt Halifax)
7 Jun	35	O. Stanley
28 May	37	Earl Stanhope
27 Oct	38	Earl De La Warr
3 Apr	40	H. Ramsbotham
20 Jul	41	R. Butler

(Minister of Education)

3 Aug	44	R. Butler
25 May	45	R. Law
3 Aug	45	Miss E. Wilkinson
10 Feb	47	G. Tomlinson
2 Nov	51	Miss F. Horsbrugh
18 Oct	54	Sir D. Eccles
13 Jan	57	Vt Hailsham (2nd)
17 Sep	57	G. Lloyd
14 Oct	59	Sir D. Eccles
13 Jul	62	Sir E. Boyle

(Secretary of State for Education and Science)

1 Apr	64	Q. Hogg
18 Oct	64	M. Stewart
22 Jan	65	A. Crosland
29 Aug	67	P. Gordon Walker
6 Apr	68	E. Short
20 Jun	70	Mrs M. Thatcher
5 Mar	74	R. Prentice
10 Jun	75	F. Mulley
10 Sep	76	Mrs S. Williams
5 May	79	M. Carlisle
14 Sep	**81**	**Sir K. Joseph**

Secretary of State for Employment and Productivity

6 Apr	68	Mrs B. Castle
20 Jun	70	R. Carr

(Secretary of State for Employment)

12 Nov	70	R. Carr

7 Apr	72	M. Macmillan
2 Dec	73	W. Whitelaw
5 Mar	74	M. Foot
8 Apr	76	A. Booth
5 May	79	J. Prior
14 Sep	**81**	**N. Tebbit**
16 Oct	**83**	**T. King**

Secretary of State for Energy

8 Jan	74	Ld Carrington
5 Mar	74	E. Varley
10 Jun	75	A. Benn
5 May	79	D. Howell
14 Sep	**81**	**N. Lawson**
11 Jun	**83**	**P. Walker**

Secretary of State for the Environment

15 Oct	70	P. Walker
5 Nov	72	G. Rippon
5 Mar	74	A. Crosland
8 Apr	76	P. Shore
5 May	79	M. Heseltine
6 Jan	**83**	**T. King**
11 Jun	**83**	**P. Jenkin**

Minister of Food Control

10 Dec	16	Vt Devonport
19 Jun	17	Ld Rhondda (Vt)
9 Jul	18	J. Clynes
10 Jan	19	G. Roberts
19 Mar	20	C. McCurdy

(*office abolished* 31 *Mar* 21)

Minister of Food

4 Sep	39	W. Morrison
3 Apr	40	Ld Woolton
11 Nov	43	J. Llewellin
3 Aug	45	Sir B. Smith
27 May	46	J. Strachey
28 Feb	50	M. Webb
31 Oct	51	G. Lloyd-George
18 Oct	54	D. Heathcoat Amory

(*and combined with Minister of Agriculture and Fisheries)*

Foreign Affairs

(*See p.* 71)

Minister of Fuel, Light and Power

3 Jun	42	G. Lloyd-George

(Minister of Fuel and Power)

25 May	45	G. Lloyd-George
3 Aug	45	E. Shinwell
7 Oct	47	H. Gaitskell
28 Feb	50	P. Noel-Baker
31 Oct	51	G. Lloyd
20 Dec	55	A. Jones

(Minister of Power)

13 Jan	57	Ld Mills
14 Oct	59	R. Wood
20 Oct	63	F. Erroll
18 Oct	64	F. Lee
6 Apr	66	R. Marsh
6 Apr	68	R. Gunter
6 Jul	68	R. Mason

(*office absorbed into Ministry of Technology* 6 *Oct* 69)

Minister of Health

(*See below, under Local Government and under Social Services*)

Minister for Health

7 May	79	G. Vaughan
5 Mar	82	K. Clarke

Home Office

(*See p.* 71)

Minister of Housing

(*See below, under Local Government)*

Secretary of State for India (and Burma 1937-48)

1900		Ld G. Hamilton
6 Oct	03	St J. Brodrick
10 Dec	05	J. Morley (Vt)
3 Nov	10	E of Crewe
7 Mar	11	Vt Morley
25 May	11	E of Crewe (M)
25 May	15	A. Chamberlain
17 Jul	17	E. Montagu
19 Mar	22	Vt Peel
22 Jan	24	Ld Olivier
6 Nov	24	E of Birkenhead
18 Oct	28	Vt Peel
7 Jun	29	W. Benn
25 Aug	31	Sir S. Hoare
7 Jun	35	M of Zetland
13 May	40	L. Amery
3 Aug	45	Ld Pethick-Lawrence
17 Apr	47	E of Listowel

(4 *Jan* 1948 *India & Burma Offices wound up)*

Minister for Industrial Development

7 Apr	72	C. Chataway

(*office abolished* 5 *Mar* 74)

Minister for Industry

15 Oct	70	Sir J. Eden
7 Apr	72	T. Boardman

(*office abolished* 8 *Jan* 74)

Secretary of State for Industry, Trade and Regional Development

20 Oct	63	E. Heath

(*office abolished* 16 *Oct* 64)

Secretary of State for Industry

5 Mar	74	A. Benn
10 Jun	75	E. Varley
5 May	79	Sir K. Joseph
14 Sep	**81**	**P. Jenkin**

(11 *Jun* 83 *office merged with Trade*)

Minister for (Industry (and Information)) Technology

5 Jan	**81**	**K. Baker**
11 Sep	**84**	**G. Pattie**

Minister of Information

10 Feb	18	Ld Beaverbrook
4 Nov	18	Ld Downham

(*office abolished* 10 *Jan* 19)

4 Sep	39	Ld Macmillan
5 Jan	40	Sir J. Reith
12 May	40	A. Duff Cooper
20 Jul	41	B. Bracken
25 May	45	G. Lloyd
4 Aug	45	E. Williams
24 Feb	**46**	**E of Listowel**

(*office abolished* 31 *Mar* 46)

Chief Secretary for Ireland

1900		G. Balfour
7 Nov	00	G. Wyndham
12 Mar	05	W. Long
10 Dec	05	J. Bryce
23 Jan	07	A. Birrell
31 Jul	16	(Sir) H. Duke
5 May	18	E. Shortt
10 Jan	19	I. Macpherson
2 Apr	20	Sir H. Greenwood

(*post vacant* 19 *Oct* 22, *office abolished* 6 *Dec* 22)

Lord Chancellor of Ireland

1900		Ld Ashbourne
12 Dec	05	Sir S. Walker
26 Sep	11	R. Barry
10 Apr	13	(Sir) I. O'Brien
4 Jun	18	Sir J. Campbell
27 Jun	21	Sir J. Ross

(*ceased to be executive office* 27 *Jun* 21)

Lord Lieutenant of Ireland

(See p. 388. *Office in Cabinet only Jun* 95-8 *Aug* 02 *and* 28 *Oct* 19-2 *Apr* 21)

Attorney-General for Ireland

1900		J. Atkinson
4 Dec	05	J. Campbell
20 Dec	05	R. Cherry
2 Dec	09	R. Barry
26 Sep	11	C. O'Connor
24 Jun	12	I. O'Brien
10 Apr	13	T. Molony
20 Jun	13	J. Moriarty
1 Jul	14	J. Pim
8 Jun	15	J. Gordon
9 Apr	16	J. Campbell
8 Jan	17	J. O'Connor
7 Apr	18	A. Samuels
6 Jul	19	D. Henry
5 Aug	21	T. Brown

(*post vacant from* 16 *Nov* 21)

Solicitor-General for Ireland

1900		D. Barton
30 Jan	00	G. Wright
8 Jan	03	J. Campbell
20 Dec	05	R. Barry
2 Dec	09	C. O'Connor
19 Oct	11	I. O'Brien
24 Jun	12	T. Molony
25 Apr	13	J. Moriarty
20 Jun	13	J. Pim
1 Jul	14	J. O'Connor
19 Mar	17	J. Chambers
12 Sep	17	A. Samuels
7 Apr	18	J. Powell
27 Nov	18	D. Henry
6 Jul	19	D. Wilson
2 Jun	21	T. Brown

(*post vacant from* 5 *Aug* 21)

Minister of Labour

10 Dec	16	J. Hodge
17 Aug	17	G. Roberts
10 Jan	19	Sir R. Horne
19 Mar	20	T. Macnamara
31 Oct	22	Sir A. Montague-Barlow
22 Jan	24	T. Shaw
6 Nov	24	Sir A. Steel-Maitland
7 Jun	29	Miss M. Bondfield
25 Aug	31	Sir H. Betterton
29 Jun	34	O. Stanley
7 Jun	35	E. Brown

(Minister of Labour and National Service)

3 Sep	39	E. Brown
13 May	40	E. Bevin
25 May	45	R. Butler
3 Aug	45	G. Isaacs
17 Jan	51	A. Bevan
24 Apr	51	A. Robens
28 Oct	51	Sir W. Monckton
20 Dec	55	I. Macleod
14 Oct	59	E. Heath

(Minister of Labour)

12 Nov	59	E. Heath
27 Jul	60	J. Hare
20 Oct	63	J. Godber
18 Oct	64	R. Gunter

(6 *Apr* 68 *office reorganised as Ministry of Employment and Productivity)*

Chancellor of the Duchy of Lancaster

1900		Ld James of Hereford
8 Aug	02	Sir W. Walrond
10 Dec	05	Sir H. Fowler (Vt Wolverhampton)
13 Oct	08	Ld Fitzmaurice
25 Jun	09	H. Samuel
14 Feb	10	J. Pease
23 Oct	11	C. Hobhouse
11 Feb	14	C. Masterman
3 Feb	15	E. Montagu
25 May	15	W. Churchill
25 Nov	15	H. Samuel
11 Jan	16	E. Montagu
9 Jul	16	T. McKinnon Wood
10 Dec	16	Sir F. Cawley
10 Feb	18	Ld Beaverbrook
4 Nov	18	Ld Downham
10 Jan	19	E of Crawford
1 Apr	21	Vt Peel
7 Apr	22	Sir W. Sutherland
24 Oct	22	M of Salisbury
25 May	23	J. Davidson
22 Jan	24	J. Wedgwood
10 Nov	24	Vt Cecil
19 Oct	27	Ld Cushendun
7 Jun	29	Sir O. Mosley
23 May	30	C. Attlee
13 May	31	Ld Ponsonby
25 Aug	31	M of Lothian
10 Nov	31	(Sir) J. Davidson
28 May	37	Earl Winterton
29 Jan	39	W. Morrison
3 Apr	40	G. Tryon
14 May	40	Ld Hankey
20 Jul	41	A. Duff Cooper
11 Nov	43	E. Brown
25 May	45	Sir A. Salter
4 Aug	45	J. Hynd
27 Apr	47	Ld Pakenham
11 May	48	H. Dalton
28 Feb	50	Vt Alexander
31 Oct	51	Vt Swinton
24 Nov	52	Ld Woolton
20 Dec	55	E of Selkirk
13 Jan	57	C. Hill
9 Oct	61	I. Macleod
20 Oct	63	Ld Blakenham
18 Oct	64	D. Houghton
6 Apr	66	G. Thomson
7 Jan	67	F. Lee
6 Oct	69	G. Thomson
20 Jun	70	A. Barber
28 Jul	70	G. Rippon
5 Nov	72	J. Davies
5 Mar	74	H. Lever
5 May	79	N. St John-Stevas
5 Jan	81	F. Pym
15 Sep	**81**	**Lady Young**
6 Apr	**82**	**C. Parkinson**
11 Jun	83	Ld Cockfield
11 Sep	84	E of Gowrie

President of the Local Government Board

1900		H. Chaplin
7 Nov	00	W. Long
12 Mar	05	G. Balfour
10 Dec	05	J. Burns
11 Feb	14	H. Samuel
25 May	15	W. Long
10 Dec	16	Ld Rhondda
28 Jun	17	W. Hayes Fisher
4 Nov	18	Sir A. Geddes
10 Jan	19	C. Addison

(24 *Jun* 19 *the Local Government Board became the Ministry of Health)*

(Minister of Health)

24 Jun	19	C. Addison
1 Apr	21	Sir A. Mond
24 Oct	22	Sir A. Griffith-Boscawen
7 Mar	23	N. Chamberlain
27 Aug	23	Sir W. Joynson-Hicks
22 Jan	24	J. Wheatley
6 Nov	24	N. Chamberlain
7 Jun	29	A. Greenwood
25 Aug	31	N. Chamberlain
5 Nov	31	Sir E. Young
7 Jun	35	Sir K. Wood
16 May	38	W. Elliot
13 May	40	M. MacDonald
8 Feb	41	E. Brown
11 Nov	43	H. Willink
3 Aug	45	A. Bevan
17 Jan	51	H. Marquand
30 Oct	51	H. Crookshank
7 May	52	I. Macleod
20 Dec	55	R. Turton
16 Jan	57	D. Vosper
17 Sep	57	D. Walker-Smith
27 Jul	60	E. Powell
20 Oct	63	A. Barber
18 Oct	64	K. Robinson

(1 *Nov* 68 *combined with Ministry of Social Security. See Social Services)*

Minister of Land and Natural Resources

17 Oct 64 F. Willey
(17 *Feb* 67 *office wound up)*

(Minister for Planning and Land)

1 Nov 68 K. Robinson
(6 *Oct* 69 *office wound up)*

Minister of Local Government and Planning

31 Jan 51 H. Dalton

(Minister of Housing and Local Government)

30 Oct 51 H. Macmillan
18 Oct 54 D. Sandys
13 Jan 57 H. Brooke
9 Oct 61 C. Hill
13 Jul 62 Sir K. Joseph
18 Oct 64 R. Crossman
11 Aug 66 A. Greenwood
31 May 70 R. Mellish
20 Jun 70 P. Walker
(15 *Oct* 70 *reorganised as Local Government and Development under Dept. of Environment)*

Minister for Local Government and Development

15 Oct 70 G. Page

Minister for Local Government and Environmental Services

6 May 79 T. King
6 Jan 83 Ld Bellwin
11 Sep 84 K. Baker

(Minister for Planning and Local Government)

7 Mar 74 J. Silkin
(*office abolished* 10 *Sep* 76)

Minister for Housing and Construction

15 Oct 70 J. Amery
5 Nov 72 P. Channon
7 Mar 74 R. Freeson
7 May 79 J. Stanley
13 Jun 83 I. Gow

Minister of Materials

6 Jul 51 R. Stokes
31 Oct 51 Vt Swinton
24 Nov 52 Sir A. Salter
1 Sep 53 Ld Woolton
(16 *Aug* 54 *office wound up*)

Minister of Munitions

25 May 15 D. Lloyd George
9 Jul 16 E. Montagu
10 Dec 16 C. Addison
17 Jul 17 W. Churchill
10 Jan 19 Ld Inverforth
(*and Minister designate for Ministry of Supply. Office abolished* 21 *Mar* 21)

Minister of National Service

19 Aug 16 N. Chamberlain
17 Aug 17 Sir A. Geddes
(*office abolished Aug* 19)

Secretary of State for Northern Ireland

24 Apr 72 W. Whitelaw
2 Dec 73 F. Pym
5 Mar 74 M. Rees
10 Sep 76 R. Mason
5 May 79 H. Atkins
14 Sep 81 J. Prior
11 Sep 84 D. Hurd

Minister of (for) Overseas Development[1]

18 Oct 64 Mrs B. Castle
23 Dec 65 A. Greenwood
11 Aug 66 A. Bottomley
29 Aug 67 R. Prentice
6 Oct 69 Mrs J. Hart
23 Jun 70 R. Wood
7 Mar 74 Mrs J. Hart
10 Jun 75 R. Prentice
21 Dec 76 F. Judd
21 Feb 77 Mrs J. Hart
6 May 79 N. Marten
6 Jan 83 T. Raison

[1]*From* 10 *Jun* 75 *the Foreign Secretary became technically Minister of Overseas Development while the Minister for Overseas Development took day-to-day charge of the Department, which ceased to be a separate Department 5 May 79.*

Paymaster-General

1900 D of Marlborough
11 Mar 02 Sir S. Crossley
12 Dec 05 R. Causton (Ld Southwark)
23 Feb 10 I. Guest (Ld Ashby St Ledgers)
23 May 12 Ld Strachie
9 Jun 15 Ld Newton
18 Aug 16 A. Henderson
15 Dec 16 Sir J. Compton-Rickett
26 Oct 19 Sir T. Walters
24 Oct 22 (*office vacant)*
5 Feb 23 N. Chamberlain
15 Mar 23 Sir W. Joynson-Hicks
25 May 23 A. Boyd-Carpenter
22 Jan 24 (*office vacant)*
6 May 24 H. Gosling
6 Nov 24 (*office vacant)*
28 Jul 25 D of Sutherland
2 Dec 28 E of Onslow
7 Jun 29 Ld Arnold
6 Mar 31 (*office vacant)*
4 Sep 31 Sir T. Walters
23 Nov 31 Ld Rochester
6 Dec 35 Ld Hutchison
2 Jun 38 E of Munster
29 Jan 39 Earl Winterton
Nov 39 (*office vacant)*
15 May 40 Vt Cranborne
3 Oct 40 (*office vacant)*
20 Jul 41 Ld Hankey
4 Mar 42 Sir W. Jowitt
30 Dec 42 Ld Cherwell
3 Aug 45 (*office vacant)*
9 Jul 46 A. Greenwood
5 Mar 47 H. Marquand
2 Jul 48 Vt Addison
1 Apr 49 Ld Macdonald
30 Oct 51 Ld Cherwell
11 Nov 53 E of Selkirk
20 Dec 55 (*office vacant)*
18 Oct 56 Sir W. Monckton
16 Jan 57 R. Maudling
14 Oct 59 Ld Mills
9 Oct 61 H. Brooke
13 Jul 62 J. Boyd-Carpenter
19 Oct 64 G. Wigg
12 Nov 67 (*office vacant)*
6 Apr 68 Ld Shackleton
1 Nov 68 Mrs J. Hart
6 Oct 69 H. Lever
23 Jun 70 Vt Eccles
2 Dec 73 M. Macmillan
7 Mar 74 E. Dell
8 Apr 76 Mrs S. Williams
5 May 79 A. Maude
5 Jan 81 F. Pym
14 Sep 81 C. Parkinson
11 Jun 83 (*office vacant*)
11 Sep 84 J. S. Gummer

Minister of Pensions

10 Dec 16 G. Barnes
17 Aug 17 J. Hodge
10 Jan 19 Sir L. Worthington-Evans
2 Apr 20 I. Macpherson
31 Oct 22 G. Tryon
23 Jan 24 F. Roberts
11 Nov 24 G. Tryon
7 Jun 29 F. Roberts
3 Sep 31 G. Tryon
18 Jun 35 R. Hudson
30 Jul 36 H. Ramsbotham
7 Jun 39 Sir W. Womersley
3 Aug 45 W. Paling

17 Apr	47	J. Hynd
7 Oct	47	G. Buchanan
2 Jul	48	H. Marquand
17 Jan	51	G. Isaacs
5 Nov	51	D. Heathcoat Amory

(Minister of Pensions and National Insurance)

3 Sep	53	O. Peake
20 Dec	55	J. Boyd-Carpenter
16 Jul	62	N. Macpherson
21 Oct	63	R. Wood
18 Oct	64	Miss M. Herbison

(6 *Aug* 66 *recast as Social Security)*

Minister of Social Insurance

8 Oct	44	Sir W. Jowitt

(Minister of National Insurance)

17 Nov	44	Sir W. Jowitt
25 May	45	L. Hore-Belisha
4 Aug	45	J. Griffiths
28 Feb	50	Edith Summerskill
31 Oct	51	O. Peake

(3 *Sep* 53 *combined with Ministry of Pensions)*

Minister without Portfolio

25 May 15-5 Dec 16
M of Lansdowne
10 Dec 16-12 Aug 17
A. Henderson
10 Dec 16-18 Apr 18
Vt Milner
22 Jun 17-10 Jan 19
J. Smuts
17 Jul 17-21 Jan 18
Sir E. Carson
13 Aug 17-27 Jan 20
G. Barnes
18 Apr 18-10 Jan 19
A. Chamberlain
10 Jan 19-19 May 19
Sir E. Geddes
2 Apr 20-13 Feb 21
Sir L. Worthington-Evans
1 Apr 21-14 Jul 21
C. Addison
7 Jun 35-22 Dec 35
A. Eden
7 Jun 35-31 Mar 36
Ld E. Percy
21 Apr 39-14 Jul 39
L. Burgin
3 Sep 39-10 May 40
Ld Hankey
11 May 40-22 Feb 42
A. Greenwood
30 Dec 42-8 Oct 44
Sir W. Jowitt
4 Oct 46-20 Dec 46
A. Alexander
17 Apr 47-29 Sep 47
A. Greenwood
18 Oct 54-11 Jun 57
E of Munster
11 Jun 57-23 Oct 58
Ld Mancroft
23 Oct 58-9 Oct 61
E of Dundee
9 Oct 61-14 Jul 62
Ld Mills
13 Jul 62-16 Oct 64
W. Deedes
20 Oct 63-16 Oct 64
Ld Carrington
19 Oct 64-6 Apr 66
E. Fletcher
21 Oct 64-7 Jan 67
Ld Champion
6 Apr 66-7 Jan 67
D. Houghton
7 Jan 67-29 Aug 67
P. Gordon Walker
7 Jan 67-16 Jan 68
Ld Shackleton
17 Oct 68-6 Oct 69
G. Thomson
6 Oct 69-19 Jun 70
P. Shore
15 Oct 70-8 Jan 74
Ld Drumalbyn
8 Jan 74-4 Mar 74
Ld Aberdare
11 Sep 84-
Ld Young of Graffham

Secretary of State for Prices and Consumer Protection

5 Mar	74	Mrs S. Williams
10 Sep	76	R. Hattersley

(Minister for Consumer Affairs)

6 May	**79**	**Mrs S. Oppenheim**
5 Mar	**82**	**G. Vaughan**

(13 *Jun* 83 *office wound up*)

Postmaster-General

1900		D of Norfolk
2 Apr	00	M of Londonderry
8 Aug	02	A. Chamberlain
6 Oct	03	Ld Stanley
10 Dec	05	S. Buxton
14 Feb	10	H. Samuel
11 Feb	14	C. Hobhouse
26 May	15	H. Samuel
18 Jan	16	J. Pease
10 Dec	16	A. Illingworth
1 Apr	21	F. Kellaway
31 Oct	22	N. Chamberlain
7 Mar	23	Sir W. Joynson-Hicks
28 May	23	Sir L. Worthington-Evans
22 Jan	24	V. Hartshorn
11 Nov	24	Sir W. Mitchell-Thomson
7 Jun	29	H. Lees-Smith
2 Mar	31	C. Attlee
3 Sep	31	W. Ormsby-Gore
10 Nov	31	Sir K. Wood
7 Jun	35	G. Tryon
3 Apr	40	W. Morrison
30 Dec	42	H. Crookshank
4 Aug	45	E of Listowel
17 Apr	47	W. Paling
28 Feb	50	N. Edwards
5 Nov	51	Earl De La Warr
7 Apr	55	C. Hill
16 Jan	57	E. Marples
22 Oct	59	R. Bevins
19 Oct	64	A. Wedgwood Benn
4 Jul	66	E. Short
6 Apr	68	R. Mason
1 Jul	68	J. Stonehouse

(*Post Office became a Public Corporation* 1 *Oct* 69)

(Minister of Posts and Telecommunications)

1 Oct	69	J. Stonehouse
24 Jun	70	C. Chataway
7 Apr	72	Sir J. Eden
9 Mar	74	A. Wedgwood Benn

(29 *Mar* 74 *office wound up)*

Minister of Public Building and Works

16 Jul	62	G. Rippon
18 Oct	64	C. Pannell
6 Apr	66	R. Prentice
29 Aug	67	R. Mellish
30 Apr	69	J. Silkin
23 Jun	70	J. Amery

(15 *Oct* 70 *reorganised as Housing and Construction under Dept. of Environment. See Local Government)*

Minister Resident in Middle East

19 Feb	42	O. Lyttelton
19 Mar	42	R. Casey

(Minister of State in Middle East)

28 Jan	44	Ld Moyne
21 Nov	44	Sir E. Grigg

(*office abolished* 27 *Jul* 45)

Minister Resident at Allied H.Q. in N.W. Africa

30 Dec 42 H. Macmillan
(*office abolished* 23 *May* 45)

Minister Resident in W. Africa

8 Jun 42 Vt Swinton
21 Nov 44 H. Balfour
(*office abolished* 27 *Jul* 45)

Minister Resident in Washington for Supply

22 Nov 42 J. Llewellin
11 Nov 43 B. Smith
(*office abolished* 23 *May* 45)

Minister of Reconstruction

17 Jul 17-10 Jan 19
C. Addison
10 Jan 19-Aug 19
Sir A. Geddes
11 Nov 43-23 May 45
Ld Woolton

Minister for Science

14 Oct 59 Vt Hailsham
(1 *Apr* 64 *combined with Dept. of Education)*

Secretary for Scotland

1900 Ld Balfour
6 Oct 03 A. Murray
2 Feb 05 M of Linlithgow
10 Dec 05 J. Sinclair (Ld Pentland)
13 Feb 12 T. McKinnon Wood
9 Jul 16 H. Tennant
10 Dec 16 R. Munro
24 Oct 22 Vt Novar
22 Jan 24 W. Adamson
6 Nov 24 Sir J. Gilmour

(Secretary of State for Scotland)

15 Jul 26 Sir J. Gilmour
7 Jun 29 W. Adamson
25 Aug 31 Sir A. Sinclair
28 Sep 32 Sir G. Collins
29 Oct 36 W. Elliot
16 May 38 J. Colville
14 May 40 E. Brown
8 Feb 41 T. Johnston
25 May 45 E of Rosebery
3 Aug 45 J. Westwood
7 Oct 47 A. Woodburn
28 Feb 50 H. McNeil
30 Oct 51 J. Stuart
13 Jan 57 J. Maclay
13 Jul 62 M. Noble
18 Oct 64 W. Ross
19 Jun 70 G. Campbell
5 Mar 74 W. Ross
8 Apr 76 B. Millan
5 May 79 G. Younger

Lord Advocate

1900 A. Murray
18 Oct 03 S. Dickson
12 Dec 05 T. Shaw
14 Feb 09 A. Ure
30 Oct 13 R. Munro
10 Dec 16 J. Clyde
25 Mar 20 T. Morison
5 Mar 22 C. Murray
24 Oct 22 W. Watson
8 Feb 24 H. Macmillan
11 Nov 24 W. Watson
23 Apr 29 A. MacRobert
17 Jun 29 C. Aitchison
2 Oct 33 W. Normand
28 Mar 35 D. Jamieson
25 Oct 35 T. Cooper
5 Jun 41 J. Reid
10 Aug 45 G. Thomson
7 Oct 47 J. Wheatley
2 Nov 51 J. Clyde
30 Dec 54 W. Milligan
5 Apr 60 W. Grant
12 Oct 62 I. Shearer
20 Oct 64 G. Stott
26 Oct 67 H. S. Wilson (Ld)
23 Jun 70 N. Wylie
8 Mar 74 R. King Murray
7 May 79 J. Mackay (Ld)
16 May 84 Lt Cameron of Lochbroom

Solicitor-General for Scotland

1900 S. Dickson
18 Oct 03 D. Dundas
30 Jan 05 E. Salvesen
16 Oct 05 J. Clyde
18 Dec 05 A. Ure
18 Feb 08 A. Dewar
18 Apr 10 W. Hunter
3 Dec 11 A. Anderson
30 Oct 13 T. Morison
25 Mar 20 C. Murray
16 Mar 22 A. Briggs Constable
24 Jul 22 W. Watson
6 Nov 22 D. Fleming
5 Apr 23 F. Thomson
18 Feb 24 J. Fenton
11 Nov 24 D. Fleming
30 Dec 25 A. MacRobert
23 Apr 29 W. Normand
17 Jun 29 J. Watson
10 Nov 31 W. Normand
2 Oct 33 D. Jamieson
15 May 35 T. Cooper
29 Nov 35 A. Russell
25 Jun 36 J. Reid
5 Jun 41 (Sir) D. Murray
10 Sep 45 D. Blades
19 Mar 47 J. Wheatley
24 Oct 47 D. Johnston
3 Nov 51 W. Milligan
10 Jan 55 W. Grant
11 May 60 D. Anderson
27 Apr 64 N. Wylie
20 Oct 64 J. Leechman
11 Oct 65 H. S. Wilson
26 Oct 67 E. Stewart
23 Jun 70 D. Brand
5 Nov 72 I. Stewart
14 Mar 74 J. McCluskey (Ld)
7 May 79 N. Fairbairn
28 Jan 82 P. Fraser

Minister of Shipping

10 Dec 16 Sir J. Maclay (Ld)
(*office abolished* 31 *Mar* 21)
13 Oct 39 Sir J. Gilmour
3 Apr 40 R. Hudson
14 May 40 R. Cross
(1 *May* 41 *combined with Ministry of Transport to form Ministry of War Transport)*

Minister of Social Security

6 Aug 66 Miss M. Herbison
26 Jul 67 Mrs J. Hart

(Secretary of State for Social Services)

17 Oct 68 R. Crossman
20 Jun 70 Sir K. Joseph
5 Mar 74 Mrs B. Castle
8 Apr 76 D. Ennals
5 May 79 P. Jenkin
14 Sep 81 N. Fowler

Minister for Social Security

10 Sep 76 S. Orme
7 May 79 R. Prentice
8 Jan 81 H. Rossi
13 Jun 83 R. Boyson
11 Sep 84 A. Newton

Solicitor-General

1900 Sir R. Finlay
7 May 00 Sir E. Carson
12 Dec 05 Sir W. Robson
28 Jan 08 Sir S. Evans
6 Mar 10 Sir R. Isaacs
7 Oct 10 Sir J. Simon
19 Oct 13 Sir S. Buckmaster
2 Jun 15 Sir F. Smith
18 Jan 16 Sir G. Cave
10 Dec 16 Sir G. Hewart
10 Jan 19 Sir E. Pollock
6 Mar 22 Sir L. Scott
31 Oct 22 Sir T. Inskip
23 Jan 24 Sir H. Slesser
11 Nov 24 Sir T. Inskip
28 Mar 28 Sir F. Merriman
7 Jun 29 Sir J. Melville
22 Oct 30 Sir S. Cripps

3 Sep	31	Sir T. Inskip
26 Jan	32	Sir F. Merriman
29 Sep	33	Sir D. Somervell
19 Mar	36	Sir T. O'Connor
15 May	40	Sir W. Jowitt
4 Mar	42	Sir D. Maxwell-Fyfe
25 May	45	Sir W. Monckton
4 Aug	45	Sir F. Soskice
24 Apr	51	Sir L. Ungoed-Thomas
3 Nov	51	Sir R. Manning-ham-Buller
18 Oct	54	Sir H. Hylton-Foster
22 Oct	59	Sir J. Simon
8 Feb	62	Sir J. Hobson
19 Jul	62	Sir P. Rawlinson
18 Oct	64	Sir D. Foot
24 Aug	67	Sir A. Irvine
23 Jun	70	Sir G. Howe
5 Nov	72	Sir M. Havers
7 Mar	74	P. Archer
5 May	79	Sir I. Percival
13 Jun	83	**Sir P. Mayhew**

Minister of State

1 May	41	Ld Beaverbrook
29 Jun	41	O. Lyttelton

(*office abolished* 12 *Mar* 42)

24 Sep	43	R. Law
25 May	45	W. Mabane
3 Aug	45	P. Noel Baker
4 Oct	46	H. McNeil
28 Feb	50	K. Younger

(*office came formally under Foreign Office May* 50)

First Secretary of State

13 Jul	62	R. Butler
18 Oct	63	(*office vacant*)
16 Oct	64	G. Brown
11 Aug	66	M. Stewart
6 Apr	68	Mrs B. Castle
19 Jun	70	(*office vacant*)

Minister of Supply

14 Jul	39	L. Burgin
12 May	40	H. Morrison
3 Oct	40	Sir A. Duncan
29 Jun	41	Ld Beaverbrook
4 Feb	42	Sir A. Duncan
3 Aug	45	J. Wilmot
7 Oct	47	G. Strauss
31 Oct	51	D. Sandys
18 Oct	54	S. Lloyd
7 Apr	55	R. Maudling
16 Jan	57	A. Jones

(*office wound up* 22 *Oct* 59)

Secretary for Technical Cooperation

27 Jun	61	D. Vosper
9 May	63	R. Carr

(*office abolished* 16 *Oct* 64)

Ministry of Technology

18 Oct	64	F. Cousins
4 Jul	66	A. Benn
20 Jun	70	G. Rippon
28 Jul	70	J. Davies

(15 *Oct* 70 *office reorganised under Trade and Industry*)

Minister of Town and Country Planning

30 Dec	42	W. Morrison
4 Aug	45	L. Silkin
28 Feb	50	H. Dalton

(*recast as Local Government and Planning* 31 *Jan* 51)

President of the Board of Trade

1900		C. Ritchie
7 Nov	00	G. Balfour
12 Mar	05	M of Salisbury
10 Dec	05	D. Lloyd George
12 Apr	08	W. Churchill
14 Feb	10	S. Buxton
11 Feb	14	J. Burns
5 Aug	14	W. Runciman
10 Dec	16	Sir A. Stanley
26 May	19	Sir A. Geddes
19 Mar	20	Sir R. Horne
1 Apr	21	S. Baldwin
24 Oct	22	Sir P. Lloyd-Greame
22 Jan	24	S. Webb
6 Nov	24	Sir P. Lloyd-Greame (changed name to Cunliffe-Lister 27 Nov 24)
7 Jun	29	W. Graham
25 Aug	31	Sir P. Cunliffe-Lister
5 Nov	31	W. Runciman
28 May	37	O. Stanley
5 Jan	40	Sir A. Duncan
3 Oct	40	O. Lyttelton
29 Jun	41	Sir A. Duncan
4 Feb	42	J. Llewellin
22 Feb	42	H. Dalton
25 May	45	O. Lyttelton
27 Jul	45	Sir S. Cripps
29 Sep	47	H. Wilson
24 Apr	51	Sir H. Shawcross
30 Oct	51	P. Thorneycroft
13 Jan	57	Sir D. Eccles
14 Oct	59	R. Maudling
9 Oct	61	F. Erroll
20 Oct	63	E. Heath[1]
18 Oct	64	D. Jay
29 Aug	67	A. Crosland
6 Oct	69	R. Mason
20 Jun	70	M. Noble

(Secretary of State for Trade and Industry)

15 Oct	70	J. Davies
5 Nov	72	P. Walker

(Secretary of State for Trade)
(*see also Industry*)

5 Mar	74	P. Shore
8 Apr	76	E. Dell
12 Nov	78	J. Smith
5 May	79	J. Nott
14 Sep	81	J. Biffen
5 Apr	82	Ld Cockfield

(Secretary of State for Trade and Industry)

11 Jun	**83**	**C. Parkinson**
16 Oct	**83**	**N. Tebbit**

Minister for Trade

15 Oct	70	M. Noble

(Minister for Trade and Consumer Affairs)

5 Nov	72	Sir G. Howe

(*office abolished* 5 *Mar* 74)

Minister of Transport

19 May	19	Sir E. Geddes
7 Nov	21	Vt Peel
12 Apr	22	E of Crawford
31 Oct	22	Sir J. Baird
24 Jan	24	H. Gosling
11 Nov	24	W. Ashley
7 Jun	29	H. Morrison
3 Sep	31	J. Pybus
22 Feb	33	O. Stanley
29 Jun	34	L. Hore-Belisha
28 May	37	L. Burgin
21 Apr	39	E. Wallace
14 May	40	Sir J. Reith
3 Oct	40	J. Moore-Brabazon

(Minister of War Transport)

1 May	41	Ld Leathers
3 Aug	45	A. Barnes

(Minister of Transport)

6 Mar	46	A. Barnes
31 Oct	51	J. Maclay
7 May	52	A. Lennox-Boyd

(Minister of Transport and Civil Aviation)

1 Oct	53	A. Lennox-Boyd
28 Jul	54	J. Boyd-Carpenter
20 Dec	55	H. Watkinson

(Minister of Transport)

14 Oct	59	E. Marples
18 Oct	64	T. Fraser
23 Dec	65	Mrs B. Castle
6 Apr	68	R. Marsh
6 Oct	69	F. Mulley
23 Jun	70	J. Peyton

[1] Also Secretary of State for Industry, Trade and Regional Development.

(Minister for Transport Industries)

15 Oct	70	J. Peyton

(Minister for Transport)

7 Mar	74	F. Mulley
12 Jun	75	J. Gilbert

(Secretary of State for Transport)

10 Sep	76	W. Rodgers

(Minister of Transport)

5 May	79	N. Fowler

(Secretary of State for Transport)

5 Jan	**81**	**N. Fowler**
14 Sep	**81**	**D. Howell**
11 Jun	**83**	**T. King**
16 Oct	**83**	**N. Ridley**

Treasury

(*see p.* 71)

Secretary of State for War

1900		M of Lansdowne
1 Nov	00	St J. Brodrick
6 Oct	03	H. Arnold-Forster
10 Dec	05	R. Haldane (Vt)
12 Jun	12	J. Seely
30 Mar	14	H. Asquith
5 Aug	14	Earl Kitchener
6 Jul	16	D. Lloyd George
10 Dec	16	E of Derby
18 Apr	18	Vt Milner
10 Jan	19	W. Churchill
13 Feb	21	Sir L. Worthington-Evans
24 Oct	22	E of Derby
22 Jan	24	S. Walsh
6 Nov	24	Sir L. Worthington-Evans
7 Jun	29	T. Shaw
26 Aug	31	M of Crewe
5 Nov	31	Vt Hailsham
7 Jun	35	Vt Halifax
22 Nov	35	A. Duff Cooper
28 May	37	L. Hore-Belisha
5 Jan	40	O. Stanley
11 May	40	A. Eden
22 Dec	40	D. Margesson
22 Feb	42	Sir J. Grigg
3 Aug	45	J. Lawson
4 Oct	46	F. Bellenger
7 Oct	47	E. Shinwell
28 Feb	50	J. Strachey
31 Oct	51	A. Head
18 Oct	56	J. Hare
6 Jan	58	C. Soames
27 Jul	60	J. Profumo
27 Jun	63	J. Godber
21 Oct	63	J. Ramsden

(*office abolished* 1 *Apr* 64)

Minister for Welsh Affairs

28 Oct	51	Sir D. Maxwell Fyfe
18 Oct	54	G. Lloyd-George
13 Jan	57	H. Brooke
9 Oct	61	C. Hill
13 Jul	62	Sir K. Joseph

(Secretary of State for Wales)

18 Oct	64	J. Griffiths
6 Apr	66	C. Hughes
6 Apr	68	G. Thomas
20 Jun	70	P. Thomas
5 Mar	74	J. Morris
5 May	79	N. Edwards

First Commissioner of Works

1900		A. Akers-Douglas
8 Aug	02	Ld Windsor
10 Dec	05	L. Harcourt
3 Nov	10	Earl Beauchamp
6 Aug	14	Ld Emmott
25 May	15	L. Harcourt (Vt)
10 Dec	16	Sir A. Mond
1 Apr	21	E of Crawford
31 Oct	22	Sir J. Baird
22 Jan	24	F. Jowett
10 Nov	24	Vt Peel
18 Oct	28	M of Londonderry
7 Jun	29	G. Lansbury
25 Aug	31	M of Londonderry
5 Nov	31	W. Ormsby-Gore
16 Jun	36	Earl Stanhope
28 May	37	Sir P. Sassoon
7 Jun	39	H. Ramsbotham
3 Apr	40	Earl De La Warr
18 May	40	Ld Tryon
3 Oct	40	Sir J. Reith (Ld)

(Minister of Works & Buildings and First Commissioner of Works)

23 Oct	40	Ld Reith

(Minister of Works and Planning)

11 Feb	42	Ld Reith
21 Feb	42	Ld Portal

(Minister of Works)

Feb	43	Ld Portal
21 Nov	44	D. Sandys
4 Aug	45	G. Tomlinson
10 Feb	47	C. Key
28 Feb	50	R. Stokes
26 Apr	51	G. Brown
18 Nov	51	(Sir) D. Eccles
1 Oct	54	N. Birch
20 Dec	55	P. Buchan-Hepburn
16 Jan	57	H. Molson
22 Oct	59	Ld J. Hope

(16 *Jul* 62 *recast as Public Building and Works*)

Leaders of the House of Commons

1900		A. Balfour
5 Dec	05	Sir H. Campbell-Bannerman
5 Apr	08	H. Asquith
10 Dec	16	A. Bonar Law
23 Mar	21	A. Chamberlain
23 Oct	22	A. Bonar Law
22 May	23	S. Baldwin
22 Jan	24	J. R. MacDonald
4 Nov	24	S. Baldwin
5 Jun	29	J. R. MacDonald
7 Jun	35	S. Baldwin
28 May	37	N. Chamberlain
11 May	40	C. Attlee[1]
19 Feb	42	Sir S. Cripps
22 Nov	42	A. Eden
27 Jul	45	H. Morrison
9 Mar	51	C. Ede
30 Oct	51	H. Crookshank
7 Apr	55	R. Butler
9 Oct	61	I. Macleod
20 Oct	63	S. Lloyd
16 Oct	64	H. Bowden
11 Aug	66	R. Crossman
6 Apr	68	F. Peart
20 Jun	70	W. Whitelaw
7 Apr	72	R. Carr
5 Nov	72	J. Prior
5 Mar	74	E. Short
8 Apr	76	M. Foot
5 May	79	N. St John-Stevas
5 Jan	**81**	**F. Pym**
5 Apr	**82**	**J. Biffen**

[1]*Although Mr Attlee fulfilled the role of Leader of the House of Commons during this period he was technically only Deputy Leader to Mr Churchill*

Leaders of the House of Lords

1900		3rd M of Salisbury
12 Jul	02	D of Devonshire
13 Oct	03	M of Lansdowne
10 Dec	05	M of Ripon
14 Apr	08	E of Crewe (M)[2]
10 Dec	16	Earl Curzon (M)
22 Jan	24	Vt Haldane
6 Nov	24	Marquess Curzon
27 Apr	25	4th M of Salisbury
7 Jun	29	Ld Parmoor
25 Aug	31	M of Reading
5 Nov	31	1st Vt Hailsham
7 Jun	35	M of Londonderry
22 Nov	35	Vt Halifax
27 Oct	38	Earl Stanhope
14 May	40	Vt Caldecote
3 Oct	40	Vt Halifax
22 Dec	40	Ld Lloyd
8 Feb	41	Ld Moyne
21 Feb	42	Vt Cranborne (5th M of Salisbury)
3 Aug	45	Vt Addison
28 Oct	51	5th M of Salisbury
29 Mar	57	E of Home
27 Jul	60	2nd Vt Hailsham
20 Oct	63	Ld Carrington
18 Oct	64	E of Longford
16 Jan	68	Ld Shackleton
20 Jun	70	Earl Jellicoe
5 Jun	73	Ld Windlesham
7 Mar	74	Ld Shepherd
10 Sep	76	Ld Peart
5 May	79	Ld Soames
14 Sep	**81**	**Lady Young**
11 Jun	**83**	**Vt Whitelaw**

[2]*During the summer of 1911 Vt Morley was temporarily Leader of the House of Lords*

Government Chief Whip

(Parliamentary Secretary to the Treasury)

1900		Sir W. Walrond
8 Aug	02	Sir A. Acland Hood
12 Dec	05	G. Whiteley
3 Jun	08	J. Pease
14 Feb	10	Master of Elibank
7 Aug	12	P. Illingworth
24 Jan	15	J. Gulland
30 May	15	{ J. Gulland
–5 Dec	16	Ld E. Talbot
14 Dec	16	{ Ld E. Talbot
–2 Mar	17	N. Primrose
2 Mar	17	{ Ld E. Talbot
–1 Apr	21	F. Guest
1 Apr	21	{ C. McCurdy
–19 Oct	22	L. Wilson
31 Oct	22	L. Wilson
25 Jul	23	B. Eyres-Monsell
23 Jan	24	B. Spoor
7 Nov	24	B. Eyres-Monsell
14 Jun	29	T. Kennedy
3 Sep	31	Sir B. Eyres-Monsell
10 Nov	31	D. Margesson
17 May	40	{ D. Margesson
–14 Jan	41	Sir C. Edwards
14 Jan	41	{ Sir C. Edwards
–12 Mar	42	J. Stuart
12 Mar	42	{ J. Stuart
–23 May	45	W. Whiteley
26 May	45	J. Stuart
3 Aug	45	W. Whiteley
30 Oct	51	P. Buchan-Hepburn
30 Dec	55	E. Heath
14 Oct	59	M. Redmayne
18 Oct	64	E. Short
4 Jul	66	J. Silkin
30 Apr	69	R. Mellish
20 Jun	70	F. Pym
2 Dec	73	H. Atkins
5 Mar	74	R. Mellish
8 Apr	76	M. Cocks
5 May	79	M. Jopling
11 Jun	**83**	**J. Wakeham**

Government Chief Whip in the House of Lords

(usually Captain of the Gentlemen at Arms—see footnotes for exceptions)

	1900	Earl Waldegrave[1]
18 Dec	05	Ld Ribblesdale[2]
29 May	07	Ld Denman[3]
15 Mar	11	Ld Colebrooke[4]
9 Jun	15	{ Ld Colebrooke[4] D of Devonshire[5]
26 Jul	16	{ Ld Colebrooke[4] Ld Hylton[6]
20 Nov	22	E of Clarendon
22 Jan	24	Ld Muir-Mackenzie[7]
1 Dec	24	E of Clarendon
26 Jun	25	E of Plymouth
1 Jan	29	E of Lucan
18 Jul	29	Earl de le Warr[7]
17 Jan	30	Ld Marley[7]
12 Nov	31	E of Lucan
31 May	40	Ld Templemore[1]
4 Aug	45	Ld Ammon
18 Oct	49	1st Ld Shepherd
5 Nov	51	Earl Fortescue
27 Jun	58	Earl St Aldwyn
21 Oct	64	2nd Ld Shepherd
29 Jul	67	Ld Beswick
24 Jun	70	Earl St Aldwyn
11 Mar	74	Lady Llewelyn-Davies
6 May	79	Ld Denham

[1]Captain of the Yeomen of the Guard.
[2]Without office.
[3]Lord in Waiting 1907; Captain of Gentlemen at Arms 1907-11.
[4]Lord in Waiting 1911; Captain of Gentlemen at Arms 1911-22.
[5]Civil Lord of the Admiralty.
[6]Lord in Waiting 1916-18; Captain of Yeomen of Guard 1918-22.
[7]Lord in Waiting.

Size of Cabinets and Governments

	1900	1910	1917	1920	1930	1940	1950	1960	:970	1980	198
Cabinet Ministers	19	19	5	19	19	9	18	19	21	22	22
Non-Cabinet Ministers	10	7	33	15	9	25	20	20	33	38	32
Junior Ministers[a]	31	36	47	47	30	40	43	43	48	47	49
Number of M.P.s in paid Government Posts	33	43	60	58	50	58	68	65	85	86	8[illegible]
Number of Peers in paid Government Posts	27	19	25	23	8	16	13	17	17	21	2[illegible]
Total paid Government Posts	60	62	85	81	58	74	81	82	102	107	10[illegible]
Parliamentary Private Secretaries in Commons	9	16	12	13	26	25	27	36	30	28	2[illegible]
Total number of M.P.s involved in Government	42	59	72	71	76	83	95	101	115	114	10[illegible]

[a] Including the political appointments of the Royal Household. In 1901 the Master of the Buckhounds ceased to be a political appointment. Since 1905 the Paymaster-General has been a non-Cabinet or Cabinet Ministerial post. Since 1924 the offices of Lord Chamberlain, Lord Steward, and Master of the House have been non-political. In 1930 the Captain Gentleman at Arms and Captain of the Yeomen of the Guard were non-political appointments. There have always been some non-political Lords in Waiting.

SOURCES.—Members of the Government from *Hansard*, the first volume of each year. P.P.S.s from *Whitaker's Almanack* (the figures for 1900-40 are only approximate), and from *H.M. Ministers and Heads of Public Departments, 1946-* (H.M.S.O.).

Social and Educational Composition of British Cabinets 1895-[1]

Date	Party	P.M.	Cabinet Size	Aristocrats	Middle Class	Working Class	Public school: All	Public school: Eton	University educated: All	University educated: Oxbridge
Aug 1895	Con.	Salisbury	19	8	11	—	16	7	15	14
Jul 1902	Con.	Balfour	19	9	10	—	16	9	14	13
Dec 1905	Lib.	Campbell-Bannerman	19	7	11	1	11	3	14	12
Jul 1914	Lib.	Asquith	19	6	12	1	11	3	15	13
Jan 1919	Coal.	Lloyd George	21	3	17	1	12	2	13	8
Nov 1922	Con.	Bonar Law	16	8	8	—	14	8	13	13
Jan 1924	Lab.	MacDonald	19	3	5	11	8	—	6	6
Nov 1924	Con.	Baldwin	21	9	12	—	21	7	16	16
Jan 1929	Lab.	MacDonald	18	2	4	12	5	—	6	3
Aug 1931	Nat.	MacDonald	20	8	10	2	13	6	11	10
Jun 1935	Con.	Baldwin	22	9	11	2	14	9	11	10
May 1937	Con.	Chamberlain	21	8	13	—	17	8	16	13
May 1945	Con.	Churchill	16	6	9	1	14	7	11	9
Aug 1945	Lab.	Attlee	20	—	8	12	5	2	10	5
Oct 1951	Con.	Churchill	16	5	11	—	14	7	11	9
Apr 1955	Con.	Eden	18	5	13	—	18	10	16	14
Jan 1957	Con.	Macmillan	18	4	14	—	17	8	16	15
Oct 1963	Con.	Home	24	5	19	—	21	11	17	17
Oct 1964	Lab.	Wilson	23	1	14	8	8	1	13	11
Jun 1970	Con.	Heath	18	4	14	—	15	4	15	15
Mar 1974	Lab.	Wilson	21	1	16	4	7	—	16	11
Apr 1976	Lab.	Callaghan	22	1	13	7	7	—	15	10
May 1979	Con.	Thatcher	22	3	19	—	20	6	18	17
Average 23 Cabinets			19½	5	12	3	13	5	13½	11½
13 Con. Cabinets			19	7	12½	—	17	7½	14	13
6 Lab. Cabinets			20½	1½	9½	9	7	½	11½	7½
2 Lib. Cabinets			19	6	11½	1	11	3	14½	12½

[1] This table is largely based on W. L. Guttsman, *The British Political Elite* (1963). Aristocrats are those who had among their grandparents the holder a hereditary title. Working class are those whose fathers appear to have had a manual occupation when they were growing up. Schools are classified as blic Schools if members of the Headmasters' Conference.

Durability of Prime Ministers 1900-

	Length of Service as P.M. Years	Months	Separate Times in Office	Age on First becoming P.M. (Years)	H. of Commons Service at First Premiership (Years)	Time in H. of Commons after Last Premier-ship (Years)	Years of life after Last Premier ship
M of Salisbury	13	9	3	55	15[1]	0	1
H. Asquith	8	8	1	55	22	6	11
(Sir) W. Churchill	8	8	2	65	38	9	10
H. Wilson	7	9	2	48	19	7	. .
S. Baldwin	6	10	3	56	15	0	11
J. R. MacDonald	6	9	2	58	14	2	2
H. Macmillan	6	9	1	62	29	1	. .
C. Attlee	6	2	1	62	23	4	16
D. Lloyd George	5	10	1	53	26	22	22
E. Heath	3	8	1	53	20	. .	. .
A. Balfour	3	5	1	53	28	17	24
J. Callaghan	3	1	1	64	31	. .	. .
N. Chamberlain	2	11	1	68	19	½	½
Sir H. Campbell-Bannerman	2	4	1	69	37	0	0
Sir A. Eden	1	9	1	57	32	0	20
Sir A . Douglas-Home	1	0	1	60	15[2]	10	. .
A. Bonar Law	0	7	1	63	22	0	0
M. Thatcher (Mrs)	. .	. .	1	53	20	. .	. .

[1] Plus 19 years in House of Lords. [2] Plus 13 years in House of Lords.

Long Tenure of Office

The following served over 20 years in ministerial office:

Years		*Period*	*Years*		*Period*
29	Sir W. Churchill	1905-55	22	Vt Swinton	1920-57
28	E of Balfour	1885-1929	21	M of Salisbury	1866-1902
26	R. Butler	1932-64	21	Sir M. Hicks-Beach	1868-1902
24	D of Devonshire	1863-1903	20	Ld Ashbourne	1877-1905
22	E of Halsbury	1875-1905	20	Sir J. Simon	1910-45
22	W. Long	1886-1921	20	Ld G. Hamilton	1874-1903
22	Sir A. Chamberlain	1895-1931			

Oldest and Youngest Ministers

The oldest M.P. to hold Cabinet office was Sir W. Churchill (80 in 1955); the oldest peers were Vt Halsbury (82 in 1905) and Vt Addison (82 in 1951) and the only other octogenarians were M of Ripon (80 in 1908) and Earl Balfour (80 in 1929). The oldest holder of any ministerial office was Ld Muir-Mackenzie (85 in 1930). The youngest Cabinet minister was H. Wilson (31 in 1947). The youngest M.P. to hold any office was H. Wilson (29 in 1945). R. Butler (1932), E. Rowlands (1969), and Mrs A. Taylor (1977) also held office at 29; the youngest peer was Earl de la Warr (23 in 1924).

Cabinet Members Dying in Office[1]

5 Jun	1916	Earl Kitchener	30 Mar	1940	Sir J. Gilmour
20 Mar	1925	Marquess Curzon	21 Sep	1943	Sir K. Wood[2]
5 Oct	1930	Lord Thomson	6 Feb	1947	Miss E. Wilkinson
13 Mar	1931	V. Hartshorn	14 Apr	1951	E. Bevin
15 Jun	1932	Sir D. Maclean	20 Jul	1970	I. Macleod
13 Oct	1936	Sir G. Collins	19 Feb	1977	A. Crosland

[1] Hugh Gaitskell, the official leader of the Opposition, died on 18 Jan 1963.
[2] Chancellor of Exchequer but not actually in War Cabinet.

Cabinet Members Suffering Electoral Defeat while Holding Office

Apr	1908	W. Churchill[1]	Nov	1935	**R. MacDonald,**[1] M. MacDonald[1]
Feb	1914	C. Masterman[1]	Jul	1945	L. Amery, B. Bracken, Sir J. Grigg, H. Macmillan, Sir D. Somervell
May	1914	C. Masterman[2]	Feb	1950	A. Creech Jones
Mar	1921	Sir A. Griffith-Boscawen[1]	Oct	1964	A. Barber
Nov	1922	Sir A. Griffith-Boscawen[1]	Jan	1965	P. Gordon-Walker[2]
Mar	1923	Sir A. Griffith-Boscawen[2]	Jun	1970	J. Diamond
Dec	1923	Sir A. Montague-Barlow	Feb	1974	G. Campbell
Oct	1924	F. Jowett	May	1979	Mrs S. Williams
May	1929	Sir A. Steel-Maitland			

[1] Sought another seat and continued in office.
[2] By-election defeat followed by resignation.

In Jan 1906 8 members of the Conservative Cabinet that left office in Dec 1905 were defeated, including A. Balfour who had been Prime Minister.

In Dec 1918 10 Asquithian Liberals who had left office in Dec 1916 were defeated including H. Asquith.

In Nov 1922 2 National Liberal members of the Coalition Cabinet that left office in Oct 1922 were defeated.

In Oct 1931 13 members of the Labour Cabinet that left office in Aug 1931 were defeated, including A. Henderson, the Party Leader.

On two occasions the Government Chief Whip was defeated (J. Pease in Jan 1910 and L. Wilson in Nov 1922). On both occasions a new seat was very speedily found.

These Ministers of Cabinet rank were found seats in by-elections: 1916; H. Fisher, Sir A. Stanley; 1917: Sir A. Geddes, Sir E. Geddes; 1924: A. Henderson; 1940: E. Bevin, O. Lyttelton, Sir J. Reith, Sir A. Duncan; 1942: Sir J. Grigg; 1963: Sir A. Douglas-Home, Q. Hogg; 1965: F. Cousins.

(See also p. 245 for defeated Ministers' attempts at re-election.)

Ministerial Resignations

Resignations from ministerial office are not easy to classify. A retirement on the ground of ill-health may always conceal a protest or a dismissal. However, there are some cases where ministers have unquestionably left office because they were not willing to continue to accept collective responsibility for some part of Government policy and some cases where the individual actions of ministers have been thought impolitic or unworthy. The following list does not include resignations made necessary because of private scandals, except when the resignation became the subject of public comment. Nor does it include even the most publicised 'refusals to serve' (e.g. I. Macleod and E. Powell in 1963).

16	Sep	03	J. Chamberlain (*Imperial preference*)
4-15	Sep	03	C. Ritchie, Ld Balfour of Burleigh, Ld G. Hamilton, D of Devonshire, A. Elliot (*Free Trade*)

6	Mar	05	G. Wyndham (*Ireland*)
30	Mar	14	J. Seely (*Curragh Mutiny*)
2	Aug	14	Vt Morley, J. Burns (*Entry into war*)
5	Aug	14	C. Trevelyan (*Entry into war*)
19	Oct	15	Sir E. Carson (*Conduct of War in the Balkans*)
31	Dec	15	Sir J. Simon (*Compulsory National Service*)
3	May	16	A. Birrell (*Irish Rebellion*)
25	Jun	16	E of Selborne (*Irish Policy*)
12	Jul	17	A. Chamberlain (*Campaign in Mesopotamia*)
8	Aug	17	N. Chamberlain (*Ministry of National Service*)
17	Nov	17	Ld Cowdray (*Conduct of the Air Ministry*)
21	Jan	18	Sir E. Carson (*Ireland*)
25	Apr	18	Ld Rothermere (*Air Force*)
22	Nov	18	Ld R. Cecil (*Welsh disestablishment*)
12	Nov	19	J. Seely (*Role of Air Ministry*)
14	Jul	21	C. Addison (*Housing*)
9	Mar	22	E. Montagu (*Turkey*)
18	Nov	23	A. Buckley (*Abandonment of Free Trade*)
28	Aug	27	Vt Cecil (*Disarmament*)
19	May	30	Sir O. Mosley (*Unemployment*)
2	Mar	31	Sir C. Trevelyan (*Education*)
6	Mar	31	Ld Arnold (*Free Trade*)
9	Oct	31	G. Lloyd-George, G. Owen (*Decision to hold a General Election*)
28	Sep	32	Sir H. Samuel, Sir A. Sinclair, Vt Snowden, M of Lothian, I. Foot, Sir R. Hamilton, G. White, W. Rea, Vt Allendale (*Free Trade*)
18	Dec	35	Sir S. Hoare (*Laval Pact*)
22	May	36	J. Thomas (*Budget leak*)
20	Feb	38	A. Eden, Vt Cranborne (*Negotiations with Mussolini*)
12-16	May	38	Earl Winterton, Vt Swinton (*Strength of Air Force*)
16	May	38	Ld Harlech (*Partition of Palestine*)
1	Oct	38	A. Duff Cooper (*Munich*)
21	Jan	41	R. Boothby (*Blocked Czechoslovakian assets*)
1	Mar	45	H. Strauss (*Treatment of Poles by Yalta Conference*)
26	May	46	Sir B. Smith (*Overwork and criticism*)
13	Nov	47	H. Dalton (*Budget leak*)
13	Dec	48	J. Belcher (*Lynskey Tribunal*)
16	Apr	50	S. Evans (*Agricultural subsidies*)
23-24	Apr	51	A. Bevan, H. Wilson, J. Freeman (*Budget proposals*)
20	Jul	54	Sir T. Dugdale (*Crichel Down*)
31	Oct	56	A. Nutting (*Suez*)
5	Nov	56	Sir E. Boyle (*Suez*)
29	Mar	57	M of Salisbury (*Release of Archbishop Makarios*)
6	Jan	58	P. Thorneycroft, E. Powell, N. Birch (*Economic policy*)
24	Nov	58	I. Harvey (*Private scandal*)
8	Nov	62	T. Galbraith (*Security: exonerated and given new office* 5 *May* 63)
5	Jun	63	J. Profumo (*Lying to the House of Commons*)
19	Feb	66	C. Mayhew (*Defence estimates*)
3	Jul	66	F. Cousins (*Incomes policy*)
26	Jul	67	Miss M. Herbison (*Social Services policy*)
16	Jan	68	E of Longford (*Postponement of raising school-leaving age*)
5	Feb	68	W. Howie (*Enforcement of Party discipline*)
16	Mar	68	G. Brown (*Conduct of Government business*)
1	Jul	68	R. Gunter (*General dissatisfaction*)
24	Sep	69	J. Bray (*Permission to publish*)
28	Jul	71	E. Taylor (*Entry into the E.E.C.*)
17	Oct	71	J. More (*Entry into the E.E.C.*)
18	Jul	72	R. Maudling (*Poulson Inquiry*)
22	May	73	Ld Lambton (*Private scandal*)
23	May	73	Earl Jellicoe (*Private scandal*)
25	Sep	74	Ld Brayley (*Inquiry into former business interests*)
17	Oct	74	N. Buchan (*Agriculture Department policy*)

9	Apr	75	E. Heffer (*speaking against E.E.C. membership in House of Commons*)[1]
10	Jun	75	Dame J. Hart (*dissatisfaction with PM*)
21	Jul	75	R. Hughes (*Incomes policy*)
21	Feb	76	Miss J. Lestor (*Education cuts*)
21	Dec	76	R. Prentice (*Disenchantment with Government policies*)
9	Nov	77	J. Ashton (*Government's handling of power dispute*)
20	Nov	78	R. Cryer (*Failure to support Kirkby Cooperative firm*)
17	Jan	79	A. Stallard (*Extra Seats for Northern Ireland*)
18	May	81	K. Speed (*Defence estimates*)[1]
21	Jan	82	N. Fairbairn (*handling of a Scottish prosecution*)
5	Apr	82	Ld Carrington, H. Atkins, R. Luce (*Falklands*)
8	May	82	N. Budgen (*Northern Ireland policy*)
11	Oct	83	C. Parkinson (*Private scandal*)

SOURCES.—R. C. K. Ensor, *England 1870-1914* (1936); C. L. Mowat, *Britain Between the Wars* (1955); *The Annual Register, 1900-; Keesing's Archives, 1931-;* S. E. Finer, 'The Individual Responsibility of Ministers', *Public Administration*, Winter 1956, pp. 377-96; P. J. Madgwick, 'Resignations', *Parliamentary Affairs*, Winter 1966, pp. 59-76; R. K. Alderman and J. A. Cross, *Tactics of Resignation* (1968).

Parliamentary Private Secretaries to Prime Ministers

1900-02	E. Cecil
1906-08	H. Carr-Gomm
1908-10	G. Howard
1910-15	C. Lyell
1915-16	Sir J. Barran
1916-17	D. Davies
1918-18	W. Astor
1918-20	(Sir) W. Sutherland
1920-22	Sir P. Sassoon
1922-23	J. Davidson
1923-24	S. Herbert
1924-24	L. MacNeil Weir
1924-27	S. Herbert
1927-29	C. Rhys
1929-31	L. MacNeil Weir
	R. Morrison
1931-32	R. Glyn
	F. Markham
1932-35	(Sir) R. Glyn
	J. Worthington
1935-35	G. Lloyd
1935-37	T. Dugdale
1937-40	Ld Dunglass
1940-41	B. Bracken
1941-45	G. Harvie-Watt
1945-46	G. de Freitas
1946-51	A. Moyle
1952-55	C. Soames
1955-55	R. Carr
1955-58	R. Allan
1958-59	A. Barber
1959-63	K. Cunningham
1963-64	F. Pearson
1964-66	P. Shore
1964-67	E. Fernyhough
1967-68	H. Davies
1968-69	H. Davies
	E. Varley
1969-70	H. Davies
1970-74	T. Kitson
1974-75	W. Hamling
1975-75	K. Marks
1975-76	J. Tomlinson
1976-76	J. Cunningham
1976-79	R. Stott
1979-83	I. Gow
1983-	M. Alison

[1] Technically a dismissal, not a resignation.

Biographical Notes

Prime Ministers, Chancellors of the Exchequer, Foreign Secretaries, and Leaders of the Opposition.[1]

Anderson, John (Sir). 1st Vt Waverley (1952)
b. 1882. *Educ.* George Watson's Coll., Edin.; Edinburgh and Leipzig Univs. Entered Col. O., 1905. Sec. to Min. of Shipping, 1917-19. K.C.B., 1919. Addit. Sec. to Loc. Govt. Bd., 1919. 2nd Sec. to Min. of Health, 1919. Ch. of Bd. of Inland Revenue, 1919-22. Joint U-S. to Ld. Lieut. of Ireland, 1920-22. P.U-S. Home O., 1922-32. Gov. of Bengal, 1932-37. M.P. (Nat.) for Scottish Univs., 1938-50. Ld. Privy S., 1938-39. Home Sec. and Min. of Home Security, 1939-40. Ld. Pres. of Council, 1940-43. Chanc. of Exch., 1943-45. d. 1958.

Asquith, Herbert Henry. 1st E of Oxford and Asquith (1925)
b. 1852. *Educ.* City of London School; Oxford. Barrister, 1876, practised M.P. (Lib.) for E. Fife, 1886-1918. M.P. for Paisley, 1920-24. Home Sec., 1892-95. Chanc. of Exch., 1905-8. P.M. and Leader of Lib. party, 1908-1916. Sec. for War, 1914. Formed Coalition Govt., 1915. Resigned as P.M., became Leader of Opposition, 1916. Resigned Leadership of Lib. party, 1926. d. 1928.

Attlee, Clement Richard. 1st Earl Attlee (1955)
b. 1883. *Educ.* Haileybury; Oxford. Barrister, 1906; practised, 1906-9. Lecturer at L.S.E., 1913-23. M.P. (Lab.) for Limehouse, Stepney, 1922-50. M.P. for W. Walthamstow, 1950-55. P.P.S. to J. R. MacDonald, 1922-24. U-S. for War, 1924. Chanc. of D. of Lanc., 1930-31. Postm.-Gen., 1931. Dep. Leader of Lab. party in Commons, 1931-35. Leader of Lab. party, 1935-55. Leader of Opposition, 1935-40. Ld Privy S., 1940-42. Sec. for Dominions, 1942-43. Ld Pres. of Council, 1943-45. Leader of Opposition, 1945. Dep. P.M., 1942-45. P.M., 1945-51. Min. of Def., 1945-46. Leader of Opposition, 1951-1955. d. 1967.

Baldwin, Stanley. 1st Earl Baldwin of Bewdley (1937)
b. 1867. *Educ.* Harrow; Cambridge. Family business. M.P. (Con.) for Bewdley div. of Worcs., 1908-37. Joint F.S. to Treas., 1917-21; Pres. of Bd. of Trade, 1921-22; Chanc. of Exch., 1922-23. Leader of Con. party, 1923-37. P.M., 1923-24 and 1924-29. Leader of Opposition, 1924, 1929-31. Ld Pres. of Council, 1931-35. Ld Privy S., 1932-33. P.M., 1935-37. d. 1947.

Balfour, Arthur James. 1st Earl of Balfour (1922)
b. 1848. *Educ.* Eton; Cambridge. M.P. (Con.) for Hertford, 1874-85. M.P. for E. Manchester, 1885-1906. M.P. for City of London, 1906-22. P.P.S. to Ld Salisbury, 1878-80. Pres. of Loc. Govt. Bd., 1885. Sec. for Scotland, 1886. (Member of Cabinet, Nov 1886.) Ch. Sec. for Ireland, 1887-91. Leader of Commons and 1st Ld of Treas., 1891-92 and 1895-1905. P.M., 1902-5. Leader of Con. party, 1902-11. Member of Committee of Imperial Defence, 1914. Attended war cabinet meetings, 1914-15. 1st Ld of Admir., 1915-16. For. Sec., 1916-19. Ld Pres. of Council, 1919-22 and 1925-29. d. 1930.

Barber, Anthony Perrinott Lysberg. Ld Barber (Life Peer 1974)
b. 1920. *Educ.* Retford G.S.; Oxford. Barrister, 1948. M.P. (Con.) for Doncaster, 1951-64. M.P. for Altrincham and Sale, 1965-74. Con. Whip, 1955-58; P.P.S. to P.M., 1958-59. Econ. S. to Treasury, 1959-62. F.S., 1962-63. Min. of Health, 1963-64. Ch. of Con. Party Organisation, 1967-70. Chanc. of D. of Lanc., 1970. Chanc. of Exch., 1970-74.

Bevan, Aneurin
b. 1897. *Educ.* Elem.; Central Labour College. Miner. M.P. (Lab.) for Ebbw Vale, 1929-60. Deputy Leader of Lab. party, 1959-60. Min. of Health, 1945-51. Min. of Lab. and Nat. Service, 1951. Resigned, 1951. Treasurer of Lab. party, 1956-60. d. 1960.

Bevin, Ernest
b. 1881. *Educ.* Elem. National Organiser of Dockers' Union, 1910-21. Gen. Sec. of T. & G.W.U., 1921-40. Member of General Council for T.U.C., 1925-40. M.P. (Lab.) for C.

[1] Virtually all the most eminent politicians of this century held one of these four positions, but common sense being more important than consistency, we have added biographies of the two most outstanding exceptions—Joseph Chamberlain and Aneurin Bevan.

Wandsworth, 1940-50. M.P. for E. Woolwich, 1950-51. Min. of Lab. and Nat. Service, 1940-45. For. Sec., 1945-51. Ld Privy S., Mar-Apr 1951. d. 1951.

Bonar Law, Andrew
b. 1858. *Educ.* Canada and Glasgow H.S. Family business. M.P. (Con.) for Blackfriars, Glasgow, 1900-6. M.P. for Dulwich, 1906-10. M.P. for Bootle, 1911-18. M.P. for C. Glasgow, 1918-23. P.S. to Bd. of Trade, 1902-5. Leader of Con. party in Commons, 1911-21. Col. Sec., 1915-16. Chanc. of Exch., 1916-19. Ld Privy S. and Leader of Commons, 1919-21. Resigned, 1921. P.M. and Leader of Con. party, 1922-23. Resigned, 1923. d. 1923.

Brown, George Alfred. Ld George-Brown (Life Peer 1970)
b. 1914. *Educ.* Secondary. M.P. (Lab.) for Belper 1945-70. P.P.S. to Min. of Lab. and Nat. Service, 1945-47, and to C. of Exchequer, 1947. Joint Parliamentary Secretary, Min. of Ag. and Fish., 1947-51. Min. of Works, Apr-Oct 1951. First Sec. of State and Sec. of State for Econ. Affairs, 1964-66. For. Sec. 1966-68. Resigned, 1968. Deputy Leader of the Labour Party, 1960-70. d. 1985.

Butler, Richard Austen. Ld Butler of Saffron Walden (Life Peer 1965)
b. 1902. *Educ.* Marlborough; Cambridge. M.P. (Con.) for Saffron Walden, 1929-65. U-S. India O., 1932-37. P.S. Min. of Lab., 1937-38. U-S. For. O., 1938-41. Pres. Bd. of Educ., 1941-44. Min. of Educ., 1944-45. Min. of Lab., 1945. Chanc. of Exch., 1951-55. Leader of Commons, 1955-61. Ld Privy S., 1955-59. Hom. Sec., 1957-62. First Sec. of State and Min. in charge of C. African O., 1962-63. For. Sec., 1963-64. Ch. of Con. party organisation 1959-61. Master of Trinity College, Cambridge, 1965-78. d. 1982.

Callaghan, (Leonard) James
b. 1912. *Educ.* Elem. and Portsmouth Northern Secondary Schools. M.P. (Lab.) for S. Cardiff, 1945-50. M.P. for S.E. Cardiff 1950-83. M.P. for Cardiff S. and Penarth 1983-. P.S. Min. of Transport, 1947-50. P.S. and F.S. Admiralty, 1950-51. Chanc. of the Exch., 1964-67. Home Sec., 1967-70. For. Sec., 1974-76. P.M., 1976-79.

Campbell-Bannerman, Henry (Sir)
b. 1836. *Educ.* Glasgow H.S.; Glasgow Univ. and Cambridge. Family business. M.P. (Lib.) for Stirling Burghs, 1868-1908. F.S. to War O., 1871-74 and 1880-82. Sec. to Admir., 1882-84. Ch. Sec. for Ireland (without seat in cabinet), 1884-85. Sec. for War, 1886 and 1892-95. G.C.B., 1895. Leader of Lib. party in Commons, 1899-1908. P.M., 1905-8. Resigned, 1908. d. 1908.

Carrington, 6th Ld (1938), Peter Alexander Rupert Carington
b. 1919. *Educ.* Eton; Sandhurst. Army 1939-45. Banker. P.S. Min. of Ag. and Fish., 1951-54. P.S. Min. of Defence, 1954-56. High Commissioner to Australia, 1956-59. 1st Ld of Admiralty, 1959-63. Leader of House of Lords, 1963-64. Sec. of State for Defence, 1970-74. Sec. of State for Energy, 1974. Ch. of Con. Party Organisation, 1972-74. For. Sec., 1979-82. Secretary-General of N.A.T.O., 1984.

Chamberlain, (Arthur) Neville
b. 1869. *Educ.* Rugby; Mason Science College, Birmingham. Birmingham and business career. Ld Mayor of Birmingham, 1915-16. Dir.-Gen. of Nat. Service, 1916-17. M.P. (Con.) for Ladywood, Birmingham, 1918-29. M.P. for Edgbaston, Birmingham, 1929-40. Postm.-Gen., 1922-23. Paym.-Gen., 1923. Min. of Health, 1923. Chanc. of Exch., 1923-24. Min. of Health, 1924-29 and 1931. Ch. of Con. party organisation, 1930-31. Chanc. of Exch., 1931-37. P.M. and Leader of Con. party, 1937-40. Ld Pres. of Council, 1940. Resigned, 1940. d. 1940.

Chamberlain, Joseph
b. 1836. *Educ.* University College School. Family business. Mayor of Birmingham, 1873-75. M.P. (Lib.) for Birmingham, 1876-85. M.P. for Birmingham W., 1885-86. M.P. (Lib. U.) for Birmingham W., 1886-1914. Pres. of Bd. of Trade, 1880-85. Pres. of Loc. Govt. Bd., 1886. Col. Sec., 1895-1903. d. 1914.

Chamberlain, (Joseph) Austen (Sir)
b. 1863. *Educ.* Rugby; Cambridge. M.P. (Con.) for E. Worcs., 1892-1914. M.P. for W. Birmingham, 1914-37. Lib. U. Whip, 1892. Civil Ld of Admir., 1895-1900. F.S. to Treas., 1900-2. Postm.-Gen., 1902-3. Chanc. of Exch., 1903-5. Sec. for India, 1915-17. Resigned, 1917. Min. without Portfolio in war cabinet, 1918-19. Chanc. of Exch., 1919-21. Ld Privy S. and Leader of Con. party in Commons, 1921-22. For. Sec., 1924-29. K.G., 1925. 1st Ld of Admir., 1931. d. 1937.

Churchill, Winston Leonard Spencer (Sir)
b. 1874. *Educ.* Harrow; Sandhurst. Army, 1895-1900. M.P. (Con.) for Oldham, 1900-4. M.P. (Lib.) for Oldham, 1904-6. M.P. (Lib.) for N.W. Manchester, 1906-8. M.P. (Lib.) for Dundee, 1908-22. M.P. (Const.) for Epping, 1924-29. M.P. (Con.) for Epping, 1929-

45; M.P. (Con.) for Woodford, 1945-64. U-S. for Col. O., 1905-8. Pres. of Bd. of Trade, 1908-10. Home Sec., 1910-11. 1st Ld of Admiralty, 1911-15. Chanc. of D. of Lanc., 1915. Min. of Munitions, 1917-19. Sec. for War and Air, 1919-21. Sec. for Air and Col., 1921. Col. Sec., 1921-22. Chanc. of Exch., 1924-29. 1st Ld of Admir., 1939-40. Min. of Def., and P.M., 1940-45. Leader of Con. party, 1940-55. Leader of Opposition, 1945-51. Min. of Def., 1951-52. P.M., 1951-55. K.G., 1953. d. 1965.

Cripps, (Richard) Stafford (Sir)

b. 1889. *Educ.* Winchester; London. Barrister, 1913. M.P. (Lab.) for E. Bristol, 1931-50. M.P. for S.E. Bristol, 1950. Kt., 1930. Sol.-Gen., 1930-31. Brit. Amb. to U.S.S.R., 1940-42. Ld Privy S. and Leader of Commons, 1942. Min. of Aircraft Prod., 1942-45. Pres. of Bd. of Trade, 1945-47. Min. for Econ. Affairs, 1947. Chanc. of Exch., 1947-50. d. 1952.

Crosland, (Charles) Anthony Raven

b. 1918. *Educ.* Highgate; Oxford. M.P. (Lab.) for South Glos., 1950-55; M.P. for Grimsby, 1959-77. Min. of State, Econ. Affairs, 1964-65. Sec. of State Educ. and Science, 1965-67. President of the Bd. of Trade, 1967-69. Sec. of State for Local Govt. and Regional Planning, 1969-70. Sec. of State for the Environment, 1974-76. For. Sec., 1976-77. d. 1977.

Curzon, George Nathaniel. Ld Curzon (1898), 1st Earl (1911), 1st Marquess Curzon of Kedleston (1921)

b. 1859. *Educ.* Eton and Oxford. M.P. (Con.) for Southport, 1886-98. U-S. India O., 1891-92. U-S. For. O., 1895-98. Viceroy of India, 1899-1905. Entered H. of Lords as Irish Representative Peer, 1908. Ld Privy Seal, 1915-16. Ld Pres. of Council, 1916-19. Member of war cabinet, Leader of Lords, 1916-24. For. Sec., 1919-24. Ld Pres. of Council, 1924-25. Leader of Con. Party, Lords, 1916-25. d. 1925.

Dalton, (Edward) Hugh John Neale. Ld Dalton (Life Peer 1960)

b. 1887. *Educ.* Eton; Cambridge, L.S.E. Barrister, 1914. Univ. Lecturer, London, 1919-36. M.P. (Lab.) for Peckham, 1924-29. M.P. Bishop Auckland, 1929-31 and 1935-59. U-S. For. O., 1929-31. Min. of Econ. Warfare, 1940-42. Pres. of Bd. of Trade, 1942-45. Chanc. of Exch., 1945-47. Chanc. of D. of Lanc., 1948-50. Min. of Town and Country Planning, 1950-51. Min. of Loc. Govt. and Planning, 1951. d. 1962.

Douglas-Home, Sir Alec (Alexander Frederick). Ld Dunglass (1918-51), 14th E of Home (1951-63). Ld Home of the Hirsel (Life Peer 1974)

b. 1903. *Educ.* Eton; Oxford. M.P. (Con.) for S. Lanark, 1931-45. M.P. for Lanark, 1950-51. M.P. for Kinross and W. Perthshire, 1963-74. P.P.S. to N. Chamberlain, 1937-40. Joint U-S. For. O., 1945. (Succ. to Earldom 1951) Min. of State Scottish O., 1951-55. Sec. Commonwealth Relations, 1955-60. Dep. Leader of Lords, 1956-57. Ld Pres. of Council, 1957 and 1959-60. Leader of Lords, 1957-60. For. Sec., 1960-63. K.T., 1962. P.M., 1963-64 (Renounced peerage 1963). Leader of Con. Party, 1963-65. For Sec., 1970-74.

Eden, (Robert) Anthony (Sir). 1st E of Avon (1961)

b. 1897. *Educ.* Eton; Oxford. M.P. (Con.) for Warwick and Leamington, 1923-57. P.P.S. to Sir A. Chamberlain (For. Sec.), 1926-29. U-S. For. O., 1931-33. Ld Privy S., 1933-35. Min. without Portfolio for League of Nations Affairs, 1935. For. Sec., 1935-38. Resigned, 1938. Sec. for Dominions, 1939-40. Sec. for War, 1940. For. Sec., 1940-45. Leader of Commons, 1942-45. Dep. Leader of Opposition, 1945-51. For. Sec., 1951-55. K.G., 1954. P.M. and Leader of Con. party, 1955-57. d. 1977.

Foot, Michael Mackintosh

b. 1913. *Educ.* Leighton Park Sch., Reading; Oxford. Journalist. M.P. (Lab) for Plymouth Devonport, 1945-55. M.P. for Ebbw Vale, 1960-83. M.P. for Blaenau Gwent, 1983-. Sec. for Employment 1974-76; Lord Pres. of Council and Leader of House of Commons, 1976-79. Leader of Opposition, 1980-83. Dep. Leader of Labour Party, 1976-80. Leader of Labour Party, 1980-83.

Gaitskell, Hugh Todd Naylor

b. 1906. *Educ.* Winchester; Oxford. M.P. (Lab.) for S. Leeds, 1945-63. Princ. Private Sec. to Min. of Econ. Warfare, 1940-42. Princ. Asst. Sec. Bd. of Trade, 1942-45. P.S. Min. of Fuel and Power, 1946-47. Min. of Fuel and Power, 1947-50. Min. of State for Econ. Affairs, 1950. Chanc. of Exch., 1950-51. Leader of Lab. party, 1955-63. d. 1963.

Gordon Walker, Patrick Chrestien. Ld Gordon-Walker (Life Peer 1974)

b. 1907. *Educ.* Wellington; Oxford. University Teacher. M.P. (Lab.) for Smethwick, 1945-64. M.P. (Lab.) Leyton, 1966-74. P.P.S. to H. Morrison, 1946. Parl. U-S., Commonwealth Relations O., 1947-50. Sec. of State for Commonwealth Relations, 1950-51. For Sec., 1964-65. Min. without Portfolio, 1967. Sec. for Educ. and Science, 1967-68. d. 1980.

Grey, Edward (Sir). 1st Vt Grey of Fallodon (1916)
b. 1862. *Educ.* Winchester; Oxford. Succ. to Btcy., 1882. M.P. (Lib.) for Berwick-on-Tweed, 1885-1916. U-S. For. O., 1892-95. For. Sec., 1905-16. (For. Sec. in Lords, 1916). Leader of Lib. party, Lords, 1923-24. d. 1933.

Halifax, 3rd Vt (1934). Edward Frederick Lindley Wood. 1st Ld Irwin (1925), 1st E of (1944)
b. 1881. *Educ.* Eton; Oxford. M.P. (Con.) for Ripon, 1910-25. U-S. Col. O., 1921-22. Pres. of Bd. of Educ., 1922-24. Min. of Agric., 1924-25. Viceroy of India, 1926-31. Pres. of Bd. of Educ., 1932-35. Sec. for War, 1935. Ld Privy S., 1935-37. Leader of Lords, 1935-38. Ld Pres. of Council, 1937-38. For. Sec., 1938-40. Leader of Lords, 1940. Brit. Amb. to U.S.A., 1941-46. d. 1959.

Healey, Denis Winston
b. 1917. *Educ.* Bradford G.S.; Oxford. M.P. (Lab.) for Leeds South-East, 1952-55. M.P. for Leeds East, 1955-. Sec. for Defence, 1964-70. Chanc. of Exch., 1974-79. Dep. Leader of Lab. Party, 1980-83.

Heath, Edward Richard George
b. 1916. *Educ.* Chatham House School, Ramsgate; Oxford. M.P. (Con.) for Bexley, 1950-74. M.P. for Sidcup 1974-. Con. Whip, 1951-55. Chief Whip, 1955-59. Min. of Labour, 1959-60. Lord Privy Seal, 1960-63. Sec. for Trade & Industry, 1963-64. Leader of the Con. Party, 1965-75. Leader of the Opposition, 1965-70. P.M., 1970-74. Leader of the Opposition, 1974-75.

Heathcoat Amory, Derick. 1st Vt Amory (1960)
b. 1899. *Educ.* Eton; Oxford. M.P. (Con.) for Tiverton, 1945-60. Min. of Pensions, 1951-53. Min. of State for Bd. of Trade, 1953-54. Min. of Ag., Fish. and Food, 1954-58. Chanc. of Exch., 1958-60. High Commissioner for the U.K. in Canada, 1961-63. d. 1981.

Henderson, Arthur
b. 1863. *Educ.* Elem. M.P. (Lab.) for Barnard Castle, 1903-18. M.P. for Widnes, 1919-22. M.P. for Newcastle E., 1923. M.P. for Burnley, 1924-31. M.P. for Clay Cross, 1933-35. Sec. of Lab. party, 1911-34. Treasurer of Lab. party, 1930-35. Leader of Lab. party in Commons, 1908-10 and 1914-17. Chief Whip, 1914. Pres. Bd. of Educ., 1915-16. Paym.-Gen., 1916. Min. without portfolio and member of war cabinet, 1916-17. Resigned from cabinet, 1917. Chief Lab. party Whip, 1920-24 and 1925-27. Home Sec., 1924. For. Sec., 1929-31. Leader of Lab. Opposition, 1931-32. d. 1935.

Hicks Beach, Michael Edward (Sir). 1st Vt St Aldwyn (1906), 1st Earl (1915)
b. 1837. *Educ.* Eton; Oxford. Succ. to Btcy., 1854. M.P. (Con.) for E. Gloucs., 1864-85. M.P. for W. Bristol, 1885-1906. Sec. of Poor Law Bd., 1868. U-S. Home O., 1868. Ch. Sec. for Ireland, 1874-78. (Seat in cabinet, 1876.) Sec. for Col., 1878-80. Chanc. of Exch. and Leader of Commons, 1885-86. Leader of Opposition in Commons, 1886. Ch. Sec. for Ireland, 1886-87. Resigned, 1887, but remained in cabinet without portfolio. Pres. of Bd. of Trade, 1888-92. Chanc. of Exch., 1895-1902. Resigned 1902. d. 1916.

Hoare, Samuel John Gurney (Sir). 1st Vt Templewood (1944)
b. 1880. *Educ.* Harrow; Oxford. M.P. (Con.) for Chelsea, 1910-44. Succ. to Btcy., 1915. Sec. for Air, 1922-24 and 1924-29. Sec. for India, 1931-35. For. Sec., 1935. 1st Ld of Admir., 1936-37. Home Sec., 1937-39. Ld Privy S., 1939-40. Sec. for Air, 1940. Brit. Amb. to Spain, 1940-44. d. 1959.

Horne, Robert Stevenson (Sir). 1st Vt Horne of Slamannan (1937)
b. 1871. *Educ.* George Watson's Coll., Edin.; Glasgow Univ. Member of Faculty of Advocates, 1896. K.B.E., 1918. M.P. (Con.) for Hillhead, Glasgow, 1918-37. Min. of Lab., 1919-20. Pres. of Bd. of Trade, 1920-21. Chanc. of Exch., 1921-22. d. 1940.

Howe, (Richard Edward) Geoffrey (Sir)
b. 1926. *Educ.* Winchester; Cambridge. Barrister. M.P. (Con.) for Bebington, 1964-66. M.P. for Reigate, 1970-74. M.P. for Surrey East, 1974-. Sol.-Gen., 1970-72. Min. for Trade and Consumer Affairs, 1972-74. Chanc. of Exch., 1979-83. For. Sec., 1983-.

Jenkins, Roy Harris
b. 1920. *Educ.* Abersychan G.S.; Oxford. Army, 1939-45. M.P. (Lab.) for Central Southwark, 1948-50. M.P. (Lab.) for Stechford, Birmingham, 1950-76. M.P. for Glasgow Hillhead, 1982-. P.P.S. Commonwealth Relations O., 1949-50. Min. of Aviation, 1964-65. Home Sec., 1965-67. Chanc. of Exch., 1967-70. Deputy Leader of Lab. party, 1970-72. Home Sec., 1974-76. President of European Economic Commission, 1977-81. Leader of SDP, 1982-83.

Kinnock, Neil Gordon
b. 1942 *Educ.* Lewis Sch., Pengam; U.C. Cardiff. M.P. (Lab.) for Bedwellty, 1970-83. M.P. for Islwyn, 1983-. P.P.S. to Sec. of State for Employment, 1974-75. Chief

Opposition Spokesman on Education, 1979-83. Leader of the Opposition, and Leader of Labour Party, 1983-.

Lansbury, George

b. 1859. *Educ.* Elem. M.P. (Lab.) for Bow and Bromley, 1910-12 and 1922-35. First Comm. of Works, 1929-31. Leader of the Opposition, 1931-35. Leader of the Labour Party, 1932-35. d. 1940.

Lansdowne, 5th M of (1866). Henry Charles Keith Petty-Fitzmaurice, Vt Clanmaurice (1845-63), E of Kerry (1863-66)

b. 1845. *Educ.* Eton; Oxford. Succ. to M. 1866. Junior Ld of Treas. (Lib.), 1869-72. U-S. for War, 1872-74. U-S. India O., 1880. Resigned and opposed Lib. Govt. in Lords, 1880. Gov.-Gen. of Canada, 1883-88. Viceroy of India, 1888-94. Sec. for War (Con.), 1895-1900. For. Sec., 1900-5. Leader of Con. party in Lords, 1903-16. Min. without portfolio, member of war cabinet, 1915-16. Left Con. party, 1917. d. 1927.

Lawson, Nigel

b. 1932. *Educ.* Westminster; Oxford. Journalist. M.P. (Con.) for Blaby, Feb. 1974-. Opposition Spokesman on Treasury and Economic Affairs, 1977-79. F.S. to Treasury, 1979-81. Sec. for Energy, 1981-83; Chanc. of Exch., 1983-.

Lloyd, (John) Selwyn Brooke. Ld Selwyn-Lloyd (Life Peer 1976)

b. 1904. *Educ.* Fettes; Cambridge. Barrister, 1930. M.P. (Con.) for Wirral, 1945-76. Min. of State For. O., 1951-54. Min. of Supply, 1954-55. Min. of Def., 1955. For. Sec., 1955-60. Chanc. of Exch., 1960-62. Lord Privy Seal and Leader of the House of Commons, 1963-64. Speaker of the House of Commons, 1971-76. d. 1978.

Lloyd George, David. 1st Earl Lloyd George of Dwyfor (1945)

b. 1863. *Educ.* Church School. Solicitor, 1884. M.P. (Lib.) for Caernarvon Boroughs, 1890-1945 (Ind. L., 1931-35). Pres. of Bd. of Trade, 1905-8. Chanc. of Exch., 1908-15. Min. of Munitions, 1915-16. Sec. for War, 1916. P.M., 1916-22. Leader of Lib. party, 1926-31. d. 1945.

MacDonald, James Ramsay

b. 1866. *Educ.* Drainie School. M.P. (Lab.) for Leicester, 1906-18. M.P. for Aberavon, Glamorganshire, 1922-29. M.P. for Seaham, 1929-35. (Nat. Lab., 1931-37.) M.P. for Scottish Univs., 1936-37. Sec. of L.R.C. and Lab. party, 1900-12. Treas. of Lab. party, 1912-29. Chairman of I.L.P., 1906-9. Ch. of Lab. party, 1911-14. Resigned Chairmanship, 1914. Ch. of P.L.P. and Leader of official Opposition, 1922. Leader of Lab. party, 1922-31. P.M. and For. Sec., 1924. P.M., 1929-31. P.M. of National Govt., 1931-35. Ld Pres. of Council, 1935-37. d. 1937.

McKenna, Reginald

b. 1863. *Educ.* St. Malo, Ebersdorf and King's Coll. School; Cambridge. Barrister, 1887. M.P. (Lib.) for N. Monmouthshire, 1895-1918. F.S. to Treas., 1905-7. Pres. Bd. of Educ., 1907-8. 1st Ld of Admir., 1908-11. Home Sec., 1911-15. Chanc. of Exch., 1915-16. Ch. of Midland Bank, 1919-43. d. 1943.

Macleod, Iain Norman

b. 1913. *Educ.* Fettes; Cambridge. Journalist. M.P. (Con.) for Enfield West, 1950-70. Min. of Health, 1952-55. Min. of Labour, 1955-59. Sec. of State for Colonies, 1959-61. Chanc. of D. of Lanc. and Leader of House of Commons, 1961-63. Ch. of Con. party organisation, 1961-63. Editor of *Spectator*, 1963-65. Chanc. of Exch., 1970. d. 1970.

Macmillan, (Maurice) Harold. 1st E of Stockton (1984)

b. 1894. *Educ.* Eton; Oxford. M.P. (Con.) for Stockton-on-Tees, 1924-29 and 1931-45. M.P. (Con.) for Bromley, 1945-64. P.S. Min. of Supply, 1940-42. U-S. Col. O., 1942. Min. resident at Allied H.Q. in N.W. Africa, 1942-45. Sec. for Air, 1945. Min. of Housing and Loc. Govt., 1951-54. Min. of Def., 1954-55. For. Sec., 1955. Chanc. of Exch., 1955-57. P.M. and Leader of Con. party, 1957-63.

Maudling, Reginald

b. 1917. *Educ.* Merchant Taylors'; Oxford. Barrister, 1940. M.P. (Con.) for Barnet, 1950-74. M.P. for Chipping Barnet, 1974-79. P.S. Min. of Civil Aviation, 1952. Econ. Sec. to Treasury, 1952-55. Min. of Supply, 1955-57. Paym.-Gen., 1957-59. Pres. Bd. of Trade, 1959-61. Sec. of State for Colonies, 1961-62. Chanc. of Exch., 1962-64. Deputy Leader of Con. party, 1965-72. Home Sec., 1970-72. Resigned, 1972. d. 1979.

Morrison, Herbert Stanley. Ld Morrison of Lambeth (Life Peer 1959)

b. 1888. *Educ.* Elem. Member of L.C.C., 1922-45. Leader of Council, 1934-40. M.P. (Lab.) for S. Hackney, 1923-34, 1929-31, 1935-45. M.P. for E. Lewisham, 1945-50. M.P. for S. Lewisham, 1950-59. Min. of Transport, 1929-31. Min. of Supply, 1940. Home Sec. and Min. of Home Security, 1940-45. Member of war cabinet, 1942-45. Dep. P.M., 1945-

51. Ld Pres. of Council and Leader of Commons, 1945-51. For. Sec., 1951. Dep. Leader of Opposition, 1951-55. d. 1965.

Owen, David Anthony Llewellyn

b. 1938. *Educ.* Bradfield; Cambridge. Doctor, 1962. M.P. (Lab.) Plymouth Sutton, 1966-74. Plymouth Devonport, 1974-. U-S. for Navy, 1968-70. U-S. Health and Social Security, 1974. Min. of State Health and Social Security, 1974-76. Min. of State For. O., 1976-77. For. Sec., 1977-79. Leader of SDP, 1983-.

Pym, Francis Leslie

b. 1922. *Educ.* Eton; Cambridge. M.P. (Con) for Cambridgeshire, 1961-83. M.P. for Cambridgeshire S.E., 1983-. Parl. Sec. to the Treasury and Government Chief Whip, 1970-73. Sec. for Northern Ireland, 1973-74. Sec. for Defence, 1979-81. Chanc. of D. of Lancaster, Paym.-Gen. and Leader of House of Commons, 1981. Lord Pres. of Council and Leader of House of Commons, 1981-82. For. Sec., 1982-83.

Reading, 1st M of (1926). Rufus Daniel Isaacs (Sir), 1st Ld (1914), 1st Vt (1916) 1st E of (1917)

b. 1860. *Educ.* Brussels, Anglo-Jewish Acad., London, University College Sch. Family business. Barrister, 1887. M.P. (Lib.) for Reading, 1904-13. Kt., 1910. Sol.-Gen., 1910. Att. Gen., 1910-13 (seat in cabinet, 1912). Ld Chief Justice, 1913-21. Brit. Amb. to U.S.A., 1918-19. Viceroy of India, 1921-26. For. Sec., 1931. Leader of Lords, 1931; Leader of Lib. party, Lords, 1930-35. d 1935.

Ritchie, Charles Thomson. 1st Ld Ritchie of Dundee (1905)

b. 1838. *Educ.* City of London School. M.P. (Con.) for Tower Hamlets, 1874-85. M.P. for St. George's in the East, 1885-92. M.P. for Croydon, 1895-1903. F.S. to Admir., 1885-86. Pres. of Loc. Govt. Bd., 1886-92. Pres. of Bd. of Trade, 1895-1900. Home Sec., 1900-2. Chanc. of Exch., 1902-3. Resigned, 1903. d. 1906.

Salisbury, 3rd M of (1868). Robert Arthur Talbot Gascoyne-Cecil, Vt Cranborne (1865-68)

b. 1830. *Educ.* Eton; Oxford. M.P. (Con.) for Stamford, 1853-68. Sec. for India, 1866. Resigned, 1867. Succ. to M. 1868. Sec. for India, 1874-76. For. Sec., 1878-80. Leader of Opposition in Lords, 1881-85. Leader of the Con. party, 1885-1902. P.M. and For. Sec., 1885-86. P.M., 1886-87. P.M. and For. Sec., 1887-92 and 1895-1900. P.M. and Ld Privy S., 1900-2. d. 1903.

Simon, John Allsebrook (Sir). 1st Vt Simon (1940)

b. 1873. *Educ.* Fettes; Oxford. Barrister, 1899. M.P. (Lib.) for Walthamstow. 1906-18. M.P. for Spen Valley, 1922-31. M.P. (L. Nat.) for Spen Valley, 1931-40. Kt., 1910. Sol.-Gen., 1910-13. Att.-Gen. (with seat in cabinet), 1913-15. Home Sec., 1915-16. For. Sec., 1931-35. Leader of L. Nat. party, 1931-40. Home Sec. and Dep. Leader of Commons, 1935-37. Chanc. of Exch., 1937-40. Ld. Chanc., 1940-45. d. 1954.

Snowden, Philip. 1st Vt Snowden (1931)

b. 1864. *Educ.* Bd. School. M.P. (Lab.) for Blackburn, 1906-18. M.P. for Colne Valley, 1922-31. Ch. of I.L.P. 1903-6 and 1917-20. Chanc. of Exch., 1924, 1929-31, and 1931. Ld Privy S., 1931-32. Resigned, 1932. d. 1937.

Stewart, (Robert) Michael Maitland. Ld Stewart of Fulham (Life Peer 1979)

b. 1906. *Educ.* Christ's Hospital; Oxford. Teacher. M.P. (Lab.) Fulham East, 1945-55 and for Fulham, 1955-79. Vice-Chamberlain, H.M. Household, 1946. Comptroller, H.M. Household, 1946-47. U-S. for War, 1947-51. P.S. Min. of Supply, 1951. Sec. for Educ. and Science, 1964-65. For. Sec., 1965-66. Sec. of State for Econ. Affairs, 1966-67. First Sec. of State, 1966-68. For. (and Commonwealth) Sec., 1968-70.

Thatcher, Mrs Margaret Hilda (née Roberts)

b. 1925. *Educ.* Grantham Girls' School; Oxford. Research Chemist. Barrister. M.P. (Con) for Finchley, 1959-. P.S. to Min. of Pensions and Nat. Insurance, 1961-64. Sec. of State for Education and Science, 1970-74. Leader of the Conservative Party, 1975-. P.M., 1979-.

Thorneycroft, (George Edward) Peter. Ld Thorneycroft of Dunston (Life Peer 1967)

b. 1909. *Educ.* Eton; Woolwich. Barrister, 1935. M.P. (Con.) for Stafford, 1938-45. M.P. (Con.) for Monmouth, 1945-66. P.S. Min. of War Transport, 1945. Pres. of Bd. of Trade, 1951-57. Chanc. of Exch., 1957-58. Resigned, 1958. Min. of Aviation, 1960-62. Min. of Defence, 1962-64. Sec. of State for Defence, 1964. Ch. of Con. party organisation 1975-81.

Wilson, (James) Harold (Sir). Ld Wilson of Rievaulx. (Life Peer 1983)

b. 1916. *Educ.* Wirral G.S.; Oxford. University teacher, Director of Economics and Statistics, Min. of Fuel and Power, 1943-44, M.P. (Lab.) for Ormskirk, 1945-50, and for Huyton (Lab.), 1950-83. P.S. Min. of Works, 1945-47. Sec. for Overseas Trade, 1947. Pres. Bd. of Trade, 1947-51. Resigned 1951. Leader, Lab. party, 1963-76. Leader of the

Opposition 1963-64. P.M., 1964-70. Leader of the Opposition, 1970-74, P.M., 1974-76. K.G., 1976.

Wood, (Howard) Kingsley (Sir)

b. 1881. *Educ.* Central Foundation Boys' School. Solicitor, 1903. Kt., 1918. M.P. (Con.) for W. Woolwich, 1918-43. P.P.S. to Min. of Health, 1919-22. P.S. Min. of Health, 1924-29. P.S. Bd. of Educ., 1931. Postm.-Gen., 1931-35 (seat in cabinet, 1933). Min. of Health, 1935-38. Sec. for Air, 1938-40. Ld Privy S., 1940. Chanc. of Exch., 1940-43. d. 1943.

SOURCES.—*Dictionary of National Biography, 1900-; Who Was Who, 1900-; Who's Who.*

Index of Ministers

This index covers every reference to a Minister given in the Tables of Ministries, pp. 1–64. It does not cover the supplementary information on Ministers and Ministries, pp. 70–94.

The educational information is necessarily incomplete. It is not always possible to trace the name or status of an elementary or secondary school. When several schools are recorded, the last is normally named here. All schools that are unstarred are 'public schools' or, more precisely, were in the 1970s members of the Headmasters' Conference. However this can be misleading, particularly for Ministers educated in the 19th century. RNC Dartmouth is also unstarred. By courtesy, we have listed the Royal Military College (Sandhurst) and the Royal Military Academy (Woolwich) in the University column. In this index promotion from a knighthood to a higher order of chivalry or to a baronetcy is not recorded.

† denotes a Privy Councillor.

When an individual appears more than once on a page, the number is indicated. Double entries are given when an individual held office under different names, and where a title was acquired after office had been held.

Name	Born	School	Univ.	Died	Page references
† Abercorn, 3rd D of (1913). J. A. E. Hamilton, M of Hamilton (1885)	1869	Eton	..	1953	3
† Aberdare, 4th Ld (1957). M. G. L. Bruce	1919	Winchester	Oxford	..	52, 53
† Acland, Sir F. D. (14th Bt 1926)	1874	Rugby	Oxford	1939	5^{2}, 6^{2}, 8
† Acland Hood, Sir A. F. (4th Bt (1892), 1st Ld St Audries (1911)	1853	Eton	Oxford	1917	3^{2}
Acton, 2nd Ld (1902). R. M. Dalberg-Acton	1870	Privately	Oxford	1924	5, 7
Adams, (H.) R.	1912	Emanuel	London	1978	36
Adamson, Mrs J. L.	1882	Elementary	..	1962	35
† Adamson, W.	1863	Elementary	..	1936	16, 19
Adamson, W. M.	1881	Elementary	..	1945	30
† Addison, 1st Vt (1945). C. Addison, 1st Ld (1937)	1869	Trinity Coll., Harrogate*	London	1951	6, 8, 10, 11^{3}, 12, 18^{2}, 32, 33^{3}, 34, 35
† Ailwyn, 1st Ld (1921). Sir A. E. Fellowes (K.C.V.O. 1911)	1855	Eton	Cambridge	1924	2, 3^{2}
Airlie, 12th E of (1900). D. L. G. W. Ogilvy	1893	Eton	..	1968	18
Aitchison, Ld (Scot, judge 1933). C. M. Aitchison	1882	Falkirk H.S.*	Edinburgh	1941	19, 22
† Akers-Douglas, A., 1st Vt Chilston (1911)	1851	Eton	Oxford	1926	2, 3
Albemarle, 8th E of (1884). A. A. C. Keppel	1858	Eton	..	1942	15
Albu, A. H.	1903	Tonbridge	London	..	45
† Aldington, 1st Ld (1962). Sir T. A. R. W. Low (K.C.M.G. 1957)	1914	Winchester	Oxford	..	38, 39
† Alexander of Hillsborough, 1st E (1963). A. V. Alexander, 1st Vt (1950)	1885	Elementary	..	1965	16, 18, 27, 33^{2}, 34^{2}
† Alexander of Tunis, 1st E (1952). H. R. L. G. Alexander, 1st Vt (1946)	1891	Harrow	Sandhurst	1969	37
Alexander of Tunis, 2nd E (1969). S. W. D. Alexander, Ld Rideau (1952)	1935	Harrow	..	..	54
† Alison, M.J.H.	1926	Eton	Oxford	..	52, 60, 62
Allan, of Kilmahew, Ld (Life Peer 1973). R. A. Allan	1914	Harrow	Cambridge	1979	40, 43
† Allendale, 1st Vt (1911). W. C. B. Beaumont, 2nd Ld Allendale (1907)	1860	Eton	Cambridge	1923	5^{2}, 7^{2}, 9
Allendale, 2nd Vt (1923). W. H. C. Beaumont	1890	Eton	Cambridge	1956	22

† Alness, 1st Ld (1934). R. Munro	1868	Aberdeen G.S.*	Edinburgh	1955	7, 9, 11, 30, 32
† Alport, Ld (Life Peer 1961). C. J. M. Alport	1912	Haileybury	Cambridge	..	39, 41^2
† Althorp, 1st Vt (1905). C. R. Spencer, Vt Althorp (1857). 6th Earl of Spencer (1910)	1857	Harrow	Cambridge	1922	5, 7
† Altrincham, 1st Ld (1945). Sir E. W. M. Grigg (K.V.C.O. 1920)	1879	Winchester	Oxford	1955	24^2, 28, 30, 32
† Alverstone, 1st Vt (1913). Sir R. E. Webster (G.C.M.G. 1893). 1st Ld Alverstone (1900)	1842	King's Coll. Sch. & Charterhouse	Cambridge	1915	3
† Amery, J.	1919	Eton	Oxford	1981	41^2, 43, 44, 51, 52, 53
† Amery, L. S.	1873	Harrow	Oxford	1955	10^2, 14, 17^2, 28, 31
† Ammon, 1st Ld (1944). C. G. Ammon	1875	Elementary	..	1960	16, 18, 36
† Amory, 1st Vt (1960). D. Heathcoat Amory	1899	Eton	Oxford	1981	37^2, 38, 39, 40
Amulree, 1st Ld (1929). Sir W. W. Mackenzie (K.B.E. 1918)	1860	Perth Academy*	Edinburgh & London	1942	19, 21
Amwell, 1st Ld (1947). F. Montague	1876	Elementary	..	1966	19, 27, 30
† Ancaster, 2nd E (1910). G. H. D. Willoughby	1867	Eton	Cambridge	1951	10, 14
Ancram (E of) (1965). M.A.J.F. Kerr	1945	Ampleforth	Oxford & Edinburgh	..	62
Anderson, Ld (Scot, judge 1913). A. M. Anderson	1862	Dundee H.S.*	Edinburgh	1936	7
Anderson, D. C.	1916	Trinity Coll. Glenalmond	Oxford & Edinburgh	..	44
† Anderson, Sir J. (K.C.B. 1919). 1st Vt Waverley (1952)	1882	George Watson's Coll., Edin.	Edinburgh & Leipzig	1958	22, 23, 26^2, 28^2, 31
Anson, Sir W. (3rd Bt 1873)	1843	Eton	Oxford	1914	2
Anstruther, H. T.	1860	Eton	Edinburgh	1926	3
† Anstruther-Gray, Sir W. J. (1st Bt 1956), Ld Kilmany (Life Peer 1966)	1905	Eton	Oxford	..	32
Archibald, 1st Ld (1949). G. Archibald	1898	Allan Glen's H.S. Glasg.*	..	1975	36
† Archer, P. K.	1926	Wednesbury Boys' H.S.*	London	..	58
† Armstrong, E.	1915	Wolsingham G.S.*	..	..	50^2, 56^2
Arnold, 1st Ld (1924). S. Arnold	1878	Manchester G.S.	..	1945	16, 19
† Arnold-Forster, H. O.	1855	Rugby	Oxford	1909	2, 3
† Ashbourne, 1st Ld (1885). E. Gibson	1837		Dublin	1913	2
† Ashby St Ledgers, 1st Ld (1910). I. C. Guest, 2nd Ld Wimborne (1914), 1st Vt Wimborne (1918)	1873	Eton	Cambridge	1939	7^2
† Ashfield, 1st Ld (1920). Sir A. H. Stanley (Kt 1914)	1874	American Schs.	..	1948	11
† Ashley, W. W. 1st Ld Mount Temple (1932)	1867	Harrow	Oxford	1939	15^2, 18
Ashton, J. W.	1933	High Storrs G.S.*	..	..	58
† Asquith, H. H. 1st E of Oxford & Asquith (1925)	1852	City of London	Oxford	1928	4, 5, 6, 8
† Assheton, R. 1st Ld Clitheroe (1955)	1901	Eton	Oxford	1984	24, 26, 27, 29
Astor, 2nd Vt (1919). W. Astor	1879	Eton	Oxford	1952	10, 12
† Atholl, 8th D of (1917). J. G. Stewart-Murray, M of Tullibardine (1871)	1871	Eton	..	1942	13
Atholl, Duchess of, K. M.	1874	Wimbledon H.S.	..	1960	17
† Atkins, Sir H. E. (K.C.M.G. 1983	1922	Wellington	..	..	53, 54, 59, 62

† Atkinson, Ld (Ld of Appeal 1905). J. Atkinson	1844	Royal Belfast Academical Institution*	Queen's Coll., Galway	1932	3
† Attlee, 1st E (1955). C. R. Attlee	1883	Haileybury	Oxford	1967	16, 19^2, 26^2, 27, 28, 32, 33
† Avon, 1st E of (1961). Sir (R.) A. Eden (K.G. 1954)	1897	Eton	Oxford	1977	20, 21, 23^2, 24, 26, 30, 31, 36^2
Avon, 2nd E of (1977). Vt Eden (1961). N. Eden	1930	Eton	..	..	61^2, 64
† Avonside, Ld (Scot. judge 1964). I. H. Shearer	1914	Dunfermline H.S.*	Glasgow & Edinburgh	..	44
† Aylestone Ld (Life Peer 1967). H. W. Bowden	1905	Secondary	..	..	36, 45, 46
† Bacon, Lady (Life Peer 1970). Miss A. M. Bacon	1911	Normanton H.S.*	London	..	46
Bagot, 4th Ld (1887). W. Bagot	1857	Eton	..	1932	3
† Baird, Sir J. L. (2nd Bt 1920). 1st Ld Stonehaven (1925), 1st Vt (1938)	1874	Eton	Oxford	1941	10, 11, 12, 15^2
† Baker, H. T.	1877	Winchester	Oxford	1960	6
† Baker, K. W.	1934	St Paul's	Oxford	..	50, 61^2, 62
† Balcarres, Ld (1880). D. A. E. Lindsay, 27th E of Crawford (1913)	1871	Eton	Oxford	1940	3, 8, 9, 12^3, 13^2
† Baldwin of Bewdley, 1st E (1937). S. Baldwin	1867	Harrow	Cambridge	1947	9, 11, 13, 14^2, 17, 20^2, 22
† Balfour, 1st E of (1922). A. J. Balfour	1848	Eton	Cambridge	1930	1^3, 8, 9, 10, 17
† Balfour, 2nd E of (1930). G. W. Balfour	1853	Eton	Cambridge	1945	2, 3^2
† Balfour of Burleigh, 6th Ld (1869). A. H. Bruce	1849	Eton	Oxford	1921	2
† Balfour of Inchrye, 1st Ld (1945). H. H. Balfour	1897	R. N. Coll., Osborne	..	..	23, 27, 28, 32
† Balniel, Ld (1940). (Life Peer 1974), 29th E of Crawford (1975). R. A. Lindsay	1927	Eton	Cambridge	..	51^2
Balogh, Ld (Life Peer 1968). T. Balogh	1905	The Gymnasium, Budapest*	Budapest, Berlin & Harvard	1985	56
† Barber, Ld (Life Peer 1974). A. P. L. Barber	1920	Retford G.S.*	Oxford	..	40^2, 42, 44, 51, 52
† Barnes, A.	1887	Northampton Institute*	..	1974	19, 35
† Barnes, G. N.	1859	Elementary	..	1940	9, 11, 12
† Barnett, Ld (Life Peer). J. Barnett	1923	Manchester Central H.S.*	..	..	55^2
Barnett, (N.) G.	1928	Highgate	Oxford	..	57
Barnston, Sir H. (1st Bt 1924)	1870	Private Schs.	Oxford	1929	13, 15, 18
Barrie, H. T.	1860	Secondary	..	1922	10
Barry, R.	1866	Secondary	Royal Univ. of Ireland	1913	5, 7^2
Barton, Sir D. P. (1st Bt 1918)	1853	Harrow	Oxford	1937	3
Bates, A.	1944	Stretford G.S.*	Manchester	..	58^2
† Bath, 5th M of (1896). T. H. Thynne, Vt Weymouth (1862)	1862	Eton	Oxford	1946	2, 15
Bathurst, 8th E (1943). H. A. J. Bathurst	1927	Canada & Eton	Oxford	..	41, 45
† Bathurst, Sir C. (K.B.E. 1917). 1st Ld Bledisloe (1918). 1st Vt (1935)	1867	Sherborne & Eton	Oxford	1958	12, 17
† Bayford, 1st Ld (1929). Sir R. A. Sanders (1st Bt 1920)	1867	Harrow	Oxford	1940	12, 13^2, 14
Beatty, 2nd E (1936). D. F. Beatty, Vt Borodale (1919)	1905	R. N. C. Osborne & Dartmouth	..	1972	31
† Beauchamp, 7th E (1891). W. Lygon	1872	Eton	Oxford	1938	5^4, 6, 7
Beaumont, W. C. B. 2nd Ld Allendale (1907), 1st Vt (1911)	1860	Eton	Cambridge	1923	5^2, 7^2, 9

† Beaverbrook, 1st Ld (1917). Sir W. M. Aitken (Kt 1911)	1879	Hawkins Acad.*	..	1964	11, 26[2], 27[3], 29[2], 31
Beck, Sir (A.) C. T. (Kt 1920)	1878	Haileybury	Cambridge	1932	7, 9, 12, 13
Beechman, (N.) A.	1896	Westminster	Oxford	1965	30, 32
Belcher, J. W.	1905	Latymer Upper	London	1964	34
† Bellenger, F. J.	1894	Elementary	..	1968	35[2]
Bellwin, Ld (Life Peer 1979) I. Bellow	1923	Leeds G.S.	Leeds	..	61[2]
† Belper, 2nd Ld (1880). H. Strutt	1840	Harrow	Cambridge	1914	4
† Belstead, 2nd Ld (1958). J. J. Ganzoni	1932	Eton	Oxford	..	52[2], 59, 60
† Benn, A. Wedgwood	1925	Westminster	Oxford	..	48, 49, 56, 57
† Benn, W. Wedgwood, 1st Vt Stansgate (1941)	1877	Paris Lycée	London	1960	7, 19, 33
Bennett of Edgbaston, 1st Ld (1953), Sir P. F. Bennett (Kt 1941)	1880	King Edward's Birmingham	..	1957	37
Bennett, Sir E. N. (Kt 1930)	1868	Durham	Oxford	1947	20, 25
Bernays, R. H.	1902	Rossall	Oxford	1945	23, 24
Berry, Sir A. G. (Kt 1983)	1925	Eton	Oxford	1984	64[3]
Bessborough, 10th E of (1956). F. E. N. Ponsonby, Vt Duncannon (1920)	1913	Eton	Cambridge	..	42[2], 53
† Beswick, Ld (Life Peer 1964). F. Beswick	1912	Elementary	..	..	33, 46[3], 50[2], 57
Bethell, 4th Ld (1967). N. W. Bethell	1938	Harrow	Cambridge	..	54
† Betterton, Sir H. B. (1st Bt 1929). 1st Ld Rushcliffe (1935)	1872	Rugby	Oxford	1949	14, 17, 20, 21
† Bevan, A.	1897	Elementary	..	1960	34[2]
† Bevin, E.	1881	Elementary	..	1951	27, 28, 33[2]
† Bevins, (J.) R.	1908	Liverpool Coll.	..	..	39, 42, 44
† Biffen (W.) J.	1930	Dr Morgan's G.S.*	Cambridge	..	59[3], 62
† Bingley, 1st Ld (1933). G. R. Lane-Fox	1870	Eton	Oxford	1947	15, 17
† Birch, (E.) N. C., Ld Rhyl (Life Peer 1970)	1906	Eton	..	1981	37, 38[2], 39, 40
Birk, Lady (Life Peeress 1967). Alma Birk	1921	Hampstead H.S.*	London	..	55, 56, 59
† Birkenhead, 1st E of (1922). Sir F. E. Smith (Kt 1915), 1st Ld Birkenhead (1919), 1st Vt (1921)	1872	Birkenhead	Oxford	1930	8, 9, 13, 17
Birkenhead, 2nd E of (1930). F. W. F. Smith, Vt Furneaux (1922)	1907	Eton	Oxford	1975	26, 39
Birnam, Ld (Scot. judge 1945). Sir (T.) D. K. Murray (Kt 1941)	1884	Hamilton Acad.* & Glasgow H.S.*	Glasgow	1955	30, 32
† Birrell, A.	1850	Amersham Hall*	Cambridge	1933	4[2], 6, 8
Bishopston, Ld (Life Peer 1981). E. S. Bishop	1920	S. Bristol C.S.*	Bristol	1984	50, 55[2]
Blades, Ld (Scot. judge 1947). D. P. Blades	1888	Berwickshire	Edinburgh	1959	36
† Blakenham, 1st Vt (1963). J. H. Hare	1911	Eton	..	1982	37, 39, 41, 42[2], 44
† Blaker, Sir P.A.R. (K.C.M.G. 1983)	1922	Shrewsbury	Toronto & Oxford	..	51[2], 59, 60
† Bledisloe, 1st Vt (1935). Sir C. Bathurst (K.B.E. 1917), 1st Ld Bledisloe (1918)	1867	Sherborne & Eton	Oxford	1958	12, 17
Blenkinsop, A.	1911	Newcastle upon Tyne Royal G.S.	..	1979	34, 35, 36
Blindell, Sir J. (Kt 1936)	1884	St. Mary's, Hitchin*	..	1937	22, 25
Boardman, Ld (Life Peer 1980). T. G. Boardman	1919	Bromsgrove	..	..	51, 53
† Bondfield, Miss M. G.	1873	Elementary	..	1953	16, 19

† Booth, A. E.	1928	St. Thomas's Sch.*, Winchester	..	..	56^2
Boothby, Ld (Life Peer 1958). Sir R. J. G. Boothby (K.B.E. 1953)	1900	Eton	Oxford	..	28
Boothroyd, Miss B.	1929	Dewsbury Tech C.*	..	..	58
Boscawen, R. T.	1923	Eton	Cambridge	..	60
Boston of Faversham, Ld (Life Peer 1976). T. G. Boston	1930	Woolwich Polytechnic Sch.*	London	..	50
† Bottomley, Ld (Life Peer). A. G. Bottomley	1907	Elementary	..	..	33, 34, 46, 47
† Bottomley, P. J.	1944	Westminster	Cambridge	..	60
Boulton, Sir W. W. (1st Bt 1944)	1873	Privately	..	1949	30, 31
Bowden, Ld (Life Peer 1964). B. V. Bowden	1910	Chesterfield G.S.*	Cambridge	..	47
† Bowden, H. W., Ld Aylestone (Life Peer 1967)	1905	Secondary	..	..	36, 45, 46
Bowles, Ld (Life Peer 1964). F. G. Bowles	1902	Highgate	London	1970	50
Bowyer, Sir G. E. W. (Kt 1929). 1st Ld Denham (1937)	1886	Eton	Oxford	1948	18, 23, 26
† Boyd, 1st Vt (1960). A. T. Lennox-Boyd	1904	Sherborne	Oxford	1983	23, 24, 27, 31, 37^2, 39, 42
Boyd-Carpenter, Sir A. B. (Kt 1926)	1873	Harrow	Oxford	1937	14^3, 15
† Boyd-Carpenter, Ld (Life Peer 1972). J. A. Boyd-Carpenter.	1908	Stowe	Oxford	..	36, 37, 39^2, 42, 43
Boyden, H. J.	1910	Tiffin's*	London	..	46, 47, 48
† Boyle, Ld Boyle of Handsworth (Life Peer 1970). Sir E. C. G. (3rd Bt 1945)	1923	Eton	Oxford	1981	36, 39, 40, 41, 42^1
Boyson, R. R.	1925	Haslingden G.S.*	Manchester & Cambridge	..	60, 61, 62
† Brabazon, 1st Ld (1942). J. T. C. Moore-Brabazon	1884	Harrow	Cambridge	1964	15, 18, 26, 27, 29
Brabazon, 3rd Ld(1974) I. A. Moore-Brabazon	1946	Harrow	..	..	64
Brabner, R. A.	1911	Felstead	Cambridge	1945	27
† Brace, W.	1865	Elementary	..	1947	8, 10
† Bracken, 1st Vt (1952). B. Bracken	1901	Sedbergh	..	1958	28
Bradford, 5th E of (1915). O. Bridgeman, Vt Newport (1898)	1873	Harrow	Cambridge	1957	13, 15
† Braine, Sir B. R. (Kt 1972)	1914	Hendon C.S.*	..	..	41, 43^2
Braithwaite, Sir J. G. (1st Bt 1954)	1895	Bootham	..	1958	39
Brand, Ld (Scot. judge 1972). D. W. R. Brand	1923	Stonyhurst	Edinburgh	..	54
Bray, J. W.	1930	Kingswood	Cambridge	..	48^2
Brayley, Ld (Life Peer 1973). Sir J. D. Brayley (Kt 1970)	1917	Secondary	..	1977	55
† Brecon, 1st Ld (1957) D. V. P. Lewis	1905	Monmouth*	..	1976	42
† Brentford, 1st Vt (1929). Sir W. Joynson-Hicks (1st Bt 1919)	1865	Merchant Taylors' Sch.	..	1932	14^2, 15^3, 17
Brentford, 3rd Vt (1958). L. W. Joynson-Hicks	1902	Winchester	Oxford	1983	38
† Bridgeman, 1st Vt (1929). W. C. Bridgeman	1864	Eton	Cambridge	1935	9, 11^3, 14, 17
Bridport, 3rd Vt (1924). R. A. H. N. Hood	1911	R.N. Coll., Dartmouth	..	1969	26
† Brittan, L.	1939	Haberdasher's Aske's	Cambridge	..	59, 60^2
† Brodrick, (W.) St J. 9th Vt Midleton (1907), 1st E of (1920)	1856	Eton	Oxford	1942	2^2, 3
Bromley-Davenport, Sir W. (K.C.B. 1924)	1862	Eton	Oxford	1949	3
† Brooke of Cumnor, Ld (Life Peer 1966). H. Brooke	1903	Marlborough	Oxford	1984	36, 41, 42^2
Brooke, P. L.	1934	Marlborough	Oxford	..	60, 63^2
Brooman-White, R. C.	1912	Eton	Cambridge	1964	42, 44, 45

† Brown, (A.) E.	1881	Torquay*	..	1962	20, 21, 24, 28^2, 29, 31
† Brown, G. A., Ld George-Brown (Life Peer 1970)	1914	Secondary	..	1985	33, 35, 45^2, 46
Brown, H. D.	1919	Whitehill S.S.*	..	..	57
Brown, R. C.	1921	Elementary	..	..	48, 56, 57
Brown, R. W.	1921	Elementary	..		50
Brown, T. W.	1879	Campbell Coll.	Belfast	1944	13^2
† Brown, Ld (Life Peer 1964). W. Brown	1908	Rossall	..	1985	48
† Browne, J. N., Ld Craigton (Life Peer 1959)	1904	Cheltenham	..	..	42^2
† Broxbourne, Ld (Life Peer 1983). Sir D. C. Walker-Smith (Bt 1960)	1910	Rossall	Oxford	..	36, 38, 43^2
Bruce-Gardyne, Ld (Life Peer 1983). J. Bruce-Gardyne	1930	Winchester	Oxford	..	59^2
Bruntisfield, 1st Ld (1942). Sir V. A. G. A. Warrender (8th Bt 1917)	1899	Eton	..	..	22^3, 23^2, 24, 27, 31
Bryan, Sir P. E. O. (Kt 1972)	1913	St John's, Leatherhead	Cambridge	..	44, 52
† Bryce, 1st Vt (1914). J. Bryce	1838	Glasgow H.S.*	Glasgow & Oxford	1922	4
Buchan, N.	1922	Kirkwall G.S.*	Glasgow	..	48, 55
† Buchan-Hepburn, P. G. T. 1st Ld Hailes (1957)	1901	Harrow	Cambridge	1974	25, 30^2, 32, 38, 39^2
† Buchanan, G.	1890	Elementary	..	1955	34, 35
† Buchanan, T. R.	1846	Sherborne	Oxford	1911	4, 6
† Buchanan-Smith, A. L.	1932	Edinburgh Acad.	Cambridge	..	53, 60, 61
Buck, Sir (P.) A. F. (Kt 1983)	1928	King's Sch., Ely	Cambridge	..	51
Buckley, A.	1877	Merchant Taylors', Crosby	..	1965	15^2
† Buckmaster, 1st Vt (1933). Sir S. O. Buckmaster (Kt 1913), 1st Ld (1915)	1861	Aldenham	Oxford	1934	7, 8
Budgen, N.	1937	St Edward's	Cambridge	..	63
Burden, 1st Ld (1950). T. W. Burden	1885	Elementary	London Sch. of Econ.	1970	36
† Burgin, (E.) L.	1887	Christ's Coll., Finchley*	Lausanne & Paris	1945	21, 24^4, 25
Burke, W. A.	1890	Secondary	..	1968	35
† Burns, J.	1858	Elementary	..	1943	4, 6^2
Burntwood, Ld (Life Peer 1970). J. W. Snow	1910	Haileybury	..	1982	36^2, 47, 48, 49
Butcher, Sir H. W. (Kt 1953)	1901	Hastings G.S.*	..	1966	39
Butcher, J. P.	1946	Huntingdon G.S.*	Birmingham & London	..	61, 62
† Butler of Saffron Walden, Ld (Life Peer 1965). R. A. Butler	1902	Marlborough	Cambridge	1982	20, 23, 24^2, 26, 28, 31, 36, 40^3, 41
† Butler, A. C.	1931	Eton	Cambridge	..	54, 60, 61, 62
† Buxton, 1st E (1920). S. C. Buxton, 1st Vt (1914)	1853	Clifton	Cambridge	1934	4, 6^2
† Buxton, N. E. N. 1st Ld Noel-Buxton (1930)	1869	Harrow	Cambridge	1948	16, 18
† Cadogan, 5th E (1873). Vt Chelsea (1864)	1840	Eton	Oxford	1915	2
Caithness, 20th E (1965). M. I. Sinclair	1948	Marlborough	..	..	64
† Caldecote, 1st Vt (1939). Sir T. W. H. Inskip (Kt 1922)	1876	Clifton	Cambridge	1947	15, 18^2, 21, 22, 23^2, 25, 28
† Callaghan, (L.) J.	1912	Portsmouth Nn*	..	..	34, 35, 45, 46, 55^2
† Cameron of Lochbroom, Ld (Life Peer 1984). K. T. Cameron	1931	Edinburgh Acad.	Oxford & Edinburgh	..	63
† Campbell, of Croy, Ld (Life Peer 1974). G. T. C. Campbell	1921	Wellington	..	..	42, 44, 52
† Campbell, Sir J. H. M. (1st Bt 1916). 1st Ld Glenavy (1921)	1851	Kingstown*	Dublin	1931	3, 9, 12, 13
† Campbell-Bannerman, Sir H. (G.C.B. 1895)	1836	Glasgow H.S.*	Glasgow	1908	4

† Caradon, Ld (Life Peer 1964). Sir H. Foot (K.C.M.G. 1951)	1907	Leighton Park	Cambridge	..	46
† Carlisle, M.	1929	Radley	Manchester	..	51^2, 60
Carmichael, Ld (Life Peer 1983). N. G. Carmichael	1921	Estbank Acad.*	..	..	48^2, 56, 57
† Carr of Hadley, Ld (Life Peer 1975). (L.) R. Carr	1916	Westminster	Cambridge	..	37, 42, 44, 50, 51, 52
† Carrington, 1st E (1895). C. R. Wynn-Carrington, 3rd Ld Carrington (1868), 1st M of Lincolnshire (1912)	1843	Eton	Cambridge	1928	4, 5, 6
† Carrington, 6th Ld (1938). P. A. R. Carington	1919	Eton	Sandhurst	..	37^2, 42, 43, 51, 52, 59
† Carson, Ld (Lord of Appeal 1921). Sir E. H. Carson (Kt 1900)	1854	Portarlington*	Dublin	1935	3, 8, 10, 11
Carter, R. J.	1935	Mortlake Co. S.S.*	..	..	57
Cary, Sir R. A. (1st Bt 1955)	1898	Ardingly	Sandhurst	1979	32
† Casey, Ld (Life Peer 1960). R. G. Casey	1890	Melbourne G.S.	Melbourne & Cambridge	1976	27
† Castle, Mrs B. A.	1911	Bradford G.G.S.	Oxford	..	45, 47^2, 48, 57
† Causton, R. K. 1st Ld Southwark (1910)	1843	Privately	..	1929	4, 7
† Cave, 1st Vt (1918). Sir G. Cave (Kt 1915)	1856	Merchant Taylors'	Oxford	1928	9, 10, 14, 17
† Cavendish, V. C. W. 9th D of Devonshire (1908)	1868	Eton	Cambridge	1938	2, 3, 8, 14
† Cawdor, 3rd E (1898). F. A. V. Campbell, Vt Emlyn (1847)	1847	Eton	Oxford	1911	2
† Cawley, 1st Ld (1918). Sir F. Cawley (1st Bt 1906)	1850	Secondary	..	1937	11
Cazalet-Keir, Mrs T.	1899	Privately	..	..	32
† Cecil of Chelwood, 1st Vt (1923). Ld R. Cecil	1864	Eton	Oxford	1958	8^2, 10, 12, 14, 17
Chadwick, Sir R. Burton (Kt 1920)	1869	Birkenhead & Privately	..	1951	17
† Chalfont, Ld (Life Peer 1964). A. Gwynne-Jones	1919	W. Monmouth S.*	..	..	46
Chalker, Mrs L.	1942	Roedean	London	..	61, 62^2
† Chamberlain, (A.) N.	1869	Rugby	Birmingham	1940	12, 14^2, 15^2, 17, 20^2, 22, 23, 26
† Chamberlain, J.	1836	University Coll. Sch.	..	1914	2
† Chamberlain, Sir (J.) A. (K.G. 1925)	1863	Rugby	Cambridge	1937	2^4, 8, 9^3, 10, 11, 17, 21
Chambers, J.	1863	Royal Acad. Institution	Queen's Coll., Belfast	1917	13
† Champion, Ld (Life Peer 1962). A. J. Champion	1897	St. John's, Glastonbury*	..	1985	33, 49
† Chandos, 1st Vt (1954). O. Lyttelton	1893	Eton	Cambridge	1972	26, 27^2, 29, 31^2, 37
† Channon, (H.) P. G.	1935	Eton	Oxford	..	52^4, 59, 60, 62, 63
† Chaplin, 1st Vt (1916). H. Chaplin	1840	Harrow	Oxford	1923	2
Chapman, A.	1897	Secondary	Cambridge	1966	29^2, 31
Charleton, H. C.	1870	Elementary	..	1959	19
† Chataway, C. J.	1931	Sherborne	Oxford	..	42^2, 53^2
† Chatfield, 1st Ld (1937). Sir A. E. M. Chatfield (K.C.M.G. 1919)	1873	H.M.S. Britannia*	..	1967	23^2
† Chelmsford, 1st Vt (1921). F. J. N. Thesiger, 3rd Ld Chelmsford (1905)	1868	Winchester	Oxford	1933	16
Cherry, R. R.	1859	Secondary	Dublin	1923	5, 7
† Cherwell, 1st Vt (1956). F. A. Lindemann, 1st Ld Cherwell (1941)	1886	Blair Lodge* & Darmstadt	Berlin	1957	29, 32, 37
Chesham, 3rd Ld (1882)	1850	Eton	..	1907	4
† Chesham, 5th Ld (1952). J. C. C. Cavendish	1916	Eton	Cambridge	..	39, 43, 44

† Chesterfield, 10th E of (1887). E. F. S.-Stanhope	1854	Eton	Oxford	1933	7, 9, 13
Chichester-Clark, Sir R. (Kt 1974)	1928	R.N. College*	Cambridge	..	44, 45, 52
† Chilston, 1st Vt (1911). A. Akers-Douglas	1851	Eton	Oxford	1926	2, 3
Chorley, 1st Ld (1945). R. S. T. Chorley	1895	Kendal*	Oxford	1978	36
Churchill, 1st Vt (1902) V. A. F. S. Churchill, 3rd Ld (1886)	1864	Eton	Sandhurst	1934	3
† Churchill, Sir W. L. S. (K.G. 1953)	1874	Harrow	Sandhurst	1965	4, 6^3, 8, 10, 11, 12^2, 17, 23, 26^2, 31^2, 36, 37
† Chuter-Ede, Ld (Life Peer 1964). J. C. Ede	1882	Dorking H.S.*	Cambridge	1965	28, 33
† Cilcennin, 1st Vt (1955). J. P. L. Thomas	1903	Rugby	Oxford	1960	27, 30, 31, 38^2
Clarendon 5th E of (1870). E. H. Villiers. Ld Hyde (1846)	1846	Harrow	Cambridge	1914	3^2
Clarendon, 6th E of (1914). G. H. H. Villiers, Ld Hyde (1877)	1877	Eton	..	1955	13, 15, 17, 18
Clark, A. K. M.	1928	Eton	Oxford	..	60,
† Clarke, K. H.	1940	Nottingham H.S.	Cambridge	..	54^2, 61, 62^2
† Cledwyn of Penrhos Ld (Life Peer 1979). C. Hughes	1916	Holyhead G.S.*	Aberystwyth	..	46^2, 48
Clegg, Sir W. (Kt 1980)	1920	Bury G.S.	Manchester	..	54^2
Clifden, 7th Vt (1930). F. G. Agar-Robartes	1883	Eton	Oxford	1966	30
† Clinton, 21st Ld (1904). C. J. R. H.-S.-F.-Trefusis	1863	Eton	..	1957	10
† Clitheroe, 1st Ld (1955). R. Assheton	1901	Eton	Oxford	1984	24, 26, 27, 29
† Clyde, Ld (Scot. judge 1920). J. A. Clyde	1863	Edinburgh Academy	Edinburgh	1944	3, 13
† Clyde, Ld (Scot. judge 1954). J. L. M. Clyde	1898	Edinburgh Academy	Oxford & Edinburgh	1975	39
† Clydesmuir, 1st Ld (1947). Sir D. J. Colville (G.C.I.E. 1943)	1894	Charterhouse	Cambridge	1954	21, 23, 24^3
† Clynes, J. R.	1869	Elementary	..	1949	12^2, 16, 18
Cobham, 9th Vt (1922). J. C. Lyttelton	1881	Eton	..	1949	24
Cochrane of Cults, 1st Ld (1919). T. H. A. E. Cochrane	1857	Eton	..	1951	2
† Cockfield, Ld (Life Peer 1978). Sir A. C. Cockfield (Kt 1973)	1916	Dover County*	London	..	59, 61, 62
† Cocks, M. F. L.	1929	Secondary	Bristol	..	58^3
† Colebrooke, 1st Ld (1906). Sir E. A. Colebrooke (5th Bt 1890)	1861	Eton	..	1939	5, 7^2, 9, 13
Coleman, D. R.	1925	Cadoxton Boys' Sch.*	..	..	58, 59
† Coleraine, 1st Ld (1954). R. K. Law	1901	Shrewsbury	Oxford	1980	26^2, 30, 32
Collick, P. H.	1897	Elementary	..	..	33
Collindridge, F.	1890	Elementary	..	1951	36^2
† Collings, J.	1831	Plymouth*	..	1920	2
† Collins, Sir G. P. (K.B.E. 1919)	1875	H.M.S. Britannia*	..	1936	13, 20, 24
† Collins, V. J. Ld Stonham (Life Peer 1958)	1903	Regent St. Poly.*	London	1971	45^2
† Colville, Sir D. J. (G.C.I.E. 1943). 1st Ld Clydesmuir (1947)	1894	Charterhouse	Cambridge	1954	21, 23, 24^3
Colville of Culross, 4th Vt. J. M. A. Colville	1933	Rugby	Oxford	..	51
† Colyton, 1st Ld (1955). H. L. D. Hopkinson	1902	Eton	Cambridge	..	37, 38, 40
† Compton-Rickett, Sir J. (Kt 1907)	1847	K. Edward VI, Bath* & privately	..	1919	12
Conant, Sir R. J. E. (1st Bt 1954)	1899	Eton	Sandhurst	1973	39
† Concannon, (J.) D.	1930	Rossington S.S.*	..	..	50, 57^2, 59

Conesford, 1st Ld (1955). H. G. Strauss	1892	Rugby	Oxford	1974	29, 30, 38
Constable, Ld (Scot. judge 1922). A. H. B. Constable	1865	Dollar*	Edinburgh	1928	13
Cook, T. F.	1908	Cardenden*	..	1952	33
† Cooper, A. Duff, 1st Vt Norwich (1952)	1890	Eton	Oxford	1954	17, 20, 21, 23^2, 24, 28^2
† Cooper of Culross, 1st Ld (1954). T. M. Cooper	1892	George Watson's Coll., Edin.	Edinburgh	1955	22, 25^2, 30
Cope, 1st Ld (1945). Sir W. Cope (1st Bt 1928)	1870	Repton	Cambridge	1946	15, 18^2
Cope, J. A.	1937	Oakham	..	..	63^2, 64
† Corfield, Sir F. V. (Kt 1974)	1915	Cheltenham	Woolwich	..	42, 53^2
† Cornwall, Sir E. (Kt 1905)	1863	Elementary	..	1953	13
† Cousins, F.	1904	Elementary	..	..	48
† Coventry, 9th E of (1843)	1838	Eton	Oxford	1930	4
† Cowdray, 1st Vt (1916). W. D. Pearson, 1st Bt (1894), 1st Ld (1910)	1856	Privately	..	1927	12
Cowley, 6th E (1968). R. F. Wellesley	1946	Eton	Birmingham	1975	54
Cox, Lady (Life Peeress 1982). Mrs C. A. Cox	1937	Channing Sch.*	London	..	64
Cox, T. M.	1930	Secondary	London	..	58^2
† Craig, C. C.	1869	Clifton	..	1960	15
† Craig, Sir J. (Bt 1918). 1st Vt Craigavon (1927)	1871	Merchiston Castle	..	1940	10, 12, 13
† Craigavon, 1st Vt (1927). Sir J. Craig (1st Bt 1918)	1871	Merchiston Castle	..	1940	10, 12, 13
Craigmyle, 1st Ld (1929). T. Shaw. Ld Shaw (Ld of Appeal 1909)	1850	Dunfermline H.S.*	Edinburgh	1937	5, 7
† Craigton, Ld (Life Peer 1959). J. N. Browne	1904	Cheltenham	..	..	42^2
† Cranborne, Vt (1865). R. A. T. Gascoyne-Cecil, 3rd M of Salisbury (1868)	1830	Eton	Oxford	1903	1^2, 2
† Cranborne, Vt (1868). J. E. H. Gascoyne-Cecil, 4th M of Salisbury (1903)	1861	Eton	Oxford	1947	1, 2, 3, 14^2, 17
† Cranborne, Vt (1903). R. A. J. Gascoyne-Cecil, 5th M of Salisbury (1947)	1893	Eton	Oxford	1972	23, 26, 27, 28^2, 29^2, 31, 36^2, 37, 40
† Crathorne, 1st Ld (1959). Sir T. L. Dugdale (1st Bt 1945)	1897	Eton	Sandhurst	1977	25, 30, 37, 38
Craven, 4th E of (1883). W. G. R. Craven	1868	Eton	..	1921	7
† Crawford, 27th E of (1913). D. A. E. Lindsay, Ld Balcarres (1880)	1871	Eton	Oxford	1940	3, 8, 9, 11, 12^3, 13^2
† Crawford, 29th E of (1975). R. A. Lindsay. Ld Balniel (1940) (Life Peer 1974)	1927	Eton	Cambridge	..	51^2
Crawley, A. M.	1908	Harrow	Oxford	..	34
† Crewe, 1st M of (1911). R. O. A. Crewe-Milnes, 2nd Ld Houghton (1885), 1st E of Crewe (1895)	1858	Harrow	Cambridge	1945	4, 5^2, 6^3, 8^2, 21
† Cripps, Sir (R.) S. (Kt 1930)	1889	Winchester	London	1952	19, 26, 27, 33^2, 34
Croft, 1st Ld (1940). Sir H. Page Croft (1st Bt 1924)	1881	Eton & Shrewsbury	Cambridge	1947	30, 31
† Cromer, 2nd E of (1917). R. T. Baring, Vt Errington (1901)	1877	Eton	..	1953	15
† Crookshank, 1st Vt (1956). H. F. C. Crookshank	1893	Eton	Oxford	1961	20, 23, 24, 26, 29, 32, 36, 37
† Crosland, (C.) A. R.	1918	Highgate	Oxford	1977	45^2, 47^2, 48, 55, 56
† Cross, 1st Vt (1886). R. Cross	1823	Rugby	Cambridge	1914	1
† Cross, Sir R. H. (1st Bt 1941)	1896	Eton	..	1968	24, 25^2, 26, 29
† Crossley, Sir S. B. (2nd Bt 1872). 1st Ld Somerleyton (1916)	1857	Eton	Oxford	1935	3, 13, 15
† Crossman, R. H. S.	1907	Winchester	Oxford	1974	45, 47^2

Crowther-Hunt, Ld (Life Peer 1973). N. C. Hunt	1920	Bellevue H.S. Bradford*	Cambridge	..	55, 56
Cryer, (G.) R.	1934	Salt H.S.*	Hull	..	57
Cullen of Ashbourne, (2nd Ld 1932). C. B. M. Cokayne	1912	Eton	..	..	64
† Cunliffe-Lister, Sir P. (K.B.E. 1920). *Born Lloyd-Greame, changed name to Cunliffe-Lister* 1924. 1st Vt Swinton (1935). 1st E of Swinton (1955)	1884	Winchester	Oxford	1972	11^{2}, 15, 17, 20, 21, 23, 27, 28, 32, 37, 38^{2}
Cunningham, J. A.	1939	Jarrow G.S.*	Durham	..	56
† Curzon, 1st M (1921). G. N. Curzon. 1st Ld Curzon of Kedleston (1898), 1st E (1911)	1859	Eton	Oxford	1925	8, 9^{2}, 10, 14, 17
Curzon, Vt (1876). R. G. P. Curzon. 4th Earl Howe (1900)	1861	Eton	Oxford	1929	3^{2}
Curzon, Vt (1900). F. R. H. P. Curzon, 5th Earl Howe (1929)	1884	Eton	Oxford	1964	18
† Cushendun, 1st Ld (1927). R. J. McNeill	1861	Harrow	Oxford	1934	14, 17^{3}
† Dalton, Ld (Life Peer 1960). (E.) H. J. N. Dalton	1887	Eton	Cambridge	1962	18, 28, 29, 33, 34^{2}, 35^{2}
† Darling of Hillsborough, Ld (Life Peer 1974). G. Darling	1905	Elementary	Liverpool & Cambridge	..	48
Darwen, 1st Ld (1946). J. P. Davies	1885	Bootham	..	1950	36
† Daryngton, 1st Ld (1923). H. Pike Pease	1867	Brighton Coll.	Cambridge	1949	9, 12
David, Lady (Life Peeress 1978). Mrs N. R. David	1913	St Felix S.	Cambridge	..	59
† Davidson, 1st Vt (1937). Sir J. C. C. Davidson (G.C.V.O. 1935)	1889	Westminster	Cambridge	1970	14, 15, 17, 21, 25
Davidson, A.	1928	King George V Sch. Southport*	Cambridge	..	58
Davies, B	1939	Redditch H.S.*	London	..	58
† Davies, (D. J.) D.	1938	Carmarthen G.S.*	Oxford	..	55
Davies, E. A.	1926	Coventry Tech. Sch.*	St. Andrews' & Cambridge	..	48
Davies, E. A. J.	1902	Wycliffe Coll.	London	..	33
Davies, Sir G. F. (Kt 1936)	1875	Uppingham	Cambridge	1950	22, 25, 26^{2}
† Davies, of Leek, Ld (Life Peer 1970). H. Davies	1904	Lewis Sch.*	London	..	48^{2}
Davies, I.	1910	Elementary	..	1984	48, 49
† Davies, J. E. H. (Life Peer 1979)[1]	1916	St. Edward's	..	1979	52, 53^{2}
Davies, R. J.	1877	Elementary	..	1954	16
Davis, S. C.	1928	Mercers' Sch.*	London	..	58
Davison, J. E.	1870	Elementary	..	1927	16
Deakins, E. P.	1932	Tottenham G.S.*	London	..	57, 58
Dean, Sir (A.) P. (Kt 1985)	1924	Ellesmere Coll.	Oxford	..	52
Dean of Beswick, Ld (Life Peer 1983). J. Dean	1923	St. Anne, Ancoats*	..	..	58
† Deedes, W. F.	1913	Harrow	..	..	37^{2}, 42
de Ferranti, B. R. Z.	1930	Eton	Cambridge	..	41
† de Freitas, Sir G. S. (K.C.M.G. 1961)	1913	Haileybury	Cambridge	1982	33, 34
† Delacourt-Smith, Ld (Life Peer 1967). C. G. P. Smith	1917	County Boys Sch. Windsor*	Oxford	1972	48
† De La Warr, 9th E (1915). H. E. D. B. Sackville, Ld Buckhurst (1900)	1900	Eton	Oxford	1976	16, 18, 19^{2}, 20, 22, 23^{4}, 25, 39
† De L'Isle, 1st Vt (1956). W. P. Sidney, 6th Ld De L'Isle & Dudley (1945)	1909	Eton	Cambridge	..	32, 38
† Dell, E.	1921	Owen's Sch.*	Oxford	..	45, 47, 48^{2}, 55
Denbigh, 9th E of (1892). R. B. A. A. Fielding	1859	Oscott Coll., Birmingham*	Woolwich	1939	3

[1] Died before grant of Letters Patent.

Denham, 1st Ld (1937). Sir G. E. W. Bowyer (Kt 1929)	1886	Eton	Oxford	1948	18, 23, 26
† Denham, 2nd Ld (1948). B. S. M. Bowyer	1927	Eton	Cambridge	..	45, 54^{2}, 64
† Denman, 3rd Ld (1894). T. Denman	1874	Wellington	Sandhurst	1954	5^{2}, 7
† Derby, 17th E of (1908). E. G. V. Stanley, Ld Stanley (1893)	1865	Wellington	..	1948	2, 3^{2}, 8, 12, 15
Derwent, 4th Ld (1949). P. V.-B. Johnstone	1901	Charterhouse	Sandhurst	..	41, 43
Desborough, 1st Ld (1905) W. H. Grenfell	1855	Harrow	Oxford	1945	18
† Devonport, 1st Vt (1917). Sir H. E. Kearley (1st Bt 1908), 1st Ld Devonport (1910)	1856	Cranleigh	..	1934	4, 6, 12
† Devonshire, 8th D of (1891). S. C. Cavendish, M of Hartington (1858)	1833	Privately	Cambridge	1908	1, 2
† Devonshire, 9th D of (1908). V. C. W. Cavendish	1868	Eton	Cambridge	1938	2, 3, 8, 14
Devonshire, 10th D of (1938). E. W. S. Cavendish, M of Hartington (1908)	1895	Eton	Cambridge	1950	23, 27, 28, 31
† Devonshire, 11th D of (1950). A. R. B. Cavendish, M of Hartington (1944)	1920	Eton	Cambridge	..	41^{2}
Dewar, Ld (Scot. judge 1910). A. Dewar	1860	Perth Academy*	Edinburgh	1917	7
† Diamond, Ld Diamond (Life Peer 1970). J. Diamond	1907	Leeds G.S.	..	..	45^{2}
Dickson, Ld (Scot. judge 1915). S. Dickson	1850	Glasgow H.S.*	Glasgow & Edinburgh	1922	3^{2}
Digby, (K.) S. D. W.	1910	Harrow	Cambridge	..	38
† Dilhorne, 1st Ld (1962). 1st Vt (1964). Sir R. E. Manningham-Buller (Kt 1951) (4th Bt 1956)	1905	Eton	Oxford	1980	32, 39^{2}, 40, 44
Dobson, R. F. H.	1925	Purbrook Park G.S.*	Oxford	1980	50
Dodds-Parker, Sir A. D. (Kt 1973)	1909	Winchester	Oxford	..	36
Donaldson, Ld (Life Peer 1967). J. G. S. Donaldson	1907	Eton	Cambridge	..	56, 57
† Donoughmore, 6th E of (1900). R. W. J. Hely-Hutchinson	1875	Eton	Oxford	1948	3
Dormand, J. D.	1919	Bede Coll.*	Oxford & Harvard	..	58^{2}
† Dorman-Smith, Sir R. H. (Kt 1937)	1899	Harrow	Sandhurst	1977	23
Douglas-Hamilton, Ld J.	1942	Eton	Oxford	..	63
† Douglas-Home, Sir A. F., Ld Dunglass (1918), 14th E of Home (1951-63). Ld Home of the Hirsel (Life Peer 1974)	1903	Eton	Oxford	..	31, 37, 38, 40^{4}, 41, 51
Doverdale, 2nd Ld (1925). O. Partington	1872	Rossall	..	1935	7
† Downham, 1st Ld (1918). W. Hayes Fisher	1853	Haileybury	Oxford	1920	2, 3, 8, 10, 11^{2}
Drewe, Sir C. (K.C.V.O. 1953)	1896	Eton	Woolwich	1971	30, 32, 39
† Drumalbyn, 1st Ld (1963). N. M. S. Macpherson	1908	Fettes	Oxford	..	38, 42, 43^{2}, 53
† du Cann, Sir E. D. L. (K.B.E. 1985)	1924	Woolbridge*	Oxford	..	40, 43
† Dudley, 2nd E (1885). W. H. Ward, Vt Ednam (1867)	1867	Eton	..	1932	2, 3
Dufferin & Ava, 4th M of (1930). B. S. H.-T.-Blackwood, E of Ava (1918)	1909	Eton	Oxford	1945	23, 26
Duffy, (A. E.) P.	1920	Secondary	L.S.E. and Columbia, N.Y.	..	56
† Dugdale, J.	1905	Wellington	Oxford	1963	33, 34

† Dugdale, Sir T. L. (1st Bt 1945). 1st Ld Crathorne (1959)	1897	Eton	Sandhurst	1977	25, 30, 37, 38
† Duke, Sir H. E. (Kt 1918). 1st Ld Merrivale (1925)	1855	Elementary	..	1939	8, 10
† Duncan, Sir A. R. (Kt 1921)	1884	Secondary	Glasgow	1952	24, 27, 29^4, 32
† Duncan-Sandys, Ld (Life Peer 1974). D. Sandys	1908	Eton	Oxford	..	29, 30^2, 32, 37, 39, 41^4
Dundas, Ld (Scot. judge 1905). D. Dundas	1854	Edinburgh Academy	Oxford & Edinburgh	1922	3
† Dundee, 11th E of (1953). H. J. Scrymgeour-Wedderburn, Vt Dudhope (1952)	1902	Winchester	Oxford	1983	24, 29, 40, 43
† Dunedin, 1st Vt (1926). A. G. Murray, 1st Ld Dunedin (1905)	1849	Harrow	Cambridge	1942	2, 3
† Dunglass, Ld (1918). Sir A. F. Douglas-Home. 14th E of Home (1951-63), Ld Home of the Hirsel (Life Peer 1974)	1903	Eton	Oxford	..	31, 37, 38, 40^4, 41, 51
Dunn, J. A.	1926	St. Theresa's Sch.*	London	..	57, 58
Dunn, R. J.	1946	Cromwell Rd., Pendlebury	Salford	..	60
† Dunrossil, 1st Vt (1959). W. S. Morrison	1893	George Watson's Coll., Edin.	Edinburgh	1961	23^2, 24, 25, 29^2, 32
Dunwoody, Mrs G.	1930	Notre Dame Convent*	..	..	48
Dunwoody, J. E. O.	1929	St. Paul's	London	..	47
Durant, (R.) T.	1928	Bryanston	..	..	63
Durbin, E. F. M.	1906	Taunton	Oxford	1948	35
Eadie, A.	1920	Buckhaven S.S.*	..	..	56
Ebury, 5th Ld (1932). R. E. Grosvenor	1914	Harrow	..	1957	26
† Eccles, 1st Ld (1962). 1st Vt (1964) Sir D. M. Eccles (K.C.V.O. 1953)	1904	Winchester	Oxford	..	37, 39, 42, 43, 53
† Ede, J. C., Ld Chuter-Ede (Life Peer 1964)	1882	Dorking H.S.*	Cambridge	1965	28, 33
† Eden of Winton, Ld (Life Peer 1983). Sir J. B. (9th Bt 1963)	1925	Eton	..	..	53^3
† Eden, Sir (R.) A. (K.G. 1954). 1st E of Avon (1961)	1897	Eton	Oxford	1977	20, 21, 23^2, 24, 26 30, 31, 36^2
Edge, Sir W. (Kt 1922)	1880	Bolton G.S.*	..	1948	13
Edmondson, Sir A. J. (Kt 1934). 1st Ld Sandford (1945)	1887	University Coll. Sch.	..	1959	25, 26, 30, 31, 32
† Edwards, Sir C. (Kt 1935)	1867	Elementary	..	1954	19, 30
† Edwards, (L.) J.	1904	Aylesbury G.S.*	Leeds	1959	33, 34^2
† Edwards, N.	1897	Elementary	..	1968	34, 35
† Edwards, (R.) N.	1934	Westminster	Cambridge	..	62
Edwards, W. J.	1900	Secondary	..	1964	34
† Elgin, 9th E of (1863). V. A. Bruce	1849	Eton	Oxford	1917	4
† Elibank, Master of (1st Ld Murray of Elibank 1912). A. W. C. O. Murray	1870	Cheltenham	..	1920	5, 6, 7^2
† Elliot, W. E.	1888	Glasgow Academy	Glasgow	1958	14, 17^2, 20^2, 23^2, 24
Elliott, A.	1846	Privately	Edinburgh & Cambridge	1923	2
Elliott of Morpeth, Ld (Life Peer 1985). Sir R. W. Elliott (Kt1974)	1920	Morpeth G.S.*	..	..	54
Ellis, J.	1934	Rastrick G.S.*	..	..	58
† Ellis, J. E.	1841	Friends' Schs.*	..	1910	4
Elton, 2nd Ld (1973). R. Elton	1930	Eton	Oxford	..	60, 61^2, 62
† Elwyn-Jones, Ld (Life Peer 1974). Sir F. E. Jones (Kt 1964)	1909	Llanelli G.S.*	Aberystwyth & Cambridge	..	49, 55
Elystan-Morgan, Ld (Life Peer 1981). (D.) E. Morgan	1932	Ardwyn G.S.*	Aberystwyth	..	46
Emery, (Kt 1982) Sir P. F. H.	1926	Scotch Plains U.S.A.*	Oxford	..	52, 53
† Emmott, 1st Ld (1911). A. Emmott	1858	Grove House, Tottenham*	London	1926	6^2
Emrys-Evans, P. V.	1894	Harrow	Cambridge	1967	28, 31

† Ennals, Ld (Life Peer 1983). D. H.	1922	Q. Mary's G.S. Walsall*	..	..	46^2, 47, 55, 57
Erne, 5th E of (1914). J. H. G. Crichton	1907	Eton	Sandhurst	1940	26
† Ernle, 1st Ld (1919). R. E. Prothero	1851	Marlborough	Oxford	1937	10
Erroll, 20th E of (1891). C. G. Hay	1852	Harrow	..	1927	3
† Erroll of Hale, 1st Ld (1964). F. J. Erroll	1914	Oundle	Cambridge	..	38, 39, 40, 42, 43^2, 44
Evans, I. L.	1927	Llanelly G.S.*	Swansea	1984	50^2
Evans, J.	1930	Jarrow Cent. S.*	..	..	58
Evans, S. N.	1898	Elementary	..	1970	35
† Evans, Sir S. T. (G.C.B. 1916)	1859	Secondary	London	1918	5, 7
Ewing, H.	1931	Beith H.S.*	..	..	57
Eyre, Sir R. E. (Kt 1983)	1924	King Edwards, Birmingham	Cambridge	..	52, 54^2, 62^2
† Eyres-Monsell, Sir B. M. (G.B.E. 1929). 1st Vt Monsell (1935)	1881	H.M.S. Britannia*	..	1969	10, 13, 14, 15, 18, 20, 21^2, 23
Fairbairn, N.	1933	Loretto	Edinburgh	..	63
Fairfax, 13th Ld (1939). T. B. M. Fairfax	1923	Eton	..	1964	39, 44
Fairgrieve, Sir (T.) R. (Kt 1981)	1924	Sedburgh	..	..	62
Fanshawe, Ld (Life Peer 1983). Sir A. H. F. Royle K.C.M.G. 1974)	1927	Harrow	Sandhurst	..	51
† Farquhar, 1st E (1922). Sir H. B. Farquhar (1st Bt 1892), 1st Ld (1898), 1st Vt (1917)	1844	Privately	..	1923	9, 13
† Fellowes, Sir A. E. (K.C.V.O. 1911). 1st Ld Ailwyn (1921)	1855	Eton	Cambridge	1924	2, 3^2
Fenner, Mrs P. E.	1922	Ide Hill Sch.*	..	..	51, 60
Fenton, Sir J. C. (Kt 1945)	1880	George Watson's Coll., Edin.	Edinburgh & Sorbonne	1951	16
† Fernyhough, E.	1908	Elementary	..	..	47^2
† Ferrers, 13th E (1954). R. W. S. Ferrers	1929	Winchester	Cambridge	...	45, 51, 54, 60
Feversham, 3rd E of (1916). C. W. S. Duncombe	1906	Eton	..	1964	22, 23, 26
Finch, Sir H. J. (Kt 1976)	1898	Elementary	..	1979	48
† Finlay, 1st Vt (1919). Sir R. Finlay (Kt 1895), 1st Ld (1916)	1842	Edinburgh Academy	Edinburgh	1929	3^2, 9
Finlay, Sir G. B. (1st Bt 1964)	1917	Marlborough	..	..	44, 45
Finsberg, Sir G. (Kt 1984).	1926	C. of London	..	..	61^2
† Fisher, H. A. L.	1865	Winchester	Oxford, Paris & Göttingen	1940	10
Fisher, Sir N. T. L. (Kt 1974)	1913	Eton	Cambridge		41
Fitch, (E.) A.	1915	Kingswood	..	..	49, 50^2
† Fitzalan, 1st Vt (1921). E. B. Fitzalan-Howard. *Assumed name of Talbot* (1876)—*Ld E. Talbot*	1855	Oratory Sch.	..	1947	3, 9, 13
† Fitzmaurice, 1st Ld (1906). Ld E. G. Fitzmaurice	1846	Eton	Cambridge	1935	4, 5, 6
Fleming, Ld (Scot. judge 1926). D. Fleming	1877	Glasgow H.S.*	Edinburgh & Glasgow	1944	15, 18
Fletcher, A. M.	1929	Greenock H.S.*	..	..	62^2
† Fletcher, Ld (Life Peer 1970). Sir E. G. M. Fletcher (Kt 1964)	1903	Radley	London	..	49
Fletcher-Cooke, Sir C. (Kt 1981)	1914	Malvern	Cambridge	..	41
Foley, M. A.	1925	St. Mary's Coll. Middlesbrough*	..	..	45, 46^2
† Foot, Sir D. M. (Kt 1964)	1905	Bembridge	Oxford	1978	28, 49
† Foot, I.	1880	Hoe G.S. Plymouth*	..	1960	21
† Foot, M. M.	1913	Leighton Park Sch	Oxford	..	55, 56
Forbes, 22nd Ld (1953). N. I. Forbes	1918	Harrow	Sandhurst	..	42

Ford, Sir P. J. (Kt 1926)	1880	Edinburgh Academy	Oxford & Edinburgh	1945	15
† Forres, 1st Ld (1922). Sir A. Williamson (1st Bt 1909)	1860	Craigmont*	Edinburgh	1931	12
† Forster, 1st Ld (1919). H. W. Forster	1866	Eton	Oxford	1936	3, 8, 12
Fortescue, 5th E (1932). H. W. Fortescue	1888	Eton	Sandhurst	1958	26, 30, 31, 32, 39, 45
Fortescue, T. V. N.	1916	Uppingham	Cambridge	..	54^2
Foster, Sir J. G. (K.B.E. 1964)	1904	Eton	Oxford	1982	37
Foster, W.	1887	Elementary	..	1947	35
Fowler, G. T.	1935	Northampton G.S.*	Oxford	..	47, 55, 56^2
† Fowler, Sir H. H. (G.C.S.I. 1895). 1st Vt Wolverhampton (1908)	1830	St Saviour's G.S., Southwark*	..	1911	4, 5, 6
† Fowler, (P.) N.	1938	K. Ed. VI, Chelmsford*	Cambridge	..	61, 62, 63
Fox, (J.) M.	1927	Wheelwright G.S., Dewsbury*	..	..	54^2, 61
† Fraser, Sir H. C. P. J. (Kt 1980)	1918	Ampleforth	Oxford & Paris	1984	41^2, 43, 44
Fraser, J. D.	1934	Sloane G.S.*	..	..	56, 57
Fraser, P. L.	1945	Loretto	Cambridge & Edinburgh	..	63
† Fraser, T.	1911	Lesmahagow*	..	..	34, 48
† Freeman, J.	1915	Westminster	Oxford	..	35^4
† Freeman-Thomas, F. 1st Ld Willingdon (1910), 1st Vt (1924), 1st E of (1931), 1st M of (1936)	1866	Eton	Cambridge	1941	5, 7
† Freeson, R. Y.	1926	Jewish Orphanage, W. Norwood*	..	..	48, 49, 56
Freeth, D. K.	1924	Sherborne	Oxford	..	42
† French, Sir J. D. P. (K.C.B. 1900). 1st Vt French of Ypres (1915), 1st E of Ypres (1921)	1852	H.M.S. Britannia*	..	1925	10
Fuller, Sir J. M. F. (1st Bt 1910)	1864	Winchester	Oxford	1915	5^2, 7
Furness, S. N.	1902	Charterhouse	Oxford	1974	25, 30
Gage, 6th Vt (1912). H. R. Gage	1895	Eton	Oxford	1982	18, 22, 26
† Gainford, 1st Ld (1917). J. A. Pease	1860	Tottenham*	Cambridge	1943	5, 6^2, 7^2, 9
† Gaitskell, H. T. N.	1906	Winchester	Oxford	1963	33^2, 34, 35^2
† Galbraith, T. D. 1st Ld Strathclyde (1955)	1891	Glasgow Acad., R.N.C. Osborne & Dartmouth	..	..	31, 38^2, 42
Galbraith, Sir T. G. D. (K.B.E. 1982)	1917	Wellington	Oxford	1982	39^3, 42, 43^2
Gammans, Sir (L.) D. (1st Bt 1955)	1895	Portsmouth G.S.	London	1957	39, 42
† Gardiner, Ld (Life Peer 1964). G. A. Gardiner	1900	Harrow	Oxford	..	45
Garel-Jones, T.	1941	King's Sch.	Canterbury	..	63^2
Garnsworthy, Ld (Life Peer 1967). C. J. Garnsworthy	1906	Wellington	..	1974	59
Garro-Jones, G. M. 1st Ld Trefgarne (1947). *Surname changed to Trefgarne in* 1954	1894	Caterham	..	1960	27
† Geddes, 1st Ld (1942). Sir A. C. Geddes (K.C.B. 1917)	1879	George Watson's Coll., Edin.	Edinburgh	1954	11^3, 12
† Geddes, Sir E. C. (Kt 1916)	1875	Merchiston Castle Sch.	..	1937	9, 10, 11, 12
† Geoffrey-Lloyd, Ld (Life Peer 1974). G. Lloyd	1902	Harrow	Cambridge	1984	23, 24, 28, 29, 32, 37^2, 38
George, Sir J. C. (K.B.E. 1963)	1901	Ballingry, Fife*	..	1972	42
† George-Brown, Ld (Life Peer 1970). G. A. Brown	1914	Secondary	..	1985	33, 35, 45^2, 46
† Gibbs, G. A. 1st Ld Wraxall (1928)	1873	Eton	Oxford	1931	13, 15, 18
† Gibson-Watt, Ld (Life Peer 1979). (J.) D. Gibson-Watt	1918	Eton	Cambridge	..	44, 53

† Gilbert, J. W.	1927	Merchant Taylors' Sch.	Oxford & New York	..	55, 56[2]
Gillett, Sir G. M. (Kt 1931)	1870	Secondary	..	1939	19, 21
† Gilmour, Sir J. (2nd Bt 1920)	1876	Trinity Coll. Glenalmond	Edinburgh & Cambridge	1940	13, 17, 20[2], 21, 24
† Gilmour, Sir I. H. J. L. (3rd Bt 1977)	1926	Eton	Oxford	..	51[4], 59
† Gladstone, 1st Vt (1910). H. J. Gladstone	1854	Eton	Oxford	1930	4, 6
Glassey, A. E.	1887	Penistone G.S.*	..	1971	22
† Glenamara, Ld (Life Peer 1976). E. Short	1912	Secondary	Durham	..	47, 49[2], 55
Glenarthur, 4th Ld (1976). S. M. Arthur	1944	Eton	..	..	60, 61, 64
† Glenavy, 1st Ld (1921). Sir J. H. M. Campbell (1st Bt 1916)	1851	Kingstown*	Dublin	1931	3, 9, 12, 13
† Glendevon, 1st Ld (1964). Ld J. A. Hope	1912	Eton	Oxford	..	37[2], 42, 44
† Glenkinglas, Ld (Life Peer 1974). M. A. C. Noble	1913	Eton	Oxford	1984	42, 44, 53[2]
† Godber, Ld (Life Peer 1979). J. B. Godber	1914	Bedford	..	1980	40[2], 41, 42, 44, 51[2]
Golding, J.	1931	Chester G.S.*	London & Keele	..	56, 58
Goodhart, Sir P. C. (Kt 1981)	1925	Hotchkiss (USA)	Cambridge	..	60[2], 62
Goodhew, Sir V. H. (Kt 1982)	1919	King's Coll. Sch.	..	..	54[2]
Goodlad, A.	1943	Marlborough	Cambridge	..	61, 63[2]
Gordon, J.	1849	Royal Acad. Institution	Queen's Coll., Belfast	1922	9
† Gordon Walker, Ld (Life Peer 1974). P. C. Gordon Walker	1907	Wellington	Oxford	1980	33[2], 46, 47, 48
Gorell, 3rd Ld (1917). R. G. Barnes	1884	Winchester & Harrow	Oxford	1963	12
† Goronwy-Roberts, Ld (Life Peer 1974), G. O. Roberts	1913	Bethesda G.S.*	Wales & London	1981	46, 47, 48[2], 55[2]
† Gorst, Sir J. Eldon (Kt 1885)	1835	Preston G.S.*	Cambridge	1916	2
† Goschen, 1st Vt (1900). G. J. Goschen	1831	Rugby	Oxford	1907	2
† Goschen, 2nd Vt (1907). G. J. Goschen	1866	Rugby	Oxford	1952	10
Goschen, 3rd Vt (1952). J. A. Goschen	1906	Harrow	Oxford	1977	45, 54
Gosford, 6th E of (1954). A. A. J. S. Acheson, Vt Acheson (1922)	1911	Harrow	Cambridge	1966	37, 40, 45
Gosling, H.	1861	Elementary	..	1930	16[2]
Gourlay, H.	1916	Kirkcaldy H.S.*	..	..	50[2]
Gow, I. R. E.	1937	Winchester	..	..	61
† Gowrie, 2nd E of (1955). A. P. G. Ruthven	1939	Eton	Oxford	..	54, 59, 60, 61, 62, 6[illegible]
Graham of Edmonton, Ld (Life Peer 1983). (T.) E. Graham	1925	Elementary	Open University	..	58
† Graham, W.	1887	George Heriot's, Edin.	Edinburgh	1932	16, 19
† Granard, 8th E of (1889). B. A. W. P. H. Forbes	1874	Oratory Sch.	..	1948	5[2], 7
Grant, Ld (Scot. judge 1962). W. Grant	1909	Fettes	Oxford	1972	39, 44[2]
Grant, Sir (J.) A. (Kt 1983)	1925	St. Paul's	Oxford	..	53[2]
Grant, J. D.	1932	Stationers' Company's Sch.*	..	..	55, 56, 58
Granville, 3rd E (1891). G. G. L. Gower	1872	Eton	..	1939	5, 7
† Gray of Contin, Ld (Life Peer 1983). (J.) H. M. Gray	1927	Inverness Royal Acad.*	..	..	54[2], 61, 62
Gray, M.	1871	Greenwich*	..	1943	20
Green, A.	1911	Brighton Coll.	London	..	40, 42, 43
† Greenwood, 1st Vt (1937). Sir H. Greenwood (1st Bt 1915). 1st Ld (1929)	1870	Canadian Sch.*	Toronto	1948	10[2], 11

† Greenwood, A.	1880	Beverley St.*	Leeds	1954	16, 19, 27, 33, 34^2
† Greenwood, of Rossendale, Ld (Life Peer 1970). A. W. Greenwood	1911	Merchant Taylors'	Oxford	1982	46, 47^2, 49
† Grenfell, D. R.	1881	Elementary	..	1968	29
† Grey of Fallodon, 1st Vt (1916). Sir E. Grey (3rd Bt 1882)	1862	Winchester	Oxford	1933	4, 5, 8
Grey, C. F.	1903	Elementary		..	50^2
† Griffith, Sir E. J. E. (1st Bt 1918)	1860	Secondary	Aberystwyth & Cambridge	1926	6
† Griffith-Boscawen, Sir A. S. T. (Kt 1911)	1865	Eton	Oxford	1946	10^2, 12, 14
Griffiths, Sir E. W. (Kt 1985)	1925	Ashton G.S.*	Cambridge	..	52^2
† Griffiths, J.	1890	Elementary	..	1975	33, 35, 48
Griffiths, T.	1867	Elementary	..	1955	16
† Grigg, Sir E. W. M. 1st Ld Altrincham (1945)	1879	Winchester	Oxford	1955	24^2, 28, 30, 32
† Grigg, Sir (P.) J. (K.C.B. 1932)	1890	Bournemouth*	Cambridge	1964	30, 31
Grimston, 1st Ld (1964). Sir R. V. (1st Bt 1952)	1897	Repton	..	1979	25, 26^2, 29, 30, 32
† Guest, F. E.	1875	Winchester	..	1937	7^2, 12, 13
† Guest, I. C., 1st Ld Ashby St Ledgers (1910), 2nd Ld Wimborne (1914), 1st Vt (1918)	1873	Eton	Cambridge	1939	7^2
† Guinness, W. E. 1st Ld Moyne (1932)	1880	Eton	..	1944	14, 15, 17^2, 27^3, 28
† Gulland, J. W.	1864	Edinburgh H.S.*	Edinburgh	1920	7^2, 9
Gummer, J. S.	1939	King's Sch. Rochester	Cambridge	..	60, 62, 63^3
† Gunter, R. J.	1909	Newbridge S.S.*	..	1977	47, 48
Gwynne, R. S.	1873	Shrewsbury	Cambridge	1924	15
† Hacking, 1st Ld (1945). Sir D. H. Hacking (1st Bt 1938)	1884	Giggleswick	Manchester	1950	15, 17^2, 18, 20, 21, 23, 24
Haden-Guest, 1st Ld (1950). L. H. Haden-Guest	1877	Hulme's G.S.*	Manchester	1960	36
† Hailes, 1st Ld (1957) P. G. T. Buchan-Hepburn	1901	Harrow	Cambridge	1974	25, 30^2, 32, 38, 39^2
† Hailsham, 1st Vt (1929). Sir D. M. Hogg (Kt 1922), 1st Ld Hailsham (1928)	1872	Eton	..	1950	15, 17^2, 21^2, 22^2
† Hailsham, 2nd Vt (1950-63). Q. M. Hogg. Ld Hailsham of St. Marylebone (Life Peer 1970)	1907	Eton	Oxford	..	27, 31, 38, 40^3, 41, 42^2, 51, 59
† Haldane, 1st Vt (1911). R. B. Haldane	1856	Edinburgh Academy	Edinburgh & Göttingen	1928	4, 5, 6, 16
† Halifax, 1st E of (1944). E. F. L. Wood. 1st Ld Irwin (1925), 3rd Vt Halifax (1934)	1881	Eton	Oxford	1959	10, 14, 17, 20, 22^2, 23, 24, 26
† Hall, 1st Vt (1946). G. H. Hall	1881	Elementary	..	1965	18, 26, 27^2, 33, 34
Hall, F.	1855	Elementary	..	1933	16
† Hall, W. G.	1887	Ellesmere	..	1962	33
Hall-Davis, Sir A. G. F. (Kt 1979)	1924	Clifton Coll.	..	1979	54
† Halsbury, 1st E (1898). H. S. Giffard, 1st Ld Halsbury (1885)	1823	Privately	Oxford	1921	1
Hamilton, A.	1941	Eton	Oxford	..	63^2
† Hamilton, M of (1885). J. A. E. Hamilton, 3rd D of Abercorn (1913)	1869	Eton	..	1953	3
† Hamilton, Ld G.	1845	Harrow	..	1927	2
Hamilton of Dalzell, 2nd Ld (1900). G. G. Hamilton	1872	Eton	Sandhurst	1952	5, 7
Hamilton, J.	1918	St. Mary's, High Wifflet*	..	..	50, 58, 59^2
Hamilton, Sir M. A. (Kt 1983)	1918	Radley	Oxford	..	44
Hamilton, Sir R. W. (Kt 1918)	1867	St Paul's	Cambridge	1946	20
Hamling, W.	1912	Liverpool Inst. H.S.*	Liverpool	1975	50
† Hanbury, R.	1845	Rugby	Oxford	1903	2^2
† Hankey, 1st Ld (1939). M. P. A. Hankey	1877	Rugby	..	1963	24, 28, 29

Hannan, W.	1906	N. Kelvinside S.S.*	..	..	36
† Hanworth, 1st Vt (1936). Sir E. M. Pollock (K.B.E. 1917), 1st Ld Hanworth (1926)	1861	Charterhouse	Cambridge	1936	13^{2}
† Harcourt, 1st Vt (1916). L. Harcourt	1863	Eton	..	1922	4^{2}, 6^{2}, 8
Hardman, D. R.	1901	Coleraine Acad. Inst.*	Cambridge	..	33
Hardwicke, 6th E (1897). A. E. P. H. Yorke. Vt Royston (1873)	1867	Eton	..	1904	2^{2}, 3
† Hare, J. H. 1st Vt Blakenham (1963)	1911	Eton	..	1982	37, 39, 41, 42^{2}, 44
† Harlech, 4th Ld (1938). W. G. A. Ormsby-Gore	1885	Eton	Oxford	1964	14, 17, 21^{3}, 23, 25
† Harlech, 5th Ld (1964). Sir (W.) D. Ormsby-Gore	1918	Eton	Oxford	1985	37, 40
Harmar-Nicholls, Ld (Life Peer 1974). Sir H. Nicholls (1st Bt 1960)	1912	Q. Mary's G.S., Walsall	..	..	37, 44
Harmsworth, 1st Ld (1939). C. B. Harmsworth	1869	Marylebone G.S.*	Dublin	1948	6, 10
Harper, J.	1914	Elementary	..	1978	49, 50, 59
Harris, 4th Ld (1872). G. R. C. Harris	1851	Eton	Oxford	1932	3
† Harris, F. L.	1864	Winchester	Cambridge	1926	12
† Harris of Greenwich, Ld (Life Peer 1974). J. H. Harris	1930	Pinner G.S.*	..	..	55
Harrison, Sir (J.) H. (1st Bt 1961)	1907	Northampton G.S.*	Oxford	1980	39, 44, 45
† Harrison, W.	1921	Dewsbury Tech*	..	..	50^{2}, 59
† Hart, Dame J. C. M. (D.B.E. 1979)	1924	Clitheroe R.G.S.*	London	..	46, 47, 48, 49^{2}, 58^{2}
Hartington, M of (1908). E. W. S. Cavendish, 10th D of Devonshire (1938)	1895	Eton	Cambridge	1950	23, 27, 28, 31
† Hartshorn, V.	1872	Elementary	..	1931	16, 18
Harvey, I. D.	1914	Fettes	Oxford	..	39, 40
Hastings, 22nd Ld (1956). E. D. H. Astley	1912	Eton	..	..	42, 45
Hastings, Sir P. (Kt 1924)	1880	Charterhouse	..	1952	16
† Hattersley, R. S. G.	1932	Sheffield City G.S.*	Hull	..	47^{3}, 55, 57
† Havers, Sir (R.) M. O. (Kt 1973)	1923	Westminster	Cambridge	..	53, 63
Hawke, 9th Ld (1939). B. W. Hawke	1901	Winchester	Cambridge	1985	39, 44
Hawkesbury, 1st Ld (1893). C. G. S. Foljambe, 1st E of Liverpool (1905)	1846	Eton	..	1907	5
Hawkins, Sir P. (Kt 1982)	1912	Cheltenham	..	..	54^{3}
Haworth, Sir A. A. (1st Bt 1911)	1865	Rugby	..	1944	6
Hay, J. A.	1919	Hove & Sussex G.S.*	..	..	41, 43^{2}
Hayes, J. H.	1889	Tech. S., Wolverhampton	..	1941	20
† Hayes Fisher, W. 1st Ld Downham (1918)	1853	Haileybury	Oxford	1920	2, 3, 8, 10, 11^{2}
† Hayhoe, B. J.	1927	Stanley T.S.*	..	..	59^{2}, 60
† Head, 1st Vt (1960). A. H. Head	1906	Eton	Sandhurst	1981	37, 39
† Headlam, Sir C. M. (1st Bt 1935)	1876	King's Sch., Canterbury	Oxford	1964	17, 21^{2}
† Heald, Sir L. F. (Kt 1951)	1897	Charterhouse	Oxford	1981	39
† Healey, D. W.	1917	Bradford G.S.	Oxford	..	46, 55
† Heath, E. R. G.	1916	Chatham House*	Oxford	..	39^{2}, 40, 42, 43, 44, 50
† Heathcoat Amory, D. 1st Vt Amory (1960)	1899	Eton	Oxford	1981	37^{2}, 38, 39, 40, 41
Heffer, E. S.	1922	Longmore Sch.*	..	..	57
† Henderson, 1st Ld (1945). W. W. Henderson	1891	Q. Elizabeth G.S., Darlington*	..	1984	33, 36
Henderson of Ardwick, 1st Ld (1950). J. Henderson	1884	Elementary	..	1950	35
† Henderson, A.	1863	Elementary	..	1935	8^{2}, 9^{2}, 11, 16, 18

† Henderson, A., Ld Rowley (Life Peer 1966)	1893	Queen's Coll., Taunton*	Cambridge	1968	30^{2}, 33, 34^{2}
Henderson, T.	1867	Elementary	..	1960	20
Henderson, Sir V. L. (Kt 1927)	1884	Uppingham	Sandhurst	1965	17
Henderson-Stewart, Sir J. (1st Bt 1957)	1897	Morrison's Acad., Crieff*	Edinburgh	1961	38
Hennessy, Sir G. R. J. (1st Bt 1927). 1st Ld Windlesham (1937)	1877	Eton	..	1953	15, 18^{3}, 22
Henry, Sir D. S. (1st Bt 1922)	1864	Mount St Mary's Coll.	Belfast	1925	13^{2}
† Herbison, Miss M. M.	1907	Bellshill Acad.*	Glasgow	..	34, 49^{2}
Herschell, 2nd Ld (1899). R. F. Herschell	1878	Eton	Oxford	1929	5, 7, 9, 13
† Heseltine, M. R. D.	1933	Shrewsbury	Oxford	..	52, 53^{2}, 60, 61
† Hewart, 1st Vt (1940). Sir G. Hewart (Kt 1916), 1st Ld (1922)	1870	Manchester G.S.	Oxford	1943	10, 13^{2}
Hewins, W. A. S.	1865	Wolverhampton G.S.	Oxford	1931	10
Hicks, (E.) G.	1879	Elementary	..	1954	30
Hicks, R.	1938	Queen Elizabeth G.S. Crediton*	London	..	54
† Hicks Beach, Sir M. E. 1st Vt St Aldwyn (1906), (9th Bt 1854), 1st E (1915)	1837	Eton	Oxford	1916	2
† Higgins, T. L.	1928	Alleyn's	Cambridge	..	51^{2}
† Hill of Luton, Ld (Life Peer 1963). C. Hill	1904	St Olave's	Cambridge	..	37, 39, 42^{2}
Hill, J. E. B.	1912	Charterhouse	Oxford	..	44
† Hills, J. W.	1867	Eton	Oxford	1938	14
Hilton of Upton, Ld (Life Peer 1965). A. V. Hilton	1908	Elementary	..	1977	50
† Hoare, Sir S. J. G. (2nd Bt 1915). 1st Vt Templewood (1944)	1880	Harrow	Oxford	1959	14, 15, 17, 20, 22, 23^{4}
† Hobhouse, Sir C. E. H. (4th Bt 1916)	1862	Eton	Oxford	1941	4, 5, 6^{2}
Hobson, Ld (Life Peer 1963) C. R. Hobson	1904	Elementary	..	1966	35, 50
† Hobson, Sir J. G. S. (Kt 1962)	1912	Harrow	Oxford	1967	44^{2}
† Hodge, J.	1855	Hutchesontown G.S.*	..	1937	11, 12
Hodges, F.	1887	Elementary	..	1947	16
† Hogg, Sir D. M. (Kt 1922). 1st Ld Hailsham (1928), 1st Vt (1929)	1872	Eton	..	1950	15, 17, 21^{2}, 22^{2}
Hogg, D. M.	1945	Eton	Oxford	..	63
† Hogg, Q. M., 2nd Vt Hailsham (1950-63), Ld Hailsham of St Marylebone (Life Peer 1970)	1907	Eton	Oxford	..	27, 31, 38, 40^{3}, 41, 42^{2}, 51, 59
Holden, 3rd Ld (1937). A. W. E. Holden	1898	Eton	Oxford	1951	33
† Holderness Ld (Life Peer 1979). R. F. Wood	1920	Eton	Oxford	..	39, 42^{2}, 43^{2}, 44, 51, 53
† Home, 14th E of (1951-63). Sir A. F. Douglas-Home, Ld Dunglass (1918), Ld Home of the Hirsel (Life Peer 1974)	1903	Eton	Oxford	..	31, 37, 38, 40^{4}, 41, 51
† Hope, Ld J. A., 1st Ld Glendevon (1964)	1912	Eton	Oxford	..	37^{2}, 42, 44
† Hope, J. F., 1st Ld Rankeillour (1932)	1870	Oratory Sch.	Oxford	1949	9, 11, 13
Hope, A. O. J., 2nd Ld Rankeillour (1949)	1897	Oratory Sch.	Sandhurst	1958	25, 26^{2}
Hopetoun, 7th E of (1873). 1st M of Linlithgow (1902). J. A. L. Hope	1860	Eton	..	1908	2, 3
† Hopkinson, H. L. D., 1st Ld Colyton (1955)	1902	Eton	Cambridge	..	37, 38
Horam, J. R.	1939	Silcoates Sch.*	Cambridge	..	58

† Hore-Belisha, 1st Ld (1954). L. Hore-Belisha	1893	Clifton	Paris, Heidelberg & Oxford	1957	20, 21^{2}, 24^{2}, 25, 32
Hornby, R.	1922	Winchester	Oxford	..	41
† Horne, 1st Vt (1937). Sir R. S. Horne (K.B.E. 1918)	1871	George Watson's Coll., Edin.	Glasgow	1940	9, 11^{2}
† Hornsby-Smith, Lady (Life Peeress 1974). Dame (M.) P. Hornsby-Smith (D.B.E. 1961)	1914	Richmond*	..	..	37, 41, 43
Horobin, Sir I. M. (Kt 1955)	1899	Highgate	Cambridge	1976	42
† Horsbrugh, Lady (Life Peeress 1959). Miss F. Horsbrugh	1889	St Hilda's Folkestone*	..	1969	23, 28, 32, 37, 38
† Houghton, of Sowerby, Ld (Life Peer 1974). (A. L. N.) D. Houghton	1898	Secondary	..	..	47, 48
Howard, G. W. A.	1877	Privately	Cambridge	1935	7, 9
Howe, 4th E (1900). R. G. P. Curzon, Vt Curzon (1876)	1861	Eton	Oxford	1929	3^{2}
† Howe, 5th E (1929). F. R. H. P. Curzon, Vt Curzon (1900)	1884	Eton	Oxford	1964	18
† Howe, Sir (R. E.) G. (Kt 1970)	1926	Winchester	Cambridge	..	53^{2}, 59^{2}
† Howell, D. A. R.	1936	Eton	Cambridge	..	50, 52^{4}, 54, 61, 62
† Howell, D. H.	1923	Handsworth G.S.*	..	..	47, 49, 56
Howie of Troon, Ld (Life Peer 1978). W. Howie	1924	Marr Coll., Troon*	..	..	50^{3}
† Hoy, Ld (Life Peer 1970), J. H. Hoy	1909	Secondary	..	1976	46
Huckfield, L.	1942	Prince Kerry's G.S.*	Oxford	..	57
† Hudson, 1st Vt (1952). R. S. Hudson	1886	Eton	Oxford	1957	20, 23, 24^{2}, 25, 27, 31
Hudson, Sir A. U. M. (1st Bt 1942)	1897	Eton	Sandhurst	1956	21, 22, 23, 24, 27, 32
† Hughes, Ld (Life Peer 1961). W. Hughes	1911	Elementary	..	..	48^{2}, 57
† Hughes, C., Ld Cledwyn of Penrhos (Life Peer 1979)	1916	Holyhead G.S.*	Aberystwyth	..	46^{2}, 48
Hughes, R.	1932	Robert Gordon's Coll., Aberdeen	..	..	57
Hughes-Hallett, J.	1901	Bedford & Osborne	Cambridge	1972	43
Hughes-Young, M. H. C. 1st Ld St Helens (1964)	1912	Harrow	Sandhurst	1981	44^{2}
Hunt, D.	1942	Liverpool Coll.	Bristol	..	61, 63^{2}
Hunter, Ld (Scot. judge 1911). W. Hunter	1865	Ayr Academy*	..	1957	7
Huntingdon, 15th E of (1939). F. J. C. W. P. Hastings, Vt Hastings (1901)	1901	Eton	Oxford	..	33
† Hurd, D. R.	1930	Eton	Cambridge	..	59, 60, 62
† Hutchison of Montrose, 1st Ld (1932). R. Hutchison	1873	Secondary	..	1950	25
Hutchison, Sir J. R. H. (1st Bt 1956)	1893	Harrow	..	1979	39
Hylton, 3rd Ld (1899). H. G. H. Joliffe	1862	Eton	Oxford	1945	9, 13, 14, 15
† Hylton-Foster, Sir H. B. H. (Kt 1954)	1905	Eton	Oxford	1965	39, 44
Hynd, J. B.	1902	St Ninian's Park*	..	1971	35^{2}
† Illingworth, 1st Ld (1921). A. H. Illingworth	1865	London International Coll.* & Switzerland	..	1942	12
Illingworth, P. H.	1869	..	Cambridge	1915	7^{2}
† Ingleby, 1st Vt (1955). O. Peake	1897	Eton	Sandhurst & Oxford	1966	23, 26^{2}, 31, 37, 38, 39
Inglewood, 1st Ld (1964). W. M. F. Vane	1909	Charterhouse	Cambridge	..	41, 43
† Inman, 1st Ld (1946). P. A. Inman	1892	Harrogate*	Leeds	1979	33

† Inskip, Sir T. W. H. (Kt 1922). 1st Vt Caldecote (1939)	1876	Clifton	Cambridge	1947	15, 17, 18^2, 21, 22, 23^2, 25, 28
† Inverforth, 1st Ld (1919). A. Weir	1865	Kirkcaldy H.S.*	..	1955	11, 13
† Irvine, Sir A. (Kt 1967)	1909	Angusfield S.,* Aberdeen	Edinburgh	1978	49
† Irving, Ld (Life Peer 1979). S. Irving	1918	Pendover*	London	..	50
† Irwin, 1st Ld (1925). E. F. L. Wood. 3rd Vt Halifax (1934). 1st E of (1944)	1881	Eton	Oxford	1959	10, 14, 17, 20, 22^2, 23, 24, 26
† Isaacs, G. A.	1883	Elementary	..	1979	34, 35
† Isaacs, Sir R. D. (Kt 1910). 1st Ld Reading (1914), 1st Vt (1916), 1st E of (1917), 1st M of (1926)	1860	University Coll. Sch.	..	1935	6, 7^2, 20
† Islington, 1st Ld (1910). J. P. Dickson-Poynder	1866	Harrow	Oxford	1936	6, 8, 10
† Ismay, 1st Ld (1947). H. L. Ismay	1887	Charterhouse	Sandhurst	1965	37
† Jackson, Sir (F.) S. (G.C.I.E. 1927)	1870	Harrow	Cambridge	1947	15
Jackson, Miss M. M. (Mrs M. M. Beckett)	1943	Notre Dame H.S. Norwich*	Manchester	..	56, 58
Jacques, Ld (Life Peer 1968). J. H. Jacques	1905	Secondary	Manchester	..	59^2
† James of Hereford, 1st Ld (1895). H. James	1828	Cheltenham	..	1911	2
† Jamieson, Ld (Scot. judge 1935). D. Jamieson	1880	Fettes	Glasgow & Edinburgh	1952	22^2, 25
† Jay, D. P. T.	1907	Winchester	Oxford	..	33^2, 48
† Jeffreys, A. F.	1848	Privately	Oxford	1906	2
† Jellicoe, 2nd E (1935). G. P. J. R. Jellicoe	1918	Winchester	Cambridge	..	41^2, 42, 43, 45, 51
† Jenkin, (C.) P. F.	1926	Clifton	Cambridge	..	51^2, 52, 61^3, 62
Jenkins, A.	1884	Elementary	..	1946	29, 33
Jenkins of Putney, Ld (Life Peer 1981). H. G. Jenkins	1908	Enfield G.S.*	..	..	56
† Jenkins, R. H.	1920	Abersychan G.S.*	Oxford	..	45, 46, 48, 55
Jersey, 8th E of (1915). G. H. R. C. Villiers, Vt Grandison (1873)	1873	Eton	Oxford	1923	13
John, B. T.	1934	Pontypridd Boys' G.S.*	London	..	55, 56
John, W.	1878	Elementary	..	1955	30
John-Mackie, Ld (Life Peer 1981). J. Mackie	1916	Aberdeen G.S.*	..	..	46
Johnson, W.	1917	Devon Ho., Margate*	..	..	58
Johnson-Smith, Sir G. (Kt 1981)	1924	Charterhouse	Oxford	..	50, 51
† Johnston, Ld (Scot. judge 1961) D. H. Johnston	1907	Aberdeen G.S.*	Oxford & Edinburgh	1985	36
† Johnston, T.	1882	Lenzie Academy*	Glasgow	1965	18, 19, 29
† Johnstone, H.	1895	Eton	Oxford	1945	29
† Jones, A.	1911	Cyfarthfa S.S.*	London Sch. of Econ.	..	38, 44
† Jones, A. Creech	1891	Elementary	..	1964	33^2
† Jones, Sir F. E. (Kt 1964). Ld Elwyn-Jones (Life Peer 1974)	1909	Llanelly G.S.*	Aberystwyth & Cambridge	..	49, 55
Jones, J. H.	1894	Rotherham*		1962	35
Jones, J. T.	1858	Elementary		1925	13
Jones, M.	1885	Elementary	Reading	1939	16, 19
Jones, (S.) B.	1938	Hawarden G.S.*	..	..	58
† Jones, (T.) A.	1924	Porth Cty G.S.*	..	1983	57, 58
Jones, W.	1860	Bangor Normal Coll.*	Aberystwyth & Oxford	1915	7
† Jopling, (T.) M.	1930	Cheltenham	Newcastle	..	54^2, 60, 63
† Joseph, Sir K. S. (2nd Bt 1944)	1918	Harrow	Oxford	..	42^2, 43, 52, 60, 61
† Jowett, F. W.	1864	Elementary	..	1944	16
† Jowitt, 1st E (1951). Sir W. A. Jowitt (Kt 1929), 1st Ld (1945), 1st Vt (1947)	1885	Marlborough	Oxford	1957	19, 21, 27, 29^3, 30, 32

† Joynson-Hicks, Sir W. (1st Bt 1919). 1st Vt Brentford (1929)	1865	Merchant Taylors' Sch.	..	1932	14^3, 15^3, 17
Joynson-Hicks, L. W. 3rd Vt Brentford (1958)	1902	Winchester	Oxford	1983	38
Judd, F. A.	1935	City of London Sch.	London	..	55, 56, 58^2
Kaberry, Ld (Life Peer 1983). Sir D. Kaberry (1st Bt 1960)	1907	Leeds G.S.	..	..	38
† Kaufman, G. B.	1930	Leeds G.S.	Oxford	..	56, 57^2
† Kearley, Sir H. E. (1st Bt 1908). 1st Ld Devonport (1910), 1st Vt (1917)	1856	Cranleigh	..	1934	4, 6, 12
† Kellaway, F. G.	1870	Bishopstoun*	..	1933	11^2, 12
† Kennedy, T.	1876	Secondary	..	1954	16, 19
† Kennet, 1st Ld (1935). Sir E. H. Young (G.B.E. 1927)	1879	Eton	Cambridge	1960	9, 20, 21
Kennet, 2nd Ld (1960). W. Young	1923	Stowe	Cambridge Harvard	..	47, 49
Kenyon, 4th Ld (1869). L. Tyrrell-Kenyon	1864	Eton	Oxford	1927	3, 13
Kerr, C. I. 1st Ld Teviot (1940)	1874	Stephen Hawtrey's, Windsor*	..	1968	25, 26
Kerr, Sir H. W. (1st Bt 1957)	1903	Eton	Oxford	1974	32
Kershaw, 1st Ld (1947). F. Kershaw	1881	Elementary	..	1962	36
Kershaw, Sir (J.) A. (Kt 1981)	1915	Eton	Oxford	..	51^2, 53
† Key, C. W.	1883	Chalfont St Giles*	..	1964	34, 35
Kidd, J.	1872	Carriden*	Edinburgh	1928	14
† Kilmany, Ld (Life Peer 1966). Sir W. J. Anstruther-Gray (1st Bt 1956)	1905	Eton	Oxford	..	32
† Kilmuir, 1st E (1962). D. P. Maxwell Fyfe, 1st Vt Kilmuir (1954)	1900	George Watson's Coll., Edin.	Oxford	1967	30, 32, 36, 37, 40
King, E. M.	1907	Cheltenham	Cambridge	..	34
King, (H.) D.	1877	Christ's Hospital	..	1930	15, 17^2
† King, T. J.	1933	Rugby	Cambridge	..	60, 61^2, 62
† Kintore, 10th E of (1880). A. H. T. Keith-Falconer	1852	Eton	Cambridge	1930	3
Kirk, Sir P. M. (Kt 1976)	1928	Marlborough	Oxford	1977	41, 44, 51
Kirkhill, Ld. (Life Peer 1975). J. F. Smith	1930	Robert Gordon's Coll., Aberdeen*	..	..	57
† Kitchener of Khartoum, 1st E (1914). H. H. Kitchener, 1st Ld (1898), 1st Vt (1902)	1850	France	Woolwich	1916	6, 8
† Lambert, 1st Vt (1945). G. Lambert	1866	Privately	..	1958	4, 6
Lambton, Vt (1941–69). A. C. F. Lambton (6th Earl of Durham, 1969, disclaimed 1970)	1922	Harrow	..	..	51
Lamont, N. S. H.	1942	Loretto	Cambridge	..	61^2, 62
Lane, Sir D. W. S. S. (Kt 1983)	1922	Eton	Cambridge	..	51
† Lane-Fox, G. R. 1st Ld Bingley (1933)	1870	Eton	Oxford	1947	15, 17
Lang, I. B.	1940	Rugby	Cambridge	..	63^2
† Lansbury, G.	1859	Elementary	..	1940	19
† Lansdowne, 5th M of (1866). H. C. K. Petty-Fitzmaurice, Vt Clanmaurice (1845). E of Kerry (1863)	1845	Eton	Oxford	1927	2, 3, 8
† Lansdowne, 8th M of (1944). G. J. C. M. N. Petty-Fitzmaurice	1912	Eton	Oxford	..	40, 41, 44
† Law, A. Bonar	1858	Glasgow H.S.*	..	1923	3, 8, 9^3, 14
† Law, R. K. 1st Ld Coleraine (1954)	1901	Shrewsbury	Oxford	1980	26^2, 30, 32
Lawrence, 2nd Ld (1879). J. H. Lawrence	1846	Wellington	Cambridge	1913	3
Lawrence, Miss (A.) S.	1871	Privately	Cambridge	1947	19
† Lawson, 1st Ld (1950). J. J. Lawson	1881	Elementary	..	1965	16, 19, 34
Lawson, G. M.	1906	Elementary	..	..	49

Lawson, Sir J. G. 1st Bt (1905)	1856	Harrow	Oxford	1919	2
† Lawson, N.	1932	Westminster	Oxford	..	59^2, 61
Leach, W.	1870	Bradford G.S.	..	1949	16
† Leathers, 1st Vt (1954). F. J. Leathers, 1st Ld (1941)	1883	Elementary	..	1965	30, 32, 37
Leburn, (W.) G.	1913	Strathallan*	..	1963	42
† Lee of Fareham, 1st Vt (1922). Sir A. Lee (K.C.B. 1916). 1st Ld (1918)	1868	Cheltenham	Woolwich	1947	2, 8, 10^2
† Lee of Newton, Ld (Life Peer 1974). F. Lee	1906	Langworthy Rd.*	..	1984	34, 46, 48, 49
† Lee of Asheridge, Lady (Life Peer 1970). Miss J. Lee (Mrs A. Bevan)	1904	Benton*	Edinburgh	..	47^2, 49
Lee, J. R. L.	1942	Hulme's G.S., Manchester	..	..	60
Leechman, Ld (Scot. judge 1965). J. G. Leechman	1906	Glasgow H.S.*	Glasgow	..	49
† Lees-Smith, H. B.	1878	Aldenham	..	1941	19^2
Legh, P. R. 4th Ld Newton (1960)	1915	Eton	Oxford	..	39, 42, 43, 44^2, 45^3
Le Marchant, Sir S. (Kt 1984)	1931	Eton	..	..	64
† Lennox-Boyd, A. T. 1st Vt Boyd of Merton (1960)	1904	Sherborne	Oxford	1983	23^2, 24, 27, 31, 37^2, 39, 41
Lennox-Boyd, M. A.	1943	Eton	Oxford	..	65
Leonard, Ld (Life Peer 1978) J. D. Leonard	1909	Boys Nat. S., Leitrim*	..	1983	59
Leonard, W.	1887	Elementary	..	1969	35
Lester, J. T.	1932	Nottingham H.S.	..	..	60
Lestor, Miss J.	1931	William Morris S.S.*	London	..	47, 55, 56
Lever, Sir (S.) H. (K.C.B. 1917)	1869	Merchant Taylors' Sch., Crosby	..	1947	9
† Lever of Manchester, Ld (Life Peer 1979) (N.) H. Lever	1914	Manchester G.S.	..	..	45^2, 57
† Lewis, Sir (J.) H. (G.B.E. 1922)	1858	Secondary	McGill & Oxford	1933	5, 6, 7, 8, 10
Lewis, T. A.	1881	Denbigh G.S.*	Cardiff	1923	13
Limerick, 6th E of (1967). P. E. Pery. Vt Glentworth (1930)	1930	Eton	Oxford	..	53
† Lincolnshire, 1st M of (1912). C. R. Wynn-Carrington, 3rd Ld Carrington (1868), 1st E (1895)	1843	Eton	Cambridge	1928	4, 5, 6
Lindgren, Ld (Life Peer 1961). G. S. Lindgren	1900	Elementary	..	1971	33, 34, 35, 48^2
Lindsay, K.	1897	St Olave's	Oxford	..	23^2
† Linlithgow, 1st M of (1902). J. A. L. Hope, 7th E of Hopetoun (1873)	1860	Eton	..	1908	2, 3
Linlithgow, 2nd M of (1908). V. A. J. Hope, E of Hopetoun (1902)	1887	Eton	..	1952	14
† Listowel, 5th E of (1931). W. F. Hare, Vt Ennismore (1924)	1906	Eton	Oxford	..	28, 33^2, 34, 35, 71
† Liverpool, 1st E of (1905). C. G. S. Foljambe, 1st Ld Hawkesbury (1893)	1846	Eton	..	1907	5
† Liverpool, 2nd E of (1907). A. W. D. S. Foljambe, Vt Hawkesbury (1905)	1870	Eton	Sandhurst	1941	7
† Llewellin, 1st Ld (1945). J. J. Llewellin	1893	Eton	Oxford	1957	23, 24, 27^2, 28, 29, 30, 32
Llewellyn, Sir D. T. (Kt 1960)	1916	Eton	Cambridge	..	37
† Llewelyn-Davies of Hastoe, Lady (Life Peeress 1967). Mrs (A.) P. Llewelyn-Davies	1915	Liverpool Coll.	Cambridge	..	50, 59
† Lloyd, 1st Ld (1925). Sir G. A. Lloyd (G.C.I.E. 1918)	1879	Eton	Cambridge	1941	27
Lloyd, 2nd Ld (1941). A. D. F. Lloyd	1912	Eton	Cambridge	..	37^2, 39
† Lloyd, G., Ld Geoffrey-Lloyd (Life Peer 1974)	1902	Harrow	Cambridge	1984	23, 24, 28, 29, 32, 38, 41

† Lloyd, (J.) S. B. Ld Selwyn-Lloyd (Life Peer 1976)	1904	Fettes	Cambridge	1978	36^2, 37, 39, 40^3
Lloyd, P. R. C.	1937	Tonbridge	Oxford	. .	65
† Lloyd George of Dwyfor, 1st E (1945). D. Lloyd George	1863	Llanystumdwy Church Sch.*	. .	1945	4, 5, 8^2, 9^2
† Lloyd-George, G. 1st Vt Tenby (1957)	1894	Eastbourne	Cambridge	1967	21, 24, 28^2, 29, 32, 37^2, 38
† Lloyd-Greame, Sir P. (K.B.E. 1920). *Changed name to Sir P. Cunliffe-Lister in* 1924, 1st Vt Swinton (1935). 1st E of Swinton (1955)	1884	Winchester	Oxford	1972	11^2, 15, 17, 20, 21, 23, 27, 28, 32, 37, 38^2
Loch, 2nd Ld (1900). E. D. Loch	1873	Winchester	. .	1942	7
† Lochee of Gowrie, 1st Ld (1908). E. Robertson	1846	Secondary	St Andrews & Oxford	1911	4
Locker-Lampson, G. L. T.	1875	Eton	Cambridge	1946	14, 17^2
† Londonderry, 6th M of (1884). C. S. Vane-Tempest-Stewart. Vt Castlereagh (1872)	1852	Eton	Oxford	1915	1, 2^2, 3
† Londonderry, 7th M of (1915). C. S. H. Vane-Tempest-Stewart. Vt Castlereagh (1884)	1878	Eton	Sandhurst	1949	12, 17, 20, 21^2, 22
† Long, 1st Vt (1921). W. H. Long	1854	Harrow	Oxford	1924	2^3, 8, 10^2
Long, 4th Vt (1967). R. G. Long	1929	Harrow	. .	. .	64
† Longford, 7th E of (1961). F. A. Pakenham, 1st Ld Pakenham (1945)	1905	Eton	Oxford	. .	33, 34^3, 35^2, 36, 45^2, 46
† Loreburn, 1st E (1911). Sir R. T. Reid (Kt 1894), 1st Ld Loreburn (1906)	1846	Cheltenham	Oxford	1923	4, 5
† Lothian, 11th M of (1930). P. H. Kerr	1882	Oratory Sch.	Oxford	1940	20, 21
Lothian, 12th M of (1940). P. F. W. Kerr	1922	Ampleforth	Oxford	. .	43, 45, 51, 54
† Lough, T.	1850	Wesleyan Sch., Dublin*	. .	1922	4
Loughlin, C. W.	1914	Elementary	. .	. .	47, 49^3
Lovat, 16th Ld (1887). S. J. Fraser	1871	Fort Augustus Abbey	Oxford	1933	17
Lovat, 17th Ld (1933). S. C. J. Fraser	1911	Ampleforth	Oxford	. .	31
Lovell-Davis, Ld (Life Peer 1974). P. L. Davis	1925	Stratford upon Avon G.S.*	Oxford	. .	56, 59
† Low, Sir T. A. R. W. (K.C.M.G. 1957), 1st Ld Aldington (1962)	1914	Winchester	Oxford	. .	38, 39
Luard, (D.) E. T.	1926	Felsted	Cambridge	. .	46, 55
† Lucan, 5th E of (1914). G. C. Bingham, Ld Bingham (1888)	1860	Harrow	Sandhurst	1949	13, 15, 18^2, 22, 26
Lucan, 6th E of (1949). G. C. P. Bingham, Ld Bingham (1914)	1898	Eton	Sandhurst	1964	33, 36
Lucas of Chilworth, 1st Ld (1946). G. W. Lucas	1896	Elementary	. .	1967	35, 36^2
Lucas of Chilworth, 2nd Ld (1967). M. W. G. Lucas	1926	Peter Symond's Winchester*	. .	. .	62, 64
Lucas & Dingwall, 8th & 11th Ld (1905). A. T. Herbert	1876	Bedford	Oxford	1916	6^4
Lucas-Tooth, Sir H. V. H. D. (Munro-) 1st Bt (1920)	1903	Eton	Oxford	. .	37
Luce, R. N.	1936	Wellington	Cambridge & Oxford	. .	59^3
Lunn, W.	1872	Elementary	. .	1942	16, 19^2
Lyell, 3rd Ld (1943). C. Lyell	1939	Eton	Oxford	. .	62, 64
Lyon, A. W.	1931	West Leeds H.S.*	London	. .	55
† Lyttelton, A.	1857	Eton	Cambridge	1913	2
† Lyttelton, O. 1st Vt Chandos (1954)	1893	Eton	Cambridge	1972	26, 27^2, 29, 31^2, 37
† Lytton, 2nd E of (1891). V. A. G. R. Lytton	1876	Eton	Cambridge	1947	8, 10^3
† Mabane, 1st Ld (1962), Sir W. Mabane (K.B.E. 1954)	1895	Woodhouse Grove*	Cambridge	1969	23, 25, 26, 28, 31
† Mabon, J. D.	1925	N. Kelvinside*	Glasgow	. .	48^2, 56

Macarthur, I.	1925	Cheltenham	Oxford	..	44
† Macartney, Sir W. (K.C.M.G. 1913)	1852	Eton	Oxford	1924	2
McBride, N.	1910	Elementary	..	1974	50^2
McCann, J.	1910	Elementary	..	1972	49, 50^2
McCluskey, Ld (Life Peer 1976). J. McCluskey	1929	Holy Cross Academy*	Edinburgh	..	58
MacColl, J. E.	1908	Sedbergh	Oxford	1971	47
† McCorquodale, 1st Ld (1955). M. S. McCorquodale	1901	Harrow	Oxford	1971	27, 31
† McCurdy, C. A.	1870	Loughboro' G.S.*	Cambridge	1941	12^2, 13
MacDermot, N.	1916	Rugby	Cambridge	..	45, 47
Macdonald, of Gwaenysgor, 1st Ld (1949). G. Macdonald	1888	Elementary	..	1966	34, 35
† MacDonald, J. Ramsay	1866	Elementary	..	1937	16^2, 18, 20, 22
† MacDonald, M. J.	1901	Bedales*	Oxford	1981	20, 23^4, 28
McElhone, F.	1929	St Bonaventure's S.S.,* Glasgow	..	1982	57
McEwen, Sir J. H. F. (1st Bt 1953)	1894	Eton	Oxford	1962	24, 30
McFarlane, (D.) N.	1936	Bancroft's Sch.	..	..	60, 61
MacGregor, J. R. R.	1937	Merchiston Castle	St. Andrews & London	..	60, 61, 63
† Mackay of Clashfern, Ld (Life Peer 1979). J. P. H. Mackay	1927	George Heriot's	Edinburgh	..	62, 63
† McKenna, R.	1863	Privately	London	1943	4^2, 6^2, 8
Mackenzie (J.) G.	1927	Queen's Park Sch.*	Glasgow	..	57^3
Mackeson, Sir H. R. (1st Bt 1954)	1905	Rugby	Sandhurst	1964	38, 39
Mackie, J., Ld John Mackie (Life Peer 1981)	1909	Aberdeen G.S.*	..	..	46
McLaren, M.	1914	Sedbergh	Oxford	1980	44
† Maclay, 1st Ld (1922). Sir J. P. Maclay (1st Bt 1914)	1857	Glasgow H.S.*	..	1951	13
† Maclay, J. S. 1st Vt Muirshiel (1964)	1905	Winchester	Cambridge	..	31, 37, 39, 42
† Maclean, Sir D. (K.B.E. 1917)	1864	Haverfordwest G.S.*	..	1932	20, 21
Maclean, Sir F. (1st Bt 1957)	1911	Eton	Cambridge	..	39
† Macleod, I. N.	1913	Fettes	Cambridge	1970	37, 38, 41, 42^2, 51
Maclennan, R. A. R.	1936	Glasgow Academy	Cambridge & Oxford	..	57
† Macmillan, Ld (Ld of Appeal 1930). H. P. Macmillan	1873		Edinburgh & Glasgow	1952	16, 24
† Macmillan, (M.) H. 1st E of Stockton (1984)	1894	Eton	Oxford	..	27, 28, 29, 31, 36^2, 37^2, 40
† Macmillan of Ovenden, Vt (1984). M. V. Macmillan	1921	Eton	Oxford	1984	40, 51, 52^2, 53
† Macnamara, T. J.	1861	St Thomas', Exeter*	..	1931	4, 6, 8, 10, 11
† McNeil, H.	1907	Woodside, Glas.*	Glasgow	1955	33^2, 34
† McNeill, R. J. 1st Ld Cushendun (1927)	1861	Harrow	Oxford	1934	14, 17^3
† Macpherson, Sir I. (1st Bt 1933). 1st Ld Strathcarron (1936)	1880	George Watson's Coll., Edin.	Edinburgh	1937	10, 12^2
† Macpherson, N. M. S. 1st Ld Drumalbyn (1963)	1908	Fettes	Oxford	..	38, 42, 43^3, 53
† MacRobert, A. M.	1873	Paisley G.S. & Acad.*	Glasgow & Edinburgh	1930	18^2
Major, J.	1943	Rutlish G.S.*	..	..	63^2
Mallalieu, Sir J. P. W. (Kt 1979)	1908	Cheltenham	Oxford	1980	46^2, 48^2
Mallet, Sir C. E. (Kt 1917)	1862	Harrow	Oxford	1947	6
Malmesbury, 5th E of (1899). J. E. Harris	1872	Privately	Oxford	1950	15
† Manchester, 9th D of (1892). W. A. D. Montagu	1877	Eton	Cambridge	1947	5
Mancroft, 1st Ld (1937). Sir A. M. Samuel (1st Bt 1932)	1872	Norwich G.S.*	..	1942	17^2
Mancroft, 2nd Ld (1942). S. M. S. Mancroft	1914	Winchester	Oxford	..	37, 39, 41, 43
† Manningham-Buller, Sir R. E. (Kt 1951), 1st Ld Dilhorne (1962), 1st Vt (1964)	1905	Eton	Oxford	1980	32, 39^2, 40, 44

Mansfield, 8th E of (1971), Vt Stormont (1935). W. D. M. J. Murray	1930	Eton	Oxford	..	62^2
† Marchamley, 1st Ld (1908). G. Whiteley	1855	Abroad	Zürich	1925	5, 7
Marchwood, 1st Vt (1945). Sir F. G. Penny (Kt 1929), 1st Ld Marchwood (1937)	1876	K. Edward VI G.S., Southampton*	..	1955	18, 22^4, 26
† Margesson, 1st Vt (1942). (H.) D. R. Margesson	1890	Harrow	Cambridge	1965	18, 21, 22, 25, 30^2
Marks, K.	1920	Central H.S.,* Manchester	..	..	57
† Marlborough, 9th D of (1892). C. R. J. Spencer-Churchill, M of Blandford (1883)	1871	Winchester	Cambridge	1934	2, 3, 10
Marley, 1st Ld (1930). D. L. Aman	1884	Marlborough & R.N.C. Greenwich	..	1952	19, 20
† Marples, Ld (Life Peer 1974). (A.) E. Marples	1907	Stretford G.S.*	..	1978	37, 39, 43, 44
† Marquand, H. A.	1901	Cardiff H.S.*	Cardiff	1972	34^2, 35^3
† Marsh, Ld (Life Peer 1981). Sir R. W. Marsh (Kt 1976)	1928	Elementary	..	..	47, 48^3
Marshall, F.	1883	Elementary	..	1962	34
Marshall, J.	1941	City G.S.,* Sheffield	Leeds	..	58
Marshall, (R.) M.	1930	Bradfield	Harvard	..	61
Marten, Sir (H.) N. (Kt 1983)	1916	Rossall	..	..	41, 59
† Mason, R.	1924	Royston*	..	..	47, 48^3, 49, 56, 57
† Masterman, C. F. G.	1873	Weymouth*	Cambridge	1927	5, 6^3
Mather, (D.) C. M.	1919	Harrow	Oxford	..	63, 64^2
† Mathers, 1st Ld (1951). G. Mathers	1886	Elementary	..	1965	30, 36
Mathew, R.	1911	Eton	Cambridge	1966	40
† Maude, Ld (Life Peer 1983). Sir A. E. U. Maude (Kt 1981)	1912	Rugby	Oxford	..	62
† Maudling, R.	1917	Merchant Taylors'	Oxford	1979	36, 39^2, 40, 41, 42, 43^2, 51
† Maugham, 1st Vt (1939). Sir F. H. Maugham (Kt 1928), Ld (Ld of Appeal 1935)	1866	Dover Coll.	Cambridge	1958	22
Mawby, R. L.	1922	Long Lawford S.*	..	..	44
† Maxwell Fyfe, D. P. 1st Vt Kilmuir (1954), 1st E (1962)	1900	George Watson's Coll., Edin.	Oxford	1967	30, 32, 36, 37, 40
Maydon, S. L. C.	1913	Twyford*	..	1971	43
Mayhew, Ld (Life Peer 1981). C. P. Mayhew	1915	Haileybury	Oxford	..	33, 46
Mayhew, Sir P. B. B. (Kt 1983)	1929	Tonbridge	Oxford	..	60^2, 63
Meacher, M. H.	1939	Berkhamsted Sch.	Oxford	..	57^2, 58
† Melchett, 1st Ld (1928). Sir A. M. Mond (1st Bt 1910)	1868	Cheltenham	Cambridge & Edinburgh	1930	10, 13
Melchett, 4th Ld (1973). P. R. H. Mond	1948	Eton	Cambridge & Keele	..	57^2, 59
Mellor, D. J.	1949	Swanage G.S.*	Cambridge	..	60, 61
† Mellish, Ld (Life Peer 1985). R. J. Mellish	1913	Elementary	..	..	47, 49^3, 55, 58
Melville, Sir J. B. (Kt 1929)	1885	Secondary	..	1931	19
† Merriman, 1st Ld (1941). Sir F. B. Merriman (Kt 1928)	1880	Winchester	..	1962	18, 22
† Merrivale, 1st Ld (1925). Sir H. E. Duke (Kt 1918)	1855	Elementary	..	1939	8, 10
† Midleton, 1st E of (1920). (W.) St. J. Brodrick, 9th Vt Midleton (1907)	1856	Eton	Oxford	1942	2^2, 3
† Millan, B.	1927	Harris Acad., Dundee*	..	..	46, 48, 57^2
† Milligan, Ld (Scot. judge 1960). W. R. Milligan	1898	Sherborne	Oxford & Glasgow	1975	39^2, 44
Miller, M. S.	1920	Shawlands Acad.*	Glasgow	..	50

† Mills, 1st Ld (1957). Sir P. H. Mills (Kt 1942)	1890	Barnard Castle	..	1968	42^{3}, 43
Mills, Sir P. M. (Kt 1982)	1921	Epsom	..	..	51, 52
† Milner, 1st Vt (1902). Sir A. Milner (K.C.B. 1895), 1st Ld (1901)	1854	German Schs.	London & Oxford	1925	9, 10, 11, 12
Mitchell, D. B.	1928	Aldenham	..	..	61, 62^{2}
† Mitchell-Thomson, Sir W. (2nd Bt 1918), 1st Ld Selsdon (1932)	1877	Winchester	Oxford	1938	11, 12, 18
Mitchison, Ld (Life Peer 1964). G. R. Mitchison	1890	Eton	Oxford	1970	49
Molony, Sir T. F. (1st Bt 1925)	1865	Secondary	Dublin	1949	7^{2}
† Molson, Ld (Life Peer 1961). (A.) H. E. Molson	1903	Lancing & R.N.C. Osborne & Dartmouth	Oxford	..	39^{2}, 44
† Monckton, 1st Vt (1957). Sir W. T. Monckton (K.C.V.O. 1937)	1891	Harrow	Oxford	1965	32, 37^{3}, 38
† Mond, Sir A. M. (1st Bt 1910). 1st Ld Melchett (1928)	1868	Cheltenham	Cambridge & Edinburgh	1930	10, 13
Money, Sir L. G. C. (Kt 1915)	1870	Privately	..	1944	13
Monro, Sir H. S. P. (Kt 1981)	1922	Canford Sch.	Cambridge	..	53, 54, 61
† Monsell, 1st Vt (1935). Sir B. M. Eyres-Monsell (G.B.E. 1929)	1881	H.M.S. Britannia*	..	1969	10, 13, 14, 15, 18, 20, 21^{2}, 23
† Montagu, E. S.	1879	Clifton & City of London	Cambridge	1924	5, 6^{2}, 8^{3}, 10
Montague, F. 1st Ld Amwell (1947)	1876	Elementary	..	1966	19, 27, 30
† Montague-Barlow, Sir (C.) A. (K.B.E. 1918)	1868	Repton	Cambridge	1951	11, 14
Moore, J. E. M.	1937	Victualler's Sch. Slough*	London	..	59^{2}, 61
† Moore-Brabazon, J. T. C. 1st Ld Brabazon (1942)	1884	Harrow	Cambridge	1964	15, 18, 26, 27, 29
More, Sir J. (Kt 1979)	1907	Eton	Cambridge	..	54
Morgan, (D.) E. Ld Elystan-Morgan (Life Peer 1981)	1932	Ardwyn G.S.*	Aberystwyth	..	46
Moriarty, J. F.	1854	Stonyhurst	Dublin	1915	7^{2}
† Morison, Ld (Scot. judge 1922). T. B. Morison	1868	Secondary	Edinburgh	1945	7, 9, 13^{2}
† Morley, 1st Vt (1908). J. Morley	1838	Cheltenham	Oxford	1923	4, 5, 6^{2}
† Morris, A.	1928	Elementary	Oxford & Manchester	..	57
† Morris, C. R.	1926	Elementary	..	..	50^{2}, 55, 56
† Morris, J.	1931	Ardwyn G.S.*	Aberystwyth & Cambridge	..	47, 48^{2}, 58
Morris-Jones, Sir (J.) H. (Kt 1937)	1884	Menai Bridge G.S.*	..	1972	25
Morrison, P. H.	1944	Eton	Oxford	..	60^{2}, 63
† Morrison, 1st Ld (1945). R. C. Morrison	1881	Aberdeen*	..	1953	35, 36
† Morrison of Lambeth, Ld (Life Peer 1959). H. S. Morrison	1888	Elementary	..	1965	19^{2}, 26, 28, 29, 32, 33
† Morrison, W. S. 1st Vt Dunrossil (1959)	1893	George Watson's Coll., Edin.	Edinburgh	1961	23^{2}, 24, 25, 29^{2}, 32
Mosley, Sir O. E. (6th Bt 1928)	1896	Winchester	Sandhurst	1980	19
† Mottistone, 1st Ld (1933). J. E. B. Seely	1868	Harrow	Cambridge	1947	6^{3}, 11, 12
Mott-Radclyffe, Sir C. E. (Kt 1957)	1911	Eton	Oxford	..	32
† Mount Temple, 1st Ld (1932). W. W. Ashley	1867	Harrow	Oxford	1939	15^{2}, 18
Mowbray and Stourton, 26th Ld (1965). C. E. Stourton	1923	Ampleforth	Oxford	..	54, 64
† Moyle, R. D.	1928	Llanidloes* County Sch.	Aberystwyth & Cambridge	..	55, 57^{2}
† Moyne, 1st Ld (1932). W. E. Guinness	1880	Eton	..	1944	14, 15, 17^{2}, 27^{3}, 28
Muir, J. W.	1879		..	1931	16

† Muir-Mackenzie, 1st Ld (1915). Sir K. A. Muir-Mackenzie (K.C.B. 1898)	1845	Charterhouse	Oxford	1930	16, 20
Muirhead, A. J.	1890	Eton	Oxford	1939	23, 24^{2}
† Muirshiel, 1st Vt (1964). J. S. Maclay	1905	Winchester	Cambridge	..	31, 37, 39, 42
† Mulley, Ld (Life Peer 1984). F. W. Mulley	1918	Warwick*	Cambridge & Oxford	..	46^{2}, 48^{2}, 49, 56^{3}
Munro, P.	1883	Leeds G.S.	Oxford	1942	25, 30
† Munro, R. 1st Ld Alness (1934)	1868	Aberdeen G.S.*	Edinburgh	1955	7, 9, 11, 30, 32
† Munster, 5th E of (1928). G. W. R. H. FitzClarence	1906	Charterhouse	..	1975	22, 24, 25, 26^{2}, 28, 31, 37, 38, 43
† Murray, Ld (Scot. judge 1922). C. D. Murray	1866	Edinburgh Academy	Edinburgh	1936	13^{2}
† Murray of Elibank, 1st Ld (1912). A. W. C. O. Murray	1870	Cheltenham	..	1920	5, 6, 7^{2}
Murray, A. G. 1st Ld Dunedin (1905). 1st Vt (1926)	1849	Harrow	Cambridge	1942	2, 3
Murray of Gravesend, Ld (Life Peer 1976). A. J. Murray	1930	Elementary	..	1980	48
Murray, Sir (T.) D. K. (Kt 1941). Ld Birnam (Scot. judge 1945)	1884	Hamilton Acad.* & Glasgow H.S.*	Glasgow	1955	30, 32
† Murray, Ld (Scot. judge 1979). R. K. Murray	1922	George Watson's Coll.	Edinburgh & Oxford	..	58
† Murton, Ld (Life Peer 1974). (H.) O. Murton	1914	Uppingham	..	..	54^{2}
† Nathan, 1st Ld (1940). H. L. Nathan	1889	St. Paul's	..	1964	34, 35
Neal, A.	1862	Wesley Coll., Sheffield*	..	1933	12
Neal, H.	1897	Elementary	..	1972	35
Neave, A. M. S.	1916	Eton	Oxford	1979	43^{2}
Neubert, M. J.	1933	Bromley G.S.*	Cambridge	..	63
Newton, A. H.	1937	Friends Sch., Saffron Walden*	Oxford	..	61^{2}, 63^{2}
Newton, 2nd Ld (1899). T. W. Legh	1857	Eton	Oxford	1942	8, 9, 10
Newton, 4th Ld (1960). P. R. Legh	1915	Eton	Oxford	..	39, 42, 43, 44^{2}, 45^{2}
Nicholls, Sir H. (1st Bt 1960). Ld Harmar-Nicholls (Life Peer 1974)	1912	Q. Mary's G.S., Walsall*	..	..	37, 44
Nicolson, Sir H. G. (K.C.V.O. 1953)	1886	Wellington	Oxford	1968	28
† Noble, Sir A. H. P. (K.C.M.G. 1959)	1908	Radley	..	1982	36, 37, 38, 40
† Noble, M. A. C. Ld Glenkinglas (Life Peer 1974)	1913	Eton	Oxford	1984	42, 44, 53^{2}
† Noel-Baker, Ld (Life Peer 1977). P. J. Noel-Baker	1889	Bootham	Cambridge	1982	30, 33^{2}, 34, 35
† Noel-Buxton, 1st Ld (1930). N. E. N. Buxton	1869	Harrow	Cambridge	1948	16, 18
† Norfolk, 15th D of (1860). H. FitzAlan-Howard, E of Arundel (1847)	1847	Oratory Sch.	..	1917	3
† Norfolk, 16th D of (1917). B. M. FitzAlan-Howard, E of Arundel (1908)	1908	Oratory Sch.	..	1975	27, 31
† Norman, Sir H. (Kt 1906)	1858	Privately	Harvard & Leipzig	1939	6
Normanby, 4th M of (1932). O. C. J. Phipps, E of Mulgrave (1912)	1912	Eton	Oxford	..	30, 32
† Normand, Ld (Ld of Appeal 1947). W. G. Normand	1884	Fettes	Oxford, Paris & Edinburgh	1962	18, 22^{2}
Northumberland, 10th D of (1940). H. A. Percy	1914	Eton	Oxford	..	32
Norton, C. W. 1st Ld Rathcreedan (1916)	1845	Abroad	Dublin & Sandhurst	1930	5, 6, 7

† Norwich, 1st Vt (1952). A. Duff Cooper	1890	Eton	Oxford	1954	17, 20, 21, 23^2, 24, 28^2
† Nott, Sir J. W. F. (K.C.B. 1983)	1932	Bradfield	Cambridge	..	51, 60, 62
† Novar, 1st Vt (1920). Sir R. C. Munro-Ferguson (G.C.M.G. 1914)	1860	Privately	Sandhurst	1935	14
† Nugent of Guildford, Ld (Life Peer 1966), Sir (G.) R. H. Nugent (1st Bt 1960)	1907	Imperial Service Coll.	Woolwich	..	37, 43
† Nutting, Sir (H.) A. (3rd Bt 1972)	1920	Eton	Cambridge	..	36^2
† Oakes, G. J.	1931	Wade Deacon Sch., Widnes	Liverpool	..	56^3
Oakshott, Ld (Life Peer 1964). Sir H. D. Oakshott (1st Bt 1959)	1904	Rugby	Cambridge	1975	39^2, 44
O'Brien, Sir I. J. (1st Bt 1916). 1st Ld Shandon (1918)	1857	Vincentian Sch., Cork*	Univ. of Ireland	1930	7^2, 12
O'Connor, C. A.	1854	St. Stanislaus Coll.*	Dublin	1928	7^2
O'Connor, Sir J. (Kt 1925)	1872	Blackrock Coll.	..	1931	7, 9, 13
O'Connor, Sir T. J. (Kt 1936)	1891	Secondary	..	1940	25
† Ogmore, 1st Ld (1950). D. R. Rees-Williams	1903	Mill Hill	Wales	1976	33^2, 34
O'Hagan, 3rd Ld (1900). M. H. T. Townley-O'Hagan	1882	Marlborough	Cambridge	1961	5, 7
Oliver, G. H.	1888	Bolton*	..	..	33
† Olivier, 1st Ld (1924). S. Olivier	1859	Tonbridge	Oxford	1943	16
† O'Malley, B. K.	1930	Mexborough G.S.*	Manchester	1976	47, 50^2, 57
† O'Neill, Sir (R. W.) H. (1st Bt 1929). 1st Ld Rathcavan (1953)	1883	Eton	Oxford	1982	24
† Onslow, 4th E of (1870). W. H. Onslow, Vt Cranley (1855)	1853	Eton	Oxford	1911	2^3
Onslow, 5th E of (1911). R. W. A. Onslow, Vt Cranley (1876)	1876	Eton	Oxford	1945	10^3, 13, 14^2, 17, 18
Onslow, 6th E of (1945). W. A. B. Onslow. Vt Cranley (1913)	1913	Winchester	Sandhurst	..	39, 45, 53
Onslow, C.	1926	Harrow	Oxford	..	59
† Oppenheim, Mrs S.	1928	Sheffield H.S.*	..	..	62
Oram, Ld (Life Peer 1975). A. E. Oram	1913	Brighton G.S.*	London	..	47, 49
† Orme, S.	1923	Elementary	..	..	57^3
† Ormsby-Gore, W. G. A. 4th Ld Harlech (1938)	1885	Eton	Oxford	1964	14, 17, 21^3, 23, 25
† Ormsby-Gore, Sir (W.) D. (K.C.M.G. 1961). 5th Ld Harlech (1964)	1918	Eton	Oxford	1985	37, 40
Orr-Ewing, Ld (Life Peer 1971). Sir C. I. Orr-Ewing (Bt 1963)	1912	Harrow	Oxford	..	43^2
† Owen, D.	1938	Bradfield	Cambridge	..	46, 55^2, 57^2
Owen, Sir G. (Kt 1944)	1881	Ardwyn G.S.*	Aberystwyth	1963	22
† Oxford & Asquith, 1st E of (1925). H. H. Asquith	1852	City of London	Oxford	1928	4, 5, 6, 8
Padley, W. E.	1916	Chipping Norton G.S.*	..	1984	46
† Page, Sir R. G. (Kt 1980)	1911	Magdalen Coll.	London	1981	52^2
Page Croft, Sir H. (1st Bt 1924). 1st Ld Croft (1940)	1881	Eton & Shrewsbury	Cambridge	1947	30, 31
† Pakenham, 1st Ld (1945). F. A. Pakenham, 7th E of Longford (1961)	1905	Eton	Oxford	..	33, 34^3, 35^2, 36, 45^2, 46
† Paling, W.	1883	Elementary	..	1971	19, 29, 30, 35^2
† Pannell, Ld (Life Peer 1974). T. C. Pannell	1902	Elementary	..	1980	49
Parker, J.	1863	Wesleyan Sch.*	..	1948	13
Parker, J.	1906	Marlborough	Oxford	..	33
† Parkinson, C.	1931	R.G.S., Lancaster*	Cambridge	..	54, 61, 62^3
Parkinson, J. A.	1870	Elementary	..	1941	16, 19^2
† Parmoor, 1st Ld (1914). Sir C. A. Cripps (K.C.V.O. 1908)	1852	Winchester	Oxford	1941	16, 18

Partington, O. 2nd Ld Doverdale (1925)	1872	Rossall	..	1935	7
† Passfield, 1st Ld (1929). S. J. Webb	1859	Switzerland & Secondary	..	1947	16, 19^2
Patten, C. F.	1944	St. Benedict's, Ealing*	Oxford	..	62
Patten, J. H. C.	1945	Wimbledon	Cambridge	..	61, 62
Pattie, G. E.	1936	Durham	Cambridge	..	60^3, 62
Pavitt, L. A.	1914	Secondary	..	..	58
† Peake, O. 1st Vt Ingleby (1955)	1897	Eton	Sandhurst & Oxford	1966	23, 26^2, 31, 37, 38, 39
Pearson, A.	1898	Elementary	..	1980	36^2
Pearson, Sir F. F. (1st Bt 1964)	1911	Uppingham	Cambridge	..	44
† Pearson, W. D. 1st Bt (1894). 1st Ld Cowdray (1910), 1st Vt (1916)	1856	Privately	..	1927	12
† Peart, Ld (Life Peer 1976). (T.) F. Peart	1914	Wolsingham G.S.*	Durham	1980 ..	45^2, 46, 55^2
Pease, Sir A. F. (1st Bt 1920)	1866	Brighton Coll.	Cambridge	1927	10
† Pease, J. A. 1st Ld Gainford (1917)	1860	Tottenham*	Cambridge	1943	5, 6^2, 7^2, 9
Peat, C. U.	1892	Sedbergh	Oxford	1979	29^2, 32
† Peel, 1st E (1929). W. R. W. Peel, 2nd Vt (1912)	1867	Harrow	Oxford	1937	10, 12^3, 13, 14, 17^2, 21
Peel, Sir J. (Kt 1973)	1912	Wellington	Cambridge	..	44
† Pembroke & Montgomery, 14th E of (1895). S. Herbert	1853	Eton	Oxford	1913	3
Pendry, T.	1934	St Augustine's*	Oxford	..	57, 58
Penny, Sir F. G. (Kt 1929), 1st Ld Marchwood (1937), 1st Vt 1945)	1876	K. Edward VI G.S., Southampton*	..	1955	18, 22^4, 26
† Pentland, 1st Ld (1909). J. Sinclair	1860	Edinburgh Acad. & Wellington	Sandhurst	1925	4, 6
Pentland, N.	1912	Elementary	..	1972	47, 49^3
† Percival Sir (W.) I. (Kt 1979)	1921	Latymer Upper Sch.	Cambridge	..	63
Percy, Earl (1871). H. A. G. Percy	1871	Eton	Oxford	1909	2^2
† Percy of Newcastle, 1st Ld (1953). Ld E. Percy	1887	Eton	Oxford	1958	14^2, 17, 24
Perkins, Sir R. D. (Kt 1954)	1903	Eton	Cambridge	..	27, 32
Perry, E. G.	1910	Elementary	..	..	58
† Perth, 17th E of (1951). Vt Strathallan (1937)	1907	Downside	Cambridge	..	41
† Pethick-Lawrence, 1st Ld (1945). F. W. Pethick-Lawrence	1871	Eton	Cambridge	1961	18, 34
Petherick, M.	1894	Marlborough	Cambridge	..	31
† Peyton, Ld (Life Peer 1983). J. W. W. Peyton	1919	Eton	Oxford	..	42, 52, 53
Phillips, Lady (Life Peeress 1964). Mrs N. M. Phillips	1910	Marist Convent*	..	..	50
† Pickthorn, Sir K. W. M. (1st Bt 1959)	1892	Aldenham	Cambridge	1975	37
Pike, Lady (Life Peeress 1974). Miss M. Pike	1918	Hunmanby Hall	Reading	..	41, 44
Pike Pease, H. 1st Ld Daryngton (1923)	1867	Brighton Coll.	Cambridge	1949	9, 12
Pilkington, Sir R. A. (K.B.E. 1961)	1908	Charterhouse	Oxford	1976	27, 31
Pim, J.	1859		Dublin	1949	7^2
Pitt, Dame E. M. (D.B.E. 1962)	1906	Bordesley Green, Birmingham*	..	1966	39, 43^2
† Plunkett, Sir H.	1854	Eton	Oxford	1932	2, 4
Plymouth, 1st E of (1905). R. G. Windsor-Clive, 14th Ld Windsor (1869)	1857	Eton	Cambridge	1923	3
Plymouth, 2nd E of (1923). I. M. Windsor-Clive	1889	Eton	Cambridge	1943	17, 18, 20, 21, 23^2
† Pollock, Sir E. M. 1st Ld Hanworth (1926), 1st Vt (1936)	1861	Charterhouse	Cambridge	1936	13^2
Polwarth, 10th Ld (1944). H. A. Hepburne-Scott	1916	Eton	Cambridge	..	52
Ponsonby of Shulbrede, 1st Ld (1930). A. A. W. H. Ponsonby	1871	Eton	Oxford	1946	16, 19^3

Popplewell, Ld (Life Peer 1966). E. Popplewell	1899	Elementary	..	1977	36
† Portal, 1st Vt (1945). Sir W. R. Portal (3rd Bt 1931). 1st Ld (1935)	1885	Eton	Oxford	1949	29, 30
† Portland, 6th D of (1879). W. J. A. C. J. Cavendish-Bentinck	1857	Eton	..	1943	4
Portland, 7th D of (1943). W. A. Cavendish-Bentinck, M of Titchfield (1893)	1893	Eton	Sandhurst	1977	18, 22
Portsmouth, 6th E of (1891). N. Wallop, Vt Lymington (1856)	1856	Eton	Oxford	1917	4
Powell, J. B.	1862		..	1923	13
† Powell, (J.) E.	1912	King Edward's, Birmingham	Cambridge	..	37, 40, 42, 43^2
Pratt, Sir J. W. (Kt 1922)	1873	S. Shields*	Glasgow	1952	11, 13
† Prentice, R. E.	1923	Whitgift	London	..	47^2, 48, 49^2, 56, 57, 61
† Pretyman, E. G.	1860	Eton	Woolwich	1931	2^2, 8, 10
Price, Sir D. E. C. (Kt 1980)	1924	Eton	Cambridge & Yale	..	43, 53^2
Price, W. G.	1934	Forest of Dean Tech. Coll.*	..	..	55, 58
Primrose, N. J. A.	1882	Eton	Oxford	1917	5, 13
† Prior, J. M. L.	1927	Charterhouse	Cambridge	..	50, 51, 60, 62
(†)Profumo, J. D.	1915	Harrow	Oxford	..	39, 40^2, 41, 44
† Prothero, R. E. 1st Ld Ernle	1851	Marlborough	Oxford	1937	10
Pybus, Sir (P.) J. (1st Bt 1934)	1880	..	..	1935	21
Pym, L. R.	1884	Bedford	Cambridge	1945	30, 32
† Pym, F. L.	1922	Eton	Cambridge	..	52, 53, 59^2, 60, 61, 62
Raglan, 3rd Ld (1884). G. F. H. Somerset	1857	Eton	Sandhurst	1921	3
† Raison, T. H. F.	1929	Eton	Oxford	..	52, 59, 60
† Ramsbotham, H. 1st Ld Soulbury (1941), 1st Vt (1954)	1887	Uppingham	Oxford	1971	20, 23^3, 25^2, 28
† Ramsden, J. E.	1923	Eton	Oxford	..	41, 44^2
† Rankeillour, 2nd Ld (1932). J. F. Hope	1870	Oratory Sch.	Oxford	1949	9, 11, 13
Rankeillour, 2nd Ld (1949). A. O. J. Hope	1897	Oratory Sch.	Sandhurst	1958	25, 26^2
Ranksborough, 1st Ld (1914). J. F. Brocklehurst	1852	Rugby	Cambridge	1921	7, 9, 13
† Rathcavan, 1st Ld (1953). Sir (R. W.) H. O'Neill (1st Bt 1929)	1883	Eton	Oxford	1982	24
Rathcreedan, 1st Ld (1916). C. W. Norton	1845	Abroad	Dublin & Sandhurst	1930	5, 6, 7
† Rawlinson of Ewell, Ld (Life Peer 1978). Sir P. Rawlinson (Kt 1962)	1919	Downside	Oxford	..	44, 53
Rea, 1st Ld (1937). Sir W. R. Rea (1st Bt 1935)	1873	University Coll. Sch.	..	1948	7, 9, 22
† Reading, 1st M of (1926). Sir R. D. Isaacs (Kt 1910), 1st Ld Reading (1914), 1st Vt (1916), 1st E of (1917)	1860	University Coll. Sch.	..	1935	6, 7^2, 20
Reading, 2nd M of (1935). G. R. Isaacs, Vt Erleigh (1917)	1889	Rugby	Oxford	1960	36^2
Redhead, E. C.	1902	Elementary	..	1967	47, 48
† Redmayne, Ld (Life Peer 1966). Sir M. Redmayne (1st Bt 1964)	1910	Radley	..	1983	39, 44^2
† Rees, M.	1920	Harrow Weald G.S.*	London	..	46^3, 55, 57
† Rees, P. W. I.	1926	Stowe	Oxford	..	59^2, 62
† Rees-Williams, D. R. 1st Ld Ogmore (1950)	1903	Mill Hill	Wales	1976	33^2, 34
† Reid, Ld (Ld of Appeal 1948). J. S. C. Reid	1890	Edinburgh Academy	Cambridge	1975	25, 30^2, 32
† Reid, Sir R. T. 1st Ld Loreburn (1906), 1st E (1911)	1846	Cheltenham	Oxford	1923	4, 5

† Reigate, Ld (Life Peer 1970). Sir J. K. Vaughan-Morgan (1st Bt 1960)	1906	Eton	Oxford	..	43^2
† Reith, 1st Ld (1940). Sir J. C. W. (Kt 1927)	1889	Glasgow Acad. & Gresham's	..	1971	24, 29, 30
† Renton, Ld (Life Peer 1979). Sir D. L. (K.B.E. 1964)	1908	Oundle	Oxford	..	38, 41^2, 42
Renton, (R.) T.	1932	Eton	Cambridge & McGill	..	59
† Reynolds, G. W.	1927	Acton G.S.*	..	1969	46^2
† Rhodes, Ld (Life Peer 1964). H. Rhodes	1895	Elementary	..	..	34, 48
† Rhondda, 1st Vt (1918). 1st Ld (1916). D. A. Thomas	1856	Privately	Cambridge	1918	11, 12
† Rhyl, Ld (Life Peer 1970). (E.) N. C. Birch	1906	Eton	..	1981	37, 38^2, 39, 40
Richard, I. S.	1932	Cheltenham	Cambridge	..	46
Richards, R.	1884	Elementary	..	1954	16
† Ridley, 1st Vt (1900). Sir M. White Ridley (5th Bt 1877)	1842	Harrow	Oxford	1904	2
† Ridley, N.	1929	Eton	Oxford	..	53^2, 59^2, 62
Ridsdale, Sir J. E. (Kt 1983)	1915	Tonbridge	London	..	41, 43
Rifkind, M. L.	1946	George Watson's	Edinburgh	..	59^2, 62
† Ripon, 1st M of (1871). G. F. S. Robinson, Vt Goderich (1833), 2nd E of Ripon (1859)	1827	Privately	..	1909	4, 5
† Rippon, (A.) G. F.	1924	King's, Taunton	Oxford	..	41, 42, 43, 44^2, 52^2, 53
† Ritchie of Dundee, 1st Ld (1905). C. T. Ritchie	1838	City of London	..	1906	2^2, 3
† Robens, Ld (Life Peer 1961). A. Robens	1910	Secondary	..	..	34, 35
Roberts, C. H.	1865	Marlborough	Oxford	1959	6, 9
† Roberts, F. O.	1876	Elementary	..	1941	16, 19
† Roberts, G. H.	1869	Elementary	..	1928	9, 11^2, 12
† Roberts, G. O., Ld Goronwy-Roberts (Life Peer 1974)	1913	Bethesda G.S.*	Wales & London	1981	46, 47, 48^2, 55
Robert, M. H. A.	1927	Neath G.S.*	Cardiff	1983	62
Roberts, (I.) W. P.	1930	Harrow	Oxford	..	62
† Robertson, E. 1st Ld Lochee of Gowrie (1908)	1846	Secondary	St Andrews & Oxford	1911	4
Robertson, J.	1867	Elementary	..	1926	6
Robertson, J. J.	1898	Elementary	..	1955	34
† Robertson, J. M.	1856	Stirling*	..	1933	6
† Robinson, Sir K. (Kt 1983)	1911	Oundle	..	..	47, 49
† Robson, Ld (Ld of Appeal 1910). Sir W. S. Robson (Kt 1905)	1852	Privately	Cambridge	1918	5^2, 7
Rochester, 1st Ld (1931). Sir E. H. Lamb (Kt 1914)	1876	Dulwich & Wycliffe Coll.	..	1955	21, 25
Rodgers, Sir J. C. (1st Bt 1964)	1906	St Peter's, York	Oxford	..	43
† Rodgers, W. T.	1928	Liverpool G.S.*	Oxford	..	45, 46, 48, 56, 58
Rogers, G. H. R.	1906	Secondary	..	1983	49
† Rosebery, 6th E of (1929). A. E. H. M. A. Primrose, Ld Dalmeny (1882)	1882	Eton	Sandhurst	1974	31
Ross, Sir J. (1st Bt 1919)	1854	Foyle Coll.*	Dublin	1935	12
† Ross of Marnock, Ld (Life Peer 1979). W. Ross	1911	Ayr Academy*	Glasgow	..	48, 57
Rossi, Sir H. A. L. (Kt 1983)	1927	Finchley Cath. G.S.*	London	..	52, 54^2, 61, 62
† Rothermere, 1st Vt (1919). Sir H. S. Harmsworth (1st Bt 1910), 1st Ld Rothermere (1914)	1868	Secondary	..	1940	12
Rothschild, J. A. de	1878	Lyceé Louis le Grand*	Cambridge	1957	29
Rowlands, E.	1940	Wirral G.S.*	London	..	48, 55^2, 58
† Rowley, Ld (Life Peer 1966). A. Henderson	1893	Queen's Coll., Taunton*	Cambridge	1968	30^2, 33, 34^2
Royle, Ld (Life Peer 1964). C. Royle	1896	Stockport G.S.*	..	1975	36

Royle, Sir A. H. F. (K.C.M.G. 1974). Ld Fanshawe (Life Peer 1983)	1927	Harrow	Sandhurst	..	51
† Runciman, of Doxford 1st Vt (1937). W. Runciman.	1870	S. Shields H.S.* & Privately	Cambridge	1949	4^{2}, 6^{3}, 8, 21, 22, 24
† Runcorn, Ld (Life Peer 1964). D. F. Vosper	1916	Marlborough	Cambridge	1968	37, 39, 41^{2}, 43, 44
† Rushcliffe, 1st Ld (1935). Sir H. B. Betterton (1st Bt 1929)	1872	Rugby	Oxford	1949	14, 17, 20, 21
Russell, 2nd E (1878). J. F. S. Russell	1865	Winchester	Oxford	1931	19^{2}
Russell, Ld (Scot. judge 1936). A. Russell	1884	Glasgow Acad.	Glasgow	1975	25
Russell, Sir T. W. (1st Bt 1917)	1841	Madras Acad., Fife*	..	1920	2, 4, 6, 8, 10
† St Aldwyn, 1st E (1915). M. E. Hicks Beach, 1st Vt St Aldwyn (1906)	1837	Eton	Oxford	1916	2
† St Aldwyn, 2nd E (1916). M. J. Hicks Beach	1912	Eton	Oxford	..	37, 41, 45, 54
† St Audries, 1st Ld (1911). Sir A. F. Acland Hood (4th Bt 1892)	1853	Eton	Oxford	1917	3^{2}
St. Helens, 1st Ld (1964). M. H. C. Hughes-Young	1912	Harrow	Sandhurst	1981	44^{2}
† St John-Stevas, N. A. F.	1929	Ratcliffe	Cambridge & Oxford	..	52^{2}, 60, 61, 63
St Oswald, 4th Ld (1957). R. D. G. Winn	1916	Stowe	Bonn & Freiburg	1984	41, 45
Sainsbury, T.	1932	Eton	Oxford	..	63
† Salisbury, 3rd M of (1868). R. A. T. Gascoyne-Cecil, Vt Cranborne (1865)	1830	Eton	Oxford	1903	1^{2}, 2
† Salisbury, 4th M of (1903). J. E. H. Gascoyne-Cecil, Vt Cranborne (1868)	1861	Eton	Oxford	1947	1, 2, 3, 14^{2}, 17
† Salisbury, 5th M of (1947). R. A. J. Gascoyne-Cecil, Vt Cranborne (1903)	1893	Eton	Oxford	1972	23, 26, 27, 28^{2}, 29^{2}, 31, 36^{2}, 37, 40
† Salter, 1st Ld (1953). Sir (J.) A. Salter (K.C.B. 1922)	1881	Oxford H.S.*	Oxford	1975	24, 29, 30, 32, 36, 38
† Salvesen, Ld (Scot. judge 1905). E. Salvesen	1857	Collegiate Sch., Edin.*	Edinburgh	1942	3
† Samuel, 1st Vt (1937). Sir H. L. Samuel (G.B.E. 1920)	1870	University Coll. Sch.	Oxford	1963	4, 6^{4}, 8^{2}, 9, 20
Samuel, Sir A. M. (1st Bt 1932). 1st Ld Mancroft (1937)	1872	Norwich G.S.*	..	1942	17^{2}
Samuels, A. W.	1852	Royal Sch., Dungannon*	Dublin	1925	13^{2}
† Sanders, Sir R. A. (1st Bt 1920). 1st Ld Bayford (1929)	1867	Harrow	Oxford	1940	12, 13^{2}, 14
Sanders, W. S.	1871	Elementary	Berlin	1941	19
Sandford, 1st Ld (1945). Sir A. J. Edmondson (Kt 1934)	1887	University Coll. Sch.	..	1959	25, 26, 30, 31, 32
Sandford, 2nd Ld (1959). Rev. J. C. Edmondson	1920	Eton	Cambridge	..	52^{3}
† Sandhurst, 1st Vt (1917). W. Mansfield, 2nd Ld Sandhurst (1876)	1855	Rugby	..	1921	7, 9, 13
† Sandys, D. Ld Duncan-Sandys (Life Peer 1974)	1908	Eton	Oxford	..	29, 30^{2}, 32, 37, 39, 41^{4}
Sandys, 7th Ld (1961). R. M. O. Hill	1931	Royal Naval Coll., Dartmouth*	..	..	54, 64
† Sankey, 1st Vt (1932). Sir J. Sankey (Kt 1914), 1st Ld (1929)	1866	Lancing	Oxford	1948	18, 20
† Sassoon, Sir P. A. G. D. (3rd Bt 1912)	1888	Eton	Oxford	1939	17, 20, 23, 25^{2}
Saye & Sele, 18th Ld (1907). G. C. T.-W.-Fiennes	1858	Eton	..	1937	7

† Scarbrough, 11th E of (1945). L. R. Lumley	1896	Eton	Sandhurst & Oxford	1969	31
† Scott, Sir L. F. (Kt 1922)	1869	Rugby	Oxford	1950	13
Scott, Sir (R.) D. (Kt 1955)	1901	Mill Hill	Cambridge	1974	31
Scott, N. P.	1933	Clapham Coll.*	..	..	52, 62
Scott-Hopkins, Sir J. S. R. (Kt 1981)	1921	Eton	Oxford	..	41
† Seely, J. E. B. 1st Ld Mottistone (1933)	1868	Harrow	Cambridge	1947	6^{3}, 11, 12
† Sefton, 6th E of (1901). O. C. Molyneux	1871		..	1930	5
† Selborne, 2nd E of (1895). W. W. Palmer, Vt Wolmer (1882)	1859	Winchester	Oxford	1942	2^{2}, 8
† Selborne, 3rd E of (1942). R. C. Palmer, Vt Wolmer (1895)	1887	Winchester	Oxford	1971	15, 18, 28
† Selkirk, 10th E of (1940). Ld G. N. Douglas-Hamilton	1906	Eton	Oxford	..	37^{2}, 38, 39, 43
† Selsdon, 1st Ld (1932). Sir W. Mitchell-Thomson (2nd Bt 1918)	1877	Winchester	Oxford	1938	11, 12, 18
† Selwyn-Lloyd, Ld (Life Peer 1976). (J.) S. B. Lloyd	1904	Fettes	Cambridge	1978	36^{2}, 37, 39, 40^{3}
Serota, Lady (Life Peeress 1967). Mrs B. S. Serota	1919	J. C. Howard Sch.*	London	..	47, 50
† Shackleton, Ld (Life Peer 1958). E. A. A. Shackleton	1911	Radley	Oxford	..	45^{2}, 46, 47, 49^{2}
† Shaftesbury, 9th E of (1886). A. Ashley-Cooper	1869	Eton	Sandhurst	1961	15
† Shakespeare, Sir G. H. (1st Bt 1942)	1893	Highgate	Cambridge	1980	20, 22, 23^{3}, 24, 28
Shandon, 1st Ld (1918). Sir I. J. O'Brien (1st Bt 1916)	1857	Vincentian Schs. Cork*	Nat. Univ.	1930	7^{2}, 12
Sharples, Sir R. C. (K.C.M.G. 1972)	1916	Eton	Sandhurst	1973	43, 44, 51
Shaw, (J.) G.D.	1931	Sedbergh	Cambridge	..	61^{2}, 62
† Shaw, Ld (Ld of Appeal 1909). T. Shaw, 1st Ld Craigmyle (1929)	1850	Dunfermline H.S.*	Edinburgh	1937	5, 7
† Shaw, T.	1872	Elementary	..	1938	16, 19
† Shawcross, Ld (Life Peer 1959). Sir H. W. Shawcross (Kt 1945)	1902	Dulwich	Geneva	..	34, 35
† Shearer, I. H. Ld Avonside (Scot. judge 1974)	1914	Dunfermline H.S.*	Glasgow & Edinburgh	..	44
† Sheldon, R. E.	1923	Secondary	..	..	55^{3}
Shelton, W. J. M.	1929	Radley	Oxford	..	60
† Shepherd, 1st Ld (1946). G. R. Shepherd	1881	Elementary	..	1954	36^{3}
† Shepherd, 2nd Ld (1954). M. N. Shepherd	1918	Friends' Sch., Saffron Walden*	..	..	46^{2}, 50, 55
Sherwood, 1st Ld (1941). Sir H. M. Seely (3rd Bt 1926)	1898	Eton	..	1971	27
Shiels, Sir (T.) D. (Kt 1939)	1881	Elementary	Edinburgh	1953	19^{2}
† Shinwell, Ld (Life Peer 1970). E. Shinwell	1884	Elementary	..	..	16, 19^{2}, 33, 34, 35
† Shore, P. D.	1924	Quarry Bank H.S., Liverpool*	Cambridge	..	45^{2}, 48^{2}, 56, 58
Short, A.	1882	Elementary	..	1938	18
† Short, E. W. Ld Glenamara (Life Peer 1976)	1912	Secondary	Durham	..	47, 49^{2}, 55
† Shortt, E.	1862	Durham	Durham	1935	10^{2}
† Sidney, W. P. 6th Ld De L'Isle & Dudley (1945). 1st Vt De L'Isle (1956)	1909	Eton	Cambridge	..	32, 38
† Silkin, 1st Ld (1950). L. Silkin	1889	Secondary	London	1972	35
† Silkin, J. E.	1923	Dulwich	Wales & Cambridge	..	49^{3}, 50^{2}, 55, 56^{2}
† Silkin of Dulwich, Ld (Life Peer 1985). S. C. Silkin	1918	Dulwich	Cambridge	..	58
Simmons, C. J.	1893	Elementary	..	1975	35, 36
† Simon, 1st Vt (1940). Sir J. A. Simon (Kt 1910)	1873	Fettes	Oxford	1954	6, 7, 8, 20, 23^{2}, 28, 32

Simon of Wythenshawe, 1st Ld (1947). Sir E. D. Simon (Kt 1932)	1879	Rugby	Cambridge	1960	20
† Simon of Glaisdale, Ld (Life Peer 1971). Simon, Sir J. E. S. (Kt 1959)	1911	Gresham's	Cambridge	..	40, 41, 44
† Simonds, 1st Vt (1954). G. T. Simonds, Ld (Ld of Appeal 1946), 1st Ld (1952)	1881	Winchester	Oxford	1971	36
† Sinclair, Sir A. H. M. (4th Bt 1912), 1st Vt Thurso (1952)	1890	Eton	Sandhurst	1970	20, 21, 27
† Sinclair, J. 1st Ld Pentland (1909)	1860	Edinburgh Academy & Wellington	Sandhurst	1925	4, 6
† Sinha, 1st Ld (1919). Sir S. P. Sinha (Kt 1914)	1864	Indian Sch.	..	1928	10
Skeffington, A. M.	1909	Streatham G.S.*	London	1971	47, 49[2]
Skelmersdale, 7th Ld (1973). R. Bootle-Wilbraham	1945	Eton	..	..	64
Skelton, (A.) N.	1880	Trinity Coll., Glenalmond	Oxford	1935	20, 24
Slater, Mrs H.	1903	Hanley H.S.*	..	1976	49
Slater, Ld (Life Peer 1970). J. Slater	1904	Elementary	..	1977	49
† Slesser, Sir H. (Kt 1924)	1883	Oundle & St Paul's	London	1979	16
† Smith, Sir B. (K.B.E. 1945)	1879	Elementary	..	1964	19, 27, 28, 35
Smith, Sir D. G. (Kt 1983)	1926	Chichester H.S.*	..	..	51, 52
Smith, E.	1896	Elementary	..	1969	34
† Smith, Sir F. E. (Kt 1915). 1st Ld Birkenhead (1919), 1st Vt (1921), Ist E of (1922)	1872	Birkenhead	Oxford	1930	8, 9[2], 13, 17
† Smith, J.	1938	Dunoon G.S.*	Glasgow	..	55, 56, 58
Smith, T.	1886	Elementary	..	1953	28
Smith, W. R.	1872	Norwich	..	1942	16, 19
Smithers, Sir P. H. B. O. (Kt 1970)	1913	Harrow	Oxford	..	40
† Smuts, J. C.	1870	S. Africa	Stellenbosch & Cambridge	1950	9, 11
† Smyth, Sir J. G. (1st Bt 1955)	1893	Repton	Sandhurst	1983	39
Snadden, Sir W. M. (1st Bt 1955)	1896	Dollar Academy*	..	1959	38
Snape, P. C.	1942	St Winifred's Sch., Stockport*	..	..	58[2]
† Snell, 1st Ld (1931). H. Snell	1865	Elementary	Nottingham	1944	19, 31
Snow, Ld (Life Peer 1964). Sir C. P. Snow (Kt 1957)	1905	Newton's*	Leicester & Cambridge	1980	48
Snow, J. W., Ld Burntwood (Life Peer 1970)	1910	Haileybury	..	1982	36[2], 47, 48, 49
† Snowden, 1st Vt (1931). P. Snowden	1864	Elementary	..	1937	16, 18, 20[2]
† Soames, Ld (Life Peer 1978). Sir (A.) C. J. Soames (G.C.M.G. 1972)	1920	Eton	Sandhurst	..	38, 41, 43, 44, 59
Soares, Sir E. J. (Kt 1911)	1864	Privately	Cambridge	1926	7
† Somerleyton, 1st Ld (1916). Sir S. B. Crossley (2nd Bt 1872)	1872	Eton	Oxford	1935	3, 13, 15
Somers, 6th Ld (1899). A. H. T. S. Cocks	1887	Charterhouse	Oxford	1944	18
† Somervell of Harrow, Ld (Ld of Appeal 1954). Sir D. B. Somervell (Kt 1933)	1889	Harrow	Oxford	1960	22, 25[2], 30, 31
Sorensen, Ld (Life Peer 1964). R. W. Sorensen	1891	Elementary	..	1971	50
† Soskice, Sir F. (Kt 1945). Ld Stow Hill (Life Peer 1966)	1902	St Paul's	Oxford	1979	35[2], 45, 46
† Soulbury, 1st Vt (1954). H. Ramsbotham, 1st Ld Soulbury (1941)	1887	Uppingham	Oxford	1971	20, 23[2], 25[2], 28

Southby, Sir A. R. J. (1st Bt 1937)	1886	H.M.S. Britannia*	..	1969	22, 25
† Southwark, 1st Ld (1910). R. K. Causton	1843	Privately	..	1929	4, 7
Speed, (H.) K.	1934	Bedfordshire	..	..	52, 54^{2}, 60
† Spencer, 6th E (1910). C. R. Spencer, Vt Althorp (1857), 1st Vt Althorp (1905)	1857	Harrow	Cambridge	1922	5, 7
Spicer, M. H.	1943	Wellington	Cambridge	..	61
† Spoor, B. C.	1878	Secondary	..	1928	16
Sproat, I. M.	1938	Winchester	Oxford	..	62
Stallard, Ld (Life Peer 1983). A. W. Stallard	1921	Hamilton Acad.*	..	..	58^{2}
† Stanhope, 7th E (1905). J. R. Stanhope, Vt Mahon (1880)	1880	Eton	Oxford	1967	12, 17, 20^{2}, 21, 22, 23^{2}, 25
† Stanley, Ld (1893). E. G. V. Stanley, 17th E of Derby (1908)	1865	Wellington	..	1948	2, 3^{2}, 8, 12, 15
† Stanley, Ld (1908). E. M. C. Stanley	1894	Eton	Oxford	1938	18, 20, 23^{3}, 24
† Stanley, Sir A. H. (Kt 1914). 1st Ld Ashfield (1920)	1874	American Schs.	..	1948	11
† Stanley, Sir G. F. (G.C.I.E. 1929)	1872	Wellington	Woolwich	1938	12, 13, 14, 18
Stanley, J. P.	1942	Repton	Oxford	..	60, 61
† Stanley, O. F. G.	1896	Eton	..	1950	20^{2}, 21, 23, 24^{2}, 27, 31
† Stanmore, 2nd Ld (1912). G. A. M. Hamilton-Gordon	1871	Winchester	Cambridge	1957	7, 9, 13
† Stansgate, 1st Vt (1941). W. Wedgwood Benn	1877	Paris Lycée	London	1960	7, 19, 33
Stedman, Lady (Life Peeress 1974). P. Stedman	1916	County G.S.,* Peterborough	..	..	57, 59
† Steel-Maitland, Sir A. H. D. R. (1st Bt 1917)	1876	Rugby	Oxford	1935	8, 10, 11, 17
Steele, T.	1905	Elementary	..	1979	35
Stewart, (B. H.) I. H.	1935	Haileybury	Cambridge	..	59, 60
Stewart, Ld (Scot. judge 1975). E. G. F. Stewart	1923	George Watson's Coll., Edin.	Edinburgh	..	49
Stewart, J.	1863	Normal Sch., Glasgow*	..	1931	16
Stewart, (J.) A.	1942	Baxter H.S., Coupar*	St Andrew's & Harvard	..	62
† Stewart of Fulham, Ld (Life Peer 1979). (R.) M. M. Stewart	1906	Christ's Hospital	Oxford	..	35^{2}, 36^{2}, 45^{2}, 46^{2}, 47
Stewart, (W.) I.	1925	Loretto	Glasgow & Edinburgh	..	54
† Stockton, 1st E of (1984). H. Macmillan	1894	Eton	Oxford	..	27, 28, 29, 31, 36^{2}, 37^{2}, 40
† Stodart of Leaston, Ld (Life Peer 1981). (J.) A. Stodart	1916	Wellington	..	..	42, 51^{2}
Stoddart of Swindon, Ld (Life Peer 1983). D. L. Stoddard	1926	Henley G.S.*	..	..	58^{2}
† Stokes, R. R.	1897	Downside	Cambridge	1957	33, 35
† Stonehaven, 1st Vt (1938). Sir J. L. Baird (2nd Bt 1920). 1st Ld Stonehaven (1925)	1874	Eton	Oxford	1941	10, 11, 12, 15^{2}
(†)Stonehouse, J. T.	1925	Taunton's, Southampton*	London	..	46, 47, 48^{3}
† Stonham, Ld (Life Peer 1958). V. J. Collins	1903	Regent St. Poly.*	London	1971	46^{2}
† Stott, Ld (Scot. judge 1967). G. Stott	1909	Edinburgh Acad.	Edinburgh	..	49
† Stow Hill, Ld (Life Peer 1966). Sir F. Soskice (Kt 1945)	1902	St Paul's	Oxford	1979	35^{2}, 45, 46
Strabolgi, 11th Ld (1953) D. M de D. K. Strabolgi	1914	Gresham's Sch.	..	..	59
Strachey, Sir E. (4th Bt 1901). 1st Ld Strachie (1911)	1858	Privately	Oxford	1936	5, 6, 7^{2}
† Strachey, (E.) J. St. L.	1901	Eton	Oxford	1963	34, 35^{2}
† Strachie, 1st Ld (1911). Sir E. Strachey (4th Bt 1901)	1858	Privately	Oxford	1936	5, 6, 7^{2}
Stradbroke, 3rd E of (1886). G. E. J. M. Rous	1862	Harrow	Cambridge	1947	17

Strang, G. S.	1943	Secondary	Edinburgh & Cambridge	..	55, 56
† Strathcarron, 1st Ld (1936). Sir I. Macpherson (1st Bt 1933)	1880	George Watson's Coll., Edin.	Edinburgh	1937	10, 12^2
† Strathclyde, 1st Ld (1914) (Scot. judge 1913). A. Ure	1853	Larchfield Acad.*	Glasgow & Edinburgh	1928	5, 7^2
† Strathclyde, 1st Ld (1955). T. D. Galbraith	1891	Glasgow Acad. & R.N.C. Osborne & Dartmouth	..	..	31, 38^2, 42
Strathcona & Mount Royal, 3rd Ld (1926). D. S. P. Howard	1891	Eton	Cambridge	1959	21, 22, 24
Strathcona & Mount Royal, 4th Ld (1959). D. E. P. Howard	1923	Eton	Cambridge & McGill	..	51, 54, 60
† Strauss, Ld (Life Peer 1979). G. R. Strauss	1901	Rugby	..	..	35^2
Strauss, H. G. 1st Ld Conesford (1955)	1892	Rugby	Oxford	1974	29, 30, 38
Stross, Sir B. (Kt 1964)	1899	Leeds G.S.	Leeds	1967	49
† Stuart, of Findhorn, 1st Vt (1959). J. G. Stuart	1897	Eton	..	1971	22, 25, 30^2, 32, 38
Studholme, Sir H. G. (1st Bt 1956)	1899	Eton	Oxford	..	39
Suffield, 6th Ld (1914). C. Harbord	1855	Eton	..	1924	9, 14
Summers, Sir (G.) S. (Kt 1956)	1902	Wellington	Cambridge	1976	29, 31
† Summerskill, Lady (Life Peeress 1961). Edith Summerskill	1901	Secondary	London	1980	35^2
Summerskill, Shirley	1931	St Paul's Girls' Sch.	Oxford	..	55
† Sutherland, 5th D of (1913). G. G. S.-L.-Gower	1888	Eton	..	1963	14, 17, 18
† Sutherland, Sir W. (K.C.B. 1919)	1880	Secondary	Glasgow	1949	12, 13
† Swingler, S. T.	1915	Stowe	Oxford	1969	47, 48^2
† Swinton, 1st E of (1955). *Sir P. Lloyd-Greame* (K.B.E. 1920) *changed name to Cunliffe-Lister in* 1924, 1st Vt Swinton (1935)	1884	Winchester	Oxford	1972	11^2, 15, 17, 20, 21, 23, 27, 28, 32, 37, 38^2
Swinton, 2nd E of (1972). J. Cunliffe-Lister, Ld Masham (1955)	1937	Winchester	..	..	64
† Talbot, Ld E. B. *E. B. Fitzalan-Howard, assumed name of Talbot in* 1876. 1st Vt Fitzalan (1921)	1855	Oratory Sch.	..	1947	3, 9, 13
Taverne, D.	1928	Charterhouse	Oxford	..	45^2, 46
Taylor, Ld (Life Peer 1958). S. J. L. Taylor	1910	Stowe	London	..	46^3
Taylor, E. M.	1937	Glasgow H.S.*	Glasgow	..	53^2
Taylor, H. B., Ld Taylor of Mansfield (Life Peer 1966)	1895	Elementary	..	..	35
† Taylor, R. J.	1881	Elementary	..	1954	35
Taylor, Mrs (W.) A.	1947	Bolton Sch.*	Bradford	..	58
Taylor, Sir W. J. (1st Bt 1963)	1902	Archb. Holgate's G.S.*	Sheffield	1972	43, 44
† Tebbit, N. B.	1931	Edmonton CGS*	..	..	60, 61, 62^2
† Templemore, 4th Ld (1924). A. C. S. Chichester	1880	Harrow	Sandhurst	1953	18, 22^2, 26, 31, 32
† Templewood, 1st Vt (1944). Sir S. J. G. Hoare (2nd Bt 1915)	1880	Harrow	Oxford	1959	14, 15, 17, 20, 22, 23^4
† Tenby, 1st Vt (1957). G. Lloyd George	1894	Eastbourne	Cambridge	1967	21, 24, 28^2, 29, 32, 37^2, 38
† Tennant, H. J.	1865	Eton	Cambridge	1935	6^3, 8^2
Teviot, 1st Ld (1940). C. I. Kerr	1874	Stephen Hawtrey's, Windsor*	..	1968	25, 26
† Thankerton, Ld (Ld of Appeal 1929). W. Watson	1873	Winchester	Cambridge	1948	13, 15, 18
† Thatcher, Mrs M. H.	1925	Grantham G.S.*	Oxford	..	43, 52, 59
Thomas, I. Bulmer	1905	W. Monmouth*	Oxford	..	33^2
† Thomas, J. H.	1874	Elementary	..	1949	16, 18, 19, 20^2, 23^2

† Thomas, J. P. L. 1st Vt Cilcennin (1955)	1903	Rugby	Oxford	1960	27, 30, 31, 38^2
Thomas, J. S.	1925	Rugby	London	..	54^2, 62, 64
† Thomas, P. J. M.	1920	Epworth Coll., Rhyl*	Oxford	..	40^2, 42, 53
† Thomas, T. G. 1st Vt Tonypandy (1983)	1909	Tonypandy Sec. S.*	Southampton	..	46^2, 48^2
Thompson, D.	1931	Hipperholme G.S.*	..	..	63^2
Thompson, Sir K. P. (1st Bt 1963)	1909	Bootle G.S.*	..	1984	41, 44
Thompson, Sir R. H. M. (1st Bt 1963)	1912	Malvern	..	..	39^2, 41, 43, 44, 45
† Thomson, 1st Ld (1924). C. B. Thomson	1875	Cheltenham	Woolwich	1930	16, 19
† Thomson, Ld (Scot. judge 1947). G. R. Thomson	1893	South African Coll.	Cape Town Oxford & Edinburgh	1962	36
Thomson, Sir F. C. (1st Bt 1929)	1875	Edinburgh Academy	Oxford & Edinburgh	1935	15^2, 18^2, 22
† Thomson of Monifieth, Ld (Life Peer 1977). G. M. Thomson	1921	Grove Academy, Dundee	..	..	46^2, 47^2, 48, 49^2
† Thorneycroft, Ld (Life Peer 1967). (G. E.) P. Thorneycroft	1909	Eton	Woolwich	..	32, 38, 40, 41^2
Thornton, E.	1905	Elementary	..	..	47
† Thurso, 1st Vt (1952). Sir A. H. M. Sinclair (4th Bt 1912)	1890	Eton	Sandhurst	1970	20, 21, 27
Thurtle, E.	1884	Elementary	..	1954	19, 28
Tilney, Sir J. (Kt 1972)	1907	Eton	Oxford	..	41
Tinn, J.	1922	Elementary	Oxford	..	58
Titchfield, M of (1893). W. A. H. Cavendish-Bentinck, 7th D of Portland (1943)	1893	Eton	Sandhurst	1977	18, 22
† Tomlinson, G.	1890	Rishton Wesleyan*	..	1952	27, 33, 35
Tomlinson, J. E.	1939	Westminster City Sch.*	Nottingham	..	55, 58
† Tonypandy, 1st Vt (1983). T. G. Thomas	1909	Tonypandy Sec. S.*	Southampton	..	46^2, 48^2
† Tranmire, Ld (Life Peer 1974) Sir R. H. Turton (Kt 1971)	1903	Eton	Oxford	..	36, 38^2, 39
Tree, R.	1897	Winchester	..	1976	32
Trefgarne, 1st Ld (1947). G. M. Garro-Jones. *Surname changed to Trefgarne in* 1954	1894	Caterham	..	1960	27
Trefgarne, 2nd Ld (1960) D. G. Trefgarne	1941	Haileybury	Princeton	..	59, 60, 61, 62, 64
Trenchard, 2nd Vt (1956) T. Trenchard	1923	Eton	..	..	60^2, 61
† Trevelyan, Sir C. P. (3rd Bt 1928)	1870	Harrow	Cambridge	1958	6, 16, 19
Trippier, D. A.	1946	Bury G. S.	..	..	62
Trumpington, Lady (Life Peeress 1980). Mrs J. A. Barker	1922	Privately	..	..	61, 64
† Tryon, 1st Ld (1940). G. C. Tryon	1871	Eton	Sandhurst	1940	12^2, 15, 18, 21, 24, 25, 29, 30
Turner, Sir B. (Kt 1931)	1863	Elementary	..	1942	19
† Turton, Sir R. H. (Kt 1971), Ld Tranmire (Life Peer 1974)	1903	Eton	Oxford	..	36, 38^2, 39
† Tweedmouth, 2nd Ld (1894). E. Majoribanks	1848	Harrow	Oxford	1909	4, 5
Tweedmouth, 3rd Ld (1909). D. C. Majoribanks	1874	Harrow	..	1935	7
† Tweedsmuir of Belhelvie, Lady (Life Peeress 1970). Lady Tweedsmuir (1948). Lady P. J. F. Grant	1915	Abroad	..	1978	42, 51, 52
Ungoed-Thomas, Sir (A.) L. (Kt 1951)	1904	Haileybury	Oxford	1972	35
† Ure, A. Ld Strathclyde (Scot. judge 1913). 1st Ld (1914)	1853	Larchfield Academy	Glasgow & Edinburgh	1928	5, 7^2
† Urwin, T.	1912	Elementary	..	..	45, 47

Valentia, 11th Vt (1863). A. Annesley (U.K. Ld Annesley 1917)	1843	Privately	Woolwich	1927	3, 9, 13, 15
Vane, W. M. F. 1st Ld Inglewood (1964)	1909	Charterhouse	Cambridge	..	41, 43
Van Straubenzee, Sir W. R. (Kt 1981)	1924	Westminster	..	..	52^2
† Varley, E. G.	1932	Poolsbrook Sec. Mod. S.*	..	..	48, 50, 56, 57
Vaughan, Sir G. F. (Kt 1983)	1933	Kenya*	London	..	61, 62
† Vaughan-Morgan, Sir J. K. (1st Bt 1960) Ld Reigate (Life Peer 1970)	1906	Eton	Oxford	..	43^2
Verney, Sir H. C. W. (4th Bt 1910)	1881	Harrow	Oxford	1974	6
Viant, S. P.	1882	Devonport*	..	1964	19
† Vosper, D. F. Ld Runcorn (Life Peer 1964)	1916	Marlborough	Cambridge	1968	37, 39, 41^2, 43, 44
Waddington, D. C.	1929	Sedbergh	Oxford	..	60^2, 63
Wakefield, Sir E. B. (1st Bt 1962)	1903	Haileybury	Cambridge	1969	39, 44^2, 45^2
† Wakeham, J.	1932	Charterhouse	..	..	59, 61, 63^3
† Waldegrave, 9th E (1859). W. F. Waldegrave	1851	Eton	Cambridge	1930	4
Waldegrave, 12th E (1936). G. N. Waldegrave, Vt Chewton (1933)	1905	Winchester	Cambridge	..	41
Waldegrave, W.	1946	Eton	Oxford & Harvard	..	60, 61
Walder, (A.) D.	1928	Latymer Upper Sch.	Oxford	1978	54
† Waleran, 1st Ld (1905). Sir W. H. Walrond (2nd Bt 1889)	1849	Eton	..	1925	2, 3^2
Walkden, 1st Ld (1945). A. G. Walkden	1873	Merchant Taylors' Sch., Ashwell	..	1951	36
† Walker, H.	1927	Secondary	..	..	47, 50, 56^2
† Walker, P. E.	1932	Latymer Upper Sch.	..	..	52^2, 53, 60, 61
† Walker-Smith, Sir D. C. (1st Bt 1960). Ld Broxbourne (Life Peer 1983)	1910	Rossall	Oxford	..	36, 38, 43^2
† Wallace, (D.) E.	1892	Harrow	Sandhurst	1941	18, 20, 22, 23^2, 24^2
Wallace of Coslany, Ld (Life Peer 1974). G. D. Wallace	1906	Central Sch.* Cheltenham Spa	..	..	59
Walrond, Sir W. H. (2nd Bt 1889). 1st Ld Waleran (1905)	1849	Eton	..	1925	2, 3^2
† Walsh, S.	1859	Elementary	..	1929	10, 12, 16
Walston, Ld (Life Peer 1961). H. D. L. Walston	1912	Eton	Cambridge	..	46, 48
† Walters, Sir (J.) T. (Kt 1912)	1868	Clitheroe G.S.*	..	1933	12, 21
Walton, Sir J. L. (Kt 1905)	1852	Merchant Taylors' Sch., Great Crosby*	London	1908	5
† Ward of Witley, 1st Vt (1960). G. R. Ward	1907	Eton	Oxford	..	38^2, 43
Ward, Sir (A.) L. (1st Bt 1929)	1875	St. Paul's	Paris & Darmstadt	1956	22^2, 26^3
† Ward, W. D.	1877	Eton	Cambridge	1946	7, 13
Wardle, G. J.	1865	Elementary	..	1947	11^2
Warne, G. H.	1881	Elementary	..	1928	16
Warrender, Sir V. A. G. A. (8th Bt 1917). 1st Ld Bruntisfield (1942)	1899	Eton	..	..	22^3, 23^2, 24, 27, 31
† Waterhouse, C.	1893	Cheltenham	Cambridge	1975	25^2, 26^2, 29^2, 31
† Watkinson, 1st Vt (1964) H. A. Watkinson	1910	Queen's Coll., Taunton*	London	..	37, 39, 41, 43
Watson, Sir J. C. (Kt 1931)	1883	Neilson Instit., Paisley*	Glasgow & Edinburgh	1944	19, 22

† Watson, W., Ld Thankerton (Ld of Appeal 1929)	1873	Winchester	Cambridge	1948	13, 15, 18
† Waverley, 1st Vt (1952). Sir J. Anderson (K.C.B. 1919)	1882	George Watson's Coll., Edin.	Edin. & Leipzig	1958	22, 23, 26^2, 28^2, 31
† Weatherill, B. B.	1920	Malvern	..	..	54^4
Webb, Sir H. (1st Bt 1916)	1866	Privately	..	1940	7
† Webb, M.	1904	Christ Ch., Lancaster*	..	1956	35
† Webb, S. J. 1st Ld Passfield (1929)	1859	Switzerland & Secondary	..	1947	16, 19^2
† Webster, Sir R. E. (G.C.M.G. 1893). 1st Ld Alverstone (1900). 1st Vt (1913)	1842	King's Coll. Sch. & Charterhouse	Cambridge	1915	3
† Wedderburn, H. J. S., 13th Vt Dudhope (1952). 11th E of Dundee (1953)	1902	Winchester	Oxford	1983	24, 29, 40, 43
† Wedgwood, 1st Ld (1942). J. C. Wedgwood	1872	Clifton & R.N.C. Greenwich	..	1943	16
† Weir, 1st Vt (1938). Sir W. D. Weir (Kt 1917), 1st Ld (1918)	1877	Glasgow H.S.*	..	1959	12
Wellbeloved, (A.) J.	1926	Elementary	..	..	56
Wells-Pestell, Ld (Life Peer 1965). R. A. Wells-Pestell	1910	Secondary	London	..	57, 59
† Westwood, 1st Ld (1944). W. Westwood	1880	Elementary	..	1953	36
† Westwood, J.	1884	Elementary	..	1948	19, 29, 34
† Wheatley, Ld (Scot. judge 1954) (Life Peer 1970). J. Wheatley	1908	Mount St Mary's Coll., Chesterfield	Glasgow	..	36^2
† Wheatley, J.	1869	Elementary	..	1930	16
Whitaker, B. C. G.	1934	Eton	Oxford	..	49
White, Lady (Life Peeress 1970). Mrs E. L. White	1909	St Paul's Girls' S.	Oxford	..	46^2, 48
White, F.	1939	Elementary	..	..	58
† White, (H.) G.	1880	Birkenhead	Liverpool	1965	20
† Whitelaw, 1st Vt (1983). W. S. I. Whitelaw	1918	Winchester	Cambridge	..	42, 44, 50, 52^2, 59, 60
† Whiteley, G. 1st Ld Marchamley (1908)	1855	Abroad	Zürich	1925	5, 7
† Whiteley, W.	1882	Elementary	..	1955	19, 30^2, 35
† Whitley, J. H.	1866	Clifton	London	1935	5, 7
Whitlock, W. C.	1918	Itchen G.S.*	Southampton	..	46^2, 49, 50^2
Whitney, R.	1930	Wellingborough	London	..	59, 61
† Wigg, 1st Ld (1967). G. Wigg	1900	Q Mary's, Basingstoke*	..	1983	49
Wiggin, (A.W.) J.	1937	Eton	Cambridge	..	60^2
† Wilkins, W. A.	1899	Elementary	..	..	36
† Wilkinson, Miss E. C.	1891	Stretford Rd.*	Manchester	1947	26, 29, 33
† Willey, F. T.	1910	Johnston Sch.*	Cambridge	..	35, 47, 49
† Williams, A. J.	1930	Cardiff H.S.*	Oxford	..	45, 48, 57^2
† Williams, Sir E. J.	1890	Elementary	..	1963	35
Williams, Sir H. G. (Kt 1939)	1884	Privately	Liverpool	1954	17
Williams, J. P.	1840	Elementary	..	1904	3
Williams, Sir R. R. (1st Bt 1918)	1865	Eton	Oxford	1955	12
† Williams, Mrs S. V. T. B.	1930	St Paul's Girls' S.	Oxford	..	46, 47^2, 55, 56, 57
† Williams of Barnburgh, Ld (Life Peer 1961). T. Williams	1888	Elementary	..	1967	27, 33
† Williamson, Sir A. (Bt 1909). 1st Ld Forres (1922)	1860	Craigmont*	Edinburgh	1931	12
† Willingdon, 1st M of (1936). F. Freeman-Thomas, 1st Ld Willingdon (1910). 1st Vt (1924), 1st E (1931)	1866	Eton	Cambridge	1941	5, 7
† Willink, Sir H. U. (1st Bt 1957)	1894	Eton	Cambridge	1973	28, 32
† Willis, (E.) G.	1903	C. of Norwich S.S.*	..	..	48
Wills, Sir G. (Kt 1958)	1905	Privately	Cambridge	1969	39, 45
† Wilmot, 1st Ld (1950). J. Wilmot	1895	Secondary	London	1964	29, 34, 35
Wilson, D. M.	1862	Royal Academical Institution, Belfast	Dublin	1932	13

† Wilson of Langside, Ld (Life Peer 1969). H. S. Wilson	1916	Glasgow H.S.*	Glasgow	..	49
† Wilson of Rievaulx (Life Peer 1983). Sir (J.) H. Wilson (K.G. 1976)	1916	Wirral G.S.*	Oxford	..	34^2, 35, 45, 55
† Wilson, Sir L. O. (G.C.I.E. 1923)	1876	St Paul's	..	1955	13^2, 15
† Wimborne, 1st Vt (1918). I. C. Guest. 1st Ld Ashby St Ledgers (1910), 2nd Ld Wimborne (1914)	1873	Eton	Cambridge	1939	7^2
Windlesham, 1st Ld (1937). Sir G. R. J. Hennessy (1st Bt 1927)	1877	Eton	..	1953	15, 18^3, 22
† Windlesham, 3rd Ld (1962). D. J. G. Hennessy	1932	Ampleforth	Oxford	..	51^2, 52
Windsor, 14th Ld (1869). R. G. Windsor-Clive, 1st E of Plymouth (1905)	1857	Eton	Cambridge	1923	3^2
Winfrey, Sir R. (Kt 1914)	1858	King's Lynn G.S.*	..	1944	10
† Winster, 1st Ld (1942). R. T. H. Fletcher	1885	H.M.S. Britannia*	..	1961	34
Winterbottom, Ld (Life Peer 1965). I. Winterbottom	1913	Charterhouse	Cambridge	..	46^2, 48, 59
† Winterton, 6th E (1907). E. Turnour (U.K. Ld Turnour 1952)	1883	Eton	Oxford	1962	10, 14, 17, 24, 25^2
† Wolmer, Vt (1895). R. C. Palmer. 3rd E of Selborne (1942)	1887	Winchester	Oxford	1971	15, 18, 28
† Wolverhampton, 1st Vt (1908). Sir H. H. Fowler (G.C.S.I. 1895)	1830	St Saviour's G.S., Southwark*	..	1911	4, 5, 6
Wolverton, 4th Ld (1888). F. G. Wolverton	1864	Eton	Oxford	1932	3
† Womersley, Sir W. J. (Kt 1934)	1878	Elementary	..	1961	22, 25^3, 29, 32
† Wood, E. F. L. 1st Ld Irwin (1925), 3rd Vt Halifax (1934), 1st E of (1944)	1881	Eton	Oxford	1959	10, 14, 17, 20, 22^2, 23, 24, 26
† Wood, Sir (H.) K. (Kt 1918)	1881	Cent. Foundation B.S.*	..	1943	17, 20^2, 21, 22, 23^2, 26, 28
† Wood, R. F. Ld Holderness (Life Peer 1979)	1920	Eton	Oxford	..	39, 42^2, 43^2, 44, 51, 53
† Wood, T. M.	1855	Mill Hill	London	1927	5^2, 6^2, 8^3
† Woodburn, A.	1890	Heriot-Watt Coll.*	..	1978	34, 35
Woodhouse, C. M.	1917	Winchester	Oxford	..	41^2
† Woolton, 1st E of (1955). Sir F. J. Marquis (Kt 1935), 1st Ld Woolton (1939), 1st Vt (1953)	1883	Manchester G.S.	Manchester	1964	23, 27, 28, 31, 36, 37, 38^2
† Worthington-Evans, Sir L. (1st Bt 1916)	1868	Eastbourne	..	1931	11^3, 12^3, 14, 15, 17
† Wraxall, 1st Ld (1928). G. A. Gibbs	1873	Eton	Oxford	1931	13, 15, 18
Wright, G.	1847		Dublin	1913	3
Wyatt, Sir W. L. (Kt 1983)	1918	Eastbourne	Oxford	..	35
† Wylie, Ld (Scot. judge 1974). N. R. Wylie	1923	Paisley G.S.*	Oxford & Glasgow	..	44, 54
† Wyndham, G.	1863	Eton	Sandhurst	1913	2, 3^2
Young, Sir A. S. L. (1st Bt 1945)	1889	Fettes	..	1950	30, 31, 32
† Young of Graffham, Ld (Life Peer 1984). D. I. Young	1932	Christ's Coll., Finchley*	London	..	62
† Young, Sir E. H. (G.B.E. 1927). 1st Ld Kennet (1935)	1879	Eton	Cambridge	1960	9, 20, 21
Young, Sir G. S. K. (6th Bt 1960) 1941	1941	Eton	Oxford	..	61^2
† Young, Lady (Life Peeress 1971). Mrs J. M. Young	1926	Headington Sch.	Oxford	..	52, 54, 59^2, 60, 61
† Younger, G. K. H.	1931	Winchester	Oxford	..	51, 53, 62
† Younger, Sir K. G. (K.B.E. 1973)	1908	Winchester	Oxford	1976	33^2
† Ypres, 1st E of (1921). Sir J. D. P. French (K.C.B. 1900). 1st Vt French (1915)	1852	H.M.S. Britannia*	..	1925	10
† Zetland, 2nd M of (1929). L. J. L. Dundas, E of Ronaldshay (1892)	1876	Harrow	Cambridge	1961	24

II

PARTIES

Conservative Party

Party Leaders

	1900	M of Salisbury	9 Oct 40	(Sir) W. Churchill
14 Jul	02	A. Balfour	21 Apr 55	Sir A. Eden
13 Nov	11	A. Bonar Law[1]	22 Jan 57	H. Macmillan
21 Mar	21	A. Chamberlain[1]	11 Nov 63	Sir A. Douglas-Home
23 Oct	22	A. Bonar Law[1]	2 Aug 65	E. Heath[3]
28 May	23	S. Baldwin	11 Feb 75	Mrs. M. Thatcher[4]
31 May	37	N. Chamberlain[2]		

Deputy Leaders

4 Aug 65-18 Jul 72	R. Maudling
12 Feb 75-	W. Whitelaw (Vt)

Leaders in the House of Lords

1900	3rd M of Salisbury	1941	Ld Moyne
1902	D of Devonshire	1942	Vt Cranborne (5th M of Salisbury)
1903	M of Lansdowne	1957	E of Home
1916	Earl Curzon (M)	1960	2nd Vt Hailsham
1925	4th M of Salisbury	1963	Ld Carrington
1930	1st Vt Hailsham	1970	Earl Jellicoe
1935	M of Londonderry	1973	Ld Windlesham
1935	Vt Halifax	1974	Ld Carrington
1938	Earl Stanhope	1979	Ld Soames
1940	Vt Caldecote	1981	Lady Young
1940	Vt Halifax	1983	Vt Whitelaw
1941	Ld Lloyd		

Principal Party Officials

Chairmen of the Party Organisation

Jun 11-Dec 16	A. Steel-Maitland	Oct 59-Oct 61	R. Butler
Dec 16-Mar 23	Sir G. Younger	Oct 61-Apr 63	I. Macleod
Mar 23-Nov 26	S. Jackson	Apr 63-Oct 63	{ I. Macleod Ld Poole
Nov 26-May 30	J. Davidson	Oct 63-Jan 65	Vt Blakenham
Jun 30-Apr 31	N. Chamberlain	Jan 65-Sep 67	E. du Cann
Apr 31-Mar 36	Ld Stonehaven	Sep 67-Jul 70	A. Barber
Mar 36-Mar 42	(Sir) D. Hacking	Jul 70-Apr 72	P. Thomas
Mar 42-Sep 44	T. Dugdale	Apr 72-Jun 74	Ld Carrington
Oct 44-Jul 46	R. Assheton	Jun 74-Feb 75	W. Whitelaw
Oct 46-Jul 55	Ld Woolton (Vt)	Feb 75-Sep 81	Ld Thorneycroft
Jul 55-Sep 57	O. Poole	Sep 81-Sep 83	C. Parkinson
Sep 57-Oct 59	Vt Hailsham	Oct 83-	J. S. Gummer

[1] A. Bonar Law, 1911-21, and A. Chamberlain, 1921-22, were Leaders of the Conservative Party in the House of Commons. Formerly, when the party was in opposition, there were separate Leaders in the Commons and the Lords; and the present title 'Leader of the Conservative and Unionist Party' did not officially exist. It was first conferred, in Oct 1922, on A. Bonar Law when he was selected for his second term of office.

[2] N. Chamberlain remained Leader of the Conservative party until 4 Oct 40, though he was succeeded as Prime Minister by W. Churchill on 10 May 40, and resigned from the Government on 30 Sep 40.

[3] In 1965 E. Heath was the first Conservative leader to be elected by a ballot of M.P.s. He received 150 votes to 133 for R. Maudling and 15 for E. Powell. Although the new rules required a larger majority, Mr Maudling instantly withdrew in favour of Mr Heath.

[4] In a first ballot on 4 Feb 75 Mrs Thatcher won 130 votes to 119 for E. Heath and 16 for H. Fraser. In a second ballot Mrs Thatcher won 146 votes; W. Whitelaw 79; J. Prior 19; Sir G. Howe 19; J. Peyton 11.

Deputy Chairmen

May 24-Jan 26	M of Linlithgow
Sep 57-Oct 59	O. Poole (Ld)
Oct 59-Oct 63	Sir T. Low (Ld Aldington)
Oct 64-Oct 75	Sir M. (Ld) Fraser
Apr 72-Jun 74	J. Prior
Feb 75-Nov 77	W. Clark
Mar 75-May 79	A. Maude
Nov 77-May 79	Lady Young
May 79-Jun 83	A. McAlpine (Ld)
Jun 83-Sep 84	M. Spicer

Principal Agents

Mar 1885-Jul 03	R. Middleton
Jul 03-Nov 05	L. Wells
Nov 05-Dec 06	A. Haig
Dec 06-Jan 12	P. Hughes
May 12-Jun 15	J. Boraston
Jun 15-Apr 20	(Sir) J. Boraston & W. Jenkins
Apr 20-Dec 20	W. Jenkins
Dec 20-Mar 23	Sir M. Fraser
Mar 23-Feb 24	Sir R. Hall
Mar 24-Jan 27	(Sir) H. Blain
Jan 27-Feb 28	Sir L. Maclachlan
Feb 28-Feb 31	R. Topping

General Directors

Feb 31-Sep 45	(Sir) R. Topping
Oct 45-Aug 57	(Sir) S. Pierssené
Aug 57-Jun 66	(Sir) W. Urton

(*office abolished Jun* 66)

Director-General

Apr 74-Mar 75	M. Wolff

Director of Organisation

Jun 66-Jan 76	(Sir) R. Webster
Feb 76-	(Sir) A. Garner

Treasurers[1]

Aug 11-Mar 23	Earl Farquhar
Mar 23-Apr 29	Vt Younger
Jan 30-Jul 31	Sir S. Hoare
Jul 31-Nov 33	Ld Ebbisham
Nov 33-Jun 38	Vt Greenwood
Jun 38-Feb 47	Vt Marchwood
Feb 47-Apr 60	C. Holland-Martin
Feb 48-Mar 52	Ld De L'Isle
Mar 52-Oct 55	O. Poole
Oct 55-Jan 62	Sir H. Studholme
Oct 60-Nov 65	R. Allan
Jan 62-Aug 66	R. Stanley
Nov 65-Apr 77	Ld Chelmer
Aug 66-Apr 74	Sir T. Brinton
Apr 74-Jul 77	Sir A. Silverstone (Ld Ashdown)
Apr 74-Mar 75	W. Clark
Aug 75-	A. McAlpine (Ld)
May 79-Jun 83	Ld Boardman
Apr 82-	Sir O. Wade
Dec 84-	Sir C. Johnston

Conservative Research Department 1929

Director

1930-39	(Sir) J. Ball
1939-45	*post vacant*
1945-51	D. Clarke (*joint from* 48)
1948-50	H. Hopkinson (*joint*)
1948-59	P. Cohen (*joint*)
1951-64	(Sir) M. Fraser (*joint to* 59)
1964-70	B. Sewill
1970-74	J. Douglas
1974-79	C. Patten
1979-82	A. Howarth
1982-84	P. Cropper
1984-85	*post vacant*
1985	R. Harris

Chairman

1930	N. Chamberlain[2]
1940	Sir K. Wood
1943	Sir J. Ball (*Acting Hon. Chairman*)
1945	R. Butler
1964	(*post vacant*)
1970	Sir M. (Ld) Fraser
1974	I. Gilmour
1975	A. Maude
1979	(*post abolished*)

SOURCES.—*Annual Conference Reports of the National Union of Conservative and Unionist Associations*, and information from the Conservative Research Department.

Chief Whips in the House of Commons

1900	Sir W. Walrond
1902	Sir A. Acland Hood
1911	Ld Balcarres
1912	Ld E. Talbot
1921	L. Wilson
1923	(Sir) B. Eyres-Monsell
1931	D. Margesson
1941	J. Stuart
1948	P. Buchan-Hepburn
1955	E. Heath

Chief Whips in the House of Lords

1900	Earl Waldegrave
1911	D of Devonshire
1916	Ld Hylton
1922	E of Clarendon
1925	E of Plymouth
1929	E of Lucan (5th)
1940	Ld Templemore
1945	Earl Fortescue
1958	Earl St Aldwyn
1977	Ld Denham

SOURCE.—*Dod's Parliamentary Companion, 1900-* . For a full list of whips see F. M. G. Wilson, 'Some Career Patterns in British Politics: Whips in the House of Commons 1906-66', *Parliamentary Affairs*, **24** (Winter 1970-1) pp. 33-42.

[1] From Feb 1948 to Jul 1977 and from May 1979 the office of Treasurer was held jointly.

[2] The Conservative Research Department was organised by Ld E. Percy in 1929 but there was no Chairman until Feb 1930.

Chief Whips in the House of Commons—*Cont.*

1959	M. Redmayne
1964	W. Whitelaw
1970	F. Pym
1973	H. Atkins
1979	M. Jopling
1983	J. Wakeham

Chairmen of 1922 Committee[1]

Jan 23-Nov 32	(Sir) G. Rentoul	Aug 45-Nov 51	Sir A. Gridley
Dec 32-Dec 35	W. Morrison	Nov 51-Nov 55	D. Walker-Smith
Dec 35-Jul 39	Sir H. O'Neill	Nov 55-Nov 64	J. Morrison
Sep 39-Nov 39	Sir A. Somerville	Nov 64-Mar 66	Sir W. Anstruther-Gray
Dec 39-Dec 40	W. Spens	May 66-Jul 70	Sir A. Harvey
Dec 40-Dec 44	A. Erskine Hill	Jul 70-Nov 72	Sir H. Legge-Bourke
Dec 44-Jun 45	J. McEwen	Nov 72-Nov 84	E. du Cann
		Nov 84-	C. Onslow

[1] Or the Conservative (Private) Members' Committee. This is an organisation of the entire backbench membership of the Conservative Party in the Commons. It acts as a sounding-board of Conservative opinion in the House, but is not authorised to formulate policy.

SOURCES.—*The Times Index, 1923-70*, information from the 1922 Committee, R. T. McKenzie, *British Political Parties* (1955), pp. 57-61, P. Goodhart, *The 1922* (1973) and Conservative Research Department.

Conservative Shadow Cabinets

Little has been published about the Conservative arrangements when in opposition. The situation appears to have been as follows:—

1906-14 After the 1906 defeat Conservative ex-ministers met regularly in what was known as a 'Shadow' Cabinet. Only after 1910 was new blood brought in, e.g. F. E. Smith and Sir A. Steel-Maitland.

1924 S. Baldwin summoned a formal Shadow Cabinet of all ex-ministers which met weekly during the Session and which had a secretariat.

1929-31 There was a Consultative Committee which met regularly and was serviced by the Research Department.

1945-51 The Chief Whip sent out notices to a regular Shadow Cabinet meeting, formally known as the Consultative Committee. Names were added but never subtracted and W. Churchill allowed the numbers to grow to about 24. No formal minutes were kept. The following seem to have attended regularly.

W. Churchill

——	A. Eden	O. Stanley
Sir J. Anderson	W. Elliot	J. Stuart
R. Assheton	R. Law	H. Willink
B. Bracken	O. Lyttelton	Vt Woolton
P. Buchan-Hepburn	H. Macmillan	
R. Butler	D. Maxwell Fyfe	*Secretary*
Ld Cherwell	W. Morrison	H. Hopkinson 1945-50
H. Crookshank	M of Salisbury	D. Clarke 1950-51

1964 A Leaders' Consultative Committee met regularly as soon as the party went into opposition and formal minutes were kept.

Sir A. Douglas-Home (1964-5)

Lord Blakenham
J. Boyd-Carpenter
Sir E. Boyle
R. Butler
Ld Carrington
Vt Dilhorne
J. Godber
E. Heath
Q. Hogg
Sir K. Joseph
S. Lloyd
I. Macleod
E. Marples
R. Maudling
M. Noble
E. Powell
M. Redmayne
D. Sandys
C. Soames
P. Thorneycroft

Secretary
Sir M. Fraser

E. Heath (1965-70)

Lord Balniel (1967-70)
A. Barber (1966-70)
J. Boyd-Carpenter (1965-6)
Sir E. Boyle (1965-9)
G. Campbell (1969-70)
R. Carr (1967-70)
Ld Carrington (1965-70)
Vt Dilhorne (1965-6)
Sir A. Douglas-Home (1965-70)
E. du Cann (1965-7)
J. Godber (1965-70)
Ld Harlech (1966-7)
Q. Hogg (1965-70)
Earl Jellicoe (1967-70)
Sir K. Joseph (1965-70)
S. Lloyd (1965-6)
I. Macleod (1965-70)
E. Marples (1965-6)
R. Maudling (1965-70)
M. Noble (1965-9)
Miss M. Pike (1966-7)
E. Powell (1965-8)
M. Redmayne (1965-6)
G. Rippon (1966-70)
D. Sandys (1965-6)
C. Soames (1965-6)
Mrs M. Thatcher (1967-70)
P. Thorneycroft (1965-6)
P. Walker (1966-70)
(W. Whitelaw, Chief Whip, 1966-70)

Secretary
Sir M. Fraser

1974 Procedures followed the general pattern of 1964-70

E. Heath (1974-5)

A. Barber (-74)
A. Buchanan-Smith
R. Carr
Ld Carrington
P. Channon
Sir A. Douglas-Home (-74)
I. Gilmour
Ld Hailsham
Sir G. Howe
P. Jenkin
Sir K. Joseph
M. Macmillan (-74)
J. Peyton
J. Prior
T. Raison
G. Rippon
N. St. John-Stevas
N. Scott
Mrs M. Thatcher
P. Thomas
W. Van Straubenzee (-74)
P. Walker
W. Whitelaw
Ld Windlesham (-74)
(H. Atkins, Chief Whip)

Secretary
Sir M. Fraser (Ld)

Mrs M. Thatcher (1975-9)

J. Biffen (1976-7, 1978-9)
A. Buchanan Smith (1975-6)
M. Carlisle (1978-9)
Ld Carrington (1975-9)
J. Davies (1976-8)
N. Edwards (1975-9)
N. Fowler (1975-6)
(Sir) I. Gilmour (1975-9)
Ld Hailsham (1975-9)
M. Heseltine (1975-9)
Sir G. Howe (1975-9)
P. Jenkin (1975-9)
Sir K. Joseph (1975-9)
T. King (1976-9)
A. Maude (1975-9)
R. Maudling (1975-6)
A. Neave (1975-9)

J. Nott (1976-9)
Mrs S. Oppenheim (1975-9)
J. Peyton (1975-9)
J. Prior (1975-9)
F. Pym (1975-9)
T. Raison (1975-6)
N. St. John-Stevas (1975-9)
E. Taylor (1976-9)
Ld Thorneycroft (1975-9)
W. Whitelaw (1975-9)
G. Younger (1975-9)
(H. Atkins, Chief Whip, 1975-9)

Secretary
Ld Fraser (1974-6)
C. Patten (1976-8)
D. Wolfson (1978-9)

Party Membership

The Conservative Party has seldom published figures of its total membership. Membership is a loose term, usually associated with the payment of an annual subscription, but exact records are not always kept locally, let alone nationally. In 1953 it was claimed that the party had reached an all-time record membership of 2,805,832, but this was a temporary peak. One estimate for 1969-70 suggests that the party's membership in Great Britain was then 1½ to 1¾ million. The Houghton Committee estimated that in 1975 the Conservatives had an average membership of 2,400 per constituency, which is equal to about 1½ million. Membership of the Young Conservatives fell from a peak of 157,000 in 1949 to 80,000 in 1959 and to 50,000 in 1968. In 1982 an internal study suggested that the membership was just under 1.2m. and a similar figure was found in 1984.

SOURCES.—*The British General Election of 1970* (1971), pp. 278-9, 287; *Committee on Financial Aid to Political Parties* (Cmnd 6601/1976 p. 31); M. Pinto-Duschinsky, *British Political Finance* (1980).

Party Finance

The Conservative Party did not publish its expenditure until 1968.[1] In 1912 Sir A. Steel-Maitland, the Party Chairman, put the party's annual income centrally at £80,000 and suggested that the extra expenses of a general election, centrally, were £80,000 to £120,000. In 1929 J. Davidson, then Chairman, put the cost of the general election at £290,000. Estimates for more recent general elections are given on p. 248.

The Houghton Committee estimated that in 1975-76 the Conservative parties raised £1.8m. at the centre and £4.5m. in the constituencies, a total of £6.3m.

In the year ending March 1983, the Conservative Party raised £4.8m. centrally and about £8.0m. locally. In the year ending March 1984 (containing a general election), central income totalled almost £10m.

[1] The routine central expenditure annually reported since 1968 has been:

1967-68	£1,071,000	1973-74	£2,134,000	1979-80	£6,200,000
1968-69	£1,054,000	1974-75	£2,867,000	1980-81	£5,500,000
1969-70	£1,052,000	1975-76	£1,874,000	1981-82	£4,200,000
1970-71	£1,668,000	1976-77	£2,177,000	1982-83	£4,700,000
1971-72	£1,249,000	1977-78	£2,754,000		
1972-73	£1,481,000	1978-79	£4,800,000		

SOURCES.—N. Blewett, *The Peers, the Parties and the People: The General Elections of 1910* (1972), p. 291; R. Rhodes James, *Memoirs of a Conservative* (1969); M. Harrison, in R. Rose and A. Heidenheimer (eds.), *Comparative Political Finance* (1963); R. Rose, *Influencing Voters* (1967), pp. 260-8; M. Pinto-Duschinsky, *The British General Election of 1970* (1971), pp. 282-3, and 'Central Office and "Power" in the Conservative Party', *Political Studies*, **20** (Mar 1972), pp. 1-16; *Committee on Financial Aid to Political Parties* (Cmnd 6601/1976 p. 31); M. Pinto-Duschinsky, *British Political Finance, 1830-1980* (1981); Conservative Party Headquarters.

National Union of Conservative and Unionist Associations—
Annual Conferences, 1900- [1]

Date	*Place*	*President*	*Chairman*
19 Dec 00	London	M of Zetland	Ld Windsor
26-27 Nov 01	Wolverhampton	Ld Llangattock	Sir A. Hickman
14-15 Oct 02	Manchester	E of Dartmouth	Sir C. Cave
1-2 Oct 03	Sheffield	E of Derby	F. Lowe
28-29 Oct 04	Southampton	D of Norfolk	H. Bowles
14-15 Nov 05	Newcastle upon Tyne	Ld Montagu of Beaulieu	Sir W. Plummer
27 Jul 06	London	D of Northumberland	H. Imbert-Terry
14-15 Nov 07	Birmingham	D of Northumberland	D of Rutland
19-20 Nov 08	Cardiff	E of Plymouth	Sir R. Hodge
17-18 Nov 09	Manchester	Earl Cawdor	Sir T. Wrightson
17 Nov 10	Nottingham	E of Derby	H. Chaplin
16-17 Nov 11	Leeds	D of Portland	Ld Kenyon
14-15 Nov 12	London	Ld Faber	Sir W. Crump
12-14 Nov 13	Norwich	Ld Farquhar	A. Salvidge
1914-16	*No conference held*	Sir A. Fellowes	Sir H. Samuel
1917	London	Sir A. Fellowes	Sir H. Samuel
1918-19	*No conference held*	Sir A. Fellowes	Sir H. Samuel
10-11 Jun 20	Birmingham	Sir A. Fellowes	J. Williams
17-18 Nov 21	Liverpool	A. Chamberlain	Sir A. Benn
15-16 Dec 22	London	E of Derby	Sir A. Leith
25-26 Oct 23	Plymouth	Ld Mildmay of Flete	Sir H. Nield
2-3 Oct 24	Newcastle upon Tyne	D of Northumberland	E of Selborne
8-9 Oct 25	Brighton	G. Loder	Sir P. Woodhouse
7-8 Oct 26	Scarborough	G. Lane-Fox	Dame C. Bridgeman
6-7 Oct 27	Cardiff	Vt Tredegar	Sir R. Sanders
27-28 Sep 28	Great Yarmouth	Ld Queenborough	J. Gretton
21-22 Nov 29	London	Ld Faringdon	G. Rowlands
1 Jul 30	London	N. Chamberlain	Countess of Iveagh
1931	*No conference held*	N. Chamberlain	G. Herbert
6-7 Oct 32	Blackpool	Ld Stanley	Earl Howe
5-6 Oct 33	Birmingham	E of Plymouth	Sir G. Ellis
4-5 Oct 34	Bristol	Ld Bayford	Miss R. Evans
3-4 Oct 35	Bournemouth	G. Herbert	Sir W. Cope
1-2 Oct 36	Margate	Ld Ebbisham	Sir L. Brassey
7-8 Oct 37	Scarborough	Ld Bingley	Mrs C. Fyfe
1938	*No conference held*	M of Londonderry	Sir E. Ramsden
1939	*No conference held*	M of Londonderry	N. Colman
1940	*No conference held*	Ld Queenborough	Lady Hillingdon
1941	*No conference held*	Ld Queenborough	Sir C. Headlam
1942	*No conference held*	M of Salisbury	R. Catterall
20-21 May 43	London	M of Salisbury	R. Catterall
1944	*No conference held*	M of Salisbury	Mrs L. Whitehead
14-15 Mar 45	London	Ld Courthope	R. Butler
3-5 Oct 46	Blackpool	O. Stanley	R. Proby
2-4 Oct 47	Brighton	H. Macmillan	Mrs Hornyold-Strickland
7-9 Oct 48	Llandudno	G. Summers	Sir H. Williams
12-14 Oct 49	London	Vt Swinton	D. Graham
12-14 Oct 50	Blackpool	Sir D. Maxwell Fyfe	A. Nutting
1951	*No conference held*	Ld Ramsden	Mrs L. Sayers
9-11 Oct 52	Scarborough	Sir T. Dugdale	C. Waterhouse
8-10 Oct 53	Margate	M of Salisbury	Mrs J. Warde
7-9 Oct 54	Blackpool	A. Eden	Sir G. Llewellyn
6-8 Oct 55	Bournemouth	Mrs L. Sayers	Mrs E. Emmet
11-13 Oct 56	Llandudno	R. Butler	Sir E. Edwards
10-12 Oct 57	Brighton	E of Woolton	Mrs W. Elliot
8-11 Oct 58	Blackpool	Sir R. Proby	Sir S. Bell
1959	*No conference held*	H. Brooke	E. Brown
12-15 Oct 60	Scarborough	H. Brooke	E. Brown
11-14 Oct 61	Brighton	Vt Hailsham	Sir D. Glover
10-13 Oct 62	Llandudno	Sir G. Llewellyn	Sir J. Howard
8-11 Oct 63	Blackpool	E of Home	Mrs T. Shepherd

[1] 1900-12, National Union of Conservative and Constitutional Associations, 1912-17 National Unionist Association of Conservative and Liberal-Unionist Associations, 1917-24, National Unionist Association, 1924- National Union of Conservative and Unionist Associations.

Date			Place	President	Chairman
		1964	*No conference held*	Vtess Davidson	Sir M. Bemrose
12-15	Oct	65	Brighton	Vtess Davidson	Sir M. Bemrose
13-16	Oct	66	Blackpool	S. Lloyd	Sir D. Mason
18-21	Oct	67	Brighton	Ld Chelmer	Mrs A. Doughty
9-12	Oct	68	Blackpool	R. Maudling	Sir T. Constantine
8-11	Oct	69	Brighton	Lady Brooke	D. Crossman
7-10	Oct	70	Blackpool	(I. Macleod)	Sir E. Leather
13-16	Oct	71	Brighton	W. Whitelaw	Miss U. Lister
11-14	Oct	72	Blackpool	Dame M. Shepherd	W. Harris
10-13	Oct	73	Blackpool	A. Barber	Mrs R. Smith
		1974	*No conference held*	P. Thomas	Sir A. Graesser
7-10	Oct	75	Blackpool	P. Thomas	Sir A. Graesser
5-8	Oct	76	Brighton	Ld Hewlett	Miss S. Roberts
11-14	Oct	77	Blackpool	Ld Carrington	D. Sells
10-14	Oct	78	Brighton	Dame A. Doughty	Sir H. Redfearn
9-12	Oct	79	Blackpool	F. Pym	D. Davenport-Handley
11-15	Oct	80	Brighton	Sir T. Constantine	Dame A. Springman
13-16	Oct	81	Blackpool	E. du Cann	F. Hardman
12-15	Oct	82	Brighton	Sir J. Taylor	D. Walters
11-14	Oct	83	Blackpool	Sir G. Howe	P. Lane
9-12	Oct	84	Brighton	Sir A. Graesser	Dame P. Hunter

SOURCES.—*National Union Gleanings 1900-12*, *Gleanings and Memoranda 1912-33*, *Politics in Review 1934-39*, all published by the National Union of Conservative Associations; *National Union of Conservative and Unionist Associations, Annual Conference Reports, 1958-*; for Conservative Party Manifestos and major recent reports, pamphlets, etc., see G. D. M. Block, *A Source Book of Conservatism* (1964). See also I. Bulmer-Thomas, *The Growth of the British Party System* (1965).

Labour Party

Party Leaders and Deputy Leaders

Chairman of the Parliamentary Party		*Vice Chairman*	
1906	K. Hardie	1906	D. Shackleton
1908	A. Henderson	1908	G. Barnes
1910	G. Barnes	1910	J. Clynes
1911	R. MacDonald	1911	W. Brace
1914	A. Henderson	1912	J. Parker
1917	W. Adamson	1914	A. Gill
1921	J. Clynes	1915	J. Hodge } *Acting Chairmen*
		1916	G. Wardle } *Acting Chairmen*
		1918	J. Clynes
		1921	J. Thomas } *joint*
			S. Walsh } *joint*

Chairman and Leader of the Parliamentary Party		*Deputy Leader*	
1922	R. MacDonald[1]	1922	S. Walsh } *joint*
			J. Wedgwood } *joint*
1931	A. Henderson[2]	1923	J. Clynes
1932	G. Lansbury	1931	J. Clynes } *joint*
			W. Graham } *joint*
1935	C. Attlee[1]	1931	C. Attlee
1955	H. Gaitskell	1935	A. Greenwood
1963	H. Wilson	1945	H. Morrison
Leader of the Parliamentary Party[1]		1956	J. Griffiths
		1959	A. Bevan
1970	H. Wilson	1960	G. Brown
1976	J. Callaghan	1970	R. Jenkins
Leader of the Labour Party		1972	E. Short
1978	J. Callaghan	1976	M. Foot
1980	M. Foot	1980	D. Healey
1983	N. Kinnock	1983	R. Hattersley

From 1922 to 1981 the Parliamentary Labour Party, when in opposition, elected its Leader and Deputy Leader at the beginning of each session. Most elections were uncontested, but there were these exceptions. (The figures in brackets show the result of the first ballot. The date is for the final ballot.)

Leader

Date		Candidate	First ballot	Final
21 Nov	22	R. MacDonald		61
		J. Clynes		56
3 Dec	35	C. Attlee	(58)	88
		H. Morrison	(44)	48
		A. Greenwood	(33)	—
14 Dec	55	H. Gaitskell		157
		A. Bevan		70
		H. Morrison		40
3 Nov	60	H. Gaitskell		166
		H. Wilson		81

Deputy Leader

Date		Candidate	First ballot	Final
11 Nov	52	H. Morrison		194
		A. Bevan		82
29 Oct	53	H. Morrison		181
		A. Bevan		76
2 Feb	56	J. Griffiths		141
		A. Bevan		111
10 Nov	60	G. Brown	(118)	146
		F. Lee	(73)	83
		J. Callaghan	(55)	—

[1] When the Labour Party was in power in 1924, 1929-31, 1940-45, 1945-51 and 1964-70, a Liaison Committee was set up. After 1970 the Parliamentary Party elected a separate Chairman. See p. 149.

[2] A. Henderson lost his seat in the 1931 election. The acting leader of the Parliamentary Labour Party in 1931 was G. Lansbury.

Leader						Deputy Leader				
2 Nov	61	H. Gaitskell		171	2 Nov	61	G. Brown		169
		A. Greenwood		59			Mrs B. Castle		56
14 Feb	63	H. Wilson	(115)	144	8 Nov	62	G. Brown		133
		G. Brown	(88)	103			H. Wilson		103
		J. Callaghan	(41)	—					
5 Apr	76	J. Callaghan	(84)(141)	176	8 Jul	70	R. Jenkins		133
		M. Foot	(90)(133)	137			M. Foot		67
		R. Jenkins	(56) —	—			F. Peart		48
		A. Wedgwood Benn	(37) —	—	17 Nov	71	R. Jenkins	(140)	140
		D. Healey	(30) (38)	—			M. Foot	(96)	126
		A. Crosland	(17) —	—			A. Wedgwood Benn	(46)	—
3 Nov	80	M. Foot	(83)	139	25 Apr	72	E. Short	(111)	145
		D. Healey	(112)	129			M. Foot	(89)	116
		J. Silkin	(38)	—			A. Crosland	(61)	—
		P. Shore	(32)	—	21 Oct	76	M. Foot		166
							Mrs S. Williams		128

At a special conference at Wembley, 24 Jan 1981, the Labour Party endorsed a procedure by which the Party's Leader and Deputy Leader should be re-elected each year by the Party Conference with 40% of the vote allocated to the Trade Unions, 30% to the Parliamentary Party and 30% to the constituency parties. The system was first used on 1 Sep 1981 when D. Healey defeated A. Benn for the Deputy Leadership.

	1st ballot				*2nd ballot*			
	TU	CLP	MP	Total	TU	CLP	MP	Total
D. Healey	24.696	5.367	15.306	45.369	24.994	5.673	19.759	50.426
A. Benn	6.410	23.483	6.374	36.627	15.006	24.327	10.241	49.574
J. Silkin	8.094	1.150	7.959	18.004				

It was used again on 1 Oct 1983 for both offices.

LEADER
1st ballot

	TU	CLP	MP	Total
N. Kinnock	29.042	27.452	14.778	71.272
R. Hattersley	10.878	0.577	7.833	19.288
E. Heffer	0.046	1.971	4.286	6.303
P. Shore	0.033	0.000	3.103	3.137

DEPUTY LEADER
1st ballot

	TU	CLP	MP	Total
R. Hattersley	35.237	15.313	16.716	67.266
M. Meacher	4.730	14.350	8.806	27.886
D. Davies	0.000	0.241	3.284	3.525
Ms G. Dunwoody	0.033	0.096	1.194	1.323

SOURCES.—*Labour Party Annual Conference Reports, Labour Year Books*; H. Pelling, *A Short History of the Labour Party* (4th ed., 1972), p. 130.

Leaders in the House of Lords

1924	Vt Haldane	1964	E of Longford
1928	Ld Parmoor	1968	Ld Shackleton
1931	Ld Ponsonby	1974	Ld Shepherd
1935	Ld Snell	1976	Ld Peart
1940	Ld (Vt) Addison	1982	Ld Cledwyn
1952	Earl Jowitt		
1955	Vt (Earl) Alexander of Hillsborough		

Chief Whips in the House of Commons

1906	D. Shackleton	1919	W. Tyson Wilson	1942	W. Whiteley
1906	A. Henderson	1920	A. Henderson	1955	H. Bowden
1907	G. Roberts	1924	B. Spoor	1954	E. Short
1914	A. Henderson	1925	A Henderson	1966	J. Silkin
1914	F. Goldstone	1927	T. Kennedy	1969	R. Mellish
1916	G. Roberts	1931	(Sir) C. Edwards	1976	M. Cocks
1916	J. Parker				

SOURCE.—For a full list of whips see F. M. G. Willson. 'Some Career Patterns in British Politics: Whips in the House of Commons 1906-66', *Parliamentary Affairs*, **24** (Winter 1970-1) pp. 33-42.

Chief Whips in the House of Lords

1924	Ld Muir-Mackenzie	1949	Ld Shepherd (1st)
1924	E De La Warr	1954	E of Lucan (6th)
1930	Ld Marley	1964	Ld Shepherd (2nd)
1937	Ld Strabolgi	1967	Ld Beswick
1941	E of Listowel	1973	Lady Llewelyn-Davies of Hastoe
1944	Ld Southwood		
1945	Ld Ammon	1982	Ld Ponsonby

SOURCES.—*Dod's Parliamentary Companion, 1900- ; Labour Party Annual Conference Reports.*

Labour Representation Committee—National Executive Officers

Chairman		*Treasurer*	
1900	F. Rogers	1902	F. Rogers
1902	R. Bell	1903	A. Gee
1904	D. Shackleton	1904	A. Henderson

Secretary

1900 R. MacDonald

Labour Party—National Executive Committee

Chairman

(listed as chairman of annual conferences at end of term of office, see p. 149)

Secretary

1906	R. MacDonald
1912	A. Henderson
1935	J. Middleton
1944	M. Phillips
(General Secretary)	
1959	M. Phillips
1962	A. Williams
1968	(Sir) H. Nicholas
1972	R. Hayward
1982	J. Mortimer
1985	L. Whitty

National Agent

1908	A. Peters
1919	E. Wake
1929	G. Shepherd
1946	R. Windle
1951	A. Williams
1962	Miss S. Barker
1969	R. Hayward
1972	R. (Ld) Underhill
1979	D. Hughes

Treasurer

1906	A. Henderson
1912	R. MacDonald
1929	A. Henderson
1936	G. Lathan
1943	A. Greenwood
1954	H. Gaitskell
1956	A. Bevan
1960	H. Nicholas
1964	D. Davies *(acting)*
1965	D. Davies
1967	J. Callaghan
1976	N. Atkinson
1981	E. Varley
1984	A. Booth
1984	S. McCluskey

Research Secretary[1]

1942	M. Phillips
1945	M. Young
1950	W. Fienburgh
1952	D. Ginsburg
1960	P. Shore
1965	T. Pitt
1974	G. Bish

SOURCES.—*Labour Representation Committee Annual Conference Reports, 1900-5*, and *Labour Party Annual Conference Reports, 1906-*.

[1] From 1922 to 1942 A. Greenwood acted as Secretary to the Research Department which was established in 1922 (at first as a Joint Research and Information Department).

Parliamentary Labour Party—Parliamentary Committee

This committee was originally known as the Executive Committee of the Parliamentary Labour Party. Its name was changed in 1951 to avoid confusion with the N.E.C. The committee was first elected in 1923 to take the place of the Policy Committee of the P.L.P. It consists of 15 (12 until 1981) Commons' members, elected at the opening of every session of Parliament by members of the P.L.P. with seats in the House of Commons. There are six *ex officio* members: the Leader and Deputy Leader of the Party, the Chief Whip in the House of Commons, the Leader of the Labour Peers, the Chief Whip of the Labour Peers and their elected representative. The elected Commons' members of the Parliamentary Committee sit on the Front Bench with the Party's Leader, Deputy Leader, Chief Whip and the Assistant Whips. Ex-Labour Ministers have the right, by custom of the House, to sit on the Front Bench, but usually prefer a place on the Back Benches. The officers and the elected 15 are joined on the Front Benches by a number of other members who have been allotted the responsibility of looking after particular subects. After 1955 it became the practice of the Leader of the P.L.P. to invite members to take charge of particular subjects, and these members included some who are not members of the Parliamentary Committee. In 1924 and 1929 when the Labour Party was in office a Consultative Committee of twelve was appointed representative of both Front and Back Benches. During the wartime coalition the P.L.P. elected an Administrative Committee of twelve, with Peers' representation, all of whom were non-Ministers. When the Labour Party was in office from 1945 to 1951, and from 1964 to 1970, the P.L.P. set up a small Liaison Committee of three elected backbench M.P.s, the Leader of the House, the Government Chief Whip, and an elected backbench Labour Peer. Until 1964 the Leader acted as Chairman at P.L.P. meetings when the party was in Opposition. Since 1970 the P.L.P. has elected a separate chairman.

Parliamentary Labour Party—Executive Committee

The figures denote the order of successful candidates in the ballot.

1923-29

	Feb 1923	Dec 1924	Dec 1925	Dec 1926	Dec 1927	1928[a]
W. Adamson	9	. .	11	11	8	
H. Dalton	. .	. .	12	3	7	
R. Davies	12	. .	. .	. .	. .	
W. Graham	. .	8	2	2	3	
A. Henderson	. .	10	. .	12	2	
T. Johnston	3	. .	. .	4	4	
F. Jowett	6	. .	. .	. .	. .	
G. Lansbury	2	1	10	9	10	
H. Lees-Smith	. .	11	4	6	6	
J. Maxton	. .	6	. .	. .	. .	
E. Morel	5	. .	. .	. .	. .	
F. Roberts	. .	12	. .	. .	. .	
T. Shaw	11	. .	7	. .	12	
E. Shinwell	7	. .	. .	. .	. .	
R. Smillie	. .	2	5	7	. .	
P. Snowden	1	3	1	1	1	
J. Thomas	4	4	3	5	5	
C. Trevelyan	. .	7	6	8	11	
S. Walsh	. .	. .	8	. .	. .	
S. Webb	10	. .	9	10	9	
J. Wedgwood	. .	9	. .	. .	. .	
J. Wheatley	8	5	. .	. .	. .	

[a] There is no record of an Executive Committee election in 1928

1931

On 28 Aug 31 officers were elected to the P.L.P.: A. Henderson (Leader), J. Clynes (Deputy Leader), W. Graham (2nd Deputy Leader), T. Kennedy (Chief Whip). On 8 Sep 31 the following were elected to the P.L.P. Committee (in order)

T. Johnston	E. Edwards
G. Lansbury	F. Pethick Lawrence
H. Dalton	E. Shinwell
A. Greenwood	H. Lees-Smith
J. Barr	D. Grenfell
C. Addison	Mary Hamilton
A. Alexander	

All but G. Lansbury and D. Grenfell were defeated in the Oct 31 election.

1931-35

	Nov 1931	Nov 1932	Nov 1933	Nov 1934
Sir S. Cripps	1	1	2	1
D. Grenfell	2	2	1	2
G. Hicks	4	3	3	5
M. Jones	7	7	4	6
W. Lunn	5	4	6	4
N. Maclean	6	6	7	7
T. Williams	3	5	5	3

1935-40

	Nov 1935	Nov 1936	Nov 1937	Nov 1938	Nov 1939
A. Alexander	6	5	2	2	1
W. Wedgwood Benn	. .	. .	7	5	2
J. Clynes	1	6	. .	. .	. .
H. Dalton	2	3	5	3	10
D. Grenfell	5	4	4	4	4
G. Hall	. .	. .	. .	. .	7
T. Johnston	3	2	3	6	. .
M. Jones	10	8	11	12	. .
J. Lawson	. .	. .	. .	. .	12
H. Lees-Smith	9	11	8	8	5
W. Lunn	11	. .	. .	. .	. .
N. Maclean	12	. .	. .	. .	. .
H. Morrison	4	1	1	1	8
P. Noel-Baker	. .	10	12	10	11
F. Pethick-Lawrence	8	9	9	9	6
D. Pritt	. .	12	. .	. .	. .
E. Shinwell	. .	. .	10	11	9
T. Williams	7	7	6	7	3

Parliamentary Labour Party (Parliamentary Committee)

(number indicates position in ballot)

1951-63

	Nov 1951	Nov 1952	Nov 1953	Nov 1954	Jun 1955	Nov 1956	Nov 1957	Nov 1958	Nov 1959	Nov 1960	Nov 1961	Nov 1962	Nov 1963
A. Bevan	. .	12	9[a]	. .	7	3	3	1	. .	. .	. .	. .	. .
A. Bottomley	. .	. .	. .	. .	. .	. .	12	9	. .	. .	. .	. .	. .
G. Brown	. .	. .	. .	. .	8	10	9	. .	8	. .	. .	. .	. .
J. Callaghan	7	6	4	10	3	5	5	5	2	1	7	1	2
R. Crossman	. .	. .	. .	. .	. .	. .	. .	. .	13[d]	. .	. .	. .	. .
H. Dalton	8	5	5	4	. .	. .	. .	. .	. .	. .	. .	. .	. .
J. Chuter Ede	5	2	6	9	. .	. .	. .	. .	. .	. .	. .	. .	. .
T. Fraser	. .	. .	. .	. .	14[c]	12	8	12	7	6	9	5	6
H. Gaitskell	3	3	2	1[b]	2[c]	. .	. .	. .	. .	. .	. .	. .	. .
P. Gordon Walker	. .	. .	. .	. .	. .	. .	11	6	9	8	11	6	5
A. Greenwood	12	. .	. .	. .	10	6	7	8	6[d]	. .	. .	. .	. .
J. Griffiths	1	1	1	1[b]	1[c]	. .	. .	. .	. .	. .	. .	. .	. .
R. Gunter	. .	. .	. .	. .	. .	. .	. .	. .	. .	7	6	10	8
W. Glenvil Hall	2	9	12	11	. .	. .	. .	. .	. .	. .	. .	. .	. .
D. Healey	. .	. .	. .	. .	. .	. .	. .	. .	12	5	4	9	7
D. Houghton	. .	. .	. .	. .	. .	. .	. .	. .	. .	10	3	4	3
D. Jay	. .	. .	. .	. .	. .	. .	. .	. .	. .	. .	. .	13[e]	11
F. Lee	. .	. .	. .	. .	. .	. .	. .	. .	5	12	12	12	10
G. Mitchison	. .	. .	. .	. .	12	4	2	3	10	3	8	7	12
P. Noel-Baker	9	8	10	8	9	8	10	10	. .	. .	. .	. .	. .
A. Robens	4	4	7	6	4	2	6	7	4	. .	. .	. .	. .
E. Shinwell	11	11	11	7	. .	. .	. .	. .	. .	. .	. .	. .	. .
Sir F. Soskice	. .	7	3	3	. .	7	4	4	3	2	2	2	4
M. Stewart	. .	. .	. .	. .	. .	. .	. .	. .	. .	4	5	8	1
R. Stokes	6	. .	. .	. .	11	. .	. .	. .	. .	. .	. .	. .	. .
E. Summerskill	10	10	8	5	6	9	. .	11	. .	. .	. .	. .	. .
F. Willey	. .	. .	. .	. .	. .	. .	. .	. .	11	11	10	11	9
H. Wilson	. .	. .	13[a]	12	5	1	1	2	1	9	1	3	. .
K. Younger	. .	. .	. .	. .	13[c]	11	. .	. .	. .	. .	. .	. .	. .

[a] A. Bevan resigned from the Parliamentary Committee on 14 Apr 54; H. Wilson, who was 13th in order of votes obtained, took his place on the Committee on 28 Apr 54.

[b] H. Gaitskell and J. Griffiths both obtained 170 votes and tied for first place.

[c] H. Gaitskell and J. Griffiths were elected Leader and Deputy Leader of the Parliamentary Labour Party on 14 Dec 55 and 2 Feb 56, K. Younger and T. Fraser as runners-up filled the vacant places on the Parliamentary Committee.

[d] A. Greenwood resigned from the Parliamentary Committee on 13 Oct 60. R. Crossman, who was 13th in order of votes obtained, took his place on the Committee for a few weeks until the 1960-61 sessional elections in November.

[e] D. Jay joined the Committee when H. Wilson was elected leader.

1970-73

	Jul 1970	Nov 1971	Nov 1972	Nov 1973
A. Benn	5	10	11	8
J. Callaghan	1	4	5	1
Mrs B. Castle	12	15[a]	..	..
A. Crosland	3	8	3	4
M. Foot	6	2	4	2
D. Healey	2	12	6	7
D. Houghton	4	..	..	..
R. Jenkins	..	..	..	5
H. Lever	8	7[a]	9	8
F. Peart	10	6	8	..
R. Prentice	..	13[a]	1	3
M. Rees	..	..	10	10
W. Ross	..[c]	5	7	12
P. Shore	..	11	12[b]	11
E. Short	9	1	..	..
J. Silkin	..	14[a]	(12[b])	(13)
G. Thomson	11	9[a]	..	..
Mrs S. Williams	7	3	1	6

[a] H. Lever and G. Thomson resigned on 10 Apr 1972. They were replaced by R. Prentice and J. Silkin, who had 13th and 14th place respectively in the original ballot. When E. Short became Deputy Leader, Mrs B. Castle beat E. Heffer 111-89, to take his place on the Committee on 3 May 1972.
[b] J. Silkin, who tied with P. Shore for 12th place, withdrew, making a second ballot unnecessary.
[c] W. Ross joined the committee in Nov 1970 when D. Houghton became Chairman of the P.L.P.

1979-

	Jun 1979	Nov 1980	Nov 1981[b]	Nov 1982	Nov 1983	Oct 1984
P. Archer	..	..	14	9	8	7
A. W. Benn	..	(13)[a]	..	..	..	..
A. Booth	7	8	8	6	..	..
R. Cook	..	..	..	..	10	15
J. Cunningham	..	..	..	..	5	3
D. Davies	..	..	..	..	..	12
D. Dewar	..	..	..	..	..	14
Ms G. Dunwoody	..	..	15	13	12	10
R. Hattersley	4	1	3	4	..	..
D. Healey	1	..	..	..	1	2
E. Heffer	..	..	13	15	11	..
B. John	..	..	10	12	..	..
B. Jones	..	..	..	..	9	8
G. Kaufman	..	3	2	1	2	1
N. Kinnock	..	12	7	2	..	..
R. Mason	11	10	..	..	..	..
M. Meacher	..	..	..	..	13	11
B. Millan	..	..	12	14	..	..
S. Orme	6	6	11	10	15	4
D. Owen	10	..	..	..	..	..
J. Prescott	..	..	..	..	6	8
G. Radice	..	..	..	..	14	13
M. Rees	9	4	6	11	..	..
W. Rodgers	8	9	..	..	..	..
P. Shore	3	5	1	3	3	6
J. Silkin	2	7	4	7	7	..
J. Smith	12	11	9	8	4	5
E. Varley	5	2	5	5	..	..

[a] A. Benn took over the place vacated by W. Rodgers when he joined the SDP.
[b] The PLP Committee was enlarged from 12 to 15 elected members in 1981.

Chairmen of Parliamentary Committee with Labour in power 1924-70

1924 *Parliamentary Executive Committee*

1924	R. Smillie

1929-31 *Consultative Committee*

1929	H. Snell
1930	J. Barr

1940-45 *Administrative Committee*

1940	H. Lees-Smith (*acting*)[1]
1941	H. Lees-Smith (*acting*)[1]
1942	F. Pethick-Lawrence (*acting*)[1]
1942	A. Greenwood (*acting*)[1]
1943	A. Greenwood (*acting*)[1]
1944	A. Greenwood (*acting*)[1]

1945-51 *Liaison Committee*

1945	N. Maclean
1946	M. Webb
1947	M. Webb
1948	M. Webb
1949	M. Webb
1950	W. Glenvil Hall

1964-70 *Liaison Committee*

1964	E. Shinwell
1967	D. Houghton

Chairmen of Parliamentary Labour Party, 1970-

1970 (Nov)	D. Houghton
1974 (Mar)	I. Mikardo
1974 (Nov)	C. Hughes
1979 (Jun)	F. Willey
1983 (Nov)	J. Dormand

Secretary Parliamentary Labour Party

1943	C. Johnson
1959	(Sir) G. Barlow
1979	B. Davies

SOURCES.—1923-29, *Daily Herald* and *Directory for National Council of Labour, TUC General Council, Labour Party and the Parliamentary Labour Party* (published annually by the Labour Party); 1931-, *Labour Party Annual Conference Reports*; *The Times*; and *Labour Party Directory*.

[1] During C. Attlee's membership of the war-time Coalition, the Labour Party appointed an Acting Chairman each session.

Labour Representation Committee—Annual Conferences, 1900-1905

Date	*Place*	*Chairman*
27-28 Feb 00	London	W. Steadman
1 Feb 01	Manchester	J. Hodge
20-22 Feb 02	Birmingham	W. Davies
19-21 Feb 03	Newcastle upon Tyne	J. Bell
4-5 Feb 04	Bradford	J. Hodge
26-29 Jan 05	Liverpool	A. Henderson

Labour Party—Annual Conferences, 1906-

Date	*Place*	*Chairman*
15-17 Feb 06	London	A. Henderson
24-26 Jan 07	Belfast	J. Stephenson
20-22 Jan 08	Hull	W. Hudson
27-29 Jan 09	Portsmouth	J. Clynes
9-11 Feb 10	Newport	J. Keir Hardie
1-3 Feb 11	Leicester	W. Robinson
24-26 Jan 12	Birmingham	B. Turner
29-31 Jan 13	London	G. Roberts
27-30 Jan 14	Glasgow	T. Fox
1915	*No conference held*	
26-28 Jan 16	Bristol	W. Anderson
23-26 Jan 17	Manchester	G. Wardle
23-25 Jan 18[1]	Nottingham	W. Purdy
26-28 Jun 18	London	W. Purdy
25-27 Jun 19	Southport	J. McGurk
22-25 Jun 20	Scarborough	W. Hutchinson

[1] Adjourned for one month. Resumed 26 Feb 18 in London.

Date			Place	Chairman
21-24	Jun	21	Brighton	A. Cameron
27-30	Jun	22	Edinburgh	F. Jowett
26-29	Jun	23	London	S. Webb
7-10	Oct	24	London	R. MacDonald
29 Sep-2	Oct	25	Liverpool	C. Cramp
11-15	Oct	26	Margate	R. Williams
3-7	Oct	27	Blackpool	F. Roberts
1-5	Oct	28	Birmingham	G. Lansbury
30 Sep-4	Oct	29	Brighton	H. Morrison
6-10	Oct	30	Llandudno	Susan Lawrence
5-8	Oct	31	Scarborough	S. Hirst
3-7	Oct	32	Leicester	G. Lathan
2-6	Oct	33	Hastings	J. Compton
1-5	Oct	34	Southport	W. Smith
30 Sep-4	Oct	35	Brighton	W. Robinson
5-9	Oct	36	Edinburgh	Jennie Adamson
4-8	Oct	37	Bournemouth	H. Dalton
		1938	*No conference held*	
29 May-2	Jun	39	Southport	G. Dallas
13-16	May	40	Bournemouth	Barbara Gould
2-4	Jun	41	London	J. Walker
25-28	May	42	London	W. Green
14-18	Jun	43	London	A. Dobbs
11-15	Dec	44	London	G. Ridley
21-25	May	45	Blackpool	Ellen Wilkinson
10-14	Jun	46	Bournemouth	H. Laski
26-30	May	47	Margate	P. Noel-Baker
17-21	May	48	Scarborough	E. Shinwell
6-10	Jun	49	Blackpool	J. Griffiths
2-6	Oct	50	Margate	S. Watson
1-3	Oct	51	Scarborough	Alice Bacon
29 Sep-3	Oct	52	Morecambe	H. Earnshaw
28 Sep-2	Oct	53	Margate	Arthur Greenwood
27 Sep-1	Oct	54	Scarborough	W. Burke
10-14	Oct	55	Margate	Edith Summerskill
1-5	Oct	56	Blackpool	E. Gooch
30 Sep-4	Oct	57	Brighton	Margaret Herbison
29 Sep-3	Oct	58	Scarborough	T. Driberg
28-29	Nov	59	Blackpool	Barbara Castle
3-7	Oct	60	Scarborough	G. Brinham
2-6	Oct	61	Blackpool	R. Crossman
2-5	Oct	62	Brighton	H. Wilson
30 Sep-4	Oct	63	Scarborough	D. Davies
12-13	Dec	64	Brighton	Anthony Greenwood
27 Sep-1	Oct	65	Blackpool	R. Gunter
3-7	Oct	66	Brighton	W. Padley
2-6	Oct	67	Scarborough	J. Boyd
30 Sep-4	Oct	68	Blackpool	Jennie Lee
29 Sep-3	Oct	69	Brighton	Eirene White
28 Sep-2	Oct	70	Blackpool	A. Skeffington
4-8	Oct	71	Brighton	I. Mikardo
2-6	Oct	72	Blackpool	A. Benn
1-5	Oct	73	Blackpool	W. Simpson
27-30	Nov	74	London	J. Callaghan
26	Apr	75[1]	London	F. Mulley
29 Sep-3	Oct	75	Blackpool	F. Mulley
27 Sep-1	Oct	76	Blackpool	T. Bradley
3-7	Oct	77	Brighton	Joan Lestor
2-6	Oct	78	Blackpool	Joan Lestor
1-5	Oct	79	Brighton	F. Allaun
29 Sep-3	Oct	80	Blackpool	Lady Jeger
27 Sep-2	Oct	81	Brighton	A. Kitson
27 Sep-1	Oct	82	Blackpool	Dame J. Hart
3-8	Oct	83	Brighton	S. McCluskey
1-5	Oct	84	Blackpool	E. Heffer

SOURCES.—*1900-5 Reports of the Labour Representation Committee Annual Conferences, Labour Party Annual Conference Reports 1906-.*

[1] Special conference on the Common Market.

Labour Party—Membership Statistics

Year	No. Constit. & Central Parties	Total Indiv. Members ('000s)	T.U.s No.	T.U.s Members ('000s)	Soc. & Co-op. Socs. No.	Soc. & Co-op. Socs. Members ('000s)	Total Membership ('000s)
1900-01	7	. .	41	353	3	23	376
1901-02	21	. .	65	455	2	14	469
1902-03	49	. .	127	847	2	14	861
1903-04	76	. .	165	956	2	14	970
1904-05	73	. .	158	855	2	15	900
1905-06	73	. .	158	904	2	17	921
1906-07	83	. .	176	975	2	21	998
1907	92	. .	181	1,050	2	22	1,072
1908	133	. .	176	1,127	2	27	1,159
1909	155	. .	172	1,451	2	31	1,486
1910	148	. .	151	1,394	2	31	1,431
1911	149	. .	141	1,502	2	31	1,539
1912	146	. .	130	1,858	2	31	1,895
1913	158	. .	[a]	[a]	2	33	[a]
1914	179	. .	10!	1,572	2	33	1,612
1915	177	. .	111	2,054	2	33	2,093
1916	199	. .	119	2,171	3	42	2,220
1917	239	. .	123	2,415	3	47	2,465
1918	389	[b]	131	2,960	4	53	3,013
1919	418	. .	126	3,464	7	47	3,511
1920	492	. .	122	4,318	5	42	4,360
1921	456	. .	116	3,974	5	37	4,010
1922	482	. .	102	3,279	5	32	3,311
1923	503	. .	106	3,120	6	36	3,156
1924	529	. .	108	3,158	7	36	3,194
1925	549	. .	106	3,338	8	36	3,374
1926	551	. .	104	3,352	8	36	3,388
1927	532	. .	97	3,239	6	55[c]	3,294
1928	535	215	91	2,025[d]	7	52	2,292[d]
1929	578	228	91	2,044	6	59	2,331
1930	607	277	89	2,011	7	58	2,347
1931	608	297	80	2,024	7	37	2,358
1932	608	372	75	1,960	9	40	2,372
1933	612	366	75	1,899	9	40	2,305
1934	614	381	72	1,858	8	40	2,278
1935	614	419	72	1,913	9	45	2,378
1936	614	431	73	1,969	9	45	2,444
1937	614	447	70	2,037	8	43	2,528
1938	614	429	70	2,158	9	43	2,630
1939	614	409	72	2,214	6	40	2,663
1940	614	304	73	2,227	6	40	2,571
1941	585	227	68	2,231	6	28	2,485
1942	581	219	69	2,206	6	29	2,454
1943	586	236	69	2,237	6	30	2,503
1944	598	266	68	2,375	6	32	2,673
1945	649	487	69	2,510	6	41	3,039
1946	649	645	70	2,635[d]	6	42	3,322[d]
1947	649	608	73	4,386	6	46	5,040

[a] Owing to the operation of the Osborne Judgement it was made impossible to compile membership statistics for 1913.
[b] Individual membership statistics were not compiled 1918-27.
[c] The Royal Arsenal Co-operative Society, through its Political Purposes Committee, continued its affiliation with the Labour Party; its membership is included in the 1927-60 totals.
[d] From 1928 to 1946 inclusive, trade unionist members of the Labour Party had to 'contract in' to payment to party political funds.

Year	No. Constit. & Central Parties	Total Indiv. Members ('000s)	T.U.s No.	T.U.s Members ('000s)	Soc. & Co-op. Socs. No.	Soc. & Co-op. Socs. Members ('000s)	Total Membership ('000s)
1948	656	629	80	4,751	6	42	5,422
1949	660	730	80	4,946	5	41	5,717
1950	661	908	83	4,972	5	40	5,920
1951	667	876	82	4,937	5	35	5,849
1952	667	1,015	84	5,072	5	21	6,108
1953	667	1,005	84	5,057	5	34	6,096
1954	667	934	84	5,530	5	35	6,498
1955	667	843	87	5,606	5	35	6,484
1956	667	845	88	5,658	5	34	6,537
1957	667	913	87	5,644	5	26	6,583
1958	667	889	87	5,628	5	26	6,542
1959	667	848	87	5,564	5	25	6,437
1960	667	790	86	5,513	5	25	6,328
1961	667	751	86	5,550	5	25	6,326
1962	667	767	86	5,503	5	25	6,296
1963	667	830	83	5,507	6	21	6,358
1964	667	830	83	5,502	6	21	6,353
1965	659	817	79	5,602	6	21	6,440
1966	658	776	79	5,539	6	21	6,336
1967	657	734	75	5,540	6	21	6,295
1968	656	701	68	5,364	6	21	6,087
1969	656	681	68	5,462	6	22	6,164
1970	656	680	67	5,519	6	24	6,183
1971	659	700	67	5,559	6	25	6,310
1972	659	703	62	5,425	9	40	6,197
1973	651	665	60	5,365	9	42	6,073
1974	623	692	63	5,787	9	39	6,406
1975	623	675	61	5,750	9	44	6,392
1976	623	659	59	5,800	9	48	6,499
1977	623	660	59	5,913	9	43	6,754
1978	623	676	59	6,260	9	55	6,990
1979	623	666	59	6,511	9	58	7,236
1980	623	348	54	6,407	10	56	6,811
1981	623	277	54	6,273	10	58	6,608
1982	623	274	50	6,185	10	57	6,515
1983	633	295	47	6,101	10	59	6,454

SOURCE.—*Labour Party Annual Conference Reports.*

The Labour Party—Organisation and Constitutions

The Labour Representation Committee was formed on 27 Feb 1900 to promote a distinct Labour group in Parliament, representing the affiliated trade unions and socialist societies. After the General Election of 1906 the L.R.C. group of M.P.s decided to assume the title of 'Labour Party' and elected their first officers and whips. Policy was determined by the Labour Party through the annual conference and its executive authority, the National Executive Committee. There was no official party leader, but an annually elected chairman of the parliamentary party. There were scarcely any official Labour Party constituency organisations (except for those provided by local trades councils, groups of miners' lodges, and local branches of the I.L.P.). In 1914 there were only two constituency associations with individual members, Woolwich and Barnard Castle, which Will Crooks and Arthur Henderson had built up on their own.

The Reorganisation of the Labour Party, 1918

The reorganisation of the Labour Party was projected by Arthur Henderson in collaboration with Sidney Webb. Their main aims were to provide local Labour Parties in every constituency or group of constituencies. These local Labour Parties were to be based fundamentally on individual subscribing membership, though representation was provided for trades councils, trade union branches, and socialist societies. The members of the N.E.C. were to be elected by the annual conference as a whole (though eleven were to be elected from candidates nominated by the trade unions and socialist societies as a single group, five were to represent the Local Labour Parties, and four were to be women). The scheme also involved an increase in affiliation fees.

The original plan was amended, so that the N.E.C. was increased to a membership of 23 (adding two to the number specified for affiliated organisations). It was agreed that the election programme should be produced by the N.E.C. and P.L.P. jointly—subject to the aims of the Party and the decisions of the annual conferences. The object of the pre-war Party had been to 'organise and maintain in Parliament and in the country a political Labour Party'. In 1918 this was changed to a new formula: 'to secure for the producers by hand and by brain the full fruits of their industry, and the most equitable distribution thereof that may be possible, upon the basis of the common ownership of the means of production and the best obtainable system of popular administration and control of each industry and service'.[1]

Modifications since 1918

The 1918 constitution was modified in 1937 in favour of the local constituency Labour Parties, which had repeatedly demanded a greater share in the control of party affairs. Representation of the constituency parties on the N.E.C. was increased from five to seven. The seven were to be elected by the vote of the constituency delegates alone. The twelve trade union representatives and one representative of the socialist societies were to be elected separately by their respective conference delegations. The five women members

[1] The 1914 and 1918 Labour Party constitutions are set out and compared in G. D. H. Cole, *A History of the Labour Party from 1914* (1948), pp. 71-81.

may be nominated by any affiliated organisation and are elected by a vote of the whole party conference. The Leader (since 1929) and the Deputy Leader (since 1953) are *ex officio* members of the N.E.C. The Treasurer of the Party may be nominated by any affiliated organisation, and is elected by the vote of the whole party conference. In 1972 a Young Socialist elected by the National Conference of Labour Party Young Socialists was added to the N.E.C. In 1981 the procedure for the election of Leader and Deputy Leader was changed (see p. 143).

SOURCES.—H. Pelling, *The Origins of the Labour Party, 1880-1900* (1954); F. Bealey and H. Pelling, *Labour and Politics, 1900-1906* (1958); P. Poirier, *The Advent of the Labour Party* (1958); G. D. H. Cole, *British Working-Class Politics, 1832-1914* (1941); G. D. H. Cole, *A History of the Labour Party from 1914* (1948); R. T. McKenzie, *British Political Parties* (1955); L. Minkin, *The Labour Party Conference* (1978). Since 1918 complete lists of Labour Party publications have been given in the Labour Party Annual Conference Reports. See also I. Bulmer-Thomas, *The Growth of the British Party System* (1965).

Sponsored M.P.s

The table on p. 155 summarises information on sponsored Labour M.P.s. M.P.s have also been sponsored by organisations which are not affiliated to the Labour Party. The two major instances of this are the National Union of Teachers and the National Farmers' Union.

Trades Union-sponsored M.P.s, 1918- (Labour)

No figures for Trades Union-sponsored M.P.s are available before 1918. Unions are here listed under their 1974 titles. M.P.s sponsored by Unions which subsequently amalgamated with other Unions and adopted other titles are listed under their present titles.

Trade Unions	1918	1922	1923	1924	1929	1931	1935	1945	1950	1951	1955	1959	1964	1966	1970	Feb 1974	Oct 1974	1979	1983
Nat. U. of Mineworkers (Miners' Federation of G.B., 1918-45)	25	41	43	40	42	26	32	34	37	36	34	31	28	26	20	18	18	16	14
Transport and General Workers' U.	3	7	10	10	13	1	7	17	16	14	14	14	21	25	19	23	22	22	25
Nat. U. of Railwaymen	1	3	4	3	8	..	5	12	10	9	8	5	6	7	5	6	6	12	10
Transport Salaried Staffs Ass. (Railway Clerks' Ass., 1918-50)	..	..	..	..	7	..	6	9	7	7	5	5	7	6	4	3	3	3	2
Nat. U. of General and Municipal Workers	4	5	5	4	6	2	6	10	6	6	4	4	9	11	12	13	13	14	11
Ass. Society of Woodworkers (UCATT 1972-)	1	1	3	2	6	1	2	3	3	3	2	1	..	..	..	2	3	1	1
U. of Shop, Distributive and Allied Workers	..	1	4	4	4	1	6	8	8	9	9	9	10	8	7	6	5	5	2
British Iron, Steel and Kindred Trades Ass.	..	2	1	3	4	1	1	2	2	2	2	2	1	1	2	2	1	2	1
United Textile Factory Workers' Ass.	4	3	3	2	4	..	..	3	2	1	1	1	1	1	..	..	..	..	..
Amalgamated Engineering U. (Amalgamated U. of Engineering Workers 1920-70)	1	7	4	4	3	2	3	4	8	8	6	8	18	18	16	22	21	21	17 ..
Nat. U. of Boot and Shoe Operatives	1	2	1	..	2	..	..	4	1	1	..	..	..	..	..	..	..	..	..
Ass. Society of Locomotive Engineers and Firemen	..	..	..	1	1	..	1	2	2	2	2	3	1	1	..	..	..	..	..
United Society of Boilermakers, etc.	1	1	2	2	1	1	1	..	..	..	..	..	..	..	..	..	..	2	..
U. of Post Office Workers	..	2	3	2	..	..	..	1	1	2	1	2	2	3	1	2	2	2	3
Nat. U. of Agricultural Workers	..	..	1	..	..	..	..	1	1	1	1	2	1	1	..	..	..	1	..
Electrical Trades U.	..	..	..	..	..	..	..	1	1	1	..	..	1	1	3	3	3	4	3
Ass. of Scientific, Technical and Managerial Staffs (A.S.S.E.T. 1951-68)	..	..	..	..	..	..	..	..	..	..	..	..	..	1	2	6	10	8	10
Clerical and Administrative Workers U. (APEX)	..	..	..	..	..	..	..	..	1	1	2	2	3	4	3	6	6	5	3
National Union of Public Employees	..	..	..	..	..	..	..	..	1	2	2	1	2	5	6	6	6	7	4
Others	8	11	18	11	13	..	8	9	4	3	2	2	8	13	11	9	7	7	9
Total T.U. M.P.s	49	86	102	88	114	35	78	120	111	108	95	92	120	127	112	127	126	134	115
Co-operative Party M.P.s	1	4	6	5	9	1	9	23	18	16	18	16	20	18	17	16	16	17	8
Total unsupported M.P.s	7	52	83	58	164	10	67	250	186	171	164	150	177	218	158	143	177	118	86
Total Labour M.P.s	57	142	191	151	287	46	154	393	315	295	277	258	317	363	287	301	319	269	209

SOURCES.—1918-24, *Labour Party Annual Conference Reports*; 1929-59, *Trade Unions and the Labour Party since 1945*, by M. Harrison (1960) (these figures are also based on the Labour Party Conference Reports but modified by examination of union accounts); J. Bailey, *The British Co-operative Movement* (1955); W. Muller, *The Kept Men* (1977), and information from Transport House.

National Union of Teachers

The N.U.T. sponsored and assisted parliamentary candidates from 1895 to 1974. The number of sponsored candidates varied, but a strict parity between the parties was always attempted. The practice ceased after 1974.

N.U.T. adopted and supported M.P.s, 1900-1974

Election	Total	Con.	Lab.	Lib.
1900	3	1	. .	2
1906	2	. .	. .	2
1910 (Jan)	1	. .	. .	1
1910 (Dec)	2	. .	1	1
1918	1	1	. .	. .
1922	3	1	2	. .
1923	3	. .	3	. .
1924	4	1	3	. .
1929	5	. .	5	. .
1931	3	1	2	. .
1935	5	1	4	. .
1945	2	. .	2	. .
1950	4	. .	4	. .
1951	4	. .	4	. .
1955	6	2	4	. .
1959	6	2	4	. .
1964	5	1	4	. .
1966	4	1	3	. .
1970	5	2	3	. .
1974 (Feb)	5	1	4	. .
1974 (Oct)	4	1	3	. .

SOURCES.—Information received from the National Union of Teachers; J. D. Stewart, *British Pressure Groups* (1958).

National Farmers' Union

In 1909 the N.F.U. set up a Parliamentary Fund with the object of sending two sponsored M.P.s to Parliament from each side of the House. Although sometimes 'independent on agricultural questions' all N.F.U. M.P.s have been Conservatives. Since 1945 the N.F.U. has not sponsored any candidates and has adopted a position of strict neutrality between the political parties.

N.F.U.-sponsored M.P.s, 1922-1935

Election	No. of M.P.s
1922	4
1923	3
1924	2
1929	No candidates
1931	No candidates
1935	2

SOURCES.—*National Farmers' Union Yearbooks, 1900-60*; P. Self and H. Storing, *The State and the Farmer* (1962), pp. 42-7, 204; J. D. Stewart, *British Pressure Groups* (1958), pp. 173-4.

Party Finance

The Labour Party has always published Accounts in its Annual Conference Reports.

Labour Party Central Income (excluding special General Election Funds):

1910*	£12,000
1920	£55,000
1930	£44,000
1940	£51,000
1950*	£197,000
1960	£225,000
1970*	£1,034,000
1980	£2,801,000

* Asterisks denote general election years. For details of the party's expenditure in recent general elections see p. 229. In 1912, the annual affiliation fee for constituency parties and trade unions was set at 1d per member. It was raised by stages (1918—2d, 1920—3d, 1931—4d, 1937—4½d, 1940—5d, 1948—6d, 1957—9d, 1963—1/-, 1970—7½p, 1972—10p, 1973—12½p, 1974—15p, 1975—17p, 1976—21p, 1978—24p, 1979—28p, 1980—32p, 1981—40p, 1982—45p, 1983—50p. In 1983 trade union affiliation fees provided 79% of the Labour Party's routine central income. The Houghton Committee estimated the income of Labour constituency parties in 1973 at £1,124,000 (£1,804 per constituency).

SOURCES.—M. Harrison, *Trade Unions and the Labour Party* (1960); R. Rose, *Influencing Voters* (1967); M. Harrison's chapter in R. Rose and A. Heidenheimer, 'Comparative Political Finance', *Journal of Politics* (1963); *Committee on Financial Aid to Political Parties* (Cmnd 6601/1976); M. Pinto-Duschinsky, *British Political Finance 1830-1980* (1981); Labour Party Annual Reports.

Liberal Party

The Liberal Party split, following D. Lloyd George's supplantation of H. Asquith as Prime Minister in 1916. The two wings merged again following the 1922 election. In 1931 the party split once more between the National Liberals (who gradually merged with the Conservatives), the Liberals, and the Independent Liberals (a Lloyd George family group); the Independent Liberals rejoined the Liberals in the mid 1930s.

After 1981 the Liberal party was linked in the Alliance with the newly formed Social Democratic Party (see p. 171).

Party Leaders[1]

	1900	Sir H. Campbell-Bannerman	4 Nov	31	Sir H. Samuel[4]
			26 Nov	35	Sir A. Sinclair
30 Apr	08	H. Asquith (E of Oxford and Asquith)[2]	2 Aug	45	C. Davies
			5 Nov	56	J. Grimond
14 Oct	26	D. Lloyd George[3]	18 Jan	67	J. Thorpe
			7 Jul	76	D. Steel[5]

Deputy Leaders

1929-31 H. Samuel　1949-51 Lady M. Lloyd George　1962-64 D. Wade　1985- A. Beith

Leaders in the House of Lords

1900	E of Kimberley	1931	M of Reading
1902	Earl Spencer	1936	M of Crewe
1905	M of Ripon	1944	Vt Samuel
1908	E (M) of Crewe	1955	Ld Rea
1923	Vt Grey	1967	Ld Byers
1924	Earl Beauchamp	1984	Lady Seear

National Liberal Federation, 1900-1936

Chairman of Committee

1900	(Sir) E. Evans	1910	F. Wright
1918	Sir G. Lunn	1923	Sir R. Hudson
1920	A. Brampton	1927	Sir F. Layland-Barratt
1931	R. Muir	1934	P. Heffer
1933	R. Walker		
1934	M. Gray		

Secretary

1893	(Sir) R. Hudson
1922	F. Barter
1925	H. Oldman
1930	H. Oldman & W. Davies
1931	W. Davies

Treasurer

1901	W. Hart
1903	J. Massie
1907	R. Bird

Liberal Party Organisation, 1936-

Head

1936	W. Davies (*Secretary*)	1966	P. Chitnis (*Head of Liberal Party Organisation*)
1952	H. Harris (*General Director*)	1970	E. Wheeler (*Head of Liberal Party Organisation*)[6]
1960	D. Robinson (*Directing Secretary*)	1977	H. Jones (*Secretary-General*)[8]
1961	P. Kemmis (*Secretary*)	1983	J. Spiller (*Secretary-General*)
1965	T. Beaumont (*Head of Liberal Party Organisation*)		

[1] All were Liberal 'Leaders in the House of Commons'. Sir H. Campbell-Bannerman from 1905 to 1908 and H. Asquith 1908 to 1926 were formally the only 'Leaders of the Liberal Party' from 1900 until the 1969 constitution came into force.

[2] After H. Asquith's defeat at the 1918 General Election, Sir D. Maclean was elected chairman of the Parliamentary Party but relinquished this post on H. Asquith's return to the Commons in Mar 1920.

[3] D. Lloyd George was Chairman of the Parliamentary Liberal Party from Dec 1924.

[4] At the General Election in 1931 there were three Liberal groups in the House of Commons. Sir H. Samuel led the main group of Liberal M.P.s. D. Lloyd George led a small family group of Independent Liberals, and Sir J. Simon (Ld) led the Liberal National Group (see *Minor Parties*). On 25 Nov 35 D. Lloyd George and the other Independent Liberals rejoined the Liberal Party in the House of Commons.

[5] An electoral college representing all constituency associations voted: D. Steel, 12,541; J. Pardoe 7,032. J. Grimond was acting Leader 12 May 76-7 Jul 76.

[6] P. Chitnis resigned in 1969. From Oct 69 to Nov 70 E. Wheeler was Director of Organisation. From Dec 69 to Jun 70 Mrs D. Gorsky was General Election Campaign Editor.

[7] In 1969 the post of Chairman of the Executive Committee was combined with the Chairmanship of the party.

[8] E. Wheeler left in 1976. From Aug 76 until Mar 77 Mrs M. Wingfield was acting head of the Liberal Party Organisation.

Chairman of Executive Committee

1936	M. Gray
1946	P. Fothergill
1949	Ld Moynihan
1950	F. Byers
1952	P. Fothergill
1954	G. Acland
1957	D. Abel
1959	L. Behrens
1961	D. Banks
1963	B. Wigoder
1965	G. Evans
1968-69[7]	J. Baker

Chairman

1966	Ld Byers
1967	T. Beaumont (Ld)
1968	Ld Henley
1969	D. Banks
1970	R. Wainwright
1972	C. Carr
1973	K. Vaus
1976	G. Tordoff
1980	R. Pincham
1983	Mrs J. Rose
1984	P. Tyler

Treasurer[1]

1937-50	Sir A. McFadyean
1937-41	P. Heffer
1941-47	Ld Rea
1942-47	H. Worsley
1947-53	Ld Moynihan
1950-58	W. Grey
1950-52	Vt Wimborne
1953-62	Sir A. Suenson-Taylor (Ld Grantchester)
1955-59	P. Fothergill
1959-62	Miss H. Harvey
1959-60	P. Lort-Phillips
1961-62	J. McLaughlin
1962-65	R. Gardner-Thorpe
1962-66	Sir A. Murray
1963-65	T. Beaumont
1966-67	J. Thorpe
1967-68	L. Smith
1968-69	J. Pardoe
1969-72	Sir F. Medlicott
1972-77	P. Watkins
1977-83	Ld Lloyd of Kilgerran
1977-83	M. Palmer
1983-	Sir H. Jones
1983-	A. Jacobs

SOURCES.—*Liberal Magazine 1900-1950*; *Liberal Year Book 1900-1939*; *Dod's Parliamentary Companion 1950-*. Annual Reports of the Liberal Party 1956-.

Chief Whips in House of Commons

1900	H. Gladstone
1905	G. Whiteley
1908	J. Pease
1910	Master of Elibank
1912	P. Illingworth
1915	J. Gulland
1919	*vacant*[2]
1923	V. Phillipps
1924	Sir G. Collins
1926	Sir R. Hutchinson
1930	Sir A. Sinclair
1931	G. Owen
1932	W. Rea
1935	Sir P. Harris
1945	T. Horabin
1946	F. Byers
1950	J. Grimond
1956	D. Wade
1962	A. Holt
1963	E. Lubbock
1970	D. Steel
1976	C. Smith
1977	A. Beith
1985	D. Alton

Coalition Liberal

1916	N. Primrose
1917	F. Guest
1921	C. McCurdy
1922	E. Hilton Young

Chief Whips in House of Lords

1896	Ld Ribblesdale
1907	Ld Denman
1911-22	Ld Colebrooke
1919	Ld Denman (*Ind. Lib.*)
1924	Ld Stanmore
1944	Vt Mersey
1949	M of Willingdon
1950	Ld Moynihan
1950	Ld Rea
1955	Ld Amulree
1977	Ld Wigoder
1984	Ld Tordoff

SOURCE.—*Dod's Parliamentary Companion 1900-*.

National Liberal Federation—Annual Conferences, 1900-1935

Date	*Place*	*President*
27-28 Mar 00	Nottingham	R. Spence Watson
14-15 May 01	Bradford	"
13-14 May 02	Bristol	A. Birrell
14-15 May 03	Scarborough	"
12-13 May 04	Manchester	"
18-19 May 05	Newcastle upon Tyne	"
23-24 May 06	Liverpool	A. Acland
6-7 Jun 07	Plymouth	"

[1] Until 1965 the post of Treasurer was held jointly by two or three officers. This practice was reverted to in 1977.
[2] J. Hogge and G. Thorne were elected joint whips, not chief whip, in Feb 1919.

Date	Place	President
18-19 Jun 08	Birmingham	Sir W. Angus
1-2 Jul 09	Southport	"
25 Nov 10	Hull	"
23-24 Nov 11	Bath	Sir J. Brunner
21-22 Nov 12	Nottingham	"
26-27 Nov 13	Leeds	"
1914-1918	*No conference held*	
27-28 Nov 19	Birmingham	Sir G. Lunn
25-26 Nov 20	Bradford	J. Robertson
24-25 Nov 21	Newcastle upon Tyne	"
17-18 May 22	Blackpool	"
30 May-1 Jun 23	Buxton	Sir D. Maclean
22-23 May 24	Brighton	"
14-15 May 25	Scarborough	"
17-18 Jun 26	Weston-super-Mare	J. Spender
26-27 May 27	Margate	Sir C. Hobhouse
11-12 Oct 28	Great Yarmouth	"
3-4 Oct 29	Nottingham	"
16-17 Oct 30	Torquay	A. Brampton
14-15 May 31	Buxton	"
28-29 Apr 32	Clacton-on-Sea	"
18-19 May 33	Scarborough	R. Muir
2-5 May 34	Bournemouth	"
23-25 May 35	Blackpool	"

Liberal Party—Assemblies[1], 1936-

Date	Place	President
18-19 Jun 36	London	Ld Meston
27-31 May 37	Buxton	"
19-20 May 38	Bath	"
11-12 May 39	Scarborough	"
1940	*No assembly held*	
18-19 Jul 41	London	"
4-5 Sep 42	London	"
15-17 Jul 43	London	"
1944	*No assembly held*	
1-3 Feb 45	London	Lady V. Bonham-Carter
9-11 May 46	London	"
24-26 Apr 47	Bournemouth	I. Foot
22-24 Apr 48	Blackpool	E. Dodds
24-26 Mar 49	Hastings	Sir A. MacFadyean
27-28 Jan 50	London	"
29-30 Sep 50	Scarborough	P. Fothergill
1951	*No assembly held*	
15-17 May 52	Hastings	R. Walker
9-11 Apr 53	Ilfracombe	L. Robson
22-24 Apr 54	Buxton	H. Graham White
14-16 Apr 55	Llandudno	Ld Rea
27-29 Sep 56	Folkestone	L. Behrens
19-21 Sep 57	Southport	N. Micklem
18-21 Sep 58	Torquay	Sir A. Comyns Carr
1959	*No assembly held*	
29 Sep-1 Oct 60	Eastbourne	H. Glanville
21-23 Sep 61	Edinburgh	E. Malindine
19-22 Sep 62	Llandudno	Sir F. Brunner
10-14 Sep 63	Brighton	Ld Ogmore
4-5 Sep 64	London	R. Fulford
22-25 Sep 65	Scarborough	Miss N. Seear
21-24 Sep 66	Brighton	Ld Henley
20-23 Sep 67	Blackpool	Ld Wade
18-21 Sep 68	Edinburgh	D. Banks
17-20 Sep 69	Brighton	Ld Beaumont of Whitley
23-26 Sep 70	Eastbourne	"

[1] Liberal Presidents normally hold office from Annual Assembly to Annual Assembly. Until 1970 they were instituted at the beginning of the Assembly which marked the beginning of their term and performed the President's duties during that Assembly. From 1970 they have been instituted at the end of an Assembly and no longer actually presided over debates. Presidents are listed on this basis here.

Date	Place	President
15-18 Sep 71	Scarborough	Mrs S. Robson
19-23 Sep 72	Margate	S. Terrell
18-22 Sep 73	Southport	T. Jones
17-21 Sep 74	Brighton	Ld Lloyd of Kilgerran
16-20 Sep 75	Scarborough	A. Holt
12 Jun 76	Manchester (Special Assembly)	Mrs M. Wingfield
14-18 Sep 76	Llandudno	"
26 Sep-1 Oct 77	Brighton	B. Goldstone
21 Jan 78	Blackpool (Special Assembly)	G. Evans
12-16 Sep 78	Southport	Ld Evans of Claughton
28-29 Sep 79	Margate	M. Steed
8-13 Sep 80	Blackpool	Mrs J. Rose
14-19 Sep 81	Llandudno	R. Holme
20-25 Sep 82	Bournemouth	V. Bingham
19-24 Sep 83	Harrogate	J. Griffiths
17-22 Sep 84	Bournemouth	Ld Tordoff
16-21 Sep 85	Dundee	A. Watson

SOURCES.—*Liberal Year Book 1902-1939*; *The Liberal Magazine 1900-1950*; *National Liberal Federation, Annual Reports 1900-1936*; *Keesing's Archives 1939-*.

The Liberal Publication Department published miscellaneous collections of *Pamphlets and Leaflets, 1908-30*. *The Liberal Magazine* was published from 1893 until 1950. J. S. Rasmussen, *The Liberal Party, A Study of Retrenchment and Revival* (1965); Alan Watkins, *The Liberal Dilemma* (1966); Trevor Wilson, *The Downfall of the Liberal Party 1914-1935* (1966); C. Cook, *A Short History of the Liberal Party* (1976); A. Cyr, *Liberal Party Politics in Britain* (1977). See also I. Bulmer-Thomas, *The Growth of the British Party System* (1965).

Minor Parties

Minor parties contesting Parliamentary Elections in England, Scotland and Wales 1900-1984

(For parties that split from major parties see pp. 164-172)

Name	Date of Founding	Principal Founder or key policy	Members elected	Candidates First	Last	No.	Lost deposit
Action Party	1953	Mosley's Union Movement (1948) renamed		1959	1972	8	8
Agricultural	1931	Formed as Norfolk farmers party 1931		1933	1933	1	0
All-Party Alliance	1967	J. Creasey		1967	1968	4	3
Anti-Partition League	1948			1950	1951	5	5
Anti Waste League	1921	Ld Rothermere	(2)	1921	1921	4	0
British Empire Party	1951			1951	1951	1	1
British Movement	1968	C. Jordan		1969	1974	3	3
British National Party (1)	1961	Merger of Whites Defence League and Nat. Lab. Party		1964	1966	4	4
British National Party (2)	1982	Merger of New National Front and other groups led by John Tyndall.		1983	1983	53	53
British People's Party	1939	D of Bedford		1939	1946	2	2
British Socialist Party	1911	H. Hyndman		1913	1918	19	2
British Union of Fascists	1932	Sir O. Mosley (see p. 170)		1940	1941	3	3
Campaign for Social Democracy	1973	D. Taverne	(1)	1974	1974	6	4
Common Wealth	1942	Sir R. Acland (see p. 164)	(4)	1943	1945	35	16
Commonwealth Land Party	1919	J. Peace		1931	1931	2	2
Communist Party of England (Marxist Leninist)	1972			1973	1974	16	16
Communist Party of G.B.	1920	(see p. 164)	(5)	1922	1983	537	500
Cooperative Party	1917	Allied with Lab. Party after 1918	(1)	1918	1918	11	0
Cornish Nationalist Party	1975	J. Whetter		1979	1983	2	2
Democratic Party (1)	1942	N. Leith-Hay-Clark		1945	1945	5	5
Democratic Party (2)	1969	D. Donnelly		1969	1970	7	6
Ecology Party	1975	Successor to People		1976	1984	170	170
Empire Free Trade Crusade	1929	Launched by Ld Beaverbrook	(1)	1930	1931	2	0
English National Party	1974	F. Hansford-Miller		1974	1976	4	4
Fellowship Party	1955			1959	1979	8	8
Fife Socialist League	1953			1959	1959	1	1
Highland Land League	1909			1918	1918	4	3
Ind. Democratic Alliance	1973	Successor to All-Party Alliance		1974	1974	6	6
Independent Labour Party	1893	Broke with Labour Party from 1930 onwards (see p. 165)	(11)	1930	1970	82	35
Ind. Nuclear Disarmament Election Committee	1962	Miss P. Arrowsmith		1964	1964	2	2
Ind. Parliamentary Group	1920	H. Bottomley	(5)	1920	1921	7	3
International Marxist Group	1966			1974	1977	4	4
Irish Civil Rights Assn.	1972			1974	1974	7	7
Irish National Movement	1882		(9)[1]	1900	1929	12	0
Labour Independent Group	1949	Expelled Lab. M.P.s		1950	1950	5	2
League of Empire Loyalists	1954	A. Chesterton, merged with Nat. Front 1967		1957	1964	4	4
Liverpool Protestant Party	c.1903			1931	1945	3	0
Mebyon Kernow	1951	Cornish Independence		1970	1983	6	6
Mudiad Gweriniaethol Cymru	1950	Welsh Republican Movement		1950	1950	1	1
National Democratic and Labour Party	1915	To support war and later the Coalition (see p. 169)	(10)	1918	1920	29	6
National Democratic Party	1963	D. Brown		1964	1974	8	7
National Farmers Union	1908	(see p. 156)		1918	1922	10	3

[1] All these victories were by T. P. O'Connor in Liverpool (Scotland).

Name	Date of Founding	Principal Founder or key policy	Members elected	Candidates First	Last	No.	Lost deposit
National Federation of Discharged and Demobilised Sailors and Soldiers	1917			1917	1918	6	3
National Fellowship	1962	E. Martell		1963	1967	1	0
National Front	1967	By merger of British National Party and League of Empire Loyalists (see p. 168)		1968	1984	546	545
National Independence Party	1972	By National Front breakaway		1972	1974	3	3
National Labour Party	1958	By J. Bean merged 1960 with White Defence League		1959	1959	1	1
National Party	1917	H. Page Croft	(2)	1917	1920	29	13
National Party	1966	E. Martell		1967	1967	1	1
National Prohibition Party	1887			1923	1923	1	1
National Socialist Party	1916	Breakaway from British Socialist Party		1918	1918	4	1
National Union of Small Shopkeepers	1943			1959	1968	3	3
New Conservative Party	1960	J. Dayton		1960	1961	4	4
New Party	1931	Sir O. Mosley (see p. 169)		1931	1931	25	3
Patriotic Party	1962	R. Hilton		1964	1966	3	3
People	1973			1974	1974	11	11
People's League for the Defence of Freedom	1956	E. Martell		1957	1957	1	1
Plaid Cymru	1925	(see p. 170)	(8)	1929	1984	258	195
Radical Alliance	1965	From supporters of C.N.D.		1966	1966	2	2
Revolutionary Communist Party (1)	1944			1945	1945	1	1
Revolutionary Communist Party (2)	1981			1983	1983	3	3
Scottish Labour Party (1)	1900			1900	1908	10	0
Scottish Labour Party (2)	1975	J. Sillars (see p. 171)		1978	1979	4	3
Scottish National Party	1928	(see p. 171)	(24)	1929	1983	378	140
Scottish Party	1932	From supporters of S.N.P.		1933	1933	1	0
Scottish Prohibition Party	1901	E. Scrymgeour	(4)	1908	1931	10	0
Social Credit	1935	J. Hargrave		1935	1950	2	2
Social Democratic Federation	1881	H. Hyndman		1900	1910	37	0
Socialist Labour Party	1903			1918	1918	3	1
Socialist Party of Great Britain	1904			1945	1979	15	15
Socialist Workers Party	1976	Formerly International Socialist Group		1976	1978	8	8
Union Movement	1948	(see Action Party) (see p. 170)					
United Country Party	1979	P. Moore		1979	1979	2	2
United Democratic Party	1974			1974	1974	13	13
United Empire Party	1930	Ld Beaverbrook. Merged with Empire Free Trade Crusade		1930	1930	3	1
Vectis National Party	1969			1970	1970	1	1
Wessex Regional Party	1979	A. Thynne		1979	1983	16	16
Women's Party	1917	Mrs Pankhurst		1918	1918	1	0
Workers' Party of Scotland	1966			1969	1969	1	1
Workers' Revolutionary Party	1959			1974	1983	101	101

SOURCE.—F. W. S. Craig, *Minor Parties at British Parliamentary Elections 1885-1974* (1975).

Notes on the Principal Minor Parties

Common Wealth

This party was founded in 1942 by Sir Richard Acland (Liberal M.P. for Barnstaple) during the war-time electoral truce. Its immediate aim was to contest all by-elections where a 'reactionary' candidate was in the field, and was not opposed by a Labour or other 'progressive' candidate. Seats were won at Eddisbury (J. Loverseed, 1943), Skipton (H. Lawson, 1944), and Chelmsford (E. Millington, 1945). In 1943 membership of Common Wealth was proscribed by the Labour Party. In the 1945 General Election Common Wealth put up twenty-three candidates but were only successful in Chelmsford, where no Labour candidate stood: the victor there, E. Millington, joined the Labour Party. Sir R. Acland joined the Labour Party as soon as the 1945 results were known. Common Wealth survived as an organisation but contested no further parliamentary elections.

Communist Party

The Communist Party of Great Britain was founded in July 1920. In its early years it sought to affiliate to the Labour Party but was rebuffed. In 1922 J. T. W. Newbold (Motherwell) was elected to Parliament; S. Saklatvala (N. Battersea) was also elected in 1922 as a Labour M.P. (although a member of the Communist Party). After defeat in 1923, he was elected again in 1924 as a Communist. Since 1924 the Labour Party has ruled that no member of the Communist Party could be an individual member of the Labour Party and in 1935, 1943, and 1946 the Labour Party turned down further Communist requests for affiliation. In 1935 and again in 1945 W. Gallacher was elected as a Communist for W. Fife; and in 1945 P. Piratin was elected for the Mile End division of Stepney.

Secretaries of the Communist Party: 1920-29 A. Inkpin, 1929-56 H. Pollitt, 1956-75 J. Gollan, 1975- G. McLennan.

Communist Candidates

1922	5	1935	2	1959	18	1974 Oct	29
1923	8	1945	21	1964	36	1979	38
1924	8	1950	100	1966	57	1983	35
1929	25	1951	10	1970	58		
1931	26	1955	17	1974 Feb	44		

SOURCE.—H. Pelling, *The British Communist Party* (1958).

Co-operative Party

In 1917 the Co-operative Congress agreed to organise as a political party. In the 1918 General Election one Co-operative M.P. was elected; he joined with the Labour Party in the House of Commons. Labour and Co-operative candidates never opposed each other at elections but it was not till

1926 that a formal understanding was reached and Co-operative Parties were made eligible for affiliation to divisional Labour Parties. In 1938 the Co-operative Party adopted a written constitution and in 1941 its representatives were invited to attend meetings of the National Council of Labour on equal terms with the Labour Party and the T.U.C. In 1946, the 1926 agreement with the Labour Party was replaced; Co-operative candidates were to run formally as Co-operative and Labour Candidates,[1] and after the General Election of 1959 it was agreed that the number of Co-operative candidates should be limited to 30.[2]

In 1951 the Co-operative Party adopted a new constitution to prevent its members from joining organisations proscribed by the Labour Party.

Co-operative M.P.s and Candidates

1918 .	1 (10)	1945 .	23 (33)	1970	17 (27)
1922 .	4 (11)	1950 .	18 (33)	1974 Feb	16 (25)
1923 .	6 (10)	1951 .	16 (37)	1974 Oct	16 (22)
1924 .	5 (10)	1955 .	18 (38)	1979	17 (25)
1929 .	9 (12)	1959 .	16 (30)	1983	8 (17)
1931 .	1 (18)	1964 .	19 (27)		
1935 .	9 (21)	1966 .	18 (24)		

SOURCES.—J. Bailey, *The British Co-operative Movement* (1955); *Reports of the Annual Co-operative Congress 1900-*; *The People's Year Book 1932.*

Independent Labour Party

The Independent Labour Party, formed in 1893, was one of the founding bodies of the Labour Representation Committee in 1900. The I.L.P. was affiliated to the Labour Party but it held its own conferences, sponsored its own parliamentary candidates, and maintained its own policies, even after the 1918 revision of the Labour Party constitution. Differences with the Labour Party grew in the late 1920's and the 37 I.L.P. Members among the 288 Labour M.P.s elected in 1929 provided some of the second Labour Government's strongest critics. At the 1930 conference of the I.L.P., it was agreed that I.L.P. members should vote against the Labour Government when its actions conflicted with I.L.P. policy. The I.L.P. was disaffiliated by the 1932 Labour Party Conference. In 1935 17 I.L.P. candidates stood, all against Labour candidates, and four (all in Glasgow) were successful. In 1945 three of the five I.L.P. candidates won but, after the death of the party's leader James Maxton in 1946, the I.L.P. M.P.s one by one rejoined the Labour Party. In the elections of 1950 and 1951 there were three I.L.P. candidates and in 1955 and 1959 two candidates. All lost their deposits. There were no candidates in 1964, 1966, 1970, 1974, 1979 or 1983.

M.P.s (since 1931)

1932-46	J. Maxton	1932-33	R. Wallhead
1932-47	J. McGovern	1935-47	C. Stephen
1932-39	G. Buchanan	1946-47	J. Carmichael
1932-33	D. Kirkwood		

SOURCE.—R. E. Dowse, *Left in the Centre* (1966).

[1] *L.P. Annual Report*, 1946, pp. 229-31. [2] *L.P. Annual Report*, 1960, p. 24.

Irish Nationalist Party up to 1922

From the days of Parnell until the First World War between 80 and 86 Irish Nationalists sat in the House of Commons—at times divided by internal frictions but with a safe control of more than three-quarters of the seats in Ireland. Divisions over support for the war and the Easter Rebellion broke the party's hold and in 1918 only 7 of its 58 candidates were elected (while Sinn Fein candidates won 73 seats). T. P. O'Connor, from 1885 the solitary Irish Nationalist Member representing an English constituency, continued to be returned unopposed for the Scotland Division of Liverpool until his death in 1929.

Chairmen of the Irish Parliamentary Party

1900	J. Redmond	1917	J. Dillon

SOURCE.—F. S. L. Lyons, *The Irish Parliamentary Party 1890-1910* (1951).

Irish Parties since 1922

Since 1922 candidates under the label 'Irish Nationalist' have fought only two or three of the Northern Ireland seats, but from 1922 to 1924 they held one of the two Fermanagh and Tyrone Seats (the other was held by Sinn Fein) and from 1929 to 1955 they held both. T. P. O'Connor continued to represent the Scotland division of Liverpool until 1929 and the Exchange division of Liverpool was fought by Nationalists on three occasions.

Sinn Fein reappeared as a political force in 1955 and 1959, contesting all 12 Northern Ireland seats. In 1955 Sinn Fein candidates won Mid-Ulster and Fermanagh and South Tyrone but they were disqualified as felons.

From 1943 to 1950, from 1951 to 1955 and from 1966 onwards Belfast West was held by candidates using the label 'Eire Labour', 'Republican Labour', and then 'Social Democratic and Labour'. The S.D.L.P. founded in 1970 became the main party representing the Republican or Nationalist aspirations of the Roman Catholic minority.

Nationalist M.P.s

1922-29	T. P. O'Connor	1929-34	J. Devlin
1922-24	T. Harbison	1934-35	J. Stewart
1922-24, 1931-35, 1950-55	(*S.F.*) C. Healy	1935-50	P. Cunningham
		1935-51	A. Mulvey
		1951-55	M. O'Neill

Sinn Fein M.P.s

1955-55	P. Clarke	1983-	G. Adams
1955-56	T. Mitchell		

Eire Labour M.P.s

1943-50	J. Beattie
1951-55	J. Beattie

Republican Labour M.P.

1966-70	G. Fitt

Independent Socialist M.P.

1979-83	G. Fitt

S.D.L.P. M.P.s

1970-9	G. Fitt
1983-	J. Hume

Independent Republican M.P.s

1969-74 Feb	Bernadette Devlin (Mrs B. McAliskey) (*Independent Unity*)
1970-74 Feb	F. McManus (*Independent Unity*)
1974 Oct-81	F. Maguire (*Independent Unity*)
1981-81	R. Sands (*Anti H-Block*)
1981-83	O. Carron (*Anti H-Block*)

After 1969 increasing fissures developed in the Ulster Unionist Party which had dominated Northern Ireland's representation at Westminster. In 1970 I. Paisley standing as a Protestant Unionist defeated the Official Unionist Candidates in North Antrim. In 1971 he formed the Democratic Unionist Party. In 1970 W. Craig formed the Vanguard Movement and in January 1974 the Unionists split further. In the February 1974 election, 11 of the 12 Ulster seats were won by candidates standing under the banner of a new United Ulster Unionist Council in opposition to those Unionists who supported Mr Faulkner's Executive Council and the Sunningdale proposals for a Council of Ireland. Of the 11, 8 were members of the Unionist party under H. West, 2 carried the Vanguard label and I. Paisley was successful as a Democratic Unionist. In October 1974 H. West who had acted as Unionist Leader was the only one of the 11 to be defeated. J. Molyneaux succeeded him as parliamentary leader. Vanguard was wound up in September 1977. In 1979 3 Paisleyites, 1 Independent Unionist (J. Kilfedder), 1 U.U.U.P. and 5 official Unionists were successful. In 1983 3 Paisleyites, 11 Official Unionists and J. Kilfedder were successful.

The non-Sectarian Alliance Party, founded in 1970, was joined by S. Mills, a Unionist M.P., in 1972. He did not stand in February 1974, when 2 of their 3 candidates lost their deposits. In October 1974 they put up 5 candidates and 4 saved their deposits. The Alliance Party Leader 1973-84 was O. Napier, followed by J. Cushnahan. In 1979 they fought all 12 N.I. seats and lost 7 deposits. In 1983 they fought 11 of the 17 N.I. seats and lost 7 deposits.

Liberal National Party (National Liberal Party after 1948)

In October 1931 23 Liberal Members broke with the party and formed the Liberal National Group. The subsequent electoral history of the Liberal National Party falls into three periods: at the 1931 General Election some of the Liberal National candidates were opposed by Conservatives but none of them by Liberals. After 1931, a Conservative only once opposed a Liberal National (Scottish Universities 1946) but they were not opposed by Liberals (except in Denbigh 1935 and St. Ives 1937) until 1945. Of 41 candidates in 1931, 35 were returned as Members of Parliament and when the 'Samuelite' Liberals left the government over the Ottawa Agreements in 1932, the 'Simonite' Liberal Nationals remained. In 1935 33 of 44 candidates were returned, and in 1945 13 of 51 candidates. E. Brown, however, who had succeeded Sir J. Simon as leader on 4 December 1940 was defeated. In May

1947 the Woolton-Teviot agreement was signed, which urged the combination of Conservative and Liberal National Constituency Associations, and in 1948 the party was renamed the National Liberal Party. After the 1966 General Election only two M.P.s styled themselves Conservative and National Liberal. Two other members of the Group were elected as Conservatives by Joint Associations. In 1966 these four M.P.s relinquished the room assigned to them in the House of Commons to the Liberal Party. The group became an integral part of the Conservative Party.

	Chairmen of the Parliamentary Party		*Chief Whips*
1931	Sir J. Simon	1931	A. Glassey
1940	E. Brown	1931	G. Shakespeare
1945	(Sir) J. Henderson-Stewart	1932	(Sir) J. Blindell
1946	Sir S. Holmes	1937	C. Kerr
1947	J. Maclay	1940	H. Holdsworth
1956	(Sir) J. Duncan	1945-66	(Sir) H. Butcher
1959	Sir J. Henderson-Stewart		
1961-4	Sir C. Thornton Kemsley		

SOURCES.—Information from the National Liberal Party, and *Dod's Parliamentary Companion, 1931-66.*

Liberal Unionist Party

The Liberal Unionist Party was based upon those Liberals who, under J. Chamberlain and the M of Hartington, broke with the party over Irish Home Rule in 1886. After they accepted office in Ld Salisbury's 1895 government, they became increasingly fused with the Conservative Party and, although they had preserved a separate organisation with separate funds, the final merger in 1912 was to some extent a recognition of a *fait accompli*. The President between 1886 and 1904 was M of Hartington (D of Devonshire) and between 1904 and 1912 J. Chamberlain. The Organising Secretary between 1895 and 1912 was J. Boraston.

Liberal Unionist M.P.s

1900	68	Jan 1910	31
1906	23	Dec 1910	35

National Democratic Party

The National Democratic Party was formed in 1915 to unite support amongst the Labour Movement for the Lloyd George Government. The N.D.P. had its origins in the dispute within the Labour Movement during the war and its greatest strength in the jingoist trade unions—the Liverpool Dockers, the Musicians' Union, some of the Textile Workers, and parts of the Miners Federation. It was also, in part, the successor to the projected anti-socialist Trade Union Labour Party and included among its members the Labour Ministers who refused to resign from the Government in 1918. G. Barnes, Labour member of the War Cabinet, was its accepted leader. In the 1918 Election the Party put up 28 candidates, all for working-class constituencies, and returned 15 to Parliament. Before the 1922 Election the surviving N.D.P. M.P.s joined the National Liberal Party, but only one (G. Roberts) was re-elected. The Party ceased to exist in 1923.

SOURCES.—G. D. H. Cole, *A History of the British Labour Party from 1914* (1945); G. N. Barnes, *From Workshop to War Cabinet* (1924); *Labour Party Annual Conference Reports, 1916-18; Trades Union Congress Reports,* 1916-18.

The National Front

The National Front was formed by a merger of the League of Empire Loyalists and the British National Party in 1966. The Greater Britain Movement joined in 1967. The leader of the League of Empire Loyalists, A. K. Chesterton, became Policy Director of the National Front; A. Fontaine, President of the British National Party, became Executive Director. In 1970 A. K. Chesterton was succeeded by J. O'Brien, who was succeeded in 1972 by J. Tyndall (previously leader of the Greater Britain Movement). In 1974 J. Read ousted J. Tyndall but the courts ruled the ouster illegal. J. Read formed the National Party and J. Tyndall resumed as leader with M. Webster as National Activities Organiser. In 1982 a breakaway faction under J. Tyndall, the New National Front, merged with other groups to form the British National Party (p. 162).

National Front Candidates

	No.	Av. % vote	Highest Vote
1970	10	3.6	5.6
1974 Feb	54	3.3	7.8
1974 Oct	90	3.1	9.5
1979	303	1.3	7.6
1983	60	1.1	2.4

National Party

A small group of dissident Conservatives led by H. Page Croft, formed this party in September 1917, with a programme described by one historian as of 'xenophobic imperialism'. Most of its members drifted back to the Conservative fold and fought under the Conservative label in 1918: only Sir H. Page Croft and Sir R. Cooper survived the election (when they made a special point of attacking the sale of honours) and in 1921 it was decided not to maintain a separate parliamentary party.

SOURCES.—Ld Croft, *My Life of Strife* (1948); M. Foot, 'Henry Page Croft, Baron Croft, *Dictionary of National Biography 1941-1950*.

National Labour Party

The party was formed in 1931 from the small group of Labour M.P.s who supported the National Government under Ramsay MacDonald. In the 1931 General Election 13 of its 20 candidates were elected. In 1935 8 of its 20 candidates were elected. The party wound itself up just before the 1945 election and in 1945 of the 7 surviving National Labour members 3 retired, 2 stood unsuccessfully as National candidates, and 2 as Independents (one, K. Lindsay, stood successfully—but in a new constituency, English Universities).

New Party, British Union of Fascists, Union Movement

Sir Oswald Mosley (Conservative, then Independent M.P. 1918-24, Labour M.P. 1926-31) resigned from the Labour Government in May 1930 after his *Memorandum* for dealing with unemployment had been rejected by the Cabinet. In October 1930 a resolution calling upon the National Executive to consider the Memorandum was narrowly defeated at the

Labour Party Conference. On 6 December 1930 the *Mosley Manifesto* summarising the main proposals in the Memorandum was published, signed by 17 Labour M.P.s. Six of the 17 signatories of the Manifesto resigned from the Labour Party to form the new Party in February 1931 (Sir Oswald and Lady Cynthia Mosley, O. Baldwin, W. J. Brown, R. Forgan, and J. Strachey), but Baldwin and Brown remained members for only one day and Strachey resigned in June. The New Party received two further recruits before the 1931 General Election, W. E. D. Allen (Conservative) and R. Dudgeon (Liberal). In the Election the New Party contested 24 seats but failed to win a single one, the New Party M.P.s all losing their seats, and, apart from Sir Oswald Mosley, their deposits.

In 1932 the New Party was renamed the British Union of Fascists after Mosley had been to Italy to study the 'modern movements'. The Director of Organisation and Deputy Leader was R. Forgan. In the 1935 General Election, the B.U.F. put up no candidates and, with the slogan 'Fascism next Time', advised their supporters not to vote. The B.U.F. fought a number of by-elections in 1939 and 1940, before it was proscribed by the Government on 30 May 1940.

In 1948, Sir Oswald Mosley formed the Union Movement. Its first Parliamentary contest was in the 1959 General Election, when he fought North Kensington, losing his deposit. The Union Movement fought two by-elections in the 1959 Parliament and in the 1966 General Election Sir Oswald Mosley and 3 other candidates stood; they gained on average 3.7% of the vote.

SOURCES.—C. Cross, *The Fascists in Britain* (1961); R. Skidelsky, *Oswald Mosley* (1975).

Plaid Cymru (Welsh Nationalist Party)

The party was founded in 1925 and has fought elections consistently since then, but without any success at the Parliamentary level until a by-election victory in Carmarthen in 1966. The seat was lost in 1970 but in the February 1974 election, two seats, Caernarvon and Merioneth were won. Carmarthen was recaptured in October 1974 but lost in 1979.

Welsh Nationalist Candidates

						Seats	% of Welsh Vote
1929	1	1951	4	1970	36	—	11.5
1931	2	1955	11	1974 Feb	36	2	10.7
1935	1	1959	20	1974 Oct	36	3	10.8
1945	6	1964	23	1979	36	2	8.1
1950	7	1966	20	1983	38	2	7.8

Plaid Cymru M.P.s

1966-70	G. Evans	1974 Feb-	D. Wigley	1974 Feb-	D. Thomas
1974 Oct-79	G. Evans				

Scottish Labour Party

The Scottish Labour Party was formed in January 1976 by Scots, mostly members of the Labour Party, who were dissatisfied with the Government's proposals for devolution to Scotland. Two Labour M.P.s, J. Sillars (Ayrshire South) and J. Robertson (Paisley), became members of the S.L.P., but did not resign the Labour Whip until 26 July 76. They then indicated that the S.L.P. would act as an independent party within Parliament.

At the S.L.P.'s first congress at Stirling in October 1976, the leadership suspended the credentials of one delegation and expelled four others for being under the influence of the extreme Left, mainly the International Marxist Group. This led to a walk-out by one third of the delegates. The S.L.P. won three district council seats in May 1977. In 1979 it fought 3 seats in the 1979 General Election. Only J. Sillars saved his deposit but he narrowly lost his seat. In 1981 the party was wound up and J. Sillars joined the Scottish National Party.

SOURCE.—H. Drucker, *Breakaway: the Scottish Labour Party* (1978).

Scottish National Party

The party was formed in 1928 as the National Party of Scotland. In 1934 it merged with a body called the Scottish Party (founded 1932) and the name was then changed to the Scottish National Party. Its first success was in the Motherwell by-election of April 1945; but the victor, R. McIntyre, was defeated in the General Election three months later. In 1967 a seat was won in the Hamilton by-election but lost in 1970. In 1970, however, a Scottish Nationalist won Western Isles. In November 1973 the Govan, Glasgow, seat was won in a by-election but lost four months later. In the General Elections of 1974 the Scottish Nationalists made great advances in votes and seats, but fell back sharply in 1979.

Scottish National Party Candidates

						% of Scottish Vote	Seats
1929	2	1951	2	1970	65	11.4	1
1931	3	1955	2	1974 Feb	70	21.9	7
1935	6	1959	5	1974 Oct	71	30.4	11
1945	8	1964	15	1979	71	17.3	2
1950	3	1966	23	1983	72	11.8	2

Scottish National Party M.P.s

1945-45	R. McIntyre	1974 Feb-79	D. Henderson	1974 Oct-79	Mrs M. Bain
1967-70	Mrs W. Ewing	1974 Feb-79	I. MacCormick	1974 Oct-79	G. Crawford
1970-	D. Stewart	1974 Feb-79	G. Reid	1974 Oct-79	G. Thompson
1973-74	Mrs M. Macdonald	1974 Feb-79	H. Watt	1974 Oct-79	A. Welsh
1974 Feb-79	Mrs W. Ewing	1974 Feb-	G. Wilson		

Social Democratic Party

The Social Democratic Party was launched by four former Labour Cabinet Ministers in protest, following the Labour Party Special Conference on 24

Jan 81. In its first year it recruited a total of 25 sitting Labour M.P.s and one Conservative M.P. and two of its founders (Mrs S. Williams and R. Jenkins) won parliamentary by-elections. It formed an alliance with the Liberal party and shared out constituencies with them in the 1983 general election, when the two parties jointly won 26% of the votes and 23 seats (6 SDP). The SDP won a further seat in a by-election (14 Jun 84).

Leader	1982	R. Jenkins
	1983	D. Owen

Independent M.P.s

The number of Independent M.P.s has been small and, even among those few elected without the label of one of the parties already listed, a substantial proportion were in fact elected with the tacit support of a major party or in default of its candidate. M.P.s elected as Independents fall into six broad categories.

Independents in University Seats

J. Butler	1922	Miss E. Rathbone	1929	Sir A. Salter	1937
G. Davies	1923	,,	1931	,,	1945
(Sir) E. Graham-Little	1924	,,	1935	T. Harvey	1937
,,	1929	,,	1945	A. Hill	1940
,,	1931	(Sir) A. Herbert	1935	K. Lindsay	1945
,,	1935	,,	1945	Sir J. Boyd Orr	1945
,,	1945	,,		W. Harris	1945

Independents emerging from war-time situations

N. Billing	1917	W. Kendall	1941	W. Brown	1942
,,	1918	,,	1945	,,	1945
H. Bottomley	1918	G. Reakes	1942	C. White[1]	1944
R. Barker	1918	T. Driberg[1]	1942		

Dissident Conservatives

T. Sloan	1902	J. Erskine[2]	1921	E. Taylor[2]	1930
,,	1906	,,	1922	D. Lipson	1937
E. Mitchell	1903	H. Becker[2]	1922	,,	1945[3]
F. Bennett-Goldney[2]	1910	G. Hall Caine[2]	1922	Sir C. Headlam[2]	1940
C. Palmer	1920	O. Mosley	1922	J. McKie[3]	1945
Sir C. Townshend	1920	,,	1923[1]	J. Little	1945
Sir T. Polson	1921	Sir R. Newman	1929	Sir D. Robertson	1959

Dissident Liberal

Sir J. Austin	1900	A. Hopkinson	1922
J. Wason	1902	,,	1923
G. Roberts[3]	1922	,,	1924[3]
		,,	1931[3]
		,,	1935[3]
		Sir T. Robinson	1929

Dissident Labour

C. Stanton	1915	D. Taverne	1972
Sir O. Thomas	1922	,,	1974 Feb
N. Maclean	1929	E. Milne	1974 Feb
D. Pritt	1945		
S. Davies	1970		

Supported by the Left

E. Scrymgeour	1922	E. Scrymgeour	1929
,,	1923	V. Bartlett	1938
,,	1924	,,	1945[1]

[1]Later accepted Labour Whip.
[2]Later accepted Conservative Whip.
[3]These later candidacies might be put into a different category.

Minor Parties—Representation in the House of Commons

	Total	Ir. Nat.	S.N.P.	P.C.	Ind. Un.	Comm.	I.L.P.	Ind. Con.	Ind. Lab.	Other
1900	82	82	. .	. .	. .	. .	. .	. .	. .	. .
1906	83	83	. .	. .	. .	. .	. .	. .	. .	. .
1910J	82	84	. .	. .	. .	. .	. .	. .	. .	. .
1910D	84	84	. .	. .	. .	. .	. .	. .	. .	. .
1918	83	80[1]	. .	. .	. .	. .	. .	. .	. .	3
1922	12	3	. .	. .	. .	1	. .	4	1	3
1923	7	3	. .	. .	. .	. .	. .	. .	. .	4
1924	5	1	. .	. .	. .	1	. .	. .	. .	3
1929	8	3	. .	. .	. .	. .	. .	1	. .	4
1931	5	2	. .	. .	. .	. .	. .	. .	. .	3
1935	9	2	. .	. .	. .	1	4	. .	. .	2
1945	22	3	. .	. .	1	2	3	4	1	8
1950	3	2	. .	. .	. .	. .	. .	. .	. .	1
1951	3	3	. .	. .	. .	. .	. .	. .	. .	. .
1955	2	2	. .	. .	. .	. .	. .	. .	. .	. .
1959	1	. .	. .	. .	. .	. .	. .	1	. .	. .
1964	. .	. .	. .	. .	. .	. .	. .	. .	. .	. .
1966	1	1	. .	. .	. .	. .	. .	. .	. .	. .
1970	6	3	1	. .	1	. .	. .	. .	1	. .
1974F	24	1	7	2	11	. .	. .	. .	2	1
1974O	26	2	11	3	10	. .	. .	. .	. .	. .
1979	16	2	2	2	10	. .	. .	. .	. .	. .
1983	21	2	2	2	15	. .	. .	. .	. .	. .

[1] There were 73 Sinn Fein candidates elected in Ireland who never took their seats. There were also 7 Nationalists elected.

SOURCES.—*The Constitutional Year Book, 1919*; D. E. Butler, *The Electoral System in Britain since 1918* (1963); G. Thayer, *The British Political Fringe* (1965); F. W. S. Craig, *British Parliamentary Election Statistics, 1918-70* (1970); F. W. S. Craig, *Minor Parties at British Parliamentary Elections 1885-1974* (1975).

III
PARLIAMENT

House of Commons

Speaker of the House of Commons

	1895	W. Gully (Vt Selby)	Lib.
20 Jun	05	J. Lowther (Vt Ullswater)	Con.
28 Apr	21	J. Whitley	Co. Lib.
21 Jun	28	E. Fitzroy[1]	Con.
9 Mar	43	D. Clifton Brown (Vt Ruffside)	Con.
1 Nov	51	W. Morrison (Vt Dunrossil)	Con.
21 Oct	59	Sir H. Hylton-Foster[1]	Con.
26 Oct	65	Dr. H. King (Ld Maybray-King)	Lab.
12 Jan	71	S. Lloyd (Ld Selwyn-Lloyd)	Con.
3 Feb	76	G. Thomas (Vt Tonypandy)	Lab.
15 Jun	83	B. Weatherill	Con.

Chairman of Ways and Means

1900	J. Lowther	Con.
1905	G. Lawson	Con.
1906	A. Emmott	Lib.
1911	J. Whitley	Lib.
1921	J. Hope	Con.
1924	R. Young	Lab.
1924	J. Hope	Con.
1929	R. Young	Lab.
1931	Sir D. Herbert	Con.
1943	D. Clifton Brown	Con.
1943	J. Milner	Lab.
1945	C. Williams	Con.
1945	J. Milner	Lab.
1951	Sir C. MacAndrew	Con.
1959	Sir G. Touche	Con.
1962	Sir W. Anstruther-Gray	Con.
1964	H. King	Lab.
1965	Sir S. Storey	Con.
1966	Sir E. Fletcher	Lab.
1968	S. Irving	Lab.
1970	Sir R. Grant-Ferris	Con.
1974	G. Thomas	Lab.
1976	O. Murton	Con.
1979	B. Weatherill	Con.
1983	H. Walker	Lab.

Deputy Chairman of Ways and Means
(*office created* 1902)

1902	A. Jeffreys	Con.
1905	L. Hardy	Con.
1906	J. Caldwell	Lib.
1910	J. Whitley	Lib.
1911	D. Maclean	Lib.
1919	Sir E. Cornwall	Lib.
1922	E. Fitzroy	Con.
1924	C. Entwistle	Lib.
1924	E. Fitzroy	Con.
1928	D. Herbert	Con.
1929	H. Dunnico	Lab.
1931	R. Bourne[1]	Con.
1938	D. Clifton Brown	Con.
1943	J. Milner	Lab.
1943	C. Williams	Con.
1945	Sir C. MacAndrew	Con.
1945	H. Beaumont	Lab.
1948	F. Bowles	Lab.
1950	Sir C. MacAndrew	Con.
1951	Sir R. Hopkin Morris[1]	Lib.
1956	Sir G. Touche	Con.
1959	Sir W. Anstruther-Gray	Con.
1962	Sir R. Grimston	Con.
1964	Sir S. Storey	Con.
1965	R. Bowen	Lib.
1966	S. Irving	Lab.
1968	H. Gourlay	Lab.
1970	Miss B. Harvie Anderson	Con.
1973	E. Mallalieu	Lab.
1974	O. Murton	Con.
1976	Sir M. Galpern	Lab.
1979	G. Irvine	Con.
1982	E. Armstrong	Lab.

Second Deputy Chairman of Ways and Means
(*office created* 1971)

1971	E. Mallalieu	Lab.
1973	O. Murton	Con.
1974	(*office vacant*)	
1974	Sir M. Galpern	Lab.
1976	G. Irvine	Con.
1979	R. Crawshaw	Lab.
1981	E. Armstrong	Lab.
1982	(Sir) P. Dean	Con.

[1] Died in office.

Officers of the House of Commons

Clerk		*Librarian*	
1900	(Sir) A. Milman	1887	R. Walpole
1902	Sir C. Ilbert	1908	A. Smyth
1921	(Sir) T. Webster	1937	V. Kitto
1930	(Sir) H. Dawkins	1946	H. Saunders
1937	(Sir) G. Campion	1950	S. Gordon
1948	(Sir) F. Metcalfe	1968	D. Holland
1954	(Sir) E. Fellowes	1976	D. Menhennet
1962	(Sir) B. Cocks		
1974	(Sir) D. Lidderdale		
1976	(Sir) R. Barlas		
1979	(Sir) C. Gordon		
1983	K. Bradshaw		

Parliamentary Sessions

In 1900 sessions of Parliament lasted from February to July or August. Occasionally Parliament sat through the summer. In 1930 both Houses agreed that they should adjourn between July and October, and that the session should last from September or October to the September or October of the following year. During the adjournments the Speaker or the Lord Chancellor has the power to give notice of an earlier meeting of his House if it is in the national interest.

Parliamentary Hours of Sitting

In 1902 the House of Commons met from 2 until 11.30 p.m., but this was altered in 1906 to 2.45 until 11.30, to allow more time for lunch. During the 1939-45 war the time for rising in the evening was changed to 10.30 p.m. Since 1945 the normal hours for sitting have been 2.30 until 10.30 p.m. on every weekday except Friday although the House usually sits later than this. From 1900 to 1939 the House met on Fridays from noon to 5.30 p.m. From 1939 the House met on Fridays at 11 a.m. and normally adjourned for the weekend at 4.30 p.m. In 1967 as an experiment, the House also met from 10 a.m. to 1 p.m. on Mondays and Wednesdays but these morning sittings were discontinued from October 1967. From 1980 the House normally met at 9.30 a.m. on Friday and adjourned at 3 p.m.

Government and Private Members' Time

Until 1939 Government business had precedence at every sitting of the House of Commons except certain Wednesdays and Fridays and Tuesday evenings after 8.15 p.m. until Easter. This generally gave Private Members about 8 Wednesdays and 13 Fridays on which they had precedence. This was always subject to the possibility that the House, or Government, might direct that the time was needed for Government business. Between 1914 and

1918 and between 1939 and 1948 Private Members' time was abolished completely. When Private Members' time was restored, the Government retained precedence on all days except for 20 Fridays. In the nine sessions 1950-51 to 1958-59 an average of ten days was allotted to Private Members' Bills and 9 days to Private Members' motions. In 1960 four extra half-days (two Mondays and two Wednesdays) were allotted for consideration of Private Members' motions in addition to the twenty Fridays. From 1967 to 1970 sixteen of the twenty Fridays were given to Bills and four to motions. Since 1970 the number of Fridays for Bills has been between ten and twelve and usually ten for motions.

SOURCES.—Sir I. Jennings, *Parliament* (2nd ed., 1957), pp. 95-9, 121-2; Sir T. Erskine May, *Parliamentary Practice* (18th ed.); Sir G. Campion, *An Introduction to the Procedure of the House of Commons* (1950); *Report of the Select Committee on the Hours of Meeting and Rising of the House*, H.C. 126 of 1930; 'The Times of Sittings of the House', *Report by Select Committee on Procedure*, Aug 1966, H.C. 153 of 1966-67; House of Commons, *Fact Sheets*.

Broadcasting of Parliament

Television cameras were first allowed into Parliament for the opening of the session and the Queen's Speech on 28 Oct 58. On 11 Dec 67 the Commons approved without a division a proposal for a closed-circuit experiment in radio only. This was carried out in Apr and May 68. In Feb 68 the House of Lords engaged in a three-day radio and television closed-circuit experiment. But the House of Commons on a free vote rejected the idea of broadcasting Parliament on 24 Nov 66 (131-130), on 19 Oct 72 (191-165) and on 30 Jan 74 (189-164).

On 24 Feb 75 the House of Commons approved (354-152) a 4-week experiment in the live radio broadcasting of its proceedings and this took place from 9 Jun to 4 Jul 75. On 16 Mar 76 the House approved (299-124) the idea of permanent sound broadcasting. A select committee of six M.P.s (Chairmen: 1978: R. Mellish; 1979: Sir A. Royle; 1983: Sir P. Goodhart) was set up on 6 Feb 78 to supervise the arrangements to be made with the broadcasting authorities. A similar Lords Committee was also set up (Chairman: 1978: Ld Aberdare). Amendments proposing the appointment of a manager of broadcasting operations and a House of Commons broadcasting unit to control the scheme were defeated (64-53) and (68-49).

Regular sound broadcasting began on 3 Apr 1978. Private members have since introduced Ten Minute Rule Bills to test opinion on televising proceedings, as follows: 4 Jul 1978: defeated (181-161). 30 Jan 1980: first reading carried (202-201) on deputy speaker's casting vote. 15 Dec 1981: defeated (176-158). 13 Apr 1983 (select committees only): first reading carried (153-138). 2 Nov 1983: first reading carried (164-159).

On 8 Dec 1983, the Lords voted (74-24) for the public televising of some of its proceedings for an experimental period, and the select committee recommended a six-month experiment which began on 23 Jan 1985.

Main Occupations of Members of Parliament 1918- (percentages)

	Conservative				Labour			
	1918-35 Average	1945	1950	1951	1918-35 Average	1945	1950	1951
Employers and managers	32	32½	30½	32½	4	9½	9½	9
Rank and file workers	4	3	3	4½	72	41	43	45
Professional workers	52	61	62	57½	24	48½	46½	45½
Unpaid domestic workers	—	½	—	—	—	1	1	½
Unoccupied	12	3	4½	5½	—	—	—	—
	100	100	100	100	100	100	100	100

	Conservative									
	1951	1955	1959	1964	1966	1970	Feb 1974	Oct 1974	1979	1983
Professional	41	46	46	48	46	45	44	46	45	45
Business	37	30	30	26	29	30	32	33	34	36
Misc.	22	24	23	25	23	24	23	20	20	19
Workers	—	—	1	1	1	1	1	1	1	1
	100	100	100	100	100	100	100	100	100	100

	Labour									
	1951	1955	1959	1964	1966	1970	Feb 1974	Oct 1974	1979	1983
Professional	35	36	38	41	43	48	46	49	43	42
Business	9	12	10	11	9	10	9	8	7	9
Misc.	19	17	17	16	18	16	15	15	14	16
Workers	37	35	35	32	30	26	30	28	36	33
	100	100	100	100	100	100	100	100	100	100

Education of Conservative and Labour M.P.s 1906- (percentages)

	Conservatives		Labour	
	Public School	University Educated	Public School	University Educated
1906	67	57	0	0
1910 Jan	74	58	0	0
1910 Dec	76	59	0	0
1918	81	49	3	5
1922	78	48	9	15
1923	79	50	8	14
1924	78	53	7	14
1929	79	54	12	19
1931	77	55	8	17
1935	81	57	10	19
1945	85	58	23	32
1950	85	62	22	41
1951	75	65	23	41
1955	76	64	22	40
1959	72	60	18	39
1964	75	63	18	46
1966	80	67	18	51
1970	74	64	17	53
1974 Feb	74	68	17	56
1974 Oct	75	69	18	57
1979	77	73	17	57
1983	70	71	14	53

SOURCES.—Data for 1906 and 1910 are based on J. A. Thomas, *The House of Commons 1906-1911* (1958). From 1918 to 1950 J. F. S. Ross provides the data on university education in *Elections and Electors* (1955) and on public school education for Conservatives. The figures for Labour public schoolboys up to 1935 have been calculated afresh for this table. All figures from 1951 onwards are taken from the Nuffield studies. See also C. Mellors, *The British M.P. 1945-1975* (1978).

House of Commons Business

Sessions		Allocation of Parliamentary Time			Parliamentary Bills		Questions to Ministers		
Parliament Met	Parliament Prorogued	Total Days on which House sat	Average length of Day	Private Members' Days[a]	Total Bills Introduced	Total Bills Receiving Royal Assent	Daily Average: Starred Questions[b]	Daily Average: Unstarred Questions	Sessional Total of all Questions
3 Dec 00	15 Dec 00	11	5h 38m	3	. .	. .	. .	. .	314
23 Jan 01	17 Aug 01[c]	121	9h 5m	14	303	127	69	. .	6,448[c]
16 Jan 02	18 Dec 02	181	8h 51m	17	300	121	. .	. .	7,168
17 Feb 03	14 Aug 03	115	9h 8m	14	311	311	28	18	4,536
2 Feb 04	15 Aug 04	124	9h 19m	13	308	121	38	18	5,933
14 Feb 05	11 Aug 05	114	9h 12m	12	309	86	47	19	6,244
Date of Dissolution 8 Jan 06. Duration of Parliament 5 yrs, 2 mths, 7 days.									
13 Feb 06	21 Dec 06	156	8h 32m	16	346	121	70	22	11,865
12 Feb 07	28 Aug 07	131	8h 28m	13	294	116	72	21	10,147
29 Jan 08	21 Dec 08	171	7h 39m	18	364	129	75	21	13,811
16 Feb 09	3 Dec 09	179	8h 38m	14	325	110	62	19	12,251
Date of Dissolution 10 Jan 10. Duration of Parliament 3 yrs, 10 mths, 28 days.									
15 Feb 10	28 Nov 10	103	6h 36m	9	289	101	81	24	8,201
Date of Dissolution 28 Nov 10. Duration of Parliament 9 mths, 3 days.									
31 Jan 11	16 Dec 11	172	7h 49m	11	373	134	87	21	15,439
14 Feb 12	7 Mar 13	206	8h 1m	14	343	101	97	19	19,913
10 Mar 13	15 Aug 13	102	7h 55m	10	315	108	88	18	8,936
10 Feb 14	18 Sep 14	130	7h 14m	16	391	168	55	16	7,705
11 Nov 14	27 Jan 16	155	6h 40m	. .	162	152	72	16	12,976
15 Feb 16	22 Dec 16	127	7h 11m	. .	112	105	108	20	15,743
7 Feb 17	6 Feb 18	181	7h 21m	. .	102	91	92	16	19,146
12 Feb 18	21 Nov 18	119	7h 16m	. .	99	86	89	15	12,025
Date of Dissolution 25 Nov 18. Duration of Parliament 7 yrs, 9 mths, 25 days.									
4 Feb 19	23 Dec 19	163	7h 16m	16	203	152	126	27	20,523
10 Feb 20	23 Dec 20	167	8h 20m	17¼	215	138	110	22	18,652
15 Feb 21	10 Nov 21	141	8h 0m	11¾	202	125	101[d]	19[d]	14,133[d]
14 Dec 21	19 Dec 21	4	6h 5m	. .	. .	. .			
7 Feb 22	4 Aug 22	113	8h 3m	11	196	105	. .[e]	. .[e]	. .[e]
Date of Dissolution 26 Oct 22. Duration of Parliament 3 yrs, 9 mths, 5 days.									
20 Nov 22	15 Dec 22	20	7h 54m	. .	10	10	103[e]	18[e]	12,860[e]
13 Feb 23	16 Nov 23	114	8h 34m	17¼	181	78	107	21	12,370
Date of Dissolution 16 Nov 23. Duration of Parliament 11 mths, 27 days.									

[a] 'Notional' days on which Private Members' business had precedence. The idea of parliamentary 'days' must be treated with caution since actua days vary in length. In recent years Private Members' days have usually been Fridays and only 5 hours long whereas Government 'days' are usually at leas 6½ hours long and are frequently extended by suspension of the ten o'clock rule and by the practice of taking the affirmative and negative resolutions afte ten o'clock.

[b] Including oral questions receiving a written reply.

[c] Although the session of 1901 was not due to begin until 14 Feb, Parliament sat for three days between 23 and 25 Jan to discuss business arising ou of the death of Queen Victoria.

[d] For both sessions in 1921.

[e] For both sessions in 1922.

House of Commons Business

Sessions		Allocation of Parliamentary Time			Parliamentary Bills		Questions to Ministers		
Parliament Met	Parliament Prorogued	Total Days on which House sat	Average length of Day	Private Members' Days[a]	Total Bills Introduced	Total Bills Receiving Royal Assent	Daily Average: Starred Questions[b]	Daily Average: Unstarred Questions	Sessional Total of all Questions
8 Jan 24	9 Oct 24	129	7h 50m	21½	248	79	101	25	13,092
Date of Dissolution 9 Oct 24. Duration of Parliament 9 mths, 1 day.									
2 Dec 24	22 Dec 25	148	8h 17m	22½	247	145	91	23	14,035
2 Feb 26	15 Dec 26	151	7h 55m	21	180	105	71	17	10,713
8 Feb 27	22 Dec 27	144	7h 53m	19¾	195	91	74	14	10,536
7 Feb 28	3 Aug 28	115	7h 34m	24½	168	79	67	13	7,559
6 Nov 28	10 May 29	100	7h 0m	. .	115	64	68	17	7,074
Date of Dissolution 10 May 29. Duration of Parliament 4 yrs, 7 mths, 2 days.									
25 Jun 29	1 Aug 30	189	7h 57m	31	237	132	93	24	18,327
28 Oct 30	7 Oct 31	187	7h 47m	21¼	212	106	78	15	14,373
Date of Dissolution 8 Oct 31. Duration of Parliament 2 yrs, 4 mths, 28 days.									
3 Nov 31	17 Nov 32	155	7h 32m	1	125	103	69	10	9,667
22 Nov 32	17 Nov 33	143	7h 33m	26½	147	92	58	8	7,559
21 Nov 33	16 Nov 34	156	7h 49m	22¼	173	111	58	9	8,768
20 Nov 34	25 Oct 35	151	7h 36m	. .	116	98	59	9	8,449
Date of Dissolution 25 Oct 35. Duration of Parliament 3 yrs, 11 mths, 21 days.									
26 Nov 35	30 Oct 36	137	7h 55m	19½	149	111	82	13	10,215
3 Nov 36	22 Oct 37	157	7h 47m	24	170	126	79	11	11,769
26 Oct 37	4 Nov 38	168	7h 42m	26¼	179	113	85	14	13,787
8 Nov 38	23 Nov 39	200	7h 34m	14	227	171	92	17	18,460
28 Nov 39	20 Nov 40	127	6h 53m	. .	80	73	84	27	13,536
21 Nov 40	11 Nov 41	113	5h 50m	. .	55	54	77	23	10,825
12 Nov 41	10 Nov 42	116	6h 23m	. .	46	46	80	23	11,592
11 Nov 42	23 Nov 43	122	7h 1m	. .	59	58	83	22	11,911
24 Nov 43	28 Nov 44	153	7h 14m	. .	55	52	77	17	11,498
29 Nov 44	15 Jun 45	95	6h 51m	. .	57	48	91	18	7,856
Date of Dissolution 15 Jun 45. Duration of Parliament 9 yrs, 5 mths, 20 days.									
1 Aug 45	6 Nov 46	212	7h 45m	. .	106	104	128	30	27,313
12 Nov 46	20 Oct 47	164	8h 38m	. .	73	71	108	22	17,310
21 Oct 47	13 Sep 48	171	8h 13m	. .	92	89	97	21	16,303
14 Sep 48	25 Oct 48	10	7h 2m	. .	. .	. .	132	41	853
26 Oct 48	16 Dec 49	208	7h 48m	10½	146	125	86	18	17,334
Date of Dissolution 3 Feb 50. Duration of Parliament 4 yrs, 4 mths, 15 days.									
1 Mar 50	26 Oct 50	105	7h 50m	5	58	57	105	19	9,861
31 Oct 50	4 Oct 51	153	8h 20m	19	107	81	108	18	15,720
Date of Dissolution 5 Oct 51. Duration of Parliament 1 yr, 7 mths, 4 days.									

House of Commons Business

Sessions		Allocation of Parliamentary Time			Parliamentary Bills		Questions to Ministers		
Parliament Met	Parliament Prorogued	Total Days on which House sat	Average length of Day	Private Members' Days[a]	Total Bills Introduced	Total Bills Receiving Royal Assent	Daily Average: Starred Questions[b]	Daily Average: Unstarred Questions	Sessional Total of all Questions
31 Oct 51	30 Oct 52	157	8h 48m	18½	113	88	99	17	14,192
4 Nov 52	29 Oct 53	162	8h 12m	20	78	62	91	16	13,878
3 Nov 53	25 Nov 54	187	8h 11m	19	113	95	89	15	15,990
30 Nov 54	6 May 55	84	7h 58m	10	72	33	90	17	7,262
Date of Dissolution 6 May 55. Duration of Parliament 3 yrs, 6 mths, 6 days.									
7 Jun 55	5 Nov 56	219	7h 57m	25½	126	101	86	16	18,285
6 Nov 56	1 Nov 57	159	7h 40m	20	93	75	90	20	14,259
5 Nov 57	23 Oct 58	156	7h 54m	20	112	89	84	18	12,734
28 Oct 58	18 Sep 59	159	7h 48m	20	113	89	89	21	14,518
Date of Dissolution 18 Sep 59. Duration of Parliament 4 yrs, 3 mths, 11 days.									
20 Oct 59	27 Oct 60	160	8h 2m	22	103	80	81	21	13,471
1 Nov 60	24 Oct 61	168	8h 30m	22	117	79	73	22	13,778
31 Oct 61	25 Oct 62	160	8h 23m	22	108	75	65	23	12,226
30 Oct 62	24 Oct 63	162	8h 15m	22	105	72	67	31	13,948
12 Nov 63	64	155	8h 14m	22	155	102	66	37	14,291
Date of Dissolution 25 Sep 64. Duration of Parliament 4 yrs, 11 mths, 5 days.									
27 Oct 64	10 Mar 66	177	9h 0m	22	158	94	74	46	19,148
9 Nov 65	8 Nov 65	65	8h 15m	22	74	21	67	56	7,978
Date of Dissolution 10 Mar 66. Duration of Parliament 1 yr, 5 mths, 13 days.									
18 Apr 66	27 Oct 67	246	9h 50m	25	210	127	69	69	33,965
31 Oct 67	25 Oct 68	176	9h 2m	22	142	76	64	77	24,910
30 Oct 68	22 Oct 69	164	9h 26m	24	158	73	81	78	23,464
28 Oct 69	29 May 70	122	8h 16m	24	152	60	81	78	17,461
Date of Dissolution 29 May 70. Duration of Parliament 4 yrs, 1 mth, 11 days.									
29 Jun 70	28 Oct 71	206	8h 16m	24	164	110	83	99	33,946
2 Nov 71	26 Oct 72	180	9h 17m	24	149	84	77	97	28,946
31 Oct 72	25 Oct 73	164	8h 53m	24	153	83	47	109	25,788
30 Oct 73	8 Feb 74	60	8h 21m	6½	77	17	41	104	8,690
Date of Dissolution 8 Feb 74. Duration of Parliament 3 yrs, 7 mths, 10 days.									
6 Mar 74	— 74	87	8h 28m	10½	86	50	48	133	15,738
Date of Dissolution 20 Sep 74. Duration of Parliament 6 mths, 14 days.									

a 'Notional' days on which Private Members' business had precedence. The idea of parliamentary 'days' must be treated with caution since actual days vary in length. In recent years Private Members' days have usually been Fridays and only 5 hours long whereas Government 'days' are usually at least 6½ hours long and are frequently extended by suspension of the ten o'clock rule and by the practice of taking the affirmative and negative resolutions after ten o'clock.

b Including oral questions receiving a written reply.

House of Commons Business

Sessions		Allocation of Parliamentary Time			Parliamentary Bills		Questions to Ministers		
Parliament Met	Parliament Prorogued	Total Days on which House sat	Average length of Day	Private Members' Days[a]	Total Bills Introduced	Total Bills Receiving Royal Assent	Daily Average: Starred Questions[b]	Daily Average: Unstarred Questions	Sessional Total of all Questions
22 Oct 74	12 Nov 75	198	9h 20m	22	183	99	47	137	36,652
19 Nov 75	22 Nov 76	191	9h 13m	22	174	100	49	167	41,460
24 Nov 76	26 Oct 77	149	9h 10m	22	141	56	46	163	31,269
3 Nov 77	24 Oct 78	169	9h 24m	24	136	60	49	175	37,775
31 Oct 78	—	86	8h 17m	15	115	50	54	153	17,851
Date of Dissolution 7 Apr 79. Duration of Parliament 4 yrs, 5 mths, 16 days.									
9 May 79	13 Nov 80	244	8h 55m	25	217	102	51	164	52,635
20 Nov 80	30 Oct 81	163	9h 7m	22	145	78	50	139	30,863
4 Nov 81	28 Oct 82	174	8h 8m	22	143	59	52	135	32,430
3 Nov 82	—	115	8h 34m	17	134	56	53	149	23,220
Date of Dissolution 13 May 1983. Duration of Parliament 4 yrs, 4 days.									
15 Jun 83	31 Oct 84	213	8h 59m	24	181	76	63	188	53,505

[a] 'Notional' days on which Private Members' business had precedence. The idea of parliamentary 'days' must be treated with caution since actual days vary in length. Private Members' days are usually Fridays and only 5 hours long whereas Government 'days' are usually at least 6½ hours long and are frequently extended by suspension of the ten o'clock rule and by the practice of taking the affirmative and negative resolutions after ten o'clock.

[b] Including oral questions receiving a written reply.

SOURCES.—Information from the *'Black Book'*, a compilation of Parliamentary statistics at the House of Commons, and the *Sessional Returns of the House of Commons*. Questions to Ministers taken from D. N. Chester and N. Bowring, *Questions in Parliament* (1962), pp. 87-8, and 316; and information from the Journal Office, House of Commons.

Fathers of the House of Commons

Name	Member of Parliament until	Length of service as M.P.		Length of service as Father	
		y.	*m.*	*y.*	*m.*
(Sir) W. Bramston Beach	August 1901	44	4	2	4
Sir M. Hicks Beach	January 1906	41	6	4	5
G. Finch	May 1907	39	6	1	4
Sir H. Campbell-Bannerman	April 1908	39	6		11
Sir J. Kennaway	January 1910	39	9	1	9
T. Burt	November 1918	44	10	8	11
T. P. O'Connor	November 1929	49	7	10	11
D. Lloyd George	December 1944	54	8	15	1
Earl Winterton	October 1951	46	11	6	10
Sir H. O'Neill	October 1952	37	8	1	0
D. Grenfell	September 1959.	37	2	6	11
Sir W. Churchill	September 1964	62	0[a]	5	0
R. Butler	January 1965	35	8		4
(Sir) R. Turton	February 1974	44	8	9	1
G. Strauss	April 1979	46	11	5	0
J. Parker	May 1983	46	7	4	1
J. Callaghan	(elected July 1945)	. .		. .	

[a] By tradition the title of Father of the House is conferred on the member who has the longest *continuous* service in the House. Churchill's service was broken in 1908 and again in 1922-4. His length of continuous service was therefore exactly 40 years.

[b] G. Strauss also served as an M.P. from May 1929 to October 1931.

SOURCES.—J. F. S. Ross, *Elections and Electors* (1955), p. 470; House of Commons, *Fact Sheets*.

Long-service M.P.s

Apart from the Fathers of the House (all but three of whom served over 38 years) the following M.P.s served 38 years or more:

Years			
49	G. Lambert	91-24,	29-45
48	A. Balfour	74-06,	06-22
47	J. Gretton	95-06,	07-43
47	H. Chaplin	68-06,	07-16
45	Sir A. Chamberlain	92-14,	14-37
42	J. Talbot	68-78,	78-10
41	Sir W. Hart Dyke	65-06	
40	Sir W. Lawson	59-65, 86-00,	68-85, 03-06
40	E. Shinwell	22-24, 35-70	28-31,
40	W. Long	80-92,	93-21
39	Sir G. Courthope	06-45	
39	W. Thorne	06-45	
39	Sir T. Moore	25-64	
39	Sir C. Taylor	35-74	
39	Sir L. Ropner	23-29,	31-64
39	**Sir H. Fraser**	**45-84**	
38	Sir J. Pease	65-03	
38	**J. Round**	**68-06**	
38	Sir J. Agg-Gardner	74-80, 00-06,	85-95, 11-28

Years			
38	J. Chamberlain	76-14	
38	J. Collings	80-86,	86-18
38	J. Lowther	83-21	
38	Ld H. Cecil	95-06,	10-37
38	W. Nicholson	97-35	
38	E. Fitzroy	00-06,	10-43
38	W. Elliot	18-23, 46-58	24-45,
38	G. Oliver	22-31,	35-64
38	H. Macmillan	24-29, 45-64	31-45,
38	Dame I. Ward	31-45,	50-74
38	G. Lloyd	31-45,	50-74
38	**Sir J. Langford-Holt**	**45-83**	
38	**A. Lewis**	**45-83**	
38	**G. Thomas**	**45-83**	
38	**J. Silverman**	**45-83**	
38	**F. Willey**	**45-83**	
38	**Sir H. Wilson**	**45-83**	
38	**Sir D. Walker-Smith**	**45-83**	

Sir J. Fergusson (55-7, 59-68, 85-06), Sir F. Powell (57-9, 63-8, 72-4, 80-1, 85-10), and Lord C. Hamilton (65-8, 69-88, 10-18) with substantially interrupted service, can be listed with Sir W. Churchill, D. Lloyd George, G. Lambert, Sir J. Agg-Gardner and G. Strauss as the only members to leave the House fifty years after entering it.

Oldest and Youngest M.P.s

The oldest M.P.s have been S. Young (96 in 1918); D. Logan (92 in 1964); Sir W. Churchill (89 in 1964); W. Thorne (88 in 1945); R. Cameron (87 in 1913); J. Collings (86 in 1918); Sir S. Chapman (86 in 1945); E. Shinwell (85 in 1970); and S. O. Davies (85 in 1972).

The youngest M.P.s have been Vt Turnour (Earl Winterton) (21 in 1904); J. Esmonde (21 in 1915); P. Whitty (21 in 1916); J. Sweeney (21 in 1918); E. Harmsworth (21 in 1919); Sir H. Lucas-Tooth (21 in 1924); and Miss B. Devlin (21 in 1969).

Family Connections of M.P.s

Many M.P.s have had extended family connections with other present or past M.P.s. Often, when through the female line, these are difficult to check. However, the following include the most outstanding examples of parliamentary families.

Acland	Sir R. Acland (1935-45, 1947-55); s. of Sir F. Acland (1906-22, 1923-4, 1932-39); s. of Sir A. Acland (1885-99); s. of Sir T. Acland (1837-47, 1865-85).
Astor	W. W. Astor (1935-45, 1951-2) and his brothers J. J. Astor (1951-9) and M. Astor (1945-51) were sons of Vtess Astor (1919-45) and W. Astor (1910-19). W. Astor's brother J. J. Astor (1922-45) and his son J. Astor (1964-74) also sat.
Baldwin	(E of Baldwin of Bewdley). O. Baldwin (1929-31, 1945-7); s. of S. Baldwin (1908-37); s. of A. Baldwin (1892-1908).
Benn	(Vt Stansgate) A. Wedgwood Benn (1950-61, 63-83, 84-); s. of W. Benn (1906-31, 1937-41); s. of Sir J. Benn (1892-5, 1904-10).
Cavendish	(D of Devonshire) M. of Hartington (1923-38); s. of V. Cavendish (1865-8, 1880-91); s. of Ld E. Cavendish (1865-74, 1880-91) b. of M of Hartington (1857-91). Three of the sisters of the M of Hartington (1923-38) were married to M.P.s – H. Macmillan (1924-9, 1931-45, 1945-64); J. Stuart (1923-59); H. Hunloke (1938-44); F. Holland-Martin (1951-60) and then Vt Hinchingbrooke (1941-62).
Cecil	(M of Salisbury) Vt Cranborne (1979-); s. of Vt Cranborne (1950-54); s. of Vt Cranborne (1929-41); s. of Vt Cranborne (1885-92, 1893-1903); s. of Vt Cranborne (1853-68); s. of Vt Cranborne (1813-23); s. of Vt Cranborne (1774-80).
Chamberlain	N. Chamberlain (1918-40); b. of Sir A. Chamberlain (1892-1937); s. of J. Chamberlain (1876-1914).
Channon	P. Channon (1959-); s. of Sir H. Channon (1935-58) and g.s. of Countess of Iveagh (1927-35) and Vt Elveden (1908-10, 1912-27). This is the only example of a seat, Southend, being held successively by four members of one family.
Churchill	(D of Marlborough) W. Churchill (1970-); s. of R. Churchill (1940-5); s. of Sir W. Churchill (1900-22, 1924-64); s. of Ld R. Churchill (1874-94); s. of M of Blandford (1844-5, 1847-5); s. of M of Blandford (1818-20, 1826-30, 1832-5, 1838-40); s. of M of Blandford (1790-96, 1802-4).
Guest	(V Wimborne) I. Guest (1935-45); s. of I. Guest (Vt Wimborne) (1906-10) who was b. of F. Guest (1910-22, 1923-9, 1931-37), O. Guest (1918-22, 1935-45) and C. Guest (1910-18, 1922-3, 1937-45).
Henderson	A. Henderson (1903-18, 1919-22, 1923, 1924-31, 1933-5), sat in the House with two sons, Arthur (1923-4, 1929-31, 1935-66) and William (1923-4, 1929-31).
Hogg	(Vt Hailsham) D. Hogg (1979-); s. of Q. Hogg (1938-50, 1963-70); s. of Sir D. Hogg (1922-8); nephew of Sir J. Hogg (1865-8, 1871-87), and grandson of Sir. J. Hogg (1835-57).
Hurd	D. Hurd (1974-); s. of Sir A. Hurd (1945-64); s. of (Sir) P. Hurd (1918-23, 1924-45).
Lloyd George	D. Lloyd George (1890-1944) sat in the House with his son Gwilym (1924-50, 1951-7) and his daughter Megan (1929-51, 1957-66).
Montagu-Douglas-Scott	(D of Buccleuch) E of Dalkeith (1960-73); s. of E of Dalkeith (1923-35) and nephew of Ld W. Scott (1935-50); s. of E of Dalkeith (1895-1906); s. of E of Dalkeith (1853-60, 1874-80).
Morrison	C. Morrison (1963-); b. of P. Morrison (1974-); s. of J. Morrison (1942-64); s. of H. Morrison (1918-23, 1924-31); b. of J. Morrison (1900-06, 1910-12).
Stanley	(E of Derby) R. Stanley (1950-66); s. of Ld Stanley (1917-18, 1922-38) and nephew of O. Stanley (1924-50); s. of Ld Stanley (1892-1900) and nephew of A. Stanley (1898-1918); s. of Ld Stanley (1865-86); s. of Ld Stanley (1824-44); s. of Ld Stanley (1796-1832).

Spouse's Succession

In the following case a wife took over at a by-election the seat being left vacant by her husband's death, or elevation to the peerage, or disqualification.

1919	Lady Astor (Plymouth, Sutton)
1921	Mrs M. Wintringham (Louth)
1923	Mrs H. Philipson (Berwick-on-Tweed)
1927	Countess of Iveagh (Southend)
1930	Lady Noel-Buxton (Norfolk North)
1937	Mrs A. Hardie (Glasgow, Springburn)
1937	Lady Davidson (Hemel Hempstead)
1941	Mrs B. Rathbone (Bodmin)
1943	Lady Apsley (Bristol Central)
1953	Mrs L. Jeger (Holborn & St. Pancras, S.)
1957	Lady Gammans (Hornsey)
1982	Mrs H. McElhone (Glasgow, Queen's Park)

In 1931 Sir O. Mosley failed to take over his wife's seat at Stoke. In 1958 Mrs W. Elliot was defeated at Glasgow, Kelvingrove, when seeking to succeed her husband. In 1969 Mrs G. Forrest was defeated in Mid-Ulster when seeking to succeed her husband.

In 1929 H. Dalton took over the seat at Bishop Auckland which his wife had won in a 1929 by-election. In 1929 W. Runciman took over the seat in Cornwall which his wife had won in a 1928 by-election.

The Duchess of Atholl (1923-38) sat for the West Perthshire seat which her husband (M of Tullibardine) had occupied (1910-17).

The only cases of husband and wife sitting together in the House of Commons have been

W. and H. Runciman	1928-9
H. and R. Dalton	1929-9
Sir O. and Lady C. Mosley	1929-31
A. Bevan and Jennie Lee	1929-31, 1945-60 (they were married in 1934)
W. and J. Adamson	1938-45
J. and F. Paton	1945-50
R. and A. Kerr	1966-70
J. and G. Dunwoody	1966-70
N. and A. Winterton	1983-
P. and V. Bottomley	1984-

Alex Lyon (1966-83) and Clare Short (1983-), though married, did not sit in the same House. Some M.P.s have married after one had left the House: N. Fisher (1950-83) and Mrs P. Ford (1953-5); J. Sillars (1970-9) and Mrs M. Macdonald (1973-4); C. Stephen (1935-47) and Miss D. Jewson (1923-4). Shirley Summerskill (1964-83) sat with her ex-husband J. Ryman (1974-).

Filial Succession

In the following cases a son or daughter was nominated to fill a vacancy left by a parent.

1908	S. Baldwin (Bewdley)
1909	T. Lundon (Limerick E.)
1913	R. McCalmont (Antrim E.)
1913	P. Meehan (Queens Co., Leix)
1914	A. Chamberlain (Birmingham)
1940	N. Grattan-Doyle (Newcastle N.) (defeated)
1945	G. Lambert (South Molton)
1946	J. Little (Down) (defeated)
1953	Mrs P. Ford (Sir W. Smiles) (Down N.)
1959	P. Channon (Southend W.)
1970	G. Janner (Leicester N.W.)
1983	S. Palmer (Bristol N.W.) (defeated)

Critical Votes in the House of Commons since 1900

Votes in the House of Commons have only rarely disturbed or threatened to disturb a government or to prevent its implementing its programme. Moreover prudent governments have retreated rather than face the risk of defeat (e.g. over *In Place of Strife*, 1969). The following occasions do not constitute an exhaustive list (e.g. only 5 of the 9 minor defeats inflicted on the Labour Government of 1924 are included) but they probably include all that caused any serious stir.

15 Feb	1904	327-276	Government majority (on Liberal Free Trade motion) cut by desertion of 26 Unionist Free Traders.
20 Jul	1905	199-196	Government defeated on Estimates for Irish Land Commission.
11 Nov	1912	227-206	Government defeated on Amendment to financial resolution of the Government of Ireland Bill.
7 Jul	1914	269-246	Government wins guillotine on Budget despite 22 Lib. abstentions, one Lib. No; setback leads to abandonment of Revenue Bill.
8 Nov	1916	213-117	Government survives challenge on sale of German property in Nigeria but 65 Cons rebelled, provoking Bonar Law to think of Cabinet reconstruction.
9 May	1918	293-106	Lloyd George victory over Maurice affair. Coupons in Dec 1918 election issued largely on basis of how Libs voted in this division.
23 Oct	1919	185-113	Amendment to Alien Restriction Bill carried on report stage against Government.
25 Feb	1920	123-57	Motion for increased police pensions carried against Government.
19 Jul	1921	137-135	Amendment to Finance Bill exempting Provident Societies from Corporation Profits Tax carried against Government.
10 Apr	1923	145-138	Government defeated on procedural motion over ex-Servicemen's salaries.
21 Jan	1924	328-256	Baldwin Government, meeting new parliament, defeated by Lib. and Lab. votes.
7 Apr	1924	221-212	Government defeated on second reading of Rent Restriction Bill.
16 Jun	1924	189-126	New Clause to London Traffic Bill carried against Government.
18 Jul	1924	171-149	Government defeated on amendment to Unemployment Insurance Bill.
8 Oct	1924	364-198	MacDonald Government defeated on Lib. amendment for enquiry into Campbell case. Dissolution follows at once.
27 Feb	1930	280-271	Government defeats key Amendment to Coal Bill, saved by support of 4 Libs and abstention of 8 Libs.
21 Jan	1931	282-249	Government defeat on Report Stage over subsidy to Catholic schools (41 Lab. Noes).
14 Mar	1931	173-168	Government survives challenge over appointment of Sir E. Gowers to chair Mines Reorganisation Commission.
16 Mar	1931	277-273	Government defeated over abolition of University M.P.s (2 Lab. M.P.s voted with Opposition and 20 abstained).
8 Sep	1931	309-250	National Government wins first vote (on procedural motion); Ayes 243 Con., 53 Lib., 12 Lab., 3 Ind.; Noes: 242 Lab., 9 Ind.
11 Feb	1935	404-133	Government wins Second Reading for Government of India Bill (with 80 Con. Noes).
1 Apr	1936	156-148	Government defeated on adjournment motion over equal pay for civil servants (vote reversed 6 Apr 1936).
8 May	1940	281-200	Chamberlain survives censure motion but Con. Noes (33) and abstentions (about 65) force his resignation.
18 Mar	1943	335-119	Government wins motion on Beveridge Report but 97 Lab. M.P.s—out of 99 non-ministers voting—defy Whip.
28 Mar	1944	117-116	Government defeated on equal pay for women (vote reversed 30 May 1944, 429-23).
13 Dec	1945	345-98	Government obtains approval for the American Loan. Cons officially abstained, but 74 Con. and 23 Lab. M.P.s voted No; 8 Cons also voted Aye.
1 Apr	1947	386-85	Government obtains Second Reading for National Service Bill (72 Lab. and one Con. Noes).

9 Mar 1950	310-296	First division in new parliament (on Steel Nationalisation) showed Government with nominal majority of five could carry on.
29 Mar 1950	283-257	Government defeated on adjournment motion following debate on Fuel and Power.
9 Apr 1951	237-219	Motion to annul a Rationing Order carried against the Government.
5 Jul 1951	157-141	Motion to annul a Prices Order carried against the Government.
16 Jul 1951	232-229	Government defeated on amendment to the Forestry Bill.
6 Dec 1956	313-260	Government wins confidence vote on Suez action (15 Con. abstentions).
17 Jun 1963	321-252	Government survives adjournment debate on Profumo Affair (27 Con. abstentions).
10 Mar 1964	287-20	Government secures Second Reading of Resale Prices Bill with Labour abstaining (20 Con. Noes and about 20 abstentions).
24 Mar 1964	204-203	Government defeats Amendment excluding medicines from Resale Prices Bill (31 Con. voting against Government and over 20 abstaining).
6 May 1965	310-306	Approval for White Paper on Steel Nationalisation.
6 Jul 1965	180-167	New Clause to Finance Bill carried against Government.
21 Dec 1965	276-48	Rhodesia oil embargo order approved. Cons officially abstained but 50 Cons voted No and 31 Aye.
30 May 1968	129-52	Reintroduction of prescription charges approved but 49 Lab. Noes and over 150 Lab. abstentions.
3 Mar 1969	224-62	Motion approving *In Place of Strife* White Paper carried but 55 Lab. Noes and 40 Lab. abstentions.
28 Oct 1971	356-244	Approval for negotiated terms on European entry. 69 Lab. M.P.s voted for and 20 abstained. 39 Con. M.P.s voted against and 2 abstained.
17 Feb 1972	309-301	Government secures Second Reading of European Communities Bill (15 Con. Noes and 4 Con. abstentions; there were 4 Lab. abstentions; Libs divided 5-1 Aye).
13 Jul 1972	301-284	Government secures Third Reading of European Communities Bill (16 Con. Noes; 4 Con. and 13 Lab. abstentions).
22 Nov 1972	275-240	Government defeated on immigration rules (7 Con. Noes and 49 Con. abstentions).
13 Jun 1973	267-250	Government defeated on new Clause to Maplin Development Bill (17 Con. Ayes and 10 Con. abstentions).
13 Jun 1973	255-246	Government secures Third Reading of Maplin Development Bill.
12 Jul 1973	285-264	Government defeated on export of live animals for slaughter (23 Cons voted Aye).
20 Jun 1974	311-290	Government defeated in debate on industrial policy.
27 Jun 1974	298-289	Opposition motion on Rates carried against Government. [The above were only two of the seventeen government defeats during the Short Parliament of 1974.]
29 Jan 1975	280-265	Government defeated on amendment to the Social Security Benefits Bill (9 Lab. Ayes).
17 Jul 1975	108-106	Government defeated on Opposition amendment to Finance Bill reducing V.A.T. on TV sets.
4 Aug 1975	268-261	Government defeated on clause to the Housing Finance (Special Provisions) Bill.
10 Mar 1976	284-256	Government defeated on motion approving public expenditure plans. (Next day Government won confidence motion 297-280.)
27 May 1976	304-303	In disputed vote Government set aside Standing Order rule on hybridity of Aircraft and Shipbuilding Nationalisation Act. (Government won retaken vote on 29 Jun 311-297 with 14 Nationalists abstaining.)
28 Jun 1976	259-0	Government defeated on motion for adjournment (through failing to contest it) following debate on its child benefits scheme.
8 Nov 1976	311-310	Government secures guillotine on Lords amendments on Aircraft and Shipbuilding Acts.
10 Nov 1976	310-308	Key clause in Dock Labour Bill defeated through two Lab. abstentions (J. Mackintosh and B. Walden).
7 Feb 1977	130-129	Government lost Second Reading of the Redundancy Rebates Bill by one vote, due to unpaired absence of the P.M. (Subsequently reintroduced in modified form.)
22 Feb 1977	312-283	Government defeated over guillotine on Scotland and Wales Bill (with 22 Lab. Noes and 21 abstentions).

17 Mar 1977	293-0	Government defeated on adjournment motion to discuss public expenditure plans (all Lab. M.P.s abstained).
23 Mar 1977	322-298	Government survives Con. motion of censure with Lib. votes, following Lib-Lab Pact.
5 Apr 1977	203-185	Government defeated on adjournment motion following debate on training colleges in Scotland, through Lab. abstentions.
22 Nov 1977	199-184	Government loses first clause of the Scotland Devolution Bill.
5 Dec 1977	158-126	Government defeated on adjournment motion on Crown Agents' affair by M.P.s demanding public inquiry.
7 Dec 1977	161-160	Government defeated over Scotland Devolution Bill provision for Secretary of State to have regard to national pay policy (2 Lab. Noes).
13 Dec 1977	319-222	Government recommendation of proportional representation for European Parliament elections rejected on Free Vote (Lab. 147 for, 115 against; Con. 61 for, 198 against).
23 Jan 1978	291-281	Motion to devalue Green Pound by 7½%, not 5%, carried against Government.
25 Jan 1978	166-151	Amendment to Scotland Devolution Bill, making 40% of electorate voting 'Yes' in referendum a precondition for the Bill taking effect carried against Government (34 Lab. in majority).
25 Jan 1978	204-118	Amendment to Scotland Devolution Bill, excluding Orkney and Shetland, carried against Government.
14 Feb 1978	298-243	Referendum decision of 25 Jan 77 confirmed on Report Stage (40 Lab. in majority).
8 May 1978	312-304	Amendment to reduce standard rate of Income Tax from 34p. to 33p. carried against Government.
10 May 1978	288-286	Amendment to raise threshold for higher tax rates from £7,000 to £8,000 carried against Government.
19 Jul 1978	293-260	Amendment to Wales Bill barring M.P.s from standing for Welsh Assembly carried against Government.
24 Jul 1978	291-281	Government defeated on clause in Dock Labour Bill giving dock workers local priority in jobs.
26 Jul 1978	276-275	Lords Amendment to Scotland Bill concerning non-Scottish legislation decided by Scottish M.P.s votes upheld against Government. (Lords amendment on Forestry powers also carried 288-266.)
13 Dec 1978	285-283	Government defeated on retention of powers to use sanctions against firms breaching pay policy.
28 Mar 1979	311-310	Government defeated on Conservative vote of No Confidence.
23 Apr 1980	477-49	Government faces rebellion on closed shop.
15 Dec 1982	290-272	Government defeated on amendment to immigration rules (51 Cons voting with Opposition or abstaining).
19 Jul 1983	226-218	Government advice on delaying M.P.s pay increase rejected.
11 Apr 1984	300-208	Government win against challenge on TU ballot rules but 90 M.P.s cross vote.

In the Parliament of 1970-4 there were 6 government defeats in the House of Commons; in Mar-Jul 1974 there were 17 defeats; in 1974-79 there were 42 defeats; in 1979-83 one defeat; and in the first session of the 1983- Parliament there was one defeat.

Sources.—P. Norton, *Dissension in the House of Commons 1945-74* (1975), *1974-9* (1980); P. Norton, 'Government Defeats in the House of Commons', *Public Law*, Winter 1978; P. Norton, *Parliament in the 1980s* (1985).

Confidence Motions since 1945

Many motions before the House of Commons are implicitly treated as questions of confidence. But since 1945 the question of confidence has only been put explicitly to the House on the following occasions. On 14 Dec 1978 the motion expressed confidence. All the other motions expressed no confidence. The only one carried was on 28 Mar 1979.

	Voting Aye	Noe		Aye	Noe
5 Dec 45	197	381	9 Jun 76	290	309
4 Dec 52	280	304	23 Mar 77	298	322
2 Aug 65	290	303	(14 Dec 78)	(300)	(290)
26 Jul 66	*no vote*		28 Mar 79	311	310
1 Dec 66	246	329	28 Feb 80	268	327
24 Jul 67	200	333	28 Oct 81	250	312
6 Mar 72	270	317	31 Jan 85	222	395
19 Nov 73	286	304			

Guillotine Motions since 1945

From 1945 to 1984 the average number of guillotine motions was less than two per year. All were carried except one (the Scotland and Wales Bill 22 Feb 1977). The session numbers are:

Session	*Guillotine motions*	*Session*	*Guillotine motions*
1946-7	2	1970-1	2
1947-8	—	1970-1	5
1948-9	1	1972-3	1
1950-1	—	1973-4	—
1951-2	2	1974-5	4
1952-3	2	1975-6	10
1953-4	2	1976-7	1
1954-5	—	1977-8	5
1955-6	—	1978-9	—
1956-7	1	1979-80	7
1957-8	1	1980-1	4
1958-9	—	1981-2	4
1959-60	—	1982-3	3
1960-1	2	1983-4	4
1960-2	5		
1962-3	2		
1963-4	—		
1964-5	—		
1965-6	—		
1966-7	1		
1967-8	2		
1968-9	1		
1969-70	1		

M.P.s Suspension

Members acting in sustained defiance of the chair can be named and suspended from the service of the House of Commons for 5 sitting days. The number of examples is limited:

18 Jul	49	E. Smith
27 Nov	51	S. Silverman
26 Mar	52	Mrs E. Braddock
23 May	68	Dame I. Ward
13 Mar	72	C. Loughlin
12 Feb	81	I. Paisley
8 Apr	81	R. Brown
15 Jul	81	R. Brown
16 Nov	81	J. McQuade, P. Robinson, I. Paisley
26 May	82	A. Faulds
2 May	84	T. Dalyell
17 Jul	84	D. Skinner
31 Jul	84	M. Flannery

Regnal Years

Until 1962 the dates of Acts of Parliament were recorded in terms of the regnal years during the session in which they were passed. Regnal years date from the accession of the sovereign. Thus the act listed as *11 & 12 Geo. VI, c. 65* was passed in the parliamentary session during the eleventh and twelfth regnal year of George VI (1948). The parliamentary session of 1948-49 covered three regnal years, and its acts appear under the style *12, 13 & 14 Geo. VI*. Since 1963 Acts of Parliament have been recorded by the calendar year and the chapter number, e.g. *Finance Act 1963, c. 25*.

Sovereign	Regnal Year	Date
Victoria	63	20 Jun 1899-19 Jun 1900
	64	20 Jun 1900-22 Jan 01
Edward VII	1	22 Jan 01-21 Jan 02
	10	22 Jan 10-6 May 10
George V	1	6 May 10-5 May 11
	26	6 May 35-20 Jan 36
Edward VIII	1	20 Jan 36-11 Dec 36
George VI	1	11 Dec 36-10 Dec 37
	16	11 Dec 51-6 Feb 52
Elizabeth II	1	6 Feb 52-5 Feb 53
	10	6 Feb 61-5 Feb 62

SOURCES.—Regnal years from 1154-1945 are listed in *Handbook of Dates*, ed. C. R. Cheney (1945), pp. 18-21; *Where to Look for Your Law* (1965).

Select Committees

Select Committees have been appointed for many purposes and have a long history in both Houses.

In the Commons Select Committees have long been used in connection with public expenditure, parliamentary procedure, legislation, and for *ad hoc* enquiries, sometimes of a quasi-judicial character. In the nineteenth century and up to 1914 Select Committees were also used for a wide range of specific enquiries, many of which would now be undertaken by a Government Inquiry or even a Royal Commission. Between the wars Select Committees were also occasionally used to examine Empire matters. Select Committees may be set up for a session or part of a session to consider a specific matter e.g. the Select Committee on Patent Medicines in 1914, the Select Committee on Tax-Credit in 1972-73, or the Select Committee on Conduct of Members in 1975-76 and 1976-77. Others are set up more regularly by custom.[1]

The Public Accounts Committee has existed continuously since 1862. An Estimates Committee now subsumed in the Expenditure Committee, has been set up in one form or another most sessions from 1912 to 1979. Although the Nationalised Industries Committee has existed since 1956 other 'specialist Committees' to consider either a subject area e.g. Race Relations and Immigration or a Department e.g. Education and Science were appointed after the 'Crossman Reforms' in 1966 for each session, for the duration of a Parliament until 1979. In 1979 a new structure of Select Committees was established to cover the work of each major Government Department.

Powers: In their order of reference, and under Standing Orders, Commons Select Committees have had powers of varying extent given to them by the House.

Except for Select Committees on Bills or procedure committees both Sessional Committees and specialist committees are now usually given powers to send for persons, papers and records (although only the House can act to punish contempt of such summons), to sit at times when the House is adjourned, to meet outside the Palace of Westminster ('to adjourn from place to place'), to report from time to time ('to report to the House and publish as many reports as they wish'), to appoint sub-committees from among their own members, and to appoint expert advisers.

Duration: Some Select Committees are more permanent than others. All share a degree of impermanence in that their membership needs to be re-appointed every session. In March 1974 for the first time the membership of a Select Committee (the Expenditure Committee) was appointed for the duration of a Parliament and the majority of Select Committees are now appointed on this basis.

Chairmen: Apart from the Public Accounts Committee, the Committee on Statutory Instruments, the Committee on the Parliamentary Commissioner and latterly the Select Committee on European Secondary Legislation, the Chairmen of the Select Committees are usually of the Government Party. This does not, however, necessarily apply to sub-committees.

Chairmen's Liaison Committee: In recent decades the practice grew up for Chairmen of Select Committees to meet in an informal Committee from time to time to discuss subjects of common interest such as the allocation of funds available for overseas visits. The Committee was not a Select Committee of the House until 1980.

[1] Since 1968-69 Select Committee returns showing Select Committees, membership, attendances, etc., have been printed by H.M.S.O.

Committee of Selection, 1840-

Chairmen (*since* 1945)

1945	T. Smith	1969	G. Rogers
1947	G. Mathers	1970	H. Gurden
1951	Sir G. Touche	1974	H. Delargy
1956	Sir R. Conant	1976	F. Willey
1960	Sir P. Agnew	1979	(Sir) P. Holland
1964	C. Kenyon	1984	M. Fox

Although the task of the Committee of Selection has for many years been predominantly the selection of Members to serve on Standing Committees on Bills, the Committee was originally set up to appoint Committees on Private Bills and is still appointed under Private Business S.O. 109. It has 11 Members.

The Committee of Selection nominates:

Public Business

(1) Members of Standing Committees;
(2) Some or all members of Select Committees on hybrid Bills (if the House orders);
(3) The Commons members of Joint Committees on hybrid Bills (if the House orders);
(4) The two members whom Mr Speaker is to consult, if practicable, before giving his certificate to a money bill.

Private Business

(1) The panel of members to serve on committees on unopposed bills;
(2) Committees on unopposed bills;
(3) Members of committees on opposed bills;
(4) Eight members to serve on the Standing Orders Committee under S.O. 103;
(5) The panel of members to act as commissioners under the Private Legislation Procedure (Scotland) Act 1936;
(6) Commons Members on Joint Committees on special procedure petitions.

Terms of Reference: The Committee would appear to interpret its instructions in S.O. 62 to have 'regard . . . to the composition of the House' by choosing Standing Committees as far as possible in direct ratio to the size of the parties in the House, except that since the 1930s the Liberal Party has usually been given a higher representation than its size would merit on this basis—a Liberal member being appointed to all Committees of 45 members and above. In the three Parliaments since the war in which the size of the Government majority has been small the Committee of Selection has usually selected Members so as to give the Government a majority of one. In the 1974 Parliament, with a minority Government, no party had a majority on any standing Committee. The Committee tends to appoint those Members who spoke on the second reading of the Bill. In recent times of heavy legislation and expanding parliamentary activity it would appear that the position of the whips to offer advice as to which members are anxious, willing, or available to serve on a particular Committee has been strengthened. Although no Government whip is appointed to the Committee a senior opposition whip was always appointed until 1974.

SOURCES.—The history of the Committee is given in Erskine May, *Parliamentary Practice* (18th ed., pp. 906-7). Details of responsibilities of Standing Committees pp. 672-3.

Committee of Public Accounts, 1862-

Chairmen

1896	A. O'Connor	1945	O. Peake
1901	Sir A. Hayter	1948	R. Assheton
1906	V. Cavendish	1950	Sir R. Cross
1908	(Sir) R. Williams	1950	C. Waterhouse
1919	F. Acland	1951	J. Edwards
1921	A. Williams	1952	(Sir) G. Benson
1923	F. Jowett	1959	H. Wilson
1924	W. Guiness	1962	D. Houghton
1924	W. Graham	1964	J. Boyd-Carpenter
1929	A. Samuel	1970	H. Lever
1931	M. Jones	1973	E. Dell
1938	F. Pethick-Lawrence	1974	E. du Cann
1941	W. Elliot	1979	J. Barnett
1943	Sir A. Pownall	1983	R. Sheldon

The Committee is made up of no more than 15 members, including the Chairman, and meets on about 30 days each session. The Chairman is usually a member of the Opposition.

Usual Terms of Reference: 'for the examination of the accounts showing the appropriation of the sums granted by parliament to meet the public expenditure', 'and of such other accounts laid before parliament as the committee may think fit' (*added 15 Nov 34*). 'The Committee shall have power to send for persons, papers and records, and to report from time to time' (*added 14 Nov 33*). The Committee is aided in its work by the Comptroller and Auditor General whose staff audit the accounts of government departments. These audits and the Comptroller's subsequent report to the House of Commons provide the basic materials for the Committee's enquiries. In 1978 the Committee began to hear evidence in public.

See also Public Accounts Commission (p. 208).

SOURCES.—*Reports of the Select Committee on Public Accounts*; *Select Committee Returns, 1900-* ; L. A. Abraham and S. C. Hawtrey, *A Parliamentary Dictionary* (1956); B. Chubb, *The Control of Public Expenditure* (1952); V. Flegman, *Called to Account* (1980).

Comptroller and Auditor-General

1896	R. Mills	1946	Sir F. Tribe
1900	D. Richmond	1958	Sir E. Compton
1904	(Sir) J. Kempe	1966	Sir B. Fraser
1911	(Sir) H. Gibson	1971	Sir D. Pitblado
1921	Sir M. Ramsay	1976	Sir D. Henley
1921	(Sir) G. Upcott	1981	(Sir) G. Downey

Estimates Committee, 1912-1970

Chairmen

1912	Sir F. Banbury	1935	Sir I. Salmon
1914	*(suspended)*	1939	*(see National Expenditure Committee)*
1917	*(see National Expenditure Committee)*	1945	B. Kirby
1920	Sir F. Banbury	1950	A. Anderson
1924	Sir J. Marriott	1951	Sir R. Glyn
1926	(Sir) V. Henderson	1953	C. Waterhouse
1927	A. Bennett	1957	R. Turton
1929	H. Charleton	1961	Sir G. Nicholson
1930	H. Romeril	1964	W. Hamilton
1931	Sir V. Henderson		

The Committee originally consisted of 15 members. In 1921 this was increased to 24, and in 1924 to 28. From 1948 to 1960 it had 36 members and from 1960 to 1970 43 members. The Chairman was usually a Government supporter.

Terms of Reference: 'to examine and report upon such of the Estimates presented to the Committee as may seem fit to the Committee' (*7 Apr 12 original terms)*, 'and to suggest the form in which the estimates shall be presented for examination, and to report what if any economies consistent with the policy implied in those estimates may be effected therein' (*added in 1921)*. Until 1939 the Estimates Committee seldom appointed sub-committees, although power to do so had been given in 1924; since 1945, however, following the example set by the Select Committee on National Expenditure, it has invariably done so. In 1956 the wording of the terms of reference was rearranged but the substance remained unchanged.

In 1960 the terms were altered to read: 'to examine such of the estimates presented to this House as may seem fit to the committee and report how, if at all, the policy implied in those estimates may be carried out more economically and, if the committee think fit, to consider the principal variations between the estimates and those relating to the previous financial year, and the form in which the estimates are presented to the House'. The committee had power to send for persons, papers, and records, and sit notwithstanding any adjournment of the House, to adjourn from place to place, and to report from time to time: to appoint sub-committees and to refer to such sub-committees any of the matters referred to the committee [each sub-committee has the same powers of sending for persons, etc., sitting and adjourning as the main committee], and to report from time to time the minutes of evidence taken before sub-committees and reported by them to the committee. In Sessions 1965 and 1966 the House gave the Estimates Committee the power 'to appoint persons with technical or scientific knowledge for the purpose of particular enquiries, either to supply information which is not readily available or to elucidate matters of complexity within the Committee's order of reference'. From 1965-70 the practice was to appoint sub-committees specialising in particular fields. The Select Committee was replaced by the Expenditure Committee in 1971.

SOURCE.—N. Johnson, *Parliament and Administration: The Estimates Committee, 1945-65* (1966).

Committee on National Expenditure, 1917-1920 and 1939-1945

Chairmen

1917	H. Samuel	1939-45	Sir J. Wardlaw-Milne
1919-20	Sir F. Banbury		

No Estimates were presented to Parliament during the two wars, and the Committee on Estimates lapsed. A Committee on National Expenditure was established each year. It consisted of 26 members 1917-20, and 32 members 1939-45. It met about 13 days a session between 1917-20, and about 19 days a session between 1939-45.

1939-45 Terms of Reference: 'to examine the current expenditure defrayed out of moneys provided by Parliament for the Defence Services, for Civil Defence, and for other services directly connected with the war, and to report what, if any, economies, consistent with the execution of the policy decided by the Government, may be effected therein'.

SOURCES.—*Reports of the Select Committee on Estimates*; *Select Committee Returns, 1900-* ; Sir I. Jennings, *Parliament* (2nd ed., 1957), pp. 303-16; E. Taylor, *The House of Commons at Work* (7th ed., 1967).

Expenditure Committee, 1971-1979

Chairmen

1970	E. du Cann	1974	J. Boyden
1973	Sir H. D'Avigdor-Goldsmid		

The Committee consists of 49 members with a quorum of 9. It has worked through six sub-committees: General; Defence and External Affairs; Trade and Industry; Education and Arts; Environment and Home; Employment and Social Services.

Terms of Reference: 'to consider how, if at all, the policies implied in the figures of expenditure and in the estimates may be carried out more economically, and to examine the form of the paper and of the estimates presented to this House'. The Committee's work was carried out through six largely autonomous sub-committees (General; Defence and External Affairs; Employment and Social Services; Trade and Industry; Environment; Education; Arts and Home Affairs).

SOURCES.—Reports of the Select Committee on Expenditure and of its Sub-committees; A. Robinson, *Parliament and Public Spending*

Nationalised Industries Committee, 1956-1979

Chairmen

1956	Sir P. Spens	1966	I. Mikardo
1957	Sir T. Low	1970	Sir H. D'Avigdor-Goldsmid
1961	Sir R. Nugent	1972	(Sir) J. Hall
1964	E. Popplewell	1974	R. Kerr

The Committee was appointed on a sessional basis; it had 13 members (1956-66), 18 members (1966-70), 14 members (1970-74), 13 members (1974-5) and 15 members (1974-9). The Chairman was always a Government supporter.

Terms of Reference: 'to examine the reports and accounts of the nationalised industries established by statute, whose controlling boards are wholly appointed by Ministers of the Crown and whose annual receipts are not wholly or mainly derived from moneys provided by Parliament or advanced by the Exchequer'. In the 1965-66 and 1966-67 Sessions the Committee's terms of reference were amended to enable them to enquire into the Post Office. From 1968-69 the Committee's terms of reference were extended to include the Independent Television Authority and Cable and Wireless Ltd the Horserace Totalisator Board and certain activities of the Bank of England.

SOURCES.—*Reports of the Select Committee on Nationalised Industries (Reports and Accounts), 1957-* ; *Select Committee Returns, 1957-* ; D. Coombes, *The Member of Parliament and the Administration, the Case of the Select Committee on Nationalised Industries* (1966). See pp. 201-5 below for a list of the Committee's *Reports*.

Committee on Agriculture, 1966-1969

Chairman 1966-69 T. Watkins

Terms of Reference: 'To consider the activities in England and Wales of the Ministry of Agriculture, Fisheries and Food.' The Committee had power to send for persons, papers, and records, to sit notwithstanding any adjournment of the House, to adjourn from place to place, and to admit strangers during the examination of witnesses unless they otherwise order. The Committee ceased to exist in Feb 1970.

Committee on Science and Technology, 1966-79

Chairmen

1966 A. Palmer
1970 A. Neave
1974 A. Palmer

Terms of Reference: 'To consider Science and Technology.' The Committee has power to send for persons, and papers.

Committee on Education and Science, 1968-1970

Chairman 1968-70 F. Willey

Terms of Reference: 'To consider the activities of the Department of Education and Science and the Scottish Education Department.' The Committee ceased to exist in 1970.

Committee on Race Relations and Immigration, 1968-79

Chairmen

1968 A. Bottomley
1970 W. Deedes
1974 F. Willey

The Committee has 12 Members, and a quorum of 4.

Terms of Reference: 'To review policies, but not individual cases, in relation to: *(a)* the operation of the Race Relations Act 1968 with particular reference to the work of the Race Relations Board and the Community Relations Commission, and *(b)* the admission into the United Kingdom of Commonwealth citizens and foreign nationals for settlement.'

Committee on Overseas Aid, 1968-1971; Overseas Development, 1973-79

Chairmen

1968	Miss M. Herbison	1974	Sir G. de Freitas
1970-71	B. Braine	1978	K. McNamara
1973	Sir B. Braine		

The first Committee had between 10 and 18 Members, with a quorum of between 4 and 9. After 1973 it had 9 Members.

Terms of Reference: 'To consider the activities of the Ministry of Overseas Development.' The Committee ceased to exist in 1971. It was re-established under a new title in 1973, 'to consider United Kingdom assistance for overseas development'.

Committee on Scottish Affairs, 1969-1972

Chairmen

1969	T. Steele
1970	Sir J. Gilmour
1971	J. Brewis

The Committee had 16 Members and a quorum of 8.

Terms of Reference: 'To consider Scottish Affairs.'

Committee on European Secondary Legislation, 1974-76; European Legislation etc., 1976-

Chairmen

1974	J. Davies	1979	J. Silverman
1976	Sir J. Eden	1983	N. Spearing

The Committee's membership since 1974 has been 16. There are currently three sub-committees.

Terms of Reference: To consider draft proposals of EEC secondary legislation and to 'report their opinion as to whether such proposals or other documents raise questions of legal and political importance' . . . 'and to what extent they may affect the law of the United Kingdom'. Expanded in 1976 to cover documents submitted to the Council of Ministers or to the European Council 'whether or not such documents originate from the Commission'. The Committee has powers to send for persons, papers and records, to sit during the Adjournment, and to adjourn from place to place.

Procedure, 1961-76; Procedure (Sessional) Committee, 1976-

Chairmen

1961	I. Macleod	1970	(Sir) R. Turton
1963	S. Lloyd	1974	S. Irving
1964	A. Irvine	1979	T. Higgins
1965	A. Blenkinsop	1983	Sir P. Emery
1966	D. Chapman		

The Committee has 15 Members and a quorum of 4.

It was long the practice of the House to set up Committees from time to time to make recommendations on its procedure. But since 1961 a Select Committee on Procedure has been appointed every Session to report on matters which the House refers to it. It came to be referred to as the 'Sessional Committee' to distinguish it from a Procedure Committee set up for the lifetime of the 1974 Parliament which reported in Aug 1978 (see p. 192). It has powers to send for persons, papers and records and to report from time to time. It lapsed between Feb 74 and Nov 74 and in the 1978-79 Session. In the 1979-83 Parliament the full committee did not meet, although T. Higgins chaired Committees on Procedure (Supply) and Procedure (Finance).

House of Commons Services Committee, 1965-

Chairmen

1965	H. Bowden	1974	A. Bottomley
1966	R. Crossman	1976	M. Foot
1968	F. Peart	1979	N. St John-Stevas
1970	W. Whitelaw	1981	F. Pym
1972	R. Carr	1982	J. Biffen
1972	J. Prior		

Terms of Reference: 'To advise Mr Speaker on the control of the accommodation and services in that part of the Palace of Westminster and its precincts occupied by or on behalf of the House of Commons and to report thereon to this House.' This Committee was set up as a result of a recommendation of the Select Committee on the Palace of Westminster of Sessions 1964-65 whose main task had been to consider the arrangements to be made by the Commons following the transfer on 26 Apr 1965 of control of the Palace from the Lord Great Chamberlain on behalf of the Crown to the two Houses.

The Committee consists of 19 members appointed by the House. It has power to send for persons, papers, and records, to sit notwithstanding the adjournment of the House, to report from time to time, and to appoint Sub-Committees, each of which consists of three members. Each Sub-Committee has similar powers to the main Committee (except of course power to nominate Sub-Committees). The Committee usually appoints four main Sub-Committees: the Accommodation and Administration Sub-Committee, the Catering Sub-Committee, the Library Sub-Committee and the Computer Sub-Committee. The Catering Sub-Committee replaced the 'Select Committee on Kitchen and Refreshment Rooms' appointed every session since the late nineteenth century.

Until 1974 the Leader of the House was always appointed Chairman of the Committee, and this practice was renewed in 1976.

See also House of Commons Commission (p. 208).

Committee on Members' Interests, 1975-

This Committee was established following a 1974 report (pp. 108/1974–5) to scrutinise a new Register of Members' outside interests.

Chairmen

1975	F. Willey
1983	(Sir) G. Johnson-Smith

Committee of Privileges, c. 1630-

The Committee of Privileges only meets when prima facie breaches of privileges are referred to it by the House. Unlike other committees it includes senior members from both the Front Benches. It is ordered to be appointed by long-standing tradition on the first day of every session. Until 1940 it was chaired by the Prime Minister. From 1940 to 1945 C. Attlee, as Deputy Prime Minister, took the chair. Since 1945 the Chairman has usually but not always been the Leader of the House.

Chairmen

1940	C. Attlee
1945	H. Morrison
1946	A. Greenwood
1947	H. Morrison
1948	C. Ede
1952	H. Crookshank
1956	R. Butler
1964	S. Lloyd
1965	H. Bowden
1967	R. Crossman
1968	F. Peart
1971	W. Whitelaw
1972	R. Carr
1973	J. Prior
1974	G. Strauss
1979	N. St John Stevas
1981	F. Pym
1982	J. Biffen

The Committee currently has 17 members.

The following include all Reports of the Select Committee of Privileges and a few from *Ad Hoc* Committees.

1902	Imprisonment of a Member: C. O'Kelly.
1902	Imprisonment of a Member: P. McHugh.
1909	D of Norfolk: alleged interference in an election.
1911	E of Aberdeen and E of Roden: alleged interference in an election.
1924	*Daily Herald*: reflection on the impartiality of the Chairman of Committees.
1926	*Daily Mail*: allegations of corrupt motives against M.P.s.
1929-30	E. Sandham: allegations of drunkenness and acceptance of bribes against M.P.s.
1932-33	H. Bowles and E. Huntsman: reflections on a Private Bill Committee's impartiality.
1933-34	Sir S. Hoare and E of Derby: alleged improper pressure on witnesses to a Committee.
1937-38	D. Sandys: summons to Military court of Inquiry.
1937-38	Official Secrets Act.

1938-39	Official Secrets Act.
1939-40	Detention of A. Ramsay under 18B of Defence of the Realm Act.
1939-40	Conduct of R. Boothby.
1940-41	Conduct of R. Boothby.
1940-41	*Observer* publication of Secret Session debate.
1940-41	Grampian electricity supply bill: Highland Development League circular to M.P.s alleging irregularities in bill procedure.
1941-42	Disclosure of Secret Session proceedings by J. McGovern.
1942-43	H. Metcalf and J. Reid: payment of expense cheque to M.P. to attend prosecution by Board of Trade.
1943-44	N.U.D.A.W.: withdrawal of Trade Union financial support from W. Robinson on ground of refusal to resign seat.
1944-45	G. Reakes and D. Henderson. Offer to make donation to constituency association in return for M.P.s' help.
1945-46	Writ of Summons served on officer of House within precincts.
1945-46	Disclosure in conversation of Secret Session information by E. Granville.
1945-46	Posters threatening publication of names of M.P.s voting for bread rationing.
1946-47	Assault on P. Piratin in precincts of the House.
1946-47	Action by Civil Service Clerical Association calculated to influence W. Brown.
1946-47	G. Schofield and S. Dobson (Editor and Political Correspondent of *Evening News*): refusal to reveal source of information to Committee.
1946-47	Article by G. Allighan alleging disclosure to newspapers of information from party meetings.
1946-47	Disclosure of party meeting information by E. Walkden in return for payment.
1947-48	H. Dalton: Budget disclosure.
1947-48	The Chairman of Ways and Means (J. Milner): personal explanation that he acted professionally as a solicitor against a Member.
1947-48	Broadcast and interview in *Daily Mail* by C. Brogan alleging that Secret Session information would be given to Russia.
1948-49	Alleged misrepresentation by *Daily Worker* of Member's speech (R. Blackburn).
1950	J. MacManaway: election of a Member, being a clergyman of the Church of Ireland.
1951	Abuse of members not related to transactions in House (S. Silverman, I. Mikardo). Comment on B.B.C. 'Any Questions' programme on matter referred to Committee.
1951	Report in *Sutton Coldfield News* of speech by Lady Mellor criticising ruling by the Chair.
1951	Obstruction of J. Lewis by the police.

1952-53	Amendment of the law relating to the disability of some clergy from sitting and voting in the House of Commons.
1953	Article by Mrs P. Ford in *Sunday Express* (Mrs Braddock).
1953	*Daily Worker* article (M.P.s vote money into their own pockets).
1955	Action by Bishop against chaplain after communication with M.P.
1956	*Sunday Graphic* advocates telephone campaign against A. Lewis.
1956	*Sunday Express* article on M.P.s' petrol rationing allowances.
1956	*Evening News* cartoon on petrol rationing.
1956-57	G. Strauss: threat of libel action by the London Electricity Board, following letter from the Member to the Paymaster General.
1957	Comment on B.B.C. 'Any Questions' programme on matter referred to Committee: report of speech in *Romford Recorder* on petrol rationing.
1957-58	Order in Council directing that the Report of the Judicial Committee on a Question of Law concerning the Parliamentary Privilege Act 1770 be communicated to the House of Commons.
1957-58	G. Strauss: recommendations of the Committee arising out of the case involving the London Electricity Board.
1958-59	Report of an Inquiry into the methods adopted by the London Electricity Board for the disposal of scrap cable.
1959-60	C. Pannell: allegation of threat in a letter from C. Jordan.
1960-61	A. Wedgwood Benn: petition for redress of grievances regarding the disqualification of peers.
1963-64	Q. Hogg: complaint by G. Wigg concerning a speech at the Town Hall, Chatham, on 19 Mar 64.
1964-65	P. Duffy: complaint concerning speech at Saddleworth on 12 Feb 65 alleging drunkenness among Conservative Members.
1964-65	F. Allaun: complaint concerning letter addressed to Members and advocating racial and anti-semitic views.
1964-65	The Chancellor of the Exchequer: complaint by Sir R. Cary concerning passages of speech reported in the *Daily Telegraph* 5 Jul 65, on Members' business interests.
1966-67	G. Fitt: complaint concerning allegations of treachery in *Protestant Telegraph*.
1967-68	E. Hooson: complaint concerning allegations of treachery in interview published in *Town* magazine.
1967-68	W. Hannan: complaint concerning letter in the *Scotsman* by Mrs W. Ewing, M.P., reflecting on the conduct of members.
1967-68	A. Palmer: complaint concerning article about biological warfare published in the *Observer* from information allegedly supplied by T. Dalyell, M.P.

1968-69 Mrs R. Short: report in *Wolverhampton Press and Star* of a speech by Alderman Peter Farmer imputing partial conduct to a Member.

1968-69 Sir D. Glover: certain events attending to a visit of a Sub-Committee of the Select Committee on Education and Science to the University of Essex.

1968-69 R. Maxwell: article published in the *Sunday Times* reflecting on the conduct of a Member as Chairman of the Catering Sub-Committee of the Select Committee on House of Commons Services and as a member of that Committee.

1969-70 J. Mackintosh: matter reported in *The Times* which disclosed a breach of privilege.

1970-71 D. Steel: report in the *Sun* of alleged attempt by a trade union to influence actions of certain Members. (Report made in following Session.)

1970-71 A. Lewis: assault upon a servant of the House.

1970-71 W. Hamilton: publication by the *Daily Mail* of an article purporting to give an account of proceedings in a Select Committee not yet reported to the House. (Report made in following Session.)

1970-71 On a Motion moved by the Leader of the House. Rights of Members detained in prison.

1971-72 On a Motion moved by a member of the Government. Matter of the style and title of the Member for Berwick upon Tweed.

1972-73 R. Carter: serving of writ within the precincts of the House of Commons.

1973-74 A. Wedgwood Benn: alleged intimidation by Aims of Industry.

1973-74 J. Ashton: allegations about Members' financial interests.

1974-75 Eric Ogden: allegations made in Liverpool and West Derby on conduct of a member.

1974-75 G. Cunningham: words alleged to have been spoken by A. Scargill and other matters relating to N.U.M. conditions to be placed on M.P.s sponsored by them.

1974-75 J. Rooker: disclosure of evidence in *The Economist* from Select Committee on a Wealth Tax, before evidence reported to House.

1975-76 Sir B. Braine: reported accusation of bias in a Select Committee by National Abortion Campaign Steering Committee and threatened refusal to give evidence.

1975-76 J. Harper: possible contempt by National Coal Board in dismissing W. Grimshaw, a witness before the Select Committee on Nationalised Industries.

1976-77 M. Lipton: newspaper report alleging interference of the Totalisation Board on members.

1976-77 R. Adley: Press Association report of threat by the National Union of Public Employees to withdraw sponsorship from 6 members if they did not take certain action.

1977-78	F. Willey: *Daily Mail* and *Guardian* reports of proceedings of the Select Committee on Race Relations and Immigration.
1977-78	M. Foot: Publication of proceedings of the House and application of the *sub judice* rule (Colonel B.).
1978-79	C. Price: Court citation of *Hansard* without permission of House.
1980-1	D. Campbell-Savours: conversation about British Steel policy towards Workington.
1980-1	R. Parry: important letter from solicitors to M.P.
1982-3	T. Davis: behaviour of witnesses before Select Committee on Abortion (Amendment) Bill.
1982-3	R. Brown: comments by K. Livingstone and other GLC members.
1982-3	Sir A. Kershaw: leak of Foreign Affairs Committee report on Falklands.
1983-4	T. Jessel: threat by GLC Chairman to penalise constituencies of London members voting in a particular way.
1984-5	Sir E. Gardner: publication by *The Times* of Home Affairs Committee draft Report on police special powers.

Statutory Instruments, 1947 (Statutory Rules and Orders, 1944-47)
(since 1972 a Joint Committee of both Houses)

Chairmen

1944	Sir C. MacAndrew	1970	A. Booth
1950	G. Nicholson	1974	G. Page
1951	E. Fletcher	1979	R. Cryer
1964	G. Page	1983	A. Bennett

The Committee has had between 7 and 11 members, meeting fortnightly on about 16 days each session. The Chairman has always been an opposition member.

Terms of Reference: The original terms of 21 Jun 44 have been considerably enlarged by additional powers conferred in subsequent years.

In 1972 the procedure for considering Statutory Instruments was changed. The vast majority of instruments are now considered by a Joint Committee of Members of both Houses. However, the Statutory Instruments Committee still exists to consider instruments on which proceedings are subject to proceedings in the House of Commons only.

The Joint Committee has power to consider every instrument which is laid before each House of Parliament and upon which proceedings may be or might have been taken in either House of Parliament in pursuance of an Act of Parliament. It also has power to draw the attention of the House of Commons to other Statutory Instruments on any of the following grounds: (i) that they involve public money; (ii) that they are immune from challenge in the courts; (iii) that they have effect retrospectively; (iv) that there seems to have been an unjustifiable delay in publication of the S.I. or in laying it before Parliament; (v) that there seems to have been an unjustifiable delay in sending notification to the Speaker; (vi) that it appears to make unusual or unexpected use of the powers conferred by the Statute under which it is made; (vii) if elucidation is considered necessary; (viii) that the drafting appears to be defective.

The Committee has powers to sit when it wishes, to report from time to time, to call for witnesses and to appoint sub-committees. It is obliged to give any government department an opportunity to explain an S.I. or other document before drawing it to the attention of the House.

Since 1890 the Statutory Rules and Orders, and since 1948 the S.I.s, have been published in annual volumes.

The distinction between 'General' and 'Local' follows that adopted between public Acts and local and personal Acts of Parliament. The documents registered as Statutory Instruments do *not* include rules of an executive character, or rules made by other bodies, e.g. local authorities, unless confirmed by a government department. Statutory Instruments also include some rules made by statutory authorities which are not government departments, e.g. the Law Society, General Dental Council, Rule Committee of Church Assembly.

Statutory Instruments

Year	Annual Total	General	Local
1900	995	174	821
1910	1,368	218	1,150
1920	2,475	916	1,559
1929	1,262	391	871
1940	2,222	1,626	596
1950	2,144	1,211	933
1960	2,495	733	1,762
1970	2,044	1,040	1,004
1980	2,051	1,197	854
1984	2,072	1,116	956

SOURCES.—*Select Committee Returns, 1944-*; *Select Committee on Statutory Instruments (Rules and Orders, 1944-47)*; Sir I. Jennings, *Parliament* (2nd ed. 1957), pp. 489-516 (quotes Sir C. Carr's figures); Ld Hewart, *The New Despotism* (1929); G. W. Keeton, *The Passing of Parliament* (1952); S. C. Hawtry and H. M. Barclay, *A Parliamentary Dictionary* (1970) and information from the Committee Office of the House of Commons; C. K. Allen, *Law and Orders* (3rd ed. 1965); Statutory Publications Office; H. C. Deb. 728, c. 1564.

Committee on Public Petitions, 1842-1974

Chairmen (*since* 1945)

1945	S. Viant	1966	D. Griffiths
1951	C. Lancaster	1970	J. Jennings
1964	G. Pargiter		

The Committee was appointed during most sessions since April 1842. It had 10 members, and a quorum of 3. It had power to send for persons, papers and records. It was abolished in 1974.

Terms of Reference: To clarify and prepare abstracts of Petitions 'in such form and manner as shall appear to them best suited to convey to the House all requisite information respecting their contents'. 'All Petitions presented to the House, with the exception of such as are deposited in the Private Bill Office' are referred to the Committee. The Committee was required in its reports to state the number of signatures to each petition. It had no power to consider the merits of the petitions.

Committee on Parliamentary Commission for Administration, 1967-

Chairmen

1967	Sir H. Munro-Lucas-Tooth	1974	C. Fletcher-Cooke
1970	M. Stewart	1974	A. Buck

The Committee has 10 members and a quorum of 4.

Terms of Reference: 'To examine the reports laid before this House by the Parliamentary Commissioner for Administration and Matters in Connection therewith.' The Committee has power to send for persons and papers.

Parliamentary Commissioner for Administration (Ombudsman)

The Parliamentary Commissioner for Administration is appointed by Letters Patent under the provisions of the Parliamentary Commissioner Act, 1967, which came into force on 1 Apr 67.

His function is to investigate complaints referred to him by Members of the House of Commons from members of the public who claim to have sustained injustice in consequence of maladministration in connection with actions taken by or on behalf of Government Departments. (Other public bodies such as the nationalised industries and local government are outside his jurisdiction.)[1] Under the Act the Commissioner is required to report the results of each investigation to the Member who referred the complaint to him and also to make an annual report to each House of Parliament on the performance of his functions. In addition he may make other reports to Parliament with respect to those functions if he thinks fit; and he may make a special report to Parliament if he considers that injustice caused to the complainant by maladministration has not been or will not be remedied.

The Commissioner may be removed from office only upon an Address from both Houses of Parliament.

Parliamentary Commissioners

1 Apr 67	Sir E. Compton
1 Apr 71	Sir A. Marre
1 Apr 76	Sir I. Pugh
3 Jan 79	(Sir) C. Clothier
1 Jan 85	A. Barrowclough

[1] Under the National Health Service (Scotland) Act, 1972, and the National Health Service Reorganisation Act, 1973, provision was made for the appointment of Health Service Commissioners for Scotland, England and Wales. Sir A. Marre was appointed to these three posts with effect from 1 Oct 73, in addition to his post as Parliamentary Commissioner for Administradition, and his successors also hold them.

Ombudsman Cases

	No. of cases completed during the year	Member informed case outside jurisdiction	Member informed case is discontinued	Investigation completed and result reported to Member
1967[1]	849	561	100	188
1968	1,181	727	80	374
1969	790	445	43	302
1970	651	362	30	259
1971	516	295	39	182
1972	596	318	17	261
1973	536	285	12	239
1974	653	374	27	252
1975	916	576	19	321
1976	863	505	29	329
1977	846	528		318
1978	1,305	927	35	343
1979	801	541	22	238
1980	927	686	16	225
1981	929	694	7	228
1982	784	574	8	202
1983	809	605	6	198
1984	850	658	9	183

[1] From 1 Apr.

SOURCES.—H.M.S.O., *The Parliamentary Commissioner for Administration* (Cmnd. 2767). H.M.S.O., *Annual Reports of the Parliamentary Commissioner for Administration*; F. A. Stacey, *The British Ombudsman* (1971); R. Gregory and P. Alexander, *The Parliamentary Ombudsman* (1975).

House of Commons Commission 1978-

Under the House of Commons (Administration) Act of 1978, a House of Commons Commission was appointed to control the internal finances of the House. Independent of Government, it comprises the Speaker, the Leader of the House, one M.P. nominated by the Leader of the Opposition, and three other non-ministerial M.P.s (including one, in practice, nominated by the minority parties).

Public Accounts Commission 1984-

The Public Accounts Commission was set up by National Audit Act 1983. It is composed of nine members of the House of Commons of whom two—the Chairman of the Public Accounts Committee and the Leader of the House—are *ex-officio*. The remaining seven, none of whom may be Ministers of the Crown, are appointed by the House. The Commission was appointed to take office on 1 Jan 1984. The Act gave the Commission three main functions: to appoint an accounting officer for the National Audit Office; to appoint an auditor for the National Audit Office; and to examine the National Audit Office Estimates and lay them before the House, with such modifications as it thinks fit. In this last capacity, the Commission can examine all the expenses of the Office, including such things as accommodation, salaries of staff, superannuation provision.

Chairman

1984 (Sir) E. du Cann

Specialist Select Committees since 1979

Fourteen Select Committees were appointed in 1979 'to examine the expenditure, administration and policy of the principle government departments . . . and associated public bodies'. In Jan 1980 a Liaison Select Committee, comprising the chairman of the Committees (and some additional members) was appointed. Their membership varied between 9 and 11 until 1983 when all Committees except Scottish Affairs (13) were allotted 11 members. Only the Foreign Affairs, Home Affairs, and Treasury Committees were empowered to appoint a sub-committee.

Agriculture (9) (11)
1979 Sir W. Elliott
1983 J. Spence

Defence (10) (11)
1979 Sir J. Langford-Holt
1981 C. Onslow
1982 Sir T. Kitson
1983 Sir H. Atkins

Education, Science and Arts (9) (11)
1979 C. Price
1983 Sir W. Van Straubenzee

Employment (9) (11)
1979 J. Golding
1982 J. Craigen
1983 R. Leighton

Energy (10) (11)
1979 I. Lloyd

Environment (10) (11)
1979 B. Douglas-Mann
1981 R. Freeson
1983 Sir H. Rossi

Foreign Affairs (11)
1979 Sir A. Kershaw

Foreign Affairs Overseas Development Sub-committee (5)
1979 K. McNamara
1982 F. Hooley
1983 (*not reconstituted*)

Home Affairs (11)
1979 Sir G. Page
1981 Sir J. Eden
1983 Sir E. Gardner

Home Affairs Sub-committee on Race Relations and Immigration (5)
1979 J. Wheeler

Scottish Affairs (13)
1979 D. Dewar
1981 R. Hughes
1982 D. Lambie

Social Services (9) (11)
1979 Mrs R. Short

Trade and Industry (11) **(Industry and Trade, 1979-83)**
1979 Sir D. Kaberry
1983 K. Warren

Transport (10) (11)
1979 T. Bradley
1983 H. Cowans
1985 G. Bagier

Treasury and Civil Service (11)
1979 E. du Cann
1983 T. Higgins

Treasury and Civil Service Sub-committee (5)
1979 R. Sheldon
1981 J. Bray
1982 M. Meacher
1983 A. Mitchell

Welsh Affairs (11)
1979 L. Abse
1981 D. Anderson
1983 G. Wardell

SOURCES.—G. Drewry (ed.), *The New Select Committees* (1985); D. Englefield (ed.), *Commons Select Committees* (1984); P. Norton (ed.), *Parliament in the 1980s* (1985); Erskine May, *Parliamentary Practice* (20th ed. 1984).

Payment of M.P.s

1912 M.P.s receive first salary; £400 per year paid to all members not receiving salaries as Ministers or officers of the House.

1913 £100 of M.P.s' salaries made tax-exempt in respect of parliamentary expenses. This remained in force until 1954.

1924 M.P.s allowed free rail travel between London and their constituencies.

1931 Salary cut to £360 as an economy measure.

1934 Salary restored to £380 and then to £400.

1937 Salary increased to £600.

1946 Salary increased to £1,000 and salaries of £500 authorised for M.P.s who, as Ministers or Leaders of the Opposition, had an official salary of less than £5,000. Free travel was granted between M.P.s' homes and Westminster as well as to their constituencies.

1953 A sessional allowance of £2 per day introduced for every day (except Friday) on which the House sat: this was payable to all M.P.s including Ministers.

1957 The sessional allowance (usually amounting to about £280 p.a.) was replaced by an annual £750 to cover parliamentary expenses. The whole £1,750 drawn by ordinary M.P.s was subject to tax but M.P.s could claim as tax free any expenses up to £1,750 incurred in respect of parliamentary duties.

1964 Salary increased to £3,250 per year, following Lawrence Committee Report.

1965 Members' Pensions Act. First comprehensive pensions scheme introduced for M.P.s and dependants. Members contribute £150 per year and the Exchequer an amount equal to the aggregate of the Members' contributions. Members receive pensions from the age of 65 or on ceasing to be an M.P. if later, provided they have served for 10 years or more. The pension of £600 per year for 10 years' service increases to £900 after 15 years' service and by £24 for each further year thereafter.

1969 Secretarial allowance of up to £500 introduced. Members to have free telephone calls within the U.K.

1972 M.P.s' pay increased to £3,500 following Boyle Committee recommendations. Secretarial allowance increased to up to £1,000. An allowance of up to £750 for additional cost of living away from main residence and London members to receive a London supplement of £175 p.a. Travel allowances extended and a terminal grant equivalent to 3 months' salary established for M.P.s who lose their seats at a General Election.

1972 Parliamentary and Other Pensions Act. Existing pensions scheme revised. Minimum qualifying period reduced from 10 years to 4. M.P.s' benefits based on 1/60th of final salary for each year of reckonable service. Contributions to be 5% of salary. Early retirement option available from 60 onwards on an actuarially reduced pension.

1974 Secretarial allowance increased to up to £1,750 and allowance for living away from main residence increased to £1,050. London supplement increased to £228 p.a.

1976 Pension scheme amended to provide for pensions to be based on a notional pensionable salary of £8,000.

1977 M.P.s' pay increased to £6,270. Secretarial allowance (also research assistance and general office expenses) increased to up to £3,687. London supplement increased to £385 p.a. Travel allowances further extended and allowance introduced for overnight stays away from home of up to £1,814.

1978 M.P.s' pay increased to £6,897; London supplement increased to £424 p.a.

1979 M.P.s pay to be increased to £9,450, with further increases to £10,725 in 1980 and £12,000 in 1981. Secretarial etc. allowance increased to £4,520, allowance for overnight stays away from home increased to up to £3,046 p.a.

1983 M.P.s pay linked to Civil Service rates. Secretarial allowance raised to £12,000 and other allowances increased.

M.P.s basic pay

1911	£400	1977	£6,270
1931	£360	1978	£6,897
1934	£380	1979	£9,450
1935	£400	1980	£11,750
1937	£600	1981	£13,950
1954	£1,250	1982	£14,510
1964	£3,250	1983	£15,308
1972	£4,500	1984	£16,106
1975	£5,750	1985	£16,904

SOURCES.—H. C. 255 of 1920, *Report of the Select Committee on Members' Expenses*, Cmd. 5624, 1937-38, *Report of the Departmental Committee on an M.P.s' Pension Scheme*; H. C. 93 of 1945–1946, *Report of the Select Committee on Members' Expenses*; H.C. 72 of 1954, *Report of the Select Committee on Members' Expenses, etc.*; *Ministerial Salaries Act, 1957*; *Report of the Committee on the Remuneration of Ministers and Members of Parliament* (Lawrence) Cmnd. 2516; *Ministerial Salaries and Members' Pensions Act* (1965); *Reports of the Committee on Top Salaries* (Cmnd. 5372/1972; Cmnd 6136/1975; Cmnd 6574/1976; Cmnd 6749/1977; Cmnd 7598/1979). Fees Office, House of Commons; House of Commons Fact Sheet (1983).

Seats Forfeited

These members left or were expelled from the House before or after their conviction and imprisonment on criminal charges.

2 Mar	03	A. Lynch	Nat.	Galway
1 Aug	22	H. Bottomley	Ind.	Hackney South
31 Jul	41	Sir P. Latham	Con.	Scarborough & Whitby
16 Dec	54	P. Baker	Con.	S. Norfolk
27 Aug	76	J. Stonehouse	Lab. (Ind)	Walsall South

These members forfeited their seats as a result of being adjudged bankrupt.

17 Sep	03	P. McHugh	Nat.	N. Leitrim (re-elected)
15 Jul	09	N. Murphy	Nat.	S. Kilkenny
1 Oct	28	C. Homan	Con.	Ashton under Lyne

In addition, H. Bottomley resigned his seat 16 May 12 after filing his bankruptcy petition.

These members forfeited their seats when it transpired that they held a government contract. All but one were re-elected in the ensuing by- election.

2 Feb	04	A. Gibbs	City of London (re-elected)
2Feb	04	V. Gibbs	St Albans (defeated)
21 Apr	12	Sir S. Samuel	Whitechapel (re-elected)
10 Feb	25	W. Preston	Walsall (re-elected)

In Nov 1924, J. Astor (Dover) forfeited his seat for inadvertently voting before taking the oath. He was re-elected unopposed in the ensuing by-election.

These members gave up their seats when under censure for some aspect of their parliamentary conduct.

26 Feb	31	T. Mardy Jones	Lab.	Pontypridd (*abuse of travel voucher)*
11 June	36	J. Thomas	Nat. Lab.	Derby (*Budget leak)*
11 June	36	Sir A. Butt	Con.	Balham & Tooting (*Budget leak)*
30 Oct	47	G. Allighan	Lab.	Gravesend (*expelled by a vote of* 187-75 *for breach of privilege)*
3 Feb	49	J. Belcher	Lab.	Sowerby (*following Lynskey Tribunal)*
5 Jun	63	J. Profumo	Con.	Stratford-on-Avon (*lying to the House)*
25 Jul	77	J. Cordle	Con.	Bournemouth E. (*Poulson affair)*

On 16 Aug 1916 C. Leach (Colne Valley) was deprived of his seat under the Lunacy (Vacating of Seats) Act 1886.

A. Ramsay, Con. Peebles and Southern, remained an M.P. from 1940 to 1945 although, being detained under Regulation 18B of the Defence of the Realm Act until Dec 1944, he was unable to sit from May 40 to Dec 44.

Various other members have resigned their seats while under the shadow of some minor private or public scandal but in almost every case it seems that they could well have remained as members had they chosen to do so.

For a list of successful election petitions, which led to the original result being disallowed by the courts see p. 250.

House of Lords

Lord Chairmen of Committees

(*Deputy Speaker of the House of Lords. The Lord Chancellor* (*see p.* 63) *acts as Speaker.*)

1889 E of Morley
1905 4th E of Onslow
1911 E of Donoughmore
1931 5th E of Onslow
1944 Ld Stanmore
1946 E of Drogheda
1957 Ld Merthyr
1965 E of Listowel
1977 Ld Aberdare

Principal Deputy Chairman of Committees

(*Salaried Chairman of Select Committee on European Communities*)

1974 Ld Diamond
1974 Lady Tweedsmuir of Belhelvie
1977 Ld Greenwood of Rossendale
1980 Lady White
1983 Lady Llewelyn-Davies

Officers of the House of Lords

Clerk of the Parliaments

1885 (Sir) H. Graham
1917 Sir A. Thring
1930 Sir E. Alderson
1934 (Sir) H. Badeley
1949 (Sir) R. Overbury
1953 (Sir) F. Lascelles
1959 (Sir) V. Goodman
1963 (Sir) D. Stephens
1974 (Sir) P. Henderson
1983 J. Sainty

Librarian

1897 A. Strong
1904 E. Gosse
1914 A. Butler
1922 C. Clay
1956 C. Dobson
1977 R. Morgan

SOURCES.—*Dod's Parliamentary Companion*; *Whitaker's Almanack*; *Hansard.*

Composition of the House of Lords
(including minors)

Year	Dukes[a]	Mar-quesses	Earls	Vis-counts	Barons	Life Peers[b]	Law Lords[c]	Representative Scotland[d]	Representative Ireland[d]	Archbps. and Bishops	Total
1901	26	22	123	32	314	. .	4	16	28	26	591
1910	25	23	124	42	334	. .	4	16	28	26	622
1920	26	29	130	64	393	. .	6	16	27	26	716
1930	24	26	134	73	428	. .	7	16	18	26	753
1939	24	28	139	84	456	. .	7	16	13	26	785
1950	23	30	137	95	503	. .	11	16	6	26	847
1960	25	30	132	111	531	31	8	16	1	26	908
1970	29	30	163	110	530	163	11	. .	. .	26	1,057
1980	28	29	157	105	477	330	19	. .	. .	26	1,171
1984	28	28	156	104	496	345	19	. .	. .	26	1,202

[a] Including Peers of the Blood Royal.
[b] Created by the Life Peerages Act, 1958.
[c] Life Peers under the Appellate Jurisdiction Acts.
[d] Scottish and Irish peers sitting by virtue of UK title are listed under the latter. In 1963 all Scottish peers became entitled to sit and are listed under their senior title.

SOURCES.—*Constitutional Year Books, 1900-39*; *Dod's Parliamentary Companion, 1940-.*

Creation of Peerages

Administration[a]		New Hereditary Creations[a]	Life Peers Law	Life Peers Other	Advanced in Rank	Total	Duration of Ministry (Yrs.)	Average Annual Creations[b]
Salisbury	1895-02	42	2	. .	n.a.	44	7	6
Balfour	1902-05	17	1	. .	5	23	3½	5
Campbell-Bannerman	1905-08	20	1	. .	. .	21	2⅓	9
Asquith	1908-15	61	6	. .	13	80	7	9
Asquith	1915-16	17	. .	. .	2	19	1½	11
Lloyd George	1916-22	90	1	. .	25	116	5¾	16
Bonar Law	1922-23	3	. .	. .	. .	3	½	6
Baldwin	1923-24	7	1	. .	1	9	⅔	10
MacDonald	1924	4	. .	. .	1	5	¾	5
Baldwin	1924-29	37	5	. .	10	52	4½	18
MacDonald	1929-31	18	2	. .	. .	20	2¼	8
MacDonald	1931-35	43	1	. .	6	50	3¾	12
Baldwin	1935-37	27	2	. .	5	34	2	14
Chamberlain	1937-40	18	2	. .	4	24	3	6
Churchill	1940-45	60	2	. .	9	71	5¼	11
Attlee	1945-51	75	11	. .	8	94	6¼	10
Churchill	1951-55	31	2	. .	6	39	3½	9
Eden	1955-57	19	. .	. .	3	22	1¾	11
Macmillan	1957-63	42	9	47	6	104	6	7
Douglas-Home	1963-64	14	1	16	1	32	1	30
Wilson	1964-70	6	2	152	1	161	5¾	29
Heath	1970-74	. .	4	30	. .	34	3½	9
Wilson	1974-76	. .	3	81	. .	84	2	40
Callaghan	1976-79	. .	2	58	. .	60	3	20
Thatcher	1979-	3	6	107	. .	116	(5½)[c]	(21)[c]

[a] These figures can be misleading as dissolution honours created by an outgoing ministry fall, in fact, into the following ministry. E.g., of H. Wilson's new creations 6 were those of Sir A. Douglas-Home.
[b] Excluding the creation of Law Lords and advancements in rank.
[c] To end of 1984.

See p. 304 for Political Honours Scrutiny Committee.

Party Organisation in the House of Lords

Since the early 1920s Conservative peers met in an Association of Independent Unionist Peers, meeting weekly, much on the lines of the 1922 Committee. In 1982 it was renamed the Association of Conservative Peers. From 1945 to 1974 Liberal peers held their weekly meetings jointly with Liberal M.P.s. After 1974 they held their own weekly meetings, but Liberal Peers who were members of the Liberal 'shadow administration' formed in 1977 met Liberal M.P.s on a regular basis.

Labour peers are entitled to attend the meetings of the Parliamentary Labour Party, but since the 1930s they have also had their own weekly meetings.

Party Strengths in the House of Lords

Year		Con.	Lib. U.	Lib.	Lab.	Irish Nat.	Not stated (inc. Bishops)	Minors	Total
1 Dec	00	354	111	69	. .	1	39	15	589
31 Mar	16	360	107	93	. .	1	51	11	623
10 Feb	20	491	. .	130	1	1	67	26	716
31 Dec	30	489	. .	79	17	. .	140	27	753
31 Oct	38	519	23	55	13	. .	141	24	785

SOURCE.—*Constitutional Year Book.*

Vacher's Parliamentary Companion, which has always been more sparing in giving party labels, suggests that in 1945 there were 400 Conservatives, 63 Liberals and 16 Labour among the 769 adult peers. For Aug 1955 the figures were Conservative 507, Liberal 42 and Labour 55 (out of 855). For Oct 1984 the figures were Conservative 524, Liberal 41, Social Democrat 43, and Labour 135 (out of 1,186). More exhaustive information on party membership was provided by the 1968 White Paper on House of Lords Reform.

Attendance at the House of Lords by Party

by those who were members on 1 Aug 68 for the period 31 Oct 67 to 1 Aug 68

Party	Peers who attended more than 33⅓% ('working House')			Peers who attended more than 5% but less than 33⅓%			Peers who attended up to 5%			Peers who did not attend[a]			Totals		
	C	S	Total	C	S	Total	C	S	Total	C	S	Total	C	S	Total
Labour	81	14	95	8	5	13	4	1	5	2	1	3	95	21	116
Conservative	38	87	125	24	86	110	9	70	79	6	31	37	77	274	351
Liberal	8	11	19	2	6	8	2	8	10	1	3	4	13	28	41
Peers not in receipt of a party whip	26	26	52	61	24	85	22	56	78	32	307	339	141	413	554
Total	163	138	291	95	121	216	37	135	172	41	342	383	326	736	1,062

C = Created peers. S = Peers by succession. Attendance at committees of the House (other than the Appellate Committee) has been taken into account.

[a] Including 192 peers with leave of absence; 81 peers without writs of summons.

SOURCE.—*House of Lords Reform* (Cmnd. 3799/1968).

The House of Lords Information Office reported that in Dec 1984, out of 972 peers who were not minors or on leave of absence 724 were in receipt of a party whip (Conservative 392, Labour 128, Liberal 39, Social Democrat 38, Association of Cross-bench peers, 227).

House of Lords Sittings and Business

Sessions and Sittings			Membership and Attendance				Work of the House					
Session[a]	Sittings	Average sitting	Total membership[b]	Without writ of summons[bc]	On leave of absence[b]	Average attendance	Public bills introduced in House of Lords	Government bills introduced into the House of Lords[d]	Divisions	Starred questions	Written questions	Unstarred (debatable questions)
L1955-56	136	3hrs 34mins	876	78	n.a.	104	20	9	26	203	82	11
1956-57	103	3hrs 54mins	871	73	n.a.	112	20	7	32	209	55	9
1957-58	103	3hrs 50mins	885	70	n.a.	124	22	8	19	184	28	6
1958-59	109	4hrs 15mins	e	e	232	134	25	8	26	244	32	11
1959-60	113	3hrs 59mins	907	76	192	136	17	9	16	264	48	12
1960-61	125	4hrs 48mins	918	57	193	142	11	7	48	290	73	12
1961-62	115	4hrs 44mins	932	74	203	143	17	8	47	275	72	12
1962-63	127	5hrs 30mins	965	100	202	140	19	5	158	297	84	9
1963-64	110	4hrs 51mins	976	85	207	151	23	11	25	340	77	23
1964-65	124	4hrs 47mins	1,018	91	186	194	34	6	34	370	73	37
S1965-66	50	5hrs 16mins	1,020	94	195	191	13	7	16	151	33	12
L1966-67	191	5hrs 17mins	1,045	99	182	241	48	18	85	660	96	61
1967-68	139	5hrs 47mins	1,061	83	190	225	44	14	72	437	92	28
1968-69	109	5hrs 03mins	1,064	91	193	235	28	9	47	363	92	35
S1969-70	83	4hrs 47mins	1,062	93	199	225	28	12	18	287	108	33
L1970-71	153	6hrs 19mins	1,078	101	171	264	37	11	196	511	283	37
1971-72	141	5hrs 46mins	1,073	98	169	249	40	15	171	494	315	26
1972-73	128	5hrs 38mins	1,080	101	173	240	32	13	73	460	281	31
S1973-74	45	5hrs 51mins	1,079	105	193	245	22	7	19	139	92	5

House of Lords Sittings and Business—*continued*

Sessions and Sittings			Membership and Attendance				Work of the House					
Session[a]	Sittings	Average sitting	Total membership[b]	Without writ of summons[bc]	On leave of absence[b]	Average attendance	Public bills introduced in House of Lords	Government bills introduced into the House of Lords[d]	Divisions	Starred questions	Written questions	Unstarred (debatable questions)
S1974	64	5hrs 28mins	1,108	100	171	246	31	13	21	192	171	23
1974-75	162	5hrs 44mins	1,121	110	170	262	49	20	119	560	350	35
1975-76	155	6hrs 15mins	1,139	95	143	275	51	27	146	553	517	41
1976-77	105	5hrs 41mins	1,140	90	135	281	40	11	45	385	380	36
1977-78	126	5hrs 51mins	1,154	88	128	282	30	22	96	439	544	46
S1978-79	59	5hrs 51mins	1,155	88	130	292	38	27	21	217	432	23
1979-80	206	6 hrs 9 mins	1,171	85	172	290	50	11	303	765	1,277	68
1980-81	143	6 hrs 43 mins	1,179	87	160	296	48	12	184	537	857	31
1981-82	147	6 hrs 20 mins	1,174	91	150	284	42	10	146	531	1,098	50
S1982-83	94	6 hrs 35 mins	1,181	97	143	294	40	11	89	357	619	36
L1983-84	178	7 hrs 13 min	1,183	99	153	321	48	14	237	691	1,350	60

a *S* beside the date of a session indicates a shortened session drawn to an early conclusion by a General Election. *L* shows a prolonged session usually following an election.
b Figures at the end of the session in question.
c Includes minors and bankrupts.
d Excludes Consolidation Bills, on average an extra 7 per session.
e Records not kept.

SOURCE.—House of Lords Information Office.

Critical Votes in the House of Lords since 1900

The following represent outstanding occasions when the House of Lords has set itself against the House of Commons. In cases of repeated defiance on the same issue the final vote alone is normally recorded. One notable instance of the Lords yielding to the Commons (10 Aug 11) is also included.

27 Nov	08	272-96	2nd Reading refused for Licensing Bill.
30 Nov	09	350-75	2nd Reading refused for Finance Bill.
(10 Aug	11)	131-114	3rd Reading for Parliament Bill.
30 Jan	13	326-69	2nd Reading refused for Government of Ireland Bill (refusal repeated 15 Jul 13 by 302-64).
13 Feb	13	251-51	2nd Reading refused for Established Church (Wales) Bill (refusal repeated 22 Jul 13 by 243-48).
24 Jul	13	166-42	2nd Reading refused for Plural Voting Bill (refusal repeated 15 Jul 14 by 119-49).
22 Jan	18	131-42	P.R. Amendment to Representation of the People Bill carried.
3 Feb	30	156-42	Insistence on one year limit to Unemployment Act.
24 Jun	30	208-13	Insistence on 'quota' amendment to Coal Mines Bill.
15 Jul	30	168-36	Insistence on 'spreadover' amendment to Coal Mines Bill.
18 Feb	31	168-22	2nd Reading refused for Education (School Attendance) Bill.
2 Jul	31	80-29	Amendment restricting Alt. Vote in Representation of the People Bill carried.
2 Jun	48	181-28	Capital punishment amendment to Criminal Justice Bill rejected.
8 Jun	48	177-81	2nd Reading refused for Parliament Bill (refusal repeated 23 Sep 48 by 204-34 and 29 Nov 49 by 110-37).
8 Jun	49	103-29	Insistence on amendment delaying Vesting Day under Iron and Steel Act (compromise later reached and Royal Assent to Act 16 Dec 49).
10 Jul	56	238-95	2nd Reading refused for Death Penalty (Abolition) Bill.
18 Jun	68	193-184	Rhodesia Sanctions Order rejected (but passed without division 18 Jul 68).
16 Oct	69	229-78	Insistence on Amendments to Bill delaying redistribution of seats.
11 Nov	75	186-86	Insistence on Amendments to Trade Union and Labour Relations Bill that barred Closed Shop in Journalism.
22 Oct	76	147-71	3rd Reading refused for British Transport Docks (Felixstowe) Bill, a Private Bill designed to bring Felixstowe Harbour into public ownership.
22 Nov	76	197-90	Insistence on Amendments to Aircraft and Shipbuilding Bill that excluded ship-repairing.
13 Mar	80	216-112	Clause of the Education (No. 2) Bill to give local authorities power to charge for home-to-school transport rejected.
9 Apr	84	235-153	Amendment to 2nd Reading of Rates Bill (stating that it would 'result in damaging constitutional changes in the relationship between central and local government', etc.) rejected.
11 Jun	84	238-217	Amendment to 2nd Reading of Local Government (Interim Provisions Bill (stating that the Bill was a 'dangerous precedent', etc.) rejected.
28 Jun	84	191-143	Amendment carried to insert a clause postponing the coming into force of the Local Government (Interim Provisions) Bill until the passing of the main Act to abolish the GLC and Metropolitan County Councils.
7 May	85	152-135	Amendment to Local Government Bill preserving some environmental powers of GLC. This was the first of four amendments to the Bill carried against the Government.

Main Landmarks in the Reform of the House of Lords, 1900-

In 1900 the legislative powers of the two Houses were in theory equal, with the exception of the privileges of the House of Commons in relation to financial measures.

1908 *Rosebery Committee's Report.* The House approved the following principal recommendations:

(1) That a strong and efficient second Chamber was necessary for the balance of Parliament;

(2) That this objective should be achieved by the reform and reconstitution of the House of Lords;

(3) That, as a necessary preliminary to reform, it should be accepted that the possession of a peerage should no longer of itself entail the right to sit and vote in the House.

No action was taken to implement these recommendations.

1911 *Parliament Act.* Provided that—

(1) Bills certified by the Speaker of the House of Commons as Money Bills were to receive the Royal Assent one month after being sent to the House of Lords, even without the consent of the latter House; and

(2) any other Public Bill (except one for extending the life of a Parliament) passed by the House of Commons in three successive Sessions and rejected by the House of Lords was nevertheless to receive the Royal Assent, provided that 2 years had elapsed between the second reading in the first session and the third reading in the third session of the House of Commons.

1918 *Bryce Report.* Recommended that the differences between the 2 Houses should be settled by some means of joint consultation. Proposed that the House should consist of two elements. (i) 246 members elected by members of the House of Commons arranged in geographical areas and voting by Proportional Representation with a single transferable vote. (ii) 80 peers to be elected for a period of 12 years by a joint Committee of both Houses of Parliament on which all parties should be represented. No action was taken to implement this Report.

1922 Government proposed House of Lords of 350 members consisting of some 'elected either directly or indirectly from the outside', hereditary peers elected by their order, and members nominated by the Crown. Resolutions criticised for vagueness, debate adjourned and not renewed.

1927 Further proposals introduced by government but later dropped.

1929 Vt Elibank's Life Peers Bill withdrawn before Second Reading.

1934 M of Salisbury's Parliament (Reform) Bill read a second time but not proceeded with in committee.

1935 Ld Rockley's Life Peers Bill read a second time but not proceeded with in committee.

1946 *Travelling Expenses.* Agreed that regular attenders at the House of Lords should be reimbursed for their travelling expenses. In practice made to apply to peers attending at least one-third of the sittings of the House.

1948 *Agreed Statement of Party Leaders.* A statement of nine principles agreed to but not acted upon. The most important of these were:
(1) The second Chamber should be complementary to and not a rival to the lower House, and
(2) The revised constitution of the House of Lords should be such as to secure as far as practicable that a permanent majority was not assured for any one political party.

1948 *Criminal Justice Act.* Privileges of Peers in Criminal Proceedings abolished.

1949 *Parliament Act.* Reduced the delaying powers of the House to two sessions and one year.

1956 *Swinton Committee Report.* Recommended provision of official Leave of Absence. This was put into effect in 1958. There are normally about 200 members of the House who have Leave of Absence at any one time.

1957 *Expenses.* Provision made for Peers to claim a maximum of three guineas a day for expenses incurred in attendance at the House. This was in addition to travelling expenses and claims were not subject to any minimum number of attendances.

1958 *Life Peerages Act.* Provided for the creation by the Sovereign, on the advice of the Prime Minister, of Life Peers and Peeresses. Women were thus for the first time enabled to become Members of the House of Lords. One of the objectives of this Act was to provide more balance of parliamentary representation in the House of Lords. This is achieved by the convention enabling recommendations for Life Peerages made by Opposition party leaders to be conveyed to the Queen through the agency of the Prime Minister.

1963 *Peerage Act.* Provided for—
(1) the option for Peers to disclaim within one year (one month in the case of Members of the House of Commons) their peerages for life without such a disclaimer affecting the subsequent devolution of the peerage;[1]
(2) the abolition of elections for Scottish Representative Peers and the admission of all Scottish Peers to membership of the House;
(3) the removal from Irish Peers of certain disabilities relating to their voting and candidature at parliamentary elections;
(4) the admission of all female holders of hereditary peerages to membership of the House of Lords.

1964 *Expenses.* Provision made for increasing the maximum expenses to which Peers were entitled from three guineas to four-and-a-half guineas per day (increased to £6 10s. in 1969, to £8.50 in 1972, and to £13.50 in 1977).

1967 The Government announced their intention of introducing legislation to reform the House of Lords and an all-party committee was established.

1968 Formal discussions were broken off after the Lords' rejection of the Southern Rhodesia Sanctions order in June and the government introduced their own Parliament (No. 2) Bill dealing with both powers and composition.

1969 The Bill was dropped in April. Though the Peers themselves approved of the proposals, it met with strong opposition in the House of Commons from sections of both the Labour and Conservative parties.

1977 At the Labour Party Conference a motion was carried by 6,248,000 votes to 91,000 for the 'total abolition of the House of Lords and the reform of Parliament into an efficient single-chamber legislating body without delay'.

[1] These peers have in fact disclaimed their titles.

1963	Vt Stansgate (A. Wedgwood Benn)
	Ld Altrincham (J. Grigg)
	E of Home (Sir A. Douglas-Home)—re-ennobled 1974
	Vt Hailsham (Q. Hogg)—re-ennobled 1970
1964	Ld Southampton (E. Fitzroy)
	Ld Monkswell (W. Collier) (d. 1980). His son reassumed the title.
	Ld Beaverbrook (Sir M. Aitken) (d. 1985). His son reassumed the title.
	E of Sandwich (V. Montagu)
1966	Ld Fraser of Allander (Sir H. Fraser)
1970	E of Durham (A. Lambton)
1971	Ld Sanderson of Ayot (A. Sanderson)
1972	Ld Reith (C. Reith)
1973	Ld Silkin (A. Silkin)
1975	Ld Archibald (G. Archibald)
1977	Ld Merthyr (T. Lewis)

SOURCES.—1908 (H.L. 234), *Select Committee Report on the House of Lords*; Cd. 9038/1918, *The Reform of the Second Chamber* (Conference: Vt Bryce); Cmd. 7380/1948, *Report of the Inner Party Conference on the Parliament Bill*; H.M.S.O. (24 Jan 56), *Report of the Select Committee on the Power of the House in Relation to the Attendance of its Members*; Cmnd. 3779/1968, *House of Lords Reform*; P. A. Bromhead, *The House of Lords and Contemporary Politics, 1911-1957* (1958); Sir I. Jennings, *Parliament* (2nd ed., 1957); *10th Report of House of Lords Select Committee on Procedure* (Aug 1971); *The House of Lords and the Labour Government, 1964-70*, J. P. Morgan (1975).

IV

ELECTIONS

General Election Statistics

IT is impossible to present election statistics in any finally authoritative way. British statutes make no acknowledgement of the existence of political parties, and in most general elections the precise allegiance of at least a few of the candidates is in doubt. This, far more than arithmetic error, explains the discrepancies between the figures provided in various works of reference.

Such discrepancies, however, are seldom on a serious scale (except, perhaps, for 1918). Election figures suffer much more from being inherently confusing than from being inaccurately reported. The complications that arise from unopposed returns, from plural voting, from two-member seats, and, above all, from variations in the number of candidates put up by each party are the really serious hazards in psephological interpretation.

In the figures which follow an attempt is made to allow for these factors by a column which shows the average vote won by each opposed candidate (with the vote in two-member seats halved, and with University seats excluded). This still gives a distorted picture, especially when, as in 1900 or 1931, there were many unopposed candidates or when, as in 1929, 1931, or 1950, there was a sharp change in the number of Liberals standing; in 1918 the situation was so complicated that any such statistics are omitted, as they are likely to confuse more than to clarify; for other elections they should be regarded as corrective supplements to the cruder percentages in the previous column rather than as substitutes for them.

The turn-out percentages are modified to allow for the distorting effect of the two-member seats which existed up to 1950.

To simplify classification, some arbitrary decisions have been made. Before 1918 candidates have been classified as Conservative, Liberal, or Irish Nationalist, even if their designation had a prefix such as Tariff Reform or Independent, but only officially sponsored candidates are classed as Labour. From 1918 onwards candidates not officially recognised by their party have been classified with 'Others' (except that in 1935 Ind. Lib. are placed with Lib.). Liberal Unionists have been listed as Conservatives throughout. Liberal National, National Labour, and National candidates are listed with Conservatives except in 1931.

General Election Results, 1900-1918

	Total Votes	M.P.s Elected	Candi-dates	Unopposed Returns	% Share of Total Vote	Average % Vote per Opposed Candidate
1900. 28 Sept-24 Oct						
Conservative	1,797,444	402	579	163	51·1	52·5
Liberal	1,568,141	184	406	22	44·6	48·2
Labour	63,304	2	15	. .	1·8	26·6
Irish Nationalist	90,076	82	100	58	2·5	80·0
Others	544	. .	2	. .	0·0	2·2
Elec. 6,730,935 Turnout 74·6%	3,519,509	670	1,102	243	100·0	. .
1906. 12 Jan-7 Feb						
Conservative	2,451,454	157	574	13	43·6	44·1
Liberal	2,757,883	400	539	27	49·0	52·6
Labour	329,748	30	51	. .	5·9	39·9
Irish Nationalist	35,031	83	87	74	0·6	63·1
Others	52,387	. .	22	. .	0·9	18·8
Elec. 7,264,608 Turnout 82·6%	5,626,503	670	1,273	114	100·0	. .
1910. 14 Jan-9 Feb						
Conservative	3,127,887	273	600	19	46·9	47·5
Liberal	2,880,581	275	516	1	43·2	49·2
Labour	505,657	40	78	. .	7·6	38·4
Irish Nationalist	124,586	82	104	55	1·9	77·7
Others	28,693	. .	17	. .	0·4	15·4
Elec. 7,694,741 Turnout 86·6%	6,667,404	670	1,315	75	100·0	. .
1910. 2-19 Dec						
Conservative	2,420,566	272	550	72	46·3	47·9
Liberal	2,295,888	272	467	35	43·9	49·5
Labour	371,772	42	56	3	7·1	42·8
Irish Nationalist	131,375	84	106	53	2·5	81·9
Others	8,768	. .	11	. .	0·2	9·1
Elec. 7,709,981 Turnout 81·1%	5,228,369	670	1,190	163	100·0	. .
1918. Sat., 14 Dec[1]						
Coalition Unionist	3,504,198	335	374	42	32·6	
Coalition Liberal	1,455,640	133	158	27	13·5	
Coalition Labour	161,521	10	18	. .	1·5	
(Coalition)	(5,121,359)	(478)	(550)	(69)	(47·6)	
Conservative	370,375	23	37	. .	3·4	
Irish Unionist	292,722	25	38	. .	2·7	
Liberal	1,298,808	28	253	. .	12·1	
Labour	2,385,472	63	388	12	22·2	
Irish Nationalist	238,477	7	60	1	2·2	
Sinn Fein	486,867	73	102	25	4·5	
Others	572,503	10	197	. .	5·3	
Elec. 21,392,322 Turnout 58·9%	10,766,583	707	1,625	107	100·0	

[1] Result announced 28 Dec 1918.

General Election Results, 1922-1931

	Total Votes	M.P.s Elected	Candi- dates	Unopposed Returns	% Share of Total Vote	Average % Vote per Opposed Candidate
1922. Wed., 15 Nov						
Conservative	5,500,382	345	483	42	38·2	48·6
National Liberal	1,673,240	62	162	5	11·6	39·3
Liberal	2,516,287	54	328	5	17·5	30·9
Labour	4,241,383	142	411	4	29·5	40·0
Others	462,340	12	59	1	3·2	28·3
Elec. 21,127,663 Turnout 71·3%	14,393,632	615	1,443	57	100·0	. .
1923. Thu., 6 Dec						
Conservative	5,538,824	258	540	35	38·1	42·6
Liberal	4,311,147	159	453	11	29·6	37·8
Labour	4,438,508	191	422	3	30·5	41·0
Others	260,042	7	31	1	1·8	27·6
Elec. 21,281,232 Turnout 70·8%	14,548,521	615	1,446	50	100·0	. .
1924. Wed., 29 Oct						
Conservative	8,039,598	419	552	16	48·3	51·9
Liberal	2,928,747	40	340	6	17·6	30·9
Labour	5,489,077	151	512	9	33·0	38·2
Communist	55,346	1	8	. .	0·3	25·0
Others	126,511	4	16	1	0·8	29·1
Elec. 21,731,320 Turnout 76·6%	16,639,279	615	1,428	32	100·0	. .
1929. Thu., 30 May						
Conservative	8,656,473	260	590	4	38·2	39·4
Liberal	5,308,510	59	513	. .	23·4	27·7
Labour	8,389,512	288	571	. .	37·1	39·3
Communist	50,614	. .	25	. .	0·3	5·3
Others	243,266	8	31	3	1·0	21·2
Elec. 28,850,870 Turnout 76·1%	22,648,375	615	1,730	7	100·0	. .
1931. Tues., 27 Oct						
Conservative	11,978,745	473	523	56	55·2 }	62·9 (Conservative, National Labour, Liberal National)
National Labour	341,370	13	20	. .	1·6 }	
Liberal National	809,302	35	41	. .	3·7 }	
Liberal	1,403,102	33	112	5	6·5	28·8
(National Government)	(14,532,519)	(554)	(696)	(61)	(67·0)	. .
Independent Liberal	106,106	4	7	. .	0·5	35·8
Labour	6,649,630	52	515	6	30·6	33·0
Communist	74,824	. .	26	. .	0·3	7·5
New Party	36,377	. .	24	. .	0·2	3·9
Others	256,917	5	24	. .	1·2	21·9
Elec. 29,960,071 Turnout 76·3%	21,656,373	615	1,292	67	100·0	. .

General Election Results 1935-1955

	Total Votes	M.P.s Elected	Candi-dates	Unopposed Returns	% Share of Total Vote	Average% Vote per Opposed Candidate
1935. Thu., 14 Nov						
Conservative	11,810,158	432	585	26	53·7	54·8
Liberal	1,422,116	20	161		6·4	23·9
Labour	8,325,491	154	552	13	37·9	40·3
Independent Labour Party	139,577	4	17	. .	0·7	22·2
Communist	27,117	1	2	. .	0·1	38·0
Others	272,595	4	31	1	1·2	21·3
Elec. 31,379,050 Turnout 71·2%	21,997,054	615	1,348	40	100·0	. .
1945. Thu., 5 Jul[1]						
Conservative	9,988,306	213	624	1	39·8	40·1
Liberal	2,248,226	12	306	. .	9·0	18·6
Labour	11,995,152	393	604	2	47·8	50·4
Communist	102,780	2	21	. .	0·4	12·7
Common Wealth	110,634	1	23	. .	0·4	12·6
Others	640,880	19	104	. .	2·0	15·4
Elec. 33,240,391 Turnout 72·7%	25,085,978	640	1,682	3	100·0	. .
1950. Thu., 23 Feb						
Conservative	12,502,567	298	620	2	43·5	43·7
Liberal	2,621,548	9	475	. .	9·1	11·8
Labour	13,266,592	315	617	. .	46·1	45·7
Communist	91,746	. .	100	. .	0·3	2·0
Others	290,218	3	56	. .	1·0	12·6
Elec. 33,269,770 Turnout 84·0%	28,772,671	625	1,868	2	100·0	. .
1951. Thu., 25 Oct						
Conservative	13,717,538	321	617	4	48·0	48·6
Liberal	730,556	6	109	. .	2·5	14·7
Labour	13,948,605	295	617	. .	48·8	49·2
Communist	21,640	. .	10	. .	0·1	4·4
Others	177,329	3	23	. .	0·6	16·8
Elec. 34,645,573 Turnout 82·5%	28,595,668	625	1,376	4	100·0	. .
1955. Thu., 26 May						
Conservative	13,286,569	344	623	. .	49·7	50·2
Liberal	722,405	6	110	. .	2·7	15·1
Labour	12,404,970	277	670	. .	46·4	47·3
Communist	33,144	. .	17	. .	0·1	4·2
Others	313,410	3	39	. .	1·1	20·8
Elec. 34,858,263 Turnout 76·7%	26,760,498	630	1,409	. .	100·0	. .

[1] Result announced 26 July 1945.

General Election Results, 1959-1970

	Total Votes	M.P.s Elected	Candi- dates	Unopposed Returns	% Share of Total Vote	Average% Vote per Opposed Candidate
1959. Thu., 8 Oct						
Conservative	13,749,830	365	625	. .	49·4	49·6
Liberal	1,638,571	6	216	. .	5·9	16·9
Labour	12,215,538	258	621	. .	43·8	44·5
Communist	30,897	. .	18	. .	0·1	4·1
Plaid Cymru	77,571	. .	20	. .	0·3	9·0
Scottish Nat. P.	21,738	. .	5	. .	0·1	11·4
Others	12,464	1	31	. .	0·4	11·0
Elec. 35,397,080 Turnout 78·8%	27,859,241	630	1,536	. .	100·0	. .
1964. Thu., 15 Oct						
Conservative	12,001,396	304	630	. .	43·4	43·4
Liberal	3,092,878	9	365	. .	11·2	18·5
Labour	12,205,814	317	628	. .	44·1	44·1
Communist	45,932	. .	36	. .	0·2	3·4
Plaid Cymru	69,507	. .	23	. .	0·3	8·4
Scottish Nat. P.	64,044	. .	15	. .	0·2	10·7
Others	168,422	. .	60	. .	0·6	6·4
Elec. 35,892,572 Turnout 77·1%	27,655,374	630	1,757	. .	100·0	. .
1966. Thu., 31 Mar						
Conservative	11,418,433	253	629	. .	41·9	41·8
Liberal	2,327,533	12	311	. .	8·5	16·1
Labour	13,064,951	363	621	. .	47·9	48·7
Communist	62,112	. .	57	. .	0·2	3·0
Plaid Cymru	61,071	. .	20	. .	0·2	8·7
Scottish Nat. P.	128,474	. .	20	. .	0·2	14·1
Others	170,569	2	31	. .	0·6	8·6
Elec. 35,964,684 Turnout 75·8%	27,263,606	630	1,707	. .	100·0	. .
1970. Thu., 18 Jun						
Conservative	13,145,123	330	628	. .	46·4	46·5
Liberal	2,117,035	6	332	. .	7·5	13·5
Labour	12,179,341	287	624	. .	43·0	43·5
Communist	37,970	. .	58	. .	0·1	1·1
Plaid Cymru	175,016	. .	36	. .	0·6	11·5
Scottish Nat. P.	306,802	1	65	. .	1·1	12·2
Others	383,511	6	94	. .	1·4	9·1
Elec. 39,342,013 Turnout 72·0%	28,344,798	630	1,837	. .	100·0	. .

General Election Results, 1974-1983

	Total Votes	M.P.s Elected	Candi-dates	Unopposed Returns	%Share of Total Vote	Average % Vote per Opposed Candidate
1974. Thu., 28 Feb						
Conservative	11,868,906	297	623	. .	37·9	38·8
Liberal	6,063,470	14	517	. .	19·3	23·6
Labour	11,639,243	301	623	. .	37·1	38·0
Communist	32,741	. .	44	. .	0·1	1·7
Plaid Cymru	171,364	2	36	. .	0·6	10·7
Scottish Nat. P.	632,032	7	70	. .	2·0	21·9
National Front	76,865	. .	54	. .	0·3	3·2
Others (G.B.)	131,059	2	120	. .	0·4	2·2
Others (N.I.)[1]	717,986	12	48	. .	2·3	25·0
Elec. 39,798,899 Turnout 78·7%	31,333,226	635	2,135	. .	100·0	. .
1974. Thu., 10 Oct						
Conservative	10,464,817	277	623	. .	35·8	36·7
Liberal	5,346,754	13	619	. .	18·3	18·9
Labour	11,457,079	319	623	. .	39·2	40·2
Communist	17,426	. .	29	. .	0·1	1·5
Plaid Cymru	166,321	3	36	. .	0·6	10·8
Scottish Nat. P.	839,617	11	71	. .	2·9	30·4
National Front	113,843	. .	90	. .	0·4	2·9
Others (G.B.)	81,227	. .	118	. .	0·3	1·5
Others (N.I.)[1]	702,094	12	43	. .	2·4	27·9
Elec. 40,072,971 Turnout 72·8%	29,189,178	635	2,252	. .	100·0	. .
1979. Thu., 3 May						
Conservative	13,697,690	339	622	. .	43·9	44·9
Liberal	4,313,811	11	577	. .	13·8	14·9
Labour	11,532,148	269	623	. .	36·9	37·8
Communist	15,938	. .	38	. .	0·1	0·9
Plaid Cymru	132,544	2	36	. .	0·4	8·1
Scottish Nat. P.	504,259	2	71	. .	1·6	17·3
National Front	190,747	. .	303	. .	0·6	1·6
Ecology	38,116	. .	53	. .	0·1	2·0
Workers Rev. P.	13,535	. .	60	. .	0·1	0·5
Others (G.B.)	85,338	. .	129	. .	0·3	1·3
Others (N.I.)[1]	695,889	12	64	. .	2·2	18·8
Elec. 41,093,264 Turnout 76·0%	31,220,010	635	2,576	. .	100·0	. .
1983. Thu., 9 Jun						
Conservative	13,012,315	397	633	. .	42.4	43.5
Liberal	4,210,115	17	322	. .	13.7	27.7
Social Democrat	3,570,834	6	311	. .	11.6	24.3
(Alliance)	(7,780,949)	(23)	(633)	. .	(25.4)	(26.0)
Labour	8,456,934	209	633	. .	27.6	28.3
Communist	11,606	. .	35	. .	0.04	0.8
Plaid Cymru	125,309	2	36	. .	0.4	7.8
Scottish Nat. P.	331,975	2	72	. .	1.1	11.8
National Front	27,065	. .	60	. .	0.1	1.0
Others (GB)	193,383	. .	282	. .	0.6	1.4
Others (NI)[1]	764,925	17	95	. .	3.1	17.9
Elec. 42,197,344 Turnout 72.7%	42,197,344 72.7%	650	2,579	. .	100.0	. .

[1]From 1974 onwards, no candidates in Northern Ireland are included in the major party totals although it might be argued that some independent Unionists should be classed with the Conservatives and that Northern Ireland Labour candidates should be classed with Labour.

Referendum on E.E.C. Membership
(Thursday 5 Jun 1975)

'Do you think that the United Kingdom should stay in the European Community (the Common Market)?'

	Total electorate[1]	Total votes[2]	% turnout[1]	% 'yes'[2]	Highest 'yes'	Lowest 'yes'
England	33,339,959	21,722,222	64·6	68·7	76·3	62·9
Wales	2,015,766	1,345,545	66·7	64.8	74·3	56·9
Scotland	3,698,462	2,286,676	61·7	58·4	72·3	29·5
Northern Ireland	1,032,490	498,751	47·4	52·1	52·1	
United Kingdom[2]	40,086,677	29,453,194	64·5	64·5	76·3	29·5

[1] The electorate and turnout figures are for the civilian electorate only. The 370,200 service votes are only included in the total votes and 'Yes' percentages.
[2] The votes were counted on a county basis, except in Northern Ireland which was treated as a single unit. In 66 of the 68 counties, there was a 'Yes' vote. (Shetland voted 56·3% 'No' and the Western Isles 70·5% 'No'.)

(For 1979 referendums in Scotland and Wales see pp. 422-3)

Direct Elections to European Parliament

1979 Thu., 7 Jun	% Turnout	% votes Con.	Lab.	Lib.	Nat.	Other	Seats Con.	Lab.	Lib.	Nat.	Other
England	31·3	53·4	32·6	13·2	—	0·8	54	12	—	—	—
Wales	34·4	36·6	41·5	9·6	11·7	0·6	1	3	—	—	—
Scotland	33·7	33·7	33·0	13·9	19·4	—	5	2	—	1	—
Great Britain	32·1	50·6	33·1	13·1	2·5	0·7	60	17	—	1	—
Northern Ireland[1]	55·7	—	—	0·2	—	99·8	—	—	—	—	3
United Kingdom	32·7	48·4	31·6	12·6	2·5	4·9	60	17	—	1	3

Electorate 41,152,763 Votes cast 13,446,083

1984 Thu., 14 June	% Turnout	% Votes Con.	Lab.	Alln.	Nat.	Other	Seats Con.	Lab.	Alln.	Other
England	31.6	43.1	35.0	20.4	—	1.5	42	24	—	—
Wales	39.7	25.4	44.5	17.4	12.2	0.5	1	3	—	—
Scotland	33.0	25.7	40.7	15.6	17.8	0.2	2	5	—	1
Great Britain	31.8	40.8	36.5	19.5	2.5	0.8	45	32	—	1
Northern Ireland[1]	63.5	—	—	—	—	100.0%	—	—	—	3
United Kingdom	32.6	39.9	36.0	19.1	2.4	5.6	45	32	—	4

Electorate 42,493,274 Votes cast 13,998,274

SOURCES.—F. W. S. Craig, *Europe Votes 2* (1985); D. Butler and D. Marquand, *European Elections and British Politics* (1981); D. Butler and P. Jowett, *Party Strategies in Britain* (1985).
[1] In Northern Ireland the election was conducted by Single Transferable vote.

General Election Results by Regions

	1900	1906	Jan 1910	Dec 1910	1918[a]	1922	1923	1924	1929	1931
County of London										
Conservative	51	19	33	30	Coal.	43	29	39	24	53
Liberal	8	38	25	26	53	9	11	3	2	4
Labour	. .	2	1	3	Op.	9	22	19	36	5
Others	. .	. .	. .	. .	9	1	. .	1	. .	1
Rest of S. England										
Conservative	123	45	107	103	Coal.	130	89	150	111	156
Liberal	32	107	46	49	149	23	48	5	18	4
Labour	. .	3	2	2	Op.	9	27	10	35	5
Others	. .	. .	. .	1	16	3	1	. .	1	. .
Midlands										
Conservative	60	27	49	50	Coal.	53	45	64	35	80
Liberal	27	59	31	30	67	17	17	2	5	3
Labour	1	2	8	8	Op.	17	25	21	47	4
Others	. .	. .	. .	. .	20	. .	. .	. .	. .	. .
Northern England										
Conservative	98	31	45	50	Coal.	82	57	101	51	146
Liberal	55	102	86	82	121	27	48	9	10	9
Labour	. .	20	22	21	Op.	60	64	59	108	15
Others	1	1	1	1	50	2	2	2	2	1
Wales										
Conservative	6	. .	2	3	Coal.	6	4	9	1	11
Liberal	27	33	27	26	20	10	12	10	9	8
Labour	1	1	5	5	Op.	18	19	16	25	16
Others	. .	. .	. .	. .	15	1	. .	. .	. .	. .
Scotland										
Conservative	36	10	9	9	Coal.	13	14	36	20	57
Liberal	34	58	59	58	54	27	22	8	13	7
Labour	. .	2	2	3	Op.	29	34	26	37	7
Others	. .	. .	. .	. .	17	2	1	1	1	. .
Ireland										
Conservative	19	16	19	17	Coal.	10	10	12	10	10
Liberal	1	3	1	1	1	. .	. .	. .	. .	. .
Labour	. .	. .	. .	. .	Op.	. .	. .	. .	. .	. .
Others	81	82	81	83	100	2	2	. .	2	2
Universities										
Conservative	9	9	9	9	Coal.	8	9	8	8	8
Liberal	. .	. .	. .	. .	13	3	2	3	2	2
Labour	. .	. .	. .	. .	Op.	. .	. .	. .	. .	. .
Others	. .	. .	. .	. .	2	1	1	1	2	2
Totals										
Conservative	402	157	273	272	Coal.	345	258	419	260	521
Liberal	184	400	275	272	478	116	159	40	59	37
Labour	2	30	40	42	Op.	142	191	151	288	52
Others	82	83	82	84	229	12	7	5	8	5
Total seats	670	670	670	670	707	615	615	615	615	615

[a] In 1918 all Coalition and all non-Coalition candidates are listed together. In fact a substantial number of the 48 Conservatives who were elected without the Coupon worked with the Government. Virtually no Coupons were issued to Irish candidates but 23 of the 101 non-University seats in Ireland went to Unionists.

The vertical lines indicate redistributions of seats.
Northern England includes Cheshire, Lancashire, Yorkshire, and all counties to their north.
Midlands includes Hereford, Worcs., Warwickshire, Northants., Lincs., Notts., Leics., Staffs., Salop, Derbyshire.
Southern England includes the rest of England, except for the County of London.

General Election Results by Regions

	1935	1945	1950	1951	1955	1959	1964	1966	1970	Feb 1974	Oct 1974	1979	1983
County of London (GLC)													
Conservative	39	12	12	14	15	18	10	6	9	42	41	50	56
Liberal/Alliance	1	. .	. .	. .	. .	. .	. .	. .	. .	. .	. .	. .	2
Labour	22	48	31	29	27	24	32	36	33	50	51	42	26
Others	. .	2	. .	. .	. .	. .	. .	. .	. .	. .	. .	. .	. .
Rest of S. England													
Conservative	147	88	144	153	163	171	157	134	169	136	128	146	168
Liberal/Alliance	3	3	1	. .	. .	1	3	4	2	5	5	3	5
Labour	15	91	54	46	42	34	46	67	34	21	29	13	3
Others	. .	3	. .	. .	1	. .	. .	1	1	. .	. .	. .	. .
Midlands													
Conservative	67	24	35	35	39	49	42	35	51	43	40	57	70
Liberal/Alliance	1	. .	. .	. .	. .	. .	. .	. .	. .	. .	. .	. .	. .
Labour	19	64	59	59	57	47	54	61	45	54	58	41	30
Others	. .	2	. .	. .	. .	. .	. .	. .	. .	1	. .	. .	. .
Northern England													
Conservative	106	43	61	69	75	77	53	44	63	47	44	53	68
Liberal/Alliance	5	2	1	2	2	2	. .	2	. .	4	3	4	6
Labour	60	128	107	99	90	88	114	121	104	112	117	107	89
Others	. .	. .	. .	. .	. .	. .	. .	. .	. .	1	. .	. .	. .
Wales													
Conservative	11	4	4	6	6	7	6	3	7	8	8	11	14
Liberal/Alliance	6	6	5	3	3	2	2	1	1	2	2	1	2
Labour	18	25	27	27	27	27	28	32	27	24	23	22	20
Others	. .	. .	. .	. .	. .	. .	. .	. .	1	2	3	2	2
Scotland													
Conservative	43	29	32	35	36	31	24	20	23	21	16	22	21
Liberal/Alliance	3	. .	2	1	1	1	4	5	3	3	3	3	8
Labour	20	37	37	35	34	38	43	46	44	40	41	44	41
Others	5	5	. .	. .	. .	1	. .	. .	1	7	11	2	2
Ireland													
Conservative	10	9	10	9	10	12	12	11	8	. .	. .	. .	. .
Liberal/Alliance	. .	. .	. .	. .	. .	. .	. .	. .	. .	. .	. .	. .	. .
Labour	. .	. .	. .	. .	. .	. .	. .	. .	. .	. .	. .	. .	. .
Other	2	3	2	3	2	. .	. .	1	4	12	12	12	17
Universities													
Conservative	9	4	. .	. .	. .	. .	. .	. .	. .	. .	. .	. .	. .
Liberal/Alliance	1	1	. .	. .	. .	. .	. .	. .	. .	. .	. .	. .	. .
Labour	. .	. .	. .	. .	. .	. .	. .	. .	. .	. .	. .	. .	. .
Other	2	7	. .	. .	. .	. .	. .	. .	. .	. .	. .	. .	. .
Totals													
Conservative	432	213	298	321	344	365	304	253	330	297	277	339	397
Liberal/Alliance	20	12	9	6	6	6	9	12	6	14	13	11	23
Labour	154	393	315	295	277	258	317	363	287	301	319	269	209
Others	9	22	3	3	3	1	. .	2	7	23	26	16	21
Total seats	615	640	625	625	630	630	630	630	630	635	635	635	650

The vertical lines indicate redistributions of seats.
Northern England includes Cheshire, Lancashire, Yorkshire, and all counties to their north.
Midlands includes Hereford, Worcs., Warwickshire, Northants., Lincs., Notts., Leics., Staffs., Salop, Derbyshire.
Southern England includes the rest of England, except for the County of London (the old L.C.C. area), but from 1974 the seats in the outer areas of the Greater London Council are classed with the County of London and not with the rest of S. England.

Party Changes between Elections

The party composition of the House of Commons changes continuously partly owing to Members changing their allegiance and partly owing to by-election results. The following table shows the net change due to both causes during the life of each Parliament. (Seats vacant at dissolution are included under the last incumbent's party.)

		Con.	Lib.	Lab.	Others
1895-1900	Dissolution	399	189	. .	82
1900-05	Election	402	184	2	82
	Dissolution	369	215	4	82
1906-09	Election	157	400	30	83
	Dissolution	168	373	46	83
1910	Election	273	275	40	82
	Dissolution	274	274	40	82
1910-18	Election	272	271	42	85
	Dissolution	281	260	39	90
1918-22[a]	Election	383	161	73	90
	Dissolution	378	155	87	87
1922-23	Election	345	116	142	12
	Dissolution	344	117	144	10
1923-24	Election	258	159	191	7
	Dissolution	259	158	193	5
1924-29	Election	419	40	151	5
	Dissolution	400	46	162	7
1929-31	Election	260	59	288	8
	Dissolution	263	57	281[b]	14
1931-35	Election	521	37	52	5
	Dissolution	512	34	59	10
1935-45	Election	432	20	154	9
	Dissolution	398	18	166	33
1945-50	Election	213	12	393	22
	Dissolution	218	10	391	21
1950-51	Election	298	9	315	3
	Dissolution	298	9	314	4

[a] In this form the 1918-22 figures are highly misleading. This amplification may help:

	Co. U.	Con.	Co. Lib.	Lib.	Co. Lab.	Lab.	O.
Election	335	48	133	28	10	63	90
Dissolution	313	65	120	35	11	76	87

[b] This figure includes 15 National Labour M.P.s.

Party Changes between Elections (*contd.*)

		Con.	Lib. (Alln)	Lab.	Others
1951-55	Election	321	6	295	3
	Dissolution	322	6	294	3
1955-59	Election	344	6	277	3
	Dissolution	340	6	281	3
1959-64	Election	365	6	258	1
	Dissolution	360	7	262	2
1964-66	Election	304	9	317	. .
	Dissolution	304	10	316	. .
1966-70	Election	253	12	363	2
	Dissolution	264	13	346	7
1970-74	Election	330	6	287	7
	Dissolution	323	11	287	9
1974	Election	297	14	301	23
	Dissolution	297	15	300	23
1974-79	Election	277	13	319	26
	Dissolution	284	14	309	28
1979-83	Election	339	11	269	16
	Dissolution	336	(42)	240	17
1983-	Election	397	(23)	209	21

M.P.s' Changes of Allegiance

The difficulties in compiling an exact and comprehensive list of all floor crossings, Whip withdrawals, Whip resignations, and Whip restorations are enormous. The list which follows is probably fairly complete as far as floor crossings go (except for 1918-22) but it certainly omits a number of Members who relinquished the Whip for a time. It also omits cases of M.P.s who stood without official party support in their constituencies but who remained in good standing with the Whips and some cases of M.P.s taking the Whip immediately before a General Election (as happened with several Members in 1918 and a few in 1945) or immediately after a General Election (as happened with the Lloyd George Group in 1935). No attempt has been made to record shifts between the various factions of Irish Nationalism. Throughout this list the test, in so far as it can be applied, is whether the M.P. was officially in receipt of the weekly documentary Whip.

Parliament of 1900-05

				from	to	
Nov	02	*J. Wason	Orkney & Shetland	L.U.	Ind.	Won by-el Nov 02 took Lib. Whip by 05
Apr	03	*J. W. Wilson	N. Worcs.	L.U.	Lib.	
Apr	03	Sir M. Foster	London Univ.	L.U.	Lib.	
Jan	04	†W. Churchill	Oldham	Con.	Ind.	Con. Whip restored after 2 weeks; Lib. Whip taken Apr 04
Jan	04	*Sir J. Dickson-Poynder	Chippenham	Con.	Ind.	
Feb	04	*T. Russell	S. Tyrone	L.U.	Lib.	
Feb	04	J. Wilson	Falkirk Burghs	L.U.	Lib.	
Mar	04	†J. Seely	I. of Wight	Con.	Ind.	Won by-el Apr 04 unop.; took Lib. Whip May 04
Apr	04	†I. Guest	Plymouth	Con.	Lib.	
Aug	04	E. Hain	St Ives	L.U.	Lib.	
Aug	04	G. Kemp	Heywood	L.U.	Lib.	
Jul	04	J. Jameson	W. Clare	I. Nat.	Con.	
Nov	04	R. Rigg	Appleby	Lib.	Ind.	Resigned seat Dec 04
Mar	05	E. Mitchell	N. Fermanagh	Ind. C.	Lib.	
Mar	05	J. Wood	E. Down	L.U.	Lib.	
Mar	05	E. Hatch	Gorton	Con.	Ind.	
Mar	05	Sir E. Reed	Cardiff D.	Lib.	L.U.	

Parliament of 1906-09

Feb.	06	*J. W. Taylor	Chester-le-Street	Lib.	Lab.	
Feb	06	A. Taylor	E. Toxteth	Con.	Lib.	
Feb	07	*R. Hunt	Ludlow	Con.	—	Whip withdrawn. Whip restored Mar 07
Nov	07	L. Renton	Gainsborough	Lib.	Con.	
Aug	08	*A. Corbett	Tradeston	L.U.	Ind. Lib.	
Mar	09	T. Kincaid Smith	Stratford-on-Avon	Lib.	Ind.	Lost by-el May 09
May	09	A. Cross	Camlachie	L.U.	Lib.	
Oct	09	C. Bellairs	King's Lynn	Lib.	L.U.	

Parliament of 1910

Nov	10	Sir J. Rees	Montgomery D.	Lib.	L.U.	

Parliament of 1911-18

Jan	14	D. Mason	Coventry	Lib.	Ind.	
Feb	14	*B. Kenyon	Chesterfield	Lab.	Lib.	Introduced as new M.P. by Lab. but resigned Whip after 2 weeks
Apr	14	W. Johnson	Nuneaton	Lab.	Lib.	Lab. Whip withdrawn
Apr	15	*J. Hancock	Mid-Derbyshire	Lab.	Lib.	Lab. Whip withdrawn
Sep	17	*H. Page Croft	Christchurch	Con.	Nat.P.	
Sep	17	*Sir R. Cooper	Walsall	Con.	Nat.P.	
Jul	18	E. John	E. Denbigh	Lib.	Lab.	
Jul	18	J. Martin	St. Pancras E.	Lib.	Lab.	

In Nov 18 a number of Liberals became Independent or Labour and some Labour members accepted the label Coalition Labour or Coalition National Democratic Party shortly before the dissolution of Parliament.

Parliament of 1919-22

Throughout this parliament the confusion of party labels and the movements within and between the Coalition and non-Coalition wings of each party make it impossible to attempt any comprehensive listing of all switches. The following changes were, however, more clear cut.

Apr	19	*J. Wedgwood	Newcastle-under-Lyme	Co.Lib.	Lab.	Lab. Whip granted May 19
Oct	19	E. Hallas	Duddeston	Co. N.D.P.	Lab.	
Nov	19	C. Malone	Leyton E.	Co.Lib.	Ind.	Joined Communist Party Jul 20
Oct	20	*O. Mosley	Harrow	Co.Con.	Ind.	
Oct	20	*Sir O. Thomas	Anglesey	Lab.	Ind.	
Feb	22	*A. Hopkinson	Mossley	Co.Lib.	Ind.	

* Re-elected for same seat at next General Election.
† Elected for different seat at next General Election.

Parliament of 1922-23

				from	to	
Jan	23	*J. Erskine	Westminster St. George's	Ind.Con.	Con.	
Jan	23	*H. Becker	Richmond-on-Thames	Ind.Con.	Con.	
Jan	23	*G. Hall Caine	Dorset E.	Ind.Con.	Con.	
Jul	23	A. Evans	Leicester E.	N.Lib.	Con.	
Oct	23	G. Roberts	Norwich	Ind.	Con.	

Parliament of 1923-24

Feb	24	G. Davies	Welsh Univ.	Ind.	Lab.	
May	24	O. Mosley	Harrow	Ind.	Lab.	

Parliament of 1924-29[1]

Jan	26	Sir A. Mond	Carmarthen	Lib.	Con.	Made peer Jun 28
Feb	26	E. Hilton Young	Norwich	Lib.	Ind.	Took Con. Whip May 26
Oct	26	*J. Kenworthy	Hull C.	Lib.	Lab.	Won by-el Nov 26
Nov	26	D. Davies	Montgomery	Lib.	Ind.	
Feb	27	G. Spencer	Broxtowe	Lab.	Ind.	Expelled from party
Feb	27	†W. Benn	Leith	Lib.	Ind.	Resigned seat Feb 27
Feb	27	L. Haden Guest	Southwark N.	Lab.	Ind.	Lost by-el Mar 27
Oct	27	*Sir R. Newman	Exeter	Con.	Ind.	
Jul	28	*Sir B. Peto	Barnstaple	Con.	—	Whip withdrawn; restored Nov 28

Parliament of 1929-31

Jun	29	Sir W. Jowitt	Preston	Lib.	Lab.	Won by-el Jul 29
Feb	30	*N. Maclean	Glasgow, Govan	Ind.Lab.	Lab.	
Feb	31	Sir O. Mosley	Smethwick	Lab.	N.P.	}
Feb	31	Lady C. Mosley	Stoke	Lab.	N.P.	}
Feb	31	R. Forgan	W. Renfrew	Lab.	N.P.	}
Feb	31	W. Allen	Belfast W.	Con.	N.P.	}
Feb	31	C. R. Dudgeon	Galloway	Lib.	N.P.	}
Feb	31	J. Strachey	Aston	Lab.	N.P.	Became Ind. Jun 31
Feb	31	O. Baldwin	Dudley	Lab.	Ind.	
Feb	31	W. Brown	Wolverhampton W.	Lab.	Ind.	
Mar	31	*Sir W. Wayland	Canterbury	Con.	—	Whip withdrawn; restored Apr 31
Jun	31	*E. Brown	Leith	Lib.	Ind.	Became L.Nat. Oct 31 (E. Brown, Sir R. Hutchison, Sir J. Simon)
Jun	31	*Sir R. Hutchison	Montrose	Lib.	Ind.	
Jun	31	*Sir J. Simon	Spen Valley	Lib.	Ind.	
Sep	31	*E. Taylor	Paddington S.	Ind.	Con.	

In Oct 31, 23 Liberal Members broke with the party to form the Liberal National Group. A further 6 Liberals, most notably the Lloyd George family, became Independent Liberals. 15 Labour members under R. MacDonald formed the National Labour Group.

Parliament of 1931-35

Nov	31	*G. Buchanan	Gorbals	Lab.	ILP.	
Nov	31	*J. McGovern	Shettleston	Lab.	ILP.	
Nov	31	J. Maxton	Bridgeton	Lab.	ILP.	
Nov	31	*D. Kirkwood	Dumbarton	Lab.	ILP.	Returned to Lab. Aug 33
Nov	31	R. Wallhead	Merthyr	Lab.	ILP.	Returned to Lab. Sep 33
Nov	32	*J. Leckie	Walsall	Lib.	L.Nat.	
Dec	32	A. Curry	Bishop Auckland	L.Nat.	Lib.	
Dec	32	F. Llewellyn Jones	Flint	L.Nat.	Lib.	
Feb	33	H. Nathan	Bethnal Green N.E.	Ind.L.	Ind.	Took Lab. Whip Jun 34
Jun	34	W. McKeag	Durham	Lib.	L.Nat.	
Jun	34	J. Hunter	Dumfries	Lib.	L.Nat.	
Jun	34	J. Lockwood	Shipley	Con.	Ind.	}
May	35	F. Astbury	Salford W.	Con.	Ind.	}
May	35	L. Thorp	Nelson & Colne	Con.	Ind.	}
May	35	A. Todd	Berwick-on-Tweed	Con.	Ind.	}

* Re-elected for same seat at next General Election.
† Elected for different seat at next General Election.

[1] The 7 members, all former Liberal M.P.s, elected under the label 'Constitutional' never voted as a group. Two, *W. Churchill and Sir H. Greenwood, took the Conservative whip from the start and one, A. Moreing, later. Three reverted during the Parliament to their former Liberalism, J. Edwards, *A. England, and J. Ward. One, *Sir T. Robinson, became an Independent.

			from	to	
May 35	*Duchess of Atholl	Kinross E. & Perth	Con.	Ind.	Whip restored Sep 35
May 35	*Sir J. Nall	Hulme	Con.	Ind.	Whip restored Nov 35
Early 35	*G. Morrison	Scottish Univ.	Lib.	L.Nat.	

Parliament of 1935-45

Jun 36	*H. Macmillan	Stockton-on-Tees	Con.	Ind.	Whip restored Jul 37
Oct 36	R. Bernays	Bristol N.	Lib.	L.Nat.	
Apr 38	Duchess of Atholl	Kinross & W. Perth	Con.	Ind.	Lost by-el Dec 38
Oct 38	H. Holdsworth	Bradford S.	Lib.	L.Nat.	
Nov 38	A. Hopkinson	Mossley	Nat.	Ind.	
Jan 39	*Sir S. Cripps	Bristol E.	Lab.	—	Expelled from party; Whip restored Feb 45
Mar 39	*A. Bevan	Ebbw Vale	Lab.	—	Expelled from party; Whip restored Dec 39
Mar 39	*G. Strauss	Lambeth N.	Lab.	—	Expelled from party; Whip restored Feb 40
May 39	*G. Buchanan	Gorbals	ILP.	Lab.	
Dec 39	*C. Davies	Montgomery	L.Nat.	Ind.	Took Lib. Whip Aug 42
Mar 40	*D. Pritt	Hammersmith N.	Lab.	—	Expelled from party
May 40	A. Ramsay	Peebles & S.	Con.	Ind.	Detained until Dec 44
Feb 42	*E. Granville	Eye	L.Nat.	Ind.	Took Lib. Whip Apr 45
Feb 42	*Sir M. Macdonald	Inverness	L.Nat.	Ind.	Whip restored by 45
Feb 42	L. Hore-Belisha	Devonport	L.Nat.	Ind.	
Feb 42	S. King-Hall	Ormskirk	N.Lab.	Ind.	
Feb 42	*Sir H. Morris-Jones	Denbigh	L.Nat.	Ind.	Whip restored May 43
Feb 42	†K. Lindsay	Kilmarnock	N.Lab.	Ind.	
May 42	C. Cunningham-Reid	St Marylebone	Con.	—	Whip withdrawn
Sep 42	Sir R. Acland	Barnstaple	Lib.	C.W.	
Mar 43	A. Maclaren	Burslem	Lab.	Ind.	
Nov 44	*J. Loverseed	Eddisbury	C.W.	Ind.	Took Lab. Whip May 45
Jan 45	*T. Driberg	Maldon	Ind.	Lab.	
May 45	*J. Little	Down	U.U.	Ind.	
May 45	*C White	W. Derbyshire	Ind.	Lab.	

Parliament of 1945-50

Apr 46	E. Millington	Chelmsford	C.W.	Lab.	
Oct 46	T. Horabin	N. Cornwall	Lib.	Ind.	Took Lab. Whip Nov 47
Mar 47	*J. McGovern	Shettleston	ILP.	Lab.	
Jul 47	C. Stephen	Camlachie	ILP.	Ind.	Took Lab. Whip Oct 47
Oct 47	*J. Carmichael	Bridgeton	ILP.	Ind.	Took Lab. Whip Nov 47
Nov 47	E. Walkden	Doncaster	Lab.	Ind.	
Mar 48	*J. McKie	Galloway	Ind.Con.	Con.	
Apr 48	J. Platts-Mills	Finsbury	Lab.	—	Expelled from party
May 48	A. Edwards	Middlesbrough	Lab.	—	Expelled from party, took Con. Whip Aug 49
Oct 48	I. Bulmer-Thomas	Keighley	Lab.	Ind.	Took Con. Whip Jan 49
Nov 48	E. Gander Dower	Caithness & Sutherland	Con.	Ind.	
May 49	L. Solley	Thurrock	Lab.	—	Expelled from party
May 49	K. Zilliacus	Gateshead	Lab.	—	Expelled from party
Jul 49	L. Hutchinson	Rusholme	Lab.	—	Expelled from party

Parliament of 1950-51

Aug 50	R. Blackburn	Northfield	Lab.	Ind.	

* Re-elected for same seat at next General Election.
† Elected for different seat at next General Election.

Parliament of 1951-55

				from	to	
Jun	54	Sir J. Mellor	Sutton Coldfield	Con.	Ind.	Whip restored Jul 54
Jul	54	*H. Legge-Bourke	Isle of Ely	Con.	Ind.	Whip restored Oct 54
Nov	54	*G. Craddock	Bradford S.	Lab.	—	Whip withdrawn; restored Feb 55
Nov	54	*S. Davies	Merthyr	Lab.	—	
Nov	54	*E. Fernyhough	Jarrow	Lab.	—	
Nov	54	*E. Hughes	S. Ayrshire	Lab.	—	
Nov	54	*S. Silverman	Nelson & Colne	Lab.	—	
Nov	54	*V. Yates	Ladywood	Lab.	—	
Nov	54	*J. McGovern	Shettleston	Lab.	—	Whip withdrawn; restored Mar 55
Mar	55	*A. Bevan	Ebbw Vale	Lab.	—	Whip withdrawn; restored Apr 55
Mar	55	Sir R. Acland	Gravesend	Lab.	Ind.	Resigned seat to fight by-el; expelled from party

Parliament of 1955-59

Nov	56	C. Banks	Pudsey	Con.	Ind.	Whip restored Dec 58
May	57	P. Maitland	Lanark	Con.	Ind.	Whip restored Dec 57
May	57	Sir V. Raikes	Garston	Con.	Ind.	Resigned seat Oct 57
May	57	A. Maude	Ealing S.	Con.	Ind.	Resigned seat Apr 58
May	57	*J. Biggs-Davison	Chigwell	Con.	Ind.	Whip restored Jul 58
May	57	*A. Fell	Yarmouth	Con.	Ind.	
May	57	*Vt Hinchingbrooke	S. Dorset	Con.	Ind.	
May	57	L. Turner	Oxford	Con.	Ind.	
May	57	P. Williams	Sunderland S.	Con.	Ind.	
Nov	57	Sir F. Medlicott	C. Norfolk	Con.	Ind.	Whip restored Nov 58
Jan	59	*Sir D. Robertson	Caithness & Sutherland	Con.	Ind.	

Parliament of 1959-64

Mar	61	A. Brown	Tottenham	Lab.	Ind.	Took Con. Whip May 62
Mar	61	*W. Baxter	W. Stirlingshire	Lab.	—	Whip withdrawn; restored May 63
Mar	61	*S. Davies	Merthyr	Lab.	—	
Mar	61	*M. Foot	Ebbw Vale	Lab.	—	
Mar	61	*E. Hughes	S. Ayrshire	Lab.	—	
Mar	61	*S. Silverman	Nelson & Colne	Lab.	—	
Mar	61	*K. Zilliacus	Gorton	Lab.	—	Whip suspended; party membership restored Jan 62
Oct	61	Sir W. Duthie	Banff	Con.	Ind.	Whip restored Nov 63
Jan	64	D. Johnson	Carlisle	Con.	Ind.	

Parliament of 1964-66

[*None*]

Parliament of 1966-70

Jul	66	G. Hirst	Shipley	Con.	Ind.	
Aug	66	*G. Fitt	Belfast W.	Rep.Lab.	S.D.L.P.	Expelled by Rep.Lab.
Dec	66	*R. Paget	Northampton	Lab.	Ind.	Whip restored Jun 67
Jan	68	D. Donnelly	Pembroke	Lab.	Ind.	Expelled from party Mar 68
Feb	68	24 M.P.s		Lab.	—	Whip suspended for one month

Parliament of 1970-74

Oct	71	*I. Paisley	N. Antrim	Prot.U.	Dem.U.	
Feb	72	R. Gunter	Southwark	Lab.	Ind.	
Oct	72	*D. Taverne	Lincoln	Lab.	Dem.Lab.	Won by-el Mar 73
Dec	72	S. Mills	Belfast N.	U.U.	Con.	Joined Alliance Party Apr 73

* Re-elected for same seat at next General Election.
† Elected for different seat at next General Election.

				from	to	
Parliament of 1974						
Jul	74	C. Mayhew	Woolwich E.	Lab.	Lib.	
Parliament of 1974-79						
Oct	75	W. Craig	Belfast E.	UUUC	Vanguard	Wound up Vanguard and rejoined UUUC Feb 78
Oct	75	*J. Kilfedder	N. Down	UUUC	Ind. U.	
Apr	76	J. Stonehouse	Walsall N.	Lab.	Ind.	
Jul	76	J. Sillars	S. Ayrshire	Lab.	Sc.Lab.	Formed Sc.Lab.P. Apr 76 rejected Lab Whip Jul 76
Jul	76	J. Robertson	Paisley	Lab.	Sc.Lab.	
May	77	*I. Paisley	N. Antrim	UUUC	Dem.U.	
May	77	J. Dunlop	Mid-Ulster	UUUC	Ind.	
Oct	77	†R. Prentice	Newham N.E.	Lab.	Con.	
Parliament of 1979-83						
Nov	79	G. Fitt	Belfast W.	SDLP	Ind. Soc.	
Feb	81	T. Ellis	Wrexham	Lab.	SDP	
Feb	81	R. Crawshaw	Liverpool Toxteth	Lab.	SDP	
Mar	81	T. Bradley	Leicester E.	Lab.	SDP	
Mar	81	*J. Cartwright	Woolwich E.	Lab.	SDP	
Mar	81	J. Horam	Gateshead W.	Lab.	SDP	
Mar	81	*R. Maclennan	Caithness & Sutherland	Lab.	SDP	
Mar	81	J. Roper	Farnworth	Lab.	SDP	
Mar	81	*D. Owen	Devonport	Lab.	SDP	
Mar	81	W. Rodgers	Teeside Stockton	Lab.	SDP	
Mar	81	N. Sandelson	Hayes & Harlington	Lab.	SDP	
Mar	81	M. Thomas	Newcastle E.	Lab.	SDP	
Mar	81	*I. Wrigglesworth	Teeside Thornaby	Lab.	SDP	
Mar	81	E. Lyons	Bradford W.	Lab.	SDP	
Mar	81	C. Brocklebank-Fowler	Norfolk N.W.	Con.	SDP	
Jul	81	J. Wellbeloved	Erith & Crayford	Lab.	SDP	
Sep	81	M. O'Halloran	Islington N.	Lab.	SDP	Became Ind. Lab. Mar 83
Oct	81	D. Mabon	Greenock and Port Glasgow	Lab.	SDP	
Oct	81	R. Mitchell	Southampton Itchen	Lab.	SDP	
Oct	81	D. Ginsburg	Dewsbury	Lab.	SDP	
Oct	81	J. Dunn	Liverpool Kirkdale	Lab.	SDP	
Oct	81	T. McNally	Stockport S.	Lab.	SDP	
Oct	81	E. Ogden	Liv. W. Derby	Lab.	SDP	
Nov	81	J. Grant	Islington C	Lab.	SDP	
Nov	81	G. Cunningham	Islington S and Finsbury	Lab.	Ind. Lab.	Became SDP Jun 82
Dec	81	R. Brown	Hackney S. and Shoreditch	Lab.	SDP	
Dec	81	J. Thomas	Abertillery	Lab.	SDP	
Dec	81	E. Hudson-Davies	Caerphilly	Lab.	SDP	
Dec	81	B. Douglas-Mann	Mitcham & Morden	Lab.	Ind. SDP	Lost by-elec. June 82
Jan	82	B. Magee	Leyton	Lab.	Ind. Lab.	Became SDP Mar 82
Aug	82	R. Mellish	Bermondsey	Lab.	Ind. Lab.	Resigned seat Jan 83

* Re-elected for same seat at next General Election.
† Elected for different seat at next General Election.

In addition to the floor crossings recorded above there are the following instances of ex-M.P.s, after an interval out of Parliament, returning to the House under a designation basically different from the ones under which they had previously sat.

(Sir) R. Acland	Lib. 35-42 C.W. 42-45 Lab. 47-55
C. Addison	Lib. 10-22 Lab. 29-31, 34-35
P. Alden	Lib. 06-18 Lab. 23-24
W. Allen	Lib. 92-00 Nat. 31-35
C. Bellairs	Lib. 06-10 Con. 15-31
(Sir) A. Bennett	Lib. 22-23 Con. 24-30
(Sir) E. Bennett	Lib. 06-10 Lab. 29-31 N. Lab. 31-45
H. Bottomley	Lib. 06-12 Ind. 18-22
T. Bowles	Con. 92-06 Lib. 10-10
J. Bright	L.U. 89-95 Lib. 06-10
W. Brown	Lab. 29-31 Ind. 42-50
C. Buxton	Lib. 10-10 Lab 22-31
N. Buxton	Lib. 05-06, 10-18 Lab. 22-24, 29-30
(Sir) W. Churchill	Con. 00-04 Lib. 04-22 Con. 24-64
(Sir) H. Cowan	Lib. 06-22 Con. 23-29
A. Crawley	Lab. 45-51 Con. 62-67
R. Denman	Lib. 10-18 Lab. 29-31 N. Lab. 31-45
(Sir) C. Entwistle	Lib. 18-24 Con. 31-45
R. Fletcher	Lib. 23-24 Lab. 35-42
(Sir) D. Foot	Lib. 31-45 Lab. 57-70
G. Garro-Jones	Lib. 24-29 Lab. 35-47
W. Grenfell	Lib. 80-82, 85-86, 92-93 Con. 00-06
Sir E. Grigg	Lib. 22-25 Con. 33-45
C. Guest	Lib. 10-18, 22-23 Con. 37-45
F. Guest	Lib. 10-22, 23-29 Con. 31-37
O. Guest	Co.Lib. 18-22 Con. 35-45
T. Harvey	Lib. 10-18, 23-24 Ind. 37-45
E. Hemmerde	Lib. 06-10, 12-18 Lab. 22-24
(Sir) B. Janner	Lib. 31-35 Lab. 45-70
R. Jenkins	Lab. 48-77 SDP 82
(Sir) W. Jowitt	Lib. 29-29 Lab. 29-31 Ind. 31-31 Lab. 39-45
E. King	Lab. 45-50 Con. 64-79
H. Lawson	Lib. 85-92, 93-95 L.U. 05-06, 10-16
H. Lees-Smith	Lib. 10-18 Lab. 22-23, 24-31, 35-42
G. Lloyd-George	Lib. 22-24, 29-50 Con. 51-57
(Lady) M. Lloyd-George	Lib. 29-51 Lab. 57-66
F. Maddison	Lib. 97-00 Lab. 06-10
E. Mallalieu	Lib. 31-35 Lab. 48-74
C. Malone	Co.Lib. 18-19 Ind. then Comm. 19-22 Lab. 28-31
(Sir) F. Markham	Lab. 29-31 N. Lab. 35-45 Con. 51-64
H. Mond	Lib. 23-24 Con. 29-30
(Sir) O. Philipps	Lib. 06-10 Con. 16-22
A. Ponsonby	Lib. 08-18 Lab. 22-30
E. Powell	Con. 50-74 U.U.U. 74-
S. Saklatvala	Lab. 22-23 Comm. 24-29
Sir A. Salter	Ind. 37-50 Con. 52-54
J. Seddon	Lab. 06-10 Co.N.D.P. 18-22
(Sir) C. Seely	L.U. 95-06 Lib. 16-18
(Sir) E. Spears	Lib. 22-24 Con. 31-45
G. Spero	Lib. 23-24 Lab. 29-31
C. Stephen	Lab. 22-31 I.L.P. 35-47 Lab. 47
J. Strachey	Lab. 29-30 N.P. 30-31 Ind. 31-31 Lab. 45-63
(Sir) C. Trevelyan	Lib. 99-18 Lab. 22-31
J. (Havelock) Wilson	Lib. 92-00 Lab. 06-10 Co.N.D.P. 18-22

M.P.s Denied Party Renomination since 1922

When a sitting M.P. does not stand again, it is often unclear whether the retirement is entirely voluntary. Irreparable conflicts with the local party may be behind formal statements about reasons of health or age or business. At least in the following cases, there is little doubt that the local party failed to renominate a sitting and willing M.P. who was still in receipt of the party whip at Westminster.[1] It is plain that in the overwhelming majority of cases the disagreement could be ascribed to personal rather than ideological considerations. In several of the 1983 cases, the M.P.s were seeking renomination in a substantially redrawn constituency, often against another sitting M.P.

Conservative

1923	Sir C. Warner (Lichfield)
1929	[a]Sir R. Newman (Exeter)
1935	[b]J. Lockwood (Shipley)
1935	H. Moss (Rutherglen)
1938	[b]Duchess of Atholl (Perth & Kinross)
1945	[a]J. McKie (Galloway)
1945	[b]C. Cunningham-Reid (St. Marylebone)
1945	H. Clifton Brown (Newbury)
1950	N. Bower (Harrow, West)
1950	C. Challen (Hampstead)
1950	A. Marsden (Chertsey)
1950	Sir G. Fox (Henley)
1951	E. Gates (Middleton & Prestwich)
1954	Lord M. Douglas Hamilton (Inverness)
1959	N. Nicolson (Bournemouth E.)
1959	Sir F. Medlicott (C. Norfolk)
1959	L. Turner (Oxford)
1964	M. Lindsay (Solihull)
1964	O. Prior-Palmer (Worthing)
1964	[b]D. Johnson (Carlisle)
1964	J. Henderson (Glasgow, Cathcart)
1970	R. Harris (Heston & Isleworth)
1974F	Sir C. Taylor (Eastbourne)
1979	B. Drayson (Skipton)
1979	R. Cooke (Bristol W.)
1983	T. Benyon (Wantage)
1983	M. Brotherton (Louth)
1983	J. Bruce-Gardyne (Knutsford)
1983	R. Mawby (Totnes)
1983	G. Morgan (Clwyd N.W.)
1983	W. Rees-Davies (Thanet North)
1983	K. Stainton (Sudbury)

Ulster Unionist

1945	[a]D. Little (Down)
1959	M. Hyde (Belfast N.)
1970	G. Currie (Down, North)

[a] Stood as Independent and won.
[b] Stood as Independent and lost.

Labour

1929	[a]N. Maclean (Glasgow, Govan)
1929	E. Davies (Ebbw Vale)
1945	[b]T. Groves (West Ham, Stratford)
1945	H. Charleton (Leeds S.)
1950	N. Maclean (Glasgow, Govan)
1951	R. Adams (C. Wandsworth)
1951	J. Mack (Newcastle-under-Lyme)
1955	J. Kinley (Bootle)
1955	J. Glanville (Consett)
1959	E. Davies (Enfield E.)
1964	J. Baird (Wolverhampton N.E.)
1966	W. Warbey (Ashfield)
1970	M. McKay (Wandsworth, Clapham)
1970	[a]S. O. Davies (Merthyr)
1973	[a]D. Taverne (Lincoln)
1974F	[a]E. Milne (Blyth)
1974O	[b]E. Griffiths (Sheffield, Brightside)
1974O	W. Baxter (W. Stirlingshire)
1979	Sir A. Irvine (Liverpool, Edge Hill)[2]
1979	F. Tomney (Hammersmith N.)
1983	J. Barnett (Heywood & Royton)
1983	S. Cohen (Leeds S.E.)
1983	S. C. Davies (Hackney C.)
1983	M. English (Nottingham W.)
1983	B. Ford (Bradford N.)
1983	R. Fletcher (Ilkeston)
1983	F. Hooley (Sheffield, Heeley)
1983	A. Lewis (Newham N.W.)
1983	Mrs H. McElhone (Glasgow, Queens Park)
1983	A. McMahon (Glasgow, Govan)
1983	C. Morris (Manchester Openshaw)
1983	F. Mulley (Sheffield Park)
1983	E. Ogden (Liverpool W. Derby)
1983	R. Race (Tottenham)
1983	J. Sever (Birmingham, Ladywood)
1983	A. Stallard (St Pancras N.)
1983	J. Tilley (Lambeth & Vauxhall)
1983	D. Watkins (Consett)
1985	R. Freeson (Brent E.)
1985	M. Maguire (Makerfield)
1985	N. Atkinson (Tottenham)

[1] Up to 1983 this list does not include M.P.s whose seats were substantially changed by redistribution and who failed to secure renomination for any part of their old seat, e.g. in Feb 1974 Sir R. Russell and E. Bullus, Con. members for Wembley N. and Wembley S., were spurned for the successor seats, Brent North and Brent South, while W. Wells, Lab. member for Walsall N., was denied renomination in the redistribution seat of the same name.

[2] Sir A. Irvine died before the 1979 election.

SOURCES.—R. J. Jackson, *Whips and Rebels* (1968); J. Pentney, 'Worms that Turned', *Parliamentary Affairs* (Autumn 1977), pp. 363-73.

By-elections

	Total[a] By-elections	Changes	Con. +	Con. −	Lib (Alln) +	Lib (Alln) −	Lab. +	Lab. −	Others +	Others −	Annual Incidence	% with Change
1900-05	113	30	2	26	20	4	3	..	5	..	22	27
1906-09	101	20	12	..	..	18	5	..	3	2	25	20
1910	20	..	..	..	..	..	..	..	..	..	20	—
1911-18	245	31	16	4	4	16	2	4	10	8	31	13
1918-22	108	27	4	13	5[b]	11[b]	14	1	4	2	27	25
1922-23	16	6	1	4	3	1	2	..	..	1	16	38
1923-24	10	3	2	1	..	1	1	1	..	..	10	30
1924-29	63	20	1	16	6	3	13	1	..	..	14	32
1929-31	36	7	4	1	..	1	2	4	1	1	15	19
1931-35	62	10	..	9	..	1	10	..	..	..	15	16
1935-45	219	30	..	29	..	..	13	1	17	..	23	14
1945-50	52	3	3	..	..	..	..	..	..	3	11	6
1950-51	16	..	..	..	..	..	..	..	..	..	10	—
1951-55	48	1	1	..	..	..	..	1	..	..	13	2
1955-59	52	6	1	4	1	1	4	..	..	1	12	12
1959-64	62	9	2	7	1	..	6	2	..	..	15	14
1964-66	13	2	1	1	1	..	..	1	..	..	9	15
1966-70	38	16	12	1	1	..	..	15	3	..	9	42
1970-74	30	9	..	5	5	..	2	3	2	1	9	30
1974	1	..	..	..	..	..	..	..	..	..	1	—
1974-79	30	7	6	..	1	..	..	7	..	..	6	23
1979-83	20	7	1	4	4	..	1	1	1	2	5	35

[a] Up to 1918, and to a lesser extent to 1926, the number of by-elections is inflated by the necessity for Ministers to stand for re-election on appointment. In 53 such cases the returns were unopposed.

[b] In 1918-22 Opposition Liberals won 5 seats and lost 2. Coalition Liberals lost 9.

SOURCES.—C. Cook and J. Ramsden, *By-elections in British Politics* (1973); F. W. S. Craig, *British Parliamentary Election Statistics 1918-1970* (1970).

Seats Changing Hands at By-elections

Date	Constituency	General Election	By-election
26 Sep 01	N.E. Lanark.	Lib.	Con.
21 Nov 01	Galway	Con.	Nat.
10 May 02	Bury	Con.	Lib.
29 Jul 02	Leeds N.	Con.	Lib.
1 Aug 02	Clitheroe	Lib.	Lab.
18 Aug 02	S. Belfast	Con.	Ind. U.
22 Oct 02	†Devonport	Lib.	Con.
19 Nov 02	Orkney & Shetland	Con.	Ind. Lib.
2 Jan 03	E. Cambs.	Con.	Lib.
1 Mar 03	Woolwich	Con.	Lab.
17 Mar 03	†E. Sussex	Con.	Lib.
20 Mar 03	†N. Fermanagh	Con.	Ind. Con.
24 Jul 03	Barnard Castle	Lib.	Lab.
26 Aug 03	Argyll	Con.	Lib.
17 Sep 03	†St Andrews	Con.	Lib.
15 Jan 04	Norwich	Con.	Lib.
30 Jan 04	†Ayr	Con.	Lib.
12 Feb 04	†Mid-Herts.	Con.	Lib.
17 Mar 04	E. Dorset	Con.	Lib.
6 Apr 04	Isle of Wight	Con.	Ind. Con.
20 Jun 04	Devonport	{ Con. 02 Lib. 00	Lib.
26 Jul 04	†W. Shropshire	Con.	Lib.
10 Aug 04	N.E. Lanark.	{ Con. 01 Lib. 00	Lib.
7 Jan 05	Stalybridge	Con.	Lib.
26 Jan 05	N. Dorset	Con.	Lib.
3 Mar 05	Bute	Con.	Lib.
5 Apr 05	Brighton	Con.	Lib.
1 Jun 05	†Whitby	Con.	Lib.
29 Jun 05	Finsbury E.	Con.	Lib.
13 Oct 05	†Barkston Ash	Con.	Lib.
	General Election 12 *Jan*-7 *Feb* 06		
3 Aug 06	Cockermouth	Lib.	Con.
31 Dec 06	Mid-Cork	Nat.	I. Nat.
30 Jan 07	N.E. Derbyshire[a]	Lib.	Lab.
26 Feb 07	†Brigg	Lib.	Con.
4 Jul 07	†Jarrow	Lib.	Lab.
18 Jul 07	†Colne Valley	Lib.	I. Lab.
31 Jul 07	N.W. Staffs[a]	Lib.	Lab.
17 Jan 08	†Mid-Devon	Lib.	Con.
31 Jan 08	S. Hereford	Lib.	Con.
24 Mar 08	Peckham	Lib.	Con.
24 Apr 08	†Manchester N.W.	Lib.	Con.
20 Jun 08	†Pudsey	Lib.	Con.
1 Aug 08	†Haggerston	Lib.	Con.
24 Sep 08	†Newcastle-o-T.	Lib.	Con.
2 Mar 09	Glasgow C.	Lib.	Con.
1 May 09	Cork City	Nat.	I. Nat.
4 May 09	Attercliffe	Lib.	Lab.
4 May 09	Stratford-on-Avon	Lib.	Con.
15 Jul 09	Mid-Derbyshire	Lib.	Lab.
28 Oct 09	†Bermondsey	Lib.	Con.

[a] Miners candidates standing as Lib-Lab, who only joined the Labour Party in 1909.
† Seats regained at subsequent General Election.

General Election 14 *Jan*-9 *Feb* 10

1910-no change

General Election 2-19 *Dec* 10

Date		Constituency	General Election	By-election
28 Apr	11	Cheltenham	Lib.	Con.
13 Nov	11	Oldham	Lib.	Con.
21 Nov	11	S. Somerset	Lib.	Con.
20 Dec	11	N. Ayrshire	Lib.	Con.
5 Mar	12	Manchester S.	Lib.	Con.
13 Jul	12	Hanley	Lab.	Lib.
26 Jul	12	Crewe	Lib.	Con.
8 Aug	12	Manchester N.W.	Lib.	Con.
10 Sep	12	Edinburghshire	Lib.	Con.
26 Nov	12	Bow & Bromley	Lab.	Con.
30 Jan	13	Londonderry	Con.	Lib.
18 Mar	13	S. Westmorland	Con.	Ind. Con.
16 May	13	E. Cambs.	Lib.	Con.
20 Aug	13	Chesterfield	Lab.	Lib.
8 Nov	13	Reading	Lib.	Con.
12 Dec	13	S. Lanarkshire	Lib.	Con.
19 Feb	14	Bethnal Green S.W.	Lib.	Con.
26 Feb	14	Leith	Lib.	Con.
20 May	14	N.E. Derbyshire	Lab.	Con.
23 May	14	Ipswich	Lib.	Con.
9 Dec	14	Tullamore	Nat.	I. Nat.
25 Nov	15	Merthyr Tydfil	Lab.	Ind.
9 Mar	16	E. Herts	Con.	Ind.
15 Nov	16	W. Cork	I. Nat.	Nat.
23 Dec	16	†Ashton-u-Lyne	Con.	Lib. (Unop.)
23 Dec	16	Sheffield, Attercliffe	Con.	Lib.
3 Feb	17	N. Roscommon	Nat.	S.F.
10 May	17	S. Longford	Nat.	S.F.
10 Jul	17	E. Clare	Nat.	S.F.
10 Aug	17	Kilkenny	Nat.	S.F.
2 Nov	17	Salford N.	Lib.	Lab.
19 Apr	18	Tullamore	{ I. Nat. 14 Nat. 10	S.F.
20 Jun	18	E. Cavan	Nat.	S.F.

General Election 14 *Dec* 18

Date		Constituency	General Election	By-election
1 Mar	19	†Leyton W.	Co. U.	Lib.
29 Mar	19	Hull C.	Co. U	Lib.
16 Apr	19	C. Aberdeen & Kincardine	Co. U.	Lib.
27 May	19	E. Antrim	Con.	Ind. U.
16 Jul	19	Bothwell	Co. U.	Lab.
30 Aug	19	†Widnes	Co. U.	Lab.
20 Dec	19	Spen Valley	Co. Lib.	Lab.
7 Feb	20	Wrekin	Co. Lib.	Ind.
27 Mar	20	†Dartford	Co. Lib.	Lab.
27 Mar	20	Stockport	Co. Lab.	Co. U.
6 Jun	20	Louth	Co. U.	Lib.
27 Jul	20	S. Norfolk	Lib.	Lab.
12 Jan	21	†Dover	Co. U.	Ind..
2 Mar	21	†Woolwich E.	Lab.	Co. U.
3 Mar	21	†Dudley	Co. U.	Lab.
4 Mar	21	†Kirkcaldy	Co. Lib.	Lab.
5 Mar	21	Penistone	Lib.	Lab.
7 Jun	21	Westminster, St George's	Co. U.	Ind.
16 Jun	21	Hertford	Ind.	Ind.
8 Jun	21	†Heywood & Radcliffe	Co. Lib.	Lab.
14 Dec	21	†Southwark, S.E.	Co. Lib.	Lab.
18 Feb	22	†Manchester, Clayton	Con.	Lab.
20 Feb	22	Camberwell N.	Co. U.	Lab.
24 Feb	22	Bodmin	Co. U.	Lib.
30 Mar	22	†Leicester E.	Co. Lib.	Lab.
25 Jul	22	Pontypridd	Co. Lib.	Lab.
18 Aug	22	Hackney S.	Ind.	Co. U.
18 Oct	22	Newport	Co. Lib.	Con.

General Election 15 *Nov* 22

Date		Constituency	General Election	By-election
3 Mar	23	†Mitcham	Con.	Lab.
3 Mar	23	Willesden E.	Con.	Lib.
6 Mar	23	Liverpool, Edge Hill	Con.	Lab.
7 Apr	23	Anglesey	Ind.	Lib.
31 May	23	Berwick on Tweed	Nat. Lib.	Con.
21 Jun	23	Tiverton	Con.	Lib.

General Election 6 *Dec* 23

Date		Constituency	General Election	By-election
22 May	24	Liverpool, W. Toxteth	Con.	Lab.
5 Jun	24	Oxford	Lib.	Con.
31 Jul	24	Holland with Boston	Lab.	Con.

General Election 29 *Oct* 24

Date		Constituency	General Election	By-election
17 Sep	25	Stockport	Con.	Lab.
17 Feb	26	Darlington	Con.	Lab.
12 Mar	26	English Univs.	Lib.	Con.
29 Apr	26	East Ham N.	Con.	Lab.
28 May	26	Hammersmith N.	Con.	Lab.
29 Nov	26	Hull C.	Lib.	Lab.
23 Feb	27	Stourbridge	Con.	Lab.
28 Mar	27	†Southwark N.	Lab.	Lib.
31 May	27	Bosworth	Con.	Lib.
9 Jan	28	Northampton	Con.	Lab.
9 Feb	28	†Lancaster	Con.	Lib.
6 Mar	28	St Ives	Con.	Lib.
4 Apr	28	Linlithgow	Con.	Lab.
13 Jul	28	Halifax	Lib.	Lab.
29 Oct	28	Ashton-u-Lyne	Con.	Lab.
29 Jan	29	†N. Midlothian	Con.	Lab.
7 Feb	29	Battersea S.	Con.	Lab.
20 Mar	29	Eddisbury	Con.	Lib.
21 Mar	29	†N. Lanark	Con.	Lab.
21 Mar	29	Holland	Con.	Lib.

General Election 30 *May* 29

Date		Constituency	General Election	By-election
31 Jul	29	Preston	Lib.	Lab.
14 Dec	29	Liverpool, Scotland	I. Nat.	Lab. (Unop.)
6 May	30	Fulham W.	Lab.	Con.
30 Oct	30	Paddington S.	Con.	Ind.
6 Nov	30	Shipley	Lab.	Con.
26 Mar	31	Sunderland	Lab.	Con.
30 Apr	31	Ashton-u-Lyne	Lab.	Con.

† Seats regained at the subsequent General Election.

General Election 27 *Oct* 31

Date		Constituency	General Election	By-election
21 Apr	32	Wakefield	Con.	Lab.
26 Jul	32	Wednesbury	Con.	Lab.
27 Feb	33	Rotherham	Con.	Lab.
25 Oct	33	†Fulham E.	Con.	Lab.
24 Apr	34	Hammersmith N.	Con.	Lab.
14 May	34	West Ham, Upton	Con.	Lab.
23 Oct	34	Lambeth N.	Lib.	Lab.
25 Oct	34	†Swindon	Con.	Lab.
6 Feb	35	†Liverpool, Wavertree	Con.	Lab.
16 Jul	35	Liverpool, W. Toxteth	Con.	Lab.

General Election 14 *Nov* 35

Date		Constituency	General Election	By-election
18 Mar	36	Dunbartonshire	Con.	Lab.
6 May	36	Camberwell, Peckham	Con.	Lab.
9 Jul	36	Derby	Con.	Lab.
26 Nov	36	Greenock	Con.	Lab.
27 Feb	37	Oxford Univ.	Con.	Ind. Con.
19 Mar	37	English Univs.	Con.	Ind.
29 Apr	37	Wandsworth C.	Con.	Lab.
22 Jun	37	Cheltenham	Con.	Ind. Con.
13 Oct	37	Islington N.	Con.	Lab.
16 Feb	38	Ipswich	Con.	Lab.
6 Apr	38	Fulham W.	Con.	Lab.
5 May	38	Lichfield	Con.	Lab.
7 Nov	38	Dartford	Con.	Lab.
17 Nov	38	Bridgwater	Con.	Ind.
21 Dec	38	Kinross & W. Perth	Con. (Ind.)	Con.
17 May	39	Southwark N.	Con.	Lab.
24 May	39	Lambeth, Kennington	Con.	Lab.
1 Aug	39	Brecon & Radnor	Con.	Lab.
24 Feb	40	Cambridge Univ.	Con.	Ind.Con.
8 Jun	40	†Newcastle N.	Con.	Ind. Con.
25 Mar	42	Grantham	Con.	Ind.
29 Apr	42	Rugby	Con.	Ind.
29 Apr	42	†Wallasey	Con.	Ind.
25 Jun	42	Maldon	Con.	Ind.
9 Feb	43	Belfast W.	U.	Eire Lab.
7 Apr	43	†Eddisbury	Con.	C.W.
7 Jan	44	†Skipton	Con.	C.W.
17 Feb	44	W. Derbyshire	Con.	Ind.
12 Apr	45	†Motherwell	Lab.	S. Nat.
13 Apr	45	Scottish Univs.	Con.	Ind.
26 Apr	45	Chelmsford	Con.	C.W.

General Election 5 *Jul* 45

Date		Constituency	General Election	By-election
18 Mar	46	English Univs.	Ind.	Con.
6 Jun	46	Down	Ind. U.	U.
29 Nov	46	Scottish Univs.	Ind.	Con.
28 Jan	48	†Glasgow, Camlachie	I.L.P.	Con.

General Election 23 *Feb* 50

1950-51—no change

General Election 25 *Oct* 51

Date		Constituency	General Election	By-election
13 May	53	Sunderland, S.	Lab.	Con.

General Election 26 *May* 55

Date		Constituency	General Election	By-election
11 Aug	55	Mid-Ulster	S.F.	U.
8 May	56	Mid-Ulster	S.F.	Ind. U.
14 Feb	57	†Lewisham N.	Con.	Lab.
28 Feb	57	Carmarthen	Lib.	Lab.
12 Feb	58	Rochdale	Con.	Lab.
13 Mar	58	†Glasgow, Kelvingrove	Con.	Lab.
27 Mar	58	†Torrington	Con.	Lib.

General Election 8 *Oct* 59

Date		Constituency	General Election	By-election
17 Mar	60	†Brighouse & Spenborough	Lab.	Con.
4 May	61	†[a]Bristol S.E.	Lab.	Con.
14 Mar	62	Orpington	Con.	Lib.
6 Jun	62	Middlesbrough W.	Con.	Lab.
22 Nov	62	Glasgow, Woodside	Con.	Lab.
22 Nov	62	†S. Dorset	Con.	Lab.
23 Aug	63	Bristol S.E.	{ Con[a] 61 Lab. 59	Lab.
7 Nov	63	Luton	Con.	Lab.
14 May	64	Rutherglen	Con.	Lab.

General Election 15 *Oct* 64

Date		Constituency	General Election	By-election
21 Jan	65	†Leyton	Lab.	Con.
24 Mar	65	Roxburgh Selkirk & Peebles	Con.	Lib.

General Election 31 *Mar* 66

Date		Constituency	General Election	By-election
14 Jul	66	†Carmarthen	Lab.	Plaid Cymru
9 Mar	67	†Glasgow Pollok	Lab.	Con.
21 Sep	67	†Walthamstow W.	Lab.	Con.
21 Sep	67	Cambridge	Lab.	Con.
2 Nov	67	†Hamilton	Lab.	S.N.P.
2 Nov	67	Leicester S.W.	Lab.	Con.
28 Mar	68	†Acton	Lab.	Con.
28 Mar	68	Meriden	Lab.	Con.
28 Mar	68	†Dudley	Lab.	Con.
13 Jun	68	†Oldham W.	Lab.	Con.
27 Jun	68	Nelson & Colne	Lab.	Con.
27 Mar	69	Walthamstow E.	Lab.	Con.
17 Apr	69	Mid-Ulster	U.U.	Ind. Unity
26 Jun	69	†Birmingham, Ladywood	Lab.	Lib.
30 Oct	69	†Swindon	Lab.	Con.
4 Dec	69	Wellingborough	Lab.	Con.

[a] Seat awarded to Con. on petition.
† Seats regained at the subsequent General Election.

Date		Constituency	General Election	By-election
General Election 18 *Jun* 70				
27 May	71	†Bromsgrove	Con.	Lab.
13 Apr	72	Merthyr Tydfil	Ind. Lab.	Lab.
26 Oct	72	Rochdale	Lab.	Lib.
7 Dec	72	†Sutton & Cheam	Con.	Lib.
1 Mar	73	Lincoln	Lab.	Dem. Lab.
26 Jul	73	Isle of Ely	Con.	Lib.
26 Jul	73	†Ripon	Con.	Lib.
8 Nov	73	†Glasgow Govan	Lab.	S.N.P
8 Nov	73	Berwick on Tweed	Con.	Lib.
General Election 28 *Feb* 74				
1974—no change				
General Election 10 *Oct* 74				
26 Jun	75	Woolwich W.	Lab.	Con.
4 Nov	76	†Walsall N.	Lab.	Con.
14 Nov	76	†Workington	Lab.	Con.
31 Mar	77	†Birmingham, Stechford	Lab.	Con.
28 Apr	77	†Ashfield	Lab.	Con.
2 Mar	78	Ilford N.	Lab.	Con.
29 Mar	79	Liverpool, Edge Hill	Lab.	Lib.
General Election 3 *May* 79				
9 Apr	81	Fermanagh & S. Tyrone	Ind.	Anti-H Block
22 Oct	81	†Croydon N.W.	Con.	Lib.
26 Nov	81	†Crosby	Con.	SDP
25 Mar	82	Glasgow, Hillhead	Con.	SDP
3 Jun	82	Mitcham & Morden	Ind. SDP	Con.
28 Oct	82	†Birmingham Northfield	Con.	Lab.
24 Feb	83	Bermondsey	Lab.	Lib.
General Election 9 June 83				
14 Jun	84	Portsmouth S.	Con.	SDP
4 Jul	85	Brecon & Radnor	Con.	Lib.

† Seats regained at the subsequent General Election.

M.P.s seeking Re-election

The following M.P.s on changing their party, or for other reasons, voluntarily resigned their seats to test public opinion in a by-election:

Date of by-election			M.P.	Constituency	Former label	New label	Whether successful
18-19	Nov	02	J. Wason	Orkney & Shetland	L.U.	Ind. L.	Yes
6	Apr	04	J. Seely	I. of Wight	Con.	Ind.	Yes (unop.)
19	Aug	04	W. O'Brien	Cork City	Nat.	Nat.	Yes
31	Dec	06	D. Sheehan	Mid-Cork	Nat.	Ind. Nat.	Yes (unop.)
21	Dec	08	C. Dolan	N. Leitrim	Nat.	Ind. Nat.	No
4	May	09	T. Kincaid-Smith	Stratford-on-Avon	Lib.	Ind.	No
26	Nov	12	G. Lansbury	Bow and Bromley	Lab.	Ind.	No
18	Feb	14	W. O'Brien	Cork City	Ind. Nat.	Ind. Nat.	Yes (unop.)
21	Jul	14	R. Hazleton	N. Galway	Nat.	Nat.	Yes (unop.)
29	Nov	26	J. Kenworthy	Hull C.	Lib.	Lab.	Yes
28	Mar	27	L. Guest	Southwark N.	Lab.	Const.	No
31	Jul	29	Sir W. Jowitt	Preston	Lib.	Lab.	Yes
21	Dec	38	Dss of Atholl	Kinross & W. Perth	Con.	Ind.	No
26	May	55[a]	Sir R. Acland	Gravesend	Lab.	Ind.	No
1	Mar	73	D. Taverne	Lincoln	Lab.	Dem. Lab.	Yes
3	Jun	82	B. Douglas-Mann	Mitcham & Morden	Lab.	Ind. SDP	No

[a] Date of General Election which overtook the by-election.

Some members have been compelled to seek re-election because they inadvertently held a government contract or appointment, or because they voted before taking the oath. This last happened in 1925.

Until the Re-election of Ministers Acts of 1919 and 1926 there were many cases of members having to seek re-election on appointment to ministerial office. In eight instances they were unsuccessful:

5 Apr	05	G. Loder	Brighton
24 Apr	08	W. Churchill	Manchester N.W.
20 Dec	11	A. Anderson	N. Ayrshire
5 Mar	12	Sir A. Haworth	Manchester S.
19 Feb	14	C. Masterman	Bethnal Green S.W.
23 May	14		Ipswich
3 Mar	21	Sir A. Griffith-Boscawen	Dudley
25 Jul	22	T. Lewis	Pontypridd

The following ministers, defeated in a general election, stayed in office until a subsequent by-election.

	Successful in by-election and continued in office		*Defeated in by-election and resigned office*
1910 Jan	J. Seely	1922	Sir A. Griffith-Boscawen
1910 Jan	J. Pease	1922	J. Hills
1910 Dec	C. Masterman[a]	1922	G. Stanley
1935	R. Macdonald	1964	P. Gordon Walker
1935	M. Macdonald		
1950	Sir F. Soskice		

[a] Unseated on petition Jun 11 but won by-election Jul 1911.

In 1959 J. Browne, a Scottish Office minister, was defeated in the general election but was given a peerage (Ld Craigton) and stayed in office.

In 1983 H. Gray, an energy minister, was defeated in the general election but was given a peerage (Ld Gray of Contin) and stayed in office.

See also p. 85 for Cabinet Ministers defeated in General Elections.

Electoral Administration

From 1900 to 1918 electoral arrangements were governed primarily by the *Representation of the People Act, 1867, as modified by the Ballot Act, 1872*, the *Corrupt Practices Act*, 1883, the *Franchise Act*, 1884, the *Registration Act, 1885*, and the *Redistribution of Seats Act*, 1885. The *Representation of the People Act, 1918*, the *Equal Franchise Act, 1928*, and the *Representation of the People Act, 1948* (consolidated in 1949), constitute the only major legislation in the century.

There have been seven major inquiries into electoral questions:

1908-10	Royal Commission on Electoral Systems
1917	Speaker's Conference on Electoral Reform
1930	Ullswater Conference on Electoral Reform
1934-44	Speaker's Conference on Electoral Reform
1965-68	Speaker's Conference on Electoral Law
1972-74	Speaker's Conference on Electoral Law
1977-78	Speaker's Conference on Electoral Law

The Franchise. From 1885 the United Kingdom had a system of fairly widespread male franchise, limited however by a year's residence qualification and some other restrictions. Voting in more than one constituency was permitted to owners of land, to occupiers of business premises, and to university graduates. The *Representation of the People Act, 1918,* reduced the residence qualification to six months and enfranchised some categories of men who had not previously had the vote. It also enfranchised women over 30. In 1928 the *Equal Franchise Act* lowered the voting age for women to 21. In 1948 the *Representation of the People Act* abolished the business and university votes for parliamentary elections; it also abolished the six months' residence qualification.

In 1969 the *Representation of the People Act* provided votes for everyone as soon as they reached the age of 18.

Electorate

Year	Population	Population over 21	Electorate	Electorate as % of Adult Population[a]	
				Male	Total
1900	41,155,000	22,675,000	6,730,935	58	27
1910	44,915,000	26,134,000	7,694,741	58	28
1919	44,599,000	27,364,000	21,755,583	. .	78
1929	46,679,000	31,711,000	28,850,870	. .	90
1939	47,762,000	32,855,000	32,403,559	. .	97
1949	50,363,000	35,042,000	34,269,770	. .	98
1959	52,157,000	35,911,000	35,397,080	. .	99
1965	54,606,000	36,837,000	36,128,387	. .	98
1970	55,700,000	40,784,000[b]	39,153,000	. .	96
1979	55,822,000	42,100,000[b]	41,769,000	. .	99
1983	56,377,000	41,300,000[b]	42,197,344	. .	102

[a] This percentage makes allowance for plural voting. In the period before 1914 this amounted to about 500,000. After 1918 the business vote reached its peak in 1929 at 370,000. The university electorate rose from 39,101 in 1900 to 217,363 in 1945. See J. Todd and P. Butcher, *Electoral Registration 1981* (1982) for an estimate of the efficiency of the registration process.

[b] Population over 18.

Redistribution. The *Redistribution of Seats Act, 1885,* left the House of Commons with 670 members. The 1885 Act, while removing the worst anomalies, specifically rejected the principle that constituencies should be approximately equal in size. This principle was, however, substantially accepted in the *Representation of the People Act, 1918,* on the recommendation of the Speaker's Conference of 1917, although Wales, Scotland and Ireland were allowed to retain disproportionate numbers of seats. The 1918 Act increased the size of the House of Commons to 707 but this fell to 615 in 1922 on the creation of the Irish Free State. Population movements produced substantial anomalies in representation and the *Redistribution of Seats Act, 1944,* authorised the immediate subdivision of constituencies with more than 100,000 electors, which led to 25 new seats being created at the 1945 election and raised the size of Parliament to 640. It also provided for the establishment of Permanent Boundary Commissioners to report every three to seven years. The Boundary Commissioners' first recommendations were enacted in the *Representation of the People Act, 1948* (with the controversial addition by the Government of 17 extra seats as well as the abolition of the 12 University seats), and the 1950 Parliament had 625 members. The next reports of the Boundary Commissioners, given effect by resolutions of the House in December 1954 and January 1955, increased the number of constituencies to 630. The controversy caused by these changes led to the *Redistribution of Seats Act, 1958*, which modified the rules governing the Boundary Commissioners' decisions and asked them to report only every 10 to 15 years. The Boundary Commissioners started their revision in 1965; they reported in 1969, but the Labour Government secured the temporary rejection of their proposals. In November 1970 the Conservative Government gave effect to the 1969 proposals. The House of Commons elected in 1974 therefore had 635 constituencies. In 1977 the Boundary Commissioners began work on a fresh general revision of boundaries and in February 1978 a Speaker's Conference recommended that the representation of Northern Ireland should be increased from 12 to 17 seats. An Act authorising the Boundary Commissioners to proceed on this basis was passed in March 1979. In 1983 the general revision resulted in a House of Commons of 650.

Election Expenses

Candidates' expenses were restricted by the *Corrupt Practices Act, 1883*, on a formula based on the number of electors. Candidates still had to bear the administrative costs of the election. The *Representation of the People Act, 1918*, removed from the candidates responsibility for the Returning Officers' fees and lowered the maximum limits on expenditure. This limit was further reduced by the *Representation of the People Act, 1948*, and only slightly increased by the *Representation of the People Act, 1969*; in February 1974 the *Representation of the People Act, 1974*, provided a further increase. In the following table the effect of variations in the number of unopposed candidates should be borne in mind (unopposed candidates seldom spent as much as £200). It is notable how the modifications in the law have kept electioneering costs stable despite a fivefold depreciation in the value of money and a fivefold increase in the size of the electorate.

Candidates' Election Expenses

Year	Total Expenditure £	Candidates	Average per Candidate £	Con.	Lib.	Lab.
1900	777,429	1,002	776	731	831	419
1906	1,166,858	1,273	917	. .	. .	. .
1910 Jan	1,295,782	1,315	985	1,109	1,075	881
1910 Dec	978,312	1,191	821	918	882	736
1918	No pub. returns	1,625	. .	. .	. .	. .
1922	1,018,196	1,443	706	. .	. .	540
1923	982,340	1,446	679	845	789	464
1924	921,165	1,428	645	. .	. .	436
1929	1,213,507	1,730	701	905	782	452
1931	654,105	1,292	506	. .	. .	. .
1935	722,093	1,348	536	777	495	365
1945	1,073,216	1,682	638	780	532	595
1950	1,170,124	1,868	626	777	459	694
1951	946,018	1,376	688	773	488	658
1955	904,677	1,409	642	692	423	611
1959	1,051,219	1,536	684	761	532	705
1964	1,229,205	1,757	699	790	579	751
1966	1,130,882	1,707	667	766	501	726
1970	1,392,796	1,786	761	949	828	667
1974 Feb	1,780,542	2,135	951	1,197	745	1,127
1974 Oct	2,168,514	2,252	963	1,275	725	1,163
1979	3,557,441	2,576	1,381	2,190	1,013	1,897
1983	6,145,264	2,579	2,383	3,320	2,520	2,927

These figures are based on the official returns from the candidates. What constitutes an election expense is a matter of judgement, particularly since there have been no petitions to test the law on expenses since 1929. Party headquarters have provided separate estimates of the amount spent centrally in general elections. (See also pp. 139 and 157.)

	Con.	Lab.
	£	£
1959	974,000	541,000
1964	992,000	314,000
1970	630,000	525,000
1974 Feb	680,000	437,000
1974 Oct	950,000	521,000
1979	2,300,000	1,038,000
1983	3,800,000	2,258,000

European Referendum Expenses

In the 1975 Referendum each side was awarded £125,000 from public funds on condition that they published their accounts from 27 Mar 1975 onwards. Britain in Europe, the pro-Market 'umbrella organisation', reported an outlay of £1,481,583. On the other side the National Referendum Campaign reported £131,354. It has been estimated that Britain in Europe actually spent £1,850,000 in all.

SOURCES.—*Accounts of Campaigning Organisations* (Cmnd 6251); D. Butler and U. Kitzinger, *The 1975 Referendum* (1976) pp. 84-6; M. Pinto-Duschinsky, *British Political Finance 1830-1980* (1981).

Lost Deposits

The Representation of the People Act provided that any Parliamentary candidate would have to deposit, on nomination, £150 in cash with the returning officer. This money would be forfeit to the state unless the candidate received one-eighth of the valid votes cast. The number of deposits lost in general elections has been as follows:

	Con.	Lab.	Lib. (Alln.)	Comm.	Other	Total	% of candidates
1918	3	6	44	—	108	161	9·9
1922	1	7	31	1	12	52	3·6
1923	—	17	8	—	2	27	1·9
1924	1	28	30	1	8	68	4·7
1929	18	35	25	21	14	113	6·5
1931	—	21	6	21	37	85	6·6
1935	1	16	40	—	24	81	6·0
1945	5	2	76	12	87	182	10·8
1950	5	0	319	97	40	461	24·6
1951	3	1	66	10	16	96	7·0
1955	3	1	60	15	21	100	7·1
1959	2	1	55	17	41	116	7·6
1964	5	8	52	36	85	186	10·6
1966	9	3	104	57	64	237	13·9
1970	10	6	184	58	150	408	22·2
1974 Feb	8	25	23	43	222	321	15·0
1974 Oct	28	13	125	29	247	442	19·6
1979	3	22	303	38	635	1,001	38·1
1983	5	119	10	35	570	739	28·7
All General Elections	110	331	1,561	491	2,383	4,876	14·7
By-elections 1918-83	21	16	94	37	400	568	22·1
Low deposits 1918-83	131	347	1,655	528	2,783	5,444	15·3

Women Candidates and M.P.s

	Conservative		Labour		Liberal (Alln.)		Other		Total	
	Cands.	M.P.s	Cands.	M.P.s	Cands.	M.P.s	Cands.	M.P.s	Cands.	M.P.s
1918	1	. .	4	. .	4	. .	8	1	17	1
1922	5	1	10	. .	16	1	2	. .	33	2
1923	7	3	14	3	12	2	1	. .	34	8
1924	12	3	22	1	6	. .	1	. .	41	4
1929	10	3	30	9	25	1	4	1	69	14
1931	16	13	36	. .	6	1	4	1	62	15
1935	19	6	35	1	11	1	2	1	67	9
1945	14	1	45	21	20	1	8	1	87	24
1950	28	6	42	14	45	1	11	. .	126	21
1951	29	6	39	11	11	. .	. .	. .	74	17
1955	32	10	43	14	12	. .	2	. .	89	24
1959	28	12	36	13	16	. .	1	. .	81	25
1964	24	11	33	18	25	. .	8	. .	90	29
1966	21	7	30	19	20	. .	9	. .	80	26
1970	26	15	29	10	23	. .	21	1	99	26
1974 Feb	33	9	40	13	40	. .	30	1	143	23
1974 Oct	30	7	50	18	49	. .	32	2	161	27
1979	31	8	52	11	51	. .	76	. .	210	19
1983	40	13	78	10	(115)	. .	87	. .	280	23

SOURCE.—F. W. S. Craig, *British Electoral Facts* (2nd ed., 1985).

Election Petitions

There have been 17 instances of election petitions leading to the original result being disallowed by the courts.

Jul	00	Maidstone (bribery by agent)	Dec	10	Hull C. (treating)
Jul	00	Monmouth (false expense statement)	Dec	10	N. Louth (irregular accounts)
Jan	06	Worcester (bribery)	Dec	10	W. Ham N. (irregular accounts)
Jan	06	Bodmin (treating by candidate)	Nov	22	Berwick on Tweed (false expense return)
Jan	10	E. Dorset (undue influence)			
Jan	10	E. Kerry (intimidation)	Dec	23	Oxford (false expense return)
Jan	10	Hartlepools (undue influence)	May	55	Fermanagh and S. Tyrone (candidate a felon)
Dec	10	Cheltenham (irregular accounts)			
Dec	10	E. Cork (treating)	Aug	55	Mid-Ulster (candidate a felon)
Dec	10	Exeter (disallowed votes)	May	61	Bristol S.E. (candidate a peer)

On 19 Oct 50 the House of Commons decided that the seat at West Belfast stood vacant because the successful candidate was ineligible as a minister of the Church of Ireland.

On 20 Jul 55 the House of Commons declared the Mid-Ulster seat vacant because the successful candidate was a felon; the same candidate was re-elected in the ensuing by-election; the defeated Unionist successfully petitioned for the seat as the only eligible candidate. However on 6 Feb 56 the seat was again declared vacant, as the Unionist too was found ineligible through holding an office of profit under the Crown.

Since 1918 there have been only two unsuccessful election petitions—by the defeated Conservative candidate in Plymouth, Drake, in 1929 and by Sir O. Mosley in Kensington North in 1959.

Sources on Electoral Matters

Official returns, listing candidates' votes and expenses, have been published as Parliamentary Papers about one year after every General Election, except 1918: *1901 (352) lix, 145; 1906 (302) xcvi, 19; 1910 (259) lxxiii, 705; 1911 (272) lxii, 701; 1924 (2) xviii, 681; 1924-5 (151) xviii, 775; 1926 (1) xxii, 523; 1929-30 (114) xxiv, 755; 1931-2 (109) xx, 1; 1935-6 (150) xx, 217; 1945-6 (128) xix, 539; 1950 (146) xviii, 311; 1951-2 (210) xxi, 841; 1955 (141) xxxii, 913; 1959-60 (173) xxiv, 1031; 1964-5 (220) xxv, 587; 1966-7 (162) liv, 1; 1970-1 (305) xxii, 41; 1974-5 (69); 1974-5 (478); 1979-80 (374); 1983 (130).*

More usable returns, identifying candidates by party and supplying supplementary data, are to be found in the following works:

Dod's Parliamentary Companion, *Vacher's Parliamentary Companion*, and *Whitaker's Almanack*, all issued annually (or more often).

Parliamentary Poll Book, by F. H. McCalmont (7th ed. 1910). This gives all returns from 1832 to 1910 (Jan). In 1971 it was reprinted and updated to 1918.

Pall Mall Gazette House of Commons, issued in paperback form after each election from 1892 to 1910 (Dec).

The Times House of Commons, issued after every election since 1880 except for 1918 and after 1906, 1922, 1923 and 1924.

The Constitutional Year Book, issued annually from 1885 to 1939. Up to 1920 it gives all results from 1885. Up to 1930 it gives the results for all post-1918 contests. Thereafter it records the latest four elections.

The Daily Telegraph Gallup Analysis of Election '66 provides an exhaustive statistical comparison of the 1964 and 1966 elections.

The most convenient and reliable source of constituency results, giving percentages as well as absolute figures, is provided by F. W. S. Craig in *British Parliamentary Election Results 1885-1918* (1973), *British Parliamentary Election Results 1918-1949* (1969), *British Parliamentary Election Results 1950-1970* (1971) and *Britain Votes III* (1984) and *Europe Votes II* (1985). All by-election results are listed in C. Cook and J. Ramsden (eds.), *By-elections in British Politics* (1973).

The 1975 Referendum results are set out in Cmnd 6105/1975.

From 1945, the results of each election have been analysed in statistical appendices to the Nuffield College series of studies, *The British General Election of 1945* (1947), by R. B. McCallum and Alison Readman, *The British General Election of 1950* (1951), by H. G. Nicholas, *The British General Election of 1951* (1952), by D. E. Butler, *The British General Election of 1955* (1955), by D. E. Butler, *The British General Election of 1959* (1960), by D. E. Butler and Richard Rose, *The British General Election of 1964* (1965), by D. E. Butler and Anthony King, *The British General Election of 1966* (1966), by D. E. Butler and Anthony King, *The British General Election of 1970* (1971), by D. E. Butler and M. Pinto-Duschinsky, *The British General Election of February 1974* (1974), by D. E. Butler and D. Kavanagh, *The British General Election of October 1974* (1975), by D. E. Butler and D. Kavanagh, *The British General Election of 1974* by D. E. Butler and D. Kavanagh, *The British General Election of 1983*, by D. E. Butler and D. Kavanagh, *The 1975 Referendum* (1975), by D. E. Butler and U. W. Kitzinger. See also A. K. Russell, *Liberal Landslide: The General Election of 1906* (1973) and N. Blewett, *The Peers, the Parties and the People; The General Elections of* 1910 (1972). For 1983 see also R. Waller, *The Almanack of British Politics* (2nd ed 1984) and I. Crewe and A. Fox, *British Parliamentary Constituencies: A Statistical Compendium* (1984).

Further data is to be found in *The Electoral System in Britain since 1918*, by D. E. Butler (2nd ed. 1963), *Parliamentary Representation*, by J. F. S. Ross (2nd ed. 1948) and *Elections and Electors*, by J. F. S. Ross (1955); *Elections in Britain*, by R. Leonard (1968); *Parliamentary Election Statistics 1918-1970*, by F. W. S. Craig (1970); *The British Voter 1885-1966*, by M. Kinnear (1968); and *Social Geography of British Elections 1885-1910*, by H. Pelling (1967). See also the *Report of the Royal Commission on Electoral Systems* (*Cd. 5163/1910)*; evidence *Cd. 5352/1910.*

Census data arranged on a constituency basis is available for 1966 in *Census* 1966; *General and Parliamentary Constituency Tables* (1969), and for 1971 in *Census 1971: General and Parliamentary Constituency Tables* (1974), and in *Census 1981: General and Parliamentary Constituency Tables* (1983).

The problems of electoral administration are also dealt with in the reports of the Speaker's Conferences on Electoral Reform of 1917, 1944, 1966, 1972-4 and 1977-8 and the Ullswater Conference of 1930 (*Cmnd. 8463/1917*; *Cmnd. 3636/1930*; *Cmnd. 6534* and *6543/1944*, *Cmnd. 2917* and *2932/1966*, *Cmnd. 3202* and *3275/1967*, *Cmnd. 3550/1968*, *Cmnd. 5363/1973*, *Cmnd. 5547/1974* (minutes of evidence are available for the 1972-3 and 1977-8 Speaker's Conferences), *Cmnd. 7110/1978* and in the reports of the Boundary Commissioners (*Cmnd. 7260, 7274, 7270, 7231 of 1947*, *Cmnd. 9311-4 of 1954* and *Cmnd. 4084-7 of 1969)*. See also H. L. Morris, *Parliamentary Franchise Reform in England from 1885 to 1918* (New York 1921), D. E. Butler, 'The Redistribution of Seats', *Public Administration*, Summer 1955, pp. 125-47, and F. W. S. Craig, *Boundaries of Parliamentary Constituencies 1885-1972* (1972).

Public Opinion Polls

Gallup Poll

The British Institute of Public Opinion was established in 1937. Its name was changed in 1952 to Social Surveys (Gallup Poll) Ltd. Its poll findings were published exclusively in the *News Chronicle* until October 1960. Since 1961 its findings have been published regularly in the *Daily Telegraph* and the *Sunday Telegraph*. As the years advanced, its questions on politics became increasingly systematic and detailed. Some of its early findings are collected in *Public Opinion, 1935-1946*, edited by H. Cantril (1951). Others may be found in the *News Chronicle*, in occasional pamphlets, in *The Gallup International Public Opinion Polls: Great Britain 1937-75*, and in the monthly *Gallup Political Index* available since 1960 from Social Surveys (Gallup Poll) Ltd. (now at 202 Finchley Road, London, N.W.3).

National Opinion Polls (N.O.P.)

National Opinion Polls were established in 1957 as an affiliate of Associated Newspapers Ltd and their address is now Tower House, Southampton Street, London W.C.2. Political findings were published in the *Daily Mail* intermittently until 1961 and then regularly until 1979. Subsequently they have been published intermittently in the *Daily Mail* and the *Mail on Sunday*. In October 1963 N.O.P. switched from quota to random sampling for its regular polls with a sample size of approximately 2,000. Findings from the regular political surveys and from other *ad hoc* political opinion polls are published in the N.O.P. Social Political and Economic Review bimonthly.

Marplan Ltd

Marplan (present address 5-13 Great Suffolk Street, London S.E.1) was founded in 1959 as a subsidiary of Interpublic and later of Research International. It published opinion polls for various newspapers from 1962 onwards. Since 1980 its polls have been reported regularly in the *Guardian*.

Opinion Research Centre (O.R.C.)

The Opinion Research Centre was founded in 1965. It has conducted private polls for the Conservative Party ever since. It published a regular monthly poll in the *Evening Standard* and other newspapers from 1967 to 1976. It merged with Louis Harris in 1983 to form the Harris Research Centre.

Louis Harris Research Ltd/Harris Research Centre

In 1969 the *Daily Express* abandoned the poll which since the 1940s it had run from within its own office and joined with the Opinion Research Centre and the American expert Louis Harris in setting up an independent new polling organisation, Louis Harris Research Ltd. In 1972 the *Daily Express* sold its shares. Louis Harris Research Ltd and the Opinion Research Centre share a single Managing Director, and merged with Opinion Research Centre in 1983 to form the Harris Research Centre. In addition to continuing to carry out private polling for the Conservative Party, it also publishes polls in the *Observer* and for *London Weekend* and Thames Television's current affairs programmes. (It is now based at Holbrooke House, Hill Rise, Richmond, Surrey.)

Market and Opinion Research International (M.O.R.I.)

M.O.R.I. (now at 32 Old Queen Street, London S.W.1), under the chairmanship of Robert Worcester, conducted extensive political surveys from 1968, including private studies for the Labour Party. From 1978 it published regular polls in the (*Evening*) *Standard* and *The Sunday Times*, as well as occasional polls for *The Times*, *Daily Express* and *Daily Star*, the *Scotsman*, the *Economist* and the B.B.C.

The following tables show in summary form the answers to the Gallup Poll question 'If there were a General Election tomorrow, how would you vote?' and to questions about approval of the government's record of the Prime Minister and of the Leader of the Opposition, as well as answers to the Party fortunes question 'Regardless of how you are going to vote yourself which party do you think is most likely to win?'

Polls on Voting Intention

Voting Intentions (Gallup Poll)

	Government %	Opposition %	Don't Know %
1939 Feb	50	44	6
1939 Dec	54	30	16
1940 Feb	51	27	22

Party Fortunes (Gallup Poll)

	Voting Intention					Approve Govt Record	Approve P.M.	Approve Opposi-tion Leader	Party thought likely to win	
	Con. %	Lab. %	Lib. %	Other %	Don't Know %	%	%	%	Con. %	Lab. %
1945 Jan	—	—	—	—	—	—	—	—	—	—
Feb	27	47	12	12	12	—	—	—	22	33
Mar	—	—	—	—	—	—	—	—	—	—
Apr	28	47	14	11	15	—	—	—	—	—
May	—	—	—	—	—	—	—	—	—	—
Jun	32	45	15	8	n.a.	—	—	—	—	—
Jul	—	—	—	—	—	—	—	—	—	—
Aug	—	—	—	—	—	—	66	—	—	—
Sep	—	—	—	—	—	—	—	—	—	—
Oct	—	—	—	—	—	57	—	—	—	—
Nov	—	—	—	—	—	—	—	—	—	—
Dec	—	—	—	—	—	—	—	—	—	—
1946 Jan	32	52	11	4	7	—	—	—	—	—
Feb	—	—	—	—	—	—	—	—	—	—
Mar	—	—	—	—	—	—	—	—	—	—
Apr	—	—	—	—	—	—	—	—	—	—
May	40	43	13	3	8	—	—	—	—	—
Jun	—	—	—	—	—	42	—	—	—	—
Jul	—	—	—	—	—	42	—	—	—	—
Aug	—	—	—	—	—	46	—	—	—	—
Sep	—	—	—	—	—	—	—	—	—	—
Oct	—	—	—	—	—	44	53	—	—	—
Nov	—	—	—	—	—	—	—	—	—	—
Dec	—	—	—	—	—	43	52	—	—	—

Party Fortunes (Gallup Poll)

		Voting Intention					Approve Govt Record	Approve P.M.	Approve Opposition Leader	Party thought likely to win	
		Con. %	Lab. %	Lib. %	Other %	Don't Know %	%	%	%	Con. %	Lab. %
1947	Jan	41	44	12	2	8	—	—	—	—	—
	Feb	—	—	—	—	—	—	—	—	—	—
	Mar	43	43	10	2	13	39	46	—	—	—
	Apr	—	—	—	—	—	—	—	—	—	—
	May	—	—	—	—	—	—	51	—	—	—
	Jun	42	42	12	2	11	42	—	—	—	—
	Jul	42	42	12	2	11	38	51	—	32	46
	Aug	44	41	11	3	17	—	—	—	—	—
	Sep	44	39	11	4	12	—	—	—	—	—
	Oct	—	—	—	—	—	36	41	—	—	—
	Nov	50.5	38	9	2	13	—	—	—	—	—
	Dec	—	—	—	—	—	41	44	—	—	—
1948	Jan	44	43	10	1	15	44	45	—	—	—
	Feb	46	42	8	3	17	—	—	—	—	—
	Mar	46	43	8	2	17	35	39	—	—	—
	Apr	42	41	10	6	15	—	—	—	—	—
	May	45	41	11	2	18	—	—	—	—	—
	Jun	—	—	—	—	—	—	—	—	—	—
	Jul	48	39	9	3	12	36	40	—	36	42
	Aug	48	41	8	2	17	—	—	—	—	—
	Sep	47	41	10	1	20	37	37	—	—	—
	Oct	46	41	9	2	18	—	—	—	—	—
	Nov	46	43	8	2	17	43	45	—	—	—
	Dec	—	—	—	—	—	—	—	—	—	—
1949	Jan	44	40	13	2	14	44	45	—	—	—
	Feb	44	43	9	2	15	—	—	—	—	—
	Mar	41	43	13	2	14	46	47	—	—	—
	Apr	42	43	13	1	15	—	—	—	—	—
	May	46	40	11	3	15	37	44	—	—	—
	Jun	46	41	10	2	18	—	—	—	—	—
	Jul	44	40	12	2	13	39	46	—	—	—
	Aug	46	40	11	1	14	—	—	—	—	—
	Sep	46	40	12	2	15	36	45	—	30	46
	Oct	45	39	12	2	19	—	—	—	—	—
	Nov	43	40	14	2	13	39	43	—	—	—
	Dec	45	41	12	1	13	—	—	—	—	—
1950	Jan	44	41	12	2	7	41	44	—	—	—
	Feb	43	44	12	—	11	—	—	—	20	40
	Mar	43	45	8	2	8	—	—	—	—	—
	Apr	45	47	7	—	9	—	—	—	—	—
	May	43	46	9	—	9	41	50	—	—	—
	Jun	43	46	9	1	9	—	—	—	—	—
	Jul	42	43	11	3	10	—	—	—	—	—
	Aug	44	46	8	1	9	44	49	—	—	—
	Sep	43	45	10	1	12	—	—	—	—	—
	Oct	42	45	10	2	11	45	47	—	—	—
	Nov	—	—	—	—	—	—	—	—	—	—
	Dec	43	44	11	1	12	38	49	—	—	—

Party Fortunes (Gallup Poll)

		Voting Intention					Approve Govt Record	Approve P.M.	Approve Opposition Leader	Party thought likely to win	
		Con. %	Lab. %	Lib. %	Other %	Don't Know %	%	%	%	Con. %	Lab. %
1951	Jan	51	38	10	1	13	—	—	—	—	—
	Feb	51	37	9	1	12	31	44	—	—	—
	Mar	51	36	10	2	14	—	—	—	—	—
	Apr	50	38	9	2	13	32	49	—	—	—
	May	49	40	9	1	13	35	57	—	—	—
	Jun	48	41	10	1	12	—	—	—	—	—
	Jul	49	39	10	—	13	31	43	—	—	—
	Aug	50	38	10	1	11	—	—	—	45	32
	Sep	52	41	6	—	11	35	44	—	44	30
	Oct	50	44	4	1	11	—	—	—	45	29
	Nov	—	—	—	—	—	—	—	—	—	—
	Dec	47	45	6	1	—	44	55	—	—	—
1952	Jan	44	48	6	1	10	—	—	—	—	—
	Feb	41	47	10	1	14	44	53	—	—	—
	Mar	41	48	9	1	9	—	—	—	—	—
	Apr	—	—	—	—	—	—	—	—	—	—
	May	43	49	7	—	—	40	51	—	—	—
	Jun	40	49	9	1	6	—	—	—	16	63
	Jul	40	50	8	1	—	—	—	—	—	—
	Aug	40	48	6	5	8	—	—	—	—	—
	Sep	41	48	9	1	9	44	48	—	25	55
	Oct	41	48	9	1	11	—	—	—	—	—
	Nov	43	46	9	1	12	47	51	—	—	—
	Dec	44	45	9	1	11	51	—	—	—	—
1953	Jan	42	46	10	1	11	46	51	—	—	—
	Feb	42	46	10	1	11	—	—	—	—	—
	Mar	46	44	8	1	11	—	—	—	—	—
	Apr	47	45	7	—	13	60	—	—	—	—
	May	47	45	7	—	12	—	—	—	38	40
	Jun	46	46	7	1	11	—	—	—	—	—
	Jul	—	—	—	—	—	—	—	—	—	—
	Aug	45	46	8	1	13	49	—	—	—	—
	Sep	44	47	7	1	12	—	—	—	43	35
	Oct	45	45	7	—	11	54	56	—	—	—
	Nov	—	—	—	—	—	—	—	—	—	—
	Dec	45	47	7	1	12	—	—	—	—	—
1954	Jan	45	46	7	1	14	50	—	—	—	—
	Feb	45	47	7	—	13	50	—	—	36	34
	Mar	46	45	7	1	12	—	—	—	—	—
	Apr	46	46	7	—	13	—	48	—	—	—
	May	45	47	6	—	12	—	—	—	—	—
	Jun	45	47	7	—	12	47	—	—	—	—
	Jul	—	—	—	—	—	—	—	—	—	—
	Aug	42	48	8	1	11	—	—	—	—	—
	Sep	43	48	8	1	11	—	—	—	33	39
	Oct	45	45	8	1	16	—	—	—	—	—
	Nov	46	47	6	1	15	—	—	—	44	26
	Dec	49	49	2	—	13	—	—	—	—	—

Party Fortunes (Gallup Poll)

		Voting Intention					Approve Govt Record	Approve P.M.	Approve Opposition Leader	Party thought likely to win	
		Con. %	Lab. %	Lib. %	Other %	Don't Know %	%	%	%	Con. %	Lab. %
1955	Jan	46	45	7	1	14	53	52	—	—	—
	Feb	46	44	8	1	13	—	—	—	—	—
	Mar	46	44	8	1	13	—	—	—	—	—
	Apr	48	44	7	1	14	—	73	—	52	22
	May	51	47	2	—	12	57	71	—	54	18
	Jun	—	—	—	—	—	—	—	—	—	—
	Jul	47	43	9	1	11	—	68	—	—	—
	Aug	44	47	7	1	14	—	—	—	—	—
	Sep	48	44	7	1	10	—	70	—	—	—
	Oct	46	44	8	1	13	—	63	—	—	—
	Nov	44	45	9	1	12	—	61	—	—	—
	Dec	45	46	7	—	12	44	60	—	—	—
1956	Jan	45	46	7	—	12	—	—	—	—	—
	Feb	44	46	9	1	12	—	50	—	—	—
	Mar	44	47	7	1	19	34	45	—	—	—
	Apr	43	48	8	1	17	—	41	—	—	—
	May	43	47	9	1	15	40	54	42	—	—
	Jun	—	—	—	—	—	—	—	—	—	—
	Jul	42	49	8	1	14	36	50	46	—	—
	Aug	43	49	6	1	16	—	—	—	—	—
	Sep	43	46	10	—	15	—	51	53	—	—
	Oct	42	47	9	1	15	—	47	—	—	—
	Nov	45	46	8	—	17	—	52	44	—	—
	Dec	45	46	8	1	15	—	56	—	—	—
1957	Jan	43	48	7	1	10	—	50	—	—	—
	Feb	42	48	8	1	19	—	—	—	—	—
	Mar	40	51	7	1	21	—	45	—	—	—
	Apr	41	51	7	1	14	—	44	—	—	—
	May	41	50	7	1	16	—	54	41	—	—
	Jun	—	—	—	—	—	—	—	—	—	—
	Jul	41	49	8	1	16	—	—	—	—	—
	Aug	40	48	10	1	17	—	—	—	—	—
	Sep	33	52	14	—	25	—	44	39	24	51
	Oct	37	49	13	1	16	37	30	—	—	—
	Nov	38	49	12	—	19	—	39	—	—	—
	Dec	41	47	9	1	16	—	—	—	26	46
1958	Jan	40	47	12	—	17	38	46	40	—	—
	Feb	36	44	18	1	19	—	35	—	—	—
	Mar	—	—	—	—	—	—	—	—	—	—
	Apr	38	46	15	—	18	30	37	—	—	—
	May	34	47	19	—	18	30	37	—	—	—
	Jun	39	43	17	—	13	40	50	—	—	—
	Jul	—	—	—	—	—	41	—	37	—	—
	Aug	42	42	15	—	14	41	53	—	40	31
	Sep	44	43	13	—	17	43	55	32	—	—
	Oct	45	41	12	1	15	47	57	41	44	29
	Nov	46	42	10	1	15	48	55	42	—	—
	Dec	47	42	9	1	15	50	55	45	43	28

Party Fortunes (Gallup Poll)

		Voting Intention								Party thought likely to win	
		Con. %	Lab. %	Lib. %	Other %	Don't Know %	Approve Govt Record %	Approve P.M. %	Approve Opposition Leader %	Con. %	Lab. %
1959	Jan	45	45	8	1	19	48	53	47	39	28
	Feb	43	47	8	1	22	41	54	43	—	—
	Mar	45	47	6	1	22	44	57	46	—	—
	Apr	44	44	10	1	14	46	60	48	—	—
	May	45	44	10	1	14	47	62	47	—	—
	Jun	45	43	11	—	14	49	58	44	—	—
	Jul	45	41	12	—	15	53	62	42	—	—
	Aug	47	41	10	1	13	56	67	46	—	—
	Sep	50	43	5	—	17	—	—	—	56	20
	Oct	48	46	5	1	16	—	—	—	51	21
	Nov	48	44	7	1	11	—	—	—	—	—
	Dec	47	44	7	1	15	—	—	—	—	—
1960	Jan	47	43	8	1	16	—	—	—	—	—
	Feb	47	43	9	—	16	—	64	43	—	—
	Mar	47	42	10	1	17	—	57	40	—	—
	Apr	45	42	11	1	17	—	56	46	—	—
	May	45	42	11	1	15	—	79	47	—	—
	Jun	45	43	10	1	14	—	70	56	—	—
	Jul	47	43	9	1	17	—	65	43	—	—
	Aug	47	42	10	—	16	59	72	48	—	—
	Sep	47	40	11	1	16	59	74	43	—	—
	Oct	50	37	12	—	19	59	72	48	—	—
	Nov	46	40	13	—	14	56	69	44	—	—
	Dec	47	37	14	1	15	—	—	—	—	—
1961	Jan	45	41	12	1	19	59	72	35	—	—
	Feb	44	42	13	1	18	48	64	45	—	—
	Mar	44	40	15	1	12	51	63	45	—	—
	Apr	43	40	15	1	18	50	64	43	—	—
	May	44	40	14	1	18	49	58	45	—	—
	Jun	43	40	15	1	16	52	58	45	—	—
	Jul	44	41	14	—	18	49	54	51	—	—
	Aug	38	43	17	2	17	38	45	47	—	—
	Sep	40	45	13	1	18	39	43	46	—	—
	Oct	43	43	12	1	14	47	55	57	—	—
	Nov	41	43	14	1	17	43	54	42	—	—
	Dec	38	43	17	1	20	—	—	—	—	—
1962	Jan	42	42	15	1	18	43	53	50	—	—
	Feb	40	42	17	—	18	41	48	45	51	23
	Mar	39	44	16	—	18	41	50	50	41	17
	Apr	33	41	25	1	12	37	46	48	—	—
	May	34	39	25	—	17	38	47	48	36	36
	Jun	35	39	25	—	14	37	46	48	31	42
	Jul	35	41	22	1	14	41	47	47	28	42
	Aug	34	43	22	1	13	37	42	47	—	—
	Sep	34	45	20	1	15	38	42	51	30	39
	Oct	34	43	20	2	17	36	43	54	37	37
	Nov	39	47	13	1	16	41	47	51	29	42
	Dec	37	46	16	1	17	36	41	52	—	—

Party Fortunes (Gallup Poll)

		Voting Intention					Approve Govt Record	Approve P.M.	Approve Opposition Leader	Party thought likely to win	
		Con. %	Lab. %	Lib. %	Other %	Don't Know %	%	%	%	Con. %	Lab. %
1963	Jan	35	48	16	—	8	34	42	49	—	—
	Feb	32	48	18	1	8	34	40	—	—	—
	Mar	33	50	15	1	9	30	35	44	26	52
	Apr	34	49	16	—	10	33	35	52	24	55
	May	36	47	16	1	10	38	41	53	25	57
	Jun	31	51	16	1	8	31	35	54	17	58
	Jul	33	51	14	1	12	32	37	57	16	68
	Aug	34	50	15	1	11	39	42	59	22	55
	Sep	33	49	16	1	10	38	40	56	23	55
	Oct	36	48	14	1	11	36	41	60	23	55
	Nov	37	49	12	1	10	44	42	67	30	53
	Dec	39	47	13	—	11	46	48	65	28	48
1964	Jan	39	47	13	—	10	41	43	63	29	45
	Feb	39	48	12	1	9	42	42	62	27	57
	Mar	39	48	12	—	9	41	44	64	31	47
	Apr	38	50	10	—	8	46	44	61	23	58
	May	39	50	10	—	7	41	44	62	21	65
	Jun	41	50	8	—	7	45	44	62	22	61
	Jul	40	49	9	—	6	43	46	56	26	56
	Aug	43	49	7	—	8	48	46	61	32	48
	Sep	44	47	8	—	7	42	47	58	41	38
	Oct	44	46	8	3	—	—	—	35	39	—
	Nov	38	50	11	—	7	49	60	39	—	—
	Dec	40	50	9	—	6	48	64	41	—	—
1965	Jan	42	46	10	—	8	39	56	38	27	46
	Feb	45	45	9	—	6	43	60	37	49	28
	Mar	43	46	9	1	8	47	58	38	41	34
	Apr	39	47	12	—	9	45	63	34	41	38
	May	44	43	12	—	9	39	56	36	40	34
	Jun	47	42	9	1	9	35	48	36	52	23
	Jul	46	45	8	—	10	36	51	32	44	30
	Aug	49	41	8	1	10	39	50	51	57	24
	Sep	42	48	8	1	6	42	54	49	56	24
	Oct	41	49	9	—	7	49	61	47	39	39
	Nov	42	48	8	1	8	50	65	48	35	44
	Dec	40	48	10	1	7	55	66	43	35	46
1966	Jan	42	47	9	1	8	51	65	48	32	42
	Feb	42	50	7	—	10	48	60	40	20	62
	Mar	40	51	8	1	7	—	—	—	11	69
	Apr	—	—	—	—	—	53	63	39	—	—
	May	35	53	10	1	6	54	69	44	—	—
	Jun	39	52	7	1	7	44	58	33	27	48
	Jul	41	48	8	2	9	42	61	33	25	55
	Aug	44	44	10	1	9	35	52	32	39	41
	Sep	42	45	11	1	8	34	49	37	37	37
	Oct	43	44	11	1	7	32	43	46	37	35
	Nov	44	42	12	1	9	33	46	32	41	34
	Dec	42	46	10	1	6	40	51	35	—	—

Party Fortunes (Gallup Poll)

		Voting Intention					Approve Govt Record	Approve P.M.	Approve Opposition Leader	Party thought likely to win	
		Con. %	Lab. %	Lib. %	Other %	Don't Know %	%	%	%	Con. %	Lab. %
1967	Jan	42	45	10	1	7	40	51	29	—	—
	Feb	37	48	13	1	5	44	57	24	—	—
	Mar	42	42	12	2	9	40	53	26	—	—
	Apr	45	41	11	2	9	44	42	33	—	—
	May	46	40	12	1	8	38	43	35	—	—
	Jun	48	41	9	1	11	36	46	37	—	—
	Jul	43	41	13	2	9	35	48	32	—	—
	Aug	43	42	13	2	11	33	45	28	—	—
	Sep	45	41	10	3	9	29	40	31	—	—
	Oct	45	38	14	3	7	—	38	39	56	19
	Nov	46	36	11	6	9	28	41	44	62	63
	Dec	49	32	12	6	9	21	34	37	—	—
1968	Jan	45	39	11	4	10	23	33	32	—	—
	Feb	52	30	12	5	12	22	36	31	—	—
	Mar	50	31	15	4	13	18	35	29	—	—
	Apr	54	30	12	3	12	17	31	28	78	7
	May	56	28	11	5	13	19	27	31	73	11
	Jun	51	28	14	6	12	19	28	28	—	—
	Jul	50	30	13	7	10	18	30	28	76	13
	Aug	49	34	11	4	11	21	30	27	—	—
	Sep	47	37	11	4	8	24	33	27	—	—
	Oct	47	39	9	4	9	29	38	27	55	25
	Nov	50	32	14	3	9	20	31	37	—	—
	Dec	55	29	11	4	11	17	28	30	—	—
1969	Jan	53	31	11	4	11	23	34	31	—	—
	Feb	54	32	11	2	13	22	32	34	—	—
	Mar	52	34	10	3	11	22	35	31	—	—
	Apr	51	30	13	5	12	21	30	29	—	—
	May	52	30	13	4	13	19	29	28	76	9
	Jun	51	35	12	2	12	24	35	29	—	—
	Jul	55	31	11	2	12	23	30	40	—	—
	Aug	47	34	15	3	12	25	26	29	—	—
	Sep	46	37	13	3	9	29	39	29	—	—
	Oct	46	44	7	2	10	34	43	33	46	33
	Nov	45	41	10	3	9	35	41	33	48	31
	Dec	50	39	9	1	12	31	38	32	54	26
1970	Jan	48	41	7	3	10	32	42	38	54	25
	Feb	48	41	9	2	10	31	42	41	53	24
	Mar	46	41	9	3	10	35	42	39	54	27
	Apr	47	42	7	3	9	40	45	34	47	31
	May	42	49	7	1	8	42	49	28	26	56
	Jun	42	49	7	1	8	40	51	28	13	68
	Jul	—	—	—	—	—	—	—	—	—	—
	Aug	47	43	7	2	9	—	—	—	—	—
	Sep	46	44	8	1	10	21	35	59	—	—
	Oct	46	46	6	—	13	29	42	62	—	—
	Nov	43	48	6	2	12	31	39	66	—	—
	Dec	46	44	6	3	12	37	45	59	—	—

Party Fortunes (Gallup Poll)

		Voting Intention					Approve Govt Record	Approve P.M.	Approve Opposition Leader	Party thought likely to win	
		Con. %	Lab. %	Lib. %	Other %	Dont't Know %	%	%	%	Con. %	Lab. %
1971	Jan	42	47	8	2	10	35	41	61	—	—
	Feb	41	49	8	1	10	31	37	61	—	—
	Mar	38	50	8	3	11	33	38	59	—	—
	Apr	44	48	6	1	10	40	43	57	—	—
	May	38	50	9	2	8	31	35	61	—	—
	Jun	36	54	8	2	11	22	31	58	—	—
	Jul	33	55	8	3	8	36	32	58	—	—
	Aug	42	46	7	2	10	35	37	51	—	—
	Sep	35	54	8	2	10	30	32	57	—	—
	Oct	40	50	8	2	8	32	35	54	—	—
	Nov	42	48	7	2	12	35	38	52	—	—
	Dec	42	48	7	2	13	34	39	54	—	—
1972	Jan	40	48	9	2	11	37	39	54	—	—
	Feb	40	49	8	2	11	34	37	53	23	57
	Mar	39	48	9	2	9	35	36	51	—	—
	Apr	43	44	10	2	10	43	41	39	—	—
	May	40	46	11	2	8	36	39	45	35	40
	Jun	41	47	10	2	9	36	40	44	—	—
	Jul	39	49	9	2	8	31	35	45	—	—
	Aug	40	49	7	3	11	32	35	47	25	56
	Sep	38	49	9	2	9	30	33	43	23	57
	Oct	40	48	8	3	10	33	34	53	28	53
	Nov	37	45	15	2	10	32	37	50	28	52
	Dec	38	46	12	3	11	36	39	44	32	42
1973	Jan	38	44	15	2	11	33	38	40	31	46
	Feb	38	47	12	2	10	33	37	45	46	—
	Mar	39	43	16	2	9	38	41	41	—	—
	Apr	38	41	17	3	11	32	37	41	26	50
	May	38	43	14	4	7	35	38	40	26	51
	Jun	41	42	14	2	10	37	43	41	34	47
	Jul	35	45	17	2	10	31	37	45	22	55
	Aug	31	38	28	2	8	29	34	39	26	47
	Sep	33	43	22	1	9	29	36	42	23	51
	Oct	33	39	25	2	11	30	36	46	29	47
	Nov	36	38	22	2	9	31	39	37	35	36
	Dec	36	42	18	3	10	34	37	31	43	—
1974	Jan	40	38	19	3	10	36	39	38	40	35
	Feb	39	37	20	2	3	32	38	38	60	20
	Mar	35	43	19	3	7	—	—	—	—	—
	Apr	33	49	15	2	7	48	53	38	19	52
	May	33	46	17	3	7	40	50	35	26	48
	Jun	35	44	17	3	9	41	49	36	25	51
	Jul	35	38	21	6	10	32	41	33	32	36
	Aug	35	30	21	4	10	37	44	35	27	44
	Sep	37	40	18	4	10	28	41	29	18	55
	Oct	36	41	19	3	5	37	45	32	18	55
	Nov	35	46	14	4	9	40	50	32	—	—
	Dec	33	47	16	3	10	42	51	31	—	—

Party Fortunes (Gallup Poll)

		Voting Intention					Approve Govt Record	Approve P.M.	Approve Opposition Leader	Party thought likely to win	
		Con. %	Lab. %	Lib. %	Other %	Don't Know %	%	%	%	Con. %	Lab. %
1975	Jan	34	48	13	4	11	37	49	29	—	—
	Feb	45	41	11	3	11	32	47	64	—	—
	Mar	42	44	11	3	7	37	51	60	—	—
	Apr	43	45	10	2	10	32	44	45	—	—
	May	45	39	11	4	11	26	40	41	45	29
	Jun	44	40	13	2	11	31	46	35	44	29
	Jul	43	40	12	4	8	27	46	37	46	28
	Aug	40	42	14	3	8	32	45	37	46	30
	Sep	38	41	16	3	10	30	45	39	44	29
	Oct	42	40	13	3	6	30	46	45	45	32
	Nov	39	44	12	4	11	31	45	42	43	35
	Dec	40	41	14	4	10	27	40	40	45	29
1976	Jan	40	42	14	3	11	29	42	42	45	32
	Feb	45	40	10	3	11	32	45	49	46	30
	Mar	44	41	9	5	9	30	46	43	49	30
	Apr	41	46	9	3	8	39	57	40	44	37
	May	44	41	10	4	11	32	43	36	51	28
	Jun	44	40	11	4	11	28	36	31	48	29
	Jul	41	41	13	5	11	32	46	33	44	32
	Aug	44	41	10	5	12	29	44	33	45	33
	Sep	42	42	11	4	10	29	46	40	44	34
	Oct	48	36	11	4	13	20	36	40	57	20
	Nov	55	30	11	3	9	19	33	41	66	18
	Dec	49	34	11	5	11	18	35	34	62	17
1977	Jan	47	34	14	4	10	21	37	39	57	21
	Feb	46	33	14	6	13	21	36	35	62	18
	Mar	49	33	13	4	10	22	37	35	62	20
	Apr	49	33	11	6	11	23	38	40	67	16
	May	53	33	8	5	10	23	43	45	74	12
	Jun	47	37	10	5	10	28	44	44	69	15
	Jul	49	34	10	6	11	24	45	42	71	13
	Aug	48	37	9	5	11	33	43	45	64	19
	Sep	45	41	8	5	8	32	49	47	54	28
	Oct	45	45	8	2	8	41	59	49	49	31
	Nov	45	42	8	4	10	41	55	47	46	35
	Dec	44	44	8	3	9	41	53	44	48	32
1978	Jan	43	43	8	4	10	43	57	42	46	38
	Feb	48	39	9	4	8	43	54	41	40	40
	Mar	48	41	8	3	9	41	51	45	52	30
	Apr	45	43	7	3	10	44	51	39	45	38
	May	43	43	8	4	9	41	54	40	48	33
	Jun	45	45	6	3	9	40	50	38	39	43
	Jul	45	43	8	3	9	40	52	38	40	42
	Aug	43	47	6	3	11	30	55	35	42	36
	Sep	49	42	6	2	10	39	51	40	42	36
	Oct	42	47	7	3	8	44	56	39	47	35
	Nov	43	48	6	3	11	44	54	33	36	41
	Dec	48	42	6	3	10	37	53	39	41	40

Party Fortunes (Gallup Poll)

		Voting Intention					Approve Govt Record	Approve P.M.	Approve Opposi-tion Leader	Party thought likely to win	
		Con. %	Lab. %	Lib. %	Other %	Don't Know %	%	%	%	Con. %	Lab. %
1979	Jan	49	41	6	3	11	34	48	38	44	35
	Feb	53	33	11	3	11	23	33	48	65	20
	Mar	51	37	8	3	11	27	39	47	61	23
	Apr	50	40	8	2	5	33	43	43	59	23
	May	43	41	13	2	5	—	—	—	—	—
	Jun	42	43	12	2	6	34	41	63	—	—
	Jul	41	46	11	1	8	34	41	61	—	—
	Aug	41	44	12	2	6	38	45	57	—	—
	Sep	40	45	12	2	9	36	45	53	—	—
	Oct	40	45	12	2	9	34	46	57	—	—
	Nov	39	43	15	2	8	38	44	55	—	—
	Dec	38	42	18	2	7	34	40	53	28	44
1980	Jan	36	45	16	3	7	33	39	53	29	45
	Feb	37	42	18	2	10	30	37	50	29	45
	Mar	37	49	11	2	6	30	38	53	27	55
	Apr	36	45	15	3	7	36	41	55	25	52
	May	39	43	15	2	7	37	44	51	24	57
	Jun	40	45	11	3	6	35	43	48	28	54
	Jul	40	43	14	2	8	33	41	46	28	55
	Aug	38	44	14	3	11	35	41	53	28	50
	Sep	35	45	16	3	6	29	37	48	22	58
	Oct	40	43	13	3	8	30	38	48	30	53
	Nov	36	47	15	1	9	29	34	38	22	60
	Dec	35	47	14	3	9	29	35	30	18	67
1981	Jan	33	46	18	2	10	26	31	26	17	65
	Feb	36	35	20	8	11	29	34	22	25	42
					Alliance begins						
	Mar	30	34	32	4	11	23	30	23	17	50
	Apr	30	34	33	2	10	24	30	21	20	44
	May	32	35	29	3	9	29	35	26	18	56
	Jun	29	37	30	2	10	26	33	28	18	60
	Jul	30	40	26	3	10	23	30	25	13	63
	Aug	28	38	32	1	11	23	28	23	18	52
	Sep	32	36	29	2	8	26	32	28	19	46
	Oct	29	28	40	2	9	24	33	27	14	39
	Nov	26	29	42	2	9	23	28	16	17	31
	Dec	23	23	50	3	11	18	25	19	12	23
1982	Jan	27	29	39	3	9	24	32	18	16	27
	Feb	27	34	36	2	10	24	29	19	21	35
	Mar	31	33	33	2	10	29	34	21	32	33
	Apr	31	29	37	2	11	32	35	23	23	27
	May	41	28	29	1	8	42	44	18	43	21
	Jun	45	25	28	1	9	48	51	14	63	13
	Jul	46	27	24	2	7	47	52	16	66	12
	Aug	44	26	27	1	10	42	49	15	58	17
	Sep	44	30	23	2	3	40	48	16	58	19
	Oct	40	29	27	3	8	40	46	20	58	20
	Nov	42	34	21	2	9	39	44	22	55	22
	Dec	41	34	22	2	10	37	44	20	54	25

Party Fortunes (Gallup Poll)

		Voting Intention					Approve Govt Record	Approve P.M.	Approve Opposition Leader	Party thought likely to win	
		Con. %	Lab. %	Alln. %	Other %	Don't Know %	%	%	%	Con. %	Lab. %
1983	Jan	44	31	22	2	9	43	49	17	61	19
	Feb	43	32	22	2	8	39	45	17	62	19
	Mar	39	28	29	3	8	41	47	19	66	11
	Apr	40	35	22	2	9	38	44	21	59	21
	May	49	31	17	2	5	45	50	18	76	11
	Jun	45	26	26	2	2	44	48	17	87	5
	Jul	44	28	26	1	6	46	52	11	49	16
	Aug	44	25	29	1	6	44	51	10	56	10
	Sep	45	24	29	1	6	47	53	9	64	12
	Oct	42	35	20	2	6	41	48	58	48	28
	Nov	43	36	19	1	7	40	49	48	53	26
	Dec	42	36	19	2	6	38	47	40	49	27
1984	Jan	41	38	19	1	7	42	49	43	58	22
	Feb	43	33	21	2	6	41	48	45	59	23
	Mar	41	38	19	1	8	41	46	47	50	35
	Apr	41	36	20		6	42	46	42	52	28
	May	38	36	23	2	6	37	41	42	50	30
	Jun	37	38	23	1	8	36	41	43	49	31
	Jul	37	38	22	2	7	36	41	43	43	37
	Aug	36	39	22	2	8	34	39	37	49	29
	Sep	37	36	25	1	9	34	40	43	54	28
	Oct	44	32	21	2	9	43	50	35	64	19
	Nov	44·5	30·5	23·5	1·5	8	41	48	59	67	17
	Dec	39·5	31	27·5	2	8	34	43	36	67	16
1985	Jan	39	33	25·5	2·5	8	33	40	36	65	16
	Feb	35	32	31·5	1·5	9	31	37	31	63	19
	Mar	33	39·5	25·5	2	8	30	37	37	53	28
	Apr	34	34·5	26·5	2	8·5	32	38	36	54	28
	May	30·5	34	33·5	2	8.5	28	36	38	46	26

Opinion Poll Accuracy in General Elections

The following is a list of all major poll predictions of general election results.

	Actual Result (G.B.)	Gallup	NOP	*Daily Express Poll*	Research Services
1945					
Con	39·5	+1·5			
Lab	49·0	−2·0			
Lib	9·2	+1·3			
1950					
Con	43·1	+0·4		+1·4	
Lab	46·8	−1·8		−2·8	
Lib	9·3	+1·2		+1·7	
1951					
Con	47·8	+1·7		+2·2	+2·2
Lab	49·3	−2·3		−3·3	−6·3
Lib	2·6	+0·4		+0·9	(+4·1)[a]
1955					
Con	49·3	+1·7		+1·9	
Lab	47·3	+0·2		−0·1	
Lib	2·8	−1·3		−0·6	

Actual Result (G.B.)		Gallup	NOP	*Daily Express Poll*	Research Services
1959					
Con	48·8	−0·3	−0·8	+0·3	
Lab	44·6	+1·9	+0·5	+0·8	
Lib	6·1	−1·6	(+2·4)[a]	−1·1	
1964					
Con	42·9	+1·6	+1·4	+1·6	+2·1
Lab	44·8	+1·2	+2·6	−1·1	+1·2
Lib	11·4	−2·9	−3·5	−0·3	−2·4
1966					
Con	41·4	−1·4	+0·2	−4·0	+0·2
Lab	48·7	+2·3	−1·9	+5·9	+1·0
Lib	8·6	−0·6	−1·2	−0·9	−0·3
				Louis Harris	ORC
1970					
Con	46·2	−4·2	−2·2	−0·2	+0·3
Lab	43·8	+5·2	+4·3	+4·2	+1·7
Lib	7·6	−0·1	−1·2	−2·6	−1·1
1974 Feb					
Con	38·6	+0·9	+0·9	+1·6	+1·1
Lab	38·0	−0·5	−2·5	−2·8	−1·3
Lib	19·8	+0·7	+2·2	+1·4	+1·4
Other	3·6	−1·1	−0·6	−0·9	−1·2
1974 Oct					
Con	36·7	−0·7	−5·7	−2·1	−2·3
Lab	40·2	+1·3	+5·3	+2·8	+1·6
Lib	18·8	+0·2	+0·7	+0·5	+0·6
Other	4·3	−0·8	−0·3	−1·2	+0·1
				MORI	
1979					
Con	44·9	−1·9	+1·1	−0·5	
Lab	37·8	+3·2	+1·2	+1·0	
Lib	14·1	−0·6	−1·6	−0·6	
Other	3·2	−0·7	−0·7	+0·1	
1983					
Con	43·5	+2·0	+3.5	+0·3	
Lab	28·3	−1·8	−3·3	−0·3	
Alln	26·0	0·0	0·0	0·0	
Other	2.2	−0·2	−0·2	−0·2	

[a] Error in Liberal and Other vote combined.

In 1970 Marplan (on a U.K. not a G.B. basis) produced a forecast for *The Times* that overestimated Labour's lead by 9·6%.

In Oct 74 a Marplan poll in the *Sun* overestimated Labour's lead by 6·2%. A Business Decisions poll in the *Observer* overestimated Labour's lead by 1·0%.

In 1979 a Marplan poll in the *Sun* underestimated the Conservative lead by 1·1%. A Research Services poll in the *Observer* overestimated the Conservative lead by 4·4%. A separate MORI poll in the *Evening Standard* overestimated the Conservative lead by 0·9%.

The Common Market Referendum on 5 Jun 75 yielded a 67·2% 'yes' vote see p. 229. On that morning the opinion poll forecasts of a 'yes' vote were: Gallup 68%; ORC 73·7%; Louis Harris 72%; Marplan (decided voted) 58% 'yes', 27% 'no'.

SOURCES.—For a comprehensive description of British opinion polling see F. Teer and J. D Spence, *Political Opinion Polls* (1973); see also R. Hodder Williams, *Public Opinion Polls and British Politics* (1970). R. Rose, *The Polls and the 1970 Election* (1970) gives full documentation about the 1970 findings. Each of the Nuffield *British General Election* Series includes analyses of the polls.

V

POLITICAL ALLUSIONS

The student of political history becomes familiar with allusive references to places, events, scandals, phrases and quotations. This chapter attempts to collect the most outstanding of these allusions.

Political Place-names

At one time or another in the twentieth century the following piace-names were sufficiently famous to be alluded to without further explanation. Any such list must necessarily be very selective. No foreign names are included here—even though that means omitting Agadir, Chanak, Munich and Suez. No venues of party conferences are included, even though that means omitting Scarborough (Labour, 1960) and Blackpool (Conservative, 1963). No constituency names are included as such, even though that means omitting some, like Bewdley or Ebbw Vale, which are indelibly associated with individuals and others where sensational elections had a lasting national impact, like Colne Valley (1907), St George's Westminster (1931), East Fulham (1933), Orpington (1962), Smethwick (1964), Lincoln (1973), and Crosby (1981).

Abbey House, Victoria St., S.W.1. Conservative Party Headquarters 1946-58.

Abingdon St., S.W.1. Site of Liberal Party Headquarters 1910-34.

Admiralty House, S.W.1. Apartments of First Lord of Admiralty until 1960. Residence of H. Macmillan during Downing St. repairs 1960-63 and since 1965 of Secretary of State for Defence and other ministers.

Aldermaston, Berkshire. Site of Atomic Weapons Research Establishment. Starting- or finishing-point of the Campaign for Nuclear Disarmament's Easter Marches 1958-63, 1967-.

Ashridge, Herts. Site of Conservative Party College, 1929-39.

Astley Hall. Worcestershire home of S. (Earl) Baldwin 1902-47.

Bachelor's Walk, Dublin. Scene (26 Jul 1914) of disturbance in which soldiers killed three rioters.

Balmoral Castle, Aberdeenshire. Summer home of the Sovereign since 1852.

Birch Grove, Sussex. Home of H. Macmillan 1906-.

Blenheim Palace, Oxfordshire. Home of Dukes of Marlborough. Birthplace of (Sir) W. Churchill.

Bowood, Wiltshire. Home of Ms of Lansdowne.

Brixton, London, S.E.24. Scene of anti-police riots in April and July 1981.

Broadstairs, Kent. Birthplace and home of Edward Heath.

Buckingham Palace. Bought by George III in 1761. Official residence of the Sovereign since 1837.

Cable Street, Whitechapel, London. Scene of confrontations with the British Union of Fascists, 1935-36.

Carlton Club. London meeting place of Conservatives. Scene (19 Oct 1922) of gathering which brought down the Lloyd George Coalition.

Carmelite House, E.C.4. Headquarters of the *Daily Mail* and *Evening News*.

Chartwell, Kent. Home of (Sir) W. Churchill 1923-65.

Chatsworth, Derbyshire. Home of Ds of Devonshire.

Chequers, Buckinghamshire. Country house given to the nation by Lord Lee of Fareham in 1917 and used as country residence for Prime Ministers from 1921.

Cherry Cottage, Buckinghamshire. Home of C. (Earl) Attlee 1951-61.

Cherkley Court, Surrey. Home of Ld Beaverbrook 1916-64.

Church House, S.W.1. Meeting place of the Church Assembly since 1920; and of both Houses of Parliament, Nov-Dec 1940, May-Jun 1941, Jun-Aug 1944. Scene of United Nations preparatory meeting 1945 and of many Conservative gatherings.

Churt, Surrey. Home of D. Lloyd George (E) 1921-45.

Clay Cross, Derbyshire. Urban District Council which refused to implement 1972 Housing Act.

Cliveden, Buckinghamshire. Home of 2nd and 3rd Vt Astor. Alleged centre of 'Cliveden Set' in 1930s. Scene (1962) of events in the Profumo affair.

Congress House, Gt. Russell St., W.C.1. Headquarters of Trades Union Congress 1960-.

Cowley St., London, S.W.1. Headquarters of the Social Democratic Party, 1981-.

Criccieth, Caernarvonshire. Welsh home of D. Lloyd George (E) 1880-1945.

Crichel Down, Dorset. The refusal to derequisition some land here led, ultimately, to the resignation of the Minister of Agriculture in Jul 1954.

Cross St., Manchester. Headquarters of the *(Manchester) Guardian* until 1970.

Curragh, The, Co. Kildare. Military camp; scene of 'mutiny' 20 Mar 1914.

Dalmeny, Midlothian. Home of Es of Rosebery.

Dorneywood, Buckinghamshire. Country house bequeathed to the nation in 1954 by Ld Courtauld-Thomson as an official residence for any Minister designated by the Prime Minister.

Downing St., S.W.1. No. 10 is the Prime Minister's official residence.[1] No. 11 is the official residence of the Chancellor of the Exchequer. No. 12 houses the offices of the Government Whips.

Dublin Castle, Offices of the Irish Administration until 1922.

Durdans, The, Epsom. Home of 5th E of Rosebery 1872-1929.

Eccleston Square, S.W.1. Site of Headquarters of the Labour Party and of the Trades Union Congress 1918-29.

Ettrick Bridge, Roxburgh. Constituency home of D. Steel since 1966. Scene of meeting of Alliance leaders, 29 May 1984.

Euston Lodge, Phoenix Park, Dublin. Residence of the Ld-Lieutenant of Ireland.

Falloden, Northumberland. Home of Sir E. (Vt) Grey 1862-1933.

Fleet St., E.C.4. Location of *Daily Telegraph* and *Daily Express*. Generic name for the London press.

Fort Belvedere, Berkshire. Country home of Edward VIII 1930-36.

Grand Hotel, Brighton. Scene of bombing on 11 Oct 1984 of Conservative Conference Headquarters.

Great George St., S.W.1. Site of the Treasury and, 1964-69, of the Department of Economic Affairs.

Greenham Common, Berkshire. Air base at which Cruise missiles were first sited (Nov 83). Women protesters camped outside it Sep 81-.

Hampstead. London suburb which, during H. Gaitskell's leadership of the Labour Party, provided a generic name for the set of intellectuals associated with him.

Hatfield House, Hertfordshire. Home of Ms of Salisbury.

Highbury, Birmingham. Home of J. Chamberlain 1868-1914.

Hirsel, The, Berwickshire. Home of Es of Home.

Holy Loch, Argyll. Site of U.S. atomic submarine base 1962-.

Howth, Co. Dublin. Scene of gun-running 26 Jul 1914.

Invergordon, Ross and Cromarty. Site of naval protest in Sep 1931 over proposed pay reductions.

Jarrow, Durham. Shipbuilding town where unemployment reached 73% in 1935. Start of Jarrow to London protest march Oct 1936.

[1]Since 1900, the only three Prime Ministers not to have lived at 10 Downing Street were M of Salisbury, up to 1902, H. Macmillan 1960-63, and H. Wilson 1974-76.

Kilmainham Jail, Dublin. Scene of execution of the leaders of the 1916 rising.

King St., W.C.2. Site of Communist Party Headquarters since early 1920s.

Knowsley, Lancashire. Home of Es of Derby.

Larne, Co. Antrim. Scene of gun-running 24 Apr 1914.

Limehouse, E.14. Scene of speech by D. Lloyd George 30 Jul 1909; became generic name for political vituperation. Also home of D. Owen 1965- and scene of meeting on 25 Jan 81, which produced 'The Limehouse Declaration' which anticipated the forming of the Social Democratic Party.

Londonderry House, W.1. London home of Ms of Londonderry until 1946.

Lord North St. Home of H. Wilson 1971-76.

Lossiemouth, Morayshire. Home of R. MacDonald, 1866-1937.

Maze, The, County Antrim (formerly Long Kesh). Prison where many convicted terrorists were held from 1968 onwards. Scene of hunger strike in which 10 IRA members died in 1981.

Molesworth, Cambridgeshire. Air base. Scene of demonstrations against Cruise missiles 1985-.

Notting Hill, W.11. Scene of racial disturbances in Aug 1958.

Old Queen St., S.W.1. Site of Conservative Party Headquarters 1941-46. Site of Conservative Research Department 1930-.

Olympia, W.14. Exhibition Hall; scene (7 Jun 1934) of Mosley meeting which provoked violence.

Palace Chambers, S.W.1. Headquarters of Conservative Party 1922-41.

Pembroke Lodge, W.8. Home of A. Bonar Law 1909-16.

Poplar. London borough whose Poor Law Guardians (including G. Lansbury) were imprisoned in 1921 for paying more than national rates of relief.

Portland Place, W.1. Headquarters of the British Broadcasting Corporation 1932-.

Printing House Square, E.C.4. Headquarters of *The Times* 1785-1974.

Relugas, Morayshire. Fishing lodge of Sir E. Grey; scene of 'Relugas Compact' with H. Asquith and R. Haldane Sep 1905.

St. James Palace, W.1. Royal Palace. Foreign Ambassadors continue to be accredited to the Court of St. James.

St. Paul's, Bristol. Scene of anti-police riot, Apr 1980.

St. Stephen's Chambers, S.W.1. Site of Conservative Headquarters 1900-18.

Sanctuary Buildings, S.W.1. Site of Conservative Headquarters 1918-22.

Sandringham House, Norfolk. Royal residence since 1861.

Scapa Flow, Orkney. Naval anchorage where German Fleet was scuttled 21 Jun 1919. Scene of trouble at the time of the Invergordon 'mutiny' Sep 1931.

Scilly Isles, Cornwall. Location of H. Wilson's country cottage 1959-.

Selsdon Park. Hotel in Croydon. Scene of Conservative Shadow Cabinet's weekend meeting, 30 Jan-1 Feb 1970.

Shanklin, Isle of Wight. Scene (Feb 1949) of meeting of Labour Party leaders.

Sidney St., E.1. Scene of police siege of anarchists 3 Jan 1911.

Smith Square, S.W.1. Location of the Labour Party Headquarters (Transport House) since 1928; of the Conservative Party Headquarters since 1958; and of the Liberal Party Headquarters 1965-68.

Southall. West London suburb with many immigrants from the Indian subcontinent. Scene of violent disturbances in anti-National Front riot, 23 Apr 1979.

Stormont, Belfast. Site of Parliament and Government of Northern Ireland.

Sunningdale, Surrey. Location of Civil Service College where a Conference on Northern Ireland 6-9 Dec 73 produced the Sunningdale Agreement on power-sharing and a Council of Ireland.

Swinton, Yorkshire. Home of E of Swinton. Conservative Party College since 1948.

Taff Vale, Glamorgan. In 1901 the Taff Vale Railway Company successfully sued a trade union for loss due to a strike.

Threadneedle St., E.C.2. Site of the Bank of England.

Tonypandy. Scene of violent miners' strike to which W. Churchill sent troops in Nov 1910.

Toxteth, Liverpool 8. Scene of rioting, Jul 1981.

Transport House, S.W.1. Headquarters of the Transport and General Workers' Union and of the Labour Party 1928-80 and of the Trades Union Congress 1928-60.

Walworth Rd, London, S.E.17. In 1980 150 Walworth Rd became the headquarters of the Labour Party.

Westbourne, Birmingham. Home of N. Chamberlain 1911-40.

Westminster, London. Parliament meets in the Palace of Westminster and Westminster has become a generic name for parliamentary activity.
Wharf, The, Sutton Courtenay, Berkshire. Home of H. Asquith 1912-28.
Whitehall, London. Many government departments are situated in Whitehall and it has become a generic name for civil service activity.
Whittingehame, East Lothian. Home of A. Balfour 1848-1930.
Windsor Castle, Berkshire. Official royal residence since 11th century.

Political Quotations

From time to time an isolated phrase becomes an established part of the language of political debate. Such phrases are frequently misquoted and their origins are often obscure. Here are a few which seem to have had an especial resonance. The list is far from comprehensive; it merely attempts to record the original source for some well-used quotations.

When was a war not a war? When it was carried on by *methods of barbarism* in South Africa?

SIR H. CAMPBELL-BANNERMAN, speech to National Reform Union, 14 Jun 01

For the present, at any rate, I must proceed alone. *I must plough my furrow alone*, but before I get to the end of that furrow it is possible that I may not find myself alone.

LORD ROSEBERY, in a speech at the City Liberal Club, 19 Jul 01

To the distinguished representatives of the commercial interests of the Empire ... I venture to allude to the impression which seemed generally to prevail among their brethren across the seas, that the old country must *wake up* if she [*England*] intends to maintain her old position of preeminence in her colonial trade against foreign competitors.

H.R.H. PRINCE OF WALES (later George V), at a lunch at the Guildhall to celebrate the recent completion of his tour of the Empire, 5 Dec 01

'What is the advice I have to offer you? ... You have to *clear* your *slate*. It is six years since you were in office. ... The primary duty of the Liberal party is to wipe its slate clean.'

E. of ROSEBERY, speaking to a Liberal audience at Chesterfield, 16 Dec 01. Sir H. Campbell Bannerman replied at Leicester 19 Feb 02, 'I am no believer in the doctrine of the *clean slate*.'

'I should consider that I was but ill performing my duty ... if we were to profess a settled conviction when *no settled conviction* exists.'

A. J. BALFOUR, House of Commons, 10 June 03

'If I believed that there was the smallest reasonable chance of success, I would have no hesitation in advising my fellow-countrymen to endeavour to end the present system of *armed revolt*.'

J. REDMOND, House of Commons, 12 Apr 05

It [the Chinese Labour Contract] cannot in the opinion of His Majesty's Government, be classified as slavery in the extreme acceptance of the word without some risk of *terminological inexactitude*.

WINSTON CHURCHILL, House of Commons, 22 Feb 06

You mean it is *Mr Balfour's poodle*! It fetches and carries for him. It barks for him. It bites anybody that he sets it on to.

LLOYD GEORGE, replying to H. Chaplin, M.P., who had claimed, in a House of Commons debate on the House of Lords (Restoration of Powers) Bill, that the Lords was the watchdog of the Constitution, 26 Jun 07

If we believe a thing to be bad, and if we have a right to prevent it, it is our duty to try to prevent it and to *damn the consequences*.

LORD MILNER, in a speech at Glasgow in opposition to Lloyd George's 1909 Finance Bill, 26 Nov 09

Wait and see.

H. ASQUITH, repeated four times to Opposition members pressing for a statement when speaking on Parliament Act Procedure Bill, House of Commons, 4 Apr 10

We were beaten by *the Bishops and the rats*.

G. WYNDHAM, on the passing of the Parliament Bill by the House of Lords, 10 Aug 11

La Grande Illusion.

Title of a book by N. ANGELL, first published in 1909 as *Europe's Optical Illusion* and republished as *The Great Illusion* in 1910

The lamps are going out all over Europe. We shall not see them lit again in our lifetime.

SIR E. GREY, 3 Aug 14, talking in his room at the Foreign Office, quoted in his autobiography *Twenty Five Years*, vol. II, p. 20

Your King and Country Need YOU.

Advertisement in *Daily Mail* and other papers 5 Aug 14. Basis for drawing on cover of *London Opinion*, 5 Sep 14, designed by A. LEETE, depicting LORD KITCHENER with arresting eyes and pointing finger above the caption 'Your Country needs you'; reproduced by Parliamentary Recruiting Committee for use as recruiting poster and issued Sep 14

The maxim of the British people is '*business as usual*'.

WINSTON CHURCHILL in a speech at the Guildhall, 9 Nov 14

To secure for the producers by hand or by brain the full fruits of their industry and the most equitable distribution thereof that may be possible upon the basis of the *common ownership of the means of production (distribution and exchange)*.

Listed under party objects in the Constitution of the Labour Party adopted at the Annual Conference in London, 26 Feb 18 (words in brackets added at the 1928 Conference)

What is our task? To make Britain *a fit country for heroes to live in*.

D. LLOYD GEORGE, speech at Wolverhampton, 24 Nov 18

We will get everything out of her [Germany] that you can squeeze out of a lemon and a bit more. . . . *I will squeeze her until you can hear the pips squeak*.

SIR E. GEDDES, in a speech at the Drill Hall, Cambridge, 9 Dec 18

They are a lot of *hard-faced men . . . who look as if they had done very well out of the war.*

A Conservative politician (often said to be Baldwin), quoted by J.M. Keynes in *Economic Consequences of the Peace* (Macmillan, 1919), p. 133

First let me insist on what our opponents habitually ignore, and indeed what they seem intellectually incapable of understanding namely the *inevitable gradualness* of our scheme of change.

S. WEBB, in his Presidential Address to the Labour Party Conference, Queen's Hall, Langham Place, 26 June 23

Until our educated and politically minded democracy has become predominantly a *property-owning democracy*, neither the national equilibrium nor the balance of the life of the individual will be restored.

A. SKELTON, in *Constructive Conservatism* (Blackwood, 1924), p. 17; subsequently used by A. EDEN at Conservative Conference, Blackpool, 3 Oct 46, and by W. CHURCHILL, 5 Oct 46

Although I know that there are those who work for different ends from most of us in this House, yet there are many in all ranks and all parties who will re-echo my prayer '*give peace in our time, O Lord*'.

S. BALDWIN speaking in House of Commons on Trade Unions (Political Fund Bill), 6 Mar 25

Not a penny off the pay, not a second on the day.

Slogan coined by A. J. COOK, Secretary of the National Union of Mineworkers, and used frequently in the run-up to the miners' strike of 1926

We can conquer unemployment.

Title of a pamphlet which was a potted version of the Liberal *Yellow Book* (1929)

Safety First. Stanley Baldwin, the man you can trust.

Slogan on election posters used by the Conservative Party in 1929; the slogan 'Safety First' was previously used by the Conservatives in the 1922 General Election

I remember when I was a child being taken to the celebrated Barnum's Circus . . . the exhibit which I most desired to see was the one described as 'the Boneless Wonder'. My parents judged that the spectacle would be too revolting for my youthful eyes, and I have waited fifty years to see *the Boneless Wonder* sitting on the Treasury Bench.

W. CHURCHILL, referring to R. MacDonald during a debate on the Amendment Bill, 28 Jan 31

What the proprietorship of these papers is aiming at is power, and *power without responsibility—the prerogative of the harlot throughout the ages.*

S. BALDWIN, attacking the Press Lords in a speech at Queen's Hall, London, during Westminster St George's by-election campaign, 18 Mar 31. The phrase was suggested by his cousin, Rudyard Kipling

I hope you have read the Election programme of the Labour Party. It is the most fantastic and impracticable programme ever put before the electors. . . . This is not Socialism. It is *Bolshevism run mad.*

P. SNOWDEN, election broadcast, 17 Oct 31

I think it is well also for the man in the street to realise that there is no power on earth that can protect him from being bombed. Whatever people may tell him, *the bomber will always get through.*

S. BALDWIN, in the House of Commons, 10 Nov 32

That this House *will in no circumstances fight for its King and Country.*

Oxford Union motion, 9 Feb 33

[You are] placing . . . the Movement in an absolutely wrong position to be *hawking your conscience round from body to body* asking to be told what you ought to do with it.

E. BEVIN, attacking G. Lansbury at the Labour Party Conference, Brighton, 1 Oct 35

My lips are not yet unsealed.

S. BALDWIN, speaking in the House of Commons, on the Abyssinian crisis, 10 Dec 35, later quoted as '*My lips are sealed*'

A Corridor for Camels.

Heading of a first leader in *The Times*, on the Hoare-Laval Pact, written by G. Dawson, 16 Dec 35

I put before the whole House my own views *with appalling frankness*. . . supposing I had gone to the country and . . . said that we must rearm, does anybody think that this pacific democracy would have rallied to the cry? I cannot think of anything that would have made the loss of the election from my point of view more certain.

S. BALDWIN, speaking in the House of Commons, 12 Nov 36

Something ought to be done to find these people employment. . . . Something will be done.

EDWARD VIII, on a visit to South Wales, 18 Nov 36

How horrible, fantastic, incredible it is that we should be digging trenches and trying on gas-masks here because of *a quarrel in a faraway country between people of whom we know nothing*.

N. CHAMBERLAIN, referring to Czechoslovakia in a broadcast of 27 Sep 38

Britain will not be involved in a European war this year, or next year either.

Daily Express headline, 30 Sep 38 inspired by LD BEAVERBROOK. Cited as basis for 'There will be no war' campaign in *Daily Express*

This is the second time in my history that there has come back from Germany to Downing Street, peace with honour. I believe that it is *peace for our time*.

N. CHAMBERLAIN, referring back to Disraeli's comment on the Congress of Berlin (1878), in a speech from a window of 10 Downing Street on return from Munich, 30 Sep 38

Speak for England, Arthur.

L. AMERY, R. BOOTHBY; shouted out as Arthur Greenwood rose to speak in the House of Commons, 2 Sep 39

Whatever may be the reason, whether it was that *Hitler* thought he might get away with what he had got without fighting for it, or whether it was that, after all, the preparations are not sufficiently complete, one thing is certain—he *has missed the bus*.

N. CHAMBERLAIN, speaking at Conservative Central Council, 4 Apr 40

You have sat too long here for any good you have been doing. Depart, I say, and let us have done with you. *In the name of God, go!*

L. AMERY, quoting Cromwell (1653) to N. Chamberlain in House of Commons, 7 May 40

I have nothing to offer but *blood, toil, tears and sweat*.

W. CHURCHILL, House of Commons, 13 May 40

We shall fight on the beaches, we shall fight on the landing grounds, we shall fight in the fields and in the streets.

W. CHURCHILL, House of Commons, 4 Jun 40

If the British nation and Commonwealth last a thousand years . . . men will still say, '*This was their finest hour*'.

W. CHURCHILL, broadcast to the nation when the fall of France was imminent, 18 Jun 40

Guilty Men. — Political tract written by Michael Foot, Frank Owen and Peter Howard, using pseudonym Cato, published Jul 40

Never in the field of human conflict was *so much owed by so many to so few.* — W. CHURCHILL, House of Commons, 20 Aug 40

Give us the tools and we will finish the job. — W. CHURCHILL, broadcast to the nation, 9 Feb 41

When I warned them [the French] that Britain would fight on alone . . . their General told their Prime Minister, . . . in three weeks England will have her neck wrung like a chicken—*some chicken, some neck.* — W. CHURCHILL, speaking to the Canadian Parliament, 30 Dec 41

I have not become the King's First Minister in order to preside over the liquidation of the British Empire. — W. CHURCHILL, speech at the Mansion House, 10 Nov 42

Pounds, shillings and pence have become quite *meaningless symbols.* — A. GREENWOOD, in the House of Commons, 16 Feb 43

Let us face the future. — Title of Labour Party Manifesto, May 45

No *Socialist* system can be established without a political police. . . . They would have to fall back on some form of *Gestapo.* — W. CHURCHILL, election broadcast, 4 Jun 45

You have no right whatever to speak on behalf of the Government. Foreign Affairs are in the capable hands of Ernest Bevin. His task is quite sufficiently difficult without the embarrassment of irresponsible statements of the kind which you are making . . . *a period of silence on your part would be welcome.* — C. ATTLEE in a letter to H. Laski, Chairman of the Labour Party NEC, 20 Aug 45

From Stettin in the Baltic to Trieste in the Adriatic, *an iron curtain* has descended across the Continent. — W. CHURCHILL, speaking at Westminster Cottage, Fulton, U.S.A., 5 Mar 46. The phrase can be traced back to Mrs Snowden's visit to Russia in 1920

We are the masters at the moment—and not only for the moment, but for a very long time to come. — SIR H. SHAWCROSS, in the House of Commons, during third reading of the Trade Disputes and Trade Union Bill, 2 Apr 46

We know that you, the organised workers of the country, are our friends. . . . As for the rest, they do not matter *a tinker's curse.* — E. SHINWELL, speaking at E.T.U. Conference, Margate, 7 May 47

For in the case of nutrition and health, just as in the case of education, *the gentleman in Whitehall really does know better* what is good for people than the people know themselves. — D. JAY, from *The Socialist Case* (1947), p. 258

No attempt at ethical or social education can eradicate from my heart a deep burning hatred for the Tory Party. . . . So far as I am concerned, they are *lower than vermin.* — A. BEVAN, speech at Manchester, 4 Jul 48

I have authorised the relaxation *of controls* affecting more than 60 commodities for which the Board of Trade is responsible. — H. WILSON, House of Commons, 4 Nov 48

Baldwin . . . confesses putting party before country. — W. CHURCHILL, entry in index to *The Gathering Storm*, vol. I of *The Second World War* (1948).

The Hon. Member asked two other questions. One of them was how many licences and permits are to be issued after the removal of the 200,000 Board of Trade licences and the 5,000 or 6,000 others which were as the result of yesterday's little *bonfire*. . . .

H. WILSON, as President of the Board of Trade, House of Commons, 5 Nov 48

The Right Road for Britain.

Conservative Party policy statement, 1949

The language of priorities is the religion of socialism.

A. BEVAN, Labour Party Conference, Blackpool, 8 Jun 49

Whose finger on the trigger?

Daily Mirror, front-page headline on eve of the election, 24 Oct 51

The right technique of economic opposition at the moment can be summed up in a slogan. The slogan is that the Opposition should keep itself on the constructive and sunny side of Mr Butskell's dilemma. Mr *Butskell[ism]* . . . is a composite of the present Chancellor and the previous one.

Article in *The Economist* referring to R. Butler and H. Gaitskell, 13 Feb 54

I know that the right kind of political leader for the Labour Party is a *desiccated calculating machine*.

A. BEVAN, taken as referring to H. Gaitskell, though Bevan subsequently denied this, at the *Tribune* meeting during Labour Party Conference at Scarborough, 29 Sep 54

There ain't gonna be no war.

H. MACMILLAN, at press conference, on return from Summit, 24 Jul 55

Reporter: Mr Butler, would you say that this is *the best Prime Minister we have?* R. Butler: Yes.

R. BUTLER, interviewed by a Press Association reporter at London Airport, Dec 55

Most Conservatives, and almost certainly some of the wiser Trade Union Leaders, are waiting to feel *the smack of firm government*.

Daily Telegraph editorial written by the Deputy Editor D. MCLACHLAN, 3 Jan 56

And all these financiers, all the little *gnomes of Zürich* and the other financial centres about whom we keep on hearing, started to make their dispositions in regard to sterling.

H. WILSON, in the House of Commons Debate on the Address, 12 Nov 56

During the past few weeks I have felt sometimes that *the Suez Canal was flowing through my drawing-room*.

LADY EDEN, opening Gateshead Conservative Association Headquarters, 20 Nov 56

Let us be frank about it, most of our people have *never had it so good*.

H. MACMILLAN, speaking at Bedford to a Conservative Party rally, 21 Jul 57

If you carry this resolution . . . you'll send the British Foreign Secretary—whoever he was—*naked into the Conference Chamber*.

A. BEVAN, Labour Party Conference, Brighton, 3 Oct 57

And you call that statesmanship. I call it *an emotional spasm*.

A. BEVAN, speaking on unilateral disarmament, Labour Party Conference, Brighton, 3 Oct 57

I thought the best thing to do was to settle up these *little local difficulties*, and then turn to the wider vision of the Commonwealth.

H. MACMILLAN, referring to resignation of Treasury Ministers in a statement at London Airport before leaving for Commonwealth tour, 7 Jan 58

Jaw-jaw is better than war-war.

H. MACMILLAN, Canberra, 30 Jan 58; echoing CHURCHILL, 'Talking jaw to jaw is better than going to war', White House lunch, 26 Jun 54

Introducing *Super-Mac.*

VICKY, caption of cartoon depicting H. Macmillan in a Superman outfit; first appeared in *Evening Standard*, 6 Nov 58

Life's better with the Conservatives. *Don't let Labour ruin it.*

Slogan on Conservative posters in the 1959 General Election

What matters is that Mr Macmillan has let Mr Lloyd know that at the Foreign Office, in these troubled times, *enough is enough.*

Article by David Wood, *The Times* Political Correspondent, 1 Jun 59

Britain belongs to you.

Title of Labour Party election manifesto, published 18 Sep 59

The wind of change is blowing through this Continent, and whether we like it or not, this growth of national consciousness is a political fact.

H. MACMILLAN, address to Joint Assembly of Union Parliament, Cape Town, 3 Feb 60

We have developed instead an *affluent*, open and democratic *society*, in which the class escalators are continually moving and in which people are divided not so much between 'haves' and 'have-nots' as between 'haves' and 'have-mores'.

R. BUTLER, at a Conservative Political Centre Summer School, 8 Jul 60

There are some of us, Mr Chairman, who will *fight and fight and fight again* to save the party we love.

H. GAITSKELL, Labour Party Conference, Scarborough, 3 Oct 60

The present Colonial Secretary . . . has been *too clever by half*. . . . I believe that the Colonial Secretary is a very fine bridge player. . . . It is not considered immoral, or even bad form to outwit one's opponents at bridge. . . . It almost seems to me as if the Colonial Secretary, when he abandoned the sphere of bridge for the sphere of politics, brought his bridge technique with him.

M OF SALISBURY, referring to I. MACLEOD and his policy in Africa in a debate in the House of Lords, 7 May 61

SCOTT: Do you think the Unions are going to respond to what amounts in effect to a '*wage freeze*' in the public sector?
LLOYD: Well, I said that I wasn't going to deal with every possible circumstance. This is a pause rather than a wage freeze.

S. LLOYD interviewed on B.B.C. Radio Newsreel by Hardiman Scott about the 'July measures', 25 Jul 61

It does mean, if this is the idea, the end of Britain as an independent European state . . . it means the end of *a thousand years of history.*

H. GAITSKELL, Labour Party Conference, Brighton, 3 Oct 62

It is a moral issue.

Heading of a *Times* first leader on the Profumo Affair, 11 Jun 63

A great party is not to be brought down because of a *squalid affair between a woman of easy virtue and a proven liar.*

LORD HAILSHAM, in a B.B.C. interview with R. McKenzie about the Profumo Affair, 13 Jun 63

He would, wouldn't he?

MISS M. RICE-DAVIES in a Magistrates Court on 28 Jun 63, referring to a peer denying knowing her

And in bygone days, commanders were taught that, when in doubt, they should march their troops towards the sound of gunfire. *I intend to march my troops towards the sound of gunfire.*

J. GRIMOND, in a speech to the Liberal Assembly at Brighton, 15 Sep 63

We are re-defining and we are re-stating our socialism in terms of *the scientific revolution* . . . the Britain that is going to be forged in *the white heat of* this revolution will be no place for restrictive practices or out-dated methods on either side of industry.

H. WILSON, Labour Party Conference, Scarborough, 1 Oct 63

I hope that it will soon be possible for the *customary processes of consultation* to be carried on within the Party about its future leadership.

H. MACMILLAN, in the letter in which he announced his resignation as P.M.; read out to the Conservative Party Conference at Blackpool by the Earl of Home, 10 Oct 63

After half a century of democratic advance, the whole process has ground to a halt with *a 14th Earl.*

H. WILSON, speech at Belle Vue, Manchester, 19 Oct 63

As far as the 14th Earl is concerned, I suppose Mr Wilson, when you come to think of it, is *the 14th Mr Wilson.*

EARL OF HOME, in a television interview by Kenneth Harris on I.T.V., 21 Oct 63

Let's go with Labour.

Labour Party slogan used in 1964

If the British public falls for this [Labour policies] I say it will be *stark, staring bonkers.*

Q. HOGG, press conference at Conservative Central Office during election campaign, 12 Oct 64

I have been given the *bed of nails.*

R. GUNTER, on his appointment as Minister of Labour, 18 Oct 64

Smethwick Conservatives can have the satisfaction of having topped the poll, of having sent a Member who, until another election returns him to oblivion, will serve his time here as *a Parliamentary leper.*

H. WILSON, referring to Peter Griffiths, M.P., who defeated Patrick Gordon Walker in an allegedly racialist election campaign at Smethwick, House of Commons, 4 Nov 64

A week is a long time in politics

Attributed to H. WILSON. Probably first used in a lobby briefing late in 1964

In this connection [use of military force in Rhodesia] the Prime Ministers noted the statement by the British Prime Minister that on the expert advice available to him, the cumulative effects of the economic and financial sanctions might well bring the rebellion to an end within a matter of *weeks rather than months.*

Final communiqué of Commonwealth Prime Ministers' Conference at Lagos, released 12 Jan 66; referring back to unreported speech by H. WILSON also on 12 Jan 66

Action not words.

Title of Conservative election manifesto, published 6 Mar 66

You know *Labour Government works.*

Labour Party slogan used in 1966 election

Now one encouraging gesture from the French Government which I welcome and the Conservative leader *rolls on his back like a spaniel.*

H. WILSON, Bristol, 18 Mar 66

It is difficult for us to appreciate the pressures which are put on men . . . in the highly organised strike committees in the individual ports by this *tightly knit group of politically motivated men* . . . who are now determined to exercise back-stage pressures . . . endangering the security of the industry and the economic welfare of the nation.

H. WILSON, House of Commons, 20 Jun 66

Sterling has been under pressure for the past two and a half weeks. After improvement in the early weeks of May, we were *blown off course* by the seven weeks seamen's strike.

H. WILSON, House of Commons, 20 Jul 66

Every dog is allowed one bite, but a different view is taken of a *dog* that goes on biting all the time. He may not get his *licence* returned when it falls due.

H. WILSON, speech to Parliamentary Labour Party, 2 Mar 67

It does not mean, of course, that *the pound* here in Britain *in your pocket* or purse or in your bank has been devalued.

H. WILSON, television and radio broadcast announcing devaluation of the pound, 20 Nov 67

As I look ahead, I am filled with foreboding. Like the Roman, I seem to see '*the River Tiber foaming with much blood*'.

E. POWELL, speech to a Conservative Political Central Meeting in Birmingham, 20 Apr 68, referring to *Aeneid* Bk. VI: 'Et Thybrim multo spumantem sanguine cerno.'

In Place of Strife.

Title of Government White Paper on industrial relations legislation, 19 Jan 69

Selsdon Man is designing a system of society for the ruthless and the pushing, the uncaring. . . . His message to the rest is: you're out on your own.

H. WILSON, at a Rally of the Greater London Party in Camden Town Hall, 21 Feb 70; referring to the Conservative policy-forming meeting at Selsdon Park, Croydon, on 31 Jan 70

Nor would it be in the interests of the Community that its enlargement should take place except with *the full-hearted consent of* the Parliament and people of the new member countries.

E. HEATH in a speech to the Franco-British Chamber of Commerce in Paris, 5 May 70

I am determined, therefore, that a Conservative Government shall introduce *a new style of government.*

E. HEATH, in foreword to Conservative manifesto, published May 70

This would, *at a stroke*, reduce the rise in prices, increase productivity and reduce unemployment.

Wrongly reported in *The Times* as having been said by E. HEATH at a press conference at Central Office, 16 Jun 70; actually taken from a Conservative Press Release (No. G.E.228) distributed at the press conference

We believe that the essential need of the country is to gear its policies to the great majority of the people, who are not *lame ducks.*

J. DAVIES, speaking in a debate on public expenditure and taxation in the House of Commons, 4 Nov 70; echoing a speech by A. BENN in the House of Commons ['the next question is what safeguards are there against the support of lame ducks'] on 1 Feb 68

Yesterday's Men.

Slogan on Labour poster caricaturing Conservative leaders, May 70; subsequently title of B.B.C. television programme about Labour leaders in opposition transmitted 17 Jun 71

We say that what Britain needs is a new *Social Contract.* That is what this document [*Labour's Programme 1972*] is all about.

J. CALLAGHAN, Labour Party Conference, Blackpool, 2 Oct 72. But A. Wedgwood Benn had used the phrase in a 1970 Fabian pamphlet *The New Politics.* J.-J. Rousseau's *Le Contrat Social* was published in 1762.

It is *the unpleasant and unacceptable face of capitalism*, but one should not suggest that the whole of British industry consists of practices of this kind.

E. HEATH, replying in the House of Commons to a question from J. Grimond about the Lonrho affair, 15 May 73

From 31 December, they [most industrial and commercial premises] will be limited [in the use of electricity] to *three* specified *days* each *week*.

E. HEATH, speaking in the House of Commons, 13 Dec 73

Looking around the House, one realises that *we are all minorities now*—indeed, some more than others.

J. THORPE, speaking in the House of Commons, after the election of the Speaker, 6 Mar 74

We believe that the only way in which the maximum degree of national cooperation can be achieved is for *a government of national unity* to be formed....

J. THORPE in a letter to E. Heath 4 Mar 74. Later in the year the phrase became a central theme in the Conservatives' October campaign.

With its [the local government world's] usual spirit of patriotism and its tradition of service to the community's needs, it is coming to realize that, for the time being at least, *the party is over*.

A. CROSLAND, at a civic luncheon at Manchester Town Hall, 9 May 1975

Ladies and Gentlemen, I stand before you tonight in my green chiffon evening gown, my face softly made up, my fair hair gently waved.... *The Iron Lady* of the Western World. Me? A cold war warrior? Well, yes—if that is how they wish to interpret my defence of values and freedoms fundamental to our way of life.

MRS M. THATCHER, speaking in her Finchley constituency, 31 Jan 76, referring to report in the Soviet newspaper *Red Star* on 23 Jan 76

That part of his speech was rather like *being savaged by a dead sheep*.

D. HEALEY, 14 Jun 78, replying to a parliamentary attack by Sir G. Howe

Labour isn't working.

Slogan on Conservative poster, designed by Saatchi and Saatchi, showing dole queue, shown in Aug 1978 and widely used in 1979 election

Crisis? What Crisis?
(Journalist: 'What . . . of the mounting chaos in the country at the moment?' Callaghan: 'I don't think that other people in the world would share the view that there is mounting chaos.')

Sun headline, 11 Jan 79, referring to J. CALLAGHAN speaking at London airport on return home from Guadaloupe summit during widespread strikes, 10 Jan 1979

The Labour Way is the Better Way.

Title of Labour election manifesto published Apr 1979

I don't see how we can talk with Mrs Thatcher . . . I will say to the lads, come on, *get your snouts in the trough*.

S. WEIGHELL, speaking in London, 10 Apr 79, echoing his speech at the Labour Party Conference, Blackpool, 6 Oct 78. 'If you want it to go out . . . that you now believe in the philosophy of the pig trough—those with the biggest snouts get the largest share—I reject it.'

There is no alternative.

A phrase widely attributed to Mrs M. THATCHER in 1979 and 1980

We are fed up with *fudging and mudging*, with mush and slush.

D. OWEN, at Labour Party Conference, Blackpool, 2 Oct 80

The Lady's not for turning	Mrs M. THATCHER, Conservative Party Conference, Brighton, 10 Oct 1980
Breaking the mould of British politics.	Phrase widely used after 1981 about the goals of the Alliance. Its origin seems to lie in R. JENKINS, *What Matters Now* (1972), quoting Andrew Marvell on Cromwell 'Casting Kingdoms' Old/Into another mould.'
He [his unemployed father in the 1930s] didn't riot. He got *on his bike* and looked for work.	N. TEBBIT, Conservative Party Conference, Blackpool, 15 Oct 81
'*GOTCHA*!'	*Sun* headline on 4 May 82 on the sinking of the Argentine cruiser *Belgrano*
Heckler: 'At least Mrs Thatcher has *got guts*.' N. Kinnock: 'And it's a pity that people had to leave theirs *on* the ground at *Goose Green* in order to prove it.'	N. KINNOCK during TV South's election programme 'The South Decides', 5 Jun 83

Political Scandals

The following list is not comprehensive but indicates most of the more celebrated examples. A few others are implicit in the list of ministerial resignations on pp. 85-86.

1904	Wyndham (Ministerial involvement with Irish Home Rule Schemes)
1912	Marconi (Ministers dealing in shares)
1918	Pemberton Billing (Libel action involving many public figures)
1918	Maurice (Army Council's disciplining of a General)
1921	Bottomley (M.P. and financial practice)
1922ff.	Maundy Gregory (Sale of honours)
1936	Budget leak (Minister telling M.P. of budget plans)
1940	Boothby (Minister influencing handling of blocked Czech assets)
1947	Allighan (M.P. leaking Parliamentary Labour Party meetings)
1948	Belcher/Stanley (Influencing peddling at the Board of Trade)
1951	Burgess/Maclean (spies fleeing to Moscow)
1955	Crichel Down (Minister's handling of sequestrated land)
1957	Bank Rate (Alleged leak)

1962	Vassall (Spy scandal)
1963	Profumo (Minister lying to the House)
1972	Poulson (Influence peddling in building)
1973	Jellicoe/Lambton (Sex scandal)
1976	Stonehouse (M.P.'s simulated drowning)
1976-9	Thorpe (Liberal Leader ultimately acquitted of conspiracy to murder).
1979	Blunt (Spy scandal)
1983	Parkinson (Sex scandal)

Major Civil Disturbances and Demonstrations (in Great Britain)

8	Nov	1910	Tonypandy
16	Aug	1911	Liverpool ('Bloody Sunday' clash between police and strikers)
		1915-16	Anti-German riots in the East End
31	Jul	1919	Glasgow ('Bloody Friday' confrontation between police and strikers)
3-10	May	1926	General Strike
	Sep	1932	Liverpool
	Feb	1934	Jarrow Hunger March
7	Jun	1934	Olympia (violence at Mosley rally)
4	Oct	1936	Cable Street (Fascist-Jewish confrontation)
24	Aug	1958	Nottingham (race riot)
31	Aug	1958	Notting Hill Gate (race riot)
15	Jun	1968	Red Lion Square (confrontation between National Front and opponents)
17	Mar	1968	Grosvenor Square
	Jan-Mar	1974	Saltley (mass picketing of the coke depot)
	Jul-Sep	1977	Grunwick, Enfield (mass picketing of photographic factory)
23	Apr	1979	Southall (confrontation between police and anti-National Front demonstrators)
2	Apr	1980	St Paul's, Bristol (anti-police riots)
11-13	Apr	1981	Brixton (anti-police riot with racial overtones; trouble continued in Jul 81)
5-6	Jul	1981	Toxteth (major riot)
		1981-	Greenham Common (women's protests against nuclear weapons)
		1984-5	Miners' Strike (many confrontations between police and pickets)

Political Assassinations
(Members of the House of Lords or House of Commons)

22	Jun	1922	Sir H. Wilson. Field Marshal and M.P. (shot on his doorstep in London by Sinn Fein).
5	Apr	1979	A. Neave (car bomb in his car at the House of Commons)
27	Aug	1979	Earl Mountbatten (killed by bomb on holiday in N. Ireland)
14	Nov	1981	Revd R. Bradford (Ulster M.P. shot in Belfast)
10	Oct	1984	Sir A. Berry (bomb at Conservative Conference)

VI

CIVIL SERVICE

Heads of Departments and Public Offices

Except where stated otherwise, all these had the title of Permanent Secretary or Permanent Under-Secretary. The Permanent Secretary is the official head and usually the accounting officer of the Department and is responsible to the Minister for all the Department's activities. In some Departments, e.g. Defence since 1964, there are also Second Permanent Secretaries who are official heads and usually accounting officers for large blocks of work. Except where stated otherwise, all the following had the title of Permanent Secretary or Permanent Under-Secretary. The name is that by which they were known while in office; if a title was acquired while in office it is placed in brackets.

Admiralty

1884	Sir E. MacGregor
1907	Sir I. Thomas
1911	Sir G. Greene
1917	Sir O. Murray
1936	Sir R. Carter
1940	Sir H. Markham
1947	(Sir) J. Lang
1961	Sir C. Jarrett
1964	(see *Defence*)

Agriculture & Fisheries

1892	(Sir) T. Elliott
1913	Sir S. Olivier
1917	(Sir) D. Hall
1920	Sir F. Floud
1927	Sir C. Thomas
1936	(Sir) D. Fergusson
1945	Sir D. Vandepeer
1952	Sir A. Hitchman

(Agriculture, Fisheries & Food)

1955	Sir A. Hitchman
1959	Sir J. Winnifrith
1968	Sir B. Engholm
1973	Sir A. Neale
1978	(Sir) B. Hayes
1983	(Sir) M. Franklin

Air

1917	Sir A. Robinson
1920	(Sir) W. Nicholson
1931	(Sir) C. Bullock
1936	Sir D. Banks
1939	Sir A. Street
1945	Sir W. Brown
1947	Sir J. Barnes
1955	Sir M. Dean
1963	(Sir) M. Flett
1964	(see *Defence*)

Aircraft Production (Director-General)

1940	Sir A. Rowlands
1943	Sir H. Scott
1945 -1945	Sir F. Tribe

Aviation

(see *Transport & Civil Aviation*)

1959	Sir W. Strath
1960	(Sir) H. Hardman
1963	Sir R. Way
1966	Sir R. Clarke
1966 -1967	Sir R. Melville

Burma

(see *India & Burma*)

Cabinet Office

(Secretary to the Cabinet)

1916	(Sir) M. Hankey
1938	Sir E. Bridges
1947	Sir N. Brook
1963	Sir B. Trend
1973	Sir J. Hunt
1979	Sir R. Armstrong

(Chief Scientific Adviser)

1964	Sir S. Zuckerman (Ld)
1971	Sir A. Cottrell
1974	(*post vacant*)

(Head of Government Statistical Service)

1968	(Sir) C. Moser
1978	(Sir) A. Boreham

(Central Policy Review Staff: Director-General)

1970	Ld Rothschild
1974	Sir K. Berrill
1980	R. Ibbs
1982	J. Sparrow
1983	(*post vacant*)

(see pp. 385-6 for *Economic Advisers*)

Civil Aviation (Director-General)

1941 Sir W. Hildred
1946 Sir H. Self
1947 Sir A. Overton
1953 (see *Transport & Civil Aviation)*

Civil Service Commission (First Commissioner)

1892 W. Courthope
1907 Ld F. Hervey
1910 (Sir) S. Leathers
1928 (Sir) R. Meiklejohn
1939 (Sir) P. Waterfield
1951 P. Sinker
1954 (Sir) L. Helsby
1959 Sir G. Mallaby
1965 Sir G. Abell
1968 J. Hunt
1971 K. Clucas
1974 F. Allen
1981 A. Fraser
1983 D. Trevelyan

Head of the Home Civil Service

1919 Sir W. Fisher
1939 Sir H. Wilson
1942 Sir R. Hopkins
1945 Sir E. Bridges
1956 Sir N. Brook
1963 Sir L. Helsby
1968 Sir W. Armstrong
1974 Sir D. Allen
1978 Sir I. Bancroft
1981 Sir R. Armstrong

Civil Service Department

1968 Sir W. Armstrong
1974 Sir D. Allen
1978 Sir I. Bancroft
1981 (*post vacant*)

Colonial Office

1897 (Sir) E. Wingfield
1900 (Sir) M. Ommaney
1907 Sir F. Hopwood
1911 Sir. J. Anderson
1916 Sir G. Fiddes
1921 Sir J. Masterton-Smith
1925 Sir S. Wilson
1933 Sir J. Maffey
1937 Sir C. Parkinson
1940 Sir G. Gater
1940 Sir C. Parkinson
1942 Sir G. Gater
1947 Sir T. Lloyd
1956 Sir J. Macpherson
1959 Sir H. Poynton
1966 (see *Commonwealth Affairs*)

Commonwealth Relations Office

1947 { Sir E. Machtig / Sir A. Carter }
1949 Sir P. Liesching
1955 Sir G. Laithwaite
1959 Sir A. Clutterbuck
1962-1966 Sir S. Garner

(Commonwealth Affairs)

1966 Sir S. Garner
1968 Sir M. James
1968 (see *Foreign & Commonwealth Office)*

Customs Establishment (Chairman)

1900 (Sir) G. Ryder
1903 (Sir) T. Pittar

(Board of Customs and Excise)

1909 (Sir) L. Guillemard
1919 Sir H. Hamilton
1927 Sir F. Floud
1930 J. Grigg
1930 (Sir) E. Forber
1934 Sir E. Murray
1941 Sir W. Eady
1942 Sir A. Carter
1947 Sir W. Croft
1955 Sir J. Crombie
1963 Sir J. Anderson
1965 Sir W. Morton
1969 Sir L. Petch
1973 (Sir) R. Radford
1978 (Sir) D. Lovelock
1983 (Sir) A. Fraser

Defence

1947 Sir H. Wilson Smith
1948 Sir H. Parker
1956 Sir R. Powell
1960 Sir E. Playfair
1961 Sir R. Scott
1964 Sir H. Hardman
1966 Sir J. Dunnett
1974 Sir M. Cary
1976 Sir F. Cooper
1983 (Sir) C. Whitmore

Defence (Procurement) (Chief Executive)

1971 (Sir) D. Rayner
1972 Sir M. Cary
1974 (Sir) G. Leitch
1975 (Sir) C. Cornford
1980 (Sir) D. Cardwell
1983 D. Perry
1985 P. Levene

Dominions Office

1925 Sir C. Davies
1930 Sir E. Harding
1940 Sir C. Parkinson
1940-1947 Sir E. Machtig
(see *Commonwealth Relations Office*)

Economic Affairs

1964 Sir E. Roll
1966 (Sir) D. Allen
1968-1969 Sir W. Nield

Economic Warfare (Director-General)

1939 Sir F. Leith-Ross
1940 { Sir F. Leith-Ross / E of Drogheda }
1942-1945 E of Drogheda

Education (and Science)

1900 Sir G. Kekewich
1903 Sir R. Morant
1911 Sir A. Selby-Bigge
1925 Sir A. Symonds
1931 Sir H. Pelham
1937 (Sir) M. Holmes
1945 Sir J. Maud
1952 (Sir) G. Flemming
1959 Dame M. Smieton
1967 Sir H. Andrew
1970 (Sir) W. Pile
1976 (Sir) J. Hamilton
1983 (Sir) D. Hancock

Employment (see *Labour)*

Energy

1974 Sir J. Rampton
1980 Sir D. Maitland
1983 Sir K. Couzens
1985 P. Gregson

Environment

1970 Sir D. Serpell

1972 Sir J. Jones
1975 Sir I. Bancroft
1978 Sir J. Garlick
1981 (Sir) G. Moseley
1985 T. Heiser

Food (Director-General)

1918 Sir C. Fielding
1919-1921 F. Coller
1939 Sir H. French
1945 Sir F. Tribe
1946 Sir P. Liesching
1949 (Sir) F. Lee
1951 Sir H. Hancock
1955 (see *Agriculture, Fisheries & Food)*

Foreign Office

1894 Sir T. Sanderson (Ld)
1906 Sir C. Hardinge (Ld)
1910 Sir A. Nicolson
1916 Ld Hardinge
1920 Sir E. Crowe
1925 Sir W. Tyrrell
1928 Sir R. Lindsay
1930 Sir R. Vansittart
1938 Sir A. Cadogan
1946 Sir O. Sargent[1]
1949 Sir W. Strang[1]
1953 Sir I. Kirkpatrick
1957 Sir F. Hoyer Millar
1962 Sir H. Caccia
1965 Sir P. Gore-Booth[2]

Foreign and Commonwealth Office)[2]

1969 Sir D. Greenhill
1973 Sir T. Brimelow
1975 Sir M. Palliser
1982 Sir A. Acland

Forestry Commission (Chairman)

1920 Ld Lovat
1927 Ld Clinton
1929 Sir J. Stirling-Maxwell
1932 Sir R. Robinson (Ld)
1952 E of Radnor
1964 Earl Waldegrave
1966 L. Jenkins
1970 Ld Taylor of Gryfe
1976 J. Mackie
1979 Sir D. Montgomery

Fuel & Power

1942 Sir F. Tribe
1945 Sir D. Fergusson
1952 Sir J. Maud

(Power)

1957 Sir J. Maud
1958 (Sir) D. Proctor
1965 Sir M. Stevenson
1966 Sir D. Pitblado
1969 (see *Technology)*

Government Accountancy Service

1984 A. Wilson

Health

1919 Sir R. Morant
1920 Sir A. Robinson
1935 Sir G. Chrystal
1940 Sir J. Maude
1945 Sir W. Douglas
1951 (Sir) J. Hawton
1960 (Sir) B. Fraser
1964-1968 (Sir) A. France

(Health & Social Security)

1968 Sir C. Jarrett
1970 Sir P. Rogers
1975 Sir P. Nairne
1981 Sir K. Stowe

Home Office

1895 Sir K. Digby
1903 Sir M. Chalmers
1908 Sir E. Troup
1922 Sir J. Anderson
1932 Sir R. Scott
1938 Sir A. Maxwell
1948 Sir F. Newsam
1957 Sir C. Cunningham
1966 Sir P. Allen
1972 Sir A. Peterson
1977 (Sir) R. Armstrong
1979 Sir B. Cubbon

Home Security

1939 Sir T. Gardiner; Sir G. Gater
1940 Sir G. Gater
1942 Sir H. Scott
1943-1945 Sir W. Brown

Housing & Local Government

(see *Town & Country Planning*)

1951 Sir T. Sheepshanks
1955 Dame E. Sharp
1966 Sir M. Stevenson
1970 (see *Environment)*

India

1883 Sir A. Godley
1909 Sir R. Ritchie
1912 Sir T. Holderness
1920 Sir W. Duke
1924 Sir A. Hirtzel
1930 Sir F. Stewart

(India & Burma)

1937 Sir F. Stewart
1941-1948 (Sir) D. Monteath

Industry

1974 Sir A. Part
1976-1983 Sir P. Carey
(see *Trade and Industry*)

Information (Director of Propaganda)

1918-1919 A. Bennett

(Director-General)

1939 Sir K. Lee
1940 F. Pick
1941 Sir C. Radcliffe
1945-1946 E. Bamford

(Central Office of Information)

(Director-General)

1946 Sir E. Bamford
1946 Sir R. Fraser
1954 (Sir) T. Fife Clark
1971 F. Bickerton
1974 H. James
1978 J. Groves
1982 D. Grant
1985 N. Taylor

Board of Inland Revenue (Chairman)

1899 Sir H. Primrose
1907 (Sir) R. Chalmers

[1]Joint Permanent Under-Secretaries—Head of the German Section: 1947-9 Sir W. Strang, 1949-50 Sir I. Kirkpatrick, 1950-1 Sir D. Gainer.
[2]Since 1968 the Permanent Under-Secretary at the Foreign Office has also been designated Head of the Diplomatic Service.

1911 Sir M. Nathan
1914 Sir E. Nott-Bower
1918 W. Fisher
1919 Sir J. Anderson
1922 Sir R. Hopkins
1927 Sir E. Gowers
1930 (Sir) J. Grigg
1934 Sir E. Forber
1938 Sir G. Canny
1942 Sir C. Gregg
1948 Sir E. Bamford
1955 Sir H. Hancock
1958 Sir A. Johnston
1968 Sir A. France
1973 (Sir) N. Price
1976 Sir W. Pile
1980 Sir L. Airey

Irish Office

1893 Sir D. Harrel
1902 Sir A. Macdonnell
1908 Sir J. Dougherty
1914 Sir M. Nathan
1916 Sir W. Byrne
1918 J. Macmahon
1920-1922 { J. Macmahon / Sir J. Anderson

Labour

1916 (Sir) D. Shackleton
1920 { Sir D. Shackleton / Sir J. Masterton-Smith
1921 Sir H. Wilson
1930 Sir F. Floud
1935 Sir T. Phillips

(Labour & National Service)

1939 Sir T. Phillips
1944 (Sir) G. Ince
1956 Sir H. Emmerson

(Labour)

1959 Sir L. Helsby
1962 Sir J. Dunnett
1966 (Sir) D. Barnes

(Employment & Productivity)

1968 Sir D. Barnes

(Employment)

1970 Sir D. Barnes
1974 (Sir) C. Heron
1975 (Sir) K. Barnes
1983 (Sir) M. Quinlan

Land & Natural Resources

1964 F. Bishop
1965-1966 Sir B. Fraser

Local Government Board

1898 (Sir) S. Provis
1910-1919 (Sir) H. Monro

Secretary to the Ld Chancellor[1]

1885 (Sir) K. Mackenzie
1915 (Sir) C. Schuster
1944 (Sir) A. Napier
1954 (Sir) G. Coldstream
1968 (Sir) D. Dobson
1977 (Sir) W. Bourne
1982 (Sir) D. Oulton

Materials

1951 A. Hitchman
1952 Sir J. Helmore
1953-1954 Sir E. Bowyer

Munitions

1915 Sir H. Llewellyn Smith
1916 E. Phipps
1917 Sir G. Greene
1920-1921 { Sir S. Dannreuther / D. Neylan

National Health Service Management Board (Chairman)

1985 V. Paige

National Insurance

1944 Sir T. Phillips
1949 Sir H. Hancock
1951 Sir G. King
1953 (see *Pensions & National Insurance)*

National Service

1917 S. Fawcett
1918-1919 W. Vaughan

Northern Ireland

1972 Sir W. Nield
1973 (Sir) F. Cooper
1976 (Sir) B. Cubbon
1979 Sir P. Woodfield
1984 R. Andrew

Overseas Development

1964 Sir A. Cohen
1968 Sir G. Wilson
1970-1974 (see *Foreign & Commonwealth Office)*
1974 (Sir) R. King
1976-1979 (Sir) P. Preston

Pensions

1916 Sir M. Nathan
1919 Sir G. Chrystal
1935 Sir A. Hore
1941 (Sir) A. Cunnison
1946 Sir H. Parker
1948 Sir A. Wilson

(Pensions & National Insurance)

1953 Sir G. King
1955 Sir E. Bowyer
1965 Sir C. Jarrett
1966 (see *Social Security)*

Post Office

1899 Sir G. Murray
1903 Sir H. Babington-Smith
1909 Sir M. Nathan
1911 Sir A. King
1914 (Sir) E. Murray

(Director-General)

1934 (Sir) D. Banks
1936 Sir T. Gardiner
1946 Sir R. Birchall
1949 (Sir) A. Little
1955 (Sir) G. Radley
1960 Sir R. German
1966-1968 (Sir) J. Wall (*Deputy Chairman of Post Office Board)*

Power

(see *Fuel & Power)*

Prices and Consumer Protection

1974-1979 (Sir) K. Clucas
(see *Trade*)

[1] Full title, Permanent Secretary to the Ld Chancellor and Clerk of the Crown in Chancery. The Clerk of the Crown is not in the ordinary sense a civil servant and is, among other things, an officer of both Houses of Parliament.

Privy Council (Clerk of the Council)

1899 (Sir) A. FitzRoy
1923 Sir M. Hankey
1938 Sir R. Howorth
1942 (Sir) E. Leadbitter
1951 F. Fernau
1953 (Sir) W. Agnew
1974 (Sir) N. Leigh
1984 G. de Deney

Production

1942 Sir H. Self
1943-1945 J. Woods

Reconstruction

1943-1945 N. Brook

General Register Office (Registrar-General for England and Wales)

1880 Sir B. Henniker
1900 R. MacLeod
1902 (Sir) W. Dunbar
1909 (Sir) B. Mallet
1921 (Sir) S. Vivian
1945 (Sir) G. North
1959 E. Firth
1964 M. Reed
1972 G. Paine
1978 A. Thatcher

Department of Scientific and Industrial Research

(Secretary)

1916 (Sir) F. Heath
1927 H. Tizard
1929 (Sir) F. Smith
1939 (Sir) E. Appleton
1949 Sir B. Lockspeiser
1956 (Sir) H. Melville

(Science Research Council (Chairman))

1965 Sir H. Melville
1967 (Sir) B. Flowers
1973 S. Edwards
1977 (Sir) G. Allen
1981 Sir J. Kingman

Office of the Minister for Science

1962-1964 F. Turnbull

Scottish Office

1892 Sir C. Scott-Moncrieff
1902 Sir R. Macleod
1909 Sir J. Dodds
1921 Sir J. Lamb
1933 Sir J. Jeffrey
1937 J. Highton
1937 Sir H. Hamilton
1946 (Sir) D. Milne
1959 Sir W. Murie
1965 (Sir) D. Haddow
1973 (Sir) N. Morrison
1978 (Sir) W. Fraser

Shipping

1917 (Sir) J. Anderson
1919-1920 T. Lodge
1939-1941 Sir C. Hurcomb

Social Security

1966 Sir C. Jarrett
1968 (see *Health & Social Security)*

Supply

1939 Sir A. Robinson
1940 Sir G. Gater
1940 Sir W. Brown
1942 Sir W. Douglas
1945 O. Franks
1946 Sir A. Rowlands
1953 Sir J. Helmore
1956 Sir C. Musgrave
1959-1959 Sir W. Strath

Technology

1964 Sir M. Dean
1966 Sir R. Clarke
1970 (see *Trade & Industry)*

Town & Country Planning

1943 Sir G. Whiskard
1946 Sir T. Sheepshanks

(Local Government & Planning)

1951 Sir T. Sheepshanks
1951 (see *Housing & Local Government)*

Board of Trade

1893 Sir C. Boyle
1901 Sir F. Hopwood
1907 (Sir) H. Llewellyn Smith
1913 { Sir G. Barnes; Sir H. Llewellyn Smith }
1916 { Sir H. Llewellyn Smith; (Sir) W. Marwood }
1919 { Sir S. Chapman; Sir W. Marwood }
1919 { Sir S. Chapman; Sir H. Payne }
1920 Sir S. Chapman
1927 Sir H. Hamilton
1937 Sir W. Brown
1941 Sir A. Overton
1945 Sir J. Woods
1951 Sir F. Lee
1960 Sir R. Powell
1968 Sir A. Part

(Trade & Industry)

1970 Sir A. Part

(Trade)

1974 Sir P. Thornton
1977 (Sir) L. Pliatzky
1979 Sir K. Clucas

(Trade and Industry)

1983 { Sir B. Hayes; Sir A. Rawlinson }
1985 Sir B. Hayes

Transport

1919 Sir F. Dunnell
1921 Sir W. Marwood
1923 Sir J. Brooke
1927 C. Hurcomb
1937 Sir L. Browett

(Director-General of War Transport)

1941 Sir C. Hurcomb

(Transport)

1946 Sir C. Hurcomb
1947 Sir G. Jenkins

(Transport & Civil Aviation)

1953 Sir G. Jenkins

(Transport) (and see *Aviation)*

1959 Sir J. Dunnett
1962 Sir T. Padmore
1968 Sir D. Serpell
1970-1976 (see *Environment)*

1976	(Sir) P. Baldwin
1982	(Sir) P. Lazarus

Treasury

1894	Sir F. Mowatt
1902	Sir F. Mowatt Sir E. Hamilton
1903	Sir E. Hamilton Sir G. Murray
1908	Sir G. Murray
1911	Sir R. Chalmers
1913	Sir T. Heath Sir J. Bradbury
1916	Sir T. Heath Sir J. Bradbury Sir R. Chalmers
1919	Sir W. Fisher
1939	Sir H. Wilson
1942	Sir R. Hopkins
1945	Sir E. Bridges
1956	Sir N. Brook Sir R. Makins
1960	Sir N. Brook Sir F. Lee
1962	Sir N. Brook W. Armstrong
1963	Sir L. Helsby (Sir) W. Armstrong
1968	Sir W. Armstrong Sir D. Allen
1968	Sir D. Allen
1974	(Sir) D. Wass
1983	(Sir) P. Middleton

Unemployment Assistance Board (Chairman)

1934	Sir H. Betterton (Ld Rushcliffe)

(Assistance Board)

1940	Ld Rushcliffe
1941	Ld Soulbury

(National Assistance Board)

1948	G. Buchanan
1954	Sir G. Hutchinson (Ld Ilford)
1964-1966	Ld Runcorn

University Grants Committee (Chairman)

1919	Sir W. McCormick
1930	Sir W. Buchanan-Riddell
1935	Sir W. Moberly
1949	(Sir) A. Trueman
1953	(Sir) K. Murray
1968	(Sir) K. Berrill
1973	Sir F. Dainton
1978	(Sir) E. Parks
1983	Sir P. Swinnerton-Dyer

War Office

1897	Sir R. Knox
1901	Sir E. Ward
1914	Sir R. Brade
1920	Sir H. Creedy
1939	Sir J. Grigg
1942	Sir F. Bovenschen Sir E. Speed
1945	Sir E. Speed
1949	Sir G. Turner
1956	Sir E. Playfair
1960	(Sir) R. Way
1963	(Sir) A. Drew
1964	(see *Defence*)

Welsh Office

1964	(Sir) G. Daniel
1969	(Sir) I. Pugh
1971	(Sir) H. Evans
1980	(Sir) T. Hughes
1985	R. Lloyd-Jones

Works

1895	Sir R. Brett (Vt Esher)
1901	Sir S. McDonnell
1912	Sir L. Earle
1933	Sir P. Duff
1941	Sir G. Whiskard
1943	Sir P. Robinson
1946	Sir H. Emmerson
1956	Sir E. Muir

(Public Building & Works)

1962	Sir E. Muir
1965	(Sir) A. Part
1968	Sir M. Cary
1970	(see *Environment)*

Salary of Permanent Secretary to the Treasury

1900	£2,500	1950	£3,750
1910	£2,500	1960	£7,450
1920	£3,500	1970	£12,700
1930	£3,500	1980	£33,500
1940	£3,500	1985	£70,000

Prime Minister's Principal Private Secretary

1900	S. McDonnell	1947	L. Helsby
1902	J. Sandars	1950	D. Rickett
1905	A. Ponsonby	1951	D. Pitblado
1908	V. Nash	1952	D. Pitblado J. Colville
1912	M. Bonham-Carter	1955	D. Pitblado
1916	J. Davies	1956	F. Bishop
1922	(Sir) R. Waterhouse	1959	T. Bligh
1928	R. Vansittart	1964	D. Mitchell
1930	P. Duff	1966	A. Halls
1933	J. Barlow	1970	A. Isserlis
1934	H. Vincent	1970	R. Armstrong
1937	O. Cleverly	1975	K. Stowe
1939	A. Rucker	1979	C. Whitmore
1940	E. Seal	1983	R. Butler
1941	J. Martin		
1945	L. Rowan		

Prime Minister's Staff

In addition to an official Civil Service Principal Private Secretary all Prime Ministers have made their own arrangements for advice and help. These cannot be consistently categorised. The following have played significant roles.

Policy advisers

W. Adams 1917-18
P. Kerr 1918-21
E. Grigg 1921-22

Personal Assistant
F. Lindermann (Ld Cherwell) 1940-45
D. Jay 1945-46
W. Gorell Barnes 1946-48

Senior Policy Adviser to the Prime Minister
B. Donoughue 1974-79
J. Hoskyns 1979-82
F. Mount 1982-84
J. Redwood 1984-

Political Secretaries

Personal Private Secretaries
H. D. Usher and
Miss R. Rosenberg 1929-35

Private Secretary
J. Wyndham 1957-63

Personal Political Secretary
Mrs M. Williams 1964-70

Political Secretary
D. Hurd 1970-74

Personal and Political Secretary
Mrs M. Williams
(Lady Falkender) 1974-76

Political Adviser
T. McNally 1976-79

Political Secretary
R. Ryder 1979-82
D. Howe 1982-3
S. Sherbourne 1983-

'Chief of Staff'
D. Wolfson 1979-

In practice T. Balogh was a senior policy adviser to H. Wilson (1964-68) although located in the Cabinet Office.

Press Officers

Chief Press Liaison Officer
G. Steward 1931-44

Adviser on Public Relations
F. Williams 1945-47
P. Jordan 1947-51
R. Bacon 1951-52
W. Clark 1955-56
S. Evans 1957-64

Press Secretary
T. Lloyd-Hughes 1964-69
J. Haines 1969-70

Chief Press Secretary
D. Maitland 1970-73
W. Haydon 1973-74

Press Secretary
J. Haines 1974-76
T. McCaffrey 1976-79

Chief Press Secretary
B. Ingham 1979-

Special or Political Advisers in Government

Many Prime Ministers have brought in unofficial advisers and secretaries but political advisers only became established in an official way after 1974 (although in 1970-74 six or seven Conservative ministers had employed assistants paid from party funds). During Mr Wilson's 1974 ministry it was agreed that any Cabinet minister could appoint two political advisers with a tenure that lasted only as long as he or she continued in office. In 1979 Mrs Thatcher limited Cabinet ministers to one political adviser.

Size of Civil Service

Adequate statistics of the number of civil servants engaged in each branch of government activity since 1900 are not readily available. Moreover, the transfer of functions between departments makes comparisons of one year with another potentially misleading. An analysis of civil service strength for certain years is to be found in *The Organisation of British Central Government, 1914-1956*, by D. N. Chester and F. M. G. Wilson. The figures in heavy type in the following table are taken from the statement *Staffs Employed in Government Departments* which has been published annually, or more frequently, by the Treasury as a Command Paper since 1919 (with retrospective figures for 1914 included in the first issue). The figures in light type in the table are taken from the *Annual Estimates* presented to Parliament by the Civil Service and Revenue Departments, and the *East India Home Accounts*. These figures are liable to slight error as they are estimates and not reports of the actual staff employed. In each case they are estimates for the year ending March 31 of the following year (e.g. under the third column headed '1 Apr 1920' the estimates are for 1920-21). The source for the 1971 and 1977 figures are departmental returns made to the Civil Service Department. The figures in this table should be used with great caution because of the considerable differences in the sources.

Number of Civil Servants

	1900-01	1 Aug 1914	1 Apr 1920	1 Apr 1930	1 Apr 1938	1 Apr 1950	1 Apr 1960	1 Apr 1971	1 Apr 1980	1 Apr 1984
otal Non-industrial Staff	n.a.	**282,420**	**380,963**	**306,154**	**376,491**	**575,274**	**637,374**	*498,425*	547,486	504,246
otal Industrial Staff	n.a.	**497,100**	n.a.	**483,100**	**204,400**	**396,900**	**358,900**	*201,660*	157,417	119,726
otal Civil Service Staff	n.a.	**779,520**	n.a.	**789,254**	**580,891**	**972,174**	**996,274**	*700,085*	704,903	623,972
dmiralty	n.a.	**4,366**	**13,432**	**7,433**	**10,609**	**30,801**	**30,731**	f	n	n
Var Office	n.a.	**1,636**	**7,434**	**3,872**	**7,323**	**33,493**	**47,244**	f	n	n
ir	. .	. .	**2,839**	**1,704**	**4,317**	**24,407**	**27,563**	f	n	n
efence (Navy)	. .	. .	. .	. .	. .	. .	. .	*33,001*	n	n
efence (Army)	. .	. .	. .	. .	. .	. .	. .	*44,732*	n	n
efence (Air Force)	. .	. .	. .	. .	. .	. .	. .	*19,976*	n	n
efence (Centre)	. .	. .	. .	. .	. .	. .	. .	*14,131*	n	n
viation Supply	. .	. .	. .	. .	. .	**5,271**	**24,756**	*16,963*	n	n
efence (including Royal Ordnance factories)	. .	. .	. .	. .	. .	. .	. .	. .	118,450	98,029
oreign Office[av]	142	**187**	885	730	902	**6,195**	**5,992**	g	9,260	8,037
iplomatic Service	. .	. .	. .	. .	. .	. .	. .	*10,353* }		
verseas Development Administration								*2,449* }	2,031	1,716
olonial Office	109	**214**	256	365	438	1,286	1,211	g	. .	. .
ominions & C.R.O.	. .	. .	. .	52	91	904	847	. .	. .	. .
dia Office	589	**554**	342	n.a.	539	. .	. .	. .	. .	. .
ish Office	559	1,007	829	. .	. .	. .	. .	i	208	170
cottish Office	159	401	517	68	n.a.	749	887	*5,651*	9,990	8,871
'elsh Office[h]	. .	. .	. .	. .	. .	. .	. .	*903*	2,324	2,050
reasury[bx]	120	**140**	291	299	344	1,396	1,322	*1,012*	1,044	2,350
ome Office[v]	297	**773**	926	1,024	1,688	**3,953**	**3,534**	*21,743*	30,289	33,344
griculture	182	**2,976**	**3,446**	**2,463**	**4,588**	**16,842**	**14,938**	*14,874*	13,273	11,391
ducation (and Science)	864	**2,187**	1,522	1,041	1,435	**3,280**	**2,738**	*4,127*	2,594	2,383
nergy	. .	. .	. .	. .	. .	. .	. .	. .	1,252	1,093
nvironment	. .	. .	. .	. .	. .	. .	. .	*38,806*[j]	28,177	21,036
ood	. .	. .	**4,142**	. .	. .	**30,785**	c	. .	. .	. .
'uel and) Power	a	a	. .	. .	. .	**6,358**	**1,768**	k	. .	. .
ealth (and Social Security)			**5,820**	**6,711**	**6,771**	**5,893**	**4,993**	*71,811*[l]	95,923	90,205
abour	. .	**4,428**	**17,835**	**18,076**	**26,934**	**29,902**	**21,394**	m	. .	. .
mployment	. .	. .	. .	. .	. .	. .	. .	*31,099*[m]	48,718	55,375
lousing and) Local Government	425	**963**	d	d	d	1,312	**2,802**	j	. .	. .
'unitions	. .	**1,250**	**11,440**	. .	. .	. .	. .	. .	. .	. .
ational Insurance	. .	**1,957**	**2,263**	n.a.	n.a.	**35,539**	e	l	. .	. .
ensions	. .	. .	24,169	6,175	3,147	10,954	36,323	l	. .	. .
ost Office	79,482	**8,889**	**209,269**	**194,933**	**224,374**	**249,869**	**254,919**	. .	. .	. .
rices and Consumer Protection[y]	. .	. .	. .	. .	. .	. .	. .	. .	. .	. .
ıpply	. .	. .	. .	. .	. .	**13,312**	. .	. .	. .	. .
oard of Trade	1,359	**2,535**	**5,410**	**4,398**	**4,611**	**10,136**	**6,735**	k	. .	. .
rade & Industry[z]	. .	. .	. .	. .	. .	. .	. .	*24,549*[k]	. .	12,188
rade[yz]	. .	. .	. .	. .	. .	. .	. .	. .	7,163	. .
idustry[z]									8,499	. .
ransport	. .	. .	876	759	2,820	**6,906**	**6,909**	. .	12,792	13,551
orks	140	**679**	580	2,054	3,584	**17,573**	**10,693**	. .	. .	. .

	1900-01	1 Aug 1914	1 Apr 1920	1 Apr 1930	1 Apr 1938	1 Apr 1950	1 Apr 1960	1 Apr 1971	1 Apr 1980	1 Apr 1984
Customs and Excise	3,792	**10,256**	**12.602**	**11,659**	**14,669**	**14,236**	**15,338**	*17,949*	27,232	25,142
Exchequer and Audit Department	230	**269**	269	331	369	501	532	*577*	. .	. .
Inland Revenue Board	**5,345**	**9,753**	**19,446**	**21,059**	**24,342**	**49,740**	**56,026**	*69.765*	78,282	69,805
National Assistance	. .	. .	. .	. .	8,105	8,516	10,509	. .[t]	. .	. .
Stationery Office	100	**517**	728	1,660	1,947	**3,241**	**2,903**	*3,480*	3,070	2,123
Civil Service Department[x]	. .	. .	. .	. .	. .	. .	. .	*2,070*[u]	3,210	. .
Cabinet Office	n.a.	n.a.	n.a.	n.a.	186	393	319	565	580	1,829

[a] Home civil servants only.
[b] Not including subordinate departments (e.g. Committee of Imperial Defence, University Grants Commission).
[c] Combined with Ministry of Agriculture and Fisheries.
[d] The functions of the Local Government Board passed to the Ministry of Health in 1919. In 1943 the Ministry of Town and Country Planning (later becoming the Ministry of Housing and Local Government) took back many of these functions from the Ministry of Health.
[e] National Insurance merged with the Ministry of Pensions, and in 1966 together with the N.A.B. became the Ministry of Social Security.
[f] In 1964 the Admiralty, War Office and Air Office were combined into the Ministry of Defence.
[g] In 1965 the Foreign Office, Commonwealth Relations Office, Trade Commission Service and attachés abroad were combined into the Diplomatic Service.
[h] The Welsh Office was set up in 1964.
[i] The Northern Ireland Office was set up in 1972.
[j] In 1970 Ministry of Housing and Local Government, Ministry of Public Building and Works, and the Ministry of Transport were combined into the Department of the Environment.
[k] In 1970 the Board of Trade and Ministry of Technology combined into the Department of Trade and Industry.
[l] In 1968 the Ministry of Social Security and Ministry of Health combined into the Department of Health and Social Security.
[m] The Ministry of Labour is now the Department of Employment.
[n] Included in Defence from 1977.
[p] In 1974 Minsitry of Overseas Development was set up independently from Foreign and Commonwealth Office.
[q] In 1971 the Office of Manpower Economics was set up within Dept. of Employment. In 1974 the Manpower Services Commission, Employment Services Agency, the Training Services Agency, and the Health & Safety Commissioners were set up within the Dept. of Employment Group.
[r] In 1974 the Dept. of Trade and Industry ceased to exist, and the Depts. of Trade, Industry, Energy, & Prices & Consumer Protection were set up.
[s] The Ministry of Transport became a separate department again in 1976.
[t] In 1970 Ministry of Housing and Local Government, Ministry of Public Building and Works, and the Ministry of Transport were combined into the Department of the Environment.
[u] The Civil Service Department was formed in 1968 by the merger of the Civil Service Commission and the pay and management side of the Treasury.
[v] From 1 Apr 1984 responsibility for the Passport Office passed from the Foreign and Commonwealth Office to the Home Office (around 900 staff were involved).
[w] Scottish Office formed on 1 Apr 1972 from central services, DAFS, SDD, SED and SHHD.
[x] The Civil Service Department was disbanded on 10 Nov 1981. Work on efficiency, personnel management, recruitment and training was discharged by a new government department—The Management and Personnel Office, now part of the Cabinet Office. Responsibility for manpower, pay, superannuation allowances and the CCTA were transferred to the Treasury.
[y] On 10 May 1979 the Department of Prices and Consumer Protection was abolished and the Civil Service Staff merged with the Department of Trade.
[z] In Jun 1983 the Department of Trade and Industry were merged to become one department.

SOURCES.—*Staffs Employed in Government Departments* (H.M.S.O., first published in 1919), figures in heavy type. *Civil Estimates, Estimates for Revenue Departments, Service Estimates*, and *East India Home Accounts* (H.M.S.O. annually), figures in light type. Figures for 1960 onwards collected by the Civil Service Department and H.M. Treasury, in italics. Departmental figures are in respect of the Non-Industrial Civil Service only.

VII

ROYAL COMMISSIONS, COMMITTEES OF INQUIRY AND TRIBUNALS

Investigatory Processes

THE public investigation of problems can take a number of forms—Royal Commissions, Tribunals, *ad hoc* departmental Committees and special parliamentary conferences or committees. We do not deal here with purely parliamentary bodies like the Speaker's Conferences (on Electoral Reform—see p. 245—and on Devolution) or like the Select Committees set up from time to time by the House of Commons and/or the House of Lords. But we attempt an exhaustive listing of all domestic Royal Commissions and of all Tribunals of Inquiry appointed under the *Tribunals of Inquiry Act, 1921*, as well as an arbitrary selection from the 1,000 or so *ad hoc* and statutory Committees of Inquiry appointed since 1900. It is, however, important to remember that the decision whether to refer a problem to a Royal Commission or a Committee is not necessarily determined by the importance of the subject. Royal Commissions are listed fully here because the number is not excessive. Departmental Committees, which have been much more numerous, often deal with relatively narrow and limited matters; we have selected only a few which seemed plainly as important as the average Royal Commission. We have also omitted any reference to committees and sub-committees appointed by Royal Commissions and by standing governmental advisory bodies, though these include some reports of importance, such as the Report to the Central Advisory Council on Education by Lady Plowden's Committee on Primary Education (1967).

Advisory Committees appointed by the Government are of two basic types (apart from those which are just internal committees of civil servants): (*a*) standing committees, set up to give advice on such matters, usually within some general class of subjects, as may from time to time be referred to them or otherwise come to their attention; and (*b*) *ad hoc* committees, which are appointed to carry out some specific mandate and which come to an end when that mandate is discharged. These committees may be appointed directly by the Minister in his own name or indirectly in the name of the Crown. Finally, standing and *ad hoc* committees may both be appointed in two different ways: namely, by virtue of conventional or (in the case of the Crown) prerogative powers, or by virtue of authority conferred by Parliament by means of a statute.

Royal Commissions

Royal Commissions are *ad hoc* advisory committees formally appointed by the Crown by virtue of its prerogative powers. All such committees appointed since the turn of the century are listed in the table below, along with the name of their chairman, their size, the dates of their appointment and adjournment, and the Command number of their final report. There is no 'official' title for a Royal Commission, so that usage may vary slightly from that given below. Where there were two successive chairmen for a single committee, both are listed. The size of a Royal Commission is given as of the date of its appointment; subsequent changes in membership are not shown. The date of appointment is the date on which the Royal Warrant appointing the committee was signed, and the date of adjournment is the date of signature of the last report issued (or, failing that, the date of its presentation to the House of Commons). Command numbers in the twentieth century form part of three successive series, each of which is marked by a different abbreviation of the word 'Command' as follows:

1900-18: Cd. 1 to Cd. 9239
1919-56: Cmd. 1 to Cmd. 9889
1956- : Cmnd. 1, which had reached Cmnd. 7500 by Mar 79

Title	Chairman	Size	Date appointed	Date of Report	Command number
Military and Civil Expenditure of India	Ld Welby	14	Aug 96	Apr 00	131
Local Taxation	Ld Balfour	14	Aug 96	May 01	638
University of London Act	Ld Davy	8	Aug 98	Feb 00	83
Newfoundland. Operation of Certain Treaties	Sir J. Bramston	2	Aug 98	*Report not published*	
Accidents to Railway Servants	Ld Hereford	14	May 99	Jan 00	41
Salmon Fisheries	E of Elgin	9	Mar 00	Jul 02	1188
Administration of the Port of London	Earl Egerton Ld Revelstoke	7	Jun 00	Jun 02	1151
South African Hospitals	Sir R. Romer	5	Jul 00	Jan 01	453
Poisoning by Arsenic (Arsenic in Beer and Other Articles of Diet)	Ld Kelvin	6	Feb 01	Nov 03	1848
University Education (Ireland)	Ld Robertson	11	Jul 01	Feb 03	1483
Tuberculosis	Sir M. Foster W. H. Power	5	Aug 01	Jun 11	5761
Coal Supplies	Ld Allerton	15	Dec 01	Jan 05	2353
Alien Immigration	Ld James	7	Mar 02	Aug 03	1741
Physical Training (Scotland)	Ld Mansfield	9	Mar 02	Mar 03	1507
Martial Law Sentences in S. Africa	Ld Alverstone	3	Aug 02	Oct 02	136
South African War	E of Elgin	7	Sep 02	Jul 03	1789
Superannuation in the Civil Service	L. Courtney	9	Nov 02	Aug 03	1744
Locomotion and Transport in London	Sir D. Barbour	12	Feb 03	Jun 05	2597

Title	Chairman	Size	Date appointed	Date of Report	Command number
Militia and Volunteer Forces	D of Norfolk	10	Apr 03	May 04	2061
Food Supply in Time of War	Ld Balfour of Burleigh	17	Apr 03	Aug 05	2643
Trade Disputes and Trade Combinations	A Murray (Ld Dunedin)	5	Jun 03	Jan 06	2825
Ecclesiastical Discipline	Sir M. Hicks Beach	14	Apr 04	Jun 06	3040
The Feeble-Minded	M of Bath	10	Sep 04	. .	. .
Churches (Scotland)	E of Elgin	3	Dec 04	Apr 05	2494
War Stores in South Africa	Sir G. Farwell	5	Jun 05	Jul 06	3127
Motor-car	Ld Selby	7	Sep 05	Jul 06	3080
Poor Laws	Ld Hamilton	18	Dec 05	Feb 09	4498
Canals and Inland Navigation of the United Kingdom	Ld Shuttleworth	15	Mar 06	Dec 09	4979
Duties of the Metropolitan Police	D. B. Jones A. Lyttelton	5	May 06	Jun 08	4156
Registration of Title	Ld Dunedin	8	May 06	Jul 10	5316
Safety in Mines	Ld Monkswell H. Cunynghame	9	Jun 06	. .	. .
Trinity College Dublin	Sir E. Fry	9	Jun 06	Jan 07	3311
Coast Erosion	I. Guest	13	Jul 06	*reconstituted*	. .
Congested Districts in Ireland	E of Dudley	9	Jul 06	May 08	4097
Lighthouse Administration	G. Balfour	5	Aug 06	Jan 08	3923
Vivisection	Ld Selby A. Ram	10	Sep 06	Mar 12	6114
Care and Control of the Feeble-Minded	E of Radnor	12	Nov 06	Jul 08	4202
Shipping 'Rings' or Conferences generally	A. Cohen	21	Nov 06	*reconstituted*	. .
Mines and Quarries	Ld Monkswell	9	May 07	Feb 11	5561
Church of England in Wales and Monmouthshire	Sir R. Vaughan-Williams	9	Jun 07	Nov 10	5432
Indian Decentralisation	Sir H. Primrose C. Hobhouse	6	Sep 07	Feb 09	4360
Whisky and other Potable Spirits	Ld Hereford	8	Feb 08	Jul 09	4796
Coast Erosion and Afforestation	I. Guest	19	Mar 08	May 11	5708
Land Transfer Acts	Ld St. Aldwyn	12	Jul 08	Jan 11	5483
Systems of Election	Ld R. Cavendish	8	Dec 08	May 10	5163
University Education in London	Ld Haldane	8	Feb 09	Mar 13	6717
Mauritius	Sir F. Swettenham	3	May 09	Apr 10	5185
Trade Relations between Canada and the West Indies	Ld Balfour	5	Aug 09	Aug 10	5369
Selection of Justices of the Peace	Ld James	16	Nov 09	Jul 10	5250
Divorce and Matrimonial Causes	Ld Gorell	14	Nov 09	Nov 12	6478
Metalliferous Mines and Quarries	Sir H. Cunynghame	9	May 10	Jun 14	7476
Public Records	Sir F. Pollock	9	Oct 10	Apr 18	367
Railways Conciliation and Arbitration Scheme of 1907	Sir D. Hamel	5	Aug 11	Oct 11	5922
Malta	Sir F. Mowatt	3	Aug 11	May 12	6090
Civil Service	Ld MacDonnell H. Smith	19	Mar 12	Nov 15	7832
The Natural Resources, Trade and Legislation of the Dominions	E. Vincent	10	Apr 12	Feb 17	8462
Public Services (India)	Ld Islington	12	Sep 12	Aug 15	8282
Housing of the Industrial Population of Scotland, rural and urban	G. Ballantyne	12	Oct 12	Sep 17	8731
Delay in the King's Bench Division	Ld St. Aldwyn	11	Dec 12	Nov 13	7177
Finance and Currency (East Indies)	A. Chamberlain	10	Apr 13	Feb 14	7236
Venereal Diseases	Ld Sydenham	15	Nov 13	Feb 16	8189
Meat Export Trade of Australia	P. Street	1	Jun 14	Apr 15	7896
The circumstances connected with the Landing of Arms at Howth July 26th, 1914	Ld Shaw	3	Aug 14	Sep 14	7631

Title	Chairman	Size	Date appointed	Date of Report	Command number
University Education in Wales	Ld Haldane	9	Apr 16	Feb 18	8991
The Rebellion in Ireland	Ld Hardinge	3	May 16	Jun 16	8729
The Arrest and subsequent treatment of Mr Francis Sheehy Skeffington, Mr Thomas Dickson, and Mr Patrick James McIntyre	Sir J. Simon	3	Aug 16	Sep 16	8376
Allegations against Sir John Jackson, Limited	A. Chamel	3	Nov 16	Mar 17	8518
Proportional Representation	J. Lowther	5	Feb 18	Apr 18	9044
Decimal Coinage	Ld Emmott	20	Aug 18	Feb 20	628
Income Tax	Ld Colwyn	21	Apr 19	Mar 20	615
Agriculture	H. Peat	23	Jul 19	Dec 19	473[1]
Oxford and Cambridge Universities	H. Asquith	19	Nov 19	Mar 22	1588
The University of Dublin (Trinity College)	A. Geikie	5	Mar 20	Nov 20	1078
Fire Brigades and Fire Prevention	Sir P. Laurence	14	Jan 21	Jul 23	1945
The Importation of Store Cattle	Ld Finlay	5	May 21	Aug 21	1139
Local Government of Greater London	Vt Ullswater	8	Oct 21	Feb 23	1830
Honours	Ld Dunedin	7	Sep 22	Dec 22	1789
Local Government	E of Onslow	12	Feb 23	Nov 29	3436
Mining Subsidence	Ld Blanesburgh	13	Jun 23	Jun 27	2899
Superior Civil Services India	H. Lee	9	Jun 23	Mar 24	2128
Lunacy and Mental Disorder	H. Macmillan	10	Jul 24	Jul 26	2700
National Health Insurance	Ld Lawrence	13	Jul 24	Feb 26	2596
Food Prices	Sir A. Geddes	16	Nov 24	Apr 25	2390
Indian Currency and Finance	E. Hilton Young	9	Aug 25	Jul 26	*Parl. paper*
The Coal Industry	Sir H. Samuel	4	Sep 25	Mar 26	2600
Court of Session and the Office of Sheriff Principal (Scotland)	Ld Clyde	9	Jan 26	Jan 27	2801
Agriculture in India	M of Linlithgow	10	Apr 26	Apr 28	3132
Cross-River Traffic in London	Ld Lee of Fareham	6	Jul 26	Nov 26	2772
Land Drainage in England and Wales	Ld Bledisloe	11	Mar 27	Dec 27	2993
National Museums and Art Galleries	Vt d'Abernon	11	Jul 27	Jan 30	3463
London Squares	M of Londonderry	14	Aug 27	Sep 28	3196
Police Powers and Procedure	Ld Lee	8	Aug 28	Mar 29	3297
Transport	Sir A. Griffith-Boscawen	12	Aug 28	Dec 30	3751
Labour in India	J. Whitley	11	Jul 29	Mar 31	3583
Licensing (England and Wales)	Ld Amulree	19	Sep 29	May 31	3988
Civil Service	Ld Tomlin	16	Oct 29	Jul 31	3909
Licensing (Scotland)	Ld Mackay	14	Oct 29	May 31	3894
Unemployment Insurance	H. Gregory	7	Dec 30	Oct 32	4185
Malta	Ld Askwith	3	Apr 31	Jan 32	3993
Lotteries and Betting	Sir S. Rowlatt	12	Jun 32	Jun 33	4341
Newfoundland	Ld Amulree	3	Feb 33	Oct 33	4480
The University of Durham	Ld Moyne	8	Mar 34	Jan 35	4815
Tithe Rentcharge in England and Wales	J. Williams	4	Aug 34	Nov 35	5095
Despatch of Business at Common Law	Earl Peel	7	Dec 34	Jan 36	5065
Private Manufacture of and Trading in Arms	J. Bankes	7	Feb 35	Sep 36	5292
Local Government in the Tyneside Area	Sir A. Scott	5	May 35	Feb 37	5402
Merthyr Tydfil	Sir A. Lowry	2	May 35	Nov 35	5039
Safety in Coal Mines	Ld Rockley	10	Dec 35	Dec 38	5890
Palestine	Earl Peel	1	Aug 36	Jun 37	5479
The Distribution of the Industrial Population	Sir M. Barlow	13	Jul 37	Dec 39	6153

[1] Interim Report only: no Final Report published.

Title	Chairman	Size	Date appointed	Date of Report	Command number
Rhodesia-Nyasaland	Vt Bledisloe	1	Mar 38	Mar 39	5949
West Indies	Ld Moyne	1	Aug 38	Dec 39	6607
Workmen's Compensation	Sir H. Hetherington	15	Dec 38	Dec 44	658
Population	Vt Simon	16	Mar 44	. .	
	Sir H. Henderson	14	May 46	Mar 49	7695
Equal Pay	C. Asquith	9	Oct 44	Oct 46	6937
Justices of the Peace	Ld du Parcq	16	Jun 46	May 48	7463
The Press	Sir D. Ross	17	Apr 47	Jun 49	7700
Betting, Lotteries and Gaming	H. Willink	13	Apr 49	Mar 51	8190
Capital Punishment	Sir E. Gowers	12	May 49	Sep 53	8932
Taxation of Profits and Income	Ld Cohen	14	Jan 51		
	Ld Radcliffe	14	. .	May 55	9474
University Education in Dundee	Ld Tedder	9	Mar 51	Apr 52	8514
Marriage and Divorce	Ld Morton of Henry-ton	18	Sep 51	Dec 55	9678
Scottish Affairs	E of Balfour	15	Jul 52	Jul 54	9212
East Africa	Sir H. Dow	8	Jan 53	May 55	9475
The Civil Service	Sir R. Priestley	12	Nov 53	Nov 55	9613
The Law Relating to Mental Illness and Mental Deficiency	Ld Percy of Newcastle	11	Feb 54	May 57	169
Common Land	Sir I. Jennings	12	Dec 55	Jul 58	462
Doctors' and Dentists' Remu-neration	Sir H. Pilkington	9	Mar 57	Feb 60	939
Local Government in Greater London	Sir E. Herbert	7	Dec 57	Oct 60	1164
The Police	Sir H. Willink	15	Jan 60	Apr 62	1728
The Press	Ld Shawcross	5	Mar 61	May 62	1811
The Penal System in England and Wales	Vt Amory	16	Jul 64	*wound up* May 66	
Reform of the Trade Unions and Employers' Associations	Ld Donovan	12	Apr 65	Jun 68	3623
Medical Education	Ld Todd	16	Jun 65	Mar 68	3569
Tribunals of Inquiry	Sir C. Salmon	7	Feb 66	Nov 66	3121
The Examination of Assizes and Quarter Sessions	Ld Beeching	8	Nov 66	Sep 69	4153
Local Government, England	Sir J. Maud (Ld)	11	May 66	Jun 69	4040
Local Government, Scotland	Ld Wheatley	9	May 66	Sep 69	4150
The Constitution	Ld Crowther Ld Kilbrandon	16	Apr 69	Oct 73	5460
Civil Liability and Compensation	Ld Pearson	16	Mar 73	Mar 78	7054
The Press	Sir M. Finer O. McGregor	11	Jun 74	Jul 77	6810
Standards of Conduct in Gov-ernment	Ld Salmon	12	Jul 74	Jul 76	6526
Gambling	Vt Rothschild	10	Feb 76	Jul 78	7200
National Health Service	Sir A. Merrison	16	May 76	Jul 79	7613
Legal Services	Sir H. Benson	15	Jul 76	Oct 79	7648
Criminal Procedures	Sir C. Philips	16	Dec 77	Jan 81	8092

Permanent and Operating Commissions

Certain Royal Commissions have an enduring existence:

The *Royal Commission on Historical Manuscripts* set up in 1869 sits under the *ex officio* Chairmanship of the Master of the Rolls. It was reconstituted with extended powers in 1959. Its task is to advise and assist in the preservation of historical manuscripts and to publish them.

The *Royal Commission on Historical Monuments* was set up for England in 1908 with similar bodies for Scotland (reconstituted 1948) and

Wales and Monmouthshire. Their task is to maintain an inventory of Ancient Monuments.

The *Royal Fine Arts Commission* was set up in 1924 (reconstituted in 1933 and 1946) and the *Royal Fine Art Commission for Scotland* in 1927 (reconstituted 1948): their task is to inquire into questions of public amenity and artistic importance.

The *Royal Commission for the Exhibition of 1851*, surviving from the winding up of the affairs of the Great Exhibitions, still distributes the income from surplus funds to promote scientific and artistic education. There was also the *Royal Commission for the Patriotic Fund (1854-1904)*. In addition, there have been operating Commissions for the *Paris Exhibition of 1900*, the *St Louis Exhibition of 1904*, and for the *International Exhibitions at Brussels, Rome and Turin in 1910 and 1911*. Another miscellaneous group of operating Royal Commissions covered *Sewage Disposal (1898-1915)*, *Horse-Breeding (1887-1911)*, and *Crofter Colonisation (1888-1906)*.

War produced another group of operating or semi-permanent Royal Commissions, *Sugar Supply* (1914-21), *Wheat Supplies* (1916-25), *Paper and Paper making materials* (1917-[1]), *Defence of the Realm Losses* (1915-20), *Compensation for Suffering Damage by Enemy Action* (1921-24), *Awards to Inventors* (1919-35, 1946-56) and *Foreign Compensation Commission* (1950-). The Royal Commission on the *Distribution of Incomes*, set up under Ld Diamond in 1974, had a continuing existence until 1979.

Other Crown Committees

The Crown has also appointed a number of other advisory committees, some of which are called 'Royal Commissions' but all of which are different from those listed above. Some of them are different because they are standing, not *ad hoc*, in nature. Two of these appointed in the nineteenth century are still in existence: the Commission on the Exhibition of 1851 (appointed in 1850) and the Historical Manuscripts Commission (appointed in 1869). In the present century there have been thirteen others appointed (see table below), of which six are still in existence. All of them were appointed by virtue of prerogative powers. Other Crown advisory committees are different from those listed above because they were appointed by virtue of statutory, not prerogative, powers. Four, all of them *ad hoc* in nature, have been appointed in this century; they dealt with Property of the Free Church of Scotland (1905-10, Cd. 5060), the Election in Worcester in 1906 (1906, Cd. 3262), the Coal Industry (1919, Cmd. 360), and Indian Government (1927-30, Cmd. 3568). Finally, the Government in Ireland prior to 1922 appointed a special kind of committee in the name of the Crown called a 'Vice-Regal Commission'; thirteen were appointed in this century (see table below).

[1] No Final Report.

Standing Advisory Committees Appointed by the Crown since 1900
(including continuing Royal Commissions producing reports)

Title	Date of appoint-ment	Date of adjourn-ment	Report
Ancient and Historical Monuments and Constructions in Scotland	Feb 08	*	Cmnd. 9404
Ancient Monuments and Constructions of Wales and Monmouthshire	Aug 08	*	Cmnd. 8645
Ancient and Historical Monuments and Constructions of England	Oct 08	*	Cmnd. 9351
Supply of Sugar	Aug 14	Apr 21	Cmd. 1300
Defence of the Realm Losses	Mar 15	Nov 20	Cmd. 1044
Supply of Paper	Feb 16	Feb 18	None issued
Supply of Wheat	Oct 16	Jul 25	Cmd. 2462
Awards to Inventors	Mar 19	Nov 37	Cmd. 5594
Compensation for Suffering and Damage by Enemy Action	Aug 21	Feb 24	Cmd. 2066
Fine Art	May 24	*	Cmnd. 4832
Fine Art for Scotland	Aug 27	*	Cmnd. 4317
Awards to Inventors	May 46	Apr 56	Cmd. 9744
Environmental Pollution	Feb 70	*	Cmnd. 9149

* Commission still in existence; report is latest issued.

Irish Vice-Regal Commissions

Title	Chairman	Size	Date appointed	Date of Report	Command number
Irish Inland Fisheries	S. Walker	7	Aug 99	Jan 01	448
Poor Law Reform in Ireland	W. L. Micks	3	May 03	Oct 06	3202
Trinity College, Dublin, Estates Commission	G. Fitzgibbon	3	Jun 04	Apr 05	2526
Arterial Drainage (Ireland)	A. Binnie	5	Sep 05	Feb 07	3374
Irish Railways, including Light Railways	C. Scotter	7	Jul 06	Jul 10	5247
Circumstances of the Loss of the Regalia of the Order of St. Patrick	J. Shaw	3	Jan 08	Jan 08	3936
Irish Milk Supply	P. O'Neill	9	Nov 11	Oct 13	7129
Primary Education (Ireland) System of Inspection	S. Dill	8	Jan 13	Jan 14	7235
Dublin Disturbances	D. Henry	2	Dec 13	Feb 14	7269
Primary Education (Ireland) 1918	Ld Killanin	17	Aug 18	Feb 19	60
Intermediate Education (Ireland)	T. Molony	14	Aug 18	Mar 19	66
Under Sheriffs and Bailiffs (Ireland)	T. O'Shaughnessy	5	Oct 18	May 19	190
Reorganisation and Pay of the Irish Police Forces	J. Ross	6	Oct 19	Dec 19	603
Clerk of the Crown and Peace, Etc. (Ireland)	J. Wakely	7	Oct 19	Jun 20	805

Departmental Committees

Departmental Committees are *ad hoc* advisory committees appointed by Ministers by virtue of their conventional powers. As such they are the direct counterpart of Royal Commissions. In the table below are listed some of the more important Departmental Committees appointed since the turn of the century. As with Royal Commissions, there is no 'official' title for a Departmental Committee, so usage may vary slightly; where there were two successive chairmen, both are listed; and the dates of appointment and report as well as the Command number are derived in the same manner as for Royal Commissions.

A Select List of Departmental Committees 1900-

In the absence of any single official title for a Committee we have tried to select the most commonly used short title. The Command number given is that of the final report.

Title	Chairman	Date appointed	Date of Report	Command number
Compensation for Injuries to Workmen	K. Digby	Nov 03	Aug 04	2208
Motor Cars	R. Hobhouse	Jan 04	Apr 04	2069
Income Tax	C. Ritchie	. .	Jun 05	2575
Company and Commercial Law and Practice	C. Warmington	Feb 05	Jun 06	3052
Accounts of Local Authorities	W. Runciman	Jan 06	Jul 07	3614
Law of Copyright	Ld Gorell	Mar 09	Dec 09	4967
Probation of Offenders Act '07	H. Samuel	Mar 09	Dec 09	5001
Procedure of Royal Commissions	Ld Balfour of Burleigh	Apr 09	Jun 10	5235
Railway Agreements and Amalgamations	R. Rea	June 09	Apr 11	5631
Alien Immigrants at the Port of London	R. Lehmann	. .	Mar 11	5575
Educational Endowments	C. Trevelyan	. .	Mar 11	5662
National Guarantee for the War Risks of Shipping	A. Chamberlain	. .	. .	7560
Local Taxation	Sir J. Kempe	Nov 12	Mar 14	7315
Retrenchment in the Public Expenditure	R. McKenna	Jul 15	Sep 15	8068
Royal Aircraft Factory	R. Burbridge	Mar 16	Jul 16	8191
Increase of Prices of Commodities since the beginning of the War	J. Robertson	Jun 16	Sep 16	8358
Summer Time	J. Wilson	Sep 16	Feb 17	8487
Commercial and Industrial Policy. Imperial Preference	Ld Balfour of Burleigh	. .	Feb 17	8482
Currency and Foreign Exchanges	Ld Cunliffe	Jan 18	Dec 19	464
National Expenditure	Ld Geddes	Aug 21	Feb 22	1589
Broadcasting	Sir M. Sykes	Apr 23	Aug 23	1951
Imperial Wireless Telegraphy	Sir R. Donald	Jan 24	Feb 24	2060
National Debt and Taxation	H. Colwyn	Mar 24	Nov 26	2800
Broadcasting	Ld Crawford and Balcarres	Aug 25	Mar 26	2599
Ministers' Powers	E of Donoughmore	Oct 29	Apr 32	4060
Finance and Industry	H. Macmillan (Ld)	Nov 29	Jun 31	3897
Regional Development	H. Chelmsford	Jan 31	Mar 31	3915
National Expenditure	Sir G. May	Mar 31	Jul 31	3920
Depressed Areas	*(3 Area Chairmen)*	Apr 34	Nov 34	4728
Broadcasting	Vt Ullswater	Apr 35	Mar 36	5091
Parliamentary Pensions	Sir W. Fisher	Jul 35	Nov 37	5624
Compensation and Betterment	Sir A. Uthwatt	Jan 41	Sep 42	6291
Social Insurance and Allied Services	Sir W. Beveridge	Jun 41	Nov 42	6404
Training of Civil Servants	R. Assheton	Feb 43	Apr 44	6525
Company Law Amendment	Sir L. Cohen	Jun 43	Jun 45	6659
Television	Ld Hankey	Sep 43	Dec 44	*N-p*
Rent Control	Vt Ridley	Nov 43	Feb 45	6621
Legal Aid and Legal Advice in England and Wales	Ld Rushcliffe	May 44	May 45	6641
Gas Industry	G. Heyworth	Jun 44	Nov 45	6699

Title	Chairman	Date appointed	Date of Report	Command number
Social and Economic Research	Sir J. Clapham	Jan 45	Jun 46	6868
Care of Children	Miss M. Curtis	Mar 45	Aug 46	6922
National Parks (England and Wales)	Sir A. Hobhouse	Jul 45	Mar 47	7121
New Towns	Ld Reith	Oct 45	Jul 46	6876
Port Transport Industry	R. Evershed	Nov 45	Dec 45	*N-p*
Shops and Non-Industrial Employment	Sir E. Gowers	Jan 46	Mar 49	7664
Resale Price Maintenance	Sir G. Lloyd-Jacob	Aug 47	Mar 49	7696
Higher Civil Service Remuneration	Ld Chorley	Jan 48	Sep 48	7635
Leasehold	Ld Uthwatt Ld Jenkins	Feb 48	Jun 50	7982
Political Activities of Civil Servants	J. Masterman	Apr 48	Apr 49	7718
Intermediaries	Sir E. Herbert	Feb 49	Oct 49	7904
Broadcasting	Ld Beveridge	Jun 49	Dec 50	8116
Fuel and Power Resources	Vt Ridley	Jul 51	Jul 52	8647
Departmental Records	Sir J. Grigg	Jun 52	May 54	9163
National Health Service	C. Guillebaud	May 53	Nov 55	9663
Air Pollution	Sir H. Beaver	Jul 53	Nov 54	9322
Crichel Down	A. Clark	Nov 53	May 54	9176
Electricity Supply Industry	Sir E. Herbert	Jul 54	Dec 55	9672
Homosexual Law Reform	Sir J. Wolfenden	Aug 54	Aug 57	247
Crown Lands	Sir M. Trustram Eve	Dec 54	May 55	9843
Dock Workers' Scheme	Sir P. Devlin	Jul 55	Jun 56	9813
Administrative Tribunals and Inquiries	Sir O. Franks	Nov 55	Jul 57	218
Children and Young People	Vt Ingleby	Oct 56	Oct 60	1191
Damage and Casualties in Port Said	Sir E. Herbert	Dec 56	Dec 56	47
Working of the Monetary System	Ld Radcliffe	May 57	Jul 59	827
Interception of Communications	Sir N. Birkett	Jun 57	Sep 57	283
Preservation of Downing Street	E of Crawford	Jul 57	Mar 58	457
The Structure of the Public Library Service in England and Wales	Sir S. Roberts	Sep 57	Dec 58	660
The Youth Service in England and Wales	Ctss of Albemarle	Nov 58	Oct 59	929
Consumer Protection	J. Molony	Jun 59	Apr 62	1781
Control of Public Expenditure	Ld Plowden	Jul 59	Jun 61	1432
Company Law Committee	Ld Jenkins	Dec 59	May 62	1749
Broadcasting	Sir H. Pilkington	Jul 60	Jun 62	1753
Higher Education	Ld Robbins	Feb 61	Sep 63	2154
Major Ports of Great Britain	Vt Rochdale	Mar 61	Jul 62	1824
Security in the Public Service	Ld Radcliffe	May 61	Nov 61	1681
Economy of Northern Ireland	Sir R. Hall	May 61	Jun 62	1835
Sunday Observance	Ld Crathorne	Jul 61	Sep 64	2528
Decimal Currency	E of Halsbury	Dec 61	Jul 63	2145
Organisation of Civil Science	Sir B. Trend	Mar 62	Sep 63	2171
The Vassall Case	Sir C. Cunningham	Oct 62	Nov 62	1871
Security Service and Mr Profumo	Ld Denning	Jun 63	Sep 63	2152
Remuneration of Ministers and M.P.s	Sir G. Lawrence	Dec 63	Oct 64	2516
Social Studies	Ld Heyworth	Jun 63	Feb 65	2660
Housing in Greater London	Sir M. Holland	Aug 63	Mar 65	2605
Port Transport Industry	Ld Devlin	Oct 64	Nov 64	2523
Aircraft Industry	Ld Plowden	Dec 64	Dec 65	2853
Shipbuilding	R. Geddes	Feb 65	Feb 66	2939
Age of Majority	Sir J. Latey	Jul 65	Jun 67	3342
Local Authority Personal Social Services	F. Seebohm	Dec 65	Jul 68	3703
Death Certification and Coroners	N. Brodrick	Mar 65	Sep 71	4810
Civil Service	Ld Fulton	Feb 66	Jul 68	3638
Prison Security	Earl Mountbatten	Oct 66	Dec 66	3175
Fire Service	Sir R. Holroyd	Feb 67	May 70	4371
Shipping	Vt Rochdale	Jul 67	Feb 70	4337
Intermediate Areas	Sir J. Hunt	Sep 67	Feb 69	3998
Civil Air Transport	Sir E. Edwards	Nov 67	Apr 69	4018
Legal Education	Sir R. Ormrod	Dec 67	Jan 71	4595
Commercial Rating	D. Anderson	Aug 68	Apr 70	4366
Overseas Representation	Sir V. Duncan	Aug 68	Jun 69	4107
Consumer Credit	Ld Crowther	Sep 68	Dec 70	4596
Adoption of Children	Sir W. Houghton F. Stockdale	Jul 69	Jul 72	5107
Small Firms	J. Bolton	Jul 69	Sep 71	4811
One-Parent Families	Sir M. Finer	Nov 69	Oct 74	5629
Rent Acts	H. Francis	Oct 69	Jan 71	4609

Title	Chairman	Date appointed	Date of Report	Command number
Privacy	K. Younger	May 70	May 72	5012
Safety and Health at Work	Ld Robens	May 70	Jun 72	5034
Defence Procurement	D. Rayner	Oct 70	Mar 71	4641
Dispersal of Government Work from London	Sir H. Hardman	Oct 70	Jun 73	5322
Lotteries	K. Witney	Jan 71	Dec 73	5506
Abuse of Social Security	Sir H. Fisher	Mar 71	Mar 73	5228
Liquor Licensing	Ld Erroll of Hale	Apr 71	Oct 72	5154
Scottish Licensing Laws	G. Clayson	Apr 71	Aug 73	5354
Official Secrets Act	Ld Franks	Apr 71	Sep 72	5104
Public Trustee Office	H. Hutton	May 71	Nov 71	4913
Contempt of Court	Ld Phillimore	Jun 71	Dec 74	5794
National Savings	Sir H. Page	Jun 71	Jun 73	5273
Brutality in Northern Ireland	Sir E. Compton	Aug 71	Nov 71	4823
Interrogation of Terrorists	Ld Parker of Waddington	Nov 71	Jan 72	4901
Probation Officers and Social Workers	J. Butterworth	Dec 71	Aug 72	5076
Psychiatric Patients	Sir C. Aarvold	Jun 72	Jan 73	5191
Mentally Abnormal Offenders	Ld Butler	Sep 72	Oct 75	6244
Legal Procedures to deal with Terrorists in Northern Ireland	Ld Diplock	Oct 72	Nov 72	5185
Handling of Complaints against Police	A. Gordon-Brown	Apr 73	Mar 74	5582
Export of Animals for Slaughter	Ld O'Brien	Jul 73	Mar 74	5566
Conduct in Local Government	Ld Redcliffe-Maud	Oct 73	May 74	5636
Broadcasting	Ld Annan	Apr 74	Mar 77	6753
Pay of Non-University Teachers	Ld Houghton	Jun 74	Jan 75	5848
Civil Liberties in Northern Ireland	Ld Gardiner	Jun 74	Jan 75	5879
Local Government Finance	F. Layfield	Jun 74	Mar 76	6543
Ministerial Memoirs	Vt Radcliffe	Apr 75	Jan 76	6386
Tape Recording Police Interrogations	W. Hyde	Apr 75	Oct 76	6630
Industrial Democracy	Ld Bullock	Dec 75	Apr 77	6706
Recruitment of Mercenaries	Ld Diplock	Feb 76	Aug 76	6569
Age of Consent	Sir G. Waller	Dec 75	Apr 81	8216
Data Protection	Sir N. Lindop	Jun 76	Dec 78	7341
Political Activities of Civil Servants	Sir A. Armitage	Aug 76	Jan 78	7057
Genetic Manipulation	Sir G. Wolstenhome	Dec 76	Sep 82	8665
Insolvency Law	Sir K. Cork	Jan 77	Jun 82	8558
Functioning of Financial Institutions	Sir H. Wilson	Jan 77	Jun 80	7937
Financing of Small Firms	Sir H. Wilson	Jan 77	Mar 79	7503
Cabinet Document Security	Ld Houghton	Jul 77	Oct 77	6677
Obscenity and Film Censorship	B. Williams	Jul 77	Nov 79	7772
Ownership of Agricultural Land	Ld Northfield	Sep 77	Jul 79	7599
Police Pay	Ld Edmund-Davies	Oct 77	Jul 78	7283
Police Interrogation in Northern Ireland	H. Bennett	Jun 78	Mar 79	7497
Public Records	Sir D. Wilson	Aug 78	Mar 81	8204
U.K. Prison Service	Sir John Douglas May	Nov 78	Oct 79	7673
Education of Ethnic Minority Children	A. Rampton Ld Swann	Mar 79	Feb 85	9403
Local Government in Scotland	Sir Anthony Stodart	Dec 79	Jan 81	8115
Post-graduate Education	Sir P. Swinnerton-Dyer	Dec 79	Apr 82	8537
University Scientific Research	Sir A. Merrison	Mar 80	Jun 82	8567
Police Complaints	Ld Plowden	Jul 80	Mar 81	8193
Brixton Disorders	Ld Scarman	Apr 81	Nov 81	8427
Civil Service Pay	Sir J. Megaw	Jun 81	Jul 82	8590
Review of 1976 Terrorism Act	Earl Jellico	Mar 82	Feb 83	8803
Cable Television	Ld Hunt of Tamworth	Apr 82	Oct 82	8679
Fertilisation of Human Embryos	Dame M. Warnock	Jul 82	Jul 84	9314
Falkland Islands Review	Ld Franks	Jul 82	Jan 83	8787
Protection of Military Information	Sir H. Beach	Feb 83	Dec 83	9112

Inquiries Held under the Tribunals of Inquiry (Evidence) Act, 1921

Tribunals of Inquiry (Evidence) Act, 1921

Upon a resolution of both Houses of Parliament on a matter of urgent public importance a tribunal might be appointed by the Sovereign or a Secretary of State with all the powers of the High Court as regards examination of witnesses and production of documents, for the objective investigation of facts.

Title	Members of Tribunal	Year	Command number
Destruction of documents by Ministry of Munitions officials	Ld Cave Ld Inchape Sir W. Plender	1921	1340
Royal Commission on Lunacy and Mental Disorder given powers under the Act	H. Macmillan *(Ch)*	1924	2700
Arrest of R. Sheppard, R.A.O.C. Inquiry into conduct of Metropolitan Police	J. Rawlinson	1925	2497
Allegations made against the Chief Constable of Kilmarnock in connection with the dismissal of Constables Hill and Moore from the Burgh Police Force	W. Mackenzie	1925	2659
Conditions with regard to mining and drainage in an area around the County Borough of Doncaster	Sir H. Monro (*Ch*)	1926/8	. .
Charges against the Chief Constable of St. Helens by the Watch Committee	C. Parry T. Walker	1928	3103
Interrogation of Miss Irene Savidge by Metropolitan Police at New Scotland Yard	Sir J. Eldon Banks H. Lees-Smith J. Withers	1928	3147
Allegations of bribery and corruption in connection with the letting and allocation of stances and other premises under the control of the Corporation of Glasgow	Ld Anderson Sir R. Boothby J. Hunter	1933	4361
Unauthorised disclosure of information relating to the Budget	Sir J. Porter G. Simonds R. Oliver	1936	5184
The circumstances surrounding the loss of H.M. Submarine 'Thetis'	Sir J. Bucknill	1939	6190
The conduct before the Hereford Juvenile Court Justices of the proceedings against Craddock and others	Ld Goddard	1943	6485
The administration of the Newcastle upon Tyne Fire, Police and Civil Defence Services	R. Burrows	1944	6522
Bribery of Ministers of the Crown or other public servants in connection with the grant of licences, etc.	Sir J. Lynskey G. Russell Vick G. Upjohn	1948	7616
Allegations of improper disclosure of information relating to the raising of the Bank Rate	Ld Parker E. Holland G. Veale	1957	350
Allegations that John Waters was assaulted on 7th December, 1957, at Thurso and the action taken by Caithness Police in connection therewith	Ld Sorn Sir J. Robertson J. Dandie	1959	718
The circumstances in which offences under the Official Secrets Act were committed by William John Christopher Vassall	Ld Radcliffe Sir J. Barry Sir E. Milner Holland	1962	2009
The disaster at Aberfan	Sir E. Davies H. Harding V. Lawrence	1967	H.C. 553
The events on Sunday, 30th January 1972 which led to loss of life in connection with the procession in Londonderry on that day	Ld Widgery	1972	H.C. 220/72
The circumstances leading to the cessation of trading by the Vehicle and General Insurance Co. Ltd	Sir A. James M. Kerr S. Templeman	1972	H.C. 133
The extent to which the Crown Agents lapsed from accepted standards of commercial or professional conduct or of public administration as financiers on their own account in the years 1967-74	Sir D. Croom-Johnson Ld Allen of Abbeydale Sir W. Slimmings	1978	

SOURCES.—P. and G. Ford, *A Breviate of Parliamentary Papers* (3 vols, 1951-61); H. M. Clokie and J. W. Robinson, *Royal Commissions of Inquiry: the Significance of Investigations in British Politics* (1937); R. V. Vernon and N. Mansergh, *Advisory Bodies* (1937); C. J. Hanser, *Guide to Decision: the Royal Commission* (1966); G. W. Keeton, *Trial by Tribunal* (1960); S. A. de Smith, *Constitutional and Administrative Law* (1971); R. Chapman, *The Role of Commissions in Policy Making* (1973); T. J. Cartwright, *Royal Commissions and Departmental Committees in Britain* (1974); and the Report of the Royal Commission on the Tribunals of Inquiry (Evidence) Act, 1921 (Cmnd. 3121, published Feb 1966).

Tribunals and Commissions

A large number of statutory tribunals, with jurisdiction to decide quasi-legal disputes, have been created since 1900. By 1960 there were over 2,000 tribunals within the supervisory role of the *Council on Tribunals*. The fifteen-member *Council on Tribunals* was set up under the *Tribunals and Inquiries Act, 1958*, following the report of the Franks Committee (Cmnd. 218/-1957). Its role is purely advisory, but it has to report annually to Parliament. The reports list the tribunals that fall within its purview and the number of cases each type of tribunal has dealt with during the past year. In the following table some categories have been merged and appeals from lower to higher tribunals are not included nor are tribunals which have had no cases to deal with. Separate Scottish tribunals are also excluded.

Category	Latest enabling legislation (1980)	Number of Tribunals (max)	Number of cases 1960	1970	1980
Agriculture	1947	8	459	402	461
Air Transport	1960	1	. .	3,537	1,002
Betting Levy	1963	1	. .	196	—
Commons	1965	4[1]	. .	—	1,514
Compensation	1958	10	27	—	—
Education	1944	*ad hoc*	1	3	—
Immigration	1969	59[2]	. .	991	11,344
Industry and Employment	(1964)	84	. .	10,318	31,736
Land	1949	1	1,121	1,511	1,237
Mental Health	1959	15	1	1,114	709
Milk and Dairies	1955	8	1	2	—
Misuse of Drugs	1971	3	. .	. .	—
National Assistance	1948	152	7,757	—	—
(Non-Contributory Benefits)	1966	151	. .	28,717	. .
(Supplementary Benefit)	1975	123	. .	. .	45,471
National Health Service	1946	204	1,235	979	1,137
National Insurance	1946	228	60,914	54,787	—
National Service	1948	83	5,954	—	—
Patents	1907	3	5,652	6,566	7,564
Pensions	1919	11	4,784	3,388	—
Performing Rights	1956	1	4	—	—
Rates	1968	42	. .	25,513	40,400
Rents	1968	53	4,652	14,923	5,086
Rent Assessment	1977	*ad hoc*	. .	. .	9,734
Revenue	1970	654	n.a.	6,562	n.a.
Road Traffic	1960	23	22,110	23,205	29,528
Social Security	1975	179	. .	. .	25,258
Vaccine Damages	1979	6	. .	. .	897
Value Added Tax	1972	5	. .	. .	61

[1] Commissioners [2] Adjudicators

SOURCES.—*Annual Reports of the Council on Tribunals, 1958-*. See also R. E. Wraith and P. G. Hutchesson, *Administrative Tribunals* (1973); J. Farmer, *Tribunals and Government* (1974); R. E. Wraith and G. B. Lamb, *Public Inquiries as an Instrument of Government* (1971); S. A. de Smith, *Constitutional and Administrative Law* (3rd ed., 1977).

Political Honours Scrutiny Committee

The Political Honours Scrutiny Committee was established in 1924, following scandals over the 'sale of honours'. It was to 'consider before they are submitted to the King, the names and particulars of persons recommended for appointment to any dignity or honours on account of political services . . . and to report . . . whether such persons . . . are fit and proper persons to be recommended'. Its activities were virtually never reported but they continued after H. Wilson announced the ending of 'political honours' in 1966 and again in 1974. In 1976, following agitation over Sir H. Wilson's resignation honours list, there was a complete change of membership. It has always had three members:

1924	Ld Buckmaster (Ch)	1925	W. Nicholson	1925	Ld Merrivale
1925	Vt Novar (Ch)	1929	Ld Buckmaster (Ch)	1929	G. Barnes
1929	H. (Ld) Macmillan	1934	M of Crewe	1938	Ld Rushcliffe
	(Ch from 1934)	1945	J. Clynes	1949	Vt Templewood
1952	Ld Asquith (Ch)	1949	Ld Pethick-Lawrence		(Ch from 1954)
1954	Vt Thurso	1961	Ld Williams	1959	Ld Crookshank (Ch)
1962	Ld Rea	1967	Bness Summerskill	1961	Ld Crathorne (Ch)
1976	Ld Franks	1976	Ld Shackleton (Ch)	1976	Ld Carr

SOURCE.—*H.M. Ministers and Heads of Public Departments.*

BIBLIOGRAPHY.—T. Cullen, *Maundy Gregory: Purveyor of Honours* (1974).

VIII

ADMINISTRATION OF JUSTICE

Major Criminal Justice Legislation 1900-

Poor Prisoners' Defence Act, 1903. This was the first Act which made provision for legal aid, which was limited to trials on indictment.

The Probation of Offenders Act, 1907. This extended courts' probation powers and allowed appointment of official probation officers.

The Criminal Appeal Act, 1907. This created the Court of Criminal Appeal.

The Prevention of Crime Act, 1908. This provided for 'borstal training' of young recidivists and 'preventive detention' for adult habitual criminals.

The Children Act, 1908. This created 'places of detention' (later 'Remand Homes') and Juvenile Courts; it also prohibited imprisonment of those under 14, restricted imprisonment of those from 14-17 and abolished death sentence for those under 17.

The Criminal Justice Administration Act, 1914. This required Summary Courts to give time for payment of fines.

Poor Prisoners' Defence Act, 1930. This Act provided a comprehensive system of legal aid, extending aid to preliminary inquiries and to cases heard summarily before magistrates' courts.

Summary Jurisdiction (Appeals) Act, 1933. This Act made provision for free legal aid for criminal cases, payable out of county or borough funds at the discretion of the magistrates.

The Children and Young Persons Act, 1933. This Act, which followed the 1927 Report of the Cecil Committee on the treatment of young offenders, codified and extended 'care and protection' law; it also raised the age of criminal responsibility from 7 to 8.

The Administration of Justice (Miscellaneous Provisions) Act, 1933. This abolished Grand Juries.

The Criminal Justice Act, 1948. Following the lines of a 1938 Bill abandoned through the onset of war, this extended the fining powers of higher courts; it further restricted imprisonment of juveniles and abolished distinction between penal servitude, imprisonment, etc.; it also improved law on probation, introduced corrective training and a new form of preventive detention and it provided for remand centres, attendance centres and detention centres. It also abolished the right of peers to be tried by the House of Lords.

Legal Aid and Advice Act, 1949. This introduced a new system of aid for civil cases. It provided for the establishment of a network of local committees, composed of solicitors and some barristers to grant legal aid under regulations made by the Lord Chancellor. By this Act, aid was extended to cover all proceedings in civil courts and civil proceedings in magistrates' courts, except for certain types of action (of which defamation and breach of promise were the most important).

Cost in Criminal Cases Act, 1952. This Act empowered the courts, in the case of an indictable offence, to order reasonable defence costs to be paid out of public funds, when the accused was discharged or acquitted.

The Homicide Act, 1957. This amended the law on murder, distinguishing capital and non-capital murder and introducing the defence of diminished responsibility.

The First Offenders Act, 1958. This restricted imprisonment of adults by Summary Courts.

Administration of Justice Act, 1960. This gave a greatly extended right of appeal to the House of Lords in criminal matters and reformed the law relating to habeas corpus and to contempt of court.

Legal Aid Act, 1960. This relates financial conditions for legal aid and makes further provision for the remuneration of counsel and solicitors.

The Criminal Justice Act, 1961. This provided compulsory supervision after release from detention centres and rationalised custodial sentences for 17-21 age-group.

The Children and Young Persons Act, 1963. This raised the age of criminal responsibility from 8 to 10, and redefined the need for 'care, protection, and control'.

The Criminal Injuries Compensation Board was set up in 1964, under an ex gratia State Scheme for compensating victims of crimes of violence.

The Murder (Abolition of Death Penalty) Act, 1965. This suspended the death penalty until 1970, and substituted a mandatory 'life' sentence. On 16 Dec 69 Parliament voted to continue the suspension indefinitely. Motions for its restoration were rejected on 11 Dec 75, 19 Jul 79 and 13 Jul 83.

Criminal Appeal Act, 1966. This amalgamated the Court of Criminal Appeal and the Court of Appeal.

The Criminal Justice Act, 1967. This introduced suspended sentences, a Parole Board (see p. 321), a new type of sentence for recidivists and further restricted imprisonment of adults. It allowed majority verdicts (10-2) by juries.

The Theft Act, 1967. This rationalised definitions of theft and other dishonesty.

The Criminal Law Act, 1967. This replaced the distinction between felonies and misdemeanours, with a distinction between arrestable and non-arrestable offences.

The Children and Young Persons Act, 1969. Redefined the circumstances in which juvenile courts could make orders dealing with children and young persons, and simplified the nature of such orders; it also provided for the raising of the minimum age of liability to prosecution (although this has not yet been implemented) and for the reorganisation of approved schools, children's homes, etc., into a system of 'community homes' controlled by local authorities.

The Courts Act, 1971, replaced Assizes and Quarter Sessions with a system of Crown Courts.

The Criminal Justice Act, 1972. Provided courts with several new means of dealing with offenders, including criminal bankruptcy orders, community service orders, deferment of sentence, day centres for probationers; and further restricted the imprisonment of adults.

The Rehabilitation of Offenders Act, 1974. This made it an offence to refer to criminal proceedings after the lapse of a certain period. This involved consequential amendments to the law of defamation.

Prevention of Terrorism (Temporary Provisions) Act, 1974. This proscribed organisations concerned in terrorism and gives power to exclude certain persons from Great Britain in order to prevent acts of terrorism.

Criminal Jurisdiction Act, 1975. This extended the jurisdiction of the criminal courts in Northern Ireland to allow them to try certain offences committed in the Irish Republic.

District Courts (Scotland) Act, 1975. This set up a new system of courts of summary jurisdiction in Scotland.

Police Act, 1976. This established a Police Complaints Board to deal with complaints from the public against members of the police.

Bail Act, 1976. This extensively reformed the law on the granting of bail, requiring reasons to be given for refusal and creating a general presumption in favour of bail, particularly for offences not punishable with imprisonment.

Criminal Law Act, 1977. This simplified the rules governing the distribution of cases between the Crown Court and magistrates courts, with a view to allowing many more cases to be tried summarily rather than on indictment. It also raised the level of fines which can be imposed for many types of offence.

Judicature (Northern Ireland) Act, 1978. This modernised the structure of the superior courts in Northern Ireland, notably by abolishing the separate Court of Criminal Appeal and by setting up a new Crown Court to try all cases of indictment.

The Criminal Attempts Act, 1981. This replaced the common law offence of attempt with a statutory offence and modified the statutory definition of criminal conspiracy. It also implemented the recommendation by the Home Affairs Committee of the House of Commons that the offence of 'sus' be repealed; it is partially replaced by a new offence of vehicle interference.

The Criminal Justice Act, 1982. This created a completely new framework of custodial offences for offenders under 21, superseding imprisonment, Borstal training and detention in detention centres. It also amended the law on suspended sentences and introduced a new scale of standard maximum fines for summary offences.

The Police and Criminal Evidence Act, 1984. This derives largely from various recommendations made by the Royal Commission on Criminal Procedure, the Criminal Law Revision Committee, and Lord Scarman's Report on the Brixton disorders. It reforms the law relating to police powers to stop and search, police powers of entry, search and seizure, powers of arrest and detention, the treatment, interrogation and identification of suspects, the admissibility of evidence obtained during police questioning, and public complaints against the police.

SOURCES.—R. M. Jackson, *Enforcing the Law* (1967); N. D. Walker, *Crime and Punishment in Britain* (1965); K. Smith and D. J. Keenan, *English Law* (1963); G. Rose, *The Struggle for Penal Reform* (1961); J. Smith and B. Hogan, *Criminal Law* (1973); L. Blom-Cooper and G. Drewry, *Final Appeal: The House of Lords in its Judicial Capacity* (1972).

Major Legislation Relating to the Administration of Civil Justice, 1900-

Industrial Courts Act, 1919. This Act provided a standing body for voluntary arbitration and inquiry in cases of industrial dispute (see p. 251).

Supreme Court of Judicature (Consolidation) Act, 1925. This is still the principal Act defining the structure, composition and jurisdiction of the High Court and the Court of Appeal.

Administration of Justice (Miscellaneous Provisions) Act, 1933. This restricted the right to jury trial in King's Bench civil proceedings.

Administration of Justice (Appeals) Act, 1934. This made it necessary to obtain leave to appeal to the House of Lords in civil matters arising in English courts.

County Courts Act, 1934. This effectively abolished jury trials in county courts and rationalised the procedure for appointing registrars.

Summary Jurisdiction (Domestic Proceedings) Act, 1937. This rationalised procedure in matrimonial, guardianship and affiliation proceedings before magistrates.

Administration of Justice (Miscellaneous Provisions) Act, 1938. This Act made important changes relating in particular to the King's Bench Division of the High Court and to Courts of Quarter Sessions.

Juries Act, 1949. This abolished special juries outside the City of London.

Justices of the Peace Act, 1949. This Act brought about the extensive revision of the functions and organisation of magistrates' courts.

County Courts Act, 1955. This fixed the general limit of county court jurisdiction at £400 (raised by successive Orders in Council to a limit, in 1977, of £2,000).

County Courts Act, 1959. This consolidated existing legislation on county courts.

Judicial Pensions Act, 1959. This fixed a retiring age of 75 for the higher judiciary and revised the system of judicial pensions.

Legal Aid Act, 1964. This gave limited powers for a non-legally aided litigant to be awarded his costs out of the legal aid fund where his unsuccessful opponent is in receipt of legal aid.

Justices of the Peace Act, 1968. This abolished *ex officio* J.P.s and redefined the powers and functions of magistrates' clerks.

Administration of Justice Act, 1969. This increased the jurisdiction of county courts to £750 and allowed certain categories of civil case in the High Court to 'leapfrog' directly to the House of Lords.

Administration of Justice Act, 1970. This Act rearranged the jurisdictions of the three divisions of the High Court (the Probate, Divorce and Admiralty Division becoming the Family Division) and abolished imprisonment for debt.

Courts Act, 1971. This replaced Courts of Assize and Quarter Sessions by Crown Courts staffed by Recorders and circuit judges; it rationalised the location of civil and criminal courts throughout England and Wales; it made sweeping changes in the administration of courts of intermediate jurisdiction and it abolished the use of juries in civil proceedings.

Industrial Relations Act, 1971. This established the National Industrial Relations Court (see p. 354).

Legal Aid and Advice Act, 1972. This Act empowered solicitors to do up to £25 worth of work for a client without the latter first having to obtain a certificate from the Law Society.

Solicitors (Amendment) Act, 1974. This made a number of changes in the administration of the solicitors' profession and made provision for a Lay Observer to examine the Law Society's handling of complaints against solicitors. The *Solicitors (Scotland) Act, 1976,* made similar changes in Scotland.

Litigants in Person (Costs and Expenses) Act, 1975. This enabled parties successfully conducting their own cases in civil proceedings to recover their costs and expenses from the other side.

The Legal Aid Act, 1979. This extended the 'green form' legal advice and assistance scheme to cover representation in inferior courts and tribunals.

The Contempt of Court Act, 1981. This implemented with modifications the Phillimore Report on Contempt of Court (Cmnd. 5794, 1974) and harmonised the law of England and Wales with the European Court's judgment in *The Sunday Times* (Thalidomide) case, 1973.

The Supreme Court Act 1981. This consolidated and significantly updated the legislation relating to the Supreme Court, superseding the Act of 1925 (see above).

SOURCES.—R. M. Jackson, *The Machinery of Justice in England* (7th ed. 1977); P. S. James, *Introduction to English Law* (8th ed. 1972); J. Griffith, *The Politics of the Judiciary* (2nd ed. 1980).

Cases of Political Significance

The number of lawsuits that have had major domestic political implications is not great. Most of the celebrated ones have involved trade unions and are listed on pp. 351-6. Successful election petitions are listed on p. 250. But these cases also seem to have left a significant mark on the political scene.

Bowles v. Bank of England [1913] 1 Ch.57 (Ch.D.). Collecting new taxes in advance of the Finance Act violates the Bill of Rights. This case led to the passage of the Provisional Collection of Taxes Act, 1913.

Viscountess Rhondda's Claim [1922] A.C. 339. The Sex Disqualification (Removal) Act 1919 did not entitle a peeress in her own right to sit in the House of Lords.

Vauxhall Estates Ltd v. Liverpool Corporation [1932] 1 K.B. 733. Parliament cannot bind its successors as to the subject matter of legislation.

Liversidge v. Anderson [1942] A.C. 206 (H.L.) A Court of law may not inquire into whether a Minister has 'reasonable grounds' for exercising a statutory discretion.

Duncan v. Cammell Laird & Co. Ltd. [1942] A.C. 624 (H.L.) The Crown may withhold documents or refuse questioning if a minister certifies that the answer would be injurious to the public interest.

R. v. Tronoh Mines Ltd. [1952] I All E.R., 697. Election expenditure has to be declared only if it is specifically directed to secure the election of a particular candidate.

MacCormick v. Lord Advocate ('The Royal Numeral Case') [1953] S.L.T. 225. A Scottish case laying down that the unlimited sovereignty of Parliament does not apply to Scotland.

Re Parliamentary Privilege Act, 1770 [1958] A.C. 331 (P.C.) (Strauss Case). Not every communication between an M.P. and a Minister is protected by parliamentary privilege.

Costa v. Enel [1964] CML Rep 425. Community law prevails over all existing inconsistent national law since 'the member States have restricted their sovereign rights, albeit within limited spheres'.

Burmah Oil Co. v. the Lord Advocate [1965] A.C. 75 (H.L.). Government held liable to compensate firm ordered to destroy its property to impede the advance of the enemy in wartime. (Reversed by the War Damage Act, 1965.)

Conway v. Rimmer [1968] A.C. 910 (H.L.). This judgement supersedes and amplifies Liversidge v. Anderson (above). The courts have a residuary power to inspect documents privately to determine whether the public interest in suppressing them outweighs the interests of parties, and of the public in the unfettered administration of justice.

Padfield v. Minister of Agriculture [1968] A.C. 997 (H.L.). Where a statute confers a discretion on a minister it is beyond his power to exercise it in such a way as to frustrate the policy of Parliament, as interpreted by the court.

John v. Rees [1969] 2 W.L.R. 1294. Chairman may not adjourn meeting without consent of majority present, majority entitled to carry on and elect a new Chairman; constituency Labour Parties not allowed to disaffiliate from the national Labour Party; a group of members may be suspended by the National Executive Committee only if natural justice is complied with by giving them an opportunity to put their case; all persons entitled to attend a meeting must be summoned or the meeting is improperly constituted and hence invalid. (The case concerned D. Donnelly and the Pembroke Constituency Labour Party.)

Anisminic Ltd. v. Foreign Compensation Commission [1969] 2 A.C. 147 (H.L.). A clause in a statute ousting the jurisdiction of the court to review administrative decisions will not be recognised and such decisions are a nullity *ab initio.*

The Hauptzollamt Hamburg Case [1970] CMLR 141. If Community law occupies a certain field in a matter within Community competence, the European Court of Justice does not recognise the right of Parliaments to pass *any* law on the matter, unless to implement this law.

McWhirter v. A.G. [1972] CMLR 882. The court will review the scope, but not the exercise, of the Crown's prerogative.

Attorney-General v. Jonathan Cape Ltd. [1976] Q.B. 752 (The Crossman Diaries case). The courts have power to prevent publication of Cabinet material in circumstances where such publication would be both a breach of confidence and a threat to the maintenance of the doctrine of collective responsibility. (In this instance injunctions were refused owing to the considerable time which had elapsed since the events described in the Diaries.)

Gouriet v. Post Office Union [1977] 3 All E.R. 70 (H.L.). The Attorney-General is not obliged to bring an action to prevent a breach of the law when required to by a member of the general public, as distinct from someone materially damaged by the breach. Neither is an injunction or declaration available without the Attorney-General's consent; and he need give no reasons for his decision. (The case concerned the blacking of mail to South Africa.)

Laker Airways v. Dept. of Trade [1977] Q.B. 643. Ministerial guidance, albeit approved by Parliament, is *ultra vires* if it conflicts with express policy objectives contained in an Act. (The case concerned the proposal for 'Skytrain' cheap flights to America.)

Sec. of State for Education v. Tameside Met B/C [1977] A.C. 1014 (H.L.). Where a statute gives a minister certain powers if he is satisfied that a local authority is acting unreasonably he may exercise them only if no reasonable authority would have done what was done, and never simply because he disagrees with the local authority's policy. (This case concerned the Tameside council's response to the Government's policy on comprehensive schools.)

Lewis v. Heffer [1978] T.L.R. 25 Jan 1978. In confirming a series of High Court judgements, arising from disputes in the Newham North-East Labour Party, the Court of Appeal ruled that the National Executive Committee of the Labour Party had the power to suspend the constituency party and, in general, argued that the courts should only be used as a very last resort in factional party controversies.

Mead v. Haringey [1979]. All E.R. 1016 A.C. The Court of Appeal held that it was arguable that a local authority might be in breach of its statutory duty to provide for children's education when it failed to do so by reason of the industrial action of School caretakers.

Duport Steels Ltd. v. Sirs [1980] 1 All E.R. 529. In the course of a pay dispute with the British Steel Corporation, the trade unions involved took secondary industrial action against private steel firms in the hope of causing a total shutdown of the industry. The Court of Appeal granted injunctions to the private steel companies, but the House of Lords reversed the decision, holding that the secondary action was 'in furtherance of a trade dispute' within the meaning of the Trade Union and Labour Relations Act, 1974. The Thatcher Government subsequently reversed the decision by legislation (see p. 355).

Williams v. Home Office [1981] 1 All E.R. 151. Following the principles laid down in *Conway v. Rimmer* (above), the judge ordered the disclosure of internal Home Office documents relating to experimental control units, in an action brought against the department by a prisoner.

Harman v. Home Office [1982] 2 All E.R. 151. A solicitor was given confidential policy documents by way of discovery in the course of a civil action brought against the Home Office, and undertook not to disclose them outside the course of the proceedings. The documents were read out in open court and the solicitor then showed them to a journalist. The House of Lords affirmed, by a 3:2 majority, the lower courts' finding that this amounted to contempt of court.

Norwich City Council v. Secretary of State for the Environment [1982] 1 All E.R. 737. The Court of Appeal upheld the exercise of default powers by a minister against a local authority in circumstances where the minister adjudged the authority to have been dilatory in fulfilling statutory obligations to sell council houses to tenants.

O'Reilly v. Mackman [1982] 3 All E.R. 1182 (H.L.) There is a fundamental distinction between private law and public law proceedings which cannot be evaded by seeking a private law remedy against a public authority in circumstances where a public law remedy is appropriate.

Bromley London Borough Council v. GLC [1983] A.C. 768 (H.L.). The GLC 'Fares Fair' case. The Council acted *ultra vires* the Transport (London) Act, 1969, and in breach of its fiduciary duty towards ratepayers by its decision to cut fares by 25%.

Pickwell v. Camden Borough Council [1983] 1 All E.R. 602. A local authority, responding to a strike by its employees, agreed a pay settlement that turned out to be more generous than the settlement agreed nationally. The Queen's Bench Divisional Court denied the district auditor's claim that the action of the council was *ultra vires.*

Air Canada v. Secretary of State for Trade [1983] 1 All E.R. 910. Action brought by foreign airlines disputing increases in fees at Heathrow Airport. The House of Lords declined to order disclosure of ministerial documents on the grounds that the plaintiffs had failed to show that the documents were likely to assist their case.

The Council of Civil Service Unions v. Minister for the Civil Service [1984] Industrial Cases Reports 1985, 15. The House of Lords decided that the 'reasonable expectations' of the Civil Service unions to be consulted before the Government banned union membership at GCHQ were overridden by considerations of national security. However, their Lordships held, contrary to the Government's contentions, that ministerial actions based on the royal prerogative could, in principle, be reviewed by the courts.

Principal Judges

Lord Chancellor
(see p. 70)

Vice Chancellor

1971	Sir J. Pennycuik
1974	Sir A. Plowman
1976	Sir R. Megarry
1985	Sir N. Browne-Wilkinson

Lord Chief Justice

1894	Ld Russell of Killowen
1900	Ld Alverstone
1913	Ld Reading (Vt) (E)
1921	Ld Trevethin
1922	Ld Hewart
1940	Vt Caldecote
1946	Ld Goddard
1958	Ld Parker of Waddington
1971	Ld Widgery
1980	Ld Lane

Lord President of the Court of Session

1899	Ld Kinross
1905	Ld Dunedin
1913	Ld Strathclyde
1920	Ld Clyde
1935	Ld Normand
1947	Ld Cooper
1954	Ld Clyde
1972	Ld Emslie

Master of the Rolls

1897	Sir N. Lindley (Ld)
1900	Sir R. Webster (Ld Alverstone)
1900	Sir A. Smith
1901	Sir R. Collins
1907	Sir H. Cozens-Hardy (Ld)
1918	Sir C. Eady
1919	Ld Sterndale
1923	Sir E. Pollock (Ld Hanworth)
1935	Ld Wright
1937	Sir W. Greene (Ld)
1949	Sir R. Evershed (Ld)
1962	Ld Denning
1982	Sir J. Donaldson

Lord Justice Clerk

1888	Ld Kingsburgh
1915	Ld Dickson
1922	Ld Alness
1933	Ld Aitchison
1941	Ld Cooper
1947	Ld Thomson
1962	Ld Grant
1972	Ld Wheatley

President of the Probate, Divorce and Admiralty Division (since 1971 the Family Division)

1892	Sir F. Jeune
1905	Sir G. Barnes
1909	Sir J. Bigham
1910	Sir S. Evans
1918	Ld Sterndale
1919	Sir H. Duke (Ld Merrivale)
1933	Sir B. Merriman (Ld)
1962	Sir J. Simon
1971	Sir G. Baker
1979	Sir J. Arnold

Lord Chief Justice of Ireland

1889	Ld O'Brien
1914	R. Cherry
1917	Sir J. Campbell
1918 1924	T. Molony

Lord Chief Justice of Northern Ireland

1921	(Sir) D. Henry
1925	(Sir) W. Moore
1937	(Sir) J. Andrews
1951	Ld MacDermott
1971	Sir R. Lowry (Ld)

Lords of Appeal in Ordinary

1887-1910	Ld Macnaghten
1894-1907	Ld Davey
1899-1909	Ld Robertson
1899-1905	Ld Lindley
1905-1928	Ld Atkinson
1907-1910	Ld Collins
1909-1929	Ld Shaw
1910-1912	Ld Robson
1912-1921	Ld Moulton
1913-1918	Ld Parker
1913-1930	Ld Sumner (Vt)
1913-1932	Ld Dunedin (Vt)
1918-1922	Vt Cave
1921-1929	Ld Carson
1923-1937	Ld Blanesburgh
1928-1944	Ld Atkin
1929-1935	Ld Tomlin
1929-1946	Ld Russell of Killowen
1929-1948	Ld Thankerton
1930-39 & 1941-47	Ld Macmillan
1932-35 & 1937-47	Ld Wright
1935-38 & 1939-41	Ld Maugham (Vt)
1935-1938	Ld Roche

1938-1944 Ld Romer
1938-1954 Ld Porter
1944-51 & 1954-62 Ld Simonds (Vt)
1944-1946 Ld Goddard
1946-1949 Ld Uthwatt
1946-1949 Ld du Parcq
1947-1951 Ld MacDermott
1947-1953 Ld Normand
1947-1957 Ld Oaksey
1947-1959 Ld Morton of Henryton
1948-1975 Ld Reid
1949-1950 Ld Greene
1949-1964 Ld Radcliffe
1950-1961 Ld Tucker
1951-1954 Ld Asquith of Bishopstone
1951-1960 Ld Cohen
1953-1961 Ld Keith of Avonholm
1954-1960 Ld Somervell of Harrow
1957-1962 Ld Denning
1959-1963 Ld Jenkins
1960-1973 Ld Morris of Borth-y-Gest
1960-1971 Ld Hodson
1961-1971 Ld Guest
1961-1964 Ld Devlin
1962-1969 Ld Pearce
1962-1965 Ld Evershed
1963-1971 Ld Upjohn
1963-1971 Ld Donovan
1964-1982 Ld Wilberforce
1965-1974 Ld Pearson
1968- Ld Diplock
1969-1980 Vt Dilhorne
1971-1977 Ld Cross of Chelsea
1971-1977 Ld Simon of Glaisdale
1971-1977 Ld Kilbrandon
1972-1980 Ld Salmon
1974-1981 Ld Edmund-Davies
1975-1985 Ld Fraser of Tullybelton
1975-1982 Ld Russell of Killowen
1977- Ld Keith of Kinkel
1977- Ld Scarman
1979-1980 Ld Lane
1980- Ld Roskill
1980- Ld Bridge of Harwich
1981- Ld Brandon of Oakbrook
1982- Ld Brightman
1982- Ld Templeman
1985- Ld Griffiths
1985- Ld Mackay of Clashfern

and such peers of Parliament as are holding, or have held, high judicial office.

Lords Justices of Appeal

1892-1900 Sir A. Levin Smith
1894-1901 Sir J. Rigby
1897-1901 Sir R. Collins
1897-1914 Sir R. Williams
1899-1906 Sir R. Romer
1900-1906 Sir J. Stirling
1901-1906 Sir J. Mathew
1901-1907 Sir H. Cozens-Hardy
1906-1912 Sir J. Moulton
1906-1913 Sir G. Farwell
1906-1915 Sir H. Buckley
1907-1915 Sir W. Kennedy
1912-1913 Sir J. Hamilton
1913-1918 Sir C. Eady
1913-1916 Sir W. Phillimore
1914-1919 Sir W. Pickford
1915-1927 Sir J. Bankes
1915-1926 Sir T. Warrington
1916-1934 Sir T. Scrutton
1918-1919 Sir H. Duke
1919-1928 Sir J. Atkin
1919-1923 Sir R. Younger
1923-1928 Sir C. Sargant
1926-1934 Sir P. Lawrence
1927-1938 Sir F. Greer
1928-1929 Sir J. Sankey
1928-1929 F. Russell
1929-1940 Sir H. Slesser
1929-1938 Sir M. Romer
1934-1935 Sir F. Maugham
1934-1935 Sir A. Roche
1935-1937 Sir W. Greene
1935-1948 Sir L. Scott
1937-1946 Sir F. MacKinnon
1938-1942 Sir A. Clauson
1938-1945 Vt Finlay
1938-1944 Sir F. Luxmoore
1938-1944 Sir R. Goddard
1938-1946 Sir H. du Parcq
1944-1947 Sir G. Lawrence
1944-1947 Sir F. Morton
1945-1950 Sir F. Tucker
1945-1951 Sir A. Bucknill
1946-1954 Sir D. Somervell
1946-1951 Sir L. Cohen
1946-1951 Sir C. Asquith
1947-1948 Sir F. Wrottesley
1947-1949 Sir R. Evershed
1948-1957 Sir J. Singleton
1948-1957 Sir A. Denning
1949-1959 Sir D. Jenkins
1950-1957 Sir N. Birkett
1951-1960 Sir F. Hodson
1951-1960 Sir J. Morris
1951-1960 Sir C. Romer
1954-1958 Sir H. Parker
1957-1968 Sir F. Sellers
1957-1963 Sir B. Ormerod
1957-1962 Sir H. Pearce
1958-1968 Sir H. Willmer
1959-1970 Sir C. Harman
1960-1961 Sir P. Devlin
1960-1965 Sir G. Upjohn
1960-1963 Sir T. Donovan
1961-1969 Sir H. Danckwerts
1961-1974 Sir W. Davies
1961-1968 Sir K. Diplock
1962-1975 Sir C. Russell
1964-1972 Sir C. Salmon
1965-1972 Sir E. Winn
1966-1974 Sir E. Davies
1966-1971 Sir E. Sachs
1968-1971 Sir J. Widgery
1968-1971 Sir F. Atkinson
1968-1974 Sir H. Phillimore
1968-1973 Sir S. Karminski

1969-1983	Sir J. Megaw
1970-1983	Sir D. Buckley
1970-1977	Sir D. Cairns
1971-1978	Sir B. Stamp
1971-1985	Sir J. Stephenson
1971-1980	Sir A. Orr
1971-1980	Sir E. Roskill
1972-	Sir F. Lawton
1973-1977	Sir L. Scarman
1973-1976	Sir A. James
1974-1983	Sir R. Ormrod
1974-1983	Sir P. Browne
1974-1979	Sir G. Lane
1975-1980	Sir W. Goff
1975-1980	Sir N. Bridge
1975-1982	Sir S. Shaw
1976-1984	Sir G. Waller
1976-1985	Sir R. Cumming-Bruce
1977-1985	Sir E. Eveleigh
1978-1981	Sir H. Brandon
1978-1982	Sir S. Templeman
1979-1982	Sir J. Donaldson
1979-1982	Sir J. Brightman
1980-	Sir D. Ackner
1980-1984	Sir R. Dunn
1980-	Sir P. Oliver
1980-	Sir T. Watkins
1980-	Sir P. O'Connor
1980-1985	Sir H. Griffiths
1981-	Sir M. Fox
1981-	Sir M. Kerr
1982-	Sir J. May
1982-	Sir C. Slade
1982-	Sir F. Purchas
1982-	Sir R. Goff
1982-	Sir G. Dillon
1983-	Sir S. Brown
1983-	Sir R. Parker
1983-1985	Sir N. Browne-Wilkinson
1984-	Sir D. Croom-Johnson
1984-	Sir J. Lloyd
1985-	Sir M. Mustill
1985-	Sir B. Neill
1985-	Sir I. Glidewell
1985-	Sir M. Nourse
1985-	Sir A. Balcombe

and ex officio *the Lord High Chancellor (President), the Lord Chief Justice, the Master of the Rolls, and the President of the Family Division.*

SOURCES.—*The Law List 1900-*; *Who Was Who 1900-*, and *Who's Who; Whitaker's Almanack 1900-*.

Other Legal and Law Enforcement Officials

Law Commission (Chairman)

1965	Sir L. Scarman
1973	Sir S. Cooke
1978	Sir M. Kerr
1981	Sir R. Gibson

Director of Public Prosecutions

1894	(H. Cuffe) E of Desart
1909	Sir C. Mathews
1920	Sir A. Bodkin
1930	Sir E. Atkinson
1944	Sir T. Mathew
1964	(Sir) N. Skelhorn
1978	(Sir) T. Hetherington

Commissioner of Metropolitan Police

1890	Sir E. Bradford
1903	Sir E. Henry
1918	Sir N. Macready
1920	Sir W. Horwood
1928	Vt Byng
1931	Ld Trenchard
1935	Sir P. Game
1945	Sir H. Scott
1953	Sir J. Nott-Bower
1958	Sir J. Simpson
1968	Sir J. Waldron
1972	(Sir) R. Mark
1977	(Sir) D. McNee
1982	Sir K. Newman

Police Complaints Board (Chairman)

1977	Ld Plowden
1981	Sir C. Philips

Monopolies and Restrictive Practices Commission (Chairman)

1948	Sir A. Carter
1954	Sir D. Cairns

(Monopolies Commission)

1956	R. Levy
1965	(Sir) A. Roskill

(Monopolies and Mergers Commission)

1973	Sir A. Roskill
1975	(Sir) J. Le Quesne

Criminal Injuries Compensation Board 1964- (Chairman)

1964	(Sir) W. Carter
1975	M. Ogden

Procurator General and Treasury Solicitor

1894 H. Cuffe (E of Desart)
1909 (Sir) J. Mellor
1923 C. Lawrence
1926 (Sir) M. Gwyer
1934 Sir T. Barnes
1953 Sir H. Kent
1964 (Sir) H. Druitt
1971 Sir H. Ware
1975 (Sir) B. Hall
1980 Sir M. Kerry

Clerk of the Crown in Chancery[1]

1885 (Sir) K. Mackenzie
1915 (Sir) C. Schuster
1944 (Sir) A. Napier
1954 (Sir) G. Coldstream
1968 (Sir) D. Dobson
1977 (Sir) W. Bourne
1982 (Sir) A. Oulton

[1] Full title, Permanent Secretary to the Chancellor and Clerk of the Crown in Chancery. *See also* p. 286.

Judge Power by Type of Judge and Population
(England and Wales)

Year	Population (aged 15-64) (millions)	Lords of Appeal Lord Justices and ex officio judges		High Court Judges		County Court Judges[a]	
		No.	No. per million of pop.	No.	No. per million of pop.	No.	No. per million of pop.
1910	23·1	12	0·52	24	1·04	57	2·47
1920	25·1	14	0·56	24	0·96	54	2·15
1930	27·5	15	0·55	26	0·95	57	2·07
1940	29·3	18	0·61	29	0·99	59	2·01
1950	29·6	20	0·68	35	1·18	60	2·03
1960	29·8	24	0·81	57	1·91	75	2·52
1970	31·1	26	0·84	68	2·19	103	3·31
1980	31.6	31	0.99	75	2.37	445	14.35

[a] From 1972 Circuit Judges with different scope.

SOURCE.—*Criminal Statistics.*

Volume of Civil Proceedings

Year	Total No. of Proceedings	Number of proceedings commenced per 100,000 population (age group 15-64)[a]				
		Chancery Division	Queen's Bench Division	Divorce (Family)	County Court	All Courts
1909	1,511,637	27	290	4	6,228	6,748
1919	512,407	32	230	28	2,188	2,524
1929	1,316,903	24	343	15	4,217	4,896
1939	1,289,755	37	281	31	3,907	4,494
1949	612,627	32	340	123	1,574	2,135
1959	1,482,188	33	314	90	4,494	5,024
1969	1,968,678	80	671	198	5,284	6,330
1979	2,072,747	41	480	835	5,309	6,683

[a] Most actions that are commenced are in fact settled or withdrawn before coming to trial.

SOURCE.—*Civil Judicial Statistics.*

Appeal Proceedings

Year	Court of Appeal (Civil Division) No. of Appeals heard	No. of reversals or variations	%	House of Lords No. of Appeals heard	No. of reversals or variations	%
1909	533	184	35	69	20	20
1919	392	135	34	60	21	35
1929	405	144	36	53	20	38
1939	433	149	34	40	20	50
1949	612	225	37	32	12	38
1959	441	147	33	58	29	50
1969	680	261	38	60	31	51
1979	445	157	35	71	36	51

SOURCE.—*Civil Judicial Statistics.*

Criminal Statistics: England and Wales

Higher Courts: All Ages

	No. for trial Total	Male	Female	No. found guilty[b]	Sentences as percentage of those found guilty: Death[k]	Custodial measure[c]	Probation	Fine	Nominal penalties[d]	Otherwise dealt with[a]
1900	10,149	8,928	1,219	7,975	0·3	90·5	—	1·1	8·1	2·2
1910	13,680	12,522	1,157	11,337	0·2	83·6	5·2	0·6	10·2	0·2
1920	9,130	8,141	989	7,225	0·5	76·5	8·1	0·8	13·4	0·7
1930	8,384	7,781	601	6,921	0·2	71·4	11·3	1·6	15·0	0·5
1938	10,003	9,322	681	8,612	0·3	62·4	19·2	1·3	16·0	0·8
1950	18,935	17,990	945	17,149	0·2	62·6	17·2	6·6	13·2	0·2
1960	30,591	29,462	1,129	27,830	0·1	53·8	22·5	13·8	9·3	0·6
1970	44,134	41,691	2,443	35,709	—	54·3 14·9†	10·7	13·9	3·5	2·7
1980	73,892	66,410	7,482	59,008	—	46.2 18.6†	6.2	14.6	5.7	8.6

For Notes see p. 320.

† Suspended prison sentences.

Summary Courts: Indictable Offences

	Adults[fg] No. proceeded against	No. found guilty or charge proved[b]	Sentences as a percentage of those found guilty: Custodial Measure[c]	Probation	Fine	Other[e]	Juveniles[i] No. proceeded against	No. found guilty or charge proved[b]
1900[h]	43,479	30,736	47·1	14·0	26·7	12·8	n.a.	n.a.
1910	40,434	36,094	47·5	11·3	22·1	19·1	12,275	10,786
1920	37,107	32,942	31·7	11·3	38·6	28·4	14,380	12,919
1930	43,464	38,709	25·6	21·1	28·3	25·0	12,198	11,137
1938	46,014	41,976	22·0	22·2	28·9	25·9	29,388	27,875
1950	61,701	57,102	18·5	11·9	48·8	20·8	43,823	41,910
1960	84,523	79,538	13·4	12·5	56·1	18·0	58,350	56,114
1970	271,187	212,467	7·8 9·3†	9·0	56·8	17·0	79,528	72,912
1980[l]	407,363	306,183	7.0 6.5†	7.9	59.2	19.4	98,028	89,192

† Suspended prison sentences. * Includes committal for sentence.

For Notes see p. 320.

Summary Offences other than Highway/Motoring Offences | TRAFFIC Highway/Motoring Offences[j] (all courts)

	Adults[g]		Juveniles[i]		TRAFFIC	
	No. proceeded against	No. found guilty or charge proved[b]	No. proceeded against	No. found guilty or charge proved[b]	No. found guilty	As % of all found guilty of non-indictable offences
1900	672,989[h]	557,489	n.a.	n.a.	2,548	0·4
1910	551,395	483,111	18,959	14,694	55,633	9·1
1920	427,556	374,565	16,953	14,956	157,875	24·9
1930	317,231	287,691	8,842	7,577	267,616	42·8
1938	236,752	216,759	16,873	15,310	475,124	60·3
1950	220,188	202,286	19,810	18,410	357,932	52·6
1960	247,133	232,992	28,025	26,337	622,551	60·1
1970	394,540	360,041	25,184	22,521	1,014,793	60.6
1980[l]	454,288	419,819	23,221	20,183	1,309,992	74.9

[a] Including the Central Criminal Court and the Crown Courts.
[b] Excluding those found guilty but insane or (since 1964) acquitted by reason of insanity.
[c] Including imprisonment, or committal to a reformatory, approved school, remand home or (since 1952) detention centre, or (in the case of Assizes and Quarter Sessions) borstal training.
[d] Includes absolute and conditional discharge and binding over with recognisances.
[e] Includes whipping (abolished 1948), fit person orders (introduced 1934), as well as days in prison cells, admission to institutions for the mentally disordered, and other miscellaneous and numerically unimportant methods of disposal.
[f] Until 1932, persons aged 16 or older were tried and sentenced as adults (although in some cases sent to establishments reserved for younger offenders, e.g. borstals). From 1933, however, 'adult' means a person aged 17 or older.
[g] Includes small numbers of juveniles tried jointly with adults.
[h] The published tables for 1900 unfortunately do not distinguish adults from juveniles, although one table shows that those found guilty include 9,450 persons under 16. Consequently the figures showing the disposal of adult offenders in 1900 include unknown numbers of juveniles. Almost certainly most of the 3,218 who were whipped in 1900 were boys.
[i] From 1908 there were in effect 'juvenile courts', although lacking many special features which were introduced later.
[j] From 1900 to 1938 'highway offences' have been taken to include all offences under the Highway Acts together with offences against regulations, etc., dealing with stage coaches, trams, trolleybuses and so on. For 1950 they have been taken to include offences numbered 123-38, 173 and 180 in the Home Office code, and for 1960 and 1968 offences numbered 124, 130, 135-8, 173 and 180.
[k] The death penalty was, in practice, confined to murder throughout this period (except for war-time executions for treason or similar offences). 'Infanticides' were excluded from 'murder' from 1922, and from 1957 murders in certain circumstances became 'non-capital': the death penalty for murder was completely suspended from 1965. A large proportion of the murderers who were sentenced to death were subsequently reprieved.
[l] Figures for 1980 are based on indictable and summary offences as redefined by the Criminal Law Act 1977, and on a new counting procedure.

SOURCE.—N. D. Walker in A. H. Halsey (ed.), *Trends in British Society since 1900* (1972).

Prison Sentences and Prison Populations, 1901-

England and Wales

	Prisoners received under sentence[a]	Daily average prison population[b]		
		Male	Female	Total
1901	149,397	14,459	2,976	17,435
1910	179,951	19,333	2,685	22,018
1920	35,439	8,279	1,404	9,683
1930	38,832	10,561	785	11,346
1940	24,870	8,443	934	9,377
1950	33,875	19,367	1,107	20,474
1960	42,810	26,198	901	27,099
1970	62,020	38,040	988	39,028
1980	75,896	40,593	1,516	42,109

[a] This column excludes those sentenced by courts martial and those under sentence of death or recalled under licence; but includes sentences of penal servitude (which were abolished in 1948), borstal training and committals to Detention Centres from 1952. Civil prisoners are not included as they are not 'under sentence'.
[b] Figures are for daily average population of penal establishments in prisons, borstals and (from 1952) detention centres.

SOURCE.—*Annual Reports* of the Prison Commissioners (changed in 1964 to the Prison Department of the Home Office).

Parole Board, 1967-

Chairman (see p. 308)

1967 Ld Hunt
1974 Sir L. Petch
1979 Ld Harris of Greenwich
1982 Ld Windlesham

Police Force

	England & Wales		Scotland		Ireland (N. Ireland only from 1930)	
	No. of forces	No. of Police	No. of forces	Authorised no. of Police	No. of forces	No. of Police
1900	179	41,900	64	4,900	1	12,300
1910	190	49,600	63	5,600	1	11,900
1920	191	56,500	59	6,500	1	11,600
1930	183	58,000	49	6,600	1	2,800
1940	183	57,300	48	6,800	1	2,900
1950	129	62,600	33	7,200	1	2,800
1960	125	72,300	33	8,700	1	2,900
1970	47	92,700	20	11,200	1	3,800
1980	43	115,900	8	13,200	1	6,900

SOURCES.—*The War Against Crime in England and Wales 1959-1964*, Cmnd. 2296/1964; C. Reith, *A Short History of the British Police* (1948); J. M. Hart, *The British Police* (1951); B. Whitaker, *The Police* (1965); M. Banton, *The Police and the Community* (1964); Sir F. Newsam, *The Home Office* (2nd ed. 1955); Sir J. Moylan, *New Scotland Yard* (1934); Ld Devlin, *The Criminal Prosecution in England* (1966); Sir C. Allen, *The Queen's Peace* (1953);) C. Reith, *A New Study of Police History* (1954); *Royal Commission on Police Powers and Procedure*, Cmd. 3297/1929; *Royal Commission on the Police*, Cmnd. 1728/1962; G. Marshall, *Police and Government* (1965). Much information on the police is available in three reports from the House of Commons Estimates Committee H.C. 307 of 1957-8, H.C. 293 of 1962-3, and H.C. 145 of 1966-7. Annual Reports of H.M. Inspectors of Constabulary for England and Wales. Further information from Scottish Office and Northern Ireland Office.

IX

SOCIAL CONDITIONS

Population

U.K. POPULATION 1901-
(thousands)

1901	41,459	1921	47,123	1941	48,216	1961	52,709	1981	56,348
1902	41,893	1922	44,372	1942	48,400	1962	53,274	1982	56,340
1903	42,237	1923	44,597	1943	48,789	1963	53,553	1983	56,377
1904	42,611	1924	44,916	1944	49,016	1964	53,885	1984	56,488
1905	42,981	1925	45,060	1945	49,182	1965	54,218		
1906	43,361	1926	45,233	1946	49,217	1966	54,500		
1907	43,738	1927	45,389	1947	49,571	1967	54,800		
1908	44,124	1928	45,578	1948	50,065	1968	55,049		
1909	44,519	1929	45,672	1949	50,363	1969	55,263		
1910	44,916	1930	45,866	1950	50,616	1970	55,421		
1911	45,222	1931	46,038	1951	50,225	1971	55,515		
1912	45,436	1932	46,335	1952	50,430	1972	55,781		
1913	45,648	1933	46,520	1953	50,593	1973	55,913		
1914	46,048	1934	46,666	1954	50,765	1974	55,922		
1915	44,333	1935	46,869	1955	50,946	1975	55,900		
1916	43,710	1936	47,081	1956	51,184	1976	55,886		
1917	43.280	1937	47,289	1957	51,430	1977	55,852		
1918	43,116	1938	47,494	1958	51,652	1978	55,822		
1919	44,599	1939	47,762	1959	51,956	1979	55,881		
1920	46,472	1940	48,226	1960	52,372	1980	55,945		

Census figures for 1901, 1911, 1921, 1931, 1951, 1961, 1971 and 1981. Figures for other years are mid-year estimates. Figures for 1901-21 inclusive include S. Ireland. Figures for 1915-20 and for 1940-50 relate to civil population only.

SOURCES.—*Annual Reports of the Registrary-General for England and Wales, Scotland, and N. Ireland*; *Annual Abstract of Statistics*; *Monthly Digest of Statistics*.

INTERCENSAL CHANGES IN POPULATION
(thousands)

	Population at beginning of period	Average Annual Change			
		Total Increase	Excess of births over deaths	Net Civilian Migration	Other Adjustments
1901-1911	38,237	385	467	−82	
1911-1921	42,082	195	286	−92	
1921-1931	44,027	201	268	−67	
1931-1951	46,038	212	190	+22	
1951-1961	50,290	252	246	−7	+13
1961-1971	52,807	280	324	−32	−12
1971-1981	55,610	64	70	−37	+32

Census enumerated population up to 1951; mid-year estimates of home population from 1951 onwards.

SOURCE.—*Annual Abstract of Statistics*.

POPULATION OF COMPONENTS OF U.K.
(thousands)

	Area (sq. kilometres)	1911	1931	1951	1961	1971	1981
England: Standard Regions[a]							
North	19,349	2,815	3,038	3,137	3,250	3,296	3,104
Yorkshire and Humberside	14,196	3,877	4,285	4,522	4,635	4,799	4,860
East Midlands	12,179	2,263	2,531	2,893	3,100	3,390	3,819
East Anglia	12,565	1,192	1,232	1,382	1,470	1,669	1,872
South East	27,408	11,744	13,539	15,127	16,271	17,230	16,796
South West	23,660	2,687	2,794	3,229	3,411	3,781	4,349
West Midlands	13,013	3,277	3,743	4,423	4,758	5,110	5,148
North West	7,993	5,796	6,197	6,447	6,567	6,743	6,414
Wales	20,763	2,421	2,593	2,599	2,664	2,731	2,792
Scotland	77,179	4,760	4,843	5,097	5,179	5,229	5,131
N. Ireland	13,570	1,251	1,280	1,371	1,425	1,536	1,482
Conurbations[a]							
Greater London	1,580	7,160	8,110	8,197	7,992	7,452	6,696
West Midlands	678	1,657	1,951	2,260	2,378	2,372	2,244
West Yorkshire	1,255	1,590	1,655	1,693	1,704	1,728	1,682
South-East Lancashire	983	2,328	2,427	2,423	2,428	2,393	2,245
Merseyside	394	1,157	1,347	1,386	1,384	1,267	1,127
Tyneside	235	761	827	836	856	805	738
Central Clydeside	778	1,461	1,690	1,759	1,802	1,728	1,718

[a]Standard Regions and Conurbations are based on 1969 boundaries.

SOURCE.—*Annual Abstract of Statistics.*

BIRTH RATES, DEATH RATES, AND MARRIAGES IN THE U.K.

	Total Births per 1000 Population	Infant Mortality (under 1 year) per 1000 live births	Total Deaths per 1000 Population	Total Marriages per 1000 Population
1900	28·2	142·0	18·4	15·1
1910	25·0	110·0	14·0	14·3
1920	25·4	82·0	12·9	19·4
1930	16·8	67·0	11·7	15·5
1940	14·6	61·0	14·4	22·2
1950	16·2	31·2	11·8	16·1
1960	17·5	22·4	11·5	15·0
1970	16·3	18·5	11·8	17·0
1980	13.1	12.2	11.9	15.0

Figures for 1900, 1910 and 1920 (except for infant mortality) include Southern Ireland.
Death rate in 1940 based on civil deaths and population only.

SOURCE.—*Annual Reports of the Registrars-General.*

AGE DISTRIBUTION OF THE POPULATION OF THE U.K.

(Percentages)

Age Groups	1901	1911	1921[a]	1931	1939	1951	1961	1971	1981
Under 10	22·2	21·0	18·2	16·1	14·1	16·0	15·1	16·6	12·6
10-19	20·3	19·1	19·0	16·8	16·3	12·9	14·9	14·6	16·3
20-29	18·3	17·3	16·2	17·1	15·6	14·2	12·7	14·3	14·1
30-39	13·9	15·1	14·5	14·5	16·0	14·5	13·7	11·6	13·8
40-49	10·5	11·4	13·1	12·9	13·1	14·8	13·5	12·3	11·3
50-59	7·3	7·9	9·6	11·1	11·3	11·9	13·2	11·9	11·7
60-69	4·7	5·1	6·0	7·3	8·5	8·9	9·4	10·6	10.2
70-79	2·2	2·5	2·7	3·4	4·1	5·3	5·6	5·9	7.2
80 and over	0·6	0·6	0·7	0·8	1·0	1·5	1·9	2·2	2.7
Total	100·0	100·0	100·0	100·0	100·0	100·0	100·0	100·0	100·0

[a] Percentages for 1921 are for England, Wales and Scotland only.

SOURCES.—Census figures for 1901, 1911, 1921, 1931, 1951, 1961, 1971, 1981. Mid-year estimate 1939 and 1978. Registrars-General of England and Wales, and Scotland, *Censuses of Population*, and the *Annual Abstract of Statistics*.

EXPECTATION OF LIFE

England and Wales
(Average future expected lifetime at birth)

Years	Male	Female	Years	Male	Female
1900-02	46	50	1950-52	66	72
1910-12	52	55	1960-62	68	74
1920-22	56	60	1969-71	69	75
1930-32	59	63	1974-6	70	76
1938	61	66	1978-80	70	77

SOURCES.—*Annual Reports of Registrars-General for England and Wales*, and the *Government Actuary's Department*, *Annual Abstract of Statistics*.

MAIN CAUSES OF DEATH

England and Wales
(thousands)

	1900	1910	1920	1930	1940	1950	1960	1970	1980
Total deaths	588	483	466	455	572	510	526	575	581
Due to:									
Tuberculosis	61	51	43	36	27	16	3	2	1
Cancer	27	35	44	57	69	83	96	114	131
Vascular lesions of the nervous system[a]	41	30	49	41	52	65	76	79	71
Heart diseases	n.a.	49	53	90	136	146	153	179	192
Pneumonia	44	40	37	28	29	18	24	43	54
Bronchitis	54	34	38	19	46	28	26	29	19
Violent causes	20	19	17	22	47[b]	19	23	23	20

[a] All diseases of the nervous system, 1900-30; cerebrovascular disease, 1970 onwards.
[b] Including 22,000 deaths of civilians due to operations of war.

Infant mortality (i.e. deaths under 1 year) per 1000 live births: 1900—154; 1910—105; 1920—80; 1930—64; 1940—57; 1950—30; 1960—22; 1970—18; 1980—12.

SOURCE.—*Annual Reports and Statistical Reviews of the Registrars-General for England and Wales.*

AVERAGE AGE AT FIRST MARRIAGE

England and Wales

Years	Bachelors	Spinsters
1901-05	26·9	25·4
1911-15	27·5	25·8
1921-25	27·5	25·6
1931-35	27·4	25·5
1941-45	26·8	24·6
1951-55	26·5	24·2
1961-65	25·5	22·9
1971-75	24·8	22·7
1981-83	25.6	24.3

SOURCES—*Annual Reports of Registrars-General for England and Wales*. 1981-3: figures are from *Population Trends*.

DIVORCES
(Great Britain)

Decrees made absolute

1910	801	1950	32,516
1920	3,747	1960	25,672
1930	3,944	1970	62,010
1940	8,396	1980	158,829

SOURCE.—*Annual Reports of Registrars-General for England, Wales and Scotland.*

The law on divorce was significantly relaxed by the *Matrimonial Causes Acts* of 1937, 1950, and 1967 and by the *Divorce Reform Act, 1969*.

NET EMIGRATION FROM GREAT BRITAIN AND IRELAND

Commonwealth citizens travelling by the long sea routes to non-European countries, 1900-59; all routes 1970-

	1900	1910	1920	1931	1938	1946	1950	1959	1970	1977	1982
All Countries	71,188	241,164	199,047	−39,056	−6,467	103,504	54,153	28,400	92,700	59,900	81,000
U.S.A.	47,978	75,021	60,067	−10,385	−1,432	45,751	8,541	4,500	4,500	5,500	7,000
Canada	7,803	115,955	94,496	−10,464	−3,974	43,414	6,464	−400	12,700	11,900	13,000
Australasia	6,259	34,657	28,405	−8,760	2,204	8,443	54,581	28,800	59,300	11,900	40,000
S. Africa	7,417	8,314	7,844	−1,263	2,037	2,242	1,912	−800	19,400	−4,100	17,000

Southern Ireland excluded from 1938 onwards.

SOURCES.—1900-1950: *External Migration 1815-1950*, N. H. Carrier and J. R. Jeffrey, *Studies on Medical and Population Subjects No. 6*, General gister Office (1953); 1959, 1970 and 1982 figures are from the *Annual Abstract of Statistics*.

PEOPLE BORN OVERSEAS[a]

Great Britain

Birthplace	1931 '000s	1931 % of population	1951 '000s	1951 % of population	1961 '000s	1961 % of population	1971 '000s	1971 % of population	1981 '000s	1981 % of population
Foreign countries[b]	347	0.8	722	1·5	842	1·6	984	1·7	1,274	2·3
Canada, Australia, New Zealand	75	0.2	99	0.2	110	0.2	136	0.4	152	0·3
Other Common-wealth	137	0.3	218	0.4	541	1.1	1,140	2.1	1,325	2·5
Irish Republic[c]	362	0.8	532	1.1	709	1.4	718	1.3	606	1·1
Total born overseas	921	2.0	1,571	3.2	2,202	4.3	2,976	5.5	3,360	6·2

[a] Persons resident in Great Britain at the time of the Census who had been born outside the United Kingdom; including United Kingdom citizens born overseas but excluding short-term visitors.
[b] Including South Africa.
[c] Including Ireland (part not stated).

SOURCES.—*Social Trends 1972*; Census for 1981.

NATURALISATION

Total certificates granted by the Home Department or oaths taken in period

1901-10	7,997	1941-50	51,132
1911-20	11,293	1951-60	44,977
1921-30	9,849	1961-70	40,252
1931-40	15,454	1971-80	28,717

SOURCES.—N. H. Carrier and J. R. Jeffrey, *External Migration 1815-1950, Studies on Medical and Population Subjects, No. 6*, General Register Office (H.M.S.O., 1953), and *Whitaker's Almanack*.

Commonwealth Immigration

Commonwealth immigration came under systematic control under the Commonwealth Immigrants Act of 1962. This Act was strengthened by the Commonwealth Immigrants Act of 1968 and largely replaced by the Immigration Act of 1971.

MAIN SOURCES OF IMMIGRATION INTO THE UNITED KINGDOM 1956-62

Year	West Indians	Indians	Pakistanis (Bangladeshis)
1956	26,400	5,600	2,100
1957	22,500	6,000	5,200
1958	16,500	6,200	4,700
1959	20,400	2,900	900
1960	52,700	5,900	2,500
1961	61,600	23,750	25,100
1962	35,000	22,100	24,900

ACCEPTANCES FOR SETTLEMENT IN THE UNITED KINGDOM 1963-

	Foreign	Old Cwth	New Cwth	Total		Foreign	Old Cwth	New Cwth & Pakistan	Total
1963	15,349	3,735	56,071	75,155	1974	26,800	3,948	42,531	68,878
1964	19,211	3,060	52,840	75,111	1975	31,477	5,387	53,265	82,405
1965	20,615	3,454	53,898	77,967	1976	31,464	5,967	55,013	80,745
1966	18,948	4,214	48,104	71,266	1977	31,917	6,572	44,155	69,313
1967	18,346	4,335	60,633	83,314	1978	34,364	7,453	30,514	72,331
1968	20,093	3,761	60,620	84,474	1979	36,600	6,960	26,110	69,670
1969	21,862	3,581	44,503	69,946	1980	38,410	6,900	24,610	69,920
1970	20,917	4,497	37,893	63,307	1981	31,280	5,380	22,400	59,060
1971	23,467	4,577	44,261	72,305	1982	26,080	5,150	22,650	53,880
1972	19,681	3,989	68,519	92,189	1983	20,120	5,800	27,550	53,460
1973	21,118	3,099	32,247	55,162					

This table covers work permit holders admitted for more than one year. Voucher holders were admitted for settlement on arrival. Work permit holders may qualify for settlement after 4 years in approved employment.

SOURCE.—Home Office.

COMMONWEALTH IMMIGRANTS IN THE U.K.

according to the 1961, 1971 and 1981 Censuses and the 1966 Sample Census

Year	W. Indians	Bangladeshis, Indians and Pakistanis	Australians	Others in British Territories	Total
1961	173,076	115,982[a]	23,390[a]	285,962[b]	596,755
1966	267,850	205,340[a]	44,480	324,640[b]	842,310
1971	302,970	462,125	32,400	496,410[b]	1,293,905
1981	295,179	628,589	61,916	280,466	1,666,120

The Office of Population and Census Statistics estimated that in 1976 1,771,000 people of Commonwealth ethnic origin were resident in the U.K., 390,000 from India, 246,000 from Pakistan, 604,000 from the West Indies, 257,000 from Africa (160,000 of these of Asian origin), and 274,000 from the rest of the New Commonwealth (Population Trends, Sep 1977, H.M.S.O.).

[a] Persons born in these countries but British by birth or descent have been deducted for 1961. No nationality data were included in the 1966 Sample Census, and therefore, on the basis of past data, the estimate for those born in the Indian subcontinent has been reduced by 100,000.
[b] The largest contributors to this total are Cypriots, New Zealanders, Maltese, Canadians and South Africans.

Race Relations Legislation

Race Relations Act, 1965, set up the Race Relations Board to receive complaints of unlawful discrimination and to investigate them.

Race Relations Act, 1968, enlarged the Race Relations Board and extended its scope. It also set up the Community Relations Commission to establish harmonious race relations.

Race Relations Act, 1976, made discrimination unlawful in employment, training, education and in the provision of goods and services and made it an offence to stir up racial hatred. It extended discrimination to include indirect discrimination and discrimination by way of victimisation. It replaced the Race Relations and the Community Relations Commission by the Commission for Racial Equality.

Race Relations Board 1966-77

Chairman

17 Feb 66	M. Bonham Carter
1 Jan 71	Sir R. Wilson (Acting)
1 Oct 71	Sir G. Wilson

Community Relations Commission 1968-77

Chairman

17 Feb 68	F. Cousins
1 Jan 71	M. Bonham Carter
1 Mar 77	Ld Pitt

Commission for Racial Equality 1977-

Chairman

13 Jun 77	(Sir) D. Lane
1 Apr 82	P. Newsam

Housing

(a) Major Housing Acts

Housing and Town Planning Act, 1909. This amended the law relating to the housing of the working classes, and provided for town-planning schemes. It also provided for the establishment of public health and housing committees of county councils.

Housing Acts, 1919, 1923, and *1924.* These Acts provided for varying subsidies to encourage the building of new houses for the working classes.

Housing Act, 1930. This Act extended subsidies and provided wider powers for slum clearance.

Housing (Financial Provisions) Act, 1933. This reduced the general subsidies, but presented subsidies for slum clearance.

Housing (Financial Provisions) Act, 1938. This Act regulated subsidies to housing.

Housing (Financial Provisions) Act, 1958. This Act provided grants for improvements to private houses.

House Purchase and Housing Act, 1959. This extended grants for improvements.

Housing Act, 1961. Laid down regulations for landlords leasing houses for less than 7 years to keep the structure, exterior, installations, etc., of the house in repair and proper working order.

Housing Act, 1964. Set up the Housing Corporation to assist Housing Societies to provide housing accommodation and conferred powers and duties on local authorities with regard to housing improvements.

Building Control Act, 1966. Controlled and regulated building and constructional work.

Housing Subsidies Act, 1967. Provided for financial assistance towards the provision, acquisition or improvement of dwellings and the provision of hostels.

Housing Act, 1969. Made further provision for grants by local authorities towards the cost of improvements and conversions; made provision as to houses in multiple occupation; altered the legal standard of fitness for human habitation; and amended the law relating to long tenancies.

Housing Act, 1971. Increased the amount of financial assistance available for housing subsidies in development or intermediate areas.

Housing Finance Act, 1972. Increased financial help to local authorities needing to clear slums, provided national rent rebate scheme for Council tenants and rent loans for private tenants of unfurnished accommodation, and based rent of public sector and private unfurnished accommodation on the 'fair rent' principle.

Housing Act, 1974. Extended functions of Housing Corporation, provided for the registration and giving of assistance to housing associations, introduced new powers for declaration of Housing Action Areas and made provisions for higher renovation grants.

Housing Finance (Special Provisions) Act, 1975. Prevented surcharges arising out of the Housing Finance Act 1972 (relating to refusal by Clay Cross Councillors to charge proper rents under the Act) and substituted other means of making up losses.

Housing Rents and Subsidies Act, 1975. Repealed provisions of Housing Finance Act 1972 relating to fixing of public sector rents; introduced new subsidies for local authorities and new town corporations and made certain housing associations eligible for housing association grant.

Housing (Homeless Persons) Act, 1977. Local authorities put under a duty to house homeless persons in 'priority need' unless the homelessness could be shown to be intentional.

Home Purchase Assistance and Housing Corporation Guarantee Act, 1978. Set up the 'Homeloan' scheme (to provide a reduction in the cost of house purchase for first-time purchasers).

Housing Act, 1980. Provided a new and much more flexible subsidy system; repealed the 'no-profit rule'; local authority tenants of 3 years' standing or more to have the right to buy their houses at discounts ranging from 33% to 50%.

Social Security and Housing Benefits Acts, 1982. Replaced rent rebates, rent allowances, rate rebates, and the 'rent' element in tenants' Supplementary Benefit by Housing Benefit.

Housing and Building Control Act, 1984. Maximum discount on 'right-to-buy' purchase increased to 60%; exercise of right to buy simplified and extended; new system of building control.

(b) **Major Rent and Mortgage Interest Restriction Acts**

Increase of Rent and Mortgage Interest (Restrictions) Acts, 1915. These acts established a limit to the rent of small houses, and protected tenants from eviction.

Rent Acts, 1919-39. These altered the exact limits on rent.

Rent and Mortgage Interest (Restriction) Act, 1939. This extended rent restriction and security of tenure to houses which had become decontrolled and to new houses.

Furnished Houses (Rent Control) Act, 1947. This Act created rent tribunals to fix the prices of furnished lettings.

Landlord and Tenant Rent Control Act, 1949. Rent tribunals were authorised to determine 'reasonable' rents, on the application of the tenants, who could also apply for the recovery of premiums. The Act applied to unfurnished houses and flats.

Housing Repairs and Rents Act, 1954. This Act authorised landlords to increase rents where sufficient repairs to their property had been carried out. Rent could also be increased to cover the increase in cost since 1939 of other services provided by the landlord.

Rent Act, 1957. This decontrolled many houses in 1958 and permitted substantial increases on controlled rents.

Protection from Eviction Act, 1964. This prevented a landlord of residential premises from recovering possession without an order of the country court. (Consolidated in *Protection from Eviction Act, 1977.*)

Rent Act, 1965. Provided for the registration of rents, introduced controls, and provided security of tenure subject to certain conditions. A landlord cannot enforce a right to possession against a tenant without a court order.

Leasehold Reform Act, 1967. Enabled tenants of houses held on long leases at low rents to acquire the freehold or an extended lease.

Rent Act, 1968. Consolidated the statute law relating to protected or statutory tenancies, rents under regulated or controlled tenancies and furnished tenancies.

Rent Act, 1974. Extended indefinite security of tenure and access to rent tribunals to furnished tenants. Landlords resident on the premises exempt from provisions of the Act. It brought most residential furnished tenancies of absentee landlords into the full protection of the Rent Acts.

Rent (Agriculture) Act, 1976. Afforded security of tenure for agricultural workers housed by their employers and imposed duties on housing authorities in respect to agricultural workers.

Housing (Homeless Persons) Act, 1977. Made local authorities more fully responsible for providing accommodation for the homeless.

Rent Act, 1977. Consolidated law relating to control and regulation of rent, security of tenure, and powers and duties of Rent Officers, Rent Assessment Committees, and Rent Tribunals.

Housing Act, 1980. All remaining rent-controlled dwellings transferred to regulation. 'Shorthold' tenure introduced, with security of tenure for limited period only.

Permanent Dwellings Completed

Great Britain: 1919-45; United Kingdom: 1945-

	Public Sector ('000s)	Private Sector ('000s)	Total ('000s)
1919/20	—	1	1
1920/21	17	23	40
1921/22	110	32	142
1922/23	67	45	112
1923/24	20	74	94
1924/25	24	120	144
1925/26	50	134	184
1926/27	84	151	235
1927/28	120	141	261
1928/29	70	119	189
1929/30	73	147	220
1930/31	64	133	197
1931/32	79	136	215
1932/33	68	151	219
1933/34	72	222	294
1934/35	57	294	351
1935/36	70	280	350
1936/37	87	283	370
1937/38	92	268	360
1938/39	122	237	359
1939/40	69	152	221

	Public Sector ('000s)	Private Sector ('000s)	Total ('000s)
1940/41	26	31	57
1941/42 to 1944/45 (annual average)	8	3	11
1945 (April-Dec)	11	1	12
1946	109	31	140
1947	148	41	189
1948	217	34	251
1949	177	28	205
1950	175	30	205
1951	176	25	202
1952	212	37	248
1953	262	65	327
1954	262	92	354
1955	208	116	324
1956	181	126	308
1957	179	129	308
1958	148	130	278
1959	128	153	282
1960	133	171	304
1961	122	181	303
1962	135	178	314
1963	130	178	308
1964	162	221	383
1965	174	217	391
1966	187	209	396
1967	211	204	415
1968	200	226	426
1969	192	186	378
1970	188	174	362
1971	168	196	364
1972	130	201	331
1973	114	191	305
1974	134	145	280
1975	167	155	322
1976	170	155	325
1977	170	144	314
1978	136	152	289
1979	108	144	252
1980	110	131	240
1981	88	116	204
1982	53	124	178
1983	55	143	198
1984	52	155	207

NOTES.—From 1919/20 to 1944/45, the figures are combinations of England and Wales financial year figures and Scottish calendar year figures.

From 1946 onwards the figures are for the United Kingdom including Northern Ireland. 'Public sector' comprises local authorities, new towns, housing associations, and public bodies in their capacity as employers. Before 1945 the last two were included in the private sector.

SOURCE.—Dept. of Environment.

Number of Houses

England and Wales

Occupied and Unoccupied
(to nearest '000)

1901	6,710	1939	11,263
1911	7,550	1951	12,389
1921	7,979	1961	14,648[a]
1931	9,400	1971	17,024[a]
		1981	17,755[a]

[a]Excluding vacant dwellings.

SOURCES.—1901, 1911, 1921, 1931, 1951, 1961, 1971, 1981 *Population Censuses*; 1939 estimates in M. E. Bowley, *Housing and the State, 1919-1944* (1945).

Housing by Tenancy

Great Britain

	Owner-Occupied %	Local Authority[a] %	Rented from Private Landlord %	Other[b]	Total Stock (millions)
1914	10[c]	—[d]	90		9·0
1938	25	10	65		12·7
1945	26	12	54	8	12·9
1951	29	18	45	8	13·9
1956	34	23	36	7	15·1
1960	42	26	26	6	16·2
1965	47	28	20	5	17·4
1970	50	30	15	5	18·7
1975	53	31	16		19.9
1980	55	32	13		21.0
1983	60	29	11		22.0

[a]Includes New Towns.
[b]Includes dwellings rented with farm and business premises, or occupied by virtue of employment.
[c]Approximate only: true figure probably lies between 8% and 15%.
[d]Included under private landlord.

SOURCES.—*Housing and Construction Statistics;* for 1976, Department of the Environment. *Encyclopaedia of Housing* (ed. A. Bramall).

Social Security

Old Age Pensions Act, 1908. This granted non-contributory pensions ranging from one to five shillings a week to be paid from national funds, subject to a means test, at the age of 70, where income was under £31 p.a.

National Insurance Act, 1911 (National Health Insurance, Pt. I). This was the first part of an act providing insurance against both ill-health and unemployment. The Act covered all those between the ages of 16 and 70 who were manual workers or earning not more than £160 p.a. (This income limit was raised in 1920 and 1942.) The self-employed, non-employed, and those already provided for by other health insurance schemes were not insurable under this Act. The scheme was administered through independent units, or 'approved societies'. Local insurance committees were set up. The insurance included benefits for sickness, maternity, and medical needs. A weekly contribution was made by the insured person, his employer, and the government. The basic weekly sickness benefit was 10s. for men, 7s. 6d. for women. It also set up general medical and pharmaceutical services.

Widows', Orphans' and Old Age Contributory Pensions Act, 1925. This provided for a contributory scheme, covering almost the same field as the national health insurance scheme. Pensions were payable to the widows of insured persons, and to insured persons and their wives over the age of 70. This age limit was reduced to 65 in 1928. The weekly rates were 10s. for widows, with additional allowances of 5s. for the first child and 3s. for each other child, 7s. 6d. for orphans and 10s. for old age pensioners.

Widows', Orphans' and Old Age Contributory Pensions Act, 1929. This

Act provided a pension at age 55 for certain widows who could not satisfy the conditions of the 1925 Act.

Widows', Orphans' and Old Age Contributory Pensions (Voluntary Contributors) Act, 1937. This Act created a new scheme of voluntary insurance for old age, widows' and orphans' benefits open to certain persons who were not within the scope of the main scheme.

Old Age and Widows' Pensions Act, 1940. This reduced to 60 the age at which a woman who was herself insured or who was the wife of an insured man could become entitled to an old age pension. The Act also introduced supplementary pensions in cases of need for widow pensioners over the age of 60 and for old age pensioners. The Unemployment Assistance Board was renamed the Assistance Board and became responsible for payment of these supplementary pensions.

National Health Insurance, Contributory Pensions and Workmen's Compensation Act, 1941. This raised the income limit for compulsory insurance of non-manual workers for pensions purposes to £420 p.a.

Family Allowances Act, 1945. This granted a non-contributory allowance, to be paid to the mother, for each child other than the first. 1945-52 5s. per week; 1952-68 8s. per week; 1956-68 10s. per week for third and subsequent children; 1968 15s. (75p) per week for second, £1 per week for third and subsequent children.

National Health Service Act, 1946. By this Act, hospitals were transferred from local authorities and voluntary bodies and were to be administered by the Minister through regional hospital boards, general medical and dental services through executive councils, and other health services by county and county borough councils. Health centres were to be provided by local authorities for general, mental, dental, and pharmaceutical services, but few were built. Almost all services under the Act were to be free.

National Health Service (Amendment) Act, 1949; National Health Service Acts, 1951 and 1952, and *National Health Service Contributions Acts, 1957-1958.* These made modifications in the original scheme by imposing charges for certain parts of the scheme (prescriptions, dental treatment, etc.).

National Insurance Act, 1946. This Act provided a new scheme of insurance replacing the national health insurance and contributory pensions schemes with effect from 5 Jul 1948. All persons over school-leaving age, except certain married women, became compulsorily insurable. In addition to provisions for unemployment (see p. 359) benefits payable were retirement pension, widow's benefit, and death grant.

National Insurance Act, 1951. This Act introduced an allowance payable with widows' benefits for each dependent child in the family.

Family Allowances and National Insurance Act, 1956. Enabled allowances for dependent children to be paid in certain cases up to the age of 18; introduced new personal rate of widowed mother's allowance, reduced length of marriage condition for widow's pension, and introduced amendments to widows' pensions.

National Insurance Act, 1957. This introduced the child's special allowance for the children of divorced parents payable on the death of the father if he had been contributing towards their support and the mother had not remarried.

National Insurance Act, 1959. This introduced a state scheme of graduated pensions, requiring that both contributions and pensions should be graduated according to salary level.

Mental Health Act, 1959. The Board of Control was abolished and its functions passed to the new Mental Health Review Tribunals, local authorities, and the Minister of Health. The Act redefined the classifications of mental disorders, provided for further safeguards against improper detention, and extended the provisions for voluntary and informal treatment of patients.

Family Allowances and National Insurance Act, 1964. This increased from 18 to 19 the age limit up to which a person could be regarded as a child for the purposes of an increase of benefit or widowed mother's allowance.

Prescription Charges were ended in 1965. They were reimposed in 1968 with exemptions for some categories.

National Insurance Act, 1966. This extended the period of widow's allowance, introduced a scheme of earnings-related supplements to unemployment and sickness benefits and included a widow's supplementary allowance.

Ministry of Social Security Act, 1966, repealed and amended much previous legislation. It provided for the abolition of the Ministry of Pensions and National Insurance and the National Assistance Board and the establishment of the Ministry of Social Security. The Act also provided for a scheme of supplementary benefits to replace the system of allowances which had previously been administered by the National Assistance Board. The benefits were paid as of right to those people whose incomes were below the levels set in the Act and not according to national insurance contribution records.

Chronically Sick and Disabled Persons Act, 1970. This placed more stringent obligations on local authorities to seek out and provide for the chronically sick and disabled.

National Insurance (Old Persons and Widows Pensions and Attendance Allowance) Act, 1970. Gave pensions to those of pensionable age in 1948. Reduced from 50 to 40 the qualifying age for widows' pensions.

Family Income Supplements Act, 1970. Created new benefit for families with small incomes.

Social Security Pensions Act, 1975. This provided for social security pensions and other related benefits to consist of a basic element and an additional component related to higher earnings and made various other provisions in relation to pensions. Made full National Insurance contributions obligatory for women except widows and women already on reduced rates.[1]

Child Benefits Act, 1975. Replaced family allowances with child benefit,

[1] For further provisions see Women's Rights Legislation on facing page.

and provided for an interim benefit for unmarried or separated parents with children.

Health Services Act, 1980. Made provision for increased access to Health Service facilities by private patients and made other alterations to the law regarding private health care.

Social Security and Housing Benefits Act, 1982. Made provision for the payment of statutory sick pay by the employers and amended rent and rate rebate procedure.

Old Age Pensions

Maximum rate for a single person

Jan 1909	5/-
Feb 1920	10/-
Oct 1946	26/-
Sep 1952	32/6
Jan 1958	50/-
Apr 1961	57/6
Mar 1963	67/6
Mar 1965	81/-
Oct 1967	90/-
Nov 1969	100/-
Sep 1971	£6·00
Oct 1972	£6·75
Oct 1973	£7·35
Jul 1974	£10·00
Apr 1975	£11·60
Nov 1975	£13·30
Nov 1976	£15·30
Nov 1977	£17·50
Nov 1978	£19·50
Nov 1979	£23.30
Nov 1980	£27.15
Nov 1981	£29.60
Nov 1982	£32.85
Nov 1983	£34.05
Nov 1984	£35.80

SOURCES.—Sir E. Wilson and G. S. Mackay, *Old Age Pensions* (1941); *Keesings Contemporary Archives 1931-*; *Report on Social Insurance and Allied Services* (Beveridge), Cmd. 6404/1944, Appendix B, *National Superannuation and Social Insurance*, Cmnd. 3883/1969, and the Department of Health and Social Security.

In 1972 a £10 Christmas bonus for pensioners was instituted.

Women's Rights

Representation of the People Act, 1918. Gave women over 30 the right to vote.

The Sex Disqualification (Removal) Act, 1919. Abolished disqualification by sex or marriage for entry to the professions, universities, and the exercise of any public function.

Matrimonial Causes Act, 1923. Relieved a wife petitioner of necessity of proving cruelty, desertion etc. in addition to adultery as grounds for divorce. (Further acts in 1927 and 1950 extended grounds for divorce and codified the matrimonial law.)

Guardianship of Infants Act, 1924. Vested guardianship of infant children in the parents jointly. If parents disagreed either could apply to court, the Court's subsequent decision being guided solely by consideration of the infant's interest.

New English Law of Property, 1926. Provided that both married and single women may hold and dispose of their property, real and personal, on the same terms as a man.

Representation of the People Act, 1928. Gave women over 21 the right to vote.

Law Reform (Married Women and Tortfeasors) Act, 1935. Empowered a married woman to dispose by will of all her property as if she were single.

British Nationality of Women Act, 1948. Gave British women the right to retain British nationality on marriage to a foreigner, and ended right of alien women to acquire automatic British nationality when marrying.

Equal Pay Act, 1970. (See p. 353.)

Matrimonial Proceedings and Property Act, 1970. Empowered courts to order either spouse to make financial provision for the other spouse or a child of the family. Laid down that if either spouse had contributed money or money's worth to property during marriage, then a share in that property had been acquired.

Finance Act, 1971. Allowed husband's and wife's earnings to be taxed separately if they so applied.

Domicile and Matrimonial Proceedings Act, 1973. Allowed women to stay in the family home.

Matrimonial Causes Act, 1973. Gave effect to recommendations of the Law Commission on Matrimonial Proceedings, validity of marriage, nationality and maintenance. Gave British women married to foreigners the same right as men for their spouses to live in Britain.

Employment Protection Act, 1975. Made dismissal because of pregnancy unlawful, and made it obligatory for employers to offer a new contract when the pregnancy was over. Also made provisions for paid maternity leave.

Sex Discrimination Act, 1975. Equal Pay Act of 1970 amended and included in this Act. Together they outlawed discrimination on grounds of sex in all aspects of employment, education, provision of professional services, recreational facilities, banking, insurance and credit. Established Equal Opportunities Commission (first chairman 29 Dec 75 Miss B. Lockwood (Lady)).

Social Security Act, 1975. Set up a special maternity allowance fund, incorporated into *Employment Protection Act, 1975,* and included income supplements for divorced women.

Social Security Pensions Act, 1975. Stipulated that pension schemes must be open on an equal basis to women doing the same or broadly similar work as men. Abolished the 'half-test' by which women had to have twenty consecutive years in employment to qualify for a full state pension.

Maternity and Child Welfare

Midwives Act, 1902. This Act sought to improve the standards of midwifery. It only became fully operative in 1910. Further Acts were passed in 1936 and 1951.

Notification of Births Act, 1908. This gave powers to local authorities to insist on compulsory notification of births.

Notification of Births Extension Act, 1915. This made notification universally compulsory.

Children Act, 1908. This Act consolidated the existing law and recognised the need for legal protection of children. It provided legislation covering negligence to children. Imprisonment of children was abolished, and remand homes were set up for children awaiting trial. This was to be only in special juvenile courts.

Education (Choice of Employment) Act, 1910. This empowered authorities to set up their own juvenile employment bureaux.

Maternity and Child Welfare Act, 1918. This empowered authorities to set up 'home help' schemes and clinics.

Children and Young Persons Act, 1933. This extended responsibility for children until the age of 17 and included a careful definition of the meaning of the need for care and protection. It established approved schools, and made detailed regulations about juvenile court procedure.

Children Act, 1948. This gave local authorities new responsibilities, with children's officers to administer the children's service (see *Local Government section).*

Children and Young Persons Act, 1963. This extended the power of local authorities to promote the welfare of children and dealt with children and young persons in need of supervision, ordered approved schools, employment of children and young persons (amended by *Children and Young Persons Act, 1969).*

Abortion Act, 1967. Made it legal for a registered medical practitioner to perform an abortion provided two registered practitioners are of the opinion termination is justifiable, either because continuance of the pregnancy would involve more risk to the life of the pregnant woman or injury to her physical or mental health or any existing children, than if the pregnancy were terminated, or because there would be a substantial risk that if the child were born it would be seriously physically or mentally handicapped.

Family Law Reform Act, 1969. This reduced the age of majority from 21 to 18. It also secured rights for illegitimate children.

Guardianship of Minors Act, 1971. Made some provision for equal rights for mothers and gave either spouse the right to appoint any person as guardian after his or her death.

Childrens Act, 1975. Gave new rights to children, foster-parents, local authorities and adoptive parents, and diminished rights of natural parents in care proceedings and adoption cases. Allowed adopted children over 18 access to information about their natural parents.

Legal Abortions, England and Wales (residents only)

	Married	Single	Other[a]	Total
1968[b]	10,090	10,302	1,840	22,332
1969	22,979	22,287	4,563	49,829
1970	34,314	34,492	7,156	75,962
1971	41,536	44,302	8,732	94,570
1972	46,894	51,115	10,556	108,565
1973	46,766	52,899	10,903	110,568
1974	45,167	53,331	10,934	109,432
1975	43,322	52,423	10,903	106,648
1976	39,868	50,481	10,934	101,003
1977	39,445	51,604	11,188	102,237
1978	42,200	56,600	13,300	112,100
1979	42,800	61,700	14,500	119,000
1980	44,300	68,800	15,900	128,900
1981	42,400	70,000	16,100	128,600
1982	40,500	71,800	16,200	128,600
1983	38,400	73,200	15,400	127,200

[a] Widowed, divorced, separated, or women whose marital status was unknown.
[b] The 1968 figures are from 27 Apr when the Act came into effect.

SOURCES.—Office of Population Censuses and Surveys. For 1978 *Population Trends*.

Children's Homes Act, 1982. Required children in the care of local authorities to be accommodated in registered and inspected homes.

Education

Education Act, 1902. This abolished school boards, gave powers to local authorities to provide secondary education, and made provisions for rate aid to voluntary schools (see Local Government section).

Education (Provision of Meals) Act, 1906. By this Act cheap school meals for children attending public elementary schools were given statutory recognition. Local authorities were to use voluntary organisations, contributing only to the cost of administration. In 1914 half the cost of the meals was provided by the Exchequer.

Education (Administrative Provisions) Act, 1907. This provided for medical inspection for elementary schools. In 1912 the Board of Education made grants to Local Education Authorities to make the treatment of children possible.

Education Act, 1918. Compulsory attendance was made universal until the age of 14. Day continuation (part-time compulsory) education was introduced for children between school-leaving age and 18. This almost disappeared under the economies proposed by Geddes but was revived in 1944.

Free milk was supplied to children in need in 1921. In 1934 it was subsidised by the Milk Marketing Board. From 1946 to 1971 it was free to all.

Education Act, 1936. Provision was made for the school-leaving age to be raised to 15 in Sep 1939 but this was not implemented. 1940-41, the school meal service was expanded and subsidised to meet war-time needs. These provisions were continued after the war, by the *Education Act, 1944*.

Education Act, 1944. This Act changed the title of the President of the Board of Education to the Minister of Education. Primary and secondary education was divided at '11-plus', and secondary education was generally provided under this Act in three types of schools, grammar, technical, and modern. Some local authorities preferred to use their powers to amalgamate these into comprehensive schools. Provision was made for compulsory part-time education between the school-leaving age and 18 in county colleges, but this has not been implemented. The minimum school-leaving age was raised to 15 (in 1947) and provision was made for raising it to 16. Powers were granted under this Act, which led to a great expansion of technical colleges. No fees were to be charged in schools which were publicly provided or aided by grants from the local authority.

School-leaving Age. It was announced in 1964 that the school-leaving age would be raised to 16 in the educational year 1970-71. In 1968 this date was put back for four years. The change was eventually made in 1973.

Comprehensive Schools. In 1965 the Department of Education asked all local authorities to submit plans for reorganising secondary education on comprehensive lines, with a view to ending selection at 11-plus and the tri-partite system. The policy of universal comprehensivisation was suspended in 1970 but revived in 1974 by Government Circular 4/74. In 1976 the Direct Grant system was phased out (119 of the 170 Direct Grant schools decided to become independent) and the *Education Act, 1976,* required Local Education Authorities to submit comprehensivisation proposals (7 had earlier refused. See the Tameside case, p. 285).

Nursery Schools. In 1972 the Department of Education (Cmnd 5174) accepted that within ten years it should provide nursery education for 90 per cent of 4-year-olds and 50 per cent of 3-year-olds.

Education Act, 1980. The Assisted Places Scheme was established to provide financial support for some students in independent education, and various other changes were made to increase parental choice and participation in the schooling of their children.

SOURCES.—*Education of the Adolescent* (Hadow) (1926); *The Primary School* (Hadow) (1931); *Secondary Education* (Spens) (1938); *The School Curriculum* (Norwood) (1943); *Education Reconstruction* (Cmd. 6458/1942-3); *Public Schools* (Fleming) (1944); *Education from 15 to 18* (Crowther) (1959); *Half Our Future* (Newsom) (1963); *Higher Education* (Robbins) (Cmnd. 2154/1963); *Primary Education* (Plowden) (1967). Since 1947 the Ministry of Education has published an *Annual Report* and *A Guide to the Educational Structure of England and Wales*. Among books on the educational system are the following: H. C. A. Barnard, *A Short History of English Education 1760-1944* (new ed. 1959); G. Baron, *A Bibliographical Guide to the English Educational System* 2nd rev. ed. 1960); H. C. Dent, *The Educational System of England and Wales* (1961); G. Kalton, *The Public Schools: a Factual Survey* (1966); J. S. McClure, *Educational Documents 1816-1963* (1965); L. Selby-Bigge, *The Board of Education* (1934); N.F.E.R., *Comprehensive Schools;* A. H. Halsey, *Educational Priority*, vol. 1, H.M.S.O. 1972; J. Vaizey and J. Sheehan, *Resources for Education* (1968). See also Annual Reports of University Grants Committee, and *Educational Statistics* published annually by the Department of Education.

Pupils in Schools

England and Wales ('000s)
(*age* 2-14)

	Public Elementary	Secondary Schools	Efficient Independent	Other Independent
1900	5,709	n.a.	n.a.	n.a.
1910	6,039	151	22	n.a.
1920	5,878	340	46	n.a.
1930	4,936	411	82	n.a.
	Primary & Secondary Maintained	Direct Grant		
1950	5,710	95	204	n.a.
1960	6,924	111	294	203
1970	7,960	143	304	110
1980	7,580	. .	500	. .

SOURCES.—G. Walford (ed.), *British Public Schools: Policy and Practice* (1984); *Annual Abstract of Statistics*; *Education Statistics*.

Percentage of Various Ages Receiving Full-time Education

Great Britain

	10-year olds	14 year olds	17-year olds	19-year olds
1870	40	2	1	1
1902	100	9	2	1
1938	100	38	4	2
1962	100	100	15	7
1970	100	100	26	13
1975	100	100	28	16
1982	100	100	30	13[a]

[a] This figure covers 19- and 20-year olds and is not therefore strictly compatible.

SOURCES.—*Report on Higher Education* (Robbins), Cmnd. 2154/1963; *Education Statistics for the U.K.* 1971-.

Students in Full-time Higher Education

Great Britain

	University	Teacher Training	Further Education[a]
1900/1	20,000	5,000	—
1924/5	42,000	16,000	3,000
1938/9	50,000	13,000	6,000
1954/5	82,000	28,000	12,000
1962/3	118,000	55,000	43,000
1970/1[b]	235,000	124,000	98,000
1976/7[b]	279,000	246,000	
1981/2	308,000	247,000	

[a] Advanced Courses only. [b] Includes N. Ireland.

SOURCES.—*Report on Higher Education* (Robbins), Cmnd. 2154/1963. Department of Education and Science and Scottish Education Department.

Expenditure on Education (U.K.)

(current prices)

	Net public current expenditure on education (£m)	(as % of National Income)	Private expenditure on education (£m)	Current expenditure of universities (£m)	% of university expenditure from parliamentary grants
1919/20	65·1	(1·2)	8·4	4·4	22
1929/30	92·8	(2·3)	8·3	6·6	29
1939/40	107·5	(2·0)	10·0	8·2	30
1949/50	272·0	(2·7)	27·8	23·0	56
1954/5	410·6	(2·8)	30·9	33·9	65
1964/5	1,114·9	(4·1)	60·0	123·9	72
1975/6	5,348·3	n.a.	n.a.	713·9[a]	78
1980/1	10,479.3	n.a.	n.a.	1381.4[a]	63[b]

[a] Excluding Oxford and Cambridge college accounts.

[b] The fall is due to changes in the payment of tuition fees from Parliament to local authorities.

SOURCES.—1919-1965 J. Vaizey and J. Sheehan, *Resources for Education* (1968); 1975-6 *Annual Abstract of Statistics* and *Education Statistics for the U.K.*

Public Library Service

	Books in stock ('000s)	No. of book issues ('000s)	Total expenditure (£'000)
1906	4,450	26,255	286
1911	10,874	54,256	805
1924	14,784	85,668	1,398
1939	32,549	247,335	3,178
1953	56,056	359,700	11,183
1962	77,200	460,504	24,431
1971-2	114,472	628,000[a]	73,436
1975-6	123,356	589,000	161,417
1982-3	133,185	632,440	375,262

[a] 1970-1.

SOURCE.—A. H. Halsey (ed.), *Trends in British Society* (1972). See also The Library Association, *A Century of Public Libraries 1850-1950* (1950), and the annual CIPFA reports. *Public Library Statistics.*

Pressure Groups

There are a large number of groups in the social field representing causes or offering voluntary services. These may seek to influence public policy by direct contact with Parliament and Government Departments or indirectly through the publication of information and research or appeals to public opinion. Some notable examples of pressure groups are listed below. They include some registered charities which have also sought to direct public funds and attention to the causes they represent (e.g. the National Council for One-Parent families); some which were founded to bring about a change in the law (e.g. Committee for Homosexual Law Reform)[1]; some which were formed to safeguard and promote the interests of a minority racial group

[1] *Sexual Offences Act, 1967*, amended the law in England and Wales relating to homosexual acts and permitted homosexual acts in private by consenting adults.

(e.g. the Indian Workers' Association) or of a profession or trade (e.g. the Road Haulage Association); and some whose main target has been industry rather than government (e.g. the Campaign for Real Ale). Most are financed by voluntary contributions but some receive grants from central or local government and may, indeed, be directly involved in the implementation of public policy.

Abortion

Abortion Law Reform Association, 1967-
Society for the Protection of Unborn Children, 1967-70. Changed name to Life, 1970-

Animal Welfare

Society for the Prevention of Cruelty to Animals, 1824. Changed name to Royal Society for the Prevention of Cruelty to Animals, 1840-
League Against Cruel Sports, 1924-
National Anti-vivisection Society, 1975-

Birth Control

Workers' Birth Control Group, 1924. Together with four other bodies became National Birth Control Council, 1930. Changed name to National Birth Control Association in 1931. Changed name to Family Planning Association, 1939-

Children

National Society for the Prevention of Cruelty to Children, 1884-
National Association of Parents of Backward Children, 1946. Changed name to The National Society for Mentally Handicapped Children, 1955-
Child Poverty Action Group, 1965-

Civil Liberties

National Council for Civil Liberties, 1934-

Consumers

Consumers Association, 1946-
Campaign for Real Ale, 1971-
National Consumer Council, 1975-

Education

Advisory Centre for Education, 1960-Confederation for the Advancement of State Education, 1961-

The Elderly

National Old People's Welfare Council, 1940. Changed name to Age

Concern, 1971-Help the Aged, 1961-British Pensions and Trade Union Action Committee, 1972-

Environment

National Trust, 1895
Council for the Protection of Rural England, 1926-
Civic Trust, 1957-
Council for Environmental Conservation (COENCO), 1969-
Friends of the Earth, 1970-
Greenpeace, 1971-
Campaign for Lead-Free Air (CLEAR), 1982-

Family Welfare

National Council for the Unmarried Mother and her Child, 1918. Changed name to National Council for One Parent Families, 1973-
National Marriage Guidance Council, 1937-
Gingerbread, 1970-

Health

British and Foreign Society for Improving the Embossed Literature for the Blind, 1868. Changed name to British and Foreign Blind Association, 1870. Changed name to National Institute for the Blind, 1914. Changed name to Royal National Institute for the Blind, 1953-
National Bureau for Promoting the General Welfare of the Deaf, 1911. Changed name to the National Institute for the Deaf, 1924. Changed name to the Royal National Institute for the Deaf, 1961-
The Voluntary Euthanasia Society, 1935-79, 1982- (Exit, 1979-82)
National Association for Mental Health, 1946. Changed name to Mind, 1973-
Samaritans, 1953-
Patient's Association, 1961-
Disablement Income Group, 1966-
Action on Smoking and Health (ASH), 1971-

Homosexuals

Committee for Homosexual Law Reform, 1967. Changed name to Campaign for Homosexual Equality, 1970-

Housing

Shelter, 1966-
Campaign for the Homeless and Rootless (CHAR), 1972-

Legal System

Howard League for Penal Reform, 1886-
Central Discharged Prisoners' Aid Society, 1924. Changed name to

National Association of Aid to Discharged Prisoners' Societies, 1960. Changed name to National Association for the Care and Resettlement of Offenders, 1966-

National Association for the Care and Rehabilitation of Offenders (NACRO), 1966-

Freedom Association, 1975-

National Campaign for the Abolition of Capital Punishment, 1955-69

National Council for Civil Liberties, 1934-

National Association of Victim Support Schemes, 1979-

Morality

Lord's Day of Observance Society, 1831-

The National Viewers' and Listeners' Council (Mary Whitehouse), 1964-

British Humanist Association, 1928- (formerly Ethical Association)

Race

Indian Workers' Association, 1956-

West Indian Standing Conference, 1958-

Runnymede Trust, 1968-

Standing Conference of Pakistani Organisations, 1975-

Social Services

Low Pay Unit, 1974-

Temperance

United Kingdom Alliance, 1853-

Transport

Royal Automobile Club, 1897-

The Automobile Association, 1905-

National Association of Railway Users, 1971-

Women's Rights

London Society for Women's Suffrage, 1866-1918 (now Fawcett Society)

Women's Freedom League, 1908-1961

National Federation of Women's Institutes, 1917-

Women's Social and Political Union, 1903-1918

Women's Liberation Workshop, 1969-

National Women's Aid Federation, 1975-

Women in Media, 1971-

SOURCES.—See P. Shipley, *Directory of Pressure Groups* (2nd ed., 1979); *Directory of British Associations* (7th ed., C.B.D., 1982).

Transport and Communications

CURRENT VEHICLE LICENCES IN GREAT BRITAIN[a]

	Cars[b]	Public Transport[c]	Goods Vehicles[d]	Total
1905	15,895	7,491[e]	9,000	32,386
1910	89,411	24,466[e]	30,000	143,877[e]
1915	277,741	44,480[e]	84,600	406,821[e]
1920	474,540	74,608[e]	101,000	650,148[e]
1925	1,151,453	113,267	259,341	1,524,061
1930	1,760,533	114,796	391,997	2,287,326
1935	1,973,945	96,419	490,663	2,581,027
1938	2,406,769	96,718	590,397	3,093,884
1940	1,701,500	88,200	542,200	2,331,900
1945	1,795,700	110,800	740,500	2,647,000
1946	2,232,279	110,704	769,747	3,112,930
1950	3,009,611	141,091	1,263,131	4,413,833
1955	4,781,741	104,664	1,581,814	6,468,219
1960	7,387,075	93,942	1,958,856	9,439,873
1965	10,623,900	96,500	2,219,500	12,939,900
1970	12,687,000	103,000	2,161,000	14,950,000
1975	15,051,000	112,000	2,337,000	17,500,000
1980	16,545,000	110,000	2,555,000	19,210,000
1983	18,448,000	113,000	1,655,000	20,216,000

a 1905-1920—Figures at 31 Mar 1925; and 1945 at 31 Aug; 1930-38 and from 1946 during quarter ending 30 Sep.
b Cars, motor-cycles, tricycles and pedestrian controlled vehicles.
c Buses, coaches, trams, and taxis.
d Goods vehicles, haulage including agricultural vehicles, exempt including Government vehicles.
e These figures do not include trams. In 1920 there were 14,000 trams.
f Figures before 1921 are estimates only, from *The Motor Industry of Great Britain, 1935*. They may be exaggerated.

SOURCES.—*Census of Mechanically Propelled Vehicles* (Ministry of Transport), 1926-62 *Highway Statistics* (Ministry of Transport), 1963 onwards, *The Motor Industry of Great Britain* (Soc. of Motor Manufacturers and Traders). Reports of the Steering Group appointed by the Ministry of Transport, *Traffic in Towns* (Buchanan Report, H.M.S.O.); D. L. Munby and A. A. Watson, *Inland Transport Statistics, Great Britain 1900-1970*, vol. II.

DRIVING LICENCES, ROAD DEATHS, AND TRAFFIC OFFENCES

	Driving licences	Road deaths involving motor vehicles or bicycles	Persons found guilty of traffic offences
1900	92,168[a]	n.a.	2,548
1910	. .	1,277	55,633
1920	. .	2,937	157,875
1930	. .	7,305	267,616
1938	(4,500,000)	6,648	475,124
1950	5,793,000	5,012	357,932
1960	11,700,000	6,970	622,551
1970	17,620,000	7,499	1,014,793
1980	24,903,000	6,010	1,319,800

a The only pre-war figures available are for 1905 in the Report of the Royal Commission on Motor Cars (Cd. 3080-1/1906).

SOURCES.—*Annual Abstract of Statistics, Transport Statistics; Offences relating to Motor Vehicles.*

RAILWAYS

Great Britain

	Standard Gauge Route Miles	Train Miles (million miles)	Passengers Carried (millions)	Freight[a] Tons (millions)	Freight[a] Ton Miles (millions)
1900	18,680	379·3	962·3	461·1	n.a.
1910	19,986	386·7	936·0	504·7	n.a.
1920	20,147	355·7	1,243·2	332·2	19·2
1930	20,243	397·5	1,238·5	304·3	17·8
1938	19,934	420·9	1,237·2	265·7	16·7
1950	19,471	384·1	981·7	281·3	22·1
1960	18,369	375·4	1,036·7	248·5	18·6
1970	11,799	195·9	823·9	199·0	15·0
1980	10,964	246.4	760.2	152.2	10.8

Excluding operations of London Electric Railway, London Passenger Transport Board, and London Transport throughout. Standard-gauge Railways only (except 1900 and 1910).

[a] Excluding free-hauled traffic.

SOURCES.—1930-38 *Railway Returns*; 1950- British Railways, *Annual Reports*.

SHIPPING

Tonnage registered
(United Kingdom)

	'000 gross tons	% of World tonnage
1900	11,514	51·5
1910	16,768	45·0
1920	18,111	33·6
1930	20,322	29·9
1939	17,891	26·1
1950	18,219	21·5
1960	21,131	16·3
1970	25,825	11·0
1980	27,135	6.4
1983	19,121	4.5

Steam and motor ships of 100 gross tons and over.

SOURCE.—*Lloyd's Register of Shipping* (Statistical Tables), published annually.

VOLUME OF POSTAL TRAFFIC

Letters, postcards, parcels, registered letters (excluding football pools). Number of inland deliveries.

millions

1903-04	4,300	1951-52	7,964
1911-12	5,508	1956-57	8,753
1922-23	5,638	1959-60	9,244
1929-30	6,622	1965-66	10,461
1935-36	7,569	1975-76	8,890
1939-40	7,624	1983-84	10,793
1946-47	6,601		

COST OF LETTER MAIL
(inland)

		First class	Second class
May	1840	1*d.*	—
Jun	1918	1½*d.*	—
Jun	1920	2*d.*	—
May	1922	1½*d.*	—
May	1940	2½*d.*	—
Oct	1957	3*d.*	—
May	1965	4*d.*	—
Sep	1968	5*d.*[a]	4*d.*
Feb	1971	3*p.*	2½*p.*
Sep	1973	3½*p.*	3*p.*
Jun	1974	4½*p.*	3½*p.*
Mar	1975	7*p.*	5½*p.*
Sep	1975	8½*p.*	6½*p.*
Jun	1977	9*p.*	7*p.*
Aug	1979	10*p.*	8*p.*
Feb	1980	12*p.*	10*p.*
Jan	1981	14*p.*	11½*p.*
Feb	1982	15½*p.*	12½*p.*
Apr	1983	16*p.*	12½*p.*
Sep	1984	17*p.*	13*p.*

[a] Two-tier postal pricing introduced.

TELEPHONES

	United Kingdom[a]
	('000s)
1900	3
1910	122
1920	980
1930	1,996
1940	3,339
1950	5,171
1960	7,864
1970	13,844
1980	27,870

[a] Including Southern Ireland, 1900-20.

SOURCES.—General Post Office, *Post Office Commercial Accounts*, published annually, and *Annual Abstracts of Statistics*. Since 1969 *Annual Reports* of the Post Office Corporation.

X

EMPLOYMENT AND TRADE UNIONS

Major Employment and Trade Union Legislation[1]

Factory and Workshop Act, 1901. This consolidated, with amendments, all previous Factory and Workshop Acts.

Unemployed Workmen Act, 1905. This established 'Distress Committees' to investigate needs and to provide employment or assistance. Funds were to be partly voluntary, and partly from the local rates.

The Trade Disputes Act, 1906, reversed the Taff Vale decision and freed trade unions from liability caused by the calling of a strike.

Labour Exchanges Act, 1909. These were established in 1909 and renamed Employment Exchanges in 1919.

National Insurance Act, 1911. This Act covered all those between the ages of 16 and 70 years, but was limited to manual workers in industries known to be subject to severe and recurrent unemployment. (The Act covered about 2¼ million people.) Within these limits it was compulsory, and financed by a triple weekly levy, from the worker, the employer, and the government. Payment of benefit continued only for a limited period, after which responsibility for the unemployed person lapsed to the poor law. In 1916 the Act was extended to include munitions workers.

The Trade Union Act, 1913, reversed the Osborne judgment and laid down the conditions under which political objects could be included in the rules of a Union by its members' consent.

Industrial Courts Act, 1919. This provided for the establishment of an Industrial Court and Courts of Inquiry in connection with Trade disputes, and made other provisions for the settlement of such disputes.

Unemployment Insurance Act, 1920. The scheme was extended to cover the same field as the National Health Insurance scheme, and included non-manual workers with an income of under £250 p.a. Workers in agriculture or domestic service were excluded from the insurance scheme until 1936-37. It was administered through the local employment exchanges of the Ministry of Labour. The basic unemployment benefit was 7*s*. in 1911, increased to 15*s*. in 1920. It was increased in 1921, and in 1924 was 18*s*. It was reduced in 1928 and 1931. Additional allowances for dependants were introduced in 1921.

[1] This list of major legislation since 1900 excludes temporary wartime measures. The most important example was the Conditions of Employment and National Arbitration Order, 1940, commonly known as Order 1305; this imposed legal restrictions upon strikes and lockouts and imposed a system of compulsory arbitration; in 1951 it was replaced by Order 1376 which retained only the compulsory arbitration system; Order 1376 was revoked in 1958.

Unemployment Insurance Act, 1927. By this Act the original scheme was completely revised in accordance with the recommendations of the Blanesburgh Committee Report. The new scheme was to provide unlimited benefits after the insured person had satisfied certain qualifying contribution conditions.

The Trades Disputes and Trade Unions Act, 1927, made a sympathetic strike or a lockout designed to coerce the government illegal; it also severed the connection between civil service organisations and other unions; and it imposed new restrictions on the unions' political activities and their conduct of trade disputes. The political levy could only be raised from workers who 'contracted in'.

Local Government Act, 1929. This Act abolished the Poor Law Guardians, and their responsibilities passed to county councils and county borough councils, who were so far as possible to administer the specialised branches through separate committees.

Poor Law Act, 1930. By this Act poor law was renamed Public Assistance. The existing law was consolidated.

Unemployment Insurance Act, 1930. This made qualification easier for transitional benefit, and abolished the requirement that the unemployed receiving benefits should be 'genuinely seeking work'. Transitional benefits were made to claimants in need of assistance, but unable to fulfil the usual qualifying conditions. Responsibility for the long-term unemployed was placed directly on the Exchequer in 1931, though receipt of benefit was made subject to a 'means test'. Dependants' benefits were increased.

Unemployment Act, 1934. An amended scheme was introduced distinguishing between 'unemployed benefit' paid from the Fund (at the basic rate of 17*s*. a week) for a limited period to those satisfying contribution conditions, and 'unemployment assistance' which was paid, subject to a 'means test', to those still needing assistance after exhausting their title to benefit, or those who were not entitled. These long-term unemployed were paid directly by the Exchequer through the newly created *Unemployment Assistance Board* (known as Assistance Board from 1940 and from 1948 until 1966 as National Assistance Board). In 1937 juveniles between the ages of 14 and 16 were brought into the scheme for medical benefits only.

Unemployment Insurance (Agriculture) Act, 1936. A separate insurance scheme was set up for agricultural workers granting lower rates of benefit than the general scheme. In 1937, the benefits of voluntary insurance for widows, orphans, etc. (see *Contributory Pensions Act, 1925)*, were extended to those with small incomes, without the qualifications of insurable employment essential to insurance under the main scheme. For the first time married women could become voluntary contributors for pensions.

Control of Employment Act, 1939. This gave the government wide powers for the organisation of labour in war-time. Its aim was to make the best use of labour and to direct it to the most vital work.

Determination of Needs Act, 1941. This abolished the household 'means test'.

National Insurance (Industrial Injuries) Act, 1946. This covered all those in insurable employment against injuries and industrial diseases arising from their employment. It was financed by contributions from the insured person, his employer, and the government.

National Insurance Act, 1946. This Act covered all contributors between school-leaving age and pensionable age, for benefits for unemployment, sickness, maternity, retirement, widows' pensions, guardians' allowances, and death grants. The self-employed and non-employed were entitled to fewer benefits. The basic weekly rate for unemployment benefit was raised to 26*s*.

The national insurance scheme was amended by Acts in 1949, 1951, 1953, 1954, 1955, 1956, 1957, 1959, 1960, 1961, 1964, 1965, 1967, 1969, 1971, and 1973 (for rates, see p. 359).

The Trade Unions Act, 1946. This repealed *The Trades Disputes and Trade Unions Act, 1927.*

National Assistance Act, 1948. This Act repealed all the poor law still in existence and it established a comprehensive scheme to be financed from government funds, to cover all the arrangements for assistance then in force. Provision was also made for those not qualified for benefits under national insurance schemes, or where the benefits were insufficient.

Local Employment Act, 1960, made provision for promoting employment in areas of persistent or threatened unemployment.

Payment of Wages Act, 1960, removed certain restrictions on methods of payment of wages and permits them to be paid otherwise than in cash by payment into a banking account in the name of the employee, by Postal Order, by Money Order or by Cheque.

The Contracts of Employment Act, 1963, laid down the notice required to be given by an employer to terminate the contract of a person who had been continuously employed for 26 weeks or more (reduced to 13 weeks in 1974), the length of notice to be given varying according to the length of continuous employment.

Offices, Shops and Railway Premises Act, 1963, contained sweeping provisions relating to the health, safety, and welfare of employees, fire precautions, accidents and other matters in connection with office, shop and railway premises.

The Industrial Training Act, 1964, gave power to establish an industrial training board for the training of persons over compulsory school age for employment in any activities of industry or commerce.

Trade Disputes Act, 1965, reversed the Rookes v. Barnard case and disallowed actions for tort or reparation being brought in respect of some kinds of activities in the conduct of industrial disputes.

Redundancy Payments Act, 1965, obliged employers in certain industries to make payment to redundant workers and set up a Redundancy fund to which employers had to contribute.

Equal Pay Act, 1970, made provision for the application to all workers of the principle of equal remuneration for men and women for work of equal value and required that terms and conditions of employment applicable to one sex should not be in any respect less favourable than those applicable to the other.

Industrial Relations Act, 1971, established new legal rights for the individual worker, mainly in relation to trade union activity but also in protection from unfair dismissal, information about the terms of employment, and long duration of notice. Most of these rights were preserved and expanded in the *Trade Unions and Labour Relations Acts* of 1974 and 1975. It also introduced fundamental and wide ranging changes in the legal framework of industrial relations. It repealed the *Trade Union Acts, 1871 and 1876*, and the *Trade Disputes Acts, 1906 and 1965*. Its provisions established new legal rights for the individual mainly in relation to trade union membership and activity, protection from unfair dismissal, information about his employment, and improved terms of notice. The Act introduced a new concept of 'unfair industrial practice'. It established a National Industrial Relations Court which, together with the industrial tribunals, was required to maintain these standards and rights by hearing complaints of unfair industrial practice and determining rights and liabilities. The Act also provided for a new system of registration and restricted legal immunities to registered trade unions; new methods of settling disputes over trade union recognition to be administered by a Commission on Industrial Relations; and new powers to be exercised by the Secretary of State for Employment to deal with emergency situations (i.e. the 'cooling off period' and ballots of membership).

Employment and Training Act, 1973, extended provisions for public authorities to provide work or training for unemployed persons.

Health and Safety at Work Act, 1974, provided a comprehensive system of law to deal with health and safety at work and established a Health and Safety Commission and Executive.

Trade Unions and Labour Relations Act, 1974, repealed the *Industrial Relations Act, 1971*, except for the provisions on unfair dismissal. The Act abolished the National Industrial Relations Court and the Commission on Industrial Relations.

Employment Protection Act, 1975, amended the law relating to workers and employers and provided redress against arbitrary dismissal. It extended the scope of redundancy payments and guaranteed suspension pay to those whose work was interrupted for external causes. It also provided for the establishment of the Advisory Conciliation and Arbitration Service as an independent statutory body and of a Central Arbitration Commission, together with a Certification Officer to take over the functions previously exercised by the Registrar of Friendly Society in monitoring Trade Unions.

Trade Union and Labour Relations (*Amendment*) *Act, 1975*, amended the 1974 Act and provided for a charter on Freedom of the Press.

Sex Discrimination Act, 1975 (see p. 338).

Race Relations Act, 1976 (see p. 329).

Employment Act, 1980, provided for payment of public funds towards the costs of ballots among Trade Union members over strike action.

Employment Act, 1982, provided for compensation from public funds for employees dismissed as a result of closed shop agreements.

Trade Union Act, 1984, made legal immunity conditional on the conduct of strike ballots and made the continued existence of political funds dependent on ten-yearly votes by the membership.

Major Trade Union Litigation

Taff Vale Railway Co. v. *Amalgamated Society of Railway Servants*, [1901] A.C. 426 (H.L.)

A trade union, registered under the *Trade Union Acts, 1871* and *1876*, may be sued in its registered name. Lord Halsbury said, 'If the legislature has created a thing which can own property, which can employ servants, or which can inflict injury, it must be taken, I think, to have impliedly given the power to make it suable in a court of law, for injuries purposely done by its authority and procurement.'

Amalgamated Society of Railway Servants v. *Osborne*, [1910] A.C. 87 (H.L.)

There is nothing in the Trade Union Acts from which it can reasonably be inferred that trade unions as defined by Parliament were meant to have the power of collecting and administering funds for political purposes. Exercise of such powers is *ultra vires* and illegal.

Bonsor v. *Musicians' Union*, [1956] A.C. 104 (H.L.)

A member of a registered trade union wrongfully expelled from it was entitled to maintain an action for damages for breach of contract against the union in its registered name.

Rookes v. *Barnard*, [1964] A.C. 1129

Threats to strike in breach of a contractual agreement for the purpose of injuring a third party were unlawful and were, even if done in furtherance of a trade dispute, not protected by the Trade Disputes Act, 1906.

Stratford v. *Lindley*, [1964] 3 All E.R. 102

Strike Action not taken in pursuance of a trade dispute about terms of employment with the plaintiff's firm was not prima facie protected by the 1906 Trade Disputes Act.

1971-4

Between 1971 and 1974 there were a series of confrontations under the terms of the Industrial Relations Act. The T.U.C. in Sep 1971 instructed all unions not to register under the Act and in Sep 1972 the 32 which had registered were suspended and 20 of them were expelled in Sep 1973.

In Apr 1972 the T.G.W.U. was fined £55,000 for contempt of the N.I.R.C. (though the fine was quashed by the Court of Appeal in Jun 1972). In Dec 1972 the A.U.E.W. refused to pay £50,000 in the Goad case (over the individual rights of a union member). In Oct 1973 £75,000 of seized A.U.E.W. assets were used to pay a further £47,000 N.I.R.C. contempt fine in the Con-Mech case. In May 1974 a further seizure of A.U.E.W. assets was ordered to pay £47,000 compensation to Con-Mech (the money was then paid by an anonymous donor).

On 17 Apr 1972 the N.I.R.C. ordered a 14-day cooling off period in a national railway dispute and on 13 May 1972 ordered a ballot which produced an 85% vote in favour of a railway strike.

On 21 Jul 1972 the N.I.R.C. committed five docker shop stewards to prison over the blacking of London container depots. They were released on 26 Jul. On 6 Aug 1974 the Industrial Relations Act was repealed.

Gouriet v. *Post Office Union*, [1977] 3 All E.R. (H.L.)

An attempt to enjoin the Post Office Union from blacking mail to South Africa was frustrated because the Attorney-General refused his *fiat* to bring the case on the ground that the plaintiff was not directly involved (see p. 313).

Grunwick Processing Laboratories Ltd. v. *Advisory Conciliation and Arbitration Service*, [1977] T.L.R. 14 Dec 77

The House of Lords ruled that an A.C.A.S. recommendation on union recognition was void because A.C.A.S. had not ascertained the opinions of two-thirds of the work-force involved (this was due to the non-cooperation of the firm's management).

B.B.C. v. *Hearn,* [1977] I.R.L.R. 273; *Beaverbrook Newspapers* v. *Keys,* [1978], I.R.L.R. 34; *Star Sea Transport* v. *Slater,* [1978] I.R.L.R. 507; *McShane* v. *Express Newspapers,* [1979] I.R.L.R. 79; *United Biscuits* v. *Fall* [1979] I.R.L.R. 110; *Associated Newspaper Group* v. *Wade* [1979] I.R.L.R. 201.

The decisions in each of these cases reduced the area of legal immunity for actions taken in furtherance of an industrial dispute.

Thomas et al. v. *Haringey* [1979]

The Court of Appeal held that it was arguable that a local authority might be in breach of its duty to provide education when it failed to do so by reason of industrial action by school caretakers.

Messenger Newspaper Group Ltd v. *NGA* [1982] (Industrial Relations Law Reports 1984, 397)

The Court of Appeal endorsed the powers of sequestrators seeking to secure control of union funds when the union had been fined for contempt for its actions in seeking to enforce a closed shop.

Mercury Communications Ltd v. *Scott Garer* (Industrial Cases Reports) 1984, 74)

The Court of Appeal ruled that it was possible under the Employment Act 1982 to secure an interlocutory injunction against union actions that were not 'wholly or mainly' related to an industrial dispute.

Dimbleby & Sons Ltd. v. *National Union of Journalists* (Industrial Cases Reports 1984, 386)

The House of Lords endorsed the granting of an interlocutory injunction against preventing a union from instructing its members to break contracts of employment in pursuits of a trade dispute that, under the Employment Act 1980, was excluded from protection.

(*See also* pp. 315 *and* 467)

National Industrial Relations Court 1971-4

President
1971 Sir J. Donaldson

Commission on Industrial Relations 1971-4

Chairman
1969 G. Woodcock
(*Made a Statutory Body, 1 Nov 71*)
1971 (Sir) L. Neal

(Advisory) Conciliation and Arbitration Service (A.C.A.S.)[1] 1974-

Chairman
1974 J. Mortimer
1981 (Sir) P. Lowry

Earnings and Hours Worked

United Kingdom

Year	Average Weekly Earnings (£)				Average Weekly Hours			
	Manual workers		Non-manual workers		Manual workers		Non-manual workers	
	Men aged 21 and over	Women aged 18 and over	Males	Females	Men aged 21 and over	Women aged 18 and over	Males	Females
1924	2·8	1·4			n.a.	n.a.		
1935	3·2	1·6			n.a.	n.a.		
1938	3·5	1·6			47·7	43·5		
1940	4·5	1·9			n.a.	n.a.		
1941	5·0	2·2			n.a.	n.a.		
1942	5·6	2·7			n.a.	n.a.		
1943	6·1	3·1			52·9	45·9		
1944	6·2	3·2			51·2	44·6		
1945	6·1	3·2			49·7	43·3		
1946	6·0	3·3			47·6	42·5		
1947	6·4	3·5			46·6	41·4		
1948	6·9	3·7			46·7	41·4		
1949	7·1	3·9			46·8	41·5		
1950	7·5	4·1			47·6	41·8		
1951	8·3	4·5			47·8	41·3		
1952	8·9	4·8			47·7	41·7		
1953	9·5	5·1			47·9	41·8		
1954	10·2	5·4			48·5	41·8		
1955	11·1	5·8			48·9	41·6		
1956	11·9	6·2			48·5	41·3		
1957	12·6	6·5			48·2	41·0		
1958	12·8	6·7			47·7	41·0		
1959	13·6	7·0	18·0	9·7	48·5	41·4		
1960	14·5	7·4	19·1	10·2	48·0	40·5		

[1] The Conciliation and Arbitration Service was established within the Department of Employment in 1974. It was made an independent statutory body by the *Employment Protection Act, 1975*.

Year	Average Weekly Earnings (£)				Average Weekly Hours			
	Manual workers		Non-manual workers		Manual workers		Non-manual workers	
	Men aged 21 and over	Women aged 18 and over	Males	Females	Men aged 21 and over	Women aged 18 and over	Males	Females
1961	15·3	7·7	20·0	10·7	47·4	39·7		
1962	15·9	8·0	21·1	11·3	47·0	39·4		
1963	16·7	8·4	22·3	12·0	47·6	39·7		
1964	18·1	9·0	23·5	12·6	47·7	39·4		
1965	19·6	9·6	25·5	13·7	47·0	38·7		
1966	20·3	10·1	26·7	14·2	46·0	38·1		
1967	21·4	10·6	27·9	14·9	46·2	38·2		
1968	23·0	11·3	29·8	15·8	46·4	38·3		
1969	24·8	12·1	32·1	17·0	46·5	38·1		
1970	26·7	13·3	35·1	17·7	45·9	38·6	39·0	36·9
1971	29·4	15·3	39·1	19·8	45·0	38·4	38·7	36·9
1972	32·8	17·1	43·5	22·2	46·0	39·9	38·7	36·8
1973	38·1	19·7	48·1	24·7	46·7	39·9	38·8	36·8
1974	43·6	23·6	54·4	28·6	46·5	39·8	38·8	36·8
1975	55·7	32·1	68·4	39·6	45·5	39·4	38·7	36·6
1976	65·1	39·4	81·6	48·8	45·3	39·3	38·5	36·5
1977	71·5	43·7	88·9	53·8	45·7	39·4	38·7	36·7
1978	80·7	49·4	100·7	59·1	46·0	39·6	38·7	36·7
1979	93.0	55·2	113·0	66·0	46·2	39·6	38·8	36·7
1980	111·7	68·0	141·3	82·7	45.4	39·6	38·7	36·7
1981	121·9	74·5	163·1	96·7	44·2	39.4	38·4	36·5
1982	133·8	80·1	178·9	104·9	44·3	39·3	38·2	36·5
1983	143·6	87·9	194·9	115·1	43·9	39·3	38·4	36·5

The figures to 1969 cover manufacturing industry and some non-manufacturing industries and services, but exclude coal mining, dock labour, railways, agriculture, shipping, distributive trades, catering, entertainments and domestic service. In 1940-5, the figures are for July but otherwise up to 1969 they are for October. The figures to 1969 come from the *Ministry of Labour Gazette British Labour Statistics: Historical Abstract 1886-1968*. From 1970 the figures come from the New Earnings Survey of a sample of all employees in *Great Britain* and are not therefore strictly comparable with those for pre-1970. They relate to April in each year.

SOURCES.—*British Labour Statistics: Historical Abstract 1886-1968; Department of Employment Gazette: New Earnings Survey.*

Size of Labour Force

Great Britain

(to nearest '000)

Year	Total	Male	Female
1901	16,312	11,548	4,763
1911	18,354	12,930	5,424
1921	19,357	13,656	5,701
1931	21,055	14,790	6,265
1939	19,750	14,656	5,094
1951	24,600	15,649	9,661
1960	24,436	16,239	8,197
1970	24,721	15,977	8,743
1980	26,176	16,595	9,581
1984	26,350	15,882	10,468

1901, 1911, and 1921 figures cover persons aged 10 years and over.

1931 and 1939 figures cover persons aged 14 years and over.

1951, 1960 and 1970 figures cover persons aged 15 years and over.

1980 and 1984 figures cover persons 16 and over.

SOURCES.—*Censuses of Population*, except 1939, 1960 and 1984; *Ministry of Labour Gazette* (-1968); *Employment (and Productivity 68-70) Gazette* (1968-).

Rates of Unemployment Benefit

(other than agricultural)

		Men over 18	Women over 18
15 Jan	13	7/-	Nil
25 Dec	19	11/-	Nil
8Nov	20	15/-	12/-
3 Mar	21	20/-	16/-
30 Jun	21	15/-	12/-
14 Aug	24	18/-	15/-
19 Apr	28	17/-	15/-
8 Oct	31	15/3	13/6
26 Jul	34	17/-	15/-
1 Aug	40	20/-	18/-
2 Nov	44	24/-	22/-
3 Jun	48	26/-	26/-
24 Jul	52	32/6	26/-
19 May	55	40/-	26/-
6 Feb	58	50/-	
6 Apr	61	57/6	
7 Mar	63	67/6	
28 Jan	65	80/-	
30 Oct	67	90/-	
6 Nov	69	100/-	
23 Sep	71	£6·00	
20 Oct	72	£6·75	
4 Oct	73	£7·35	
22 Jul	74	£8·60	
7 Apr	75	£9·80	
20 Nov	75	£11·10	
15 Nov	76	£12·90	
14 Nov	77	£14·70	
13 Nov	78	£15·75	
12 Nov	79	£18·50	
16 Nov	80	£20·65	
2 Dec	81	£22·50	
8 Nov	82	£25·00	
17 Nov	83	£27·05	
11 Nov	84	£28·45	

After 6 Oct 66 flat rate unemployment benefit was supplemented by earnings related benefit.

SOURCE.—Dept. of Health and Social Security.

Industrial Analysis of the Occupied Population

Great Britain

('000s)

	1911	1921	1931	1951	1961	1971	1981
Total Working Population[a]	18,351	19,369	21,074	22,610	24,014	25,021	26,548
Total Out of Employment	n.a.	n.a.	2,524	476	676	1,289	2,395
Total in Employment	n.a.	n.a.	18,550	22,013	23,501	24,615	24,153
Agriculture & Fishing	1,493	1,373	1,180	1,126	855	635	n.a.
Mining & Quarrying	1,308	1,469	1,040	841	722	391	336
Manufacturing Industries	6,147	6,723	5,981	7,902	8,383	8,136	5,974
Building & Contracting	950	826	970	1,404	1,600	1,669	1,117
Gas, Electricity & Water	117	180	224	358	377	362	338
Transport & Communications	1,260	1,359	1,430	1,705	1,673	1,564	1,422
Distributive Trades	n.a.	n.a.	2,697	2,742	3,189	3,016	2,715
Insurance, Banking & Finance[b]	n.a.	328	388	489	722	952	1,295
Public Administration:							
National (inc. Defence)	452	480	368	1,036	798	812	589
Local	555	457	541	602	629	760	931
Professional and Scientific Services	n.a.	868	1,018	1,536	2,120	2,901	3,649
Miscellaneous Services	n.a.	n.a.	2,713	2,393	2,270	2,534	2,522[c]
(of which private domestic service)	n.a.	(1,390)	(1,509)	(499)	(362)	(239)	(n.a.)

The Table shows only the changes in the general pattern of industry over the period. The figures are based on the Census of Population figures published by the Registrar-General. The figures for 1911 and 1921 are not completely comparable with those for the later years due to changes in classification and the inclusion of the unemployed who are excluded in the analysis from 1931 onwards.

[a] 1911, 12 and over; 1921, 1931, 14 and over; 1951, 15 and over.
[b] Including Business Services.
[c] Not including private domestic service.

SOURCES.—*Annual Abstract of Statistics.*

Trades Union Congresses 1900-

Date	Place	President	General Secretary	No. of Delegates	Members represented ('000s)
3-8 Sep 00	Huddersfield	W. Pickles	S. Woods	386	1,250
2-7 Sep 01	Swansea	C. Bowerman	,,	407	1,200
1-6 Sep 02	London	W. Steadman	,,	485	1,400
6-11 Sep 03	Leicester	W. Hornidge	,,	460	1,500
5-10 Sep 04	Leeds	R. Bell	,,	453	1,423
4-9 Sep 05	Hanley	J. Sexton	W. Steadman	457	1,541
3-8 Sep 06	Liverpool	D. Cummings	,,	491	1,555
2-7 Sep 07	Bath	A. Gill	,,	521	1,700
7-12 Sep 08	Nottingham	D. Shackleton	,,	522	1,777
6-11 Sep 09	Ipswich	,,	,,	598	1,705
12-17 Sep 10	Sheffield	J. Haslam	,,	505	1,648
4-9 Sep 11	Newcastle	W. Mullin	C. Bowerman	523	1,662
2-7 Sep 12	Newport	W. Thorne	,,	495	2,002
1-6 Sep 13	Manchester	W. Davis	,,	560	2,232
6-11 Sep 15	Bristol	J. Seddon	,,	610	2,682
4-9 Sep 16	Birmingham	H. Gosling	,,	673	2,851
3-8 Sep 17	Blackpool	J. Hill	,,	697	3,082
2-7 Sep 18	Derby	J. Ogden	,,	881	4,532
8-13 Sep 19	Glasgow	G. Stuart-Bunning	,,	851	5,284
6-11 Sep 20	Portsmouth	J. Thomas	,,	955	6,505
5-10 Sep 21	Cardiff	E. Poulton	,,	810	6,418
4-9 Sep 22	Southport	R. Walker	,,	723	5,129
3-8 Sep 23	Plymouth	J. Williams	F. Bramley	702	4,369
1-6 Sep 24	Hull	A. Purcell	,,	724	4,328
7-12 Sep 25	Scarborough	A. Swales	,,	727	4,351
6-11 Sep 26	Bournemouth	A. Pugh	W. Citrine	696	4,366
5-10 Sep 27	Edinburgh	G. Hicks	,,	646	4,164
3-8 Sep 28	Swansea	B. Turner	,,	621	3,875
2-6 Sep 29	Belfast	B. Tillett	,,	592	3,673
1-5 Sep 30	Nottingham	J. Beard	,,	606	3,744
7-11 Sep 31	Bristol	A. Hayday	,,	589	3,719
5-9 Sep 32	Newcastle	J. Bromley	,,	578	3,613
4-8 Sep 33	Brighton	A. Walkden	,,	566	3,368
3-7 Sep 34	Weymouth	A. Conley	,,	575	3,295
2-6 Sep 35	Margate	W. Kean	Sir W. Citrine	575	3,389
7-11 Sep 36	Plymouth	A. Findlay	,,	603	3,615
6-10 Sep 37	Norwich	E. Bevin	,,	623	4,009
5-9 Sep 38	Blackpool	H. Elvin	,,	650	4,461
4-5 Sep 39	Bridlington	J. Hallsworth	,,	490[a]	4,669
7-9 Oct 40	Southport	W. Holmes	,,	667	4,867
1-4 Sep 41	Edinburgh	G. Gibson	,,	683	5,079
7-11 Sep 42	Blackpool	F. Wolstencroft	,,	717	5,433
6-10 Sep 43	Southport	Anne Loughlin	,,	760	6,024
16-20 Oct 44	Blackpool	E. Edwards	,,	730	6,642
10-14 Sep 45	Blackpool	,,	,,	762	6,576
21-25 Oct 46	Brighton	C. Dukes	V. Tewson	794	6,671
1-5 Sep 47	Southport	G. Thomson	,,	837	7,540
6-10 Sep 48	Margate	Florence Hancock	,,	859	7,791
5-9 Sep 49	Bridlington	Sir W. Lawther	,,	890	7,937
4-8 Sep 50	Brighton	H. Bullock	Sir V. Tewson	913	7,883

[a] Actual attendance owing to the outbreak of war. Credentials were issued to 659 delegates.

Date	Place	President	General Secretary	No.of Delegates	Members represen-ted ('000s)
3-7 Sep 51	Blackpool	A. Roberts	Sir V. Tewson	927	7,828
1-5 Sep 52	Margate	A. Deakin	,,	943	8,020
7-11 Sep 53	Douglas	T. O'Brien	,,	954	8,088
6-10 Sep 54	Brighton	J. Tanner	,,	974	8,094
5-9 Sep 55	Southport	C. Geddes	,,	984	8,107
3-7 Sep 56	Brighton	W. Beard	,,	1,000	8,264
2-6 Sep 57	Blackpool	Sir T. Williamson	,,	995	8,305
1-5 Sep 58	Bournemouth	T. Yates	,,	993	8,337
7-11 Sep 59	Blackpool	R. Willis	,,	1,017	8,176
5-9 Sep 60	Douglas	C. Bartlett	G. Woodcock	996	8,128
4-8 Sep 61	Portsmouth	E. Hill	,,	984	8,299
3-7 Sep 62	Blackpool	A. Godwin	,,	989	8,313
2-6 Sep 63	Brighton	F. Hayday	,,	975	8,315
7-11 Sep 64	Blackpool	G. Lowthian	,,	997	8,326
6-10 Sep 65	Brighton	H. Collison	,,	1,013	8,771
5-9 Sep 66	Blackpool	J. O'Hagan	,,	1,048	8,868
4-8 Sep 67	Brighton	Sir H. Douglass	,,	1,059	8,787
2-6 Sep 68	Blackpool	Ld Wright	,,	1,051	8,726
1-5 Sep 69	Portsmouth	J. Newton	,,	1,034	8,875
7-11 Sep 70	Brighton	Sir S. Greene	V. Feather	1,064	9,402
6-10 Sep 71	Blackpool	Ld Cooper	,,	1,064	10,002
4-8 Sep 72	Brighton	G. Smith	,,	1,018	9,895
3-7 Sep 73	Blackpool	J. Crawford	,,	991	10,001
2-6 Sep 74	Brighton	Ld Allen	L. Murray	1,032	10,002
1-5 Sep 75	Blackpool	Marie Patterson	,,	1,030	10,364
6-10 Sep 76	Brighton	C. Plant	,,	1,114	11,036
5-9 Sep 77	Blackpool	Marie Patterson	,,	1,148	11,516
4-8 Sep 78	Brighton	D. Basnett	,,	1,172	11,865
3-7 Sep 79	Blackpool	T. Jackson	,,	1,200	12,128
1-5 Sep 80	Brighton	T. Parry	,,	1,203	12,173
7-11 Sep 81	Blackpool	A. Fisher	,,	1,188	11,601
6-10 Sep 82	Brighton	A. Sapper	,,	1,163	11,006
5-9 Sep 83	Blackpool	F. Chapple	,,	1,155	10,810
3-7 Sep 84	Brighton	R. Buckton	N. Willis	1,121	10,082

SOURCE.—*Trades Union Congress Report, 1900-.*

The Largest Unions

(Unions which, at some time, have had over 200,000 members)

Amalgamated Union of Engineering Workers (AUEW)	1920 (1970)	Amalgamated Society of Engineers (founded 1851) merged with other unions to form the Amalgamated Engineering Union (A.E.U.) in 1920. In 1968 the A.E.U. merged with the Amalgamated Union of Foundry Workers (A.E.F.) which in 1970 merged with the Construction Engineering Workers and the Draughtsmen and Allied Technicians Association.

President

1920	J. Brownlie	1954	R. Openshaw
1930	W. Hutchinson	1956	(Sir) W. Carron (Ld)
1933	J. Little	1967	H. Scanlon
1939	J. Tanner	1978	T. Duffy

Amalgamated Weavers' Association — 1884-1974 — An association of many small local unions in the Cotton Trade. In 1974 it merged with the National Union of Textile and Allied Workers to form the Amalgamated Textile Workers Union.

Secretary

1907	J. Cross	1953	L. Wright (Ld)
1925	J. Parker	1969	H. Kershaw
1929	(Sir) A. Naesmith	1972	F. Hague

Association of Scientific Technical and Managerial Staffs (ASTMS) — 1917 (1968) — National Foreman's Association became Association of Supervisory Staff, Executives and Technicians (ASSET) in 1941 and ASTMS in 1968 when it merged with the Association of Scientific Workers (founded in 1918 as National Union of Scientific Workers and became AScW in 1925). NFA joined TUC in 1919; AScW in 1942.

Secretary

1917	H. Reid (NFA)	1960	C. Jenkins (ASSET)
1939	T. Agar (NFA)	1968	J. Dutton C. Jenkins
1945	W. Bretherton (ASSET)	1970	C. Jenkins
1946	H. Knight (ASSET)		

Civil and Public Service Association (CPSA) — 1902 (1969) — Assistant Clerks Association became Clerical Officers Association in 1919 and Civil Service Clerical Association in 1922. Changed name to CPSA in 1969 (not in TUC 1927-1946).

Secretary

1916	W. Brown	1967	W. Kendall
1942	L. White	1976	K. Thomas
1955	G. Green	1982	A. Kendall
1963	L. Wines		

Confederation of Health Service Employees (COHSE) — 1946 — Formed by a merger of various small hospital unions.

Secretary

1946	G. Gibson	1967	A. Akers
1948	C. Comer	1969	F. Lynch
1953	J. Waite	1974	A. Spanswick
1959	W. Jepson	1983	D. Williams

Electrical Trades Union (EETU) 1889 Electrical Trades Union and others. In 1968 following mergers it became the Electrical, Electronic and Telecommunications Union—Plumbing Trades Union and then the Electrical, Electronic Telecommunication and Plumbing Union.

President

1907	J. Ball	1963	(Sir) L. Cannon
1931	E. Bussey	1971	F. Chapple
1940	H. Bolton	1984	E. Hammond
1944	F. Foulkes		

General Municipal Boilermakers and Allied Trades Union (GMBATU) 1924 National Union of General Workers (founded 1889 as the National Union of Gasworkers and General Labourers of G.B. and Ireland), National Amalgamated Union of Labour (founded 1889 as Tyneside and General Labourers' Union), and Municipal Employees' Association (founded 1894). Became National Union of General and Municipal Workers in 1924. Changed name to General and Municipal Workers Union for popular use in 1965. Merged with Amalgamated Society of Boilermakers, Shipwrights, Blacksmiths and structural workers to form GMBATU in 1982.

Secretary

1924	W. Thorne	1962	J. (Ld) Cooper
1934	C. Dukes	1972	D. Basnett
1946	(Sir) T. Williamson		

National and Local Government Officers' Association (NALGO) 1905 National Association of Local Government Officers. 1930 amalgamated with National Poor Law Officers' Association and in 1963 with the British Gas Staffs Association. 1952 changed name to National and Local Government Officers' Association (Joined TUC 1965.)

Secretary

1905	F. Ginn	1946	J. Warren
1909	L. Hill	1957	W. Anderson
1943	J. Simonds	1973	G. Drain
1945	H. Corser (*Acting*)	1983	J. Daly

National Union of Mineworkers (NUM) 1889 (1945) Formed as the Miners' Federation of G.B., amalgamated with specialist unions, and renamed NUM in 1945.

President		Secretary	
1912	R. Smillie	1920	F. Hodges
1921	H. Smith	1924	A. Cook
1929	T. Richards	1932	E. Edwards
1931	E. Edwards	1946	A. Homer
1932	P. Lee	1959	W. Paynter
1934	J. Jones	1969	L. Daly
1938	W. Lawther	1984	P. Heathfield
1954	W. Jones		
1960	S. Ford		
1971	J. Gormley		
1982	A. Scargill		

National Union of Public Employees (NUPE)	1888 (1928)	Formed as London County Council Protection Association; in 1894 became Municipal Employees Association; in 1920 the MEA and the National Union of Corporation Workers jointly affiliated to the TUC but in 1924 MEA was absorbed by NUGMW. The National Union of Corporation Workers became NUPE in 1928.

Secretary

1926	J. Wills	1968	A. Fisher
1934	B. Roberts	1982	R. Bickerstaffe
1962	S. Hill		

National Union of Railwaymen (NUR)	1913	Amalgamated Society of Railway Servants, and General Railway Workers' Union, and others.

Secretary

1920	J. Thomas and C. Cramp	1948	J. Figgins
1931	C. Cramp	1953	J. Campbell
1933	*(Acting Secretary)*	1958	(Sir) S. (Ld) Greene
1934	J. Marchbank	1975	S. Weighell
1943	J. Benstead	1982	J. Knapp

National Union of Teachers (NUT)	1870	Originally National Union of Elementary Teachers (till 1890). Affiliated to TUC in 1970.

Secretary

1892	(Sir) J. Yoxall	1947	(Sir) R. Gould
1924	F. Goldstone	1970	(Sir) E. Britton
1931	(Sir) F. Mander	1975	F. Jarvis

Society of Graphical and Allied Trades (SOGAT) (SOGAT 82)	1847 (1968)	Established by amalgamation of the National Union of Bookbinders and Machine Rulers and the National Union of Printing and Paper Workers as the National Union of Printing, Bookbinding and Paper Workers (NUPBPW). In 1968 merged with the National Society of Operative Printers (NATSOPA) to form SOGAT. In 1971 merger was dissolved but NUPBPW section kept name of SOGAT.

Secretary

1921	T. Newland	1959	T. Smith (1968-71 jointly with R. Briginshaw)
1938	E. Spackman	1974	W. Keys
1946	V. Flynn	1985	Ms B. Dean
1947	W. Morrison		

Transport and General Workers' Union (TGWU)	1922	Dock, Wharf, Riverside and General Workers' Union, National Union of Dock Labourers and other dockers' unions, United Vehicle Workers, National Union of Vehicle Workers and others. 1928 amalgamated with the Workers' Union.

Secretary

1921	E. Bevin	1966	F. Cousins
1940	A. Deakin (*Acting* till 1946)	1969	J. Jones
1955	A. Tiffin	1977	M. Evans
1956	F. Cousins	1985	R. Todd
1964	H. Nicholas (*Acting*)		

Union of Construction Allied Trades and Technicians (UCATT)	1860 (1971)	Amalgamated Society of Carpenters and Joiners became, in 1921 after mergers, Amalgamated Society of Woodworkers (ASW). ASW merged in 1971 with the Amalgamated Union of Building Trade Workers (formed 1921), the Amalgamated Society of Painters and Decorators and the Association of Building Technicians.

Secretary

1919	A. Cameron	1959	(Sir) G. Smith
1925	F. Wolstencroft	1978	L. Wood
1949	J. MacDermott		

Union of Communication Workers (Union of Post Office Workers: UCW)	1920	Postal Telegraph Clerks' Association. U.K. Postal Clerks Association merged in 1914 to form Postal and Telegraph Clerks' Association. This merged in 1920 with Fawcett Association and other unions to form UPW. Name changed to Union of Communication Workers in 1980. (Legally banned from membership of TUC 1927-1946.)

Secretary

1920	J. Bowen	1957	R. Smith
1936	T. Hodgson	1966	T. Jackson
1944	C. Geddes	1982	A. Tuffin

Union of Shop, Distributive and Allied Workers (USDAW)	1921 (1946)	Co-operative Employees, and Warehouse and General Workers amalgamated in 1921 to form the National Union of Distributive and Allied Workers. 1946 fusion with National Amalgamated Union of Shop Assistants, Warehousemen and Clerks.

Secretary

1921	J. Hallsworth and W. Robinson	1949	(Sir) A. Birch
1924	(Sir) J. Hallsworth	1962	A. (Ld) Allen
1947	*(Acting Secretary)*	1979	W. Whatley
		1985	G. Davies

SOURCE.—*Trade Union Congress Reports*, 1920-.

Membership

(to nearest '000) (at 31 December)

The Eight Largest Unions (in 1960)

Year	AUEW	ETU	NALGO	(NU)GMW	NUM	NUR	T & GWU	USDAW
1920	407	57	36	. .	900	458	. .	. .
1921	357	46	36	. .	800	341	300	100
1922	256	31	33	. .	750	327	300	90
1923	246	26	33	. .	750	327	300	90
1924	206	28	34	327	800	327	300	93
1925	205	29	37	320	800	327	300	95
1926	162	29	40	300	800	327	300	94
1927	146	26	44	278	725	327	300	100
1928	151	26	46	258	600	313	286	109
1929	155	29	49	261	600	310	389	115
1930	154	31	61	258	600	321	384	119

Year	AUEW	ETU	NALGO	(NU)GMW	NUM	NUR	T & GWU	USDAW
1931	146	31	65	240	600	310	390	121
1932	136	31	68	220	500	285	390	127
1933	135	31	73	230	500	272	370	131
1934	146	34	79	252	500	291	403	134
1935	164	40	86	280	500	306	460	145
1936	248	48	93	340	518	338	523	158
1937	299	58	101	405	538	365	611	172
1938	334	64	106	417	584	367	635	183
1939	376	70	114	430	589	350	648	194
1940	454	80	111	441	589	362	650	223
1941	550	97	113	548	580	376	680	234
1942	645	113	121	721	599	394	806	254
1943	825	124	127	726	603	406	1,089	268
1944	811	132	133	661	605	404	1,017	272
1945	704	133	134	605	533	410	975	275
1946	723	162	146	795	538	414	1,230	374
1947	742	170	171	824	572	448	1,264	343
1948	743	182	176	816	611	455	1,271	342
1949	714	188	189	805	609	421	1,253	340
1950	716	192	197	785	602	392	1,242	343
1951	756	198	212	809	613	396	1,285	348
1952	796	203	222	808	641	397	1,277	346
1953	810	212	225	790	669	378	1,259	339
1954	823	216	230	787	675	372	1,240	344
1955	854	223	236	805	675	368	1,278	347
1956	860	228	243	808	674	369	1,264	349
1957	900	239	247	804	681	371	1,244	352
1958	888	230	252	775	674	355	1,225	353
1959	908	233	263	769	639	334	1,241	351
1960	973	243	274	769	586	334	1,302	355
1961	982	253	285	786	545	317	1,318	351
1962	986	257	295	781	529	311	1,331	356
1963	981	272	226	782	501	283	1,374	355
1964	1,011	282	338	785	479	264	1,426	352
1965	1,049	293	349	796	446	255	1,444	349
1966	1,055	293	361	793	413	220	1,428	336
1967	1,107	352	367	782	380	218	1,451	321
1968	1,136	365	373	798	344	199	1,476	311
1969	1,195	392	397	804	297	191	1,532	316
1970	1,295	421	440	853	279	198	1,629	330
1971	1,284	420	464	842	276	194	1,643	319
1972	1,340	417	498	848	271	184	1,747	325
1973	1,173	420	518	864	261	174	1,785	326
1974	1,211	414	542	884	255	173	1,857	353
1975	1,429	420	625	881	262	180	1,856	377
1976	1,412	420	683	916	260	180	1,930	413
1977	1,423	420	709	945	258	180	2,023	441
1978	1,484	420	729	965	255	180	2,073	462
1979	1,499	420	753	967	253	180	2,086	470
1980	1,381	405	782	916	257	170	1,887	450

Year	AUEW	ETU	NALGO	(NU)GMW	NUM	NUR	T & GWU	USDAW
1981	1,290	395	796	865	250	160	1,696	438
1982	1,238	380	784	940	245	150	1,633	417
1983	1,220	365	780	875	208	143	1,547	403

SOURCE.—*Trade Union Congress Reports*, 1920-.

Other Unions Which Have Exceeded 200,000 Members

	ASTMS	CPSA	COHSE	NUPE	NUT	SOGAT	UCATT	UCW
1950	12	134	53	175	192	124	197	149
1960	25	140	54	200	225	158	192	166
1970	221	185	90	373	311	192	221	209
1980	491	224	213	692	249	206	348	203
1983	390	191	223	689	210	214	260	196

The Amalgamated Weavers' Association had 219,000 members in 1920. It fell to 89,000 by 1940.

SOURCE.—*Trade Union Congress Reports*, 1920-.

Income, Expenditure and Funds of Registered Trade Unions

(in shillings per member)

Year	Income from members	Expenditure: Dispute benefit	Unemployment benefit	Other Welfare benefits	Political	Working Expenses	Funds
1910	27·8	5·3	6·8	11·1	. .	8·1	59·3
1920	32·4	9·3	4·5	5·1	0·5	17·2	45·8
1930	37·6	1·6	9·7	12·1	0·5	16·6	62·0
1940	36·0	0·2	3·0	10·4	0·4	14·8	92·2
1950	39·6	0·6	0·4	10·4	1·1	22·8	156·4
1960	58·8	1·1	0·4	15·5	1·2	34·9	211·6
1970	104·9	8·6	0·6	25·9	3·7	72·4	322·6
1982	507·6	12·2	3·0	45·8	12·2	400·4	734·2

SOURCES.—A. Flanders, *Trade Unions* (1967), and *Department of Employment Gazette*.

Density of Union Membership in Total Labour Force

United Kingdom

1901	12·6%	1951	44·1
1911	17·7	1961	43·1
1920	45·2	1970	47·7
1933	22·6	1974	49·6
1938	29·5%	1981	43·7

SOURCES.—G. S. Bain, *The Growth of White-Collar Unionism* (1970); G. S. Bain and R. Price, 'Union Growth and Employment Trends in the U.K., 1964-70', *British Journal of Industrial Relations* (1972), pp. 366-81 and 'Union Growth Revisited 1948-70', *British Journal of Industrial Relations* (1976), pp. 339-55; *Annual Reports of Certification Officer*.

White-Collar Unions

Much of the expansion of union membership during the twentieth century has occurred among white-collar workers. Prior to 1900 few of these workers were unionised, but by 1920 the Webbs estimated that close to three-quarters of a million white-collar employees belonged to trade unions. More recently, there has been a further dramatic increase in union membership among white-collar employees. While union membership among manual workers decreased by 6·8 per cent between 1948 and 1974 union membership among white-collar workers increased by 104·7 per cent. In 1974 there were approximately 300 unions catering for white-collar employees with a total membership of 3·5 million, and union density among white-collar workers was 38 per cent compared with 53 per cent among manual workers.

SOURCES.—G. S. Bain, *The Growth of White-Collar Unionism* (1970) and G. S. Bain and R. Price, 'Union Growth Revisited 1948-70', *British Journal of Industrial Relations* (1976), pp. 339-55.

Major Industrial Disputes

(in which more than 500,000 working days were lost)

Dispute Began		*Industrial group*	*Area*	*Numbers affected ('000s)*	*Working days lost ('000s[a])*
1900	Apr	Potters	N. Staffs.	20	640
	Nov	Quarrymen	Bethesda	3	505
1902	Jul	Miners	Federated districts	103	872
1906	Oct	Shipyard workers	Clyde	15	592
1908	Feb	Shipyard workers	Humber, Barrow, Birkenhead, Clyde, E. Scotland	35	1,719
	Feb	Engineers	N.E. Coast	11	1,706
	Sep	Cotton operatives	Lancs., Cheshire, Derby	120	4,830
1909	Jul	Miners	S. Wales and Mon.	55	660
1910	Jan	Miners	Durham	85	1,280
	Jan	Miners	Northumberland	30	1,080
	Apr	Miners	Rhondda	13	2,985
	Jun	Cotton operatives	Lancs. and Cheshire	102	600
	Sep	Shipyard workers	N.E. Coast and Scotland	35	2,851
1911	Jun	Seamen and dockers	U.K.	120	1,020
	Aug	Dockers and carters	London	22	500
	Aug	Railwaymen	U.K.	145	500
	Dec	Cotton weavers	N.E. Lancs.	160	2,954
1912	Feb	Miners	U.K.	1,000	30,800
	Feb	Jute workers	Dundee	28	726
	May	Dockers and carters	Port of London and Medway	100	2,700
1913	Jan	Cab drivers	London	11	637
	Apr	Tube and metal workers	S. Staffs. and N. Worcs.	50	1,400
	Aug	Transport workers	Dublin	20	1,900
1914	Jan	Builders	London	20	2,500
	Feb	Miners	Yorks.	150	2,654
1915	Jul	Miners	S. Wales	232	1,400
1916	Mar	Jute workers	Dundee	30	500
1917	May	Engineers	U.K.	160	2,880
1918	May	Miners	S. Wales and Mon.	40	760
	Dec	Cotton spinners	Lancs. and Cheshire	100	900

Dispute Began	Industrial group	Area	Number affected ('000s)	Working days lost ('000s[a])
1919 Jan	Miners	Yorks.	150	1,950
Jan	Shipyard workers	N.E. Coast	40	820
Mar	Miners	Various districts	100	600
Jun	Cotton operatives	Lancs. and adjoining counties	450	7,500
Jul	Miners	Yorks.	150	4,050
Sep	Ironfounders	England, Wales, and Ireland	50	6,800
Sep	Railwaymen	U.K.	500	3,850
1920 Sep	Cotton operatives	Oldham and district	400	620
Oct	Miners	U.K.	1,100	16,000
1921 (Dec 1920)	Shipyard carpenters	U.K.	10	2,200
Apr	Miners	U.K.	1,100	72,000
Jun	Cotton operatives	Lancs. and adjoining counties	375	6,750
1922 Mar	Engineers	U.K.	250	13,650
Mar	Shipyard workers	Various districts	90	3,400
1923 Feb	Jute workers	Dundee	29	950
Apr	Boilermakers	Clyde, E. Scotland, N.E. Coast, Hull, Southampton, Birkenhead, Barrow	30	5,725
1924 Jan	Railwaymen	U.K.	69	500
Feb	Dockers	U.K.	110	510
Jul	Builders	U.K.	100	2,970
1925 Jul	Wool textile workers	W. Riding of Yorks. and part of Lancs.	165	3,105
1926 May	Miners	U.K.	1,050	145,200
May	General Strike	U.K.	1,580[b]	15,000[b]
1928 May	Cotton weavers	Nelson	17	600
1929 Jul	Cotton operatives	Lancs. and adjoining counties	388	6,596
1930 Apr	Wool textile workers	W. Riding of Yorks. and part of Lancs.	120	3,258
1931 Jan	Cotton weavers	Lancs. and adjoining counties	145	3,290
Jan	Miners	S. Wales and Mon.	150	2,030
1932 Aug	Cotton weavers	Lancs. and Yorks.	148	4,524
Oct	Cotton spinners	Lancs. and adjoining counties	130	760
1937 May	Busmen	London	24	565
1944 Mar	Miners	Wales and Mon.	100	550
Mar	Miners	Yorkshire	120	1,000
1945 Sep	Dockers	Birkenhead, Liverpool, Hull, Manchester, London	50	1,100
1953 Dec	Engineers and Shipyard workers	U.K.	1,070	1,070
1954 Sep	Dockers	Port of London and sympathy strikes	45	726
1955 May	Dockers	Various ports of England	21	673
May	Railwaymen	U.K.	70	865
1957 Mar	Engineers	U.K.	615	4,000
Mar	Shipyard workers	U.K.	165	2,150
Jul	Busmen	Provinces	100	770
1958 Apr	Dockers, transport and market workers	London	24	515
May	Busmen	Greater London	49	1,604
1959 Jun	Printing workers	U.K.	120	3,500
1962 Feb	Engineering & Shipbuilding	U.K.	1,750	1,750
Mar	Engineering & Shipbuilding	U.K.	1,750	1,750
1966 May	Shipping	U.K.	30	850

Dispute Began	Industrial group	Area	Number affected ('000s)	Working days lost ('000s[a])
1968 May	Engineering	U.K.	1,500	1,500
1969 Feb	Motor Vehicles	Various districts	38	561
Oct	Miners	Various districts	121	979
1970 Jul	Dockers	U.K.	42	502
Sep	Local authority workers	England and Wales	134	1,216
Oct	Miners	Various	99	1,050
1971 Jan	Motor vehicles	Various districts	42	1,909
Jan	Post Office workers	U.K.	180	6,229
1972 Jan	Miners	U.K.	309	10,726
Jun	Construction	England and Wales	120	2,904
Jun	Construction	Scotland	36	933
Jul	Dockers	U.K.	35	548
1974 Feb	Miners	U.K.	250	5,567
1977 Nov	Firemen	U.K.	30	1,250
1978 Oct	Motor Vehicles (Ford)	U.K.	56	2,529
Dec	Printworkers	London	3	592
1979 Jan	Lorry drivers	U.K.	85	950
Jan	Public employees	U.K.	1,500	3,239
Feb	Civil servants	U.K.	279	508
Jul	Television staff	U.K.	12	600
Aug	Engineers	U.K.	1,500	16,000
1980 Jan	Steelworkers	U.K.	151	8,800
1981 Mar	Civil servants	U.K.	318	867
1982 Jan	Railway footplatemen	U.K.	59	814
Apr	Health service employees	U.K.	180	781
May	All workers	U.K.	948	672
1983 Jan	Water workers	England, Wales, and Northern Ireland	35	766
1984 Mar	Miners	U.K.	130	26,100

[a] Where figures for working days lost are not given in the *Gazettes*, they have been estimated.
[b] Excluding Miners.

SOURCES.—*The Board of Trade Labour Gazette, 1900-17*; *The Ministry of Labour Gazette* (1918-68); *Employment and Productivity Gazette* (1968-).

Emergency Powers

Under the *Emergency Powers Act, 1920,* the government may proclaim a State of Emergency if the essentials of life of the country are threatened. The Act then empowers the government to make regulations by Order-in-Council which have the full force of law. All the occasions on which States of Emergency have been proclaimed under the Act have been associated with strikes.

31 Mar	21	Coal
26 Mar	24	London Transport[1]
2 May	26	General Strike
29 Jun	48	Docks
11 Jul	49	Docks
31 May	55	Rail
23 May	66	Seamen
16 Jul	70	Docks
12 Dec	70	Electricity
9 Feb	72	Coal
3 Aug	72	Docks
13 Nov	73	Coal and Electricity (also Middle East oil crisis)

[1] It is doubtful whether this proclamation was ever made.

Unemployment, Industrial Disputes, and Trade Union Statistics

	Unemployment[b]		Industrial Disputes[c]						
	Maximum ('000s)	Minimum ('000s)	Working Days Lost[d] ('000s)	No. of Stoppages beginning in year[e]	Workers involved[d] ('000s)	Total No. of Trade Unions	Total No. of Trade Union Members ('000s)	Total No. of Trade Unions affiliated to T.U.C.	Total No. of members of Trade Unions affiliated to T.U.C. ('000s)
1900			3,088	633	185	1,325	1,911	184	1,250
1901			4,130	631	179	1,323	2,022	191	1,200
1902			3,438	432	255	1,322	2,025	198	1,400
1903			2,320	380	116	1,297	2,013	204	1,500
1904			1,464	346	87	1,285	1,994	212	1,423
1905			2,368	349	92	1,256	1,967	205	1,541
1906			3,019	479	218	1,244	1,997	226	1,555
1907			2,148	585	146	1,282	2,210	236	1,700
1908			10,785	389	293	1,283	2,513	214	1,777
1909			2,687	422	297	1,268	2,485	219	1,705
1910			9,867	521	514	1,260	2,477	212	1,648
1911			10,155	872	952	1,269	2,565		
1912			40,890	834	1,462	1,290	3,139	202	1,662
1913			9,804	1,459	664	1,252	3,416	201	2,002
1914			9,878	972	447	1,269	4,135	207	2,232
1915			2,953	672	448	1,260	4,145	215	2,682
1916			2,446	532	276	1,229	4,359	227	2,851
1917			5,647	730	872	1,225	4,644	235	3,082
1918			5,875	1,165	1,116	1,241	5,499	262	4,532
1919			34,969	1,352	2,591	1,264	6,533	266	5,284
1920			26,568	1,607	1,932	1,360	7,926	215	6,505
1921	2,038[a]		85,872	763	1,801	1,384	8,348	213	6,418
1922	2,015 Jan	1,443 Oct	19,850	576	552	1,275	6,633	206	5,129
1923	1,525 Jan	1,229 Dec	10,672	628	405	1,232	5,625	194	4,369
1924	1,374 Jan	1,087 Jun	8,424	710	613	1,192	5,429	203	4,328
1925	1,443 Aug	1,243 Dec	7,952	603	441	1,194	5,544	205	4,351
1926	1,432 Dec	1,094 Apr	162,233	323	2,734	1,176	5,506	207	4,366
1927	1,451 Jan	1,059 May	1,174	308	108	1,164	5,219	204	4,164
1928	1,375 Aug	1,127 Mar	1,388	302	124	1,159	4,919	196	3,875
1929	1,466 Jan	1,164 Jun	8,287	431	533	1,142	4,866	202	3,673
1930	2,500 Dec	1,520 Jan	4,399	422	307	1,133	4,858	210	3,744
1931	2,880 Sep	2,578 May	6,983	420	490	1,121	4,842	210	3,719
1932	2,955 Jan	2,309 Nov	6,488	389	379	1,108	4,624	209	3,613
1933	2,407 Jan	1,858 Dec	1,072	357	136	1,081	4,444	208	3,368
1934	2,295 Jan	2,080 Sep	959	471	134	1,081	4,392	210	3,295
1935	2,333 Jan	1,888 Dec	1,955	553	271	1,063	4,590	211	3,389
1936	2,169 Jan	1,640 Aug	1,829	818	316	1,049	4,867	214	3,615
1937	1,739 Dec	1,373 Sep	3,413	1,129	597	1,036	5,295	214	4,009
1938	1,912 Dec	1,818 Apr	1,334	875	274	1,032	5,842	216	4,461
1939	2,032 Jan	1,230 Aug	1,356	940	337	1,024	6,053	217	4,669
1940	1,471 Jan	683 Dec	940	922	299	1,019	6,298	223	4,867
1941	653 Jan	151 Dec	1,079	1,251	360	1,004	6,613	223	5,079
1942	162 Jan	100 Dec	1,527	1,303	456	996	7,165	232	5,433
1943	104 Jan	. .	1,808	1,785	557	991	7,867	230	6,024
1944	84 Jan	. .	3,714	2,194	821	987	8,174	190	6,642
1945	111 Jan	. .	2,835	2,293	531	963	8,087	191	6,576
1946	408 Jan	360 Jan	2,158	2,205	526	781	7,875	192	6,671
1947	1,916 Feb	262 Sep	2,433	1,721	620	757	8,803	187	7,540
1948	359 Dec	299 Jun	1,944	1,759	424	734	9,145	188	7,791
1949	413 Jan	274 Jul	1,807	1,426	433	735	9,319	187	7.937
1950	404 Jan	297 Jul	1,389	1,339	302	726	9,274	186	7,937
1951	367 Jan	210 Jul	1,694	1,719	379	732	9,289	186	7,828
1952	468 Apr	379 Jan	1,792	1,714	415	735	9,535	183	8,020
1953	452 Feb	273 Jul	2,184	1,746	1,370	719	9,583	183	8,088
1954	387 Feb	220 Jul	2,457	1,989	448	717	9,523	184	8,094
1955	298 Jan	185 Jul	3,781	2,419	659	703	9,556	183	8,107
1956	297 Dec	223 Jun	2,083	2,648	507	694	9,726	186	8,264

Unemployment, Industrial Disputes, and Trade Union Statistics

	Unemployment[b]		Industrial Disputes[c]						
	Maximum ('000s)	Minimum ('000s)	Working Days Lost[a] ('000s)	No. of Stoppages beginning in year	Workers involved[e] ('000s)	Total No. of Trade Unions	Total No. of Trade Union Members ('000s)	Total No. of Trade Unions affiliated to T.U.C.	Total No. of members of Trade Unions affiliated to T.U.C. ('000s)
1957	383 Jan	244 Jul	8,412	2,859	1,356	685	9,829	185	8,305
1958	536 Nov	395 Jan	3,462	2,629	523	675	9,639	185	8,337
1959	621 Jan	395 Jul	5,270	2,093	645	668	9,623	186	8,176
1960	461 Jan	292 Jul	3,024	2,832	817	664	9,835	184	8,128
1961	419 Jan	259 Jul	3,046	2,686	771	646	9,897	183	8,299
1962	566 Dec	397 Jun	5,795	2,449	4,420	626	9,887	182	8,313
1963	878 Feb	449 Jul	1,755	2,068	591	607	9,934	176	8,315
1964	501 Jan	318 Jul	2,277	2,524	871	598	10,079	175	8,326
1965	376 Jan	276 Jun	2,925	2,354	871	630	10,325	172	8,771
1966	564 Dec	261 Jun	2,398	1,937	530	622	10,261	170	8,868
1967	603 Feb	497 Jul	2,787	2,116	734	603	10,110	169	8,787
1968	631 Jan	515 Jul	4,690	2,378	2,255	584	10,193	160	8,726
1969	595 Jan	499 Jun	6,846	3,116	1,654	563	10,472	155	8,875
1970	628 Jan	547 Jun	10,980	3,906	1,793	540	11,179	150	9,402
1971	868 Dec	655 Jan	13,551	2,228	1,776	523	11,128	142	10,002
1972[f]	929 Jan	745 Dec	23,909	2,497	1,722	503	11,353	132	9,895
1973	785 Jan	486 Dec	7,197	2,873	1,513	513	11,449	126	10,001
1974	628 Aug	515 Jun	14,750	2,922	1,622	498	11,756	109	10,002
1975	1,152 Dec	738 Jan	6,012	2,282	789	488	12,184	111	10,364
1976	1,440 Aug	1,220 Jun	3,284	2,016	882	462	12,376	113	11,036
1977	1,567 Aug	1,286 May	9,985	2,627	1,143	485	12,719	112	11,516
1978	1,608 Aug	1,364 Dec	9,306	2,349	939	485	..	..	..
1979	1,464 July	1,299 May	29,474	4,583	2,080	462	13,112	112	865
1980	2,244 Dec	1,471 Jan	11,964	830	1,330	453	13,289	112	12,128
1981	2,772 Oct	2,271 Jan	4,266	1,499	1,338	438	12,947	109	12,173
1982	3,097 Dec	2,770 June	5,313	2,101	1,528	414	12,106	108	11,601
1983	3,225 Jan	2,984 June	3,754	571	1,352	401	11,445	105	11,006
1984								102	10,510

[a] Figures for Dec available only.
[b] 1900-20, unemployment figures for certain skilled trade unions available in *Ministry of Labour Gazettes*, figures are given as percentages. No comparable figures of total unemployed before 1921. Figures for insured workers registered as unemployed. Agricultural workers, insurable in 1936, are included from that date. Numerous changes in coverage throughout.
[c] Disputes involving less than 10 work-people and those lasting less than one day are omitted, except where aggregate duration exceeded 100 working days.
[d] S. Ireland included from 1900 to 1907.
[e] Workers involved directly and indirectly. 'Indirectly' involved means those unable to work at establishments where disputes occurred, though not themselves parties to the dispute.
[f] After the passage of the *Industrial Relations Act, 1971*, many trade unions ceased to be registered and as a result many trade union statistics for the following four years are non-existent or non-comparable.

SOURCES.—*Annual Abstract of Statistics, Ministry of Labour Gazette, Employment Gazette* and *Abstract of Labour Statistics. T.U.C. Congress Reports.*

BIBLIOGRAPHY: For a general introductory survey of industrial relations see: A. Flanders, *Trade Unions* (1967) (contains a useful bibliography); H. A. Clegg (ed.), *The Changing System of Industrial Relations in Great Britain* (1979); B. C. Roberts (ed.), *Industrial Relations: Contemporary Problems and Perspectives* (1962); Ministry of Labour, *Industrial Relations Handbook* (H.M.S.O., 1961); Ministry of Labour, *Evidence to the Royal* *Commission on Trade Unions and Employers' Associations* (H.M.S.O., 1965); G. D. H. Cole, *An Introduction to Trade Unionism* (1953); G. S. Bain, *The Growth of White-Collar Unionism* (1970); G. S. Bain (ed.), *Industrial Relations in Britain* (1983).

A comprehensive study of the whole field is to be found in the *Report* of the Royal Commission on Trade Unions and Employers' Associations (Cmnd. 3623/1968) and the eleven *Research Papers* which were published in connection with it.

For a discussion of contemporary problems see: A. Flanders, *Industrial Relations: What Is Wrong with the System?* (1965); A. Flanders, *Collective Bargaining: Prescription for Change* (1967); PEP, 'Trade Unions in a Changing Society', *Planning*, No. 472 (1963); J. Hughes, *Change in the Trade Unions*, Fabian Research Series 244 (1964); W. E. J. McCarthy, *The Future of the Unions*, Fabian Tract No. 339 (1962); E. Wigham, *What's Wrong with the Unions?* (1961); and the research papers published by the Royal Commission on Trade Unions and Employers' Associations.

The definitive history of British trade unionism is H. A. Clegg *et al.*, *A History of British Trade Unions Since 1889* (vol. 1, 1889-1910 (1964), vol. 2, 1911-1933 (1985)). For the period prior to 1889 see S. and B. Webb, *The History of Trade Unionism* (1920). The most useful short history is H. Pelling, *A History of British Trade Unionism* (1963) (contains an excellent bibliography, including references to the histories of individual unions).

For recent developments, see *In Place of Strife* (Cmnd. 3888/1969); P. Jenkins, *The Battle of Downing Street* (1970); W. E. J. McCarthy and N. D. Ellis, *Management Agreement; An Alternative to the Industrial Relations Act* (1973); H. A. Clegg, *How to Run an Incomes Policy* (1971); the report of the Bullock Committee on Industrial Democracy (Cmnd. 6706/1977); *Trade Union Immunities* (Cmnd. 8128/1981); *Democracy in Trade Unions* (Cmnd. 8778/1973).

For the legal aspects of trade unionism and industrial relations see K. W. Wedderburn, *The Worker and the Law* (1972) (contains a very comprehensive bibliography); C. Grunfeld. *Modern Trade Union Law* (1970); O. Kahn-Freund, *Labour and the Law* (3rd ed., 1984); R. W. Rideout, *Principles of Labour Law* (4th ed., 1983); P. A. Davies, *Labour Law* (2nd ed., 1984).

The most extensive work on trade union government and administration is B. C. Roberts, *Trade Union Government and Administration* (1956). See also: H. A. Clegg *et al.*, *Trade Union Officers* (1961); V. L. Allen, *Power in Trade Unions* (1954); PEP, 'The Structure and Organisation of British Trade Unions', *Planning*, No. 477 (1963); PEP, 'Trade Union Membership', *Planning*, No. 463 (1962); and TUC, *Written Evidence to the Royal* *Commission on Trade Unions and Employers' Associations* (1966). See also K. Coates and T. Topham, *Trade Unions in Britain* (1984) and R. Undy *et al.*, *Change in Trade Unions* (1981).

For the relations between trade unions and the government see: D. F. Macdonald, *The State and the Trade Unions* (1960); V. L. Allen, *Trade Unions and the Government* (1960); and M. Harrison, *Trade Unions and the Labour Party Since 1945* (1960).

Other useful books include: W. E. J. McCarthy, *The Closed Shop* (1964); F. J. Bayliss, *British Wages Councils* (1962); and K. G. J. C. Knowles, *Strikes* (1952); B. Wootton, *The Social Foundations of Wage Policy* (1955); J. Corina, *Incomes Policy—Problems and Prospects*, Institute of Personnel Management (1966), Parts 1 and 2. A. Marsh, *Industrial Relations in Engineering* (1965); E. H. Phelps Brown, *The Growth of Industrial Relations* (1959); H. A. Turner, *Trade Union Growth, Structure and Policy* (1962); R. Hyman, *Strikes* (1972); W. Brown, *Piecework Bargaining* (1973); R. B. Mackenzie and L. C. Hunter, *Pay, Productivity and Collective Bargaining* (1973); E. Batstone, *Working Order* (1984); J. Durcan, *Strikes in Post-War Britain* (1983); W. Daniel and N. Millward, *Workplace Industrial Relations* (1983).

Bibliographies and details of current work on labour history and industrial relations may be found in the *Bulletin* of the Society for the Study of Labour History. Useful articles on various aspects of industrial relations as well as a chronicle of events may be found in the *British Journal of Industrial Relations*. Most of the basic statistics of industrial relations are to be found in the *Ministry of Labour/Employment Gazette*.

XI

THE ECONOMY

Some Landmarks in the British Economy

1 Aug	14	War emergency measures, including temporary increase in Bank Rate to 10%.
Dec	16	Exchange rate pegged at \$4·77 to £.
15 Aug	18	Report of Cunliffe Committee on Currency and Foreign Exchanges (Cd. 9182) recommended eventual return to an effective gold standard at pre-war par value.
20 Mar	19	Withdrawal of official peg from sterling-dollar exchange; exchange rates allowed to fluctuate.
Jan	21	Post-war trade slump. Unemployment exceeded 1 million (it remained above that level until 1939).
28 Apr	25	Return to fixed gold parity, at pre-1914 level (\$4·86 = £1). Britain now on gold bullion standard.
3 May	26	General Strike.
23 Jun	31	Report of Macmillan Committee on Finance and Industry (Cmd. 3897).
24 Jul	31	Report of May Committee on National Expenditure (Cmd. 3920), recommended big cuts in Government expenditure.
21 Sep	31	Gold Standard suspended; sterling on fluctuating rate.
29 Feb	32	Import Duties Act set up Import Duties Advisory Council.
25 Apr	32	Exchange Equalisation Fund established to smooth variations in exchange rates.
30 Jun	32	Bank rate reduced to 2% and held at this level until 1939.
21 Aug	32	Ottawa Agreements on Imperial Preference.
21 Dec	33	Agricultural Marketing Act authorises quota controls on agricultural imports.
21 Dec	34	Special Areas (Development and Improvement) Act recognised problems of distressed areas.
3 Feb	36	Publication of J. M. Keynes, *General Theory of Employment, Money and Interest*.
12 Oct	36	Tripartite Agreement between Britain, France, and the U.S.A. to promote greater exchange stability by inter-Treasury Co-operation.
4 Sep	39	War emergency measures including imposition of exchange control with formal definition of the Sterling Area. Exchange rate fixed at \$4.03 = £1.
21 Aug	41	Start of Lend-Lease.
22 Jul	44	Bretton Woods agreement leading to establishment of International Monetary Fund. (27 Dec 1945).
26 Aug	44	White Paper on Employment Policy (Cmd. 6527) accepts Government responsibility for 'maintenance of a high and stable level of employment'.
21 Aug	45	End of Lend-Lease followed by U.S. and Canadian loans to Britain.
1 Jan	46	Nationalisation of Bank of England.
Feb	47	Fuel Crisis.
5 Jun	47	Gen. Marshall's speech leading to establishment of Marshall Aid (Jul 48) and of Organisation for European Economic Co-operation (Apr 48).
15 Jul	47	Sterling made convertible. Convertibility suspended 20 Aug.
4 Oct	47	Agriculture Act put the policy of agricultural subsidy and protection on a permanent basis.
4 Feb	48	'Wage Freeze' and dividend restraint.
30 Jul	48	Monopolies and Restrictive Practices (Inquiry and Control) Act established Monopolies Commission.
18 Sep	49	Devaluation of £ from \$4·03 to \$2·80.
13 Dec	50	Marshall Aid suspended as no longer necessary.
7 Nov	51	Bank rate increase from 2% to 2½% signals the revival of use of monetary policy. Import liberalisation rescinded to check record dollar drain.
25 Oct	55	Autumn budget following balance-of-payments crisis.
2 Aug	56	Restrictive Trade Practices Act established Restrictive Trade Practices Court.

11 Dec	56	Stand-by credits arranged following post-Suez balance-of-payments crisis.
12 Aug	57	Council on Prices Productivity and Incomes ('Three Wise Men') set up. (Disbanded 1961.)
19 Sep	57	Bank rate raised to 7% to meet sterling crisis.
27 Dec	57	Convertibility announced for non-resident sterling on current account.
20 Aug	59	Report of Radcliffe Committee on the working of the monetary system (Cmnd. 827).
20 Nov	59	European Free Trade Association Treaty signed.
4 Dec	60	O.E.E.C. reconstituted and broadened to include U.S.A. and Canada and retitled O.E.C.D.
20 Jul	61	Plowden Report on Control of Public Expenditure.
25 Jul	61	'Pay Pause' measures of S. Lloyd following balance-of-payments crisis. Establishment of National Economic Development Council.
10 Aug	61	Britain applies to join European Economic Community (negotiations terminated Jan 63).
16 Jul	64	Resale Prices Act greatly limits resale price maintenance.
26 Oct	64	New Government meets balance-of-payments deficit by imposing 15% import surcharge (reduced to 10% in Apr 65 and ended Nov 66).
18 Mar	65	Establishment of Prices and Incomes Board.
5 Aug	65	Monopolies and Mergers Act extended 1948 Monopolies Act to cover services as well as goods.
13 Sep	65	Publication of first National Economic Plan (Cmnd. 2764).
25 Jan	66	Industrial Reorganisation Corporation established to encourage 'concentration and rationalisation and to promote the greater efficiency and international competitiveness of British Industry'. (Cmnd. 2889.)
6 Mar	66	Announcement that Decimal Currency would be adopted in 1971.
20 Jul	66	Sterling crisis leads to Bank rate 7%, tax increases, credit restraints, and prices and incomes standstill (Cmnd. 3073).
12 Aug	66	Prices and Incomes Act becomes law (Part IV actuated 6 Oct 66).
7 Mar	67	First landing of North Sea Gas.
11 May	67	Britain applies (for second time) to join European Economic Community. (De Gaulle gives second veto 27 Nov 67.)
18 Nov	67	Devaluation of £ from \$2·80 to \$2·40. Bank Rate 8%.
19 Jan	68	Major cuts in Government expenditure announced, followed by drastically deflationary Budget 19 Mar.
17 Mar	68	Two-tier gold system announced by World Central Banks.
30 Mar	68	Agreement on Special Drawing Rights in International Monetary Fund.
27 Oct	70	Expenditure cuts of £330m. announced, together with tax cuts.
15 Feb	71	Changeover to decimal currency.
30 Mar	71	Budget announces switch from surtax to graduated tax and to adopt Value Added Tax in 1973.
15 Aug	71	U.S.A. ends dollar-gold convertibility and, thereby, the Bretton Woods era.
23 Aug	71	£ floated.
19 Dec	71	General currency realignment under the Smithsonian agreement.
18 Feb	72	Wilberforce Court of Enquiry (Cmnd. 4903) ends six-week miners' strike with 22% pay increase recommendation.
26 Sep	72	Anti-inflation programme announced including pay and prices freezes and establishment of Prices Commission and Pay Board.
1 Jan	73	Britain joins European Economic Community.
4 Mar	73	European currencies floated against £.
1 Apr	73	Value Added Tax supplants other excise duties and Selective Employment Tax.
6 Oct	73	Outbreak of Middle East War followed by short term cut in Middle East oil supplies and quadrupling of world oil prices.
8 Oct	73	Announcement of 'Phase 3' anti-inflation proposals.
13 Dec	73	Announcement of 3-day week for industry, starting in January, to cope with miners' overtime ban since 12 Nov.
11 Feb	74	Complete mine stoppage until 11 Mar. 3-day week ended 8 Mar.
31 Dec	74	End of year during which retail prices rose by 19% and wage rates by 29% while total industrial production fell by 3% (each figure a post-war record).
30 Jan	75	*Financial Times* Index of leading shares prices touched 252 having been at 146 on 9 Jan 75 and at 339 on 28 Feb 74.
5 Jun	75	Referendum on continued British membership of the EEC. 67·2% vote to stay in Community.
18 Jun	75	First landing of North Sea Oil.
11 Jul	75	Government publishes White Paper, *The Attack on Inflation*, which introduces a universal pay rise limit of £6 per week from 1 Aug 75. (In the year up to June 1975 earnings for manual workers had risen by 33.3%.)
12 Aug	75	Monthly retail price index shows a 26·9% increase in a year—a post-war record.

20 Nov	75	Announcement that cash limits will be applied to most public expenditure in the financial year 1976/7.
19 Feb	76	Public expenditure White Paper published, showing cuts in spending of £1·0 billion in 1977/8 and £2·4 billion in 1978/9 compared with previous plans.
2 Mar	76	Sterling falls below $2 for first time.
6 Apr	76	In Budget £1·3 billion tax cuts are announced but made dependent on agreement by the T.U.C. to a new low pay norm in Stage 2. 4½% pay formula agreed on 5 May and endorsed at special T.U.C. meeting on 16 Jun.
22 Jul	76	Announcement of further £1,000m. cut in public expenditure in 1977/8.
29 Sep	76	Government approaches IMF for a $3·9 billion stand-by credit.
7 Oct	76	Minimum Lending Rate increased to 15%.
28 Oct	76	Sterling closes at $1·5675—its lowest ever.
15 Dec	76	A further cut in public expenditure of £1,000m. in 1977/8 and £1,500m. in 1978/9 is announced as part of the agreement with the IMF.
11 Aug	77	Unemployment reaches peak of 1,635,800.
7 Sep	77	T.U.C. supports 12-month rule for Stage 3. Government continues to seek voluntary 10% limit on earnings increases.
4 Jan	78	U.K. official reserves rise to $20·6 billion—the highest ever.
5 Jan	78	U.S. Treasury announces it will intervene in foreign exchange markets to halt decline in dollar.
17 Feb	78	Inflation (year on year) falls below 10% for first time since 1973.
12 Mar	79	European Monetary system starts.
12 Jun	79	New Conservative Government's budget cuts income tax from 33% to 30% and raises VAT from 8% to 15%.
24 Oct	79	Abolition of exchange controls.
15 Nov	79	Minimum lending rate touches 17%.
26 Mar	80	Announcement of Medium Term Financial Strategy (MFTS).
Jun	80	Britain becomes net exporter of oil.
2 Jun	80	Agreement on reduction of Britain's EEC budget contribution.
21 Nov	80	Youth Opportunities Programme doubled.
Oct	80	£ reaches peak exchange with $ (2.39).
Jan	81	Bottom of worst post-war slump for Britain.
20 Aug	81	Minimum lending rate abolished.
27 Jul	82	Hire purchase controls abolished.
9 Sep	82	Unemployment reaches three million.
13 Mar	84	Beginning of miners' strike.
26 Jun	84	Fontainebleau summit agrees permanent settlement of Britain's EEC contribution.
28 Nov	84	Government sells 33% of British Telecom.
3 Dec	84	Br Telecom Shares (sold in Nov) gain 45% premium in first Stock Exchange dealings.
19 Dec	84	Hong Kong Agreement for 1997 handover.
4 Mar	85	End of year-long miners' strike (26.1m. days lost).
7 Mar	85	£ touches bottom level of $1.05.

SOURCES.—A. Shonfield, *British Economic Policy since the War* (1958); J. C. R. Dow, *The Management of the British Economy 1945-60* (1964); A. C. Pigou, *Aspects of British Economic History 1918-1925* (1948); E. V. Morgan, *Studies in British Financial Policy 1914-1925*; S. Brittan, *Steering the Economy* (1971); R. S. Sayers, 'Co-operation between Central Banks', *The Three Banks Review* (Sep 1963); R. S. Sayers, *Central Banking after Bagehot* (1959). Since 1960 an economic chronology has been provided in successive issues of the *National Institute Economic Review*.

Sources of Government Economic Advice

The Treasury and, from 1964-69, the Department of Economic Affairs have provided governments with their main official guidance (see p. 262 for Permanent Secretaries). In addition, under the Cabinet Office or the Treasury, there have been the following official economic advisers.

Economic Section of the Cabinet Office (1941-53)

Director

1941	J. Jewkes	1946	J. Meade
1941	L. Robbins	1947	R. Hall

Economic Adviser to the Government (1953-64)

1953	(Sir) R. Hall	1961	A. Cairncross

Head of Government Economic Service (1964-)

1964	(Sir) A. Cairncross	1974	Sir B. Hopkin
1969	Sir D. MacDougall	1976	Sir A. Atkinson
1973	Sir K. Berrill	1980	(Sir) T. Burns

Outside the Civil Service there have been the following official bodies:

Bank of England (1696-)
Governor

1899	S. Gladstone	1920	M. Norman (Ld)
1901	(Sir) A. Prevost	1944	Ld Catto
1903	S. Morley	1949	C. Cobbold (Ld)
1905	A. Wallace	1964	E of Cromer
1908	R. Johnston	1966	(Sir) L. O'Brien (Ld)
1913	W. Cunliffe (Ld)	1973	G. Richardson (Ld)
1918	Sir B. Cokayne (Ld Cullen of Ashbourne)	1983	R. Leigh-Pemberton

Economic Advisory Council (1930-39)

(No full meeting of this body was held after the first year, but until 1939 its Standing Committee on Economic Information was active under Sir J. Stamp (Ld).)

Import Duties Advisory Council (1932-39)
Chairman

1932 Sir F. May (Ld)

Economic Planning Board (1947-62)
Chairman

1947-53 Sir E. Plowden

(After 1953, when some of its functions were merged with the Economic Section of the Treasury, the Permanent Secretary of the Treasury was made *ex officio* Chairman of the Board of outside advisers.)

National Economic Development Council (1961-)
Director-General of National Economic Development Office

1962	Sir R. Shone	1973	(Sir) R. McIntosh
1966	(Sir) F. Catherwood	1983	J. Cassels
1966	Sir F. Figgures		

Council on Pay, Productivity, and Incomes (1957-61)
Chairman

1957	Ld Cohen	1960	Ld Heyworth

National Incomes Commission (1961-64)
Chairman

1962 Sir G. Lawrence

Prices and Incomes Board (1965-70)
Chairman

1965 A. Jones

Prices Commission (1973-79)
Chairman

1973	Sir A. Cockfield	1976	C. Williams

Pay Board (1973-74)
Chairman
1973 Sir F. Figgures

Industrial Adviser to the Government (1974-75)
1974 Sir D. Ryder (Ld)

Commission on Pay Comparability (1979-80)
Chairman
H. Clegg

(See also Monopolies Commission, p. 288; Royal Commissions and Committees of Inquiry, pp. 268-71; Central Policy Review Staff, p. 257.)

Economic Interest Groups

Industrial and Commercial Organisations

Federation of British Industry (1916-1965)

President

1916 F. Docker
1917 Sir R. Vassar-Smith
1918 Sir V. Gaillard
1919 Sir P. Rylands
1921 O. Armstrong
1923 Sir E. Geddes
1925 V. Willey
1927 Sir M. Muspratt
1928 Ld Ebbisham
1929 L. Lee
1930 Sir J. Lithgow
1931 Sir A. Duckham
1932 Sir G. Beharrell
1933 Sir G. Macdonough
1934 Ld H. Scott
1935 Sir F. Joseph
1936 Ld Hirst
1937 (Sir) P. Bennett
1940 Ld D. Gordon
1943 Sir G. Nelson
1945 Sir C. Ballieu
1947 Sir F. Bain
1949 Sir R. Sinclair
1951 Sir A. Forbes
1953 Sir H. Pilkington
1955 Sir G. Hayman
1957 Sir H. Beaver
1959 Sir W. MacFadzean
1961 Sir C. Harrison
1963 Sir P. Runge

Director

1916 R. Nugent
1917 E. Hill
1919 (Sir) R. Nugent
1932 (Sir) G. Locock
1946 (Sir) N. Kipping

Confederation of British Industry (1965)

Formed by a merger of the Federation of British Industries (FBI) (founded 1916), the National Association of British manufacturers (1915) and the British Employers Confederation (1919). It held its first Annual Conference at Brighton 13-15 Nov 77.

President

1965 Sir M. Laing
1966 Sir S. Brown
1968 Sir A. Norman
1970 Sir J. Partridge
1972 Sir M. Clapham
1974 Sir R. Bateman
1976 Vt Watkinson
1978 Sir J. Greenborough
1980 Sir R. Pennock
1982 Sir C. Fraser
1984 Sir J. Cleminson

Director-General

1965 J. Davies
1969 (Sir) C. Adamson
1976 (Sir) J. Methven
1980 Sir T. Beckett

Economic Pressure Groups

Adam Smith Institute (1977)
Aims of Industry (1942)
Association of British Chambers of Commerce (1860)
British Institute of Management (1947)
Building Societies Association (1860)
Free Trade League (1873)
National Chamber of Trade (1897)
National Farmers' Union (1908)
Tariff Reform League (1903)
Trades Union Congress (1868) (see p. 361)

Consumer Organisations

(a) **Official**

Consumer Council (1963-1970). Director 1963: (Dame) E. Ackroyd.
Office of Fair Trading (1973-). Director General: 1973 J. Methven; 1977 (Sir) G. Borrie.
National Consumer Council (1975-). Director: 1975 A. Kershaw; 1975 J. Hosker; 1975- J. Mitchell.

In 1972 Sir G. Howe was appointed Minister for Trade and Consumer Affairs in the Department of Trade and Industry, but with a seat in the Cabinet.

In 1974 the Department of Prices and Consumer Protection was established. (Secretaries of State: 1974, Mrs S. Williams; 1976, R. Hattersley) but in 1979 it was absorbed into the Department of Trade.

(b) **Unofficial**

Consumers' Association (1956-)

Select Statistics

	Net National Income (at factor cost)[a] (£m.)	Income Tax (Standard Rate in £)	Amount Retained of Bachelor's £10,000 earned income after Income Tax and Surtax	Wholesale Price Index Number (1963 = 100)	Retail Price Index Number (1963 = 100)	Purchasing Power of £ (1900 = 20/-)	Real gross domestic product per head (1963 = 100)
	1	2	3	4	5	6	7
1900	1,750	8	9,667	22	19	20/-	53
1901	1,727	1/-	9,500	21	19	19/9	54
1902	1,740	1/2	9,417	21	19	19/7	54
1903	1,717	1/3	9,375	21	19	19/4	52
1904	1,704	11	9,542	22	19	19/1	52
1905	1,776	1/-	9,500	21	19	19/4	53
1906	1,874	1/-	9,500	22	19	19/4	53
1907	1,966	1/-	9,500	23	20	18/8	53
1908	1,875	1/-	9,500	23	20	18/4	49
1909	1,907	1/-	9,500	23	20	18/4	51
1910	1,984	1/2	9,242	24	20	18/1	52

	Net National Income (at factor cost)[a] (£m.)	Income Tax (Standard Rate in £)	Amount Retained of Bachelor's £10,000 earned income after Income Tax and Surtax	Wholesale Price Index Number (1963 = 100)	Retail Price Index Number (1963 = 100)	Purchasing Power of £ (1900 = 20/-)	Real gross domestic product per head (1963 = 100)
	1	2	3	4	5	6	7
1911	2,076	1/2	9,242	24	21	17/11	53
1912	2,181	1/2	9,242	25	21	17/3	53
1913	2,265	1/2	9,242	26	21	17/3	54
1914	2,209	1/2	9,242	26	21	17/5	54
1915	(2,591)	1/8	8,669	31	26	14/2	. .
1916	(3,064)	3/-	7,721	41	30	11/11	. .
1917	(3,631)	5/-	6,721	53	37	9/11	. .
1918	(4,372)	5/-	6,721	59	42	8/7	. .
1919	(5,461)	6/-	5,813	66	46	8/1	. .
1920	5,664	6/-	5,813	79	52	7/-	. .
1921	4,460	6/-	5,672	50	47	7/8	48
1922	3,856	6/-	5,672	41	38	9/6	48
1923	3,844	5/-	6,150	41	37	10/-	49
1924	3,919	4/6	6,389	43	37	9/11	49
1925	3,980	4/6	6,389	41	37	9/11	54
1926	3,914	4/-	6,968	38	36	10/1	50
1927	4,145	4/-	6,968	36	35	10/5	54
1928	4,154	4/-	6,968	36	35	10/6	56
1929	4,178	4/-	6,968	35	35	10/7	57
1930	3,957	4/-	6,968	30	33	11/-	56
1931	3,666	4/6	6,487	27	31	11/10	52
1932	3,568	5/-	6,103	26	30	12/1	52
1933	3,728	5/-	6,103	26	30	12/5	52
1934	3,881	5/-	6,103	27	30	12/4	56
1935	4,109	4/6	6,340	27	30	12/2	59
1936	4,388	4/6	6,341	29	31	11/10	60
1937	4,616	4/9	6,222	33	32	11/4	63
1938	4,671	5/-	6,103	30	33	11/2	65
1939	5,037	5/6	5,867	31	34	10/10	. .
1940	5,980	7/-	4,965	42	38	8/11	. .
1941	6,941	8/6	3,921	47	42	8/-	. .
1942	7,664	10/-	3,138	48	45	7/5	. .
1943	8,171	10/-	3,138	50	47	7/2	. .
1944	8,366	10/-	3,138	51	47	7/-	. .
1945	8,340	10/-	3,138	53	49	6/10	. .
1946	7,974	10/-	3,138	58	51	6/7	. .
1947	8,587	9/-	3,637	67	54	6/2	. .
				. . . .			
1948	9,669	9/-	3,501	63	57	5/9	72
1949	10,240	9/-	3,587	66	59	5/7	73
1950	10,784	9/-	3,587	71	61	5/5	75
1951	11,857	9/-	3,598	80	67	5/-	78
1952	12,763	9/6	3,361	84	73	4/8	78
1953	13,766	9/6	3,411	84	75	4/8	81
1954	14,573	9/-	3,646	83	76	4/7	84
1955	15,511	9/-	3,646	86	80	4/5	86

	Net National Income (at factor cost)[a] (£m.)	Income Tax (Standard Rate in £)	Amount Retained of Bachelor's £10,000 earned income after Income Tax and Surtax	Wholesale Price Index Number (1963 = 100)	Retail Price Index Number (1963 = 100)	Purchasing Power of £ (1900 = 20/-)	Real gross domestic product per head (1963 = 100)
	1	2	3	4	5	6	7
1956	16,861	8/6	3,873	89	84	4/2	87
1957	17,863	8/6	3,873	92	87	4/1	89
1958	18,615	8/6	4,341	93	90	4/-	88
1959	19,559	8/6	4,341	93	90	4/-	90
1960	20,809	7/9	4,648	94	91	3/11	94
1961	22,268	7/9	4,648	97	94	3/10	97
1962	23,267	7/9	4,648	99	98	3/8	97
1963	24,810	7/9	4,648	100	100	3/7	100
1964	26,953	7/9	4,845	103	103	3/6	105
1965	28,807	8/3	5,922	107	108	3/5	107
1966	30,423	8/3	5,922	110	112	3/3	108
1967	32,037	8/3	5,715	111	115	3/2	111
1968	34,177	8/3	5,715	115	121	3/-	114
1969	36,056	8/3	5,715	120	127	2/10	116
1970	39,567	7/9	5,715	128	135	2/8	118
1971	44,674	38·75%	6,188	140	148	12½p	121
1972	49,984	38·75%	6,141	147	159	11½p	122
1973	58,588	30%	6,377	158	173	10½p	130
1974	67,379	33%	6,088	195	201	9p	129
1975	83,958	35%	5,930	242	250	7½p	127
1976	99,504	35%	5,966	281	291	6½p	132
1977	111,285	34%	6,580	335	337	5½p	134
1978	128,001	33%	7,013	365	365	5p	138
1979	146,586	30%	7,387	. .	414	4½p	141
1980	167,042	30%	7,413	. .	488	3½p	138
1981	181,179	30%	7,413	. .	546	3½p	137
1982	202,509	30%	7,470	. .	593	3p	139
1983	222,947	30%	7,536	. .	621	3p	143
1984	. .	30%	7,602	. .	647[b]	3p	145

[a] Changes in sources at 1914 and 1947.

[b] Average for first nine months.

SOURCES.—

1. 1900-14, C. H. Feinstein, 'Income and Investment in the U.K. 1856-1914', *Economic Journal*, June 1961. 1914-46, A. R. Prest, 'National Income of the U.K. 1870-1946', *Economic Journal*, March 1948. 1947 onwards, *National Income and Expenditure* Annual Blue Books.
2. *Reports of the Commissioners for Inland Revenue.*
3. *Reports of the Commissioners for Inland Revenue* and information received from the Inland Revenue.
4 and 5. *The British Economy: Key Statistics 1900-1970* and *Annual Abstract of Statistics.*
6. 1900-14 based on unofficial price index compiled by G. H. Wood, in W. T. Layton and G. Crowther, *An Introduction to the Study of Prices* (1938); 1914-38 based on Ministry of Labour *Cost of Living Index* (*Min. of Labour Gazette*); 1938 onwards based on figures in *Annual Abstract of Statistics.*
7. Based on *The British Economy: Key Statistics 1900-1970* and *Economic Trends.*

	Index Number of Industrial Production (1963 = 100)	Steel Production[a] ('000 tons)	Coal Production[b] (million tons)	Raw Cotton Consumption[c] U.K. (million lbs.)	Agriculture			Price of 2½% Consols (Average for year)	Bank Rate % (Maximum and Minimum for year)
					Cultivated Areas[d] ('000 acres)	Agricultural Output[e] (1963 = 100)	Employment in Agriculture[e] ('000)		
	1	2	3	4	5	6	7	8	9
1900	27	4,900	225	1,737	47,795	52	2,243	99·6	6 3
1901	27	4,900	219	1,569	47,761	52	. .	94·3	5 3
1902	28	4,910	227	1,633	47,753	53	. .	94·4	4 3
1903	28	5,030	230	1,617	47,708	52	. .	90·8	4 3
1904	28	5,030	232	1,486	47,671	52	. .	88·3	4 3
1905	28	5,810	236	1,813	47,673	54	. .	89·8	3 2½
1906	29	6,460	251	1,855	47,193	54	. .	88·3	6 3½
1907	30	6,520	268	1,985	46,998	53	. .	84·1	7 4
1908	28	5,290	262	1,917	47,002	53	. .	86·0	7 2½
1909	29	5,880	264	1,824	46,888	55	. .	83·9	5 2½
1910	29	6,370	264	1,632	46,932	56	. .	81·1	5 3
1911	30	6,460	272	1,892	46,927	54	2,205	79·3	4½ 3
1912	31	6,800	260	2,142	46,794	55	. .	76·2	5 3
1913	33	7,664	287	2,178	46,741	56	. .	73·6	5 4½
1914	31	7,835	266	2,077	46,643	54	. .	74·8	10 3
1915	. .	8,550	253	1,931	46,554	. .	. .	65·5	5
1916	. .	8,992	256	1,972	46,564	. .	. .	58·0	6 5
1917	. .	9,717	249	1,800	46,212	. .	. .	54·7	6 5
1918	. .	9,539	228	1,499	46,142	. .	. .	56·9	5
1919	30	7,894	230	1,526	46,206	51	. .	54·1	6 5
1920	33	9,067	230	1,726	45,953	49	1,553	47·0	7 6
1921	27	3,703	163	1,066	45,581	50	1,488	48·0	7 5
1922	31	5,801	250	1,409	45,458	50	1,453	56·5	5 3
					. . . .				
1923	33	8,482	276	1,362	33,106	52	1,415	58·0	4 3
1924	36	8,201	267	1,369	33,057	50	1,423	57·0	4
1925	38	7,385	243	1,609	32,920	53	1,420	56·3	5 4
1926	36	3,596	126	1,509	32,830	55	1,407	55·0	5
1927	41	9,097	251	1,557	32,724	55	1,389	54·8	5 4½
1928	40	8,520	238	1,520	32,617	58	1,380	55·9	4½
1929	42	9,636	258	1,498	32,547	58	1,372	54·3	6 4½
1930	40	7,326	244	1,272	32,459	60	1,340	55·8	5 3
1931	38	5,203	220	985	32,374	54	1,312	56·9	6 2½
1932	37	5,261	209	1,257	32,284	57	1,300	66·8	6 2
1933	46	7,024	207	1,177	32,193	62	1,296	73·7	2
1934	44	8,850	221	1,322	32,096	62	1,279	80·6	2
1935	47	9,859	222	1,261	32,024	60	1,260	86·6	2
1936	52	11,785	228	1,366	31,932	60	1,232	85·1	2
1937	55	12,984	240	1,431	31,827	59	1,213	76·3	2
1938	53	10,398	227	1,109	31,755	58	1,180	74·1	2
1939	. .	13,221	231	1,317	31,679	. .	1,168	67·2	4 2
1940	. .	12,975	224	1,389	31,430	. .	1,128	73·5	2
1941	. .	12,312	206	965	31,353	. .	1,177	80·0	2
1942	. .	12,942	205	939	31,204	. .	1,192	82·6	2
1943	. .	13,031	199	885	31,058	. .	1,235	80·7	2
1944	. .	12,142	193	804	31,008	. .	1,226	79·6	2
1945	. .	11,824	183	717	31,023	. .	1,207	85·5	2

	Index Number of Industrial Production (1963 = 100)	Steel Production[a] ('000 tons)	Coal Production[b] (million tons)	Raw Cotton Consumption[c] U.K. (million lbs.)	Agriculture: Cultivated Areas[d] ('000 acres)	Agriculture: Agricultural Output[e] (1963 = 100)	Agriculture: Employment in Agriculture[e] ('000)	Price of 2½% Consols (Average for year)	Bank Rate[f] % (Maximum and Minimum for year)
	1	2	3	4	5	6	7	8	9
1946	55	12,695	190	813	31,010	65	1,240	96·3	2
1947	58	12,725	197	815	31,022	62	1,231	90·7	2
1948	62	14,877	209	977	31,062	67	1,274	78·0	2
1949	66	15,553	215	979	31,056	72	1,274	75·9	2
1950	70	16,293	216	1,017	31,126	73	1,258	70·5	2
1951	72	15,639	223	1,024	31,131	75	1,232	66·1	2½ 2
1952	71	16,418	227	686	31,163	77	1,203	59·1	4 2½
1953	75	17,609	224	831	31,177	79	1,177	61·3	4 3½
1954	79	18,520	224	892	31,128	81	1,164	66·6	3½ 3
1955	83	19,791	222	778	31,103	80	1,155	60·0	4½ 3
1956	83	20,659	222	714	31,092	84	1,121	52·8	5½ 4½
1957	85	21,699	224	744	31,030	86	1,111	50·2	7 5½
				. . . .					
1958	84	19,566	216	628	31,001	84	1,091	50·2	7 4
1959	88	20,186	206	623	30,873	87	1,044	51·8	4
1960	95	24,305	194	599	30,854	93	1,017	46·1	6 4
1961	96	22,086	192	536	30,637	93	985	46·1	7 5
1962	97	20,491	199	473	30,655	96	951	407	6 4½
1963	100	22,520	197	483	30,644	100	929	44·8	4½ 4
1964	108	26,230	195	508	30,686	104	890	41·5	7 4
1965	112	27,006	187	492	30,660	107	846	39·0	7 6
1966	114	24,315	175	454	30,683	106	814	36·7	7 6
1967	115	23,895	175	384	30,653	110	789	37·4	8 5½
1968	122	25,862	167	382	30,437	109	757	33·8	8 7
1969	125	26,422	153	376	30,291	110	727	28·2	8 7
1970	125	27,868	145	366	30,005	116	707	27·3	7½ 7
1971	126	23,792	147	316	30,029	123	. .	27·6	7 5
1972	128	24,921	120	291	29,978	126	709	27·5	9 5
1973	138	26,228	130	278	29,848	130	713	23·2	13 7½
1974	133	22,072	109	245	29,835	131	681	16·8	13 11½
1975	126	19,879	127	218	29,722	119	664	17·1	11¾ 9¾
1976	129	21,922	122	249	29,789	110	660	17·6	15 9
1977	134	20,088	120	212	29,628	130	658	20·4	14¼ 5
1978	139	19,989	122	184	29,702	138	366	21.0	12½ 6½
1979	144	21,125	121	192	29,751	137	350	22.1	17 12
1980	135	11,077	128	138	30,031	151	345	21.1	17 14
1981	128	15,327	125	92	29,904	152	334	19.3	16 12
1982	131	13,488	122	90	29,900	167	331	21.4	14½ 9
1983	134	14,986	116	90	29,824	159	326	24.5	11 9
1984	135	. .	. .	. .	. .	. .	. .	. .	12 8½

. . . . Change in basis of calculation.

[a] Great Britain only. [b] including S. Ireland, 1900-21 inclusive.

[c] From 1958 a revised bale weight was used in calculations.

[d] Total area under all crops and grass. For Great Britain excluding all holdings under one acre before 1970, for N. Ireland excluding all holdings under ¼ acre until 1953, and under one acre from 1954 to 1972.

[e] Includes forestry and fishing. From 1978 onwards the figures include only employees and not farmers themselves.

[f] Minimum Lending Rate from 13 Oct 1972.

SOURCES.—

1. *The British Economy, Key Statistics 1900-1970* and *Annual Abstract of Statistics.*
2. British Iron and Steel Federation, *Annual Abstract of Statistics.*
3. Ministry of Power, *Annual Abstract of Statistics.*
4. R. Robson, *The Cotton Industry in Britain* (1957), p. 332. Statistics table, 1, and information supplied by the Cotton Board.
5. Figures for June each year, 1900-13 including Isle of Man and Channel Islands. 1914 onwards excluding Isle of Man and Channel Islands. 1900-22 including S. Ireland. *Annual Abstract of Statistics*, Agriculture Department.

6 and 7. *The British Economy, Key Statistics 1900-1970* and *Annual Abstract of Statistics.* 1972 onwards *Economic Trends.*

8 and 9. Bank of England and *Annual Abstract of Statistics.*

	Net Balance of Payments of the U.K. on current account[a] (£m.)	Terms of Trade[b] Index No. (1963 = 100)	Imports and Exports of the U.K.			Imports and Exports of the U.K. Volume Indices		Foreign Exchange Rates		
			Imports[c] c.i.f. (£m.)	Exports of U.K. Products[c] f.o.b. (£m.)	Re-exports f.o.b. (£m.)	Imports[d]	Exports[d]	U.S.A. ($ to £)	France (Francs to £)	Germany (Marks to £)
	1	2	3	4	5	6	7	8	9	10
1900		72	523	291	63	48	44	4·84	25·1	20·4
1901		71	522	280	68	49	44	4·85	25·2	20·4
1902		69	528	283	66	51	47	4·85	25·2	20·5
1903		67	543	291	70	51	48	4·85	25·1	20·4
1904		69	551	301	70	52	49	4·85	25·2	20·4
1905		68	565	330	78	53	54	4·85	25·2	20·5
1906		68	608	376	85	54	58	4·82	25·1	20·5
1907		68	646	426	92	55	63	4·84	25·1	20·5
1908		69	593	377	80	53	58	4·85	25·1	20·4
1909		65	625	378	91	54	60	4·86	25·2	20·4
1910		65	678	430	104	56	65	4·84	25·2	20·4
1911		67	680	454	103	57	68	4·84	25·3	20·4
1912		66	745	487	112	61	72	4·85	25·2	20·5
1913	237	69	769	525	110	64	75	4·83	25·2	20·4
1914		. .	697	431	95	. .	. .	4·87	25·2	20·5
1915		. .	852	385	99	. .	. .	4·77	26·3	. .
1916		. .	949	506	98	. .	. .	4·76	28·2	. .
1917		. .	1,064	527	70	. .	. .	4·76	27·4	. .
1918		. .	1,316	501	31	. .	. .	4·76	27·2	. .
1919	−128	79	1,626	799	165	56	41	4·60	29·7	. .
1920	235	86	1,933	1,334	223	56	53	3·97	47·9	145
1921	119	87	1,086	703	107	47	37	3·73	46·7	268
1922	173	90	1,003	720	104	54	51	4·41	52·8	1,654
			. . . .	. . . .	. . . .					
1923	169	89	1,096	767	119	59	56	4·58	75·2	720,000
1924	72	86	1,277	801	140	66	57	4·33	81·8	18 billion
1925	46	85	1,321	773	154	69	56	4·86	106·1	20·4
1926	−15	87	1,241	653	125	70	50	4·87	167·5	20·4
1927	82	86	1,218	709	123	72	58	4·85	124·0	20·5
1928	123	82	1,196	724	120	69	60	4·87	124·2	20·4
1929	103	85	1,221	729	110	73	61	4·84	124·0	20·4
1930	28	92	1,044	571	87	71	50	4·86	123·7	20·4
1931	−104	102	861	391	64	72	38	4·86	124·2	20·5
1932	−51	102	702	365	51	63	38	3·58	91·1	15·0
1933	—	104	675	368	49	63	39	4·30	86·2	14·3
1934	−77	103	731	396	51	66	41	5·04	76·6	13·3
1935	32	100	756	426	55	67	45	4·94	74·5	12·2

	Net Balance of Payments of the U.K. on current account[a] (£m.)	Terms of Trade[b] No. (1963 = 100)	Imports and Exports of the U.K.			Imports and Exports of the U.K. Volume Indices		Foreign Exchange Rates		
			Imports[c] c.i.f. (£m.)	Exports of U.K. Products[e] f.o.b. (£m.)	Re-exports[c] f.o.b. (£m.)	Imports[d] (1963 = 100)	Exports[d] (1963 = 100)	U.S.A. ($ to £)	France (Francs to £)	Germany (Marks to £)
	1	2	3	4	5	6	7	8	9	10
1936	−18	99	848	441	61	72	45	5·01	75·7	12·4
1937	−56	93	1,028	521	75	76	49	4·94	120	12·3
	. . . .									
1938	−70	102	920	471	62	72	43	4·95	178	12·3
1939	−250	99	886	440	46	69	40	4·68	177	11·7
1940	−804	85	1,152	411	26	61	31	4·03	177	. .
1941	−816	93	1,145	365	13	50	21	4·03	. .	. .
1942	−663	94	997	271	5	47	16	4·03	. .	. .
1943	−680	94	1,234	234	6	50	12	4·03	. .	. .
1944	−659	100	1,309	266	16	54	13	4·03	. .	. .
1945	−875	94	1,104	399	51	44	20	4·03	203·8	. .
1946	−230	95	1,298	912	50	49	43	4·03	480·0	. .
1947	−381	88	1,798	1,142	59	55	47	4·03	480·0	. .
1948	26	85	2,075	1,578	61	57	60	4·03	[f]	. .
1949	−1	86	2,279	1,789	58	61	66	[e]	[g]	. .
1950	307	80	2,609	2,174	85	61	75	2·80	980·0	. .
1951	−369	73	3,905	2,582	127	69	74	2·80	979·7	. .
1952	163	80	3,456	2,567	142	63	69	2·79	981·5	West Germany only
1953	145	87	3,328	2,558	103	68	71	2·81	982·8	11·7
1954	117	87	3,359	2,650	98	69	74	2·81	981·6	11·7
1955	−155	84	3,861	2,877	116	76	80	2·79	978·1	11·7
1956	208	86	3,862	3,143	144	75	84	2·80	982·7	11·7
1957	233	87	4,044	3,295	130	78	86	2·79	[h]	11·7
1958	346	95	3,748	3,176	141	79	83	2·81	[i]	11·7
1959	158	97	3,983	3,330	131	84	86	2·81	13·77[j]	11·7
1960	−244	97	4,557	3,536	141	94	90	2·81	13·77	11·7
1961	27	99	4,398	3,682	158	93	93	2·80	13·74	11·17
1962	130	101	4,492	3,792	158	96	95	2·81	13·76	11·22
1963	129	100	4,820	4,080	154	100	100	2·80	13·72	11·16
1964	−358	99	5,696	4,412	153	111	103	2·79	13·68	11·10
1965	−45	101	5,751	4,724	173	111	108	2·80	13·70	11·17
1966	109	103	5,949	5,047	194	114	112	2·79	13·72	11·17
1967	−294	104	6,437	5,029	185	123	111	2·79[k]	13·68[l]	11·10[m]
1968	−286	101	7,897	6,182	220	136	126	2·39	11·86	9·56
1969	463	101	8,315	7,039	259	138	140	2·39	12·43[n]	9·38
1970	731	103	9,051	7,741	323	144	143	2·40	13·24	8·74
1971	1,090	104	9,799	9,071		153	154	2·44	13·47	8·61
1972	135	106	11,073	9,602		171	154	2·50	12·61	7·97
1973	−979	93	15,724	12,087		195	175	2·45	10·90	6·54
1974	−3,278	81	23,139	16,309		196	187	2·34	11·25	6·05
1975	−1,523	87	24,046	19,607		179	180	2·22	9·50	5·45
1976	−846	85	31,084	25,277		190	197	1·80	8·61	4·55
1977	53	87	36,219	31,990		193	213	1·75	8·57	4·05
1978	1,162	92	39,533	35,330		202	218	1·92	8·65	3·85
1979	−525	96	46,925	40,637		224	229	2·12	9·03	3·89
1980	3,629	100	49,773	47,364		212	231	2·33	9·83	4·23

	Net Balance of Payments of the U.K. on current account[a] (£m.)	Terms of Trade[b] No. (1963 = 100)	Imports and Exports of the U.K.			Imports and Exports of the U.K. Volume Indices		Foreign Exchange Rates		
			Imports[c] c.i.f. (£m.)	Exports of U.K. Products[c] f.o.b. (£m.)	Re-exports[c] f.o.b. (£m.)	Imports[d] (1963 = 100)	Exports[d] (1963 = 100)	U.S.A. ($ to £)	France (Francs to £)	Germany (Marks to £)
	1	2	3	4	5	6	7	8	9	10
1981	7,221	100	51,169	50,998		204	229	2·03	10·94	4·56
1982	5,206	99	56,978	55,558		213	234	1·75	11·48	4·24
1983	2,916	98	66,101	60,684		228	236	1·52	11·55	3·87
1984	51	97	78,705	70,511		245	255	1·34	11·54	3·79

. . . . Change in basis of calculation.

[a] Changes in sources and methods in 1924.
[b] Export price index as a percentage of the import price index. A fall indicates an adverse movement.
[c] 1900-22 inclusive, S. Ireland is included. From 1923 direct foreign trade of S. Ireland is excluded, and Imports and Exports include trade of Great Britain and N. Ireland with S. Ireland. There are small changes in coverage from time to time.
[d] 1900-23 inclusive, including S. Ireland.
[e] 4·03 to 19 Sep, 2·80 thereafter:
[f] 480 to 25 Jan, 864 from 26 Jan to 17 Oct, 1,062 thereafter.
[g] 1,062 to 26 Apr, 1,097 from 27 Apr to 20 Sep, 980 therafter.
[h] 984·9 to 19 Aug, 1,117·1 thereafter.
[i] 1,775·5 to 24 Dec, 13·74 from 29 Dec (in units of 100 francs).
[j] In units of 100 francs (100 francs = 1 New Franc).
[k] 2·79 to 18 Nov, 2·40 thereafter.
[l] 13·68 to 18 Nov, 11·88 thereafter.
[m] 11·10 to 18 Nov, 9·50 thereafter.
[n] 11·86 to 11 Aug., 13·31 thereafter.

SOURCES.—

1. *Key Statistics* and *Balance of Payments Pink Books*.
2. *The British Economy, Key Statistics 1900-70*.
3, 4, and 5. *Trade and Navigation Accounts of the U.K.*, Board of Trade, annually. From 1965 *Overseas Trade Accounts of the U.K.*
6 and 7. *The British Economy, Key Statistics 1900-1970*.
8, 9, 10. 1900-39, *The Economist*, figures for the end of June; 1940-1970 *Annual Abstract of Statistics*. 1970– *Financial Statistics:* Figures are average for the year.

	Total Central Government Revenue[a] (£m.)	Main Sources of Revenue				
		Income tax[b] (£m.)	Surtax (£m.)	Profits Tax (£m.)	Customs and Excise (£m.)	Death Duties (£m.)
	1	2	3	4	5	6
1900	140	28	. .	. .	65	17
1901	153	35	. .	. .	68	19
1902	161	39	. .	. .	72	18
1903	151	31	. .	. .	71	17
1904	153	31	. .	. .	72	17
1905	154	31	. .	. .	70	17
1906	155	31	. .	. .	69	19
1907	157	31	. .	. .	68	19
1908	152	34	. .	. .	63	18
1909	132	13	. .	. .	61	22
1910	204	60	3	. .	73	25
1911	185	42	3	. .	72	25
1912	189	41	4	. .	71	25
1913	198	44	3	. .	85	27
1914	227	59	10	. .	81	28
1915	337	112	17	. .	121	31
1916	573	186	19	140	127	31
1917	707	216	23	220	110	32
1918	889	256	36	285	162	30
1919	1,340	317	42	290	283	41
1920	1,426	339	55	220	334	48

	Total Central Government Revenue[a] (£m.)	Main Sources of Revenue				
		Income tax[b] (£m.)	Surtax (£m.)	Profits Tax (£m.)	Customs and Excise (£m.)	Death Duties (£m.)
	1	2	3	4	5	6
1921	1,125	337	62	48	324	52
1922	914	315	64	21	280	57
1923	837	269	61	23	268	58
1924	799	274	63	19	234	59
1925	812	259	69	14	238	61
1926	806	235	66	8	240	67
1927	843	251	61	2	251	77
1928	836	238	56	2	253	81
1929	815	238	56	2	247	80
1930	858	256	68	3	245	83
1931	851	287	77	2	256	65
1932	827	252	61	2	288	77
1933	809	229	53	2	286	85
1934	805	229	51	2	290	81
1935	845	238	51	1	303	88
1936	897	257	54	1	321	88
1937	949	298	57	1	335	89
1938	1,006	336	63	22	340	77
1939	1,132	390	70	27	400	78
1940	1,495	524	76	96	529	81
1941	2,175	770	75	269	704	91
1942	2,922	1,007	75	378	885	93
1943	3,149	1,184	76	500	1,043	100
1944	3,355	1,317	74	510	1,076	111
1945	3,401	1,361	69	466	1,111	120
1946	3,623	1,156	76	357	1,184	148
1947	4,011	1,189	91	289	1,421	172
1948	4,168	1,368	98	279	1,557	177
1949	4,098	1,438	115	297	1,520	190
1950	4,157	1,404	121	268	1,630	185
1951	4,629	1,669	130	315	1,752	183
1952	4,654	1,736	131	376	1,764	152
1953	4,606	1,731	132	188	1,764	165
1954	4,987	1,893	135	173	1,872	188
1955	5,160	1,943	139	193	2,014	176
1956	5,462	2,114	158	195	2,101	169
1957	5,679	2,208	157	251	2,149	171
1958	5,850	2,322	167	274	2,191	187
1959	6,016	2,243	181	261	2,282	227
1960	6,344	2,433	189	263	2,390	236

	Total Central Government Revenue[a] (£m.)	Main Sources of Revenue						
		Income tax[b] (£m.)	Surtax (£m.)	Profits (Corporation) Tax[c] (£m.)	Customs and Excise (£m.)	Death Duties[d] (£m.)	Capital Gains Tax[d] (£m.)	Capital Transfer Tax (£m.)
	1	2	3	4	5	6	7	8
1961	6,644	2,727	224	335	2,595	262	. .	. .
1962	6,794	2,818	184	383	2,668	270	. .	. .
1963	6,890	2,745	177	390	2,766	310	. .	. .
1964	8,157	3,088	184	423	3,174	297	. .	. .
1965	9,144	3,678	203	438	3,401	292	. .	. .
1966	10,219	3,246	242	1,118	3,536	301	7	. .
1967	11,177	3,826	239	1,253	3,721	330	15	. .
1968	13,363	4,337	225	1,354	4,601	382	47	. .
1969	15,266	4,900	255	1,689	4,933	365	127	. .
1970	15,843	5,728	248	1,591	4,709	357	139	. .
1971	16,932	6,449	348	1,560	5,325	451	156	. .
1972	17,178	6,475	341	1,533	5,744	459	208	. .
1973	18,226	7,136	307	2,263	6,220	412	324	. .
1974	23,570	10,239	186	2,851	7,407	338	380	. .
1975	29,417	15,054	109	1,998	9,176	212[d]	387	118[d]
1976	33,778	17,013	62	2,655	10,900	124[d]	323	260[d]
1977	38,773	17,420	30	3,343	12,284	87[d]	340	310[d]
1978	43,088	18,748	15	3,940	13,835	46[d]	353	317[d]
1979	54,331	20,599	11	4,646	18,032	32[d]	431	404[d]
1980	66,213	24,295	5	4,645	22,095	27[d]	508	423[d]
1981	76,754	28,725	4	4,926	25,248	17[d]	525	480[d]
1982	83,270	30,474	2	5,564	27,895	12[d]	632	499[d]
1983	88,364	31,306	2	6,011	31,435	9[d]	671	571[d]

[a] Total national revenue includes Ordinary and Self-Balancing Revenue. Figures relate to year ending 31 Mar of following year.

[b] 1900-10, 'Income tax' covers Property and Income tax. 1910 figure includes arrears for 1909.

[c] Corporation Tax replaced Profits Tax and Income Tax on Companies from 1966. Some profits tax is included in the figures for the subsequent years (£85m. in 1966-7 and £32m. in 1967-8 but negligible thereafter).

[d] Capital Transfer Tax began to replace Estate Duty in 1975.

SOURCE.—*Annual Abstract of Statistics and Financial Statistics.*

	Main Heads of Expenditure			Specimen Tariffs			
	Defence (£m.)	Health, Labour and Insurance[a] (£m.)	Pensions[b] (£m.)	Sugar[c] (per cwt.)	Tea[c] (per lb.)	Excise Duty on Beer[d] (per barrel of 36 gallons)	National Debt[e] (£m.)
	1	2	3	4	5	6	7
				s. d.	s. d.	s. d.	
1900	121	. .	. .	. .	6	6/9	628·9
1901	124	. .	. .	4/2	6	7/9	689·5
1902	101	. .	. .	4/2	6	7/9	745·0
1903	72	. .	. .	4/2	6	7/9	770·8
1904	66	. .	. .	4/2	8	7/9	762·6
1905	62	. .	. .	4/2	6	7/9	755·1

	Main Heads of Expenditure			Specimen Tariffs			
	Defence (£m.)	Health, Labour and Insurance[a] (£m.)	Pensions[b] (£m.)	Sugar[c] (per cwt.)	Tea[c] (per lb.)	Excise Duty on Beer[d] (per barrel of 36 gallons)	National Debt[e] (£m.)
	1	2	3	4	5	6	7
				s. d.	s. d.	s. d.	
1906	59	..	..	4/2	5	7/9	743·3
1907	58	..	..	4/2	5	7/9	724·5
1908	59	..	..	1/10	5	7/9	709·0
1909	63	..	..	1/10	5	7/9	702·7
1910	67	..	..	1/10	5	7/9	713·2
1911	70	..	..	1/10	5	7/9	685·2
1912	72	..	..	1/10	5	7/9	668·3
1913	77	14	1	1/10	5	7/9	656·5
1914	437	14	1	1/10	5	7/9	649·8
1915	1,424	14	1	1/10	8	23/-	1,105·0
1916	2,007	14	1	14/-	1/-	24/-	2,133·1
1917	2,436	14	1	14/-	1/-	25/-	4,011·4
1918	2,238	15	1	25/8	1/-	50/-	5,871·9
1919	692	74	100	25/8	1/-	70/-	7,434·9
							. . . . .
1920	292	73	110	25/8	1/-	100/-	7,828·8
1921	189	73	96	25/8	1/-	100/-	7,574·4
1922	111	61	83	25/8	8	100/-	7,654·3
1923	105	59	72	25/8	8	100/-	7,742·2
1924	114	65	71	11/8	4	100/-	7,641·0
1925	119	65	70	11/8	4	100/-	7,597·8
1926	116	75	65	11/8	4	100/-	7,558·6
1927	117	73	62	11/8	4	100/-	7,554·6
1928	113	76	59	11/8	4	100/-	7,527·8
1929	113	86	56	11/8	..	100/-	7,500·3
1930	110	108	55	11/8	..	103/-	7,469·0
1931	107	121	52	11/8	..	103/-	7,413·3
1932	103	155	49	11/8	4	134/-	7,433·9
1933	107	151	49	11/8	4	24/-	7,643·8
1934	113	151	47	11/8	4	24/-	7,822·3
							. . . . .
1935	136	162	46	11/8	4	24/-	6,763·9
1936	186	162	45	11/8	6	24/-	6,759·3
1937	197	162	44	11/8	6	24/-	6,764·7
1938	254	166	43	11/8	8	24/-	6,993·7
1939	626	167	42	11/8	8	24/-	7,130·8
1940	3,220	165	41	23/4	8	90/-	7,899·2
1941	4,085	170	41	23/4	8	90/-	10,366·4
1942	4,840	186	40	23/4	8	118/1½	13,041·1
1943	4,950	199	39	23/4	8	138/4½	15,822·6
1944	5,125	208	40	23/4	8	140/7½	18,562·2
1945	4,410	219	42	23/4	8	140/7½	21,365·9
1946	1,653	334	97	23/4	8	140/7½	23,636·5
1947	854	380	91	23/4	8	140/7½	25,630·6
1948	753	598	96	23/4	8	178/10½	25,620·8
		. . . .					
1949	741	806	97	11/8	2	157/10½	25,167·6
1950	777	835	94	11/8	2	155/4½	25,802·3

. . . . . Change in basis of calculation.

	Main Heads of Expenditure			Specimen Tariffs			
	De-fence (£m.)	Health, Labour and In-surance[a] (£m.)	Pen-sions[b] (£m.)	Sugar[c] (per cwt.)	Tea[c] (per lb.)	Excise Duty on Beer[d] (per barrel of 36 gallons)	National Debt[e] (£m.)
	1	2	3	4	5	6	7
				s. d.	s. d.	s. d.	
1951	1,110	810	91	11/8	2	155/4½	25,921·6
1952	1,404	884	100	11/8	2	155/4½	25,890·5
1953	1,365	903	97	11/8	2	155/4½	26,051·2
1954	1,436	619	419	11/8	2	155/4½	26,583·0
1955	1,405	652	433	11/8	2	155/4½	26,933·7
1956	1,525	750	463	11/8	2	155/4½	27,038·9
1957	1,430	782	490	11/8	2	155/4½	27,007·5
1958	1,468	794	575	11/8	2	155/4½	27,232·0
1959	1,475	1,209	610	11/8	2	111/9½	27,376·3
1960	1,596	1,384	634	11/8	2	111/9½	27,732·6
1961	1,689	1,417	659	11/8[f]	2	111/9½	28,251·7
1962	1,767	1,549	705	. .	2	123/-	28,674·4
1963	1,792	1,716	772	. .	2[g]	123/-	29,847·6
1964	1,909	1,897	792	. .	. .	147/-	30,226·5
1965	2,055	. .[h]	. .[h]	. .	. .	171/-	30,440·6
1966	2,145	. .	. .	. .	. .	171/-	31,340·2
1967	2,274	. .	. .	. .	. .	188/8	31,935·6
1968	2,232	. .	. .	. .	. .	188/8	34,193·9
1969	2,204	. .	. .	. .	. .	207/6	33,982·6
1970	2,493	. .	. .	. .	. .	207/6	33,079·4
1971	2,799	. .	. .	. .	. .	£10·37½	33,441·7
1972	3,083	. .	. .	. .	. .	£10·37½	35,839·1
1973	3,495	. .	. .	. .	. .	£6.90[i]	36,910·0
1974	4,228	. .	. .	. .	. .	£9·36[i]	40,124·5
1975	5,458	. .	. .	. .	. .	£13·68[i]	45,925·5
1976	6,282	. .	. .	. .	. .	£15·84[i]	56,581·6
1977	6,965					£17·42[i]	67,165·8
1978	7,701[j]	. .	. .	. .	. .	£17·42[i]	79,179·9
1979	9,431	. .	. .	. .	. .	£21·35	86,884·9
1980	11,759	. .	. .	. .	. .	£29·45	95,314·2
1981	12,968	. .	. .	. .	. .	£33·37	113,036·0
1982	14,796	. .	. .	. .	. .	£35.33	118,390·4
1983	16,007	. .	. .	. .	. .	£35.33	125,326·0

[a] 1900-13, the system of classification prevents entries comparable with those for later years. 1949-53, figures cover Housing, Local Government, Health, Labour, National Insurance and National Assistance. From 1954 figures cover Health, Housing and Local Government.

[b] 1900-13, the system of classification prevents entries comparable with those for later years. Before 1954, 'Pensions' equivalent to 'non-effective' charges. 1954 onwards figures cover Pensions, National Insurance and National Assistance.

[c] Full Customs duty given. In many cases preferential rates apply to Commonwealth trade. Sugar: exceeding 98° of polarisation.

[d] 1900-32 beer of 1,055° specific gravity. 1933-49 beer of 1,027° specific gravity. 1950 beer of 1,030° specific gravity.

[e] Debt of U.K. Exchequer, debt created by N. Ireland Exchequer excluded. Bonds tendered for death duties and held by National Debt Commissioners excluded from 1920. External debt arising out of 1914-18 war, excluded from 1935, when it was £1,035·5 m. at 31 Mar.

[f] April 1962 Excise Duty on sugar was repealed.

[g] June 1963 tariffs on tea ceased to be direct revenue and became chargeable under the Import Duties Act 1958.

[h] From 1965 onwards figures no longer collected in this form.

[i] Subject to VAT at standard rate from 1/4/73.

[j] From 1978, Defence figures cover expenditure in the year ending in April the following year.

SOURCES.—

1. *Annual Abstract of Statistics.* From 1970 *Financial Statistics.*

2 and 3. *Annual Abstract of Statistics. Central Statistical Office.*

4 and 5. *Customs Tariff of the U.K. (Annual Reports of Commissioners for Customs and Excise.)*

6. *Reports of Commissioners for Customs and Excise.*

7. *Finance Accounts of the U.K.*, from 1969 *Consolidated Fund and National Loans Fund Accounts* and *Financial Statistics.*

PERCENTAGE SHARES IN NET NATIONAL INCOME (BASED ON CURRENT PRICES)

United Kingdom (percentages)

Year	Wages	Salaries	Income from self-employment	Gross Trading Profits of: Private companies	Gross Trading Profits of: Public corporation	Rent
1900	41·4	9·1		36·4		12·5
1910	39·0	10·6		34·6		12·1
1921	43·6	17·9	13·4	5·7	0·5	5·8
1930	39·4	21·1	14·8	11·3	1·2	8·5
1938	40·8	21·9	13·4	14·3	1·4	9·3
1950	44·8	25·5	12·8	19·6	3·0	4·9
1960	42·8	29·2	9·5	17·7	3·4	5·9
1970	68·6		8·3	12·0	3·5	7·5
1980	68.9		8.8	14.6	3.1	6.8
1983	65.5		8.9	16.0	3.7	6.7

SOURCE.—*National Income and Expenditure Blue Books.*

SELECTED ITEMS OF CONSUMER EXPENDITURE AS PERCENTAGES OF TOTAL CONSUMER EXPENDITURE

United Kingdom

Year	Food	Alcoholic drink	Tobacco	Furniture, electrical and other durables	Cars and motor-cycles[a]	Clothing and footwear
1900	27·3	20·8	3·7	2·5	0·0	10·0
1910	28·7	16·0	4·0	2·5	0·1	10·1
1921	29·9	12·4	6·0	3·4	0·2	9·4
1930	30·2	8·4	5·7	4·7	0·8	9·8
1938	29·0	7·2	6·3	4·7	1·2	9·3
1950	31·1	6·2	6·6	4·0	0·7	9·8
1960	24·9	5·9	7·0	4·8	2·7	9·6
1970	20·3	7·4	5·5	4·3	3·1	8·5
1980	16·7	7·3	3·5	5·1	4·6	7·2

[a] This does not include running costs.

INCOME DISTRIBUTION AFTER TAX

United Kingdom

(tax units—000's)

Year	£50-£250	£250-£500	£500-£750	£750-£1,000	£1,000-£2,000	£2,000-£6,000	£6,000-£10,000	£10,000 and over
1938	n.a.	1,940	375	132	142	66	7	0
1949	13,040	10,140	2,020	442	368	90	0	0
1959	6,200	7,440	6,630	3,880	2,052	295	3	0
1967	2,338	5,906	5,418	4,822	8,298	954[a]	63[b]	1
1972/3		7,465		4,164	11,138	5,474	101	9
1975/6		1,862		2,738	9,738	13,432	511	60
1978/8			1,446		7,580	16,709	2,988	353

[a] £2,000-£5,000 [b] £5,000-£10,000 [c] Under £750 SOURCE.—*National Income and Expenditure,* Blue Books.

DISTRIBUTION OF PERSONAL WEALTH AMONG ADULT[c] POPULATION

Percent of total wealth owned by top groups

Wealth Group	1911-13[a]	1924-30[a]	1936[a]	1951-56[a]	1960[b]	1970[b]	1980
Top 1%	65·5	59·5	56·0	42·0	37·6	29·6	23
Top 5%	86·0	82·5	81·0	56·7	63·6	54·4	43
Top 10%	90·0	89·5	88·0	79·8	76·1	70·1	58
Top 20%	..	96·0	94·0	89·0	..	..	..
Top 25%	..	..	..	..	93·2	92·9	8·1

[a] England and Wales [b] Great Britain [c] Over 25, 1911-56, over 18, 1960-.

SOURCES.—H. F. Lydall and D. G. Tipping, 'The Distribution of Personal Wealth in Britain', *Bulletin of the Oxford University Institute of Statistics* (1961); *Inland Revenue Statistics* (1978).

OUTPUT PER MAN 1900-1970

(1913 = 100)

	U.K.	U.S.	France	Germany (F.R.)	Italy	Sweden
1900	98·1	79·8	90·0	85·5	77·3	70·1
1913	100·0	100·0	100·0	100·0	100·0	100·0
1929	121·6	126·7	135·6	96·5	126·3	101·6
1938	143·6	136·0	125·7	122·4	145·2	127·5
1950	159·4	177·1	146·1	124·1	153·2	171·1
1960	193·1	217·3	215·8	207·5	229·4	223·6
1970	247·6	271·8	352·8	321·2	418·2	315·1
1970 (U.K. = 100·0)	100·0	251	146	142	100	166

SOURCE.—Adapted from A. Maddison, *Economic Growth in the West* (1964) and updated with O.E.C.D. data.

INDUSTRIAL OUTPUT OF THE U.K.

(Census of Production figures)

All census Industries	Value of Production (Gross Output) (£m.)
1907[a]	1,765
1924	3,747[b]
1930	3,371[b]
1935	3,543[b]
1948[c]	12,961
1951	18,733
	- - -[d]
1958	26,980
1963	34,467
1968	48,216
1973	68,472[e]
1982	212,640[e]

[a] Including firms in the Irish Republic.
[b] Firms employing more than 10 persons only. [c] Great Britain only.
[d] Prior to 1951 classified according to the 1948 edition of the *Standard Industrial Classification*. For 1958 and 1963 according to the 1958 edition, and 1968 and 1973 according to the 1968 edition.
[e] Excludes construction.

SOURCE.—*Annual Abstract of Statistics*.

SURTAX, 1909-1972

Year of Change	Income Level at which Surtax Payable Exceeding	Maximum Rate in £ Payable			
	£				£
1909	5,000	6d. on amount in excess of 3,000			
1914	3,000	1/9½	,,	,,	8,000
1915	3,000	3/6	,,	,,	10,000
1918	2,500	4/6	,,	,,	10,000
1920	2,000	6/-	,,	,,	30,000
1929	2,000	7/6	,,	,,	50,000
1930	2,000	8/3	,,	,,	50,000
1938	2,000	9/6	,,	,,	30,000
1939	2,000	9/6	,,	,,	20,000
1946	2,000	10/6	,,	,,	20,000
1951	2,000	10/-	,,	,,	15,000
1961	2,000[a]	10/-	,,	,,	15,000
1969	2,500	50%	,,	,,	15,000
1971	3,000	50%	,,	,,	15,000

[a] In 1961 special reliefs introduced for earned incomes made the surtax threshold effectively £5,000.

In 1973 the system of personal income tax and surtax was replaced by a single graduated tax. In consequence surtax ceased to be charged after 1972-3.

SOURCE.—*Annual Reports of Commissioners of Inland Revenue.*

ESTATE DUTY

Payable on estate of net capital value £100,000

Death occurred in Period	Rate of Duty %	Duty Payable £
Before 1909	5·5	5,500
1909-1914	8	8,000
1914-1919	9	9,000
1919-1925	14	14,000
1925-1939	19	19,000
1939-1939	20·9	20,900
1939-1940	22·8	22,800
1940-1946	24·7	24,700
1946-1949	30	30,000
1949-1969	45	45,000
1969-1972	65[a]	47,125
1972-1974	55[a]	37,250

Where death occurred before 30 Jul 49 additional legacy and succession duties were also payable. [a] Marginal rate.

SOURCE.—*Annual Reports of Commissioners of Inland Revenue.*

MAXIMUM RATES OF DEATH DUTY

Death occurred in Period	Rate of Duty	Net Capital Value of Estate
	%	£m.
1894-1907	8	1
1907-1909	15	3
1909-1914	15	1
1914-1919	20	1
1919-1925	40	2
1925-1930	40	2
1930-1939	50	2
1939-1939	55	2
1939-1940	60	2
1940-1946	65	2
1946-1949	75	2
1949-1969	80	1
1969-1972	85	0·75
1972-1974	75	0·5

SOURCE.—*Annual Reports of Commissioners of Inland Revenue.*

CAPITAL TRANSFER TAX

Following the abolition of Estate Duty in 1974, a Capital Transfer Tax of 45% became payable on property transferred from a £100,000 estate on death or within three years preceding death. The maximum rate of Capital Transfer Tax reached 75% for an estate over £2m. However, from 1984 the top brackets were abolished, leaving the highest rate at 60% on estates over £285,000.

HIRE PURCHASE 1947-76

Hire Purchase and other instalment credit (Finance Houses, Durable Goods, Shops and Department Stores)—total outstanding business at end of period (£m).

1947	68	1962	887	1977	4,184
1948	105	1963	959	1978	5,499
1949	128	1964	1,115	1979	6,901
1950	167	1965	1,196	1980	7,844
1951	208	1966	1,104	1981	8,481
1952	241	1967	1,058	1982	9,693
1953	276	1968	1,089	1983	12,221
1954	384	1969	1,063		
1955	461	1970	1,127		
1956	376	1971	1,377		
1957	448	1972	1,769		
1958	556	1973	2,151		
1959	849	1974	1,944		
1960	935	1975	1,892		
1961	934	1976	2,163		

SOURCES.—*Key Statistics 1900-1970*; *Annual Abstract of Statistics 1970-76*; *Economic Trends* (1977). The basis of calculations is different from 1977.

BUDGET DATES

1900	5	Mar	1926	26	Apr	1949	6	Apr		12	Nov
1901	18	Apr	1927	11	Apr	1950	18	Apr	1975	15	Apr
1902	14	Apr	1928	24	Apr	1951	10	Apr	1976	6	Apr
1903	23	Apr	1929	15	Apr	1952	11	Apr	1977	29	Mar
1904	19	Apr	1930	14	Apr	1953	14	Apr	1978	11	Apr
1905	10	Apr	1931	27	Apr	1954	6	Apr	1979	3	Apr
1906	30	Apr		10	Sep	1955	19	Apr		12	Jun
1907	18	Apr	1932	19	Apr		26	Oct	1980	26	Mar
1908	7	May	1933	25	Apr	1956	17	Apr	1981	10	Mar
1909	29	Apr	1934	17	Apr	1957	9	Apr	1982	9	Mar
1910	30	Jun	1935	15	Apr	1958	15	Apr	1983	15	Mar
1911	16	May	1936	21	Apr	1959	7	Apr	1984	13	Mar
1912	2	Apr	1937	20	Apr	1960	4	Apr	1985	19	Mar
1913	22	Apr	1938	26	Apr	1961	17	Apr			
1914	4	May	1939	25	Apr	1962	8	Apr			
	17	Nov		27	Sep	1963	3	Apr			
1915	4	May	1940	23	Apr	1964	14	Apr			
	21	Sep		23	Jul		11	Nov			
1916	4	Apr	1941	7	Apr	1965	6	Apr			
1917	3	May	1942	14	Apr	1966	5	May			
1918	22	Apr	1943	12	Apr	1967	11	Apr			
1919	30	Apr	1944	25	Apr	1968	19	Mar			
1920	19	Apr	1945	24	Apr	1969	15	Apr			
1921	25	Apr		23	Oct	1970	14	Apr			
1922	1	May	1946	9	Apr	1971	30	Mar			
1923	17	Apr	1947	15	Apr	1972	21	Apr			
1924	29	Apr		12	Nov	1973	6	Mar			
1925	28	Apr	1948	6	Apr	1974	26	Mar			

Occasionally *ad hoc* statements by the Chancellor of the Exchequer on revised fiscal and economic arrangements have been referred to by the media as 'Budgets', although not so regarded by the Treasury. Such statements or 'mini-Budgets' occurred on 22 Jul 74, 12 Nov 74, 11 Jul 75, 19 Feb 76, 22 Jul 76, 15 Dec 76, 15 Jul 77, 26 Oct 77, 8 Jun 78, and 15 Nov 80.

In 1982 the forecast required under the *Industry Act, 1975* for decisions on public expenditure plans and proposed changes to National Insurance contributions were brought together in one 'Autumn Statement' (8 Nov 82, 17 Nov 83, 11 Nov 84).

XII

NATIONALISATION

Publicly owned enterprises involved in industrial or commercial activities can be divided into two broad categories: public trading bodies and limited companies. The first category can be further subdivided into public corporations, central government trading bodies and local authority trading bodies; all three are grouped as 'public sector' organisations for government statistical purposes. Limited companies with government shareholdings, for example Rolls-Royce and British Leyland, were not in 1979 treated as 'public sector' organisations.

Public corporations, defined as public trading bodies which have a substantial degree of financial independence of the public authority which created them, include not only the major nationalised industries, but also a number of other bodies listed on pp. 374-5. For practical purposes 'nationalised industries' can be defined as public corporations whose assets are in public ownership, whose boards are appointed by a Secretary of State, whose employees are not civil servants, which are engaged in trading activities, and which derive the greater part of their revenue directly from customers.

This definition is used in practice by the Treasury, but it does not cover all the public corporations which have been investigated by the Select Committee on Nationalised Industries.

Main Landmarks

1908 **The Port of London Authority** was set up in 1909 under the *Port of London Act, 1908* (but it only followed the pattern of the Mersey Docks and Harbour Board, set up in 1874).

1926 **The Central Electricity Board** was set up by the *Electricity (Supply) Act, 1926*, to control generation by purchasing all electricity output.

1926 **The British Broadcasting Corporation** was granted its first charter as a public corporation.

1933 **The London Passenger Transport Board** was established.

1943 **The North of Scotland Hydro-Electricity Board** was established.

1946 **The Bank of England** was taken into public ownership.

1946 **The Coal Industry** was nationalised by the *Coal Industry Nationalisation Act, 1946*, which set up the National Coal Board.

1946 **Civil Aviation** was reorganised by the *Civil Aviation Act, 1946*. This covered the British Overseas Airways Corporation (set up in 1939), and two new corporations, British European Airways and British South American Airways. B.S.A.A. was merged with B.O.A.C. in 1949. B.O.A.C. and B.E.A. were merged into British Airways in 1972-74.

1947 **Electricity** was fully nationalised by the *Electricity Act, 1947*, which set up the British Electricity Authority. The *Electricity Act, 1957*, set up the Electricity Council and the Central Electricity Generating Board. The twelve area boards remained financially autonomous.

1948 **Railways, Canals** (and some other transport) were nationalised by the *Transport Act, 1947*. The British Transport Commission was established, and the Docks and Inland Waterways, Hotels, Railways, London Transport, Road Haulage, and Road Passenger Transport were administered by six executive boards. The *Transport Act, 1953,* denationalised Road Haulage. *The Transport Act, 1962,* reorganised nationalised transport undertakings and provided for the establishment of separate Boards for Railways, London Transport, Docks and Waterways, and for a Transport Holding Company, as successors to the British Transport Commission.

1948 **Gas** was nationalised by the *Gas Act, 1948*, which established twelve Area Gas Boards and the Gas Council. *The Gas Act, 1972*, established the British Gas Corporation which replaced the Gas Council and Area Boards.

1949 **Iron and Steel** were nationalised by the *Iron and Steel Act, 1949*, and the Iron and Steel Corporation of Great Britain was established. The vesting date of the Act was 15 Feb 51. The *Iron and Steel Act, 1953*, denationalised the industry, and set up the Iron and Steel Board. In 1967 the *Iron and Steel Act* renationalised the industry, as from 28 Jul 67.

1954 **The U.K. Atomic Energy Authority** was established by the *U.K. Atomic Energy Authority Act, 1954*.

1969 **The Post Office** ceased to be a Government Department and became a public corporation.

1971-73 **Hiving-off.** The Conservative Government began to hive-off some concerns of nationalised industries. In 1971-72 some B.O.A.C. routes were allotted to British Caledonian. In 1973 Thomas Cook's travel agency and the Carlisle state breweries (which was nationalised in 1916) were sold to the private sector.

1971 **Rolls-Royce Ltd** was established following the company's bankruptcy. The shares were vested in the National Enterprise Board in February 1976.

1975 **British Leyland.** The majority of shares were acquired by the Government and later vested in the National Enterprise Board.

1975 **The National Enterprise Board** established by *Industry Act, 1975*.

1976 **British National Oil Corporation** established by *Petroleum and Submarines Pipelines Act, 1975*.

1977 **British Aerospace** and **British Shipbuilders** established by *Aircraft and Shipbuilding Industries Act, 1977*.

Privatisation

1979 The Conservative government came to power promising to privatise large segments of nationalised industry. Parts of BP, ICL and Suez Finance Co. were, in due course, sold to private investors.

1980 Ferranti, Fairey, North Sea Oil Licenses, British Aerospace, and smaller NEB holdings were sold.

1981 British Sugar, Cable and Wireless holdings, Amersham International and the National Freight Consortium, and miscellaneous Crown Agent and Forestry holdings were sold.

1982 Parts of Britoil and Associated British Ports, BR Hotels, and more oil licenses and stockpiles were sold, together with Amersham International, a biotechnology enterprise.

1983 Further parts of Britoil, BP and Cable and Wireless were sold.

1984-5 Enterprise Oil (British Gas's offshore oil assets), British Telecom, British Airways were sold.

1985 The government confirmed plans to sell off British Airports, British Gas, Royal Ordnance factories, Sealink, National Bus, Jaguar, Land Rover, Rolls-Royce, Unipart, British Nuclear Fuels, naval shipbuilding yards, and parts of British Steel and British Shipbuilders.

Nationalised Industries

Air

		Responsible Minister		*Chairman/Deputy-Chairman*	
				Chairman	
ritish verseas irways orpora- on B.O.A.C.) 939-74	1939	Sec. of State for Air	26 May 43	Vt Knollys	Established under the *Air Corporations Act, 1939,* as successor to Imperial Airways. In 1946 became one of the three corporations set up under the *Civil Aviation Act, 1946,* to provide passenger and cargo flights to all parts of the world, other than Europe and Latin America. Under the *Civil Aviation Act, 1971,* merged with BEA in April 1974 to form British Airways.
	1944	Min. for Civil Aviation	1 Jul 47	Sir H. Hartley	
	1951	Min. of Transport and Civil Aviation	1 Jul 49	Sir M. Thomas	
			1 May 56	(Sir G. d'Erlanger	
	1959	Min. of Civil Aviation			
	1964	Min. of Aviation	29 Jul 60	Sir M. Slattery	
	1968	Min. of State at Board of Trade	1 Jan 64	Sir G. Guthrie	
			1 Jan 69	(Sir) C. Hardie	
	1970	Min. of Aviation at the Dept. of Trade and Industry	1 Jan 71	K. Granville	
			1 Sep 72	J. Stainton	
				Deputy Chairman	
	1971	Min. for Aerospace (and Shipping 1972) at the Dept. of Trade and Industry	1 Aug 46	Sir H. Howitt	
			1 Apr 48	Sir M. Thomas	
			1 Jul 49	W. Straight	
	1974	Sec. of State for Trade	(1 Aug 49-30 Apr 50, *additional Deputy Chairman*, J. Booth)		
			21 Nov 55	Ld Rennell	
			1 May 56	Sir G. Cribbett	
			20 Jun 60	Sir W. Neden	
			3 Apr 64-31 Dec 68	K. Granville / C. Hardie	
			1 Jan 68	K. Granville	
			1 Apr 71	Sir A. Norman	
			21 Dec 71	J. Stainton	
			1 Sep 72	W. Bray	

		Responsible Minister		*Chairman/Deputy-Chairman*	
British European Airways Corporation (B.E.A.) 1946-74	1946 1951 1959 1968 1970 1971 1974	Min. for Civil Aviation Min. of Transport and Civil Aviation Min. of Aviation Min. of State at the Board of Trade Min. of Aviation Supply Min. for Aerospace (and Shipping 1972) at the Dept. of Trade and Industry Sec. of State for Trade	1 Aug 46 1 Apr 47 14 Mar 49 3 May 56 1 Jan 71 1 Sep 72 1 Aug 46 1 Apr 47 1 Oct 65 22 Dec 71 1 Dec 72	*Chairman* Sir H. Hartley G. d'Erlanger Ld Douglas (Sir) A. Milward H. Marking P. Lawton *Deputy Chairman* W. Straight (Sir) J. Keeling (Sir) K. Keith K. Wilkinson R. Watts	Established under the *Civil Aviation Act, 1946,* to take over European, domestic and some North African flights. In April 1974, under the *Civil Aviation Act, 1971,* merged with BOAC to form British Airways.
British South American Airways Corporation (B.S.A.A.) 1946-49	1946	Min. for Civil Aviation	1 Aug 46 1 May 50 1 Aug 46 1 Apr 49	*Chairman* J. Booth Sir M. Thomas *Deputy Chairman* (Sir) J. Stephenson Sir F. Brake	Established under the *Civil Aviation Act, 1946,* to take over Central and South American routes from BOAC. Merged with BOAC 1949.
British Airways Board 1974-	1972 1974 1983	Min. for Aerospace and Shipping at the Dept. of Trade and Industry Sec. of State for Trade Sec. of State for Transport	7 Oct 71 1 Jul 76 1 Jul 79 3 Jan 81 1 Sep 72-30 Nov 74 1 Sep 72-1 Nov 77 1 Jan 78 1 Jun 79 1 Dec 80-30 Sep 83 1 Feb 81-	*Chairman* D. Nicolson Sir F. McFadzean Sir R. Stainton J. (Ld) King *Deputy Chairman* (Sir) K. Granville H. Marking R. Stainton K. Wilkinson R. Watts A. Dibbs	Established under the *Civi Aviation Act, 1971,* to take overall responsiblility for the activities of BEA and BOAC from 1 Apr 72. Became fully operational from 1 Apr 74.
British Airports Authority 1966-	1966 1968 1970 1971 1974 1983	Min. of Aviation Min. of State at the Board of Trade Min. of Aviation Supply at the Dept. of Trade and Industry Min. for Aerospace (and Shipping 1972) at the Dept. of Trade and Industry Sec. of State for Trade Sec. of State for Transport	3 Jun 65 9 Jan 72 1 Mar 77 2 Aug 65 15 Dec 75	*Chairman* (Sir) P. Masefield N. Foulkes (Sir) N. Payne *Deputy Chairman* R. MacLellan W. Gregson	Established under *Airport Authority Act, 1965,* to ru Gatwick, Heathrow an Stansted, and since 1971, Edir burgh Turnhouse airport Aberdeen and Glasgow wer acquired in 1975.
British Aerospace 1977-	1977 1983	Sec. of State for Industry Sec. of State for Trade and Industry	22 Mar 77 22 Mar 80 29 Mar 77 30 Jun 83	*Chairman* Ld Beswick (Sir) A. Pearce *Deputy Chairman* A. Greenwood (*office vacant*)	Established under the *Aircra and Shipbuilding Industri Act, 1977,* to promote th efficient and economical desig development, production, sal repair and maintenance of civ and military aircraft, of guide weapons and of space vehicle In 1981 51% of British Aero space shares were sold to th private sector and employees.

		Responsible Minister	Chairman/ Deputy-Chairman		

Fuel and Power

		Responsible Minister		Chairman/ Deputy-Chairman	
				Chairman	
British Electricity Authority (Central Electricity Authority 1955-57) 1947-55	1947	Min. of Fuel and Power	15 Aug 47-31 Dec 57	Ld Citrine	Established under the *Electricity Act, 1947*, to be responsible for generation and main transmission throughout Great Britain excluding the North of Scotland. There were 14 Area Boards responsible for distribution. Under *Electricity Reorganisation (Scotland) Act, 1954*, two of these Area Boards (S.E. Scotland and S.W. Scotland) merged and took over generation in their areas from British Electricity Authority which was now renamed Central Electricity Authority.
	1957	Min. of Power			
				Deputy Chairman	
			15 Aug 47-16 Dec 53	Sir H. Self / Sir J. Hacking	
			16 Dec 53-31 Aug 57	Sir H. Self / J. Eccles	
				Chairman	
Electricity Council 1957-	1957	Min. of Power	1 Sep 57	Sir H. Self	Established under the *Electricity Act, 1957*, to co-ordinate development of the industry. Consists of 14 statutory corporations: the Electricity Council, the CEGB and 12 Area Electricity Boards.
	1969	Min. of Technology	1 Sep 59	(Sir) R. King	
	1970	Sec. of State for Trade and Industry	1 Jan 66	Sir R. Edwards	
	1974	Sec. of State for Energy	1 Nov 68	Sir N. Elliott	
			1 Apr 72	Sir P. Menzies	
			1 Apr 77	(Sir) F. Tombs	
			1 Jan 81	(Sir) A. Bunch	
			1 Apr 83	T. Jones	
				Deputy Chairman	
			1 Sep 57	Sir J. Eccles	
			1 Sep 57	R. Edwards	
			1 Jan 66	N. Marsh	
			1 Jan 66	Sir A. Wilson	
			1 Jan 72-30 Jun 76	Sir A. Wilson	
			1 Jan 72-31 Mar 76	R. Richardson	
			1 Dec 76-31 Dec 80	A. Bunch	
			1 Feb 81	A. Plumpton	
				Chairman	
Central Electricity Generating Board (C.E.G.B.) 1957-	1957	Min. of Power	1 Sep 57	Sir C. Hinton	Established under the *Electricity Act, 1957*, to own and operate the power stations and to provide electricity in bulk to the Area
	1969	Min. of Technology	1 Jan 65	(Sir) S. Brown	
	1970	Sec. of State for Trade and Industry	1 Jul 72	A. Hawkins	
	1974	Sec. of State for Energy	9 May 77	G. England	
			9 May 82	(*office vacant*)	
			1 Jul 82	Sir W. (Ld) Marshall	
				Deputy Chairman	
			1 Sep 57	C. King	
			1 Sep 59	S. Brown	
			1 Jan 65	O. Francis	
			15 May 72	W. Fenton	
			16 Apr 75	F. Bonner	

				Chairman	
North of Scotland Hydro-Electricity Board 1943-	1943	Sec. of State for Scotland	1 Sep 43	E of Airlie	Established under the *Hydro-Electric Development (Scotland) Act, 1943*, to supply electricity and to develop water power in the Highlands and Islands. In 1947 became responsible for all public generation and distribution of electricity in the North of Scotland.
			1 Apr 46	T. Johnston	
			1 Jul 59	Ld Strathclyde	
			1 Sep 69	T. Fraser	
			30 Apr 73	Sir D. Haddow	
			1 Jan 79	Ld Greenhill	
			1 Jan 84	M. Joughin	
				Deputy Chairman	
			1 Sep 43	Sir E. McColl	
			1 Jun 51	Sir H. Mackenzie	
			1 Jan 60	Sir J. Erskine	
			1 Jan 62	A. Mackenzie	
			1 Jan 70	I. Duncan Millar	
			1 Jan 73	K. Vernon	
				Chairman	
South of Scotland Electricity Board 1955-	1955	Sec. of State for Scotland	1 Dec 54	(Sir) J. Pickles	Established under the *Electricity Reorganisation (Scotland) Act, 1954*, to generate and distribute electricity throughout S of Scotland.
			20 Feb 62	N. Elliot	
			1 Apr 67	C. Allan	
			1 Jan 74	F. Tombs	
			1 Apr 77	D. Berridge	
			22 Mar 82	D. Miller	
				Deputy Chairman	
			1 Dec 54	Sir N. Duke	
			1 Feb 56	W. Hutton	
			1 Jan 64	C. Allan	
			1 Apr 67	A. Christianson	
			1 Jan 73	F. Tombs	
			1 Jan 74	D. Berridge	
			1 Apr 77	*(office vacant)*	
			1 Jan 80	D. Miller	
			22 Mar 82	*(office vacant)*	
			22 Dec 82	I. Preston	
				Chairman	
National Coal Board (N.C.B.) 1946-	1946	Min. of Fuel and Power	15 Jul 46	Ld Hyndley (Vt)	Established under the *Coal Industry Nationalisation Act, 1946*, to own and run the coal industry and certain ancillary activities.
	1956	Min. of Power	1 Aug 51	Sir H. Houldsworth	
	1969	Min. of Technology	1 Feb 56	(Sir) J. Bowman	
	1970	Sec. of State for Trade and Industry	1 Feb 61	A. Robens (Ld)	
			3 Jul 71	(Sir) D. Ezra	
	1974	Sec. of State for Energy	3 Jul 82	(Sir) N. Siddall	
			1 Sep 83	I. MacGregor	
				Deputy Chairman	
			15 Jul 46	Sir A. Street	
			1 Aug 51	(Sir) W. Drummond & Sir E. Coates	
			1 Feb 55	J. Bowman	
			21 Feb 56	(Sir) J. Latham	
			1 Sep 60-30 Apr 67	(Sir) E. Browne	
			1 Oct 60-31 Jan 61	A. Robens	
			3 May 67	D. Ezra	
			8 Jul 71-2 Jul 75	W. Sheppard	
			1 Oct 73-3 Jul 82	N. Siddall	
			3 Jul 82-31 Mar 84	L. Mills	
			3 Jul 82-	J. Cowan	

		Responsible Minister	Chairman/Deputy-Chairman		Notes
Gas Council and Boards 1948-73	1948	Min. of Fuel and Power		*Chairman*	Established by the *Gas Act, 1948*, to co-ordinate 12 Area Gas Boards which were set up to manufacture and retail town gas. The Gas Council was responsible for the purchase and distribution of natural gas. Under the *Gas Act, 1972*, replaced by British Gas Corporation.
	1957	Min. of Power	23 Nov 48	Sir E. Sylvester	
	1969	Min. of Technology	1 Jan 52	(Sir) H. Smith	
	1970	Sec. of State for Trade and Industry	1 Jan 60	Sir H. Jones	
			1 Jan 72	A. Hetherington	
				Deputy Chairman	
			25 Nov 48	H. Smith	
			1 Feb 52	(Sir) H. Jones	
			1 Jan 60	(Sir) K. Hutchison	
			1 Jan 67	A. Hetherington	
			1 Jan 72	D. Rooke	
British Gas Corporation 1973-	1973	Sec. of State for Trade and Industry		*Chairman*	Established under the *Gas Act, 1972*, to take over responsibilities of Gas Council and Area Gas Boards. In 1984 British Gas's offshore oil interests were hired off to form Enterprise Oil.
	1974	Sec. of State for Energy	1 Jan 73	(Sir) A. Hetherington	
			1 Jul 76	(Sir) D. Rooke	
				Deputy Chairman	
			1 Jan 73	D. Rooke	
			1 Jul 76	J. Smith	
			30 Sep 83	(*office vacant*)	
United Kingdom Atomic Energy Authority (U.K.A.E.A.) 1954-	1954	Ld President		*Chairman*	Established under the *Atomic Energy Authority Act, 1954*, to be responsible for the development of nuclear energy and its applications.
	1956	Prime Minister	1 Aug 54	Sir E. Plowden (Ld)	
	1959	Min. of Science	1 Jan 60	Sir R. Makins	
	1963	Ld President	10 Feb 64	Sir W. Penney (Ld)	
	1964	Min. of Technology	16 Oct 67	(Sir) J. Hill	
	1970	Sec. of State for Trade and Industry	7 Jul 82	Sir W. Marshall	
	1974	Sec. of State for Energy	1 Oct 82	Sir P. Hirsch	
			1 Oct 84	A. Allen	
				Deputy Chairman	
			16 Dec 75	W. Marshall	
			1 May 81	A. Allen	
			1 Oct 84	(*office vacant*)	
British National Oil Corporation (B.N.O.C.) 1976-82	1976	Sec. of State for Energy		*Chairman*	Established under the *Petroleum and Submarines Pipelines Act, 1975*, to search for and get, move, store and treat, buy, sell, and deal in petroleum. In Nov 1982 the government sold its majority shareholding to the private sector.
			1 Jan 76	Ld Kearton	
				Deputy Chairman	
			1 Jan 76	Ld Balogh	
			31 Dec 77	(*office vacant*)	
			1 Sep 78	Ld Croham	
			1 Nov 82	(*office vacant*)	

Transport

		Responsible Minister	Chairman		Notes
London Passenger Transport Board (L.P.T.B.) 1933-47	1933	Min. of Transport	1933	Ld Ashfield	Established under the *London Passenger Transport Act, 1933*, to take over railway, tramway, bus and coach undertakings within the London area. Under the *Transport Act, 1947*, responsibilities transferred to the British Transport Commission operating through a London Transport Executive.
	1941	Min. of War Transport			
	1946	Min. of Transport			

		Responsible Minister	Chairman/Deputy-Chairman	
London Transport Board 1963-70	1963	Min. of Transport	*Chairman* 1 Jan 63 (Sir) A. Valentine 1 Apr 65 (Sir) M. Holmes *Vice-Chairman* 1 Jan 63 A. Grainger 1 Oct 65 A. Bull	Established under the *Transport Act, 1962*, to replace part of the British Transport Commission, to provide an adequate and properly co-ordinated system of passenger transport for the London area. Under the *Transport (London) Act, 1969*, responsibilities transferred to the Greater London Council.
London Regional Transport (L.R.T.) 1984-	1984	Sec. of State for Transport	*Chairman* 29 Jun 84 K. Bright *Deputy Chairman* 29 Jun 84 D. Hardy	Established under the *London Regional Transport Act* to take over London Transport from the G.L.C.
British Transport Commission (B.T.C.) 1947-62	1947 1953 1959	Min. of Transport Min. of Transport and Civil Aviation Min. of Transport	*Chairman* 8 Sep 47 Sir C. Hurcomb (Ld) 15 Sep 53 Sir B. Robertson 1 Jun 61 R. Beeching (Ld) *Deputy Chairman* 1 Jan 49 (Sir) J. Benstead 1 Oct 61 Sir P. Warter *Chairman of Executives of BTC* *Docks and Inland Waterways Executive* 1947-53 Sir R. Hill *Hotels Executive* 1948-51 Ld Inman (*part-time from* 1950) 1951-53 Sir H. Methven (*part-time*) *Railway Executive* 1947-51 Sir E. Missenden 1951-53 J. Elliot *Road Haulage Executive* 1948-53 G. Russell *London Transport Executive* 1947-53 Ld Latham 1953-59 (Sir) J. Elliot 1959-62 A. Valentine *Road Passenger Service* 1948-52 G. Cardwell	Established under the *Transport Act, 1947*, to provide an integrated system of transport facilities (excluding air). The separate executives were wound up in 1953. The *Transport Act, 1962*, transferred the whole of the B.T.C. to new separate Corporations.
British Railways Board (B.R.) 1963-	1962 1970 1976	Min. of Transport Sec. of State for the Environment Sec. of State for Transport	*Chairman* 1 Jan 63 R. Beeching (Ld) 1 Jun 65 (Sir) S. Raymond 1 Jan 68 (Sir) H. Johnson 13 Sep 71 (Sir) R. Marsh 12 Sep 76 (Sir) P. Parker 12 Sep 83 (Sir) R. Reid *Deputy Chairman* 1 Oct 72 M. Bosworth 1 Oct 83 (Sir) R. Cave	Established under the *Transport Act, 1962*, to take over the B.T.C.'s rail services.

		Responsible Minister	*Chairman / Deputy Chairman*	
British Transport Docks Board 1963-84	1962 1970 1976	Min. of Transport Sec. of State for the Environment Sec. of State for Transport	*Chairman* 3 Dec 62 Sir A. Kirby 15 Jun 67 S. Finnis 6 Aug 69 R. Wills 25 Sep 69 C. Cory (*acting*) 19 Jan 70 Sir C. Dove 1 May 71 Sir H. Browne 1 May 82 K. Stuart *Vice-Chairman* 10 Dec 62 Sir A. Crichton 1 Jan 68 R. Wills 15 Sep 69 C. Cory 1 Jan 80 K. Stuart 1 May 82 D. Stringer	Established under the *Transport Act, 1962*, to administer publicly owned ports throughout the country. Under *Docks and Harbours Act, 1966*, became licensing authority for all but three ports. Sold off in 1983 and 1984 under the *Transport Act, 1981*, to form Associated British Ports.
British Waterways Board 1963-	1963 1970	Min. of Transport Sec. of State for the Environment	*Chairman* 1 Jan 63 F. Arney 1 Jul 63 Sir J. Hawton 1 Jul 68 Sir F. Price 1 Jul 84 Sir L. Young *Vice-Chairman* 1 Jan 63 Sir J. Hawton 11 Aug 63 Sir F. Parham 1 Jul 68 Sir J. Hawton 1 Jul 74 Ld Feather 1 Mar 77 C. Plant (Ld) 1 Mar 80 Sir F. Corfield 15 Aug 83 A. Robertson	Established under the *Transport Act, 1962*, to take over inland waterways from the B.T.C. The *Transport Act, 1968*, extended its powers particularly in regard to recreation and amenities.
National Bus Company 1968-	1968 1970 1976	Min. of Transport Sec. of State for the Environment Sec. of State for Transport	*Chairman* 28 Nov 68 A. Todd 1 Jan 72 F. Wood 1 Jan 79 Ld. Shepherd 1 Jan 85 R. Brook *Deputy Chairman* 1 Jan 77 R. Brook 1 Jan 85 (*office vacant*)	Established under the *Transport Act, 1968*, to take over responsibility for state-owned bus companies and bus manufacturing interests from the Transport Holding Company.
National Freight Company Ltd. (National Freight Corporation 1968-82)	1968 1970 1976	Min. of Transport Sec. of State for the Environment Sec. of State for Transport	*Chairman* 1 Jan 69 Sir R. Wilson 1 Jan 71 (Sir) D. Pettit 1 Jan 79 Sir R. Lawrence *Deputy Chairman* 15 Feb 77 V. Paige	Established under the *Transport Act, 1968*, to take over road haulage and shipping interests of the Transport Holding Company. Shipping interests terminated in 1971. Sold to the National Freight Consortium in 1982.
Scottish Transport Group 1968-	1968	Sec. of State for Scotland	*Chairman* 18 Nov 68 (Sir) P. Thomas 1 Jan 78 A. Donnet (Ld) 1 Jan 81 W. Stevenson	Established under the *Transport Act, 1968*, to control various transport activities in Scotland, including road passenger, insurance, tourism and shipping.

		Responsible Minister		*Chairman/Deputy Chairman*	
				Chairman	
Transport Holdings Company	1962	Min. of Transport	15 Nov 62	Sir P. Warter	Established by the *Transport Act, 1962*, to take over all B.T.C. investments not given to British Rail, London Transport, Docks or Waterways Boards. The *Transport Act, 1968*, transferred its road interests to the National Freight Corporation and the National Bus Company. Its residual interests (Thos. Cook, Lunn-Poly, etc.) were sold 1970-72.
1962-72	1970	Sec. of State for Environment	15 Nov 67	Sir R. Wilson	
			1 Jan 71	L. Whyte	
				Deputy Chairman	
			16 Nov 62-15 Nov 67	Sir R. Wilson	

Miscellaneous

				Chairman	
Iron and Steel Corporation	1950	Min. of Supply	2 Oct 50	S. Hardie	Established under the *Iron and Steel Act, 1949*, to take over 298 Companies in the Iron and Steel Industries. Wound up by the *Iron and Steel Act, 1953*.
1950-53			25 Feb 52	Sir J. Green	
				Deputy Chairman	
			2 Oct 50	Sir J. Green	
			25 Feb 52	*(vacant)*	
				Chairman	
British Steel Corporation	1967	Min. of Power	28 Jul 67	Ld Melchett	Established under the *Iron and Steel Act, 1967*, to take over the management of the major part of the steel industry.
1968-	1969	Min. of Technology	18 Jun 73	(Sir) M. Finniston	
	1970	Sec. of State for Trade and Industry	10 Sep 76	Sir C. Villiers	
	1974	Sec. of State for Industry	1 Jul 80	I. MacGregor	
	1983	Sec. of State for Trade and Industry	1 Sep 83	(Sir) R. Haslam	
				Deputy Chairman	
			9 Sep 76	M. Littman	
			10 Sep 76	R. Scholey	
				Chairman	
Cable and Wireless Ltd.	1947	Postmaster-General	1 Jan 47	Sir A. Augwin	Under the *Cable and Wireless Act, 1946*, the Government acquired all those shares of Cable and Wireless Ltd. not already in its possession. The company's U.K. assets were integrated into the Post Office and it continued to own and operate telecommunications services outside the U.K. In 1981 the Government sold the majority of its shares.
1947-81	1969	Min. of Posts and Telecommunications	1 Apr 51	(Sir) L. Nicholls	
	1970	Sec. of State for Trade and Industry	1 Feb 56	Sir G. Ince	
	1974	Sec. of State for Industry	1 Jan 62	Sir J. Macpherson	
			1 Nov 67	D. McMillan	
			1 Mar 72	H. Lillicrap	
			1 Nov 76	E. Short (Ld Glenamara)	
			15 Oct 80	(Sir) E. Sharp	
				Deputy Chairman	
			1 Sep 77	P. McCunn	
				Chairman	
Post Office Corporation	1970	Min. of Posts and Telecommunications	1 Oct 69	Vt Hall	Established under the *Post Office Act, 1969*, to take over from the office of the Postmaster General, responsibility for postal services, Giro and remittance services and telecommunications throught the U.K. In March 1974 all broadcasting functions transferred to Home Office supervision. In 1981 all telecommunications services were transferred to British Telecom.
1970-	1974	Sec. of State for Industry	22 Apr 71	(Sir) W. Ryland	
	1983	Sec. of State for Trade and Industry	31 Oct 77	Sir W. Barlow	
			1 Sep 80	Sir H. Chilver	
			1 Oct 81	(Sir) R. Dearing	
				Deputy Chairman	
			1 Oct 69	W. Straight	
			10 Mar 75	Sir E. Fennessy	
			1 Jan 78	P. Benton	
			1 Jan 79	(*office vacant*)	
			1 Oct 81	S. Wainwright	

	Responsible Minister	*Chairman/Deputy Chairman*	
British Telecom 1981-84	1983 Sec. of State for Industry 1983 Sec. of State for Trade and Industry	*Chairman* 27 Jul 81 Sir G. Jefferson *Deputy Chairman* 1 Oct 83 D. Vander Weyer	Established under the *British Telecommunications Act, 1981*, to take over the telecommunication functions of the Post Office prior to their sale to the private sector in Nov 1984.
British Shipbuilders 1977-	1977 Sec. of State for Industry 1983 Sec. of State for Trade and Industry	*Chairman* 1 Jul 77 Sir A. Griffin 1 Jul 80 (Sir) R. Atkinson 1 Sep 83 J. Day *Deputy Chairman* 1 Jul 77-22 Mar 83 K. Griffin 18 Aug 81-17 Aug 83 W. Richardson 1 Jul 83-1 Sep 83 G. Day	Established under the *Aircraft and Shipbuilding Industries Act, 1977*, to promote the efficient and economical design, development, production, sale, repair and maintenance of ships.
British Technology Group 1981-	1981 Sec. of State for Industry 1983 Sec. of State for Trade and Industry	*Chairman* 20 Jul 81 Sir F. Wood 1 Nov 83 C. Barker	Established in 1981 as an umbrella organisation for the National Enterprise Board and the National Research Development Corporation, which retain separate legal identities.
Rolls-Royce Ltd 1971-	1971 Min. for Aerospace at the Dept. of Trade and Industry 1974 Sec. of State for Industry 1983 Sec. of State for Trade and Industry	*Chairman* 22 May 71 Ld Cole 5 Oct 72 Sir K. Keith (Ld) 22 Jan 80 Ld McFadzean 31 Mar 83 Sir W. Duncan 13 Nov 84 Sir A. Hall (*acting*) 31 Jan 85 Sir F. Tombs *Vice-Chairman* 1 Apr 74-30 Jun 80 Sir D. Spotswood 1 Dec 76-31 Mar 83 D. Pepper 1 Jan 78-17 Dec 82 A. Raeburn	Established in Feb 1971 under the *Companies Act, 1960*, with the Government as the sole shareholder to ensure the continuance of those activities of Rolls-Royce Ltd. which are essential to national defence and to main air forces and airlines all over the world. Shares vested in N.E.B. from 1 Feb 76 to 12 Aug 80. Now under British Technology Group.
British Leyland 1975-	1975 Sec. of State for Industry 1983 Sec. of State for Trade and Industry	*Chairman* 30 Oct 75 Sir R. Edwards 14 Apr 76 Sir R. Dobson 1 Nov 77 (Sir) M. Edwardes 8 Nov 82 Sir A. Bide *Deputy Chairman* *(office vacant)* 1 Nov 77 I. MacGregor 15 May 80 Sir A. Bide 8 Nov 82 Sir R. Hunt	Majority of shareholdings were purchased in 1975, using *Companies Act, 1960*, following financial problems. Shares vested in N.E.B. from 30 Oct 75 to 31 Mar 81.

Nationalised Industries: Assets and Employees, 1950-

	1950		1960		1970		1980	
	Net Assets[a] (£m.)	Total Em-ployed ('000)	Net Assets (£m.)	Total Em-ployed ('000)	Net Assets (£m.)	Total Em-ployed ('000)	Net Assets (£m.)	Total Em-ployed ('000)
British Overseas Airways Corporation	42	16	132	21	251	23	—	—
British European Airways	6	7	58	13	116	25	—	—
British Airways Board	—	—	—	—	—	—	880	57
British Airports Authority	—	—	—	—	73	4	748	7
British Aerospace	—	—	—	—	—	—	992	78
British Electricity Authority / Electricity Council[b] and Area Boards	686	161	1,948	189	4,921	197	7,179	159
North of Scotland Hydro-Electricity Board	53	3	197	3	267	4	610	4
South of Scotland Electricity Board	—	—	153	13	418	15	828	14
Area Gas Boards and Gas Council, British Gas	269	132	585	127	1,658	119	2,576	104
National Coal Board	337	749	910	631	666	356	2,128	294
U.K. Atomic Energy Authority	—	—	488	39	256	30	98	14
British National Oil Corporation	—	—	—	—	—	—	1,000	2
British Transport Commission	1,226	889	1,828	729	—	—	—	—
British Rail	—	—	—	—	850	273	1,230	238
National Bus Company	—	—	—	—	93	84	214	51
National Freight Company	—	—	—	—	116	65	74	31
British Transport Docks	—	—	—	—	123	11	166	11
Iron and Steel Corporation / British Steel Corporation	492[c]	292[c]	—	—	1,222	250	2,056	121
Post Office Corporation	—	—	—	—	2,521	407		
Cable and Wireless	38	13	46	10	70	10	248	12
British Shipbuilders	—	—	—	—	—	—	88	70

[a] Net assets should be treated with caution, as accounting methods and the definition of net assets vary from industry to industry.
[b] Including Central Electricity Generating Board. [c] Figures for 1951.

SOURCE.—*Annual Reports and Accounts* of the individual Boards and from additional information supplied by the Boards themselves.

Inquiries into Nationalised Industries

The nationalised industries have been the subject of a number of Government inquiries into different aspects of their organisation and performance. Recent examples include *Report of the Post Office Review Committee*, July 1977 (Cmnd 6850), and *The Structure of the Electricity Supply Industry in England and Wales,* January 1976 (Cmnd 6388). In addition, the National Economic Development Office in June 1975 were invited to undertake a wide-ranging inquiry into the role of nationalised industries in the economy and 'the way in which they are to be controlled in future'. Their report published in 1976, together with an appendix volume and 7 background papers, add up to the most comprehensive analysis of the industries' post-war performance.

Between 1965 and 1970 the National Board for Prices and Incomes produced reports which, while primarily concerned with prices and wages, considered the efficiency of the industries. From 1967-70 all major price increase proposals by the nationalised industries were referred to the National Board for Prices and Incomes.

The Select Committee on Nationalised Industries (see also p. 182), established in 1956, has also produced the following major reports:

Reports of the Select Committee on Nationalised Industries 1957-79

Date	*H of C Reference*	*Title*
Oct 1957	304 of 1956-57	Ministerial Control of the Nationalised Industries
		Reports and Accounts of the North of Scotland Hydro-Electric Board and the South of Scotland Electricity Board
Apr 1958	187-I of 1957-58	National Coal Board
May 1959	213 of 1958-59	The Air Corporations
Jul 1960	241-I of 1959-60	British Railways
Jul 1961	280 and 280-I of 1960-61	The Gas Industry (2 vols)
Feb 1962	116 of 1961-62	Reports of Former Select Committees on Nationalised Industries: Outcome of Recommendations and Conclusions
May 1963	236-I, II and III of 1962-63	The Electricity Supply Industry (3 vols)
Jun 1964	240 and 240-I of 1963-64	B.O.A.C. (2 vols)
Aug 1965	313 and 313-I of 1964-65	London Transport (2 vols)
Feb 1966	77 of 1965-66	Gas, Electricity and Coal Industries
Feb 1967	340 and 340-I of 1966-67	The Post Office (2 vols)
Oct 1967	673 of 1966-67	B.E.A.
Jul 1968	371-I, II and III of 1967-68	Ministerial Control of the Nationalised Industries (3 vols)
Oct 1969	471-I and II of 1968-69	National Coal Board (2 vols)
May 1970	258 of 1969-70	Bank of England
Feb 1971	275 of 1970-71	British Airports Authority
Jul 1971	514 of 1970-71	Relations with the Public
Jul 1972	312 of 1971-72	British Transport Docks Board
Aug 1972	465 of 1971-72	Independent Broadcasting Authority
Feb 1973	141 of 1972-73	British Steel Corporation
Oct 1973	461 of 1972-73	National Freight Corporation
Dec 1973	65 of 1973-74	Capital Investment Procedures
May 1974	129 of 1974	The Purchasing of Powered Roof Supports and Spares by the N.C.B.
Jul 1975	345 of 1974-75	Nationalised Industries and the Exploitation of North Sea Oil and Gas
Sep 1975	346 of 1974-75	The Ownership, Management and Use of Shipping by Nationalised Industries
Feb 1976	56 of 1975-76	British Airways: The Merger of B.E.A. and B.O.A.C.
Feb 1976	73 of 1975-76	The Post Office's Letter Post Services
Jul 1976	353 of 1975-76	Gas and Electricity Prices
Jul 1976	472 of 1975-76	Cable and Wireless Limited
Jul 1976	508 of 1975-76	Report and Accounts 1974-75 of the National Water Council, Yorkshire Water Authority and Welsh National Water Development Authority
Oct 1976	672 of 1975-76	The Bank of England
Apr 1977	305-I, II and III of 1976-77	The Role of British Rail in Public Transport (3 vols)
May 1977	344 of 1976-77	The Horserace Totalisator Board
Nov 1977	26-I, II and III of 1977-78	The British Steel Corporation
Dec 1977	127-I and II of 1977-78	The British Steel Corporation
Dec 1977	128 of 1977-78	Reports and Accounts of the Regional Water Authorities
Feb 1978	239 of 1977-78	British Waterways Board
Feb 1978	238 of 1977-78	Financial Forecasts of the British Steel Corporation
Jul 1978	582 of 1977-78	Reports and Accounts of the Transport Industries

Date	H of C Reference	Title
Jul 1978	583 of 1977-78	Reports and Accounts of the Energy Industries
Jul 1978	635 of 1977-78	Innovations in Rural Bus Services
Jul 1978	636 of 1977-78	Re-organising the Electricity Supply Industry; Pre-Legislative Hearings
Jul 1978	637-I and II of 1977-78	Independent Broadcasting Authority
		(*Committee abolished* 1979)

Other Public Corporations

There are a number of other public corporations which, while they cannot be placed into the category of nationalised industries, have been treated in an identical way to the industries in the Public Expenditure White Papers. They are:

British Broadcasting Corporation 1926- (see p. 501)
Independent Broadcasting Authority 1954- (see p. 505)
Civil Aviation Authority 1971-
Cable and Wireless Ltd 1947-81
Covent Garden Market Authority 1961-
Development Commission 1909-
National Dock Labour Board 1947-
National Film Finance Corporation 1949-84
Industrial Reorganisation Corporation 1966-70
National Research Development Corporation 1967-
National Enterprise Board 1975- (see p. 409)
Scottish Development Agency 1975-
Welsh Development Agency 1976-
Northern Ireland Development Agency 1976-
Northern Ireland Electricity Service 1973-
Northern Ireland Transport Holding Company 1968-

A number of other corporations are treated somewhat differently for expenditure purposes as they are closely integrated in departmental spending programmes:

Colonial Development Corporation 1948-63
Commonwealth Development Corporation 1963-
Housing Corporation 1964-
National Ports Council 1964-81
New Town Development Corporations and Commission (see p. 441)
Passenger Transport Executives
Public Trust Ports
Regional Water Authorities

Central Government Trading Bodies

Some central government trading bodies raise revenue through the sales of goods and services, but are not answerable to a Minister or organised as public corporations:

Export Credits Guarantee Department 1975-
Forestry Commission 1918-
Her Majesty's Stationery Office (HMSO) 1786-
National Savings Bank 1969-
Land Authority for Wales 1975-
Defence Procurement Agency 1971-
Royal Mint 11th cent, reorganised 1870-
Royal Ordnance Factories
Crown Estate Commission 1762, reorganised 1961-
Land Registry 1862-

Other Quasi-governmental Organisations

It has been suggested that the number of quasi-governmental organisations defies classification. Most official and academic studies indicate that there are between 250 and 350 central non-Departmental bodies of a permanent nature in the U.K. However, in addition to those already listed a number of categories have been identified by C. C. Hood and W. J. M. Mackenzie in Appendix III of *Public Policy and Private Interests*, ed. D. Hague, A. Barber and W. J. M. Mackenzie (1975), and these have been used to set out the examples given below:

1. **Those which are self-financing through fees or levies**
Agricultural Marketing Boards (wool, hops, milk, potato)
Industrial Training Boards
Herring Industry Board 1935-
White Fish Authority 1951-
British Film Fund Agency 1957-84
Corporation of Trinity House 1514-

2. **Statutory monopolies**
Racecourse Betting Control Board 1928-60
Horse Race Totalisator Board 1960-

3. **Those which act as agencies for the spending of government money**
Regional Hospital Boards
Regional Health Authorities
University Grants Committee 1919-
The Family Fund 1972-
Manpower Services Commission 1974-
Sports Council 1972-
Agricultural Research Council 1931-

Medical Research Council 1920-
National Environment Research Council 1965-
Arts Council 1946-
Highlands and Islands Development Board 1965-
Social Science Research Council 1965-83
Economic and Social Research Council 1983-

4. Advisory, regulatory and adjudicative bodies

a) Quasi-judicial bodies
Prices and Incomes Board 1965-70
Monopolies Commission 1956-73
Monopolies and Mergers Commission 1973-
Price Commission 1973-79
Criminal Injuries Compensation Board 1964-
Review Board for Government Contracts 1969-
General and Special Commissioners of Income Tax
Parole Board 1967-

b) Bodies with statutory powers of regulation and licensing
Horserace Betting Levy Board 1961-
Agricultural Marketing Boards
H.M. Land Registry 1925-
Area Traffic Commissioners
Charity Commission 1853-
Transport Tribunals

c) Statutory advisory or consultative bodies nominated wholly or in part by Ministers
Gaming Board for Great Britain 1968-
Metrication Board 1969-80
Cinematograph Films Council 1938-
Consumer Councils of the Nationalised Industries
Equal Opportunities Commission 1975-
Co-operative Development Agency 1978-

5. Special clientele agencies
Uganda Resettlement Board 1972-74

Policy for Nationalised Industries

Four important White Papers on the control of Nationalised Industries have been issued since the war. They are:

Nationalised Industries: Financial and Economic Obligations (Cmnd 1337, 1961)
Nationalised Industries: A Review of Economic and Financial Objectives (Cmnd 3437, 1967)
Ministerial Control of Nationalised Industries (Cmnd 4027, 1969)
The Nationalised Industries (Cmnd 7131, 1978)

In addition a series of White Papers have been published on both Fuel Policy (1965, 1967) and Transport Policy (1952, 1966, 1977) which have had an important impact on the operation of the nationalised industries in these sectors.

SOURCES.—For an analysis of the statutory provisions of the nationalised industries, see D. N. Chester, *The Nationalised Industries* (1951). Other studies of the nationalised industries include: Acton Society Trust, *Twelve Studies on Nationalised Industries* (1950-3); H. A. Clegg and T. E. Chester, *The Future of Nationalisation* (1953); W. A. Robson (ed.), *Problems of Nationalised Industries* (1952); W. A. Robson, *Nationalised Industry and Public Ownership* (1960); A. H. Hanson (ed.), *Nationalisation: A Book of Readings* (1963); D. Coombes, *The Member of Parliament and the Administration: The Case of the Select Committee on Nationalised Industries* (1966); G. L. Reid and K. Allen, *The Nationalised Industries* (1970); R. Pryke, *Public Enterprise in Practice* (1971); L. Tivey (ed.), *The Nationalised Industries since 1960* (1973); M. Rees, *The Public Sector in the Mixed Economy* (1973); D. N. Chester, *The Nationalisation of British Industry 1945-51* (1975); R. Kelf-Cohen, *British Nationalisation 1945-73* (1973); M. Sloman, *Socialising Public Ownership* (1978); I. G. Anderson, *Councils, Committees and Boards* (3rd ed. 1977); R. Pryke, *The Nationalised Industries: Policy and Performance since 1968* (1981).

XIII

ROYALTY

British Kings and Queens, 1900-

Name	Accession	Coronation	Died	Age	Reigned
Victoria	20 Jun 1837	28 Jun 1838	22 Jan 1901	81	63 yrs
Edward VII	22 Jan 1901	9 Aug 1902	6 May 10	68	9 yrs
George V	6 May 10	22 Jun 11	20 Jan 36	70	25 yrs
Edward VIII	20 Jan 36	. .	(Abdicated)	. .	325 days
George VI	11 Dec 36	12 May 37	6 Feb 52	56	15 yrs
Elizabeth II	6 Feb 52	2 Jun 53	. .	. .	. .

Use of Royal Power

Throughout this century great efforts have been made to avoid involving the Crown in politics. But there have been a few occasions when, unavoidably or deliberately, the Sovereign has been involved in decision making. No list of such occasions can be very satisfactory. It may omit times when in private audience the Sovereign expressed strong views to the Prime Minister. It may include times when, despite all the formality of consultation, the Sovereign had no real opportunity of affecting the outcome. The following list of incidents is compiled primarily from *Cabinet Government*, by Sir Ivor Jennings, *King George V,* by Sir Harold Nicolson, *King George VI,* by Sir J. W. Wheeler-Bennett, and *The Political Influence of the Monarchy 1868-1952,* by F. Hardie.

Dec	1909	Edward VII's refusal to promise to create peers until after a second general election.
Jul	1910	George V's sponsorship of the Constitutional Conference.
Nov	1910	George V's secret pledge to create peers, if necessary.
Jul	1914	George V's sponsorship of Buckingham Palace Home Rule Conference.
Mar	1917	George V's support for General Haig, when in danger of being dismissed.
May	1923	George V's summons of S. Baldwin as Prime Minister.
Jan	1924	George V's request to R. MacDonald to form government.
Aug	1931	George V's invitation to R. MacDonald to form National Government.
May	1940	George VI's invitation to W. Churchill to form Coalition Government.
Jul	1945	George VI's advice on switching appointment of Bevin and Dalton (a disputed allegation).
Jan	1957	Elizabeth II's summons of H. Macmillan as Prime Minister.
Oct	1963	Elizabeth II's invitation to E of Home to form a Government.
Nov	1965	Elizabeth II's award of G.C.V.O. to Governor of Rhodesia.
May	1977	Elizabeth II's Silver Jubilee Speech to Parliament stressing her Coronation oath as Queen of the United Kingdom.

Regency Acts, 1937 and 1953

These Acts provide that if the Sovereign is under 18 years of age, the royal functions shall be exercised by a Regent appointed under the provisions of the Acts. (Formerly the appointment of a Regent was *ad hoc.*) The Regent may not give assent to Bills altering the succession to the throne or repealing the Acts securing the Scottish Church.

The Acts provide for Counsellors of State to be appointed during the Monarch's absence from the U.K., or infirmity; and empower certain high officials of the state to declare that 'the Sovereign is by infirmity of mind or body incapable for the time being of performing the royal function'.

The Royal Family

Children of Queen Victoria

1. H.R.H. Princess Victoria (Princess Royal). Born 21 Nov 1840, married Prince Frederick of Prussia (1858), afterwards Kaiser Frederick III, died 5 Aug 1901.
2. **H.M. King Edward VII.** Born 9 Nov 1841, married H.R.H. Princess Alexandra (eldest daughter of King Christian IX of Denmark), 10 Mar 1863, succeeded to the throne 22 Jan 1901, crowned at Westminster Abbey 9 Aug 1902, died 6 May 1910 *(for children, see below)*.
3. H.R.H. Princess Alice. Born 25 Apr 1843, married Prince Louis (1862), afterwards Grand Duke of Hesse, died 14 Dec 1878.
4. H.R.H. Prince Alfred, D of Edinburgh. Born 6 Aug 1844, married Marie Alexandrovna (1874) only daughter of Alexander II, Emperor of Russia. Succeeded as D of Saxe-Coburg and Gotha 22 Aug 1893, died 30 Jul 1900.
5. H.R.H. Princess Helena. Born 25 May 1846, married H.R.H. Prince Christian of Schleswig-Holstein (1866), died 9 Jun 1923.
6. H.R.H. Princess Louise. Born 18 Mar 1848, married M of Lorne (1871), afterwards 9th D of Argyll, died 3 Dec 1939.
7. H.R.H. Prince Arthur, D of Connaught. Born 1 May 1850, married H.R.H. Princess Louisa of Prussia (1879), died 16 Jan 1942.
8. H.R.H. Prince Leopold, D of Albany. Born 7 Apr 1853, married Princess Helena of Waldeck (1882), died 28 Mar 1884.
9. H.R.H. Princess Beatrice. Born 14 Apr 1857, married H.R.H. Prince Henry of Battenberg (1885), died 26 Oct 1944.

Children of Edward VII

1. H.R.H. Prince Albert, D of Clarence and Avondale (1891). Born 8 Jan 1864, died 14 Jan 1892.

2. **H.M. King George V.** H.R.H. Prince George, D of York (1893), Prince of Wales (1901-1910). Born 3 Jun 1865, married (6 Jul 1893) H.R.H. Princess Mary of Teck (Queen Mary, died 24 Mar 1953), succeeded to the throne 6 May 1910, crowned at Westminster Abbey 22 Jun 1911, assumed by Royal Proclamation (17 Jun 1917) the name of Windsor for his House and family, died 20 Jan 1936 (*for children, see below*).
3. H.R.H. Princess Louise (Princess Royal). Born 20 Feb 1867, married to 1st D of Fife (1889), died 4 Jan 1931. Children: (i) H.H. Princess Alexandra, Duchess of Fife. Born 17 May 1891, married H.R.H. Prince Arthur of Connaught (1913), died 26 Feb 1959. Child: Alastair, D of Connaught, born 9 Aug 1914, died 26 Apr 1943. (ii) H.H. Princess Maud. Born 3 Apr 1893, married to 11th E of Southesk (1923), died 14 Dec 1945. Child: D of Fife, born 23 Sep 1929, married (1956) Hon. Caroline Dewar.
4. H.R.H. Princess Victoria. Born 6 Jul 1868, died 2 Dec 1935.
5. H.R.H. Princess Maud. Born 26 Nov 1869, married Prince Charles of Denmark (1896), afterwards King Haakon VII of Norway, died 20 Nov 1938. Child: H.M. Olaf V, King of Norway. Born 2 Jul 1903, married (1929) H.R.H. Princess Marthe of Sweden. Children: (i) H.R.H. Princess Ragnhild, born 9 Jun 1930, married (1953) to E. Lorentzen. (ii) H.R.H. Princess Astrid, born 12 Feb 1932. (iii) H.R.H. Harald, Crown Prince of Norway, born 21 Feb 1937, married (1968) Miss S. Haraldsen. Children: (i) H.R.H. Princess Martha Louise, born 22 Sep 1971. (ii) H.R.H. Prince Haakon Magnus, born 20 Jul 1973.

Children of George V

1. H.R.H. Prince Edward, D of Windsor (1936), Prince of Wales (1910-36). Born 23 Jun 1894, succeeded to the throne as **King Edward VIII** on 20 Jan 1936, abdicated 11 Dec 1936. Married Mrs W. Simpson on 3 Jun 1937. Died 28 May 1972.
2. **H.M. King George VI.** H.R.H. Prince Albert, D of York (1920). Born 14 Dec 1895, married Elizabeth Bowes-Lyon, daughter of 14th E of Strathmore and Kinghorne on 26 Apr 1923, succeeded to the throne on 11 Dec 1936, crowned at Westminster Abbey 12 May 1937, died 6 Feb 1952 (*for children, see below*).
3. H.R.H. Princess Victoria (Princess Royal). Born 25 Apr 1897, married (1922) to 6th E of Harewood, died 28 Mar 1965. Children: (i) George, 7th E of Harewood. Born 7 Feb 1923, married (1949) Marion, daughter of E. Stein. Divorced, 7 Jul 1967. Married (1967) Patricia Tuckwell. Children: David, Vt Lascelles, born 21 Oct 1950; J. Lascelles, born 5 Oct 1953; R. Lascelles, born 14 Feb 1955; M. Lascelles, born 5 Jul 1964. (ii) G. Lascelles, born 21 Aug 1924, married (1952) Miss A. Dowding. Child: H. Lascelles, born 19 May 1953. Divorced July 1978. Married Mrs E. Colvin 1979.

4. H.R.H. Prince Henry, D of Gloucester (1928). Born 31 Mar 1900, married (1935) Lady A. Montagu-Douglas-Scott, daughter of 7th D of Buccleuch, died 10 Jun 1974. Children: (i) H.R.H. Prince William, born 18 Dec 1941, died 28 Aug 1972. (ii) H.R.H. Prince Richard, born 26 Aug 1944, married (1972) Birgit Van Deurs. Children: Alexander, Earl of Ulster, born 28 Oct 1974. Lady Davina Windsor, born 19 Nov 1977. Lady Rose Windsor, born 1 Mar 1980.
5. H.R.H. Prince George, D of Kent (1934). Born 20 Dec 1902, married (1934) H.R.H. Princess Marina of Greece and Denmark, killed on active service 25 Aug 1942. Children: (i) H.R.H. Prince Edward, D of Kent, born 9 Oct 1935, married (1961) Katherine, daughter of Sir W. Worsley. Children: George, E of St Andrews, born 26 Jun 1962; Lady Helen Windsor, born 28 April 1964; Lord Nicholas Windsor, born 25 Jul 1970. (ii) Princess Alexandra, born 25 Dec 1936, married (1963) Hon. Angus Ogilvy. Children: James Ogilvy, born 29 Feb 1964, Marina Ogilvy, born 31 Jul 1966. (iii) H.R.H. Prince Michael, born 4 July 1942, married (1978) Baroness Marie-Christine von Reibnitz. Child: Lord Frederick Windsor, born 6 Apr 1979. Lady Ella Windsor, born 23 Apr 1981.
6. H.R.H. Prince John. Born 12 Jul 1905, died 18 Jan 1919.

Children of George VI

1. **H.M. Queen Elizabeth II.** Born 21 Apr 1926, married to Philip, D of Edinburgh on 20 Nov 1947, succeeded to the throne 6 Feb 1952, crowned at Westminster Abbey 2 Jun 1953. Children: (i) H.R.H. Prince Charles, Prince of Wales (26 Jun 1958), D of Cornwall, born 14 Nov 1948, married Lady Diana Spencer 29 Jul 1981. Children: Prince William Arthur Philip Louis, born 21 Jun 1982; Prince Henry Charles Albert David, born 15 Sep 1984. (ii) H.R.H. Princess Anne, born 15 Aug 1950, married Mark Phillips 14 Nov 1973. Children: Peter Mark Andrew Phillips, born 15 Nov 1977; Zara Anne Elizabeth, born 15 May 1981. (iii) Prince Andrew, born 19 Feb 1960. (iv) Prince Edward, born 10 Mar 1964.
2. H.R.H. Princess Margaret. Born 21 Aug 1930, married on 6 May 1960 to Antony Armstrong-Jones (created E of Snowdon, 1961). Divorced 24 May 1978. Children: (i) David, Vt Linley, born 3 Nov 1961. (ii) Lady Sarah Armstrong-Jones, born 1 May 1964.

Private Secretaries to the Sovereign

1895-1901	Sir A. Bigge (Ld Stamfordham)
1901-13	Sir F. Knollys (Ld) (Vt)[1]
1910-31	Ld Stamfordham[1]
1931-36	Sir C. Wigram (Ld)
1936-43	Sir A. Hardinge
1943-52	Sir A. Lascelles
1953-72	Sir M. Adeane
1972-77	Sir M. Charteris
1977-	Sir P. Moore

[1] Ld Stamfordham and Ld Knollys were joint private secretaries 1910-13 to King George V.

Lord Chamberlains

1898	E of Hopetoun
1900	5th E of Clarendon
1905	Vt Althorp (Earl Spencer)
1912	Ld Sandhurst (Vt)
1921	D of Atholl
1922	E of Cromer
1938	6th E of Clarendon
1952	E of Scarborough
1963	Ld Cobbold
1971	Ld Maclean
1984	E of Airlie

Poets Laureate

1896	A. Austin
1913	R. Bridges
1930	J. Masefield
1968	C. Day Lewis
1971	Sir J. Betjeman
1984	E. Hughes

Civil List of the Crown

The annuities payable to the Sovereign and Members of the Royal Family are known as the Civil List which is granted by Parliament upon the recommendation of a Select Committee.

Year	Privy Purse	Total
1900	£60,000	£385,000
1901	£110,000	£470,000
1931[a]	£97,000	£420,000
1938	£110,000	£410,000
1952	£60,000	£475,000
1972	. .[b]	£980,000
1975	. .	£1,400,000
1976	. .	£1,614,575
1977	. .	£1,905,000
1978	. .	£2,394,962
1979	. .	£2,609,200
1980	. .	£3,527,550
1981	. .	£3,964,200
1982	. .	£4,308,183
1983	. .	£4,515,600
1984	. .	£4,686,000
1985	. .	£5,180,000

[a] By Command of the King the Civil List was reduced by £50,000 p.a. as from 1 Oct 1931, in view of the national economic situation.
[b] In 1972 the Privy Purse, as a separate head, was abolished.

SOURCES.—*Imperial Calendar*; *Whitaker's Almanack*; *Dictionary of National Biography*; *Who Was Who*; *Who's Who*.

XIV

THE BRITISH ISLES

Scotland

Under the Treaty of Union, 1707, Scotland preserved her independent legal and judicial systems, under which developed her system of education and local government which have never been assimilated to those of England and Wales. The established (Presbyterian) Church was also recognised by the Union settlement. After the abolition of the post of Secretary of State for Scotland in 1746 and between the date of the establishment of the Secretaryship for Scotland in 1885 (which became a full *Secretaryship of State* in 1926), Scotland had been controlled into the nineteenth century by a 'Manager', then the Lord Advocate acting through the Home Secretary, and, for a short period from 1881, by an Under Secretary at the Home Office with responsibility for Scottish Affairs, as well as by the developing system of Boards.

The continued existence of the Boards was criticised as anachronistic, maintaining a system of patronage and lacking direct responsibility to Parliament in practice, if not in theory, in Reports of the Royal Commission on the Civil Service in 1914[1] and the Haldane Committee on the Machinery of Government in 1918.[2] Under the Reorganisation of Offices (Scotland) Act, 1928, the Boards of Agriculture and Health for Scotland became Departments statutorily defined independent of, though in reality responsible to, the Scottish Secretary of State.

This constitutional peculiarity disappeared along with the remaining Boards after a general review of the Scottish administration by the Gilmour Committee[3] which led to the Reorganisation of Offices (Scotland) Act, 1939. This Act brought into being four Departments of the Scottish Offices: Agriculture, Education, Health, and Home Affairs, each with their permanent head and with a Permanent Under Secretary of State over them. Further responsibilities were allocated to the Scottish Office during and after the Second World War such as the Crown Estates in 1943 and Forestry in 1945. Following the Report of the Royal Commission on Scottish Affairs,[4] published in 1954, there were further transfers to the Scottish Departments such as the responsibility for roads, bridges and ferries, Justices of the Peace, animal health, and the duties of the defunct

[1] Cmnd. 7338/1914. [2] Cmnd. 9320/1918. [3] Cmnd. 5563/1936-37. [4] Cmnd. 9212/1953-4.

Ministry of Food. Functions withdrawn from the Scottish Office have been fewer; roads were lost to the Ministry of Transport in 1911, though regained in 1956, but the most notable function transferred from the Scottish Office was that of pensions and national insurance in 1948.

In 1962 the Scottish Development Department was created and the Scottish Economic Planning Department was established in 1973. A Scottish Development Agency, responsible to the Scottish Office, was set up in 1975. By 1977 most 'United Kingdom' Departments had regional offices in Scotland. Over the period from 1885, the Scottish Office has gained additional Ministers including Under Secretaries in 1919, 1940, and 1952. A Minister of State was added to assist the Secretary of State in 1952. By 1983 the Scotttish Office was organised into five Departments; the Department of Agriculture and Fisheries for Scotland, the Scottish Development Department, the Scottish Economic Planning Department, the Scottish Education Department, and the Scottish Home and Health Department. The office's headquarters in Edinburgh is complemented by a liaison office in Dover House, Whitehall.

Scotland has its own separate legal and judicial systems, its bar, its established church, and its heraldic authority, Lord Lyon King-at-Arms. A Scottish Grand Committee was established by the House of Commons on an experimental basis in 1894/5 and then from 1907 had a continued existence. Scottish Standing Committees dealing with peculiarly Scottish legislation were created in 1957 and 1962, and a Select Committee on Scottish Affairs was established in 1969 (see p. 199), although it went into abeyance in 1972, but in 1979 the Select Committee on Scottish Affairs was reconstituted (see p. 209). After the passage of the Scotland Act, 1978, a referendum was held on 1 Mar 1979 to ascertain the electorate's views on the provisions for legislative devolution contained in the Act. In the referendum 1,230,937 voted 'Yes' and 1,153,502 voted 'No' but as the 'Yes' majority represented 32.9% of the registered electorate, failing to overcome the 40% provision of the enactment, an Order to Repeal the Scotland Act, 1978, was successfully moved on 20 Jun 1979, following the General Election of 3 May.

SOURCES.—Sir D. Milne, *The Scottish Office* (1957); G. Pryde, *Central and Local Government in Scotland Since 1707* (1960); J. Wolfe (ed.), *Government and Nationalism in Scotland* (1969); H. J. Hanham, *Scottish Nationalism* (1969); J. G. Kellas, *The Scottish Political System* (3rd ed., 1985); C. M. Harvie, *Scotland and Nationalism* (1977); J. Brand, *The National Movement in Scotland* (1977); J. Knox and E. Wilson, *Scotland '78* (1977); H. M. Drucker and N. L. Drucker, *The Scottish Government Yearbook* (1976-83); M. Keating and D. Bleiman, *Labour and Scottish Nationalism* (1979); G. Pottinger, *The Secretaries of State for Scotland* (1979); J. G. Kellas, *Modern Scotland* (2nd ed., 1980); C. Archer and J. Main, *Scotland's Voice in International Affairs* (1980); J. Bochel, D. Denver and A. Macartney, *The Referendum Experience* (1981); M. Keating and A. Midwinter, *The Government of Scotland* (1983); see also Governmental Reports: (Gilmour) Scottish Administration, Cmnd. 5563/1937; (Balfour) Royal Commission on Scottish Affairs, Cmnd. 9212/1954; (Wheatley) Royal Commission on Local Government in Scotland, Report, Cmnd. 4150/1969; Kilbrandon) Royal Commission on the Constitution, Report, Cmnd. 5460-1/1973.

Wales

The only significant devolution of administrative responsibility from Westminster to Wales has taken place since 1950, and this to a much more limited extent than in Scotland. In 1907 a Welsh Department of the Board of Education (now part of the Ministry of Education) was established. A Welsh Board of Health was set up in 1919, but was only to exercise such powers in Wales as the Minister thought fit. A Welsh Office in the Ministry of Housing and Local Government was also established. In 1951 a Minister for Welsh Affairs was appointed, holding the office jointly with the Home Office from 1951 to 1957. From 1957 to 1964 the Minister for Welsh Affairs was also the Minister of Housing and Local Government. A second parliamentary secretary was appointed at the Home Office from 1951 to 1957 to be responsible for Welsh Affairs; in 1957 a Minister of State for Welsh Affairs was appointed and in 1964 a Welsh Office was established with a Secretary of State for Wales. Since 1964 in many detailed ways powers have been devolved from Whitehall to the Welsh Office in Cardiff. In 1960 a Welsh Grand Committee analogous to the Scottish Grand Committee was appointed by the House of Commons to consider all Bills and other parliamentary business relating exclusively to Wales. In 1979 a Select Committee on Welsh Affairs was appointed (see p. 209).

Welsh national or separatist feeling has, however, expressed itself in forces other than the movement for home rule or devolution. The most important aspects of this have been the campaigns on such matters as the Church, education, land, temperance reform and the Welsh language. The 1881 Welsh Sunday Closing Act and the 1889 Intermediate Education (Wales) Act were the beginning of separate legislation for Wales. In 1961, 1968, 1975 and 1982 referendums were held throughout Wales on Sunday opening of licensed premises. The Elections (Welsh Forms) Act, 1964, provided for the use of Welsh on election forms and following the recommendations of the Hughes Parry committee, the Welsh Language Act, 1967, paved the way for the removal of restrictions on the use of the Welsh language in official documents and in the administration of justice in Wales. In 1978 the Wales Act provided for the establishment of a devolved Welsh Assembly in Cardiff, subject to a referendum. In the referendum on 1 Mar 1979 243,048 (11.9 per cent or 20.2 per cent of valid votes) voted 'yes', 956,330 (46.9 per cent or 79.8 per cent of valid votes) voted 'no' and 41.2 per cent did not vote; the highest 'yes' vote (34.5 per cent) was in Gwynedd and the lowest (12.1 per cent) was in Gwent.

In 1901 50 per cent of the population spoke Welsh; in 1931 the figure was 37 per cent; in 1951, 29 per cent; in 1961, 26 per cent; in 1971, 21 per cent; and in 1981, 19 per cent. A Welsh language television channel was established in 1982.

SOURCES.—D. Williams, *History of Modern Wales* (1950); K. O. Morgan, *Wales in British Politics, 1868-1972* (2nd ed. 1980); K. O. Morgan, *Rebirth of a Nation: Wales 1880-1980* (1981); A. Butt-Philip, *The Welsh Question* (1974); B. Jones (ed.), *Anatomy of Wales* (1972); *Report on the Status of the Welsh Language* (Cmnd 2785); *Report of Commission on the Constitution* (Cmnd 5460-1, 1973); D. Balsam and M. Burch, *A Political and Electoral Handbook for Wales* (1980); P. Madgwick and R. Rose, *The Territorial Dimension in U.K. Politics* (1982).

Ireland 1900-1922

From 1900 to 1921 the Lord-Lieutenant of Ireland was responsible for the administration of Irish affairs, with an office in Dublin. His Chief Secretary was a member of the House of Commons, and assisted him in carrying on the parliamentary business of the department, for which he was the responsible minister. At the same time there were several departments in Dublin, working under the presidency of the Chief Secretary: the Department of Agriculture and Technical Instruction, the Irish Congested Districts Board, and the Local Government Board for Ireland. There were three boards of education commissioners, all of whom were appointed by the Lord-Lieutenant or the Government, and there was the Irish Land Commission. The Irish Public Works Board was controlled by the Treasury in London, and not by the Irish Government. There was scarcely any further devolution of administrative authority to Ireland between 1900 and 1922.

The Irish Office remained in existence until 1924 after the partition of Ireland, though the posts of Chief Secretary and Lord-Lieutenant lapsed in 1922, with the recognition of the Irish Free State. The functions previously exercised by the Irish Office became the responsibility of the Home Office (for Northern Ireland) and the Colonial Office handled relations with the Free State (in 1937 renamed Eire). When Ireland became a republic in 1949, the Commonwealth Relations Office continued to be the department responsible for relations with her. In 1966 this responsibility was transferred to the Commonwealth Affairs Office (since 1968 the Foreign and Commonwealth Office).

Lord-Lieutenant of Ireland 1900-22

	1895	Ld Cadogan
8 Aug	02	E of Dudley
3 Feb	06	E of Aberdeen
19 Feb	15	Ld Wimborne
12 May	18	Vt French
2 May	21	Vt FitzAlan

(Office in cabinet only June 95-8 Aug 02 and 28 Oct 19-2 Apr 21)

Chief Secretary for Ireland 1900-22

	1900	G. Balfour
7 Nov	00	G. Wyndham
12 Mar	05	W. Long
10 Dec	05	J. Bryce
23 Jan	07	A. Birrell
31 Jul	16	(Sir) H. Duke
5 May	18	E. Shortt
10 Jan	19	I. Macpherson
2 Apr	20	S. H. Greenwood

(Irish Office wound up 1922)

(See pp. 74-5 for Lord Chancellor of Ireland and Irish Law Officers.)

Northern Ireland 1922-1972

The Northern Ireland Parliament was created by the *Government of Ireland Act*, 1920. The powers of the Crown were exercised by the Governor, appointed by the Crown. Provision was made in the Act for the continued representation of Northern Ireland constituencies in the House of Commons of the United Kingdom. The constitutional position of Northern Ireland was thus unique in that it was part of the United Kingdom and sent representatives to the United Kingdom Parliament but was subject in most internal matters to the jurisdiction of a Parliament and Government of its own. The Government of Ireland Act conferred on that Parliament extensive powers for the regulation of the affairs of Northern Ireland, but excluded a number of specified matters from its jurisdiction. In respect of these excluded matters executive power remained with the United Kingdom Government, and only the United Kingdom Parliament could legislate. Consequently Northern Ireland was subject to two jurisdictions, and although most of Northern Ireland's public services were administered by Ministers who were members of the Northern Ireland Government, there were some public services, such as, for example, the Post Office services, the Customs and Excise service, and the Inland Revenue service, for which Ministers of the United Kingdom Government were responsible.

In respect of all matters on which the Northern Ireland Parliament was empowered to make laws, executive powers were exercisable by the Government of Northern Ireland. At the head of this Government was the Governor appointed by the Crown who formally summoned, prorogued and dissolved the Parliament, appointed the members of the Privy Council, and appointed Ministers to administer such Government departments as the Northern Ireland Parliament might establish. The departments were the Prime Minister's Department, the Ministry of Finance, the Ministry of Home Affairs, the Ministry of Development, the Ministry of Education, the Ministry of Agriculture, the Ministry of Commerce, and the Ministry of Health and Social Services. The Ministers in charge of these eight departments (together with the Minister in the Senate, the Minister of State in the Ministry of Development, and the Minister who was Leader of the House) formed an Executive Committee of the Privy Council which aided and advised the Governor in the exercise of his executive powers.

The Parliament of Northern Ireland consisted of a Senate and a House of Commons. The House of Commons had 52 members. Proportional Representation was used in the elections of 1921 and 1925 but after 1929, except for 4 members for Queen's University, Belfast, they were chosen directly by single-member constituencies. In 1969 the University constituency was abolished and four new territorial seats were created. The Senate had 26 members, 24 being elected by the House of Commons by proportional representation, and two being *ex officio*, the Lord Mayor of Belfast and the Mayor of Londonderry. The main differences between the Northern Ireland law relating to elections to the Northern Ireland Parliament and the United Kingdom law relating to elections to the United Kingdom Parliament were that, after 1950, Northern Ireland law retained the University seats (until 1963) and the 'business premises' qualification for a vote (until 1968), and required qualified electors either to have been born in Northern Ireland or to have been resident in the U.K. for seven years and to possess the requisite residence, business premises or service qualification. The Parliament of Northern Ireland could legislate on all matters except certain fields that were permanently excepted by the 1920 Act, such as the succession to the Crown, making of peace or war, the armed forces of the Crown, the making of treaties, honours, naturalisation and aliens, and certain functions that were reserved such as postal and telegraph services, the Supreme Court, and the important forms of taxation. It was also prohibited from making laws which would interfere with religious freedom or might discriminate against any religious body, and until 1961, from taking property without compensation. All United Kingdom bills applied to Northern Ireland unless there was express provision to the contrary. In general, legislation at Stormont followed very closely legislation in Westminster. The revenue of the Government of Northern Ireland was derived partly from taxes imposed by the

United Kingdom Parliament (known as 'reserved' taxes) and partly from taxes imposed by the Northern Ireland Parliament (known as 'transferred taxes'). The powers of the Northern Ireland Parliament were similar to those of the United Kingdom Parliament as regards the appropriation of revenue. The Treasury was responsible for financial relations with Northern Ireland, and other departments were concerned with trade, commerce, and employment, but the Home Office retained the major responsibility for Northern Ireland.

Governors of Northern Ireland 1922-73

11 Dec 22	D of Abercorn
7 Sep 45	Earl Granville
1 Dec 52	Ld Wakehurst
1 Dec 64	Ld Erskine
2 Dec 68	Ld Grey

(*office abolished* 19 *Jul* 73)

Prime Ministers of Northern Ireland 1921-72

7 Jun	21	Sir J. Craig (1927 Vt Craigavon)
26 Nov	40	J. Andrews
6 May	43	Sir B. Brooke (1952 Vt Brookeborough)
25 Mar	63	T. O'Neill
1 May	69	J. Chichester-Clark
23 Mar	71	B. Faulkner

(*office suspended* 30 *Mar* 72)

Members of Northern Ireland Cabinet 1921-72

Minister of Finance

1921	H. Pollock
1937	J. M. Andrews (also PM 1940-1)
1941	J. Barbour
1943	J. Sinclair
1953	W. Maginess
1956	G. Hanna
1956	T. O'Neill
1963	J. L. Andrews
1964	I. Neill
1965	H. Kirk

Minister of State (Finance)

1971	J. Brooke

Minister of Education

1921	M of Londonderry
1926	Vt Charlemont
1937	J. Robb
1943	R. Corkey
1944	S. Hall-Thompson
1950	H. Midgely
1957	W. May
1962	I. Neill
1964	H. Kirk
1965	W. Fitzsimmons
1966	W. Long
1969	P. O'Neill
1969	W. Long

Minister of Health (and Local Government)

1944	W. Grant
1949	Dame D. Parker
1957	J. L. Andrews
1961	W. Morgan
1964	W. Craig

(1965 became *Minister of Development)*

1965	W. Craig
1966	W. Fitzsimmons
1968	I. Neill
1969	W. Long
1969	B. Faulkner
1971	R. Bradford

Minister of State (Development)

1966	B. McConnell
1969	N. Minford

Minister of Home Affairs

1921	(Sir) D. Bates
1943	W. Lowry
1944	J. Warnock
1949	W. Maginess
1953	G. Hanna
1956	T. O'Neill
1956	W. Topping
1959	B. Faulkner
1963	W. Craig
1964	R. McConnell
1966	W. Craig
1968	W. Long
1969	R. Porter
1970	J. Chichester-Clark (PM)
1971	B. Faulkner (PM)

Minister of State (Home Affai

1971	J. Taylor

Minister of Agriculture (and Commerce 1921-5)

1921	(Sir) E. Archdale
1933	Sir B. Brooke
1941	Ld Glentoran (1st)
1943	R. Moore
1960	H. West
1967	J. Chichester-Clark
1969	P. O'Neill
1971	H. West

Minister in the Senate

1949-50	Sir R. Nugent
1951	A. Gordon
1961	Ld Glentoran (2nd)
1964	J. L. Andrews

Minister of Public Security

1940 J. MacDermott
1941 W. Grant
1943 H. Midgely
-4

Minister of Labour (and National Insurance 1949)

1921 J. M. Andrews
1938 J. Gordon
1943 W. Grant
1944 H. Midgely
1945 W. Maginess
1949 W. McCleery
1949 H. Midgely
1950 I. Neill
1962 H. Kirk
1964 W. Morgan
(1965 became *Minister of Health and Social Services)*
1965 W. Morgan
1969 R. Porter
1969 W. Fitzsimmons

Minister of Community Relations

1970 R. Simpson
1971 D. Bleakley
1971 B. McIvor

Minister of Commerce

1925 J. Barbour
1941 Sir B. Brooke
(also PM 43-5)
1945 Sir R. Nugent
1949 W. Maginess
1949 W. McCleery
1953 Ld Glentoran
(2nd)
1961 J. L. Andrews
1963 B. Faulkner
1969 R. Bradford
1971 R. Bailie

Minister without Portfolio

1944 Sir R. Nugent
-44
1966 J. Chichester-Clark
-67
1969 J. Dobson
-71

Minister of State (PM's Office)

1971 G. Newe

General Elections of Northern Ireland 1921-69

Date	Unionist	Ind. Unionist	Lib.	Lab.	Nat.	Sinn Fein Republican Abstentionist	Irish Lab. Rep. Lab. Soc. Rep. Ind. Lab.	Ind. & Other
24 May 21	40	. .	. .	. .	6	6	. .	. .
28 Apr 25	32	4	. .	3	10	2	. .	1
22 May 29	37	3	. .	1	11	. .	. .	. .
30 Nov 33	36	2	. .	2	9	2	. .	1
9 Feb 38	39	3	. .	1	8	. .	1	. .
14 June 45	33	2	. .	2	9	. .	3	3
10 Feb 49	37	2	. .	. .	9	. .	2	2
22 Oct 53	38	1	. .	. .	7	2	3	1
20 Mar 58	37	. .	. .	4	8	. .	2	1
31 May 62	34	. .	1	4	9	. .	3	1
25 Nov 65	36	. .	1	2	9	. .	2	2
24 Feb 69	36	3	. .	2	6	. .	2	3

Northern Ireland 1972-

After sectarian troubles and terrorist activities which from 1969 onwards cost several hundred lives and led to the sending of substantial British military forces, the British Government on 30 Mar 72 passed the *Northern Ireland (Temporary Provisions) Act*. This Act suspended Stormont and transferred all the functions of the Government and Parliament of Northern Ireland to a new Secretary of State for Northern Ireland, acting by Order-in-Council, for one year (extended in Mar 1973 for a further twelve months). From Mar 1972 to Dec 1973 the Secretary of State was William Whitelaw. He was succeeded by F. Pym (Dec 1973); M. Rees (Mar 1974); R. Mason (Apr 1976); H. Atkins (May 1979), J. Prior (Sep 1981); D. Hurd (Sep 1984).

On 8 Mar 73 on a 58.1% poll, the electors of Northern Ireland voted, 591,820 for the province to remain part of the U.K. and 6,463 for it to be joined with the Republic of Ireland, Eire. Following a White Paper (Cmnd. 5259 published on 2 Mar 73) the *Northern Ireland Constitution Act 1973* was passed; this abolished the office of Governor and the Northern Ireland Privy Council; vested the executive power in the Crown, exercisable by the Secretary of State; provided for a complex system of power-sharing in a new Assembly (to be elected by proportional representation from multi-member constituencies) with an Executive to be appointed by the Secretary of State after consulting with the parties, and also authorised any department in Northern Ireland 'to consult' or 'enter into agreements with any authority of the Republic of Ireland in respect of any transferred matter'. Local elections were held on 30 May 1973 for 26 district councils (using proportional representation) in place of the old local government bodies. On June 28 1973 the 78-member Assembly was elected; its composition was 22 Ulster Unionist (B. Faulkner) 13 other Unionist (12 anti-White Paper) 15 Loyalist Coalition (7 Vanguard (W. Craig) 8 Democratic Unionist (I. Paisley)), 3 Alliance (O. Napier) 1 Northern Ireland Labour Party (D. Bleakley) and 19 Social Democratic and Labour Party (G. Fitt).

The election was followed by prolonged negotiations over the formation of a Northern Ireland Executive, which was finally agreed in December. The Executive which took over on 1 Jan 1974 consisted of 6 Ulster Unionists accepting the Leadership of B. Faulkner, the Chief Executive, 4 Soc. D.L.P. members under G. Fitt, the Deputy Chief Executive, and 1 Alliance Party member. Opposition to the Sunningdale agreement of Dec 1973 (which provided, among other things, for the establishment of a Council of Ireland) led to Mr Faulkner's repudiation by the Unionist Party. In May 1974 a strike of Protestant workers forced the ending of the Northern Ireland Executive and the return to direct rule from Westminster.

On 1 May 75 elections were held for a Northern Ireland constitutional Convention. 46 of the 78 seats went to the Ulster Unionists (H. West), 5 to the Unionist Party of Northern Ireland (B. Faulkner) and one to an Independent Loyalist; there were 8 Alliance members, one from the Northern Ireland Labour Party and 17 from the Social Democratic and Labour Party. The Convention discussions proved abortive.

On 7 Nov 75 it submitted a majority (42-31) draft final report to the Secretary of State, and then adjourned. It reconvened 3 Feb 76, at the request of the Secretary of State, to reconsider the report. The Convention was finally dissolved by Order in Council on 6 Mar 76 because, as reported in the House of Commons on 5 Mar (H. C. Deb. 906 c.1715-1727), the debates and resolutions in the Convention had made it plain that there was no prospect of agreement between the parties and that no further progress could be made.

The Northern Ireland Act, 1982, again attempted to restore devolved institutions to the province. On 25 Oct 1979, the Secretary of State, H. Atkins had announced that the new Conservative Government favoured devolution in Northern Ireland. In Nov 1979 a White Paper was published,

The Government of Northern Ireland: A Working Paper for a Conference (Cmnd. 7763) setting out principles to be observed in the transfer of power, and issues for discussion at a round-table conference. The conference held between Jan and Mar 1980 failed to reach agreement. A further White Paper, *The Government of Northern Ireland: Proposals for Further Discussion* (Cmnd. 7950), published in Jul 1980 put forward further proposals for discussion.

In Feb 1982, J. Prior, the new Secretary of State, held further discussions with the Northern Ireland parties, and in Apr 1982, a third White Paper, *Northern Ireland: A Framework for Devolution* (Cmnd. 8451), was published, proposing a scheme of 'rolling devolution' given legislative effect by the Northern Ireland Act which was placed on the statute book on 23 Jul 1982. This provided for the election of a Northern Ireland Assembly whose functions would initially be limited to scrutiny, deliberation and advice, pending cross-community agreement on the transfer of certain legislative powers.

The election for the Assembly was held on 20 Oct 1982, and of the 78 seats, 26 went to the Official Unionists, 21 to the Democratic Unionists, 14 to the SDLP, 10 to Alliance, 5 to Sinn Fein, 1 to a Popular Unionist and 1 to an Independent Unionist. However, Sinn Fein and the SDLP refused to take their seats in the Assembly, whole on 21 Nov 83 most of the Official Unionists withdrew after some murders in Armagh.

The SDLP took part in a New Ireland Forum with the leaders of the three main parties in Northern Ireland—Fine Gael, Fianna Fail and the Labour Party—which met for the first time on 30 May 1983 in Dublin, and produced a report on 2 May 84 advocating fresh approaches.

(See p. 477 for Army activities.)

SOURCES.—N. Mansergh, *The Government of Northern Ireland* (1936); T. Wilson (ed.), *Ulster under Home Rule* (1955); Sir F. Newsam, *The Home Office* (1954) pp. 167-70; R. J. Lawrence, *The Government of Northern Ireland* (1965); M. Wallace, *Northern Ireland: 50 Years of Self-Government* (1971); F. S. L. Lyons, *Ireland since the Famine* (1971); R. Rose, *Governing without Consensus: An Irish Perspective* (1971); I. Budge and C. O'Leary, *Belfast: Approach to Crisis; A Study of Belfast Politics 1613-1970* (1973); S. Elliott, *Northern Ireland Parliamentary Election Results 1921-72* (1973); A. Maltby, *The Government of Northern Ireland, 1922-72: a Catalogue and Breviate of Parliamentary Papers* (1974); R. Rose, *Northern Ireland, a Time of Choice* (1976); M. Farrell, *Northern Ireland: The Orange State* (1976); P. Buckland, *The Factory of Grievances; Devolved Government in Northern Ireland 1921-1939* (1979); P. Bew, P. Gibbon and H. Patterson, *The State in Northern Ireland 1921-1972* (1979); P. Buckland, *Northern Ireland: A Short History* (1980); W. D. Flackes (ed.), *Northern Ireland: A Political Directory 1968-79* (1980); M. Wallace, *British Government in Northern Ireland from Devolution to Direct Rule* (1982); D. Harkness, *Northern Ireland since 1920* (1983).

The Channel Islands

The Channel Islands which were originally part of the Duchy of Normandy have been associated with England since 1066. They have their own legislative assemblies, systems of local administration, fiscal systems, and courts of law. The Islanders have general responsibility for the regulation of their local affairs subject to the prerogative of the Crown over appointment to the chief posts in the local administrations and the necessity of Royal Assent to legislative measures passed by the insular assemblies. Most of the laws by which they are governed emanate from their representative assemblies and although they cannot be regarded as local authorities most of their public services are provided by these assemblies in the same way as local government services are provided and administered in Great Britain.

The Channel Islands are divided into 2 Bailiwicks, one comprising Jersey and the other, Alderney, Sark, and Guernsey with its dependants, Herm and Jethou. Each Bailiwick has a Lieutenant Governor appointed by the Crown for a period of 5 years, through whom all official communications between the U.K. Government and the Islands pass, and in whom certain executive functions are vested. A Bailiff also appointed by the Crown presides over the local legislatures, the States, and over the sittings of the Royal Court. Since 1948 all members of the States who have the right to vote are elected directly or indirectly by the electorate. The Islands have their own Courts of Law, but there remains leave to appeal to the Judicial Committee of the Privy Council.

The Island Assemblies may initiate legislation but they must then petition the Sovereign in Council to give these measures force of law. Acts of the U.K. Parliament do not apply to the Channel Islands unless by express provision or necessary application. As a general rule Parliament refrains from legislating on matters with which these assemblies can deal unless for some special reason a U.K. act must be preferred to local legislation.

The public revenues of the Islands are raised by duties on imported goods, by income taxes and other taxes. Proposals made by the States for raising revenue require authorisation by Order in Council but responsibility for determining how the revenue shall be spent is, in practice, left to the States. Immunity from taxation for Crown purposes has been a privilege of the Islanders since the time of Edward VI.

SOURCE.—*Report of Commission on the Constitution* (Cmnd. 5460-1/1973).

Jersey

Lieutenant-Governor

1895	(Sir) E. Hopton	1939	R. Harrison
1900	H. Abadie	1940	(*Office vacant*)
1904	H. Gough	1945	Sir A. Grassett
1910	(Sir) A. Rochfort	1953	Sir R. Nicholson
1916	Sir A. Wilson	1958	Sir G. Erskine
1920	Sir D. Smith	1963	Sir M. Villiers
1924	Sir F. Bingham	1969	Sir J. Davis
1929	Ld Ruthven	1974	Sir D. Fitzpatrick
1934	(Sir) H. Martelli	1979	Sir P. Whiteley
		1985	Sir W. Pillar

Bailiff

1899	(Sir) W. Venables-Vernon	1962	(Sir) R. le Masurier
1931	C. Malet de Carteret	1973	(Sir) F. Ereaut
1935	(Sir) (Ld) A. Coutanche		

Guernsey

Lieutenant-Governor

1899	M. Savard	1934	(Sir) E. Broadbent
1903	B. Campbell	1939	J. Minshull-Ford
1908	R. Auld	1940	(*Office vacant*)
1911	Sir E. Hamilton	1945	Sir P. Neame
1914	Sir R. Hart	1953	Sir T. Elmhirst
1918	Sir F. Kiggell	1958	Sir G. Robson
1920	Sir J. Capper	1964	Sir C. Coleman
1925	Sir C. Sackville-West (Ld Sackville)	1969	Sir C. Mills
		1974	Sir J. Martin
1929	E. Willis	1980	Sir P. Le Cheminant

Bailiff

1895	(Sir) T. Carey	1935	(Sir) V. Carey
1902	W. Carey	1946	(Sir) A . Sherwill
1915	(Sir) E. Chepnell Ozanne	1960	(Sir) W. Arnold
1922	Sir H. de Sausmarez	1973	(Sir) J. Loveridge
1929	A. Bell	1982	(Sir) C. Frossard

The Isle of Man

This island was successively under the rule of Norway, of Scotland, of the Stanley family and of the Dukes of Atholl before it became a Crown Dependency in 1765. For over 1000 years the internal affairs of the island have been regulated by the Tynwald, which has evolved from the Lord of Man's Council composed of his chief officials and other persons of importance and the House of Keys. The latter comprises 24 representatives elected by all over the age of 18 who have resided in the island for 6 months. The consent of both the Legislative Council and the Keys is requisite for any Act of Tynwald except when in two successive sessions of a Parliament the Keys pass the same Bill, or a essentially similar one, which is once rejected by the Council. In that case the Bill is deemed to have been passed by the Council. All legislation by Tynwald depends for its validity on confirmation by Royal Assent granted by the Lieutenant Governor or, in certain rare cases, in the form of orders made by the Queen in Council.

Most of the public services are provided by Tynwald and administered by Boards of Tynwald, but the Lieutenant Governor is still the executive authority for certain services, including the administration of justice. In 1866, Tynwald was granted certain financial powers which had been removed from it in 1765. This process continued through the following decades until, by Tynwald's Isle of Man Contribution Act of 1958 the Treasury's control over the Island's finance was removed enabling the Tynwald to regulate its own finances and Customs, although under the Act, the Island continues to make an annual contribution to the Exchequer for defence and common services. There is a statutory body of members of

Tynwald known as the Executive Council the duty of which is to consider and advise the Lieutenant Governor upon all matters of principle and policy and legislation.

Lieutenant-Governor

1899	Ld Henniker	1945	Sir G. Bromet
1902	Ld Raglan	1952	Sir A. Dundas
1919	(Sir) W. Fry	1959	Sir R. Garvey
1926	Sir C. Hill	1966	Sir P. Stallard
1933	Sir M. Butler	1973	Sir J. Paul
1937	W. Leveson-Gower (Earl Granville)	1980	Sir N. Cecil
		1985	L. New

SOURCES.—*Report of Commission on the Constitution* (Cmnd. 5460-1/1973); D. Kermode, *Devolution at Work: A Case Study of the Isle of Man* (1979).

Devolution

Main Landmarks

1906-14	Scottish Home Rule Bills given First or Second Readings 6 times in House of Commons, though never reaching Committee Stage.
1912	First draft of Government of Ireland Bill proposed that all Bills referring exclusively to England, Scotland, or Ireland should be dealt with by national Grand Committees. This was to be a prelude to full legislative devolution but was abandoned to avoid overloading the Government of Ireland Bill.
4 Jun 19	Resolution in favour of devolution carried by 187 to 34.
12 May 20	Speaker's Conference reported (Cmd 692/1920) in favour of either full legislative devolution or devolution to Grand Committees.
7 Jun 21	Devolved powers transferred to Northern Ireland government at Stormont under Government of Ireland Act 1920.
12 Apr 45	First Scottish Nationalist M.P. elected (defeated 5 Jul 45).
1949-51	Scottish Covenant attracts 1,100,000 signatures in Scotland.
1950	Parliament for Wales Campaign.
14 Jul 66	First Plaid Cymru M.P. elected.
2 Nov 67	S.N.P. win Hamilton by-election.
19 May 68	E. Heath in Declaration of Perth proposes directly elected Scottish Assembly. (Endorsed by Douglas-Home Committee 1970)
11 Jun 69	Royal Commission on Local Government (Redcliffe-Maud, Cmnd 4040/1969) envisages eight provincial Councils for England.
15 Apr 69	Committee on the Constitution set up under Ld Crowther (Lord Kilbrandon from 1970).
30 Mar 72	Suspension of Stormont.
18 Jul 73	Northern Ireland Constitution Act provides for a power-sharing Executive.
31 Oct 73	Kilbrandon Commission report (Cmnd 5460/1973) rejects separatism or federation but unanimously favours directly elected Scottish Assembly and approves devolution in general.
1 Jan 74	Power-sharing Executive established in Northern Ireland.
28 Feb 74	General Election results in 7 S.N.P. and 2 Plaid Cymru M.P.s.
28 May 74	Power-sharing Executive resigns, following strike (see p. 392).
3 Jun 74	Privy Council Office publishes discussion document *Devolution in the U.K.*
17 Jul 74	Northern Ireland Act confirms suspension of Northern Ireland Executive.
17 Sep 74	Government announces decision to set up elected assemblies (Cmnd 5732/1974).
10 Oct 74	General Election results in 11 S.N.P. M.P.s (with 30% of Scottish vote) and 3 Plaid Cymru M.P.s.
27 Nov 75	Government outlines detailed proposals in *Our Changing Democracy* (Cmnd 6348/1975, modified by Cmnd 6585/1976).
16-19 Jan 76	Four-day debate on devolution in House of Commons.
9 Dec 76	Consultative document published, *Devolution: the English Dimension.*
16 Dec 76	Second Reading of Scotland and Wales Bill carried 292-247.
22 Feb 77	Government fails (312-283) to secure guillotine on Scotland and Wales Bill.
5 Mar 77	Abortive all-party talks on devolution started.

16 Jun	77	Scotland and Wales Bill 1976 withdrawn by government.
14 Nov	77	Second Reading of Scotland Bill carried 307-263.
15 Nov	77	Second Reading of Wales Bill carried 295-264.
23 Nov	77	House of Commons rejects Proportional Representation for Scottish Assembly Elections 290-107.
25 Jan	78	Amendments setting referendum condition (40% of electorate voting Yes) carried against Government (confirmed 298-243 15 Feb 78).
22 Feb	78	Scotland Bill gets Third Reading, 297-257.
31 Jul	78	Scotland Bill and Wales Bill receive Royal Assent.
1 Mar	79	Scotland votes 'yes' in Referendum (33% to 31% with 36% not voting); Wales votes 'no' (12% to 47% with 41% not voting).
28 Jun	79	Parliament passes resolution nullifying Scotland Act, 1978.
5 Jul	79	Parliament passes resolution nullifying Wales Act, 1978.
5 Apr	82	Government outlines new Northern Ireland proposals in *Northern Ireland: A Framework for Devolution* (Cmnd. 8451).
26 Oct	82	Northern Ireland Assembly elected (see p. 392a).
2 May	84	Irish Forum proposals published in Dublin.

SOURCES.—Wan-Hsuan Chiao, *Devolution in Great Britain* (1926); J. P. Mackintosh, *The Devolution of Power* (1968); H. Calvert, *Constitutional Law in Northern Ireland* (1968); J. C. Banks, *Federal Britain* (1973); A. H. Birch, *Political Integration and Disintegration in the British Isles* (1977); T. Dalyell, *Devolution: The End of Britain* (1977); V. Bogdanor, *Devolution* (1979); see also White Papers listed in Chronology above.

XV

LOCAL GOVERNMENT

Structure

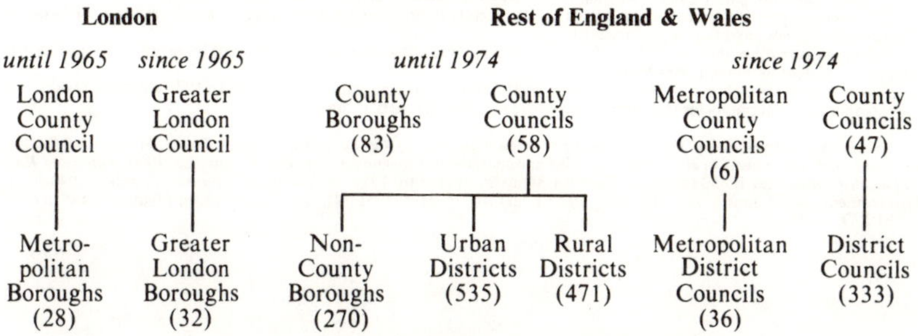

Scotland

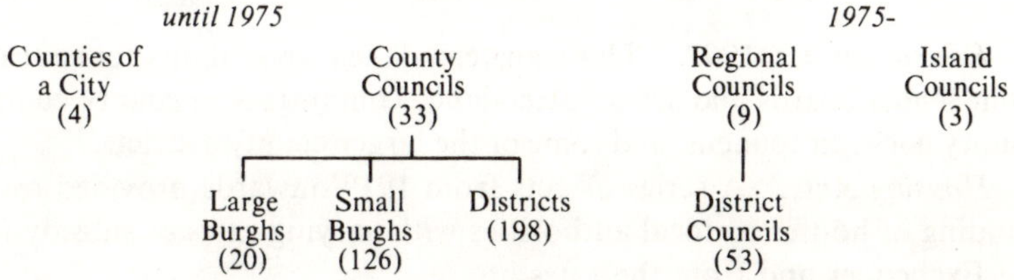

Number of Councils: England & Wales

	County Councils inc. London	County Boroughs[a]	Non-County Boroughs	Urban District Councils	Rural District Councils	London Boroughs and City of London
1900	62	67	250	800	663	29
1910	62	75	249	812	657	29
1920	62	82	246	799	649	29
1930	62	83	300	780	638	29
1940	61	83	256	581	476	29
1950	61	83	309	572	475	29
1960	62	83	319	564	473	29
1973	58	83	270	535	471	33
	County Councils inc. London			District Councils		
1974	54			369		33

[a] The figures in this column are deceptively constant. In the 1960s a few County Boroughs disappeared through local government amalgamation (almost all in Greater London), while a few more non-County Boroughs were promoted to county status.

Parish Councils. This table does not include parish councils. No exact figures for their numbers are available. In 1900 there were about 8,000, in 1920 about 7,000 and in 1966 about 7,700. Following the 1973 reorganisation of local government a number of the smaller authorities that had been abolished applied for parish council status.

Local Government Finance—England and Wales

Year (ending 31 Mar)	Total Receipts from Rates (£000s)	Assessable Value of all Rateable Property (£000s)	Average Rates collected per £ of Assessable Value	Government Grants (£000s)[b]	Total Expenditure (£000s)
1900	40,734	175,623	4s. 11·8d.	12,249	100,862
1910	63,261	215,310	6s. 2·8d.	20,915	166,105
1920	105,590	220,714	9s. 6·8d.	48,263	289,353
1930	156,312	284,937	11s. 6·8d.	107,828	423,655
1940	200,567	318,834	12s. 7·5d.	181,900	578,798[c]
1950	280,195	325,262	17s. 3·0d.	294,358	849,099[c]
1960	646,608	687,618	18s. 10·0d.	705,590	1,865,718[c]
1965	988,054	2,099,034	9s. 6·0d.[a]	1,102,989	2,902,829[c]
1970	1,515,184	2,440,500	12s. 4·8d.[a]	1,954,931	5,405,264[c]
1975	2,927,262	6,659,700	43·95p.[d]	5,651,767	12,253,941[c]
1980	6,122,518	7,441,233	100.3p	11,845,505	18,688,038

[a] Spectacular fall partly due to re-rating of industry and partly to general revaluation 1 Apr 63.
[b] Consisting partly of grants in aid, and partly of receipts from Local Taxation Account and from the local Taxation Licence Duties, not including capital receipts.
[c] Expenditure other than out of loans for capital works. Including the repayment of loans by various local authorities to the L.C.C. Consolidated Loans Fund.
[d] A revised system of returns after 1969 may invalidate comparisons with earlier years. In 1973 a general revaluation of rateable values accounts for the sharp change in the third and fourth columns for 1975.

SOURCES.—*Annual Local Taxation Returns*; *Annual Reports of the Local Government Board, Ministry of Health, and Ministry of Housing and Local Government*; also summarised in the *Annual Abstract of Statistics, 1900. Rates and Rateable Values in England and Wales* (annually from the Ministry of Health, 1919-43. Town and Country Planning, 1943-51, Local Government and Planning, 1951, Housing and Local Government, 1951-74); *Local Government Financial Statistics* 1974-5 (H.M.S.O. 1978).

Major Legislation Affecting Local Government

Education Act, 1902. This transferred the responsibility for education from school boards and school attendance committees to county councils, county borough councils, and some of the larger county districts.

Housing Acts. A series of acts from 1919 onwards provided for the building of houses by local authorities with varying rates of subsidy from the Exchequer and from the rates.

Local Government Act, 1929. This abolished the guardians of the poor, and transferred their responsibilities for poor law and registration to county councils and county borough councils. It also reorganised the system of grants in aid, creating the general grant, partly as compensation for the complete de-rating of agriculture and the de-rating of industry to 25%.

Town and Country Planning Act, 1932. This established a general system of planning control which could be adopted by second tier local authorities.

Local Government Act, 1933. This was a codifying Act covering the structure and constitution of local authorities of all sorts, but making no fundamental change in the law.

Local Government (Boundary Commission) Act, 1945. This provided for the establishment of a local government boundary commission, which was later abolished by the *Local Government Boundary Commission (Dissolution) Act, 1949*. (But see *Local Government Boundary Commission Act, 1958*.)

New Towns Act, 1946. This provided for the establishment of new towns to be built by development corporations appointed by the Ministry, and was succeeded by further Acts which were consolidated in the *New Towns Act, 1965.*

National Health Service Act, 1946. This transferred local authority hospitals to the Ministry of Health. It made counties and county boroughs responsible for ambulance service, maternity and child welfare, health visiting, home helps, prevention of illness, and after-care, etc.

Town and Country Planning Act, 1947. This applied planning control to the whole country, transferred responsibility to county councils and county borough councils, and introduced development charges balanced by a compensation fund of £300m. Development charges and the £300m. fund were abolished by the *Town and Country Planning Act, 1953.*

Children Act, 1948. After the Curtis Committee Report, this Act made counties and county boroughs responsible for all children without proper homes.

National Assistance Act, 1948. This repealed the existing poor law. It made counties and county boroughs responsible for accommodation of the aged and those temporarily homeless, also for welfare services for the blind, deaf, dumb, etc. Financial assistance and residual responsibilities were passed to the National Assistance Board.

Local Government Act, 1948. This replaced the block grant by the Exchequer Equalisation grant. It transferred responsibility for valuation from local authorities to Inland Revenue and it provided for revaluation: small houses being valued on pre-war building costs, other houses by reference to pre-war rents.

Local Government Act, 1958. This abolished most percentage grants and the Exchequer Equalisation grant, substituting a general grant and a rate deficiency grant.

Local Government Boundary Commission Act, 1958. This set up local boundary commissions, producing a number of reports before being wound up in 1966. The main recommendations put into effect were in the Black Country and Tees-side.

Town and Country Planning Act, 1959. This Act altered the basis of compensation for compulsory acquisition.

Public Bodies (Admission to Meetings) Act, 1960. This extended the rights of members of the public and press to be admitted to local authority meetings. These have since been extensions to meetings of Regional Water Authorities, Regional Health Authorities and Community Councils.

Rating and Valuation Act, 1961. This Act ended the derating of industrial and freight-transport property, empowered the Minister to reduce by order the rateable value of dwellings in valuation lists, offered 50% relief from rates on property occupied by charities, and introduced a new method of rating statutory water undertakings. Industry and Commerce re-rated to 100% values.

Town and Country Planning Act, 1962. This consolidated enactments for England and Wales from 1944 onwards and incorporated planning sections of other Acts.

Local Authorities (Land) Act, 1963. This introduced a new 'positive planning'—power for local authorities to acquire land by agreement in advance of requirements; and powers to develop their land and to make advances to promote developments by others on land released by them.

London Government Act, 1963. This Act replaced the old LCC with a Greater London Council which covered, in addition to the old LCC area, almost all of Middlesex and some suburban portions of Surrey, Kent, Essex, and Hertfordshire. All the existing 85 local authorities in the GLC area were merged into 32 new boroughs (the City of London alone preserved its complete independence). The first GLC election took place on 9 Apr 64, two, three and four councillors being chosen *en bloc* from each of the 32 boroughs. The GLC formally took over from the LCC on 1 Apr 65.

Local Government (Financial Provision) Act, 1963. This extended the powers of local authorities to defray expenses incurred by their members and officers, and to contribute to other local authorities and to bodies having activities connected with local government, and made further provision with respect to borrowing by local authorities; the management of local authority debt, the application by local authorities of capital funds, renewal and repair funds, unexpected balances of loans, and capital money received by way of financial adjustment.

Housing Act, 1964. This set up a new Housing Corporation to assist Housing Societies, conferred new compulsory powers on local authorities to secure improvement of houses, amended the improvement grant system and strengthened the powers of local authorities in dealing with houses in multi-occupation.

Rating Act, 1966. This conferred on rateable occupiers of dwellings the right to pay rates in monthly instalments and provided for the granting of rebates in respect of such rates.

Town and Country Planning Act, 1968. This introduced a fundamental change in the land-use planning system in the direction of greater flexibility and speed of action and a greater degree of public participation. The development plan was replaced by the 'structure, action area' and 'local' plans.

Local Authority Social Services Act, 1970. This required counties and county boroughs to combine, under one social services department, the child care, personal health, and welfare services.

Local Government Act, 1972. This was the first full-scale reorganisation of the local government structure of England and Wales since 1889. It abolished the existing system entirely (outside Greater London) and replaced it with a top tier of metropolitan counties in the six conurbations and 47 non-metropolitan counties in the rest of the country. The new second tier comprised 36 metropolitan districts within the areas of the metropolitan counties and 333 districts in the rest of the country.

Local Government Act, 1974. This provided for a Commissioner for Local Administration (an Ombudsman) to be established (see p. 440).

Lotteries Act, 1975. This gave power to local authorities to conduct lotteries under certain restricted conditions.

Inner Urban Areas Act, 1978. This provided for designated urban districts to lend money for land acquisition or for works on land within their areas. Other powers are exercisable in declared 'improvement areas' and by 'partnership' authorities (to make loans for site preparation, grants for industrial and commercial rents, and for small firms' interest payments).

Local Government, Planning and Land Act, 1980. This complex and diverse Act relaxed certain Ministerial controls on authorities and required them to publish reports and information about the performance of their functions (as prescribed by the Secretary of State). It brought the operations of direct labour organisations under control—to secure more regulated working, separate accounting, open tendering, and prescribed rates of return. It extended arrangements for the payment of rates by instalments and added rate rebates for the disabled. It provided for registers of under-used land owned by public authorities in designated areas. The Act also provided for a new control system for local authority capital expenditure—giving expenditure allocations a switching of resources between authorities and between financial years. A new system for the distribution of rate support grant—with a single block grant in place of the previous 'needs' and 'resources' elements—was a major change.

Local Government Finance Act, 1982. This provided for the abolition of supplementary rates and precepts and required them to be levied for complete financial years. By amendment of the 1980 Act it provided expressly for adjustments in block grant payable to an authority to be made by reference to central government guidance. This was designed to encourage reductions in expenditure on account of general economic conditions. The Act also established the Audit Commission for Local Authorities in England and Wales—which will appoint the auditors (whether from the private sector or from the Commission). The Commission is also responsible for studies of the economy, efficiency and effectiveness of local services (and the impact on them of statutory provisions and Ministerial initiatives). It is appointed by the Security of State, who may direct it in the discharge of its functions.

Local Authority (Expenditure Powers) Act, 1983. This was intended to facilitate the aid which local authorities could give to industry—in particular to top up expenditure by the 'free two pence' powers in S.137 of the Local Government Act 1972.

Rate Act, 1984 This allowed for rate limitation—'rate capping'—by a selection scheme or by one of general limitation. It also required authorities to consult industrial and commercial ratepayers before reaching decisions on expenditure and its financing and to provide additional information to ratepayers.

Local Government Act, 1985. This abolished the Greater London Council and the six Metropolitan County Councils and distributed their functions and responsibilities among their component boroughs and some joint authorities.

(*See also Housing,* pp. 330–4.)

Local Authority Interest Groups

The interests of the local authorities have been represented by two main kinds of groups. First, there are the associations of each tier of local authorities. Most powerful amongst these have been the Association of Municipal Corporations (1873-1974) and the County Councils Association (1889-1974). They were replaced in 1974 by the Association of Metropolitan Authorities and the Association of County Councils; a new District Council Association was also formed. In addition, there are associations representing each of the professions in local government services. Examples would be the Institute of Municipal Engineers (1873) and the Institute of Municipal Treasurers and Accountants (1885), renamed in 1973 the Chartered Institute of Public Finance and Accountancy. All kinds of municipal employees are represented by the National and Local Government Officers Association (1905). The National Union of Public Employees (1886) and other Unions.

Many pressure groups which have focused on Local Authorities are listed on pp. 344-60.

SOURCES.—*Municipal Year-Book*; A. Barber, *The Local Authority Movement* (1976).

Commission for Local Government in England

Chairman

1974 Lady Serota
1982 D. Yardley

Commission for Local Government in Wales

Chairman

1974 D. Jones-Williams
1979 A. Jones

Commission for Local Government in Scotland

Chairman

1975 R. Moore
1978 J. Russell
1982 E. Gillett

New Towns

The *New Towns Act, 1946,* with subsequent amendments as consolidated in the *New Towns Act, 1965*, provided for New Towns to be built by development corporations appointed by the Minister. The *New Towns Act, 1959*, set up a Commission for the New Towns to take over responsibility for New Towns as soon as the development corporations' purposes were substantially achieved. The *New Towns (Amendment) Act, 1976,* provided for the transfer in April 1978 to local authorities of certain of the New Towns Commission's housing and related assets.

New Towns	Development Corporation Formed	Handed over to Commission	Area (acres)	Population ('000s) 1951	1961	1971	1981
Aycliffe, Durham	1947		2,508	0·6	12	24	26
Basildon, Essex	1949		7,818	24	54	85	100
Bracknell, Berks.	1949	1982	3,303	5	20	34	48
Central Lancs.	1970		35,225			25	247
Corby, Northants.	1950	1980	4,296	15	36	48	48
Crawley, Sussex	1947	1962	6,047	10	54	68	76
Cwmbran, Gwent	1949		3,157	13	30	46	45
Harlow, Essex	1947	1980	6,395	5	53	71	79
Hatfield, Herts.	1948	1966	2,340	9	20	26	25
Hemel Hempstead, Herts.	1947	1962	5,910	21	55	70	81
Milton Keynes, Bucks.	1967		22,000			46	97
Northampton	1968		19,966			148	162
Peterborough	1968		15,940			87	121
Peterlee, Durham	1948		2,799	0·2	14	22	23
Redditch, Worcs.	1964		7,200			38	64
{ Runcorn, Cheshire (merged	1964		7,234			36 }	198
{ Warrington, Lancs 1981)	1968		19,000			125 }	
Skelmersdale, Lancs.	1962		4,100			27	41
Stevenage, Herts.	1946	1980	6,256	7	42	68	74
Telford, Salop	1963		10,243			80	104
Warrington (see Runcorn)							
Washington, Durham	1964		5,300			25	52
Welwyn, Herts.	1948	1966	4,317	19	35	44	42
Cumbernauld, Dunbarton	1956		4,017		5	32	51
East Kilbride, Lanarks.	1947		13,679	6	32	64	76
Glenrothes, Fife	1948		5,696	2	13	27	38
Irvine, Ayrshire	1966		3,989			42	60
Livingston, W. Lothian	1962		3,641			14	39

In 1973 Stonehouse, Lanarks., was designated a New Town, but its status was cancelled in 1977. In 1967 Newtown, Powys, was designated a New Town, but in 1977 its status was cancelled and it fell under the Development Board for Rural Wales.

New Towns Commission

Chairman

1961 Sir D. Anderson
1964 Sir M. Wells
1971 (Sir) D. Pilcher
1978 C. Macpherson
1982 Sir N. Shields

SOURCE.—F. J. Osborn and A. Whittick, *The New Towns* (1963). See also *Annual Reports* of *New Towns*.

Local Government Elections

After the Second World War the results of Local Government Elections became increasingly accepted as barometers to the national political mood. They could be misleading. The custom of fighting under national party labels spread only gradually and sporadically. The fact that, under the triennial system, only a third of the seats on borough and district councils were fought each year caused much confusion (a party might claim a great trend in its favour because it was gaining compared to three years before, even though it was losing compared to the previous year). Moreover the results were very patchily reported and no altogether satisfactory statistics are available. However, the results in the boroughs of England and Wales (excluding London), both county and non-county, provided some pointer to the national mood (even though the smaller non-county boroughs introduced a very distorting element). Between 3,300 and 3,500 seats used to be fought each year, usually on a party basis; after 1964 the number of seats at risk was between 3,000 and 3,200 owing to the merging of councils under the London Government Act. After 1946 the outcome of these borough contests was fairly accurately reported, although it was not until 1965 that the first really detailed analyses of the voting figures appear (see *The Economist* for the Saturday nine days after the elections each year since 1945).

Borough Council Election Results 1949-72

	Conservative and Conservative-supported Independent	Independent without Conservative Support	Labour	Liberal	Total	Labour % of vote (County Boroughs only)	Turnout % (County Boroughs only)
1947	1,892	359	776	97	3,124	41·7	52·6
1949	1,749	426	1,091	79	3,345	43·2	52·2
1950	1,610	510	1,132	72	3,324	46·2	45·5
1951	1,893	548	883	79	3,403	n.a.	44·4
1952	1,138	488	1,718	53	3,397	55·4	49·9
1953	1,571	447	1,448	60	3,562	52·0	45·2
1954	1,498	511	1,438	74	3,521	49·2	42·8
1955	1,604	514	1,470	56	3,644	47·6	43·8
1956	1,358	454	1,614	72	3,498	51·1	37·6
1957	1,292	435	1,642	89	3,458	50·0	40·0
1958	1,307	460	1,705	118	3,590	49·3	40·3
1959	1,545	441	1,399	103	3,488	45·5	41·0
1960	1,750	449	1,137	130	3,466	40·0	35·4
1961	1,453	470	1,387	196	3,506	43·3	40·6
1962	995	465	1,571	454	3,485	42·4	40·2
1963	973	524	1,733	255	3,485	46·0	41·3
1964	967	474	1,494	149	3,084	47·0	40·5
1965	1,140	476	1,027	154	2,797	38·3	37·7
1966	1,107	467	1,259	151	2,984	43·1	35·6
1967	1,690	466	846	148	3,150	36·4	40·3
1968	2,184	436	450	152	3,222	29·8	35·8
1969	1,972	453	542	168	3,135	33·1	35·6
1970	1,382	406	1,207	133	3,128	44·0	37·6
1971	823	391	1,848	128	3,180	55·7	39·2
1972	890	375	1,643	155	3,063	52·6	36·7

SOURCE.—Conservative Central Office. Turnout figures are drawn from the Annual Reports of the Registrar-General for England and Wales

Party Control in Major Cities 1945-

Party politics in many cities goes back to the first half of the nineteenth century but, although in most sizeable towns (practically all over 50,000) councillors have worn political labels throughout this century, in only a few larger councils did a majority of councillors of one party mean that that party exercised control. Labour successes after the First World War introduced a more organised form of party politics into some councils. After the Second World War, the local government franchise was extended to practically the same basis as that for parliamentary elections (it had hitherto been confined to ratepayers) and, with sweeping Labour successes in the 1945 municipal elections and an organised Conservative counter-attack in the succeeding years, party politics extended their hold to most urban authorities, including practically all those with more than 20,000 inhabitants. Here is the record since 1945 of the party control in cities which in 1972 had more than 200,000 inhabitants: 'Citizen' in Bristol, 'Ratepayers' in Southampton and 'Progressive' (also called 'Moderate') in Scottish cities and Newcastle refers to local anti-Socialist, Conservative-supported parties. For England and Wales the 1974 entries refer to the district councils elected in 1973 (in some cases on enlarged boundaries).

Belfast. 1945- Unionist.

Birmingham
1945 No clear majority.[1] 1946-47 Labour. 1947-49 No majority. 1949-52 Conservative. 1952-66 Labour. 1966-72 Conservative. 1972-75 Labour. 1975-76 No clear majority. 1976-79 Conservative. 1979-80 No clear majority. 1980-82 Labour. 1982-84 Conservative. 1984- Labour.

Bradford
1945-51 Labour. 1951-52 No clear majority. 1952-59 Labour. 1959-61 No clear majority. 1961-62 Conservative and National Liberal. 1962-63 No clear majority. 1963-67 Labour. 1967-72 Conservative. 1972-74 Labour. 1974-80 Conservative. 1980-82 Labour. 1982 No clear majority.

Bristol
1945-49 Labour. 1949-51 No clear majority. 1951-52 Citizen. 1953-60 Labour. 1960-63 Citizen. 1963-67 Labour. 1967-72 Citizen. 1972-83 Labour. 1983- No clear majority.

Cardiff
1945-58 anti-Labour coalition. 1958-61 Labour. 1961-63 No clear majority. 1963-66 Labour. 1967-74 Conservative. 1974-76 Labour. 1976-79 Conservative. 1973-83 Labour. 1983- Conservative.

Coventry
1945-67 Labour. 1967-72 Conservative. 1972-75 Labour. 1975-79 Conservative. 1979- Labour.

Edinburgh
1945-62 Progressive. 1962-65 No clear majority. 1965-71 Progressive[2]. 1971- No clear majority. 1977-84 Conservative. 1984- Labour.

Glasgow
1945-47 Labour. 1947-50 No clear majority. 1950-52 Progressive. 1952-68 Labour. 1968-69 No clear majority. 1969-70 Progressive. 1970-77 Labour. 1977-80 No clear majority. 1980- Labour.

Leeds
1945-51 Labour. 1951-53 Conservative. 1953-67 Labour. 1967-72 Conservative. 1972-74 Labour. 1974-76 No clear majority. 1976-79 Conservative. 1979-80 No clear majority. 1980 Labour.

[1] 'No clear majority' is shown wherever no party had a clear overall majority of seats; frequently a party holding half the seats was able to exercise some control in this situation with the aid of the mayoral vote and in other cases a party exercised control in alliance with a minor group.

[2] The position in Edinburgh and Glasgow is complicated by two *ex-officio* councillors who make clear definition of overall majority difficult.

Leicester

1945-49 Labour. 1949-52 Conservative. 1952-61 Labour. 1961-62 Conservative. 1962-63 No clear majority. 1963-66 Labour. 1966-67 No continuous majority. 1967-72 Conservative. 1972-76 Labour. 1976-79 Conservative. 1979- Labour.

Liverpool

1945-54 Conservative. 1954-55 Conservative with Protestant support. 1955-61 Labour. 1961-63 Conservative. 1963-67 Labour. 1967-72 Conservative. 1972-74 Labour. 1974-83 No clear majority (Liberal largest party 1974-76. Labour 1976). 1983- Labour.

Manchester

1945-47 Labour. 1947-49 No clear majority. 1949-52 Conservative. 1952-53 No clear majority. 1953-67 Labour. 1967-71 Conservative. 1971- Labour.

Newcastle

1945-49 Labour, 1949-58 Progressive. 1958-67 Labour. 1967-74 Conservative. 1974- Labour.

Nottingham

1945-50 Labour. 1950-51 No clear majority. 1951-52 Conservative. 1952-53 No clear majority. 1953-60 Labour. 1960-61 No clear majority. 1961-63 Conservative. 1963-67 Labour. 1967-72 Conservative. 1972-76 Labour. 1976-79 Conservative. 1979- Labour.

Plymouth

1945-53 Conservative. 1953-59 Labour. 1959-63 Conservative. 1963-66 Labour. 1966- Conservative.

Portsmouth

1949-64 Conservative. 1964-65 Labour. 1965- Conservative.

Sheffield

1945-68 Labour. 1968-69 Conservative. 1969- Labour.

Southampton

1945-50 Labour. 1950-54 Ratepayers. 1954-61 Labour. 1961-62 Conservative. 1962-67 Labour. 1967-72 Conservative. 1973-76 Labour. 1976-84 Conservative. 1984- Labour.

Stoke on Trent

1945-70 Labour. 1970-71 Conservative. 1971- Labour.

Sunderland

1945-68 Labour. 1968-72 Conservative. 1972- Labour.

Teesside (created 1967, abolished 1974)

1967-72 Conservative. 1972-74 Labour.

Wolverhampton

1945-49 Labour. 1949-52 Conservative and allies. 1952-67 Labour. 1967-72 Conservative. 1972-78 Labour. 1978-79 No clear control. 1979- Labour.

Local Government Elections 1973-

		Party Control				Seats				
		Con.	Lab.	Lib./Alln	No clear control or Ind.	Con.	Lab.	Lib./Alln	Other	Nat.
Metropolitan Counties[1]	12 Apr 73	—	6	—	—	141	402	49	9	—
	5 May 77	4	2	—	—	360	213	19	8	—
	7 May 81	—	6	—	—	122	425	50	3	—
Other Counties	12 Apr 73	18	11	—	18	1484	1397	210	513	18
	5 May 77	36	3	—	8	2524	641	71	445	37
	7 May 81	19	14	1	13	1560	1376	340	371	23
	2 May 85	10	9	1	27	1370	1269	640	160	21
Metropolitan Districts	10 May 73	5	26	—	5	716	1566	183	48	—
	7 May 75[2]	9	22	—	5	919	1361	173	58	—
	6 May 76[2]	15	18	—	3	1088	1199	151	75	—
	4 May 78[2]	18	14	—	4	1169	1127	124	82	—
	3 May 79[2,4]	11	18	—	7	986	1317	116	87	—
	1 May 80	6	27	—	3	770	1548	133	75	—
	6 May 82	7	24	—	5	751	1457	222	42	—
	5 May 83	7	24	—	5	745	1481	213	39	—
	3 May 84	5	25	—	6	690	1523	228	40	—
Other Districts (England)	7 Jun 73	86	73	—	137	4286	4327	919	3983	—
	6 May 76	176	29	—	91	6783	2758	550	3191	—
	4 May 78[3]	176	30	—	90		[3]			
	3 May 79[3,4]	166	49	—	81					
	1 May 80	148	53	3	82					
	6 May 82	139	59	2	96					
	5 May 83	145	55	3	93					
	3 May 84	140	53	3	100					
Other districts (Wales)	7 Jun 73	1	19	—	17	136	648	42	658	46
	6 May 76	4	9	—	24	199	425	36	644	122
	3 May 79[4]	2	16	—	17	197	604	45	604	67
	5 May 83	3	14	—	20	184	620	58	562	69
Scottish Regions	9 May 74	1	2	—	6	115	171	11	18	19
	2 May 78	2	4	—	3	135	174	7	96	17
	6 May 82	2	3	—	4	119	186	25	88	23
Scottish Districts	9 May 74	5	17	—	31	241	428	17	335	62
	3 May 77	8	5	—	40	277	299	31	335	170
	1 May 80	6	24	—	23	229	494	40	307	54
	3 May 84	4	25	1	23	189	545	78	278	59

[1] Not including GLC.

[2] From 1975 onwards one-third of Metropolitan District Councillors came up for re-election in each year, except those in which there are county elections. The seats are the totals for both continuing and newly elected councillors.

[3] 44 of the 316 non-metropolitan districts in England opted that after 1976 one-third of their councillors would retire at a time. 1978 saw the first such elections.

[4] The 1979 elections took place simultaneously with the General Election.

SOURCES.—D. Clark, *Battle for the Counties* (1977); and the series by J. Bochel and D. Denver, *The Scottish Local Government Elections* (1974, 1977, 1980, 1984); *The Scottish Regional Elections* (1978, 1982).

Metropolitan Counties

	Seats				Votes (%)			
2 Apr 1973	Con.	Lab.	Lib.	Other	Con.	Lab.	Lib.	Other
Greater Manchester	24	69	13	—	38·7	45·1	14·9	1·3
Merseyside	26	53	19	1	33·7	41·3	22·0	3·0
South Yorkshire	13	82	1	4	25·5	55·8	11·3	7·4
Tyne & Wear	27	74	1	2	36·3	55·7	4·6	3·4
West Midlands	27	73	4	—	48·3	42·5	7·7	1·5
West Yorkshire	25	51	11	1	37·3	44·8	14·6	3·3
Greater London	32	58	2	—	38·0	47·4	12·5	2·1
5 May 1977								
Greater Manchester	82	23	—	1	56·6	34·6	7·5	1·9
Merseyside	67	26	6	—	47·7	32·0	19·1	1·2
South Yorkshire	31	62	2	5	39·7	44·7	6·3	9·4
Tyne & Wear	44	54	4	2	49·4	40·7	6·4	3·4
West Midlands	82	18	3	1	56·5	31·7	4·1	6·1
West Yorkshire	54	30	4	—	50·3	35·4	10·3	4·1
Greater London	64	28	—	—	52·6	32·9	7·8	6·3
7 May 1981								
Greater Manchester	19	78	9	—	30·6	49·8	18·0	1·7
Merseyside	27	56	15	—	29·3	45·6	24·2	1·0
South Yorkshire	14	82	3	1	25·8	58·2	12·8	3·2
Tyne & Wear	23	72	7	2	29·4	55·9	12·2	2·5
West Midlands	25	74	5	—	36·0	50·3	9·8	3·9
West Yorkshire	14	63	11	—	30·2	47·5	21·0	1·3
Greater London	41	50	1	—	39·4	41·4	15·0	4·2

Party Representation on the London County Council, 1898-1964

Year	Councillors (elected) Pr.	MRM	Lab.	Ind.	Total	Aldermen Pr.	MRM	Lab.	Ind.	Total	Majority
1898	84	34	. .	. .	118	13	6	. .	. .	137	Pr.
1901	87	31	. .	. .	118	14	5	. .	. .	137	Pr.
1904	83	35	. .	. .	118	15	4	. .	. .	137	Pr.
1907	38	79	. .	1	118	9	10	. .	. .	137	MRM
1910	55	60	3	. .	118	2	15	. .	2	137	MRM
1913	50	67	1	. .	118	3	14	. .	2	137	MRM
1919	40	68	15	1	124	6	12	2	. .	144	MRM
1922	25	82	17	. .	124	5	12	3	. .	144	MRM
1925	6	83	35	. .	124	3	13	4	. .	144	MRM
1928	5	77	42	. .	124	1	12	6	1	144	MRM
1931	6	83	35	. .	124	. .	13	6	1	144	MRM
1934	. .	55	69	. .	124	. .	9	11	. .	144	Lab.
1937	. .	49	75	. .	124	. .	8	12	. .	144	Lab.
	Lib.	Con.	Lab.	Comm.		Lib.	Con.	Lab.	Comm.		
1946	2	30	90	2	124	. .	6	14	. .	144	Lab.
1949	1	64	64	. .	129	. .	5	16	. .	150[a]	Lab.
1952	. .	37	92	. .	129	. .	6	15	. .	150	Lab.
1955	. .	52	74	. .	126	. .	8	13	. .	147	Lab.
1958	. .	25	101	. .	126	. .	7	14	. .	147	Lab.
1961	. .	42	84	. .	126	. .	7	14	. .	147	Lab.

[a] Plus Chairman, an outsider and Labour nominee.

Pr.—Progressives (Lib.).
MRM—Municipal Reform Moderates (Con.).
Lab.—Labour.
Ind.—Independent.
Comm.—Communist.
Lib.—Liberal.

SOURCES.—Sir G. Gibbon and R. W. Bell, *History of the London County Council, 1889-1939* (1939); *General Election of County Councillors* (published after each election by the L.C.C.), 1919-61.

Greater London Council, 1964-1981

Year	Councillors Con.	Lab.	Lib.	Aldermen Con.	Lab.	Lib.
1964	36	64	—	5	11	—
1967	82	18	—	10	6	—
1970	65	35	—	11	5	—
1973	32	58	2	6	9	—
1977	64	28	—	(*Aldermen abolished*)		
1981	41	50	1			

Control and Representation in London Boroughs, 1964-

Year	Control			Councillors			
	Con.	Lab.	No clear control	Con.	Lab.	Lib./Alln	Other
1964	9	20	3	668	1,112	13	66
1968	27	4	1	1,441	350	10	57
1971	10	21	1	601	1,221	9	32
1974	13	18	1	713	1,090	27	37
1978	17	14	1	960	882	30	36
1982	17	12	3	984	781	124	25

SOURCES.—J. Redlich and F. W. Hirst (ed. B. Keith-Lucas), *The History of Local Government in England* (1958); *Report of Royal Commission on Local Taxation 1901*, XXIV; *Report of Royal Commission on the Poor Law 1909*, XXXVII; *Report of Royal Commission on Local Government 1924-25*, XIV; *1928-29*, VIII, *1929-30*, XV; *Proposals for Reform in Local Government 1928*, XIX; *Social Insurance and Allied Services 1942-43* (The Beveridge Report); *A National Health Service 1943-44*, VIII; *Report of Interdepartmental Committee on the Care of Children 1945-46*, X (The Curtis Report); *Report of the Local Government Boundary Commission for the year 1947, 1947-48*, XIII; *Local Government: Areas and Status of Local Authorities in England and Wales, 1956*, Cmnd. 9831; *Local Government: Functions of County Councils and County District Councils in England and Wales 1957*, Cmnd. 161; *Local Government Finance (England and Wales) 1957*, Cmnd. 209. T. W. Freeman, *The Conurbations of Great Britain* (1966). *Report of the Royal Commission on Local Government in Greater London* (1960) Cmnd. 1164. *Staffing of Local Government* (Mallaby) (1967), *Management of Local Government* (Maud) (5 vols 1967). *Report of the Royal Commission on Local Government in England*, Cmnd. 4040, 1969; *The New Local Authorities: Management and Structure* (H.M.S.O., 1972); P. G. Richards, *The Reformed Local Government System* (1973); J. Stanger, *Understanding Local Government* (1976). For details of local voting trends see *The Economist* for the middle of May in each year since 1964.

XVI

THE COMMONWEALTH

Main Territories under British Rule since 1900

Commonwealth Status 1 Jan 1985		Original entry into British rule and Status in 1900	Changes of Status
—	Aden	Colony (1839) and adjacent Protectorate	Acceded to South Arabian Federation 1963. Became People's Republic of South Yemen 1967
Dependency	Anguilla	*See* St. Kitts	Became separate Dependency 1980
Member	Antigua and Barbuda	Colony (1663)	*See* Leeward Isles
Dependency of St. Helena	Ascension	Admiralty administered territory (1815)	Became dependency of Colony of St Helena 1922
Member	Australia	First settled 1788 6 self-governing colonies (1855 and later)	Federal government formed 1901. Dominion status recognised 1907
Member	Bahamas	First settled 1646 Colony (1783)	Independence granted 1973
Member	Bangladesh	—	Became East Pakistan 1947. Broke away from Pakistan 1971. Commonwealth Member 1972
Member	Barbados	Settled 1627 Colony (1662)	Part of West Indies Federation 1958-62; Independence granted 1966
—	Basutoland	Protectorate (1871) Colony (1884)	Independence granted 1966. Now Lesotho
—	Bechuanaland	Protectorate (1885)	Independence granted 1966. Now Botswana
Member	Belize		Formerly British Honduras. Independence granted 1981
Colony	Bermuda	First settled 1609 Colony (1684)	
Member	Botswana	—	Formerly Bechuanaland Protectorate. Independence granted 1966 as Republic
Dependency	British Antarctic Territory	Discovered (1819)	Became a Territory 1982. Part was devolved to Australia 1933
—	British Guiana	Ceded Colony (1814)	Independence granted 1966. Now Guyana
—	British Honduras	First settled 1638 Colony (separated from Jamaica 1884)	Changed name to Belize 1973
Dependency	British Indian Ocean Territory	Dependencies of Mauritius or Seychelles	The Chagos Archipelago and Aldabra, Farquhar and Desroches Islands were formed into a single British Dependency in 1965
—	British North Borneo	Protectorate (1888)	Administered by Chartered Company 1882-1946. Became part of North Borneo Colony 1946. Entered Malaysian Federation as Sabah 1963
Member	British Solomon Islands	Protectorate (1893)	Independence granted 1978 as Solomon Islands

Commonwealth Status 1 Jan 1985		Original entry into British rule and Status in 1900	Changes of Status
—	British Somaliland	Protectorate (1887)	Independence granted 1960 when it became part of Somalia, a Republic outside the Commonwealth
—	British Togoland	—	Administered by Britain under League of Nations mandate 1922-46 and U.N. Trusteeship 1946-57. Merged with Ghana 1957
Member	Brunei	Protectorate (1888)	Independence granted 1984 as Indigenous Monarchy
—	Burma	Indian Province (1852)	Separated from India 1937. Independence granted in 1948 when it became a Republic outside the Commonwealth
—	Cameroons (British)	—	Administered as part of Nigeria under League of Nations mandate 1922. Northern Cameroons incorporated in Nigeria 1961. Southern Cameroons joined Cameroun Republic, outside the Commonwealth
Member	Canada	Ceded Colonies from 1714 onwards. Self-governing Federation (1867)	Dominion status recognised 1907
—	Cape of Good Hope	Ceded Colony (1814)	Dominion status recognised 1907. Province of Union of South Africa
Dependency	Cayman, Turks, and Caicos Islands	Ceded (1670) Dependencies of Jamaica (1848)	Separate dependencies under Colonial Office following Jamaican Independence 1962
Member	Ceylon	Ceded Colony (1802)	Independence granted 1948. Became Republic and changed name to Sri Lanka 1972
—	Christmas Island	Annexed (1888)	Part of Straits Settlements 1900 by incorporation with Singapore. Separate Colony Jan 1958. Transferred to Australia Oct 1958
—	Cocos-Keeling Islands	Annexed (1857)	Part of Straits Settlement 1903. Incorporated in Singapore Colony 1946. Transferred to Australia 1958
Ass. state of N.Z.	Cook Islands	Protectorate (1888)	Annexed 1900. Administered by New Zealand since 1901
Member	Cyprus	British administered territory (1878)	Annexed by Britain 1914. Colony 1925. Independence granted as Republic 1960
Member	Dominica	Colony (1763)	Part of Leeward Islands till 1940. Separate Colony 1940. Associated State 1967. Independent Republic 1978
—	East African Protectorate	Protectorate (1895)	Became a Colony and protectorate of Kenya 1920. *See* Kenya
—	Egypt	Occupied by British since 1882	British Protectorate 1914-22
—	Eire (*see Ireland*)		
Dependency	Falkland Islands	Colony (1833)	Invaded by Argentina, then recaptured 1982
Member	Fiji	Colony (1874)	Independence granted 1970
Member	Gambia	Settlement began 1618. Colony (1843) and adjacent Protectorate (1888)	Independence granted 1965. Republic 1970
Member	Ghana	—	Formerly Gold Coast. Independence granted 1957. Republic 1960
Dependency	Gibraltar	Ceded Colony (1713)	
Member	Gilbert (and Ellice) Islands	Protectorate (1892)	Colony 1915. Ellice Islands separated 1975. *See* Tuvalu. Independence granted to Gilbert Islands as Republic 1979 with name of Kiribati
—	Gold Coast	Settlement began 1750. Colony (1821 and 1874)	Independence granted 1957. Now Ghana

Commonwealth Status 1 Jan 1985		Original entry into British rule and Status in 1900	Changes of Status
Member	Grenada	Ceded Colony (1763)	Part of Leeward Isles 1871-1974. Independence granted 1974
Member	Guyana	—	Formerly British Guiana. Independence granted 1966. Republic 1970
Dependency	Hong Kong	Ceded Colony (1843)	Kowloon ceded to Britain in 1860. New Territories leased to Britain for 99 years in 1898. 1997 reversion to China agreed 1984
Member	India	Settlement began 1601. Indian Empire (1876)	Independence granted 1947. Republic 1950
—	Iraq	—	Administered by Britain under League of Nations Mandate 1932-32
—	Ireland	Union with Great Britain (1801)	26 counties became Irish Free State 1922 with Dominion Status, 1937 Constitution asserted Sovereign Independence. Became Republic of Ireland (Eire) outside Commonwealth in 1949
Member	Jamaica	Colony (seized 1655 and ceded 1670)	Part of West Indies Federation 1958-62. Independence granted 1962
Member	Kenya	—	Formerly East African Protectorate. Colony and Protectorate of Kenya (1920). Independence granted 1963. Republic 1964
Member	Kiribati	—	Formerly Gilbert Islands. Independence granted as Republic 1979
—	Labuan	Colony (1848) governed by North Borneo Company (1890)	Administered by Straits Settlement 1907. Became separate Straits Settlement 1912. Part of North Borneo (1946) now Sabah (1963)
—	Lagos	Colony (1861)	Amalgamated with protectorate of Southern Nigeria 1906
—	Leeward Isles	Colonies federated (1871)	Federated Colony dissolved 1956. (Antigua, Montserrat, St Kitts-Nevis and until 1940 Dominica and Virgin Is.) Part of West Indies Federation (except for Virgin Is.) 1958-62. *See* separate entries
Member	Lesotho	—	Formerly Basutoland Colony. Independence granted 1966 with indigenous monarch
Member	Malawi	—	Formerly Nyasaland. Part of Federation of Rhodesia and Nyasaland 1953-63. Independence granted 1964. Republic 1966
—	Malay States	9 Protectorates, 4 of which were federated	
—	Malaya	—	Formerly Malay States (federated and unfederated) and Straits Settlements. Independence granted in 1957 as elective monarchy. Merged in Malaysia Federation 1963
Member	Malaysia	—	Formed in 1963 by a federation of Malaya, Singapore, Sabah (North Borneo), and Sarawak; Singapore seceded in 1965. An indigenous elective monarchy
Member	Maldives	Protectorate (1887)	Independence granted 1965. Republic 1980
Member	Malta	Ceded Colony (1814)	Independence granted 1964. Republic 1974
Member	Mauritius	Ceded Colony (1814)	Independence granted 1968
Dependency	Montserrat	First settled (1642) as Colony	*See* Leeward Isles. Separately administered since 1962
—	Natal	Colony (1843)	Province of South Africa 1910
Member	Nauru	—	Administered by Australia under League of Nations mandate 1920-47 and under U.N. Trusteeship 1947-68. Independent Republic 1968
—	New Guinea	—	Administered by Australia under League of Nations mandate 1921-46 and under U.N. Trusteeship since 1946. United with Papua 1946 as Papua-New Guinea

Commonwealth Status 1 Jan 1985		Original entry into British rule and Status in 1900	Changes of Status
Member	New Hebrides	—	Administered as Anglo-French condominium 1906. Independence granted as Republic of Vanuatu 1980
Member	New Zealand	Colony (1840)	Dominion status recognised 1907
—	Newfoundland	Settlement began 1623. Self-governing Colony (1855)	Dominion status recognised 1907. Under U.K. Commission of government 1933-1949. Acceded to Canada 1949
Member	Nigeria	Protectorates (1900)	Colony of Lagos joined Southern Nigeria 1906. Protectorates of Northern and Southern Nigeria joined 1914. Independence granted 1960. Republic 1963
—	Norfolk Island	Settled 1788. Under New South Wales (1896)	Became dependency of Australian Government 1914
—	North Borneo	—	Colony created in 1946 mainly from British North Borneo. Entered Malaysian federation as Sabah 1963
—	Northern Rhodesia	Chartered Company territory (1889)	Administered by British South Africa Company. Became Protectorate 1924. Part of Federation of Rhodesia and Nyasaland 1953-63. Independence granted 1964. Now Zambia
—	Nyasaland	Protectorate (1891)	Part of Federation of Rhodesia and Nyasaland 1953-63. Independence granted 1964. Now Malawi
—	Orange Free State	—	Colony 1902. Province of Union of South Africa 1910
—	Pakistan	—	Part of Indian Empire. Independence granted 1947. Republic 1950. Left Commonwealth 1972
—	Palestine	—	Administered by Britain under League of Nations mandate 1922-48. Achieved Independence as State of Israel 1948
—	Papua	Protectorate (1884) Colony (1888)	Administered by Australia since 1906. United with New Guinea 1946
Member	Papua-New Guinea	—	Papua and New Guinea were united under Australian Trusteeship 1946. Independence granted 1975
Dependency	Pitcairn Island Group	Settled 1790 Colony (1898)	
Member	Rhodesia	—	Formerly Southern Rhodesia. Part of Federation of Rhodesia and Nyasaland 1953-63. Resumed status as a self-governing colony with name of Rhodesia 1964. Unilateral declaration of 'independence' 1965. Granted independence as Zimbabwe 1980.
—	Rhodesia and Nyasaland	—	Federation of Northern Rhodesia, Nyasaland, and Southern Rhodesia established in 1953 and dissolved in 1963
—	Sabah	—	Formerly North Borneo. Part of Malaysian Federation since 1963
Member	St Christopher (St Kitts) and Nevis	Colony (1625)	*See* Leeward Isles
Colony	St Helena	Administered by E. India Co. 1673 Colony (1834)	Ascension 1922 and Tristan da Cunha 1938 are its dependencies
Member	St Lucia	Ceded Colony (1814)	(*See* Windward Isles) Independence granted 1979
Member	St. Vincent and the Grenadines	Ceded Colony (1763)	*See* Windward Isles
—		Protectorate (1888)	Ceded to Britain in 1946 as Colony. Part of Malaysian Federation since 1963
Member	Seychelles	Dependency of Mauritius (1810)	Separate Colony 1903. Independence granted 1976. Republic 1976

Commonwealth Status 1 Jan 1985		Original entry into British rule and Status in 1900	Changes of Status
Member	Sierra Leone	Colony (1808) and adjacent Protectorate (1896)	Independence granted 1961. Republic 1971
Member	Singapore	Under Indian government 1824. Became Independent Colony (1946)	Separate Colony 1946. Part of Malaysian Federation 1963-65. Seceded to form Republic 1965
Member	Solomon Islands	Protectorate (1893)	Formerly British Solomon Islands. Independence granted 1978
—	South Africa, Union of	—	Formed 1910 from the Colonies of Cape of Good Hope, Natal, Orange Free State, and Transvaal. Dominion status 1910. Became Republic 1961 and left the Commonwealth
—	South Arabia	—	Federation formed in 1959 from 6 states or sheikhdoms. A further 16 subsequently acceded together with (1963) the Colony of Aden. Became Republic of South Yemen 1967
—	South-West Africa	—	Administered by South Africa under League of Nations mandate 1920-46 and under U.N. Trusteeship since 1946. Unilaterally incorporated in South Africa 1949
—	South Yemen	—	Formerly Aden Protectorate
—	Southern Rhodesia	Chartered Company (1889)	Administered by British South Africa Company. Self-governing Colony 1923. Part of Federation of Rhodesia and Nyasaland 1953-63. Rhodesia 1963-80. Now Zimbabwe
Member	Sri Lanka	—	Formerly Ceylon. Independence granted 1948. Became Republic and changed name 1972
—	Straits Settlements (Singapore, Penang, Malacca)	Colonies (1867)	Part of Straits Settlements. Malacca, Labuan added 1912. Labuan and Penang joined Malay States 1948. Singapore joined Malaysian Federation 1963 but seceded 1965
—	Sudan	Condominium with Egypt (1899)	Independence granted 1956 when it became Republic outside the Commonwealth
Member	Swaziland	—	British Protectorate 1903. Independence granted 1968. Indigenous monarchy
—	Tanganyika	—	Administered by Britain under League of Nations mandate 1920-46 and under U.N. Trusteeship 1946-61. Independence granted 1961. Republic 1962. Merged with Zanzibar to form Tanzania 1964
Member	Tanzania	—	Formed by merging Tanganyika and Zanzibar 1964
Dependency of N.Z.	Tokelau	Protectorate (1877)	Annexed by U.K. 1916. Administration transferred to New Zealand 1925
Member	Tonga	Protectorate (1900)	Independence granted under indigenous monarchy 1970
—	Transjordan	—	Administered by Britain under League of Nations mandate 1922-28. Full independence recognised 1946
—	Transvaal	Annexed 1902	Responsible Government 1906. Province of Union of South Africa 1910
Member	Trinidad and Tobago	Ceded (1802 and) 1814) Colony (combined 1889)	Part of West Indies Federation 1958-62. Independence granted 1962
—	Tristan da Cunha	British settlement (1815)	Dependency of Colony of St Helena 1938. (Evacuated 1961-63)
Dependency	Turks and Caicos Islands	Annexed 1766 Dependency of Jamaica (1873)	Dependency under Colonial Office following Jamaican independence 1962

Commonwealth Status 1 Jan 1985		Original entry into British rule and Status in 1900	Changes of Status
Member	Tuvalu	Protectorate (1892)	Formerly Ellice Islands. Part of Gilbert and Ellice Islands. Separated 1975. Independence granted 1978
Member	Uganda	Protectorate (1894)	Independence granted 1962. Sovereign State 1963
Member	Vanuatu	—	Formerly New Hebrides. Administered as Anglo-French condominium 1906. Independence granted as Republic of Vanuatu 1980
Dependency	Virgin Islands	Colonies (1666)	*See* Leeward Isles
—	West Indies Federation	—	Independence was granted in 1958 to a Federation of the colonies of Jamaica, Trinidad and Tobago, Barbados, the Leeward Isles (except for the Virgin Isles) and the Windward Isles. The Federation broke up in 1962 when Jamaica and Trinidad and Tobago became Independent. Some common institutions were continued by the other members of the Federation
Member	Western Samoa	—	Administered by New Zealand under League of Nations mandate 1920-46 and under U.N. Trusteeship 1946-62. Independent Republic 1962. Full Commonwealth member 1970
Members	Windward Isles	Colonies (1763 and 1814 federated in 1885)	The colonies Grenada, Dominica, St Lucia, and St Vincent. Part of West Indies Federation 1958-62. Attained Associated Statehood 1967. Independence granted to Grenada 1974; Dominica 1978; St Lucia 1979; St Vincent 1979
Member	Zambia	—	Formerly Northern Rhodesia. Part of Federation of Rhodesia and Nyasaland 1953-63. Independence granted as Republic 1964
—	Zanzibar	Protected State (1890)	Independence granted 1963. Republic 1964. Merged with Tanganyika as Tanzania 1964
Member	Zimbabwe	Chartered Company (1889)	Formerly Rhodesia. Independence granted as Republic 1980

Independent Self-Governing Members of the Commonwealth

United Kingdom
New Zealand[1] 1856
Canada[1] 1867
Australia[1] 1901
South Africa[1] 1909-61
Newfoundland[1 2] 1907-33
Ireland (Eire) 1922-49
India[3] 1947 (Republic 1950)
Pakistan 1947-72 (Republic 1956)
Ceylon (Sri Lanka 1972) 1948 (Republic 1972)
Federation of Rhodesia and Nyasaland 1953-63[4]
Ghana 1957 (Republic 1960)
Malaya 1957 (Malaysia 1963) (Elective Monarchy)
West Indies Federation 1958-62[5]
Nigeria 1960 (Republic 1963)
Cyprus 1961 (Republic 1960)
Sierra Leone 1961 (Republic 1971)
Tanganyika (Tanzania 1965) 1961 (Republic 1962)
Jamaica 1962
Trinidad and Tobago (Republic 1976) 1962
Uganda 1962 (Republic 1963)
Zanzibar 1963-64
Kenya 1963 (Republic 1964)
Zambia 1964 (Republic 1964)
Malta 1964 (Republic 1974)
Malawi 1964 (Republic 1966)
The Gambia 1965 (Republic 1970)
Singapore 1965 (Republic 1965)
Guyana 1966 (Republic 1970)
Botswana 1966 (Republic 1966)
Lesotho 1966 (Indigenous Monarchy)
Barbados 1966
Mauritius 1968
Swaziland 1968 (Indigenous Monarchy)
Nauru 1968 (Republic 1968)[6]
Fiji 1970
Tonga 1970 (Indigenous Monarchy)
Western Samoa 1970 (Indigenous Monarchy)
Bangladesh 1972 (Republic 1971)
Bahamas 1973
Grenada 1974
Papua-New Guinea 1975
Seychelles 1976 (Republic 1976)
Dominica 1978
Solomon Islands 1978[6]
Tuvalu 1978
St Lucia 1979

Kiribati 1979 (Republic 1979)
St Vincent and the Grenadines 1979
Zimbabwe 1980 (Republic 1980)
Vanuatu 1980 (Republic 1980)
Belize 1981
Antigua and Barbuda 1981
Maldive Islands 1982 (Republic 1982)[6]
Brunei 1984 (Indigenous Monarchy)

[1] These were recognised as having 'Dominion Status', in 1907.
[2] From 1933 to 1949 Newfoundland was governed by a U.K. Commission of Government. In 1949 Newfoundland joined the Canadian confederation as the tenth Province.
[3] Indian representatives were invited to attend Imperial Conferences and Prime Ministers' Meetings 1917-47.
[4] Although the Central African Federation, set up in 1953, and composed of N. Rhodesia, S. Rhodesia, and Nyasaland, was not a fully independent member of the Commonwealth, her Prime Ministers were invited to the Prime Ministers' Meetings 1955-62 and the Prime Minister of Rhodesia was invited 1962-1965.
[5] Barbados, Jamaica, Trinidad, Tobago, the Leeward and the Windward Islands all formed the West Indies Federation between 1958 and 1962.
[6] Special membership.

Commonwealth Prime Ministers' Meetings, 1900-
(Commonwealth Heads of Government Meetings 1971-)

(All have taken place in London unless otherwise stated)

30 Jun-11 Aug 02	Colonial Conference
15 Apr-9 May 07	Colonial Conference
23 May-20 Jun 11	Imperial Conference
Mar-May 17	Imperial War Conference
Jun-Aug 18	Imperial War Conference
1 Oct-8 Nov 23	Imperial Conference
19 Oct-23 Nov 26	Imperial Conference
1 Oct-14 Nov 30	Imperial Conference
14 May-15 Jun 37	Imperial Conference
1-16 May 44	Commonwealth Prime Ministers' Meeting
23 Apr-23 May 46	Commonwealth Prime Ministers' Meeting
11-22 Oct 48	Commonwealth Prime Ministers' Meeting
21-28 Apr 49	Commonwealth Prime Ministers' Meeting
4-12 Jan 51	Commonwealth Prime Ministers' Meeting
3-9 Jun 53	Commonwealth Prime Ministers' Meeting
31 Jan-8 Feb 55	Commonwealth Prime Ministers' Meeting
27 Jun-6 Jul 56	Commonwealth Prime Ministers' Meeting
26 Jun-5 Jul 57	Commonwealth Prime Ministers' Meeting
3-13 May 60	Commonwealth Prime Ministers' Meeting
8-17 Mar 61	Commonwealth Prime Ministers' Meeting
10-19 Sep 62	Commonwealth Prime Ministers' Meeting
8-13 Jul 64	Commonwealth Prime Ministers' Meeting
17-25 Jan 65	Commonwealth Prime Ministers' Meeting
6-15 Sep 66	Commonwealth Prime Ministers' Meeting
7-15 Jan 69	Commonwealth Prime Ministers' Meeting
14-22 Jan 71	Commonwealth Heads of Government Meeting (Singapore)
2-10 Aug 73	Commonwealth Heads of Government Meeting (Ottawa)
29 Apr-6 May 75	Commonwealth Heads of Government Meeting (Kingston, Jamaica)
8-15 Jun 77	Commonwealth Heads of Government Meeting (London)
1-10 Aug 79	Commonwealth Heads of Government Meeting (Lusaka)
30 Sep-7 Oct 81	Commonwealth Heads of Government Meeting (Melbourne)
23-29 Nov 83	Commonwealth Heads of Government Meeting (New Delhi)

Certain other meetings of comparable status have been held

20 Jun-5 Aug 21	Conference of Prime Ministers and London Representatives of the United Kingdom, the Dominions, and India	London
Jul-Aug 32	Imperial Economic Conference	Ottawa
4-13 Apr 45	British Commonwealth Meeting	London
27 Nov-11 Dec 52	Commonwealth Economic Conference	London
11-12 Jan 66	Commonwealth Prime Ministers' Conference on Rhodesia	Lagos

SOURCES.—*Commonwealth Relations Office List 1951*, pp. 56-58; *Annual Register 1900-*; *Keesing's Archives 1931-*.

Commonwealth Secretariat

As a result of the Commonwealth Prime Ministers' Meeting of Jul 1964 a Commonwealth Secretariat was established in London with its own civil servants seconded from Commonwealth Governments.

Secretary-General

Aug 65 A. Smith (Canada)
Jul 75 (Sir) S. Ramphal

Viceroys and Governors-General

Antigua and Barbuda 1981-

1 Nov	81	Sir W. Jacobs

Australia 1901-

1 Jan	01	E of Hopetoun
9 Jan	03	Ld Tennyson
21 Jan	04	Ld Northcote
9 Sep	08	E of Dudley
31 Jun	11	Ld Denman
18 May	14	Sir R. Munro-Ferguson
6 Oct	20	Ld Forster
8 Oct	25	Ld Stonehaven
22 Jan	31	Sir I. Isaacs
23 Jan	36	Ld Gowrie
30 Jan	45	D of Gloucester
11 Mar	47	Sir W. McKell
8 May	53	Sir W. Slim
2 Feb	60	Vt Dunrossil
3 Aug	61	Vt de L'Isle
22 Sep	65	Ld Casey
30 Apr	69	Sir P. Hasluck
11 Jul	74	Sir J. Kerr
8 Dec	77	Sir Z. Cowan
29 Jul	82	Sir N. Stephen

Bahamas 1973-

10 Jul	73	Sir J. Paul
1 Aug	73	Sir M. Butler
22 Jan	79	Sir G. Cash (*acting*)
24 Sep	79	Sir G. Cash

Barbados 1966-

30 Nov	66	Sir J. Stow
15 May	67	Sir W. Scott
17 Nov	76	Sir D. Ward
23 Jan	79	Sir G. Cash (acting)
Feb	84	Sir H. Springer

Belize 1981-

21 Sep	81	Ms M. Gordon

Canada 1900-

	1898	E of Minto
10 Dec	04	Earl Grey
13 Oct	11	D of Connaught
11 Nov	16	D of Devonshire
11 Aug	21	Ld Byng
2 Oct	26	Vt Willingdon
4 Apr	31	E of Bessborough
2 Nov	35	Ld Tweedsmuir
21 Jun	40	E of Athlone
12 Apr	46	Vt Alexander
28 Feb	52	V. Massey
15 Sep	59	G. Vanier
4 Apr	67	R. Michener
14 Jan	74	J. Leger
22 Jan	79	E. Schreyer
14 May	84	Jeanne Sauvé

Ceylon 1948-72

4 Feb	48	Sir H. Moore
6 Jul	49	Ld Soulbury
17 Jul	54	Sir O. Goonetilleke
2 Mar	62	W. Gopallawa

22 May 72 Declared Republic (Sri Lanka)

Fiji 1970-

10 Oct	70	Sir R. Foster
13 Jan	73	Sir G. Cakobau
12 Feb	83	Sir P. Ganilau

The Gambia 1965-70

18 Feb	65	Sir F. Singhateh

24 Apr 70 Declared Republic

Ghana 1957-60

6 Mar	57	E of Listowel

1 Jul 60 Declared Republic

Grenada 1974-

7 Feb	74	(Sir) L. de Gale
30 Sep	78	Sir P. Scoon

Guyana 1966-70

26 May	66	Sir R. Luyt
16 Dec	66	Sir D. Rose

23 Feb 70 Declared Republic

Viceroys of India 1900-47

	1899	Ld Curzon
30 Apr	04	Ld Ampthill (*officiating*)
13 Dec	04	Ld Curzon
18 Nov	05	E of Minto
23 Nov	10	Ld Hardinge of Penshurst
4 Apr	16	Ld Chelmsford
2 Apr	21	E of Reading
10 Apr	25	E of Lytton (*officiating*)
3 Apr	26	Ld Irwin
29 Jun	29	Vt Goschen (*officiating*)
24 Oct	29	Ld Irwin
18 Apr	31	E of Willingdon
16 May	34	Sir G. Stanley (*officiating*)
18 Apr	36	M of Linlithgow
25 Jun	38	Ld Brabourne (*officiating*)
25 Oct	38	M of Linlithgow
20 Oct	43	Vt Wavell
24 Mar	47	Vt Mountbatten (Earl)

Dominion of India—Governors-General 1947-50

15 Aug	47	Earl Mountbatten
21 Jun	48	C. Rajagopalachari

26 Jan 50 Declared Republic

Ireland 1922-37

6 Dec	22	T. Healy
15 Dec	27	J. McNeill
30 Nov	32	D. O'Buachalla

29 Dec 37 Declared Republic

Jamaica 1962-

6 Aug	62	Sir C. Campbell
27 Jun	73	(Sir) F. Glasspole

Kenya 1963-64

12 Dec	63	M. Macdonald

12 Dec 64 Declared Republic

Malawi 1964-66

6 Jul	64	Sir G. Jones

6 Jul 66 Declared Republic

Malta 1964-74

21 Sep	64	Sir M. Dorman
5 Jul	71	Sir A. Mamo

13 Dec 74 Declared Republic

Mauritius 1968-

1 Sep	68	Sir A. Williams
27 Dec	72	Sir R. Osman
19 Nov	77	Sir W. Garrioch *(acting)*
Mar	78	(Sir) D. Burrenchobay
27 Dec	83	Sir S. Ramgoolam

New Zealand 1900

(Governors)

1897		E of Ranfurly
20 Jun	04	Ld Plunkett
22 Jun	10	Ld Islington
19 Dec	12	E of Liverpool

Governors-General

28 Jun	17	E of Liverpool
27 Sep	20	Earl Jellicoe
13 Dec	24	Sir C. Fergusson
18 Mar	30	Ld Bledisloe
12 Apr	35	Vt Galway
21 Feb	41	Ld Newall
16 Jun	46	Ld Freyberg
1 Dec	52	Sir C. Norrie (Ld)
3 Sep	57	Vt Cobham
9 Nov	62	Sir B. Fergusson
19 Oct	67	Sir A. Porritt
26 Sep	72	Sir D. Blundell
26 Oct	77	Sir K. Holyoake
26 Oct	80	(Sir) D. Beattie
Sep	85	Sir P. Reeves

Nigeria 1960-63

1 Oct	60	N. Azikwe

1 Oct 63 Declared Republic

Dominion of Pakistan 1947-56

15 Aug	47	M. Jinnah
14 Sep	48	Khwaja Nazimuddin
19 Oct	51	Ghulam Mohammed
6 Oct	55	Iskander Mirza

23 Mar 56 Declared Republic

Papua-New Guinea 1975-

15 Sep	75	Sir J. Guise
1 Mar	76	Sir T. Lokoloko
28 Feb	83	Sir K. Dibela

Federation of Rhodesia and Nyasaland 1957-63

8 Oct	57	E of Dalhousie

31 Dec 63 Federation dissolved

St Christopher-Nevis 1983

19 Sep	83	Sir C. Arrindell

St Lucia 1979-

22 Feb	79	Sir A. Lewis

St Vincent and the Grenadines 1979

27 Oct	79	Sir S. Gun-Munro

Sierra Leone 1961-71

27 Apr	61	Sir H. Lightfoot-Boston

(In Mar 67 the Constitution was suspended)

7 Apr	68	B. Tejan-Sie (acting)

19 Apr 71 Declared Republic

Solomon Islands 1978-

7 Jul	78	(Sir) B. Devesi

South Africa 1910-61

31 May	10	Vt Gladstone
8 Sep	14	Vt Buxton
20 Nov	20	Prince Arthur of Connaught
21 Jan	24	E of Athlone
26 Jan	31	E of Clarendon
5 Apr	37	Sir P. Duncan
1 Jan	46	G. van Zyl
1 Jan	51	E. Jansen
25 Nov	59	C. Swart

The Union of South Africa became an independent republic outside the British Commonwealth on 31 May 61.

Tanganyika 1961-62

9 Dec	61	Sir R. Turnbull

9 Dec 62 Declared Republic

Trinidad and Tobago 1962-

31 Aug	62	Sir S. Hochoy
31 Jan	73	Sir E. Clarke

1 Aug 76 Declared Republic

Tuvalu 1978-

1 Oct	78	(Sir) P. Teo

Uganda 1962-63

9 Oct	62	Sir F. Crawford

9 Oct 63 Declared Republic

West Indies 1957-62

10 May	57	Ld Hailes

Feb 62 Federation dissolved

SOURCES.—C. Cook and J. Paxton, *Commonwealth Political Facts*; *Statesman's Year-Book* (1900-).

XVII

INTERNATIONAL RELATIONS

Major Treaties and Documents Subscribed to by Britain since 1900[1]

30 Jan	02	Anglo-Japanese Alliance
8 Apr	04	Anglo-French Entente
31 Aug	07	Anglo-Russian Entente
18 Mar	15	Anglo-Russian Agreement over Constantinople
25 Apr	15	Treaty of London (Italy)
May	16	Sykes-Picot Agreement (Middle East)
31 Oct	17	Balfour Declaration (Palestine)
28 Jun	19	Treaty of Versailles (Germany) and League of Nations Covenant[2]
10 Sep	19	Treaty of St Germain (Austria)
27 Nov	19	Treaty of Neuilly (Bulgaria)
9 Feb	20	Spitsbergen Treaty (status and sovereignty of Spitsbergen Archipelago)
4 Jun	20	Treaty of Trianon (Hungary)
10 Aug	20	Treaty of Sèvres (Turkey)
6 Dec	21	Articles of Agreement for an Irish Peace
13 Dec	21	Washington Four Power Treaty (Pacific)
6 Feb	22	Washington Nine Power Treaty (China)
6 Feb	22	Washington Five Power Treaty (Naval)
23 Aug	23	Treaty of Lausanne (Middle East and the Straits)
17 June	25	Geneva Protocol on the use of Asphyxiating and Poisonous Gases
15 Oct	25	Locarno Pact
27 Aug	28	General Pact for the Renunciation of War (Briand-Kellogg)
22 Apr	30	London Naval Treaty
18 Jun	35	Anglo-German Naval Agreement
25 Mar	36	London Naval Treaty
20 Jul	36	Montreux Agreement (Straits)
7 Aug	36	Non-Intervention Agreement (Spain)
26 Aug	36	Anglo-Egyptian Treaty
29 Sep	38	Munich Agreement
31 Mar	39	Franco-British Guarantee to Poland
13 Apr	39	British Guarantee to Roumania and Greece
12 May	39	British Guarantee to Turkey
25 Aug	39	Anglo-Polish Agreement of Mutual Assistance
14 Aug	41	Atlantic Charter
23 Feb	42	Anglo-American Aid Mutual Agreement (Lend-Lease 'Master Agreement')
26 May	42	Anglo-Soviet Treaty
22 Jul	44	Bretton Woods Agreement (International Finance)
7 Dec	44	Chicago Convention on International Civil Aviation
11 Feb	45	Yalta Agreement
26 Jun	45	United Nations Charter[3]
2 Aug	45	Potsdam Agreement
16 Oct	45	Institution of the Food and Agriculture Organisation
6 Dec	45	Anglo-American Financial Agreement
9 Feb	47	Peace Treaties with Italy, Hungary, Roumania, Bulgaria, and Finland
17 Mar	48	Brussels Treaty Organisation
16 Apr	48	Organisation for European Economic Co-operation
6 Jul	48	Economic Co-operation Agreement (Marshall Aid)
4 Apr	49	North Atlantic Treaty Organisation (Nato)
5 May	49	Council of Europe
12 Aug	49	Red Cross Convention on the protection of civilians in war-time

[1] See also the section on the Commonwealth (pp. 449-54) and on Britain and Europe (pp. 465-70).

[2] The *International Labour Organisation* (I.L.O.) was created by the Treaty of Versailles, as a semi-autonomous organisation associated with the League of Nations. On 16 Dec 20 a statute was drawn up for the establishment of the *Permanent Court of International Justice* at the Hague. The Hague Court had its preliminary session on 30 Jan 22. It was dissolved by resolution of the League Assembly in Apr 1946.

[3] The Charter made provision for the continuance of the International Court of Justice at the Hague. The I.L.O. continued to function as one of the specialised agencies of the United Nations. (Among the other subsidiary organisations were F.A.O., U.N.E.S.C.O., W.H.O., I.M.F., etc. See *The Statesman's Year-Book, 1973-74*, pp. 10-23, for a brief summary of the organisations and their member countries.)

4 Nov	50	Convention for the protection of Human Rights and Fundamental Freedom (U.N. Declaration on Human Rights)
28 Nov	50	Colombo Plan (South and South-East Asia)
8 Sep	51	Treaty of Peace with Japan
20 Jul	54	Geneva Conventions on Indo-China
8 Sep	54	South-East Asia Defence Treaty (Seato)
3 Oct	54	London Nine Power Agreement (European security and integration)
23 Oct	54	Western European Union (formerly Brussels Treaty Organisation)
21 Dec	54	European Coal and Steel Community (Britain made an agreement of association). Community formed on 18 Apr 51
4 Apr	55	Special agreement whereby Britain joined the Baghdad Pact (defence). (Pact signed 24 Feb 55)
5 May	55	Bonn/Paris Conventions terminating the Occupation Regime in West Germany
15 May	55	Austrian State Treaty (occupation ended and declaration of neutrality)
29 Jul	57	International Atomic Energy Agency
29 Apr	58	Law of the Sea Convention (Continental Shelf)
4 Feb	59	European Atomic Energy Community (Euratom). Britain made an agreement of association. (Euratom formed 1 Jan 58)
21 Aug	59	Central Treaty Organisation (Cento). Formerly the Baghdad Pact
20 Nov	59	European Free Trade Association
31 May	59	Antarctic Treaty
14 Dec	60	Organisation for Economic Co-operation and Development (formerly Organisation for European Economic Co-operation)
18 Apr	61	Vienna Convention on Diplomatic Relations
30 Sep	62	Convention on the High Seas
6 Apr	63	Polaris Sales Agreement with the U.S.A.
5 Aug	63	Test-ban Treaty
30 Aug	63	European Space Research Organisation
9 Mar	64	European Fisheries Convention
20 Aug	64	INTELSAT agreement (interim arrangements for a global commercial communications satellite system)
27 Jan	67	Outer Space Treaty
25 Aug	67	'Hotline' Agreement with U.S.S.R.
22 Apr	68	Agreement on the Rescue and Return of Astronauts and Space Vehicles
1 Jul	68	Nuclear Non-Proliferation Treaty
13 Aug	70	Ratification by U.K. of the Hague Convention on the Pacific Settlement of International Disputes (originally signed 29 Jul 1889)
11 Feb	71	Treaty on prohibition of weapons of mass destruction on sea-bed
20 Aug	71	Revised INTELSAT Agreement and INTELSAT operating Agreement
3 Sep	71	Quadripartite Agreement on Berlin
22 Jan	72	Treaty of Accession to European Economic Community and European Atomic Energy Community
10 Apr	72	Convention on the Prohibition of the Development, Production and Stockpiling of Bacteriological (Biological) and Toxic Weapons
9 Nov	72	Quadripartite Declaration on the entry of the Federal Republic of Germany and the German Democratic Republic into the U.N.
28 Feb	75	Lomé Convention (E.E.C. with 46 African, Caribbean and Pacific Territories)
1 Aug	75	Final Act of Conference on Security and co-operation in Europe (Helsinki Conference)
20 May	76	International (U.N.) Covenants on Economic and Social Rights and on Civil and Political Rights
18 May	77	Convention on the Prohibition of military or any other hostile use of environmental modification techniques
21 Dec	79	Lancaster House agreement between Britain and the leaders of the main parties in Zimbabwe-Rhodesia.
19 Dec	84	Hong Kong treaty between Britain and China signed in Peking.

League of Nations, 1919-1946

Britain was a founder member of the League of Nations. Between 1919 and 1922 the British Government conducted its relations with the League through its cabinet secretariat. After 1922 the Foreign Office was responsible for British representation at the League. A member of the Government was generally deputed to act as British representative at meetings of the League. No permanent national delegation stayed at Geneva. A. Eden was the only Minister appointed officially for League of Nations Affairs (7 Jun-22 Dec 35). Vt Cranborne was Parliamentary Under-Secretary at the Foreign Office with special responsibility for League of Nations Affairs from 6 Aug 35 until 20 Feb 38. The League was formally dissolved in 1946 although in practice it ceased to meet during the war.

United Nations, 1946-

Britain was one of the original signatories of the Charter of the United Nations. Since 1946 the British Government has had a permanent representative at the United Nations in New York. In addition, a Minister of State at the Foreign Office has usually been given special responsibility for United Nations affairs. From 1964 to 1970 the permanent representative was a Minister of State at the Foreign Office.

Foreign Affairs Pressure Groups

The League of Nations Union (1920-45) and the United Nations Association (1945-) have provided nationwide forums for the discussion of foreign affairs. Other bodies concerned with the country's international involvements include the Royal Institute of International Affairs (Chatham House) (1920), the European Movement (1949), Amnesty International (1960) and the Campaign for Nuclear Disarmament (1958).

British Ambassadors to Leading Powers, 1900-

Austria-Hungary (-1914)

1896		Sir H. Rumbold
9 Sep	00	Sir F. Plunkett
7 May	05	Sir W. Goschen
1 Nov	08	Sir F. Cartwright
1 Nov	13	Sir M. de Bunsen
2 *Aug*	14	*War declared by G.B. on Austria-Hungary*

France

1896		Sir E. Monson
1 Jan	05	Sir F. Bertie (Ld)
9 Apr	18	E of Derby
7 Nov	20	Ld Hardinge of Penhurst
1 Dec	22	M of Crewe
0 Jul	28	Sir W. Tyrrell (Ld)
7 Apr	34	Sir G. Clerk
4 Apr	37	Sir E. Phipps
1 Nov	39	Sir R. Campbell
24 *Jun*	40	*Diplomatic mission withdrawn*
23 Oct	44	A. Duff Cooper
9 Jan	48	Sir O. Harvey
13 Apr	54	Sir G. Jebb
11 Apr	60	Sir P. Dixon
11 Feb	65	Sir P. Reilly
17 Sep	68	(Sir) C. Soames
13 Nov	72	Sir E. Tomkins
8 Dec	75	Sir N. Henderson
20 Apr	79	Sir R. Hibbert
4 Mar	82	Sir J. Fretwell

Germany

1895		Sir F. Lascelles
1 Nov	08	Sir W. Goschen
4 *Aug*	14	*War declared by G.B. on Germany*
10 Jan	20	Ld Kilmarnock (*ch. d'aff.*)
29 Jun	20	Ld D'Abernon
12 Oct	26	Sir R. Lindsay
1 Aug	28	Sir H. Rumbold
2 Aug	33	Sir E. Phipps
29 Apr	37	Sir N. Henderson
3 *Sep*	39	*War declared by G.B. on Germany*

(Military Governors)

1945	Sir B. Montgomery
1946	Sir S. Douglas
1947	Sir B. Robertson

(British High Commissioners)

1949	Sir B. Robertson
1950	Sir I. Kirkpatrick
1953	Sir F. Hoyer Millar

(Ambassadors to West Germany)

5 May	55	Sir F. Hoyer Millar
7 Feb	57	Sir C. Steel
15 Feb	63	Sir F. Roberts
15 May	68	Sir R. Jackling
25 Jul	72	Sir N. Henderson
30 Sep	75	Sir O. Wright
17 Mar	81	Sir J. Taylor
1 Sep	84	Sir J. Bullard

Italy

	1898	Sir P. Currie (Ld)
17 Jan	03	Sir F. Bertie
1 Jan	05	Sir E. Egerton
1 Dec	08	Sir J. Rennell Rodd
21 Oct	19	Sir G. Buchanan
25 Nov	21	Sir R. Graham
26 Oct	33	Sir E. Drummond (E of Perth)
1 May	39	Sir P. Loraine
11 *Jun*	40	*War declared by Italy on G.B.*
5 Apr	44	Sir N. Charles (1944, *High Commissioner*; 1945, *Representative of H.M. Government with the personal rank of Ambassador)*
9 Oct	47	Sir V. Mallet
12 Nov	53	Sir A. Clarke
19 Sep	62	Sir J. Ward
17 Dec	66	Sir E. Shuckburgh
16 Sep	69	Sir P. Hancock
14 Oct	76	Sir A. Campbell
12 Jul	79	Sir R. Arculus
1 Mar	83	Ld Bridges

Russia (U.S.S.R.)

	1898	Sir C. Scott
28 Apr	04	Sir C. Hardinge (Ld)
10 Feb	06	Sir A. Nicolson
23 Nov	10	Sir G. Buchanan
	1917	*Diplomatic mission withdrawn*
1 Feb	24	Sir R. Hodgson (*ch. d'aff.*)
3 *Jun*	27	*Suspension of diplomatic relations*
7 Dec	29	Sir E. Ovey
24 Oct	33	Vt Chilston
19 Jan	39	Sir W. Seeds
12 Jun	40	Sir S. Cripps
4 Feb	42	Sir A. Kerr (Ld Inverchapel)
17 May	46	Sir M. Peterson
22 Jun	49	Sir D. Kelly
18 Oct	51	Sir A. Gascoigne
1 Oct	53	Sir W. Hayter
19 Feb	57	Sir P. Reilly
29 Apr	60	Sir F. Roberts
27 Nov	62	Sir H. Trevelyan
27 Aug	65	Sir G. Harrison
3 Oct	68	Sir D. Wilson
9 Sep	71	Sir J. Killick
13 Nov	73	Sir T. Garvey
18 Jan	76	(Sir) H. Smith
1 Apr	78	(Sir) C. Keeble
16 Sep	82	Sir I. Sutherland
Sep	85	Sir B. Cartledge

Turkey

	1898	Sir N. O'Conor
1 Apr	08	Sir G. Barclay (*Min. plen. ad. int.*)
1 Jul	08	Sir G. Lowther
10 Oct	13	Sir L. Mallet
5 *Nov*	14	*War declared by G.B. on Turkey*
1 Nov	20	Sir H. Rumbold
2 Feb	24	(Sir) R. Lindsay *(H.M. Representative)*
1 Mar	25	Sir R. Lindsay *(Ambassador)*
12 Nov	26	Sir G. Clerk
16 Dec	33	Sir P. Loraine
25 Feb	39	Sir H. Knatchbull-Hugessen
29 Sep	44	Sir M. Peterson
10 May	46	Sir D. Kelly
20 Apr	49	Sir N. Charles
6 Dec	51	Sir K. Helm
13 Jan	54	Sir J. Bowker
15 Nov	58	Sir B. Burrows
7 Mar	63	Sir W. Allen
16 Mar	67	Sir R. Allen
8 Feb	73	Sir H. Phillips
15 Jun	77	Sir D. Dodson
30 Jan	80	Sir P. Laurence
28 Feb	83	(Sir) M. Russell

U.S.A.

	1893	Sir J. Pauncefote (Ld)
4 Jun	02	(Sir) M. Herbert
23 Oct	03	Sir M. Durand
3 Feb	07	J. Bryce
19 Apr	13	Sir A. Spring-Rice
1 Jan	18	E of Reading
25 Mar	20	Sir A. Geddes
2 Feb	24	Sir E. Howard
11 Mar	30	Sir R. Lindsay
29 Aug	39	M of Lothian
24 Jan	41	Vt Halifax (E of)
23 May	46	Ld Inverchapel
22 May	48	Sir O. Franks
31 Dec	52	Sir R. Makins
2 Nov	56	Sir H. Caccia
18 Oct	61	Sir W. Ormsby-Gore (Ld Harlech)
6 Apr	65	Sir P. Dean
21 Feb	69	J. Freeman
4 Jan	71	E of Cromer
3 Mar	74	Sir P. Ramsbotham
21 Jul	77	P. Jay
9 Jul	79	Sir N. Henderson
2 Sep	82	Sir O. Wright

North Atlantic Council

1953	Sir C. Steel
1957	Sir F. Roberts
1960	Sir P. Mason
1963	Sir E. Shuckburgh
1966	Sir B. Burrows
1970	Sir E. Peck
1975	Sir J. Killick
1979	Sir C. Rose
1982	Sir J. Graham

The United Nations

1946	Sir A. Cadogan
1950	Sir G. Jebb
1954	Sir P. Dixon
1960	Sir P. Dean
1964	Ld Caradon
1970	Sir C. Crowe
1973	Sir D. Maitland
1974	I. Richard
1979	Sir A. Parsons
1982	Sir J. Thomson

SOURCES.—*United Nations Year-books, 1946-; Foreign Office List 1953-66; Diplomatic Service List 1967-.*

Among the major works on international relations since 1900 are: A. J. P. Taylor, *Struggle for Mastery in Europe, 1848-1918* (1954); C. R. M. F. Cruttwell, *A History of the Great War, 1914-18* (1936); C. B. Falls, *The First World War* (1960); G. M. Gathorne-Hardy, *A Short History of International Affairs, 1920-39* (1950); E. H. Carr, *International Relations between the Two World Wars* (1947); E. H. Carr, *Twenty Years' Crisis* (1947); G. F. Hudson, *Far East in World Politics* (1939); W. M. Jordan, *Great Britain, France and the German Problem, 1919-39* (1943); A. J. P Taylor, *Origins of the Second World War* (1961); J. W. Wheeler-Bennett, *Munich: Prologue to Tragedy* (1948); A. Wolfers, *Britain and France between the two Wars* (1940); Sir L. Woodward, *British Foreign Poiicy in the Second World War* (1962); W. McNeill, *America, Britain and Russia: Their Co-operation and Conflict 1941-46* (1953); F. S. Northedge, *The Troubled Giant, Britain among the Great Powers 1916-1939* (1967); R. E. Jones, *The Changing Structure of British Foreign Policy* (1974); J. Frankel, *British Foreign Policy 1945-1973* (1975); W. Wallace, *The Foreign Policy Process in Britain* (1976).

Among the main works on Britian and the international organisations are: F. P. Walters, *History of the League of Nations* (2 vols. 1951); G. L. Goodwin, *Britain and the United Nations* (1957); and A. H. Robertson, *European Institutions* (1966).

The Royal Institute of International Affairs has published the *Survey of International Affairs* annually since 1920. The main British documents of the period are edited by G. P. Gooch and H. Temperley, *British Documents on the Origin of the War* (11 vols, 1927-39), and edited by R. Butler and Sir E. L. Woodward (later J. P. T. Bury), *Documents on British Foreign Policy, 1919-39* (three series, still in course of publication).

Since 1915 the texts of major public documents have been printed in the *Annual Register*. For reference only, see *The Statesman's Year-Book*, and the *Year Book of International Organisations, 1951-*.

XVIII

BRITAIN AND EUROPE

A Chronology of Events

17 Mar	48	Treaty signed establishing Western European Union
7 May	48	Churchill's speech at Hague Congress leads to formation of European Movement
5 May	49	Council of Europe established at Strasbourg
9 May	50	Schuman Plan launched leading to establishment of Coal and Steel Community
30 Aug	54	Final abandonment of Pleven Plan for European Defence Community
2 Jun	55	Messina meeting at which Economic Community negotiations begin (British observer withdrawn Nov 55)
25 Mar	57	Treaty of Rome signed by the Six establishes E.E.C. and Euratom
20 Nov	59	EFTA established following failure to agree with E.E.C. on free-trade area
31 Jul	61	Conservative Government initiates negotiations to join E.E.C.
14 Jan	62	E.E.C. agrees Common Agricultural Policy
14 Jan	63	General de Gaulle vetoes British entry
29 Jan	66	'Luxembourg Compromise' preserves national veto.
2 May	67	Labour Government announces intention to apply following winter exploratory talks
27 Nov	67	General de Gaulle gives second veto
1 Dec	69	Hague E.E.C. summit agrees in principle to open negotiations for British entry
8 Jun	70	E.E.C. invites Britain to apply and negotiations start on 30 Jun
7 Jul	71	White Paper (Cmnd 4715) sets out agreement reached on almost all major points
28 Oct	71	Parliament endorses (by 356 to 244) decision in principle to join on the terms negotiated
22 Jan	72	Treaty of Accession signed
17 Oct	72	Royal Assent to European Communities Act
1 Jan	73	Britain becomes member of E.E.C. and Euratom
1 Apr	74	'Renegotiation' of British membership opened at Brussels
11 Mar	75	'Renegotiation' concluded at Dublin meeting of E.E.C. Heads of Government
9 Apr	75	Parliament endorses (by 396 to 170) 'renegotiation'
5 Jun	75	Britain votes 67·2% 'Yes' in Referendum on continued E.E.C. membership
7 Jul	75	Labour party delegates take seats in European Parliament for first time
29 Jun	76	Foreign ministers agree to start negotiations with Greece
13 Jul	76	Heads of Governments agree to 410 seat Parliament with direct elections in 1978
7 Jul	77	House of Commons gives Second Reading to European Elections Bill 394-147. Vote repeated in new session Nov 77 by 381-98
13 Dec	77	Proportional representation for European elections defeated 319-222
31 Dec	77	Transitional period for U.K. ends
7 Apr	78	Copenhagen summit decides on Jun 79 for first Direct Elections to European Parliament
5 May	78	Royal Assent to European Elections Bill
6 Dec	78	Brussels summit approves European Monetary System (commenced 12 Mar 79) but Britain does not participate
7 Jun	79	60 Con; 17 Lab; 4 Other U.K. members elected to European Parliament
2 Dec	79	Dublin summit: Mrs Thatcher asks for her money back
14 Dec	79	European Parliament rejects the Community budget for spending too much on agriculture and not enough on the Regional and Social Funds
18 May	80	EEC states impose economic sanctions against Iran in support of the United States
30 May	80	Agreement is reached among EEC foreign ministers in dispute over Britain's budget contribution (Britain gets $\frac{2}{3}$ rebate for three years). The Commission is asked to report on long-term reform (the Mandate)

1 Jan 81	Greece enters the Community. New Commission takes office under Gaston Thorn
27 Nov 81	London summit of EEC leaders fails to reach agreement on the Commission's Mandate report. Britain's hopes of getting a long-term solution to her budget problems fade
2 Apr 82	Argentina invades the Falklands. The EEC states swiftly back Britain in a programme of economic sanctions against Argentina
18 May 82	The British veto over farm price increases is overruled in the Farm Council, but West Germany and France state that Luxembourg protest still stands
24 Dec 82	European Parliament rejects supplementary budgets containing British and West German rebates
9 Jun 83	Mrs Thatcher's Government returned with an increased majority
3 Oct 83	Labour make withdrawal 'an option' rather than a certainty should Labour Government be returned
20 Dec 83	The European Parliament freezes British and West German rebates again after the failure of the Athens summit to come to a long-term solution to the budget problem
14 Jun 84	Second direct elections to the European Parliament. Conservatives lose 15 seats: Con. 45, Lab. 32, SNP 1
26 Jun 84	British Budget settlement agreed at Fontainebleau
1 Jan 85	New Commission takes office under Jacques Delors

European Organisations with British Membership

Western European Union (W.E.U.), 1947-

The U.K., France, the Netherlands, Belgium and Luxembourg signed a 50-year treaty in Brussels, 17 Mar 48, for collaboration in economic, cultural and social matters and for collective self-defence. Western Union's defence functions were formally transferred to NATO 20 Dec 50. In 1954 Italy and West Germany were invited to join and W.E.U. was formally inaugurated 6 May 55. Its social and cultural functions were transferred to the Council of Europe 1 Jul 60 but the W.E.U. Council continued to hold regular consultative meetings.

European Free Trade Association (EFTA), 1960-72

After failure to agree on a Free Trade Area with the European Economic Community in 1959 Britain joined with Austria, Denmark, Norway, Portugal, Sweden and Switzerland in EFTA under the Stockholm Convention, 20 Nov 59 signed in May 1960. Iceland joined EFTA 27 Mar 70 and Finland became an Associate on 27 Mar 61. All inter-EFTA tariffs were removed by 31 Dec 67, three years earlier than planned. Britain and Denmark left EFTA 1 Jan 73 on joining the Common Market—but on 27 Jul 72 the remaining EFTA countries had signed Free Trade Agreements with the E.E.C. and by 1 Jul 77 there was a complete free trade area between E.E.C. and EFTA.

Council of Europe, 1949-

Following the 1948 Congress of Europe at the Hague, the Council of Europe came into being in May 1949. Its founder members were Belgium, Denmark, France, Ireland, Italy, Luxembourg, the Netherlands, Norway, Sweden and the U.K. Turkey and Greece joined later in 1949, Iceland in 1950, West Germany in 1951, Austria in 1956, Cyprus in 1961, Switzerland in 1963 and Malta in 1965.

It is run by a Committee of Ministers and Consultative Assembly (147 members, 18 from U.K. in 1976).

The Council of Europe aims to foster European co-operation in every field and about 80 Conventions have been concluded, ranging from extradition rules to equivalence of degrees. One of its main achievements was the European Convention on Human Rights signed in 1950 (with violations examinable by the European Court of Human Rights set up in 1959).

European Court of Human Rights, 1959-

Britain has been involved in a number of cases brought under the European Convention of Human Rights. In all but one of the cases below (Handyside, 1976) some part of the complainant's argument has been found proved against the British authorities.

Golder, 1975 (rights of prisoners)
Handyside, 1976 (obscenity—the Little Red Schoolbook)
Ireland vs U.K., 1978 (torture and degrading treatment of prisoners in Northern Ireland)
Tyrer, 1978 (birching in Isle of Man)
Sunday Times, 1979 (contempt of court—the thalidomide case)
Young, James & Webster, 1981 (closed shop)
Dudgeon, 1981 (homosexual rights in Northern Ireland)
X vs United Kingdom, 1981 (detention of mental health patients)
Campbell & Cosans, 1982 (use of tawse in Scottish schools)
Silver & Others, 1983 (rights of prisoners)
Malone, 1984 (interception of communications—the telephone tapping case)
Campbell & Fell, 1984 (rights of Irish prisoners in U.K.)
Abdulaziz, Cabales & Balkandali, 1985 (rights of spouses of female U.K. residents to enter Britain).

(See *European Human Rights Reports* for detail of cases; see also P. Sieghart, *The International Law of Human Rights*, 1983.)

European Communities, 1973-

Britain subscribed to the Treaty of Rome 22 Jan 72 and joined the Communities 1 Jan 73. British membership was confirmed in a nationwide Referendum 5 Jun 75 (see p. 229).

European Economic Community (E.E.C.), 1973-

The E.E.C. was established 1 Jan 1958 (under the Treaty of Rome 25 Mar 1957) with France, Germany, Italy, Belgium, Holland and Luxembourg as Members. It achieved a complete customs union by 1 Jul 1968. On 1 Jan 1973 Britain, Denmark and Ireland joined and, following transitional arrangements, the customs union of the enlarged Community was complete by 1 Jul 1977.

The Community's day-to-day affairs are managed by the European Commission situated in Brussels (with 13 commissioners since 1973) subject to a Council of Ministers, one from each of the member nations,[1] working under a unanimity rule, and, in some ways, also to the European Parliament and to the European Court of Justice. Regulations promulgated by the Commission are subject to Parliamentary scrutiny at Westminster (see p. 199).

The Community's main functions have been promoting agreement on a customs union, on economic union (harmonising trade, transport and financial policies), on a common agricultural policy (CAP) and on external relations, particularly on trade with the developing world.

The Community was originally financed entirely by direct contributions from member states but following a Council decision 21 Apr 70 from 1971 onwards moved towards an independent revenue system based on 90% of all import duties and levies and a value added tax levy of up to 1%.

United Kingdom's contributions to and receipts from Community Budget (£ million)

	Gross Contribution	Receipts	Net Contribution
1973	181	79	102
1974	181	150	31
1975	342	398	–56
1976	463	296	167
1977	737	368	368
1978	1,348	544	804
1979	1,606	659	947
1980	1,767	1,061	706
1981	2,174	1,777	997
1982	2,863	2,257	606
1983	3,120[a]	2,473[a]	647

These figures refer to transfers through the Community budget at UK prices. They are much affected by the transitional arrangements for the first five years of British membership. They do not include monies received from the European Investment Bank or the European Coal and Steel Community.

SOURCE.—*The Government's Expenditure Plans 1979-80 to 1982-83* (Cmnd 7439/1979)
[a]The 1983 figures for Gross Contributions and Receipts are estimates.

European Coal and Steel Community (E.C.S.C.), 1973-

E.C.S.C. was established 10 Apr 52 (following Paris Treaty 18 Apr 51) with France, West Germany, Italy and the Benelux countries as members. Britain, Denmark and Ireland joined on 1 Jan 73.

European Atomic Energy Community (Euratom), 1973-

Euratom was established 1 Jan 58 for E.E.C. members to cooperate in the peaceful uses of atomic energy. Britain joined 1 Jan 73 on joining the E.E.C.

[1] The Presidency of the Council of Ministers rotates alphabetically between the member states every six months. The United Kingdom's first turn was Jan-Jun 77.

European Parliament, 1973-

Under the Treaty of Rome, each member country's Parliament nominated delegates from its own members to serve in a European Parliament which meets monthly in Strasbourg or Luxembourg. Its main functions have been advisory and supervisory. It has to be consulted on the Community Budget and it can, by a two-thirds majority, dismiss the Commissioners en bloc.

After the enlargement of the Community in 1973 it had 198 members. The U.K. was entitled to send 36 members but, in the absence of Labour representation, it at first sent only 22 (18 Conservatives, 2 Liberal, 1 Scottish National Party and 1 Independent). After the 1975 Referendum a Labour delegation was selected and until 1979 there were 18 Labour, 16 Conservative, 1 Liberal and 1 Scottish National representative. (26 were M.P:s and 10 peers.)

On 7-10 Jun 1979 and on 15-18 Jun 1984 Community-wide elections took place for a 410 member directly elected Parliament (see p. 229).

Leaders of the British Party Groups

Conservative

Jan 73	(Sir) P. Kirk
Feb 77	G. Rippon
Jun 79	J. Scott-Hopkins
Jun 82	Sir H. Plumb

Labour

Jul 75	M. Stewart
Nov 76	J. Prescott
Jun 79	Mrs B. Castle

European Court of Justice, 1973-

This was established under the Treaty of Rome to adjudicate on disputes arising out of the application of the Community treaties. Its regulations are enforceable on all member countries. After 1973 it had 9 judges and 4 advocates-general. It ruled against Britain on fishing regulations (1979) and on the use of tachographs (1979).

British Members of European Commission

1 Jan	73	Sir C. Soames
1 Jan	73	G. Thomson
1 Jan	77	R. Jenkins (*President*)
1 Jan	77	C. Tugendhat
1 Jan	81	C. Tugendhat
1 Jan	81	I. Richard
1 Jan	85	Ld Cockfield
1 Jan	85	S. Clinton Davies

British Ambassadors to the European Communities (1960-72)

17 Jul	60	Sir A. Tandy
18 Apr	63	Sir C. O'Neill
7 Apr	65	Sir J. Marjoribanks
30 May	71	*post vacant*
Oct	72	(Sir) M. Palliser

Ministers with special E.E.C. Responsibilities

(Cabinet Ministers)

19 Sep 57-14 Oct 59	R. Maudling
27 Jul 60-20 Oct 63	E. Heath
7 Jan 67-29 Aug 67	G. Thomson
19 Jun 70-25 Jul 70	A. Barber
28 Jul 70-5 Nov 72	G. Rippon
5 Nov 72-4 Mar 74	J. Davies
5 May 79-11 Sep 81	Sir I. Gilmour
11 Sep 81-5 Apr 82	H. Atkins

(Ministers of State at the Foreign Office)

Mar 74-Aug 76	R. Hattersley
Aug 76-Feb 77	D. Owen
Feb 77-May 79	F. Judd
May 79-Jun 83	D. Hurd
Jun 83-	M. Rifkind

Permanent British Representative to the European Communities

1 Jan 73	(Sir) M. Palliser
1 Jan 76	Sir D. Maitland
Nov 80	Sir M. Butler

British Member of the European Court

1 Jan 73-	Ld Mackenzie-Stuart

SOURCES.—On Britain and Europe see M. Camps, *Britain and the European Communities 1955-63* (1964); U. W. Kitzinger, *The Second Try* (1968); U. W. Kitzinger, *Diplomacy and Persuasion* (1973); C. Cosgrove, *A Reader's Guide to Britain and the European Communities* (1970); D. Butler and U. Kitzinger, *The 1975 Referendum* (1976); A. King, *Britain Says 'Yes'* (1977); P. Goodhart, *Full Hearted Consent*, (1976); R. Jackson, *The Powers of the European Parliament* (1977); Hansard Society, *The British People: Their Voice in Europe* (1977); R. Jowell and G. Hoinville, *Britain into Europe, Public Opinion on the EEC 1961-75* (1976); J. Paxton, *A Dictionary of the European Economic Community* (1977); *The European Community: A Brief Reading List* (EEC London Office, 1977); R. Jackson and J. Fitzpatrick, *The European Parliament* (1979); V. Herman and J. Lodge, *The European Parliament and the European Community* (1978); D. Marquand, *Parliament for Europe* (1979); D. Butler and D. Marquand, *European Elections and British Politics* (1980); S. Henig, *Power and Decision in Europe: The Institutions of the European Community* (1980); J. Lodge (ed.), *Institutions and Policies of the European Community* (1983); J. Lodge and V. Herman, *Direct Elections to the European Parliament: A Community Perspective* (1982); G. Pridham and P. Pridham, *Transnational Party Cooperation and European Integration: The Process Towards Direct Elections*; G. Denton, *The British Problem and the Future of the EEC Budget* (1982); D. Strasser, *The Finances of Europe* (1981); H. Wallace, *Budgetary Politics: The Finances of the European Communities* (1980); D. Butler and P. Jowett, *Party Strategies in Britain: A Study of the 1984 European Elections* (1985). See also *The Times Guides to the European Parliament* (1979 and 1984).

XIX

ARMED FORCES

Service Chiefs

Royal Navy

First Naval Lord

1899 Ld W. Kerr

First Sea Lord

1904 Sir J. Fisher (Ld)
1910 Sir A. Wilson
1911 Sir F. Bridgeman
1912 Prince Louis of Battenberg
1914 Ld Fisher
1915 Sir H. Jackson
1916 Sir J. Jellicoe
1917 Sir R. Wemyss
1919 Earl Beatty
1927 Sir C. Madden
1930 Sir F. Field
1933 Sir E. Chatfield (Ld)
1938 Sir R. Backhouse
1939 Sir D. Pound
1943 Sir A. Cunningham (Ld)
1946 Sir J. Cunningham
1948 Ld Fraser of North Cape
1951 Sir R. McGrigor
1955 Earl Mountbatten[1]
1959 Sir C. Lambe
1960 Sir C. John
1964 Sir D. Luce
1966 Sir V. Begg
1968 Sir M. Le Fanu
1970 Sir P. Hill-Norton
1971 Sir M. Pollock
1974 Sir E. Ashmore
1977 Sir T. Lewin
1979 Sir H. Leach
1982 Sir J. Fieldhouse
1985 Sir W. Stareley

Army

Commander in Chief

1895 Vt Wolseley
1900 Ld Roberts (Earl)

Chief of General Staff

1904 Sir N. Lyttelton
1908 Sir W. Nicholson

Chief of Imperial General Staff

1909 Sir W. Nicholson
1912 Sir J. French
1914 Sir C. Douglas
1914 Sir J. Wolfe-Murray
1915 Sir A. Murray
1915 Sir W. Robertson
1918 Sir H. Wilson
1922 E of Cavan
1926 Sir G. Milne
1933 Sir A. Montgomery Massingberd
1936 Sir C. Deverell
1937 Vt Gort
1939 Sir E. Ironside
1940 Sir J. Dill
1941 Sir A. Brooke (Ld Alanbrooke)
1946 Vt Montgomery
1948 Sir W. Slim
1952 Sir J. Harding
1955 Sir G. Templer
1958 Sir F. Festing
1963-4 Sir R. Hull

Chief of General Staff

1964 Sir R. Hull
1965 Sir J. Cassels
1968 Sir G. Baker
1971 Sir M. Carver
1973 Sir P. Hunt
1976 Sir R. Gibbs
1979 Sir E. Bramall
1982 Sir J. Stanier
1985 Sir N. Bagnall

Royal Air Force

Chief of Air Staff

1918 Sir H. Trenchard
1918 Sir F. Sykes
1919 Sir H. Trenchard
1930 Sir J. Salmond
1933 Sir G. Salmond
1933 Sir E. Ellington
1937 Sir C. Newall
1940 Sir C. Portal
1946 Sir A. Tedder (Ld)
1950 Sir J. Slessor
1953 Sir W. Dickson[1]
1956 Sir D. Boyle
1960 Sir T. Pike
1964 Sir C. Elworthy
1968 Sir J. Grandy
1971 Sir D. Spotswood
1973 Sir A. Humphrey
1976 Sir N. Cameron
1977 Sir M. Beetham
1982 Sir K. Williamson
1985 Sir D. Craig

Defence Staff

Chief of Defence Staff[1]

1964 Earl Mountbatten
1965 Sir R. Hull
1967 Sir C. Elworthy
1971 Sir P. Hill-Norton
1973 Sir M. Carver
1976 Sir A. Humphrey
1977 Sir E. Ashmore
1979 Sir T. Lewin
1982 Sir E. Bramall
1985 Sir J. Fieldhouse

[1] Before the post of Chief of Defence Staff was established in 1964 Sir W. Dickson (1956-9) and Earl Mountbatten (1959-64) acted as Chairmen of the Chiefs of Staffs Committee.

Defence Organisation

Committee of Imperial Defence, 1904-1946

The committee was first established in 1902 on a temporary basis to advise the Prime Minister, as a result of British experience in the Boer War of the need for planning and co-ordination of the Empire's defence forces. The C.I.D. was established permanently in 1904, as a small flexible advisory committee to the Prime Minister. Members were usually cabinet ministers concerned with defence, military leaders, and key civil servants. The Dominions also had representatives sitting on the committee occasionally. The Prime Minister was the chairman of the committee, which had no executive power, but exercised considerable influence. A secretariat was set up to assist the C.I.D., which was later adopted by the cabinet itself. During the First World War the C.I.D. was suspended. Its functions between 1914 and 1919 were taken over by the War Council (Nov 1914), the Dardanelles Committee (May 1915), the War Committee (Nov 1916), and finally the War Cabinet (Dec 1916-Nov 1919). The C.I.D. resumed plenary sessions in 1922. In the 'thirties the membership of the C.I.D. rose from about 11 to 18, and the committee became unwieldy. This led to the establishment of a Minister for the Co-ordination of Defence (1936-40), who was without a department, but worked through the Committee Secretariat. On the outbreak of the Second World War the C.I.D. was again suspended, and its responsibilities taken over by the War Cabinet. In 1946 the decision to make the suspension permanent was published in a White Paper on the C.I.D. (Cmd. 6923).

Secretaries to the C.I.D. 1904-1946

1904	G. Clarke	1912	(Sir) M. Hankey[1]
1907	Sir C. Ottley	1938	(Sir) H. Ismay (Ld)

Ministry of Defence. The C.I.D. was replaced by a cabinet defence committee, with executive power, and the Ministry of Defence was set up as a regular department on 1 Jan 47. It existed as an administrative body, responsible for liaison between the Service Ministries and co-ordination of defence policy until 31 Mar 64.

On 1 Apr 64 the complete reorganisation of the three Service Departments (Admiralty, War Office and Air Ministry) under the Secretary of State for Defence took place. A Defence Council was also established under the Secretary of State to exercise the powers of command and administrative control previously exercised by the separate Service councils, which became subordinate to it. Further reorganisation on 6 Jan 67 reduced the status of the administrative heads of the three Services from Ministers to Under-Secretaries of State, while creating two new posts: Minister of Defence (Administration) and Minister of Defence (Equipment). In June 1970 fur-

[1] Sir M. Hankey (later Ld Hankey) became the Joint Secretary to the C.I.D. and the Cabinet in 1916, and in 1923 he was also appointed Clerk to the Privy Council.

ther reorganisation of these two posts later reduced them to that of a single Minister of State for Defence. In May 1981 a major reorganisation abolished the three Service Under-Secretaries of State and divided the Ministry of Defence between a Minister of State and Under-Secretary of State for Defence Procurement, and a Minister of State and Under-Secretary of State for Armed Forces. The present membership of the Defence Council consists of the Secretary of State for Defence, the two Ministers of State and their Parliamentary Under-Secretaries, the Chiefs of Defence, Naval, General and Air Staffs, the Chief of Personnel and Logistics, the Chief Scientific Adviser, the Chief Executive of the Procurement Executive and the Permanent Under-Secretary of State.

SOURCES.—F. A. Johnson, *Defence by Committee* (1960); D. N. Chester and F. M. G. Willson, *The Organisation of British Central Government* (1957); J. Ehrman, *Cabinet Government and War, 1890-1940* (1958). *Whitaker's Almanack.*

Defence Pressure Groups

Pressure on the Service Departments and the Cabinet about the nature and scale of forces and armaments has always been informal. But arguments for the expansion of particular services has been sustained by the Navy League (founded 1895) and the Air League (1909). More recently the Institute of Strategic Studies (1958) has provided an influential forum for the discussion of defence questions. See also the Foreign Affairs pressure groups listed on p. 421.

Total Forces Serving[a] (year ending 31 March)

(to nearest '000)

	1900	1910	1920	1930	1940[b]	1950[b]	1960	1970	1980	1985
Army	661	522	435	333	1,688	360	252	174	159	162
Royal Navy[d]	98	128	133	97	282	135	93	86	64	70
Royal Air Force	. .	. .	28	33	303	193	158	113	90	93
Total Forces	759[c]	650	596	463	2,273[e]	688	503	373	321	326

[a] Men locally enlisted abroad are excluded, except that the figures for the army include those whose documents are held in the U.K.
[b] Including Women's Auxiliaries. The figures for the war years include a number of casualties that had not been reported on the dates to which the figures relate. They also include men and women locally enlisted abroad.
[c] Including 278,000 non-regulars.
[d] Excluding the Royal Marine Police, except in 1940.
[e] The total strength of the Armed Forces reached its war-time peak in 1945 with 5,098,100 men and women serving.

Total Expenditure on Defence[a] (year ending 31 March)

(£ millions)

	1899-1900	1909-10	1919-20	1929-30	1939-40	1949-50	1959-60	1969-70	1978-79	1984-85
Army	43·6	27·2	395·0	40·5	81·9	291·8	428·2	n.a.	n.a.	4,073
Navy	26·0	35·8	156·5	55·8	69·4	186·8	364·6	n.a.	n.a.	4,007
Air Force	. .	. .	52·5	16·8	66·6	201·6	485·1	n.a.	n.a.	4,339
Defence Total[b]	69·8	63·0	604·0	113·1	626·4[c]	740·7	1,475·7	2,266·0	6,918·8	16,817·8

[a] The figures refer to the Exchequer of the U.K. and included Northern Ireland up to 1972 only to the extent that services, taxes, etc., are reserved to the U.K. Parliament.
[b] The discrepancies between the service votes and the totals are due to the expenditures of the Ministries of Defence and Civil Aviation (1950 and 1960), and the Army Ordnance Factories.
[c] Including votes of credit of £408·5 m. Defence expenditure reached its war-time peak in 1944-5 at £5,125·0 m.

SOURCES.—The *Annual Abstract of Statistics*, 1900-; for a brief summary of the statistics. The *Army*, *Navy* and *Air Estimates* giving the full figures are published annually as government white papers up to 31 Mar 64. From 1 Apr 64 figures are those given in Ministry of Defence Estimates.

Conscription

After a long controversy about conscription, H. Asquith announced the introduction of the first *Military Service Bill* on 5 Jan 16. Military service lapsed in 1919. It was first introduced in peace time on 26 Apr 39. The period of compulsory service was to have been six months, but war intervened. Conscription was extended to women from Dec 1941 until Jan 1947, but few women were called up after Nov 1944. The *National Service Act, 1947,* provided for the continuation of military service after the war. The period of service was twelve months. It was increased to eighteen months in Dec 1948, and to two years in Sep 1950. A government White Paper published on 5 Apr 57[1] announced a progressive reduction in the national service intake. No men were to be called up after the end of 1960, so that by the end of 1963 there were no national servicemen left in the forces. (This was slightly modified by the *Army Reserves Bill*, introduced in 1962.)

Rationing

The first national rationing scheme in this country came into operation on 31 Dec 17, with the rationing of sugar. This was followed in Jul 1918 by national schemes for meat, lard, bacon, ham, butter and margarine. The abolition of rationing began on 28 Jul 18 and was completed on 29 Nov 20. Butter and meat rations were most severely restricted in Apr-May 1918 and sugar in 1919. There was much controversy during the course of World War I over the form that rationing should take. National rationing was preceded by local schemes and even after Jul 1918 rationing was, in many cases, wider in extent locally than nationally. The characteristic feature of the World War I scheme was the tie to the retailer of each customer.

When World War II broke out in Sep 1939, prearranged plans for commodity control were at once put into effect. Rationing was introduced on 8 Jan 40 when bacon, butter, and sugar were put under control and extended during the following two years to meat, tea, margarine, lard, jam, marmalade, cheese, eggs, and milk. In Dec 1941 the 'points' system was introduced to ration such items as tinned meat and biscuits and from Jul 1942 sweets and chocolate were rationed under a system of 'personal points'. During the war animal feedstuffs, fertilizers, farm machinery, petrol, domestic coal, clothing and textiles were also rationed. Rationing was at its most stringent, however, in the immediate post-war years. In Jul 46, bread rationing, which in 1939 the Minister of Food had described as 'the last resort of a starving nation', was introduced for the first time ever and this was followed in Nov 1947 by the rationing of potatoes. In Dec 1947 the distribution of nearly all important foods was controlled with the exception of some fresh fruit and vegetables, fish and coffee; the bacon, butter, meat and fats rations were at their lowest ebbs and the basic petrol ration had been suspended altogether. The gradual abolition of rationing began in Apr 1948; it was not completed until the abolition of butter rationing in May 1954, of meat rationing in July 1954 and of coal rationing in 1958.

[1] Cmnd. 124/1957

During the Suez crisis of 1956, petrol rationing was re-introduced. It lasted from 17 Dec 56 to 14 May 57.

Principal Military Operations

Boer War, 1899-1902

Following the rejection by the British Government of the Boer ultimatum, the Transvaal and Orange Free State declared war on Britain in October 1899. Major operations against the Boers ended in the summer of 1900, but guerrilla warfare continued. Peace was finally concluded at Vereeniging on 31 May 02.

Costs and Casualties

1. *Total Engaged* ('000s)	2. *Killed*[a] ('000s)	*Percentage* *Col. 2* to *Col. 1*	*Cost* (£m)
448	22	4·9	217

[a] Including those dying of wounds, of disease, and while prisoners of war.

First World War, 1914-1918

4 Aug	14	Britain declares war on Germany
12 Aug	14	Britain declares war on Austria-Hungary
23 Aug	14	Retreat from Mons begins
12 Oct	14	First Battle of Ypres
20 Jan	15	First Zeppelin Raid on Britain
22 Apr	15	Second Battle of Ypres
25 Apr	15	Gallipoli landing
6 Sep	15	Bulgaria joins Central Powers
25 Sep	15	British attack at Loos
8 Jan	16	Evacuation of Gallipoli completed
31 May	16	Battle of Jutland
1 Jul	16	Battle of the Somme
27 Mar	17	Turks defeated at Gaza
6 Apr	17	U.S.A. enters War
4 Oct	17	British victory at Passchendaele
20 Nov	17	Tanks used in Cambrai victory
21 Nov	17	Russia asks for peace
9 Dec	17	Jerusalem captured by British
21 Mar	18	German Somme offensive
15 Jul	18	Last German offensive
11 Sep	18	Allies break Hindenburg Line
2 Oct	18	British capture Damascus
30 Oct	18	Turkey signs Armistice
3 Nov	18	Austria-Hungary signs Armistice
11 Nov	18	Germany signs Armistice
28 Jun	19	Treaty of Versailles

Military Costs and Casualties
(Empire figures)

1. *Total Engaged* ('000s)	2. *Killed*[a] ('000s)	*Percentage* *Col. 2* to *Col. 1*	*Cost* (£m)
9,669	947	9·8	3,810

[a] Including those dying of wounds, of disease, and while prisoners of war.

Intervention in Russia, 1918-1919

British troops landed at Murmansk and Archangel in June and August of 1918. Troops also entered the Transcaucasus in August 1918. The withdrawal of troops from the Transcaucasus was completed by 5 Apr 19; and from Murmansk and Archangel by 28 Sep 19.

Second World War, 1939-1945

1 Sep	39	Germany invades Poland
3 Sep	39	Britain and France declare war
17 Sep	39	Russia invades Poland
30 Nov	39	Russia invades Finland
9 Apr	40	Germany invades Denmark and Norway
10 May	40	Germany invades Holland and Belgium
4 Jun	40	Dunkirk evacuation complete
22 Jun	40	France capitulates
10 Jul	40	Italy declares war on Britain
15 Sep	40	Climax of Battle of Britain
20 Nov	40	Hungary joins axis powers
7 Feb	41	Britain reach Benghazi
1 Mar	41	Bulgaria joins axis powers
27 May	41	*Bismarck* sunk
29 May	41	German N. Africa offensive halted
22 Jun	41	Germany invades Russia
16 Jul	41	British occupy Syria
18 Nov	41	Second British Libyan offensive
7 Dec	41	Japan attacks Pearl Harbour
8 Dec	41	U.S. and Britain declare war on Japan
9 Dec	41	British relieve Tobruk
11 Dec	41	Germany and Italy declare war on U.S.A. and vice versa
15 Feb	42	Japanese take Singapore
21 Jan	42	German offensive in Libya
30 Jun	42	German held at El Alamein
19 Aug	42	Dieppe raid
23 Oct	42	British attack at El Alamein
23 Jan	43	British enter Tripoli
12 May	43	Axis surrenders N. Africa
10 Jul	43	Allies invade Sicily
3 Sep	43	Allies invade Italy
22 Jan	44	Allied landing at Anzio
4 Jun	44	Allies take Rome
6 Jun	44	D Day landing in Normandy
13 Jun	44	V1 Bombardment begins
25 Aug	44	Allies enter Paris
17 Sep	44	Arnhem assault
16 Dec	44	German Ardennes offensive
22 Mar	45	Rhine crossing
8 May	45	VE day, final German surrender
6 Aug	45	Atomic bomb on Hiroshima
9 Aug	45	Second atomic bomb on Nagasaki
14 Aug	45	VJ Day (Britain), cessation of hostilities between the Allies and Japan
2 Sep	45	Final Japanese surrender signed

Military Costs and Casualties
(Great Britain)

1. *Total Engaged* ('000s)	2. *Killed*[a] ('000s)	*Percentage Col. 2* to *Col. 1*	*Cost* (£m)
5,896	265	4·5	34,423

[a] Including those dying of wounds, of disease and while prisoners of war.

Korean War, 1950-1953

Britain declared her support for the United States' action in Korea on 28 Jun 50, following the invasion of South Korea by North Korean troops, and the call for a cease fire by an emergency session of the United Nations Security Council. The intervention of Chinese troops fighting with the North Koreans was confirmed on 6 Nov 50. An armistice was signed between the United Nations and the Communist forces on 27 Jul 53. British casualties in the Korean war were 749 killed (H.C. Deb., 1952-53, Vol. 518, Cols. 221-222). The total expenditure incurred by Britain was about £50m. (H.C. Deb., 1952-53, Vol. 517, Col. 1218).

Suez, 1956

Following the Egyptian nationalisation of the Suez Canal on 26 Jul 56, tension grew in the Middle East. The Israeli army attacked the Egyptians on 29 Oct 56 in the Sinai peninsula. The rejection of a British and French ultimatum by Egypt resulted in a combined British and French attack on Egypt on 1 Nov 56. Operations were halted at midnight on 6-7 Nov 56. On 26 Jan

61 full diplomatic relations were resumed between Britain and Egypt. British casualties were 21 men killed (H.C. Deb., 1956-57, Vol. 561, Col. 36). The military expenditure incurred was about £30m. (H.C. Deb., 1956-57, Vol. 575, Col. 51).

Northern Ireland, 1969-

On 14 Aug 69 the Government of Northern Ireland informed the U.K. Government that as a result of the severe rioting in Londonderry it had no alternative but to ask for the assistance of the troops at present stationed in Northern Ireland to prevent a breakdown in law and order. British troops moved into Londonderry that day, and into Belfast on 15 Aug 69. On 19 Aug 69 G.O.C. Northern Ireland assumed overall responsibility for security in the Province.

Costs and Casualties

	Regular Army (as at 31 Dec)	*Deaths*	*Ulster Defence Regiment*[a] (as at 31 Dec)	*Deaths*	*Expenditure*[b] (as at 31 Mar) (£m)	*Civilian Deaths*	*R.U.C. Deaths*
1969	7,495	0	. .	. .	. .	11	1
1970	7,170	0	4,008	0	1·5	21	2
1971	13,762	43	6,786	5	6·5	104	11
1972	16,661	103	9,074	24	14	305	17
1973	15,342	58	7,982	8	29	158	13
1974	14,067	28	7,795	7	33	151	15
1975	13,913	14	7,861	6	45	205	11
1976	13,672	14	7,769	15	60	222	23
1977	13,632	15	7,843	14	65	55	14
1978	13,600	14	7,862	7	69	40	10
1979	13,000	38	7,623	10	81	37	14
1980	12,000	8	7,373	8	96	41	9
1981	10,000	10	7,479	13	111	36	21
1982	9,000	21	7,130	7	149	45	12
1983	8,000	5	7,026	10	143	44	19
1984	8,000	9	6,929	10	141	36	8

[a] The Ulster Defence Regiment was formed on 1 Apr 70. The figures include permanent, part-time, male and female members.

[b] Military expenditure only. Up to March 79 £45m. had been awarded as damages for criminal injuries to persons in Northern Ireland and £276m. for criminal damage to property.

SOURCES.—Ministry of Defence and Northern Ireland Office. For expenditure see H.C. Deb. 1976-77, Vol. 915, Col. 123. For further statistics on the security operation in Northern Ireland see H.C. Deb. 1977-8, Vol. 943, Col. 236.

Falklands, 1982

On 2 Apr 1982 Argentine forces landed on the Falklands and took over the Islands and South Georgia. An expeditionary force was despatched and on 25 Apr South Georgia was recaptured. British forces landed on West Falkland on 20 May and by 14 Jul Port Stanley was recaptured and all the Argentine forces surrendered. The British forces under Rear-Admiral J. Woodward lost six ships and twenty aircraft. The total casualties were 254 killed and 777 wounded. The cost of the operation from Apr to Jun was estimated at £350m.

Major War Commanders

World War I

Allenby, E. 1st Vt (1919). 1861-1936
Field-Marshal. C-in-C Egyptian Expeditionary Force 1917-19.

Beatty, D. 1st E (1919). 1871-1936
Admiral of the Fleet. Commanded Grand Fleet 1916-19.

Fisher, J. 1st Ld (1909). 1841-1920
Admiral of the Fleet. 1st Sea Lord 1914-15.

French, J. 1st E of Ypres (1922). 1852-1925
Field-Marshal. C-in-C British Expeditionary Force in France 1914-15. C-in-C Home Forces 1916.

Haig, D. 1st E (1919). 1861-1928
Field-Marshal. Commanding 1st Army 1914-15. C-in-C Expeditionary Forces in France and Flanders 1915-19.

Hamilton, I. Sir (1915). 1853-1947
General. C-in-C Mediterranean Expeditionary Force 1915.

Jellicoe, J. 1st E (1925). 1859-1935
Admiral of the Fleet. Commanded Grand Fleet 1914-16.

Plumer, H. 1st Vt (1929). 1857-1932
Field-Marshal. General Officer Commanding Italian Expeditionary Force 1917-18. 2nd Army British Expeditionary Force 1918-19.

Robertson, W. Sir. 1st Bt (1919). 1860-1933
Field-Marshal. Chief of Imperial General Staff 1915-18. C-in-C Eastern Command 1918. Great Britain 1918-19. B.A.O.R. 1919-20.

Trenchard, H. 1st Vt (1936). 1873-1956
Marshal of the RAF. Assistant Commandant Central Flying School 1913-14. G.O.C. Royal Flying Corps in the Field 1915-17. Chief of Air Staff 1918. Commanded Independent Force 1918. Chief of Air Staff 1919-29.

Wilson, H. Sir. 1st Bt (1919). 1864-1922
Field-Marshal. Assistant Chief of General Staff to Ld French 1914. Commanded 1st Army Corps 1915-16. Eastern Command 1917. British Military Representative Versailles 1917. Chief of Imperial General Staff 1918-22.

World War II

Alanbrooke, 1st Ld (1945). 1st Vt (1946). 1883-1963, Sir A. Brooke.
Field-Marshal. G.O.C.-in-C Southern Command 1939 and 1940. C of Second Army Corps B.E.F. 1939-40. C-in-C Home Forces 1940-41. Chief of Imperial General Staff 1941-46.

Alexander, H. 1st E (1952). 1891-1969
Field-Marshal. C-in-C Middle East 1942-43. C-in-C North Africa 1943. C-in-C Allied Armies in Italy 1943-44. Supreme Allied Commander Mediterranean Theatre 1944-45.

Auchinleck, C. Sir. 1884-1981.
Field-Marshal. C-in-C India 1941 and 1943-47. C-in-C Middle East 1941-42.

Cunningham, A. 1st Vt of Hyndhope (1946). 1883-1962
Admiral of the Fleet. Ld Commissioner of the Admiralty and Deputy Chief of Naval Staff 1938-39. C-in-C Mediterranean 1939-42. Naval C-in-C Expeditionary Force North Africa 1942. C-in-C Mediterranean 1943. 1st Sea Ld and Chief of Naval Staff 1943-46.

Dill, J. Sir. 1881-1944
Field-Marshal. Commanded 1st Corps in France 1939-40. Chief of Imperial General Staff 1940. British Representative on Combined Chief of Staffs' Committee in U.S. 1941.

Douglas, W. 1st Ld (1948). 1893-1969
Marshal of the RAF. C-in-C Fighter Command 1940-43. Air Officer C-in-C Middle East 1943-44. Air Officer C-in-C Coastal Command 1944-45. Air C-in-C British Air Forces of Occupation in Germany 1945-46.

Dowding, H. 1st Ld (1943). 1882-1970
Air Chief Marshal. Air Officer C-in-C Fighter Command 1936-1940.

Fraser, B. 1st Ld (1946). 1888-1981
C-in-C Home Fleet 1943-44. C-in-C Eastern Fleet 1944-45.

Gort, J. 6th Vt (Ireland) (1902). 1st Vt (U.K.) (1945) 1886-1946
Field-Marshal. C-in-C British Expeditionary Force 1939-40. Commanded B.E.F. in withdrawal towards Dunkirk 1940.

Harris, A. Sir. 1st Bt (1953). 1892-1984.
Marshal of the RAF. Air Officer. C-in-C Bomber Command 1942-45.

Ironside, W. 1st Ld (1941). 1880-1959
Field-Marshal. C.I.G.S. 1939-40. C-in-C Home Forces 1940.

Leigh-Mallory, T. Sir. 1892-1944
Air Chief Marshal. Air Officer C-in-C Fighter Command 1942. Air C-in-C Allied Expeditionary Force 1943-44. Lost while flying to take up appointment as Allied Air C-in-C South-East Asia.

Montgomery, B. 1st Vt of Alamein (1946). 1887-1976
Field-Marshal. Commander 8th Army 1942 in N. Africa, Sicily and Italy. C-in-C British Group of Allied Armies N. France 1944. British Commander Allied Expeditionary Forces in Europe 1944-46.

Mountbatten, L. 1st E of Burma (1947). 1900-1979
Admiral of the Fleet. Chief of Combined Operations 1942-43. Supreme Allied Command S.E. Asia 1943-46.

Newall, C. 1st Ld (1946). 1886-1963
Marshal of the RAF. Chief of Air Staff 1937-40. Governor-General and C-in-C New Zealand 1941-46.

Park, K. Sir. 1892-1975
Air Chief Marshal. Air Officer Commanding RAF Malta 1942-43. Air Officer C-in-C 1944. Allied Air C-in-C South-East Asia Command 1945-6.

Peirse, R. Sir. 1892-1970
Air Chief Marshal. Air Officer C-in-C Bomber Command 1940-42. Air

Officer C-in-C India 1942-43. Allied Air C-in-C South-East Asia Command 1943-44.

Percival, A. 1887-1966

Lieutenant-General. G.O.C. Malaya 1941-42.

Portal, C. 1st Vt (1946). 1893-1971

Marshal of the RAF. Air Officer C-in-C Bomber Command 1940. Chief of the Air Staff 1940-45.

Pound, D. Sir. 1877-1943

Admiral of the Fleet. C-in-C Mediterranean 1936-39. 1st Sea Lord 1939-43.

Ramsay, B. Sir. 1883-1945

Admiral. Flag Officer commanding Dover 1939-42. Naval Commander Eastern Task Force Mediterranean 1943.

Ritchie, N. Sir. 1897-1984.

General. Commander of 8th Army, Libya, 1941-42.

Slessor, J. Sir. 1897-1979

Marshal of the RAF. Air Officer C-in-C Coastal Command 1943-44. C-in-C RAF Mediterranean and Middle East 1944-45.

Slim, W. 1st Vt (1960). 1891-1970

Field-Marshal. C-in-C Allied Land Forces S.E. Asia 1945-46.

Tedder, A. 1st Ld (1946). 1890-1967

Marshal of the RAF. Air Officer C-in-C Middle East 1941-43. Air C-in-C Mediterranean Air Command 1943. Deputy Supreme Commander under Gen. Eisenhower 1943-45.

Wavell, A. 1st E (1947). 1883-1950

Field-Marshal. Formed Middle East Command 1939. C-in-C India 1941. Supreme Commander S.W. Pacific 1941-43.

Wilson, H. 1st Ld (1946). 1881-1964

Field-Marshal. C-in-C Egypt 1939-41. C-in-C Greece 1941. C-in-C Persia—Iraq Command 1942-43. C-in-C Middle East 1943. Supreme Commander Mediterranean Theatre 1944.

XX

THE PRESS[1]

National Daily Newspapers

(British Gazette), 5-13 May 1926
Proprietors: His Majesty's Stationery Office. Printed at offices of *Morning Post*.
Policy: Strong opposition to the general strike.
Editor: W. Churchill.

(Daily Chronicle), 1869-1930
Proprietors: E. Lloyd, 1871-1918. Frank Lloyd and family trading as United Newspapers Ltd. Lloyd family parted with their interest in 1918. Bought by D. Lloyd George and associates 1918. Sold to Sir T. Catto and Sir D. Yule, 1926. Bought by Inveresk Paper Co., 1928. Sold and incorporated with *Daily News* as the *News Chronicle*, 1930.
Policy: Liberal.
Editors: W. Fisher, 1899. R. Donald, 1902. E. Perris, 1918-30.

(Daily Citizen), 1912-Jan 1915
Proprietors: Labour Newspapers Ltd.
Policy: Official Labour.
Editor: F. Dilnot, 1912-15.

Daily Express, 1900
Proprietors: A. Pearson, Daily Express (1900) Ltd. Acquired by London Express Newspaper Ltd, 1915. Ld Beaverbrook assumed control in 1916. In 1954 he relinquished it to Beaverbrook Newspapers Ltd and transferred controlling shares to the Beaverbrook Foundations. In 1977 Beaverbrook Newspapers were taken over by Trafalgar House property group (Chairman: V. (Ld) Matthews).
Policy: Independent conservative.
Editors: A. Pearson, 1900. R. Blumenfeld, 1902. B. Baxter, 1929. A. Christiansen, 1933. E. Pickering, 1957. R. Wood, 1962. R. Edwards, 1964. D. Marks, 1965. I. MacColl, 1971. A. Burnet, 1974. R. Wright, 1977. D. Jameson, 1977. A. Firth, 1980. C. Ward, 1981. Sir L. Lamb, 1983.

(Daily Graphic), 1890-1926. 1946-52
Proprietors: Founded by W. L. Thomas. Owned by H. Baines & Co. Amalgamated with *Daily Sketch* in 1926 (Kemsley Newspapers). Appeared as *Daily Sketch and Daily Graphic* 1926-46, as *Daily Graphic* 1946-52, then as *Daily Sketch*.

[1] The policies of national newspapers between 1900 and 1985 have inevitably fluctuated. Policy should here be taken only as a general indication of the nature of the paper. In very few cases have newspapers been the official organs of a political party.

Policy: Independent conservative.
Editors: H. Hall, 1891. H. White, 1907. W. Ackland, 1909. A. Hutchinson, 1912. A. Netting, 1917. H. Lawton, 1919. E. Tebbutt, 1923. H. Heywood, 1925-26. A. Thornton, 1946. N. Hamilton, 1947. H. Clapp, 1948-52 (see *Daily Sketch*).

(Daily Herald), 1912-1964
Proprietors: Daily Herald Printing and Publishing Society in association with Odhams Press Ltd. Formed Daily Herald (1929) Ltd (Chairman: Ld Southwood). 49% of shares held by T.U.C., 51% by Odhams Press. 1960 new agreement between Odhams Press and T.U.C. 1961 Daily Mirror Newspapers, Ltd take over Odhams Press. T.U.C. sign agreement for the paper to be published by the Mirror Group (International Publishing Corporation). 1964 T.U.C. sold their 49% holding to I.P.C. 1964, replaced by the *Sun*.
Policy: General support to Labour Movement, 1912-23, 1960-. Official Labour 1923-60.
Editors: R. Kenny, 1912. W. Seed, 1912. S. Jones, 1912. C. Lapworth, 1913. G. Lansbury, 1913. W. Ryan, 1922. H. Fyfe, 1923. W. Mellor, 1926. W. Stevenson, 1931. F. Williams, 1937. P. Cudlipp, 1940. S. Elliott, 1953. D. Machray, 1957. J. Beavan, 1960. S. Jacobson, 1962-64. (Issued as a weekly paper during 1st World War, launched again as a daily in 1919.)

Daily Mail, 1896
Proprietors: A. Harmsworth (Ld Northcliffe), Associated Newspapers Ltd (Chairman: 1st (1922), 2nd (1932), 3rd (1971) Lds Rothermere).
Policy: Independent. Right-wing Conservative.
Editors: T. Marlowe, 1899. W. Fish, 1926. O. Pulvermacher, 1929. W. McWhirter, 1930. W. Warden, 1931. A. Cranfield, 1935. R. Prew, 1939. S. Horniblow, 1944. F. Owen, 1947. G. Schofield, 1950. A. Wareham, 1955. W. Hardcastle, 1959. M. Randall, 1963. A. Brittenden, 1966. (Sir) D. English, 1971.

Daily Mirror, 1903
Proprietors: A. Harmsworth, Sir H. Harmsworth (Ld Rothermere), 1914. Pictorial Newspaper (1910) Co. Daily Mirror Newspapers Ltd. 1961, bought by International Publishing Corporation (Chairman: C. King. H. Cudlipp, 1968). Control acquired by Reed International 1970 (Chairman: (Sir) D. Ryder). (Sir) A. Jarratt, 1974). Control acquired by British Printing and Publishing Co., 1984 (Chairman: R. Maxwell).
Policy: Independent. Since 1940s Labour-supporting.
Editors: Mary Howarth, 1903. H. Fyfe, 1904. A. Kinealy, 1907. E. Flynn, 1915. A. Campbell, 1919. L. Brownlee, 1931. C. Thomas, 1934. S. Bolam, 1948. J. Nener, 1953. L. Howard, 1960. A. Miles, 1971. M. Christiansen, 1974. M. Molloy, 1975.

(Daily News), 1846-1930
Proprietors: Daily News Ltd, 1901 (Chairman: G. Cadbury, 1901-11). Amalgamated with *Morning Leader*, as *Daily News and Leader*, 1912. Amalgamated with *Westminster Gazette*, 1928. Amalgamated with *Daily Chronicle*, 1930. Continued as *News Chronicle* (see below).
Policy: Liberal.
Editors: E. Cook, 1896. R. Lehmann, 1901. A. Gardiner, 1902. S. Hodgson, 1920-30.

(Daily Paper), 1904 (32 issues only)
Proprietor: W. Stead.
Policy: 'A paper for the abnormally scrupulous'.
Editor: W. Stead.

(Daily Sketch), 1908-1971
Proprietors: E. Hulton and Co. Ltd. Daily Mirror Newspapers Ltd, and Sunday Pictorial Newspapers (1920) Ltd. Bought by the Berry brothers, 1926, and merged with the *Daily Graphic.* Name changed to *Daily Graphic,* 1946-52. Subsidiary of Allied Newspapers Ltd. Kemsley Newspapers Ltd. Bought by Associated Newspapers Ltd, 1952. Renamed *Daily Sketch,* 1953. Merged with *Daily Mail,* 1971.
Policy: Independent Conservative.
Editors: J. Heddle, 1909. W. Robinson, 1914. H. Lane, 1919. H. Gates, 1922. H. Lane, 1923. A. Curthoys, 1928. A. Sinclair, 1936. S. Carroll, 1939. L. Berry, 1942. A. Thornton and M. Watts, 1943. A. Thornton, 1944. N. Hamilton, 1947. H. Clapp, 1948. H. Gunn, 1953. C. Valdar, 1959. H. French, 1962. D. English, 1969-71.

Daily Star, 1978
Proprietors: Beaverbrook Newspapers (Chairman: V. Matthews). At first printed in Manchester and distributed only in North.
Policy: Independent.
Editor: P. Grimsditch, 1978. L. Turner, 1982.

Daily Telegraph, 1855
Proprietors: Ld Burnham and family. Sold to Sir W. Berry (Ld Camrose), Sir G. Berry (Ld Kemsley) and Sir E. Iliffe (Ld) in 1928. Absorbed *Morning Post,* as *Daily Telegraph and Morning Post* in 1937. Ld Camrose acquired Ld Kemsley's and Ld Iliffe's interests in 1937. M. Berry (Ld Hartwell) succeeded him as Editor-in-Chief in 1968.
Policy: Conservative.
Editors: (Sir) J. le Sage, 1885. F. Miller, 1923. A. Watson, 1924. (Sir) C. Coote, 1950. M. Green, 1964. W. Deedes, 1974.

(Daily Worker), 1930-1966
Proprietors: Daily Worker Cooperative Society Ltd. Descendant of the *Sunday Worker,* 1925-30. Publication suppressed 1941-42. Changed name to *Morning Star,* 1966.
Policy: Communist.
Editors: W. Rust, 1930. J. Shields, 1932. I. Cox. 1935. R. Palme Dutt, 1936. W. Rust, 1939. J. Campbell, 1949. G. Matthews, 1959-1966.

(Financial News), 1884-1945
Proprietors: Financial News Ltd, 1898 (H. Marks). Incorporated with the *Financial Times* in 1945.
Policy: Finance, independent.
Editors: H. Marks, 1884. Dr Ellis, 1916. H. O'Neill, 1921. W. Dorman and W. Lang, 1921. Sir L. Worthington-Evans, 1924. Sir E. Young, 1925. O. Hobson, 1929. M . Green, 1934. H. Parkinson, 1938-45.

Financial Times, 1888
Proprietors: Financial Times Ltd. Incorporated *Financier and Bullionist.* Incorporated the *Financial News* in 1945. Merged with Westminster Press Ltd, as Financial and Provincial Publishers, Ltd, 1967.
Policy: Finance, independent.

Editors: W. Lawson. A. Murray, 1901. C. Palmer, 1909. D. Hunter, 1924. A. Chisholm, 1938. A. Cole, 1940. H. Parkinson, 1945. (Sir) G. Newton, 1950. F. Fisher, 1973. G. Anderson, 1981.

(Manchester) Guardian, 1821
Proprietors: The Manchester Guardian & Evening News Ltd. Renamed *Guardian*, 1959. The Scott Trust.
Policy: Independent liberal.
Editors: C. P. Scott, 1872. E. Scott, 1929. W. Crozier, 1932. A. Wadsworth, 1944. A. Hetherington, 1956. P. Preston 1975.

(Majority), 1906 (10-14 Jul only)
Proprietors: Majority Ltd.
Policy: 'The organ of all who work for wage or salary'.

Morning Advertiser, 1794
Proprietors: Incorporated Society of Licensed Victuallers.
Policy: Defence of the interests of licensed trade.
Editors: F. Doney, 1894. H. Fyfe, 1902. G. Talbot, 1903. H. Byshe, 1913. A. Jackson, 1924. H. Bennett, 1927. F. Millman, 193?. E. Hopwood, 1947. D. Quick, 1954. L. Forse, 1956. T. Cockerell, 1971.

(Morning Herald), 1892-1900
Proprietors: Morning Newspaper Co. Became *London Morning* in 1898, and *Morning Herald* in 1899. Merged with *Daily Express* in 1900.
Policy: Independent.
Editor: D. Murray, 1892-1900.

(Morning Leader), 1892-1912
Proprietors: Colman family of Norwich. Merged with *Daily News*, as *Daily News and Leader* in 1912 (see *Daily News*).
Policy: Liberal.
Editor: E. Parke, 1892-1912.

(Morning Post), 1772-1937
Proprietors: Sir A. Borthwick (Ld Glenesk), 1876-1908. Lady Bathurst, 1908-24. Absorbed in *Daily Telegraph* in 1937 (Ld Camrose).
Policy: Conservative.
Editors: J. Dunn, 1897. S. Wilkinson, 1905. F. Ware, 1905. H. Gwynne, 1911-37.

(Morning Standard), 1857-1917
Proprietors: Bought from Johnston family by A. Pearson, 1904. Sold to D. Dalziel (Ld) in 1910.
Policy: From 1904 supporter of tariff reform.
Editors: W. Mudford, 1874. G. Curtis, 1900. H. Gwynne, 1904. H. White, 1911-17.

Morning Star, 1966
Proprietors: Morning Star Co-operative Society. Successor to the *Daily Worker*.
Policy: Communist.
Editor: G. Matthews, 1966. T. Chater, 1974.

(New Daily), 1960-1966
Proprietors: The British Newspaper Trust Ltd. Sponsored by the People's League for the Defence of Freedom, the Free Press Society, and the Anti-Socialist Front.

Policy: 'The only daily newspaper in Great Britain independent of combines and trade unions'.
Editor: E. Martell, 1960-66.

(News Chronicle), 1930-60
Proprietors: Amalgamation of *Daily News and Leader* and *Daily Chronicle* in 1930 (Cadbury family). Bought by Associated Newspapers Ltd in 1960, and merged with *Daily Mail.*
Policy: Liberal.
Editors: T. Clarke, 1930. A. Vallance, 1933. G. Barry, 1936. R. Cruikshank, 1948. M. Curtis, 1954. N. Cursley, 1957.

(Recorder), 27 Oct 1953-17 May 1954
Proprietors: The Recorder Ltd. (Managing Director: E. Martell). A weekly suburban newspaper 1870-1939, continued as a weekly after 1954.
Policy: Independent. 'Keynote: pride in Britain and the British Empire.'
Editor: W. Brittain, 1953-4.

Sun, 1964
Proprietors: International Publishing Corporation (Chairman: C. King. H. Cudlipp, 1968). 1969 News International Ltd (R. Murdoch).
Policy: Labour. Independent since 1969.
Editors: S. Jacobson, 1964. R, Dinsdale, 1965. A. Lamb, 1969. B. Shrimsley, 1972. (Sir) L. Lamb, 1975. K. McKenzie, 1981.

The Times, 1785[1]
Proprietors: Founded as the *Daily Universal Register*, became *The Times* in 1788. Owned by the Walter family, 1785-1908. Bought by Ld Northcliffe in 1908. Owned by J. Astor and J. Walter in 1922. 7 Aug 24, Times Association formed (comprising Lord Chief Justice, Warden of All Souls, Oxford, President of the Royal Society, President of the Institute of Chartered Accountants and Governor of the Bank of England). 21 Dec 66, Monopolies Commission approved common ownership of *The Times* and *The Sunday Times* by the Thomson Organisation. Times Newspapers Ltd formed. President: G. Astor (Ld). Chairman: Sir W. Haley. 1967 K. Thomson (Ld). Acquired by News International, 1981 (Chairman: R. Murdoch).
Policy: Independent conservative.
Editors: G. Buckle, 1884. G. Dawson, 1912. H. Steed, 1919. G. Dawson, 1922. R. Barrington-Ward, 1941. W. Casey, 1948. Sir W. Haley, 1952. W. Rees-Mogg, 1967. H. Evans, 1981. C. Douglas-Home, 1983.

(Tribune), 1906-1908
Proprietors: F. Thomasson.
Policy: Liberal.
Editors: W. Hill and S. Pryor, 1906.

(Westminster Gazette), 1921-1928 issued as a morning paper.
(See *Evening Papers).*

[1] *The Times* suspended publication from 1 Dec 1978 to 12 Nov 1979.

National Sunday Newspapers
(excluding all those not published in London)

((Illustrated) Sunday Herald), 1915-1927

Proprietors: Sir E. Hulton. Renamed *Illustrated Sunday Herald.* Bought by Berry family in 1926 and renamed *Sunday Graphic* in 1927 (see below).
Policy: Independent conservative.
Editors: J. E. Williams. T. Hill, 1926-27.

Mail on Sunday, 1982

Proprietors: Associated Newspapers Ltd (Chairman: 3rd Ld Rothermere).
Policy: Independent Conservative.
Editors: B. Shrimsley, 1982. Sir D. English, 1982. S. Stevens, 1983.

(National News), 1917-1918

Proprietors: Odhams Press Ltd.
Policy: Independent.
Editor: A. de Beck, 1917-18.

News of the World, 1843

Proprietors: News of the World Ltd. (Sir) G. Riddell (Ld), 1903-34. The Carr family 1934-69. 1969 News International Ltd (R. Murdoch).
Policy: Independent conservative.
Editors: Sir E. Carr, 1891. D. Davies, 1941. R. Skelton, 1946. A. Waters, 1947. R. Cudlipp, 1953. S. Somerfield, 1959. C. Lear, 1970. P. Stephens, 1974. B. Shrimsley, 1975. K. Donlan, 1980. B. Askew, 1981. D. Jameson, 1981. N. Lloyd, 1984.

The Observer, 1791

Proprietors: F. Beer. Bought by Ld Northcliffe in 1905. Bought by W. Astor (Vt) in 1911. Sold to Atlantic Richfield, 1976. 10 shares to remain with *Observer* Trustees. Sold to Lonrho, 1980 (Chairman: R. Rowland).
Policy: Conservative. Independent since 1942.
Editors: F. Beer, 1894. A. Harrison, 1905. J. Garvin, 1908. I. Brown, 1942. D. Astor, 1948. D. Trelford, 1976.

People, 1881 (since 1972 **Sunday People**)

Proprietors: W. Madge and Sir G. Armstrong. Sir W. Madge, 1914-22. M. L. Publishing Co. Ltd. The People Ltd. Odhams Press. 1961 amalgamated with International Publishing Corporation (Chairman: C. King. H. Cudlipp, 1968). Control acquired by Reed International 1970 (Chairman: (Sir) D. Ryder. A. Jarratt, 1974). Control aquired by British Printing and Publishing Co., 1984 (Chairman: R. Maxwell).
Policy: Independent.
Editors: J. Hatton. J. Sansome 1913. H. Swaffer, 1924. H. Ainsworth, 1925. S. Campbell, 1958. R. Edwards, 1966. G. Pinnington, 1972. R. Stott, 1984.

(Reynolds News), 1850-1967

Proprietors: Originally *Reynold's Weekly Newspaper,* and later *Reynold's Illustrated News.* Owned by J. Dicks and family since 1879. H. Dalziel (Ld)[1] appointed business manager in 1907. He became the sole pro-

[1] Ld Dalziel of Kirkcaldy, not to be confused with Ld Dalziel of Wooler, who was proprietor of the *Evening Standard* 1910-15.

prietor in 1914. Bought by the National Co-operative Press Ltd. Incorporated the *Sunday Citizen.* 1962. Changed name to *Sunday Citizen and Reynolds News.*

Policy: Support for the Labour and Co-operative movements.

Editors: W. Thompson, 1894. H. Dalziel, 1907. J. Crawley, 1920. S. Elliott, 1929. (Sir) W. Richardson, 1941-67.

(Sunday Citizen), 1962-1967. *(See above, Reynolds News)*

(Sunday Dispatch), 1801-1961

Proprietors: Sir G. Newnes (1900-10). Originally the *Weekly Dispatch* until 1928. Bought by the Harmsworth family. Ld Northcliffe, Ld Rothermere from 1928. Associated Newspapers Ltd. Absorbed by the *Sunday Express* in 1961.

Policy: Independent conservative.

Editors: M. Cotton, H. Swaffer, 1915. B. Falk, 1919. W. McWhirter, 1930. H. Lane, 1933. W. Brittain, 1934. C. Brooks, 1936. C. Eade, 1938. H. Gunn, 1959-61.

Sunday Express, 1918

Proprietors: Sunday Express Ltd. (Ld Beaverbrook; from 1954 Beaverbrook Newspapers Ltd.) Taken over by Trafalgar House property group, 1977. Chairman: V. (Ld) Matthews.

Policy: Independent conservative.

Editors: J. Douglas, 1920. J. Gordon, 1928. (Sir) J. Junor, 1954.

(Sunday Graphic (and Sunday News)), 1915-60

Proprietors: Sir E. Hulton. Originally called the *Sunday Herald*, renamed the *Illustrated Sunday Herald*. Bought by the Berry family in 1926, and renamed the *Sunday Graphic* in 1927. Daily Graphic and Sunday Graphic Ltd., a subsidiary of Ld Kemsley's newspapers. Incorporated the *Sunday News* in 1931. Bought by R. Thomson in 1959. Ceased publication in 1960.

Policy: Independent.

Editors: T. Hill, 1927. A. Sinclair, 1931. R. Simpson, 1935. M. Watts, 1947. N. Hamilton, 1947. I. Lang, 1948. A. Josey, 1949. B. Horniblow, 1950. P. Brownrigg, 1952. M. Randell, 1953. G. McKenzie, 1953. A. Hall, 1958. R. Anderson, 1959. A. Ewart, 1960.

(Sunday Illustrated), 1921-23

Proprietor: H. Bottomley.

Policy: Independent.

Editor: H. Bottomley.

(Sunday (Illustrated) News), 1842-1931

Proprietors: Originally *Lloyd's Sunday News*. Sunday News Ltd. United Newspapers Ltd (W. Harrison). Merged with the *Sunday Graphic* in 1931.

Policy: Independent liberal.

Editors: T. Catling. W. Robinson, 1919. E. Perris, 1924. E. Wallace, 1929-31.

Sunday Mirror, 1963

Proprietors: International Publishing Corporation (Chairman: C. King. H. Cudlipp, 1968) Control acquired by Reed International 1970 (Chairman: (Sir) D. Ryder, 1974. A. Jarratt). Control acquired by British Printing and Publishing Co., 1984 (Chairman: R. Maxwell).

Policy: Independent.
Editor: M. Christiansen, 1963. R. Edwards, 1972.

(Sunday Pictorial), 1915-1963
Proprietors: The Harmsworth family. Taken over by Ld Rothermere in 1922. Sunday Pictorial Newspapers (1920) Ltd. 1961 absorbed by International Publishing Corporation (Cecil King). 1963. Became *Sunday Mirror* (*see above*).
Policy: Independent.
Editors: F. Sanderson, 1915. W. McWhirter, 1921. D. Grant, 1924. W. McWhirter, 1928. D. Grant, 1929. H. Cudlipp, 1938. R. Campbell, 1940. H. Cudlipp, 1946. P. Zec, 1949. H. Cudlipp, 1952. C. Valdar, 1953. L. Howard, 1959. R. Payne, 1960.

((Sunday) Referee), 1877-1939
Proprietors: Printed by the Daily News Ltd. Owned by I. Ostrer. Incorporated in the *Sunday Chronicle* in 1939 (which was published in Manchester and ceased independent publication in 1955).
Policy: Conservative.
Editors: R. Butler. (Sir) R. Donald, 1922. A. Laber, 1924. M. Joulden, 1933.

(Sunday Special), 1897-1904
Proprietor: H. Schmidt.

Sunday Telegraph, 1961
Proprietors: The Sunday Telegraph Ltd (M. Berry (Ld Hartwell)).
Policy: Independent conservative.
Editor: D. McLachlan, 1961. B. Roberts, 1966. J. Thompson, 1976.

Sunday Times, 1822[1]
Proprietors: Mrs. F. Beer. Bought by H. Schmidt. Amalgamated with the *Sunday Special* in 1904. Bought by the Berry family in 1915. Bought by R. Thomson in 1959. Thomson Allied Newspapers. 1967, Times Newspapers Ltd, formed to run *The Times* and *Sunday Times*. Control acquired by News International, 1981 (Chairman: R. Murdoch)
Policy: Independent conservative.
Editors: L. Rees, 1901. W. Hadley, 1932. H. Hodson, 1950. C. D. Hamilton, 1961. H. Evans, 1967. F. Giles, 1981. A. Neil, 1983.

(Sunday Worker), 1925-30
Proprietors: The Communist Party through nominees. Published daily as the *Daily Worker* from 1930.
Policy: Communist.
Editors: W. Paul, 1925. W. Holmes, 1927.

London Evening Newspapers

(Evening Echo and Chronicle), 22 Mar-4 May 1915
Proprietor: E. Lloyd. Merged with *Star*.
Policy: Liberal.

[1]Publication suspended 1 Dec 1978-

(Echo), 1868-1905

Proprietors: Consolidated Newspapers. F. Pethick-Lawrence in control, 1901-5.

Policy: Radical, progressive.

Editors: W. Crook, 1898. T. Meech, 1900. P. Alden, 1901. F. Pethick-Lawrence, 1901-5.

(Evening News, 1881-1980**)**

Proprietors: A. Harmsworth (Evening News Ltd), 1894. Associated Newspapers Ltd, 1905. Merged with *Evening Standard,* 1980.

Policy: Conservative.

Editors: W. Evans, 1896. C. Beattie, 1922. F. Fitzhugh, 1924. G. Schofield, 1943. J. Marshall, 1950. R.Willis, 1954. J. Gold, 1967. D. Boddie, 1973. L. Kirby, 1974.

(Evening) (New) Standard, 1827

Proprietors: Bought by A. Pearson from Johnston family in 1904. Absorbed *St James' Gazette* in 1905. D. Dalziel (Ld)[1], 1910. Hulton and Co. 1915-23. Incorporated with *Pall Mall Gazette* and *Globe*, 1923. Bought by Ld Beaverbrook in 1923. In 1954 he relinquished it to Beaverbrook Newspapers Ltd and transferred controlling shares to the Beaverbrook Foundations. In 1977 Beaverbrook Newspapers were taken over by Trafalgar House property group. Chairman: V. Matthews. Sold to Associated Newspapers, 1980 (Chairman: Ld Rothermere) and merged with *Evening News* as *(New) Standard.*

Policy: Independent conservative.

Editors: S. Pryor, 1897. W. Woodward, 1906. J. Kilpatrick, 1912. D. Sutherland, 1914. A. Mann, 1916. D. Phillips, 1920. E. Thompson, 1923. G. Gilliat, 1928. P. Cudlipp, 1933. R. Thompson, 1938. F. Owen, 1939. M. Foot, 1942. S. Elliott, 1943. H. Gunn, 1944. P. Elland, 1950. C. Wintour, 1959. S. Jenkins, 1977. C. Wintour, 1978. L. Kirkby, 1980.

(Evening Times), 1910-1911

Proprietors: London Evening Newspaper Co. (J. Morrison, Sir S. Scott, J. Cowley).

Policy: Conservative.

Editors: C. Watney, E. Wallace.

(Globe), 1803-1921

Proprietors: (Sir) G. Armstrong, 1871-1907. H. Harmsworth, 1907-11. W. Madge, 1912-14. Absorbed by *Pall Mall Gazette* in 1921, incorporated with *Evening Standard* in 1923.

Policy: Conservative.

Editors: Sir G. Armstrong, 1895. P. Ogle, 1907. J. Harrison, 1908. C. Palmer, 1912. W. Peacock, 1915-21.

(Pall Mall Gazette), 1865-1923

Proprietors: W. Astor (Ld), 1892. Sir H. Dalziel, 1917. Sir J. Leigh, 1923. Incorporated with *Evening Standard* in 1923.

Policy: Conservative.

Editors: Sir D. Straight, 1896. F. Higginbottom, 1909. J. Garvin, 1912. D. Sutherland, 1915-23.

[1] Later Ld Dalziel of Wooler, not to be confused with Ld Dalziel of Kirkcaldy who was proprietor of *Reynolds News,* 1914-29.

(St James's Gazette), 1880-1905

Proprietors: E. Steinkopff, 1888. W. Dallas Ross. A. Pearson, 1903. Amalgamated with *Evening Standard* in 1905.

Policy: Conservative.

Editors: H. Chisholm, 1897. R. McNeill, 1900. G. Fiennes, 1903. S. Pryor, 1904-5.

(Star), 1887-1960

Proprietors: Star Newspaper Co. Owned by Daily News Ltd. Bought by Associated Newspapers Ltd, and incorporated in *Evening News*, 1960.

Policy: Liberal.

Editors: E. Parke, 1891. J. Douglas, 1908. W. Pope, 1920. E. Chattaway, 1930. R. Cruikshank, 1936. A. Cranfield, 1941. R. McCarthy, 1957-60.

(Sun), 1893-1906

Proprietors: T. P. O'Connor. H. Bottomley, 1900. Sir G. Armstrong and W. Madge, 1904-6.

Policy: Literary, non-political.

Editors: T. P. O'Connor. T. Dahle.

(Westminster Gazette), 1893-1928

Proprietors: Sir G. Newnes, 1893. Liberal Syndicate (Chairman: Sir A. Mond), 1908-15. A. Pearson, 1915-28. Last issue as evening paper 5 Nov 21. First issue as morning paper 7 Nov 21. Incorporated with *Daily News* in 1928.

Policy: Liberal.

Editors: J. Spender, 1896. J. Hobman, 1921-28.

National Newspapers Printing in More than One City

	London	Manchester	Glasgow
Daily Chronicle	1869-1930	1925-1930[1]	—
Daily Express	1900-	1927-	1928-1974
Daily Herald (Sun)	1912-	1930-1969	—
Daily Mail	1896-	1900-	1946-1966[2]
Daily Mirror[3]	1903-	1955-	—
Daily News	1846-1930	{ 1921-1924 1929-1930	— —
Daily Star	1978-	1978-	—
Daily Sketch (Graphic)	1911-1971	1908-1953	—
Daily Telegraph	1855-	1940-	—
News Chronicle	1930-1960	1930-1960	—
(Manchester) Guardian	1961-	1821-	—
News of the World	1843-	1941-	—
Sunday Dispatch	1801-1961	1930-1961	—
Sunday Express	1918-	1927-	1927-1974
Sunday Graphic	1915-1960[4]	1932-1952	—
Sunday Pictorial/Sunday Mirror	1955-	1955-	—
(Sunday) People	1881-	1930-	—
Sunday Times	1822-	1940-1964	—
Sunday Chronicle	1939-1955	1885-1955	—

[1] The *Daily Chronicle* was printed in Leeds, not Manchester, 1925-1930.
[2] The *Scottish Daily Mail* was printed in Edinburgh, not Glasgow, 1946-66.
[3] The *Daily Mirror* was also printed in Belfast, 1966-1971.
[4] The Manchester printing of the *Sunday Graphic* was suspended from 1936-1950.

Partisan Tendencies and Circulations of National Daily Newspapers in British General Elections, 1945-74

Newspaper	Circulation in thousands; Party support											
	1945	1950	1951	1955	1959	1964	1966	1970	Feb 1974	Oct 1974	1979	1983
Daily Express	3,300 Con	4,099 Con	4,169 Con	4,036 Con	4,053 Con	4,190 Con	3,954 Con	3,607 Con	3,227 Con	3,081 Con	2,458 Con	1,936 Con
Daily Herald/ The Sun[1]	1,850 Lab	2,030 Lab	2,003 Lab	1,759 Lab	1,465 Lab	1,300?* Lab	1,248 Lab	1,509 Lab	3,303 Con	3,457 All-Pty Coalition	3,942 Con	4,155 Con
Daily Mail	1,704 Con	2,215 Con	2,267 Con	2,068 Con	2,071 Con	2,400 Con	2,381 Con	1,916 Con	1,768 Con	1,738 Con-Lib Coalition	1,973 Con	1,834 Con
Daily Mirror	2,400 Lab	4,603 Lab	4,514 Lab	4,725 Lab	4,497 Lab	5,085 Lab	5,077 Lab	4,697 Lab	4,192 Lab	4,218 Lab	3,783 Lab	3,267 Lab
Daily Sketch/ Daily Graphic[2]	896 Con	777 Con	794 Con	950 Con	1,156 Con	847 Con	849 Con	839 Con	—	—	—	—
Daily Telegraph	813 Con	984 Con	998 Con	1,055 Con	1,181 Con	1,324 Con	1,354 Con	1,402 Con	1,427 Con	1,385 Con	1,358 Con	1,284 Con
(*Manchester*) *Guardian*[3]	83 Lib	141 Lib	139 Lib/Con	156 Lib/Con	183 Lab/Lib	278 Lab	283 Lab/Lib	303 Lab/Lib	365 Con/Lab/ Lib Balance	354 More Lib Influence	275 Lab	417 Alln/Con
News Chronicle[4]	1,549 Lib	1,525 Lib	1,507 Lib	1,253 Lib	1,207 Lib	—	—	—	—	—	—	—
The Times	204 Lab	258 Con	232 Con	222 Con	254 Con	255 Con	273 ?/Lib	402 Con/Lib	351 Con/Lib	340 Con-Lib Coalition	—	321 Con
Daily Star	—	—	—	—	—	—	—	—	—	—	n.a. Neutral	1,313 Con

Total circulation	12,799	16,632	16,623	16,224	16,067	15,679	15,419	14,642	14,633	14,573	13,789[5]	14,527
Total Conservative circulation	6,713 (52%)	8,333 (50%)	8,599† (52%)	8,487† (52%)	8,715 (54%)	9,016 (57%)	8,538 (55%)	8,133† (55%)	10,441† (71%)	6,898† (47%)	9,731 (71%)	11,260† (78%)
Total Conservative vote	9,578 (40%)	12,503 (43%)	13,718 (48%)	13,312 (50%)	13,750 (49%)	12,001 (43%)	11,418 (42%)	13,145 (46%)	11,872 (38%)	10,465 (36%)	13,698 (44%)	13,012 (42%)
Total Labour circulation	4,454 (35%)	6,633 (40%)	6,517 (39%)	6,484 (40%)	6,145† (38%)	6,663 (42%)	6,608† (43%)	6,509† (44%)	4,557† (31%)	4,572† (31%)	4,058 (29%)	3,267 (22%)
Total Labour vote	11,633 (48%)	13,267 (46%)	13,949 (49%)	12,405 (46%)	12,216 (44%)	12,206 (44%)	13,065 (48%)	12,178 (43%)	11,646 (37%)	11,457 (39%)	11,532 (37%)	8,457 (28%)
Total Liberal circulation	1,632 (13%)	1,666 (10%)	1,646† (10%)	1,409† (9%)	1,390† (9%)	— —	556† (4%)	705† (5%)	716† (5%)	2,432† (17%)	— —	417 (3%)
Total Liberal vote	2,197 (9%)	2,622 (9%)	731 (2%)	722 (3%)	1,639 (6%)	3,093 (11%)	2,327 (8%)	2,117 (7%)	6,059 (19%)	5,347 (18%)	4,314 (14%)	7,781 (25%)

[1] Name changed to *The Sun* in 1964.
[2] Named *Daily Graphic*, 1946-52.
[3] 'Manchester' dropped from title in 1959.
[4] Ceased publication in 1960.
[5] Not including the *Daily Star*.
* Figure uncertain due to relaunching at that time.
† Includes paper(s) with divided support, but omits *The Sun* in October 1974.

Source of circulation figures: 1945, 1950: Nuffield election studies; thereafter, Audit Bureau of Circulation, excepting *The Daily Telegraph* figures for 1951, 1955, 1959 (London Press Exchange). Circulation figures are for the period of the year in which the election was held.

The *Daily Worker*, the Communist daily paper, which changed its name to the *Morning Star* in 1966, is omitted: comparable circulation figures are not available. The number of Communist candidates at general elections was as often as not under fifty.

SOURCES.—*Royal Commission on the Press*; Working Paper No. 3. Cmnd 6810.

Circulations of National Newspapers, 1910-

National Daily Newspapers

(to nearest '000)

	1910	1930	1939	1951	1960	1965	1970	1980
D. Express	400	1,603	2,486	4,193	4,130	3,981	3,607	2,325
D. Herald/Sun	. .	750[b]	2,000	2,071	1,467	1,274	1,509	3,837
D. Mail	900	1,968	1,510	2,245	2,084	2,464	1,917	1,985
D. Mirror[h]	630	1,071	1,367[d]	4,567	4,545	4,957[i]	4,697	3,651
D. News	320	900	. .	. .	. .	. .	. .	. .
D. Sketch	750[a]	1,013	850[d]	777	1,152	844	806	. .
D. Telegraph	230	222[c]	640[d]	976[e]	1,155[e]	1,351	1,402	1,456
D. Worker/ M. Star	. .	n.a.	100[d]	115	73[f]	. .	. .	34
Guardian	40	47	51	140	190	270	303	375
M. Leader	250	. .	. .	. .	. .	. .	. .	. .
M. Post	n.a.	119	. .	. .	. .	. .	. .	. .
N. Chronicle[g]	800[a]	967	1,317	1,583	1,206	. .	. .	. .
Times	45	187	213	254	255	258	402	316
D. Star	. .	. .	. .	. .	. .	. .	. .	1,033

Unless otherwise stated the figures are taken from *T. B. Browne's Advertiser's ABC*, 1910-40, and figures after 1950 are from the Audit Bureau of Circulation, published in the *Newspaper Press Directory. Benn's Press Directory, 1981.*

[a] Circulation figure for 1915, *T. B. Browne*.
[b] P.E.P.: *Report on the British Press* (1938) gives 1082 for 1930.
[c] From the P.E.P. *Report*.
[d] From the P.E.P. *Report*. Figure for 1938.
[e] *Daily Telegraph* audited circulation figures.
[f] *ABC* circulation in 1956. Latest available figure.
[g] 1910 and 1930 figures are for *Daily Chronicle*.
[h] This does not include circulation of *Daily Record* (Glasgow), acquired by the *Daily Mirror* in 1955.
[i] For a period in 1964 the *Daily Mirror* became the only daily newspaper ever to top 5m. circulation.

National Sunday Newspapers

(to nearest '000)

	1900	1910	1930	1937	1951	1960	1965	1970	1980
Lloyd's Weekly Newspaper	1,250	1,250	1,450[b]	. .	. .	. .	. .	. .	. .
News of the World	400	1,500	3,250[b]	3,850	8,407	6,664	6,176	6,215	4,472
Observer	60	n.a.	201	208	450	738	829	848	1,018
People	n.a.	n.a.	2,535	3,406	5,181	5,468	5,538	5,242	3,856
Reynolds News	2,000[a]	2,000[a]	420	426	712	329	236	. .	. .
Sunday Dispatch	n.a.	n.a.	1,197	741	2,631	1,520	. .	. .	. .
Sunday Express	. .	. .	958	1,350	3,178	3,706	4,187	4,281	3,100
Sunday Graphic	. .	. .	1,100[b]	651	1,121	890	. .	. .	. .
Sunday Mirror	. .	. .	. .	. .	. .	. .	5,022	4,885	3,856
Sunday Pictorial	. .	. .	1,883	1,345	5,170	5,461	. .	. .	. .
Sunday Referee	n.a.	n.a.	73	342	. .	. .	. .	. .	. .
Sunday Telegraph	. .	. .	. .	. .	. .	. .	662	756	1,032
Sunday Times	n.a.	n.a.	153	270	529	1,001	1,290	1,464	1,419

Unless otherwise stated, the figures are taken from *T. B. Browne's Advertiser's ABC*, 1900-30; the figures for 1937 are from the *Report of the Royal Commission on the Press, 1947-49* (Cmd. 7700 and 7690/1949); from 1951 they are the Audit Bureau of Circulations' figures quoted in the *Newspaper Press Directory*.

[a] These figures should be treated with caution. They are from an advertisement in *T. B. Browne's Advertiser's ABC* for 1901 and 1911.
[b] From *Sell's World Press*.

London Evening Newspapers

(to nearest '000)

	1905	1910	1930	1939	1951	1960	1965	1970	1980
E. News	300	300	667	822	1,752	1,153	1,238	1,017	. .
E. Standard	n.a.	160	n.a.	390	862	586	680	550	608
Star	250	327	744	503	1,228	744	. .	. .	. .

All circulation figures for evening newspapers exclude Sporting Editions. 1905-39 figures from *T. B. Browne's Advertiser's ABC*; from 1951 figures are from the Audit Bureau of Circulations, published in the *Newspaper Press Directory*. Information on the circulations of other evening papers is not available.

Provincial Morning Daily Newspapers, 1900-

Sporting newspapers and publications such as the *Hull Shipping Gazette* and the Hartlepool *Daily Shipping List* have been omitted. Bold type indicates newspapers still being published on 1 Jan 1985.

BATH—*Bath Daily Argus* (1870). Merged with local evening paper, *Bath Daily Chronicle*, in Jan 1900.

BEDFORD—*Bedford Daily Circular* (1903). Merged with *Bedford Record* July 1939.

BIRMINGHAM—*Daily Argus* (1891). Merged with local evening paper, *Birmingham Evening Dispatch*, Jan 1902.

Birmingham Daily Post (1857). Changed name to *Birmingham Post* May 1918. Became *Birmingham Post and Gazette* Nov 1956. Changed name to **Birmingham Post** 1973.

Birmingham Daily Gazette (1862). Merged with *Midland Express* and changed name to *Birmingham Gazette and Express* 1904. Merged with *Birmingham Post* Nov 1956.

BRADFORD—*Bradford Observer* (1834). Changed name to *Yorkshire Daily Observer* Nov 1901. Changed name to *Yorkshire Observer* Jan 1909. Merged with local evening paper, *The Telegraph and Argus*, Nov 1956.

BRIGHTON—*Morning Argus* (1896). Ceased publication as morning paper May 1926.[1]

Sussex Daily News (1868). Merged with *Evening Argus* Mar 1956.

BRISTOL—*Bristol Western Daily Press* (1858). Changed name to **Western Daily Press** 1928.

Bristol Mercury (1790). Changed name to *Bristol Daily Mercury* Dec 1901. Ceased publication Nov 1909.

Bristol Times and Mirror (1713). Merged with *Western Daily Press* 1932.

CROYDON—*Surrey Morning Echo* (1908). Ceased publication Jan 1910.

DARLINGTON—*North Star* (1881). Merged with *Newcastle Daily Journal* 1926. **Northern Echo** (1870).

EXETER—*Devon and Exeter Daily Gazette* (1772). Merged with *Western Morning News* Mar 1932.

Western Times (1827). Became weekly paper 1922.

HUDDERSFIELD—*Huddersfield Daily Chronicle* (1871).[2] Ceased publication Dec 1915.

HULL—*Daily Mail* (1787). Became an evening paper 1902.

Eastern Morning News (1864). Ceased publication Nov 1929.

IPSWICH—**East Anglian Daily Times** (1874).

LEAMINGTON—*Leamington, Warwick, Kenilworth and District Morning News* (1896). Originally *Leamington, Warwick, Kenilworth and District Daily Circular*. Changed name and started morning publication in 1919.

LEEDS—*Leeds Mercury* (1718). Changed name to *Leeds and Yorkshire Mercury* Oct 1901-Nov 1907. Merged with *Yorkshire Post* Nov 1939.

Yorkshire Post (1754).

LEICESTER—*Leicester Daily Post* (1872). Ceased publication Mar 1921.

LIVERPOOL—*Liverpool Courier* (1808). Changed name to *Liverpool Daily Courier* Sep 1922. Changed name to *Daily Courier* Oct 1922. Ceased publication Dec 1929.

Liverpool Mercury (1811). Merged with *Liverpool Daily Post* Nov 1904.

Liverpool Daily Post (1855).

Journal of Commerce (1861).

MANCHESTER—*Manchester Courier* (1825). Ceased publication Jan 1916.

Daily Dispatch (1900). Merged with *News Chronicle* Nov 1955.

(**Manchester**) **Guardian** (1821). (*See under National Daily Newspapers.*)

Manchester Journal of Commerce. Ceased publication 1911.

Telegraphic News. Ceased publication 1901.

Daily Citizen (1912). Ceased publication June 1915.

Daily Sketch (1909). Ceased publication Apr 1911.

NEWCASTLE—*Illustrated Chronicle* (1910). Ceased publication June 1925.

Newcastle Daily Chronicle (1858). Merged with *North Mail* Mar 1923.

Newcastle Daily Journal (1832). Became *Newcastle Journal and North Mail* Sep 1939. Changed name to **Journal** Jul 1958.

North Mail (1901). Incorporated *Newcastle Daily Chronicle* Mar 1923 and became *North Mail and Newcastle Daily Chronicle*. Merged with *Newcastle Journal* in Sep 1939.

Newcastle Morning Mail (1898). Changed name to *Morning Mail* Feb 1901. Ceased publication Aug 1901.

NORWICH—**Eastern Daily Press** (1870).

Norfolk Daily Standard (1855). Became an evening paper in 1900.

[1] Localised editions of the *Argus* were published at Battle, Chichester, Eastbourne, East Grinstead, Hastings, Horsham, Hove, Lewes, Littlehampton, Rye, Tunbridge Wells, and Worthing. Those still publishing in 1926 were merged with the Brighton *Morning Argus* into the *Evening Argus*.

[2] Not published on Saturdays.

NOTTINGHAM—*Nottingham Daily Express* (1860). Changed name to *Nottingham Journal and Express* Apr 1918. Changed name to *Nottingham Journal* 1921. Merged with *Nottingham Guardian* Sep 1953 to become *Nottingham Guardian Journal*. Ceased publication Jan 1973.

Nottingham Daily Guardian (1861). Changed name to *Nottingham Guardian* Oct 1905. Merged with *Nottingham Journal* Sep 1953.

OXFORD—*Oxford Morning Echo* (1860). Ceased publication Jan 1900.

PLYMOUTH—*Western Daily Mercury* (1860). Merged with *Western Morning News* Jan 1921.

Western Morning News (1860).

PORTSMOUTH—*Southern Daily Mail* (1884). Ceased publication 1905.

SHIELDS—*Shields Morning Mail* (1889). Ceased publication Feb 1901.

SHEFFIELD—*Yorkshire Early Bird* (1899). Became morning paper in 1929. Changed named to *Early Bird* Mar 1938. Merged with local evening paper, *Chronicle Midday*, May 1950.

Sheffield Daily Telegraph (1855). Changed name to *Sheffield Telegraph* Jun 1934; to *Sheffield Telegraph and Daily Independent* Oct 38-May 39; to *Telegraph and Independent* Jun-Jul 42; to *Sheffield Telegraph* Jul 42-Sep 65; to **Sheffield Morning Telegraph** Sep 65.

Sheffield and Rotherham Independent (1819). Changed name to *Sheffield Independent* Jan 1901. Changed name to *Sheffield Daily Independent* Feb 01-Oct 09. Changed name to *Daily Independent* June 1922. Amalgamated with *Sheffield Telegraph* Oct 1938.

YORK—*Yorkshire Herald* (1790). Became weekly 1936.

CARDIFF—*South Wales Daily News* (1872). Changed name to *South Wales News* Apr 1928. Merged with *Western Mail* Aug 1928.

Western Mail (1869).

Cardiff Journal of Commerce (1904). Changed name to *Cardiff and South Wales Journal of Commerce* July 1914. Changed name to *South Wales Journal of Commerce* June 1918. Ceased publication Apr 1935.

NEWPORT—*South Wales Daily News* (1872). Changed name to *South Wales News* 1928. Merged with *Western Mail* 1928.

SWANSEA—*Swansea Gazette*. Changed name to *Swansea Daily Shipping Register* 1900. Ceased publication 1918.

ABERDEEN—*Aberdeen Daily Journal* (1746). Merged with *Aberdeen Free Press* Nov 1922 and became **Aberdeen Press and Journal.**

Aberdeen Free Press (1853). Merged with *Aberdeen Daily Journal* Nov 1922.

GLASGOW—**Glasgow Herald** (1783).

North British Daily Mail (1847). Became *Glasgow Daily Mail* 1901. Merged with *Glasgow Record* 1901.

Daily Record (1895). Incorporated *Glasgow Daily Mail* 1901 and became *Daily Record and Daily Mail*. Changed name to *Daily Record and Mail* 1902. Changed name to **Daily Record** 1954.

Bulletin (1915). Became *Bulletin and Scots Pictorial* Jan 1924. Ceased publication July 1960.

Scottish Daily News (Apr 75). Workers' Cooperative, using *Scottish Daily Express* plant. Ceased publication Nov 1975.

DUNDEE—*Dundee Advertiser* (1861). Merged with *Courier and Argus* 1926 and became *Dundee Advertiser and Courier*.

Courier and Argus (1861). Merged with the daily edition of *Dundee Advertiser* 1926 and became *Dundee Advertiser and Courier*.

Dundee Advertiser and Courier (1926). Changed name to **Courier and Advertiser** 1926.

EDINBURGH—**Scotsman** (1817).

BELFAST—**Belfast News-Letter** (1737).

Northern Whig (1824). Changed name to *Northern Whig and Belfast Post* June 1919. Ceased publication 1963.

Irish Daily Telegraph (1904). Merged with local evening paper, *Belfast Telegraph*, Apr 1952.

Irish News and Belfast Morning News (1881).

SOURCES.—*Willing's Press Guide 1900-*; the catalogue of the British Museum Newspaper Library at Colindale.

Main Political Weeklies

Economist, The, 1843

Proprietors: The Economist Newspaper Limited. (Since 1928 50% of shares held by Financial Newspaper Proprietors Limited, later Financial News Ltd.)

Policy: Independent.

Editors: E. Johnstone, 1883. F. Hurst, 1907. H. Withers, 1916. W. Layton, 1922. G. Crowther, 1938. D. Tyerman, 1956. A. Burnet, 1965. A. Knight, 1974.

(Nation), 1907

Proprietors: The *Nation.* 1931 Amalgamated with the *New Statesman.*

Policy: Independent radical.

Editors: H. Massingham, 1907. H. Henderson, 1923. H. Wright, 1930-1931.

New Statesman, 1913

Proprietors: Statesman Publishing Company. 1931 Amalgamated with the *Nation*, The Statesman and Nation Publishing Company.

Policy: Independent radical.

Editors: C. Sharp, 1913. K. Martin, 1931. J. Freeman, 1961. P. Johnson, 1965. R. Crossman, 1970. A. Howard, 1973. B. Page, 1978, H. Stephenson, 1982.

The Spectator, 1828

Proprietors: The Spectator Limited since 1898. J. St. L. Strachey, 1898. (Sir) E. Wrench, 1925. I. Gilmour, 1954. H. Creighton, 1967. H. Keswick, 1975. A. Clough, 1981.

Policy: Independent conservative.

Editors: J. St. L. Strachey, 1897. (Sir) Evelyn Wrench, 1925. W. Harris, 1932. W. Taplin, 1953. I. Gilmour, 1954. B. Inglis, 1959. I. Hamilton, 1962. I. Macleod, 1963. N. Lawson, 1966. G. Gale, 1970. H. Creighton, 1973. A. Chancellor, 1975. C. Moore, 1984.

(Time and Tide), 1920[1]

Proprietors: Lady Rhondda, 1920-1958. L. Skevington, 1958. T. Beaumont, 1960. W. Brittain, 1962. Time and Tide Ltd, 1977. Re-named Time and Tide Business News 1977 and published fortnightly. From 1978 published monthly.

Policy: Independent.

Editors: Lady Rhondda, 1920. A. Lejeune, 1957. L. Skevington, 1958. J. Thompson, 1960. W. Brittain, 1962. I. Lyon, 1977.

[1] Published monthly 1971-6.

Tribune, 1937

Proprietors: Tribune Publications, Ltd.

Policy: Left-wing.

Editors: W. Mellor, 1937. J. Hartshorn, 1938. R. Postgate, 1940. A. Bevan, 1942. J. Kimche, 1945. M. Foot, 1948. R. Edwards, 1952. M. Foot, 1956. R. Clements, 1959. C. Mullin, 1982. N. Williamson, 1984.

Newspaper Readership

(percentage of population over the age of 16)[1]

	National Dailies	National Sundays
1939	67	82
1947	73	89
1961	85	93
1972	75	87
1977	74	82

[1] Since 1970, percentage of population over the age of 15.

The Press Council

Chairmen

(General Council of the Press)

1953 W. Astor (Ld)
1955 Sir L. Andrews
1959 G. Murray

(The Press Council)

1963 Ld Devlin
1969 Ld Pearce
1974 Ld Shawcross
1978 (Sir) P. Neill
1983 Sir Z. Cowan

The General Council of the Press was formed in 1953 in response to a recommendation of the Royal Commission on the Press (Cmd. 7700). It consisted of 15 editorial representatives and 10 managerial representatives. Its objects were to preserve the freedom of the press, to review any developments likely to restrict the supply of information of public interest and importance, to encourage training of journalists and technical research and to study developments in the press tending towards greater concentration or monopoly.

In 1963 it was reorganised to bring in lay members and the title was changed to the Press Council. The objects of the Council were extended to include considering complaints about the conduct of the press or the conduct of persons and organisations towards the press, and publishing relevant statistical material.

In 1977 the Press Council accepted the recommendation of the Royal Commission on the Press that in addition to its independent lay Chairman, it should consist of equal numbers of press and lay members. Since 1978, the composition has been 18 representatives from the newspaper and magazine industry, both management and trade union, 18 lay representatives, 8 non-voting consultative members and a lay Chairman. Lay members are appointed by an independent body, the Press Council Appointments Commission (Chairman: Ld Briggs).

SOURCES.—*The Cambridge Bibliography of English Literature,* Vol. III. pp. 797-8, lists all press directories, pp. 798-846 lists newspapers and magazines. *The History of the Times,* Pt II, pp. 1130-36 gives a chart of the Metropolitan morning and evening press from 1884-1947. There are several press directories which cover all or part of the period: *T. B. Browne's Advertiser's ABC, 1900-1932; Sell's Dictionary of the World's Press, 1900-1921* (including a *Who's Who* of notabilities of the British Press in 1914-21 editions); *Mitchell's Newspaper Press Directory* (became *Benn's* in 1946), 1900-61; *Willing's Press Guide, 1900-*. PEP: *Report on the British Press* (1938); *Report of the Royal Commission on the Press* (Cmd. 7700 of 1949, Minutes of Evidence, Cmd. 7317 of 1948); *Report of the Royal Commission on the Press* (Cmnd. 1811 of 1962); N. Kaldor and R. Silverman, *A Statistical Analysis of Advertising Expenditure and of the Revenue of the Press* (1948); A. P. Wadsworth, 'Newspaper Circulations' (in *Proceedings of the Manchester Statistical Society* 1954). J. L. Hammond, *C. P. Scott of the Manchester Guardian* (1934); J. W. Robertson Scott, *The Life and Death of a Newspaper (The Pall Mall Gazette)* (1952); A. Gollin, *The Observer and J. L. Garvin* (1960); F. Williams, *Dangerous Estate* (1957); C. Seymour-Ure, *Politics, the Press and the Public* (1968); C. Seymour-Ure, *The Political Impact of Men's Media* (1974); J. Whale, *The Politics of the Media* (1977); Press Council Annual Reports, *The Press and the People;* H. P. Levy, *The Press Council* (1967). *Hutton Readership Surveys,* J. W. Hobson and Harry Henry, came out annually between 1947 and 1955. *National Readership Surveys* were first published in 1947 by the Institute of Practitioners in Advertising and again in 1954: they have appeared bi-annually since 1957 and were taken over in 1967 by the Joint Industry Committee for National Readership Surveys (JICNARS). See also *Royal Commission on the Press* (Cmnd. 6810) and companion papers Cmnd. 6811-16; D. McQuail, *Review of Sociological Writing on the Press* (1976); C. Seymour-Ure, Oliver Boyd Barrett and Jeremy Tunstall, *Studies on the Press* (1977); J. Tunstall, *The Media in Britain* (1983); S. Jenkins, *Newspapers* (1980).

XXI

BROADCASTING AUTHORITIES

The British Broadcasting Corporation

The British Broadcasting Company Ltd was formed by some 200 manufacturers and shareholders on 18 Oct 22, registered on 15 Dec 22, and received its licence on 18 Jan 23. A system of paid licences for owners of radio receivers was started in 1922. London, Manchester, Birmingham, and Newcastle stations began to operate in November and December, 1922. This was followed by the establishment of the *British Broadcasting Corporation* under royal charter (20 Dec 26), which came into operation on 1 Jan 27. It was to be a public service body 'acting in the national interest' and financed by licence fees paid by all owners of radio receivers. (A formal agreement with the Postmaster General had been drawn up on 9 Nov 26.) Under the royal charter the B.B.C. was granted a licence for ten years and was to be directed by a board of governors nominated by the government. The charter was renewed and modified 1 Jan 37, 1 Jan 47, 1 Jul 52, 30 Jul 64. It was extended until 31 July 1979 in 1976 (Cmnd. 6581). In Jul 1979 it was extended for a further period until 31 Jul 1981, when it was replaced by a new charter to last until 31 Dec 1996.

British Broadcasting Company, 1923-1926

Chairman: Ld Gainford

Managing Director: (Sir) J. Reith (formerly **General Manager**)

Board members:

G. Isaacs (Marconi)[1]
B. Binyon (Radio Communication Co.)
A. McKinstry (Metropolitan Vickers)
J. Gray (British Thomson-Houston Co.)
Sir W. Noble (General Electric)
H. Pease (Western Electric)
W. Burnham (Burndept)
Sir W. Bull (M.P.)

British Broadcasting Corporation, 1927-

Board of Governors

Chairmen

1 Jan	27	E of Clarendon
2 Jun	30	J. Whitley
28 Mar	35	Vt Bridgeman
3 Oct	35	R. Norman
19 Apr	39	Sir A. Powell
1 Jan	47	Ld Inman
9 Jun	47	Ld Simon
1 Aug	52	Sir A. Cadogan
1 Dec	57	Sir A. fforde
1 Feb	64	Sir J. Duff (*acting*)
14 May	64	Ld Normanbrook
1 Sep	67	Ld Hill of Luton
1 Jan	73	Sir M. Swann
1 Aug	80	G. Howard (Ld)
1 Aug	83	S. Young

Vice-Chairmen

1 Jan	27	Ld Gainford
1 Jan	33	R. Norman
25 Oct	35	H. Brown
8 Jun	37	C. Millis
1 Jan	47	Marchioness of Reading
7 Jan	51	Ld Tedder
1 Jul	54	Sir P. Morris
1 Jul	60	Sir J. Duff
19 Sep	65	Ld Fulton
11 Jun	66	R. Lusty
31 Jul	67	Ld Fulton
1 Jan	68	R. Lusty
15 Feb	68	Ld Fulton
12 Nov	70	Lady Plowden
26 Jun	75	M. Bonham Carter
1 Aug	81	Sir W. Rees-Mogg

[1]On the resignation of G. Isaacs, Marconi was represented by F. Kellaway.

Governors

1927-31	Sir G. Nairne
1927-32	M. Rendall
1927-32	Mrs P. Snowden (Vtess)
1932-36	H. Brown
1933-35	Vt Bridgeman
1933-37	Mrs M. Hamilton
1935-39	Lady Bridgeman
1935-39	H. Fisher
1937-39	Sir I. Fraser
1937-39	J. Mallon
1938-39	Miss M. Fry
1939-41[1]	
1941-46	Lady V. Bonham-Carter
1941-46	Sir I. Fraser
1941-46	J. Mallon
1941-46	A. Mann
1941-46	H. Nicolson
1946-49	Miss B. Ward
1946-49	G. Lloyd
1946-49	Sir R. Peck
1946-50	E. Whitfield
1946-50	Marchioness of Reading
1947-52	J. Adamson
1950-54	Ld Tedder
1950-52	Ld Clydesmuir[2]
1951-52	F. Williams
1950-56	Mrs Barbara Wootton
1952-54	Sir P. Morris
1951-55	I. Stedeford
1952-56	Lady Rhys Williams
1954-59	Ld Rochdale
1955-60	Sir E. Benthall
1956-61	Mrs T. Cazalet-Keir
1956-62	Dame F. Hancock
1959-60	Sir J. Duff (*Vice-Chairman* 60-65)
1960-62	E of Halsbury
1960-65	R. Lusty (*Vice-Chairman* 66-67)
1961-66	G. Cooke
1962-68	Dame A. Godwin
1962-67	Sir A. Clarke
1966-67	Ld Fulton
1966-68	J. Trower
1967-73	Sir R. Murray
1968-71[3]	Sir R. Bellenger
1968-72[3]	P. Wilson
1968-73[3]	T. Jackson
1968-71	Sir L. Constantine (Ld)
1968-73	Dame M. Green
1969-71	Sir H. Greene
1971-76	R. Allan (Ld)
1972-79	R. Fuller
1972-76	T. Morgan
1972-80	G. Howard
1973-76	V. Feather (Ld)
1973-78	Sir D. Greenhill (Ld)
1974-81	Mrs S. Clarke
1976-81	P. Chappell
1976-82	Ld Allen
1977-82	Lady Serota
1978-	Sir J. Johnston
1979-84	C. Longuet-Higgins
1981-83	P. Moores
1981-83	S. Young
1981-	Miss J. Barrow
1982-	Miss D. Park
1982-	Sir J. Boyd
1983-	M. McAlpine
1984-	Lady Parkes
1985-	E of Harewood

Governors appointed to represent national interests

	N. Ireland
1952-58	Sir H. Mulholland
1958-62	J. McKee
1962-67	Sir P. Pim
1968-73	Ld Dunleath
1973-78	W. O'Hara
1978-	Lady Faulkner
	Scotland
1952-55	Ld Clydesmuir
1955-56	T. Johnston
1956-60	E of Balfour
1960-65	Sir D. Milne
1965-71	Lady Baird
1971-76	Lady Avonside
1976-79	A. Thompson
1979-	(Sir) R. Young
	Wales
1952-60	Ld Macdonald
1960-65	Mrs R. Jones
1965-71	G. Williams
1971-79	G. Hughes
1979-	A. Roberts
1984-	W. Peat

Directors-General

1 Jan	27	Sir J. Reith
1 Oct	38	F. Ogilvie
1 Jan	42	Sir C. Graves & R. Foot
24 Jun	43	R. Foot
31 Mar	44	(Sir) W . Haley
17 Jul	52	B. Nicholls (*acting*)
1 Dec	52	Sir I. Jacob
31 Dec	59	(Sir) H. Greene
1 Apr	68	(Sir) C. Curran
1 Oct	77	(Sir) I. Trethowan
1 Aug	82	A. Milne

[1] 5 Sep 39, the Board was reduced to 2 members (Chairman and Vice-Chairman) by Order in Council. The Board was reconstituted to its full strength of 7 members in 1941.

[2] 1 Aug 52, appointed Governor to represent Scottish interests.

[3] In 1967 the Board's strength was increased to 12 members.

SOURCE.—*B.B.C. Handbooks*, published annually since 1928.

B.B.C. Radio

The B.B.C. originally offered one basic radio service, known as the National Programme, together with variant Regional Services. In 1939 these services were all replaced by a single Home Service; the Forces Programme, providing a lighter alternative, began in 1940. In 1945 Regional Home Services, as variants of the Home Service, were restarted, and the Light Programme replaced the Forces Programme. In 1946 the Third Programme was introduced to provide a second alternative service. Very high frequency (VHF) transmissions began in 1955, in order to improve the quality and coverage of the existing services. In 1964 the Music Programme was added, using the Third Programme wavelengths in the daytime, and in 1967 a fourth network came into being to provide a pop music service replacing the offshore 'pirate' stations; this was called Radio 1, and the existing national services were renamed Radio 2 (Light Programme), Radio 3 (Third and Music Programmes) and Radio 4 (Home Service).

In 1970 the radio networks were reorganised as 'generic' services following publication of the B.B.C.'s proposals in *Broadcasting in the Seventies*, and the English regional radio services were then gradually wound down, though the regional centres continued to provide programmes for the networks. The regional radio broadcasts in the three National Regions started to develop as autonomous services with the opening of Radio Ulster in 1975. In 1978 there was a major reorganisation of the radio frequencies used for the national networks, and Radio 4 became available throughout the United Kingdom on the long-wave band. This enabled the national services—Radio Scotland, Radio Wales, Radio Cymru (Welsh language, on VHF only) and Radio Ulster—to become fully independent on Radio 4. Regular network services of sports programming were carried on Radio 2 and, for cricket, on Radio 3. Radios 3 and 4 carried Open University programmes on their VHF-FM bands and Radio 4 also carried Schools and Continuing Education output. In 1978 also the B.B.C. began regular broadcasting on radio of recorded material from Parliamentary proceedings (see p. 177).

B.B.C. Local Radio

The B.B.C. began a limited experiment in Local Radio in 1967. The following stations broadcast in England and the Channel Islands.

Radio Bristol	1970	Radio Lincolnshire	1980
Radio Cambridgeshire	1982	Radio London	1970
Radio Cleveland	1970	Radio Manchester	1970
Radio Cornwall	1983	Radio Merseyside	1967
Radio Cumbria	1975	Radio Newcastle	1971
Radio Durham	1968-72	Radio Norfolk	1980
Radio Derby	1971	Radio Northampton	1982
Radio Devon	1983	Radio Nottingham	1968
Radio Furness	1982	Radio Oxford	1970
Radio Guernsey	1982	Radio Sheffield	1967
Radio Humberside	1971	Radio Solent	1970
Radio Jersey	1982	Radio Stoke-on-Trent	1968
Radio Kent	1970	Radio Sussex[1]	1968
Radio Lancashire	1971	Radio WM (West Midlands)	1970
Radio Leeds	1968	Radio York	1983
Radio Leicester	1967		

[1] Formerly Radio Brighton.

B.B.C. Television

On 2 Nov 1936 the first scheduled public service television was started from Alexandra Palace. The service was suspended from September 1939 until June 1946. The first stations outside London, in the Midlands and the North, began transmitting in 1949 and 1951 respectively. By 1966, with more than 100 transmitting stations, B.B.C. Television was within the range of more than 99 per cent of the population of the United Kingdom on a 405-line standard. In April 1964 a second B.B.C. Channel was opened in the London area and by 1967 it was available to more than two-thirds of the population of the U.K. It was transmitted on 625 lines. In 1969 the first channel began to be transmitted on 625 lines as well as 405, and colour transmissions were started. By 1985, 99% of the U.K. population were within range of 625-line transmissions.

	Licences ('000s)				B.B.C. expenditure on revenue account £000s	
	Total	Sound only	Sound and Television (Mono-chrome)	Colour Television		
1925	1,654	1,654	. .	. .	. .	
1927	2,270	2,264	. .	. .	902	
1930	3,092	3,076	. .	. .	1,224	
1935	7,012	6,970	. .	. .	2,473	
1940	8,951	8,898	. .	. .	4,350	
1945	9,710	9,663	. .	. .	9,001	
					Home	External
1947	10,778	10,713	15	. .	7,273	3,878
1950	12,219	11,819	344	. .	9,579	4,471
1955	13,980	9,414	4,504	. .	17,964	5,093
1960	15,005	4,480	10,470	. .	30,560	6,408
1965	16,047	2,759	13,253	. .	55,642	8,499
1970	18,184	2,279	15,609	273	81,134	10,565
1975	17,701	. .	10,120	7,580	152,771	19,625
1980	18,285	. .	5,383	12,902	363,400	40,100
1984	18,361	. .	3,261	15,370	616,100	64,500

The difference between the total and other licences column is explained by the issue of free licences to the blind.

The expenditure figures from 1940 onwards are for the year ending the following 31 Mar. The figures from 1947 onwards are for operational expenditure only.

Broadcast Receiving Licences and B.B.C. Expenditure

Broadcasting receiving licences were first issued for 10s. a year in 1922; the price for sound-only licences was raised to £1 in 1946 and to £1 5s. in 1965; it was abolished in 1971. Licences for television were introduced in 1946 when a combined radio and television licence cost £2; this was raised to £3 in 1954, to £4 in 1957, to £5 in 1965, to £6 in 1969, to £7 in 1971, to £8 in 1975, to £9 in 1977 and to £10 in 1978. Since 1968 owners of colour sets have had to pay a supplementary £5, raised in 1975 to £10, in 1977 to £12, and in 1978 to £15.

In 1939-45 all licence revenue went to the Government and the B.B.C. was financed by an annual grant-in-aid. The external services have continued to be financed in this way. Except for 1950-51 the Treasury retained part of the licence fee every year until 1961.

Independent Broadcasting

The Independent Television Authority was set up by the Postmaster-General under section 1 (3) of the *Television Act, 1954*, on 4 Aug 1954 for a period of ten years. The Authority was to licence programme contracting companies and to regulate their output. The whole of the finance of Independent Television was to depend on advertising revenue though the Act specifically prohibited the 'sponsoring' of programmes by advertisers. The first Independent Television programmes were transmitted on 22 Sep 1955. The following Acts have since been passed significantly affecting Independent Broadcasting:

Television Act, 1963. This extended the life of the I.T.A. until 1976.

Television Act, 1964. This consolidates the *Television Acts* of 1954 and 1963 and increased the I.T.A.'s power over programmes and advertising.

Sound Broadcasting Act, 1972. This Act renamed the I.T.A. the Independent Broadcasting Authority and extended its functions to include the provision of local commercial sound broadcasting services.

Independent Broadcasting Authority Act, 1973. This consolidated the *Television Act, 1964* and the *Sound Broadcasting Act, 1972.*

Independent Broadcasting Authority Act, 1974. This Act made provision for 'additional payments' to be made by television programme contractors to the I.B.A.

Independent Broadcasting Authority Act (No 2), 1974. This extended the I.B.A.'s life until July 1979.

Independent Broadcasting Authority Act, 1978. This further extended the I.B.A. until the end of 1981.

Independent Broadcasting Authority Act, 1979. This Act gave the I.B.A. responsibility for establishing a fourth television channel.

Broadcasting Act, 1980. This Act extended the life of the I.B.A. until 1996. It laid down the operating condition of the fourth television channel, which was to be separately established in Wales by the Welsh fourth Channel Authority, and also established a Broadcasting Complaints Commission.

Broadcasting Act, 1981. This consolidated the *Independent Broadcasting Authority Acts*, 1973, 1974, and 1978, and the *Broadcasting Act, 1980.*

Cable and Broadcasting Act, 1984. This made provision for the establishment of a Cable Authority to provide cable programmes and amended the Broadcasting Act, 1981, to provide for the establishment of a Satellite Broadcasting Board.

Members of the Independent Television Authority 1954-1972 and Independent Broadcasting Authority 1972-

		Chairman			*Deputy Chairman*
31 Mar	55	Sir K. Clark	4 Aug	54	Sir C. Colston
8 Nov	57	Sir I. Kirkpatrick	3 Jan	55	Sir R. Matthews
6 Nov	62	Sir J. Carmichael (*acting*)	22 Jun	60	Sir J. Carmichael
1 Jul	63	Ld Hill of Luton	29 Jul	64	Sir S. Caine
1 Sep	67	Ld Aylestone	1 Jul	67	Sir R. Gould
1 Apr	75	Lady Plowden	29 Jun	72	C. Bland
1 Jan	81	Ld Thomson of Monifieth	1 Feb	80	Ld Thomson of Monifieth
			1 Jan	81	Sir J. Riddell

Director-General

1 Oct	54	Sir R. Fraser
15 Oct	70	(Sir) B. Young
Nov	82	J. Whitney

National Members

N. Ireland

1955-60	A. Chichester
1960-65	Sir L. O'Brien
1965-71	D. Gilliland
1971-74	H. McMullan
1974-79	W. (Ld) Blease
1980-	Mrs J. McIvor

Scotland

1955-58	T. Honeyman
1958-64	T. Talbot Rice
1964-70	W. MacFarlane Grey
1970-79	T. Carbery
1979-85	W. Morris
1985-	J. Purvis

Wales

1955-56	Ld Aberdare
1956-63	J. Alban Davies
1964-70	Sir B. Bowen Thomas
1970-76	T. Glyn Davies
1976-82	H. Morris-Jones
1982-	G. Peregrine

Other Members

1955-56	Ld Layton
1955-56	Miss M. Popham
1955-57	Miss D. Powell
1955-58	G. Thorneycroft
1955-59	Sir H. Hinchliffe
1956-60	Miss D. Reader Harris
1957-60	T. Summerson
1957-61	Dame F. Farrer
1958-61	W. Beard
1960-60	Sir J. Carmichael
1960-64	Sir S. Caine
1960-65	Mrs I. Graham-Bryce
1960-64	A. Cropper
1961-64	Sir T. Williamson (Ld)
1961-66	Dame A. Bryans
1964-69	Lady Burton
1964-69	Sir P. Hamilton
1964-69	H. Hunt
1964-69	Sir O. Saunders
1964-69	Sir V. Tewson
1965-70	Mrs M. Adams
1965-71	Lady Plummer
1966-73	Lady Sharp
1969-73	Sir F. Hayday
1969-74	S. Keynes
1969-74	J. Meek
1970-76	A. Page
1971-75	Lady Macleod
1973-78	W. Anderson
1973-81	Mrs M. Warnock
1974-81	J. Ring
1975-75	Lady Stedman
1976-81	Mchness of Anglesey
1976-81	Mrs A. Coulson
1976-81	A. Purssell
1978-83	A. Christopher
1979-	G. Russell
1981-83	Sir D. Hamilton
1981-	Mrs J. Jowitt
1982-	A. Cullen
1982-	Mrs P. Ridley
1982-	Mrs Y. Conolly
1984-	R. Grantham
1984-	M. Caine

SOURCES.—*Independent Television Authority Report and Accounts 1954-72*; *Independent Broadcasting Authority Report and Accounts 1972-*.

Programme Contracting Companies—Television

The following programme companies have been under contract to the Authority.

They are listed together with their original date of appointment and their major controlling interests. In 1964 all were re-appointed to provide programmes until July 1968. On 11 June 1967 new contractors were announced to operate from 30 July 1968 to 29 July 1974.[1] In 1972 the Authority made plain its intention to renew the existing contracts with the programme companies for two years from 31 July 1974, subject to satisfactory performance and subject to review of rentals and areas. A further reallocation of contracts was announced on 28 Dec 1980, and took effect in Jan 1982.

[1] Most of the existing contractors were reappointed for the new contract period commencing 30 Jul 68, although Harlech Television replaced T.W.W., and Rediffusion and A.B.C. Television came together to form Thames Television. The 7-day companies were appointed to serve the Midlands, Lancashire and Yorkshire, while the new London Weekend Television took over Friday evening, Saturday and Sunday in London.

A.B.C. Television. 1956-68 (Weekends North and Midlands). Chairman, 1956: Sir P. Warter. A wholly owned subsidiary of Associated British Picture Corporation (see Thames Television).

Anglia Television. 1958 (East Anglia). Chairman, 1958: Marquess Townshend of Raynham. Significant minority interests held by the *Guardian* and *Manchester Evening News* and Romulus and Remus Films.

A.T.V. Network. (1955-1966 Associated TeleVision) 1955-81. (1955-68 Midlands, Monday to Friday; London, Saturday and Sunday; 1968-82 Midlands, all week). Chairman, 1955: P. Littler, 1960: Sir R. Renwick (Ld), 1973: Sir L. Grade (Ld), 1977: J. Gill. Originally Associated Broadcasting Development Co., then renamed Associated Broadcasting Co. Later wholly controlled by A.T.V. Corporation Ltd., in which substantial shareholdings were in the hands of the *Daily Mirror* and IPC group until 1976 and Beaverbrook Newspapers (1965-77) and (formerly) Moss Empires; Trafalgar House Ltd. became major shareholders in 1977.

Border Television. 1961 (Carlisle). Chairman: (Sir) J. Burgess. 1984, E. Wright. Shares widely held.

Central Independent. 1982 (Midlands). Chairman, 1982: Sir G. Hobday. Ladbrokes, D. C. Thomson, Pergamon, B.P.C.C. and Sears Holdings major shareholders.

Channel Four. 1982. Chairman, 1982: E. Dell. A wholly owned subsidiary of the I.B.A.

Channel Television. 1962 (Channel Islands). Chairman, 1962: Senator G. Troy, 1963: Senator W. Krichefski, 1971: E. Collas, 1982: J. Riley. Controlling interest (formerly) held by a subsidiary of A.B.P.C. (see A.B.C. Television). Shares now widely held.

Grampian Television. 1960 (Aberdeen). Chairman, 1960: Sir A. King, 1968: I. Tennant. Shares widely held.

Granada Television. 1955 (North Monday to Friday); 1968 (Lancashire all week). Chairman, 1955: S. Bernstein, 1971: (Ld) Bernstein, 1974: Sir D. Forman. A wholly owned subsidiary of the Granada group. Shares widely held.

H.T.V. (formerly **Harlech Television**). 1968 (Wales and West of England). Chairman, 1968: Ld Harlech, 1985: R. Wordley. Shares widely held.

London Weekend Television. 1968 (London Friday 7 p.m. to Sunday).

Chairman, 1968: A. Crawley, 1971: J. Freeman, 1982: B. Tesler. Shares widely held.

Rediffusion Television (Associated Rediffusion 1955-64). 1955-68 (London Monday to Friday). Chairman, 1955: (Sir) J. Wills. Majority interests held by British Electric Traction and Rediffusion (see Thames Television).

Scottish Television. 1956 (Central Scotland). Chairman, 1957: R. Thomson (Ld), 1969: J. Coltart, 1972: (Sir) J. Campbell Fraser. Controlling interest (formerly) held by The Thomson Organisation Ltd which disposed of its holding in 1977. Shares now widely held.

Sianel Pedwar Cymru (S4C). Welsh Fourth Channel Authority. Chairman, 1982: Sir G. Daniel.

Southern Television. 1958-81 (South of England). Chairman, 1958: (Sir) J. Davis, 1976: C. Wilson. Main shareholders, the Rank Organisation, the Amalgamated Press, and Associated Newspapers. The Amalgamated Press holding passed to the *Daily Mirror* group when the latter acquired the Amalgamated Press in Nov 1958. The *Television Act, 1954*, requirement of 'adequate competition' forced the *Daily Mirror* holding to be sold to Associated Newspapers, the Rank Organisation and D. C. Thomson Ltd.

Thames Television. 1968 (London Monday to Friday 7 p.m.). Chairman, 1968: Sir P. Warter, 1969: Ld Shawcross, 1974: H. Thomas, 1978: H. Dundas. Controlling shares held by Thames Television Holdings, and since 1982 A.R. Rediffusion and Thorn E.M.I.

T.S.W. 1982 (South-West). Chairman, 1982: (Sir) B. Bailey. Shares widely held.

TV-AM. 1983 (breakfast time). Chairman, 1982: P. Jay, 1983: Ld Marsh, 1984: T. Aitkin. Controlling shares held by Fleet Holdings, Consolidated Press and Aitken Telecommunications.

T.V.S. 1982 (South of England). Chairman, 1982: Ld Boston. Significant minority interests held by Whitbread & Co. p.l.c. and London Trust Company Ltd.

T.W.W. 1958-68 (Wales and the West of England). Chairman, 1958: E of Derby. Main shareholders *News of the World*, *Liverpool Daily Post*, E of Derby and J. Hylton (after 1965 his executors).

Tyne-Tees Television. 1956 (North-East). Chairman, 1956: Sir R. Pease, 1963: E. Fairburn, 1968: G. Daysh, 1972: Sir G. Cox, 1974: Sir R. Carr-Ellison. Significant shareholdings formerly held by the *Daily News* Ltd.,

Black Brothers, William Baird & Co. and in 1968 by Mercantile Investment Trust. In 1970 Trident Television acquired the share capital of Tyne-Tees Television and Yorkshire Television. Since 1982 substantial shareholdings by Trident T.V., Vaux Breweries and I.C.F.C.

Ulster Television. 1959 (Northern Ireland). Chairman, 1959: E of Antrim, 1977: J. MacQuitty, 1983: R. Henderson. Shares widely held.

Wales (West and North) Television. 1962-4. Chairman, 1962: H. Hayden Williams, 1963 (*acting*): C. Traherne. Shares widely held. In 1964 this company was absorbed by T.W.W.

Westward Television. 1960-1981 (South-West). Chairman: P. Cadbury. Shares widely held.

Yorkshire Television. 1968 (Yorkshire). Chairman, 1968: Sir R. Graham, 1982: D. Palmar. Significant minority interests held by Telefusion and *Yorkshire Post*. In 1970 Trident Television acquired the share capital of Tyne-Tees Television and Yorkshire Television. Substantial shareholdings by Bass, W. H. Smith and P. L. Publishing.

Independent Television News Ltd. 1955, Editor and chief executive: A. Crawley, 1955. (Sir) G. Cox, 1956. Managing director: D. Edwards, 1968-71. Editor: N. Ryan, 1968 (and Chief Executive, 1971). D. Nicholas, 1977. This is an independent non-profit making company, to provide a common news service for all the contracting companies. The appointment of the editor and chief executive must have the approval of the I.T.A. (now the I.B.A.).

Programme Contracting Companies—Radio

These companies have operated under the Sound Broadcasting Act, 1972.

Aberdeen	Jul	81	North South Radio
Ayr	Oct	81	West Sound
Belfast	Mar	76	Downtown Radio
Birmingham	Feb	74	BRMB Radio
Bournemouth	Sep	80	Two Counties Radio
Bradford	Sep	75	Pennine Radio
Brighton	Aug	83	Southern Sound
Bristol	Oct	81	Radio West
Bury St Edmunds	Nov	82	Saxon Radio
Cardiff	Apr	80	CBC
Coventry	May	80	Mercia Sound
Doncaster	late	85	Radio Hallam
Dundee	Oct	80	Radio Tay
East Kent	Oct	84	Invicta Radio
Edinburgh	Jan	75	Radio Forth
Exeter	Nov	80	Devon Air Radio
Glasgow	Dec	73	Radio Clyde
Gloucester	Oct	80	Severn Sound
Great Yarmouth	Oct	84	Radio Broadland
Guildford	Apr	83	County Sound
Hereford	Oct	82	Radio Wyvern
Humberside	Apr	84	Viking Radio
Inverness	Feb	82	Moray Firth Radio
Ipswich	Oct	75	Radio Orwell
Leeds	Sep	81	Radio Aire
Leicester	Sep 81-Oct	83	Centre Radio
Leicester	Sep	84	Leicester Sound
Liverpool	Oct	74	Radio City
London	Oct	73	Capital Radio
London	Oct	73	LBC
Luton	Oct	81	Chiltern Radio
Maidstone	Oct	84	Invicta Radio
Manchester	Apr	74	Piccadilly Radio
Newport	Jun Apr	'83- 85	Gwent Broadcasting
Northampton	Oct	84	Hereward Radio
Nottingham	Jul	75	Radio Trent

Peterborough	Apr 79	Hereward Radio	Southend	Sep 81	Essex Radio
Plymouth	May 75	Plymouth Sound	Stoke-on-Trent	Sep 83	Signal Radio
Portsmouth	Oct 75	Radio Victory	Swansea	Sep 74	Swansea Sound
Preston	Oct 82	Red Rose Radio	Swindon	Oct 82	Wiltshire Radio
Reading	Mar 76	Thames Valley Broadcasting	Teesside	Jun 75	Radio Tees
			Tyne-Wear	Jul 75	Metro Radio
Reigate	Oct 84	Radio Mercury	Wolverhampton	Apr 76	Beacon Radio
Sheffield	Oct 74	Radio Hallam	Wrexham	Sep 83	Marcher Sound

Independent Radio News (IRN), a wholly owned subsidiary of LBC, has since October 1973 provided a news service, available to all the independent local radio stations.

Inquiries into Broadcasting

Committee Chairman	Date appointed	Date of report	Command Number	Estimated Cost
Sir F. Sykes	Apr 23	Aug 23	1951	£320
E of Crawford and Balcarres	Aug 25	Mar 26	2599	£106
Ld Selsdon	May 34	Jan 35	4793	£965
Ld Ullswater	Apr 35	Mar 36	5091	£564
Ld Hankey	Sep 43	Dec 44	Non-parl	. .
Ld Beveridge	Jun 49	Dec 50	8116	£15,415
Sir H. Pilkington	Jul 60	Jun 62	1753	£45,450
Ld Annan	Apr 74	Mar 77	6753	£315,000
Ld Hunt of Tamworth	Apr 82	Oct 82	8679	£47,388
Sir A. Part	Jul 82	Nov 82	8751	£34,625
A. Peacock	May 85			

SOURCES.—*Annual Reports and Accounts of the B.B.C. 1927-; Annual Reports and Accounts of the I.T.A. (I.B.A.) 1954-; B.B.C. Handbook 1927-.*

Sir G. Beadle, *Television: a Critical Review* (1963); A. Briggs, *The History of Broadcasting in the United Kingdom*, Vol. I: *The Birth of Broadcasting* (1961); Vol. II: *The Golden Age of Radio* (1965); Vol. III: *The War of Words* (1970); Vol. IV: *Sound and Vision* (1979); E. G. Wedell, *Broadcasting and Public Policy* (1968); R.H. Coase, *British Broadcasting: a Study in Monopoly* (1950); B. Paulu, *British Broadcasting* (1956); B. Paulu, *British Broadcasting in Transition* (1961); Ld Reith, *Into the Wind* (1949); Ld Simon of Wythenshawe, *The B.B.C. from Within* (1953); H. H. Wilson, *Pressure Groups: the Campaign for Commercial Television* (1961); M. Gorham, *Broadcasting Sound and Television since 1900* (1952); S. Hood, *A Survey of Television* (1967); J. Scupham, *Broadcasting and the Community* (1967).

XXII

RELIGION

Church Membership Statistics

EXTREME caution should be observed in making use of church membership statistics, as no entirely reliable sources exist giving information about membership or attendance. The last reasonably authoritative figures of religious affiliations in Britain were taken from the 1851 census, though even then there was no compulsion to answer the questions on religion. Since then no census has included questions on religious affiliation. Strictly comparable figures are impossible to obtain for church membership and church attendance between 1900 and 1984. The definition of membership varies greatly from one denomination to another, as does the minimum age for reception into the church. At one extreme, the Roman Catholic Church officially records the Roman Catholic population of all ages, regardless of church attendance. Nonconformist churches with adult baptism, and in the case of the Methodists a probationary period before baptism, are the most exclusive. These statistics give no indication how frequently 'members' of the churches attended services. Moreover even within the denominations different figures are quoted at different times and in different sources. E.g. Church of England membership can be variously defined by figures for baptised membership, those for Easter communicants, and the Electoral Roll. In a report prepared by Gallup Poll for A.B.C. Television (University of London Press, 1964), *TV and Religion*, it was stated that in the three television areas of London, Midlands, and the North only 1 in 17 of those aged 16 and over, i.e. 6%, say that they have no religious affiliation, yet the total of all the religious statistics available do not add up to anything like 94% of the population. A further problem is the definition of churchgoing. J. K. Lawton in an article in the British Council of Churches bulletin, *The Church in the World*, said that if church attendance was to be judged by the criterion of twice a month churchgoing the figure was 15%, if the criterion was one attendance in three months it rose to 40%. A Gallup survey done for the magazine *Sunday* (May 1966) suggested that about 10 million people go to church most Sundays or at least once a month. No precise information is available on the effect of religious broadcasting on attendance at church services. Some studies of church attendance and religious affiliations that have attempted to fill out these necessarily very inadequate figures are: *Religious Broadcasts and the Public*, by the B.B.C. Audience Research Department (1955); 'How Many in the Pew?' in *The Economist* of 20 Aug 58; *Puzzled*

People, by Mass Observation (1948); *A Survey of Social Conditions in England and Wales*, chapter 18, by A. M. Carr-Saunders, D. C. Jones, and C. M. Moser (1958); R. F. Neuss, *Facts and Figures about the Church of England No. 3* (1966); H.M.S.O., *Social Trends;* and Gallup Poll figures for church membership and attendance.

More general works on religion in Britain in the twentieth century are: R. B. Braithwaite, *The State of Religious Belief* (1927); E. O. James, *History of Christianity in England* (1949); R. Lloyd, *The Church of England in the Twentieth Century* (2 vols, 1948-50); G. Spinks (ed.), *Religion in Britain since 1900* (1952); R. F. Wearmouth, *The Social and Political Influence of Methodism in the Twentieth Century* (1957); J. Highet, *The Scottish Churches* (1960). Maps on the strength of religion in Britain are given in *The Reader's Digest Atlas of Britain* (1965), and in John D. Gay, *The Geography of Religion in England* (1971).

The most convenient summary of facts and statistics is to be found in R. Currie and A. Gilbert's chapter in A. H. Halsey (ed.), *Social Trends in Britain since 1900* (1972).

THE CHURCH OF ENGLAND

Principal degrees of membership for the Provinces of Canterbury and York.

(Totals for 43 dioceses)[a]

Year	Home population of the two provinces ('000s)	Estimated baptised membership		Estimated confirmed membership		Membership of parochial electoral rolls	
		('000s)[d]	Per 1,000 home pop.	('000s)[d]	Per 1,000 pop. aged 13 and over[e]	('000s)	Per 1,000 pop. of appropriate age
1901	30,673[b]	n.a.		n.a.		n.a.	
1911	33,807[b]	n.a.		n.a.		n.a.	
1921	35,390[b]	22,000	622	8,100	301	3,537[f]	140
1931	37,511[b]	23,800	634	9,000	302	3,686	145
1941	39,173[c]	24,900	636	9,200	294	3,423[g]	120
1951	41,330[b]	25,800	624	9,400	284	2,923[h]	95
1960	43,296	27,323	631	9,792	281	2,862	89
1970	46,429	27,736	597	9,514	205	2,559	73
1980	46,323	26,500	571	8,700	185	1,815	52

a In 1910 there were 15,864 parochial churches; in 1966 there were 17,755.
b Enumerated in the Registrar General's censuses of ecclesiastical areas.
c Estimates based on the Registrar General's annual estimates of population at 30th June.
d Calculated by the Statistical Unit of the Central Board of Finance of the Church of England by reference to the age composition of the home population, born and resident in the two provinces, and to the respective rates of infant baptisms at Anglican fonts per 1,000 live births; and to the respective rate of Anglican confirmations per 1,000 males and females living at age 15 years. (It is not possible to include in these estimates baptised and confirmed Anglicans who were born abroad but are now resident in the two provinces.)
e In the Church of England very few boys and girls are confirmed before the age of 13 years.
fgh Figures for 1924, 1940, and 1953, respectively.
i 1957 was the first year that persons of 17 years and over were included in the electoral rolls. In previous years the minimum age was 18 years.

SOURCES.—*Facts and Figures about the Church of England*, Nos. 1-3. Edited by R. F. Neuss, published by the Church Information Office (1966). The Statistical Unit, Central Board of Finance of the Church of England.

Archbishops and leading Bishops of the five principal Dioceses in the Church of England[1]

(These are the only Sees automatically represented in the House of Lords)

Archbishops of Canterbury

1896	F. Temple (*Frederick Cantuar:*)
1903	R. Davidson (*Randall Cantuar:*)
1928	C. Lang (*Cosmo Cantuar:*)
1942	W. Temple (*William Cantuar:*)
1945	G. Fisher (*Geoffrey Cantuar:*)
1961	A. Ramsey (*Michael Cantuar:*)
1974	F. Coggan (*Donald Cantuar:*)
1980	R. Runcie (*Robert Cantuar:*)

Archbishops of York

1891	W. Maclagan (*Willem Ebor:*)
1909	C. Lang (*Cosmo Ebor:*)
1929	W. Temple (*William Ebor:*)
1942	C. Garbett (*Cyril Ebor:*)
1956	A. Ramsey (*Michael Ebor:*)
1961	F. Coggan (*Donald Ebor:*)
1974	S. Blanch (*Stuart Ebor:*)
1983	J. Habgood (*John Ebor:*)

Bishops of London

1897	M. Creighton (*Mandell Londin:*)
1901	A. Winnington-Ingram (*A. F. London:*)
1939	G. Fisher (*Geoffrey Londin:*)
1945	J. Wand (*William Londin:*)
1956	H. Campbell (*Henry Londin:*)
1961	R. Stopford (*Robert Londin:*)
1973	G. Ellison (*Gerald Londin:*)
1981	G. Leonard (*Graham Londin:*)

Bishops of Durham

1890	B. Westcott (*B. F. Dunelm:*)
1901	H. Moule (*Handley Dunelm:*)
1920	H. Henson (*Herbert Dunelm:*)
1939	A. Williams (*Alwyn Dunelm:*)
1952	A. Ramsey (*Michael Dunelm:*)
1956	M. Harland (*Maurice Dunelm:*)
1966	I. Ramsey (*Ian Dunelm:*)
1973	J. Habgood (*John Dunelm:*)
1984	D. Jenkins (*David Dunelm:*)

Bishops of Winchester

1895	R. Davidson (*Randall Winton:*)
1903	H. Ryle (*Herbert E. Winton:*)
1911	E. Talbot (*Steuart Edward Winton:*)
1924	F. Woods (*Theodore Winton:*)
1932	C. Garbett (*Cyril Winton:*)
1942	M. Haigh (*Mervyn Winton:*)
1952	A. Williams (*Alwyn Winton:*)
1961	S. Allison (*Falkner Winton:*)
1974	J. Taylor (*John Winton:*)
1984	C. James (*Colin Winton:*)

[1] Names in brackets are those used as signature.

THE CHURCH IN WALES

The Church in Wales was disestablished from 31 March 1920

Year	Parochial Easter Day Communicants Estimated No. ('000s)	No. of Churches
1920	160	1,755
1930	167	1,774
1940	175	1,766
1950	n.a.	n.a.
1960	183	1,783
1970	155[a]	1,780
1975	133[b]	1,720

[a] 1968 Easter attendance.

[b] 1976 Easter attendance.

SOURCE.—H.M.S.O. *Social Trends* No. 8 (1977) and the Secretary, the Representative Body of the Church in Wales.

EPISCOPAL CHURCH IN SCOTLAND

Year	Communicants ('000s)	No. of Church Buildings
1900	46	354
1910	52	404
1920	57	416
1930	60	415
1940	62	404
1950	57	397
1960	57	369
1970	49	341
1976	45	302
1980	41	n.a.
1983	40	286

SOURCES.—*The Year Book for the Episcopal Church in Scotland; Whitaker's Almanack* (figures for 1910, 1920 and 1976); *The Statesman's Year-Book* (figures for 1930 and 1940).

BAPTIST UNION

British Isles[a]

Year	Members ('000s)	No. of Places of Worship[b]
1900	366	2,579
1910	419	2,889
1920	405	2,866
1930	406	2,965
1940	382	3,044
1950	338	3,110
1960	318	3,053
1970	293	3,657
1975	256	3,560
1980	187	n.a.
1983	222	n.a.

[a] These are statistics actually received from the churches; no estimates are made for churches omitting to return figures.
[b] England and Wales only.

SOURCE.—*The Baptist Handbook, 1900-.*

CONGREGATIONAL UNION

United Kingdom[a]

Year	Members ('000s)	No. of Places of Worship
1900	436	4,607[b]
1910	494	4,721
1920	n.a.	n.a.
1930	490	3,556
1939	459	3,435
1950	387	3,173
1959	212	2,984
1965	198	2,799
1971	165	2,266

On 5 Oct 72 the Congregational Union merged with the Presbyterian Church in England to form the United Reformed Church.

[a] 1900 and 1910 figures for British Isles.

[b] Figure for 1901.

SOURCE.—*The Congregational Year Book, 1900-1972.*

PRESBYTERIAN CHURCH

England

Year	Members ('000s)
1900	76
1911	87
1922	84
1930	84
1940	82
1950	82
1960	71
1965	70
1971	57

On 5 Oct 1972 the Presbyterian Church in England merged with the Congregational Union to form the United Reformed Church.

SOURCES.—1900 and 1911, *The Official Handbook of the Presbyterian Church of England;* 1922-72, *The Statesman's Year-Book.*

UNITED REFORMED CHURCH

	Members (000s)	No. of Church Buildings
1973	192	2,139
1977	175	2,068
1984	140	n.a.

SOURCE.—*Whitaker's Almanack.*

METHODIST CHURCH[a]

Great Britain and Ireland

Year	Members and Probationers ('000s)	No of Church Buildings
1900	520	9,037
1910	544	n.a.
1920	512	9,013
1930	548	9,070
1940	823	n.a.
1950	776	n.a.
1960	734	n.a.
1970	657	9,972
1980	510	7,990[b]
1984	459	7,659[b]

[a] Up to 1930 these figures are for the Wesleyan Methodist Church. The Methodist Church was formed in 1932 by a union of the Wesleyan, Primitive, and United Methodist Churches. The United Methodists were themselves formed by a union of three separate bodies in 1905.

[b] Figures for Great Britain only.

SOURCES.—*The Minutes of the Methodist Conference, 1900-.* W. S. F. Pickering, *Anglo-Methodist Relations* (1961) gives figures (for England only) for all bodies (1906-1957). H.M.S.O. *Social Trends*, No. 8 (1977).

THE CHURCH OF SCOTLAND[a]

(Presbyterian)

Year	Total Communicants on Rolls ('000s)	No. of Places of Worship
1901	1,164	n.a.
1911	1,220	1,703
1921	1,278	1,704
1931	1,281	2,795
1941	1,269	2,507
1951	1,273	2,348
1961	1,293	2,212
1971	1,134	2,088
1981	919	1,805

[a] In 1929 the United Free Church of Scotland rejoined the Church of Scotland.

SOURCE.—*The Church of Scotland Year Book.*

THE ROMAN CATHOLIC CHURCH

Great Britain

Year	Estimated Catholic Population ('000s)[a]	Catholic Baptisms ('000s)	No. of Public Churches and Chapels[f]
1900	5,415	n.a.	1,536
1910	5,515	n.a.	1,773
1920	5,704	n.a.	1,408
1930	6,024[b]	66	1,564
1940	3,444[c]	70	1,802
1950	3,884[c]	87	1,971
1960	4,818	112[d]	3,204
1971	5,447	105[e]	3,668
1976	5,004	85[eg]	3,753
1983	5,056	n.a.	3,874

[a] These figures include England and Wales, Scotland, Ireland, 1900-30, and N. Ireland, 1940-1971. 1976 England, Wales and Scotland.
[b] This figure is made up of the English estimate for 1930, the Scottish estimate for 1926, and the Irish estimate for 1911.
[c] The figures for 1940 and 1950 include the N. Irish Catholic population taken from the 1937 census.
[d] Figure for 1959. [e] Up to 7 years.
[f] England and Wales. [g] England, Wales and Scotland.

SOURCE.—Census reports quoted in *The Statesman's Year-Book, 1900-.*

Roman Catholic Archbishops of Westminster

1892 H. Vaughan (Cardinal, 1893)
1903 F. Bourne (Cardinal, 1911)
1935 A. Hinsley (Cardinal, 1937)
1943 B. Griffin (Cardinal, 1946)
1956 W. Godfrey (Cardinal, 1958)
1963 J. Heenan (Cardinal, 1965)
1976 B. Hume (Cardinal, 1976)

SOURCE.—*The Catholic Directory, 1900-.*

NORTHERN IRELAND

Religious Affiliations

(to nearest '000)

Year	Roman Catholic	Presbyterian	Protestant Episcopalian	Methodist	Others
1911	430	395	327	46	52
1937	428	391	345	55	60
1951	471	410	353	67	69
1961	498	413	345	72	98
1971	478	406	334	71	88
1981	415	340	284	59	n.a.

SOURCE.—*Census*.

OTHER CHRISTIAN DENOMINATIONS

Data on the smaller denominations is of very uneven quality. However, some recent figures are worth recording.

Welsh Independents	92,990 (1968)[a]		
Plymouth Brethren	80,000 (1971)[b]		
Assemblies of God	65,972 (1966)[a]		
Jehovah's Witnesses	55,876 (1969)[a]	57,000 (1975)[c]	
Salvation Army	1,812 (1983)[b]		
Elim Four Square Gospel Alliance	44,800 (1967)[a]		
Society of Friends	29,909 (1968)	19,689 (1977)[b]	18,303 (1984)
Seventh-Day Adventists	12,145 (1971)	12,680 (1977)	15,500 (1984)
Mormons	11,400 (1966)[a]	100,000 (1975)[c]	

The Unitarians claimed 250 places of worship in 1984[b] and the Christian Scientists had 260 branches.[b]

SOURCES.—[a] A. H. Halsey (ed.), *Social Trends in Britain since 1900* (1973).
[b] *Whitaker's Almanack*.
[c] H.M.S.O. *Social Trends*, No. 8 (1977).

THE JEWISH COMMUNITY[a]

Great Britain

Year	Estimated No. of Jews ('000s)	Approx. No. of Synagogues
1900	160	80[d]
1910	243	200[d]
1920	287	200[d]
1929[b]	297	300[e]
1940	385[c]	200[e]
1950	450	240[e]
1960	450	240[e]
1970	450	240[e]
1980	410	240
1983	354	240

[a] Statistics for 1900 for G.B. and Ireland, 1910 for the British Isles, 1920 for U.K., 1929 for G.B., 1940-60 for G.B. and N. Ireland.
[b] No Jewish statistics available, 1930-34.
[c] Including about 35,000 refugees.
[d] From *Whitaker's Almanack*.
[e] From *The Statesman's Year-Book*.

SOURCE.—*The Jewish Year Book, 1900-*.

BUDDHISTS, HINDUS, MUSLIMS AND SIKHS

United Kingdom

	Members ('000s)		Ministers		Church buildings	
	1970	1975	1970	1975	1970	1975
Buddhists	6[a]	21[a]	38	172	8[a]	30[a]
Hindus	50[a]	100[a]	80[b]	100	60[a]	120[a]
Muslims	250[a]	400[a]	. .	1,000	. .	800[a]
Sikhs	75[a]	115[a]	—	—	40[a]	75
Total	754[a]	1,053	. .	14,329	. .	3,695

[a] Estimate.
[b] Including part-time Ministers.

SOURCE.—H.M.S.O. *Social Trends*, No. 8 (1977).

Marriages by Manner of Solemnisation

England and Wales

	1901	1911	1919	1934	1952	1962	1967	1974	1981
No. of marriages ('000s)	259	275	369	342	349	348	386	384	352
					Percentage				
Church of England	66·6	61·1	59·7	53·5	49·6	47·4	44·9	35·8	33·6
Roman Catholic	4·1	4·4	5·2	6·5	9·4	12·3	11·2	8·8	7·4
Jewish	0·7	0·7	0·5	0·7	0·5	0·4	0·4	0·4	0·3
Baptist	12·8 (Baptist, Congregationalist, Methodist, Other Religion)	13·0 (Baptist, Congregationalist, Methodist, Other Religion)	1·9	1·8	1·5	1·7	1·4	1·2	1·2
Congregationalist[a]			2·3	2·1	2·0	1·9	1·7	1·6	2·2
Methodist			5·6	5·3	4·8	4·9	4·5	4·1	4·8
Other Religion			1·6	1·8	1·6	1·8	1·7	1·6	1·5
Religious Marriage	84·2	79·1	76·9	71·6	69·4	70·4	65·9	53·5	51·0
Secular Marriage	15·8	20·9	23·1	28·4	30·6	29·6	34·1	46·5	49·0
	100	100	100	100	100	100	100	100	100

[a] The Congregationalist figure for 1974 and 1981 includes United Reformed Church.

SOURCE.—*Annual Reports of the Registrar-General.*

XXIII

BIBLIOGRAPHICAL NOTE

THIS book does not attempt to provide an extensive bibliography of works on British politics since 1900. That would demand a separate volume and much of its contents would duplicate bibliographies already available. The main sources of factual data used in compiling this book are listed separately in the appropriate sections. There are, however, some works of reference of such major importance and reliability that it seems useful to collect them together as a help or reminder to those involved in research.

Many of the standard and most useful sources for reference are Stationery Office publications. Summaries, guides, and short-cuts to these publications are provided in the Stationery Office: *Catalogue of Government Publications* (annually), the *Sectional Lists of Government Publications*, published by the Stationery Office for individual departments, the *List of Cabinet Papers 1880-1914* (P.R.O. handbook), the *General Index to Parliamentary Papers, 1900-1949* (H.M.S.O.), the three volumes by P. and G. Ford, *Breviate of Parliamentary Papers* (1900-16, 1917-39, 1940-54), and C. Hughes, *The British Statute Book* (1957). An H.M.S.O. *Guide to Official Statistics* has been published biennially since 1976. J. G. Ollé, *An Introduction to British Government Publications*, although dated, is still very useful.

For reference to day-to-day political events the *Official Index to 'The Times'* is the most complete guide, though before 1906 *Palmer's Index to 'The Times'* is difficult to use successfully and is by no means complete. *Keesing's Contemporary Archives* since 1931 give a concise summary of news reported in the national Press, though they were not published in their present fuller form until 1937. Brief chronologies of the year's major events (including some very minor ones) are printed in the *Annual Register* (since 1954 the *Annual Register of World Events)*, which also covers them in greater detail in the main text of the book. Still briefer summaries of the year's events are to be found in *Whitaker's Almanack*.

For biographical details of leading figures in British politics since 1900 the main sources are the *Dictionary of National Biography* (1901-11, 1912-21, 1922-30, 1931-40, 1941-50, 1951-60), the *Concise Dictionary of National Biography, 1901-50*, *Who Was Who* (1897-1915, 1916-28, 1929-40, 1941-50, 1951-60, 1961-70) and *Who's Who*, for those still alive. As supplements to these, for lesser-known figures in the Labour and Co-operative movement see also the *Labour Who's Who*, 1924 and 1927 (The Labour Publishing Company), the *Herald Book of Labour Members* (1923, with a supplement in 1924, ed. S. Bracher), and *The Dictionary of Labour Biography* (eds J. Bellamy and J. Saville). Appointments are recorded in many official sources. The major annual publications are: the *Imperial Calendar and Civil Service List* (replaced in 1973 by two works, *Civil Service Year Book* and *Diplomatic List), H.M. Ministers and Heads of Public Departments* (published 1946–77, from four to six times a year and after 1973 renamed *H.M. Ministers and Senior Staff in Public Departments*), and the *London Gazette*, where appointments are announced officially, which appears about once a fortnight. Since 1978 the House of Commons has published a *Weekly Information Bulletin*. Official appointments are also recorded in the annual *Lists of the Foreign Office*, the *Colonial Office*, and the *Commonwealth Relations Office*, the *Army*, *Navy* and *Air Force Lists*, the *Law Lists*, and the *Annual Estimate* of the civil, revenue, and service departments. There are three handbooks on Parliament, giving the names of M.P.s, details of procedure and officials: *Dod's Parliamentary Companion* (annually), *Vacher's Parliamentary Companion* (published from four to six times a year) and F. W. S. Craig's *The Political Companion* (published quarterly since 1968). Up to 1931 *Debrett's Illustrated House of Commons and the Judicial Bench* is particularly useful. Extremely valuable sources of reference for the House of Commons are the books *House of Commons* published by the *Pall Mall Gazette* in 1906, 1910 and 1911, and since 1885 by *The Times* after each General Election (1922-4 excepted)—in 1885-1900 as *The New House of Commons* and since 1970 as *The Times Guide to the House of Commons*. M. Stenton and S. Lees, *Who's Who of British Members of Parliament*, vols 2-4: *1886-1979* (1978-81) offers the most compact single source of M.P.s' biographies. Other sources of biographical information are *Debrett's* and *Burke's Peerage*, *Burke's New Extinct Peerages* (1972) and *Burke's Dictionary of the Landed Gentry*, L. G. Pine, *The New Extinct Peerage, 1884-1971* (1972), the *Directory of Directors*, the *Authors' and Writers' Who's Who*, and other directories or registers devoted to the members of particular professions, or to the alumni of particular schools and universities. C. Hazlehurst and C. Woodland, *A Guide to the Papers of British Cabinet Ministers 1900-51* (1975) can lead to much recherché material.

The annual almanacks are also an extremely useful source of information. Amongst these the most notable are: the *Constitutional Year Book* (published until 1939), *Whitaker's Almanack*, *The Statesman's Year-Book*, the *Yearbook of International Organisations*, the *United Nations Yearbook*, and *Britain: An Official Handbook* (published by the Central Office of Information). Another valuable source is *Committees, Councils and Boards* (3rd ed. 1977).

The major sources for British statistics are already quoted in notes to the tables throughout the book. The most readily available is the *Annual Abstract of Statistics* (H.M.S.O.). This appears both annually, and in a form covering ten-year periods since 1945. The *Monthly Digest of Statistics* is also very helpful. The *Censuses of Population*, *Industry* and *Production* though infrequent provide the firmest figures. Much of the information in annual publications is only estimated. The reports of the major revenue departments, the *Commissioners for Customs and Excise*, the *Commissioners for Inland Revenue*, and the *Registrars-General for England and Wales* and for *Scotland*, are major sources of statistical information—as are the reports of the other Government Departments, and especially the *Ministry of Labour Dept. of Employment (and Productivity)* with its monthly *Gazette* (until 1917 this was the *Board of Trade Labour Gazette)*, and *Annual Abstract of Labour Statistics*. Other major sources of information are *The London and Cambridge Economic Service* published about three times a year in the '*Times*' *Review of Industry* and the *Abstract of British Historical Statistics* by B. R. Mitchell and P. Deane (1962). Much statistical information is presented in A. H. Halsey (ed.), *Trends in British Society since 1900* (1972).

A useful guide to works on British politics is the subject index of the British Museum Library (which covers the period up to 1960). Bibliographical references can be checked through the *British National Bibliography* and the *Cumulative Book Index*; there is also the *London Bibliography of the Social Sciences* (published annually since 1931) and the *International Bibliography of the Social Sciences* (annually since 1953). For information on many aspects of British politics the *Encyclopaedia Britannica* or *Chambers's Encyclopaedia* may give a lead. Weekly journals, especially the *Economist*, may provide much additional information. Apart from *The Times*, the national dailies are not indexed, which makes reference a slow process. But newspaper libraries generally have their own index system and may be of much help.

The learned journals with most material on British politics are *The Political Quarterly* (1930-), *Parliamentary Affairs* (1947-), *Political Studies* (1953-), and the *British Journal of Political Science* (1971-). *The Table* (the Journal of the Commonwealth Parliamentary Association, 1931), *Government and Opposition* (1965-) and the *Journal of Contemporary History* (1966-) also contain much that is relevant. *International Political Science Abstracts* published annually since 1951 gives a classified abstract of journal articles.

No attempt has been made to provide a bibliography for this century. But for the early years, a valuable guide is H. J. Hanham, *Bibliography of British History 1851-1914* (1976). An extensive bibliography is available for the middle of the period by C. L. Mowat in his book *Britain between the Wars* (1955) and in his article, 'Some Recent Books on the British Labour Movement', *Journal of Modern History*, xvii, No. 4, Dec 1945. He also published *British History since 1926: A Select Bibliography* (The Historical Association, 1960). Another critical bibliography is supplied by A. J. P. Taylor, *English History 1914-45* (1966). See also R. M. Punnett, *British Government and Politics* (1971). Other bibliographies include J. Palmer, *Government and Parliament in Britain: A Bibliography* (1964, The Hansard Society), E. J. Hobsbawm, 'Twentieth-Century British Politics', *Past and Present*, No. 11, Apr 1957, and H. R. Winkler, 'Some Recent Writings on Twentieth-Century Britain', *Journal of Modern History*, xxxii, No. 1, Mar

1960. See also 'Bibliography of British Labour History' in the *Journal of Modern History*, Vol. 41, No. 3, Sep 1969, compiled by William H. Maehl Jr. Perhaps the best recent bibliographies are to be found in A. F. Havinghurst, *Modern England 1901-70* (1976), B. Stevenson, *Reader's Guide to Great Britain* (1977), and J. Westergaard, A. Weyman and P. Wiles, *Modern British Society, a Bibliography* (1977).

INDEX

This index lists all major items in the book, but it is not exhaustive; it does not include individual names of people or places, the names of publications, of Bills or Acts of Parliament, or separate entries in bibliographies. References to important items are grouped together, with sub-headings in the order in which they appear for the first time in the book. The Index of Ministers on pp. 95–134 supplements this index, and should be used for finding details of Ministries on pp. 1–64.

Abortions, 339–40, 344
Aden, 449
Admiralty:
  First Lords of, 2–43, 68, 71
  Permanent Secretaries, 283
  number of civil servants, 291
Aerospace, Minister for, 53, 68, 71, 398, 399, 400; *see also* Air, Transport *and* Aviation
Africa, Ministers in, 28, 78
Age Concern, 344–5
Age of ministers, 84
Agriculture (*see also* Food):
  (Fisheries and Food) Ministry of, 2–60, 68, 71, 198, 283, 291
  policy, resignations over, 86
  National Farmers' Union, 156, 380
  Select Committee on, 198, 209
  Royal Commission on, 296
  Committees on, 302
  Unemployment Insurance Scheme, 352
  employment, 360, 383–4
  import controls, 375
  acreage, 383–4
  output, 383–4
  Marketing Boards, 411, 412
  as a pressure group, 380
  Research Council, 411
Air (*see also* Aviation, British Airports Authority, British Airways Board *and* Aerospace):
  Board, 12, 68, 72
  Council, 12, 68, 72
  Ministry, 12–43, 68, 86, 283, 291, 399
  Aircraft Production, Ministry of, 27–31, 68, 72, 283
  Force, strength, 46–60, 86, 471, 473; resignations over, 86; *see also* Defence
  Aircraft Industry, Committee on, 301
  Civil air transport, Committee on, 301
  Nationalisation, 397, 399 400, 408
  Airways (B.O.A.C., B.E.A., etc.), 397, 399, 400, 408, 409
Alliance Party, 167, 428
Alliance, Liberal/SDP, 158, 172, 228
Amalgamated Union of Engineering Workers, 155, 362, 366–8
Amalgamated Weavers' Association, 363, 368
Ambassadors, 461–2, 469–70
Amersham International, 399
Animal welfare, 344
Archbishops:
  C. of E., 513
  R.C., 516
Army (*see also* Defence *and* War):
  Under-Secretary for, 46–60
  Commanders-in-Chief, 471
  Chiefs of General Staff, 471
  total forces, serving, 473
  expenditure, 473
  war commanders, 478–80
Arts, Minister for, 47, 52, 53, 56, 63, 68, 72
Arts Council, 412
Assassinations, 281
Assistance Board, National, 288, 352
Association of County Councils, 440
Association of Scientific, Technical and Managerial Staffs, 155, 363, 368
Atomic Energy Authority, 398, 403, 408, 468
Attorneys-General, 3–60, 68, 72, 75
Australia, 326–9, 449, 454, 456
Austria-Hungary, 461
Aviation (*see also* Transport and Aerospace)
  Ministry of, 41–8, 68, 72, 283
  Supply, Ministry of, 53, 68, 72, 291, 400
  Civil Authority, 397, 410

Bahamas, 449, 454, 456
Balance of Payments, 375, 385–7
Bangladesh, 328–9, 449, 454
Bank of England, 198, 378, 397, 409
Bank rate, 303, 375–7, 383–4
Baptist Union, 514, 518
Barbados, 449, 454, 456
Beer, 294, 389–91
Belize, 449, 455, 456
Bibliographical Note, 519–21
Bills, parliamentary, 180–3, 188–90
Biographies of Ministers, 88–94
Birth control, 344
Birth rates, 324
Bishops, 513
Blockade, Minister of, 12, 68, 72
Boer War, 475
British Aerospace, 398, 400
British Airports Authority, 400, 408

British Airways Board, 400, 408, 409
British Broadcasting Company, 501
British Broadcasting Corporation:
  Headquarters, 269
  formation, 410, 501
  Governors, 501–2
  Directors-General, 502
  radio, 503
  television, 504
  licences, 504
  expenditure, 504
British Employers' Confederation, 379
British European Airways Corporation, 397, 400, 408, 409
British Leyland, 398, 407
British National Oil Corporation, 398, 403, 408
British Overseas Airways Corporation, 397, 399, 400, 408
British Shipbuilders, 398, 407, 408
British South American Airways Corporation, 397, 400
British Steel Corporation, *see* Steel
British Telecom, 407 (*see also* Post Office)
British Waterways Board, 405, 409
Broadcasting (*see also* British Broadcasting Corporation and Independent Television):
  of parliament, 177
  quotations from broadcasts, 270–80
  departmental committees, 300–2, 510
  nationalisation, 397
  British Broadcasting Company, 501
  British Broadcasting Corporation, 501–4
  Independent Broadcasting, 505–9
  legislation, 505
Bryce Report, 219
Budgets, 86, 303, 375, 395
Burma, 24–34, 68, 74, 285, 450
Bus Company, 405, 408
Business pressure groups, 379
By-elections, 241–4

Cabinet (*see also* Ministers):
  death in office, 85
  defeat in office, 85
  Ministers, 1–64
  size, 82
  social composition, 83
  secretary to, 283
  Office staff, 292
  Office, Economic Section, 377
Cable and Wireless Ltd, 198, 399, 406, 410
Canada, 326–9, 375, 450, 454, 456
Capital punishment, 308, 319, 346
Capital transfer tax, 394
Cars, *see* Motor cars
Central Electricity Generating Board, 397, 401, 408
Central Policy Review Staff, 283
Ceylon, 450, 453, 454, 456
Chancellors of the Exchequer, 1–59, 70–1, 88–94; *see also* Treasury
Channel Islands, 429–31
Children (*see also* Education):
  departmental committees on, 301
  legislation (criminal justice), 307–8
  offenders, 320
  legislation (welfare), 339–41
  pressure groups, 344
Churches:
  Assembly, 268
  Royal Commissions, 295
  in Wales, 423, 513
  membership statistics, 511–18
  Church of England, 511–13, 518
  buildings, 513–16
  Episcopal, in Scotland, 514
  Baptist, 514
  Congregational, 514
  Presbyterian, 515
  United Reformed, 515
  Methodist, 515
  of Scotland, 516
  Roman Catholic, 516
  in Northern Ireland, 517
  other Christian denominations, 517
  marriages in, 518
Civil Aviation, *see* Aviation
Civil Liability, 297, 310–11
Civil Liberties, 302, 344
Civil List, 419
Civil & Public Service Association, 363, 368
Civil Service:
  Department of, 68, 72, 284, 292
  heads of departments, 283–8
  size of, 290–2
  salary levels, 288; committee on, 301–2
  Royal Commissions, 295
  Select Committee, 209
  political activities of, 301
  training, 300
  Fulton Committee on, 301
  Clerk of the Crown in Chancery, 318
Coal (*see also* Mines *and* National Union of Mineworkers):
  disputes, 269, 369–71, 376–7
  Royal Commissions, 294–6
  production, 383–4
  nationalisation, 397, 402
  National Coal Board, 402, 408–9
  European Coal and Steel Community, 465, 468
Coalition Labour, 224
Coalition Liberal, 224
Coalition Unionist, 224
Colonial Office, 2–46, 68, 72, 284, 291
  Development Corporation, 410
  see also Dominions *and* Commonwealth
Commission for Racial Equality, 329
Committees:
  Nineteen Twenty-Two, 137
  Labour Representation, 152
  National Executive, 153–4
  Ways and Means, 175
  of Selection, 194

Committees:–*continued*
Public Accounts, 195
Estimates, 196
on National Expenditure, 197
on Nationalised Industries, 197
Agriculture, 198
Science and Technology, 198
Services, 200
of Privileges, 201
on Parliamentary Commissioner, 207–8
Specialist Select Committees, 209
of Inquiry, 293, 302–3
Departmental, 299–302
Standing Advisory, 299
Political Honours Scrutiny, 304–5
of Imperial defence, 472
Common Wealth Party, 162, 164
Commons, House of (*see also* Parliament *and* Members of Parliament):
Leaders, 1–59, 81
Speakers, 175
Chairmen of Ways and Means, 175
Officers of, 176
Sessions, 176
hours of sitting, 176
broadcasting, 177
allocation of time, 180–3
dates of dissolution, 180–3
prorogations, 180–3
Fathers of, 183
critical votes in, 188–90
Government and Private Members time, 176
confidence motions, 191
guillotine motions, 191
suspension of Members, 191–2
Select Committees of, 192–209
quotations from, 270–80
Commonwealth (*see also* Colonial Office *and* Dominions Office):
Relations, Ministry of, 33–46, 68, 73, 284, 291
emigration to, 326–8
Development Corporation, 410
territories since 1900, 449–54
Members, 454–5
Prime Ministers' Meetings, 455
Secretariat, 456
Viceroys and Governors-General, 456–7
Communist Party:
history, 162, 164
election results, 225–8
lost deposits, 162, 249
headquarters, 269
on the L.C.C., 447
Community Relations Commissions, 298; *see also* Race
Compensation, legal, 297, 308, 310–11, 317
Conduct of M.P.s, 191–2
Confederation of British Industry, 379
Confederation of Health Service Employees, 363, 368
Confidence votes, 188–91
Congregational Church, 514, 518
Conscription, 86, 474
Conservative Party (*see also* National Party):
Leaders, 135; in the House of Lords, 135
Deputy Leaders, 135
officials, 135–6
Chief Whips, 136
Research Departments, 136
Nineteen Twenty-Two Committee, 137
Shadow Cabinet, 137–9
membership, 139
finance, 139
annual conferences, 140–1, 267
in the House of Lords, 215
election results, 224–31
M.P.s changes of allegiance, 233–9
in by-elections, 241–5
election expenses, 247–8
lost deposits, 249
women candidates and M.P.s, 249
rating in opinion polls, 255–65
headquarters, 267–8
quotations from, 270–80
in local elections, 443–7
in the press, 481–99
sponsored M.P.s, 156
Consols, 383–4
Constitution, Commission on, 297
Consumers:
(Trade and) Consumer Affairs, Minister of, 53, 69, 77, 79
Prices and Consumer Protection, Ministry of, 57, 69, 77, 286
protection, 301, 380
credit, 301
expenditure, 392
pressure groups, 344, 380
councils, 412
Cook, Thomas, 398
Co-operative Party, 162, 164–5
Co-ordination of Defence, 68, 73
Co-ordination of Transport, Secretary of State, 37, 68
Copyright, 300
Cotton, 369–70, 383–4
Council of Europe, 466
Council for the Protection of Rural England, 345
Councils, *see* Local Government
Covent Garden Market Authority, 410
Crime statistics, 319–20
Criminal procedure, 297, 307–10
Criminal Injuries Compensation Board, 308, 317
Critical votes, 180–90, 218
Crown Lands, 301, 411
Customs and Excise:
Board, 284
civil servants, 292
revenue, 387–8
tariffs, specimen, 389–91

Cultivated acres, 383–4
Cyprus, 450, 454

Death:
certification, committee on, 301
penalty, 308, 319, 346
rates, 324
main causes of, 325
on the road, 347
duties, 387–9, 394
Decimal currency, 296, 301, 376
Defence (*see also* War, Army, Navy *and* Air):
Co-ordination of, Minister for, 23, 68, 73
Ministry of, 26–60, 68, 73, 472–3
Minister of, for Administration, 47, 68, 73, 472–3
Minister of, for Equipment, 68, 73, 472–3
Air Force, Minister for, 68, 73
Army, Minister for, 68, 73
Navy, Minister for, 68, 73
Procurement, Minister of, 51, 68, 73; Agency, 411; committee on, 302
Select Committee, 209
permanent secretaries, 284
civil servants, 291
of the Realm, Standing Advisory Committee, 299
expenditure, 389–91, 473
Service Chiefs, 471
Committee of Imperial Defence, 472
pressure groups, 473
total forces serving, 473
military operations, 475–7
war commanders, 478–80
Democratic Labour, 237, 244
Democratic Unionist Party, 237–8, 427–9
Demonstrations, 281
Departmental Committees, 300–2
Development Commission, 410
Devolution, 421–33
Diplomatic Service, 461–2
Disturbances and demonstrations, major civil, 281
Divorce, 295, 297, 326, 337–8
Docks, 294, 301, 310, 397–8, 405, 408, 409; *see also* Ports, Transport and Transport and General Workers' Union
Dominica, 450, 454
Dominions Office, 17–33, 68, 73, 284, 291; *see also* Commonwealth
Duchy of Lancaster, 2–65, 68, 71

Earnings, 357–8; *see also* Pay
Economic:
Warfare, Ministry of, 25–8, 68, 73, 284
Affairs, Ministry of, 33–45, 68, 70, 284,
policy, resignations over, 85–6
Departmental Committees, 300–1
statistics, 357–8, 380–95
landmarks, 375–7
policy, 375–9
National Plan, 378
European Economic Community, 378, 465–70
and Social Research Council, 412
advice, sources of, 377–9
National Economic Development Council, 376, 378; Service, Head of, 378
Advisory Council, 378
Planning Board, 378
Section of the Cabinet Office, 377
Education:
Board of, 2–28, 68, 73, 341
Ministry of, 28–42, 68, 73, 341
and Science, Ministry of, 42–60, 68, 73, 284, 301
policy, resignations over, 85–7
and Science, Select Committee on, 198
Select Committee on, 209
Central Advisory Council on, 293
departmental committees on, 300–2
legislation, 340–1, 436
finance, 341, 343
statistics, 342–3
expenditure, 343
pressure groups, 344
Eire, 423–4, 451; *see also* Ireland
Elderly, *see* Pensions
Elections:
resignations over, 86
statistics, 223–31
results, 224–8
European Parliament, 229
regional results, 230–1
party changes between elections, 232–3
by-elections, 241–4
administration, 245
Speakers' Conferences, 245
franchise, 246
redistribution, 246–7
expenses, 247–8
lost deposits, 249
women candidates and M.P.s, 249
petitions, 250
Royal Commissions, 295
women's rights in, 337–8
Local Government, 442–8
Electrical Trades Union, 155, 364, 366–8
Electricity:
Union, 155, 364, 366–8
Departmental Committees on, 301
employees, 360, 408
nationalisation, 397–9
British Electricity Authority, 401, 408, 409
Central Electricity Generating Board, 397, 401
Council, 401, 408
North of Scotland Hydro-Electricity Board, 402, 408, 409
South of Scotland Electricity Board, 402, 408, 409
Central Electricity Board, 397
Emergency Powers, 371

Emigration, 326
Employment (*see also* Labour *and* Unemployment):
(and Productivity), Ministry of 47–60, 68, 73
Select Committee on, 209
Permanent Secretaries, 286
civil servants, 291
legislation, 351–5
statistics, 357–60, 372–3
government responsibility for, 375
Energy (*see also* Fuel and Power):
Department of, 52–60, 68, 74, 284, 291
Select Committee on, 209
atomic, 398, 403, 408
Environment (*see also* Housing, Local Government *and* Transport):
Department of, 52–60, 68, 74, 404–5
Select Committee on, 209
Permanent Secretaries, 284–5
civil servants, 291
Environmental Pollution, Standing Advisory Committee, 299
pressure groups, 345, 440
Equal pay, 297, 338
Equal Opportunities Commission, 338
Estate Duty, 394
Estimates Committee, 196
European:
Economic Community, 86–7, 376, 465–70
Secondary Legislation, Select Committee on, 199
Referendum on, 229, 248
Parliament, 229, 465, 469
Free Trade Association, 376, 465, 466
European Economic Co-operation, Organisation for, 376, 465, 466
Council of Europe, 465, 466–7
Coal and Steel Community, 468
Atomic Energy Community, 468
Budgetary contribution, 468
Court of Justice, 469–70
Commission, British members of, 469
Cabinet Ministers, 469
ambassadors, 469–70
Exchange rates, 376, 385–7
Exchequer and Audit Department, 292
Excise (*see also* Customs and Excise):
Board, 284
revenue, 387–9
duty on beer, 389–91
Exports, 385–7
Export Credits Guarantee Department, 411

Factory Acts, 351
Falkland Islands, 87, 450, 477
Family Allowances, 334–6
Family Division, 315
Family Fund, 411
Family Welfare, 345
Farmers, 156, 380
Fascists, British Union of, 162, 169–70
Fathers of the House of Commons, 183
Federation of British Industries, 379
Fiji, 450, 454, 456
First Secretary of State, 40, 68, 79
Fisheries, *see* Agriculture *and* White Fish Authority
Food:
Ministry of Food Control, 12, 68, 74
Ministry of, 23–38, 68, 74, 285, 291
Directors-General, 285
Royal Commissions, 295
specimen tariffs, 389–91
percentage of consumer expenditure, 392
Foreign:
Office, 2–46, 68, 71, 285
Secretaries, 2–58, 68, 71, 88–93
(and Commonwealth Office), 46–58, 68, 71, 285
policy, resignations over, 86
Affairs, Select Committee, 209
pressure groups, 461
policy quotations, 271–6
Permanent Secretaries, 285
civil servants, 291
United Nations affairs, 461, 462
Forestry Commission, 285, 411
France, 375, 385–7, 393, 461, 465
Franchise, 246
Free Trade, 85
Fuel (*see also* Gas, Electricity, Coal *and* Power):
(Light and Power), Ministry of, 28, 68, 74
(and Power), Ministry of, 32–8, 68, 74, 285, 291
Co-ordination of Transport, Fuel & Power, Secretary of State for, 37, 68
Resources, Committee on, 301
work force, 360
crises, 371, 375–6
nationalised industries, 397–8, 401–3, 408–10
rationing, 474

Gallup Poll, 252–65
Gambia, 450, 454, 456
Gambling, 296, 297, 302, 411, 412
Gas:
Industry, Committee on, 300
employees, 360
nationalisation, 398, 403, 408, 409
Council, 403, 408
Area Gas Boards, 398, 403, 408, 409
Corporation, 398, 403
General and Municipal Workers' Union, 155, 364, 366–8
General Dental Council, 206
General Elections, *see* Elections
General Register Office, 287
General Strike, 370, 371, 375
Germany, 385–7, 393, 461–2, 466
Ghana, 450, 454, 456
Gibraltar, 450

Gold, 375
Government (*see also* Cabinet *and* Ministers):
  in chronological order, 1–65
  size of, 82
  Economic Service, 378
Accountancy
  revenue, 387–9
  expenditure, 389–91
Greater London Council, 435, 446–8
Grenada, 451, 454, 456
Gross Domestic Product, 380–2
Guernsey, 429–31
Guyana, 451,454, 456

Harris Poll, *see* Public Opinion Polls
Health (and Social Security) (*see also* Social Services, Secretary of State for):
  Department of, 10–61, 68, 69, 75, 78
  ministerial salaries, 67
  policy, resignation over, 86
  Permanent Secretaries, 285, 287
  civil servants, 291
  Royal Commission, 294–7
  Departmental Committees, 301
  tribunals, 304
  legislation, 334–7; industrial, 351–3
  expenditure, 389–91
  local authority responsibility for, 437
  pressure groups, 440
Her Majesty's Stationery Office, 411
Hindu religion, 518
Hire Purchase, 395
'Hiving-off' of nationalised industries, 398–9
Home Office:
  Ministers, 1–59, 68
  Secretaries, 1–59, 71
  Select Committee on, 209
  Permanent Secretaries, 285
  civil servants, 284, 291
Home Security, Ministry of, 23–8, 68, 285
Homosexuals, 345
Hong Kong, 451, 460
Honours scrutiny, 296, 304–5
Horserace Totalisator Board, 412
House of Commons, *see* Commons, House of
House of Lords, *see* Lords, House of
Housing:
  (and Local Government), Ministry of, 37–52, 68, 74, 76
  and Construction, Ministry of, 52–9, 68, 76
  policy, resignation over, 86
  Permanent Secretaries, 285
  civil servants, 285
  Royal Commission, 295
  Departmental Committee on, 301–2
  legislation, 330–2
  Corporation, 330, 331, 410
  Local Authorities, 331, 436–8
  statistics, 332–3
  pressure groups, 345
Immigration, 294; *see also* Race, 328–9
Imperial Preference, 85–6
Imports:
  Duties Advisory Council, 378
  statistics, 385–7
India:
  Office, 2–24, 68, 74, 285, 291
  and Burma Office, 24–34, 68, 74, 285
  Royal Commissions, 295–6
  immigration from, 328–9
  independence, 451, 454
  Governors-General, 456
  Viceroys, 456
Independent Broadcasting Authority, 410, 505–9
Independent Labour Party (I.L.P.), 162, 165, 226
Independent M.P.s, 171, 233–9
Independent Television (*see also* Television *and* Independent Broadcasting Authority):
  Select Committee investigation, 198
  Authority, 505
  programme contracting companies, 506–9
  News Ltd, 509
Industry (*see also* Trade):
  (and Trade) Department of, 53–6, 68, 74, 400–7
  Industrial Development, Ministry of, 53, 68, 74
  Department of, 56, 68, 74, 285, 291, 400–7
  Select Committee on, 209
  Training Boards, 411
  Finance and, Committee on, 300–1, 375
  Courts of Inquiry, 303, 304
  industrial relations, 303, 351–4, 357
  industrial injuries, 353–4
  work force, 360
  disputes, 369–71
  Reorganisation Corporation, 376, 410
  production, 383–4
  output, 393
  nationalised, 397–408
  Confederation of British Industry, 379
Inflation, 376–7, 380–2
Information:
  Ministry of, 11, 24–32, 68, 74, 285
  Central office of, 285
  Ministry of Information-Technology, 68
Inland Revenue, 285, 292, 387–9
Insurance, *see* National Insurance *and* Social Insurance
Interest groups: *see* Pressure groups
International:
  Monetary Fund, 375, 377
  relations, 459–63
Ireland (*see also* Eire *and* Northern Ireland):
  Chief Secretaries for, 2–10, 68, 74, 424
  Lord Chancellors, 2–12, 69, 74
  Lords Lieutenant of, 2, 10, 75, 424
  Attorneys-General, 3–13, 68, 75

Ireland:–*continued*
Solicitors-General, 3–13, 69, 75
Permanent Secretaries, 286
Civil Service, 291
Ministerial resignations over, 86, 87
parties, 166–7
election results, 224, 228–31
Royal Commission, 296
Vice-Regal Commissions, 299
Lords Chief Justice, 315
emigrations from, 326–7
government of, before independence, 424
Governors-General, 456
independence of, 451, 454
Irish Nationalist Party, 162, 166, 211–2, 224
Irish Office, *see* Ireland
Iron, *see* Steel
Italy, 393, 462, 467

Jamaica, 451, 454, 457
Jersey, 429–30
Jewish community, 517, 518
Judges, 315–17
number, 318
Junior Lords of the Treasury, *see* Whips
Justice (*see also* Judges, Law *and* Legislation):
Royal Commission relating to, 295–7
administration of, 307–22
criminal legislation, 307–10
civil legislation, 310–11
Statute Law Commission, 317
statistics, 318–20

Kenya, 451, 454, 457
Kings, 415–18; *see also* Royal
Kirbati, 451, 455
Korean War, 476

Labour (*see also* Employment):
(and National Service) Ministry of, 11–47, 68, 75, 286, 291
force, size of, 359
Labour Party (*see also* Independent Labour Party *and* National Labour Party):
leaders, 142–3
Chief Whips, 144
Representation Committee, 144
National Executive Committee, 144
Parliamentary Committee, 145–9
Annual Conferences, 149–50
membership, 151–2
organisation and constitutions, 152–4
sponsored M.P.s, 154–6
Labour Party finance, 157
in the House of Lords, 215
election results, 224–31
M.P.s' changes of allegiance, 233–9
in by-elections, 241–4
election expenses, 247–8
lost deposits, 249
women candidates and M.P.s, 249
rating in opinion polls, 254–65
headquarters, 267–70
quotations from, 270–80
in local elections, 443–8
and the press, 481–2, 485, 487, 492–3
Lancaster, Duchy of, 1–60, 68, 75
Land:
and National Resources, Ministry of, 49, 69, 76
Permanent Secretaries, 286
Royal Commissions, 295, 297
Lands tribunal, 304
Committees on, 362
Registry, 411, 412
Law (*see also*) Judges, Justice *and* Legislation):
Officers, 3–65, 68–9, 70, 72, 74–5, 78–9
Society, 206
Company, Committees on, 301
Commission, 317
pressure groups, 345–6
League of Nations, 461
Leasehold, 301, 330
Leeward Islands, 411
Legal, Aid, 308, 311
Legal System, *see* Law
Legislation:
criminal justice, 307–10
civil justice, 311–12
housing, 330–2
rent and mortgage interest restriction, 330–2
social security, 334–7
women's rights, 337–8
maternity and child welfare, 339
education, 340–1
employment, 351–5
trade union, 351–5
monopolies, 375–6
economic, 375–7
Local Government, 436–9
Lend-Lease, 375, 459
Liberal National Party, 167–8, 225
Liberal Party:
Leaders, 158
National Liberal Federation, 158
party organisation, 158–9
Chief Whips, 159
Annual Conferences, 159–61
in the House of Lords, 215
election results, 224–31
M.P.s' changes of allegiance, 233–9
sponsored M.P.s, 156
in by-elections, 241–3
election expenses, 247–8
lost deposits, 249
women candidates and M.P.s, 249
rating in opinion polls, 254–65
headquarters, 267–9
quotations, 270–80
in local elections, 443–8
in the press, 481–8, 492–3
Liberal Unionist Party, 168, 215, 223, 234
Libraries, 301, 343
Licensing laws, 295, 296, 302

Life, expectation of, 325
Litigation:
political, 311–15
Trade Union, 355–6
Local Government (*see also* National and Local Government Officers' Association *and* Town and Country Planning):
Board, President of, 2–11, 69, 75
and Planning, 34, 56, 69, 76
and Housing, Ministry of, 37–52, 69, 74
and Regional Planning, 47, 69, 74
and Development, 52, 69, 76
and Environmental Services, 69, 76
Permanent Secretaries, 285, 286, 287
civil servants, 291
Royal Commissions, 297
committees on, 300–2
finance, 300–2, 436
housing, responsibilities, for, 330–2, 436–9
children, responsibilities for, 339
industrial dispute, 371
structure, 435
legislation, 436–9
health, responsibilities for, 437
elections, 443–8
pressure groups, 440
London, 297, 397, 404, 447
Long tenure of office, 84
Lords Advocate, 3–60, 69, 78
Lord Chancellors, 1–59, 67, 69, 70
Secretaries to, 286, 318
Lord Chancellors of Ireland, 2–12, 69, 74
Lord Chief Justices, 315
Lords, House of:
Leaders, 81
Officers, 213
Lord Chairmen of Committees, 213
composition of, 213
attendance, 215
Party organisation, 214
Party strengths, 215
sittings, 216–17
business, 216–17
critical votes, 218
reform of, 218–21
appeals heard, 319
Lords in Waiting, *see* Whips
Lord Justice Clerk, 315
Lords Justices of Appeal, 316–17
Lords of Appeal in Ordinary, 315
Lord Presidents of the Council, 1–58, 69, 70
Lord Presidents of the Court of Session, 315
Lords Privy Seal, 1–59, 69, 70

Malawi, 451, 454, 457
Malaya, 451, 454
Malta, 295, 451, 454, 457
Man, Isle of, 431–2
Manpower Services Commission, 411
Market & Opinion Research International, 253, 265
Marplan Ltd, 253
Marriage (*see also* Divorce):
Royal Commission, 295–7
rates, 324
average age at, 326
legislation, 337–8
by solemnisation, 518
Marshall Aid, 375
Master of the Rolls, 315
Materials, Ministry of, 38, 69, 76, 286
Maternity and child welfare, 339–40
Mauritius, 451, 454, 457
Members of Parliament:
sponsored, 154–6
education, 179
occupations, 178
longest serving, 184
oldest, 184
youngest, 184
family connections of, 185
spouse's succession, 186
final succession, 186–7
payment of, 210–11, 301
pensions, 210–11, 301
seats forfeited, 211–12
suspensions, 191–2
changes of allegiance, 233–9
seeking re-election, 244–5
women, 249
creation of peerages, 214
denied renomination, 239–40
Methodist Church, 515, 517, 518
Metrication Board, 412
Metropolitan Police, 317
Military operations, 475–7
Mines, 11, 24, 69, 295, 296, 360, 364–71, 376–7; *see also* Coal *and* National Union of Mineworkers
Ministers (*see also* Government *and* Cabinet):
by Governments, 1–62
salaries, 67, 301
Ministerial officers, 68–9
holders of Ministerial office, 70–83
number of, 82
longest serving, 84
dying in office, 85
losing seats, 85
powers, 300
resignations, 86–7
biographical notes, 88–94
index of, 95–134
re-election of, 245
memoirs of, 302
Northern Ireland, 426–7
resident overseas, 27–8, 69, 77–8
Minor parties, 162–72
representation, 173
election results, 223–31
Monetary system, 301, 377
Monopolies:
Commission, 317, 375, 376, 412
and Restrictive Practices Commission, 317, 376

Monopolies:–*continued*
and Mergers Commission, 412
legislation, 376
Morality pressure groups, 346
Mortgage Interest (Restriction) Acts, 331
Motor cars (*see also* Transport *and* Traffic):
Royal Commission, 295
licences, 347
industrial disputes, 371
percentage of consumer expenditure, 392
Munitions, Ministry of, 8–11, 69, 76, 286, 291
Museums, 296
Muslim religion, 518

National and Local Government Officers' Association, 364, 366–8
National Assistance, 288, 292, 335–6, 437
National Association of British Manufacturers, 379
National Bus Company, 405, 408
National Debt, 300, 389–91
National Democratic Party, 162, 169
National Dock Labour Board, 410
National Economic Development Council, 376, 378
National Enterprise Board, 398, 410
National Executive Committee, 144
National Expenditure Committee, 197, 300
National Farmers' Union, 156, 380
National Film Finance Corporation, 410
National Freight Corporation, 399, 405, 408
National Front, 163, 168
National Health Service, 296–7, 301, 304; *see also* Health and Social Security
Management Board, 286
National Income, 380–2, 392
Commission, 378
National Insurance (*see also* Social Insurance *and* Pensions):
(and Pensions) Ministry of, 29–49, 69, 77
Permanent Secretaries, 286
civil servants, 291
Royal Commission, 296
committee on, 300
tribunals, 304
legislations, 334–7, 351–4
expenditure, 390–1
National Labour Party, 163, 169, 225, 235
National Opinion Poll, 252, 264–5
National Party, 163, 169
National Research Development Corporation, 410
National Savings Bank, 411
National Service:
Ministry of, 12, 69, 75, 76
(Labour and) Ministry of, 24–42, 69
resignation over, 86
Permanent Secretaries, 286
history of, 474
National Union of General and Municipal Workers, 364, 366–7
National Union of Mineworkers (N.U.M.), 155, 364, 366–8
National Union of Public Employees (N.U.P.E.), 365, 368
National Union of Railwaymen (N.U.R.), 155, 365, 366–8
National Union of Teachers (N.U.T.), 156, 365, 368
Nationalisation, 397–414
main landmarks, 397–8
Nationalised Industries, Select Committee, 197, 408–10
policy for, 412–13
Naturalisation, 327
Nauru, 451, 454
Navy (*see also* Admiralty *and* Defence)
Under-Secretaries for, 46–55
First Sea Lords, 471
total forces serving, 473
expenditure, 473
war commanders, 478–80
New Party, 163, 169–70, 225, 235
New Towns, 334n., 410, 437, 441
New Zealand, 327–9, 452, 454, 457
Newfoundland, 296, 454, 452
Newspapers (*see also* Press):
headquarters, 267–9
national daily, 481–5, 491–4
national Sunday, 486–8, 495
London evening, 488–90, 495
printing in more than one city, 491
partisan tendencies, 492–3
circulation, 492–5
provincial morning daily, 495–8
readership,
weekly, 498–9
Nigeria, 452, 454, 457
Nineteen Twenty-Two Committees, 137
North Atlantic Council, 462
North Atlantic Treaty Organisation (N.A.T.O.), 459
Northern Ireland (*see also* Stormont, S.D.L.P., Sinn Fein *and* Ulster Unionist Party):
Department, 52–60, 69, 76, 286, 427–8
resignation over, 87
committees, on, 302
tribunals of inquiry, 303
Lords Chief Justice, 315
judicature, 309
quangos, 410
Government of, 424–9
Governors of, 426
Prime Ministers, 426
Ministers, 69, 76, 426–7
General Elections, 230–1, 427
civil disturbances, 428, 477
B.B.C., Governor for, 502
I.B.A., Governor for, 505–6
religious affiliations, 517

Oil, 374, 398–9, 403; *see also* Power
Oldest M.P.s, 184

Oldest Ministers, 84
Ombudsman, *see* Parliamentary Commissioner for the Administration
One-parent families, 301, 339, 345
Opinion Research Centre, 253, 265
Opposition, Leader of, 67
Organisation for European Economic Co-operation (and Development), 376, 460
Output per man, 393
Overseas:
  Trade Department of, 11–38, 69
  Development, Ministry of, 47–60, 69, 76, 286, 291
  Development, Select Committee, 199, 209
  Aid, Select Committee, 199
  people born, 327

Pakistan, 328–9, 452, 454, 457
Palestine, 86, 296, 452
Papua-New Guinea, 451, 454, 457
Parliament; 175–222; *see also* Members of Parliament, Commons, House of *and* Lords, House of
Parliamentary Commissioner for the Administration, 207–8
Parliamentary Labour Party, 142–9
Parliamentary Private Secretaries, 82, 87
Parliamentary Secretary to the Treasury, *see* Whips
Parliamentary time, allocation of, 176–7, 180–3
Party Conferences:
  Conservative, 140–1
  Labour, 149–50
  Liberal, 159–61
  quotations from, 271–8
Party finance, 139, 157, 248
Pay:
  Board, 376, 379, 412
  Productivity and Incomes, Council on, 378
  percentage of national income, 392
  Comparability Commission, 379
Paymaster-General, 3–64, 69, 76
Peerages, 213–14, 221
Pensions:
  Ministry of, 12–39, 69, 76
  and National Insurance, Ministry of, 37–49, 69, 77
  Permanent Secretaries, 286
  civil servants, 291
  tribunals, 304
  legislation, 334–6
  old age, 334–7
  widows', 335
  pressure groups, 344–5
  expenditure, 389–91
Permanent Secretaries, 283–8; salary, 288
Petroleum Department, 29, 69; *see also* Fuel
Place-names, political, 267–9
Plaid Cymru, 163, 170, 227–9
Planning and Land, Minister for, 69, 76
Planning and Local Government, *see* Local Government
Poets Laureate, 419
Police, 295, 297, 302, 303, 310, 317, 321
Police Commissioners, 317
Police Complaints Board, 309, 317
Political advisers, 290
Political honours, 296, 304–5
Political litigation, 311–15
Polls, *see* Public Opinion Polls
Pollution, 299, 301
Population:
  Royal Commissions, 297
  regional distribution, 296, 324
  in prison, 320
  statistics, 323
  intercensal change, 323
  main conurbations, 324
  age distribution, 325
  wealth distribution, 393
  in agriculture, 360, 383–5
  percentage reading newspapers, 499
Portfolio, Minister without, 8–11, 24–9, 34, 38–48, 53, 69, 77
Ports (*see also* Docks):
  Royal Commissions on, 294
  Departmental Committees on, 301
  Port of London Authority, 397
  nationalised, 405, 408
Post Office:
  Postmaster General, 2–49, 69, 77, 501
  Posts and Telecommunications, Ministry of, 49–53, 69, 77, 406
  Union, 155, 366, 368
  Permanent Secretaries, 286
  Directors-General, 286
  civil servants, 291
  postal traffic, 348; costs, 349
  telephones, 349
  industrial dispute, 371
  nationalisation, 398, 406
  Corporation, 406, 407, 408
Power (*see also* Fuel):
  Ministry of, 42–8, 69, 74, 285, 291
  crises, 371, 375–7
  nationalised industries, 397–9, 401–3, 408
Presbyterian Church, 515, 516, 517
Prescription charges, 336
Presidents of Probate, Divorce and Admiralty Division, 315
Press, 297; *see also* Newspapers
Press Council, 499–500
Pressure groups, 343–6, 379–80, 440, 461, 473
Prices:
  and Consumer Protection, Ministry of, 56, 69, 77, 286, 291
  Royal Commissions, 297
  departmental committees, 300
  Council on, 376, 378
  Commission, 376, 378, 412
  and Incomes Board, 376, 378, 412
  indices, 380–2

Prime Ministers:
by Government, 1–60, 69, 83
salary, 67
chronological list of, 70
P.P.S.s to, 87
biographical details, 88–94
homes of, 267–9
Private Secretaries to, 289
staff, 289
Atomic Energy, responsibility for, 403
durability of, 84
Prisons:
Committee on, 301, 302
sentences, 318, 319, 320
prisoners, 320
reform, 345–6
Privacy, Committee on, 302
Privatisation, 398–9
Privileges, Select Committee on, 201–5
Privy Council:
Minister of State for, 54, 69
Counsellors, 91–134
Clerk of the Council, 287
Probate, Divorce and Admiralty Division, 315
Probation, 300, 302, 307–11, 319
Procedure, Parliamentary Committee on, 200
Procurator-General, 318
Production, Ministry of, 27, 69, 287
Proportional representation, 296
Prorogations of Parliament, 180–3
Prosecutions, Director of Public, 317
Public Accounts Committee, 193–5
Public Building and Works, Ministry of, 43–9, 69, 77, 288; *see also* Works
Public opinion polls:
Gallup Poll, 252–65
National Opinion Poll, 252, 264–5
Opinion Research Centre, 253, 265
Louis Harris Research Ltd, 253, 265
Marplan Ltd, 253
Market & Opinion Research International, 253, 265
Public Petitions, Select Committee on, 206–7
Public schools:
ministers educated at, 83, 88–93; *see also* Index of Ministers, 95–134
M.P.s educated at, 179
Public Trustee Office, 302

Quakers, 517
Quangos, 410–12
Queens, 415–18; *see also* Royal
Questions, parliamentary, 180–3
Quotations, political, 270–80

Race:
Select Committee on Race Relations and Immigration, 198–9, 209
riots, 281
quotations, 278
Relations Board, 329
pressure groups, 346
Radio, 503, 509; *see also* Broadcasting
Railways (*see also* Transport):
unions, 155, 355, 365, 366–8
Royal Commissions on, 295, 296
departmental committees on, 300
statistics, 348
disputes, 369–71
nationalisation, 397–8
British Railways Board, 404, 408
Rationing, 474–5
Reconstruction, Ministry of, 12, 27, 69, 78, 287
Redistribution of seats, 246–7
Re-election, 244–5
Referendums:
on Europe, 229, 248, 465
in Scotland, 422
in Wales, 423
in Northern Ireland, 428
Regional Development, 300
Registrars-General, 287
Regnal years, 192
Religion (*see also* Churches *and* Sunday Observation):
Christian, 511–17
other, 517–18
Rent:
departmental committees, 300–1
tribunals, 304
legislation, 331–2
percentage of national income, 392
Resale Price Maintenance, 301, 376
Resident Overseas, Ministers, 27–8, 69, 77–8
Resignations, Ministerial, 85–7
Restrictive Trade Practices Court, 375
Retail Trade Associations, 378
Rhodesia (*see also* Zimbabwe), 452, 454, 457, 460
Rolls-Royce Ltd, 398, 407
Roman Catholics, 516, 517, 518
Rosebery Committee Report, 219
Royal:
Household, 3–64, 82, 419
Assent, 180–3, 219, 415, 425
homes, 267–9
quotations from, 270, 275
power, 415
Regency Acts, 416
family, 415–18
Private Secretaries, 419
Chamberlains, 419
payment, 419
Royal Commissions:
description, 293–4
lists of, 294–7
permanent and operating commissions, 297–8
Irish and Vice-Regal Commissioners, 299
Royal Mint, 411
Royal Ordnance Factories, 411
R.S.P.C.A., 344

Rule Committee of Church Assembly, 206
Runnymede Trust, 346; *see also* Race
Russia, 459, 462, 475

Safety and Health at Work, Committee on, 302
St Lucia, 452, 454, 457
Salaries:
  Ministers, 67
  M.P.s' 210–11
  Permanent Secretaries to the Treasury, 288
Salvation Army, 517
Scandals, political, 280–1
Schools, 340–2; *see also* Public Schools *and* Education
Science (*see also* Education):
  Ministry of, 42, 69, 78, 287, 403
  and Technology, Committee on, 198
  Chief Scientific Advisers, 283
  Research Council, 287
  Scientific and Industrial Research Department, 287
Scotland:
  Secretary (of State) for, 2–64, 69, 78, 421–2
  Lords Advocate, 3–64, 69, 78
  Solicitors-General, 3–64, 69, 78
  Scottish Affairs, Committee on, 199, 209
  election results, 230–1, 422, 443–5
  Scottish Office, Permanent Secretaries, 287; civil servants, 291
  Electricity Boards, 402, 408
  Scottish Transport Group, 405
  Local Government, 435, 440, 443–5
  Development Agency, 410
  government of, 421–2
  B.B.C. Governors for, 502
  I.B.A. Governors for, 506
  Scottish Television, 508
  churches in, 514, 516
Scottish Labour Party, 163, 171, 238
Scottish National Party, 163, 171
Seats forfeited, 211–12
Select Committees, 192–209, 422
Selection, Committee of, 194
Service Chiefs, 471
Seychelles, 452, 454
Shadow Cabinets:
  Conservative, 137–9
  Labour (Parliamentary Committee), 146–9
Shipbuilding, 398, 399, 407, 408
Shipping:
  Ministry of, 13, 24–9, 69, 78, 287
  Royal Commission, 295
  departmental committees, 300
  tonnage registered, 348
  industrial disputes, 369–70
  nationalisation proposals, 398, 399
Sierra Leone, 453, 454, 457
Sikh religion, 518
Singapore, 453, 454
Sinn Fein, 163, 166, 173
Social Democratic Party, 171–2, 228, 238, 244, 269
Social Democratic and Labour Party, 166, 237–8, 428–9
Social Insurance (*see also* Pensions and National Insurance):
  Ministry of, 29, 69, 77
  Beveridge Committee on, 300
  tribunals, 304
  legislation, 334–7, 351–5
Social Security, *see* Health and Social Security
Social Services, Secretary of State for, 47–56, 69, 78; *see also* Health and Social Security
  Select Committee on, 209
  Pressure groups, 346
Society of Friends, 517
Society of Graphical & Allied Trades, 365, 368
Solicitors-General, 3–64, 69, 78
  for Ireland, 3–13, 69, 75
  for Scotland, 3–64, 69, 678
Solomon Isles, 449, 453, 454, 457
South Africa, 294–5, 454, 457; *see also* Boer War
Speaker of House of Commons, 175
Speakers' Conferences, 245, 252
Sponsored M.P.s, 154–6
Sport and Recreation, Minister of State for, 56, 69
Sri Lanka, *see* Ceylon
Standing Advisory Committees, 299
State:
  Ministers of, 26, 69, 79
  First Secretary of, 40, 45, 69, 79
Statistical Service, 283
Statute Law Commission, *see* Law Commission
Statutory Instruments Committee, 205–6
Steel:
  production, 383–4
  nationalisation, 398, 399
  Iron and Steel Corporation, 406, 408
  British Steel Corporation, 406, 408, 409
  European Coal and Steel Community, 465, 468
Sterling, 375–7, 385–7
Stormont, 424–7
Strikes, 369–74; *see also* General Strike
Students (*see also* Universities *and* Education):
  in full-time higher education, 342
Suez, 86, 275, 476–7
Sugar:
  Royal Commission, 296
  tariffs on, 389–91
Summer time, 300
Sunday observance, 301, 346
Sunningdale Agreement, 428
Supplementary benefits:
  tribunals, 304

Supply, Ministry of, 11–13, 24–44, 69, 79, 287, 291
Sweden, 393
Swinton Committee Report, 220

Tanganyika, 453, 454, 457
Tanzania, 453
Tariffs, specimen, 389–91
Taxation (*see also* Inland Revenue):
  Income Tax, 295, 300, 377, 380–2, 387–9
  Royal Commission, 294, 296, 297
  local, 294, 295, 296, 302
  departmental committees on, 300, 302
  Value Added Tax, 376, 377
  Profits Tax, 388–9
  Capital Transfer Tax, 389
  Capital Gains Tax, 389
  Selective Employment Tax, 376
  Surtax, 376, 380–2, 387–9, 394
  Death Duty, 388–9, 394
  Estate Duty, 394
Tea tariffs, 389–91
Technical Cooperation, Secretary for, 69
Technology, Minister of, 48–53, 69, 79, 287, 401, 403
Telephones, 349
Television:
  Independent, 198, 410, 505–9
  Committees on, 300, 301, 302, 510
  B.B.C., 397, 410, 501–4
  pressure groups, 346
Temperance, 346
Town and Country Planning, Ministry of, 29–34, 69, 79, 287, 436–7; *see also* Local Government
Trade (*see also* Restrictive Trade Practices Court):
  Board of, 3–53, 69, 79
  and Industry, Department of, 53, 69, 79, 399–403
  and Consumer Affairs, Minister of, 53, 69, 79
  Department of, 56, 69, 79, 287
  Free, 85–6
  Permanent Secretaries, 287
  civil servants, 291
  Royal Commission, 295
  statistics, 385–7
  terms of, 385–7
  Central Government Trading Bodies, 411
  Select Committee, 209
Trade Unions (*see also* Employment *and* Industry):
  M.P.s, 154–6
  places associated with, 267–9
  quotations from and about, 272–9
  Royal Commissions, 295–7
  legislation, 354–5
  Litigation, 355–6
  Congresses, 361–2
  largest unions, 362–6
  income, expenditure and funds, 368
  membership statistics, 366–8, 372–3
  white collar, 369
Traffic (*see also* Transport):
  offences, 320, 347
  road, 347
  railway, 348
  postal, 349
Transport (*see also* War Transport, Railways, Motor cars *and* Traffic):
  Ministry of, 12–29, 35–9, 43–9, 56–60, 69, 79, 80, 399–400, 403–6
  Co-ordination of Transport, Fuel & Power, Secretary of State for, 37, 68
  and Civil Aviation, Ministry of, 39–43, 68, 72, 79, 287, 399–400
  Industries, Minister for (under Environment), 52, 69, 80
  Minister for (under Environment), 56, 69
  Select Committee on, 209
  and General Workers' Union, 155, 365, 366–8
  Permanent Secretaries, 287–8
  civil servants, 291
  Royal Commissions, 294, 295
  tribunals, 304, 412
  pressure groups, 346
  statistics, 347–8
  employment in, 360
  industrial disputes, 369–71
  nationalisation, 397–8, 404–6, 408–10
  privatisation, 398–9
  London Passenger Transport Board, 397, 403
  London Transport Board, 404
  British Transport Commission, 404, 408
  British Transport Docks Board, 405, 408
  Scottish Transport Group, 405
  Transport Holdings Company, 406
Treasury (*see also* Chancellors of the Exchequer, Whips *and* Economic):
  Ministers, 1–61, 67, 69–71
  Select Committee on, 209
  Permanent Secretaries, 288
  civil servants, 291
  Solicitor, 318
  role in economic policy, 375–7
  Economic Section of, 377
  definition of nationalised industries, 397
Treaties, 459–60
Tribunals of Inquiry, 293–4, 297, 301, 302–4
Trinidad and Tobago, 453, 454, 457
Turkey, 86, 462
Tuvalue, 453, 454, 457
Tynwald, 431–2

Uganda, 412, 454, 457
Ullswater Conference on Electoral Reform, 245
Ulster Unionist Party, 167, 238–9, 427–9
Unemployment:
  resignation over, 86

Unemployment:–*continued*
Assistance Board, 288, 352
benefits, 301, 351–4, 359, 368
legislation, 351–4
statistics, 372–3, 375
Union of Construction, Allied Trades and Technicians, 155, 366, 368
Union of Shop, Distributive and Allied Workers, 155, 366–8
Union Movement, 163, 169–70
United Kingdom Atomic Energy Authority, 398, 403, 408
United Nations, 459, 461, 462
United Reformed Church, 514, 515
United States of America, 326, 375–6, 385–7, 393, 459, 462
United Ulster Unionist Council, 167, 428
Universities:
Ministers educated at, 83, 88–94, *see also* Index of Ministers, 95–134
University seats, 172, 230–1
M.P.s educated at, 179
University Grants Committee, 288, 411
Royal Commissions, 294–6
Committee on, 301
removal of sex disqualification, 337
students at, 342
expenditure on, 343
Urban Affairs, Minister of State, 69
U.S.S.R., 459, 462

Value Added Tax, 376
Vanguard Movement, 167, 428
Vivisection, 295, 346
Voting intention, 252–65

Wales (*see also* entries for subjects where England and Wales are taken together):
Minister for Welsh Affairs, 37–42, 69, 80, 422–3
Secretary of State for, 48–63, 69, 80, 422–3
disestablishment, 86
election results, 230–1
Welsh Office, Permanent Secretaries, 288; civil servants, 291
government of, 422–3
Church in, 423, 513
B.B.C. Governors for, 502
I.B.A. Governors for, 506
Development Agency, 410
Land Authority, 411
Commission for Local Government, 440
Select Committees, 209
War (*see also* Economic Warfare, Defence *and* Army):
Office, 3–44, 69, 80, 288, 291, 472
Transport Ministry, 30–2, 69, 79, 287
ministerial resignations over, 86–7
quotations, (1914–18) 271, (1939–45) 273–4
Royal Commissions, 294
emergency measures, 375, 474
Boer, 475
First World, 475
intervention in Russia, 475
Second World, 476
Korean, 476
Suez, 476–7
commanders, 478–80
costs and casualties in, 475–7
Falklands, 477
Water Authorities, 410
Waterways, 398, 405, *see also* Transport
Ways and Means Committee, 175
Welsh, *see* Wales
Welsh Nationalist Party, *see* Plaid Cymru
Wesleyan, *see* Methodist
West Indies, 328–9, 454, 457
Western European Union, 465–6
Western Samoa, 454
Whips:
P.S. to Treasury (Chief Whips), 1–63, 81
Junior Lords of Treasury (Government Whips), 1–63
Government Chief Whip in the Lords (Capt. Gents at Arms), 1–64, 82
Lords in Waiting (Government Whips in the Lords), 64
Assistant Government Whips, 50, 54, 58, 63
Opposition, 67
Conservative, 136–7
Labour, 144
Liberal, 159
White Fish Authority, 411
Women (*see also* Marriage, Divorce *and* Abortion):
candidates and M.P.s, 249
votes for, 246
rights of, 337–9
pressure groups, 346
welfare legislation, 339–40
Works:
First Commissioner of, 3–30, 69, 80
Ministry of, 30–44, 69, 77, 80
and Buildings, Ministry of, 30, 69, 80
and Planning, Ministry of, 30, 69, 80
Public Building and Works, Ministry of, 43–53, 69, 77
Permanent Secretaries, 288
civil servants, 291

Youngest M.P.s, 184
Youngest Ministers, 84

Zambia, 454
Zimbabwe, 454, 455, 460; *see also* Rhodesia